THE ROUGH GUIDE TO

Morocco

There are more than two hundred Rough Guide titles
covering destinations from Alaska to Zimbabwe
and subjects from Acoustic Guitar to Travel Health

Forthcoming travel guides include
The Algarve • The Bahamas • Bolivia • Cambodia
Caribbean Islands • Costa Brava • Zanzibar

Forthcoming reference guides include
Chronicles series: China, England, France & India
Cult TV • Elvis

Rough Guides Online
www.roughguides.com

ROUGH GUIDE CREDITS

Text editor: Clifton Wilkinson
Series editor: Mark Ellingham
Editorial: Martin Dunford, Jonathan Buckley, Jo
Mead, Kate Berens, Amanda Tomlin, Ann-Marie Shaw,
Paul Gray, Helena Smith, Judith Bamber, Orla Duane,
Olivia Eccleshall, Ruth Blackmore, Geoff Howard, Claire
Saunders, Gavin Thomas, Alexander Mark Rogers, Polly
Thomas, Joe Staines, Andrew Tomičić, Richard Lim,
Duncan Clark, Peter Buckley, Sam Thorne, Lucy
Ratcliffe, David Glen (UK); Andrew Rosenberg, Mary
Beth Maioli, Stephen Timblin, Yuki Takagaki (US)
Production: Susanne Hillen, Andy Hilliard, Link Hall,
Helen Ostick, Julia Bovis, Michelle Draycott, Katie
Pringle, Robert Evers, Mike Hancock, Zoë Nobes

Cartography: Melissa Baker, Maxine Repath, Ed
Wright, Katie Lloyd-Jones
Picture research: Louise Boulton, Sharon Martins
Online: Kelly Cross, Anja Mutić-Blessing, Jennifer
Gold, Audra Epstein, Suzanne Welles (US)
Finance: John Fisher, Gary Singh, Edward Downey,
Mark Hall, Tim Bill
Marketing & Publicity: Richard Trillo, Niki Smith,
David Wearn, Chloë Roberts, Birgit Hartmann, Claire
Southern (UK); Simon Carloss, David Wechsler,
Kathleen Rushforth (US)
Administration: Tania Hummel, Demelza Dallow, Julie
Sanderson

ACKNOWLEDGEMENTS

The main **researchers** for this sixth edition of *The
Rough Guide to Morocco* were Don Grisbrook,
Daniel Jacobs, and, in the Atlas Mountains, Hamish
Brown. Hamish also provided many of the **photos**,
as did long-term contributor Dan Eitzen, along with
his fellow Agadir-based photographer, D. Britel.

The researchers on this edition would like to thank the
following: Laghmir Abdelmoula; Abdelillah Alami;
Annie Austin of CLM; Tony Andrews; Jamal
Belouchi; Ali El Kasmi and Hassan Benlamlih of the
Moroccan Tourist Board in London; Stephen Brown;
Michael Butterfield; Robin Cluley; Don Cruckshank;
Bert Flint; Abderresak Labiad; Najim Lahcen; Annie
Lambton; Kristy Larson; Houssine Laroussi;
Mohammed Ben Madani; Roger Mimó; Sabir

Mohammed; Samir Mustapha; Nioua Noureddine;
Cherie Nutting; ONTT staff in Meknes; Abdessadek
Rhorza; Andrew Rosenberg; Benzianme Saïd;
Mohammed Ouhammou Sahnoun; Jill Swift; Badi
Taoufik; the *Hôtel Tiout* in Taroudannt; the Tourist
Office and Municipal Museum in Melilla; Ian
Twilley; and Jasper Winn.

The editor would like to thank Jo and Helena for their
explanatory skills and enduring patience, Rob for
his typesetting expertise, Sharon for photography,
Katie Lloyd-Jones and Sam Kirby for maps, Louise
for the cover, David Price for proofreading, Dan
Richardson for indexing, Narrell Leffman and Kate
Davis for extra Basics research, and Tim Bremner
for the box on "Mountain biking in the High Atlas".

PUBLISHING INFORMATION

This sixth edition published April 2001 by
Rough Guides Ltd, 62–70 Shorts Gardens,
London WC2H 9AH. Reprinted May 2002
Distributed by the Penguin Group:
Penguin Books Ltd, 80 Strand, London WC2R ORL
Penguin Putnam, Inc. 375 Hudson Street, New York,
NY 10014, USA
Penguin Books Australia Ltd, 487 Maroondah Highway,
PO Box 257, Ringwood, Victoria 3134, Australia
Penguin Books Canada Ltd, 10 Alcorn Avenue, Toronto,
Ontario, Canada M4V 1E4
Penguin Books (NZ) Ltd, 182–190 Wairau Road,
Auckland 10, New Zealand
Typeset in Linotron Univers and Century Old Style to an
original design by Andrew Oliver.
Printed in England by Clays Ltd, St Ives Plc
Illustrations in Part One and Part Three by Edward Briant.

Illustrations on p.1 & p.547 by Henry Iles
© Mark Ellingham 2001
No part of this book may be reproduced in any form
without permission from the publisher except for the
quotation of brief passages in reviews.
656pp – Includes index
A catalogue record for this book is available from the
British Library
ISBN 1-85828-601-8

The publishers and authors have done their best
to ensure the accuracy and currency of all the
information in *The Rough Guide to Morocco*;
however, they can accept no responsibility
for any loss, injury, or inconvenience sustained by
any traveller as a result of information or advice
contained in the guide.

THE ROUGH GUIDE TO

Morocco

written and researched by

Mark Ellingham, Shaun McVeigh,
Daniel Jacobs, Hamish Brown
and Don Grisbrook

with additional contributions from

Tim Bremner, Dan Eitzen, Jon Marks, Peter Morris,

David Muddyman and Chris Overington

ROUGH
GUIDES

THE ROUGH GUIDES

TRAVEL GUIDES • PHRASEBOOKS • MUSIC AND REFERENCE GUIDES

 We set out to do something different when the first Rough Guide was published in 1982. Mark Ellingham, just out of university, was travelling in Greece. He brought along the popular guides of the day, but found they were all lacking in some way. They were either strong on ruins and museums but went on for pages without mentioning a beach or taverna. Or they were so conscious of the need to save money that they lost sight of Greece's cultural and historical significance. Also, none of the books told him anything about Greece's contemporary life – its politics, its culture, its people, and how they lived.

So with no job in prospect, Mark decided to write his own guidebook, one which aimed to provide practical information that was second to none, detailing the best beaches and the hottest clubs and restaurants, while also giving hard-hitting accounts of every sight, both famous and obscure, and providing up-to-the-minute information on contemporary culture. It was a guide that encouraged independent travellers to find the best of Greece, and was a great success, getting shortlisted for the Thomas Cook travel guide award,

and encouraging Mark, along with three friends, to expand the series.

The Rough Guide list grew rapidly and the letters flooded in, indicating a much broader readership than had been anticipated, but one which uniformly appreciated the Rough Guide mix of practical detail and humour, irreverence and enthusiasm. Things haven't changed. The same four friends who began the series are still the caretakers of the Rough Guide mission today: to provide the most reliable, up-to-date and entertaining information to independent-minded travellers of all ages, on all budgets.

We now publish more than 150 titles and have offices in London and New York. The travel guides are written and researched by a dedicated team of more than 100 authors, based in Britain, Europe, the USA and Australia. We have also created a unique series of phrasebooks to accompany the travel series, along with an acclaimed series of music guides, and a best-selling pocket guide to the Internet and World Wide Web. We also publish comprehensive travel information on our Web site:

www.roughguides.com

HELP US UPDATE

We've gone to a lot of effort to ensure that the sixth edition of *The Rough Guide to Morocco* is accurate and up-to-date. However, things change — places get "discovered", opening hours are notoriously fickle, restaurants and rooms raise prices or lower standards. If you feel we've got it wrong or left something out, we'd like to know, and if you can remember the address, the price, the time, the phone number, so much the better.

We'll credit all contributions, and send a copy of the next edition (or any other Rough Guide if you prefer) for the best letters. Please mark letters: "Rough Guide Morocco Update" and send to:
Rough Guides, 62–70 Shorts Gardens, London WC2H 9AH, or Rough Guides, 4th Floor, 345 Hudson St, New York, NY 10014.
Or send email to: mail@roughguides.co.uk
Online updates about this book can be found on Rough Guides' Web site at www.roughguides.com

THE AUTHORS AND CONTRIBUTORS

Hamish Brown is a mountain writer, guide and photographer, who has spent much of the past two decades walking and climbing in Morocco's Atlas Mountains.

Mark Ellingham originated the *Rough Guide* series and continues to work as Series Editor. His most recent book was the two-volume *Rough Guide to World Music*.

Dan Eitzen is an American writer, walker, and photographer, based in Agadir.

Don Grisbrook discovered *Rough Guides* when on the verge of retirement – and has injected the series with his extraordinary research skills ever since. He makes several trips to Morocco each year.

Daniel Jacobs has contributed to many *Rough Guides*, and is author of the titles on *Israel and the Palestinian Territories* and *Jerusalem*.

Jon Marks covers North Africa for the *Middle East Economic Digest*. He wrote the section on modern history and politics.

Shaun McVeigh co-wrote the first edition of this book and has since moved on from travel writing to the mysteries of jurisprudence, which he teaches in Brisbane, Australia.

Peter Morris works in banking, currently. He is author of *The Rough Guide to Tunisia* and wrote the section on Islam for this book.

David Muddyman wrote the piece on music in "Contexts". He is a London-based musician, playing mainly with the group Loop Guru.

Chris Overington is a naturalist and writer. He contributed the "Wildlife" overview and bird-watching feature-boxes.

READERS' LETTERS

As ever, research on this edition of *The Rough Guide to Morocco* has been helped enormously by readers who wrote in with comments, changes and discoveries. The letters we receive about Morocco are consistently the best of all those sent to Rough Guides – detailed and wonderfully generous in their sharing of knowledge and experiences.

A **thousand thanks** to the following: Sonia Alexandrian; Tamara Atkinson; Tom Bass; Irene and Rienzi Beckett; Jason Bedford; Ahdan Benelhadj; Vivien Billington; Tricia Brady; Andrew Bruce; Margaret Casserly; Jean Cobb; J.V. Connor; Bob Crittenden; Chris Davies; Isabel De Jesus; Tanya De Weymarn; Deborah Fink; Sam Grace; Tim Hayward; Phil Hodgkiss; Jimmy & Anneke Jansen; George Jones; Julie Jones; Anne Kay; Maureen Keenoy; John Kelly; J.E. Lafene; Abdelmoula Laghmir; Mohssine Laroussi; Chris Lawrence; Anthony Lawton; Peter Mann; Frank Marker; Duncan Matthews; Roger Mimo; Lahbib Naamani; George Packard; Robert Patterson; Catriona Picken; S.E. Powell; Gary Pulsifer; Alex Rankin; Alan Rhodes; Chloe Roberts; Chris Saffell; Anthony Simpson; Stephanie Sweet; Said Tazi; Tooria Haji Temsamani; Mohamed Temsamani; Mary Thale; Janet Warren; Mary Whelan; Catherine Wilde; John James Wood; Antony Woods; Chris Wright; Tom Wylie.

CONTENTS

Introduction x

PART ONE — BASICS — 1

Getting there from Britain and Ireland 3
Getting there from North America 14
Getting there from Australia & New Zealand 18
Travellers with disabilities 20
Visas and red tape 22
Costs and money 23
Health and insurance 27
Information, maps and trekking guides 30
Hustle, hassle, kids and guides 34
Security, the police and consulates 38

Getting around 39
Accommodation 49
Eating and drinking 52
Communications: post, phones and the media 57
Festivals: Ramadan, holidays and moussems 61
Sports and activities 65
Souks and Moroccan crafts 68
Mosques and monuments 70
Directory 72

PART TWO — THE GUIDE — 75

● CHAPTER 1: TANGIER, TETOUAN AND THE NORTHWEST 77–135

Tangier 79
Around Tangier 100
Asilah 102
Larache and around 107
Ancient Lixus 110
South towards Fes or Rabat 111

Ceuta 114
Tetouan 118
Tetouan beaches: Mdiq to Oued Laou 125
Chaouen 127
Ouezzane 133

● CHAPTER 2: THE MEDITERRANEAN COAST AND THE RIF 136–172

Chaouen to Al Hoceima 139
Ketama to Fes 142
Taza 144
Djebel Tazzeka 144
Taza to Oujda 149

Al Hoceima 150
Nador 155
Melilla 159
The Zegzel Gorge: Berkane and Saïdia 164
Oujda and around 166

● CHAPTER 3: MEKNES, FES AND THE MIDDLE ATLAS 173–267

Meknes 176
Volubilis and Moulay Idriss 191
Around Meknes 197
Fes 198
Sefrou and around 238
Immouzer du Kandar, Ifrane and Mischliffen 242
Azrou 245

Aïn Leuh and the waterfalls of Oum er Rbia 248
Azrou to Midelt and Er Rachidia 249
Azrou to Kasba Tadla 255
Beni Mellal 259
Cascades d'Ouzoud 262
Azilal to Marrakesh: Demnate 265

● CHAPTER 4: THE WEST COAST: FROM RABAT TO ESSAOUIRA 268–341

Kenitra to Rabat 269
Rabat 274
Salé 292
Rabat to Casablanca 295
Casablanca 299
Casablanca to Marrakesh: Settat 314

Casablanca to El Jadida 315
El Jadida 317
El Jadida to Safi 321
Safi 324
Essaouira 328
South to Agadir 339

● CHAPTER 5: MARRAKESH 342–379

History 343
Arrival and orientation 346
Transport 347
Accommodation 348
The Djemaa El Fna 352
The Koutoubia 353

The Souks and northern Medina 354
The Lower Medina, Saadian Tombs and
  Mellah 362
The gardens 370
Eating, drinking and nightlife 372
Listings 376

● CHAPTER 6: THE HIGH ATLAS 380–414

Ourika Valley and Oukaïmeden 383
Djebel Toubkal Massif 387
Tizi n'Test 399

Telouet and the Tizi n'Tichka 406
Marrakesh to Agadir: Tizi Maachou 410
Western High Atlas: Tichka Plateau 410

● CHAPTER 7: THE GREAT SOUTHERN OASIS ROUTES 415–470

Ouarzazate 416
Aït Benhaddou 423
South to Zagora: the Drâa oases 425
Zagora 427
Zagora to M'hamid 430
Desert pistes east and west from Zagora 433
The Skoura oasis 435
El Kelâa des Mgouna 438
Boumalne du Dadès 438
Djebel Sarhro 440
The Dadès Gorge 444

Tinerhir 446
The Todra Gorge 449
Beyond Todra: over the Atlas 451
Tinerhir to Er Rachidia and Erfoud 454
Er Rachidia 456
Meski and the Ziz valley 459
Erfoud 459
The dunes of Merzouga 462
Rissani and around 465
East to Figuig 467

● CHAPTER 8: AGADIR, THE SOUSS AND ANTI-ATLAS 471–528

Agadir 473
Inezgane 485
The Coast to Cap Rhir 485
Paradise Valley and Immouzer 488
Massa lagoon 490
Taroudannt 491

Taliouine and Djebel Sirwa 498
The Tata circuit 502
Tiznit 509
Tafraoute 513
Tiznit to Goulimine and Sidi Ifni 520
Goulimine 523

• CHAPTER 9: THE DEEP SOUTH AND WESTERN SAHARA 529–546

Goulimine to Tan Tan 531
Tan Tan 531
A loop through Smara 534
Tan Tan to Laayoune 538

Laayoune 539
Laayoune to Dakhla 543
The road to Mauritania 545

PART THREE CONTEXTS 547

History 549
Chronology 566
Islam 569
Wildlife 573
Music 580
Moroccan storytelling 590

Index 626

Writers on Morocco 599
Books: further reading 607
Glossary of Moroccan terms 616
Glossary of street names 618
Language 621

LIST OF MAPS

Morocco	x
Major roads and rail network	xii–xiii
Temperature chart	xiv
Chapter divisions map	75
Tangier, Tetouan and the Northwest	78
Tangier	82–83
Tangier: The Medina and Kasbah	87
Asilah	103
Larache	108
Ceuta	115
Tetouan	120–121
Chaouen	128
The Mediterranean Coast and the Rif	136–137
Taza	145
Al Hoceima	151
Nador	156
Melilla	160
Oujda	167
Meknes, Fes and the Middle Atlas	174–175
Meknes	178–179
Meknes: Ville Nouvelle	180
Meknes: Medina	186
Volubilis	193
Fes Ville Nouvelle	200–201
Around Bab Boujeloud	206
Fes El Bali	210–211
Around the Kairaouine Mosque	219
Fes El Djedid	228
Sefrou	239
Azrou	246
Midelt	251
Beni Mellal	260
The West Coast: From Rabat to Essaouira	270–271
Rabat	276–277
Kasbah des Oudaïas	282
Chellah: The Sanctuary	287
Salé Medina	293
Mohammedia	298
Casablanca	300–301
El Jadida	318
Safi	325
Essaouira	330–331
Marrakesh	344–345
Marrakesh: Medina Hotels & Restaurants	349
The Souks	355
Marrakesh: Lower Medina	363
The High Atlas	381
Toubkal Massif	392–393
Western High Atlas	
Tichka Plateau	412–413
The Great Southern Oasis Routes	416–417
Ouarzazate	420–421
Zagora	428
Skoura Kasbahs	436
Boumalne du Dadès	439
Djebel Sarhro	441
Tinerhir	447
Tinerhir and Todra Palmeries	449
Over the Atlas: Beyond Todra and Dades	452
Er Rachidia	458
Erfoud	460
Tafilalt and the roads to Merzouga	463
Agadir, the Souss and High Atlas	472
Agadir	474–475
Taroudannt	492–493
Djebel Sirwa (Siroua) Trek	501
Tata	503
Akka Oasis	505
Aït Herbil	506
Souk Ifrane and Ifrane de l'Anti-Atlas	508
Tiznit	510
Tafraoute	515
Around Tafraoute: The Ameln Valley	517
Sidi Ifni	521
Goulimine	524
The Deep South and Western Sahara	530
Tan Tan	532
Smara	536
Laayoune	540

MAP SYMBOLS

Railway	★ Bus/taxi Stop	◉ Eating place
Motorway	∴ Ruins	▣ Accommodation
Road	▲ Tower	Lighthouse
Pedestrianized road	∩ Arch	ⓘ Tourist office
Track/trail	Hill	⊠ Post office
Footpath	☾ Dunes	⭕ Stadium
Ferry route	Cave	Building
Waterway	▲ Peak	Church
Chapter division boundary	Mountain range	Mosque
International borders	Spring	Christian cemetery
Wall	Waterfall	Muslim cemetery
Points of interest	Oasis	Jewish cemetery
Viewpoint	⚠ Campsite	Park
Ⓟ Parking	Refuge hut	Beach

INTRODUCTION

For Westerners, **Morocco** holds an immediate and enduring fascination. Though just an hour's ride on the ferry from Spain, it seems at once very far from Europe, with a culture – Islamic and deeply traditional – that is almost wholly unfamiliar. Throughout the country, despite the years of French and Spanish colonial rule and the presence of modern and cosmopolitan cities like Rabat or Casablanca, a more distant past constantly makes its presence felt. **Fes**, perhaps the most beautiful of all Arab cities, maintains a life still rooted in medieval times, when a Moroccan empire stretched from Senegal to northern Spain, while in the mountains of the **Atlas** and the **Rif**, it's still possible to draw up tribal maps of the Berber population. As a backdrop to all this, the country's physical make-up is also extraordinary: from a Mediterranean coast, through four mountain ranges, to the empty sand and scrub of the Sahara.

All of which makes **travel** here an intense and rewarding experience. It's not always easy-going – there can be problems in coming to terms with your privileged position as a tourist, and in dealing with self-appointed guides eager to offer their services. However, in recent years the worst of the hustlers have been cleared off the streets (anyone who visited in the early 1990s will be amazed at the change) and the unofficial guides you encounter are fewer and more discreet. If you find things too much of a struggle, you can take refuge in low-key resorts like Essaouira or Asilah, or in the more cosmopolitan holiday destination of Agadir, built very much in the image of its Spanish counterparts. Or you could make things easy on yourself with a small-group tour, travelling by Landrover or going on an organized trek.

But Morocco is really an ideal place for independent travel. A week's hiking in the Atlas, a journey through the southern oases or into the pre-Sahara, or leisured strolls around Tangier, Fes or Marrakesh – once you adapt to a different way of life, all your time will be well spent. It's also a safe and politically stable country to visit: the death in 1999 of King Hassan II, the Arab world's longest serving leader, was followed by an easy transition to his son, Mohammed VI. And it's difficult for any traveller to go for long without running into Morocco's equally powerful tradition of hospitality, generosity and openness. This is a country people return to again and again.

Regions

Geographically, the country divides into four basic zones: the **coast**, Mediterranean and Atlantic; the great cities of the **plains**; the **Rif** and **Atlas** mountains; and the oases and desert of the pre- and fully-fledged **Sahara**. With two or three weeks – even two or three months – you can't expect to cover all of this, though it's easy enough (and highly recommended) to take in something of each aspect.

You are unlikely to miss the **mountains**, in any case. The three ranges of the Atlas, with the Rif a kind of extension in the north, cut right across the interior – physical and historical barriers, and inhabited for the most part by the indigenous Moroccan **Berbers**. Contrary to general preconceptions, it is actually the Berbers who make up most of the population (only around ten percent of Moroccans are "pure" Arabs) although with the shift to the industrialized cities, such distinctions are becoming less and less significant.

A more current distinction, perhaps, is the legacy of Morocco's colonial occupation over the fifty-odd years before it reasserted its independence in 1956. The colonized country was divided into **Spanish** and **French** zones – the former contained Tetouan and the Rif, the Mediterranean and the northern Atlantic coasts, and parts of the Western Sahara; the latter comprised the plains and the main cities (Fes, Marrakesh, Casablanca and Rabat), as well as the Atlas. It was the French, who ruled their "protectorate" more closely, who had the most lasting effect on Moroccan culture, Europeanizing the cities to a strong degree and firmly imposing their language, which is spoken today by all educated Moroccans (after Moroccan Arabic or the three local Berber languages).

Highlights

The attractions of the individual regions are discussed in the chapter introductions. Broadly speaking, **the coast** is best enjoyed in the north at **Tangier**, beautiful and still shaped by its old "international" port status, **Asilah** and **Larache**, and in the south at **El Jadida**, at **Essaouira**, perhaps the most easy-going resort, or at remote **Sidi Ifni**. **Agadir**, the main package tour resort, is less worthwhile – but a functional enough base for exploration.

Inland, where the real interest of Morocco lies, the outstanding cities are **Fes** and **Marrakesh**. The great imperial capitals of the country's various dynasties, they are almost unique in the Arab world for the chance they offer to witness some city life which, in patterns and appearance, remains in large part medieval. For monuments, Fes is the highlight, though Marrakesh, the "beginning of the south", is for most visitors the more enjoyable and exciting.

Travel in the **south** – roughly beyond a line drawn between Casablanca and Meknes – is, on the whole, easier and more relaxing than in the sometimes frenetic north. This is certainly true of the **mountain ranges**. The **Rif**, which can feel disturbingly

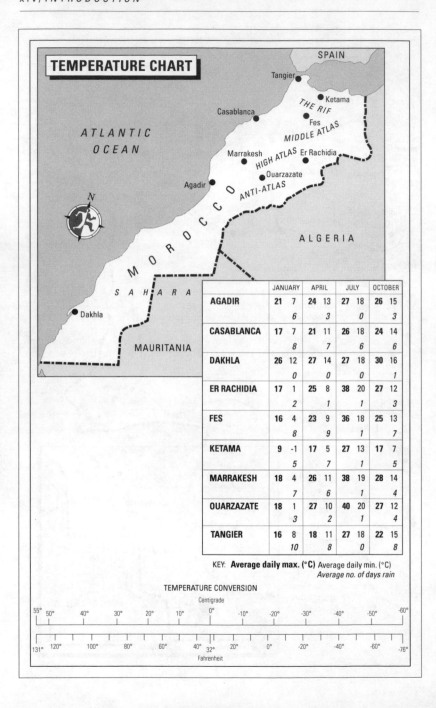

TEMPERATURE CHART

	JANUARY		APRIL		JULY		OCTOBER	
AGADIR	**21**	7	**24**	13	**27**	18	**26**	15
		6		*3*		*0*		*3*
CASABLANCA	**17**	7	**21**	11	**26**	18	**24**	14
		8		*7*		*6*		*6*
DAKHLA	**26**	12	**27**	14	**27**	18	**30**	16
		0		*0*		*0*		*1*
ER RACHIDIA	**17**	1	**25**	8	**38**	20	**27**	12
		2		*1*		*1*		*3*
FES	**16**	4	**23**	9	**36**	18	**25**	13
		8		*9*		*1*		*7*
KETAMA	**9**	-1	**17**	5	**27**	13	**17**	7
		5		*7*		*1*		*5*
MARRAKESH	**18**	4	**26**	11	**38**	19	**28**	14
		7		*6*		*1*		*4*
OUARZAZATE	**18**	1	**27**	10	**40**	20	**27**	12
		3		*2*		*1*		*4*
TANGIER	**16**	8	**18**	11	**27**	18	**22**	15
		10		*8*		*0*		*8*

KEY: **Average daily max. (°C)** Average daily min. (°C)
Average no. of days rain

TEMPERATURE CONVERSION

Centigrade

55° 50° 40° 30° 20° 10° 0° -10° -20° -30° -40° -50° -60°

131° 120° 100° 80° 60° 40° 32° 20° 0° -20° -40° -60° -76°

Fahrenheit

STATISTICS

Morocco's area of 710,000 square kilometres is as great as that of France, Spain or Italy. The population – over half of which is under 20 years of age – is around 30 million, a dramatic increase compared with just eight million at independence in 1956.

---

anarchic, is really for hardened travellers, only **Chaouen**, on its periphery, could be counted a "holiday spot". But the **Atlas ranges** (Middle, High and Anti) are beautiful and accessible.

Hiking in the **High Atlas**, especially around North Africa's highest peak, **Djebel Toubkal**, is in fact something of a growth industry. Even if you are no more than a casual walker, it's worth considering, with summer treks possible at all levels of experience and altitude. And, despite inroads made by commercialization, it remains essentially "undiscovered" – like the Alps must have been in the nineteenth century.

Equally exploratory in mood are the great **southern routes** beyond – and across – the Atlas, amid the **oases** of the pre-Sahara. Major routes here can be travelled by bus, minor ones by rented car or local taxi, the really remote ones by four-wheel-drive vehicles or by getting lifts on local *camions* (lorries), sharing space with the market produce and livestock.

The oases, around **Tinerhir**, **Zagora** and **Erfoud**, or (for the committed) **Tata** or **Figuig**, are classic images of the Arab world, vast palmeries stretching into desert horizons. Equally memorable is the architecture that they share with the Atlas – bizarre and fabulous *pisé* (mud) **kasbahs** and **ksour**, with Gothic-looking turrets and multi-patterned walls.

Further south, you can follow a route through the **Western Sahara** all the way down to Dakhla, just 20km short of the Tropic of Cancer, where the weather is scorching even in midwinter.

Climate

As far as the **climate** goes, it would be better to visit the south – or at least the desert routes – outside **midsummer**, when for most of the day it's far too hot for casual exploration, especially if you're dependent on public transport. But July and August, the hottest months, can be wonderful on the coast, and in the mountains, there are no set rules.

Spring, which comes late by European standards (around April to May), is perhaps the best overall time, with a summer climate in the south and in the mountains, and water warm enough to swim in on both the Mediterranean and Atlantic coasts. **Winter** can be perfect by day in the south, though be warned that desert nights can get very cold – a major consideration if you're staying in the cheaper hotels, which rarely have heating. If you're planning to **hike** in the **mountains**, it's best to keep to the months from April to October unless you have some experience of snow conditions.

Weather conditions apart, the **Islamic religious calendar** and its related festivals will have the most seasonal effect on your travel. The most important factor is **Ramadan**, the month of daytime fasting; this can be a problem for transport, and especially hiking, though the festive evenings do much to compensate. See "Festivals" in the *Basics* section following for details of its timing, as well as that of other festivals.

PART ONE

THE

BASICS

EVITEZ LA FATIGUE
ET LES RISQUES
D'UN LONG VOYAGE

Maroc

FAITES VOS CALCULS ET PRENEZ LE TRAIN.

You tell me you are going to Fes.
Now, if you say you are going to Fes,
that means you are not going.
But I happen to know that you are going to Fes.
Why have you lied to me, you who are my friend?

Moroccan saying quoted in Paul Bowles' *The Spider's House*

GETTING THERE FROM BRITAIN AND IRELAND

The simplest way to get to Morocco is, of course, to fly. There are scheduled flights from Britain direct to Tangier (2hr 50min), Casablanca (3hr 15min) and Marrakesh (3hr 40min) and connections from Casablanca to other Moroccan airports. Charters generally go to Tangier and Agadir. From Ireland you can only fly direct on charters, though scheduled routes via London and other European cities offer a much wider choice of destinations and fares. Alternatively, you can travel overland (or fly) to France, Spain or Gibraltar and pick up a ferry to Morocco. All-in package deals are worth considering too, either for specialist holidays or off-season bargains.

BUYING A TICKET

For the best deals on **fares** to Morocco, contact a **flight agent** – see the box on p.4. You should also check the ads in the travel pages of weekend national newspapers, local listings magazines such as *Time Out* in London and *City Life* in Manchester, and Teletext and Ceefax for special deals and last-minute offers. The **Internet** often has good deals, and Web sites worth looking at include *www.cheapflights.co.uk*, *www.ebookers.com*, *www.lastminute.com* and *www.bargainholidays.com* Whoever you buy from, check that they belong to the travel industry bodies ABTA or IATA, so that you'll be covered if the agency goes bust before you receive your ticket. **Students** and those under 26 can often get discounts through agents such as Campus and STA.

High season for Morocco flights is Christmas/New Year, Easter and July/August, when fares for charter flights can double and seats become hard to find. Fares quoted here give the range you can expect to find for return tickets during the year and include airport departure taxes, currently £20 from the UK and around £7 from Morocco.

SCHEDULED FLIGHTS

The cheapest **scheduled flights** have fixed, unchangeable dates and demand a minimum stay

AIRLINES

Air France ☎0845/0845 111, *www.airfrance.co.uk* Several daily flights to Casablanca, and also less frequently to Agadir, Oujda, Rabat, Marrakesh and Tangier, all via Paris.

EasyJet ☎0070/600 0000, *www.easyjet.com* Twice daily flights from Luton to Málaga.

GB Airways contact British Airways ☎0845/773 3377, *www.britishairways.com* This BA franchisee flies daily from Gatwick to Casablanca, three times a week to Marrakesh and twice a week to Tangier, and can be booked through their Travel Shops nationwide.

Go ☎0845/605 4321, *www.go-fly.com* Daily flights from Stansted to Málaga.

KLM ☎08705/074 074, *www.klm.com* Casablanca via Amsterdam with a very wide choice of connections from British airports through their subsidiary, KLM UK.

Royal Air Maroc (RAM) ☎020/7439 4361 or 7439 8854, *www.royalairmaroc.com/ver_en/index.htm* Daily flights from London Heathrow to Casablanca and twice weekly to Tangier. Also twice weekly from Stansted to Marrakesh. There are daily connections from Casablanca to Agadir and Fes, and less frequently to Essaouira, Laayoune, Ouarzazate and Oujda. RAM also has flights via Paris to all the above airports plus Rabat.

Sabena ☎0845/758 1291, *www.sabena.com* Indirect flights to Casablanca via Brussels.

of one Saturday night and a maximum of one month. Others allow more flexibility with stays of up to three months and the option of flying into one airport and out of another.

Only two airlines have direct scheduled flights; **Royal Air Maroc (RAM)**, and the British Airways franchisee **GB Airways**, whose services are generally a cut above both RAM and regular BA flights, with prices from London ranging from £230 to £350 to Tangier and Casablanca, and £210 to £400 for Marrakesh, depending on season. Add-on flights are available from various UK regional airports.

An alternative is to take an **indirect flight** via Europe and if you are flying from a UK airport other than Heathrow, Gatwick or Stansted, this can turn out cheaper and easier than changing planes in London. The most obvious route is via **Paris** which has many more connections with Morocco than

London does, and both **Royal Air Maroc** and **Air France** have several daily flights to the major Moroccan cities, and weekly flights to smaller ones. Prices with Air France to Casablanca via Paris start at £335.

CHARTER FLIGHTS

The main Moroccan destinations for British-run charter flights are **Tangier** in the north and **Agadir** in the south, although a few operators also offer **Marrakesh**. The cheapest flights are invariably from London but there are also direct charter flights from Manchester, Birmingham, Newcastle and Glasgow. If you're lucky, outside the high season you might find return flights to Tangier or Agadir for as low as £120–170 return. In peak season you should expect to pay £240–300 return – and you may well have problems finding a seat.

FLIGHT AGENTS

Alecoss Travel, 3a Camden Rd, London NW1 (☎020/7267 2092). Discount fares on scheduled flights to Morocco.

North South Travel, Moulsham Mill Centre, Parkway, Chelmsford, Essex (☎01245/608291). Friendly, competitive travel agency, offering discounted fares worldwide – profits are used to support projects in the developing world, especially the promotion of sustainable tourism.

STA Travel, www.statravel.co.uk 86 Old Brompton Rd, London SW7; 117 Euston Rd, London NW1; 38 Store St London WC1 (☎020/7361 6262); 27 Forrest Road, Edinburgh (☎0131/226 7747); 30 Upper Kirkgate, Aberdeen (☎0122/465 8222); 38 North St, Brighton (☎01273/728 282); 25 Queens Rd, Bristol (☎0117/929 4399); 184 Byres Rd, Glasgow (☎0141/338 6000); 38 Sidney St, Cambridge (☎01223/366966); 78 Bold Street, Liverpool (☎0151/707 1123); 75 Deansgate, Manchester (☎0161/834 0668); 88 Vicar Lane, Leeds (☎0113/244 9212); 9 St Mary's Place, Newcastle-upon-Tyne (☎0191/233 2111); 36 George St, Oxford (☎01865/792800); on university campuses throughout Britain. Worldwide specialists in low-cost flights and tours for students and under-26s, though other customers welcome.

Trailfinders, www.trailfinders.co.uk 1 Threadneedle Street, London EC2 (☎020/7628 7628); 194 Kensington High St, London, W8

(☎020/7938 3939); 58 Deansgate, Manchester (☎0161/839 6969); 254–284 Sauchiehall St, Glasgow (☎0141/353 2224); 22–24 The Priory, Queensway, Birmingham (☎0121/236 1234); 48 Corn St, Bristol (☎0117/929 9000). One of the best-informed and most efficient agents.

Travel Bug, www.flynow.com 597 Cheetham Hill Rd, Manchester (☎0161/721 4000); 125a Gloucester Road, London SW7 (☎020/7835 2000). Large range of discounted tickets.

Travel Cuts, www.travelcuts.co.uk 295a Regent Street, London W1 (☎020/7255 2082); 33 Prince's Square, London W2 (☎020/7792 3770). British branch of Canada's main youth and student travel specialist.

UsitCampus, www.usitcampus.co.uk 52 Grosvenor Gardens, London SW1 (☎020/7730 3402); 541 Bristol Rd, Selly Oak, Birmingham (☎0121/414 1848); 61 Ditchling Rd, Brighton (☎01273/570226); 37–39 Queen's Rd, Clifton, Bristol (☎0117/929 2494); 5 Emmanuel St, Cambridge (☎01223/324283); 53 Forrest Rd, Edinburgh (☎0131/668 3303); 122 George St, Glasgow (☎0141/553 1818); 166 Deansgate, Manchester (☎0161/833 2046); 105–106 St Aldates, Oxford (☎01865/484730); national call centre ☎0870/240 1010. Student/youth travel specialists, with branches also in YHA shops and on university campuses all over Britain.

UsitCouncil, 28a Poland St, London W1V 3DB (☎020/7437 7767). Flights and student discounts.

UK SPECIALIST AND PACKAGE OPERATORS

Morocco is covered by a variety of UK travel agents and operators, offering everything from straight **package holidays**, through mountain **trekking** or **desert overland "exploration" safaris** in customized trucks and Landrovers, to **tailor-made itineraries**, with flights, car rental and hotels booked to your specifications.

Prices start from £350 for packages, depending on length of visit, season and standard of accommodation.

MOROCCO SPECIALISTS

Best of Morocco, Seend Park, Seend, Wilts SN12 6NZ (☎01380/828533, *www.morocco-travel.com*). One of the best Moroccan specialists, with accommodation in quality hotels and upmarket "designer" trekking in the High Atlas and Djebel Sarhro. Knowledgeable about alternatives to the traditional tourist traps. The owner's son, Max Lawrence, is on hand at their Marrakesh office to help clients in person.

CLM ("Morocco Made to Measure"), 69 Knightsbridge, London SW1X 7RA (☎020/7235 0123) This reliable and highly flexible agency, run by the redoubtable Annie Austin, will arrange flights and tailor holidays from a wealth of personal knowledge. Accommodation on offer ranges from the country's top hotels, through individual gems like the *Villa Maroc* in Essaouira, to more modest, out of the way *auberges*.

Naturally Morocco Ltd, Hill House, Llansteffan, Carmarthen SA33 5JG (☎01267/241999, *www.naturallymorocco.com*). Ecologically oriented tours of Morocco based at Taroudannt, with vegetarian food if desired and a variety of special services available, including Arabic, Berber or French tuition and even Moroccan cookery lessons.

Panorama, Panorama House, Vale Road, Portslade Sussex BN41 1HP (☎01273/427777, *www.panoramaholidays.co.uk*). Package holidays from a company well established in Tunisia, where they have an excellent reputation, now offering a Moroccan brochure too, with holidays based at Agadir and/or Marrakesh, and optional extensions to Essaouira, Ouarzazate and Taroudannt.

TREKKING AND BIKING TOURS

Most trekking companies run High Atlas tours in spring, summer and autumn, which are fine for the averagely fit walker and require no actual climbing. In winter these areas are for experienced hikers only, and alternatives further south such as the Djebel Sarhro, Anti-Atlas (Tafraoute region) and Djebel Sirwa are offered instead. Prices range from £500 to £800, depending on accommodation and season, including flights.

AMIS (Atlas Mountain Information Services), 26 Kircaldy Road, Burntisland, Fife KY3 9HQ (☎01592/873546). This small agency is run by Hamish Brown, author of the High Atlas chapter in this book. He leads prearranged treks and climbing trips (summer/winter) in most Atlas areas, and occasional bird/flower tours.

Acacia Adventure Holidays, Lower Ground Floor, 23A Craven Terrace, London W2 3QH (☎020/7706 4700). Offers a fifteen-day Moroccan Experience tour and a fifteen-day High Atlas Trek.

Exodus Expeditions, 9 Weir Rd, London SW12 0LT (☎020/8675 5550, *www.exodus.co.uk*). One-, two- and three-week High Atlas, Anti-Atlas and Djebel Sarhro treks. Highlight is the three-week "Atlas Grand Traverse", a crossing of the Middle and High Atlas ranges (summer only). Also two-week truck tours and one-week mountain-bike trips. Recently introduced is the one-week ascent of Djebel Toubkal (April–Oct).

Explore Worldwide, 1 Frederick St, Aldershot, Hants GU11 1LQ (☎01252/319448, *www.explore.co.uk*). An imaginative range of treks including fifteen days in the High Atlas or Djebel Sarhro. Also desert and Imperial City truck tours.

Mountain Treks, 125 Coombes Lane, Longbridge, Birmingham B31 4QU (☎0121/680 3507, *www.mountaintreks.co.uk*). Offers various two-week treks, and can arrange camel riding and whitewater rafting, plus surfing and mountain-biking holidays.

Ramblers Holidays, PO Box 43, Welwyn Garden City, Herts AL8 6PQ (☎01707/331133, *info@ramblersholidays.co.uk*). A long-established operator offering hiking rather than trekking holidays, as well as sightseeing tours. Options include a two-week Atlas hike, a two-week Imperial Cities tour, and eleven days in Chaouen and the Rif.

Continued overleaf

UK SPECIALIST AND PACKAGE OPERATORS continued

TREKKING AND BIKING TOURS continued

Sherpa Expeditions, 131a Heston Rd, Hounslow, Middlesex TW5 0RD (☎020/8577 2717, *www.sherpa-walking-holidays.co.uk*). Choice of three two-week tours in the High Atlas (Toubkal area and little-explored Mgoun Massif), and Djebel Sarhro, plus a week-long self-guided trip from Asni in the Djebel Toubkal.

Walks Worldwide, 25 Mt Carmel St, Derby DE23 6TB (☎01332/230883, *www.walksworldwide.com*). Fifteen-day treks in the High Atlas, plus an easier eight-day option suitable for those travelling with kids.

Wildcat Bike Tours, Stirling Enterprise Park, Unit 102, John Player Building, Stirling FK7 7RP (☎01786/464333, *www.wildcat-bike-tours.co.uk*). Eight- to fifteen-day mountain-biking tours.

Wilderness Wheels, Deneside, Ravenworth, Gateshead, Tyne and Wear NE11 0HQ (☎0191/496 0869, *www.wildernesswheels.com*); c/o Peter Gray, BP 278, Ouarzazate 45000 (☎04/488 5863). One- and seven-day trailbiking tours in the desert and High Atlas, based at Ouarzazate. Bikes, meals and accommodation included (motorcycle licence required).

Worldwide Journeys, 25–27 Vanston Place, London SW6 1AZ (☎020/7381 8638, *wwj@wjournex.demon.co.uk*). Fairly upmarket operator which runs High Atlas and Djebel Sarhro treks, plus desert safaris as part of tailor-made itineraries.

OVERLAND EXPEDITION TOURS

Discover, Timbers, Oxted Rd, Godstone, Surrey RH9 8AD (☎01883/744392, *www.discover.ltd.uk/net*).Discover runs three or four Morocco tours each year, taking in some Atlas trekking and overland transit down to Zagora and the desert. They have (very beautifully) restored an old kasbah above Imlil as an expedition base and field study centre.

Dragoman Overland Expeditions, 63 Camp Green, Kenton Rd, Debenham, Stowmarket, Suffolk IP14 6LA (☎01728/861133, *www.dragoman.co.uk*). Trips from three to thirty weeks overland through Morocco to West and East Africa.

Encounter Overland, 267 Old Brompton Rd, London SW5 9JA (☎020/7370 6845, *www.encounter-overland.com*). A fifteen-day tour of Morocco including Fes, High Atlas, Todra Gorge, Meski, Zagora and Marrakesh, starting and ending in Casablanca; or Morocco as part of a thirteen-week overland trip to West Africa.

Guerba, Wessex House, 40 Station Rd, Westbury, Wiltshire BA13 3JN (☎01373/826611, *www.guerba.co.uk*). One- and two-week tours in small buses using budget hotels: Morocco Deserts and Mountains (Mar–Oct); Trekking in the High Atlas (July–Sept); Imperial Cities (Oct–May); eight-day Essential Morocco visiting Fes, Rabat and Essaouira (May–Oct).

Headwater Holidays, 146 London Rd, Northwich, Cheshire CW9 5HH (☎01606/813333, *www.headwater.com*). Easy walking trips based on Marrakesh and Ouarzazate oriented to local culture and nature.

The Imaginative Traveller, 14 Barley Mow Passage, London W4 4PH (☎020/8742 8612, *www.imaginative-traveller.com*). A "soft" adventure operator, offering hikes, camel treks and jeep safaris in the High Atlas and the desert.

Tribes Travel, 7 The Business Centre, Earl Soham, Woodbridge, Suffolk IP13 7SA (☎01728/685971, *www.tribes.co.uk*). Winner of Tourism Concern's award for "most responsible tour operator" offering a week's hiking and camel trekking in the desert, or a two-week "Moroccan Summer" taking in Fes and Marrakesh as well as the Atlas and the Sahara.

Nomadic Expeditions, 263 Barkham Rd, Wokingham, Berkshire RG41 4BY (☎0118/978 0800, *www.nomadic.co.uk*). A small firm running overland tours in Morocco and West Africa with groups of six to eighteen people. Journeys include a two- or three-week "Morocco Explorer", starting and finishing in Casablanca, and a five-week "Nomadic

Meets Nomadic" desert trip from Morocco through the Western Sahara and Mauritania to Senegal.

Steppes East, Castle Eaton, Cricklade, Wiltshire, SN6 6JU (☎01285/810267, *www.steppeseast.co.uk*). A few set itineraries such as "Call of the Coast" to Essaouira, Immouzer des Ida Outanane and Taroudannt; "Journey Across the Atlas" from Marrakesh to Taroudannt. Also tailor-made and special interest holidays (notably textiles and embroidery). Worth sending off for the current brochure.

Top Deck Tours 131/135 Earls Court Rd, London SW5 9RH (☎020/7244 8641, *www.topdecktravel.co.uk*). Coach/camping tours of Morocco; nine days starting and finishing at Casablanca. The double-decker buses have been pensioned off, but the tours are still a perennial favourite with Australians in Europe. Age limit 18–38.

Travel Bag Adventures, 15 Turk St, Alton, Hampshire GU34 1AG (☎01420/541007, *www. travelbag-adventures.co.uk*). Small groups, off the beaten track around Taroudannt and Merzouga. Four trips a year, of eight–fifteen days each.

BIRD-WATCHING TOURS

Birdquest, Two Jays, Kemple End, Stonyhurst, Lancashire BB7 9QY (☎01254/826317). Upmarket bird-watching with winter and/or spring tours visiting the classic birding sites from Larache to Erfoud, and staying in the best hotels.

Naturetrek, Cherlton Mill, Cheriton, Alresford, Hants SO24 0NG (☎01962/733051,

www.naturetrek.co.uk). Four trips a year: High Atlas – birds and flowers (end of May; 2 weeks) and Southern Morocco – birds (February, March and September; 10 days).

Country Connoisseurs, 2 Wey Lodge Close, Liphook, Hants GU30 7DE (☎01428/727929, *www.odspain.com*). Tailor-made bird-watching holidays.

MAINSTREAM PACKAGE TOUR OPERATORS

The advantage of mainstream operators rests in getting a good-value deal on flight plus resort accommodation; some can offer excellent rates, too, on stays at top hotels like the Mamounia in Marrakesh, El Minzah in Tangier, and Palais Jamai in Fes. The best of the operators include:

Aardvark Safaris (☎01980/849160, *www.aardvarksafaris.com*). Imperial cities tours, High Atlas treks, Landrover safaris, beach holidays and sea fishing. For "discriminating clients".

Abercrombie & Kent (☎020/7730 9600, *www.abercrombiekent.co.uk*). Major hotels and "Morocco à la carte". Upmarket.

British Airways (☎0870/242 4243, *www.baholidays.co.uk*). City breaks to Marrakesh (three nights or more) in 3- and 4-star hotels.

Cadogan Holidays (☎023/8082 8304, *www.cadoganholidays.com*). Tangier, Marrakesh, Agadir, Essaouira, Ouarzazate. Moderate/upmarket.

CVTravel (☎020/7581 0851, *cv.travel@dial.pipex.com*). Upmarket and often extraordinary villa rentals.

Hayes & Jarvis (☎0870/89 89 890, *www.Hayes-Jarvis.com*). Marrakesh, Taroudannt and Agadir; southern and "Imperial City" tours. Recommended by several readers. Moderate.

Martin Randall, 10 Barley Mow Passage, London W4 4PH (☎020/8742 3355, *info@martinrandall.co.uk*). Upmarket escorted cultural tours focusing on art, architecture, archeology and music.

Prestige (☎01425/480400). Marrakesh, Agadir, Essaouira, Taroudannt and Ourgane. Moderate.

Travelscene (☎0870/777 4445, *www.travelscene.co.uk*). Short breaks to Marrakesh, Casablanca, Fes and Rabat. Moderate.

Looking for a charter fare, it is worth keeping an eye out for full **package holidays**, which may work out little more expensive than a flight-only option. See pp.5–7 for details of tour operators.

VIA SPAIN

Cheap flights to Spain are usually easier to come by than those to Morocco, especially if you want to travel from one of the smaller regional British airports. Fares can drop as low as £75–100 return to Málaga or Almería – the best destinations for travelling on to Morocco.

If you get a flight to **Málaga**, you've a choice of onward travel to Morocco: a ferry direct to **Melilla** or a bus trip down to **Algeciras** and the crossings to **Ceuta** or **Tangier** (see box on pp.12–13 for prices). From the airport, take the train into Málaga (20–30min; service starts at 7.30am), where a bus (there's no direct train) from the terminal opposite the train station makes the journey to Algeciras in 3–5 hours depending on traffic. Iberia flies from Málaga and Almería to Melilla, while Regional Air Lines runs flights from Málaga to Casablanca, though a direct flight to Morocco from the UK will cost somewhat less than buying a flight from Britain to Spain and then another one across to Morocco, and this option is really only for those interested in seeing Andalucian-Moorish architecture as well as its Moroccan counterpart.

If you fly to **Almería**, you'll probably want to make use of the direct ferry to Melilla. For **more on the crossings**, see "Ferry Routes and Agents" on pp.12–13.

VIA GIBRALTAR/LA LINEA

Gibraltar is another possible starting point for travelling on to Morocco. Scheduled return flights from London on GB Airways (handled by British Airways – see p.3) go for around £190–260 including tax and depending on season, and there are also charter flights from major regional British airports. From Gibraltar, **ferries** sail direct to Tangier twice a week, or you can take a local bus to pick up a ferry from Algeciras, half an hour round the bay (see the "Ferry Routes and Agents" box on pp.12–13).

FLIGHTS FROM IRELAND

Charter flights direct from Ireland to Morocco are operated by Sunway Travel (see box opposite)

with prices from IR£199–399 (€250–500), depending on season. There are no direct scheduled flights, but you have a number of choices for an **indirect flight**. You can fly from Dublin or Belfast to **London** with British Airways to connect with the GB Airways flight to Casablanca, or with Aer Lingus or British Midland to connect with the Royal Air Maroc flight (see p.3 for details of flights out of London). Alternatively, you can go with Air France from Dublin or Belfast to **Paris** to connect with that airline's onward flights to Morocco, or with Aer Lingus from Dublin or British Airways from Belfast to connect with Royal Air Maroc flights. The advantage of the Paris route is that it gives you a wider choice of destinations in Morocco, with daily RAM flights to Casablanca, Marrakesh and Rabat, plus two or more weekly to Agadir, Fes, Ouarzazate, Oujda and Tangier, and several daily Air France flights to Casablanca, plus others to Agadir, Oujda, Rabat, Marrakesh and Tangier. Alternative routes include Dublin to Casablanca via **Brussels** with Sabena (though it's a tight 40-minute connection), or via **Madrid** with Iberia. You could also fly from Dublin to **Málaga** with Iberia and travel on to Morocco from there (see above), or get a through air ticket to Melilla or Casablanca with Iberia, changing planes at Málaga.

As far as organized tours are concerned, Ireland does not have as wide a choice of operators as Britain, though many of the British-based operators listed on pp.5–7, will also accept bookings from the Republic. For details on specialist Irish operators see box opposite.

BY TRAIN

London to Morocco by train and ferry takes the best part of three days, but it's a great trip if you have the time to stop en route and take in something of France and Spain. Paris, the Pyrenees, Madrid, Seville, Córdoba and Granada all lie pretty much on the route. Córdoba's Great Mosque and Granada's Alhambra are arguably the two finest achievements of medieval Moorish architecture, and a visit to the classic cities of Andalucia would fit very well with a trip to Morocco. However, unless you are under 26 (the age qualification for discount BIJ tickets or rail passes), you will probably end up paying a higher fare than for a flight.

The cheapest train departures (to Europe by ferry) are from London's **Victoria Station**, with faster but pricier services available via the

AIRLINES, FLIGHT AGENTS & SPECIALIST OPERATORS

AIRLINES

Aer Lingus, Northern Ireland reservations ☎0645/737 747; 40–41 O'Connell St, Dublin 1; 13 St Stephen's Green, Dublin 2; 12 Upper St George's St, Dun Laoghaire (centralized reservations at Dublin airport ☎01/705 3333/☎8444777); 2 Academy St, Cork (☎021/327 155); 136 O'Connell St, Limerick (☎061/474 239); Minicom/Text telephone (☎01/705 3994), *www.aerlingus.ie*.

Air France, Dublin Airport ☎01/844 5633.

British Airways, 1 Fountain Centre, College St, Belfast BT1 6ET (reservations ☎0345/222 111,

bookings and travel agency services ☎0345/326 566). BA doesn't have a Dublin office, for reservations from Eire, call ☎0141/2222345

British Midland, Belfast airport ☎0345/554 554; Dublin airport ☎01/283 8833, *www.iflybritishmidland.com*.

Iberia, Second Floor, 54 Dawson St, Dublin 2 (☎01/677 9846).

Ryanair, Phoenix House, Conyngham Rd, Dublin 8 (☎01/609 7800, *www.ryanair.com*).

Sabena Airlines, Dublin airport (☎01/844 5454).

FLIGHT AGENTS & SPECIALIST OPERATORS

Exodus, c/o Silk Road Travel, 64 South William St, Dublin 2 (☎01/677 1029). Trekking tours.

Explore, c/o Maxwells Travel, D'Olier Chambers, 1 Hawkins Street, Dublin 2 (☎01/677 9479). Organized package tours.

Panorama, 3 College Green, Dublin 2 (☎01/670 7666). Ireland's main Moroccan package holiday specialists.

Student & Group Travel, 1st floor, 71 Dame St, Dublin 2 (☎01/677 7834). Student and group specialists.

Sunway Travel, 114 Lower George Street, Dun Laoghaire, Co. Dublin (☎01/288 6828, *www.sunway.ie*). Charter flights direct from Ireland to Agadir, Essaouira, Marrakesh, Ouirgane and Taroudannt.

Trailfinders, 4-5 Dawson Street, Dublin 2 (☎01/677 7888). Competitive rates out of all Irish airports, as well as deals on hotels, tours and car hire.

USIT, O'Connell Bridge, 19-21 Aston Quay, Dublin 2 (☎01/602 1777); Fountain Centre, College St, Belfast (☎028/9032 4073); 10–11 Market Parade, Patrick St, Cork (☎021/270900); 4 Ship Quay Place, Derry (☎028/7137 1888); Victoria Place, Eyre Square, Galway (☎091/565177); Central Buildings, O'Connell St, Limerick (☎061/415064); 36-37 Georges St, Waterford (☎051/872601). Student/youth deals on scheduled flight combinations.

Channel Tunnel from **Waterloo**. For details see box overleaf.

TICKETS

Through rail tickets from London to Morocco are no longer available, but the full price of the journey inclusive of the ferries en route, works out at around £225 return (slightly less if you are under 26). Tickets as far as Algeciras are available from European Rail or RailEurope (see box below), and ferry tickets can be bought from there; onward train tickets can be bought once you're in Tangier.

BIJ youth tickets – available to anyone under 26 years – discount standard rail fares by 20–35 percent, with a return ticket to Algeciras going for £163 as opposed to the full fare of £195. The tickets allow any number of stopovers along a pre-

specified route and can be used on all standard European trains (some express services have a surcharge). The period of validity is two months.

THE INTERRAIL PASS

Morocco is covered by the European **InterRail pass**. To get from Britain or Ireland to Morocco, you will need a three-zone pass (£195 if you're under 26, £269 if you're over 26), which buys one month's unlimited travel on trains in France, Spain and Morocco. If bought in Ireland, it also gives free travel across Britain. However, as you have to pay half the fare in the country where you buy it, it may be more worthwhile in Britain to buy a two-zone pass (£169 under-26, £235 over-26), and pay the full fare as far as Dover. The pass also gives a fifty-percent discount on the price of most ferries across the English Channel (though only

INTERNATIONAL RAIL TRAVEL OFFICES

European Rail ☎020/7387 0444, fax 7387 0888. Phone and fax bookings only.
Eurostar ☎0870/518 6186, *www.eurostar.com/eurostar*
Irish Rail, 35 Lower Abbey St, Dublin 1, ☎01/836 6222.

Northern Ireland Railways, Great Victoria Station, Belfast, ☎028/9023 0671.
RailEurope (SNCF French Railways), 179 Piccadilly, London W1, ☎08705/848848, *www.raileurope.co.uk/interrail.htm*

around ten per cent on Eurostar services) and the Straits of Gibraltar. Note that although the InterRail pass is supposed to give you free travel on the railways of all the countries it covers, most of the trains you'll want to use in fact carry a supplement, often a hefty one, or a compulsory reservation fee. To be eligible for a pass, you must have been resident in one of the countries covered by InterRail for at least six months, and be able to prove that, if you are not a citizen; in practice you may find a place where they don't ask, but don't count on it.

The pass is available through youth/student travel agencies or from any major British or Irish train station, or from the firms listed in the box above.

BY COACH

There are regular **coach services from London to Morocco**, changing buses in Paris and travelling via the ferry at Algeciras. Be warned though that it is a 48-hour journey to Tangier and another 11 hours to Marrakesh, 15 to Agadir – quite an endurance test.

The coaches are operated jointly by the British and Spanish companies, **Eurolines** and **Iberbus**. They run twice weekly to Agadir, Casablanca, Fes, Marrakesh, Meknes, Nador, Rabat, Tangier, Tiznit, and Oujda. Fares from London are £93–121 one-way, £166–202 return, depending on destination and season; there are no student/youth reductions on these routes.

For details contact Eurolines 52 Grosvenor Gardens, London SW1W 0AU (☎0870/514 3219, *www.eurolines.co.uk*). **Departures** are from London's **Victoria Coach Station** which is served by National Express coaches from throughout the UK and by Victoria train station.

DRIVING

If you plan to **drive down to Morocco through Spain and France**, you'd be well advised to set aside a minimum of four days for the journey. The

buses detailed above cover the route to Algeciras in 48 hours but they are more or less nonstop, with two drivers and just a few short meal breaks.

There are **car ferries** across to Morocco from Spain at **Almería and Málaga** (to Melilla), at **Algeciras** (to Ceuta or Tangier), and at **Tarifa** and **Gibraltar** (to Tangier). Ferries also sail from **Sète** in France to Tangier (year round) and Nador (June–Sept). The Algeciras–Ceuta crossing is the shortest, easiest and most frequent. For more details, see the box on "Ferry Routes and Agents" on pp.12–13.

DRIVING ROUTES

Heading through France for the ferries from Spain, there is much to be said for getting off at least some of the main routes. However, if time is all important, the most direct **route** is:

London – Dover/Folkestone (Channel ferry to Calais/Boulogne); Calais/Boulogne – Paris – Tours – Poitiers – Bordeaux – Bayonne; San Sebastian – Madrid – Jaen/Córdoba; then Jaen – **Almería**, Córdoba – **Málaga**, or Córdoba – **Algeciras**.

It is possible to cut off the French section of the route by using the **car ferries to northern Spain**. These cost rather more than the shorter crossings to France, but they save on fuel, motorway tolls and an overnight stop en route. For further information contact the operators, see box below. It is also possible to drive south through France to Sète and take a ferry to Morocco from there. You could even load your car onto a motorail train for part of the journey (Calais to Avignon or Narbonne for example – for further details, contact RailEurope (see rail box).

VEHICLE RED TAPE

Driving to (and within) Morocco you must take out **Green Card Insurance**; some insurance companies don't cover Morocco, so you may need to shop around; it speeds things up if the reference to Morocco is prominent and in French.

CROSSING TO FRANCE AND SPAIN

Brittany Ferries, Wharf Rd, Portsmouth PO2 8RU; Millbay, Plymouth PL1 3EW (☎0870/901 2400, *www.brittany-ferries.com*). Portsmouth to Caen and St Malo; Poole to Cherbourg; Plymouth to Roscoff and Santander (March to November only).

Hoverspeed, International Hoverport, Marine Parade, Dover, Kent CT17 9TG (☎0870/524 0241, *www.hoverspeed.co.uk*). Dover to Calais and Ostend; Folkestone to Boulogne; Newhaven to Dieppe.

P&O Portsmouth, Peninsular House, Wharf Road, Portsmouth PO2 8TA

(☎0870/242 4999, *www.poportsmouth.com*). Portsmouth to Bilbao, Cherbourg and Le Havre.

P&O Stena, Channel House, Channel View Rd, Dover, Kent CT17 9TJ (☎087/0600 0600, *www.posl.com*). Dover to Calais.

SeaFrance, Eastern Docks, Dover CT16 1JA (☎0870/571 1711, *www.seafrance.com*). Dover to Calais.

Eurotunnel, Customer Service Centre, jct #12 off M20; PO Box 300, Dept 302, Folkestone, Kent CT19 4QD (☎0870/535 3535, *www.eurotunnel.com*).

Entering Morocco, you will need to present the card, along with your vehicle registration document – which must be in your name or accompanied by a letter from the registered owner. **Trailer caravans** need temporary importation documents, which are obtainable at the frontier for no charge.

Entering Morocco through the Spanish enclaves of Ceuta or Melilla (the most economic crossings for vehicles), try to avoid arriving at the weekend. If there are any problems, you may well be sent back to Ceuta or Melilla to wait until the Monday to sort them out. Some visitors choose to tip at the frontier, leaving a note in their passport to get them through more quickly.

EU, Australasian and North American **driving licences** are recognized and valid in Morocco, though an **International Driving Licence**, with its French translations (available from the AA or equivalent motoring organizations) is a worthwhile investment, especially if your domestic licence does not have a photograph on it (Moroccan police will find that strange). The **minimum age** for driving in Morocco is 21 years. For further details, see "Driving", p.44.

FERRIES TO MOROCCO

Crossing to Morocco by **ferry** – sailing from Europe to Africa – is an enjoyably scenic way to arrive in the country. From Spain the trip is just a couple of hours by ferry – or half an hour on the (passenger-only) hydrofoils.

ROUTES

Routes are covered in the box opposite. Your main choice is in deciding which port to head for. Most

overland travellers cross (and services are most frequent) on the routes from Algeciras to Ceuta (a Spanish enclave) and Tangier. **Ceuta** is the cheaper crossing with considerable savings for cars – but for pedestrians it is time-consuming, as you need to get a bus to the Moroccan border and another from there to the rather intimidating town of Tetouan. If you are heading for Ceuta, a handy shortcut is the direct catamaran service from Málaga. **Tangier** has the advantage of being already in Morocco, an interesting city in its own right, and much better placed than Ceuta for onward public transport to the rest of Morocco, since it is located at the beginning of the railway line, and has direct intercity bus connections nationwide. Tangier can also be reached by catamaran from Gibraltar, and in summer by both ferry and catamaran from there and from the small port of Tarifa. Unless you particularly want to visit those places, however, they are rather less convenient to get to than Algeciras or Málaga.

Further east, the crossings from Málaga and Almería to **Melilla**, another Spanish enclave, are most useful for drivers heading for Fes and southern Morocco, while the ferry from Sète in southern France to Tangier offers a convenient (if expensive) short cut, avoiding Spain entirely.

Note that for the first and last weeks of **August** the ferries to/from Ceuta, Tangier and Melilla are **booked solid**, when virtually the entire population of Spain and France (including expatriate Moroccans) have their **summer holidays** at exactly the same time. Ferries are also packed out at either end of the **Easter week** (Semana Santa) holiday, so booking in advance is essential.

FERRY ROUTES AND AGENTS

Ferry **frequencies** are given below for peak season (in general, mid-June to early September) and off-peak (mid-September to mid-June). **Fares** quoted are the sterling and US dollar equivalents of the cheapest adult passenger fares (steerage if available, shared cabin if not), the lowest car fares (usually for a vehicle up to 2.5m long), and lowest motorcycle fares (usually up to 250cc, but 125cc on COMANAV services), with seasonal variations shown. Children (up to 12 years) normally pay half fare. Most lines offer discounts (usually 20 percent) to holders of youth and student cards, some to senior citizens too, and Trasmediterranea and Buquebus do not charge for bicycles. Certain firms (COMANAV for example) may refuse to take women over six months pregnant. Note that all departures are subject to **weather conditions**, especially out of Algeciras, Tarifa and Gibraltar. For detailed schedules and prices, contact the operators, or **Southern Ferries**, 179 Piccadilly, London W1V 9DB (☎020/7491 4968, fax 020/7491 3502), who are the UK agents for Trasmediterranea and COMANAV. Most passenger tickets can be bought at boat stations on departure, but for vehicles, especially at times of high demand, and for departures out of Sète, it is best to book in advance – for vehicles on ferries out of Sète, make that *well* in advance.

ALGECIRAS

Tickets can be bought in Algeciras from any travel agent (there are dozens along the seafront and on the approach roads to the town) or at the boat station itself. Ticket prices are standard, wherever you buy them.

Algeciras–Ceuta ferry Operated by Trasmediterranea. 3–10 crossings daily. Crossing time 1hr 30min. Passenger fare £7.50/$11, cars from £34.70/$50.30, motorbikes from £7.50/$11.

Algeciras–Ceuta fast ferry (passenger only) Operated by Trasmediterranea. 12–13 crossings daily in winter, 14–18 in summer. Crossing time 40min. Passenger fare £12/$17.40.

Algeciras–Ceuta catamaran Operated by Buquebus. 8–10 crossings daily. Crossing time 30min. Tourist class passenger fare £12.70/$18.40, cars from £20.70/$30, motorbikes from £8.10/$11.75. Special car-plus-passenger fares sometimes available.

Algeciras–Tangier ferry Operated in collaboration by the Spanish companies Trasmediterranea, EuroFerrys and Lineas Maritimas Europeas, and the Moroccan companies COMANAV, Limadet and Comarit. Up to 20 crossings daily in summer, depending on demand; 11–12 daily in winter. Crossing time 2hr 30min. Passenger fare £13.20/$19.15, cars from £40.50/$58.70, motorbikes from £12.60/$18.25.

Algeciras–Tangier fast ferry (passenger only) Operated by Trasmediterranea. 1–2 daily. Crossing time 1hr 30min. Passenger fare £11.85/$17.20.

CADIZ

Cadiz–Tangier ferry Operated by IMTC. 2 daily. Crossing time 3hr. Passenger fare £11.85/$17.20, cars from £36.70/$53.20, motorbikes from £11.85/$17.20, bicycles £8.90/$12.90.

TARIFA

Tarifa–Tangier ferry Operated by Southern Ferries. 1–3 daily, depending on demand. Crossing time 1hr. Passenger fare £12.50/$18.10; cars from £37.50/$54.40; bicycle or motorbike £12.50/$18.10.

Tarifa–Tangier catamaran Operated by FRS Maroc. 1 or more daily. Crossing time 35min. Passenger fare £10.60/$15.40.

GIBRALTAR

Gibraltar–Tangier ferry Operated by Southern Ferries. 2 weekly. Crossing time 2hr. Passenger fares £18/$26; cars from £40/$58; bicycle or motorbike £15/$21.75.

Gibraltar–Tangier hydrofoil Operated by Bland Line. 7 weekly Apr–Oct, 4 weekly Nov–Mar. Crossing time 1hr 15min. Passenger fare £18/$26.

Gibraltar–Tangier hydrofoil Operated by FSR Maroc. 2 weekly. Crossing time 1hr 10min. Passenger fare £15/$21.75.

MÁLAGA

Málaga–Melilla ferry Operated by Trasmediterranea. Daily (usually 1pm, but may depart Sunday and Monday evenings instead). Crossing time 7–8hr. Passenger fare £15.60/$22.60, cars from £42.80/$62, motorbikes from £17.50/$25.40.

Málaga–Ceuta catamaran Operated by Buquebus. 2–3 daily year-round. Crossing time 1hr 30min. Tourist class passenger fare £21.50/$31.20, cars from £23.70/$34.35, motorbikes from £11.65/$18.60.

ALMERÍA

Almería–Melilla ferry Operated by Trasmediterranea. Crossing time 6hr–8hr 30min. 6 weekly in winter, 2 daily in summer. Passenger fare £15.60/$22.60, cars from £42.80/$62, motorbikes from £17.50/$25.40.

Almería–Nador ferry Operated by Ferrimaroc. 2–3 daily in summer, 6 weekly in winter. Crossing time 6–7hr. Passenger fare £19–21/$27.50–30.50, cars from £47–53/$68.15–78.85, motorbikes from £19–21/$27.50–30.50.

Almería–Nador ferry Operated by Trasmediterranea. Daily. Crossing time 7hr. Passenger fare £17/$24.65, cars from £37.22/$54, motorbikes from £15.16/$22.

SETE

Bookings well in advance are essential for Sète ferries – COMANAV's central offices for reservations from abroad are those in Casablanca and Sète, or you can book through Southern Ferries in London.

Sète–Tangier ferry The ferry *Marrakech* operated by COMANAV, runs every four to eight days, leaving Sète at 7pm. Crossing time 36hr (arrives 8am winter, 9am summer). Cheapest passenger fare £99–149/$144–216, including meals, cars from £126–210/$182.70–304.50, bicycles and motorbikes from £42–60/$61–87. Youth and student reductions available. Special fare deals for a vehicle and four passengers.

Sète–Nador ferry The ferry *Captain Zamani*, operated by COMANAV, runs from Sète to Nador's port at Beni Enzar, by the Morocco/Melilla border, once every four days from mid-June to end September. Crossing time 36hr. Cheapest passenger fare £95–119/$137.75–172.50, including meals, cars from £156–224/$226.20–324.80, bicycles and motorbikes from £48–59/$69.60–85.55. Youth and student reductions available. Special fare deals for a vehicle and four passengers.

FERRY OPERATORS

Bland Line, Cloister Building, Irish Town, Gibraltar (☎76155); c/o MedTravel, 22 Bd. Mohammed V, Tangier (☎03/922 2334 or 35). Gibraltar to Tangier.

Buquebus, *www.buquebus.es* Estación Maritima, Algeciras (☎956 666 909); Estación Maritima, Málaga (☎952 227 905); 8 Rue Youssoufia, Immeuble Youssoufia, Entre-Sol Apt. 9B, Tangier (☎03/934 2384); Estación Maritima, Ceuta (☎956 521 193). Algeciras and Málaga to Ceuta.

COMANAV, 7 Bd. de la Résistance, Casablanca (☎02/230 2412, fax 230 0790); c/o SNCM Ferryterranée, 4 Quai d'Alger, Sète (☎04/67.46.68.00, fax 67.74.93.05); c/o Transbull, Paseo de la Conferencia 13, 7º K, Algeciras (☎956 570 420 or 428); 43 Ave Abou el Alâa el Maârri, Tangier (☎03/994 0488); c/o Southern Ferries, 179 Piccadilly, London W1V 9DB (☎020/7491 4968). Sète to Nador and Tangier. Algeciras to Tangier.

Comarit, 7 Ave. de Mexique, Tangier (☎03/993 1220). Algeciras to Tangier.

EuroFerrys, Recinto del Puerto, Algeciras (☎956 651 178); 31 Ave. de la Résistance, Tangier (☎03/932 2253). Algeciras to Tangier.

Ferrimaroc, BP 96, Nador Port, Beni Enzar (☎05/634 8100); Muelle de Ribera, Almería (☎950 274 800, *www.ferrimaroc.com*). Almería to Nador.

FRS Maroc, Estación Maritima, Tarifa (☎956 627 180); c/o Turner & Co, 65–67 Irish Town, Gibraltar (☎78305); 18 Rue el Farabi, Tangier (☎03/994 2612). Tarifa and Gibraltar to Tangier.

IMTC, 122 Bd. Anfa, Casablanca (☎02/29.92.09); 2 Rue Pasteur, Tangier (☎03/933 6002 or 03); Avenida del Puerto 1, 6º, Cadiz (☎956 282 111). Cadiz to Algeciras.

Lineas Maritimas Europeas, Recinto del Puerto, Algeciras. Algeciras to Tangier.

Limadet 31 Ave de Mexique, Tangier (☎03/993 1142). Algeciras to Tangier.

Southern Ferries, (not to be confused with the London agents of Trasmediterranea and COMANAV, who have the same name) c/o TourAfrica, Unit G10, 2a Main St, Gibraltar (☎77666). Tarifa and Gibraltar to Tangier.

Trasmediterranea, Recinto del Puerto, Algeciras (☎956 583 444); Parque Nicolás Salmerón 19, Almería (☎950 257 390); Local E-1, Estación Maritima, Málaga (☎95 206 1218); 3 Rue Ibn Rochd, Tangier (☎03/993 2913); Muelle Cañonero Dato 6, Ceuta (☎956 507 257); General Marina 1, Melilla (☎952 690 170); c/o Southern Ferries, 179 Piccadilly, London W1V 9DB (☎020/7491 4968), *www.trasmediterranea.es* Algeciras to Tangier and Ceuta; Málaga to Melilla; Almería to Melilla and Nador.

RED TAPE

It's important to note that for **all ferries from Spain to Morocco** (but not to Ceuta or Melilla) you must collect an exit stamp (in Algeciras from a lone official in a passport kiosk) before boarding. Then, once on board, you have to complete a **disembarkation form** and have your **passport stamped** at the ship's purser's office.

Announcements to this effect are not always made in English, but if you don't have a stamp, you'll have to wait until everyone else has cleared frontier and customs controls before being attended to.

Returning from Morocco to Spain, you need to collect an embarkation form and departure card and have these stamped by the port police prior to boarding your ferry.

GETTING THERE FROM NORTH AMERICA

Although there are direct flights from Montreal and New York to Casablanca, most North Americans travel to Morocco via Europe. Flights across the Atlantic to London, Paris or Amsterdam can be purchased with an add-on connection to a number of Moroccan destinations. Alternatively, if time is not your main concern, you could fly to Europe and travel overland through Spain and cross over to Morocco on the ferry (see "Getting There From Britain and Ireland", p.3).

SHOPPING FOR TICKETS

The cheapest **fares** to Morocco are usually found through **specialist flight agents** – see box on p.16, though once you get a quote, it can still be worth checking with the airlines, who occasionally turn up an even better deal.

Student/youth discount fares are not particularly promising for direct flights, though **Council**, **STA**, and **Travel Cuts** (see box for addresses) may turn up the occasional budget fare to Casablanca. All three of these agencies, however,

are likely to come up with much better deals on **flights to London, Paris or Amsterdam**. Given that the cheapest and most frequent flights to Morocco are from France, Nouvelles Frontières should probably be your first call if you are planning to holiday purely in Morocco (see box for details). Note that although Council, STA, CIEE and Travel Cuts specialize in the student/youth market, they offer **low-cost fares to all travellers** – irrespective of age or student status.

Discounted tickets aside, your best bet will probably be an **Apex** (Advance Purchase Excursion) ticket, although this carries certain restrictions: you'll most likely have to book – and pay – up to 45 days before departure, be restricted as to the time you spend abroad (minimum seven days, maximum stay three months, must include a Saturday night) and pay heavy surcharges if you want to change your schedule.

At certain times of year, you may find direct **charter flights** to Morocco from the East Coast. Check the Sunday travel section of the *New York Times* and phone around. For cheaper flights from the Midwest and West Coast also check the travel pages in the local press, including the *LA Times* and *San Francisco Chronicle*, which may produce the occasional charter or a good deal to London, Paris or Amsterdam.

The **Internet** is also an increasingly popular, and often more convenient, option for purchasing tickets. All of the airlines, as well as most of the discount agents, consolidators and travel clubs listed, have Web sites offering all sorts of ticket information, and can usually take your reservation online. Discount Airfares Worldwide at *www.etn.nl/discount.htm* and International Travel Network/Airlines of the Web at *www.flyaow.com* both specialize in online booking and have useful links to other sites that offer all sorts of travel information, including hotel and car rental booking.

Regardless of where you buy your ticket, fares will depend on the time of year and **high season** for Morocco flights is Christmas/New Year, Easter and July/August.

FLIGHTS FROM THE USA

The Moroccan national airline, **Royal Air Maroc** (**RAM**), operates nonstop flights to Casablanca from New York (flight time 6hr 40min) on Tuesday, Thursday, Saturday and Sunday, with fares ranging from $700 to $900, depending on season; weekend flights are around $20 extra. Tickets can be bought in conjunction with one or more add-on flights to other Moroccan airports, or, if you are embarking on a trip across North Africa, with flights east to Tunisia or Egypt.

Alternatives to the RAM route include flights on **British Airways** (to Casablanca), **Air France** (to Casablanca, Marrakesh and Agadir), **KLM** (to Casablanca) routed through the airlines' respective hubs of London, Paris and Amsterdam. APEX return fares from New York go from $800 to $1100 to Casablanca and Marrakesh; $1000 to $1500 to Agadir.

West Coast scheduled flights to Morocco via Europe from LA or San Francisco cost around $300 more than the New York fares. Cheaper flights from the **Midwest** generally involve transiting via New York with an add-on fare of $250.

FLIGHTS FROM CANADA

Royal Air Maroc has four weekly flights **from Montreal to Casablanca** via New York, on Tuesday, Thursday, Saturday and Sunday, with a flight time of nine hours forty minutes. They currently offer a Super Apex seven-day advance midweek fare of Can$880/1340 (low/high season). Weekend supplements range from Can$20 to Can$40.

Other airlines with scheduled flights to **Casablanca via Europe** are **KLM** and **Air France**, flying from Toronto and Montreal for Can$960/1400, or from Vancouver for Can$1300/1750 (low/high season). Shopping round the **discount agents** you may be able to get better prices.

VIA BRITAIN

If you decide to make your own way to Morocco via Britain, you have a wide range of flights to London to choose from. **From the US** many airlines fly nonstop to London from the major East and West Coast cities and Midwestern hubs. Flight time from the West Coast is around nine to ten hours, compared to around six to seven hours from East Coast cities. There is heavy competition on these routes, and consolidators and discounters often have cheap, last-minute fares. The best midweek, round-trip fares in, respectively, low and high season, cost around $350 or $660 from **New York**; $450 or $850 from **Chicago**; $560 or $770 from **Miami**; $420 or $820 from **Atlanta**; and $500 or $900 from **Los Angeles**.

From the West Coast, some of the best fares are on flights connecting through Midwest and East Coast cities, but occasionally there will be sales on nonstops, so check around before assuming you'll have to take a connecting flight. Contact the **discount travel agents** in the box on p.16 who have been known to find flights to London for as low as $290 low season, and $430 high season from New York and $450 low season, and $600 high season from LA.

From Canada the cheapest flights to the UK are from the gateway cities of **Toronto** and **Montreal**, where competition between the major carriers drives midweek return fares as low as Can$679 in the off-season, or Can$1533 in the

---

TOLL-FREE AIRLINE NUMBERS

American Airlines ☎800/433-7300, *www.aa.com*

British Airways, US ☎800/247-9297, Canada 800/668-1059, *www.britishair.com*

Continental ☎800/231-0856, *www.flycontinental.com*

Delta ☎800/241-4141, *www.delta-air.com*

Air France, US ☎800/237-2747, Canada 800/667-2747, *www.airfrance.com*

Iberia, US ☎800/772-4642, Canada 800/423-7421, *www.iberia.com*

KLM, US ☎800/374-7747, Canada 800/361-5073, *www.klm.com*

Royal Air Maroc, US ☎800/344-6726, Canada 514/285-1937, *www.royalairmaroc.com*

Virgin Atlantic ☎800/862-8621, *www.virgin.com*

DISCOUNT AGENTS, CONSOLIDATORS AND TRAVEL CLUBS

Air Brokers International, 150 Post St, Suite 620, San Francisco, CA 94108 (☎1-800/883-3273 or 413/397-1383, *www.airbrokers.com*). Consolidator and specialist in RTW tickets.

Air Courier Association, 15000 W 6th Ave, Suite 203, Golden, CO 80401 (☎1-800/282-1202 or 303/279-3600, *www.aircourier.org*). Low-cost courier fares to London and other parts of Europe.

Airtreks.com, 442 Post St, Suite 400, San Francisco, CA 94102 (☎1-800/350-0612, *www.airtreks.com*). Specialists in round-the-world tickets.

Council Travel, Head Office 205 E 42nd St, New York, NY 10017 (☎212/822-2700 or 1-800/226-8624 to find the branch nearest to you, *www.counciltravel.com*). Specialist in student travel.

Educational Travel Centre, 438 N Frances St, Madison, WI 53703 (☎1-800/747-5551 or 608/256-5551, *www.edtrav.com*). Student/youth discounts.

New Frontiers/Nouvelles Frontières, 12 E 33rd St, New York, NY 10016 (☎1-800/366-6387 or 212/779-0600); 1001 Sherbrook East, Suite 720, Montréal, PQ H2L 1L3 (☎514/526-8444). French discount travel firm, offering charter flights to France. Other branches in LA, San Francisco and Quebec City.

Now Voyager, 74 Varick St, Suite 307, New York, NY 10013 (☎212/431-1616, *www.nowvoyagertravel.com*). Courier-flight broker and consolidator.

Skylink, 265 Madison Ave, 5th Floor, New York, NY 10016 (☎1-800/247-6659 or 416-922-1000 in Canada). Consolidator with branches in Chicago, Los Angeles, Montreal, New York, Toronto and Washington D.C.

STA Travel, *www.sta-travel.com* 10 Downing St, New York, NY 10014 (☎212/627-311); 7202 Melrose Ave, Los Angeles, CA 90046 (☎323/934-8772); 429 S Dearborn St, Chicago, IL 60605 (☎312/786-9050); branches nationwide call (☎1-800/777-0112) to find the branch nearest you. Worldwide specialists in student/youth fares.

TFI Tours International, 34 W 32nd St, 12th Floor, New York, NY 10001 (☎1-800/745-8000 or 212/736-1140). Consolidator.

Travac, 989 6th Ave, 16th Floor, New York, NY 10018 (☎1-800/872-8800 or 212/563-3303, *www.thetravelsite.com*. Consolidator and charter broker.

Travel Avenue, 10 S Riverside Plaza, Suite 1404, Chicago, IL 60606 (☎1-800/333-3335 or 312/876-6866, *www.travelavenue.com*). Discount-travel company.

Travel CUTS, 187 College St, Toronto, ON M5T 1P7 (☎1-800/667-2887 or 416/979-2406, *www.travelcuts.com*) plus branches on most Canadian university campuses call 1-800/954-2666 to find the location nearest you. Student/youth and general discount agency.

UniTravel, 11737 Administration Drive, Suite 120, St Louis, MO 63146 (☎1-800/325-2222 or 314/569-250, *www.flightsforless.com*). Consolidator.

high season; direct flights from Ottawa and Halifax cost only slightly more. From Vancouver, Edmonton and Calgary, flights start at Can$957 in the off season, Can$1257 in the high season. It's also worth checking discount agents and consolidators, which can often find London flights from Toronto or Montreal for as low as Can$575 low season, Can$1200 high season, and from Vancouver or Calgary for Can$850 low season and Can$1150 high season.

For details of onward travel from the UK to Morocco, see "Getting there from Britain and Ireland", p.3.

ROUND-THE-WORLD TICKETS

If Morocco is only one stop on a longer journey, you might want to consider buying a **Round-**

the-World (RTW) ticket. Some travel agents can sell you an "off-the-shelf" RTW ticket that will have you touching down in several cities. Others will assemble one for you, which can be tailored to your needs but is apt to be more expensive. Some sample itineraries are: Los Angeles – Casablanca – Bangkok – Bali – Sydney – Auckland – Los Angeles for $2095 or Toronto – Vancouver – Auckland – Bangkok – Moscow – Casablanca – Paris – Toronto for Can$2425.

PACKAGE TOURS

For ease and convenience, **package tours** make a lot of sense: you get to see the country without worrying too much about the hassles of getting to and from each place. Among available tours, some cover Morocco exclusively, others in combination with Spain and Portugal, or beyond.

See boxed listings for recommended North American agencies and check also the **UK spe-** **cialist tours** detailed on pp.5–7; many of these are sold by American travel agents, and if you contact the UK companies direct, they will put you in touch with their North American agent.

SPECIALIST TOUR OPERATORS

All prices quoted below exclude taxes and are subject to change; return flights are quoted from New York.

Abercrombie & Kent, 1520 Kensington Rd, Oak Brook, IL 60523 (☎1-800/323-7308).Ten-day fully escorted tour with luxurious accomodation from $4495.

Adventure Center, 1311 63rd Street, Suite 200, Emeryville, CA 94608 (☎1 800/228 8747. *www.adventurecenter.com*). Budget adventure travel including an eight-day "Essential Morocco" tour starting at $430.

Backroads, 801 Cedar St, Berkeley, CA 94710-1800 (☎1-800/462-2848, *www.backroads.com*). Ten-day mountain-biking, walking & camel-riding adventure holiday. From $3398.

Crystal Cruises, 2049 Century Park East, Suite 1400, Los Angeles, CA 90067 (☎1-310/785-9300, *www.crystalcruises.com*). "Moroccan Memories" ten-day cruise from Barcelona to Lisbon. From $4845.

Heritage Tours, 216 W 18ᵗʰ St, Suite 1001, New York, NY 10011 (☎1-212/206-8400, *www.heritagetoursonline.com*). Customized tours and packages exploring the 2500-year Jewish experience and the tradition of Muslim/Jewish coexistence in Morocco.

Homeric Tours, 55 E 59th St, New York, NY 10022 (☎1-800/223-5570 or 212/753-1100, *www.homerictours.com*). Several Morocco packages. Eight-day Marrakesh & Agadir Super Winter Specials from $899 (land/air); eleven-day "Discovery of Morocco" from $1569 (land/air).

Maupintour, 1515 St. Andrews Drive, Lawrence KS 66047 (☎1-800/255-6162, *www.maupintours.com*). "Moroccan Highlights".

Fully escorted ten-day package from $2700 (land/air).

Morocco Travel International, 5146 Leesburgh Pike, Alexandria, VA 22302 (☎1-800/428-5550). Customized tours and packages. Seven-day "Imperial Cities" tour to Fes, Meknes, Casablanca, Rabat & Marrakesh from $1399 (land/air).

Mountain Travel-Sobek, 6420 Fairmount Av, El Cerrito, CA 94530 (☎1-888/MT SOBEK (687-6235, *www.mtsobek.com*). Fifteen-day winter "Camel Trek", $3190. (land only).

Overseas Adventure Travel, 625 Mount Auburn St, Cambridge, MA 02138 (☎1-800/221-0814, 617/876-0533, *www.aottravel.com*). Fifteen-day "Morocco Sahara Odyssey" includes a tour of the Imperial Cities and a trip to the desert. From $2290 (land/air).

Questers Worldwide Nature Tours, 381 Park Av. South, New York, NY 10016 (☎1-800/468-8668, *www.questers.com*). Fifteen-day Natural History tours of Morocco. $3800 (land only).

Saga Holidays, 222 Berkeley St, Boston, MA 02116 (☎1-800/343-0273, *www.sagaholidays.com*). Specialists in group travel for the over 50s. Eleven-night tour of Morocco and Egypt (six days in Morocco) from $2599 (land/air).

Wilderness Travel, 1102 9ᵗʰ St, Berkeley, CA 94710 (☎1-800/368-2794 or 510/548-0420, *www.wildernesstravel.com*). "High Atlas Trek" fifteen days from $2495 (land only). "Camels to Casbahs" fourteen days from $2895 (land only).

GETTING THERE FROM AUSTRALIA AND NEW ZEALAND

Although there are no direct flights from Australia and New Zealand to Morocco it's possible to get there with the minimum of hassle. The most "direct route" to Casablanca is with Alitalia via Bangkok and Milan, or Air France via Singapore and Paris from Sydney and Auckland. Most Australian and New Zealand travellers however, make their way to Morocco via London, with a tag-on flight or overland transport to Tangier or Agadir – although more time-consuming this can be a cheaper option if funds are tight (see "Getting there from Britain and Ireland", p.3). Given the high cost of flights from Australia and New Zealand, a round-the-world (RTW) fare could also be worth considering.

Air fares vary throughout the year with **low season** to Europe from mid-January to the end of February and October to the end of November; **high season** mid-May to the end of August, and December to mid-January; shoulder seasons cover the rest of the year. Seat availability on most international flights out of Australia and New Zealand is often limited so it's best to book several weeks ahead.

Tickets purchased direct from the airlines tend to be expensive, with published **fares** from eastern cities/Auckland to Casablanca listed at

AIRLINES

Air France, Australia ☎02/9244 2100, New Zealand ☎09/308 3352, *www.airfrance.fr* Several flights a week to Casablanca via Paris and Singapore. Teams up with Qantas for links from major Australasian cities and Auckland.

Alitalia, Australia ☎02/9244 2400, New Zealand ☎09/302 1452, *www.alitalia.it* Three flights a week to Casablanca via Bangkok and a transfer or stopover in Milan from Sydney. Teams up with Qantas for links from major Australian and New Zealand cities.

British Airways, Australia ☎02/8904 8800, New Zealand ☎09/356 8690, *www.british-airways.com* Daily to London from major Australian and New Zealand cities. One World Alliance member offering RTW fares.

Garuda Indonesia, Australia ☎1300/365 330, New Zealand ☎09/366 1862 or ☎1800/128 510. Several flights a week to London Gatwick with either a transfer or stopover in Jakarta or Denpasar from major Australian and New Zealand cities.

KLM, Australia ☎1300 303 747, *www.klm.com*. No NZ office. Two flights a week to Casablanca via Amsterdam and Singapore from Sydney.

Qantas, Australia ☎13 1211, New Zealand ☎09/357 8900 or 0800/808 767, *www.qantas.com.au*s One World Alliance member, offering RTW tickets.

Royal Brunei Airlines, Australia ☎07/3221 7757, no NZ office, *www.bruneiair.com* Three flights a week to London from Sydney, Brisbane and Cairns via a transfer or stopover in Brunei.

Singapore Airlines, Australia ☎13/10 11 & ☎02/ 9350 0262, New Zealand ☎09/303 2129, ☎0800/808 909, *www.singaporeair.com* Daily flights to Madrid from Brisbane, Sydney, Melbourne, Perth and Auckland with either a transfer or overnight stop in Singapore, and on some flights a transfer in Zurich.

Thai Airways International, Australia ☎1300/651 960, New Zealand ☎09/377 3886, *www.thaiair.com* Several flights weekly to Madrid from Sydney, Melbourne, Brisbane and Auckland via either a transfer in Rome or Frankfurt and with either a transfer or overnight stop in Bangkok.

DISCOUNT TRAVEL AGENTS

All the agents listed below offer competitive discounts on air fares and a good selection of package holidays and tours

Anywhere Travel, 345 Anzac Parade, Kingsford, Sydney (☎02/9663 0411, *anywhere@ozemail.com.au*).

Budget Travel, 16 Fort St, Auckland, plus branches around the city (☎09/366 0061 & 0800/808 040).

Destinations Unlimited, 220 Queen St, Auckland (☎09/373 4033).

Flight Centres, *www.flightcentre.com.au* Australia: 82 Elizabeth St, Sydney, plus branches nationwide (☎02/9235 3522, nearest branch ☎13 1600). New Zealand: 350 Queen St, Auckland (☎09/358 4310), plus branches nationwide.

Northern Gateway, 22 Cavenagh St, Darwin (☎08/8941 1394, *oztravel@norgate.com.au*).

STA Travel, *www.statravel.com.au* Australia: 855 George St, Sydney; 256 Flinders St, Melbourne; other offices in state capitals and major universities (nearest branch ☎13 1776, fastfare telesales ☎1300/360 960). New Zealand: 10 High St, Auckland (☎09/309 0458, fastfare telesales ☎09/366 6673), plus branches in Wellington, Christchurch, Dunedin,

Palmerston North, Hamilton and at major universities.

Student Uni Travel, 92 Pitt St, Sydney (☎02/9232 8444, *sydney@backpackers.net*) plus branches in Brisbane, Cairns, Darwin, Melbourne and Perth.

Thomas Cook, *www.thomascook.com.au* 175 Pitt St, Sydney (☎02/9231 2877); 257 Collins St, Melbourne (☎03/9602 3811); plus branches in other state capitals (local branch ☎13 1771, Thomas Cook Direct telesales ☎1800/801 002); 191 Queen St, Auckland (☎09/379 3920).

Trailfinders, *www.travel.com.au* 8 Spring St, Sydney (☎02/9247 7666); 91 Elizabeth St, Brisbane (☎07/3229 0887); Hides corner, Shield St, Cairns (☎07/4041 1199).

Travel.com.au, 76-80 Clarence St, Sydney (☎02/9249 5444 & 1800 000 447, *www.travel.com.au*).

USIT Beyond, *www.usitbeyond.co.nz* cnr Shortland St and Jean Batten Place, Auckland (☎09/379 4224 or ☎0800/788 336) plus branches in Christchurch, Dunedin, Palmerston North, Hamilton and Wellington.

A$2399/NZ$2699 (low season) and A$2999/NZ$3399 (high season). **Travel agents** offer better deals on fares and have the latest information on special offers. Flight Centres and STA (which offer fare reductions for ISIC card holders and under 26s) generally offer the lowest fares. You might also want to have a look on the **Internet**; *www.travel.com.au* offers discounted fares online, as does *www.sydneytravel.com*

From **Australia**, Alitalia has a scheduled service to Casablanca via Bangkok and Milan three times a week which, if booked through a specialist agent, can go from A$1799 low season to A$2499 high season. You also have the option of Air France and KLM who can get you there via a transfer in their home cities (Paris and Amsterdam respectively) for A$1999–2499. Fares from major eastern cities are common rated, from Perth and Darwin they are usually between $100–200 less.

From **New Zealand**, Qantas-Alitalia fly from Auckland to Casablanca via Sydney and Milan from NZ$2199 low season to NZ$2899 high season.

To European gateways you'll find the cheapest fares are to **London**, with Sri Lankan Airlines, Royal Brunei, Philippine Airlines and Garuda all starting at A$1499/NZ$1800 low season while Malaysia Airlines, Thai Airways, and Singapore Airlines all fly to **Paris** and **Madrid** for A$1899–2499/NZ$2099–2799 from where you can continue on to Morocco either by air or overland, see "Getting there from Britain and Ireland", p.3.

There are several **RTW fares** that take in Casablanca, with the cheapest offered by Qantas-Air France allowing a limited number of stops in each direction for around A$1699/NZ$2099; prices are distance-based.

Package holidays are few and far between – and organized tours may seem a little expensive, but can be well worth it, especially if your time is limited, you're unfamiliar with the country's customs and language or you just don't like travelling alone. Specialist travel agents and operators offer a range of itineraries, and though most tours don't include airfares from Australia or New Zealand, the specialists can usually assist with flight arrangements too.

Abercrombie and Kent, 90 Bridport St, Albert Park, Melbourne (☎03/9699 9766 & 1800 331 429), plus branches in Brisbane and Sydney; 1/88 Rockfield Rd, Penrose, Auckland (☎09/579 3369). Seven-night luxury tours of Morocco's imperial cities of Marrakesh, Casablanca, Rabat, Meknes and Fes for A$2,600/NZ$3,300 land only.

The Adventure Travel Company, 164 Parnell Rd, Parnell, Auckland (☎09/379 9755; *advakl@hot.co.nz*). NZ agent for Peregrine. All travel arrangements and a wide selection of adventure tours in Morocco. Fifteen-day trek through remote parts of the High Atlas Mountains. From A$1300/NZ$1390 land only.

Adventure Specialists, 1/69 Liverpool St, Sydney (☎02/9261 2927). Overland and adventure tour agent for a variety of adventure wholesalers that offer one- and two-week treks and camping holidays throughout Morocco.

Adventure World, 73 Walker St, North Sydney (☎02/9956 7766 & 1300/363 055, *www.adventureworld.com.au*) plus branches in Adelaide, Brisbane, Melbourne and Perth; 101 Great South Rd, Remuera, Auckland (☎09/524 5118). Accommodation, treks, discount air fares. Agents for Explore's fourteen-night round trip out of Marrakesh through the Anti Atlas Mountains by coach, from A$800/NZ$1050 plus US$100 expenses land only.

Africa Travel Centre, 456 Kent St, Sydney (☎02/9267 3048 or 1800/622 984); 21 Remuera Rd, Auckland (☎09/520 2000). Specialists in camping holidays in Morocco.

IB Tours, 1/47 New Canterbury Road, Petersham, Sydney (☎02/9560 6932, *petersham@harveyworld.com.au*). Individually tailored holidays in Morocco, plus accommodation from A$60–130/NZ$75–150 per night.

Ibertours, 1/84 William St, Melbourne (☎03/9670 8388 & 1800/500 016, *www.ibertours.com.au*) Fully escorted small group and private tours in Morocco.

Intrepid Adventure Travel, 12 Spring St, Fitzroy, Melbourne (☎1300 360 667 or 03/9473 2626, *www.intrepidtravel.com.au*). Agents for Imaginative Traveller's small-group tours to Morocco with an emphasis on cross-cultural contact and low-impact tourism.

Peregrine, 258 Lonsdale St, Melbourne (☎03/9662 2700 & 1300 655 433, *www.peregrine.net.au*), plus offices in Brisbane, Sydney, Adelaide and Perth. Small-group hiking and archeological trips with an emphasis on local contact such as for Exodus's biking and trekking expeditions (see UK Specialist Operators box on p.5).

Yalla Tours, 661 Glen Huntley Rd, Caulfield, Melbourne (☎1300/362 844, *www.yallatours.com.au*). Guided six- to nine-day tours include "Crown of Morocco" tour from Marrakesh. From A$1375/2530, city accommodation from A$93 (twin share half-board).

TRAVELLERS WITH DISABILITIES

Facilities for people with disabilities are little developed in Morocco, and, although families are usually very supportive, many disabled Moroccans are reduced to begging. Despite this, able-bodied Moroccans are, in general, far more used to mixing with disabled people than their Western counterparts, and are much more likely to offer help without embarrassment if you need it.

Blindness is more common than in the West, and sighted Moroccans are generally used to helping blind and visually impaired people find their way around and get on and off public transport at the right stop.

Wheelchairs, though often ancient, do exist, but there is little in the way of wheelchair access. Some package **hotels**, especially in Agadir, do attempt to cater for wheelchair-users. Some may have ramps, for example, but no accessible toilets. Depending on your mobility, you may also want to book ground-floor rooms to avoid having to climb a staircase, since many places lack lifts. You should always check that the hotel can cater for your specific needs.

Bus and train **travel** will be difficult because of the steps that have to be negotiated, but grands taxis are a more feasible mode of transport if you can stake a claim on the front seat (maybe paying for two places to get the whole of it) – if you don't have a helper travelling with you, and you require assistance, the driver or other passengers will almost certainly be happy to help you get in and out.

You're likely to find travelling on a **package tour** much easier than fully independent travel, but all the same you should contact any tour operator in advance and inform them of your exact needs before making a booking. Cheap city accommodation will often have narrow staircases to negotiate, while beach hotels are more able to cater for visitors with mobility difficulties. Some upmarket hotels claim that they have facilities for disabled visitors and these include the *Agadir Beach Club* in Agadir, the *Holiday Inn* and the *Sheraton* in Casablanca, the *Sheraton* and *La Mamounia* in Marrakesh, and the *Hilton* in Rabat, but it's always best to check exactly what they have to match your requirements. It's also important to ensure you are covered by any insurance policy you take out.

It's impossible for us to detail facilities for disabled visitors for everywhere we list in the

CONTACTS FOR TRAVELLERS WITH DISABILITIES

BRITAIN AND IRELAND

Holiday Care Service, 2nd floor, Imperial Building, Victoria Rd, Horley, Surrey RH6 7PZ (☎01293/774535, minicom ☎01293/776943, *www.freespace.virgin.net/hol-care*). Provides free lists of accessible accommodation and information on financial help for holidays

Tripscope, The Courtyard, Evelyn Rd, London W4 5JL (☎020/8994 9294, *www.justmobility.co.uk/tripscope*). A national telephone and online information service offering free travel advice for anyone with mobility problems.

RADAR, 12 City Forum, 250 City Rd, London EC1V 8AF (☎020/7250 3222, minicom ☎020/7250 4119, *www.radar.org.uk*). A good source of advice on holidays.

Disability Action Group, 2 Annadale Ave, Belfast BT7 3JH (☎028/9049 1011).

Irish Wheelchair Association, Blackheath Drive, Clontarf, Dublin 3 (☎01/833 8241, *www.iwa.ie*). National voluntary organization for people with disabilities, including services for holidaymakers.

NORTH AMERICA

AccessAbility Travel, 186 Alewife Brook Pkwy, Cambridge, MA 02138-1102 (☎1-800/610 5640, TTY 1-800/228 5379). A division of FPT Travel Management Travel Group with travel information and tips for disabled travellers.

Access First, 45A Pleasant St, Malden, MA 02148 (☎1-800/557 2047; TTY 617/397-8610). Current information for disabled travellers.

Directions Unlimited, 123 Green Lane, Bedford Hills, NY 10507 (☎1-800/533-5343). Tour operator specializing in custom tours for people with disabilities.

Jewish Rehabilitation Hospital, 3205 Place Alton Goldbloom, Chomedy Laval, PQ H7V 1R2 (☎514/688 9550, ext. 226). Guidebooks and travel information.

Mobility International USA, PO Box 10767, Eugene, OR 97440 (Voice and TDD: ☎541/343 1284). Information and referral services, access guides, tours and exchange programmes. Annual membership $35 (incl. quarterly newsletter).

Society for the Advancement of Travel for the Handicapped (SATH), 347 5th Ave, New York, NY 10016 (☎212/447-7284, *www.sath.org*). Nonprofit-making travel-industry referral service that passes queries on to its members as appropriate (allow plenty of time for a response).

Travel Information Service (☎215/456 9603). Telephone only information and referral service.

Twin Peaks Press, Box 129, Vancouver, WA 98666 (☎360/694 2462 or 1-800/637 2256). Publisher of the *Directory of Travel Agencies for the Disabled* ($19.95), listing more than 370 agencies worldwide; *Travel for the Disabled* ($19.95); the *Directory of Accessible Van Rentals* ($9.95) and *Wheelchair Vagabond* ($14.95), loaded with personal tips.

Wheels Up! PO Box 5197 Plant City, FL 33564-5197 (☎1-888/389-4335, *www.wheelsup.com*). Provides discounted air fare, tour and cruise prices for disabled travellers, also publishes a free monthly newsletter and has a comprehensive Web site.

AUSTRALIA AND NEW ZEALAND

ACROD, PO Box 60, Curtin, ACT 2605 (☎02/6282 4333). Offers advice and keeps a list of tour operators catering for people with disabilities.

Disabled Persons Assembly, PO Box 10, 138 The Terrace, Wellington (☎04/472 2626). Provides lists of travel agencies and tour operators catering for people with disabilities.

Wheelchair Travel, 29 Ranelagh Drive, Mt Eliza Vic 3930 (☎03/9787 8861, *www.travelability.com*).

guide; nor can we detail the best and worst of the operators. For more **information on disabled travel abroad** you should contact the organizations listed in the box. As well as their publications, look out for *The World Wheelchair Traveller* (AA Publications) by Susan Abbott and Mary Ann Tyrrell, which includes basic hints and advice.

VISAS AND RED TAPE

If you hold a full passport from the UK, Ireland, any other EU country, the US, Canada, Australia or New Zealand, you require no visa to enter Morocco for up to ninety days. Note, however, that your passport must be valid for at least six months beyond your date of entry, and always double check your visa requirements before departure as the situation can change. South African citizens are among those who need a visa; applications should be made to the nearest Moroccan embassy or consulate (see box opposite).

When **entering the country**, formalities are fairly straightforward, though you will have to fill in a form stating personal details, purpose of visit and your **profession**. In recent years, Moroccan authorities have shown an occasional reluctance to allow in those who categorize themselves as "journalist"; an alternative profession on the form might be wise.

Note that items such as **electronic equipment and video cameras** may be entered on your passport. If you lose them during your visit, they will be assumed "sold" when you come to leave and (unless you have police documentation of theft) you will have to pay 100 percent duty. All goods on your passport should be "cleared" when leaving to prevent problems on future trips. Vehicles need a Green Card (see p.46).

VISA EXTENSIONS

To **extend your stay** in Morocco you should – officially – apply to the Bureau des Etrangers in the nearest main town for a residence permit (see below). This is, however, a very complicated procedure and it is usually possible to get round the bureaucracy by simply leaving the country for a brief time when your three months are up. If you decide to do this – and it is not foolproof – it is best to make a trip of at least a few days outside Morocco. Spain is the obvious choice and some people just go to the enclave of Ceuta; the more cautious re-enter the country at a different post. If you are very unlucky, you may be turned back and asked to obtain a **re-entry visa** prior to your return. These can be obtained from any Moroccan consulate abroad (see opposite).

OFFICIAL BUSINESS

Extending a stay officially involves opening a bank account in Morocco (a couple of days' procedure in itself) and obtaining an *Attestation de Résidence* from your hotel, campsite or landlord. You will need a minimum of 20,000dh (£1250/$1820) deposited in your bank account before making an application.

Once you have got through these two stages, you need to go to the **Bureau des Etrangers** in the central police station of a large town,

CHILDREN ON PARENTS' PASSPORTS

If travelling as a family, note that **children travelling on their parents' passports** must have their photographs affixed to the passport. If this is not done, it is possible that you will be refused entry to Morocco. This is not just a piece of paper bureaucracy: families are regularly refused entry for failing to comply.

MOROCCAN EMBASSIES AND CONSULATES ABROAD

Algeria 8 Rue des Cèdres, al-Mouradia, 12070 Algiers (☎02/60.74.08).

Australia 11 West Street, North Sydney, NSW 2060 (☎02/9922 4999).

Canada 38 Range Rd, Suite 1510, Ottawa, ON K1N 8J4 (☎613/236-7391); 1010 Sherbrooke St W, Montreal, PQ H3A 2R7 (☎514/288-8750).

Denmark Øregårrds Allé 19, 2900 Hellerup, Copenhagen (☎3962 4511).

Mauritania Tevragh Zeina 634, BP621, Nouakchott (☎25.23.99).

Netherlands Oranjestraat 9, 2514 The Hague (☎070/360 2900); Vondelstraat 65–67, 1054 Amsterdam (☎020/618 1616).

Spain c/Serrano 179, Madrid (☎91 458 0950); Rambla de Catalunya 78, Barcelona (☎93 215 3470); c/Teniente Maroto 2, Algeciras (☎956 661 803).

South Africa 799, Schoeman St, PO Box 12382, Arcadia, Pretoria 0083 (☎012/243 0230).

Sweden Kungsholmstorg 16, Stockholm (☎08/5455 1139).

UK 49 Queens Gate Gardens, London SW7 5NE (☎020/7581 5001).

USA 1601 21st St NW, Washington DC 20009 (☎202/462-7979); 10 E 40th St, 24th Floor, New York, NY 10016 (212/758-2625).

Morocco has no diplomatic mission in **Ireland** or **New Zealand**, which are covered by the embassy in London and the consulate in Sydney respectively. For foreign embassies and consulates in Morocco, see p.38.

equipped with: your passport; seven passport photos; two copies of the *Attestation de Résidence*; two copies of your bank statement (*Compte de Banque*); and a 60dh stamp (available from any *Tabac*). If the police are not too busy they'll give you a form to fill out in duplicate and, some weeks later, you should receive a plastic-coated permit with your photo laminated in.

For anyone contemplating this labyrinthine operation, the *Bureau des Etrangers* in **Agadir** is perhaps the simplest place to approach, since a number of expatriates live in the city and banking facilities there (try the Banque Populaire) are fairly efficient. The Bureau is located at the Commissariat behind the fire station on Rue du 18 Novembre.

COSTS AND MONEY

For visitors, Morocco is inexpensive and in most respects excellent value, with costs for food, accommodation and travel low by European or North American standards. If you stay in the cheaper hotels (or camp out), eat local food, and share expenses and rooms with another person, £80/$125 each a week would be enough to survive on. On £110–140/$175–225 each you could live pretty well, while with £300–400/$450–600 a week split between two people you would be approaching luxury.

SOME BASIC COSTS

Accommodation costs range from £4/$6 a night – sometimes even less – for a double room in a basic hotel to £150/$200 a night in the country's half-dozen top-range luxury palaces. On a limited budget, you can expect to get a decent double room in a mid-range hotel for around £12–25/ $20–40 a night, while the occasional splurge in a more up-market hotel, with a swimming pool, will set you back around £25–50 /$40–80 for a double, depending on season and location.

The price of a **meal** reflects a similar span. Basic Moroccan staples such as brochettes (small kebabs) or tajine (casserole) are available at cheap restaurants or cafés for around £2/$3. More substantial Moroccan meals can be had for around £4/$6 and European-style meals in restaurants from around £7.50/$11; it's worth bearing in mind that comparable meals in a hotel can cost twice as much. **Drinks** are really the only things that compare unfavourably with Western prices: a bottle of Moroccan wine costs upwards of £4/$6, a can of local beer about 70p/$1 in the shops, very slightly more in a normal bar, or £2.50/$4 in hotel bars and discos.

Beyond accommodation and food, your major outlay will be for **transport** – expensive if you're renting a car (£250/$360 a week plus petrol), but very reasonable if you use the local trains, buses and shared taxis. The 475km trip from Fes to Marrakesh, for instance, costs around £7/$10 by ordinary bus, £8/$12 on the express CTM service, £10/$15 by train in second class, £12.50/$18 in first class.

REGIONAL VARIATIONS

To some extent, all of these costs are affected by where you are and when. Inevitably, larger **cities** and **resorts** (Agadir especially) prove more expensive, with bottom-line hotel prices from around £6/$8 a night for a basic double. In **remote parts** of the country, too, where all goods have to be brought in from some distance and where transport (often only lorries or Landrovers) has to be negotiated, prices can be steep. This is particularly true of the popular trekking region of Djebel Toubkal in the High Atlas.

In the Spanish enclaves of Ceuta (Sebta in Arabic) and Melilla, prices for most things are the same as they are in mainland Spain, except that there is no duty on alcohol, tobacco, electronic goods and, most importantly, petrol – so these are good places to fill up. For everything else, Ceuta and Melilla are around twice as expensive as Morocco proper. The other place where petrol is cheap is in the Saharan provinces of the far south (roughly the Western Sahara), where it is subsidized by the state.

HIDDEN COSTS

Hidden costs in Morocco are twofold. The most obvious, perhaps, is that you'll almost certainly end up buying a few things. Moroccan **crafts** are very much a part of the fabric of the towns and cities, with their labyrinthine areas of souks (markets). Rugs, blankets, leather and jewellery are all outstanding – and few travellers leave without at least one of these items.

A harder aspect to come to terms with is that you'll be confronting real **poverty**. As a tourist, you're not going to solve any problems, but with a labourer's wages at little more than 5dh (30p/45¢) an hour, and an unemployment rate in excess of 25 percent, even a small **tip** to a guide can make a lot of difference to individual family life. For Moroccans, giving alms is a natural function – and a requirement of Islam, especially since there is no social security here. For tourists, rich by definition, local poverty demands at least some response. Do not, however, dispense money indiscriminately to **children**, which simply promotes a dependence on begging.

CURRENCY

Morocco's basic unit of **currency** is the **dirham** (dh). The dirham is not quoted on international money markets, a rate being set instead by the Moroccan government. The present rates are approximately **16dh to £1, 11dh to US$1, 9.5dh to €1**. As with all currencies there are fluctuations, though in the long term the dirham tends to fall against Western currencies.

The dirham is divided into 100 **centimes**, and you may find prices written or expressed in centimes rather than dirhams. Confusingly, centimes may also be referred to as **francs** or, in former Spanish zones of the country, as **pesetas**. You may also hear prices quoted in **rials**, or *reales*. In most parts of the country a dirham is considered to be 20 rials, though in Tangier and the Rif there are just 2 rials to the dirham. These are forms of expression only: there are no actual physical Moroccan rials. Coins of 10, 20 and 50 centimes, and 1, 5 and 10 dirhams are in circulation, along with bills of 20, 50, 100 and 200 dirhams, plus some old ones of 10 dirhams.

It is possible to buy a small amount of dirhams at the bank exchange desks in the Algeciras ferry terminal or from moneychangers in Gibraltar (where you'll usually get a very slightly better rate than in Morocco itself), and in Ceuta and Melilla.

When you're nearing the end of your stay, it's best to get down to as little Moroccan money as possible. You can change back dirhams at the airport on departure, but you may be asked to produce bank exchange receipts – and you can change back only fifty percent of sums detailed on these. You'll probably be offered re-exchange into French francs only, though from January 2002 this will be euros, usable in much of continental Europe, as well as Ireland. You can also change dirhams into pesetas (also due to be superseded by euros) in Ceuta and Melilla.

CARRYING YOUR MONEY

Arriving in Morocco it is useful to have at least two days' survival money in **cash**, especially as you cannot always count on airport banks/bureau de change offices being open. English pounds, US and Canadian dollars, and all euro zone currencies including Irish pounds, are easy to exchange at banks, hotels and some travel agents and tourist shops. Gibraltarian banknotes fetch a very slightly lower rate of exchange than English ones, but Scottish and Northern Irish notes are not negotiable in Morocco. Also note that Australian and New Zealand dollars, and South African rand are not accepted for exchange in Morocco, so they should be changed into US dollars, sterling or euros before arrival. The rest of your money should ideally, for the sake of security, be spread around different forms, such as traveller's cheques, "travel money" (see below) and plastic.

Traveller's cheques are easily exchanged at most Moroccan banks, and at the more upmarket hotels, travel agencies and tourist shops. However, a surcharge (currently 10.70dh) is levied on each cheque by almost all banks with the exception of the state-run Bank al Maghrib (also called the Banque du Maroc). Banks may also on occasion demand to see the original receipt for the cheques, even though you are not supposed to carry that and the cheques together – if you do show it, don't let the bank keep it. Thomas Cook, VISA and American Express are the best-known and most widely accepted cheques. In the event that your cheques are lost or stolen, the issuing company will expect you to report the theft to them and to local police immediately. Most companies claim to replace lost or stolen cheques within 24 hours, though they may drag their feet if fraud is suspected.

A new option from VISA (and their competitors will no doubt soon be offering the same kind of service) is **Visa travel money**, a disposable prepaid debit card with a PIN that you can use in ATM machines worldwide. It's a sort of electronic version of traveller's cheques, where you can buy as much credit as you think you'll need, and throw the card away when it runs out. You can carry up to eight spare cards in case you lose one, or for a family or group with a common pool of money. There is a 24hr toll-free global customer assistance services centre in Baltimore, which you can in theory call collect (☎001-410/581-9091), or via AT&T USA Direct (dial ☎002/11.00.11 and ask the operator for 1-800-847-2399). The card is available from, among other places, Thomas Cook in the UK and Colombus Bank in the US, and can be ordered in the United States on ☎1-877/394-2247. For further information, check VISA's Web site at *www.visa.com*

VISA and **Mastercard** can also be used to obtain cash at some banks (see below), as well as in payment at the more upmarket hotels, restaurants and shops, and for car rental. It's wise to make sure your card is in good condition, as banks will refuse cash advances if machines reject the card. The weekly limit varies according to what type of account you have, but is typically around 5000dh per week.

BANKS AND EXCHANGE

For exchange purposes, by far the most useful and efficient chain of banks is the **BMCE** (Banque Marocaine du Commerce Exterieur). There is at least one BMCE in all major cities and they are dotted about in smaller towns (see listings in the text of the guide). They handle cash or travellers' cheques with the minimum of hassle (though they do charge the standard 10.70dh for changing the latter), and give cash advances on VISA and Mastercard, as well as currency exchange.

The **Banque Credit du Maroc** (BCM) also handles VISA and Mastercard, as do the generally efficient **Citibank**, and larger branches of the **Banque Populaire**. Most other banks don't tend to have facilities for credit card transactions, despite the stickers in their windows, though they will exchange cash and travellers' cheques. In the far south, you may find that Banque Populaire and BMCE are your only choices.

Standard banking hours for most of the year are Monday to Thursday 8.15am–11.30am and 2.15pm–4.30pm, Friday 8.15am–11.15am and 2.45pm–4.45pm. Some branches of WAFA Bank are open an hour later, until 5.30pm (5.45 on

Friday). In summer (usually 15 June – 30 September), banks open from 8am to 2pm, and during Ramadan (see "Festivals" on p.61) from 9am to 2pm. In major resorts there is usually one or more bank that keeps extended hours on bureau de change transactions to meet tourist demand, and BMCE often has a separate bureau de change open longer hours and at weekends. In some places you may find travel agents with exchange facilities, and most large hotels will also change money for nonresidents out of banking hours.

In most **exchange transactions** at banks, customers fill in forms at one desk, then join a second queue for the cashier. You'll usually need to show your passport as proof of identity. Cheque/cash transactions usually get dealt with in 10 to 15 minutes, but it's wise to allow up to an hour if you need to draw cash on a credit card. Obviously, if you can change money at a hotel or travel agent, or a bureau de change, the whole procedure will be quicker and easier.

ATMs (cashpoints/cash dispensers) are to be found outside more and more banks in the bigger towns, and accept major systems, though be warned; they can be unreliable and occasionally swallow cards.

AMERICAN EXPRESS

American Express is represented by the Voyages Schwartz agencies in Tangier, Casablanca, Rabat and Marrakesh. Note that Voyages Schwartz are only agents, and not every American Express service is available at their offices. They can issue Amex traveller's cheques (but often won't cash them), and hold clients' mail, but they cannot cash personal cheques or receive wired money. Offices are located at:

Tangier Voyages Schwartz, 54 Bd. Pasteur (☎03/933 0372).

Casablanca Voyages Schwartz, 112 Rue Prince Moulay Abdallah (☎02/222 2947).

Rabat Av. Omar ben Khattab, cnr Rue Daraa 5 (☎02/222 2947).

Marrakesh Voyages Schwartz, Immeuble Moutoukil, 1 Rue Mauritania (☎04/433 3022).

Opening hours vary, but they are open at least Monday to Friday 9am–noon and 3pm–6pm, though banking services are sometimes mornings only.

EMERGENCY CASH

Despite travellers' tales, very few people lose (or are conned out of) all their money in Morocco – but it does happen. Access to an **emergency source** of money – whether it be a credit card or an arrangement with your bank or family to wire you money after a phone call – is reassuring and may prove invaluable.

The quickest and easiest way to wire money is via **MoneyGram** or **Western Union**. Transfer is pretty well instantaneous, and fees depend on the amount being transferred, but as a guide, wiring £700/$1000 will cost around £40/$60. Funds should be available for collection (usually in dirhams) from the company's local agent within minutes of being sent. This can be done in person at the company's nearest office (see box below – in the UK, all post offices are agents for MoneyGram), and with Western Union it can be done over the phone using a credit card. Western Union is also the more convenient of the two since money can be received from them at most large post offices and some small ones too (MoneyGram's local agent will usually be a branch of Credit du Maroc). It's also possible, and slightly cheaper, to have money wired from a bank in your home country to a bank in Morocco, but this is much slower and somewhat less reliable because it involves two separate

WIRING MONEY

To find the location of your nearest agent or branch call:

MONEYGRAM (*www.moneygram.com*)
Australia ☎1800/230 100
Ireland ☎1850/205800
New Zealand ☎09/379 8243 or ☎0800/262263
UK ☎0800/8971 8971
USA and Canada ☎1-800/543 4080

WESTERN UNION (*www.westernunion.com*)
Australia ☎1800/649565
Ireland ☎1800/395395
New Zealand ☎09/270 0050
UK ☎0800/833833
USA and Canada ☎1-800/325 6000

institutions. If you go this route, the person wiring the funds to you will need to know the routeing number of the bank the funds are being wired to. From the UK, a compromise option is **Thomas Cook**'s Telegraphic Transfer service

(☎01733/318922), which costs £15 plus one percent of the amount to be sent (minimum charge £25), and takes one to two days to arrive. They can also credit foreign bank accounts for the same fee (2–3 days).

HEALTH AND INSURANCE

For minor health complaints, a visit to a pharmacy is likely to be sufficient. Moroccan pharmacists are well trained and dispense a wide range of drugs, including many available only on prescription in Europe or North America. If pharmacists feel you need a full diagnosis, they can recommend a doctor – sometimes working on the premises. Addresses of English- and French-speaking doctors can also be obtained from consulates and large hotels.

If you need **hospital treatment**, contact your consulate at once and follow their advice. If you are near a major city, reasonable treatment may be available locally. Morocco, however, is no country in which to fall seriously ill.

The latest advice on health in Morocco can be found on the British government's travel health Web site at *www.ukhealthnet.co.uk/travel/country/morocco.htm* or the US government's equivalent site at *www.cdc.gov/travel/nafrica.htm*

INOCULATIONS

There are no **inoculations** officially required of travellers, although you should always be up to date with polio and tetanus. Jabs against hepatitis A, typhoid and cholera are worthwhile, too – although some doctors doubt the effectiveness of

the cholera jab. Those intending to stay a long time in the country, especially if working with animals or in the healthcare field, are also advised to consider vaccinations against TB, hepatitis B, diphtheria and rabies, though these are not worth your while if just going on holiday.

Moroccan authorities deny the existence of **malaria** anywhere on Moroccan territory, including the Western Sahara, but other authorities report occasional cases between May and October in the region to the north of Beni Mellal and Khenifra, in the area between Chaouen and Larache, and in the province of Taza. Local strains of malaria are not life-threatening and malaria pills are not normally considered necessary unless you actually fall ill with it (in which case they are easy enough to get at any pharmacy), but if you really want to be on the safe side, you could take a course of chloroquine (brands include Resochin, Nivaquin and Avlaclor). Note that chloroquine should not be taken if pregnant, and is best not taken for stretches of more than six months at a time. The dose is two tablets weekly for adults, to be taken from a week before entering a malarial zone until four weeks after leaving it. More importantly, avoid bites; use mosquito repellent on all exposed areas of skin, especially feet, and especially around dusk. Repellents using DEET are usually recommended for adults, though alternatives are citronella oil and Avon's Skin So Soft bath oil, both of which are highly effective, safe for children, and don't contain nasty chemicals, though citronella oil is only effective for a few hours, not all night. Electric mosquito repellent scent diffusers are also effective indoors, but require a socket. Mosquito "buzzers" are useless.

If you haven't had a typhoid jab then buy some Intétrix capsules (available from any pharmacy in Morocco). These are excellent antibacterial medication – useful for diarrhoea as well as typhoid prevention – and some doctors consider them more effective than inoculation. They are certainly valuable if you are travelling for any length of time in the south.

WATER AND HEALTH HAZARDS

The **tap water** in northern Morocco is generally safe to drink (in Chaouen, for example, it is pumped straight from a well), though in the south it's best to stick to bottled mineral water.

A more serious problem in the south is that many of the **river valleys and oases** are infected with **bilharzia**, also known as **schistosomiasis**, caused by a tiny fluke worm that lives part of its life cycle in a freshwater snail, and the other part in the blood and internal organs of a human or other mammal which bathes in or drinks the water. The snails only live in stagnant water, but the flukes may be swept downstream. Staying clear of slow-flowing rivers and oasis water is the best way to avoid it. If infected while bathing, you'll probably get a slightly itchy rash an hour or two later where the flukes have entered the skin. Later symptoms may take several months to appear, and are typified by abdominal pains, and blood in faeces or even urine. If you suspect that you might have it, seek medical help. Bilharzia is easily cured, but can cause permanent intestinal damage if untreated. Care should be taken, too, in drinking water from **mountain streams**. In areas where there is livestock upstream **giardiasis** may be prevalent and is a common cause of travellers' diarrhoea. Other symptoms include nausea, weight loss and fatigue which usually last no more than two weeks and settle without treatment. If they continue for longer then a course of **metronidazole** (Flagyl) generally leads to effective eradication. Using iodine water purification tablets, or boiling any drinking or cooking water (remember that you'll have to boil it for longer at high altitudes, where the boiling point is lower) is the simplest way to avoid putting yourself at risk from either of these illnesses.

DIARRHOEA

At some stage in your Moroccan travels, it is likely that you will get **diarrhoea**. As a first stage of treatment it's best simply to adapt your diet. Yoghurt is an effective stomach settler and prickly pears (widely available in summer) are good too, as are bananas, but other fruit is best avoided, along with greasy food, dairy products, (except yoghurt), caffeine and alcohol. It's important if you have diarrhoea to replace the body fluids and salts lost through dehydration (this is especially the case with children) and dissolving rehydration salts in water will help. Failing that, half a teaspoon of salt plus three of sugar per litre of water should do the trick. Water (at least two litres per adult daily) should be drunk constantly throughout the day, rather than all in one go.

If this doesn't shake it off in a couple of days, you could obtain **carbosylate capsules** (such as Carbosylane) from a pharmacist. If symptoms persist for several days – especially if you get painful cramps, or if blood or mucus appear in your stools – you could have something more serious (see above) and should seek medical advice.

OTHER HAZARDS

There are few natural hazards in northern Morocco, where wildlife is not very different from that of Mediterranean Europe. If you venture into the Sahara however, be aware of the very real dangers of a bite from a **snake**, **palm rat** or **scorpion**. Several of the Saharan snakes are deadly, as is the palm rat. Bites should be treated as medical emergencies.

Certain scorpions (for instance, a black one with a fat tail and thin claws known as *Androctonus Mauretanicus*), are very dangerous; their sting can be fatal if not treated. Avoid going barefoot or in flip-flops in the bush, or turning over stones. In the desert, shake out your shoes before putting them on in the morning.

Never underestimate Morocco's **heat**, especially in the south. A hat – preferably light in both weight and colour – is an essential precaution and, especially if you have very fair skin, you should also consider taking a sunblock cream with a very high screening factor, as the sun really is higher (and therefore stronger) in Morocco than in northern latitudes. Resulting problems include **dehydration** – make sure that you're drinking enough (irregular urination such as only once a day is a danger sign) – and **heatstroke**, which is potentially fatal. Signs of heatstroke are a very high body temperature without a feeling of fever, but accompanied by headaches, nausea and/or disorientation (irrational behaviour by your travelling companions may be due to this). Lowering body temperature, with a tepid shower or bath, for example, is the first step in treatment, after which medical help should be sought.

AIDS

There is little awareness in Morocco of AIDS (or *SIDA*, as it is called in French), although the

Moroccan Health Ministry has been represented at recent AIDS conferences. At present, official statistics of AIDS sufferers in Morocco are very low but if the European experience is anything to go by, the reality is likely to be much higher – and rising.

As throughout the world, the need for extreme caution, and safe sex, cannot be overstressed. That applies as much to holiday romances with other travellers as it does to any sexual contact you may have with Moroccans. Moroccan condoms are less reliable than Western ones, so be on the safe side, take some with you, and insist on using them. Casual heterosexual contact is nowadays the most common way of getting HIV.

INSURANCE

Wherever you're travelling from, it's a very good idea to have some kind of **travel insurance**. A typical travel insurance policy usually provides cover for the loss of baggage, tickets and – up to a certain limit – cash or cheques, as well as cancellation or curtailment of your journey. Most of them exclude so-called **dangerous sports** unless an extra premium is paid: in Morocco this could include mountaineering, skiing, water rafting or paragliding. Read the small print and benefits tables of prospective policies carefully; coverage can vary wildly for roughly similar premiums. Many policies can be chopped and changed to exclude coverage you don't need – for example, sickness and accident benefits can often be excluded or included at will. If you do take **medical coverage**, ascertain whether benefits will be paid as treatment proceeds or only after returning home, and whether there is a 24-hour medical emergency number. When securing **baggage cover**, make sure that the per-article limit – typically under £500 equivalent – will cover your most valuable possession. If you need to make a claim, you should keep **receipts** for medicines and medical treatment, and in the event you have anything stolen, you must obtain an official statement from the police. Bank and credit cards often have certain levels of medical or other insurance included and you may automatically get travel insurance if you use a major credit card to pay for your trip.

If you have a good all-risks home insurance policy it may cover your possessions against loss or theft even when overseas. Many private medical schemes also offer coverage plans for abroad, including baggage loss, cancellation or curtailment and cash replacement as well as sickness or accident.

Canadian provincial health plans usually provide partial cover for medical mishaps overseas. North American holders of official student/ teacher/youth cards are entitled to meagre accident coverage and hospital in-patient benefits. Students will often find that their student health coverage extends during the vacations and for one term beyond the date of last enrolment.

REIMBURSEMENT

Most insurance policies work by **reimbursing you** once you return home, so be sure to keep all your receipts from doctors and pharmacists.

If you have had to undergo serious medical treatment, and incur major hospital bills, contact your consulate. They will normally be able to arrange for an insurance company, or possibly relatives, to cover the fees, pending a claim.

ROUGH GUIDES TRAVEL INSURANCE

Rough Guides now offer their own travel insurance, customized for our readers by a leading UK broker and backed by a Lloyds underwriter. It's available for anyone, of any nationality, and any age, travelling anywhere in the world.

There are two main Rough Guide insurance plans: Essential, for effective, no-frills cover, starting at £11.75 (or the equivalent) for two weeks; and Premier, from £12.50 with more generous and extensive benefits. Both can be supplemented with a "Hazardous Activities Premium" if you plan to indulge in sports considered dangerous, such as skiing or trekking. Unlike many policies, the Rough Guides schemes are calculated by the day, so if you're travelling for 27 days rather than a month, that's all you pay for. You can alternatively take out annual multi-trip insurance, which covers you for all your travel throughout the year (with a maximum of 60 days for any one trip).

For a policy quote in the UK, call the Rough Guides Insurance Line toll-free on ☎0800/015 0906; from outside Britain call ☎(+44)1243/621046. Alternatively, get an online quote or buy your policy at *www.roughguides.com/insurance*

INFORMATION, MAPS AND TREKKING GUIDES

Morocco's national tourist board (ONMT) has offices in around 25 Moroccan cities and towns. In addition, there are local tourist information offices known as Syndicats d'Initiatives. There are also – and this is a very mixed blessing – local, often self-appointed guides (for more on which see p.34).

TOURIST OFFICES

The **ONMT** (*www.tourism-in-morocco.com*) maintains general information offices in several Western capitals (see box), where you can pick up a number of pamphlets on the main Moroccan cities and resorts, and a few items on cultural themes.

In Morocco itself, you'll find an **ONMT** office or **Syndicat d'Initiative** bureau in all towns of any size or interest – often both; their addresses are detailed in the relevant sections of the Guide. Occasionally, these offices can supply you with particular local information sheets and they can of course try to help out with specific questions.

But don't expect too much from them; their main function, from their point of view, is to gather statistics and to put you in touch with an officially recognized guide (for more on which, read on).

ROAD MAPS

The **maps of Moroccan towns** in this book should be sufficient for most needs. Local commercial ones exist but add little to those we've printed; the most authoritative local series, the **Plan-Guides** published by Editions Gauthey, look impressive but are next to useless in trying to find your way round the twists and turns of a Medina. They may, however, be useful if you need to find places way out on the edge of town.

One thing you will probably want, though, is a **road map**. Very good ones are in fact given out free at ONMT tourist offices, and these are adequate for most purposes. Should you wish to buy one, the best is Michelin's (sheet #959), on a scale of 1:1,000,000 with 1:600,000 insets of the Casa–Rabat area, the Fes–Meknes–Rif area, the Marrakesh area and the Middle Atlas, though much of the Western Sahara is only on a 1:4,000,000 inset. Michelin's is generally the most accurate. Another good one is Hildebrand's at 1:900,000, with the Western Sahara on 1:1,500,000. This is less dense with information and so sometimes clearer than Michelin. Geo Center's 1:800,000 (Western Sahara 1:2,500,000) is also good, and has the advantage of being available in Morocco, as is Carima's 1:1,850,000 map, which is cheaper but not as good.

Note that maps (or guidebooks) which do not show the **former Spanish Sahara (Western Sahara)** as Moroccan territory are liable to confiscation. Even maps showing a reduced-scale version of the territory are frowned upon.

TRAVEL BOOK AND MAP OUTLETS

UK AND IRELAND
London Daunt Books, 83 Marylebone High St, W1 (☎020/7224 2295), 193 Haverstock Hill, NW3 (☎020/7794 4006); National Map Centre, 22–24 Caxton St, SW1 (☎020/7222 2466, www.mapsworld.com), Stanfords, 12–14 Long Acre, WC2 (☎020/7836 1321), in the UsitCampus shop at 52 Grosvenor Gardens, SW1 (☎020/7730 1314), and in the British Airways shop at 156 Regent St, W1 (☎020/7434 4744); The Travel Bookshop, 13–15 Blenheim Crescent, W1 (☎020/7229 5260, www.thetravelbookshop.co.uk).
Dublin Eason's, 40 O'Connell St, Dublin 1 (☎01/873 3811); Waterstone's, 7 Dawson St, Dublin 2 (☎01/679 1415).
Belfast Waterstone's, Queens Bldg, 8 Royal Ave (☎028/9024 7355).
Bristol Stanfords, 29 Corn Street (☎0117/929 9966).
Cambridge Heffers Map Shop, 3rd Floor, 19 Sidney St (☎01223/568467, www.heffers.co.uk).
Cardiff Blackwell's, 13–17 Royal Arcade (☎029/2039 5036).
Cork Waterstone's, 69 Patrick St (☎021/276522).
Fife Atlas Maps, 26 Kirkcaldy Road, Burntisland (☎01592/873546; mail order only; sae with all correspondence; closed Feb–May).
Inverness James Thin Melven's Bookshop, 29 Union St (☎01463/233500, www.jthin.co.uk).
Leicester The Map Shop, 30a Belvoir St (☎0116/247 1400).
Manchester Waterstone's, 91 Deansgate (☎0161/837 3000, www.waterstones-manchester-deansgate.co.uk).
Newcastle Newcastle Map Centre, 55 Grey St (☎0191/261 5622, www.traveller.com).
Oxford Blackwell's Map and Travel Shop, 53 Broad St (☎01865/792792, www.bookshop.blackwell.co.uk).
Worcestershire The Map Shop, 15 High St, Upton-upon-Severn (☎01684/593146, www.themapshop.co.uk).

Maps by mail or phone order are available from Stanfords (☎020/7836 1321; sales@stanfords.co.uk), Atlas Maps and several of the other listed suppliers.

USA
Chicago Rand McNally, 444 N Michigan Ave, IL 60611 (☎312/321-1751, www.randmcnally.com).
New York The Complete Traveler Bookstore, 199 Madison Ave, NY 10016 (☎212/685-9007, www.completetraveller.com); Rand McNally, 150 East 52nd St, NY 10022 (☎212/758-7488,

www.randmcnally.com); Traveler'sChoice Bookstore, 2 Wooster St, New York, NY 10013 (☎212/941-1535; tvlchoice@aol.com).
Palo Alto Phileas Fogg's Books & Maps, #87 Stanford Shopping Center, Palo Alto, CA 94304 (☎1-800/533-FOGG, www.foggs.com).
Portland Powell's Travel Store, 701 West 6th Street, Pioneer Courthouse Square, Portland (☎503/228-1108, www.powells.com).
San Francisco The Complete Traveler Bookstore, 3207 Fillmore St, CA 94123 (☎415/923-1511, www.completetraveller.com) Rand McNally, 595 Market St, CA 94105 (☎415/777-3131, www.randmcnally.com).
Santa Barbara Map Link Inc., 30 S La Patera Lane, Unit 5, Santa Barbara, CA 93117 (☎805/692-6777, www.maplink.com).
Seattle Elliott Bay Book Company, 101 S Main St, Seattle, WA 98104 (☎206/624-6600, www.elliottbaybook.com).
Washington DC Travel Books & Language Center, 4437 Wisconsin Ave, Washington, DC 20016 (☎1-800/220-2665); ADC Map and Travel Center, 1636 I St NW, Washington DC 20006 (☎202/628-2608); Rand McNally, 1201 Connecticut Ave NW, Washington DC 20036 (☎202/223-6751, www.randmcnally.com).

Rand McNally have stores across the US; call ☎1-800/333 0136 (ext 2111) for the address of your nearest store, or for direct mail maps.

CANADA
Montreal Ulysses Travel Bookshop, 4176 St-Denis, Montreal, PQ H2W 2M5 (☎514/843 9447, www.ulyssesguides.com)
Toronto Open Air Books and Maps, 25 Toronto St, ON M5C 2R1 (☎416/363 0719).
Vancouver International Travel Maps and Books, 552 Seymour St, Vancouver, BC V6B 3J5 (☎604/687 3320, www.itmb.com).

AUSTRALIA AND NEW ZEALAND
Adelaide The Map Shop, 16a Peel St, SA 5000 (☎08/8231 2033).
Auckland Specialty Maps, 58 Albert St (☎09/307 2217).
Brisbane Worldwide Maps and Guides, 187 George St, Qld 4000 (☎07/3221 4330).
Melbourne Bowyangs, 372 Little Bourke St, Vic 3000 (☎03/9670 4383).
Perth Perth Map Centre, 891 Hay St, WA 6000 (☎08/9322 5733).
Sydney Travel Bookshop, Shop 3, 175 Liverpool St, NSW 2000 (☎02/9261 8200).

MOROCCO ON THE INTERNET

There are scores of Web sites on Morocco, both in English and French, run from within and without the country, and more than twenty local ISPs. There is also an ever-increasing number of cybercafés and Internet clubs in the major cities, where you can browse the Web, send email, or check your own if you have a Hotmail or similar account. Places where you can do this are detailed under "Internet access" in "Listings" in this book. There is also a small directory of Moroccan cybercafés on the Al Akhawayn University resources page (see below), but it is far from comprehensive.

NEWS GROUPS

The following newsgroups are good for reading and posting travel and cultural questions, and for discussions about Morocco:

rec.travel.africa

soc.culture.maghreb

soc.culture.berber

An excellent **Morocco FAQ** compiled from Morocco postings on *rec.travel* is maintained by Jey Burrows on a number of Web sites, including:

*www.geocities.com/TheTropics/4896/
    morocco.html*

This contains a multitude of links across the Web and should be your first port of call.

WEB SITES

Al Akhawayn University
www.alakhawayn.ma
The Ifrane International University Web site has details on their language and other courses and an excellent resource section of links to other sites.

Anas's Moroccan WWW Sites
www.utoledo.edu/~achraibi/morocco.html
A good page of miscellaneous links to sites of Moroccan interest.

Arab.net
www.arab.net/morocco
Arab.net includes a range of info on Moroccan government, culture, history and much more.

Barbarity
www.maroc.net/barraka
Barbarity is an adventurous record label, mixing Moroccan singers and rhythms in a dance context.

City.net: Morocco
www.city.net/countries/morocco
City.net's Web indexes usually unearth the interesting new sites. This one is a bit sparse, but still worth checking.

Channel#Maroc
www.mines.u-nancy.fr/~mhamdi/maroc.html
IRC (chat) channel, used mainly by Moroccans living abroad. Multilingual discussions take place.

TREKKING MAPS AND GUIDES

At present, the vital **topographical maps** needed by trekkers, climbers, skiers, etc (1:50,000 and 1:100,000) are very difficult to find in Morocco. You have to go in person to the *Division de la Cartographie*, 31 Av. Moulay El Hassan, Rabat (☎03/776 5192), show your passport, and submit an order which is then available for collection several days later – if the request is approved. The only exceptions are the maps of Toubkal (both scales) which will be served over the counter. These are also sporadically available at the *Hôtel Ali*, Marrakesh, or in Imlil, the trailhead for treks in the area. However, if you are planning to go trekking, it is best to try and get maps through a **specialist map outlet** before you leave home (see box on p.31). Look for 1:100,000 (and if you're lucky 1:50,000) maps of the Atlas and other moun-

tain areas. Stanfords in London does a good pack of four maps covering the Djebel Toubkal area.

Atlas Maps (see box on p.31) produce brief **map-guides** to the Asni-Toubkal, Western High Atlas (Taroudannt) and Sirwa (Taliouine), Anti-Atlas (Tafraoute), Aklim (Igherm) and Djebel Bou Iblane/Bou Naceur (Middle Atlas) areas. Written by our High Atlas contributor, Hamish Brown, these are useful complements to the coverage in this guide. Atlas Maps do mail order worldwide, and are definitely the best place to try for Moroccan maps that you cannot obtain elsewhere.

Also worth acquiring is a **booklet** called *Maroc: Tourisme en Montagnes et au Désert*. It comes out annually in French, English, Spanish and other European languages, and contains listings for guides, transport and even mule hire, as well as their tariffs – essential for knowledgeable

Discover
www.discover.ltd.uk
Homepage of the adventure tour company, including notes from its High Atlas kasbah field centre.

Hotels on the Net
www.hotelstravel.com/morocco.html
Links to Moroccan hotel Web sites.

La Maison du Maroc
www.maroc.net/kiosque
A "kiosque" of local press, including daily news from Radio Casablanca in Real Audio.

Marrakesh Express
uslink.net/ddavis/meintr.html
This US-based Moroccan carpet store has a gallery of photos, plus illuminating text on weaving techniques.

Maroc Hebdo
www.maroc hcbdo.press.ma
French-language weekly magazine covering political and economic issues.

Moroccan Links
www.maroc.net/ipm/maroc.html
An attempt to list and link to all the sites of Moroccan interest on the Internet. It doesn't, of course, but it does have a very varied and useful selection of links nonetheless.

Sephardic-Moroccan Page
www.jewishglobe.com/morocco
From Moroccan synagogues around the world to music and cooking. There is more on Sephardic Moroccan music (including sound samples) at Sylvian's Judeo-Arabic Melodies Page
www.geocities.com/Paris/6256/judeo.htm

La Rennaissance Amazigh
http://www.multimania.com/aza/ugzil.htm
An excellent site on Berber language and culture run by the Amazigh Movement Association, but unfortunately plagued with annoying pop-ups.

US Consular Travel Advisory
http://travel.state.gov/morocco.html
A fairly cautionary warning sheet on matters such as crime and health, as well as more mundane details.

INTERNET CONNECTIONS (ISPs)

The following ISPs (the Al Akhawayn resource pages – see opposite – have full lists) have English-speaking staff and are recommended.

Cybermania
www.cybermania.net.ma (☎03/970 4987).

MTDS
www.mtds.net.ma (☎03/767 4861 or 767 4862).

---

bargaining. It should be available through ONMT outlets in Morocco; they often deny having any copies, but persevere or, better still, pick one up from their office in your country before leaving home.

More **detailed trekking guidebooks** are also available in both English and French. The most useful are Michael Peyron's *Grand Atlas Traverse* (West Col, UK; 2 vols), Robin Collomb's *Atlas Mountains* (West Col, UK) and Karl Smith's *Atlas Mountains: A Walker's Guide* (Cicerone Press, UK). Also available from West Col, in English, is a map guide to the Mgoun Massif at 1:100,000, which is useful for a wide region, sec-

ond only to Toubkal in popularity. In Morocco, Rabat has some good bookshops. In Marrakesh, there are two on Av. Mohammed V (see p.377); Librairie Chatr at no.19 has the best selection of titles. Guidebooks are also on sale at the CAF refuge at Oukaïmeden.

If you pass through London en route to Morocco, you might also want to consult some of the Expedition Reports at the **Royal Geographical Society** (1 Kensington Gore, London SW7); the RGS's **Expeditionary Advisory Centre** (☎020/7591 3030) will help locate relevant material, maps and reports.

HUSTLE, HASSLE, KIDS AND GUIDES

The question of whether to employ a guide will be one of your first (and most frequent) decisions in Morocco. With tourism so important a part of the economy, guiding has become quite a business – especially in the major cities of Fes and Marrakesh. In addition to the guides authorized by the local *Délégation du Tourisme*, there are scores of young Moroccans offering their services to show you round the souks (markets) and sights. These "unofficial guides" are not, strictly speaking, legal, and there are occasional crackdowns by the police on offenders. However, they remain very much a factor (and bane) of tourist life.

With all guides, official or otherwise, it is important to establish at the outset what you want to see. You may well find it useful to agree an itinerary – perhaps showing your guide the points you want to visit on the maps in this book. Do not be pushed into a tour of the craft stores or you will see nothing else. If you do want to visit shops, make it clear what kind of goods you are interested in seeing, and equally clear that you do not want to purchase on an initial visit. Remember that any purchase you make with a guide in tow will add to the price of whatever you are buying, since the guide will want a commission from the shopkeeper on whatever you buy. This is especially true in the case of official guides, who can demand a higher commission than unofficial ones (40 percent is quite normal). It is better to come back and do your shopping later, without a guide.

Would-be guides, moreover, are not the only people who will be on your case in Morocco. You are also likely to be accosted by hustlers of various sorts, often posing as potential guides. This particularly applies to the north of the country, much less so in the more laid-back south (apart from Marrakesh). Hustlers range from outright thieves and confidence tricksters, through dope dealers, to people hoping for a commission by steering you (sometimes with the most amazing deviousness) into carpet shops where you will be subjected to hours of hard-sell. Other people who approach you, on the other hand, are simply trying to be friendly – they may want to help you, or to practise their English, or think that you are able to get them a visa to work abroad.

OFFICIAL GUIDES

Official guides, engaged through tourist offices (or some of the larger hotels), are paid at a fixed rate of 120dh (£7.50/$12) for a half-day. The rate is for the guide's time, and can be shared by a group of people – though the latter would be expected to make some additional tip.

Taking an introductory tour of a new city with an official guide can be a useful exercise in orientation – especially in the vast Medinas (old quarters) of Fes and Marrakesh. Your guide may well be an interesting and entertaining presence, too. Some are highly knowledgeable. There is an advantage also in that, if you are accompanied by an official guide, you won't be approached or hassled by any of their (sometimes less than reputable) unauthorized equivalents.

Official guides can identify themselves by a large, brass "sheriff's badge".

UNOFFICIAL GUIDES AND HUSTLERS

Unofficial guides will approach you in the streets of any sizeable town, offering to find you a hotel, show you the sights, or perhaps, if you look a likely customer, sell you some *kif* or hashish. You will need to develop a strategy to deal with these approaches, otherwise you are unlikely to enjoy urban Morocco.

The most important point to realize is that there are **good** and **bad guides**. Some are genuine students, who may want to earn a small fee, but may equally be interested (as so many claim) in practising their English. Others are out-and-out

FRIENDSHIPS

Following clampdowns on "unofficial guides", there are laws in effect that can make relationships with Moroccans problematic. In theory, any Moroccan – without a guide's permit – seen "accompanying" a tourist can be arrested and imprisoned. In practice this is rarely enforced but friendships, especially with young Moroccans in tourist cities like Tangier, Agadir or Marrakesh, should be discreet. On the whole, once invited to a home, and having met a family, you are unlikely to encounter problems, and your hosts will deal effectively with any enquiries from curious local policemen.

ATTITUDES AND BEHAVIOUR

If you want to get the most from a trip to Morocco, it is vital not to start assuming anyone who approaches or talks to you is a hustler. Too many tourists do, and end up making little contact with what must be one of the most hospitable peoples in the world.

Behaviour and attitude are equally important on your part. If some Moroccans treat tourists with contempt, and exploit them as a simple resource, it has much to do with the way the latter behave. It helps everyone if you can avoid **rudeness** or aggressive behaviour in response to insistent offers from guides. And be aware, too, of the importance of **dress**: many Moroccans, especially in rural areas, may well take exception to (or get the wrong idea from) clothes that do not fully cover parts of the body considered "private". That may include both legs and shoulders, especially for women. It is true that in cities Moroccan women wear short-sleeved tops and knee-length skirts (and may suffer more harassment as a result), and men may wear sleeveless T-shirts and above-the-knee shorts. However, the Muslim idea of "modest dress" (such as would be acceptable in a mosque for example) requires women to be covered from wrist to ankle, and men from below the shoulder to below the knee. In rural areas at least, it is a good idea to follow these codes, and definitely a bad idea for women to wear skirts or shorts above the knee, or sleeveless T-shirts, and for members of either sex to wear only very short shorts. Even ordinary T-shirts may be regarded as underwear. The best guide is to note how Moroccans dress locally – and not how other tourists choose to.

Photography needs to be undertaken with care. If you are obviously taking a photograph of someone, ask their permission – especially in the more remote, rural regions where you can cause genuine offence. On a more positive front, taking a photograph of someone you've struck up a friendship with and sending it on to them, or exchanging photographs, is often greatly appreciated. In fact, while in Morocco, you may be surprised to find yourself dragged off by new friends or acquaintances to a street or studio photographer for a photo session. This is quite common practice and has no untoward ends.

When **invited to a home**, you normally take your shoes off before entering the reception rooms – follow your host's lead on that. It is customary to take a gift: sweet pastries or tea and sugar are always acceptable, and you might even take meat (by arrangement – a chicken from the countryside for example, still alive of course) to a poorer home.

hustlers, preying on first-visit innocence and paranoia. Your task is to distinguish between offers, to accept (perhaps limited) services from those who seem friendly and enjoyable company, and to deal as humanly as possible with approaches you wish to decline. Politeness is essential, or you'll find things unpleasant, and silence is taken as rudeness; mutual preservation of **dignity** is important.

In general, don't agree to a guide showing you to a **hotel**; they will only take you to those which pay them a commission, meaning not only a higher bill for you, but also that the hotels you are being taken to are more likely to be dodgy – decent hotels shouldn't pay commission to guides for bringing them tourists. It is best to know in advance which you want to go to – check our listings before arrival. Letting someone guide you to a **café** or **restaurant** won't increase the price of a meal (although waiters will generally make a small tip to the guide).

Offers of a **tour of the town**, however, you may want to avoid. To do so, it is a golden rule to

look as if you know where you are going. Never admit to this being your first visit to Morocco. If you feel confident enough, say that you have visited the town before and that you are glad to be back. You will be on your way to setting the parameters of discussion. The most exploitative guides will probably drop you to look elsewhere. If you are unsure of a guide, suggest taking a mint tea together in a café. Don't make any agreement to employ him prior to this, or any suggestion of an agreement. In addition, never allow yourself to be bullied into going with someone with whom you don't feel at ease – there is no shortage of candidates. And if you feel genuinely threatened or harassed, don't hesitate to threaten or indeed to go to the police: hustlers tend to vanish fast at the prospect of police involvement.

If you do decide to hire an unofficial guide, be sure to **fix the rate**, as well as the **itinerary**, in advance. You should make it clear that you know the official rates for guides and should agree on these as a maximum. Many unofficial guides will attempt to charge a rate per person.

SEXUAL HARASSMENT

Different women seem to have vastly different experiences of **sexual harassment** in Morocco. Some travellers find it persistent and bothersome, while others have little or no trouble with it at all. Many women compare Morocco favourably with Spain and other parts of southern Europe, but there is no doubt that, in general, harassment of tourists here is more persistent than it is in northern Europe or the English-speaking world.

Harassment will usually consist of men simply trying to chat you up or even asking directly for sex, and it can be constant and sometimes intimidating. In part this is to do with Moroccan men's misunderstanding of Western culture and sexual attitudes, and some think they can get away with taking liberties with tourists that no Moroccan woman would tolerate.

The obvious **strategies** for getting rid of unwanted attention are the same ones that you would use at home: appear confident and assured and you will avoid a lot of trouble. Moroccan women are traditionally coy and aloof, and uninhibited friendliness – especially any kind of physical contact between sexes – may be seen as a come-on, therefore being formal but polite when talking to men will diminish the chances of misinterpretation. The negative side to this approach is that it can also make it harder for you to get to know people, but after you've been in the country for a while, you will probably develop a feel for the sort of men with whom this tactic is necessary.

How you **dress** is another thing that may reduce harassment. Wearing "modest" clothes (long sleeves, long skirts, baggy rather than tight clothes) will give an impression of respectability. Wearing a headscarf to cover your hair and ears will give this impression even more. One reader, agreeing with this advice, wrote to say that she felt a headscarf was "the single most important item of dress", and added that you can pull it over your face as a veil if unwanted male attention makes you feel uncomfortable. Indeed, Western women often forget that the purpose of wearing a veil is to protect women rather than to oppress them. However, you will notice that many Moroccan women totally ignore the traditional dress code, and do not suffer excessive harassment as a result. Making it clear that you, like your Moroccan counterparts, are not willing to accept such behaviour will usually deter all but the most insistent of men.

Other strategies include avoiding eye contact, mentioning a husband who is nearby, and, if travelling with a boyfriend or just with a male friend, giving the impression that he is your husband. You should also avoid physical contact with Moroccan men, even in a manner that would not be considered sexual at home, since it could easily be misunderstood. If a Moroccan man touches *you*, on the other hand, he has definitely crossed the line, and you should not be afraid to **make a scene**. Shouting "*Shooma!*" ("Shame on you!") is likely to result in bystanders intervening on your behalf, and a very uncomfortable situation for your assailant.

It is often said that women are second-class citizens in Morocco and other Islamic countries, though educated Muslim women are usually keen to point out that this is a misinterpretation of Islam. It is certainly true that feminism and sexual equality have a long way to go in Morocco, but in some ways, at least in theory, the sexes are not as unequal as they seem. Men traditionally rule in the street, which is their domain, the woman's being the home. One result of this is that Moroccan women will receive their friends at home rather than meet them in, say, a café, and this can make it difficult for you to get to know Moroccan women. One place where you *can* meet up with them easily is the hammam (see p.50). It may also be that if you are travelling with a man, Moroccan men will address him rather than you – but this is in fact out of respect for you, not disrespect, and you will not be ignored if you join in the conversation. In any case, however interpreted, Islam most certainly does not condone sexual harassment, and nor do any respectable Moroccans. Being aware of that fact will make it seem a lot less threatening.

CON MEN AND SCAMS

Hustlers and con men are a distinct minority in Morocco, as anywhere else. In recent years, they have been largely cleaned off the streets by police action, and those who remain are less persistent. Many seem to have moved on to smaller places rather than remain in the classic hustler cities – Tangier, Tetouan, Fes or Marrakesh – where you will, on your first day, encounter just about all those available. On the second and subsequent days, they'll know your face and approaches will notably drop off. However, forewarned is forearmed, so a few notes on the **most common scams**:

As stressed in the introduction, all guides (including official ones) have an interest in getting you into craft shops, where they can earn commission of thirty to fifty percent. Even if you say you're not interested, they may suggest taking tea with a cousin who owns a shop. Don't be afraid to keep to your agreed itinerary; keep moving and show interest in the next place on the agreed itinerary.

A favourite line is that there is a Berber market taking place – and this is the only day of the week to see it. This is rarely true. You will probably visit everyday shops and souks.

Some of the more exploitative hustlers will guide you into the Medinas, then, when you have no idea where you are, charge a large fee to take you back out and to your hotel. If this happens to you, don't be afraid to appeal to people in the street; your hustler will not want attention.

A few tales are told each year of people approaching visitors with a letter or package to mail to the USA or Europe when you leave Morocco. Never agree to this; you may be involving yourself in a drugs plant.

Many more hustlers will simply use the excuse of a letter ("Could you help translate or write one?") as a means of attaching themselves to you; it's best to decline assistance.

Another favourite way for hustlers to introduce themselves is by pretending to be someone you have met but forgotten, so if someone you don't remember says, "Hey, remember me?" it's probably a hustler trying to lure you into a carpet shop or practise some scam on you.

A common line from hustlers if you don't want to buy their wares or engage their services as a guide is that you must be paranoid or racist. They are appealing quite cynically here to the guilty conscience of the Western liberal.

On the trains, especially at Tangier, hustlers sometimes pose as porters or railway staff, demanding an extortionate fee for carrying baggage or payment of supplements. Genuine rail staff wear beige overalls and have ID cards, which, if suspicious, you should ask to see.

Drivers should beware of hitchhiking hustlers, who spend all day hitching between a pair of towns and can get highly obnoxious in their demands for money when you approach one or other destination. Alternatively, they may wish to thank you for the lift by taking you home for a cup of tea – except that "home" turns out to be a carpet shop, where you are then subjected to hours of hard-sell. We've even heard of people who seem to have broken down on the road flagging down passing tourists and asking them to take a note to a "mechanic", who turns out to be a carpet salesman.

In the south, be wary of offers to meet "Blue Men" (desert Touareg nomads) in the "desert". The "nomads" are almost invariably rogues.

In a number of towns, con merchants have been posing as students, working alone or in couples, befriending tourists, and then, after a day or two, telling some sad tale about needing money for getting a passport off a corrupt official, or to look after sick relatives, or some such. You may feel a little foolish if you give money and then meet six other travellers with identical tales to tell.

Heading for the beach, especially in Tangier, leave most of your money back at your hotel. Thefts and pickpocketing are common and on the increase, particularly in the Medinas and by juveniles; mugging is rare but alas on the increase, especially in Tangier and Marrakesh.

DEALING WITH CHILDREN

In the countryside, and especially along the major southern routes, you will find fewer hustlers and guides, but many more children, eager in their demands for a dirham, *un cadeau* (present) or *un stylo* (a pen/pencil).

Working out your own strategy is all part of the game, but, whatever else you do, be sure to keep a good humour: smile and laugh, or kids can make your life hell. Faced with **begging from children**, we strongly recommend not obliging, as this ties them to a begging mentality.

SECURITY, THE POLICE AND CONSULATES

Keeping your luggage and money secure is an important consideration in Morocco. For all the tales, the situation is probably no worse than in Spain or Italy, but it is obviously unwise to carry large sums of cash or valuables on your person – especially in the main tourist cities like Fes, Marrakesh and Tangier.

Hotels, generally, are secure and useful for depositing money before setting out to explore; larger ones will keep valuables at reception and some will have safes. **Campsites** are considerably less secure, and many campers advise using a **money belt** – to be worn even while sleeping. If you do decide on a money belt (and many people spend time quite happily without), leather or cotton materials are preferable to nylon, which can irritate in the heat.

If you are **driving**, it almost goes without saying, you should not leave anything you cannot afford to lose visible or accessible in your car.

THE POLICE

There are two main types of Moroccan **police**: the *Gendarmerie* (who wear grey uniforms and man the checkpoints on main roads, at junctions and the entry to towns), and the *Police* (*Sûreté*), who wear navy blue uniforms or plain clothes. Either force may demand to see your passport (and/or driving papers). The carrying of ID cards or passports is obligatory, though you should not

FOREIGN EMBASSIES AND CONSULATES IN MOROCCO

Algeria 46–48 Bd. Tariq Ibn Ziad, Rabat (☎03/776 5474); 159 Bd. Moulay Idriss I, Casablanca (☎02/280 4177); Rue de Taza, Oujda (☎05/668 3740 or 41).

Canada 13 bis Rue Jaâar As-Saddik, Agdal, Rabat (☎03/767 2880).

Denmark 4 Rue de Khémisset, Rabat (☎03/776 9293); 719 Bd. Modiboukeita, Rue d'Indre, Casablanca (☎02/228 1706); 3 Rue Ibn Rochd, Tangier (☎03/993 8727).

Mauritania 266 Quartier O.I.M., Souissi, Rabat (☎03/765 6678).

Netherlands 40 Rue de Tunis (☎03/773 3512); 26 Rue Nationale, Casablanca (☎02/222 1820); Immeuble Miramonte, 47 Av. Hassan II, Tangier (☎03/993 1245).

Norway 9 Rue de Khenifra, Agdal (☎03/776 4084 or 85); 44 Rue Mohammed Smitha,

Casablanca (☎02/231 9732); c/o *Hôtel Kamal*, Bd. Hassan II, Agadir (☎04/884 2817).

South Africa 34 Rue des Saadiens, Rabat (☎07/70.67.60).

Sweden 159 Av. John Kennedy, Souissi, Rabat (☎03/775 9303); 3 Rue du Lt. Sylvestre, Casablanca (☎02/230 2533); 31 Rue Prince Heritier, Tangier (☎03/993 8730); c/o *Hôtel Adrar*, Bd. Mohammed V, Agadir (☎04/884 0417).

UK 17 Bd. Tour Hassan, Rabat (☎03/772 0996); 41 Bd. Mohammed V, BP 2122, Tangier (☎03/994 1557); 60 Bd. d'Anfa, BP 13 762, Casablanca (☎02/222 1653); c/o Complet Tours, 1 Immeuble Beausouss (opposite campsite entrance), Agadir (☎04/882 3401 or 02).

USA 2 Av. de Marrakech, Rabat (☎03/762 2265); 8 Bd. Moulay Youssef, Casablanca (☎02/226 4550).

New Zealanders can use UK consular facilities while in Morocco. **Australians** can use Canadian consular facilities. **Irish** citizens are in theory covered by their embassy in Lisbon, Portugal (Rua da Imprensa à Estrela 1–4°, 1200 Lisboa; ☎00-351-1/392 9440), but might be able to get help from British consular authorities in cases of dire emergency.

For Moroccan embassies and consulates abroad, see p.23.

have any problems if you leave yours in a hotel safe while wandering around town, especially if you carry a photocopy of the important pages.

The **Gendarmes** have jurisdiction outside built-up areas, but you will find their prominent headquarters in, or on the edge of, most towns; they are generally better educated and more polite than the police. You can report any kind of crime to them – or turn to them if you need help.

The **Police**, who operate within towns, are usually polite and helpful to visitors, although they are more concerned with public order and petty crime in the towns. There is now a *Brigade Touristique* in cities such as Marrakesh and Fes, specifically set up to protect tourists, though there have been reports that the *Brigade Touristique* in Fes will turn a blind eye to the activities of pick-pockets, who pay them off for the favour.

In addition to these, there is a green-uniformed **Force Auxiliaire**, who wear berets and look more like the army. Their role is as a back-up to the regular police and *gendarmes*, and you are unlikely to have any contact with them.

If you do need to **report a theft**, try to take along a fluent French- or Arabic-speaker if your own French and Arabic are not too hot. You may only be given a scrap of paper with an official stamp to show your insurance company, who then have to apply themselves to a particular police station for a report (in Arabic). If you cannot prove that a theft has taken place, the police may decline to make any report, especially if the theft is of money only. They will always give you a report, however, if you have lost any official document (passport, driving licence, etc).

The **police emergency number** is ☎19.

GETTING AROUND

Moroccan public transport is, on the whole, pretty good. There is an efficient rail network linking the main towns of the north, the coast and Marrakesh, and elsewhere you can travel easily enough by bus or collective taxi. In the mountains and over the more remote desert routes, where roads are often just dirt tracks (pistes), local people maintain a network of market-day lorries – uncomfortable but fun.

Renting a car can be a good idea, at least for a part of your trip, opening up routes that are time-consuming or difficult on local transport.

Most major companies allow you to rent a car in one city and return it to another.

FLIGHTS

Royal Air Maroc (RAM) operates **domestic flights** from their Casablanca hub to major cities nationwide, as does domestic rival **Regional Air Lines**. Between any other two points, however, you will have to change planes at Casablanca, unless both points are stops on a single Casa-bound flight (Dakhla to Agadir, for example). In general, flying is not really worthwhile except for long-distance routes such as to Laayoune or Dakhla in the Western Sahara, when they can save you a lot of time. A flight from Casablanca to Laayoune would set you back 1480dh (£92.50/$148) and take just over an hour and a half (plus journey time to the airport and check-in time), compared to nineteen hours by bus. If you're very pressed for time, you might want to use the services between Casablanca and places like Agadir or even Oujda. On shorter routes, the speed of a flight is counterbalanced by factors such as the price, the time taken travelling between airports and town centres, and the relative infrequency of flights compared to buses.

A summary of flights available is given in the "Travel Details" section at the end of each chapter of this book, along with details of train and bus services. RAM offices are detailed in the "Listings" or "Practicalities" sections for each major town. The airlines can also be contacted through their head office and reservation centres at Casablanca airport (RAM ☎0900 0800; Regional Air Lines ☎02/253 8080). RAM also has a Web site at *www.royalairmaroc.com* Remember that you must always confirm flights at a RAM office 72 hours before departure. Student and under-26 youth **discounts** of 25 percent are available on all RAM domestic flights but only if the ticket is bought in advance from one of their offices.

TRAINS

Trains cover a limited network of routes, but for travel between the major cities they are easily the best option – reliable, comfortable, efficient and fairly fast.

The **map** at the beginning of this book shows all the passenger train routes in the country, and services are summarized in the "Travel Details" at the end of each chapter. There are basically two lines which carry passengers: from Tangier in the north down to Marrakesh, and from Oujda in the northeast, also to Marrakesh, joining with the Tangier line at Sidi Kacem. There are plans to extend the railway south to Agadir, and on to Laayoune in the Western Sahara, but it's anyone's guess when that project will reach fruition. Schedules change very little from year to year, but it's wise to check times in advance at stations. **Timetables**, printed by ONCF, the national railway company, are usually available at major train stations and tourist offices – if they don't have a full timetable at the station, they'll print you off a mini-timetable of services between any two stations. You can also check schedules and fares on the ONCF Web site at *www.oncf.org.ma*

There are two **classes** of tickets – first and second. **Costs** for a second-class ticket are slightly more than what you'd pay for buses; on certain "express" services ("express" refers to the level of comfort rather than the speed), they are around thirty percent higher. In addition, there are **couchettes** (50dh extra) available on the Tangier–Marrakesh and Tangier–Oujda night trains; these are worth the money for the sake of security, as passengers are locked into a carriage with a guard. If you intend to use the railways a lot, it might just about be worth your while buying a "EuroDomino" or "Freedom Pass". These are available from youth travel agencies and international rail travel centres in the British Isles or North America (Wasteels or RailEurope for example), and give three to eight days' free travel on Moroccan railways for £23–53/$33–77 (£22–48/$31–75 for under-26s) in second class, or £31–71/$45–103 in first.

Most of the **stations** are located reasonably close to the modern city centres, in the French-built quarters – the Villes Nouvelles. They generally have **left luggage** depots, though these accept only luggage that can be locked (effectively excluding rucksacks). An alternative is usually provided by nearby cafés, who will look after your luggage for a small tip.

GRANDS TAXIS

Collective **grands taxis** are one of the best features of Moroccan transport. They operate on a wide variety of routes, are much quicker than

---

FARES

Fares for train, bus and grand taxi journeys follow a reasonably consistent pattern.

For **bus** journeys, reckon on around 1.50–2.50dh for each 10km.

For **trains**, expect to pay around 3dh per 10km in second class, depending on the train.

Grands taxis charge around 2–4dh per person for each 10km. Fares tend to be lower for more popular routes, when the taxi will get passengers more quickly, and higher for routes where the taxi needs to wait a long time for passengers before setting off. Chartering a taxi for yourself or a group, you will have to pay for six places.

For **comparison**, on the Marrakesh to Casablanca route, a train will take three hours and cost 73dh second class/100dh first class on an "express" (seven out of eight services), or 56dh/84dh on the single daily "ordinary" train. A CTM bus will cost 65dh and take three and a half hours, while an ordinary bus will cost 34dh and take around four. A shared grand taxi will cost 80dh and take two and a half hours (though on most routes in fact the difference between grand taxi and ordinary bus fares is a good deal less).

buses (usually quicker than trains, too), and fares are very reasonable. They are also a good way of meeting people and having impromptu Arabic lessons.

The taxis are usually big Peugeot or Mercedes cars carrying six passengers (Peugeots are less common but have a slightly less cramped seating arrangement). Most business is along specific routes, and the most popular routes have more or less continuous departures throughout the day. Consequently, you don't have to worry about timetables. You just show up at the terminal (locations are detailed, city by city, in the guide) and ask for a place to a specific destination. As soon as six (or, if you're willing to pay extra, four or five) people are assembled, the taxi sets off. Make sure, however, when asking about grands taxis, that it is clear you only want a place (*une place*) in a collective taxi (*collectif*), as drivers often "presume" that a tourist will want to charter the whole taxi, which means paying for all six places.

Most collective grands taxis run over a fairly short route, from one large town to the next. If you want to travel further, you will have to change taxis from time to time. Some routes are covered routinely in **stages** (eg Agadir–Taroudannt, or Agadir–Taliouine) and taxi drivers will generally assist you in finding a connecting taxi and in settling the fare with the driver. Picking up a grand taxi on the road is much more problematic, since they will only stop if they have a place free (if a passenger has already alighted in other words).

Fares for set routes are fixed, and drivers do not usually try to overcharge tourists for a place. If you think that you are being overcharged, ask the other passengers, or check the price with your hotel before leaving – or, as a general guideline, consult the "Fares" box opposite. Occasionally, five passengers may agree to split the cost of the last place to hasten departure, or one passenger may agree to pay for two places. You will normally be expected to pay the full fare for the journey even if travelling only part of the way.

If you want to take a **non-standard route**, or an excursion, it is possible to charter a whole grand taxi (*une course*). In theory this should be exactly six times the price of a place in a shared taxi, but you'll often have to bargain hard to get that. Hotels can sometimes be useful in helping to charter grands taxis.

Some people consider grands taxis **dangerous**. It is certainly true that they are prone to practices such as speeding, and overtaking on blind curves or the brows of hills, and they have more than their fair share of accidents. Drivers may work all day and into the night, and it seems a large number of accidents involve grand taxi drivers falling asleep at the wheel while driving at night, so you may wish to avoid using them for night-time journeys. Note also that with the seating arrangements, it is not usually possible to wear a seat belt.

BUSES

Bus travel is marginally cheaper than taking a grand taxi, and there are far more **regular routes**. Travelling on public transport for any length of time in Morocco, you are likely to make considerable use of the various networks.

Grands taxis are likely to do a journey in about two thirds of the time a bus would take (though CTM now run a few nonstop express buses). Buses, on the other hand are safer and more comfortable, though on some older buses legroom is extremely limited and long journeys can be rather an endurance test for anyone approaching six feet or more in height. In summer, it can be worthwhile taking **night buses** on the longer journeys. Though still not very comfortable, many long-distance buses run at night and they are both quicker and cooler. Although most buses are fitted with reading lights these are invariably turned off, so you will not be able to read on buses after dark.

When travelling during the day, especially in summer, it pays to sit on the side away from **the sun**. Travelling from north to south, this means sitting on the right in the morning, on the left in the afternoon, vice-versa if going the other way. Travelling from east to west, sit on the right, or on the left if going from west to east. Note too, especially on rural services, that some passengers may be unused to road travel and a lot of people may vomit on the journey.

CTM AND PRIVATE LINES

There are a variety of bus services and companies. In all sizeable towns, you will generally find both CTM (the national company) and a number of other companies, privately owned and operated.

The **CTM buses** are faster and more reliable, with numbered seats and fixed departure schedules. Their services are often referred to as the rapide, and buses come equipped with videos on the longer routes. Some of the **larger private**

company buses, such as SATAS (which operates widely in the south) and Trans Ghazala (which runs in the north) are of a similar standard. By contrast, many other private companies are tiny outfits, with a single bus which leaves only when the driver considers it sufficiently full. On the other hand, such private buses are much more likely to stop for you if you flag them down on the open road, whereas CTM services will only pick up and set down at official stops.

BUS TERMINALS

Most towns have a main **bus station** (*gare routière*), often on the edge of town. CTM buses usually leave from the company's office, which may be quite a way from the main bus station, though in one or two places CTM and the private companies share a single terminal. In a few places, there might be two or more separate terminals (these are detailed in the guide), sometimes even one for daytime departures and another for night-time ones.

Bus stations usually have a number of ticket windows, one for each of the companies operating out of it. There is often a departures board, but it may be in Arabic only, and it may be out of date anyhow, so you should always check departure times at the appropriate window. Bus conductors or ticket sellers may be calling out destinations in the bus station in any case, or may greet you as you come in by asking where you want to go. On the more popular trips (and especially with CTM services, which are often just once a day in the south), it is worth trying to buy **tickets in advance**; this may not always be possible on

smaller private-line services, but it's worth enquiring about.

You can sometimes experience problems getting tickets at **small towns** along major routes, where buses often arrive and leave already full. It's sometimes possible to get round this problem by taking a local bus or a grand taxi for the next section of the trip (until the bus you want empties a little), or by waiting for a bus that actually starts from the town you're in. Overall, the best policy is simply to arrive early in the day (ideally 5.30–6am) at a bus station.

On private-line buses, you generally have to pay for your **baggage** to be loaded into the hold (or onto the roof). The standard fee is 5dh, but this may be forgone on short hops. On CTM buses your luggage is weighed and you are issued with a receipt for the baggage charge (usually also about 5dh). On arrival, porters with wheeled box-carts (*chariots*) may offer their services, but always agree a price before engaging one.

ONCF BUSES

An additional service, on certain major routes, is the **Supratour express buses** run by the train company, **ONCF**. These are fast and very comfortable, and run from Nador, from Tetouan, and from Essaouira, Agadir and the Western Sahara to connect with rail services at, respectively, Taourirt on the line from Oujda to Fes and Casablanca, Tnine Sidi Lyamani on the Tangier–Casablanca line near Asilah, and Marrakesh for train services northwards. ONCF/Supratours services are more expensive than regular buses and compare, both in terms of time and cost, with

---

POLICE CHECKS ON TRAVEL

Police checks take place on travellers throughout the country. They come in three forms. One is a check on local transport; European cars, or rental cars, are usually waved through. Buses (other than CTM services) are much more likely to be stopped, but usually only briefly. The second kind of police check is a routine but simple passport check – most often polite and friendly, with the only delay due to a desire to relieve boredom with a chat.

The third kind of check is more prolonged and involves being stopped by police stationed at more or less permanent points on the roads, who will conduct a fairly detailed inquisition into all nonresident travellers. There is a considerable amount of form-filling and delay. This occurs most commonly entering the major towns of the Western Sahara (Laayoune, Smara, Boujdour and Dakhla), but such checks are diminishing in number and are really now just a formality as the situation gradually becomes more and more stable.

In the **Rif mountains**, especially around the cannabis-producing region of Ketama, you may also come across police checks – concerned, obviously enough, with just the one substance. Buses are usually delayed more than grands taxis at such checkpoints. There are also several and sometimes lengthy checks for duty-free contraband on buses from Nador to Fes.

CTM buses. They do not use the main bus stations, but depart from outside their own town-centre offices (detailed in the text). Through tickets to and from connecting rail stations are available (Nador through to Fes, for example), and travellers with rail tickets for connecting services have priority. It's best to book tickets in advance if possible.

TRUCKS AND HITCHING

In the countryside, where buses may be sporadic or even nonexistent, it is standard practice for **vans** and **lorries** (*camions*), **pick-up trucks** (*camionettes*) and **transit-vans** (*transits*) to carry and charge passengers. You may be asked to pay a little more than the locals, and you may be expected to bargain over the price – but it's straightforward enough.

In parts of the **Atlas**, local people run more or less scheduled truck or transit services, generally to coincide with the pattern of local souks. If you plan on traversing any of the more ambitious Atlas pistes, you'll probably be dependent on these vehicles, unless you walk.

HITCHING

Hitching is not very big in Morocco. Most people, if they own any form of transport at all, have mopeds – which are said to outnumber cars by something like five hundred to one. However, it is often easy to get rides from other **tourists**, particularly if you ask around at the campsites, and for **women travellers** this can be an effective and positive option for getting around – or at least a useful respite from the generally male preserves of buses and grands taxis.

Out on the road, it's inevitably a different matter – and hitching is definitely not advisable for women travelling alone. Hitchers should not be surprised to be asked to **pay for a ride** if picked up by country Moroccans. Local rides can operate in much the same way as truck taxis (see above).

CAR RENTAL

Car rental is expensive, from around £250/$400 per week or £40/$65 a day for a basic car with unlimited mileage. You will be expected to leave a large deposit, and petrol prices are high, too (see p.45). However, having a car does pay obvious dividends if you are pushed for time, allowing you to explore unusual routes and take in much more in a lot less time. This is especially true in the **south**, where getting around can be quite an effort if you have to rely on local buses. Driving yourself also gives a certain sense of invulnerability, if Morocco's hustling ways are a bit too much for you.

Many visitors choose to rent a car in Casablanca, Marrakesh or Agadir, expressly for the southern routes. If you're organized, however, it usually works out cheaper to **arrange car rental in advance** through the travel agent who arranges your flight. If you have problems, try one of the Morocco specialists detailed on p.5. Major international firms such as Hertz, Budget, Europcar, National and Avis have facilities for booking from home on toll-free or cheap-rate numbers or via the Internet (see box).

Details of **car rental companies in Morocco** are given where relevant in city listings in the guide. The best-value places are mostly in Casablanca and Agadir. Deals to go for are unlimited mileage and daily/weekly rates; paying by the kilometre invariably works out more expensive. Local firms have the advantage that the price is more likely to be negotiable, though the condition of the vehicle should be well checked. The cheapest car on offer is usually a **Renault 4**

CAR RENTAL PHONE NUMBERS AND WEB SITES

Avis US & Canada ☎1-800/331 1084; UK ☎0870/590 0500; Ireland ☎01/874 5844; Australia ☎1800/225533; New Zealand ☎0800/655111 or ☎09/579 5231. *www.avis.com*
Budget US & Canada ☎1-800/527 0700; UK ☎0800/181181; Ireland ☎0800/973159; Australia ☎1300/362848; New Zealand ☎0800/652227 or ☎09/375 2222. *www.budgetrentacar.com*
Europcar US & Canada ☎1-800/800 6000; UK ☎0845/722 2525; Ireland ☎01/874 5844;
Australia ☎02/9223 1444; New Zealand ☎0800/486677. *www.europcar.com*
Hertz US & Canada ☎1-800/654 3001; UK ☎0870/848 4848; Ireland ☎01/676 7476; Australia ☎1800/550067; New Zealand ☎0800/655955 or ☎09/309 0989. *www.hertz.com*
National US & Canada ☎1-800/CAR RENT; UK ☎0870/536 5365; Ireland ☎1800/301401; Australia ☎13 1908; New Zealand ☎09/537 2582. *www.nationalcar.com*

– well designed for unsurfaced piste roads, with its high suspension and sturdy frame. If you can't or don't want to drive, car rental companies can usually arrange a **driver** for around 250dh (£15/$25) a day all in.

Before making a booking, be sure to find out if you can pick the car up in one city and return it to another. Most companies will allow this if they have more than one office. Check also, if booking in Morocco, whether you will be charged extra for payment with a credit card; there is often a (negotiable) six percent fee for this. Before setting out, make sure the car comes with spare tyre, tool kit and full documentation – including insurance cover, which is compulsory issue with all rentals.

DRIVING

There are few real problems driving in Morocco, but be aware that **accident rates** are high – in large part because much of the population is not yet tuned in to looking out for motorized vehicles. You should treat all pedestrians with the suspicion that they will cross in front of you, and all cyclists with the idea that they may well swerve into the middle of the road. Your fellow motorists may also be rather haphazard in their driving, particularly in towns, which can make negotiating city streets a rather hair-raising experience.

However, with those caveats in mind, daytime and certainly long-distance driving can be as good as anywhere. Good road surfaces, long straight roads, and little traffic between inhabited areas allow for high average speeds. The usual **speed limit** outside towns is 100km per hour (62mph), which is difficult to keep down to in desert areas, where perceptions of speed change. In built-up areas, the speed limit is generally 40km per hour (25mph). Signs indicate speed limits other than those. There is an on-the-spot fine of 30dh for

DRIVING REQUIREMENTS

Note that the **minimum age** for driving in Morocco is 21 years.

You must **carry your driving licence and passport** at all times. International Driving Licences are useful though not mandatory; they are particularly advisable if your domestic licence does not bear a photograph, since police expect to see one on all identification documents.

You **drive on the right**.

speeding offences, and oncoming motorists flashing their headlights at you may well be warning you to slow down for a police check ahead. The French rule of giving priority to traffic from the right is observed at roundabouts and junctions – meaning that cars coming onto a roundabout have priority over those already on it.

Be very wary about driving **after dark**. It is legal to drive without lights at up to 20km per hour, which allows all cyclists and mopeds to wander at will; donkeys, goats and sheep do not carry lights, either.

By law, drivers and passengers are required to wear **seatbelts**. Almost no one does, but if you're stopped by the police, you may have a small fine or *cadeau* (present) extracted.

PISTE DRIVING

On the pistes (rough, unpaved tracks in the mountains or desert), there are special problems. Here you do need a good deal of driving and mechanical confidence – and if you don't feel your car's up to it, don't drive on these routes. Obviously, a 4x4 vehicle, albeit expensive, is best suited to the pistes, but the cheaper Renault 4L is still a sturdy favourite with old hands. On mountain roads, beware of gravel, which can be a real danger on the frequent hairpin bends, and, in spring, flash-floods caused by melting snow.

EQUIPMENT

Whether you rent a car or drive your own, always make sure you're carrying a spare tyre in good condition (plus a jack and tools). Flat tyres occur very frequently, even on fairly major roads, and you can often be in for a long wait until someone drives along with a possible replacement.

Carrying an emergency windscreen is also useful, especially if you are driving your own car for a long period of time. There are lots of loose stones on the hard shoulders of single-lane roads and they can fly all over the place.

If you're not mechanically minded, be sure to bring a car maintenance manual with you – a useful item, too, for anyone planning to rent a vehicle.

FUEL AND BREAKDOWNS

Petrol stations are to be found in towns of any size but can be few and far between in rural areas: always fill your tank to the limit. Premium is the standard brand for cars; unleaded is available at larger stations, including most of the

MOTORBIKING IN MOROCCO

Each year an increasing number of **motorcyclists** travel to Morocco and find that it has all the major attractions sought by the enthusiast. The first choice to make when planning a trip is between going with an escorted group or on an independent journey. If you have never taken a bike abroad before and want to go to Morocco, seriously consider the group option. For those on their own, the following are some practical tips to help organize a trip. Read the comments on driving on p.44, too, particularly in relation to the absence of lights at night.

RENTING A MOTORBIKE – AND PAPERWORK

There is a fair bit of bureaucracy involved in taking a motorbike to Morocco. One way of getting around the hassles is to **rent a motorbike** there (see "Useful Contacts" below).

If you take your own motorbike, you will need **special insurance**. Most companies, especially those based outside Europe, will not cover motorcycling as part of a holiday overseas, particularly when off-road riding is contemplated or inevitable (as it often is in Morocco). You'll have to shop around and remember to take the policy with you, together with your bike registration certificate, biker's licence and international licence. The British Automobile Association's Web site, *www.theaa.co.uk* can provide up-to-date advice.

Even large insurance companies don't give clear answers about "**Green Cards**" for motorcycling in Morocco and cannot understand that you may encounter up to a dozen police roadblocks a day where the first language is Arabic, the second French and the third Baksheesh.

When **entering Morocco**, try to arrive as early in the day as possible. If you are a lone traveller and speak neither Arabic nor French, you may be left queuing until those without queries have been dealt with. If the office then closes, you may have to return the next morning. In these circumstances, it might be worth investing in a tout who, for a fee, will take your papers to a friendly officer. It's also worth picking up a couple of (free) extra immigration forms for the return journey.

ROADS AND POLICE

Surfaced roads over the Atlas are easy to navigate – although most are only one lorry wide, bends are likely to be gravelly, and the edge of precipices rarely have barriers. The shoulder on either side is used by whichever approaching vehicle is the smaller – and this is usually the motor cycle. It's important to keep an eye on petrol consumption, especially in remote areas, and know distances between fuel stops.

The general style of driving is unpredictable and only the red roads on the Michelin map will have two lanes. Overtaking on these is no problem (traffic density is low) but police radar is active and on the spot cash fines for speeding are common.

WHAT TO TAKE AND WHEN TO GO

Don't take a model of bike likely to be unfamiliar in Morocco. Previous bikers recommend that you take all cables and levers, inner tubes, puncture repair kit, tyre levers, pump, fuses, plugs, chain, washable air filter, cable ties, good tape and tool kit. For riding off-road, take knobbly tyres and rim locks, brush guards, metal number plate and bashplate. In winter, take tough fabric outer clothing. In summer, carry lighter-weight clothing, wool pullovers and waterproofs. Drying out leathers takes a long time.

Travelling during Ramadan can pose problems; strict observance of the period can mean a long wait if anything goes wrong with the bike. Summer in the Deep South is also best avoided, as the heat can be overwhelming, making travelling a far from enjoyable experience.

For further information, see Chris Scott's *The Adventure Motorbiking Handbook* (Compass Star), which claims to be the first world guide to overlanding on two wheels.

USEFUL CONTACTS

Moto Aventures (☎ & fax 376/835472, *www.motoaventures.com*). Andorra-based company with trips from Casablanca into High Atlas or desert. Bikes provided.

H–C Travel, 16 High Street, Overton, Hampshire, RG25 3HA, UK (☎01256 770775, *www.hctravel.com*). Off-road tours, through Middle and High Atlas. Bikes provided, previous off-road experience necessary.

Afriquia branches. Prices are pretty much in line with Western Europe, at 8.50dh (53p/77¢) a litre for leaded petrol (*super*), and 5.50dh (35p/50¢) for diesel (*gasoil*). Fuel costs for a Renault 4 work out at around 6dh for every 10km. Fuel is much cheaper however in the Saharan provinces (basically the Western Sahara), where it is subsidized, costing 3dh (18p/27¢) per litre for *super*, 5dh (31p/45¢) for diesel, and in the Spanish enclaves of Ceuta (Sebta) and Melilla, where it is duty-free, at 92ptas/€0.55 (33p/48¢) for *super*, 70ptas/€0.42 (26p/37¢) for diesel.

Moroccan mechanics are usually excellent at coping with breakdowns and all medium-sized towns have garages (most with an extensive range of spare parts for Renaults and other French cars). But be aware that if you break down miles from anywhere you'll probably end up paying a fortune to get a lorry to tow you back.

If you are driving your own vehicle, there is also the problem of having to re-export any car that you bring into the country (even a wreck). You can't just write off a car: you'll have to take it out of Morocco with you.

VEHICLE INSURANCE

Insurance must by law be sold along with all rental agreements. Driving your own vehicle, you should obtain Green Card cover from your insurers. If you don't have it on arrival, you can buy it from Assurance Frontière for around £25/$36 a month, at Tangier port, Nador port, or the land frontiers at Ceuta and Melilla; to renew it, the main AF office is at 28 Bd. Moulay Youssef, Casablanca (☎02/247 0810).

PARKING: GARDIENS AND HOTELS

In almost every town of at least moderate size, you will find a *gardien de voitures* makes an appearance. *Gardiens* are often licensed by local authorities to look after cars, claiming a few dirhams by way of parking fees. Red and white striped kerbs mean no parking.

Most of the larger hotels in the Ville Nouvelle quarters of cities have parking space (and occasionally garaging) available.

CYCLING

Cycling – and particularly **mountain biking** – is becoming an increasingly popular pursuit for Western travellers to Morocco. The country's regular roads are well maintained and by European standards very quiet, while the extensive network of **pistes** – dirt tracks – makes for exciting mountain bike terrain, leading you into areas otherwise accessible only to trekkers or four-wheel drive expeditions.

The biggest negative factor is the pest of **local kids** in the countryside, who for some reason have developed a fondness for the sport of **throwing stones** at cyclists. You need to keep your wits about you, wherever you cycle, and your eyes wide open. The heat and the long stretches of dead straight road across arid, featureless plains – the main routes to (or beyond) the mountain ranges – can all too easily drain your energy. Additionally, public **water** is very rare – there are very few roadside watering places such as are found in Europe – and towns and villages are often a long way apart.

Regular roads – are generally surfaced (*goudronné* or *revêtue*) but narrow, and you will often have to get off the tarmac to make way for traffic. Beware also of open land-drains close to the roadsides, and loose gravel on the bends.

Cycling on the **pistes**, mountain bikes come into their own with their "tractor" tyres and wide, stabilizing handlebars. There are few pistes that could be recommended on a regular tourer. By contrast, some intrepid mountain bikers cover footpaths in the High Atlas, though for the less than super-fit this is extremely heavy going. Better, on the whole, to stick to established pistes – many of which are covered by local trucks, which you can pay for a ride if your legs (or your bike) give out.

GETTING YOUR BIKE TO MOROCCO

Most **airlines** – even charters – carry bikes free of charge, so long as they don't push your baggage allowance over the weight limit. When buying a ticket, register your intention of taking your bike and check out the airline's conditions. They will generally require you to invert the handlebars, remove the pedals, and deflate the tyres; some (like KLM) provide/sell a cardboard **box** to enclose the bike, as protection for other passengers' luggage as much as for the bike; you are, however, unlikely to be offered a box for the return journey. A useful alternative, offering little protection but at least ensuring nothing gets lost, is to customize an industrial nylon sack, adding a drawstring at the neck.

If you plan to fly to Spain and cross over **by ferry to Morocco**, things couldn't be simpler. You ride on with the motor vehicles (thus avoiding the long queues of foot passengers) and the bike is secure during the voyage. At time of writing, bicycles travel for free on Trasmediterranea ferries from Algeciras to Ceuta or Tangier, and Málaga or Almería to Melilla but not on COMANAV services from Sète to Tangier or Nador.

CYCLES AND LOCAL TRANSPORT

Cycling around Morocco, you can make use of local transport to supplement your own wheels. **Buses** will generally carry cycles on the roof. CTM usually charge around 10dh per bike – make sure you get a ticket. On other lines it's very much up to you to negotiate with the driver and/or baggage porter (who will probably expect at least 5dh at each end – don't pay both ends in advance). If you're riding, and exhausted, you can usually flag down private-line buses (but not usually CTM services) on the road.

Some **grands taxis** also agree to carry cycles, if they have space on a rack. The fare will be about the same as for a place in the taxi: again, you may well have to bargain. In mountain or desert areas, you can have your bike carried with you on **truck or transit services** (see p.43). Prices for this are highly negotiable, but should not exceed your own passenger fare.

Cycles are carried on **trains** for a modest handling fee, though it's not really worth the hassle. Bikes have to be registered in advance as baggage and won't necessarily travel on the same train as you (though they will usually turn up within a day).

ACCOMMODATION

Accommodation doesn't present any special problems. The cheaper **hotels** will almost always let you keep your bike in your room – and others will find a disused basement or office for storage. It's almost essential to do this, as much to deter unwelcome tampering as theft, especially if you have a curiosity-inviting mountain bike. At **campsites**, there's usually a *gardien* on hand to keep an eye on your bike, or stow it away in his chalet.

ROUTES

Rewarding areas for biking include:

Tizi n'Test (High Atlas): **Asni to Ijoukak**, and an excursion to Tin Mal.

Asni to Setti Fatma (High Atlas: Ourika Valley) and beyond if you have a mountain bike.

Northern and Western (well-watered) **side of the Middle Atlas**.

Djebel Sarhro and Djebel Bani: a choice of good east–west routes from Tafilelt to Tata.

In summer, at least, it wouldn't be a good idea to go much **beyond the Atlas**, though given cooler winter temperatures, rewarding long routes exist in the **southern oasis routes**, such as **Ouarzazate to Zagora** or **Ouarzazate to Tinerhir**, and the **desert routes** down to **Er Rachidia**, **Erfoud** and **Rissani**.

See box on p.400 for more on mountain biking in the High Atlas.

REPAIRS

Most towns reveal a wealth of **general repair shops** in their Medina quarters, well used to servicing local bikes and mopeds. Though they are most unlikely to have the correct spare parts for your make of bike, they can usually sort out some kind of temporary solution.

It is worth bringing with you **spare spokes** (and tool), plus **brake blocks** and **cable**, as the mountain descents can take it out on a bike.

Tyres and **tubes** can generally be found for tourers, though if you have anything fancy, best bring at least one spare, too.

Obviously, before setting out, you should make sure that your brakes are in good order, renew bearings, etc, and ensure that you have decent quality (and condition) tyres.

PROBLEMS AND REWARDS

All over Morocco, and particularly in rural areas, there are stray, wild and semi-cared-for **dogs**. A cyclist pedalling past with feet and wheels spinning seems to send at least half of them into a frenzied state. Normally, cycling in an equally frenzied state is the best defence, but on steep ascents and off-road this isn't always possible. In these situations, keep the bike between you and the dog, and use your pump or a shower from your water bottle as defence. If you do get bitten, a rabies inoculation is advisable.

Another factor to be prepared for is your susceptibility to unwanted attentions of locals. Small **children** will often stand in the road to hinder your progress, or even chase after you in gangs. This is normally good-natured but it can become intimidating if they start throwing stones. Your attitude is important: be friendly, smile, and maintain strong eye contact. On no account attempt to mete out your own discipline. Small children always have big brothers.

Lastly, the dreaded **hustlers** – for more on whom see p.36. As a cyclist you will avoid the customary hassle at ports and train stations but you are vulnerable to motorbike hustlers who pull alongside tourists in Fes and Marrakesh. Some of these characters can be pretty unpleasant if you decline their services of guiding you to hotels.

So – as one correspondent put it – after all these warnings, and the extra expense and hassle, **is it worth cycling in Morocco**? His answer was a definite yes: "I felt an extra intimacy with the country by staying close to it, rather than viewing it from car or bus windows. And I experienced unrivalled generosity, from cups of tea offered by policemen at roadside checkpoints to a full-blown breakfast banquet from a farming family whose dog had savaged my leg. People went out of their way to give me advice, food, drink and lifts, and not once did I feel seriously threatened. Lastly, the exhilaration I felt on some of the mountain descents, above all the Tizi n'Test in the High Atlas, will remain with me forever. I was not an experienced cycle tourer when I arrived in Morocco, but the grandeur of the scenery helped carry me over the passes."

FURTHER INFORMATION

In the UK, the British **Cycle Touring Club**, Cotterell House, 69 Meadrow, Godalming, Surrey GU7 3HS (☎01483/417217, *www.ctc.org.uk*) keep members' reports on past tours in Morocco, which are available to other members, who can also get good-value **insurance** among other services from the club. In the US, **Adventure Cycling** (☎800/755-2453, *www.adventurecycling.org*) can help find general information about biking and produce the Cyclist Yellow Pages which offers listings of all sorts of bike-related information (suppliers, tour operators) but no specific information about Morocco tours.

Inspiration for mountain bikers can be found in Nick Crane's **book**, *Atlas Biker* (Oxford Illustrated Press, UK, an adventurous account of a traverse of the High Atlas on – or at times carrying – mountain bikes. For general advice on equipment and clothing, *Bicycle Expeditions* by Paul Vickers (available from the Expedition Advisory Service, Royal Geographical Society, Kensington Gore, London SW7 2AR, UK; ☎020/7591 3030) is useful.

CITY TRANSPORT

You'll spend most time exploring Moroccan cities on foot. The alleys of the old Medina quarters, where the sights and souks are to be found, will rarely accommodate more than a donkey. In the newer quarters, you may want to make use of city taxis and occasionally a bus. In the new city quarters, you should be aware that pedestrian crossings don't count for very much, except perhaps at junctions "controlled" by traffic lights. And even then, cycles and mopeds pay scant attention to traffic lights showing red.

Petits taxis, usually Fiats or Simcas, carry up to three passengers and (unlike grands taxis) are limited to trips within city limits. Officially, all of them should have meters, but in practice you're unlikely to find one that works (at least for tourists) outside Rabat or Fes. It is then a matter of bargaining for a price – either before you get in (wise to start off with) or by simply presenting the regular fare when you get out. If you are a lone passenger, your taxi driver may pick up one or two additional passengers en route, each of whom will pay the full fare for their journey, as of course will you. This is standard practice.

Fares vary enormously (in Marrakesh and Agadir, demands can often be excessive), though everywhere it depends to a large extent on what you look like, how you act, and where you're going. Don't be afraid to argue with the driver if you feel you're being unreasonably overcharged. After 8pm, standard fares rise by 50 percent.

ACCOMMODATION

Hotels in Morocco are cheap, good value, and usually pretty easy to find. There can be a shortage of places in the major cities and resorts (Tangier, Fes, Marrakesh and Agadir) in August, and in Rabat or Casablanca when there's a big conference on. Other times, you should be able to pick from a wide range.

The most important distinction among Moroccan hotels is between **classified hotels** (which are given star-ratings by the tourist board) and **unclassified hotels** (which are not). The latter tend to be cheap places, with few facilities, in the old Medina quarters. For any level of comfort, you'll want a classified hotel.

If you're on a limited budget, a good course is to **alternate between the extremes**, spending most nights in basic Medina hotels but going for the occasional blast of grandeur. At any rate don't limit yourself to the middle categories – these are mostly dull, and staying all the time in the Villes Nouvelles will cut you off from the most interesting aspects of traditional Moroccan life.

UNCLASSIFIED HOTELS

Unclassified (non-classé) hotels, (① in our price code box), are mainly to be found in the older, Arab-built parts of cities – the **Medinas** – and are almost always the cheapest accommodation options. They offer the additional advantage of being at the heart of things: where you'll want to spend most of your time, and where all the sights and markets are concentrated. The disadvantages are that the Medinas can at first appear daunting – with their mazes of narrow lanes and blind alleys – and that the hotels themselves can be, at worst, dirty flea traps with tiny, windowless cells and half-washed sheets. At their best, they're fine: traditional "caravanserai" buildings with whitewashed rooms round a central patio.

One other minus point for unclassified Medina hotels is that they often have a problem with **water**. Most of the Medinas remain substantially unmodernized, and many cheap hotels are without hot water, with squat toilets that are sometimes pretty disgusting. On the plus side,

HOTEL PRICE CODES

The basis of our **hotel price codes**, set out below and keyed throughout the guide, is the price currently quoted for the cheapest double room in high season (June–September).

Note that cheaper prices in the lower categories are generally for rooms with just a washbasin – you always pay extra for **en-suite** shower and WC – and that double rooms can generally be converted into **triples/family rooms**, with extra beds, for a modest extra charge. Single occupancy usually costs about two thirds the price of a double, though in some places a single person will pay the same rate for a room as two people sharing, and in other places exactly half as much. Prices quoted are for bed only, without breakfast, but including local taxes.

① 40–100dh	③ 150–200dh	⑤ 400–800dh
② 100–150dh	④ 200–400dh	⑥ over 800dh

In Spanish Ceuta and Melilla

① 1000–3000ptas/€6–18	③ 5000–7500ptas/€30–45	⑤ 10,000–15,000ptas/€60–90
② 3000–5000ptas/€18–30	④ 7500–10,000ptas/€45–60	⑥ over 15,000ptas/over €90

there is usually a hammam (Turkish bath – see box below) nearby.

Unclassified hotel **rates** fluctuate widely, depending on their location, sometimes varying with season, and being more or less negotiable depending on demand. The cost of a double room in high season ranges from 40dh (£2.50/$4) to 100dh (£6.25/$10).

CLASSIFIED HOTELS

Classified (classé) hotels are almost always in a town's **Ville Nouvelle** – the "new" or administrative quarters, built by the French and usually set slightly apart from the old Medina quarters.

Since 1993, classified hotels have been allowed, regardless of **star-rating**, to set their own prices – and to vary them according to season and depending on demand. Prices and ratings should be on display at reception and behind the bedroom door, but if in doubt about value for money, don't hesitate to ask to see the room in question; indeed, you will normally be invited to do so.

At the bottom end of the scale – a **one-star hotel** (② to ③ in our price code) – a basic double room with a washbasin will cost around £7–10/$10–15 a night, with a shower and WC around £12/$18. Moving into **two- and three-star hotels** (price codes ③ to ④), you will be paying around £25/$40 for a double with shower and WC, at the top end of the scale. You get a fair bit more comfort for your money and there are a scattering of elegant, old hotels in these categories – places which used to be the grand hotel in town but have since declined.

For European/American standards of comfort, you need to look, on the whole, at **four-star hotels**. These are used by most foreign tour operators and charge around £25–50/$40–80 (price codes ④ to ⑤), for a double. If you can afford the

---

HAMMAMS

The absence of hot showers in some of the cheaper Medina hotels is not such a disaster. Throughout all the Medina quarters, you'll find local **hammams**. A hammam is a Turkish-style steam bath, with a succession of rooms from cool to hot, and endless supplies of hot and cold water, which you fetch in buckets. The usual procedure is to find a piece of floor space in the hot room, surround it with as many buckets of water as you feel you need, and lie in the heat to sweat out the dirt from your pores before scrubbing it off. A plastic bowl is useful for scooping the water from the buckets to wash with. You can also order a **massage**, in which you will be allowed to sweat, pulled about a bit to relax your muscles, and then rigorously scrubbed with a rough flannel glove (*kiis*). Alternatively, buy a *kiis* and do it yourself. For many Moroccan women, who would not drink in a café or bar, the hammam is a social gathering place, in which tourists are made very welcome too. Indeed, hammams turn out to be a highlight for many women travellers, and an excellent way to make contact with Moroccan women.

Several hammams are detailed in the text, but the best way of finding one is always to ask at the hotel where you're staying. You will often, in fact, need to be led to a hammam, since they are usually unmarked and can be hard to find. In some towns, you find a separate hammam for women and men; at others the same establishment offers different hours for each sex – usually mornings and evenings for men, afternoons (typically noon to 6pm) for women.

For both sexes, there's more **modesty** than you might perhaps expect: it's customary for men (always) and women (generally) to bathe in **swimming costume** (or underwear), and men will undress facing the wall. Women may be surprised to find their Moroccan counterparts completely shaven and may (in good humour) be offered this service; there's no embarrassment in declining.

As part of the Islamic tradition of cleanliness and ablutions, hammams sometimes have a **religious element**, and non-Muslims may not be welcome (or allowed in) to those built alongside mosques, particularly on Thursday evenings, before the main weekly service on Friday. On the whole, though, there are no restrictions against *Nisara* ("Nazarenes", or Christians).

Finally, don't forget to bring your own **soap, shampoo and towels** along to hammams; the latter are rented but can be a bit dubious. Moroccans often bring a **plastic mat** to sit on, too, as the floors can get a bit clogged. These can be bought easily enough in any town. Most Moroccans use a pasty, olive oil-based soap (*sabon bildi*), sold by weight in Medina shops. On sale at the same shops, you'll find *kiis* flannel gloves, a fine mud (*ghasoul*), used by some instead of shampoo, pumice stones (*hazra*) for removing dead skin, and a white crystalline substance (*chebba*), used as an antiperspirant and to stop shaving cuts from bleeding.

upper end of this scale, you'll be moving into real style, with rooms looking out onto palm-shaded pools and gardens – at their best in buildings that have been converted from old palace residences. But even here, you are advised to check what's on offer. The plumbing, heating and lighting are sometimes unreliable; restaurants are often closed and swimming pools empty. Many of these hotels were state-owned and are now privatized, which has led to some improvements.

Hotels accorded the **five-star-luxury rating**, (price code ⑥) more or less guarantee style, either in a historic conversion (the most famous of which are the *Hôtel Mamounia* in Marrakesh and the *Palais Jamai* in Fes) or in a modern building with a splendid pool and all the international creature comforts.

YOUTH HOSTELS

Morocco has expanded its **youth hostel** organization in recent years, and there are now eleven *Auberges de Jeunesse* scattered around the country. Most are clean and reasonably well run, and charges vary from 20dh (£1.25/$2) to 45dh (£2.80/$4.50) per person per night in a dorm. HI membership cards are not required but you may have to pay a little extra if you do not have one. The hostels are located at Asni (High Atlas), Azrou (Middle Atlas), Casablanca, Chaouen, Fes,

Laayoune, Marrakesh, Meknes, Rabat, Rissani and Tangier. Addresses and details are given for all of these in the relevant sections of the guide; those at Casablanca, Marrakesh and Tangier recommend booking in advance. One general attraction is the opportunity for meeting other travellers, including young Moroccans on holiday. Further information on Moroccan Youth hostels can be found in Hostelling International's guide to Africa, the Americas, Asia and the Pacific (£6.99/$10.95), which can be consulted in most public libraries. Alternatively, contact the *Fédération Royale Marocaine des Auberges de Jeunesse*, Parc de la Ligue Arabe, BP No 15998, Casa Principale, Casablanca 21000 (☎02/247 0952, fax 222 7677).

REFUGES AND GITES D'ETAPES

In the **Djebel Toubkal** area of the High Atlas mountains, the Club Alpin Français (CAF) maintain five huts, or **refuges**, equipped for mountaineers and trekkers. These provide bunks or bedshelves for sleeping at 48–96dh (£3–£6/$4.80–9.60) per person, depending on the refuge, and in the case of two of them the season, with discounts for members of CAF or its affiliates, and for HI youth hostel cardholders. Some refuges can provide meals and/or cooking facilities. They are detailed in the relevant sections.

YOUTH HOSTEL ASSOCIATIONS

AUSTRALIA Level 3, 10 Mallett St, Camperdown, NSW 2050 (☎02/9565 1699, fax 9565 1325, *www.yha.com.au*). Adult membership rate A$47

CANADA Hostelling International/Canadian Hostelling Association, Room 400, 205 Catherine St, Ottawa, ON K2P 1C3 (☎1-800/663-5777 or ☎613/237-7884, *www.hostellingintl.ca*). Annual membership adults $26.75, children under 18 free when accompanied by parents; two-year memberships cost $35, or become a lifetime member for $175.

ENGLAND AND WALES Youth Hostel Association (YHA), Trevelyan House, 8 St Stephen's Hill, St Albans, Herts AL1 2DY (☎01727/845 047, *www.yha.org.uk*). Also London membership desk and booking office: 14 Southampton St, London WC2 7HY (☎020/7836 8541). Annual membership £11, (£5.50 under 18).

IRELAND An Oige, 61 Mountjoy St, Dublin 7 (☎01/830 4555, *www.irelandyha.org*). Annual membership IR£10, IR£4

NEW ZEALAND 173 Gloucester St, Christchurch (☎03/379 9970, *www.yha.co.nz*). Adult membership rate NZ$40.

NORTHERN IRELAND Youth Hostel Association of Northern Ireland, 22 Donegall Rd, Belfast BT12 5JN (☎028/9032 4733, *www.hini.org.uk*). Annual membership £8.

SCOTLAND Scottish Youth Hostel Association, 7 Glebe Crescent, Stirling, FK8 2JA (☎01786/891 400; fax 01786/891 333, *www.syha.org.uk*). Annual membership £6.

USA Hostelling International-American Youth Hostels (HI-AYH), 733 15th St NW, Suite 840, PO Box 37613, Washington, DC 20005 (☎202/783-6161, *www.hiayh.org*). Annual membership for adults (18-55) is $25, for seniors (55 or over) is $15, and for under 18's is free. Lifetime memberships are $250.

Also in trekking areas, a number of locals offer rooms in their houses: an informal scheme which the Moroccan tourist authorities have begun promoting as **gîtes d'étape**. Lists of these *gîtes* are to be found in the pamphlet *La Grande Traversée des Atlas Marocains*. Current charges are set at 20dh (£1.25/$2) per person per night for "*non-classé*"; 30dh (£18.75/$3) per person per night for "*2e classe*"; 40dh (£2.50/$4) for "*1e classe*"; breakfast is charged at 15dh and an evening meal at 30–40dh.

CAMPSITES

Campsites are to be found at intervals along most of the developed Moroccan coast and in most towns or cities of any size. They are inexpensive and often quite informal and makeshift, advertised from season to season on roadside signs.

Most sites are very cheap, at around 10dh (65p/$1) per person, plus a similar charge for a motorcaravan or campervan; they usually have basic (and sometimes very basic) washing and toilet facilities. A few more upmarket places, in Meknes or Fes, for example, offer swimming pools and better facilities at around double the cost – sometimes more. Details and addresses are given in relevant sections of the guide.

Note that campsites don't tend to provide much **security**, and you should never leave valuables unattended. Camping **outside official sites**, this obviously applies even more, and if you want to do this, it's wise to ask at a house if you can pitch your tent alongside – you'll usually get a hospitable response. If you're trekking in the Atlas, it is often possible to pay someone to act as a *gardien* for your tent.

EATING AND DRINKING

Like accommodation, food in Morocco falls into two basic categories: ordinary Moroccan meals served in the Medina cafés (or bought from stalls), and French-influenced tourist menus in most of the hotels and Ville Nouvelle restaurants. There are exceptions – cheap local cafés in the new cities and occasional palace-style places in the Medina. Whatever your budget, don't be afraid to try both options. The Medina places are mostly cleaner than they look and their food is usually fresh and tasty.

BASIC CAFÉ FOOD

Basic Moroccan meals may begin with a thick, very filling soup – most often the spicy, bean and pasta **harira** (which is a meal in itself, and eaten as such to break the Ramadan fast). Alternatively, you might start with a **salad** (often very finely chopped), or have this as a side dish with your main course, typically a plateful of **kebabs** (either *brochettes* – small pieces of lamb on a skewer – or *kefta*, made from minced lamb). Some small places also offer fried fish, a stew of beans (*loobia*), or a plate or kebab of offal such as liver or brain, which many Western tourists prefer to avoid, though in fact it can be very tasty. A few hole-in-the wall places specialize in soup, which they sell by the bowlful all day long – such places are usually indicated by a pile of soup bowls at the front. As well as *harira*, and especially for breakfast, some places sell a thick pea soup called *baisara*, topped with full-flavoured green olive oil.

Alternatively, you could go for a **tajine**, which is essentially a stew, steam-cooked slowly in an earthenware dish, with a conical earthenware "lid", over a charcoal fire. Like "casserole", the term "tajine" actually refers to the dish and lid rather than the food cooked in it. Classic tajines include lamb/mutton with prunes and almonds, or

VEGETARIAN/VEGAN OPTIONS

Moroccan cuisine presents distinctly limited options for vegetarians – a preference which will meet with little comprehension in most of Morocco, though restaurants in some places are becoming more aware that tourists may be vegetarian. Tajines can be requested without meat (and, with some difficulty, without meat stock), but beyond these vegetarian casseroles, and ubiquitous omelettes and sandwiches, the menus don't present very obvious choices. *Harira* (bean soup) may or may not be made with meat stock, while most foods are cooked in animal fats.

It's possible, however, to maintain a balanced and reasonably interesting diet, so long as you're not too strict, and are prepared for a few problems outside the cities. If you're vegan, however, you will really need to come equipped and do a fair bit of cooking for yourself.

Provisions that most vegetarians will feel grateful to have brought include yeast extract, peanut butter, veggie pâtés/spreads, and stock cubes – which you can present to cafés (preferably a couple of hours in advance) for preparing your tajine. You might also take along a small Camping Gaz stove and pan – canisters are cheap and readily available, and in the cheaper hotels a lot of Moroccan people cook in their rooms.

Locally, there are plenty of beans, grains, seeds and pulses available, basic cheeses, excellent yoghurts, and a great selection of fruit and nuts; dates, figs, almonds and pistachio nuts can all enliven dishes. In the countryside, you may find fresh fruit and vegetables hard to obtain except during the weekly souk, but you can often buy from locals, who grow a small stock on their terraces.

In cafés and restaurants, asking for a dish *sans viande ou poisson* (without meat or fish) can still result in your being served chicken or lamb, so you'll need to take the trouble to explain matters very clearly. It often helps to talk of being a vegetarian in terms of religious restrictions or rules: concepts that Moroccans are themselves familiar with.

The most difficult situations are those in which you are invited to eat at someone's house – a common occurrence in the countryside. You may find people give you meat when you have specifically asked for vegetables because they think you can't afford it: a scenario in which you might decide that it's more important not to offend someone showing you kindness than to be dogmatic about your own principles. Picking out vegetables from a meat tajine won't offend your hosts; declining the dish altogether, on the other hand, may well end up with the mother/sister/wife in the kitchen getting the flak.

chicken with olives and lemon. Less often, you may get a tajine of fish or just vegetables. A popular alternative is *kefta*, a tasty tajine of meatballs topped with eggs. A tajine is to Moroccan cuisine what a curry is to Indian, and you'll find a whole variety of different ones on offer at Moroccan eateries through from the very cheapest to the most expensive place in town. Mopped up with bread, they can be unbelievably delicious.

Kebabs or a tajine would in all likelihood set you back little more than 25dh (£1.50/$2.50) at one of the hole-in-the-wall places in the Medina, with their two or three tables. You are not expected to bargain for cooked food, but prices can be lower in such places if you enquire how much things cost before you start eating. There is often no menu – or a board written in Arabic only.

If you're looking for **breakfast or a snack**, you can buy a half-**baguette** – plus butter and jam, cheese or eggs, if you want – from many bread or grocery stores, and take it into a café to order a coffee. Many cafés, even those which serve no other food, may offer a breakfast of

bread, butter and jam (which is also what you'll get in most hotels), or maybe an omelette. Some places also offer soup, such as *harira*, with bread, and others have stalls outside selling by weight traditional griddle breads such as *harsha* (quite heavy with a gritty crust), *melaoui* (sprinkled with oil, rolled out thin, folded over and rolled out again several times, like an Indian paratha) and *baghira* (full of holes like an English crumpet). If that is not sufficient, supplementary foods you could buy include dates or olives, yoghurt, or soft white cheese (*cjbcn*).

RESTAURANT MEALS

More expensive dishes, available in some of the Medina cafés as well as in the dearer restaurants, include **fish**, particularly on the coast, and **chicken** (*poulet*), either spit-roasted (*rôti*) or in a tajine with lemon and olives (*poulet aux olives et citron*).

You will sometimes find **pastilla**, too, a succulent pigeon (in cheaper versions chicken may be used) pie, prepared with filo pastry dusted with

A GLOSSARY OF MOROCCAN FOOD

Note that where food/dishes are commonly available in all kinds of restaurants, both **French** and **Arabic** words are given; in Arabic words, the letters printed in **bold italics** should be stressed.

BASICS

Pain	l-***khobz***	Bread	Sauce	l-merga	Sauce
Oeufs	l-***bayd***	Eggs	Sucre	soukar	Sugar (sanida is
Poissons	l-***hout***	Fish			granulated
Viande	l-***hem***	Meat			sugar; soukar,
Huile	zit	Oil			lump sugar)
Poivre	lebzar	Pepper	Légumes	l-khoudra	Vegetables
Salade	shalada	Salad	Vinaigre	l-khel	Vinegar
Sel	l-melha	Salt			

SOUPS, SALADS AND VEGETABLES

–	Bai***sara***	Thick pea soup	Frites	l'batata	Fried potatoes
Potage	***Hari***ra	Thick soup	Haricots	loobia	Beans
Bouillon	–	Thin soup	Tomates	matecha	Tomatoes
Salade	Salata	Mixed salad	Epinards	salk	Spinach
marocaine	Maghrebia		Oignons	l-basla	Onions

MAIN DISHES

Tajine de viande	l-***hem***	Meat stew	–	Djaja mahamara	Chicken stuffed with almonds,
Tajine des poissons	l-***hout***	Fish stew			semolina and raisins
Couscous (aux sept légumes)	Couscous bidaoui	Couscous (with seven vegetables)	Boulettes de viande	***kef***ta	Meatballs
Poulet aux olives et citron	–	Chicken with olives and lemon	Biffteck	l-habra	Steak
			Agneau rôti	Mechoui	Roast lamb
			Pastilla	B'stilla	Pigeon pie

MEAT, POULTRY AND FISH

Poulet	djaj	Chicken	Merlan	l-mirla	Whiting
Pigeon	lehmama	Pigeon	Crevettes	qambri	Shrimps
Lapin	qniya	Rabbit	Langouste	–	Crayfish
Mouton	l-houli	Mutton			(rock lobster)
Sardines	sardile	Sardines			

sugar and cinnamon; it is a particular speciality of Fes.

And, of course, there is **couscous**, perhaps the most famous Moroccan dish, based on a huge bowl of steamed semolina piled high with vegetables and mutton, chicken, or occasionally fish. Couscous, however, tends to be disappointing. There is no real tradition of going out to eat in Morocco, and this is a dish that's traditionally prepared at home for a special occasion (on Friday, the holy day, in richer households; perhaps for a festival in poorer ones). As a general rule, you'll need to give two or three hours' notice for it to be cooked in a restaurant. In the home, remember that every Moroccan's mother cooks the finest couscous in the kingdom.

At festivals, which are always good for interesting food, and at the most expensive tourist restaurants, you may also come across **mechoui** – roast lamb, which may even take the form of a whole sheep roasted on a spit.

To supplement these standard offerings, most tourist restaurants add a few **French dishes** – steak, liver, various fish and fowl, etc – and the

SWEETS AND FRUITS

Cornes de gazelles	kab l-ghazl	Marzipan-filled pastry horns	Bananes	banane	Bananas
–	m'hencha	Coiled, almond-filled pastry	Fraises	l-fraise	Strawberries
			Cerises	hblmluk	Cherries
			Pêches	l-khoukh	Peaches
Briouats au miel	–	Similar – but covered in honey	Oranges	limoune	Oranges
			Melon	l-battikh	Melon
			Pasteque	dellah	Watermelon
–	fekkas	Sweet aniseed biscuits	Raisins	la'anb	Grapes
			Pommes	tufaah	Apples
Fromage	ejben	Cheese	Abricots	mishmash	Apricots
Dattes	tmer	Dates	Figues de Barbarie	hendiya	Prickly pear (cactus fruit)
Figues	kermous	Figs			
Amandes	louze	Almonds			

DRINKS

Eau (minerale)	l-ma (mazdini)	(Mineral) water	Café (au lait)	qahwa (bi lahlib)	Coffee (with milk)
Jus	'asir	Juice			
Thé (à la menthe)	atay (deeyal naanaa)	Tea (with mint)	Bière	birra	Beer
			Vin	sh-rab	Wine

SOME ARABIC PHRASES

What do you have . . .	Ashnoo kane . . .	Without meat	Ble l-hem
. . . to eat?	. . . f'l-makla?	This is not what I asked for!	Hedee meshee heea li tlubt!
. . . to drink?	. . . f'l- mucharoubat?		
What is this?	Shnoo hada?	This is not fresh/ clean!	Hedee meshee treea/ n'qeea!
Can you give me . . .	Ateenee . . .		
. . . a knife/fork/ spoon?	moos/forsheta/ malka?	This is (not) good!	Hedee (meshee) mezyena!
. . . a plate/glass/ napkin?	. . . t'b-sil/kess/ l-fota?	The bill, please.	l'h'seh minfadlik.
		Please write it down.	Minfadlik, k'tib'h.
Less/without sugar	Shweeya/ble soukar		

EATING MOROCCAN STYLE

Eating in local cafés, or if **invited to a home**, you may find yourself using your hands rather than a knife and fork. Muslims eat only with the **right hand** (the left is used for the toilet), and you should do like-wise. Hold the bread between the fingers and use your thumb as a scoop; it's often easier to discard the soft centre of the bread and to use the crust only – as you will see many Moroccans do.

Eating from a **communal plate** at someone's home, it is polite to take only what is immediately in front of you, unless specifically offered a piece of meat by the host.

ubiquitous **salade marocaine**, actually very dif ferent from the Moroccan idea of salad, since it's based on a few tomatoes, cucumbers and other greens. You'll also probably have the choice of fruit, yoghurt, or sometimes even crème caramel for dessert.

In the text we have indicated what kind of **price range** a restaurant falls into. At restau-rants described as "cheap", a typical meal (starter, main course, dessert and drink) will cost less than 80dh (£5/$8). At places described as "moderate", you can expect to pay 80–150dh (£5–9.50/$8–15), while anywhere likely to cost over 150dh (£9.50/$15) is described as "expen-sive". Obviously, though, you'll get more and bet-ter food in general at a moderate or expensive restaurant than you will at a cheap one.

CAKES, DESSERTS AND FRUIT

Cakes and desserts are available in some Moroccan café-restaurants, though you'll find them more often at pastry shops or street stalls. They can be excellent, not generally too sickly and often made with nuts, especially almonds;

there are infinite variations, like *m'hencha* (almond-filled pastry coils which sometimes appear covered in honey) and *cornes de gazelles* (banana-shaped pastries filled with a kind of marzipan).

Yoghurt (*yaourt*) is also delicious, and Morocco is surprisingly rich in seasonal **fruits**. In addition to the various kinds of **dates** – sold all year but at their best fresh from the October harvests – there are grapes, melons, strawberries, peaches and figs, all advisably washed before eaten. Or for a real thirst-quencher (and a good cure for a bad stomach), you can have quantities of **prickly pear**, cactus fruit, peeled for you in the street for a couple of dirhams in season.

TEA AND OTHER DRINKS

The national drink is **mint tea** (*atay deeyal naanaa* in Arabic, *thé à la menthe* in French, "Whisky Marocain" as locals boast), Chinese gunpowder green tea flavoured with sprigs of mint (*naanaa* in Arabic: the gift of Allah) and sweetened with a minimum of four cubes of sugar per cup, or four lumps knocked off a sugar loaf – something you won't find nowadays in many other parts of the world. It tastes a little sickly at first (you can ask for it with little or no sugar – *shweeya soukar* or *ble soukar*) but is worth getting used to. It's perfect in the summer heat and a ritual if you're invited into anyone's home or if you're doing any serious bargaining in a shop. In cafés, it is usually cheaper to ask for a pot (*une théière*) for two or three people.

In winter, Moroccans often add *chiba* (Arabic for wormwood, *absinthe* in French) to their tea to 'keep out the cold'. You can also get black tea (*atai ahmar* in Arabic, *thé rouge* in French, literally meaning "red tea") – inevitably made with the ubiquitous Lipton's tea bags, a brand fondly believed by Moroccans to be typically English. **Herbal infusions** include aniseed (*anis*) and verbena (*verveine*).

Also common at cafés and street stalls are a range of wonderful fresh-squeezed **juices**: orange juice (*jus d'orange* in French, *'asir burtuqal* in Arabic – if you don't want sugar in it, remember to say so), almond mik (*jus d'amande* or *'asir louze*), banana "juice", meaning milk-shake (*jus des bananes* or *'asir mooz*) and apple milk-shake (*jus de pomme* or *'asir tufah*). *Leben* – soured milk – is tastier than it sounds, and does wonders for an upset stomach.

Other **soft drinks** inevitably include Coke, Fanta and other fizzy soda pops – all pretty inexpensive and sold in large bottles. **Mineral water**, which is a worthwhile investment throughout the country, is usually referred to by brand name, ubiquitously the still *Sidi Harazem* or *Sidi Ali* (some people claim to be able to tell one from the other), or the naturally sparkling *Oulmès*.

Coffee (*café*) is best in French-style cafés – either *noir* (black), *cassé* (with a drop of milk), or *au lait* (with a lot of milk). Instant coffee is known, like teabag tea, after its brand – in this case *Nescafé*.

Lastly, do not take risks with **milk**: buy it fresh and drink it fresh. If it smells remotely off, don't touch it.

WINE AND BEER

As an Islamic nation, Morocco gives **drinking alcohol** a low profile. It is in fact not generally possible to buy any alcohol at all in the Medinas, and for beer or wine you always have to go to a tourist restaurant or hotel, or a bar in the Ville Nouvelle. Outside of tourist hotels, **bars** – which are often called **brasseries**, though they serve no food – are very much **all-male preserves**, in which women travellers may feel uneasy (bartenders may be female, but female Moroccan customers are likely to be on the game).

On the drinks front, Moroccan **wines** can be palatable enough, if a little heavy for drinking without a meal. The best to be found is the pinkish red *Clairet de Meknès*, made purposefully light in French claret style. *Beauvallon* is another good one, but usually reserved for export. Other varieties worth trying include the strong red *Cabernet*, *Ksar* and *Siraoua*, which are also red, the rosé *Gris de Boulaoune* and the dry, white *Spécial Coquillages*.

Those Moroccans who drink in bars tend to stick to **beer**, usually the local *Stork* or *Flag*, which are about 50 percent cheaper than imported European brands. The most popular imported beer is *Heineken* from the Netherlands.

KIF AND HASHISH

The smoking of **kif** (marijuana) and hashish ("*chocolate*") has for a long time been a regular pastime of Moroccans and tourists alike. Indeed, in the 1960s and 1970s (or further back, in the 1930s), its ready availability, good quality and low cost made *kif* a major tourist attraction. It is, however, illegal, or, as the ONMT puts it:

Tourists coming to Morocco are warned that the first article in the Dahir of April 24th 1954 prohibits the POSSESSION, the OFFER, the DISTRIBUTION, the PURCHASE, the SALE and the TRANSPORTATION as well as the EXPORTATION of CANNABIS IN WHATEVER FORM. The Dahir allows for a penalty of IMPRISONMENT from three months to five years and a fine of 2400 to 240,000 dirhams, or only one of these. Moreover the law court may ordain the SEIZURE of the means of transport and the things used to cover up the smuggling as well as the toxic products themselves.

In practice, there is no real effort to stop Moroccans from using *kif*, but as a tourist you are rather more vulnerable. Not so much because of the **police**, as because of the **dealers**. Many have developed aggressive tactics, selling people hash (or, occasionally, even planting it) and then returning or sending friends to threaten to turn you in to the police (or just doing so themselves in return for a cut of the backsheesh you have to pay to extricate yourself). Either way, it can all become pretty paranoiac and unpleasant – and large fines (plus prison sentences for substantial amounts) do get levied, though you should be aware if arrested for cannabis that the police normally expect to be paid off, and that this should be done as quickly as possible while the minimum number of officers are involved.

What can you do to avoid all this trouble? Most obviously, keep well clear – above all, of the *kif*-growing region of **Ketama** in the Rif mountains – and always reply to hustlers by saying you don't smoke. If you are going to indulge, don't buy anything in the first few days (definitely not in Tangier and Tetouan). And above all **do not try to take any out** of the country, even to Spain (where attitudes to possession are relaxed but there's nearly always a prison sentence for importing).

If you do get in trouble there are **consulates** for most nationalities in Rabat, Casablanca and, to a lesser extent, in Tangier and Agadir (see lists on p.38). All of the consulates are notoriously unsympathetic to drug offenders – the British one in Rabat has an old French poster on the wall, *"Le kif détruit l'esprit"* – but they can help with technical problems and find you legal representation. For more on *kif* traditions and the hash industry in the Rif, see the box on p.142.

COMMUNICATIONS: POST, PHONES AND THE MEDIA

emptied fairly efficiently, even in out-of-the-way places.

Stamps can sometimes be bought alongside postcards, or from some *Tabacs* as well as at the PTT, where there may be a dedicated window or counter (labelled *timbres*), and where stamps should be sold too in the phone section, if there is one.

At the PTT, there is a separate window for **parcels**, where the officials will want to examine the goods you are sending. Always take them unwrapped; alongside the parcels counter, there is usually someone (on a franchise) to supply wrapping paper, string and all the trimmings, or wrap your parcel, if you want.

Post office hours are Monday to Friday, 8am–12.15pm (11.30am on Friday) & 3–6.30pm in winter, 8am–3.30pm in summer (usually 15 July to 30 September), 9am–3.30pm during Ramadan; closed Saturday and Sunday. Central post offices in big cities will be open longer hours (typically 8am–6.30pm Monday to Friday, 8am–noon

MAIL AND POSTE RESTANTE

Letters between Morocco and Western Europe generally take around a week to ten days, around two weeks for North America or Australasia. There are postboxes at every post office (**PTT** aka *La Poste*) and on the wayside; they seem to get

Saturday, but the same weekday hours as small offices in summer and during Ramadan), and they usually have a separate phone section, open longer hours, where stamps and phonecards are sold too.

POSTE RESTANTE

Receiving letters **poste restante** can be a bit of a lottery, as Moroccan post office workers don't always file letters under the name you might expect. Ask for all your initials to be checked (including *M* for Mr or Ms, etc) and, if you're half-expecting anything, suggest other letters as well.

To pick up your mail you need your passport. To have mail sent to you, it should be addressed (preferably with your surname underlined) to Poste Restante at the PTT Centrale of any major city (Marrakesh is notoriously inefficient).

Alternatives to sending poste restante to post offices are to pick a big **hotel** (anything with three or more stars should be reliable) or have things sent **c/o American Express** – represented in Morocco by Voyages Schwartz in Tangier, Casablanca, Rabat and Marrakesh (see p.26 for addresses).

PHONES

There is a **telephone section** in each city's main post office (PTT Centrale), which often has a separate entrance and stays open longer hours – 24 hours a day in some of the main cities, but it is usually easier to use **téléboutiques**, which you'll find in abundance in all towns, great and small. You can dial abroad from almost all of these (some use coins, others have their own cards), the exception being in the Western Sahara, where

you either have to use the PTT, or else (in Smara) call the operator from a *téléboutique* and ask for a connection. Some public phone boxes (*cabines*), especially in the Villes Nouvelles of large cities, will take **phonecards** issued by Itissalat al-Maghrib (the main phone company), which are available from some newsagents and tobacconists, and from post offices. These work out cheaper than calling from a PTT or *téléboutique*, but the phones don't usually seem to work (except for those outside the PTT itself). Alternatively, you can **make calls through a hotel**. Even fairly small places will normally do this; however, it'll cost you, so be sure to ask in advance both of possible surcharges and the chargeable rate. Note that international calls from a PTT or a hotel are usually charged for each **three-minute period**. If you go one second over, you're charged for the next period. If phoning from a PTT, you can request the operator to cut you off after a three-minute period.

To **make a call from a cabine**, you place the phonecard – or coins – into the slot on the phoneset and then dial. Using coins, a few dirhams are enough for a call within Morocco; for international calls you need at least four 5dh coins for Europe or the British Isles, and eight or more for North America or Australasia. Some phones take the old 5dh coins, others use the new ones (*téléboutiques* will supply whichever ones you need); a few take 10dh coins.

Some *téléboutiques* will send a **fax** for you – and, by arrangement, receive one for you. A few also have a **photocopier**, but they are not well maintained and you may have to visit several to find one which works. Newsagents, stationers and bookshops may also do photocopies.

PHONE NUMBERS

All Moroccan phone numbers, even local ones, must now be dialled in full. In addition, some codes have changed; new ones are listed below:

Mobiles that were ☎01/xxxxx are now ☎06/1xx xxxx.

Numbers that were ☎02/xxxxxx are now ☎02/2xx xxxx.

Numbers that were ☎03/xxxxxx are now ☎02/3xx xxxx.

Numbers that were ☎04/xxxxxx are now ☎04/4xx xxxx.

Numbers that were ☎05/xxxxxx are now ☎05/5xx xxxx.

Numbers that were ☎06/xxxxxx are now ☎05/6xx xxxx.

Numbers that were ☎07/xxxxxx are now ☎03/7xx xxxx.

Numbers that were ☎08/xxxxxx are now ☎04/8xx xxxx.

Numbers that were ☎09/xxxxxx are now ☎03/9xx xxxx.

PHONING MOROCCO FROM ABROAD

Phoning Morocco from abroad, you dial the international access code (00 from Britain, Ireland, Spain, the Netherlands and New Zealand; 0011 from Australia; 011 from the USA and most of Canada), then the country code (212), the second digit of the local code (omitting the initial zero), and the full seven-digit number. Note that for Ceuta and Melilla, the country code is 34 instead of 212, and the number has 9 digits, including the former area code.

HOME COUNTRY DIRECT

Toll-free numbers for home country direct services (not available from all phones) are:

UK (BT)	☎211 0044	**USA (AT&T)**	☎211 0011
UK (MCL)	☎211 0144	**USA (MCI)**	☎211 0012
Ireland	☎211 0353	**Canada**	☎211 0010

Mobile phones can be used from most places in Morocco (the country now has about 90 percent coverage), but note that prepaid cards from abroad cannot be charged up or replaced in Morocco, so remember to bring enough credit with you.

MOROCCAN CALLS AND NUMBERS

All landline phone numbers in Morocco are prefixed by one of four **area zones**:

02 Casablanca-Settat area (including Azilal, Beni Mellal, El Jadida, Kasba Tadla and Mohammedia)

03 Rabat-Tangier area (including Al Hoceima, Asilah, Chaouen, Kenitra, Khemissat, Larache, Ouazzane, Salé, Sidi Kacem and Tetouan)

04 Marrakesh-Agadir area (including Bou Izakarn, Demnate, Essaouira, Goulimine, Inezgane, Ouarzazte, Safi, Sidi Ifni, Tafraoute, Tan Tan, Tarfaya, Taroudannt, Tata, Tiznit and Zagora)

05 Fes-Oujda area (including Azrou, Berkane, Erfoud, Er Rachidia, Figuig, Ifrane, Immouzer, Khenifra, Meknes, Nador, Oujda, Rissani, Saidia and Taza)

Area code prefixes are given with all phone numbers quoted in the text of this book, from which you should be able to work out the area code for any town you're not sure about. Mobiles are all prefixed 06.

When dialling, the **ringing tone** consists of one-and-a-half-second bursts of tone, separated by a three-and-a-half-second silence. The **engaged tone** is a series of short tones (pip-pip-pip-pip), as in most other parts of the world. A short series of very rapid pips may also indicate that your call is being connected.

As in mainland Spain, the area codes for the **Spanish enclaves** in Morocco are now part of the number and must be dialled even locally. All numbers are now nine-digit, starting with the former area codes (956 for **Ceuta**, 952 for **Melilla**). To call from mainland Spain, you will only need to dial the nine-digit number. To call from Morocco proper, add 00 34 in front.

INTERNATIONAL CALLS

For an **international call** from Morocco, dial the international access code **00**, followed by the **country code**:

Australia 61	Canada 1
Ireland 353	Netherlands 31
New Zealand 64	South Africa 27
Spain 34	UK 44
USA 1	

Then dial the **individual number**, leaving out the initial 0 of its local code (except to the USA and Canada, which have no initial 0). Note that the initial 9, formerly left out in international calls to Spain, including Ceuta and Melilla, is now part of the actual number and must be dialled.

If you are successfully connected you will hear the local tones for your number. If not, you will hear either a busy signal, a recording in Arabic and then French informing that lines are "saturated", or silence. Persevere: it may well take three or four attempts to get through.

The peak **rate for international calls** is currently 12dh a minute to the UK, 13.70dh to Ireland, 20dh to the USA and Canada, and 32dh to Australia, New Zealand and South Africa. There is a 40 percent discount on these rates from midnight to 7am, plus Saturdays after 12.30pm and all day Sunday; a 20 percent discount rate applies on weekdays from 10pm to midnight. To reverse call charges, a good policy is to phone someone briefly and get them to ring you back. Actual collect (reverse charge) calls are hard to arrange, though home country direct services to the British Isles and North America are available from some phones (usually at card phones if they work, especially those outside main post offices, or in the post office phone sections if all else fails). Charge cards from your phone company at home can be used in the same places.

EMAIL AND THE INTERNET

Internet clubs and cybercafés are springing up all over Morocco, and can be found in any town (the most convenient are listed in the "Practicalities" or "Listings" sections of places in this book). You can send, and usually receive, email at any of these. A useful way of keeping in touch is to set up a email account with a firm like Yahoo or Hotmail that can be accessed via the Internet from anywhere. To set up such or access an account, visit the Web sites *www.yahoo.com* or *www.hotmail.com*. For a list of useful Web sites on Morocco, see pp.32–33.

THE MEDIA

A selection of European **newspapers** (usually including some British dailies) and the *International Herald Tribune* are available in all the main cities. *Le Monde* is the most common. The British *Guardian Weekly* is also usually available, as occasionally is *USA Today*, and more commonly *Time*, *Newsweek* and *The Economist*. Also often available, though of limited value as a serious source of news, is the *Saudi Gazette*, whose content is, needless to say, slavishly favourable to the Saudi regime.

If you take a short-wave radio, you can pick up the **BBC World Service**, which is broadcast on various frequencies through the day, from 6am to midnight local time. The most consistent reception is generally on 9.41 and 12.095 MHz (31m and 25m bands), plus 3.955, 6.195 and 7.325 MHz after dark, 15.485, 17.64 and 17.705 MHz during the day; full programme listings are available from the BBC or the British Council in Rabat. You can also pick up the **Voice of America** during the day on 1.197MHz, at night on 15.205MHz, afternoons on 1.548MHz, and evenings on 9.76MHz, among other frequencies.

Some of the pricier hotels these days can receive **satellite TV** – CNN, the French TV5, and occasionally the UK Sky channels. In the north of the country you can also get Spanish TV stations and, in Tangier, the English-language **Gibraltar TV** and radio broadcasts.

Morocco's own two TV channels broadcast in Arabic, but include some French programmes – plus news bulletins in Arabic, French, Spanish and, more recently, Berber.

Note that **videotapes** recorded in Morocco use the French SECAM system which means that they won't be playable on machines in Britain, Ireland, North America, Australasia and most of western Europe.

THE MOROCCAN PRESS

The **Moroccan press** encompasses a reasonable range of papers, published in French and Arabic. Of the **French-language** papers, the most accessible is the official – and somewhat rigorously pro-government – French-language daily, *Le Matin du Sahara* (circulation 100,000). Others include *L'Opinion* (Istiqlal party, circulation 60,000), *Maroc Soir* (independent, circulation 50,000), and *Al-Bayannne* (communist, circulation around 5,000). Among periodicals, *L'Economiste*, a news weekly with a 24,000 circulation, is the most influential, and publishes a digest on its Web site at *www.l'economiste.press.ma*.

Arabic daily newspapers include *El Alam* (circulation 100,000), which supports the Istiqlal party, and *El Ittihad el Ichtiraki* (circulation 110,000), which supports the socialist USFP party.

FESTIVALS: RAMADAN, HOLIDAYS AND MOUSSEMS

If the popular image of Islam is somewhat puritanical and ascetic, Morocco's festivals – the moussems and amouggars – do their best to contradict it. The country abounds in holidays and festivals of all kinds, both national and local, and coming across one can be the most enjoyable experience of travel in Morocco – with the chance to witness music and dance, as well as special regional foods and market souks.

Perhaps surprisingly, there are rewards, too, in coinciding with one of the major Islamic celebrations – above all Ramadan, when all Muslims (which means almost all Moroccans) observe a total fast from sunrise to sunset for a month. This can pose some problems for travelling but the celebratory evenings are again good times to hear music and to share in hospitality.

RAMADAN

Ramadan, in its observance, parallels the traditional Christian Lent. The ninth month of the Islamic calendar, it commemorates the time in which the Koran was revealed to Muhammad. In contrast to the Christian West, the Muslim world observes the fast rigorously – indeed Moroccans are forbidden by law from "public disrespect" of the fast, and a few are jailed for this each year.

The Ramadan fast involves abstention from food, drink, smoking and sex during daylight hours throughout the month. With most local cafés and restaurants closing during the day, and people getting on edge towards the month's end, it is in some respects an unsatisfactory time to travel: efficiency drops, drivers fall asleep at the wheel (hence airline pilots are excused fasting), and guides and muleteers are unwilling to go off on treks.

But there is compensation in witnessing and becoming absorbed into the pattern of the fast. At sunset, signalled by the sounding of a siren and the lighting of lamps on the minarets, an amazing calm and sense of wellbeing fall on the streets, as everyone drinks a bowl of *harira* and possibly a glass of milk, and maybe eats dates. You will also see almsgiving (*zakat*) extended to offering *harira* to the poor and homeless.

After breaking their fast, everyone – in the cities at least – gets down to a night of celebration and **entertainment**. This takes different forms. If you can spend some time in Marrakesh during the month, you'll find the Djemaa El Fna square there at its most active, with troupes of musicians, dancers and acrobats coming into the city for the occasion. In Rabat and Fes, there seem to be continuous promenades, with cafés and stalls staying open until 3am. Urban cafés provide venues for live music and singing, too, and in the southern towns and Berber villages you will often come across the ritualized *ahouaches* and *haidus* – circular, trance-like dances often involving whole communities.

If you are a **non-Muslim** outsider you are not expected to observe Ramadan, but it is good to be sensitive about breaking the fast (particularly smoking) in public. In fact, the best way to experience Ramadan – and to benefit from its naturally purifying rhythms – is to enter into it. You may lack the faith to go without an occasional glass of water, and you'll probably have breakfast later than sunrise, but it is worth an attempt.

OTHER ISLAMIC HOLIDAYS

At the end of Ramadan comes the feast of **Aïd es Seghir**, a climax to the festivities in Marrakesh, though observed more privately in most communities. Equally important to the Muslim calendar is **Aïd el Kebir**, which celebrates the willingness of Abraham to obey God and to sacrifice Isaac. Aïd el Kebir is followed, about two months later, by **Moharem**, the Muslim new year.

Both *aïds* are traditional family gatherings. At the Aïd El Kebir every household that can afford it

RAMADAN AND ISLAMIC HOLIDAYS

Islamic religious holidays are calculated on the **lunar calendar**, so their dates rotate throughout the seasons (as does Ramadan's), losing about eleven days a year against the Western (Gregorian) calendar. Exact dates in the lunar calendar are impossible to predict – they are set by the Islamic authorities in Fes – but approximate dates for the next few years are:

	2001	**2002**	**2003**	**2004**
Aïd el Kebir	5 Mar	22 Feb	11 Feb	31 Jan
Moharem	26 Mar	15 Mar	4 Mar	21 Feb
Mouloud	4 June	24 May	13 May	1 May
1st Ramadan	16 Nov	5 Nov	25 Oct	13 Oct
Aïd es Seghir	16 Dec	5 Dec	24 Nov	12 Nov

FETES NATIONALES

Secular *fêtes nationales*, all celebrated to some extent, are tied to Western calendar dates:

January 1	New Year's Day
January 11	Anniversary of Istiqlal Manifesto (see p.559)
May 1	Labour Day
May 23	Fête Nationale
July 30	Feast of the Throne (probable date)
August 14	Allegiance Day
August 20	King's Birthday and Youth Day
November 6	Anniversary of the Green March
November 18	Independence Day

The **Feast of the Throne** is the largest secular holiday, a colourful affair, celebrated throughout Morocco, over two to three days, with fireworks, parades and music.

will slaughter a sheep. You see them tethered everywhere, often on rooftops, for weeks prior to the event; after the feast, their skins are to be seen, being cured on the streets. Note that, on both *aïd* days, shops and restaurants close and buses don't run; on the following day, all transport is packed, as people return to the cities from their family homes.

The fourth main religious holiday is the **Mouloud**, the Prophet's birthday. This is widely observed, with a large number of moussems (see next column) timed to take place in the weeks around it. There is also a music festival, **Ashorou**, which takes place thirty days after Aïd el Kebir, when people gather to play whatever traditional instrument they feel capable of wielding, and the streets are full of music.

PUBLIC HOLIDAYS

Nowadays each of the big **religious feasts** is usually marked by **two days off**. These are announced or ratified by the king, each time, on TV and radio the preceding day.

On these public holidays, and on the secular *fêtes nationales* (see box above), all **banks**, **post offices** and most **shops** are closed; **transport** is reduced, too, but never stops completely.

MOUSSEMS AND AMMOUGARS

Moussems – or ammougars – are held in honour of saints or marabouts. They are basically local, and predominantly rural, affairs. Besides the Aïd Es Seghir and Aïd El Kebir, however, they form the main religious and social celebrations of the year for most Moroccans, especially for the country Berbers.

Some of the smaller moussems amount to no more than a market day with religious overtones; others are essentially harvest festivals, celebrating a pause in agricultural labour after a crop has been successfully brought in. A number, however, have developed into substantial occasions – akin to Spanish fiestas – and a few have acquired national significance. If you are lucky enough to be here for one of the major events, you'll get the chance to witness Moroccan popular culture at its

MOULOUD MOUSSEMS

MEKNES: BEN AISSA MOUSSEM

The largest of all the moussems, this includes a spectacular **fantasia** (a charge of horses with riders firing guns at full gallop) if weather conditions permit, held near Place El Hedim. With this, the enormous conical tents, and crowds of country people in white *djellabahs* beneath the city walls, it has the appearance of a medieval tournament. At least, that is, until you see the adjoining fairground, which is itself fun, with its illusionists and riders of death.

In the past, this moussem was the principal gathering of the **Aissoua** brotherhood, and the occasion for them to display their extraordinary powers of endurance under trance – cutting themselves with daggers, swallowing glass and the like. Their activities today are more subdued, though they still include going into trance, and of course playing music. Their focus is the marabout tomb of Ben Aissa, near the road in from Rabat.

Accommodation in Meknes is a problem at this time unless you arrive two or three days in advance. However, you could quite easily visit on a day-trip from Fes.

OTHER POPULAR MOUSSEMS

SALÉ: WAX CANDLE MOUSSEM

As the name suggests, this festival centres on a procession of wax candles – enormous lantern-like creations, carried from Bab El Rih to the Grand Mosque on the eve of the *Mouloud*. The candle bearers (a hereditary position) are followed by various brotherhoods, dancing and playing music.

The **procession** starts about 3pm and goes on for three or four hours; the best place to see it is at Bab Bou Hadja, where the candles are presented to local dignitaries.

May	**Moulay Bousselham** moussem of Sidi Ahmed Ben Mansour.
June	**Goulimine** Traditionally a camel traders' fair, elements of which remain.
	Tan Tan Moussem of Sidi Mohammed Ma El Ainin. Large-scale religious and commercial moussem. Saharan "Guedra" dance may be seen performed.
July	**Tetouan** Moussem of Moulay Abdessalem. A very religious, traditional occasion with a big turnout of local tribesmen. Impressive location on a flat mountain top south of the town.
August	**Setti Fatma** Large and popular moussem in the Ourika valley, southeast of Marrakesh.
	El Jadida Moussem of Moulay Abdallah. Located about 9km west of the city at a village named after the saint. Features displays of horse-riding, or fantasias.
	Tiznit Moussem of Sidi Ahmed ou Moussa. Primarily religious.
September	**Chaouen** Moussem of Sidi Allal Al Hadh. Located in the hills out of the town.
	Moulay Idriss Zerhoun Moussem of Moulay Idriss. The largest religious moussem, but visitable only for the day as a non-Muslim. Impressive display by brotherhoods, and a highly charged procession of gifts to the saint's tomb. Also a large fantasia above the town.
	Imilchil Marriage moussem. Set in the heart of the Atlas mountains, this is the most celebrated Berber moussem – traditionally the occasion of all marriages in the region, though today also a tourist event. In fact there now seem to be two moussems, with one laid on specifically for package tours from Marrakesh and Agadir; the real event is held in the last week in September or the first in October.
	Fes Moussem of Moulay Idriss II. The largest of the moussems held inside a major city, and involving a long procession to the saint's tomb. The Medina is packed out, however, and you will have a better view if you stand at Dar Batha or Place Boujeloud before the procession enters the Medina proper.

richest, with horse-riding, music, singing and dancing, and of course eating and drinking.

AIMS AND FUNCTIONS

The ostensible aim of the moussem is religious: to obtain blessing, or *baraka*, from the saint and/or to thank God for the harvest. But the social and cultural dimensions are equally important. Moussems provide an opportunity for country people to escape the monotony of their hard working lives in several days of festivities. They may provide the year's single opportunity for friends or families from different villages to meet. Harvest and farming problems are discussed, as well as family matters – marriage in particular – as people get the chance to sing, dance, eat and pray together.

Music and singing are always major components of a moussem and locals will often bring tape recorders to provide sounds for the rest of the year. The different religious brotherhoods, some of whom may be present at larger moussems, each have their own distinct styles of music, dancing and dress.

Moussems also operate as **fairs**, or markets, with artisans offering their produce to a wider market than is available at the weekly souk. Buyers in turn can inform themselves about new products and regional price differences, as the moussem attracts people from a much wider area than the souk. There is a welcome injection of cash into the local economy, too, with traders and entertainers doing good business, and householders renting out rooms.

At the **spiritual level**, people seek to improve their standing with God through prayer, as well as the less orthodox channels of popular belief. Central to this is *baraka*, good fortune, which can be obtained by intercession of the saint. Financial contributions are made and these are used to buy a gift, or *hedia*, usually a large carpet, which is then taken in procession to the saint's tomb; it is deposited there for the local *shereefian* families,

the descendants of the saint, to dispose of as they wish. Country people may seek to obtain *baraka* by attaching a garment or tissue to the saint's tomb and leaving it overnight to take home after the festival.

The procession which takes the gift to the tomb is the high point of the more **religious** moussems, such as that of **Moulay Idriss**, where an enormous carpet is carried above the heads of the religious **brotherhoods**. Each of these brotherhoods will be playing its own music, hypnotic in its rhythms; spectators and participants may go into a trance, giving themselves up to the music. If you witness such events, it is best to keep a low profile (and certainly don't take photographs); the presence of foreigners or non-Muslims at these times is sometimes considered to impede trance.

Release through trance probably has a therapeutic aspect, and indeed some moussems are specifically concerned with **cures** of physical and psychiatric disorders. The saint's tomb is usually located near a freshwater spring, and the cure can simply be bathing in and drinking the water. Those suffering from physical ailments may also be treated at the moussem with herbal remedies, or by recitation of verses from the Koran. Koranic verses may also be written and placed in tiny receptacles fastened near the affected parts. The whole is reminiscent of the popular remedies found at European pilgrimage centres like Lourdes.

PRACTICALITIES

There are enormous numbers of moussems. An idea of quite how many can be gathered from the frequency with which, travelling about the countryside, you see *koubbas* – the square, white-domed buildings covering a saint's tomb. Each of these is a potential focal point of a moussem, and any one region or town may have twenty to thirty separate annual moussems. Establishing when they take place, however, can be difficult for out-

HARVEST MOUSSEMS			
February	Tafraoute (almonds)	July	Al Hoceima (sea produce)
March	Beni Mellal (cotton)	August	Immouzer du Kandar (apples/pears)
May	Berkane (clementines)		Immouzer des Ida Outanane (honey)
	El Kelâa des Mgouna (roses)	November	Erfoud (dates)
July	Sefrou (cherries)		Rhafsaï (olives)

siders; most local people find out by word of mouth at the weekly souks.

Many moussems are held around religious occasions such as the **Mouloud**, which change date each year according to the lunar calendar (see box p.62). Others, concerned with celebrating the **harvest**, have their date decided at a local level according to when the harvest is ready. Moussems of this type are obviously more difficult to plan a visit around than those which occur at points in the Islamic year. **August** and **September** are the most promising months overall, with dozens of moussems held after the grain harvest when there is a lull in the agricultural year before sowing starts prior to the first rains in October or November.

The **lists** on pp.63 & 64 give an approximate idea (sometimes an exact one) of when the moussems are, but you will generally need to ask at a local level for information. Sometimes tourist offices may be able to help, though often not.

The **accommodation** situation will depend on whether the moussem is in the town or countryside. In the country, the simplest solution is to take a tent and camp – there is no real objection to anyone camping wherever they please during a moussem. In small towns there may be hotels – and locals will rent out rooms in their houses. **Food** is never a problem, with dozens of traders setting up stalls, though it is perhaps best to stick to the grills, as stalls may not have access to running water for cleaning.

SPORTS AND ACTIVITIES

Morocco is doing much to keep up with the increasing interest in activity and sporting holidays. In addition to its magnificent trekking opportunities, the country offers impressive golf and tennis facilities, a couple of ski resorts (plus some adventurous off-piste skiing) and excellent fishing. The national sporting obsession, however, is football; enthusiasts can join in any number of beach kick-about games, or watch local league and cup matches.

TREKKING

Trekking is one of the very best things Morocco has to offer. In the High Atlas, the country boasts one of the most rewarding mountain ranges in the world – and one of the least spoilt. If you are used to the Pyrenees or Alps, here you will feel you are moving a century or so back in time.

A number of **long-distance Atlas routes** can be followed – even a "Grand Traverse" of the full range. Most people, however, limit themselves to **shorter treks** round the **Djebel Toubkal** area (best in spring or autumn; conditions can be treacherous in winter). Other promising areas include the **Djebel Sirwa**, **Western High Atlas**, or in winter the **Djebel Sarhro** and **Tafraoute** region of the Anti-Atlas. The **Middle Atlas** has much attractive walking too, from such places as **Tazzeka** (Taza), the **Djebel Iblane** range, **Kerrouchen** and **Azrou**.

Each of these areas is featured in some detail in this guide. For further information, check the **trekking books** detailed on p.33. And if you haven't had much experience or feel a little daunted by the lack of organized facilities, try one of the **specialist trekking companies** offering Moroccan trips (see box on pp.5–7).

For general **trekking practicalities**, see the Toubkal section (p.388). For details of survey-style **maps**, see p.32.

FOOTBALL (SOCCER)

Football is important in Morocco and the country is a growing force. The national team qualified for the **World Cup** finals in 1986 (when they reached the quarter finals), 1994 and 1998, and are important participants in the annual **African Nations Cup** championship.

Moroccan clubs play at the top level in the various African club tournaments too, and at home compete in an annual **league** and the (knock-out) **Throne Cup**. For a long time there was just one full-time professional team, **FAR** (the army), but the 1990s saw the introduction of sponsorship and other semiprofessional sides, the best of which are **WIDAD** and **RAJA**, the two big Casablanca teams, **MAS** from Fes and **KAC** from Kenitra. The result is a fairly high standard of skill in the Moroccan league, but unfortunately Moroccan clubs are unable to afford the money commanded by top players in Europe, with the result that the best Moroccan players are to be found playing for clubs in France, Belgium, the Netherlands, Spain and England.

One negative aspect of Moroccan league games is a tendency towards defensive play – the points system gives two points for a draw and three for a win. But there is always the potential for displays of individual dynamism and inspiration – a parallel, so Moroccans would have it, with the Brazilian style of play.

Brazilian comparisons could certainly be made with the social background of Moroccan football, players developing their game in unstructured **kick-arounds** on the beach, street or patches of wasteland. The lack of a team strip in these games (and hence easy recognition of team mates) discourages long balls and intricate passing, and encourages individual possession and quick one-twos. The same conditions produced Pelé and Maradona.

SKIING

Morocco isn't immediately thought of as a skiing destination, but the High Atlas mountains are reliably snow-covered from late January to early April, and occasionally the Middle Atlas, too, has sufficient snows for the sport.

In the High Atlas, the only resort is **Oukaïmeden** (see p.385), two hours' drive from Marrakesh. It is quiet, well appointed and inexpensive, with pleasant chalet hotels, seven piste runs, a ski lift, local instructors, and equipment for hire. In the Middle Atlas, **Mischliffen** (see p.245) – in a volcanic crater – has rather more limited facilities, with three lifts, a shorter and unreliable season, and very old-fashioned equipment rental. A third prospective ski centre is at **Djebel Bou Iblane** in the eastern Middle Atlas (see p.241), which offers little more than an approach road (often blocked by snow) and a single ski lift.

Off-piste skiing is popular in the High Atlas, particularly in the **Toubkal massif**, where the Toubkal Refuge (see p.395) is often full of groups. Most off-piste activity is ski mountaineering, but skinny skis (*langlang*) are good in the Middle Atlas if there is snow, in which case the Azilal–Bou Goumez–Ighil Mgoun area is possible. Experienced off-piste skiers may relish the challenge of trekking to remote peaks. For further information on skiing and mountaineering, contact the Fédération Royale Marocaine du Ski et du Montagnisme, Parc de la Ligue Arabe, BP 15899, Casablanca (☎02/247 4979; *frmsm@hotmail.com*).

RIDING

The established base for **riding holidays** is *La Roseraie* hotel at **Ouirgane** on the Tizi n'Test road (see p.401). The hotel runs trekking tours into the **High Atlas**, offering anything from one-day excursions to extended trips staying at villages en route. You should bring your own helmet. Firms specializing in horseback riding holidays from the UK include In The Saddle (☎01256/851665, *www.inthesaddle.com*), Motion Travel (☎020/7629 9777, *www.motion-europe.com*) and Peregrine Holidays (☎01425/480400, *eqtours@aol.com*). Stays or packages can be arranged through most of the Moroccan specialist agents detailed on pp.5–7.

You might also want to visit the **Haras de Meknes** (see p.184), Morocco's largest National Stud Farm, where you can both exercise and ride the horses.

FISHING

French visitors to Morocco have long appreciated the possibilities for fishing. The country offers an immense Atlantic (and small Mediterranean) **coastline**, with opportunities to arrange boat trips at Safi, Essaouira, Moulay Bousselham (near Asilah), and elsewhere.

Inland, the **Middle Atlas** shelters beautiful **lakes** and **rivers**, many of them well stocked with trout. Good bases could include **Azrou** (near the Aghmas lakes), **Ifrane** (near Zerrrouka), **Khenifra** (the Oum Er Rbia River) and **Ouirgane** (the Nfis River). Pike are also to be found in some Middle Atlas lakes (such as Aguelmame Azizgza, near Khenifra), and a few of the huge artificial **barrages**, like **Bin El Ouidaine** (near Beni Mellal), are said to contain enormous bass.

For the really determined and adventurous, the most exciting Moroccan fishing is along the coast of the **Western Sahara**, where catches weigh in regularly at 20–30 kilos. The best places to make enquiries about this are the fishing ports of Dakhla, Boujdour and the territory's capital, Laayoune.

For all fishing in the country, you need to take your own **equipment**. For coarse or fly fishing you need a **permit** from the Administration des Eaux et Fôrets (11 Rue du Devoir, Rabat). For trout fishing, you are limited to the hours between 6am and noon; the season starts on March 31.

WATER SPORTS AND SWIMMING

Agadir has **sailing, yachting, windsurfing** and **diving** on offer, with Taghazoute, just north of the resort, developing a growing reputation among **surfers and windsurfers**. The biggest surfing and windsurfing destination, however, is **Essaouira**, on the coast west of Marrakesh, which draws devotees of the sport all year round, with lesser surfing centres at Mirhleft (north of Sidi Ifni), Kenitra, Bouznika Plage (between Rabat and Casablanca), El Jadida, Safi, and even Rabat.

Anywhere on the Atlantic coast, however, surfers and **swimmers** alike should beware of strong undertows. The Atlantic can be very exposed, with crashing waves, and you'll often see Moroccan bathers venturing rather timidly into the water in formation.

Inland, most towns of any size have a municipal **swimming pool** – they're always very cheap and addresses are given in the guide. In the south, you'll be dependent on campsite pools or on those at the luxury hotels (which often allow outsiders to swim, either for a charge or if you buy drinks or a meal).

The High and Middle Atlas have also become a popular destination for **whitewater rafting** and **kayaking** enthusiasts. One UK firm specializing in these sports is Nature Rafting Journeys (☎020/7431 6898; *waterbynature.com*).

GOLF AND TENNIS

The British opened a golf course in Tangier as far back as 1917 – a rather more refined alternative to their then-favoured sport of pig-sticking. Today the country has an international-level course at **Rabat** (Royal Dar-Es-Salam Royal Golf), a 27-hole course in **Agadir** (Royal Golf), further 18-hole courses at **Mohammedia** (Royal Golf), **Marrakesh** (Amelkis; Palmeraie Golf; Royal Golf), **Tangier** (Royal Golf Club), **El Jadida** (Royal Golf), and nine-hole courses at **Casablanca** (Royal Anfa), **Agadir** (Dunes Golf Club), **Fes** (Royal Golf), **Cabo Negro** (Royal Golf), **Beni Slimane** (Royal Golf), **Ouarzazate** (Royal Golf), and **Meknes** (Royal Golf – actually within the confines of the Royal Palace gardens).

For a **golf-centred holiday** package from Britain, or details (and photos) of the courses, consult the golf brochure issued by Best of Morocco (☎01380/828533, *www.morocco-travel.com*). Other firms offering golfing holidays from the UK include Destination Golf (☎020/8891 5151, *www.destinationgolf.co.uk*), Exclusive Golf Tours (☎020/8679 6571, *www.exclusivegolf.co.uk*) and Cadogan Holidays (☎023/8082 8304, *www.cadoganholidays.com*).

Tennis courts are to be found at most four-star and five-star hotels, especially in Agadir (which now has a total of over 120 courts) and Marrakesh. Tennis equipment can often be loaned from hotels but it is not often up to much and you'd be advised to take rackets and balls.

OTHER SPORTS

The Marrakesh International Marathon takes place each second Sunday in January. It starts on Place Djemaa El Fna, passes through the Hivernage, encircles the Palmeraie and finishes a couple of hours later back at the Djemaa El Fna. The Marrakesh Marathon is not to be confused with the (even more gruelling) Maraton des Sables, the world's toughest race, covering 240km on the edge of the Moroccan Sahara (see p.432).

The more creative tour operators are always eager to exploit new markets, and the market for exciting sports is currently one of the hottest. Best of Morocco (☎01380/828533, *www.morocco-travel.com*) now offer desert **go-karting. Paragliding** is increasingly popular in the south of Morocco, around Tafraoute and Sidi Ifni in particular, where the hotels *Tafraout* and *Suerte Loca* respectively keep some information on good paragliding spots.

SOUKS AND MOROCCAN CRAFTS

Souks – markets – are a major feature of Moroccan life, and among the country's greatest attractions. They are to be found everywhere: each town has its special souk quarter, large cities like Fes and Marrakesh have labyrinths of individual souks (each filling a street or square and devoted to one particular craft), and in the countryside there are hundreds of weekly souks, on a different day in each village of the region.

SOUK DAYS

Some of the villages, or areas between villages, are in fact named after **their market days**, so it's easy to see when they're held.

The souk days are:

Souk El Had – Sunday (literally, "first market")

Souk El Tnine – Monday market

Souk El Tleta – Tuesday market

Souk El Arba – Wednesday market

Souk El Khamees – Thursday market

Souk Es Sebt – Saturday market

There are very few village markets on **Friday** (El Djemaa – the "assembly", when the main prayers are held in the mosques), and even in the cities, souks are largely closed on Friday mornings and very subdued for the rest of the day.

In general, village souks begin on the afternoon preceding the souk day, as people travel from all over the region; those who live nearer set out early in the morning of the souk day. As a consequence, the souk itself is usually over by noon and people disperse in the afternoon. You should therefore arrange to arrive by mid-morning at the latest.

CRAFT TRADITIONS

Moroccan **craft**, or *artesanie*, traditions are still highly active, and even goods mass-produced for tourists are surprisingly untacky. To find pieces of real quality, however, is not that easy – some crafts have become dulled by centuries of repetition and others have been corrupted by modern techniques and chemical dyes.

In general, if you're planning on buying anything, it's always worth getting as close to the source of the goods as possible, and to steer clear of the main tourist centres. **Fes** might have the richest traditions, but you can often find better work at much cheaper prices elsewhere; **Tangier** and **Agadir**, neither of which has imaginative workshops of their own, are generally poor bets. As stressed throughout the guide, the best way to get an idea of standards and quality is to visit the various **traditional crafts museums** spread round the country: there are good ones in Fes, Meknes, Tangier, Rabat and Marrakesh.

CARPETS, RUGS AND BLANKETS

Moroccan **carpets** are not cheap – you can pay £1000/$1500 and more for the finer Arab designs in Fes or Rabat. However, it is possible to find **rugs** or **kellims** (which are woven rather than knotted) at more reasonable prices, with a range of strong, well-designed weaves from £30–50/$45–75.

Most of these kellims will be of Berber origin and the most interesting ones usually come from the High and Middle Atlas; if you're looking seriously, try to get to the town souk in **Midelt** or the weekly markets in **Azrou** and other villages around **Marrakesh**. The chain of Maison Berbère shops in Ouarzazate, Tinerhir and Rissani are good hunting grounds, too. In fact, one of the best ways to find carpets is to wander around villages or parts of town where they are made, listen for the tell-tale sound of the loom in use, and ask at the weavers' homes if they have any carpets for sale.

On a simpler and cheaper level, the **Berber blankets** (*foutahs*, or *couvertures*) are imaginative, and often very striking with bands of reds and blacks; for these, **Tetouan** and **Chaouen**, on the edge of the Rif, are promising.

JEWELLERY

Silver jewellery went into decline with the loss to Israel of Morocco's Jewish population, the country's traditional workers in precious metals and crafts in general; in the **south**, however, you can pick up some fabulous Berber necklaces and bracelets, always very chunky, and characterized by bold combinations of semiprecious (and sometimes plastic) stones and beads. There are particularly good jewellery souks in Essaouira, Marrakesh and Tiznit.

MINERALS AND FOSSILS

You'll see a variety of **semiprecious stones** on sale throughout Morocco, and in the High Atlas they are often aggressively hawked on the roadsides. If you're lucky enough to be offered genuine **amethyst** or **quartz**, prices can be bargained to very tempting levels. Be warned, however, that all that glitters is not necessarily the real thing. Too often, if you wet the stone and rub, you'll find traces of dye on your fingers.

Fossils too are widely sold in Morocco, and sometimes as beautiful as they are fascinating. The fossil-rich black marble of the Erfoud region, for example, is sold in the form of anything from ashtrays to table tops. But again, things aren't always what they seem, and a lot of fossils are in fact **fakes**, made out of cement. This is particularly true of trilobites, or any black fossil on a grey background. For more on fossils and minerals, see the box on p.453.

WOOD AND POTTERY

Marquetry is one of the few crafts where you'll see genuinely old pieces – inlaid tables and shelves – though the most easily exportable objects are boxes and chess sets, beautifully inlaid in thuja and cedar woods in **Essaouira**.

Pottery is colourful if fairly crudely made on the whole, though the blue-and-white designs of **Fes** and the multicoloured pots of **Chaouen** (both produced largely for the tourist trade) are highly attractive. The essentially domestic pottery of **Safi** – Morocco's major pottery centre – is worth a look, too, with its colourful plates, tajines and garden pots. Safi tajines are nice to look at, but for practical use, the best are those produced by the Oulja pottery at **Salé**, near Rabat, in plain red-brown earthenware.

CLOTHING AND LEATHER

Moroccan clothes are easy to purchase, and though Westerners – men at least – who try to imitate Moroccan styles by wearing the cotton or wool *djellaba* (a kind of cloak) tend to look a little silly, there are some highly desirable items. Some of the cloth is exquisite in itself, and walking down the dyers' souks is an inspiration.

Leather is also excellent, and here you can buy and wear goods with perhaps greater confidence. The classic Moroccan shoes are **babouches**, open at the heel, immensely comfortable, and produced in yellow (the usual colour), white, red (for women) and occasionally

grey or (for the truly fetishistic) black; a good pair – and quality varies enormously – can cost £6–15/$9–22. Marrakesh and Tafraoute are especially good for *babouches*.

FOODSTUFFS

You'll find quite a variety of **food products** in Morocco that you would be hard pressed to find at home, and which make excellent and inexpensive gifts or souvenirs (assuming your country's customs allow their importation). Locally produced **olive oil** can be excellent, with a distinctive strong flavour, and in the Souss Valley there's delicious sweet **argan oil** too (see p.487). Olives themselves come in numerous varieties, and there are also almonds, walnuts and spices available, notably **saffron**, which is grown in the area east of Taliouine (see p.499). A jar of lemons preserved in brine is not only useful (if you want to try your hand at making a tajine back home), but also attractive on any kitchen shelf, and excellent **honey** of various varieties can be found too. The honey shop in Agadir (see p.484) is particularly recommended for the latter. The word for quality in traditional foods of this sort is *bildi*, meaning "country-style".

Cakes, sweets and biscuits are tempting but won't keep for long, while Moroccan wines are generally mediocre at best compared to those produced in California, Australia or Europe. Of more everyday **groceries** not easily available at home, cans of spiced sardines are worth considering, as is Knorr's surprisingly good instant fish soup.

For those with transport, **hypermarkets** run by the French firms Macro and Marjane are located on major approach roads at the edge of most big cities, offering a wide choice of Moroccan and imported foods and other goods at discount prices.

BARGAINING

Whatever you buy, and wherever you buy it, you will want (and be expected) to **bargain**. There are no hard and fast rules – it is really a question of paying what something is worth to you – but there are a few general points to keep in mind.

First, **bargaining is entirely natural** in Morocco. If you ask the price in a market, the answer, as likely as not, will come in one breath – "Twenty; how much will you pay?"

Second, don't pay any attention to **initial prices**. These are simply a device to test the limits of a particular deal or situation. Don't think, for example, in terms of paying one-third of the asking price (as some guides suggest) – it might well turn out to be a tenth or even a twentieth. Equally, though, it might not – some sellers actually start near the price they have in mind and will bustle you out of their shop for offering an "insulting" price. Don't feel intimidated by either tactic; if you return the following day for some coveted item, you will most likely be welcomed as an old friend. Take your chances.

Third, **don't ever let a figure pass your lips** that you aren't prepared to pay – nor start bargaining for something you have absolutely no intention of buying – there's no better way to create bad feelings.

Fourth, **take your time**. If the deal is a serious one (for a rug, say), you'll probably want to sit down over tea with the vendor, and for two cups you'll talk about anything but the rug and the price. If negotiations do not seem to be going well, it often helps to have a friend on hand who seems – and may well be – less interested in the purchase than you and can assist in extricating you from a particularly hard sell.

Fifth, remember that even if you're **paying more than local people**, it doesn't necessarily mean you're being "ripped off". As a Westerner, your earning power is well above that of most Moroccans and it's rather mean to force traders down to their lowest possible price just for the sake of it.

The final and most golden rule of them all is never to go shopping with a **guide** or a hustler, even "just to look" – the pressures will be either too great or it'll be too boring, depending on how long you've been in the country and how you've learned to cope with these people.

In the villages – and with beach traders – you might find **bartering goods** to be more satisfactory than bargaining over a price. This way you know the value of what you're offering better than your partner (though they'll have a pretty good idea), and in a sense you're giving a fairer exchange. Items particularly sought after are training shoes (even if they're well worn), printed T-shirts (rock designs – especially Prince – are favourites), football shirts (British or American) and other sports clothes, bandannas (especially sought after by girls in the High Atlas to tie back their hair), basic medicines (in country areas), and Western department-store clothes (Marks & Spencer has particularly good currency).

An approximate idea of what you should be paying for handicrafts can be gained from checking the **fixed prices** in the state- or co-operative-run *Ensembles Artisanals*, which are slightly higher than could be bargained for elsewhere.

MOSQUES AND MONUMENTS

Without a doubt, one of the major disappointments of travelling in Morocco if you are not Muslim is not being allowed into its mosques – as is permitted in many other Muslim countries. In Morocco, all non-Muslims are excluded and the rule is strictly observed.

However, there is much architecture to be admired in the form of Medersas – medieval "colleges" attached as teaching institutions to urban mosques – and in the numerous, elaborately decorated gateways (babs) to be found in any well-preserved city walls. Cities also reveal some beautiful fondouks – caravanserais – and the occasional palace. There is a scattering of remains, too, from Morocco's ancient civilizations under Roman and even Phoenician rule.

Most public monuments, including Medersas, museums and archeological sites, levy a standard 10dh admission fee and usually open from 8.30am to noon and 2.30pm to 5.30pm, though some may open a little earlier, close a little later, and stay open at lunchtime. Museums are usually closed on Tuesdays, and everything opens a little later and closes a little earlier during Ramadan.

MOSQUES AND KOUBBAS

The only "mosques" that non-Muslims *are* allowed to visit are the ruined Almohad structure of **Tin Mal** in the High Atlas (see p.404), the courtyard of the sanctuary-mosque of Moulay Ismail in **Meknes** (see p.183), the sanctuary of Mohammed V in **Rabat** (see p.285), the Bou

Inania Medersa in **Fes** (see p.214) and the new Grand Mosquée Hassan II in **Casablanca** (see p.306). Elsewhere, if you are not a believer, you'll have to be content with an occasional glimpse through open doors, and even in this you should be sensitive: people don't seem to mind tourists peering into the Kairaouine Mosque in Fes (the country's most important religious building), but in the country you should never approach a shrine too closely.

This rule applies equally to the numerous domed and whitewashed **koubbas** – the tombs of marabouts, or local saints – and the "monastic" **zaouias** of the various Sufi brotherhoods. It is a good idea, too, to avoid walking through **graveyards**, as these also are regarded as sacred places.

OTHER ISLAMIC MONUMENTS

As some compensation, many of the most beautiful and architecturally interesting of Morocco's monuments are open to view – the great imperial gateways, or **babs**, of the main cities, for example, and, of course, the **minarets** (towers from which the call to prayer is made) attached to the mosques.

Of buildings that can be visited, highlights must include the **Berber Kasbahs** (fortified castle residences) of the south; a series of city **palaces** and **mansions** – many of them converted into hotels, restaurants or craft shops – in Fes and Marrakesh; and the intricate **Medersas** of Fes, Meknes, Salé, and Marrakesh.

The **Medersas**, many of them dating from the thirteenth and fourteenth centuries, are perhaps the most startling – and certainly the most "monumental" – of all Moroccan buildings, each displaying elaborate decoration and designs in stucco (gypsum or plaster), cedar and tile mosaics (known in Morocco as zellij). Originally, these buildings served as religious universities or student residences for a neighbouring mosque school, but by the turn of the century they had largely fallen into decay and disuse. Today, they have almost all become secularized. Their role is discussed in the chapter on **Fes**, which is where you'll find the richest and most varied examples.

ANCIENT REMAINS

Unlike Tunisia and Algeria, Morocco never saw extensive **Roman** colonization – and indeed, the south of the country remained unconquered by any outside force until the French invasion of the 1920s. Ancient sites are, therefore, limited. The most interesting, and really the only one worth going out of your way to visit, is **Volubilis**, close to Meknes (see p.192). For enthusiasts, **Lixus** (near Larache – see p.110) is worthwhile, and there are good bronze collections and statuary at the Archeological Museum in **Rabat** (see p.286).

A number of **prehistoric sites**, with well-preserved **rock carvings** (*gravures rupestres* in French), survive in the south of the country, though most are extremely difficult to reach – and to find. The most rewarding and easily accessible ones are around **Oukaïmeden** and **Djebel Yagour**, near Marrakesh (see p.385). More significant, but remote, sites are scattered among the hills near the desert town of **Foum El Hassan** (see p.506), and in the region between there and Tafraoute. Enthusiasts might seek out the book *Gravures Rupestres du Haut Atlas* by Susan Searight and Danièle Hourbette, available at bookshops in Marrakesh.

DIRECTORY

ADDRESSES Arabic names – Derb, Zankat, etc – are gradually replacing French ones. The main street or square of any town, though, is still invariably Avenue or Place Hassan II (the last king) or Mohammed V (his father). Older street signs are usually in French and Arabic lettering; new ones are often Arabic only.

ANIMAL WELFARE Animals – and especially pack animals – have a tough life in Morocco. The **Society for the Protection of Animals Abroad** (SPANA) works throughout North Africa to improve conditions, replacing painful, old-style bits on donkeys and horses, employing vets, and running animal clinics and refuges. They have centres in Rabat, Marrakesh, Meknes, Khémisset, Khenifra, Had Ouled Frej, Chemaia, Midelt and Tangier – all of which can be contacted if you are are concerned about animals you've come across, or if you are interested in their work and would like to visit. The best initial contact address in Morocco is SPANA's administrative office in Temara (☎03/774 7209), 14km south of Rabat. The Society also has a British office at 15 Buckingham Gate, London SW1E 6LB (☎020/7828 0997) which can provide you with details of the Moroccan centres listed above.

CONSULATES AND EMBASSIES are mostly in Rabat, Tangier, Agadir and Casablanca; see p.38 for lists. For Moroccan embassies abroad, see p.23.

CONTRACEPTIVES Somewhat poor quality and unreliable condoms (*préservatifs*) can be bought in most pharmacies, and so can the pill (officially by prescription, but this isn't essential). If you're suf-

fering from diarrhoea, the pill (or any other drug) may not be in your system long enough to be absorbed, and consequently may become ineffective.

CULTURAL SOCIETIES OVERSEAS British residents may be interested in the British Moroccan Society (c/o Embassy of Morocco, 49 Queens Gate Gdns, London SW7 5NE), which organizes various Moroccan-oriented events and discussions, usually in London. Also of interest is the Maghreb Society, run pretty much single-handed by the indefatigable Ifnian Londoner, C Larousst from the Maghreb Bookshop, 45 Burton St, London WC1H 9AL (☎020/7388 1840). The society publishes the *Maghreb Review*, the most important English-language journal on the Maghrebian countries, and members get a discount on books.

CUSTOMS ALLOWANCES You're allowed to bring a litre of spirits into Morocco, which is well worth doing. Up to 200 cigarettes are also permitted, which saves money on American brands.

ELECTRICAL VOLTAGE Most of the country runs on 220v but some towns still have 110v sockets and it's not uncommon to have both in the same building. Electric shavers work OK, but heat-producing items like hairdryers need converters to function properly.

EMERGENCIES Fire ☎15; police (within towns) ☎19; gendarmes (police force with jurisdiction outside towns) ☎177.

GAY ATTITUDES Male homosexuality is common in Morocco, although attitudes towards it are a little schizophrenic. No Moroccan will declare himself gay – which has connotations of femininity and weakness; the idea of being a passive partner is virtually taboo, while a dominant partner may well not consider himself to be indulging in a homosexual act. Private realities, however, are rather different from public show. (On which subject, note that Moroccan men often walk hand-in-hand in public – a habit which has nothing to do with homosexuality and is simply a sign of friendship.)

If you are visiting Morocco specifically as a "gay destination" be warned that the legendary Joe Orton days of Tangier – and Marrakesh – as gay resorts are long gone. Gay sex is, of course, still available, and men travelling alone or togeth-

USEFUL THINGS TO BRING

Alarm clock Vital for early-morning buses.

Bartering gifts If you want to bargain for handicrafts, bring things to barter with; hiking in the Atlas, spare gear is always appreciated by local guides.

Camping gear If you are planning on a lot of camping, a sleeping bag and foam pad are invaluable, but it is worth considering whether you will make enough use of campsites to justify the weight, as hotels are remarkably cheap. A good compromise is to pack a **sheet sleeping bag** – reassuring in those hotels that don't relentlessly pursue cleanliness awards. **Camping gas** is widely available in larger towns (but not Epigas).

Clothes Keep both practicality and sensitivity in mind. Morocco is a deeply conservative nation: the more modest your dress the less hassle you will attract

On the practicalities front, keep in mind that the mountain areas and Sahara alike can get distinctly **chilly** at night, even in spring and autumn. A warm sweater, or even lightweight tracksuit, is invaluable. So, too, in winter and spring, is some kind of waterproof clothing and a solid pair of shoes: mountain storms (and resulting flash floods) are commonplace and wandering round a muddy Medina in sodden sandals is a miserable experience. For advice on **trekking gear**, see Chapter Six.

Condoms Moroccan ones are less reliable than those brought from home.

Film Kodak and Fuji film is available in most towns and major resorts, but it's relatively expensive and may well be pretty old stock. It's best to bring adequate supplies. For photography in the Medinas – all dark alleyways and hidden corners – fast film (400–800 ASA) is useful. If you're looking for good landscape photographs, especially in the south, slow film (and/or early rising) is a must. See also notes on behaviour (p.35).

Medicines Salt tablets, some insect repellent, iodine water purifying tablets, rehydration salts, aspirin and plasters are all useful. You may also find yourself dispensing them to locals, especially in mountain areas, where they are in very short supply.

Needle and thread Useful for tears and lost buttons. Wily travellers patch up torn baggage using dental floss instead of cotton.

Penknife multipurpose, handy for all sorts of things.

Plug If you like your water to fill a basin, it is worth packing an omnisize plug; few hotels (even relatively upmarket ones) supply such equipment or replace it when it disappears. As for the other sort of plug (electric), you will need an adaptor if carrying an appliance with a British, North American or Australasian one.

Sunblock, preferably high-factor, especially for sun-sensitive skin.

Toiletries and (rough) **toilet paper** (*papier hygénique*) are easy enough to obtain in all but the most remote parts of the country. Despite this, many hotels fail to supply it.

Towels Some hotels do not provide towels and you will certainly need one if you are hostelling or camping. It's wise to bring one that's large enough to wrap around you for modest beach or hammam changing.

---

er may be propositioned. But attitudes are tending increasingly towards hustling and exploitation on all sides. Cafés called "Renaissance" are frequently meeting places for gay Moroccan men, certainly in Fes and Marrakesh.

Despite the sexual segregation which makes it common, however, gay sex is officially illegal under Moroccan law. Article 489 of the Moroccan penal code prohibits any "shameless or unnatural act" with a person of the same sex and allows for imprisonment of six months to three years, plus a fine. There are also various provisions in the penal code for more serious offences, with correspondingly higher penalties in cases involving, for example, corruption of minors.

As emphasized under "Health and Insurance", p.28, AIDS is a real threat in Morocco, despite a lack of reported cases. There is some awareness of AIDS among Moroccans but most are steadfast in seeing it as a "disease for foreigners" and the concept, let alone practice, of "safe sex" is yet to emerge.

There is no public perception of lesbianism.

LAUNDRIES in the larger towns will take in clothes and wash them overnight, but you'll usually find it easier to ask at hotels – even basic places will be able to offer the service.

LEFT LUGGAGE You can deposit baggage at most train stations, but it will have to be locked or padlocked (so unlockable rucksacks for example will not be accepted); if you are catching a late train, make sure that the office will be open on your return. There are similar facilities at the main bus stations, CTM offices and ferry stations (Tangier, Ceuta, Melilla). Where no left luggage facilities are available, café proprietors will generally agree to look after baggage for you, sometimes for a small fee, more often for free in out-of-the-way places.

OPENING HOURS follow a reasonably consistent pattern: **banks** (Mon–Thurs 8.15–11.30am & 2.15–4.30pm, Fri 8.15–11.15am & 2.45–4.45pm); **Medersas** (daily 8.30am–5.30pm); **museums** (Wed–Mon 9am–noon & 3–6pm); **offices** (Mon–Thurs 8.30am–noon & 2.30–6.30pm; Fri 8.30–11.30am & 3–6.30pm); **shops** (Mon–Sat 8.30am–noon & 2–6.30pm). These hours may vary in the height of summer or during Ramadan (when banks, for example, open 8am–2pm and 9am–2pm respectively).

TAMPONS can be bought at general stores, not pharmacies, in most Moroccan cities. Don't expect to find them in country or mountain areas.

TIME Morocco keeps Greenwich Mean Time the whole year. Ceuta and Melilla keep Spanish time, which is GMT+1 in winter and GMT+2 in summer. The hour's difference – two hours' in summertime – is something to keep in mind when coming from Morocco to catch ferries out of Ceuta or Melilla, or trains out of Algeciras. Morocco is on the same time as Britain, Ireland and the Canary Islands in winter, an hour behind in summer. It's five hours ahead of the US east coast (EST) and eight ahead of the west coast (PST), an hour less in summer; and it's eight hours behind Western Australia, ten hours behind eastern Australia, and twelve hours behind New Zealand, an hour more during summer in those places.

TIPPING You're expected to tip – among others – waiters in cafés (1dh per person) and restaurants (5dh or so); museum and monument curators (3dh); *gardiens de voitures* (4–5dh; see p.46); petrol pump attendants (2–3dh); and bus porters (5dh).

WORK Your only chance of paid work in Morocco is **teaching English**. For information, try the following schools: The British Council in Morocco at 36 Rue de Tanger, Rabat (☎03/776 0836, *britcoun.morocco@bcmor.org.ma*) or in London at 10 Spring Gardens, London SW1A 2BN (☎020/7930 8466, *www.britcoun.org/english/engvacs.htm*), The American Language Centre (1 Place de la Fraternité, Casablanca; also in Rabat, Kenitra, Tangier, Tetouan, Meknes, Fes and Marrakesh) or The American School (Rue Al Amir Abdelkader, Agdal, Rabat; also in Casablanca and Tangier). Reasonable spoken French and an EFL qualification are normally required by all of these, and they usually do their recruiting at home. Smaller schools in Casablanca may be a better bet therefore if you are actually in Morocco.

WORK CAMPS If you are interested in taking part in a work camp, a number of possibilities exist. The United Nations Association (UK head office: 3 Whitehall Court, London SW1; ☎020/7930 2931) recruit international teams to work on manual and community projects for two or three weeks in the summer; applicants pay their own travel costs but are provided with accommodation. In the US, Volunteers for Peace (1034 Tiffany Rd, Belmont, VT 05730–0202; ☎802/259 2759, *www.vfp.org*) recruit volunteers for projects that are detailed on their Web site. Alternatively, there are four Moroccan organizations: Les Amis des Chantiers Internationaux de Meknes (PO Box 8, Meknes), whose projects generally involve agricultural or construction work around Meknes – three weeks in July and August, accommodation and food provided; Chantiers Jeunesse Maroc (BP 1351, Rabat; ☎03/772 2140); Chantiers Sociaux Marocains (BP 456, Rabat; ☎03/729 7184) and Pensés et Chantiers (26 Rue de Pakistan, BP 1423, Rabat). Most of the work camps are open to all-comers over 17 years of age; travel costs have to be paid by the participant, but you generally receive free accommodation (take a sleeping bag) and meals.

PART TWO

THE

GUIDE

CHAPTER 1
TANGIER, TETOUAN
& THE NORTH WEST

CHAPTER 2
MEDITERRANEAN
COAST & THE RIF

CHAPTER 4
THE WEST COAST:
FROM RABAT TO
ESSAOUIRA

CHAPTER 3
MEKNES, FES &
THE MIDDLE ATLAS

CHAPTER 5
MARRAKESH

CHAPTER 6
THE HIGH ATLAS

CHAPTER 7
THE GREAT
SOUTHERN
OASIS ROUTES

CHAPTER 8
AGADIR, THE
SOUSS &
ANTI-ATLAS

CHAPTER 9
THE DEEP SOUTH
& WESTERN SAHARA

ATLANTIC

OCEAN

SPAIN

MEDITERRANEAN SEA

ALGERIA

MAURITANIA

MALI

N

0   250km

CHAPTER ONE

TANGIER, TETOUAN AND THE NORTHWEST

The northwest can be an intense introduction to Morocco. Its two chief cities, **Tangier** and **Tetouan**, are the country's blackspots for hustlers and unofficial guides preying on first-time travellers. However, once clear of the port, trains or bus stations, and having set your bags down in a hotel, it doesn't take long to get the measure of the cities – and to begin to enjoy the experience. Tangier, hybridized and slightly seedy from its long European contact, has a culture distinct from any other Moroccan city, and a setting and skyline the equal of any Mediterranean resort. Difficult it may be, but it is compelling, too, in its age-old role as meeting point of Europe and Africa. Tetouan, in the shadow of the wild Rif mountains, feels more Moroccan – its Medina a glorious labyrinth, dotted with squares, souks and buildings from its fifteenth-century founding by Muslim refugees from Spanish Andalucia.

Moving on from either city, the most popular destination is the mountain town of **Chaouen** – a small-scale and enjoyably laid-back place to come to terms with being in Morocco. It is most easily reached via Tetouan. Heading south from Tangier – which is the terminus for the railway lines to Meknes, Fes, Rabat, Casablanca and Marrakesh – the best places to get acclimatized are the seaside resorts of Asilah and Larache. **Asilah** is a low-key, though growing tourist resort, and in August hosts an **International Festival**, northern Morocco's major cultural event of the year. **Larache** is less well

---

HOTEL PRICE CODES

The basis of our **hotel price codes**, set out below and keyed throughout the guide, is the price currently quoted for the cheapest double room in high season (June–September).

Note that cheaper prices in the lower categories are generally for rooms with just a washbasin – you always pay extra for **en-suite** shower and WC – and that double rooms can generally be converted into **triples/family rooms**, with extra beds, for a modest extra charge. Single occupancy usually costs about two thirds the price of a double, though in some places a single person will pay the same rate for a room as two people sharing, and in other places exactly half as much. Prices quoted are for bed only, without breakfast, but including local taxes.

In Morocco

① 40–100dh	③ 150–200dh	⑤ 400–800dh
② 100–150dh	④ 200–400dh	⑥ over 800dh

In Spanish Ceuta

① 1000–3000ptas/€6–18	④ 7500–10,000ptas/€45–60
② 3000–5000ptas/€18–30	⑤ 10,000–15,000ptas/€60–90
③ 5000–7500ptas/€30–45	⑥ over 15,000ptas/over €90

known, but no less enjoyable, with its relaxed feel, fine beach and proximity to the ancient Carthaginian-Roman site of **Lixus**.

International zones

Northern Morocco has an especially quirky **colonial history**, having been divided into three separate zones. Tetouan was the administrative capital of the **Spanish zone**, which

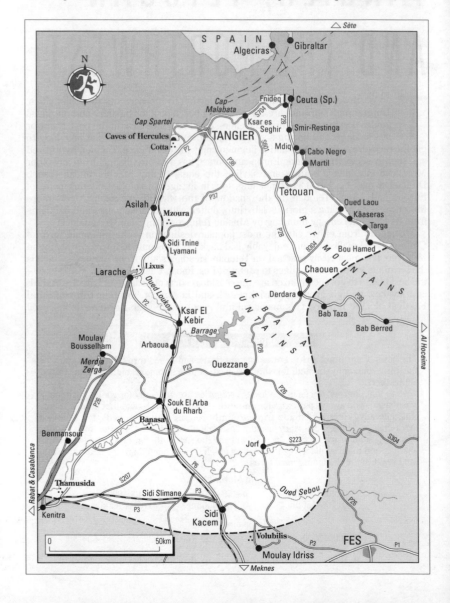

encompassed Chaouen and the Rif, spreading south through Asilah and Larache – itself a provincial centre. The **French zone** began at Souk El Arba du Rharb, the edge of rich agricultural plains sprawling south towards the French Protectorate's capital, Rabat. **Tangier**, meanwhile, experienced **International Rule** under a group of European legations.

One modern consequence of this past is that, although French is the official second **language** (after Arabic) throughout Morocco, most adults in the northwest are equally, or more, fluent in **Spanish** – a basic knowledge of which can prove extremely useful. Adding to and perpetuating the colonial legacy is the fact that Spanish TV and radio can be received (and attract enthusiastic audiences) throughout much of northern Morocco.

TANGIER AND THE COAST

Tangier has an international airport at Ibn Batouta (previously known as Boukhalef), and ferry connections with Algeciras, Gibraltar and the French port of Sète. Unless you are bringing a car over from Spain, it's a better point of arrival than Ceuta: both for the town's own attractions, and for the convenience of moving straight on into Morocco. Asilah is a mere forty minutes' ride on the train; Meknes, Fes, Rabat and Casablanca are all comfortably reached within the day, while if you are in a hurry to get south, there is an overnight train for Marrakesh.

The **coast** detailed in this section is the **Atlantic** stretch south towards Rabat. **Asilah**, on the train line, is the easiest destination; **Larache** can be reached by bus or grand taxi only, either from Tangier or (simpler) from Asilah. A more distinctively Moroccan resort is **Moulay Bousselham**, south of Larache and accessible by bus or grand taxi via Ksar El Kebir or Souk El Arba du Rharb.

Tangier (Tanja, Tanger)

For the first half of the twentieth century **TANGIER** was one of the stylish resorts of the Mediterranean – an international city with its own laws and administration, plus an eclectic community of exiles, expatriates and refugees. It was home, at various times, to Spanish and Central European refugees; to Moroccan nationalists; and – drawn by loose tax laws and free-port status – to over seventy banks and 4000 companies, many of them dealing in currency transactions forbidden in their own countries. Writers were also attracted to the city. Paul Bowles, the American novelist who knew Tangier in the thirties and called it his "dream city", settled here after 1945. William Burroughs spent most of the 1950s here, and most of the Beats – Jack Kerouac, Allen Ginsberg, Brion Gysin and the rest – passed through. Tangier was also the world's first and most famous gay resort, a role it maintains to a lesser degree today.

At the **International Zone**'s peak in the early 1950s, Tangier's foreign communities numbered 60,000 – then nearly half the population. When Moroccan independence was gained in 1956, however, Tangier's special status was removed. Almost overnight, the finance and banking businesses shifted their operations to Spain and Switzerland. The expatriate communities dwindled too (today there are under 2000, including 800 Spanish, 600 French, and 150 Britons and Americans, in a city of 425,000), as the new national government imposed bureaucratic controls and instituted a "clean-up" of the city. Brothels – previously numbering almost a hundred – were banned, and in the early 1960s "The Great Scandal" erupted, sparked by a number of paedophile convictions and escalating into a wholesale closure of the once outrageous gay bars.

These ghosts have left a slight air of decay about the city, still tangible in the older hotels and bars, and despite a recent flurry of development and, especially, apartment building, Tangier's future is uncertain. It is never likely to become a mainstream tourist destination – although it is increasingly popular with holidaying Moroccans.

As a port, ranked second only to Casablanca, it still has a future. There are also plans to build another, goods-only port, Tanger Atlantique, on the Atlantic coast financed by the private sector and leaving Tangier a passenger-only port.

Tangier has two other sources of wealth, neither of which appears in official statistics. Cannabis is widely cultivated in the Rif and, until an alternative cash crop is found, will continue to be so; and there is also a lucrative business in ferrying would-be immigrants across the Straits to Spain, with money made in these ways being invested in apartments and other speculative ventures. You will be unlikely to see any cannabis in Tangier, but you will certainly see young men and women from sub-Saharan countries, waiting their opportunity to share in Europe's perceived wealth.

And, as previously noted, Tangier is still a tricky place for first-time arrivals – hustling and mugging stories here should not be discounted and the characters you run into at the port are as objectionable as any you'll find in Morocco – but once you get the hang of it, Tangier is lively and very likeable, highly individual and with an enduring eccentricity.

Orientation, arrival and city transport

After the initial confusion of an unfamiliar Arab city, Tangier is surprisingly easy to find your way around. As with all the larger Moroccan cities, it's made up of two parts: the **Medina**, the original Moroccan town, and the **Ville Nouvelle**, built by its several European colonizers. Inside the Medina, a classic web of alleyways and stepped passages, is the old fortified quarter of the **kasbah**, with the former Sultanate's palace at its centre.

Together with the **beach** and the seafront **Avenue d'Espagne**, the easiest reference points are the city's three main squares – the Grand Socco, Petit Socco and Place de France. **Place de France** is a conventional, French-looking square at the heart of the Ville Nouvelle, flanked by kerbside cafés and a **terrace-belvedere** looking out over the straits to Spain with the city of Tarifa often visible. From here, **Boulevard Pasteur** (the main city street) leads off past the ONMT **tourist office**, a couple of blocks up, towards the main PTT (post office).

In the other direction from Place de France, **Rue de la Liberté** runs down to the **Grand Socco**, an amorphous open space in front of the Medina. The north side of the square opens onto the Medina's principal street, **Rue es Siaghin**, which culminates in the **Petit Socco**, a tiny square of old cafés and cheap hotels.

Arrival

Disembarking by **ferry** at Tangier can be a slow process, with long queues for passport control and customs: be prepared. Most importantly, make sure that you have your **passport stamped** (and departure card collected) while *on board the ferry*; announcements to this effect are not always made in English, so make your way to the purser's office during the journey. If you miss out on this, you'll be left until last by the officials in Tangier. If you arrive on the **hydrofoil** things are a little easier, as they dock by their own individual passport office.

Once ashore, and through customs, ferry arrivals pass into the **ferry terminal building**. There's a **bureau de change** here and outside the building is a branch of the Banque Populaire; both sell dirhams at regular rates and accept most currencies and traveller's cheques. There is also a Trans-Med shipping office just outside the port gates, which changes currency and traveller's cheques, and sells ferry tickets for the return journey. (For credit card exchange or a cash dispenser you need a bank in the city proper – see p.98).

Be warned that unofficial guides – or **hustlers** – can be incredibly persistent around the port entrance, telling you some fairly amazing tales: the hotels are full, the Medina is dangerous, the trains and buses are on strike. Don't take too much of this at face value, and don't feel in any way duty bound to employ anyone's services – you don't need a guide in Tangier.

From the port, it's possible to walk into the centre, or, if laden with luggage, get a petit taxi.

Tangier's **airport** is 15km outside the city. If you arrive on a package tour you'll be met by a hotel shuttle (try to get a transfer with your ticket, if you're on flight only). If you're on your own, either bargain with the **taxi** drivers, who *should* charge 100dh for up to six passengers (get a group together before leaving the terminal building, or they will charge each person 100dh), or if you want to pick up a local bus (#17 and #70 run to the Grand Socco), you'll need to walk 2km to the main road.

There are two **banks** at the airport which are usually open to meet incoming flights; one – or sometimes both – of them will cash travellers' cheques or eurocheques. There is no cash dispenser.

The **Gare du Port** and **Gare de Ville**, centrally located by the port and Medina, are both closed – the reason given being the number of fatalities caused by people crossing the tracks. **Trains** now arrive and depart from **Tanger Morora** (on the outskirts of town, 4km from the port), from where petits taxis will take you into town.

Bus services from most towns generally arrive at **Tangier Gare Routière** (Bus Station), south of the Ville Nouvelle. **CTM** has buses from Rabat, Casablanca, Fes, Marrakesh and the other major cities some of which continue on from the *gare routière* to the **Port Entrance**.

City transport

Grands taxis (large cream/beige Mercedes) are permitted to carry up to six passengers. The price for a ride should be fixed in advance – 15-20dh per person is standard for any trip within the city, including tip. Small blue/green **petits taxis** (which carry just three passengers) can be flagged down around the town. Most of these are metered – standard rate for a city trip is 10dh per person. On the streets you can **hail a taxi**, whether it has passengers or not; if it is going in your direction it will generally take you. If you join a taxi with passengers, you pay the full fare, as if it were empty. **After 8pm** both grand and petit taxi rates increase by fifty percent.

Minibuses operated by Bourghaz run to a number of useful destinations – including the bus station and Cap Spartel; there is a stop just outside the port gates. Regular bus services (Tingis or Raihini) serve mainly the city suburbs.

STREET NAME CHANGES

Spanish colonial names are still in use alongside their Arabicized successors. In addition, both *Rue* and *Calle* are sometimes replaced by *Zankat*, and *Avenue* and *Boulevard* by *Charih*.

Local maps tend to use the new Arabic versions, though not all of the street signs have been changed. In the text and maps of this guide, we have used new names only when firmly established. Among the main street-name changes, note:

Main squares	**Medina**
Place de France – Place de Faro	Rue des Chrétiens – Rue des
Grand Socco – Place du 9 Avril 1947	Almouahidines
Petit Socco – Place Souk Dakhil	Rue de la Marine – Rue Djemaa Kebir
	Rue des Postes – Rue Mokhtar Ahardane

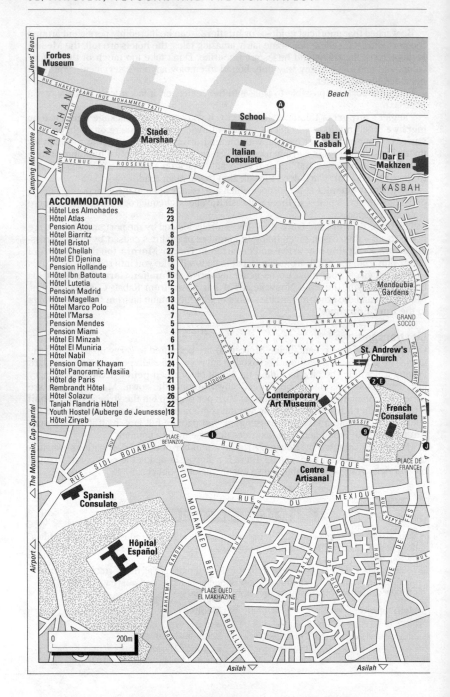

ACCOMMODATION

Hôtel Les Almohades	25
Hôtel Atlas	23
Pension Atou	1
Hôtel Biarritz	8
Hôtel Bristol	20
Hôtel Chellah	27
Hôtel El Djenina	16
Pension Hollande	9
Hôtel Ibn Batouta	15
Hôtel Lutetia	12
Pension Madrid	3
Hôtel Magellan	13
Hôtel Marco Polo	14
Hôtel l'Marsa	7
Pension Mendes	5
Pension Miami	4
Hôtel El Minzah	6
Hôtel El Muniria	11
Hôtel Nabil	17
Pension Omar Khayam	24
Hôtel Panoramic Masilia	10
Hôtel de Paris	21
Rembrandt Hôtel	19
Hôtel Solazur	26
Tanjah Flandria Hôtel	22
Youth Hostel (Auberge de Jeunesse)	18
Hôtel Ziryab	2

TANGIER

Gare du Port
(closed)

Ferry
Terminal

PORT

See 'Tangier: The Medina
and Kasbah' map

MEDINA

PETIT
SOCCO

Port
Entrance

Gare de Ville
(closed)

Gran Teatro
Cervantes

Belvedere

BOULEVARD

RUE MAGELLAN

RUE IBN RACHID

RUE MARCO POLO

RUE MOULA

RUE DE LA PLAGE (R. SALAH EL AYOURI)

RUE DU PORTUGAL

RUE

PASTEUR

AVENUE D'ESPAGNE

RUE TARIK

RUE EL FARABI

Beach

RUE EL

MOUSSA BEN NOUSSAIR

RUE ABDALLAH BEN

RUE OMAR

RUE ZERKTOUNI

RUE ABOU
ALLA

RUE EL ANTAKI

RUE EL MAARI

AVENUE YOUSSEF BEN TACHFINE

PTT

BOULEVARD

MOHAMMED

PRINCE

HERITIER

RUE ALLAL BEN ABDALLAH

RUE DE PORTUGAL

R. OMAR IBN KHATTAB

RUE DE LA RESISTANCE

AVENUE LAFAYETTE

PLACE DES
NATIONS

& 'Tangier Morora'▷

RESTAURANTS, BARS & CAFÉS

Restaurant Africa	C
Restaurant Agadir	Z
Café Atlas	O
Restaurant Bab Al Maghreb	B
Hôtel Biarritz	H
Restaurant Le Coeur de Tanger	K
Las Conchas	X
El Dorado	u
Emma's BBC Bar	V
Pâtisserie Florence	b
Guitta's	I
Café Halfa	A
El Korsan	F
Restaurant Mendes	G
Café Metropole	N
Hôtel Miramar	Y
Le Mogador	E
Restaurant Number One	U
Restaurant Osso Buco	L
Restaurant Pagode	R
Restaurant-Bar La Paix	D
Café de Paris	K
Pâtisserie Rahmouni	J
Restaurant Raihani	P
Restaurant Romero	M
Rubis Grill	T
Restaurant San Remo	S
Traiteur: Laiterie Al Mouatamid Ibn Abbad	Q
Restaurant Valencia	W

Accommodation

Tangier has dozens of **hotels and pensions**, and finding a room is rarely much of a problem: if the first place you try is full, ask them to phone and reserve you a place elsewhere – most will be happy to do so. The city does, however, get crowded during July and August, when many Moroccan families holiday here, or spend a few days en route to and from Europe. Cheaper hotels and *pensions* hike up their prices at this time of year, and if you want an inexpensive room you'll often do best by going for one of the middle-range hotels.

Of the **hotels** listed below, a few of the more expensive places are detailed simply because they are regular package choices (which you may be booked into); the rest, however, are all to some extent recommended. As always, there is a choice between the **Medina** or **Ville Nouvelle**. If it's your first time in Tangier, you will probably prefer the easier, more familiar feel (and greater comforts) of the Ville Nouvelle places.

Tangier also has two campsites, *Camping Miramonte* aka *Camping Marshan,* and *Camping Tingis*; both are some distance from the town centre, with poor access to the beaches and equally poor facilities. Campers are better advised to consider *Camping Ashakar*, 16km from town and 5km south of the Cap Spartel lighthouse, and close to the Caves of Hercules and several beaches (see p.100), or the well-maintained campsites north of **Asilah**, 35km from Tangier (see p.102).

Seafront hotels

All the places below are along or just off the seafront **Avenue d'Espagne** and its continuation **Avenue des F.A.R.** (Avenue des Forces Armées Royales); the name change takes place, it seems, after Avenue Youssef Ben Tachfine, though maps differ. Several hotels are on Rue Magellan, which is easy to miss: it zigzags up from the seafront alongside the *Hôtel Biarritz* towards Boulevard Pasteur in the Ville Nouvelle. A number of others are on Rue Salah Eddine El Ayoubi (aka Rue de la Plage), which runs uphill from the port to the Grand Socco and is lined with small *pensions*.

On the whole, the seafront places get pricier and fancier as you move around the bay away from the port, though note that you may find some closed for renovation or lack of tourists. All those listed below are within walkable distance of the port, though you may prefer to take a petit taxi to the further ones.

CHEAP

Pension Atou, 45 Rue Salah Eddine El Ayoubi (☎03/993 6333). Halfway up the street, on the right, this used to be one of the friendliest places on this pension-packed street, but recent reports are less enthusiastic. It's basic, with shared facilities, but a bargain at the price, and there's a great rooftop terrace overlooking the Jewish cemetery and the port. ①.

Pension Madrid, 140 Rue Salah Eddine El Ayoubi (☎03/993 1693). One of several old Spanish town houses, now turned into *pensions* – and this is one of the most popular. ①.

Hôtel Magellan, 16 Rue Magellan (☎03/937 2319). A tad tatty nowadays and breakfast is no longer included, but it's quiet and the front rooms have a fine view. ①.

Hôtel L'Marsa, 92 Av. d'Espagne (☎03/993 2339). Better known as a café-restaurant with street-level patio and a roof terrace, the accommodation is adequate and value for money. ①.

Hôtel Panoramic Masilia, 11 Rue Targha (formerly Marco Polo) (☎03/337 0703). Below the *Rembrandt Hôtel*, the superb view of the straits justifies its inclusion as a seafront hotel. It's a friendly and popular place, despite poor maintenance. ②.

Pension Mendes, 80 Av. d'Espagne (☎03/993 3159). Just uphill from *L'Marsa*; look out for the 1920s Spanish tiles by the entrance depicting Don Quixote. Toilets and showers (5dh) on the corridor. Pavement café below. ①.

Pension Miami, 126 Rue Salah Eddine El Ayoubi (☎03/993 2900). Beautifully tiled old Spanish town house, said to be over one hundred years old. Pleasant rooms and bathrooms on each corridor. ①.

Hôtel El Muniria, 1 Rue Magellan (☎03/993 5337). Owned originally by an Englishman, this place has seen William Burroughs, Jack Kerouac and Allen Ginsberg amongst its guests, and Burroughs is said to have written *The Naked Lunch* in room 9. This room is no longer available, but the rest have bathrooms, with toilets on the corridor. ②.

Pension Omar Khayam, 28 Rue El Antaki (☎03/994 3393). A charming Andalucian, two-storey, white-and-pink building, some distance uphill from the *Hôtel Bristol*. ③.

Youth Hostel (Auberge de Jeunesse), 8 Rue El Antaki (☎03/994 6127). Ahmed Laroussi, the current warden, is maintaining the high reputation of this well-established hostel. Sixty beds (27dh with YHA card, 35dh without). Open 8–10am & noon–11pm (midnight in summer).

MODERATE TO EXPENSIVE

Hôtel Les Almohades, Av. des F.A.R. (☎03/994 0026, fax 994 6371). A luxury hotel at one end of the town beach, with 138 rooms, four restaurants, nightclub, sauna and pool. ⑤.

Hôtel Biarritz, 102–104 Av. d'Espagne (☎03/993 2473). An old hotel with comfortable rooms, all en suite. Reductions for long stays. ④.

Hôtel Bristol, 14 Rue El Antaki (☎03/994 2914). This well-managed hotel, 100m uphill from the beach, is a good bet, with en-suite baths, plus a bar and restaurant (you may be obliged to have half board in midsummer). ④.

Hôtel El Djenina, 8 Rue El Antaki (☎03/994 2244, fax 994 2246). Recently refurbished and with 21 rooms, a restaurant and bar, it's a serious competitor in its price range. ④

Hôtel Ibn Batouta, 8 Rue Magellan (☎03/993 9311, fax 993 9368). Hidden from the street, facing the sea, this hotel has a noble facade, and the visitor comments in its Golden Book suggest it offers value for money. Breakfast on the terrace is included. ④

Hôtel Marco Polo, corner of Av. d'Espagne/Rue El Antaki (☎03/994 1124, fax 994 2476). A dozen comfortable rooms, popular restaurant and lively bar (both open to nonresidents) keep this place ahead of the field, though it could do with a face-lift. ④.

Hôtel Nabil, 11 Rue Magellan (☎03/937 5407). A refurbished warehouse converted into a first-class hotel. All rooms are en suite, and it has stunning views from the front top-floor rooms. Good parking. ④.

Hôtel Solazur, Av. des F.A.R. (☎03/932 0759, fax 932 5286). On the next block after Av. Yacoub El Mansour. One of the older beach hotels which was used by the late Malcolm Forbes for his seventieth birthday bash (see p.91). Attempts have been made to modernize it but it still feels like time has passed it by. ⑤.

Central Ville Nouvelle hotels

Most of these recommendations are within a few blocks of Place de France/Place de Faro and the central Boulevard Pasteur; coming up from the port, if you've got much luggage, a taxi could be useful as it's a steep climb.

Hôtel Atlas, 50 Rue Moussa Ben Noussair (☎03/993 6435, fax 993 3095). A bit out of the way but the rooms, suites and apartments are good value for money. ④.

Hôtel Chellah, 47-49 Rue Allal Ben Abdellah (☎03/932 4457, fax 994 3346). A regular tour-group hotel, with a small pool and garden, and its own club on the beach, *El Cavabo*. Slightly isolated from shops and banks on Bd. Pasteur but otherwise good value for money. ⑤.

Pension Hollande, 139 Rue de Hollande (☎03/993 7838) A big airy house, shaded by trees, behind the French Consulate; simple rooms but a nice place and good value. ②.

Hôtel Lutetia, 3 Rue de Prince Moulay Abdellah (☎03/993 1866). This has seen better days but is still value for money. Safe parking. ②.

Hôtel El Minzah, 85 Rue El Houria (aka Rue de la Liberté) (☎03/993 5885). Built in 1931, this remains Tangier's most prestigious hotel, with a wonderful garden, a pool overlooking the sea and town, and elegant (if pricey) bar. Past guests have included Cecil Beaton, Jean Genet and Mick Jagger, and tradition has it that it was from here that World War II Allied agents spied on their German counterparts at the *Hôtel Rif*. ⑥.

Hôtel de Paris, 42 Bd. Pasteur (☎03/993 1877). A pleasant and functional hotel, centrally located, and which acted as a temporary tourist office while the latter was being renovated. It has large spacious rooms, good breakfast and helpful reception. ④.

Rembrandt Hôtel, corner of Bd. Pasteur/Bd. Mohammed V (☎03/993 7870, fax 993 0443). Luxurious and prestigious, but cheaper than the *El Minzah*. ⑥.

Tanjah Flandria Hôtel, 6 Bd. Mohammed V (☎03/993 3279, fax 993 4347). Slightly superior modern package tour hotel, with a pool on the roof, disco and sauna. ⑤.

Hôtel Ziryab, Complexe Istiraha, 42 Rue de Hollande (☎03/933 1812, fax 933 1823). Facing the once-elegant but now-ruined *Grand Hôtel Villa de France,* this new establishment, with twenty rooms, pool and cafeteria, is part of the new complex which also includes a cinema and boutiques. ⑤.

Medina hotels

With the exception of the *Continental* and the *Mamora,* these listings – the best of the thirty-five Medina hotels – are fairly basic; they do, however, have a distinct character and are safe enough as long as you have the initial confidence for the area. To reach the Medina from the port, there's a choice of routes: either up Rue du Portugal to the Grand Socco, or up the steps behind the port entrance, round to the Grand Mosque and the junction of Rue des Postes/Rue Dar El Baroud. If you're unsure of yourself – and the Medina can be intimidating if this is your first visit to Morocco – it's best to take a petit taxi.

Hôtel Continental, 36 Rue Dar El Baroud (☎03/993 1024, fax 993 1143). By far the best choice in the Medina, it was founded in 1865 and was once the most fashionable hotel in Tangier with Queen Victoria's son Alfred as its first official guest. Other notable guests include Degas and Churchill, but it now has a ragged feel and, despite renovations, is showing its age. However, nothing can detract from the view of the harbour from its terrace – captured in Bertolucci's *The Sheltering Sky.* Taking a taxi is the easiest way to get to the hotel, or, if on foot, make your way from Petit Socco along Rue de la Marine, past the Grand Mosque, and then along Rue Dar El Baroud to the hotel gates. ④.

Pension Fuentes, 9 Petit Socco, at the heart of the Medina (☎03/993 4669). One of the first hotels in Tangier, and boasting, over the years, the likes of Saint-Saëns and the Beat people, though there is little residual glamour and the noisy café below can be annoying. ①.

Hôtel du Grand Socco, Grand Socco, entrance on Rue Imam Layti (☎03/993 3126). The oldest hotel in Tangier; it was in Jewish hands before 1912 and the arrival of the Spanish. It's seen better times but there are a number of large rooms which are good value if shared by three to five people. ①.

Hôtel Mamora, 19 Rue des Postes (☎03/993 4105). Centrally located at the heart of the Medina, the *Mamora*'s reception area is a bit shabby, but the rooms are clean and pleasant, and all have showers. ④.

Pension Mauretania, 2 Rue des Chrétiens – aka Rue des Almouahidines, just off the Petit Socco (☎03/993 4674). Cold showers, but otherwise fairly well kept, and cheap. ①.

Hôtel Olid, 12 Rue des Postes (☎03/993 6128). Slightly tatty but still reasonable value for money. ①.

Pension Palace, 2 Rue des Postes (☎03/993 6128). A touch of past splendours – balconies and a central court with fountain – led Bertolucci to shoot part of his film of Paul Bowles' novel *The Sheltering Sky* here. Some rooms are quite pleasant, including a few en suite. ①.

The beach and Ville Nouvelle

Tangier's interest and attraction lies in the city as a whole: its café life, beach, and the tumbling streets of the Medina. The handful of "monuments", with the notable exception of the Dar El Makhzen palace, are best viewed as adding direction to your wanderings, rather than as unmissable sights.

The town beach

It was the beach and mild climate which drew in Tangier's first expatriates, the Victorian British, who used to amuse themselves with afternoon rides along the sands and weekends of "pig-sticking" in the wooded hills behind. Today's pleasures come a little more packaged on the **town beach**, with camel rides, windsurfing, and a string of club-like beach bars. It's no Acapulco, nor even an Agadir, but by day the sands are diverting and fun, with Moroccans entertaining themselves with acrobatics and football.

It is easier, safer and some say compulsory to change in a cabin, so when you arrive at the beach you might like to attach yourself to one of the **beach bars**, most of which offer showers and deck chairs, as well as food and drink. Some of these are institutions, like *Emma's BBC Bar* (still serving up English breakfasts), *The Sun Beach*, where Tennessee Williams wrote a first draft of *Cat on a Hot Tin Roof*, and *The Windmill*, where Joe Orton hung out. One of the most pleasant is *Chez Miami*, with its gardens to

TANGIER:
THE MEDINA
AND KASBAH

ACCOMMODATION

Hôtel Continental	1
Pension Fuentes	3
Hôtel du Grand Socco	7
Hôtel Mamora	4
Pension Mauretania	2
Hôtel Olid	6
Pension Palace	5

RESTAURANTS

Restaurant Ahlen	G
Restaurant Andaluz	C
Chez Hammadi	F
Greg Restaurant	B
Restaurant Ibn Batouta	D
Restaurant Marhaba	A
Ray Charley	E

△ Ferry Terminal & Gare du Pont

laze around in, but the favourites change each year, so look around and take your pick. All are open in summer only.

By day, don't leave anything on the beach unattended. By night, limit your exploration to the beach bars (a few of which offer evening cabarets – if Arabic Country & Western appeals), as the beach itself becomes dangerous, with muggings fairly common.

The Grand Socco and Place de France

The **Grand Socco** is the obvious place to start a ramble around the town. Its name, like so many in Tangier, is a French–Spanish hybrid, proclaiming its origins as the main market square. The markets have long gone, but the square remains a meeting place and its cafés are good points to sit around and absorb the city's life. The Grand Socco's official but little-used name, **Place du 9 avril 1947**, commemorates the visit of Sultan Mohammed V to the city on that date – an occasion when, for the first time and at some personal risk, he identified himself with the struggle for Moroccan independence.

A memorial to this event (in Arabic) is to be found amid the luxuriant **Mendoubia Gardens**, flanking the square. These enclose the former offices of the Mendoub – the Sultan's representative during the international years – which are nowadays used for registering weddings. The gardens, a welcome shade from the midday sun, are open daily except Sundays; besides the memorial and some old cannons, they include a spectacular banyan tree, said to be 800 years old.

The old **markets** of the Grand Socco were moved out in the 1970s, onto the Rue de Portugal (running down to the port) and to some cramped terraces beside the Rue d'Angleterre, southwest of the square. More interesting, however, is the little **Fondouk Market**, which is to be found by following **Rue de la Liberté** from the Grand Socco towards Place de France, then turning left down a series of steps, past the *El Minzah* hotel. The stalls here offer everything from pottery to spectacle repairs, from fruit and vegetables to junk.

Over in the **Place de France**, the cafés are the main attraction – and at their best in the late afternoon and early evening, when an interesting mix of local and expatriate regulars turn out to watch and be watched. The seats to choose are outside the *Café Paris*, a legendary rendezvous throughout the years of the International Zone. During World War II, this was notorious as a centre of deal making and intrigue between agents from Britain, America, Germany, Italy and Japan; later the emphasis shifted to Morocco's own politics: the first nationalist paper, *La Voix du Maroc*, surfaced at the café, and the nationalist leader Allal El Fassi, exiled in Tangier from the French-occupied zone, set up his Istiqlal party headquarters nearby.

Saint Andrew's church and the Musée d'Art Contemporain

Just south of the Grand Socco, on Rue d'Angleterre, is the nineteenth-century Anglican church of **Saint Andrew**, one of the city's odder sights in its fusion of Moorish decoration and English country churchyard. The congregation has fallen to around fifteen but the church is still used for a Sunday morning service (11am), when the numbers are swollen by worshippers from sub-Saharan countries, particularly Nigeria, en route to a better life in Europe. On weekdays, the caretaker, Mustapha Cherqui, is generally around to show off the church, whose interior is notable for its rendition of the Lord's Prayer in Arabic script around the chancel arch.

In the graveyard, among the laments of early deaths from malaria, you come upon the tomb of **Walter Harris** (see "Contexts"), the most brilliant of the chroniclers of "Old Morocco" in the closing decades of the nineteenth century and the beginning of the twentieth. Other graves reveal epitaphs to **Caid Sir Harry Maclean**, the Scottish military adviser to Sultan Moulay Abd El Aziz at the turn of the twentieth century; to **Dean** of *Dean's Bar* ("Missed by all and sundry"), a bit of a legend himself from the 1940s and 50s; and to a number of Allied aircrew who died over the straits in the last days of World War II. Inside the church another eccentric Briton, **Emily Keane**, is commemorated. A contemporary of Harris, she lived a very different life, marrying in 1873 the Shereef of Ouezzane – at the time one of the most holy towns of the country (see p.133). The most recent grave is that of David Herbert, second son of the Earl of Pembroke and a notable eccentric and keen churchgoer. His tombstone reads simply "He loved Morocco" and its position by the south porch is so that, as he threatened, he could check on latecomers for the morning service.

A little further along Rue d'Angleterre is a large white-walled villa, formerly the British Consulate and now the **Musée d'Art Contemporain de la Ville de Tanger** (Tues–Sun 9am–12.30pm & 3–6pm; 10dh). Devoted to contemporary Moroccan artists, it often has interesting exhibitions, while permanent displays include works by Moroccan artists Chabia Tallal, Fatimi Hassani and Mohammed Hamidi, and are concerned with the reality and meaning of Moroccan life.

The American Legation and Gran Teatro Cervantes

If you follow Rue de la Plage out of the Grand Socco, then turn left down towards the port on the Rue du Portugal, you come to a small gate in the Medina wall on the left; climb the steps to the gate and, just through it, is the **Old American Legation** (Mon–Fri 10am–1pm & 3–5pm; free; other times by appointment, ☎03/993 5317), a former palace given to the US government by the Sultan Moulay Slimane, and preserved today as an American Historic Landmark. Morocco was the first overseas power to recognize an independent United States and this was the first American ambassadorial residence, established in 1777. A fascinating three-storey palace, bridging an alleyway (the Rue d'Amerique) below, it houses excellent historical exhibits on the city's history – including the correspondence between Sultan Moulay Ben Abdallah and George Washington – and has displays of paintings by, in the main, Moroccan-resident American artists.

Over to the southeast of the Grand Socco, off the Rue de la Plage, is another interesting relic of Tangier's international past, the **Gran Teatro Cervantes** – the old Spanish theatre. Located on a side street still labelled in Spanish as Calle Esperanza Orellana (the wife of its architect), it is an unmistakable building, with its tiled, Art Deco front and impressive glass dome. It was due to be restored with the help of European Union and Spanish funds, but the proposal seems to be have been dropped, and the building continues to decay.

The Medina

The Grand Socco offers the most straightforward **approach to the Medina**. The arch at the northwest corner of the square opens onto Rue d'Italie, which becomes Rue de la Kasbah, the northern entrance to the kasbah quarter. To the right, there is an opening onto Rue es Siaghin, off which are most of the souks and at the end of which is the Petit Socco, the Medina's principal landmark and little square. An alternative approach to the Medina is from the seafront: follow the steps up, walk round by the Grand Mosque, and Rue des Postes (aka Rue Mokhtar Ahardane) will lead you into the Petit Socco.

Rue es Siaghin

Rue es Siaghin – Silversmiths' Street – was Tangier's main thoroughfare into the 1930s, and remains an active one today, with a series of fruit, grain and cloth markets opening off to its sides. Halfway along from the Grand Socco (on the right), locked and decaying, is the **old Spanish Cathedral** and **Mission**. It is now the Convent of the Sisters of Mother Theresa and the present cathedral is on Rue Side Boua (Mass

Mon–Sat 7pm, Sun 11am). Behind the convent was formerly the **Mellah**, or Jewish quarter, centred around Rue des Synagogues. Moroccan Jews traditionally controlled the silver and jewellery trade – the "Siaghin" of the street name – but few remain in Tangier, having left at Moroccan independence in 1956 for Gibraltar, France and Israel. The street itself has long been taken over by tourist stalls.

The Petit Socco

The **Petit Socco** or Zoco Chico (Little Market) seems too small ever to have served such a purpose. Old photographs, in fact, show it almost twice its present size: it was only at the turn of the twentieth century that the hotels and cafés were built. These, however, give the place its atmosphere: seedy and slightly conspiratorial, and the location for many of the Moroccan stories of Mohammed Mrabet (see "Contexts").

In the heyday of the "International City", with easily exploited Arab and Spanish sexuality a major attraction, it was in the alleys behind the Socco that the straight and gay brothels were concentrated. William Burroughs used to hang out around the square: "I get averages of ten very attractive propositions a day," he wrote to Alan Ginsberg, ". . . no stasis horrors here." The Socco cafés (the *Central* was the prime Beat location) lost much of their allure at independence, when the sale of alcohol was banned in the Medina, but they remain diverting places to sit around, people watch, talk and get some measure of the town.

Towards the kasbah

It is beyond the Petit Socco that the Medina proper seems to start, "its topography", to quote Paul Bowles, "rich in prototypal dream scenes: covered streets like corridors with doors opening into rooms on either side, hidden terraces high above the sea, streets consisting only of steps, dark impasses, small squares built on sloping terrain so that they looked like ballet sets designed in false perspective, with alleys leading off in several directions; as well as the classical dream equipment of tunnels, ramparts, ruins, dungeons and cliffs".

Walking up from the Petit Socco, you can follow **Rue des Chrétiens** (aka Rue des Almouahidines) and its continuation **Rue Ben Raisuli** and emerge, with luck, around the lower gate to the kasbah. Heading past the Socco towards the sea walls are two small streets straddled by the Grand Mosque. If you want to get out and down to the beach, follow **Rue des Postes** and you'll hit the flight of steps (known as the "American Steps") down to the port. If you feel like wandering, take the other one, **Rue de la Marine**, which curls into **Rue Dar El Baroud** and the entrance to the old *Hôtel Continental* – another fine place to sit and drink tea. From here it's relatively simple to find your way across to the square below the Kasbah Gate.

The **Grand Mosque** itself is screened from public view – and, as throughout Morocco, entrance is strictly forbidden to non-Muslims. Enlarged in the early nineteenth century, the mosque was originally built on the site of a church by the Sultan Moulay Ismail in celebration of the return of Tangier to Moroccan control in 1685. Prior to this, the city had seen some two centuries of European rule: it was first conquered by the Portuguese in the aftermath of the Moors' expulsion from Andalucia and the Algarve, and in 1663 it passed to the British as part of the dowry of Catherine of Braganza, bride to Charles II.

It was the British – in just 22 years of occupation – who destroyed the city's medieval fortifications, including a great upper castle which covered the entire site of the present-day kasbah. Under virtually constant siege, they found it an expensive and unrewarding possession: "an excrescence of the earth", according to Samuel Pepys, who oversaw the garrison's withdrawal, shocked at the women of the town ("generally whores") and at the governor ("with his whores at the little bathing house which he has furnished with jade a-purpose for that use"). Dining alone with the chaplain, Pepys had "a great deal of discourse upon the viciousness of this place and its being time for God Almighty to destroy it".

The kasbah and beyond

The **kasbah**, walled off from the Medina on the highest rise of the coast, has been the palace and administrative quarter since Roman times. It is a strange, somewhat sparse area of walled compounds, occasional colonnades, and a number of luxurious villas built in the 1920s, when this became one of the Mediterranean's most chic residential sites. Richard Hughes, author of *A High Wind in Jamaica* (and of a book of Moroccan tales), was the first European to take a house here – his address fabulously titled "Numéro Zero, La Kasbah, Tangier".

Among those who followed was the eccentric Woolworths heiress, Barbara Hutton, who reputedly outbid General Franco for her mini-palace, Sidi Hosni. Her parties were legendary – including a ball where thirty Reguibat racing camels and their drivers were brought 1000 miles from the Sahara to form a guard of honour. The mini-palace is now for sale – but unless you have $2.5 million to offer, you are unlikely to see beyond the high walls and cast-iron gates.

Local guides point with some pride to these locations, but the main point of interest here is the former **Sultanate Palace**, or **Dar El Makhzen**, now converted to an excellent **museum of crafts and antiquities** (open daily except Tues, 9am–1pm & 3–6pm; 10dh). It stands near the main gateway to the Medina, the **Bab El Assa**, to the rear of a formal court, or mechouar, where the town's pashas held public audience and gave judgement well into the twentieth century. The entrance to the palace, a modest-looking porch, is in the left-hand corner of the court as you enter from the Medina – scores of children will probably direct you.

MALCOLM FORBES: TANGIER'S LAST TYCOON

The American publishing tycoon, **Malcolm Forbes**, bought the **Palais du Mendoub** in 1970. His reason, ostensibly at least, was the acquisition of a base for launching and publishing an Arab-language version of *Forbes Magazine* – the "millionaires' journal". For the next two decades, until his death in 1990, he was a regular visitor to the city, and it was at the Tangier palace that he decided to host his last great extravagance, his **seventieth birthday party**, in 1989.

This was the grandest social occasion Tangier had seen since the days of Woolworths heiress Barbara Hutton (see above), whose scale and spectacle Forbes presumably intended to emulate and exceed. Spending an estimated $2.5m, he brought in his friend Elizabeth Taylor as co-host and chartered a 747, a DC-8 and Concorde to fly in 800 of the world's rich and famous from New York and London. The party entertainment was on an equally imperial scale, including 600 drummers, acrobats and dancers, and a *fantasia* – a cavalry charge which ends with the firing of muskets into the air – by 300 Berber horsemen.

In the media, Malcolm's party was a mixed public relations exercise, with even the gossip press feeling qualms about such a display of American affluence in a country like Morocco, and, despite Liz Taylor's presence at Forbes's side, using the choice of location to hint at the tycoon's sexual preferences (a story that broke in full cry after Forbes' death). However, Forbes most likely considered the party a success, for his guests included not just the celebrity rich – Gianni Agnelli, Robert Maxwell, Barbara Walters, Henry Kissinger – but half a dozen US state governors and the chief executives or presidents of scores of multinational corporations likely to advertise in his magazine. And, of course, it was tax deductible.

Just before the entrance to the palace, you pass (on your left) the ramshackle club-house of the *Orquesta Andalusi de Tanger*, a fine group of musicians who play Andalous music with a lot of swing. If they're around practising, they'll probably invite you in to watch them play.

The Dar El Makhzen and Café Detroit

The **Dar El Makhzen** – built, like the Grand Mosque, by Moulay Ismail – last saw royal use in 1912, with the residence of the Sultan Moulay Hafid, who was exiled to Tangier after his forced abdication by the French. The extraordinary negotiations which then took place are chronicled in Walter Harris's *Morocco That Was*. According to Harris, the ex-Sultan found the building "uncomfortable, out-of-date, and out-of-repair and by no means a satisfactory place of residence, for it was not easy to install 168 people within its crumbling walls with any comfort or pleasure". Most of this extended entourage seem to have been members of the royal harem and well able to defend their limited privileges. Moulay Hafid himself ended up with "only a couple of very shabby rooms over the entrance", where he apologetically received visitors and played bridge with a small circle of Americans and Europeans.

However out of date and uncomfortable the palace may have been, it is by no means a poor example of Moroccan craftsmanship and architecture. The design is centred on two interior courtyards, each with rich arabesques, painted wooden ceilings and marble fountains. Some of the flanking columns are of Roman origin, particularly well suited to the small display of **mosaics and finds from Volubilis** (see Chapter Three). The main part of the museum, however, is devoted to **Moroccan arts**, laid out according to region and including an exceptional collection of ceramics from Meknes and Fes.

At the entrance to the main part of the palace is the **Bit El Mal**, the old treasury, and adjoining is a small private **mosque**, near to which is the entrance to the herb- and shrub-lined palace **gardens**, shaded by jacaranda trees. If you leave this way, you will come out by the stairway to the **Café Detroit**, set up in the early 1960s by Beat writer Brion Gysin. Gysin created the place partly as a venue for the **Master Musicians of Jajouka**, drummers and pipe-players from a village in the foothills of the Rif, who achieved cult fame through an LP recorded by his friend, Rolling Stone Brian Jones; the group resurfaced on the Stones' 1990 *Steel Wheels* album and these days still appear at festivals in the US and Europe. The café itself is now a rather shabby tourist spot, though worth the price of a mint tea for the views. Its main entrance is on Rue Riad Sultan, the street running alongside the outer walls of the kasbah.

Café Halfa, Palais du Mendoub and Jews' Beach

Leaving the Medina by the Kasbah Gate, a ten- to fifteen-minute walk along Rue Asad Ibn Farrat and then Rue Mohammed Tazi will bring you to the quarter known as *la Marshan*, an exclusive residential quarter with a rich spread of villas, consulates and royal properties. After the grand **Italian Consulate**, and opposite the stadium, is a large school, to the right of which a lane, too narrow for a car, leads to the **Café Halfa**. The steep hillside is terraced and from the café, shaded by shrubs and trees, there are stunning views over the straits. Serving coffee, mint tea, sandwiches and cakes, this is just the place to spend the late afternoon – as did Paul Bowles and his friends, Tennessee Williams, Truman Capote and Jack Kerouac.

Going along Rue Mohammed Tazi you come to the **Palais du Mendoub** on the right. From the 1920s, this was the residence of the Mendoub, the Sultan's representative during the international years and more recently was owned by Malcolm Forbes (see box p.91). Between 1970 and 1990, it housed his unrivalled collection of toy soldiers and battle tableaux, including the 1578 Battle of the Three Kings near Ksar El Kebir, in which virtually the entire Portuguese nobility was killed or imprisoned (see

---

GARDENS ON THE MOUNTAIN

The two most prestigious addresses in Tangier are **La Marshan**, the area west of the Palais du Mendoub, and **La Montagne**, the 'Mountain' behind the Spanish Consulate, on the inland route to Cap Spartel (see p.100). The Mountain, less imposing than its name suggests, was a rebel base against the British and Portuguese occupations of Tangier, but is now thoroughly tamed. Its cork and pine woods shield two vast royal palaces: one, built by the Victorian British consul Sir John Hay, which was (until her recent death), the residence of King Hassan's mother; the other, heavily guarded, among the numerous retreats of the Saudi royal family. It is also peppered with villas, many of which have beautiful gardens with stunning views of the bay, and several of which are owned by expats who are prepared to show serious garden-lovers around. One such is Anne Lambton, Villa Palma, La Vielle Montagne (☎03/993 1393), who asks only for a donation to SPANA, the animal welfare charity. Like many who live on the Mountain, Anne is an artist and occasionally exhibits at the Lawrence Arnott Art Gallery (see p.96).

To reach La Montagne you'll need to drive or take a taxi. From Place de France take Rue Belgique to its end, where it becomes the Rue de la Montagne and begins winding its way up. If you want to make a day-trip of it, you can continue, over the mountain, towards the Caves of Hercules (see "Around Tangier", p.100).

---

p.554), and the 1975 Marche Verte when 350,000 unarmed Moroccans, led by the late King Hassan II, "reclaimed" the former Spanish Sahara.

Continuing past *Café Halfa* for a further 1km, you reach *Camping Miramonte*, and a track down to the **Jews' Beach** – so called from its role as the landing stage for Spanish Jews fleeing the Inquisition. There is a pleasant little **beach café** open here in summer.

Eating, drinking and nightlife

Tangier is not really a night-time city, and if you're looking for international resort-style action, or the Tangier of sin-city legend, you'll be disappointed. There are nevertheless good and generally inexpensive **restaurants**, a fair scattering of **bars** and **discos**, and possibilities for films and the occasional concert.

Restaurants

As with most Moroccan cities, the cheapest places to eat are in the **Medina**, though note that alcoholic drinks are not served in this quarter. For fancier meals – and drinks – you'll need to try the **Ville Nouvelle** or the **seafront**; for late-night snacks, several of the cafés around the Grand Socco stay open all night. All of our **out of town** recommendations will require use of a car.

Opening hours are generally noon–2.30pm for lunch, and 7–10pm for dinner.

MEDINA

Restaurant Ahlen, 8 Rue des Postes. Simple but well-cooked food – roast chicken, grilled beef, harira soup – and a warm welcome. Cheap.

Restaurant Andaluz, 7 Rue de Commerce. The best of the cafés on this street – the first alley to the left off Rue de la Marine (the street running from the Petit Socco to the Grand Mosque). With a trio of tables, it is about as simple as it's possible to be – and excellent, serving impeccably fried swordfish and grilled brochettes. Cheap.

Chez Hammadi, 2 Rue d'Italie. This is actually just outside the west wall of the Medina: a rather kitsch salon, where traditional Moroccan dishes are served to entertainment from a worthwhile band of Andalous musicians. Moderate.

Greg Restaurant, 21 Rue de Commerce. This is a rival and neighbour to the *Andaluz* – and there's little to choose between them. Moroccan dishes. Cheap.

Restaurant Ibn Batouta, Rue es Siaghin. Small, unpretentious restaurant on the main street of the Medina, not far from the Petit Socco. Cheap.

Restaurant Marhaba, 67 Palais Ahannar, off Rue de la Kasbah (inside the Kasbah Gate, take the first small alley to the left). A splendid old palace, stacked with antiques, and with good music and food. Moderate.

Ray Charley, corner of Place Petit Socco. A good little café serving big portions of egg, tomato and chips. (Very) cheap.

VILLE NOUVELLE

Restaurant Africa, 83 Rue Salah Eddine El Ayoubi (aka Rue de la Plage). Best of the many restaurants on this street, which leads down from the Grand Socco. It's at the bottom of the hill, opposite *Hôtel Valencia*. It was a Spanish town house and a tiled Goya of the Duchess of Alba still looks down on proceedings. Regular Moroccan dishes, well prepared, and there's beer and wine. Moderate.

Restaurant Agadir, 21 Rue Prince Heritier, off Place de France. This small and friendly restaurant, run by a Tafraouti, with accomplished French and Moroccan cooking, is a personal favourite. Moderate.

Las Conchas, Rue Ahmed Chaouki. Good French menu, though the chef who made its name has defected to the *Osso Buco* (see below). Moderate.

Restaurant Le Coeur de Tanger, 1 Rue Annoual, off Place de France (it's above the *Café Paris*, though the entrance is on a side street). Moroccan dishes served in some style. Moderate to expensive.

El Dorado, 21 Rue Allal Ben Abdallah, by the *Hôtel Chellah*. Dependable Jewish-Moroccan/Spanish cooking; try the fish dishes. Moderate.

Guitta's, 110 Sidi Bouabid, near the modern Hassan II Mosque on Place de Koweit (☎03/993 7333). This is a little hard to find, and its dismal exterior offers little promise. However, this is a relic of old Tangier and a favourite of the expats, redolent of the 1950s International Zone. An Italian family serves up simple European dishes – and Sunday roasts. Moderate. Closed Mon

El Korsan, in the *Hôtel El Minzah*, 85 Rue de la Liberté (☎03/993 5885). The hotel's Moroccan restaurant has a reputation as one of the country's best, serving authentic and traditional specialities to the accompaniment of a group of musicians. However, it has the occasional lapse and if you want classic Moroccan cooking you may feel your money is better spent at *Raihani's* (see below). Expensive.

Le Mogador, Complexe Istiraha, 42 Rue de Hollande (☎03/993 1821). New but already gaining a good reputation for its Moroccan and European dishes. Expensive.

Restaurant Number One, 1 Bd. Mohammed V, across the side street from the *Hôtel Rembrandt* (☎03/994 1674). A restaurant and cocktail bar which attracts a business crowd at lunchtime and tends to be fairly quiet in the evenings. French-Moroccan menu. Good cooking. Expensive.

Restaurant Osso Buco, on the ground floor of the *Maroc Hôtel*, 1 Rue du Prince Moulay Abdallah. Excellent Italian dishes from an extensive menu, presided over by an Englishwoman. Moderate.

Restaurant Pagode, just off Rue Prince Héritier, facing the *Carousel Bar*. The best Chinese food in Tangier, though the service is pretty joyless. Expensive.

Restaurant Raihani, 10 Rue Ahmed Chaouki, a side street opposite the terrace-belvedere on Bd. Pasteur (☎03/993 4866). This is an excellent restaurant, serving traditional Moroccan food – it's worth at least one meal here for the superb couscous and pastilla – as well as a decent French-based menu. Moderate.

Restaurant Romero, 12 Rue du Prince Moulay Abdallah, off Bd. Pasteur (☎03/993 2277). Spanish fish and seafood. Not as good as it was, following a change of ownership, but it's an attractive place and still worth a try. Moderate.

Restaurant San Remo, 15 Rue Ahmed Chaouki – see *Raihani's* above. Credible, good-value Italian cooking, and with a cheaper pizzeria across the road. Moderate.

Rubis Grill, 3 Rue Ibn Rochd, off Av. Prince Moulay Abdallah. Long established, serving Spanish and other European dishes; the candle-lit hacienda decor is a bit over the top, but the food and service is exemplary. Moderate.

SEAFRONT

Restaurant Bab Al Maghreb, 30 Av. d'Espagne, facing the former Gare de Ville. The best restaurant along this rather elegant front which featured at the beginning and end of Bertolucci's *The Sheltering Sky*. Moderate.

Hôtel Biarritz, 102–104 Av. d'Espagne. One of the nicer hotel restaurants, with old-style service and a limited but reliable menu. Moderate.

Emma's BBC Bar, on the beach facing the *Hôtel Miramar*. The only one of the beach-cafés where food is a significant attraction. Open summer only – and until late. Moderate.

L'Marsa, Av. d'Espagne. Superb pizzas and spaghetti, with home-made ice cream to follow, served (slowly) on a roof terrace, patio or inside. Moderate.

Hôtel Marco Polo, corner of Av. d'Espagne/Rue El Antaki. Very noisy ground floor bar, with restaurant on the first and top floors, and views of the bay. Limited menu, but generous helpings. Cheerful and swift service. Moderate.

Restaurant Mendes, 80 Av. d'Espagne. Pavement restaurant under awnings which specializes in grills. Friendly and value for money. Moderate.

Hôtel Miramar, 168 Av. d'Espagne. There are good-value set meals in this popular and often very crowded hotel restaurant. Moderate.

Restaurant-Bar La Paix, 66 Av. d'Espagne, at the junction with Rue Salah Eddine El Ayoubi. More of a bar than a restaurant, but if that's what you're after you can eat on the first floor and watch the action. Cheap.

Restaurant Valencia, 6 Av. Youssef Ben Tachfine (☎03/994 5146). A relatively new fish restaurant which is very popular with locals and tourists alike. Worth making a reservation. Moderate. Closed Tues.

OUT OF TOWN

Chez Abdou, 17km out of town, on the coast road leading south towards Asilah, in the so-called Fôret Diplomatique. Recommended for seafood. Expensive.

Club Le Mirage, near the Caves of Hercules (see p.100) in the area known as Ashakar, 5km south of the Cap Spartel lighthouse. The old, friendly hotel here, with its camel rides and resident apes, has been replaced by an international-style restaurant. But the food is still pretty good and the views fabulous. Moderate to expensive.

Le Riad Restaurant, 7km along the Malabata road, amid the trees to the right of the road. A pleasant lunchtime stop. Moderate.

Cafés

Like all Moroccan towns, Tangier has many cafés, each with its particular clientele and daily rhythm, some good for breakfast, others popular late morning or evening. Following are a few long-standing favourites.

Café Atlas, by the *Hôtel Rembrandt*. Open until midnight and often beyond, this is a good fall-back for late-night snacks.

Pâtisserie Florence, corner of Rue Lafayette and Rue du Portugal, near *Hôtel Chellah*. This place serves fine European and Moroccan pastries and cakes.

Café Halfa, Marshan. This cliff-top café is the perfect late-afternoon locale to gaze across the straits and write your postcards. For help finding it, see p.92.

L'Marsa, 92 Av. d'Espagne. Recommended for its pizzas, this serves equally delicious croissants, *pains chocolats* and cakes for breakfast or tea.

Café Metropole, 27 Bd. Pasteur – next to the synagogue. This serves the best *café au lait* in town and pastries can be bought across the road at *Patisserie Le Petit Prince* and consumed at your table.

Café de Paris, Place de France. Tangier's most famous café, from its conspiratorial past, is a little dull these days, though still an institution for expats.

Pâtisserie Rahmouni, 35 Rue du Prince Moulay Abdallah. The rival to *Florence* for the best pastries and cakes in town.

Traiteur: Laiterie Al Mouatamid Ibn Abbad, 16 Rue Al Mouatamid Ibn Abadd. New caterers selling Moroccan sweetmeats and fancy cakes.

Bars

Tangier's **bars** are much depleted from past glories. The legendary *Parade* died with its owner in 1987, and most of those that do survive have fallen into a not very interesting seediness. The better options remaining are to be found in or alongside the older hotels, supplemented in summer by the beach bars, which stay open till 1am or so (though take care in this area after dark).

Caid's Bar in the *Hôtel Minzah*, 85 Rue de la Liberté. Long the chi-chi place to meet – ritzy decor and very pricey drinks. Over the bar is a grand painting of Caid Harry Aubrey Maclean, former Commander in Chief of the Sultan's army (see p.88).

Carousel Bar, opposite the Chinese Restaurant, *Le Pagode*, off Rue Prince Heritier. Comfortable British-run wine bar.

Hôtel Chellah, Rue Allal Ben Abdallah. Lively, with music some evenings, and a sporadic happy hour from 6–7pm.

Dean's Bar, Rue d'Amerique du Sud. The closest bar to the Medina – a tiny shop-room that was once the haunt of people like Tennessee Williams, Francis Bacon and Ian Fleming. It is now frequented more or less exclusively by Moroccans and tourists are not really welcomed.

Chez Miami – aka Miami Beach, on the beach – nearest Rue Salah Eddine Al Ayoubi turning. The liveliest of the beach bars and one of the most easily accessible, too.

Hôtel Marco Polo, Av. d'Espagne. The ground floor is popular with tourists, especially hard-drinking Scandinavians and Germans getting through its range of European beers.

Negresco – aka **English Bar**, 14 Rue du Mexique. A small, somewhat down-at-heel bar serving draught beer and tapas, alongside the *Restaurant Negresco*.

Le Pub, 4 Rue Sorolla – behind the *Hôtel Tanjah Flandria*, off Bd. Mohammed V. British-run pub, with hunting scenes on the walls and bar food. Daily 9pm–1am.

Tanger Inn, 16 Rue Magellan – below the *Hôtel Muniria*. Deadpan imitation of a Brighton pub, circa 1955, with the (British) Queen's portrait on the wall. One of Tangier's last surviving International Zone relics. Daily 9pm–2am.

Discos and clubs

The principal area for **discos** is a grid of streets off Place de France, in particular Rue Sanlucar (aka Zankat Moutanabi) and Rue du Méxique, and Rue du Prince Moulay Abdallah (off Boulevard Pasteur). Admission is usually 100dh, drinks are two or three times regular bar prices and take care if leaving late at night as the streets are none too safe hereabouts; the best idea is to tip the doorman 5dh to call you up a taxi.

Borsalino, 30 Rue du Prince Moulay Abdalah. A small and usually quite lively disco, with a mixed crowd, screened by the doorman.

Morocco Palace, 13 Rue du Prince Moulay Abdallah. A clear winner among Tangier's nightspots, this strange, sometimes slightly manic, place puts on traditional Moroccan music and dance (plus a couple of Egyptian belly-dancing sets) each night from around 9pm until 4am. Customers are predominantly Moroccan and expect – and get – a good show.

Radio Club, Rue du Prince Moulay Abdallah. Attractively sleazy club which sometimes puts on Moroccan bands.

Regine Club, Rue El Mansour Dahbi (opposite the Roxy Cinema). Mainstream disco, larger and a little cheaper than most. Open from 10pm.

Scott's, Rue El Moutanabi (aka Rue Sanlucar). Traditionally (though not exclusively) a gay disco, this is worth a look if only for its very particular choice of paintings – Berber boys in Highland military uniform. It's usually very quiet until after midnight.

Concerts, art and films

Music concerts – traditional and popular – are sporadic events in Tangier. The old Spanish bullring, out beyond the bus station in the Ville Nouvelle, has had a major refurbishment as an open-air concert hall, so it might be worth asking about events there. Cultural events are also hosted by the **Old American Legation** (see p.89) and the **Institut Français de Tangier**.

You can pick up a programme for Institut Français events from the **Galerie Delacroix**, 86 Rue de la Liberté (closed Mon), where there is usually an interesting exhibition by contemporary artists. Two other **galleries** are also worth a look for work by local artists: the Lawrence Arnott Art Gallery, 68 Rue Amr Ibn Ass, near *Hôtel*

Chellah (closed Sun), and the Volubilis Art Gallery, 6 Sidi Boukouja (in the kasbah; closed Mon), under the same management as the Volubilis Boutique below.

There are a dozen or so **cinemas** scattered about the Ville Nouvelle, in the grid around Boulevard Pasteur. Films are frequently shown in their original language, with Arabic subtitles, though some are dubbed into French. The Cinéma Rif on the Grand Socco shows an exclusive and entertaining diet of Indian and Kung Fu films.

More upmarket are the Cinéma Flandria, Rue Ibn Rochd, and the two-screen Dawliz cinema in the Istiraha tourist complex, opposite the old *Grand Hôtel Villa de France* on Rue de Hollande.

Up-to-date **information** on local events can be found in the weekly *Les Nouvelles du Nord*, out on Fridays, available in cafés and hotel receptions.

Shops and stalls

Many of the Tangier **market stalls and stores** are eminently avoidable, geared to selling tourist goods that wouldn't pass muster elsewhere. But a few are worthwhile, unique, or both; a half-hour preliminary browse at the more "fixed price" outlets on Boulevard Pasteur is useful for establishing roughly what you should pay for things.

There are fruit and vegetable stalls in a couple of central locations. One is at the bottom of the **steps beyond the Hôtel El Minzah**. Another is the **Fes Market**, between Rue de Fes and Rue de Hollande in the Ville Nouvelle, where you can also buy groceries. **Beer and wine** is sold in supermarkets in the Ville Nouvelle.

Crafts and antiques

Ensemble Artisanal, Rue Belgique (left-hand side, going up from Place de France). Modern Moroccan crafts are displayed in this small government-run store, as in other major cities. They are rarely the best or the cheapest available but prices are (more or less) fixed, so this can be a useful first call to get an idea of quality and costs before bargaining elsewhere. The only problem being that it keeps very unpredictable hours.

Perfumerie Madini, 14 Rue Sebou, in the Medina; from the Petit Socco take the alley between the *Tingis* and *Centrale* cafés, which leads into Rue Sebou, and look for the shop on your left. Madini makes inspired copies of brand-name perfumes from natural oils, which he sells at a fraction of the "real" price, as well as musk and traditional fragrances. Given a couple of days and a sample, he will reproduce any scent you like. Closed 1–4pm and Friday.

Bazaar Tindouf, 64 Rue de la Liberté, opposite the *Hôtel El Minzah*. One of the better quality junk-antique shops, with a good array of cushion-carpets and old postcards. Bargaining is difficult but essential.

Rue Touahin, first right off Rue Siaghin, entering the Medina from the Grand Socco. This line of jewellery stalls may turn up something appealing, though don't take silver, gold or most stones at face value: judge on aesthetics.

Volubilis Boutique, 15 Place Petit Socco. A more than usually interesting mix of traditional Moroccan and Western fashion.

Listings

Airlines GB Airways, 83 Rue Houria aka Rue de Liberté (☎03/993 5211 or 993 5877) has flights to Casablanca, Marrakesh, Gibraltar and London, and handles British Airways business. For domestic flights (and some international destinations) contact Royal Air Maroc at 1 Place de France (☎03/993 4722). For flights to Spain (cheapest departures are from the Spanish enclave of Melilla, see Chapter Two) try Iberia at 35 Bd. Pasteur (☎03/993 6177), or the Moroccan-run Regional Air Lines (☎03/939 3536) which has three flights weekdays to Málaga, and two flights at weekends. Three other airline offices are to be found at 7 Rue du Mexique: Air France (☎03/993 6477), KLM (☎03/993 8926) and Lufthansa (☎03/993 1327).

Airport Tangier's airport at Ibn Batouta (previously Boukhalef), is 15km west of the city (information ☎03/993 5129).

Banks Most are grouped along Bd. Pasteur/Bd. Mohammed V. The BMCE bureau de change on Bd. Pasteur is the most efficient, changing cash and traveller's cheques, and handling cash advances on Visa and Mastercard; daily 10am–1pm & 3–7pm and there is a cash dispenser outside. The SGMB at 58 Bd. Mohammed V (opposite the main post office) takes some bank cheques backed by credit cards. Crédit du Maroc, Bd. Pasteur, also handles Visa transactions.

Books The long-established Librairie des Colonnes at 54 Bd. Pasteur (Mon–Fri 9.30am–1pm & 2–7pm, Sat 9.30am–noon) has a fair selection of English-language books, including some of Paul Bowles' Moroccan translations.

Car parking The *Hôtel Tanjah Flandria* (see main map key) has an underground garage open to nonresidents (10dh for 24hr).

Car rental Most of the big companies have offices along Bd. Pasteur/Bd. Mohammed V. Avis, 54 Bd. Pasteur (☎03/993 3031, fax 933 0624); Europcar/InterRent, 87 Bd. Mohammed V (☎03/994 1938, fax 934 0394); Hertz, 36 Bd. Mohammed V (☎03/993 3322); and Tourist Cars, 84 Bd. Mohammed V (☎03/993 5493). Also centrally located are Budget, 7 Rue du Prince Moulay Abdallah (☎03/993 7994). Avis, Europcar/InterRent and Hertz also have desks at the airport. A local agency, offering a more personal service, is Harris Rent-a-Car, 1 Rue Zerktouni, off Bd. Mohammed V (☎03/994 2158).

Car repairs Most repairs can be undertaken – or arranged – by Garage Lafayette, 27 Rue Mohammed Abdou (☎03/993 2887).

Consulates Britain, 41 Bd. Mohammed V – 7th floor (Mon–Thurs 8.30am–12.30pm & 1.30–4pm, Fri 8.30am–12.30pm; ☎03/994 1557, fax 994 2284); Denmark, 3 Rue Ibn Rochd (☎03/993 8183); France, 2 Place de France (☎03/993 2039); Italy, 37 Rue Asad Ibn Farrat (☎03/993 7647); Portugal, 9 Place des Nations (☎03/993 1708); Spain, 85 Rue Sidi Bouadid (☎03/993 5625, fax 993 2381); and Sweden, 31 Rue Prince Héritier (☎03/993 8730). Despite the presence of the old American Legation, there is no USA consulate and the nearest USA diplomatic representation is in Rabat.

Ferry companies You can buy ferry tickets from any travel agent (see our recommendations below) and also from the ferry companies themselves. All crossings are Tangier to Algeciras, unless otherwise stated. Bland Line, 22 Bd. Mohammed V (☎03/922 2334; Gibraltar); COMANAV, 43 Av. Abou Alla El Maari (☎03/994 0488; Sète); Comarit, 7 Rue du Mexique (☎03/993 1220); Euro Ferrys, 31 Av. de la Résistance (☎03/932 2253); IMTC, 2 Bd. Pasteur (☎03/933 6002; Cadiz); Intercona, 31 Av. de la Résistance (☎03/993 4883); Limadet, 13 Rue du Prince Moulay Abdallah (☎03/993 3626); Trasmediterranea, 3 Rue Ibn Rochd (☎03/993 2913).

Golf The area around Tangier offers two options for golf enthusiasts: Tangier Royal Golf Club, B.P. 41, Tangier (☎03/994 4484, fax 994 5450); and Cabo Negro Royal Golf, B.P. 696 G Tetouan (☎03/997 8303, fax 997 8305).

Internet access *Cybercafé Adam*, 4 Rue Ibn Rochd (off Bd. Pasteur); *Futurescope*, 8 Rue Youssoufia (off Bd, Mohammed V).

Newspapers English-language newspapers are sold outside the post office, in various stores along Bd. Pasteur, and by vendors around the *Café Paris*.

Pharmacies There are several English-speaking pharmacies in the Place de France (try the Pharmacie de Paris, opposite the *Café Paris*) and along Bd. Pasteur. A roster of all-night and weekend pharmacies is displayed in every *pharmacie* window. Pharmacists are happy to recommend local doctors.

Photographic developing Studio Farah, opposite the *Hôtel El Minzah* on Rue de la Liberté, offers a good quality one-hour service for Kodak film; Studio Flash, further down Rue de la Liberté on the same side as the *Minzah*, does the same for Fuji film.

Police Main station is on Rue Ibn Toumert. Emergency ☎19.

Post The main PTT is at 33 Bd. Mohammed V and has a *poste restante* service; open Mon–Sat 8.30am–12.15pm & 2.30–6.45pm.

Telephones The post office (see above) phone section is open 24hr. As Tangier has direct dialling you can phone (internationally) from any phone box or from one of the new *téléboutiques* – look out for their blue and white lettering and logos.

Tourist office There's an ONMT office at 29 Bd. Pasteur (☎03/993 8239), just down from Place de France and open (in theory) Mon–Sat 8am–2pm. It is in fact open very erratically, and doesn't have a lot to offer in any case, save a few leaflets.

Travel agencies There are many travel agents, particularly along the seafront; they handle ferry and flight bookings and most will advise on – and book – travel and hotels in Morocco. Three reliable agents are: Voyages Marco Polo, 72 Av. d'Espagne – by the *Hôtel Valencia* (☎03/993 4345); Transalpino Maroc, 100 Av. d'Espagne (☎03/993 2594); and Koutoubia, 112 bis Av. d'Espagne (☎03/993 5540).

Moving on

Travelling on **into Morocco** from Tangier is simplest either by **train** (the lines run to Meknes/Fes/Oujda or to Rabat/Casablanca/Marrakesh; all trains stop at Asilah en route), or, if you are heading east to Tetouan, by **bus** or shared **grand taxi**. Leaving the country, **ferries** run to Algeciras, Tarifa, Gibraltar, Cadiz and Sète (France).

By train

At present there is only one train station in Tangier, Tanger Morora (see p.81), with three trains a day: the 7.15am, 4.30pm and 10.30pm all going to **Casablanca**, where connections can be picked up for Marrakesh. For Meknes, Fes, Taza and Oujda change at Sidi Slimane. For further information on journey times see Travel Details, p.134.

Beware of hustlers on trains leaving Tangier, who insist that it's necessary to change trains at Asilah (the first stop) – it's not, and they use the time you spend waiting for the next train trying to sell you carpets from their shops.

By bus and grand taxi

Since the closure of Gare du Port and Gare de Ville, many more **CTM long-distance buses** leave from the Port Entrance (see p.81), including those for Tetouan and Chaouen.

All other long-distance services start from **Gare Routière**, 2km from the centre of town, by the large, modern Syrian Mosque, Sahat Al Jamai Al Arabia. It's better to take a petit taxi (15dh) but if on foot, from the seafront, take Av. Youssef Ben Tachfine, cross Bd. Mohammed V and continue a further 400m to the *gare routière*. Useful departures include, again, Tetouan and Chaouen (the latter doesn't involve a change of bus, though you stop in Tetouan for 20 min; don't pay extra to hustlers there who might just suggest your ticket covers only a "reservation fare" for the Chaouen stage).

There are **grands taxis** leaving through the day to **Tetouan**, again from the *gare routière* by the Syrian Mosque. To get a place in a taxi, just announce yourself to the driver at the head of the rank. You will then be crammed (with five other passengers) into the car. The cost is only slightly more than going by bus and journey time is considerably less. Taxis can also be chartered here for expeditions further afield, direct to **Chaouen** or **Asilah** for example, and work out relatively economical shared between a group. On your own, heading for Chaouen, it's a lot cheaper to get a bus on from Tetouan. The cost of a place to Tetouan is a standard tariff (currently 25dh); all other destinations are negotiable.

For destinations in the immediate **vicinity of Tangier**, such as the Caves of Hercules or Cap Malabata, you need to negotiate a grand taxi at the rank on the Grand Socco.

By ferry and hydrofoil

Although **ferries** invariably depart an hour or so late, you should **check in** at the port at least one hour before official sailing time to get through the chaos of official business. At the ferry terminal, you have to get an embarkation card and departure card from the *départ* desk of the ferry companies, then you must take this, along with your passport, to the police *visa de passeport* desk on the same floor (opposite the bar), and have your passport stamped before going through customs to the boat. Arrive later than an hour before official departure time and you may find the visa police have knocked off – which means waiting for the next ferry. **Hydrofoils** have a separate *visa de passeport* desk and departures are normally on time.

Two **periods to avoid** the ferries from Tangier are the end of the **Easter week** (Semana Santa) holiday, and the **last week of August**, when the ferries can be full for days on end with Moroccan workers returning to northern Europe. If possible avoid travelling during this period, but if that's not possible then reservations are essential.

Details of **ferry/hydrofoil routes** are to be found in the "Basics" section of this book (see pp.12–13). **Tickets and timetables** can be obtained from any travel agent in Tangier or from the ferry company's agents (see our "Listings").

Around Tangier: capes, caves and coast

The **Bay of Tangier** curves around to a pair of capes – Malabata to the east, Spartel to the west. Either makes a pleasant detour or afternoon's trip, if you have a day to fill waiting for a ferry or flight.

West: the Caves of Hercules and "Atlantic Beach"

The **Caves of Hercules** (Grottes d'Hercule) are something of a symbol for Tangier, with its strange sea window, shaped like a map of Africa. The name, like Hercules' legendary founding of Tangier, is purely fanciful, but the caves, 16km outside the city and above the "Atlantic Beach", make an attractive excursion, together with the minor Roman site of Cotta. If you feel like staying for a few days by the sea, the beach can be an attractive base, too; outside of July and August only stray groups of visitors share the long surf beaches. Take care with currents, however, which can be very dangerous even near the shore.

If you have your own transport, you can head out to the caves via La Montagne and make a round trip by continuing along the S701 and then taking either the minor S702 or the faster P2 back to Tangier. If you don't, the cheapest access is a local **bus** (unnumbered but with a placard reading Ashakar – in Arabic – in its window) which runs throughout the day from the local bus station near the Grand Socco; this takes the S702 out of Tangier, turns onto the S701 and runs past *Camping Ashakar*, close by the caves, then carries on 5km to the Cap Spartel lighthouse. An alternative is to charter a **grand taxi** (from the Grand Socco or by the Port Entrance); this should cost around 120dh for the return trip – for which price most drivers can be persuaded to drop you in the morning and pick you up late afternoon; you should, obviously enough, pay at the end.

Cap Spartel and the Caves

The most interesting route to the caves and Cap Spartel runs around and above the coast via the quarter known as La Montagne (see box on p.93). Follow this road for around 14km and you'll reach a short turn off to the lighthouse at **Cap Spartel** – a dramatic and fertile point, known to the Greeks and Romans as the "Cape of the Vines". The lighthouse, which you can visit and sometimes, if the keeper is around, climb, was built in 1864 by Sultan Mohammed III, who then persuaded Britain, France, Italy and Spain to pay for its maintenance; they did, until Moroccan independence in 1956.

To the south of Cap Spartel begins the vast and wild "Atlantic Beach", known locally as **Robinson Plage**. It is broken only by a rocky spit – 5km from the Cape – and then rambles off for as far as you can see. On the spit are located the **Caves of Hercules**. Natural formations, occupied in prehistoric times, they are most striking for a manmade addition – thousands of disc-shaped erosions created by centuries of quarrying for millstones. There were still Moors cutting stones here for a living until the 1920s, but by that time their place was beginning to be taken by professional guides and discreet sex hustlers; it must have made an exotic brothel. Today, there's a standard admission charge of 5dh (9am–sunset), though you're unlikely to get away without a

guide, too, whose descriptive abilities tend to be somewhat dwarfed by the utter obvi-
ousness of all there is to see ("wet cave", "dark cave", "sea", etc). In midsummer there
are usually a couple of stalls nearby, serving grilled fish caught on the rocks below.

Ancient Cotta

Five minutes' walk past the caves, a track turns inland from the beach and leads you to
the rather scant ruins of **Ancient Cotta**, a small Roman town, founded in the second
century AD and occupied for 200 years or so. Like Lixus to the south (see p.110), the
town produced *garum* (a kind of anchovy paste) for export. Parts of the factory, and of
a temple and baths complex, can be made out, while nearby have been found the ruins
of several Roman farms which cultivated olives for oil. Even before the Romans, and
certainly afterwards, this was a well-populated and prosperous area.

The most remarkable feature, these days, is the modern factory plant you see just
beyond the site, with its tall, thin red-and-white chimneys discharging hot air and flames.
This is the point where the **Maghreb-Europe Gazodue pipeline**, carrying natural gas
from Hassi Rimel in Algeria and across Morocco, goes under the straits of Gibraltar to
Spain and beyond. The 45km submarine section was a unique challenge, given that the
strait has a rocky, mountainous seabed, and strong currents, often in three layers, with
the top and bottom flowing in one direction, the middle in the opposite direction.

Inspired by its success, and perhaps by the Channel Tunnel between Britain and
France, Spain and Morocco agreed, in 1996, to build a rail tunnel along much the same
course. The project, costed at £2.5bn/$4bn, is still very much at planning stage but if
funds materialize, it is planned to have trains running by 2010.

Between the gas plant and Ancient Cotta, a Saudi prince has built a **royal palace**; you
may see one of his servants rolling out a carpet across the beach to the water's edge
for a royal party to bathe.

Accommodation

Close by the caves, on the same rocky spit, are two **hotels**, the *Hôtel Robinson*
(☎03/937 2345, fax 937 5452; ④), a pleasant old-established place, and the *Club Le
Mirage* (☎03/993 3332, fax 933 3452; ⑥), an upmarket cliff top complex with swimming
pool and satellite TV, which has replaced the old *Mirage* restaurant. On the landward
side of the hotels there is the **campsite**, *Camping Ashakar*, a pleasant, well-wooded site
with showers, café, restaurant and small shop, but really only for those with transport.
Next to the site is the *Cuevas* night club and bar.

East: Cap Malabata and Ksar es Seghir

The best beaches in the immediate vicinity of Tangier are to be found at **Cap
Malabata**, where much wealthy villa development has been taking place. Beyond here,
Ksar es Seghir offers a pleasant day by the sea, or a stop on the recently resurfaced
and much improved coast road to Ceuta, if you have your own transport to get there.

Cap Malabata and Villa Harris

The bay east of Tangier is flanked by a gritty strip of beach and a chain of elderly villas
and new apartment blocks until you reach the "complexe touristique" of **Cap Malabata**.
This has a couple of hotels, intermittently open, and a *Club Med* "village" which occasionally takes guests without a reservation (recently *Club Med* has seen falling membership and a subsequent softening of its image to attract a wider age range). Membership
does carry some advantages and with seven "villages" in Morocco it may be worthwhile
considering joining. For further information contact **Club Med**, Kennedy House, 115
Hammersmith Road, London, W14, ☎0700 007 007 007). Its buildings encompass the

splendid turn-of-the-century **Villa Harris** and its gardens, built by the writer Walter Harris (see "Contexts", p.607) and given by him to the people of Tangier. Harris's wife decently cited his obsession with the garden (rather than his predilection for boys) in her case for divorce. If you're interested in visiting the villa and gardens, you may be able to talk your way in at the gates, even if you're not staying at the Club.

You can get to Cap Malabata on bus #11 from the local bus station near the Grand Socco, or by petit taxi, but once **around the cape** the buses give out (save for a single daily bus from Tangier to Ksar es Seghir), along with the hotels and villas. There is in fact virtually no development the whole way round the coast to Ceuta: just a road winding through the hills above enticing stretches of beach.

Ksar es Seghir and Djebel Moussa

KSAR ES SEGHIR, halfway to Ceuta, makes a pleasant stop. The picturesque little fishing port attracts a fair number of Moroccan beach campers in summer, but few Europeans. There are a few ruined walls which date from Portuguese times, and legend has it that Tarik Ibn Ziyad invaded Spain from here in 711. The *Café-Restaurant Diamant Bleu* (☎03/994 6832, fax 994 6831; ④) has rooms overlooking the sea, and you can eat here or at the *Restaurant Luna Mar* by the petrol station.

From Ksar es Seghir the road to Fnideq climbs around the windy **Djebel Moussa** – the mountain which, with Gibraltar, forms the so-called Pillars of Hercules, gateway to the Classical world. Mythologies aside, the twin pillars effect remarkable thermal currents, speeding passage for **migratory birds** at this, the shortest crossing between Africa and Europe. A spring or autumn visit should ensure sightings, as up to 200 species make their way across the Straits, as well as providing sightings of a new addition to the landscape of Djebel Moussa, a line of 35m-high wind machines producing electricity for the area.

Asilah

The first town south of Tangier – and first stop on the train line – **ASILAH** is one of the most elegant of the old Portuguese Atlantic ports, ranking with El Jadida and Essaouira to the south of Casablanca, and is small, easy to manage, and exceptionally clean. First impressions are of wonderful square stone ramparts, flanked by palms, and an outstanding beach – an immense sweep of sand stretching to the north halfway to Tangier. Further exploration reveals the Medina, which is one of the most attractive in the country, colourwashed at every turn, and with a series of murals painted for the town's **International Festival**. The first International Festival was in 1978 and it has been held most years since. It always takes place in August and runs for three to four weeks, with a programme usually including art, dance, film, music and poetry, attracting performers from around the world.

Arrival and accommodation

The **train station** is 2km north of the town; there is occasionally a taxi to meet arrivals but don't count on it. It's an easy enough walk into town, so long as you're not weighed down with bags. Arriving by **grand taxi** (40min from Tangier), or by **bus**, you're dropped in or around **Place Mohammed V**, a small square at the edge of the Medina, a short walk from the ramparts and a prominent gate, **Bab El Kasaba**.

Hotels

Asilah can be packed during its festival but at other times, even high season, there's usually space to be found in the dozen or so *pensions* and hotels. There is a string of

ASILAH

Hôtel de Ville

PTT

Cinéma Magali

San Bartolome

Campsites, Train Station, Tangier & 1

Laroche

P2

AVENUE MOHAMMED V

RUE ALLAL BEN ABDALLAH

RUE TARFAYA

AVENUE PRINCE HERITIER

RUE MELILIA

RUE MANSOUR EDDAHBI

RUE MOULAY HASSAN BEN MEHDI

RUE AHMED M'DIM

RUE ASSILI

AVENUE IMAM

RUE ZELLACA

RUE HASSAN BEN TABIT

PLACE MOHAMMED V

BMCE

PLACE ZELLACA

Bab El Kacaba

Grand Mosque

Centre Hassan II

El Hamra

Bab El Homar

HASSAN II

RUE IBN BATOUTA

Palais de Raisuli

MEDINA

Mosque

N

0   100m

ACCOMMODATION

Al Khaima Hôtel	1
Hôtel Belle Vue	12
Hôtel Ennasr	7
Pension Karam	4
Hôtel Las Palmas	9
Hôtel Mansour	3
Hôtel Marhaba	11
Mounia Apartments	8
Hôtel Oued El Makhazine	5
Hôtel Patio de la Luna	10
Hôtel Sahara	2
Hôtel Zelis	6

RESTAURANTS

Al Kasabah	G
Café-Restaurant Al Najoum	E
Casa Gracia	C
El Espigón	A
El Oceano	F
Restaurant Ifrane	B
Café-Restaurant Le Pont	D
Restaurant Sevilla	H

campsites between the town and the train station, of which **Camping Echrigui** (☎03/941 7182) is the closest – and probably the best. Located about 400m from the town, it is well maintained, with thatched "bungalows" as well as pitches for tents, and has hot showers, a small shop and a cafeteria. Open all year.

CHEAP

Hôtel Belle Vue, Rue Hassan Ben Tabit (☎/fax 03/941 7747). A newish hotel which is quite difficult to find (follow the signs) and has bizarre decor. Reasonably priced though, with breakfast included. ②.

Hôtel Ennasr, 3 Rue Ahmed M'dem (☎03/941 7385). Rooms around a courtyard; plain but clean. The sign is small – look for it on the right-hand side of the street, behind a row of banks, walking from Place Mohammed V. ②.

Pension Karam, 39 Rue Mansour Eddahbi (☎03/941 8852). A small pension close to the seafront (and behind the prominent *Hôtel Oued El Makhazine*). ②.

Hôtel Marhaba, 9 Rue Zellaca (☎03/941 7144). A friendly place, close by the town gate; small, simple rooms but good value for your money. ②.

Hôtel Sahara, 9 Rue Tarfaya (☎03/941 7185). A little way from the action, behind the Cinéma Magali, but quiet, clean and comfortable. Hot showers 5dh extra. ②.

MODERATE

Hôtel Las Palmas, 7 Rue Imam Assili (☎03/941 7694). Another newish hotel – comfortable and good value. ④.

Hôtel Mansour, 49 Av. Mohammed V (☎03/991 7390). This is probably the best mid-range hotel in Asilah, and the change of owner has, by all reports, not meant any decline in service. There is also a travel agency, Jaouharat El Haram Voyages. ④.

Mounia Apartments, 14 Rue Moulay Hassan Ben Mehdi (☎03/941 7815). A range of apartments with kitchenettes, next to *Restaurant Casa Garcia* on the promenade. The owner also has other apartments elsewhere. ③.

Hôtel Patio de la Luna, 12 Rue Zellaca (☎03/941 6074). A small house, beautifully converted into a hotel, with a small patio and garden – very central. ④.

Hôtel Oued El Makhazine, Av. Melilla (☎03/941 7090). A pleasant and comfortable hotel. It may not be the most exciting in town, but it's close to the seafront and has a swimming pool and bar. ③.

EXPENSIVE

Al Khaima Hôtel, Route de Tanger – 1km north of town on the Tangier road (☎03/941 7428, fax 941 7098). This modern, comfortable hotel is built around a pool and has always had very positive reports. It has a pleasant bar, open to all-comers, which can be a little noisy in high season. ⑤.

Hôtel Zelis, 10 Rue Mansour Eddahbi (☎03/941 7029, fax 941 7098). Opened in 1995, this is a good-looking, very comfortable hotel, which perhaps has a slight edge over the *Al Khaima*. ⑤.

The town

Before the tourists and the International Festival, Asilah was just a small fishing port, quietly stagnating after the indifference of Spanish colonial administration. Whitewashed and cleaned up, it now has a prosperous feeling to it – the Grand Mosque, for example, has been rebuilt and doubled in size and a marina complex is planned.

The ramparts and Medina

The Medina's circuit of **towers and ramparts** – built by the Portuguese military architect Botacca in the sixteenth century – are pleasant to wander around. They include two main gates: **Bab El Homar**, on Avenue Hassan II, and **Bab El Kasaba**. If you enter by the latter, you pass the **Grand Mosque** and the **Centre Hassan II des Rencontres Internationales**, a venue and accommodation centre for the festival, with a cool open courtyard.

Further on is a small square overlooked by the "red tower", **El Hamra**. This is used for exhibitions, particularly during the festival. Turn right past here, along a tiny network of streets, and down towards the platform overlooking the sea, and you'll come upon at least a half-dozen **murals** painted (and subsequently repainted) during the festivals; they form an intriguing mix of fantasy-representational art and geometric designs. In turn, these offset the whitewashed walls of the houses, with their doors and windows picked out in cool pastel shades. It's quite an entrancing quarter.

Palais de Raisuli

The town's focal sight – stretching over the sea at the heart of the Medina – is the **Palais de Raisuli**, built in 1909 with forced tribal labour by one Er Raisuli, a local bandit. One of the strangest figures to emerge from what was an almost routinely bizarre period of Moroccan government, he began his career as a cattle rustler, achieved notoriety with a series of kidnappings and ransoms (including the British writer Walter Harris and a Greek-American millionaire, Perdicaris, who was bailed out by Teddy Roosevelt), and was eventually appointed governor over practically all the tribes of northwest Morocco. Harris described his captivity in *Morocco That Was* as an "anxious time", made more so by being confined in a small room with a headless corpse. Despite this, captor and captive formed a friendship, Harris finding Raisuli a "mysterious personage, half-saint, half-blackguard", and often entertaining him later in Tangier.

Another British writer, Rosita Forbes, visited Raisuli at his palace in 1924, later writing his biography. She described the rooms, today mostly bare, as hung with rugs "of violent colours, embroidered with tinsel", their walls lined with cushions stuffed with small potatoes. The decoration seems logical enough – the palace today still looks more like a glittering Hollywood set than anything real. The great reception room, a long glass terrace above the sea, even has dialogue to match: Raisuli told Forbes that he made murderers walk to their death from its windows – a 27m drop to the rocks. One man, he said, had turned back to him, saying, "Thy justice is great, Sidi, but these stones are more merciful."

The palace overhangs the sea ramparts towards the far end of the Medina (away from the beach). It is not officially open to visitors but if you're interested – and the interior is worth seeing – knock or enlist the help of a local and you may strike lucky with

---

ROADSIDE BIRD-WATCHING: TANGIER TO LARACHE

When travelling between Tangier and Larache, there are interesting bird habitats to be seen on both sides of the road.

A few kilometres **north of Asilah**, the dry flatlands attract wintering **great bustards** and large numbers of **common cranes**, and you're also likely to see **callandra** and **crested larks**. Hereabouts, too, and particularly between Asilah and Larache, there are wetlands and salt pans which attract the **water pipit**, **black-winged stilt**, and **greater flamingo**.

To the southeast of Larache, and accessible by car, are the **Loukos wetlands**. These marshes and pools are said to be the best spot in Morocco for spotting the **little bustard** and in winter there are four species of rails to look out for – moorhen, coot, crested coot, and purple gallinule. Amongst other birds recorded here are the squacco heron, white stork, glossy ibis, and greater flamingo. Bird-watching historians might like to note that it was close to here, around the confluence of the Oued Loukous and its tributary, the Oued El Makhazine, that the **Battle of the Three Kings** (see p.112) was fought.

A little further south of Larache is the major bird habitat in this part of Morocco, Merdja Zerga, the **Moulay Bousselham lagoon**; see p.111.

the caretaker. If you are really determined you could visit the Hôtel de Ville (the town hall) beforehand and ask them to give you a note in Arabic for the caretaker.

The **Hôtel de Ville** is to be found inland on the Tangier-Rabat road as it bypasses Asilah. Nearby is a modern, massive **monument** commemorating the passage of Mohammed V on his way to Tangier in April 1947, when he identified himself with the struggle for Moroccan independence.

There's a villagers' **market**, at its liveliest on Thursday and Sunday, held on the near side of the Tangier–Rabat road.

The beaches and the harbour

As with Tangier, the **beach** is the main focus of life in summer. The most popular stretches are to the north of the town, out towards the campsites. For more isolated strands, walk south, past the Medina ramparts, for about fifteen minutes.

For some years now there have been plans to extend the small **harbour**, providing anchorage for fishing boats and a marina for yachts. In 1995 there was even extensive advertising of the new facilities and adjoining apartment blocks, but a subsequent change of plan will now see separate provision for commercial and leisure craft – as shown on the map (p.103). At time of writing however, though the sea walls are there, they are incomplete, and the apartment block which had been built has been subsequently demolished.

Saint Bartolome

At the junction of Avenue Mohammed V and Avenue Prince Heritier, is the Church of San Bartolome, built by Franciscan priests from Galicia, in northwest Spain. The cool and airy colonial-Spanish-style interior is complemented by the nuns' own small chapel in Moorish style, with prayers common to Islam and Christianity carved in Arabic. One of the few church bells allowed to be used in Morocco is rung for Mass at 11am on Sundays and the Sisters, from a teaching order founded by Mary Ward in Yorkshire in 1585, train local girls in dressmaking, embroidery and literacy. Visitors are welcome at any time – ring the bell by the door alongside the church.

Restaurants, cafés, discos and baths

The town's most prominent **restaurants** are *El Oceano* (aka *Casa Pepe*) and *Al Kasabah,* side by side in the Place Zellaca, just outside the ramparts. Both have outdoor tables and Spanish-style fried fish; *Al Kasabah* scores for its site, with tables shaded by palms, across the road, and a roof terrace overlooking the ramparts and harbour; *El Oceano* has, alas, acquired a microwave. Further north along the seafront are a couple of similar restaurants, *Casa Gracia* and *El Espigón*, again specializing in fish and seafood, and, between the two, the popular *Café-Restaurant Le Pont.*

In the town the *Restaurant Ifrane*, on Place Mohammed V, and the *Restaurant Sevilla*, near the *Hôtel Las Palmas* at 18 Ave. Imam Assili, both serve generous helpings of Spanish-style dishes; the *Ifrane* also has the distinction of table flowers fashioned from old plastic bags. A new venture, *Café-Restaurant Al Najoum,* 11 Place Zellaca, below the *Hôtel Marahaba,* so far looks promising, serving Moroccan dishes.

Asilah's other diversions include a couple of lively **cafés,** *Café Haddou,* by the old *Hôtel Asilah,* and *Café Salam,* further along Avenue Hassan II as it turns inland. Neither café has a sign but anyone will direct you. In summer, there are **discos** at the *Hôtel Al Khaima* and at several of the campsites. Much further afield, and calling for transport, are the *Club Solitaire* and the *Atlantis* nightclub, beyond the last campsite north of town, towards the Mohammed V bridge.

Finally, ask directions to the town's small **hammam**, tucked down an alleyway in the north of the Medina. Unusually, the keeper charges Westerners a group rate and gives you the place to yourselves.

Mzoura

If you have an interest in ancient sites, you might devote a half-day to explore the pre-historic **stone circle of Mzoura**, south of Asilah. The site, whose name means "Holy Place" in Arabic, originally comprised a tumulus, assumed to be the tomb of some early Mauritanian king, enclosed by an elliptical circle of some 167 standing stones. It was excavated in 1935 and the mound is now reduced to a series of watery hollows. To the north of the circle, there still stands a tall, upright stone known as El Uted, where, legend has it, Sebastian, the young king of Portugal, lunched on his way from Asilah, where he had landed, to his death the following day at the cataclysmic Battle of the Three Kings near Ksar El Kebir. There are photographs of Mzoura, pre-excavation, in the archeological museum in Tetouan.

To reach Mzoura, follow the P2 south of Asilah for 16km, then turn left along the P37 towards Tetouan. After crossing the railway line, and 4km from the junction with the P2, turn left by the Somepi petrol station and onto a side road signposted El Yamini (aka Tnine Sidi Lyamani). From here the site is 5km northeast, across a confusing network of sandy tracks; it would be wise to enlist a guide at El Yamini.

Larache and around

LARACHE is a relaxed, easy-going town, its summer visitors primarily Moroccan tourists, who come to enjoy the beaches to the north of the estuary of the River Loukos. You'll see as many women around as men – a reassuring feeling for women travellers looking for a low-key spot to bathe. Nearby, and accessible, are the ruins of **ancient Lixus**, legendary site of the Gardens of the Hesperides.

Physically, the town looks like an amalgam of Tangier and Tetouan: an attractive place, if not spectacularly so. It was the main port of the northern Spanish zone and, though the central Plaza de España has since become Place de la Libération, it still bears much of its former stamp. There are faded old Spanish hotels, Spanish-run restaurants and Spanish bars, even an active Spanish cathedral (Mass Sat 7pm, Sun 11am) for the small colony who still work at the docks. In its heyday it was quite a metropolis, publishing its own Spanish newspaper and journal, and drawing a cosmopolitan population that included the French writer Jean Genet, who spent the last decade of his life here and is buried in the old Spanish cemetery.

Before its colonization in 1911, Larache was a small trading port, its activities limited by dangerous offshore sand bars. Without these, it might have rivalled Tangier, for it is better positioned as a trade route to Fes. Instead, it eked out a living by building pirate ships made of wood from the nearby Forest of Mamora for the "Barbary Corsairs" of Salé and Rabat.

The town and beach

The town's circular main square, **Place de la Libération** – originally Plaza de España – is a striking piece of Spanish colonial architecture. It is set just back from the sea and a straightforward 400-metre walk from the bus station and grand taxi stand.

A high archway, **Bab El Khemis**, at the centre of the square leads into the **Medina**, a surprisingly compact wedge of alleys and stairways leading down towards the port. It is now the poorest area of Larache – better-off families have moved out to the new parts of town, leaving their houses here to the elderly – but it doesn't seem so bad a place to live, artfully shaded and airy in its design. The colonnaded market square, just inside the archway, was again built by the seventeenth-century Spanish.

If you carry on through the Medina, you can reach the small Place de Makhzen, below the **Château de la Cigogne** (Castle of the Stork), a hulking, three-sided fortress from the original Spanish occupation. Standing back from here, to the right, is a palace, built by the Spanish in 1915 and now used as a music school. Opposite, overlooking the Oued Loukos and across to Lixus, is a fine esplanade and a small **museum** (daily except Mon 9am–noon & 3–6pm; 10dh), converted from a prison and containing a few Roman coins and other relics from Lixus.

The beach and coastline

If you walk from the Place de la Libération, directly to the seafront, you find yourself on another and longer promenade, Avenue Moulay Ismail. The shore below here is wild and rocky, but cross the estuary of the Oued Loukos and there are miles of fine sandy **beach** sheltered by trees and flanked by a handful of café-restaurants. You can get there by bus (#4 from the port, every 20min – some buses start from the square), a circuitous seven-kilometre route, or, more fun, from the port in a flotilla of small **fishing boats** (5–15dh per person depending on whether you haggle) which shuttle across from the base of a flight of stone steps and help you out in the shallows on the other side. From the square, the quickest route down to the **port** is along the promenade and under the crumbling ruins of the **Fort Kebibat** (Little Domes), built by Portuguese merchants in the sixteenth century.

In summer, an oddity on the beach is the variety of foreign languages you hear – yet with so few foreigners around. The explanation is the number of migrant families, scattered about Europe, who return to the town for the holiday. As well as being part of

LARACHE

Loukos Estuary

Fort Kebibat

PORT

Boats to beach

Bab El Khemis

MEDINA

PLACE DE LA LIBERATION

A

B

BCM

PLACE DE MAKHZEN

C

1

2

PTT

D

Château de la Cigogne

3

D

E

4

Archeological Museum

Spanish Cemetery

5

Lighthouse

Grands Taxis

Bus Station

RUE ALLAH BEN ABDALLAH

N

ACCOMMODATION
Pension Amal	4
Hôtel Cervantes	1
Hôtel España	2
Pension Essalama	3
Hôtel Riad	5

RESTAURANTS
Restaurant Al Khozama	E
Restaurant Larache	D
Restaurant Lixus	A
Estrella del Mar	C
Restaurant Sekala	B

0   100m

Ksar El Kebir (P2) ▽   ▽ Lixus & Asilah (P2)

communities in Barcelona, Naples and Paris, people from Larache account for most of the Moroccan community in London, and on the beach you're likely to come upon kids with disarming English accents.

For an alternative walk, head southwest of the town, **along the cliffs** towards the jail and the **lighthouse**. Before you reach the jail, you will pass the neglected Spanish Christian cemetery where **Jean Genet** is buried; the gravestone, regularly white-washed, is marked by a small handwritten card.

Larache also has a link with **Thor Heyerdahl** of Kon-Tiki expedition fame. Planning to cross the Atlantic in a vessel made of papyrus reeds, re-creating voyages believed to have been undertaken by ancient Egyptian mariners, Heyerdahl was intrigued to hear about similar craft being used in Larache. He visited the town in 1969 to find out more about the **reed boats**, known as madia, which he knew had been in use as recently as 1913 on the Oued Loukos. Anticipation turned to disappointment however, when local fishermen told him "You've come a generation too late. Here we can show you only boats of plastic." For more information on Heyerdahl's trip, see p.327.

Practicalities

Long-distance **buses**, including CTM, continue to use the town bus station, just off Avenue Hassan II (see map). There are few **banks** around Place de la Libération, but no tourist office.

Accommodation

Larache has some decent accommodation, but there's not a lot of choice. In summer, you'd be well advised to book ahead.

CHEAP

Pension Amal, 10 Rue Abdallah Ben Yasin (☎03/991 2788). Clean, quiet and friendly, this is sign-posted – off to the left down an alleyway – on the street from the bus station to the Place de la Libération. Hot showers 6dh extra and there is a hammam just down the street. ①.

Hôtel Cervantes, 3 Rue Tarik Ibnou Ziad, off Place de la Libération (☎03/991 0874). Once listed only as a fallback, this place has since been redecorated and is worth considering. ①.

Pension Essalama, 50 Av. Moulay Mohammed Ben Abdallah (☎03/991 0192). Welcoming and refurbished hotel – though the plumbing's still a problem. ①.

Hostal-Camping Flora, 3km from Larache on the P2 towards Ksar El Kebir (☎03/991 2250). This modest little hotel has a camping patch beside it, shaded and secure. It also has a restaurant. ②

MODERATE

Hôtel España, Place de la Libération/entrance at 6 Av. Hassan II (☎03/991 3195, fax 991 5628). The Grand Hotel in Spanish days – much decayed but retaining a touch of elegance. It has a range of rooms (with and without bathrooms) and prices. ③.

Hôtel Riad, Av. Moulay Mohammed Ben Abdallah (☎03/991 2626, fax 991 2629). The town's grand hotel was the former mansion of the Duchesse de Guise, mother of the current pretender to the French throne. Most of the big airy rooms overlook the gardens, tennis courts and a swimming pool, and there's a restaurant indoors, and a bar at the bottom of the garden – both open to nonresidents. ④.

Eating and drinking

Meals in Larache, except at the Medina cafés, or the sardine grills down by the port, remain resolutely Spanish. The cheapest cafés are in Place de la Libération around Bab El Khemis, the entrance archway of the Medina. The *Restaurant Sekala*, here, serves fine paella, fish and chicken tajine.

A little more upmarket, and worth trying for seafood, are *Restaurant Larache* at 18 Avenue Moulay Mohammed Ben Abdallah, next door to the *Hôtel Saada*, and the *Estrella del Mar* at 68 Avenue Mohammed Zerktouni (the other end from Place de la Libération). Take a look, too, at the *Lixus*, a grand old restaurant on Place de la Libération/Avenue Mohammed Zerktouni, and, a little further afield, *Restaurant Al Khozama* at 114 Avenue Mohammed V.

For **drinks**, the choice is between the *Hôtel Riad* bars and the downmarket *Bar Hillal*, near the *Hôtel Saada*, where you can play pinball and video games with the locals; the latter looks a dive but is friendly enough – and prices are half those in the *Riad*.

Ancient Lixus

Ancient Lixus is one of the oldest – and most continuously – inhabited sites in Morocco. It had been settled in prehistoric times, long before the arrival of Phoenician colonists around 1000 BC, under whom it is thought to have become the first trading post of North Africa. Later, it was in turn an important Carthaginian and Roman city, and was deserted only in the fifth century AD, two hundred years after Diocletian had withdrawn the empire's patronage. There are remains of a church from this period, and Arabic coins have also been found.

As an archeological site, then, Lixus is certainly significant, and its legendary associations with Hercules (see box below), are rich soil for the imagination. It has to be said, though, that the visible ruins are not especially impressive, and only around a quarter of the site has ever been excavated. Even so, if you're spending any amount of time in Larache, or passing through by car, the Lixus ruins are good for an hour or two's exploration. They lie upon and below the summit of a low hill on the far side of the estuary, at the crossroads of the main Larache–Tangier road and the narrow lane to Larache beach. It's a four- to five-kilometre walk to the ruins from either the beach or town, or you can use the bus which runs between the two; alternatively, for about 75dh you could charter one of the boats to row you over from Larache, wait an hour or so, and then row you back to the town or beach. The site is not effectively enclosed, so there are no real opening hours.

The site

The site's **Lower Town**, spreading back from the modern road, consists largely of the ruins of factories for the production of salt – still being panned nearby – and, as at Cotta, anchovy-paste *garum*. The factories seem to have been developed in the early years of the first century AD and they remained in operation until the Roman withdrawal.

A track, some 100m down the road to Tangier, leads up to the Acropolis (upper town), passing on its way eight rows of the Roman **theatre** and **amphitheatre**, unusu-

---

LIXUS AND HERCULES

The **legendary associations** of Lixus – and the site's mystique – centre on the Labours of Hercules. For here, on an island in the estuary, Pliny and Strabo record reports of the palace of the "Libyan" (by which they meant African) King Antaeus. Behind the palace stretched the **Garden of the Hesperides**, to which Hercules, as his penultimate Labour, was dispatched.

In the object of Hercules' quest – the **Golden Apples** – it is not difficult to imagine the tangerines of northern Morocco, raised to legendary status by travellers' tales. The site, too, seems to offer reinforcement to conjectures of a mythic pre-Phoenician past. Megalithic stones have been found on the Acropolis – they may have been linked astronomically with those of Mzoura (see p.107) – and the site was known to the Phoenicians as Makom Shemesh (City of the Sun).

ally combined into a single structure. Its deep, circular arena was adapted for circus games and the gladiatorial slaughter of animals. Morocco, which Herodotus knew as "the wild-beast country", was the major source for these Roman *venationes*, and local colonists must have grown rich from the trade. Amid **baths** built into the side of the theatre, a mosaic remains *in situ*, depicting Neptune and the Oceans.

Climbing above the baths and theatre, you pass through ramparts to the main fortifications of the **Acropolis** – a somewhat confused network of walls and foundations – and **temple sanctuaries**, including an early **Christian basilica** and a number of **pre-Roman buildings**. The most considerable of the sanctuaries, with their underground cisterns and porticoed priests' quarters, were apparently rebuilt in the first century AD, but even then retained Phoenician elements in their design.

Heading south towards Fes or Rabat

Heading **south from Larache**, the main road and most of the buses bypass **Ksar El Kebir** on their way towards Meknes, Fes or Kenitra/Rabat. You'll probably do likewise, though the town does have one of the largest weekly markets in the region (on Sundays). Just past here, you cross the old border between Spanish and French colonial zones. Beyond, Roman enthusiasts may want to explore the minor sites at **Banasa** and **Thamusidia**, while **bird-watchers** should head for the lagoon and local bathing resort of **Moulay Bousselham**.

Ksar El Kebir

As its name – in Arabic, "the Great Enclosure" – suggests, **KSAR EL KEBIR**, 36km southeast of Larache, was once a place of some importance. Founded in the eleventh century, it became an early Arab power base and was enlarged and endowed by both

---

WETLAND WILDLIFE

Adjoining the Moulay Bousselham lagoon is a large wetland area – recently given protected wildlife status – known as **Merdja Zerga** ("Blue Lake"). This open barren space is used for grazing by nomadic herds of sheep, cattle and goats, while around the periphery are lines of dwarf palm and the giant succulent agave.

This diversity of habitat, and the huge extent of the site, ensures rewarding **birdwatching** at all times of year. There are large numbers of waders, including a large colony of flamingoes, plus little ringed plovers, black-winged stilts and black-tailed godwits. These can be seen most easily by taking a boat trip – though at 120dh an hour this can be expensive, and make sure that you arrange to set off at least an hour before high tide or you will run aground a tantalizing distance from the birds.

For serious bird-watchers, it is the **gulls and terns** that roost on the central islands which are worthy of the closest inspection, as, among the flocks of lesser black-backed gull and black tern, it is possible to find rarer species such as **Caspian tern**. However, the campsite at Moulay Bousselham is probably the best place in Morocco to see pairs of North African **marsh owl** which usually appear hunting over the adjacent grassland ten to fifteen minutes after sunset, and the same vantage point is also a good spot for seeing **Barbary partridge**. One bird you'll certainly see wintering here, usually around cattle (and sometimes sitting on their backs), is the **cattle egret**.

The *Café Milano* in Moulay Bousselham keeps a **bird log** and will put you in touch with a local bird guide if you wish. For rarity-spotters, the grail is the **slender-billed curlew**, an endangered species, spotted once or twice in recent years; it is smaller than the European curlew with distinct spade-like markings on its flanks.

Almohads and Merenids, and perennially coveted by the Spanish and Portuguese of Asilah and Larache. It was about 12km north of here where, in August 1578, the Portuguese fought the disastrous **Battle of the Three Kings**, the most dramatic and devastating in their nation's history – a power struggle disguised as a crusade, which saw the death or capture of virtually the entire nobility. For the Moroccans it resulted in the fortuitous accession to power of Ahmed El Mansour, the greatest of all Merenid sultans.

The town fell into decline in the seventeenth century, after a local chief incurred the wrath of Moulay Ismail, causing him to destroy the walls. Neglect followed, although its fortunes revived to some extent under the Spanish protectorate, when it served as a major barracks.

Practicalities

The easiest way to get to Ksar El Kebir is by train; most of those travelling north from Rabat or south from Tangier stop at the edge-of-town station. As the motorway bypasses the town, few long-distance buses serve Ksar El Kebir – your best option is a local bus or grand taxi.

The **Sunday souk** is held right by the bus and grand taxi terminals. On any morning of the week, however, there are lively **souks** around the main **kissaria** (covered market) of the old town – in the quarter known as Bab El Oued (the Gate of the River). There is also an active **tannery** on the south side of the Medina and a handful of minor Islamic monuments scattered about. It doesn't amount to much, but if you've time to spare you might get a local to show you around – especially the souks.

If you want to stay, the *Hôtel Ksar Al Yamana*, 8 Av. Hassan II (☎03/990 7960, fax 990 4954; ②) is good value. For **meals**, the *Café-Restaurant Manar*, on the central square with the fountain, is popular and good.

Arbaoua and Souk El Arba du Rharb

Beyond Ksar El Kebir, a decaying customs post at **ARBAOUA** marks the old colonial frontier between the Spanish and French zones. There is a row of worthwhile **pottery stalls** at the border post, while two kilometres from the main road is the *Hostellerie Route de France* (no phone at present; ③).

South again, **SOUK EL ARBA DU RHARB** is the first settlement of any size, though it is little more than its name suggests (Wednesday Market of the Plain), a roadside sprawl of market stalls, with some grill-cafés and a few **hotels**, the best of which is the *Gharb Hôtel* (☎03/790 2615; ①). On the Tangier side of town is the *Grand Hôtel* (☎03/790 2020; ②), with a popular bar on the ground floor. The town is not a very compelling place to stay, though you may want to head here for transport connections to Ouezzane (a standard grand taxi run, or infrequent buses) or Moulay Bousselham (regular grands taxis take 20min; buses, if they stop at all villages en route, up to two hours).

While in Souk El Arba Du Rharb there is the opportunity to visit **Basra**, the summer retreat of Idriss II, the sultan who created Fes. To get there, head north on the P6 towards Ksar El Kebir, turning right after 9km towards Ouezzane, and, after another 12km, you arrive at a village with the ruins of Basra standing on hills above it. The tenth-century walls were demolished in the sixteenth century, but can still be traced, along with the town gates. Now it's now a pleasant viewpoint and a great place for a picnic.

Moulay Bousselham

MOULAY BOUSSELHAM, 55km from Ksar El Kebir, is a very low-key resort, popular almost exclusively with Moroccans. It comprises little more than a single street, crowded with grill-cafés and sloping down to the sea at the side of a broad lagoon and wetland area, known as **Merdja Zerga**. This is one of northern Morocco's prime **bird-watching** locations (see p.111), and any foreign visitor will be encouraged to see the lagoon's flamingo and other bird colonies in one of the locals' fishing boats. The **beach** itself is sheltered by cliffs – rare along the Atlantic – and has an abrupt drop-off, which creates a continual crash of breaking waves. While a lot of fun for swimming, the currents can be highly dangerous and the beach is strictly patrolled by lifeguards. Take care.

For Moroccans, the village is part summer resort, part pilgrimage centre. The saint from which the village takes its name, the **Marabout Moulay Bousselham**, was a tenth-century Egyptian, whose remains are housed in a koubba prominently positioned above the settlement. In July this sees one of the largest **moussems** in the region.

Practicalities

Most Moroccan visitors to Moulay Bousselham stay at the lagoon **campsite**, which is beautifully positioned but is very run-down and plagued by mosquitoes; it is open in summer only. If you don't want to camp, the alternatives in town are limited to **rooms** above the cafés.

The best of the area's **accommodation** is the *Villanora* (☎03/743 2017; ③), a family-run villa overlooking the beach and the Atlantic rollers. It's 2km out of town but an attractive place, with English owners, Alan Gabriel and his sister Jean Oliver, who are knowledgeable on local birdlife and in summer have exhibitions of Moroccan art. To get there, turn right off the main street running down to the sea, and after 2km look for the house on the left.

Most of the **grill-cafés** will fix you a mixed platter of fish – served in copious quantity and at very reasonable prices. For more of a **restaurant** meal, *L'Océan* and *La Jeunesse*, both on the main street, are good bets.

Moulay Bousselham has a **post office** and a **téléboutique** but no bank.

Banasa and Thamusida

This pair of minor Roman sites is really of specialist interest only – and for those with transport. **Banasa** lies south of Souk El Arba du Rharb, and **Thamusida** just west of the main P2 road to Kenitra.

Banasa

BANASA was settled from around 250 BC, but later enlarged by Octavian (the future Emperor Augustus) as a colony for veterans. It was linked by both land and water with Lixus (see p.110) and prospered into the second and third centuries AD, the period from which most of the visible ruins date. Within the traces of the city walls, the central feature is a forum, around which stood the capitol, a basilica (or law courts) and municipal buildings. In the town, among the houses and shops, were two public baths.

The custodian, who lives nearby, will probably notice your arrival and add a little life to the stones. He can point out a few mosaics, though most, he claims, have been removed to museums.

The site is easy to find. Leave Souk El Arba by the main road (P2) to Kenitra, then, just after Souk Tleta, turn left onto a minor road, crossing the Oued Sebou by a bridge. After 2km you reach a T-junction with the S210: turn left and, after another 2km, look for a track on the left (better signposted coming the other way, from Mechra Ben Ksiri). This leads to the ruins, which are overlooked by a marabout dedicated to Sidi Ali Boujnoun.

Thamusida

THAMUSIDA is more or less contemporary with Banasa, some 45km to the north. A Roman camp and small town, it was occupied from around 200 BC, fortified fifty years later, and abandoned by 250 AD, after fire damage. You can trace the walls of the camp and barracks, and make out a temple and baths, though the site as a whole is less extensive – and less interesting – than Banasa; its setting, however, closer to the Oued Sebou, is impressive.

There are several possible approaches to the site, which is quite tricky to find, and it's probably best to ask the help of a local. If you enquire at **Sidi Aïche** on the main road (P2), someone will be able to direct you.

Near the site there is a prominent koubba, dedicated to Sidi Ali Ben Ahmed, and a favourite picnic spot for locals. The site lies between this koubba and the river.

CEUTA, TETOUAN AND CHAOUEN

The Spanish enclave of **Ceuta** is a slightly frustrating port of entry. Although in Africa, you are not yet in Morocco, and you must make your way to the border at Fnideq, then on from there to **Tetouan**, the first Moroccan town. It can be a time-consuming business. However, if you are making for **Chaouen**, Tetouan has the advantage of regular bus connections.

The Mediterranean coast between **Fnideq** and **Martil**, Tetouan's home beach, has been developed over the past ten years, its sands colonized by large hotels, a golf course (see listings), a couple of marinas and a clutch of tourist complexes (including a *Club Med* at Smir). **Mdiq** and **Martil** are the only resorts here with much charm, though **Oued Laou**, in the shadow of the Rif, remains a "travellers' resort", with basic facilities. All are easily reached from Tetouan.

Ceuta (Sebta)

A Spanish enclave since the sixteenth century, **CEUTA** (Sebta in Arabic) is a curious political anomaly. Along with Melilla, east along the coast, it was retained by Spain after Moroccan independence in 1956 and today functions largely as a military base, its economy bolstered by a limited duty-free status. It is something of an embarrassment for the Spanish government, in the light of its own claims to Gibraltar, visible just a few sea

---

BORDER TRADE: PEOPLE AND DRUGS

Until recently, the economies on both sides of the border seemed to benefit from the enclave, spurred by Ceuta's duty-free status, but there has been growing political friction of late, aggravated by Spain's membership of the European Union (EU). The border here is the frontier between Africa and Europe and the EU is increasingly concerned about traffic in drugs and illegal immigrants, financing a £15m ($22m) hi-tech "wall" with closed circuit TV and sensors along the eight-kilometre boundary.

The money to be made from outflanking these defences has attracted equally hi-tech smugglers, trading in hash, hard drugs, disadvantaged Moroccans, and refugees from as far south as Liberia and Rwanda. The refugees are sent over to Spain nightly, often in small boats unsuited to the short but difficult crossing. Hundreds have drowned, hundreds more are arrested as soon as they land. However, many immigrants make it, either slipping away into Spain, or claiming statelessness, hence making it impossible for the Spanish authorities to return them to Morocco.

The Moroccan government, keen to gain some form of member status in the EU itself, has made efforts to stamp out the trade in both people and drugs. In the past few years, numbers of customs and police officers have been arrested and jailed. The trade, however, continues little affected.

miles across the straits. They would find it hard politically to return the colony to Morocco, and, in many ways, nobody is much interested in their so doing. Large numbers of Moroccans live and/or work in Ceuta; the local police and taxi drivers are fluent in both Spanish and Arabic; and both pesetas and dirhams are used and accepted in shops and restaurants, (though dirhams can't be used on buses, so when travelling into Ceuta from the frontier you need 75ptas/€0.5).

Note that Ceuta works to Spanish time, which is one hour (in winter) and two hours (in summer) ahead of Morocco. When **phoning Ceuta** from Morocco (or anywhere else outside Spain), you must prefix phone numbers with the international code (☎00 34). Dialling numbers within Ceuta you must include the old local code 956 as part of the new nine-digit number. To **phone Morocco from Ceuta**, you need to dial ☎00 212, followed by the local code (minus the initial zero) and number.

The town

Ceuta has a long and eventful history, with occupation by Phoenicians, Romans, Visigoths and Byzantines, prior to the Moors, who from the eighth century onwards used it as a springboard for invasions of Andalucia. The Europeans only regained

CEUTA

ACCOMMODATION

Hôtel Africa	1
Pension Charito	5
Gran Hôtel La Muralla	3
Hôtel Puerta de Africa	4
Pension Real	8
Hôtel-Residencia Skol	2
Gran Hôtel Ulises	7
Youth Hostel	6

RESTAURANTS & CAFÉ'S

China Town	A
Club Nautico	B
Gran Muralla	E
Restaurante Marina	D
Café Pizzeria Roma	C
Marisqueria Silva	F

0   200m

pre-eminence in the fifteenth century, with Portugal first taking control, and ownership passing to Spain in 1580. In 1936, the port and airstrip were used by Franco, then commanding the Spanish army garrison at Tetouan, to launch his revolt against the Spanish Republic, igniting the Spanish Civil War.

All of this notwithstanding, there's not a great deal to see – or do. The town is modern, functional and provincial in the lacklustre Spanish manner, and its most attractive part is within a couple of hundred metres of the ferry dock, where the **Plaza de Africa** is flanked by a pair of Baroque churches, **Nuestra Señora de Africa** (Our Lady of Africa – open most days) and the **Cathedral** (usually locked). Bordering the square, to the west, is the **Foso de San Felipe**, a walled moat that is all that survives of the town's fortress.

To the south of Avenida Alcalde Sánchez Prado, the ground plan of the Roman city is being revealed, whilst to the east of Plaza de la Constitución, an oldish quarter rambles up from the bottom of the long **Paseo del Revellín**. To the south, the **Museo de la Legión** (daily 10am–1.30pm & 4–6pm; free), on the Paseo de Colón, offers an intriguing glimpse of Spanish-African military history, crammed with uniforms, weapons and paraphernalia of the infamous Spanish Foreign Legion.

If you walk to the end of the Paseo del Revellín, you can continue along a circuit of the peninsula, which is known as **Monte Acho**, in little over an hour. As the buildings, three to a dozen blocks in width, gradually disappear from view, the land swells into a rounded, pine-covered slope, offering fine views out to the Rock of Gibraltar. Around midway, signs direct you to the **Ermita de San Antonio**, an old convent rebuilt during the 1960s and dominated by a monument to Franco.

And that's about it, as far as diversions go. The local authorities plan to create a town beach, but at present there are no sands to speak of – locals go by bus to **Playa**

ENTERING MOROCCO FROM CEUTA

Since the Algeciras–Ceuta ferries and hydrofoils are quicker than those to Tangier (and the ferries significantly cheaper for cars or motorbikes), Ceuta is a popular **point of entry**. Coming over on a first visit to Morocco, however, try to arrive early in the day so that you have plenty of time to move on to Tetouan – and possibly beyond. There is no customs/passport check at the port. You don't officially enter Morocco until the border at **Fnideq**, 3km out of town. This can be reached by local bus from the centre of Ceuta (turn left as you come off the ferry or hydrofoil and it is about 800m away, in Plaza de la Constitución).

At **the border**, formalities are brief on the **Spanish side** (at least, if you are leaving Spain: searches are common for those coming back – and there are long tailbacks of cars on Sunday evenings). On the **Moroccan side**, they are often convoluted and time-consuming, especially for drivers. You need a registration form (yellow or photocopied white) for yourself, and, if you have a car, an additional green form; these are available – if you ask for them – from the security *chefs* outside the frontier post. The car form requires inconvenient details such as chassis number and date of registration. If you despair of getting a form and having it processed, you can always enlist an official porter (they have badges – ask to see them) for a 10dh tip; don't get hooked up with an unofficial tout if you can avoid it. The whole business can take ten minutes on a good day, an hour or two on a bad one.

Once across and into Morocco proper, the easiest form of public transport is a shared **grand taxi** to **Tetouan** (20dh per person) or **Chaouen** (60dh per person); buses also run infrequently to Tetouan. There are **exchange facilities**, including BMCE and Banque Populaire bank offices, which accept cash and travellers' cheques, at the frontier.

Drivers should note that **petrol** in Ceuta is about 40 percent cheaper than in Morocco, so stock up as best you can.

Benzou, 6km out of town on the northern coast of the peninsula. The duty-free status of the port draws many of the Tangier expatriates on day-trips to buy cheap spirits, and Spanish day-trippers to buy radios and cameras, but neither are very compelling pursuits for casual visitors. If you do want a cheap bottle for Moroccan travels, stop at the Dumaya or Spar supermarkets opposite the Mobil petrol station on Avenida Muelle Cañonero Dato, by the port, or the Roma supermarket on Paseo del Revellin.

Practicalities

There are two **tourist offices** in Ceuta: one at the exit from the ferry terminal (☎956 501 410, fax 956 528 248) and the other a breeze-block box near the local bus terminal at the start of Paseo del Revellin. For more detailed information – or ferry tickets – you will do better at the **Flandria travel agency** at Calle de la Independéncia 1 (Mon–Sat 9am–2pm & 4.30–8.30pm; ☎956 512 074).

Accommodation

If you plan to stay overnight in Ceuta, book ahead; with its large garrison and its consumer goods, the town has a constant flow of Spanish families. Accommodation problems are compounded at **festival times**, the main events being Carnival (February), Holy Week, the Fiesta de Nuestra Señora de Monte Carmel (July 16), and the Fiesta de Nuestra Señora de Africa on August 5.

Most of the dozen or so hotels and *hostales*, and cheaper *pensiones, casas de huespedes* and *fondas* are to be found along the main thoroughfare, Paseo del Revellin, or its extensions, Calle Camoens and Calle Real. Some of the cheaper places are, as on the Spanish mainland, easy to miss, distinguished only by their blue and white signs (H for *Hostal*; P for *Pension*; CH for *Casa de Huespedes*; F for *Fonda*). There is at present no town **campsite** – ignore signs for *Camping Marguerita*, which has been closed for some time.

Hotel Africa, 9 Avda. Muelle Cañonero Dato (☎956 509 467). A comfortable, air-conditioned three-star hotel, sited right opposite the ferry terminal. ④.

Pensión Charito, Calle Arrabal 5 (☎956 513 982). The best and most welcoming of a number of small, cheap lodgings in this area (ask to be directed elsewhere if it is full). Cold showers. ①.

Gran Hotel La Muralla, Plaza de Africa 15 (☎956 514 940, fax 956 514 947). Ceuta's characterful old *parador* remains the prime choice if you can afford it. ⑥.

Hotel Puerta de Africa, Gran Via 2 (☎956 517 191). A new four-star hotel with a gleaming white atrium and quite luxurious rooms. ⑤.

Pensión Real, Calle Real 1 (☎ & fax 956 511 449). A shift upmarket from the average place in this list; a pleasant, comfortable little pensión. ②.

Hotel-Residencia Skol, Avda. Reyes Catolicos 6 (☎956 504 161). A quiet two-star hotel, 1km uphill from the centre – off our map to the west. ③.

Gran Hotel Ulises, Calle Camoens 5 (☎956 514 540, fax 956 514 546). An old and respectable four-star business hotel on a rather busy street. ⑤.

Youth Hostel (Pousada de Juventud), Plaza Rafael Gilbert 27 (☎956 515 148, fax 956 510 318). Centrally placed: take the steps up from Paseo de Revellin, past the Gran Muralla Chinese restaurant, and turn right at the top. Dormitory beds and rooms for two to six people. It is definitely open in July and August, but may also open earlier and/or later in the year. IYHFA cards are advisable. ①.

Eating and drinking

Ceuta's main concentration of restaurants is around the Plaza de la Constitución.

China Town, Marina Club (☎956 509 053). A new, cheerful and busy Chinese restaurant by the ferry terminal. Cheap to moderate.

Club Nautico, Calle Edrissis (☎956 514 400). A small fish restaurant, just off Paseo de las Palmeras and overlooking the fishing harbour. Open 1–4pm and 7pm till late. Moderate.

Gran Muralla, Plaza de la Constitución 4 (☎956 517 625). A popular, long-established Chinese restaurant with extensive menu and sweeping views over the harbour. It's located up the steps from the square and near the youth hostel. Moderate.

Restaurante Marina, on Calle Alferez Bayton, between the Paseo del Revellin and Paseo de la Marina Española. Good place for coffee and *tostadas* to start the day, or for full meals later on. Moderate to expensive.

Café Pizzeria Roma, at the junction of Calle Arrabal and Paseo de la Marina Española. A friendly pizza/pasta place. Cheap to moderate.

Marisqueria Silva, Calle Real 67 (☎956 513 715). A tiny restaurant (it's actually squeezed between nos. 65 and 67) with fish and seafood specialities. Moderate to expensive.

Restaurant La Torre, in the *Hotel La Muralla*, Plaza de Africa (☎956 514 949). Generally reckoned to be the best restaurant in town, serving Andalucian classics. Expensive.

Moving on

Leaving Ceuta **by ferry** for Algeciras, you can normally turn up at the port, buy tickets, and board a ferry within a couple of hours. The two periods to avoid, as at Tangier, are the end of the **Easter week** (Semana Santa) holiday and the **last week of August**, when the ferries can be full for days on end with Moroccan workers and their families returning to northern Europe.

If you plan to use the quicker **hydrofoil service** to Algeciras, it's best to book the previous day – though you should be OK outside the high season; details and tickets are available from the agents at Muelle Cañonero Dato 6 (☎956 516 041), by the ferry terminal.

For details of ferry services, see p.12. Be aware that all arrivals from Ceuta need to go through customs at Algeciras – and drug suspects are very thoroughly searched.

Tetouan

If you're a first-time visitor to Morocco, coming from Ceuta, **TETOUAN** will be your introductory experience to a Moroccan city with its crowded streets and noisy souks. The Medina here seems – initially – overwhelming and totally unfamiliar, and the hustlers, often dealing large quantities of *kif* from the nearby Rif mountains, have one of the worst reputations in Morocco. On the positive side, the city boasts a new university, albeit based at Martil, 11km to the east, on the coast, so people you meet are just as likely to be genuine students. Nonetheless, you do need to keep your wits about you for the first few hours, especially at the bus station where pickpockets and con men await.

Approaching Tetouan from the landward side it looks strikingly beautiful, poised atop the slope of an enormous valley against a dark mass of rock. Its name (pronounced *Tet-tá-wan*) means "open your eyes" in Berber, an apparent reference to the town's hasty construction by Andalucian refugees in the fifteenth century. The refugees, both Muslims and Jews, brought with them the most refined sophistication of Moorish Andalucia – an aristocratic tradition that is still reflected in the architecture of the Medina. Their houses, full of extravagant detail, are quite unlike those of other Moroccan towns; indeed, with their tiled lintels and wrought-iron balconies, they seem much more akin to the old Arab quarters of Córdoba and Seville.

The Spanish connection was reinforced by colonization in the early years of this century, Tetouan becoming a provincial capital of the Spanish northern protectorate, encompassing the Rif Mountains. Spanish is still the second language of older Tetouanis and there are many other reminders of mainland Spain, particularly in the cuisine and in *el paseo* – the summer evening stroll.

Orientation, arrival, information and accommodation

Tetouan is not too hard a city in which to get your bearings – or to find your own way around. Arriving by bus, or by grand taxi, you'll find yourself on the edge of the **Ville Nouvelle** at the *gare routière*. Built by the Spanish in the 1920s, this quarter of town follows a straightforward grid. At its centre is **Place Moulay El Mehdi**, with the Spanish consulate, post office and main banks. From there the pedestrianized Boulevard Mohammed V runs east **to Place Hassan II** and the **Royal Palace**, beyond which lies the Medina, still partially walled and entered through the Bab Rouah gateway.

The **Medina** is not as large as it appears and, by day at least, you won't get lost for long without coming to an outer wall or gate – beyond which you can loop back to the Ville Nouvelle. If this is your first foray into Morocco you might want to consider arranging an **official guide** at the helpful **tourist office** (☎03/996 1916; Mon–Fri 8.30am–noon & 2.30–6.30pm), a few metres from Place El Mehdi at 30 Boulevard Mohammed V.

Accommodation

Try to ignore all offers from touts and head for one of the recommendations below. You're likely to get the best deal at the **hotels**, as most of the thirty-or-so **pensions** (including the few we've listed) raise their prices well above basic rates in summer and offer little security against touts and hustlers. The high *pension* prices are partly because newly arrived tourists will pay whatever they're asked but also reflect demand. With its excellent local beaches, Tetouan is a popular Moroccan resort and rooms in July or August can be in short supply. If at all possible, phone ahead and make a booking.

There is no **campsite** in the city. The nearest which can be useful fallbacks if you have problems finding a room – are on the beach or nearby at **Martil**, 11km out (see p.125 for transport details).

CHEAP

Hôtel Bilbao, 7 Bd. Mohammed V (☎03/996 4114). This is one of the cheapest *pensions* but is centrally placed and reasonably clean, with cold showers in the rooms. ①.

Pension Iberia, 5 Place Moulay El Mehdi, third floor (☎03/996 3679). Above the BMCE bank, this place is central and clean. Hot showers extra. ①.

Hôtel Nacional, 6/8 Rue Mohammed Ben Larbi Torres (☎03/996 3290). Reasonable, old-fashioned hotel with a café and restaurant. Some of the rooms are a little dark but most have bath or shower, and the best overlook the street. ①.

Principe Hôtel, 20 Av. Youssef Ben Tachfine (no phone). A decent cheapie but gloomy rooms, some of them with shower. Midway up from the bus station to Place Moulay El Mehdi, just off the pedestrianized strip of Bd. Mohammed V. Has a ground-floor café for breakfast and snacks. ②.

Hôtel Rio Jana, 2 Av. 10 Mai (☎03/996 3677). A fallback if similar places are full – at least it's cheap and central. ①.

Hôtel Trebol, 3 Av. Yacoub El Mansour (☎03/996 2018). Right behind the bus station so very noisy if you get a room at the front; still, it's safe, clean, and has showers in some rooms. ①.

MODERATE TO EXPENSIVE

Hôtel Oumaima, Av. 10 Mai (☎03/996 3473). Central, clean and functional, offering decent value for money. There's a ground floor café for breakfast. ③.

Paris Hôtel, 31 Rue Chkil Arssalane (☎03/996 6750). An adequate if rather drab hotel in a central (and sometimes noisy) location. Still, it's clean and prices are reasonable. The restaurant opens summer only. ④.

Hôtel Regina, 8 Rue Sidi Mandri (☎03/996 2113). A small hotel with en-suite rooms, though hot water is restricted to 6am–noon. A small café serves breakfast. ④.

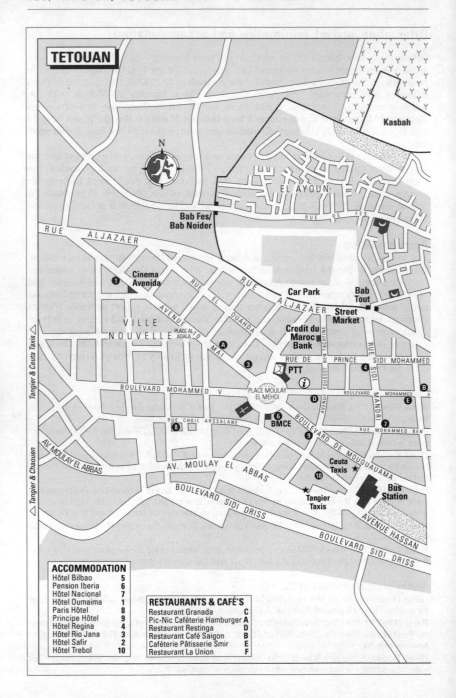

TETOUAN

Kasbah

EL AYOUN

RUE DE FES

Bab Fes/
Bab Noider

RUE ALJAZAER

Cinema
Avenida

RUE EL OUAHDA

RUE ALJAZAER

Car Park

Bab
Tout

Street
Market

VILLE
NOUVELLE

AVENUE AL 10 MAI

PLACE AL 10
ADALA

Credit du
Maroc
Bank

A

RUE DE PRINCE SIDI MOHAMMED

RUE SIDI MANDRI

Tangier & Ceuta Taxis

3

PTT

i

BOULEVARD MOHAMMED V

AVENUE YOUSSEF BEN TACHFINE

PLACE MOULAY
EL MEHDI

D

BOULEVARD MOHAMMED V

B

E

RUE CHKIL ARSSALANE

8

6
BMCE

9

RUE MOHAMMED BEN

7

AV. MOULAY EL ABBAS

BOULEVARD DE MOUQAUAMA

Tangier & Chaouen

AV. MOULAY EL ABBAS

AV. MOULAY EL ABBAS

Ceuta
Taxis

10

Tangier
Taxis

Bus
Station

BOULEVARD SIDI DRISS

AVENUE HASSAN

BOULEVARD SIDI DRISS

N

ACCOMMODATION

Hôtel Bilbao	5
Pension Iberia	6
Hôtel Nacional	7
Hôtel Oumaima	1
Paris Hôtel	8
Principe Hôtel	9
Hôtel Regina	4
Hôtel Rio Jana	3
Hôtel Safir	2
Hôtel Trebol	10

RESTAURANTS & CAFÉ'S

Restaurant Granada	C
Pic-Nic Cafétérie Hamburger	A
Restaurant Restinga	D
Restaurant Café Saigon	B
Cafétérie Pâtisserie Smir	E
Restaurant La Union	F

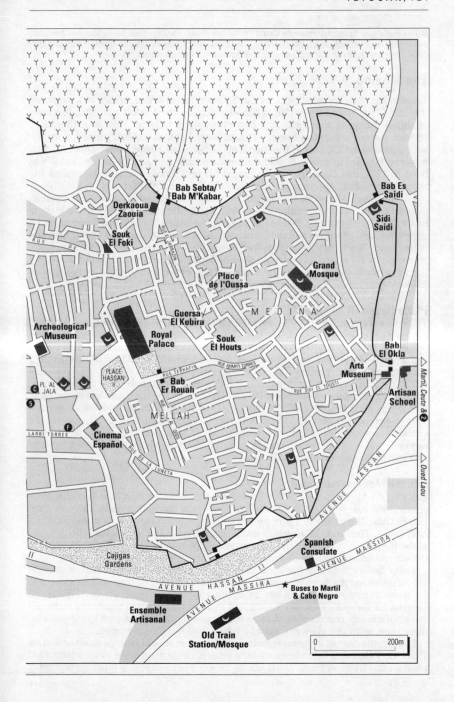

Bab Sebta/
Bab M'Kabar

Bab Es
Saidi

Derkaoua
Zaouia

Sidi
Saidi

Souk
El Foki

RUE DE FES

Grand
Mosque

Place
de l'Oussa

M E D I N A

Archeological
Museum

Guersa
El Kebira

Royal
Palace

Souk
El Houts

Bab
El Okla

PLACE
HASSAN II

Arts
Museum

RUE TERHAFIN

RUE AHMED TORRES

Artisan
School

△ Martil, Ceuta & ②

PL. AL
JALA

C

Bab
Er Rouah

RUE SIDI EL YOUSTI

⑤

MELLAH

△ Oued Laou

LARBI TORRES

F

Cinema
Español

RUE DE LA LUNETA

AVENUE HASSAN II

Spanish
Consulate

AVENUE MASSIRA

Cajigas
Gardens

AVENUE HASSAN II

★ Buses to Martil
& Cabo Negro

AVENUE MASSIRA

Ensemble
Artisanal

Old Train
Station/Mosque

0   200m

Hôtel Safir Rue Kennedy/Route de Ceuta (☎03/996 7044). Package tour hotel, 3km out from the city centre on the Ceuta road. Comfortable – with recently renovated rooms, pool, tennis and gardens – but hardly worth the extra money and out-of-town inconvenience. ⑨.

The Medina

Tetouan has been occupied twice by the Spanish. It was seized, briefly, as a supposed threat to Ceuta, from 1859 to 1862, a period which saw the Medina converted to a town of almost European appearance, complete with street lighting. Then in 1913 a more serious, colonial occupation began. Tetouan served first as a military garrison for the subjugation of the Rif, later as the capital of the **Spanish Protectorate Zone**. As such it almost doubled in size to handle the region's trade and administration, and it was here, in 1936, that **General Franco** issued his proclamation of uprising against the Spanish Republican government, beginning the Spanish Civil War.

For Tetouan's Moroccan population, there was little progress during the Spanish colonial period. "Native tradition" was respected to the extent of leaving the Medina intact, and even restoring its finer mansions, but Spanish administration retained a purely military character and only a handful of schools was opened throughout the entire zone. This legacy had effects well beyond independence in 1956, and the town, alongside its Rif hinterland, adapted with difficulty to the new nation, dominated by the old French zone. It was at the centre of anti-government rioting as recently as 1984.

Place Hassan II and the Mellah

To explore Tetouan, the place to start is **Place Hassan II**, the old meeting place and former market square. Completely remodelled in 1988, this is a squeaky-clean public square, with a shiny pavement of Islamic motifs, minaret-like floodlights at each corner and a brand-new Royal Palace – replacing the old Spanish consulate and incorporating parts of a nineteenth-century Caliphal Palace that stood beside it.

The usual approach to the Medina is through **Bab Er Rouah** (Gate of the Winds), the archway just south of the Royal Palace. The lane on the right, just before the archway, opens on to Rue Al Qods, the main street of the **Mellah**, the old Jewish quarter. This was created as late as 1807, when the Jews were moved from an area around the Grand Mosque. Very few of the population remain today, although if you ask around someone will point out the old synagogues, the oldest of which, the eighteenth-century **Yitzhak Benoualid**, remains in use.

Into the Medina: the souks

Entering the Medina proper, at Bab Er Rouah, you find yourself on **Rue Terrafin**, a relatively wide lane which (with its continuations) cuts straight across to the east gate, Bab El Okla. Along the way a series of alleys give access to most of the town's food and craft souks. The **Souk El Houts**, a small shaded square directly behind the grounds of the Royal Palace, is one of the most active: devoted to fish in the mornings, meat in the afternoons, and with an all-day smattering of local pottery stalls.

From the north side of the Souk El Houts, two lanes wind up through a mass of alleys, souks and passageways towards Bab Sebta. Following the one on the right (east) for about twenty metres you'll see an opening to another small square. This is the **Guersa El Kebira**, essentially a cloth and textile souk, where a number of stalls sell the town's highly characteristic *foutahs* – strong and brilliantly striped lengths of rug-like cotton, worn as a cloak and skirt by the Djebali and Riffian women.

Leaving the Guersa at its top right-hand corner, you should emerge more or less on **Place de l'Oussa**, another beautiful little square, easily recognized by an ornate, tiled fountain and trellis of vines. Along one of its sides is an imposing nineteenth-century

Xharia, or almshouse; on another is an artesania shop, elegantly tiled and with good views over the quarter from its roof.

Beyond the square, still heading up towards Bab Sebta, are most of the specific **craft souks** – among them copper and brass workers, renowned makers of *babouches* (pointed leather slippers), and carpenters specializing in elaborately carved and painted wood. Most of the shops along the central lane here – **Rue El Jarrazin** – focus on the tourist trade, but this goes much less for the souks themselves.

So, too, with the nearby souks around **Rue de Fes**, which is reached most easily by following the lane beside the Royal Palace from Place Hassan II. This is the main thoroughfare of a much more mundane area selling ordinary everyday goods, with the occasional villagers' **Joutia**, or flea market. At its main intersection – just to the right as you come out onto the lane up from Place Hassan II – is **Souk El Foki**, once the town's main business sector, though it's little more than a wide alleyway. Following this past a small perfume souk and two sizeable mosques, you meet up with Rue El Jarrazin just below **Bab Sebta** (also known as Bab M'Kabar).

Walk out this way, passing (on your left) the superb portal of the **Derkaoua Zaouia** (no admission to non-Muslims), headquarters of the local Derkaoua brotherhood, and you enter a huge **cemetery**, in use since at least the fifteenth century and containing unusually elaborate Andalucian tombs. Fridays excluded, non-Muslims are tolerated in most Moroccan cemeteries, and walking here you get illuminating views over the Medina and across the valley to the Rif.

Had you proceeded along the newly re-roofed main drag of Rue Terrafin/Rue Ahmed Torres/Rue Sidi El Yousti, you would have reached the eastern edge of the Medina at **Bab El Okla**. The quarter to the north of here, below the Grand Mosque, was the Medina's most exclusive residential area and contains some of its finest mansions. Walking towards the gate you see signs for a *Palais*, one of the best of the buildings, but converted into a carpet and crafts warehouse aimed at tourists.

On the far side of the Medina, and most easily accessed from the Ville Nouvelle, there is a regular **street market** by Bab Tout, spilling out of the gates and along Rue Aljazaer. This is well worth a stroll and is only a couple of blocks north of Boulevard Mohammed V.

The Moroccan Arts Museum and Artisan School

Considerably more authentic, and an interesting comparison for quality, is the **Moroccan Arts Museum** (Musée d'Art Marocain), the entrance to which is a gate in the wall just below Bab El Okla. A former arms bastion, the museum has one of the more impressive collections around of traditional crafts and ethnographic objects. Take a look particularly at the zellij – enamelled tile mosaics – and then, across the road from the gateway, is the **Artisan School** (Ecole des Métiers), where you can see craftsmen working at new designs in the old ways, essentially unmodified since the fourteenth century. Perhaps owing to its Andalucian heritage, Tetouan actually has a slightly different zellij technique to other Moroccan cities – the tiles are cut before rather than after being fired. A slightly easier process, it is frowned upon by the craftsmen of Fes, whose own pieces are more brittle but brighter in colour and closer fitting.

Both museum and school are open Mon–Fri 8.30am–noon and 2.30–6.30pm (10dh for each); the times can vary so check the clock faces outside which display opening times. The school is often closed (for most of August, for example).

The Ensemble Artisanal and Archeological Museum

Outside the Medina the most interesting sight is the **Ensemble Artisanal** on the main road below the town. The regular exhibits on the ground floor are well worth a check if you're planning to make purchases in the souks and want to assess prices and quality first. But where it scores most highly is in the displays of craftworking. Go up the stairs, at either the front or back of the main building, and you come to a fascinating array of carpet and embroidery workshops, while outside the building there are metalwork, basketry and musical instrument artisans at work.

The **Archeological Museum** is off Place Al Jala at the eastern end of Boulevard Mohammed V. It was founded during the Spanish protectorate, so it features exhibits from throughout their zone, including rock carvings from the Western Sahara. Highlights, as so often in North Africa, are the Roman mosaics, mostly gathered from Lixus and the oft-plundered Volubilis.

Other than these, the most interesting exhibits are concerned with the stone circle at Mzoura (see p.107), including a model and aerial photographs.

The Old Train Station

On the main road below the town and not far from the Ensemble Artisanal, is the **Old Train Station**. It's a singular building looking like an Aladdin's palace and was in use when a narrow gauge line connected Tetouan with Ceuta and Martil. It closed when the Spanish left, and is now a mosque with a little café beside it.

Eating, drinking and entertainment

Tetouan is a fairly small city but it offers a good spread of restaurants, some (generally dive-like) bars, a scattering of cinemas, and the chance to catch one of the best music groups in the country.

Eating and drinking

As ever, the cheapest food is to be found in the **Medina**, particularly the stalls inside Bab Er Rouah and along Rue de la Luneta in the old Mellah quarter. For variety, try one of the many places on or around Boulevard Mohammed V or Rue Mohammed Ben Larbi Torres in the **Ville Nouvelle**.

RESTAURANTS

Restaurant Granada, at the junction of Bd. Mohammed V and Place Al Jala. Spotless and cheap café-restaurant with the usual soups and tajines, and above average couscous.

Restaurant La Union (formerly known as *Restaurant Moderno*), 1 Pasaje Achaach, off Rue Mohammed Ben Larbi Torres – to find it, go through the arcades opposite Cinema Español. Excellent budget meals from an extensive menu – and with fast, friendly service. No alcohol. Open daily 9am–9pm.

Restaurant Restinga, 21 Bd. Mohammed V. Eat indoors or in a courtyard at this very pleasant restaurant that's been serving tajine, couscous and fried fish twelve hours a day (11.30am–11.30pm) since 1968. Beer available with meals. Moderate.

Restaurant Café Saigon, 2 Rue Mohammed Ben Larbi Torres. Mainstream Spanish-Moroccan cooking, despite the name. But it's a popular place, and does a good paella. Open daily 6am–midnight. Moderate.

CAFÉS AND SNACK BARS

Pic-Nic Caféterie Hamburger, 6 Av. 10 Mai. A lively snack bar for breakfast and snacks. Open 8am–10pm. Cheap.

Caféterie Pâtisserie Smir, 17 Bd. Mohammed V. Rich gateaux, sweets and soft drinks. Open 6am–11pm. Cheap.

Entertainment

The Orquesta Andalusi de Tetouan is one of the best-known groups playing Moroccan-Andalous music, a seductive style awash with oriental strings. It was founded, and is still conducted, by Abdessadaq Chekana, and his brother Abdellah leads on lute. They often play in Tetouan and you may be able to catch them locally at an official reception, or at a wedding or festival; ask at the tourist office, who may be able to help.

The orchestra has recorded with Spanish flamenco singer Juan Peña Lebrijano and has toured with British composer Michael Nyman (best known for his soundtracks for Peter Greenaway's films – and for *The Piano*). Despite such collaborations, none of them reads music; everything is committed to memory.

Two good **cinemas** are the Avenida, on Place Al Adala (off Avenue 10 Mai) and the Monumental, near the *Hôtel Principe*. The Español, near the *Restaurant La Union*, has an exclusive diet of kung fu and Indian epics.

Moving on

From the main **bus station** there are regular departures to Chaouen, Meknes, Fes and Tangier; ask around for times at the various windows, as both CTM and private companies operate on all of these routes (if it's convenient, best take the CTM). Beware of con men at the station. Tales abound of youths posing as bus officials and demanding "supplements" or "booking fees" on top of your ticket – often on the bus itself; resist and, if needs be, appeal to your fellow passengers.

Heading for **Tangier** or **Ceuta** it's easiest to travel by **grand taxi**; these are routine runs – just go along to the ranks (see map) and get a place (currently 30dh and 20dh, respectively); it's also possible to negotiate a price for **Chaouen** (around 250dh – for up to six passengers). Ceuta taxis (or buses) will drop you at the border; once there, you can walk across and pick up a Spanish bus for the 3km into town.

For the **beaches** at Martil and Mdiq – all easy day-trips – buses leave frequently through the day in summer from behind the ornate Old Train Station on the road to Ceuta, or from the bus station in winter. For **Oued Laou**, there are two buses daily from the main station (7am and 5pm), or – considerably easier – you can share a grand taxi (from the Oued Laou road junction).

If you prefer to travel by **train**, an **ONCF office** (☎03/996 7559) on Avenue 10 Mai, opposite the *Hôtel Oumaima*, sells through tickets to Fes, Rabat, Marrakesh and beyond, including a connecting bus service (currently leaving at 8.45am and 4pm) to the station of Tnine Sidi Lyamani, just south of Asilah. The Supratours bus leaves from outside the ONCF office in Tetouan.

The Tetouan beaches: Mdiq to Oued Laou

Despite the numbers of tourists passing through, Tetouan is above all a resort for Moroccans, rich and poor alike – a character very much in evidence on the extensive beaches to the east of the town. Throughout the summer whole villages of family tents appear at **Martil, Mdiq** and, particularly, around **Restinga-Smir**, further north. At **Oued Laou**, 40km southeast of Tetouan, there's a younger and slightly alternative atmosphere with summer colonies of German, French and, to a lesser extent, British and American travellers. All these places are accessible by bus from Tetouan (see above).

West: Martil and Mdiq

MARTIL, essentially Tetouan's city beach, was its port as well until the river between the two silted up. From the fifteenth to eighteenth centuries, it maintained an active corsair fleet, twice provoking Spanish raids to block the harbour. Today it is a small semi-active fishing village with a slightly ramshackle appearance, owing to unmade roads and the rows of tourist huts along the seafront. The beach, stretching all the way around to the headland of Cabo Negro, is superb – a stretch of fine, yellow sand that is long enough at 8km to remain uncrowded, despite its summer popularity and colonization by *Club Med* and other tourist complexes.

There are various options for accommodation. Arriving from Tetouan, there is a new hotel on the right, *Hôtel Café Addiafa* (☎03/968 8010; ②). Somewhat more expensive, but good value for money, is the *Hôtel Etoile de la Mer* (☎03/996 9276; ④), on the seafront by the grand taxi stand; known locally as the *Nejuna El Bahr*, it has a popular café and restaurant.

Of the **campsites**, *Camping Martil*, on the town beach, has had several unfavourable reports from readers and is not recommended. *Camping Al Boustane*, one block inland (☎03/968 8822) is small, but well maintained and friendly. A third site, *Camping Oued El Maleh*, is further out to the north (signposted from town), reached along a river bank. It's a dusty site but safe enough and has some shade and a useful shop; the beach is just 200m away, through a wood.

There are many cafés and restaurants; recommended for seafood are *Restaurant Rio Martil*, opposite *Hôtel Etoile de la Mer*, and *Café Restaurant Avenida*, 102 Avenue Mohammed V. Five kilometres towards Mdiq is the *Restaurant La Lampe Magique* (☎03/997 0822), an extraordinary place complete with cupolas, one of which is made up of nine thousand Heineken bottles and illuminated at night.

Mdiq

MDIQ is a lovely coastal village and fishing port, which can be approached via Martil or direct from Tetouan (18km on the P28). Though it is getting a little overdeveloped, its beach is superb and there are some nice places to stay. The best of the cheaper options is the seafront *Hôtel Playa* (☎03/997 5166; ②), which has a bar and a good restaurant. Nearby, but at the other extreme, is a major resort hotel, the *Golden Beach* (☎03/997 5077, fax 997 5096; ⑤). There is no campsite.

Restinga-Smir and Fnideq

RESTINGA-SMIR is more a collective name for a length of beach than for an actual place or village: an attractive strip of the Mediterranean, dominated by package hotels and holiday villages, eg *Kabila*, (☎03/966 6013, fax 966 6203) and *Club Med Smir*, (☎03/997 7146, fax 997 7046).

Many Moroccan families still camp in the woods between here and Fnideq. The rather spartan but inexpensive *Al Fraja* **campsite**, opposite the *El Andalouz* tourist complex and 15km from Fnideq, makes a good first or last stop in the country in summer; in winter it's closed.

In addition, there are several **hotels** in **Fnideq**, just 2km from the Ceuta border. The best of these is the *Hôtel Ceuta* (☎03/997 6140; ②), on the main street, Avenue Mohammed V. Fnideq, however, has little to recommend it, except a busy market for cheap Spanish goods; Moroccans from Tetouan and even Tangier come here regularly for household items and clothes.

Southeast: in the shadow of the Rif

Southeast of Tetouan the coastline almost immediately changes. For a few kilometres, the road (S608) follows the sea and the still more or less continuous beach, dotted in summer with communities of tents. Very soon, however, it begins to climb into the foothills of the Rif, a first taste of the zigzagging Moroccan mountain roads, though in this case always with the sea down below, and including the occasional swoop down to cross the estuary of a mountain stream, dry in summer but often destructive in winter

– watch out for diversions around broken bridges. Alongside the beach, near Cap Mazari, is the nicely shaded *Camping Azla* (14km from Tetouan) with a small café/shop.

Oued Laou

Tetouan is connected to **Oued Laou**, 44km away, by local **bus** (#9) and **grand taxi**, and when you finally arrive, you're unlikely to want to return immediately. A stay, in any case, is a positive option. Oued Laou is not an especially pretty place – Riffian villages tend to look spread out and lack any core. However, it has a near-deserted beach, which extends for miles on each side, particularly to the southeast, where the river has created a wide, fertile bay down to Kâaseras, 8km distant. Equally important, Oued Laou is a very easy-going sort of place and one of the best parts of the Rif to meet and talk with local people. Hustlers have nothing to hustle except *kif* and rooms, and aren't too bothered about either.

There is one **hotel** and a campsite in the area. The *Hôtel-Restaurant Oued Laou* (☎ mobile 06/182 0032; ②) is open all year round and has hot showers in winter. It's one block from the beach on Boulevard Massira and if it's full, or you want to pay less, they can find you **rooms** elsewhere – everyone knows everyone here. *Camping Oued Laou* (☎/fax 03/999 3995; open all year), alongside the municipal building, is a secure site, a hundred metres back from the beach. Camping fees are reasonable (tent 7dh) and there are also three bungalows (150dh a night). There's a small restaurant and shops nearby, and an unusual octagonal minaret. On Saturdays, there is a **souk**, held 3km inland from Oued Laou, which draws villagers from all over the valley; look for the terracotta pottery, fired locally.

East: Kâaseras, El Jebha and the roads to Chaouen

Heading east from Oued Laou is complicated without your own transport. The coast road is sealed all the way to El Jebha (see below), but only one bus a day, leaving Tetouan at 7am, travels the full six-hour-plus, 137km, route, via Oued Laou, Kâaseras, Targha and Bou Hamed.

It's no problem getting a taxi as far as **KÂASERAS**, twenty minutes from Oued Laou – and in similar mould. A tiny resort, it is geared towards Moroccans camping on the beach, though there are usually a few rooms to be had, if you ask around. If heading from Oued Laou to Chaouen, it's possible to drive along the minor road (8304) up the Oued Laou valley – which includes some impressive peaks and gorges – but it's not advisable when the road is wet, and never on a motorbike. At present, a bus from Kâaseras leaves for Chaouen at 6am, and returns in the afternoon, leaving Chaouen at 5pm.

It's also possible to keep to the coast and make a circuit to Chaouen via Bou Hamed (38km from Oued Laou) or, further on, via El Jebha (93km from Oued Laou). Bou Hamed is a largish village on a broad alluvial plain. The road from here into the Rif calls for a Fiat Uno or better still a 4x4. The Rif road (8310) from El Jebha is easier and shorter but El Jebha itself is not the most appealing of destinations – a shabby sort of place, with little beyond a lighthouse and a few fishermen's cottages.

Chaouen (Chefchaouen, Xaouen)

Shut in by a fold of mountains, **CHAOUEN** becomes visible only once you have arrived – a dramatic approach to a town which, until the arrival of Spanish troops in 1920, had been visited by just three Westerners. Two of these were missionary explorers: Charles de Foucauld, a Frenchman who spent just an hour in the town, disguised as a rabbi, in 1883, and William Summers, an American who was poisoned by the townsfolk here in

1892. The third, in 1889, was the British journalist Walter Harris (see "Contexts"), whose main impulse, as described in his book, *Land of an African Sultan*, was "the very fact that there existed within thirty hours' ride of Tangier a city in which it was considered an utter impossibility for a Christian to enter".

This impossibility – and Harris very nearly lost his life when the town was alerted to the presence of "a Christian dog" – had its origins in the foundation of the town in 1471. The region hereabouts was already sacred to Muslims due to the presence of the tomb of Moulay Abdessalam Ben Mchich – patron saint of the Djebali tribesmen and one of the "four poles of Islam" – and over the centuries acquired a considerable reputation for pilgrimage and marabouts – "saints", believed to hold supernatural powers. The town was actually established by one of Moulay Abdessalam's *shereefian* (descendant of the Prophet) followers, Moulay Rachid, as a secret base from which to attack the Portuguese in Ceuta and Ksar es Seghir. In the ensuing decades, as the population was boosted by Muslim and Jewish refugees from Spain, Chaouen grew increasingly anti-European and autonomous. For a time, it was the centre of a semi-independent Emirate, exerting control over much of the northwest, in alliance with the Wattasid sultans of Fes. Later, however, it became an almost completely isolated backwater. When the Spanish

ACCOMMODATION				RESTAURANTS	
Pension Abie Khancha	10	Hôtel Madrid	15	Restaurant Ali Baba	F
Hôtel Ahrazem	2	Hôtel Marrakesh	12	Restaurant Assada	G
Hôtel Andaluz	7	Hôtel Mauretania	11	Restaurant El Baraka	E
Hôtel Asmaa	1	Hôtel Parador de Chaouen	8	Restaurant Ben Rachid	D
Hôtel Bab El Ain	9	Hôtel Rif	14	Restaurant Marbella	A
Pension La Castellana	6	Hôtel Salam	13	Restaurant Nakhlil	H
Hostal Gernika	3	Hôtel Sevilla	16	Restaurant Tissemlal	C
Pension Ibn Batouta	5	Pension Znika	4	Restaurant Zouar	B

arrived in 1920, they were astonished to find the Jews here speaking, and in some cases writing, medieval Castilian – a language extinct in Spain for nearly four hundred years.

These days, Chaouen is well established on the excursion routes and indeed becoming a little over-concerned with tourism. There are the inevitable souks and stalls for the tour groups and a major hotel disfigures the twin peaks (*ech-Chaoua*: the horns) from which the town takes its name. But local attitudes towards tourists are generally relaxed, the Medina pensions are among the friendliest and cheapest around, and to stay here a few days and walk in the hills remains one of the best possible introductions to Morocco.

As the centre of so much *maraboutism*, Chaouen and its neighbouring villages have a particularly large number of **moussems**. The big events are those in Moulay Abdessalam Ben Mchich (40km away: usually in May) and Sidi Allal El Hadj (in August). There are dozens of others, however – ask around and you should come upon something.

Orientation, arrival and accommodation

With a population of around 36,000 – a tenth of Tetouan's – Chaouen is more like a large village in size and feel, and confusing only on arrival. **Buses** drop you at the new *gare routière*, 20–30 minutes' walk from the town centre; **grands taxis** from Tetouan and Ouezzane drop much more centrally, close to the *Hôtel Sevilla*. The marketplace and a straggle of modern buildings arc to be found in the Ville Nouvelle alongside Avenue Hassan II, which is dominated by the Ben Rachid mosque. You'll find a **PTT** and three **banks** here, all of which change money and traveller's cheques.

To reach the Medina, walk up across the marketplace to the tiny arched entrance, **Bab El Ain**, just beyond the prominent *Hôtel Magou*. Through the gate a clearly dominant lane winds up through the town to the main square, **Place Outa El Hammam** (flanked by the gardens and ruined towers of the **kasbah**) and, beyond, to a second, smaller square, **Place El Makhzen**.

Both along and just off this main route in the Medina are a number of small, **pensions**, most of them converted from private houses – rooms can be a bit cell-like, but most are exceptionally clean and remarkably inexpensive. For more comfort (and less "community life"), several of the **hotels** in the Ville Nouvelle are good value, too, and there's also an old Spanish parador in the heart of the Medina.

Chaouen's **campsite**, *Camping Azilan* (☎03/998 6979), is on the hill above the town, by the *Hôtel Asmaa* (see below), whose signs you can follow along the road; on foot, there is a shortcut through the cemetery. It is shaded and inexpensive, with a café and small shop, but can be crowded in summer, and with pensions so cheap it hardly seems worth the 2km climb.

Alongside the campsite is the *Youth Hostel*, but the warden works in the *Maison de la Jeunesse* in town. If he is not around, wait at the campsite until he arrives. 15dh per person per night.

Medina

All the recommendations below are grouped close together in the Medina and – with the exception of the *Hôtel Parador* – all charge much the same prices.

The uncertain showers in some of the pensions are mitigated by the ease of visiting the local **hammams**. The town, unusually, has separate hammams for men and women. The male one is next door to the *Pension Castellana,* off Place Outa El Hammam; the one for women, which is older and much more elaborate, is in the quarter of the souks – ask someone to show you the way because it totally defies written directions. In recent years, entrance to the hammams for tourists has been limited, and sometimes refused unless you have a group and book the hammam together. Ask your *pension*/hotel for advice, or for someone to accompany you.

CHEAP

Pension Abie Khancha, 57 Rue Lalla El Hora (☎03/998 6879). An excellent new *pension*, 30m up on the right from the Bab El Ain. A converted house, it has an open courtyard, salon and a high terrace. ①.

Hôtel Andaluz, 1 Rue Sidi Salam (☎03/998 6034). Small, basic *pension*, whose rooms face an inner courtyard – not too airy, but otherwise fine, and with a friendly management. It is signposted off to the left at the near end of Place Outa El Hammam. ①.

Hôtel Bab El Ain, 77 Rue Lalla El Hora (☎03/998 6935). A well-maintained modern conversion, just inside the Bab El Ain on the right. It charges a bit more than most of the *pensions* but the rooms are comfortable. ②.

Pension La Castellana, 4 Rue Bouhali (☎03/998 6295). Just to the left at the near end of Place Outa El Hammam – follow the signs. Aficionados return loyally to the *Castellana* each year, creating a distinctly laid-back and youthful atmosphere; others take one look at the poky rooms and leave. The key is the manager, Mohammed Nebrhout, who arranges communal meals and excursions on request. In addition, there is a hammam right next door. ①.

Hostal Gernika, 49 Onsar (☎03/998 7434). This excellent new conversion of an old house by a Spanish woman owner deserves a look. It's in the higher quarter of the Medina, going up towards Bab Onsar. Includes some en-suite rooms. ②.

Pension Ibn Batouta, 31 Rue Abie Khancha (☎03/998 6044). One of the quietest of the *pensions*, with less feel of a "travellers' hangout"; located in an alley to the left, about 70m along from Bab El Ain, beyond the *Restaurant El Baraka*. Cold showers only. ①.

Hôtel Mauretania, 15 Hadi Alami (☎03/998 6184). For the participatory: communal dormitories, as well as individual rooms, and awash with rock music most hours. Located down a maze of alleys to the southeast of Place Outa El Hammam. ①.

Pension Znika, 14 Rue Znika (☎03/998 6624). Another excellent-value *pension*, with welcoming management, and plans to add a café-restaurant on its panoramic terrace. ①.

EXPENSIVE

Hôtel Parador de Chaouen, Place El Makhzen (☎03/998 6136, fax 998 7033). The former Spanish "grand hotel", once part of the Parador chain, now reconstructed for the package trade. The bar and swimming pool help justify the expense and there are stunning views from the terrace. However, if you're only having an occasional splurge, this isn't special enough. ⑤.

Ville Nouvelle

There is more comfort in the Ville Nouvelle's purpose-built hotels and a few of them have the character to match the Medina *pensions*. None is far from the Medina, except for the hilltop *Hôtel Asmaa*.

Hôtel Ahrazem, 76 Rue Sidi Abdelhamid (☎03/998 7384, fax 998 8941). Below *Camping Azilan* this was originally the *Auberge Granade* but now is in the hands of Dr Agrazem, whose Golden Book testifies to the high standards he has established. ①.

Hôtel Asmaa (☎03/998 6002, fax 998 7158). An ugly modern building on the site of an old fort, half an hour's walk above the town. The views of the town and valley, and a swimming pool (50dh for nonresidents), are its best features. Comfortable rooms geared for package trade but not a very welcoming place. ④.

Hôtel Madrid, Av. Hassan II (☎03/998 7496, fax 998 7498). Tastefully decorated, and with a fine panoramic rooftop breakfast terrace. Fitful hot water ②; or en suite ③.

Hôtel Marrakesh, Av. Hassan II (☎03/998 7113). A bright, modern hotel, small but comfortable rooms, some en suite, plus a decent restaurant. ③.

Hôtel Rif, 29 Av. Hassan II (☎03/998 6982). This has been a popular hotel for some years. In the past, the restaurant let it down, but it is now under new management – and we await reports. ②.

Hôtel Salam, 39 Av. Hassan II (☎03/998 6239). Just below Bab El Hammam and long a favourite with individuals and groups. Back rooms and a shady roof terrace overlook the valley. Meals are served in a salon or on the terrace, which can get a bit crowded with groups at times. Overall, highly recommended. ①.

Hôtel Sevilla, Av. Allal Ben Abdellah (☎03/998 7285). A little out of the way, and quite a climb from the Medina, but a well-run place with good rooms – most en suite. ②.

The town and river

Like Tetouan, Chaouen's architecture has a strong Andalucian character: less elaborate (and less grand), perhaps, but often equally inventive. It is a town of extraordinary light and colour, its whitewash tinted with blue and edged by soft, golden, stone walls – and it is a place which, for all its present popularity, still seems redolent of the years of isolation. The roofs of its houses, tiled and with eaves, are an obvious physical assertion, in contrast to the flat ones found everywhere else in Morocco. But it is something you can sense about life in general here, even about the people themselves – inbred over many generations.

The souks and Mellah

Since the Medina is so small, it is more than ever a place to explore at random: the things which draw your attention are not so much "sights" as unexpected strands of detail. At some point, though, head for the two main squares, and for the **souks** – just below Place Outa El Hammam.

There are basic town souks held on Mondays and Thursdays in the market square, and these, to some degree, have been set up for, or at least geared to, the tourist industry. But both the quality and variety are surprising. When the Spanish arrived in 1920 Chaouen craftsmen were still working leather in the manner of twelfth-century Córdoba, tanning with bark, and hammering silver to old Andalucian designs. Although you won't see any of this today, the town's carpet and weaving workshops remain active and many of their designs unchanged. Vendors are well used to haggling with travellers, and if you're staying for a few days, prices can fall dramatically.

It's interesting, too, to observe the contrasts in feel between the main, Arab part of Chaouen and the still modestly populated Jewish quarter of the **Mellah**. This is to be found behind the jewellers' souk, between the Bab El Ain and the kasbah.

Place Outa El Hammam and the kasbah

The elongated **Place Outa El Hammam** is where most of the town's evening life takes place. It's a pretty square, with its cafés overhung by upper rooms (some the preserve of *kif* smokers), though by day, alas, it's virtually obscured by massed ranks of tour buses. On one side of the square is the town's **kasbah**, a quiet ruin with shady gardens, and a little museum of crafts and old photos (Mon–Sat 9am–1pm & 3–7pm; 10dh). The kasbah was built, like so many others in northern Morocco, by Moulay Ismail. Inside, and immediately to the right, in the first of its compounds, are the old town prison cells, where Abd El Krim (see p.138) was imprisoned after his surrender in nearby Targuist in 1926. Five years earlier, he had driven the Spanish from the town, a retreat which saw the loss of several thousand of their troops.

The *place* was once the main market square, and off to its sides are a number of small **fondouks**; one of the more visible is at the beginning of the lane opposite the kasbah. The local Djebala tribesmen, who form most of the town's population, have a particular tradition of homosexuality, and there were boy markets held here until as recently as 1937, when they were officially banned by the Spanish administration.

Place El Makhzen and Ras El Ma

Place El Makhzen – the old "government square" – is in some ways a continuation of the marketplace, an elegant clearing with an old fountain, and pottery stalls set up for the package tourists.

If you leave the Medina at this point, it's possible to follow **the river**, the Oued El Kebir, around the outside of the walls, with Bab Onsar up to your left. Here, past a couple of traditional flour-mills, you reach **Ras El Ma** (the water-head), a small, seasonal cascade in the mountainside with water so clear and cold that, in the local phrase, "it knocks your teeth out to drink it". It has long been a favourite picnic spot – and is to an extent a holy place, due to the nearby marabout's tomb of Sidi Abdallah Habti.

Over to the southeast of the town, an enjoyable, fifteen-minute walk brings you to the ruined "**Spanish Mosque**". It is set on a hilltop, with exterior patterned brickwork and an interior giving a good sense of the layout of a mosque – normally off-limits in Morocco.

Up into the hills

Alongside the path to the Spanish Mosque are some spectacular rock-climbing pitches, frequented by European climbers; and in the limestone hills behind there are active cave systems – the source of local springs.

Further afield, a good **day's hike** is to head east, up over the mountains behind Chaouen. As you look at the "two horns" from town, there is a path winding along the side of the mountain on your left. A four-hour (or more) hike will take you up to the other side, where a vast valley opens up, and if you walk further, you'll see the sea. The valley, as even casual exploration will show, is full of small farms cultivating *kif* – as they have done for years. Walking here, you may occasionally be stopped by the military, who are cracking down on foreign involvement in the crop. For more ambitious hikes – and there are some wonderful paths in the area – ask at the *pensions* about hiring a **guide**. Someone knowledgeable can usually be found to accompany you, for around 50 to 100dh a day; the harder the climb, the more it costs.

Restaurants and cafés

Compared with the hotels, Chaouen is not overstocked with **restaurants**. However, there are some good choices to search out, most of them in the back streets of the Medina.

Medina

Restaurant Ali Baba, Place Outa El Hammam. Best of the café-restaurants around the square but recommended more for the location than the food. Cheap.

Restaurant Assada, on a nameless lane just north of Bab El Ain, opposite the *Hôtel Bab El Ain*. A tiny, three-table joint, very friendly, and with fine tajines. Cheap.

Restaurant El Baraka, near *Pension Andaluz*. This is a great little place: a beautiful 150-year-old house, built for a judge and sensitively converted; the food's good, too. Cheap.

Restaurant Marbella, opposite the fountain on the square between the pensions *Valencia* and *Cordoba* (neither of which we list – ask for Rue Granada). Good simple dishes. Cheap.

Restaurant Tissemlal, again near the *Pension Valencia* (see above). For our money, the best restaurant in the Medina: a beautifully decorated old house with French-Moroccan menus. There are a few rooms here, too, if you take a liking to the place; a double room with half board costs 250dh.

Ville Nouvelle

Restaurant Ben Rachid and **Restaurant Zouar**, Rue Moulay Ali Ben Rachid – up from the Bab El Ain. Two decent small places with inexpensive, simple menus. Given the choice, the *Ben Rachid* seems more popular with the locals than the *Zouar*. Both cheap.

Restaurant Nakhlil, Av. Hassan II. A modest place, popular with locals. Cheap.

Moving on

The new **gare routière** is a 20–30 minute walk (or a taxi ride) southwest from the town centre, and problems are compounded in that CTM and most other lines start their Chaouen routes elsewhere so that buses can (despite promises) arrive full, with no available space. The best advice is to visit the bus station the evening before you plan to leave and, if possible, book a ticket in advance.

Fes is the most difficult place to get to and you may have to settle for a bus to Meknes and change there, or alternatively take a local bus or grand taxi to Ouezzane, which has a lot more bus and grand taxi traffic (including regular grand taxi runs to Fes). If all else fails, you could always backtrack to Tetouan by bus or grand taxi and travel on from there. Availability tends to be better on the routes to Tetouan, or on the daily departures to the border at Fnideq, to the coast at Oued Laou, and east to Al Hoceima and beyond.

Grands taxis can be **chartered** – a stylish way to travel to Tangier or to Fes. The cost for either trip should be around 450dh, for up to six passengers.

Ouezzane (Wazzan)

OUEZZANE, 60km southwest of Chaouen, has a fine, mountainous site, looping around an outreach of the Djebala mountains. It stands virtually at the edge of the Rif and formed the old traditional border between the *Bled es-Makhzen* (the governed territories) and the *Bled es-Siba* (those of the lawless tribes). As such, the town was an important power base, and particularly so under the last nineteenth-century sultans, when its local sheikhs became among the most powerful in Morocco.

The sheikhs – the *Ouezzani* – were the spiritual leaders of the influential **Tabiya brotherhood**. They were *shereefs* (descendants of the Prophet) and came in a direct line from the Idrissids, the first and founding dynasty of Morocco. This, however, seems to have given them little significance until the eighteenth century, when Moulay Abdallah es-Shereef established a zaouia at Ouezzane. This religious centre acquired a huge following, becoming one of the great places of pilgrimage and an inviolable sanctuary.

Unlike Chaouen, the town that grew up around this centre was not itself sacred, but until the beginning of the twentieth century Jews and Christians were allowed to take only temporary residence in one of the fondouks set aside for this purpose. Walter Harris, who became a close friend of the Ouezzani *shereefs* in the late nineteenth century, found the town "the most fanatical that Europeans may visit" and the zaouia a virtually autonomous religious court. Strange to relate, however, an Englishwoman, Emily Keane, married in 1877 the principal *shereef*, Si Abdesslem, whom she had met while out riding. For several decades she lived in the town, openly as a Christian, dispensing medical care to the locals. Her *Life Story*, published in 1911 after her husband's death, ends with the balanced summing up: "I do not advise anyone to follow in my footsteps, at the same time I have not a single regret." She is commemorated in the Anglican church in Tangier.

The Town

The **Zaouia**, distinguished by an unusual octagonal minaret, is the most striking building in the town, and though the Tabiya brotherhood now maintain their main base elsewhere, it continues to function and is the site of a lively spring **moussem**, or pilgrimage festival. (As in the rest of Morocco, entrance to the zaouia area is forbidden to non-Muslims.)

The older quarters of Ouezzane – many of their buildings tiled, gabled and sporting elaborate doors – enclose and rise above the zaouia, newer suburbs sprawling into the hills on each side. There is a grandeur in the site, though with the zaouia off limits, little of specific interest.

The main **souks** climb up from an archway on the main square, Place de l'Indépendance, behind the *Grand Hôtel*. Ouezzane has a local reputation for its woollen rugs – most evident in the weavers' souk, around Place Rouida near the top end of the town. Also rewarding is the metalworkers' souk, a covered lane under the Mosque of Moulay Abdallah Shereef; to find it, ask directions for the pleasant (and adjacent) *Café Bellevue*. The town also has a couple of Centres Artesanal – one facing Place de l'Indépendance, the other on Avenue Hassan II.

There is a large **Thursday souk** on the Place de l'Indépendance.

Practicalities

Few tourists stay in Ouezzane, as it is only a couple of hours out of Chaouen, but there are worse places to be stranded. The bus and grand taxi terminal is about 50m below the **Place de l'Indépendance**, where you'll also find three basic **hotels**, the *Marhaba*, *Horloge* and *El Elam* (all ①). There is little to choose between them though all are preferable to the *Grand Hôtel* just off the square. There is a **hammam** on Avenue Mohammed V and grill-cafés on the square.

Ouezzane provides a useful link if you're travelling by public **transport** (bus or grand taxi) between **Chaouen and the Atlantic coast**, or vice versa, or if you're moving on to Meknes or Fes (there are regular grand taxi runs to both). There are also a fair number of **buses** to Meknes and Fes, but if you're stopping or staying, buy onward tickets in advance; as with Chaouen it's not unusual for them to arrive and leave full.

travel details

Trains

Tangier Morora to: Asilah (5 daily; 50 min); Casablanca Voyageurs (3 direct and 2 connecting daily; 6hr); Fes (1 direct and 4 connecting daily; 5hr 40min); Marrakesh (1 direct and 4 connecting daily; 9hr 30min); Meknes (1 direct and 4 connecting daily; 3hr 50min); Oujda (1 direct and 2 connecting daily; 11hr); Rabat (3 direct and 2 connecting daily; 5hr); Souk El Arba (5 daily; 1hr 50min); Taza (1 daily; 8hr).

Buses

Asilah to: Larache (5 daily; 1hr).

Chaouen to: Al Hoceima (3 CTM and 8 others daily; 4hr 30min); Fes (2 CTM and 8 others daily; 5hr) via Ouezzane (2hr); Meknes (5 daily; 5hr 30min); Tangier (1 CTM and 7 others daily; 4hr 30min); Tetouan (3 CTM and 8 others daily; 1hr 30min).

Larache to: Ksar El Kebir (3 daily; 40min); Souk El Arba (5 daily; 1hr); Rabat (4 daily; 3hr 30min); Meknes (2 daily; 5hr 30min).

Ouezzane to: Meknes (2 daily; 4hr); Fes (2 daily; 5hr 30min); Chaouen (4 daily; 1hr 20min).

Souk El Arba to: Moulay Bousselham (5 daily; 35min); Ouezzane (3 daily; 1hr 30min).

Tangier to: Agadir (3 CTM and 1 other daily; 16hr); Al Hoceima (1 CTM and 5 others daily; 6hr); Asilah (30 daily; 1hr); Casablanca (37 daily; 6hr 30min); Chaouen (1 CTM and 7 others daily; 4hr 30min); Fes (3 CTM and 7 others daily; 5hr 45min); Fnideq (for Ceuta) (16 daily; 1hr); Marrakesh (2 CTM and 3 others daily; 10hr); Meknes (3 CTM and 7 others daily; 7hr); Nador (1 CTM and 7 others daily; 12hr); Rabat (6 CTM and 28 others daily; 5hr); Tetouan (3 CTM and 17 others; 1hr 30min).

Tetouan to: Agadir (4 CTM buses daily; 15hr); Al Hoceima (3 CTM and 9 others daily; 5hr 30min); Casablanca (3 CTM and 16 others daily; 6hr); Chaouen (3 CTM and 8 others daily; 1hr 30min); Fes (3 CTM and 12 others daily; 5hr 20min); Fnideq (for Ceuta) (18 daily; 1hr); Meknes (2 CTM and 7 others daily; 6hr); Larache (5 daily; 3hr); Marrakesh (5 CTM buses daily; 10hr); Nador (1 CTM and 7 others daily; 9hr 30min); Rabat (4 CTM and 28 others daily; 5hr); Tangier (3 CTM and 17 others daily; 1hr 30min).

Grands Taxis

Asilah to: Larache (40min); Tangier (40min).

Chaouen to: Bab Bered (50min); Ouezzane (1hr 15min); Tangier (2hr); Tetouan (1hr).

Fnideq (Ceuta border) to: Tangier (1hr); Tetouan (20min).

Larache to: Asilah (40min); Souk el Arba (50min).

Ouezzane to: Chaouen (1hr 15min); Jorf (change for Fes) (45min); Souk el Arba (1hr).

Souk el Arba to: Larache (50min); Moulay Bousselham (30min); Ouezzane (1hr).

Tangier to: Asilah (40min); Chaouen (2hr); Fnideq (for Ceuta) (1hr); Tetouan (1hr).

Tetouan to: Chaouen (1hr); Fnideq (for Ceuta) (20min); Oued Laou (1hr 20min); Tangier (1hr).

Ferries

Ceuta to: Algeciras (22–33 daily; 30min–1hr 30min); Málaga (2–3 daily; 1hr 30min).

Tangier to: Algeciras (12–22 daily; 1hr 30min–2hr 30min); Cádiz (2 daily; 3hr); Gibraltar (5–11 weekly; 1hr 10min–2hr 30min); Sète (1–2 weekly; 36hr); Tarifa (2–3 daily; 35min–1hr).

Flights

Tangier to: Al Hoceima (weekly; 55min); Casablanca (6 weekly; 50min).

Tetouan to: Al Hoceima (weekly; 35min); Casablanca (4 weekly; 1hr 5min)

CHAPTER TWO

THE MEDITERRANEAN COAST AND THE RIF

Morocco's Mediterranean coast extends for nearly 500km – from the Spanish enclave of Ceuta east to Saïdia on the Algerian border. The westerly reaches around Tetouan, described in the previous chapter (see pp.125–127), shelter the only established resorts. Beyond Tetouan you enter the shadow of the Rif Mountains, which restrict access to the sea to a very few points. Such beaches as there are here remain almost entirely undeveloped and for a seaside stop you really need to head east to the fishing harbour and small-time resort of Al Hoceima, or to Saïdia, beach playground for the city of Oujda, at the end of the road. Neither is much visited by foreigners, particularly since the closure of the Moroccan/Algerian frontier, though if you're making a loop east, you'll find Oujda a pleasant, relaxed city, with a scenic side-trip through the Zegzel gorges, and further gorges, cutting into the Middle Atlas, at Taza, on the Fes–Oujda road.

Between Al Hoceima and Oujda is a second Spanish enclave, **Melilla**, which with its flights and ferries to Málaga and Almería on "the mainland" sees a fair bit of traffic. Though pleasant and interesting in its way, Melilla will not tempt many for a detour if not travelling through, other than bird-watchers, who will find the dunes and lagoons spreading around nearby **Nador** among the richest sites in Morocco.

The **Rif Mountains** themselves are even less on the tourist trail than the coast – and with some reason. This is wild, isolated country, and always has been, with a tradition of dissent from central government and little relationship with the authorities. A vast, limestone mass, over 300km long and up to 2500m in height, the Rif is in fact the natural boundary between Europe and Africa, and with the Sahara it cuts off central Morocco from Algeria and the rest of the Maghreb. In the past this was a powerful barrier – it took the first recorded European traveller three months to travel from Al

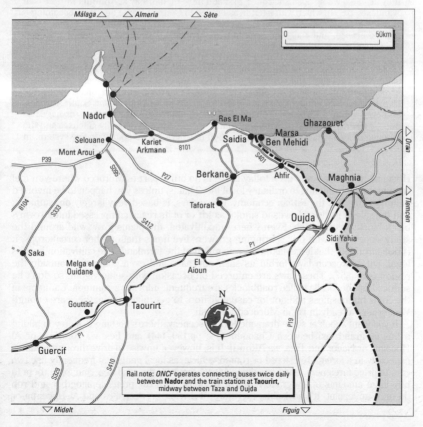

Rail note: *ONCF* operates connecting buses twice daily between **Nador** and the train station at **Taourirt**, midway between Taza and Oujda

ABD EL KRIM AND THE REPUBLIC OF THE RIF

Until the establishment of the Spanish protectorate in 1912, the **tribes of the Rif** existed outside government control – a northern heartland of the *Bled es Siba*. They were subdued temporarily by *harkas*, the burning-raids with which sultans asserted their authority, and for a longer period under Moulay Ismail; but for the most part, bore out their own name of *Imazighen*, or "Free Ones".

Closed to outside influence, the tribes developed an isolated and self-contained way of life. The Riffian soil, stony and infertile, produced constant problems with food supplies, and it was only through a complex system of alliances (*liffs*) that outright wars were avoided. Blood feuds, however, were endemic, and a major contributor to maintaining a viably small population. Unique in Morocco, the Riffian villages are scattered communities, their houses hedged and set apart, and where each family maintained a pillbox tower to spy on and fight off enemies. They were different, too, in their religion: the *salat*, the prayers said five times daily – one of the central tenets of Islam – was not observed. *Djinns*, supernatural fire spirits, were widely accredited, and great reliance was placed on the intercession of local marabouts.

It was an unlikely ground for significant and organized rebellion, yet for over five years (1921–27) the tribes forced the Spanish to withdraw from the mountains. Several times they defeated whole Spanish armies, first and most memorably at **Annoual** in 1921 (see "Contexts, p.558), which with later disasters led to General Primo de Rivera becoming – with the king's blessing – the virtual dictator of Spain. It was only through the intervention of France, and the joint commitment of nearly half a million troops, that the Europeans won eventual victory.

In the intervening years, **Abd El Krim El Khattabi**, the leader of the revolt, was able to declare a **Republic of the Rif** and to establish much of the apparatus of a modern state. Well educated, and confident of the Rif's mineral reserves, he and his brother, Mohammed, manipulated the *liff* system to forge an extraordinary unity among the tribes, negotiated mining rights in return for arms with Germany and South America, and even set up a Riffian State Bank. Still more impressive, the brothers managed to impose a series of social reforms – including the destruction of family pillboxes and the banning of *kif* – which allowed the operation of a fairly broad administrative system. In

Hoceima to Melilla – and even today there is no other part of Morocco where you feel so completely incidental to ordinary local life. That is, unless you happen to be involved in smuggling. For the Riffian economy, these days, is based very largely on cannabis, and the sale of its dried leaves to smoke as **kif** or of its resin, compressed into browny-black blocks, as **hashish**. Even where uncultivated, the plants grow wild around the stony slopes, and with prices bringing growers five times that of other cereal crops, it is not surprising that it has taken over so much of the farmland. The cultivation itself is legal, but Moroccan laws forbid its sale, purchase and even possession outside the region (see p.57). These laws are enforced on occasion with some vigour, so don't be seduced by the locals: police roadblocks are frequent, informers common. Cannabis in the Rif is big business and not for casual visitors to get mixed up in; there are enough Westerners already in jail in Morocco for hash.

If you want a look at some dramatic Riffian scenery, there's nothing to stop you taking a bus or grand taxi between Chaouen (see pp.139–144) and Fes, via **Ketama**, or Al Hoceima or Nador and Taza, via **Aknoul**. It is, however, unwise to drive through Ketama, especially in a foreign-registered or rented vehicle, as local gangsters frequently use two cars to drive foreigners (and sometimes Moroccans) off the road here and force them to buy large amounts of low-grade hash, or dispense with the pretence altogther and rob them at knifepoint. It's advisable, therefore, if driving between Fes and Al Hoceima or

their success, however, was the inevitability of defeat. It was the first nationalist movement in colonial North Africa, and although the Spanish were ready to quit the zone in
1925, it was politically impossible for the French to allow that. Intervention by French
troops tipped the balance against the rebels.

Defeat for the Riffians – and the capture of Abd El Krim at Targuist – brought a virtual
halt to social progress and reform. **The Spanish** took over the administration en bloc,
governing through local *caids* (district administrators), and although they exploited some
mineral deposits there was no road-building programme nor any of the other "civilizing
benefits" introduced in the French zone. There were, however, two important changes:
migration of labour (particularly to French Algeria) replaced the blood feud as a form of
population control, and the Riffian warriors were recruited into Spain's own armies. The
latter had immense consequences, allowing General Franco to build up a power base in
Morocco. It was with **Riffian troops** that he invaded Andalucia in 1936, and it was probably their contribution which ensured the Fascist victory in the Spanish Civil War.

Abd El Krim was a powerful inspiration to later nationalists, and the Riffians themselves played an important guerrilla role in the 1955–56 **struggle for independence**.
When, in April 1957, the Spanish finally surrendered their protectorate, however, the
Berbers of the former Spanish zone found themselves largely excluded from government. Administrators were imposed on them from Fes and Casablanca, and in October
1958, the Rif's most important tribe, the Beni Urriaguel, rose in open **rebellion**. The
mutiny was soon put down, but necessitated the landing at Al Hoceima of then-Crown
Prince Hassan and some two-thirds of the Moroccan army.

Nearly half a century later, the Rif is still perhaps the most unstable part of Morocco,
remaining conscious of its under-representation in government and its underdevelop-
ment, despite substantial school-building programmes, improved road communications
and a large, new, agricultural project in the plains south of Nador and Al Hoceima.
Labour **emigration**, too, remains high – with Western Europe replacing Algeria as the
main market – and (as in the rest of Morocco) there is widespread resentment at the difficulty of obtaining a passport and then a visa for this outlet. With the growth of more
sophisticated government systems, further tribal dissidence now seems unlikely,
though there were riots in the Riffian towns of Nador, Al Hoceima and Tetouan as
recently as 1984.

Melilla to use the main road (P1) via Taza instead; between Fes and Chaouen go via
Ouezzane (P26/P28); and between Chaouen and Al Hoceima, take the long way round via
Ouezzane, Aïn Aïsha and Aknoul (P28/P26/S304). On no account stop within the region
of Ketama for hitchhikers or people who appear to be asking for help, and if you are pursued by a vehicle while driving through the region, do not stop or allow it to overtake you,
since with one vehicle in front and another behind, you can easily be forced off the road.

On top of the Rif: the road from Chaouen to Ketama and Al Hoceima

There are very few journeys in Morocco as spectacular as that from **Chaouen** (see
p.127) **to Al Hoceima**. The road precisely – and perversely – follows the backbone of
the Western Rif, the highest peaks in the north of the country. You can look down on
one side to the Mediterranean coast, and on the other across the southern range; "big
mountains and more big mountains" – as Paul Bowles put it in a wonderful travel piece,
"The Rif, to Music", in *Their Heads are Green* – "mountains covered with olive trees,
with oak trees, with bushes, and finally with giant cedars".

HOTEL PRICE CODES

The basis of our **hotel price codes**, set out below and keyed throughout the guide, is the price currently quoted for the cheapest double room in high season (June–September).

Note that cheaper prices in the lower categories are generally for rooms with just a washbasin – you always pay extra for **en-suite** shower and WC – and that double rooms can generally be converted into **triples/family rooms**, with extra beds, for a modest extra charge. Single occupancy usually costs about two thirds the price of a double, though in some places a single person will pay the same rate for a room as two people sharing, and in other places exactly half as much. Prices quoted are for bed only, without breakfast, but including local taxes.

In Morocco

① 40–100dh	③ 150–200dh	⑤ 400–800dh
② 100–150dh	④ 200–400dh	⑥ over 800dh

In Spanish Melilla

① 1000–3000ptas/€6–18	④ 7500–10,000ptas/€45–60
② 3000–5000ptas/€18–30	⑤ 10,000–15,000ptas/€60–90
③ 5000–7500ptas/€30–45	⑥ over 15,000ptas/over €90

This is not a route to be undertaken by inexperienced drivers; although in good condition, it seems constructed entirely of zigzags and hairpin turns. More importantly, drivers of foreign or rented vehicles are very likely to be stopped and robbed.

Bab Taza, Bab Berred and Ketama

BAB TAZA, 23km out of Chaouen, is the first village of any size – an attractive place surrounded by rolling, green, flower-strewn countryside and outcrops of claret thyme. It has a Wednesday souk and a café. Ten kilometres further on is **Cheferat**, a small hamlet with a noted spring and a small waterfall which rushes under the road. Like Bab Taza, it has no hotel, though there are two cafés, one on the roadside serving grilled brochettes.

Once beyond Bab Taza, you wind around the tops of ridges, sheer drops on either side to gorges and isolated valleys. **BAB BERRED**, a smallish market village and former Spanish administrative centre, has a reasonable *pension*, the *Tizirane* (①), near the grand taxi stand. The village also signals the real beginning of *kif* country – it is surrounded, in fact, by the plants – and at **ISSAGUEN** (usually marked on maps simply as "Ketama"), 30km to the east, where the P39 from Chaouen to Al Hoceima meets the S302 Route de l'Unité, you arrive at the epicentre.

The region, **KETAMA**, even in transit, is an initiation because absolutely everybody seems to be involved in "Business". If you get off the bus at Issaguen you will immediately be offered large amounts of hash – and few locals will believe that you are here for any other purpose. Anywhere in Morocco, if people introduce themselves as "from Ketama", there is no ambiguity about what they are offering. Small-time dealers or growers here may invite you to stay at their farms – not to be recommended, even if you've got an insatiable appetite and curiosity for *kif* production – travellers tend to leave parted from their money and possessions, sometimes at knife-point. Issaguen, and the region's main village – **TLETA KETAMA**, 8km down the road to Fes – are full of gangsters and best avoided. If travelling by grand taxi from Fes or Chaouen to Al Hoceima, or vice-versa, you will probably have to change vehicles at Issaguen; if that happens, make sure you arrive early enough to be certain of getting a vehicle out. Grands taxis for Chaouen and for Targuist and Al Hoceima leave from, respectively, just west and just east of the road junction, which is where buses also stop; grands taxis for Taounate, where you change for Fes, leave 300m south of the junction. Just walking that 300m or waiting for a connecting vehicle, you are sure to be accosted by several unpleasant "hello my friend" types wanting to sell you hash. Even if you want to buy some, this is not the place to do it, and these are not the people to buy it from. If you do get stuck here, you can stay in the old Spanish *parador*, the *Hotel Tidighine*, just south of the junction (☎03/981 3016; ④), where once upon a time tourists stayed to ski or hunt wild boar on **Djebel Tidirhine**. There are also two cheap hotels just south of the *Tidighine*, towards the Taounate taxi stand, the better of which is the *Hôtel Saada* (☎03/986 3161; ①).

Roads to the coast lead off 23km before and 12km beyond Issaguen, cutting through the mountains to El Jebha (see p.127). This is a memorable trip but there are much better resorts at Torres de Alcala and Kalah Iris, accessible from the next junction (see below).

Continuing east from Ketama, with the cedar forests giving way to barren, stony slopes, you reach the town of **TARGUIST**, Abd El Krim's HQ and last stronghold (see box on pp.138–139) and the site of his surrender to the French. Paul Bowles described the place, almost forty years ago, in "The Rif, to Music", as "a monstrous excrescence with long dirty streets, the wind blowing along them, whipping clouds of dust and filth against the face, stinging the skin". It has not improved and, despite a trio of **small hotels** (all ①), would be a perverse place to stay. It does, however, have a lively **Saturday souk**, which draws villagers from the dozens of tiny communities in the neighbouring hills.

Back on the main road, 1km beyond the junction to Targuist and alongside the Shell petrol station, there is a good, modest **restaurant**, the *Targuist*, favoured by long-distance buses.

Torres de Alcala and Kalah Iris

A pair of temptingly low-key beach resorts, **Torres de Alcala** and **Kalah Iris** can be reached by a road (signposted Beni Boufrah and Torres de Alcala) 5km west of Targuist. They can be reached by grand taxi from Targuist or Al Hoceima, but no longer by bus.

Torres de Alcala

TORRES DE ALCALA is a simple, whitewashed hamlet, 250m from a small, pebbly beach. Cliffs frame its beach and on the western headland is a deserted fort, probably Spanish, with stunning views along the Mediterranean coast. It's a perfect resort-in-embryo, with – as yet – no hotel. In summer there are a few rooms available for rent and rough camping behind the small café on the beach. Other than that, there's just a bakery and the smallest of shops.

Along a rocky cliff-path, 5km to the east, are the **ruins of Badis**, which from the fourteenth to the early sixteenth century was the main port of Fes, and used for trade with the western Mediterranean states, in particular Venice. A once-considerable caravan route ran across the Rif, following the course of the modern S302 road, the so-called Route de l'Unité (see next page).

Offshore from Badis is a small island, the **Peñon de Velez de la Gomera**, which – like the islands off Al Hoceima, and Chafarinas further east – remains Spanish territory. It was this that caused the port's decline. The Spaniards occupied it in 1508, then in 1522 it passed to the Turks, who used it as a base for raids along the Spanish coast. Philip II of Spain tried to regain it, failed to do so, but destroyed Badis in the process. Subsequently, the island was used by Turkish and other pirates before, in the twentieth century, the Spanish took possession, using it until recent years as a penitentiary.

Kalah Iris

At **KALAH IRIS**, 4km east of Torres de Alcala, along a paved road, there's a longer beach, with a natural breakwater, formed by a sandspit which runs out to one of two

THE TRADITIONS OF KIF . . .

Smoking *kif* or consuming hashish is an age-old tradition in the Rif and northern Morocco. Its effects were enthusiastically described by James Grey Jackson in *An Account of the Empire of Marocco*, published in 1809:

The plant called Hashisha *is the African hemp plant; it grows in all the gardens and is reared in the plains of Marocco for the manufacture of string, but in most parts of the country it is cultivated for the extraordinary and pleasing voluptuous vacuity of mind which it produces in those who smoke it; unlike the intoxication from wine, a fascinating stupour pervades the mind, and the dreams are agreeable. The* kief, *which is the flower and seeds of the plant, is the strongest, and a pipe of it half the size of a common English tobacco pipe, is sufficient to intoxicate. The infatuation of those who use it is such that they cannot exist without it.*

The Kief *is usually pounded, and mixed with an invigorating confection which is sold at an enormous price; a piece of this as big as a walnut will for a time entirely deprive a man of all reason and intellect: they prefer it to opium from the voluptuous sensations which it never fails to produce. Wine or brandy, they say, does not stand in competition with it.*

The Hashisha, *or leaves of the plant, are dried and cut like tobacco, and are smoked in very small pipes, but when the person wishes to indulge in the sensual stupour it occasions, he smokes the* Hashisha *pure, and in less than half an hour it operates: the person under its influence is said to experience pleasing images: he fancies himself in company with beautiful women; he dreams that he is an emperor, or a* bashaw, *and that the world is at his nod.*

. . . AND THE MODERN INDUSTRY

Although many of the Riffian tribes in the mountains had always smoked *kif*, it was the Spanish who really encouraged its cultivation – probably as an effort to keep the peace. This situation was apparently accepted when Mohammed V came to power, though the

islets in the bay. There is no village as such here but a few facilities: a good, year-round **campsite** (☎03/980 8727), plus a restaurant, café, and a shop with fresh food. It is not totally undiscovered, with excursions being offered to European holidaymakers in Al Hoceima, but it's still a delightful spot.

The Route de L'Unité: Ketama to Fes

At the end of the Spanish Protectorate in 1957, there was no north–south route across the Rif, a marked symbol both of its isolation and of the separateness of the old French and Spanish zones. It was in order to counteract these aspects – and to provide working contact between the Riffian tribes and the French-colonized Moroccans – that the **Route de l'Unité** was planned, cutting right across the range from Ketama south to Fes.

The Route, completed in 1963, was built with volunteer labour from all over the country – Hassan II himself worked on it at the outset. It was the brainchild of Mehdi Ben Barka, first President of the National Assembly and the most outstanding figure of the nationalist Left before his exile and subsequent "disappearance" in Paris in 1965. Ben Barka's volunteers, 15,000-strong for much of the project, formed a kind of labour university, working through the mornings and attending lectures in the afternoons.

Today the Route de l'Unité sees little traffic – travelling from Fes to Al Hoceima, it's quicker to go via Taza; from Fes to Tetouan, via Ouezzane. Nevertheless, it's an impressive and very beautiful road, certainly as dramatic an approach to Fes as you could hope for. However, see the **warning** about driving through here on p.138.

reasons for his doing so are obscure. There is a story, probably apocryphal, that when he visited Ketama in 1957, he accepted a bouquet of cannabis as a symbolic gift.

Whatever, Ketama continued to supply the bulk of the country's cannabis, and in the early 1970s it became the centre of a significant drug industry, exporting to Europe and America. This sudden growth was accounted for by the introduction, by an American dealer, of techniques for producing hash resin. Overnight, the Riffians had access to a compact and easily exportable product, as well as a burgeoning world market for dope. Inevitably, big business was quick to follow and a quarter of a century on, Morocco is reckoned to be the world's leading producer of cannabis, supplying the vast majority of Europe's demand, and contributing an estimated US$2bn (£1.2bn) to the Moroccan economy. Even bigger money, however, is made by the dealers – mainly British, Dutch, Spanish, and Italians – who organize the shipments and sell the hash on the streets at prices fifty times higher than those paid to the Riffian growers.

The Moroccan authorities are caught between a rock and a hard place over the cannabis industry. They are pressured by Western European governments – and the UN – to take action against growers and dealers, and, given their aspirations to join the EU, have made efforts to co-operate. But the cultivation and sale of cannabis are important items in the local economy. Short of radically diversifying the agriculture of the Rif, and paying large subsidies to the local farms, little can be done to limit the cultivation. Hassan II actually announced such a scheme as long ago as 1994, promising to devote US$2.2 billion to the economy of the Rif in a programme developed with the European Union.

The EU, thus far, has come up with grants of around £50m to improve the north's infrastructure, but with an estimated 800 square kilometres of land devoted to cannabis, there is an awful long way to go. Meantime, the area under cultivation has been expanding beyond the Ketama region into neighbouring areas of the Rif, and each year the harvest seems to break all previous records, despite a drought in the region over recent years.

Taounate and Tissa

Going by bus, the village which most tempts a halt is **TAOUNATE**. The largest community along the Route, it stands on a hill above the valley of the Oued Ouerrha. If you can make it for the huge **Friday market** here, you should be able to get a lift out to any number of villages in the region. If you choose to stay overnight, there's quite a pleasant little hotel, the *Entente* (☎05/568 8291; ①), halfway down the hill on the left-hand side, with panoramic views. There are also a couple of cafés in the village.

Continuing south along the Route, there is a turning, 33km from Taounate, to **TISSA**, announced by a sign at the entrance to the village as the "Berceau des Chevaux". The region around Tissa is known for its thoroughbred Hayani horses. Here, in late September/early October, horses and riders from the region gather to compete at the annual **horsefair**. The climax is the competitive **fantasias** judged on speed, discipline and dress. Elsewhere, *fantasias* – traditional cavalry charges culminating in firing of muskets in the air – are put on largely for tourists, but these are the real thing, for aficionados.

West of Taounate

To the west of Taounate lies **RAFSAÏ**, the last village of the Rif to be overrun by the Spanish, and the site of a December **Olive Festival**. Until recently this was reached by taking the S304 towards the village of Fes El Bali – as marked on most maps – but this road has been diverted due to construction of a new reservoir, the Barrage al Wahda (see below). If you are into scenic roads and have transport, you might consider taking a forty-kilometre dirt road out from here to the **Djebel Lalla Outka**, the peak reputed to offer the best view of the whole Rif range. The road is reasonable as far as the village of Tamesnite, but thereafter is very rough *piste* – accessible only in summer.

FES EL BALI is, since 1997, to be found only on the maps. The Oued Ouerrha has been dammed – the **Barrage Al Wahda** – at Mjara, 20km downstream of the old village of Fes El Bali. The lake formed by the dam is 34km long, designed to irrigate 2000 square kilometres of the **Gharb** coastal plain and protect them from floodwaters, as well as adding ten percent to the national electricity grid.

East: Aknoul

Going **east from Taounate**, an attractive though less spectacular route heads through cork and holm oak forests towards the scattered and rather grim village of **AKNOUL**. From here you can pick up a bus or grand taxi down to Taza, or the one bus a day over to Nador or Al Hoceima.

Taza and the Djebel Tazzeka

TAZA was once a place of great importance: the capital of Morocco for periods of the Almohad, Merenid and Alaouite dynasties, and controlling the Taza Gap, the only practicable pass from the east. It forms a wide passage between the Rif and Middle Atlas and was the route to central power taken by Moulay Idriss and the first Moroccan Arabs, as well as the Almohads and Merenids, both of whom successfully invaded Fes from Taza. Each of these dynasties fortified and endowed the city but as a defensive position it was never very effective: the local Zenatta tribe were always willing to join an attack by outsiders and, in the nineteenth century, they managed to overrun Taza completely, with centralized control returning only with the French occupation of 1914.

Modern Taza seems little haunted by this past, its monuments sparse and mostly inaccessible to non-Muslims. It is, however, a pleasant market town – an easy place to get acclimatized if you have arrived in Morocco at Melilla – and its Medina is saved from anonymity by a magnificent hilltop terrace site, flanked by crumbling Almohad walls. In addition, there is a considerable attraction in the surrounding countryside – the national park of **Djebel Tazzeka**, with its circuit of waterfalls, caves and schist gorges.

Taza splits into two parts, the **Medina** and the French-built **Ville Nouvelle**, distinct quarters separated by 2km of road. The Ville Nouvelle was an important military garrison in the Riffian war and retains much of the barrack-grid character. Its focal point, **Place de l'Indépendance**, actually serves a population of 70,000, but it's so quiet you'd hardly know it.

The Medina

Buses from Place de l'Indépendance run up to **Place Ahrrache**, a busy little square overlooking the Ville Nouvelle, or you can climb up to it on the steps from the main road junction opposite the gendarmerie. Lab Photo Touzani in the southwest corner of the square sells some interesting prints from photos of Taza taken in the early days of French colonization. The **Medina**, to the west of the square, is a compact, modernized quarter – easy enough to navigate, though you may need to ask directions for the few scattered sites. The quarter spreads out from a long main street, called the **Mechouar** on its initial stretch and changing name to Rue Koubet and Rue Cherkiyne as it approaches the **Grand Mosque**.

The Andalous Mosque and Palais Bou Hamra

From between Place Ahrrache and its southern extension, **Place Moulay Hassan**, Zenqat El Andalous, which starts roughly opposite the post office, runs west to the

ACCOMMODATION

Grand Hôtel du Dauphiné	3
Hôtel de l'Étoile	6
Hôtel Friouato	5
Hôtel de la Gare	1
Hôtel de la Poste	4
Hôtel Quillaum Tell	2

RESTAURANTS

Restaurant du Jardin	A
Café-Restaurant Majestic	B
Restaurant Youm-Youm	C

TAZA

▽ *Djebel Tazzeka Circuit*

twelfth century **Andalous Mosque**. The mosque is the largest building in the southern section of the Medina – though its courtyards are characteristically well concealed from outside view. The minaret is best viewed from the Mechouar. Close by the mosque, just west of the Mechouar, is the Merenid-era **Bou Abul Hassan Medersa**. An inconspicuous building, it is usually kept locked; if you can locate the *gardien*, there are rewards to be had in a classic court and beautiful mihrab.

To the rear of the Andalous Mosque is the **Palais Bou Hamra**, the largely ruined residence of Bou Hamra, the *Rogui* or pretender to the throne, in the early years of the twentieth century. There is little to see today, but for a decade or so this was a power base controlling much of eastern Morocco. Like most protagonists of the immediate pre-colonial period, Bou Hamra was an extraordinary figure: a former forger, conjurer and saint, who claimed to be the legitimate Shereefian heir and had himself proclaimed Sultan at Taza in 1902.

The name Bou Hamra – "man on the she-donkey" – recalled his means of travel round the countryside, where he won his followers by performing "miracles". One of these involved talking to the dead, which he perfected by the timely burying of a disciple, who would then communicate through a concealed straw; the pronouncements over, Bou Hamra flattened the straw with his foot (presumably not part of the original deal) and allowed the amazed villagers to dig up the by-then-dead witness.

Bou Hamra's own death – after his capture by Sultan Moulay Hafid – was no less melodramatic. He was brought to Fes in a small cage on the back of a camel, fed to the court lions (who refused to eat him), and was eventually shot and burned. Both Gavin Maxwell and Walter Harris give graphic accounts (see "Books" in Contexts).

The souks and Grand Mosque

Taza's **souks** branch off to either side of the main street (by now Rue Koubet), midway between the Andalous and Grand Mosques. Since there are few and sporadic tourists, these are very much working markets, free of the artificial "craft" goods so often found. In fact, one of the most memorable is a souk for used European clothing – a frequent feature of country and provincial markets, the more fortunate dealers having gained access to the supplies of international charities. The **granary** and the covered stalls of the **kissaria** are also worth a look, in the shadow of the **Market Mosque** (Djemaa Es Souk).

Taza's **Grand Mosque** is historically one of the most interesting buildings in the country, though, like that of the Andalous, it is so discreetly screened that it's difficult for non-Muslims to gain any glimpse of the interior. Founded in the twelfth century by the Almohad sultan Abd El Moumen, it is probably the oldest Almohad structure in existence, predating even the partially ruined mosque at Tin Mal (see p.404), with which it shares most stylistic features. If you are Muslim, you will be able to pop in for a look at the sumptuous stucco work on the mihrab and on the domed ceiling in front of it. Like the ivory-inlaid *minbar* and the magnificent pagoda-like brass lamp overhanging the main aisle, these date from the end of the thirteenth century when the mosque was enlarged and endowed by the Merenids. For non-believers, on the other hand, even the outside of the mosque is elusive, shielded by a net of buildings; you have to walk up towards Bab Er Rih for a reasonable impression of its ground plan.

Bab Er Rih and the bastions

Above the Medina, at **Bab Er Rih** (Gate of the Winds), it is possible to get some feeling for Taza's historic and strategic significance. You can see up the valley towards the Taza Gap: the Djebel Tazzeka and the Middle Atlas on one side, and the reddish earth of the Rif behind on the other. The only drawback to this vantage point is the smell of rubbish thrown down the hillside below.

The actual gate now leads nowhere and looks somewhat lost below the road, but it is Almohad in origin and design. So, too, is most of the circuit of walls, which you can follow round by way of a **bastion** (added by Moulay Ismail, in Spanish style) back to Place Moulay Hassan.

Practicalities

City bus #1 runs between **Place de l'Indépendance** and **Place Ahrrache**, in the Medina. The train station and adjacent bus and grands taxis terminals are at the north end of the Ville Nouvelle, 2km from Place de l'Indépendance (bus #3 or #4 from Place Ahrrache), which is where CTM services will drop you. Petits taxis are available for rides between the stations, Ville Nouvelle and Medina.

Accommodation

Taza doesn't have a great choice of accommodation – and there's no longer a campsite – but you should find a room any time of year. If you're not too fussy about comfort, Place de l'Indépendance is the best location, with a scattering of cafés and restaurants nearby, but the best hotel choices are a way away, one in the Medina, the other by the station.

Hammams are to be found off Place de l'Indépendance at 34 Avenue d'Oujda (two blocks north of the *Grand Hôtel du Dauphiné*), where men and women can get clean simultaneously, though not together, with separate entrances and sections. In the Medina, the main hammam also has separate entrances, but also separate times. Men enter through the tiled doorway at 13 Zenkat Khtitl (first right up Zenqat El Andalous, the street off Place Ahrrache opposite the post office) and bathe 6pm–midnight; women enter via a similarly tiled doorway at 10 Zenqat Hadj Mimoune (second right up Zenqat El Andalous), and bathe noon–6pm.

Grand Hôtel du Dauphiné, Place de l'Indépendance (☎05/567 3567). An old Art Deco hotel, once grand as the name proclaims, though now somewhat down-at-heel. Nonetheless, the rooms are decent-sized and it's reasonable value for money. Some rooms are en suite, there's hot water mornings and evenings, and you'll find a cross-sectional plan of the Friouato cave (see p.149) in the lobby, along with some photos of French explorers visiting the cave back in 1951. ②.

Hôtel de l'Étoile, Place Moulay Hassan, the southern extension of Place Ahrrache (☎05/567 0179). This is a bargain cheapie, a friendly, family-run place with twelve decent rooms off a tiled courtyard. There are no showers but a hammam is nearby, though not much, it must be said, in the way of places to eat. ①.

Hôtel Friouato (☎05/567 2593, fax 567 2244). A rather charmless concrete outpost, set in its own grounds amid the scrubland between the Ville Nouvelle and Medina. Still, there's a functional swimming pool, a bar, and reasonable restaurant, and the rooms are pleasant, comfortable, and heated in winter. ④.

Hôtel de la Gare, Av. Prince Sidi Mohammed – opposite the train station (☎05/567 2448, fax 567 0686). Handy for transport though a long haul from the Medina. Rooms off a small courtyard with a banana tree, many with shower and toilet, and 24hr hot water. Attached are a *téléboutique*, and a café for breakfast. ①.

Hôtel Quillaum Tell, Place de l'Indépéndance (☎05/567 2347). More or less opposite the *Dauphiné*, this second-floor lodging house is a tad grim, though friendly, with grubby rooms and no showers (there's a hammam round the corner). It was here that Paul Bowles, "feverish and depressed", ended his adventures in search of the music of the Rif. ①.

Eating and drinking

Most of the **cafés and restaurants** are to be found around **Place de l'Indépendance**. The *Café-Restaurant Majestic*, a block north of the square on Avenue de Fes (daily 5am–11pm; cheap), is a good choice for brochettes, chicken or tajine, while the Restaurant du Jardin, a block northeast at 46 Rue Sultan Abou El Hassan, opposite the Bank al Maghrib (daily 11am–2am; cheap) offers pizzas as well as tasty tajines. The nicely named *Restaurant Youm-Youm* on Avenue Moulay Youssef, around the corner from the *Hôtel de la Poste* (daily 10am–10pm; cheap), has burgers and steaks along with brochettes and tajines.

In the **Medina**, you won't find any restaurants as such, though shops around Place Ahrrache will sort you a sandwich. A good place for a mint tea or a coffee and croissant breakfast is the *Andalousia* café, above *Laitrie Ahrrache* on the south side of Place Ahrrache and overlooking the square. Down below the Medina, there's a bar – and a passable restaurant – at the rather forlorn *Hôtel Friouato*.

Moving on

Taza is quite a transport junction, with good connections west to Fes, east to Oujda and north to Nador and Al Hoceima. Grands taxis and all buses other than CTM services leave from right by the train station, so virtually all transport leaves from pretty much the same place.

For **Fes** there's a wide choice of options. Grands taxis run throughout the day (just ask and wait for a place), arriving in Fes at Bab Ftouh (where you'll need to pick up a city taxi or bus to get to the hotels at Bab Boujeloud or the Ville Nouvelle). Fes is also served by four daily trains, plus a number of buses, but note that buses which originate from Nador will be subject to numerous police and customs checks en route, making the journey time rather longer. **Oujda** is easiest reached by train – a quick route across the eastern steppes, through Guercif and Taourirt (see p.150), though there are buses too.

For the **Rif**, most buses leave very early in the morning. There are plenty to **Nador** (most leaving in the morning), but only one going via **Aknoul**, the others over a more direct road via Taourirt (on the P1). There are also one or two buses each morning to **Al Hoceima**, via Aknoul. From Aknoul you can catch sporadic local buses across the southern slopes of the Rif to Taounate on the Route de l'Unité. Travelling to Al Hoceima by grand taxi, you may have to change vehicles at Kassita.

CTM buses leave from Place de l'Indépendance with daily services to Al Hoceima, Oujda and Tangier, plus two to Rabat and Casablanca, and four to Fes.

The Djebel Tazzeka and beyond

A loop of some 123km around Taza, the **Cirque du Djebel Tazzeka** is really a car-driver's route, with its succession of mountain views, marking a transition between the

---

WILDLIFE IN THE DJEBEL TAZZEKA

The **Djebel Tazzeka National Park** is one of northern Morocco's most rewarding wildlife sites, positioned, as it is, at the point where the Rif merges with the Middle Atlas. The range's lower slopes are covered in cork oak, the prime commercial crop of this area, and interspersed with areas of mixed woodland containing holm oak, the pink-flowered cistus and the more familiar bracken.

These woodland glades are frequented by a myriad of **butterflies** from late May onwards; common varieties include knapweed, ark green fritillaries and Barbary skippers. The forest floor also provides an ideal habitat for **birds** such as the multicoloured hoopoe, with its identifying crest, and the trees abound with the calls of wood pigeon, nuthatch, short-toed treecreeper and various titmice. The roadside telegraph lines also provide attractive hunting perches for such brightly coloured inhabitants as rollers and shrikes, both woodchat and great grey, who swoop on passing insects and lizards with almost gluttonous frequency.

Rif and Middle Atlas. However, it has a specific "sight" in the immense **Friouato Cave** (Gouffre du Friouato), 22km from Taza, and the whole route is fertile ground for bird-watching and other wildlife (see box). If you don't have transport, you could negotiate a grand taxi in Taza (at the rank by the train station) to take you to the cave and back, either waiting while you visit or picking you up later in the day; obviously, you'll want to pay at the end of the trip.

The cirque – and the Friouato cave

The **Cirque du Djebel Tazzeka road** starts out curling around below Taza's Medina before climbing to a narrow valley of almond and cherry orchards. About 10km out of Taza you reach the **Cascades de Ras El Oued**, a series of small waterfalls reduced to a trickle in the dry summer months. Beyond this point, you loop up towards the first pass (at 1198m) and emerge onto the Chiker Plateau. Here, in exceptional years, the **Dayat Chiker** appears as a broad, shallow lake. More often than not, though, it is just a fertile saucer, planted with cereals; geographers will recognize its formation as a classic limestone polje.

At this point, the road divides; to reach the Friouato cave, take the right fork – the left leads to Meghraoua and Midelt, see below for details. After 4km, midway along the polje, you'll pass a sign to the **Gouffre du Friouato**, 500m to the right of the road. The cave complex, explored down to 180m, is said to be the deepest in North Africa – and it feels it – entered by descending into a huge 'pot', over 30m wide, with wall-clinging steps down to a scree-filled base. From there, it's a tight squeeze through the entrance to a maze of passages which go deeper and deeper. Warm clothing is essential, as are sturdy shoes (it can be muddy), and more than one flashlight if exploring alone. If you are unused to potholing, it would be wise to employ the services of the *gardien*, who charges 75dh per person. The complex has hardly been developed but there is a small café, and a map of the system is on sale. The entrance is kept locked when the *gardien* is not in.

Beyond Friouato, the road runs up through the dark schist gorges of the Oued Zireg. At **Bab Bou Idir**, a low-key *éstivage* site 8.5km from Friouato, there is an office (sporadically open) for the **Tazzeka National Park** (see box opposite); more or less alongside, a small café and campsite operate in summer.

The most dramatic and scenic stretch of the cirque is undoubtedly the **ascent of Djebel Tazzeka** itself. It can be climbed by walking up the *piste* that turns off some 15km beyond Bab Bou Idir and serves a communication mast at the summit. The view from the top, encased in forests of cedars, stretches to the Rif, to the mountains around Fes and to much of the eastern Middle Atlas.

The road wends on pleasantly, through cork oak forests where cork production is much in evidence, to rejoin the Fes–Taza road at Sidi Abdallah Des Rhiata.

A route to Midelt

For anyone with sturdy transport (a Renault 4L should do the job), there is an adventurous route **through the Middle Atlas to Midelt**. The start of this is the left fork (route 4822) at the beginning of the Chiker plateau described above; it is paved road as far as Meghraoua, where a dirt road (very rough) takes over to Talzemt, eventually joining the P20 to Midelt at Enjil Des Ikhatarn.

Taza to Oujda

The route from **Taza to Oujda** is as bare as it looks on the map: a semi-desert plain, broken by little more than the odd roadside town. Nonetheless, if you've got time to spare, and transport, there are a trio of recommendable detours.

Msoun and Guercif

MSOUN, 29km east of Taza, and 3km north of the main road, is the first point of interest. The village, inhabited by a hundred or so members of the semi-nomadic Haoura tribe, is built within a **kasbah**, dating to the reign of Moulay Ismail (1672–1727) which is still turreted and complete on three sides. You can view its original rainwater cistern and grain silos, alongside the settlement's shop, post office and mosque. Visitors are a curiosity here and you're likely to be guided around and possibly taken off to meet the *mukhtar* (headman).

Back on the main road, just opposite the track to Msoun, is the *Motel La Kasbah* (①), a friendly place for a meal or overnight stop.

Guercif, Gouttitir, and the Cascades

At the agricultural centre of **GUERCIF**, at 37km from Taza, is another small **hotel**, the *Hôtel Howary* (☎05/567 5062; ①); it's a modest, friendly place with a reasonable restaurant at street level. Midway between here and Taourirt, you might consider a brief detour from the main road, off to the left, to the hamlet of **GOUTTITIR**. Signposted "Thermal Spring", this comprises a few buildings set around a **hot spring**, in a rocky, steep-sided gully, whose waters are pumped up to supply a hammam (used by men during the day; women after dusk). There are very basic **rooms** (no beds) and **meals** to be had nearby at the *Café Sidi Chaffi*.

There's another possible detour: north of the road, 12km on from the Gouttitir turning, are the **Bou Mazouz Cascades**. These can be reached by turning left (north) for 9km along the road to the Melga El Ouidane barrage. In contrast to the barren landscape either side of the main Taza road, this takes you past orange and olive orchards watered by the Oued Za. Look for a small mosque, with prominent loudspeaker, on the right; leave the road at this point and follow a rough track to the waterfalls – you can swim in a natural pool here, and camp beside it if you want.

Taourirt

TAOURIRT, the largest town along the route, was the crossroads between the old north–south caravan route linking Melilla and the ancient kingdom of Sijilmassa (see p.466), and the Taza corridor between Morocco and Algeria. The presence of the army (who occupy the old kasbah) and of prominent radio aerials confirms its continuing strategic importance, and for travellers it is a useful train and road junction, with buses north to Nador connecting reasonably well with train arrivals from Oujda or Fes. The town itself is of little interest, however, save for its large **Sunday souk**. There are two **hotels**, much the better of which is the *El Mansour* (☎05/669 4003; ①), just off the roundabout in the middle of the town.

Al Hoceima and on to Nador

Coming from the Rif, **AL HOCEIMA** can be a bit of a shock. It may not be quite the "exclusive international resort" the tourist board claims, but it is truly Mediterranean and has developed enough to have little in common with the farming hamlets and tribal markets of the mountains around.

If you're travelling through the Rif, you will probably want to stop here and rest a couple of days – maybe longer. It is a relaxing place, with none of the hassle of Tangier or Fes or Tetouan, and the cafés and streets full of people going about their business or pleasure. In late spring, or September, when the beaches are quiet, it's near idyllic. In midsummer, though, be warned that the town and its beaches get pretty crowded under the weight of Moroccan families and French and German tourists, and rooms can be difficult to find. It is, after all, a small town and not geared to tourism on the scale of, say, Tangier or Agadir.

The Town

Al Hoceima's compact size is one of its charms. Until the 1950s, it consisted of just a small fishing port to the north of the bay, and a fringe of white houses atop the barren cliffs to the south. At the heart of this older quarter is the **Place du Rif**, enclosed by café-restaurants and *pensions*, and the terminal for CTM and private-line buses.

The newer part of town, with its neat grid of boulevards and occasional palms, occupies the land sloping down to the cliffs above the town beach, **Plage Quemado** – between the harbour and the original village – and at every turn you can see either the wooded hills behind the town, or the sea. If this quarter can be said to have a heart, it

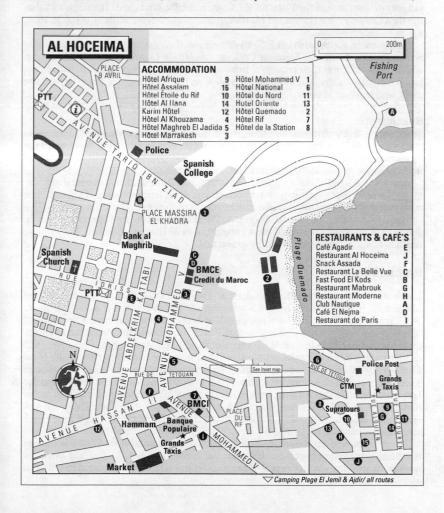

AL HOCEIMA

0   200m

Fishing Port

ACCOMMODATION
Hôtel Afrique	9	Hôtel Mohammed V	1
Hôtel Assalam	15	Hôtel National	6
Hôtel Étoile du Rif	10	Hôtel du Nord	11
Hôtel Al Ilana	14	Hôtel Oriente	13
Karim Hôtel	12	Hôtel Quemado	2
Hôtel Al Khouzama	4	Hôtel Rif	7
Hôtel Maghreb El Jadida	5	Hôtel de la Station	8
Hôtel Marrakesh	3		

RESTAURANTS & CAFÉ'S
Café Agadir	E
Restaurant Al Hoceima	J
Snack Assada	F
Restaurant La Belle Vue	C
Fast Food El Kods	B
Restaurant Mabrouk	G
Restaurant Moderne	H
Club Nautique	A
Café El Nejma	D
Restaurant de Paris	I

PLACE 9 AVRIL

PTT

AVENUE TARIQ IBN ZIAD

Police

Spanish College

PLACE MASSIRA EL KHADRA

Bank al Maghrib

Spanish Church

RUE IDRISS

PTT

BMCE
Credit du Maroc

AVENUE ABDELKRIM KATTABI

AVENUE MOHAMMED V

Plage Quemado

RUE DE TETOUAN

N

See Inset map

Police Post

RUE DE TETOUAN

CTM

Grands Taxis

Supratours

RUE ABBOUYEN

RUE IMOUREN

AVENUE HASSAN

RUE DE TETOUAN

BMCI

AVENUE MOHAMMED V

PLACE DU RIF

Hammam

Banque Populaire

Grands Taxis

MOHAMMED V

Market

▽ *Camping Plage El Jemil & Ajdir/ all routes*

is the **Place Massira El Khadra**, a squeaky-clean square on the cliff top, at the upper end of **Avenue Mohammed V**, the principal boulevard.

From some vantage points, you get a view of the **Peñon de Alhucemas**, another of the Spanish-owned islands off this coast (and another former penitentiary), over in the bay to the east of town. It's a pretty focal point, topped with sugar-white houses, a church and tower. The Spanish took it in 1673 and have held it ever since – a perennial source of dispute between Morocco and Spain. Some Moroccan patriots refer to it as the *Ile de N'Kor*, after the Oued Nekor, which flows into the bay.

There seems, however, no lobby for a change of name for Al Hoceima itself, which was developed by the Spanish after their counter-offensive in the Rif in 1925 (see pp.138–139), and was known by them as **Villa Sanjuro**. The name commemorated the Spanish General José Sanjuro, who landed in the bay, under the cover of Spanish and French warships, with an expeditionary force – and it is still occasionally used for the old part of town around the Place du Rif. Coincidentally, it was at Al Hoceima, too, that the then Crown Prince Hassan led Moroccan forces to quell the Riffians' revolt in 1958, following independence.

Names aside, the Spanish left little to distinguish their occupation. The only notable architectural feature is the **Spanish College**, the *Misión Cultural Española Marruecos*, which, until 1956, was their provincial headquarters. It is the custard cream and chocolate building, with blue and white *azulejos* tiles, on the north edge of town, beyond the main square, Place Massira.

Beaches

Swimming – and walking in the olive-groved hills if you want a change – is the main attraction of Al Hoceima. If you wake early enough it is worth going down to **Plage Quemado**, the town beach, to watch the lamparo fishermen coming in; they work at night using acetylene lamps to attract and dazzle the fish.

Besides Quemado, there is a less crowded beach at **Asfiha**, a kilometre west of town, along the Ajdir road (a cheap petit taxi ride, if you don't fancy walking). This stretches right round the bay to Djebel Hadid, the headland to the east.

There are further beaches at Torres de Alcala and Kalah Iris (see p.141), which, although 60km away, are nevertheless thought of as Al Hoceima beaches. They can be reached along a minor inland road by grand taxi.

Practicalities

There is a helpful **tourist office** on Avenue Tariq Ibn Ziad, 300m northwest of Place Massira El Khadra (Mon–Thurs 8.30am–noon & 2.30–6.30pm, Fri 8.30–11.30am & 3–6.30pm; ☎03/998 1185). There are plenty of **banks** in town, including the Bank al Maghrib in Place Massira El Khadra, and BMCE and Credit du Maroc next to each other on Avenue Mohammed V. Numerous hotels and travel agents, however, will change money faster, at the same rates, and at times when banks are closed (the *Hotel Étoile du Rif* for example, 8am–9pm daily), so you shouldn't need to waste your time in a bank here at all, unless trying to extract cash from your plastic. If you need to use the **Internet**, the cheapest and most convenient place is Club Computer Al Hoceima just of Place du Rif at 46 Rue Tetouan (daily 9am–noon & 3–10pm; 10dh/hr). There are several **pharmacies** around town – one on Avenue Hassan II, 50m east of the *Karim Hôtel*, stays open all night.

The most convenient **hammam** is at 12 Rue Azzalaga, parallel with Avenue Hassan II behind the Banque Populaire. It's near the centre and easy to find and open for women 10am–5pm, and for men 5–10am & 5–9pm – a picture hung outside tells you which sex is in occupation.

Accommodation

Most of the cheaper *pensions* are grouped in and around the Place du Rif; they are reasonable, if basic; there are also a couple of more upmarket options.

CHEAP

Hôtel Afrique, 20 Rue Al Alaouiyine (☎03/998 3065). An old *pension* with bright, airy rooms, and showers on the corridor. It's just off the Place du Rif, so reasonably quiet. ①.

Hôtel Assalam, 10 Place du Rif (☎03/998 1413). A larger *pension* than most, and not the cleanest in town, with a café on the ground floor. Some rooms have balconies and some have showers, which are cold, though hot common ones are available. ①.

Hôtel Etoile du Rif, 40 Place du Rif (☎03/984 08 47 or 48, fax 998 5696). The former *Hotel Florido*, an ornate Spanish building in the middle of the square, with a lively café downstairs. Now refurbished, this is still the best-value hotel in town, though not as cheap as it was, with bright, clean, en suite rooms, the best ones overlooking the square. ②.

Hôtel al Hana, 17 Rue Imzouren (☎03/998 1642). A decent place with simple but clean rooms. ①.

Karim Hôtel, 27 Av. Hassan II (☎03/998 2184, fax 998 1903). An old but comfortable hotel near the covered market, with small en-suite rooms, a restaurant and a bar (which can be noisy). ②.

Hôtel Marrakesh, 2 Rue Abdallah Hammou (☎03/998 3025, fax 998 1058). A small hotel, whose clean, comfortable rooms are all en suite, with reliable hot water; all in all, pretty good value for money. ②.

Hôtel du Nord, 20 Rue Imzouren (☎03/998 3079). Cleaner than a lot of the cheapies. Some rooms have balconies and hot showers are available. ①.

Hotel Oriente, Place du Rif (☎03/998 2246). Not a bad place for the price. Not all rooms have external windows, but some which do also have balconies. ①.

Hôtel Rif, 13 Rue Moulay Youssef (☎03/998 2268). Quite a large place, off the Place du Rif, in the jewellers' quarter. Simple but clean rooms with showers on the corridor. ①.

Hôtel de Station, Place du Rif (☎03/998 3096). A friendly place with lower prices than any of the above. Rooms #7, #14 and #20 have balconies overlooking the square. Showers are cold but there's a hammam not far away. ①.

MODERATE TO EXPENSIVE

Hôtel Al Khouzama, Rue Al Andalous (☎03/998 5669 or 81, fax 998 5696). A modern hotel, with en-suite rooms and a pool room. Windows facing onto the street are much brighter than those facing into a light well. ④.

Hôtel Maghreb El Jadida, 56 Av. Mohammed V (☎03/998 2504, fax 998 2505). The best upmarket choice: a central hotel, with a top-floor restaurant and bar. ④.

Hôtel Mohammed V, Place Massira El Khadra (☎03/998 2233 or 34, fax 998 3314). The old state-run grand hotel, privatized and reopened in 1995, with all mod cons, great beach views, and a terrace restaurant to enjoy them from over breakfast. ⑤.

Hôtel National, 23 Rue de Tetouan (☎03/998 2681, fax 998 1123). A central location, close to buses in Place du Rif, ensures the popularity of this oldish hotel, with a/c and heating in all rooms, TV in some. ④.

Hôtel Quemado, Plage Quemado (☎03/998 3315 or 16, fax 998 3314). Four ugly barrack blocks plus thirty bungalows and chalets constitute this package hotel, open summer only, the only hotel on the beach. It is used by tour groups, so book ahead. Includes a bar, restaurant and disco. ④.

CAMPSITES

Camping Plage El Jamil (aka Camping Cala Bonita), 500m east of town along the Ajdir road (☎03/998 4026). A small, friendly site, open year-round, and backing onto a stony beach, with pedalos on offer; there is also a bar and restaurant and, in summer, a café and a grocery store, plus a firm doing water-skiing on the beach.

Club Méditerranée, 10km out of town, past Ajdir, off the Ketama–Nador road (☎03/980 2013 or 41, fax 980 2014). The largest *Club* in Morocco, with space for 1250 campers, sleeping two to a straw-roofed, concrete-based hut. Extensive facilities. Very French atmosphere. You generally have to book ahead, and for at least a week, through the *Club* offices in Casablanca (☎02/231 1906) or London (☎020/7581 1161). Open mid-June to mid-September.

Restaurants and nightlife

Al Hoceima has quite a lot of good, cheap eateries, though nothing very upmarket, nor much in the way of nightlife, beyond the Hôtel Quemado's Jupiter **disco** at the main beach (open year-round, 11pm–3am or later) or discreet **bars** on the top floors of the hotels Quemado and Maghreb El Jadida. **Cafés** offering omelettes, croissants, or bread and jam for breakfast include the *Hôtel Etoile du Rif* in Place du Rif, the *Café Agadir* on the corner of Avenue Abdelkrim Kattabi and Rue Idriss I, and the *Café El Nejma* next door to the *Belle Vue* (see below) on Avenue Mohammed V by Place Massira El Khadra.

Restaurant Al Hoceima, Place du Rif. A reliable place for inexpensive fare at any time – mainly brochettes and tajines. Open 24hr. Cheap.

Snack Assada, 24 Av. Hassan II. A small place but with a good selection of snacks or basic meals. Daily 9am–10pm. Cheap.

Restaurant La Belle Vue, Av. Mohammed V by Place Massira El Khadra. A café all year, and a fully fledged restaurant in summer, with fish, meat, tajines and paella, plus great views. Daily 5am–11pm. Cheap.

Club Nautique, by the fishing port (☎03/998 1461). The best place in town to tuck into freshly landed, freshly cooked fish and seafood of various sorts. Licensed. Daily 7am–1am. Moderate.

Fast Food El Kods, Place Massira El Khadra. A snack bar offering portions of various meats sold, as in many cheap places here, by weight. Daily 11am–10pm. Cheap.

Restaurant Mabrouk, 18 Rue Alouien. Another small basic restaurant, serving fish, tajine and chicken. Daily 7am–11pm. Cheap.

Hôtel Maghreb El Jadida, 56 Av. Mohammed V (☎03/998 2504). This hotel's top-floor licensed restaurant is a good choice for upmarket eating. Daily noon–3pm & 7–10pm. Moderate.

Restaurant Moderne, 15 Place du Rif. Big platefuls of meat or fish with vegetables – good hearty fare. Daily 10am–11pm. Cheap.

Restaurant de Paris, 21 Av. Mohammed V (upstairs). A good, friendly and homely family-run restaurant with a choice of several differently priced (but all good-value) set menus. Daily 7.30am–11.30pm. Cheap.

Moving on

Buses tend to leave Al Hoceima early, especially heading eastward. All depart from Place du Rif, where CTM and various other companies have offices. All Oujda buses leave in the morning, plus one very late at night indeed, while the last bus for Nador currently leaves at 3.30pm. Some of the Nador buses continue to the Melilla border. For Targuist, Ketama, Chaouen, Tetouan and Tangier, there are departures both morning and evening, as there are (though fewer) for Fes, Meknes, Rabat and Casablanca. **Grands taxis** hang out in two posses: those bound for Nador, Oujda and Taza gather in Rue Alouien, just east of Place du Rif, while those with destinations like Targuist, Issaguen, Beni Ahdiba and Kalah Iris are to be found in Rue Raya al Maghribia, off Avenue Mohammed V by the *Paris* restaurant. For Chaouen, you have to change at Issaguen, a place that you can avoid if travelling to Fes by going via Taza instead, though the latter is the less scenic route.

The local **airport**, Aeroport Charif Al Idriss, is 17km east of Al Hoceima on the Nador road (P39), just before the village of Imzouen (☎03/998 2560). It caters largely for charter flights from France and Germany – used as much by Moroccan workers as tourists – although RAM has a couple of flights each week to Casablanca (one of which stops at Tetouan), and to Amsterdam, Brussels, Rotterdam and Cologne in summer.

East to Nador and Melilla

There is little of apparent interest to slow your progress over the 164km stretch of the P39 from **Al Hoceima to Nador**. For anyone who has read about the events of the Rif

War, however, the names of the villages will be familiar. This was the territory of Abd El Krim's first, dramatic rising – the so-called **Rout of Annoual** – of July–August 1921. In those two months, the Spanish were forced back to Melilla, losing over 18,000 of their troops along the way.

Al Hoceima to Selouane

The road from Al Hoceima climbs inland alongside the Oued Nekor, crossing a high pass before arriving at **KASSITA** (60km), and the friendly *Hôtel-Restaurant Andalous* (②). Here you can take the S312 south to Taza, via Aknoul. Heading east towards Nador, if you drive into the hills north of the road, at Midar or Driouch, there is still the occasional lookout post and barracks to be seen from the Rif War.

At **MONT ARAOUI**, where the road crosses the Oued Moulouya, there is a large and wonderful **Sunday souk**, plus several café-restaurants and a spotless **hotel**, the *Hassan* (☎05/626 2433, fax 636 2823; ③), with a choice of cheaper ordinary rooms, or pricier ones with en-suite bathrooms.

SELOUANE, 9km further east (and 11km short of Nador), stands at a rather complex junction of the roads to Al Hoceima and Oujda. It hosts a Saturday souk but is worth a short visit on any day of the week. There is an interesting **kasbah**, built by Moulay Ismail, used as a base by the bizarre pretender to the throne, Bou Hamra (see "History" in Contexts), and now adapted as a storehouse. But the main reason to stop is for a **meal** at the *Restaurant Brabo*, 110 Avenue Mohammed V (☎05/660 9033; Tues–Sat noon–4pm & 8pm–midnight, Sun noon–4pm only; expensive), the best **place to eat** in this entire area. A superlative restaurant, run by a Belgian chef (it is named after the Brabo Fountain in Antwerp) and his Moroccan wife, it is the only restaurant for hundreds of miles around that can boast a *Collier d'Or* from the *Gastronomique Internationale*. Phone ahead and splash out.

South to Guercif

The road **south to Guercif** (S333), heading off 8km west of Mont Araoui, is narrow and sealed. It makes an interesting alternative to Taza or Oujda, with its vistas of palms and scrub, and the occasional wandering camel.

Nador and the coast

Entering or leaving Morocco at the Spanish enclave of Melilla you will have to pass through **NADOR**. If you're a bird-watcher, the marshes and dunes of Kariet Arkmane and Ras El Ma, 30–40km east of the town, may well entice a stay of several days (see box on p.158). If not, you will probably want to move straight out and on. Nador itself, fringed by a shallow lagoon, is earmarked as a centre for economic development and has little to offer conventional tourists.

When the Spanish left in 1957, Nador was just an ordinary Riffian village, given work and some impetus by the port of Melilla. Its later choice as a provincial capital was perhaps unfortunate. There was little to do for the local university students, while the iron foundry proposed to fuel the Rif's mining industry never materialized: two reasons that explain why the 1984 riots started in this town. The past decade saw some attempt to address these problems, along with much new building, but the effective closure of the Algerian border has hit local business and tourism. A success story, however, is the Marost fish farm, whose tower is visible across the lagoon. Set up in the 1980s, this specializes in sea perch, dorado, shrimps and oysters, which are mainly exported to France and Italy. It employs over 250 people, including a number of technicians engaged on research projects, whom you may well run across in the local restaurants.

The bulk of Nador lies between the **Selouane–Melilla road** (P39), to the west, and the **lagoon** of **Sebgha bou Areq** (or Mar Chica – "small sea"), to the east.

Driving in from Selouane, turn right at the first sign to "Centre Ville" and you'll find yourself at the **Municipalité** and the landmark *Hôtel Riyad*. From there, **Avenue Mohammed V**, with its palms and orange trees, runs down to a little jetty on the lagoon corniche. Parallel, and to the south, **Avenue Youssef Ibn Tachfine** runs past the **Grand Mosque** with its tall, thin minaret down to the *Hôtel Rif* on the corniche. Halfway down, it is bisected by **Avenue Hassan II**, where you will find the two-storey **Grand Souk**.

Practicalities

If you're arriving by **bus** or **grand taxi**, you'll likely be dropped at the ranks nearby the Grand Souk on the town's third main avenue, **Avenue des F.A.R**; these terminals include connections to the Melilla border. CTM buses and night-time services (mostly to Casablanca via Fes, Meknes and Rabat) use a terminal across the avenue from the *Hôtel Riyad* on Rue General Meziane. Nador's ONMT **tourist office** is at 80 Boulevard Ibn Rochd (☎05/633 0348).

Leaving Nador, if you are heading for Tetouan or Chaouen, it's best to break the trip in Al Hoceima (3hr 30min): from there, either town is still an eight-hours-plus journey.

If you are heading for **Fes**, **Taza** or **Oujda**, the best course is to take the *Supratours* buses run by **ONCF**, the rail company, to **Taourirt**, on the Fes–Oujda train line. They leave from outside the ONCF office on Avenue Sidi Mohammed. Buses from Nador to Fes are invariably used for smuggling duty-free goods (Nador is a duty-free port), and therefore subject to numerous police and even customs checks en route, which may lengthen journey times somewhat.

Details of the Nador–Almería and (summer only) Nador–Sète **ferries** are to be found on p.172; the boats leave from Beni Enzar, the Moroccan side of the Melilla border.

Accommodation, eating and drinking

There is a wide choice of **hotels**, many of them built in the more optimistic climate of the late 1980s/early 1990s, with most of the cheapies grouped around the two bus stations (and often full).

For **meals**, besides the hotel-restaurants below, the *Restaurante Romero* at 48/50 Avenue Youssef Ben Tachfine, overlooking the Grand Souk (daily noon–10pm; cheap), is highly recommended for fish dishes. If you have your own transport, you should definitely take the opportunity to try *Restaurant Brabo at Selouane* (see p.155).

CHEAP

Hôtel Annoual, 16 Rue No. 20 – off Av. des F.A.R. (☎05/660 2828). Cheap 1-star hotel, near the bus station, with a restaurant and café. ②

Hôtel Ibn Khaldoun, 91 Av. Ibn Rochd (☎05/660 7042). A reasonable *pension*, with some en-suite rooms, and hot showers in the evenings. ①

Hôtel Maghreb, 72 Av. Youssef Ben Tachfine (☎05/660 4664). A very basic option, and not tremendously clean, but cheap. ①.

Hôtel al Mahatta, 38 Av. Abbas Mohammed Akkad (☎05/660 2777). The town's largest hotel, with 200 very reasonable rooms on three floors. Before the border closure, it used to cater for Algerian and Tunisian visitors. ②.

Hôtel Nador, Rue 22, 49 Hay el Khattabi (☎05/660 7071) The best cheap hotel in town by far, with low prices, clean en-suite rooms and hot water round the clock. ①.

MODERATE TO EXPENSIVE

Hôtel Mansour Eddahbi, 105 Rue de Marrakesh (☎05/660 6583). A modern hotel, with a restaurant, café and bar. ④.

Hôtel Méditerranée, 2/4 Av. Youssef Ibn Tachfine (☎05/660 6495, fax 660 6611). A good-value choice, opposite the prominent *Hôtel Rif*. Friendly, with comfortable rooms, the best of which have a balcony. ④.

Hôtel Rif, Av. Youssef Ibn Tachfine (☎05/660 6535, fax 633 3384). An outpost of the *Maroc-Tourist* chain, overlooking the lagoon. Equipped with a swimming pool, restaurant and bar, but with a rather sad, empty air about proceedings. ⑤.

Hôtel Riyad, Av. Mohammed V (☎05/660 7715 to 18, fax 660 7719). A modern and spectacular wedding cake of a hotel, with air-conditioning, restaurant, two bars, and underground car park. ⑤.

The coast

For a quick swim, the closest **beach** to Nador is at Boukana, 10km out of town, on the road towards Melilla. A nicer beach is at **Kariet Arkmane**, 25km southeast of Nador, at the end of the lagoon (see below), which in summer becomes a popular campground for Moroccan families.

Moroccans also set up camp at the beaches to the northwest of Nador, beyond Boughafar (30km northwest), and at the **Cap des Trois Forches**, the cape 35km north of Nador on the continuation of the Melilla road. There are no official campsites at either resort but you'd have no problem in joining the locals.

BIRDS AND DUNES: EAST OF NADOR

The coast east of Nador (described below) offers compelling sites for bird-watching – and plant wildlife – with a series of highly frequented freshwater and saline sites.

At **KARIET ARKMANE** a path leads out, opposite the village mosque, past salt pans and a pumping station (right-hand side) to an **extensive area of salt marsh**. This is covered by the fleshy-stemmed **marsh glasswort** or *salicornia*: a characteristic "salt plant" or *halophyte*, it can survive the saline conditions through the use of glands which excrete the salt. The **insect life** of the salt marsh is abundant, including damselflies, brightly coloured grasshoppers and various ants and sand spiders. The **birds** are even more impressive, with black-winged stilt, greater flamingo, coot, great-crested grebe, and various gulls and terns wheeling overhead.

Further along the coast, a walk east of the resort of **RAS EL MA** demonstrates the means by which plants invade **sand dunes**: a sequential colonization is known as "**succession**", where one plant community gradually cedes to the next as a result of its own alteration of the environment. Typical early colonizers are marram grass and sea couch, which are eventually ousted by sea holly and sea spurge and finally by large, "woodier" species such as pistacihu, juniper and cistus species. Whole sequences can be seen occurring over time along the beach. The area attracts a variety of interesting **sea birds** as well, including the internationally rare **Audouin's gull** (thought to breed on the adjacent offshore Chafarinas Islands – see below). Other more familiar birds include dunlin, Kentish plover and oystercatcher.

Even further along the coast is the freshwater lagoon system which marks the mouth of the **OUED MOULOUYA**. The lagoons here are separated from the sea by a remarkable series of sand spits, no more than fifty metres across, and the **birdlife** is outstanding. Secluded among the reedbeds, it is possible to locate grey heron, white stork and little egret while the water's surface is constantly patrolled by the ever-alert black terns and kingfishers. Other varieties which you should manage to spot, wading in the shallows, are redshank, spotted redshank (in summer) and black-tailed godwit.

The Spanish-owned **Islas Chafarinas**, incidentally, are another important wildlife site, which Spanish ecologists are attempting to have declared a nature park. The three small islets support the Mediterranean's largest seabird colonies, and are home to the only known pair of **monk seals** surviving anywhere in Spanish waters. These are strictly protected as only about five hundred pairs exist in the world.

The coast to the east of Nador has some of the most interesting **wildlife** sites in Morocco (see box), and good beaches in addition. To get the most out of this area, a car would be a great help. However, you can make use of the grands taxis, or the daily bus from Nador (which runs along road 8101 to Kariet Arkmane and Ras El Ma, then turns round and heads back to town).

Kariet Arkmane

The village of **KARIET ARKMANE**, 30km from Nador, gives access to a sand and shell-packed **road along the spit of the lagoon**. This is a desolate area but picturesque in its own way, with saltmarshes that provide manifold attractions for birdwatchers. The road out follows the edge of the lagoon from Kariet, passing an old Spanish lookout post en route to a shell-beach – a popular weekend spot with Spaniards from Melilla – before giving out at a tiny fishing village. On the beach, 1km beyond Kariet, is a **campsite**, *Camping Karia Plage* (☎05/636 0241), and a ribbon of easy and relaxed café-restaurants and holiday homes.

Ras El Ma and the Oued Moulouya

The road **east of Kariet** is a pleasant drive, too, twisting into the hills, never far from the sea, and eventually bringing you to **RAS EL MA** (or Ras Kebdana, as it is also known), 70km from Nador – and closer to Saïdia and Berkane (see p.164). Facing another of Spain's offshore island possessions on this coast, the three tiny **Islas Chafarinas**, this is a mix of resort and fishing village, with a good **beach**, a smattering of cafés and street vendors, and a year-round **campsite**, *Camping Ras El Ma*, which has a small shop. Beyond the resort, dunes run virtually undisturbed to the Algerian border.

If you have your own transport, you could complete a loop back towards Nador from Ras El Ma, trailing the **Oued Moulouya** on road 8100 – or take the road across the river (once the border between the French and Spanish Protectorates) to the beaches around Saïdia (see p.165).

Melilla (Mlilya)

Spanish-occupied **MELILLA** is a friendly little place, much more so than Ceuta, with a new-found pride in its mix of cultures, and an interesting selection of early twentieth-century architecture. More conventional tourist pleasures are to be found, too, in an exploration of the walled old town, **Medina Sidonia**, with its stunning views out across the Mediterranean.

Together with Ceuta, Melilla is the last of Spain's Moroccan enclaves on Moroccan soil – a former penal colony which saw its most prosperous days under the Protectorate, when it was the main port for the Riffian mining industry. Since Moroccan independence in 1956, the city's population has halved to a little over 60,000, split two-to-one between Christians and Muslims, along with 3000 Jews and a few hundred Indian Hindus. Many of the Christians are Romanies, and all the enclave's various religious and ethnic communities get along reasonably well together, despite an episode of rioting in 1986, after the enactment of Spain's first real "Aliens Law" threatened to deprive certain Muslim families of their residence rights. There were further riots in 1996, when 400 Spanish Foreign Legionnaires, a tough bunch posted here by the Madrid authorities out of harm's way, went on the rampage after one of their number had been killed in a bar brawl.

Along with Ceuta, Melilla achieved autonomous status in 1995 after years of shilly-shallying on the issue by Madrid for fear of offending Morocco. The autonomous

---

THE NADOR-MELILLA BORDER

On a good day you can cross the **Nador–Melilla border** in ten or fifteen minutes. At other times, you may need considerable time and patience. During the summer it's often extremely crowded, with Moroccans returning from (or going to) jobs in Europe, as well as travellers off the ferry. If you want to avoid the queues, it is a good idea to spend a couple of hours in Melilla after arriving off a ferry, to let the main traffic get through. Or travel on the next morning: Melilla is worth a stay.

It is also possible to **stay** in Beni Enzar, just over the border on the Moroccan side: the *Hôtel les Quatre Saisons* right by the border post was closed at our last check, but the *Hôtel de la Marine*, some 500m further on at 23 Avenue Hassan II (☎05/660 8939; ①) is basic but clean, and pretty reasonable for the price.

If you are **driving**, be aware that smuggling goes on at the border, with periodic police crackdowns; in recent years, trading has included both drugs and people, with Moroccans (and sub-Saharan Africans) attempting to cross illegally into mainland Spain. Driving at night, keep an eye out for road checks – not always well lit but usually accompanied by tyre-puncturing blockades.

If driving to Nador, beware of the local police, eager to pounce and demand large "fines" from newly arrived foreigners for the slightest infraction.

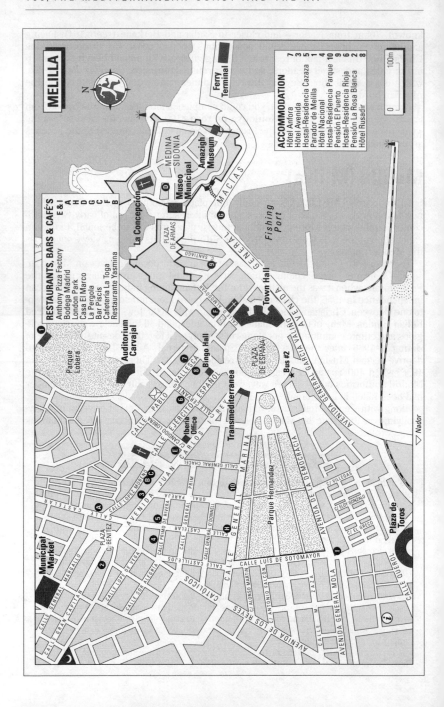

MELILLA

Ferry Terminal

MEDINA SIDONIA

Amazigh Museum

Museo Municipal

La Concepción

PLAZA DE ARMAS

Fishing Port

AVENIDA GENERAL MACIAS

SANTIAGO

Town Hall

AVENIDA GENERAL

RESTAURANTS, BARS & CAFÉS

Anthony Pizza Factory	E & I
Bodega Madrid	A
London Park	H
Casa El Marco	D
La Pergola	G
Bar Piscis	C
Cafetería La Toga	F
Restaurante Yasmina	B

Parque Lobera

Auditorium Carvajal

CALLE CASTIELAR

CALLE LOPEZ MORENO

PLAZA C. BENITEZ

Municipal Market

CALLE GENERAL MARISCAL

CALLE GRAN CAPITÁN

CALLE GENERAL

CALLE LOPE DE VEGA

CALLE SOR ALEGRIA

CALLE

CALLE CASTIELAR

CATOLICOS

CALLE DE LOS REYES

AVENIDA GENERAL MOLA

CALLE ZAZA

CALLE M

C/ ALONSO MARTIN

C/ ANTONIO FALCON

Plaza de Toros

CALLE QUEROL

C/ EL GRECO

C/ ELOY GONZALO

C/ VILLEGAS

Parque Hernandez

AVENIDA DE LA DEMOCRACIA

CALLE LUIS DE SOTOMAYOR

CALLE GENERAL MARINA

CALLE GENERAL O'DONNELL

CALLE GENERAL CHACEL

GRAL PAREJA

CALLE GENERAL PRIM

AVENIDA JUAN CARLOS I

CALLE CANDIDO LOBERA

CALLE PABLO VALLESCA

CALLE EJERCITO ESPANOL

Bingo Hall

Transmediterranea

Iberia Office

PLAZA DE ESPAÑA

Bus #2

AVENIDA GENERAL GARCIA VALIÑO

Nador

ACCOMMODATION

Hôtel Anfora	7
Hôtel Avenida	3
Hostal-Residencia Cazaza	5
Parador de Melilla	1
Hôtel Nacional	4
Hostal-Residencia Parque	10
Pensión El Puerto	9
Hostal-Residencia Rioja	6
Pensión La Rosa Blanca	2
Hôtel Rusadir	8

0   100m

assembly is dominated as in Ceuta by the maverick right-wing Grupo Independiente Liberal, whose initials spell out the name of its leader, controversial businessman and Atlético Madrid chairman Jesús Gil. Meanwhile, the mainstay of the economy, as at Ceuta, remains the double anomaly of an army garrison plus the duty-free status of the port.

The Town

Melilla centres on **Plaza de España**, overlooking the port, and **Avenida Juan Carlos I Rey**, leading inland off it. This is the most animated part of town, especially during the evening *paseo*, when everyone promenades up and down, or strolls through the neighbouring **Parque Hernandez**, which on the town's numerous festival days hosts a fairground late into the night.

To the northeast, occupying a walled promontory, and adjacent to the ferry terminal, is the old part of town, **Medina Sidonia**. It is here that you should head, if you have time to fill waiting for a ferry – or you want to avoid queueing at the border after disembarking (see box on the Nador–Melilla border, p.159).

Medina Sidonia

Until the beginning of the twentieth century, the walled "Old Town" of **Medina Sidonia**, wedged in above the port, was all there was of Melilla. This was the site of the original Phoenician colony of Rusadir around the tenth century BC, which the Spanish took it in 1497, a kind of epilogue to the expulsion of the Moors from Spain after the fall of Granada in 1492. As an enclave, its security was always vulnerable, and at various periods of expansionist Moroccan rule – it was blockaded throughout the reign of Moulay Ismail – the Spanish population was limited to their fortress promontory and its sea approaches. The quarter's streets suggest the Andalucian Medinas of Tetouan or Chaouen, though inside, the design is much more formal; it was in fact laid out along the lines of a Castilian fort, following a major earthquake in the sixteenth century.

Steps near the fishing port lead up to the quarter's main square, **Plaza Maestranza**, entered by the Gothic **Puerta de Santiago**, a gate flanked by a chapel to Saint James the Apostle – known to Spaniards as *Matamoros*, "the Moor-Slayer". Beyond the square, which is in the throes of restoration, you come to an old barracks and armoury, and, if you follow the fortifications round from here, you'll come to a small fort, below which is the church of **La Concepción**, crowded with baroque decoration, including a revered statue of *Nuestra Señora de Victoria* (Our Lady of Victory), the city's patroness. A small **Museo Municipal** (Tues–Sat mid-Sept–May 10am–2pm & 4–8.30pm, June–mid-Sept 10am–2pm & 5–9.30pm, Sun all year 10am–2pm only; free), nearby, houses a miscellany of historical documents, coins and ceramics. More interesting, especially for a traveller in Morocco, is the new **Amazigh Museum** of Berber culture and ethnography in the southern corner of the Medina (Tues–Sat 10am–2pm & 5–9pm, Sun 10am–2pm; free), with exhibits on Berber arts such as ceramics and jewellery, and a big map showing the original extent of Berber culture in North and West Africa, and the pockets where it remains today.

The new town: Art Nouveau

In the new town, many of the buildings around **Plaza de España** were designed by **Enrique Nieto**, a modernista (Art Nouveau) disciple of the renowned Catalan architect, Gaudí. Nieto arrived in 1909 at the age of 23 and proceeded, over the next four decades, to transform Melilla's architecture. The tile and stucco facades left by Nieto and his imitators – in a style more flowery than Gaudí's – are a quiet delight of the New Town if you cast your eyes above the shops.

A short, circular **walk** taking in these delights starts in Plaza de España with Melilla's most famous Art Deco building, the town hall, a Nieto building of 1947. Avenida Juan Carlos I Rey, leading away from the Plaza de España, begins with the 1917 Trasmediterranea building on the left, followed by another fine piece of Art Nouveau at no. 9, built in 1915. Crossing the street, head up a block behind the Iberia office for a look at Ejército Español 16, and the cinema just next to it, and continue up Calle Lopez Moreno, checking out the modernista buildings on the right-hand side, among them Nieto's Or Zoruah Synagogue, built in 1924, and, opposite, the Polygon Mosque, also by Nieto, and dating to 1945. Back on Avenida Juan Carlos I Rey, you have quite a selection around Plaza Comandante Benitez and, just down Calle Reyes Catolicos, have a look at those on Calle Sor Alegría, before heading along Avenida General Prim for a look at the building on the corner of Castelar. The last building, the bingo hall, has another fine stucco facade, in Art Deco style this time, on the corner of Comandante Emperador and Ejército Español, just off Plaza de España, and bringing you back to the start.

Practicalities

The local **bus and grands taxis** from Nador (from the eastern end of Avenue des F.A.R., or from the P39 main road, just north of the town hall) drop you at the border post of **Beni Enzar**, and from there, once the often time-consuming process of crossing the border is out of the way, buses on the Melilla side will take you to Plaza de España (#2; every 15min; takes 15min; accepts dirhams or pesetas/euros). **Rented cars**, incidentally, are not allowed across the border, so if you want to take a day-trip to Melilla from Morocco, you'll have to use public transport. Arriving at the **airport** (☎952 673 800), southwest of the town, means a 500pta or so taxi ride into the centre. The ferry terminal is no more than a ten-minute walk from Plaza de España.

Accommodation in Melilla is not easy to find; rooms tend to be in short supply – and are expensive by Moroccan standards. If you have problems, the **tourist office** (Mon–Fri mid-Sept–June 8.30am–3pm; July–mid-Sept 8am–2pm) in the Palacio de Exposiciones y Congresos, c/Fortuny 21, near the Plaza de Toros, might be able to suggest alternatives. If possible, it's worth booking ahead. When **phoning Melilla** from Morocco (or anywhere else outside Spain), you must prefix phone numbers with the international code (☎00 34). Dialling numbers within Melilla you must include the old local code 952 as part of the new nine-digit number. To **phone Morocco from Melilla**, you need to dial ☎00 212, followed by the local code (minus the initial zero) and number. Note that Melilla works to Spanish time, which is one hour (in winter) and two hours (in summer) ahead of Morocco.

There are a number of **banks** on or near Avenida Juan Carlos I Rey which will change cheques, sterling, dollars or dirhams. Banco Central is at c/Ejército Español 1 and Banco de España is on Plaza de España itself. Note that some banks in Melilla (Mon–Fri 9am–2pm) charge outrageous rates of commission for changing small amounts of cash, while others charge none at all, so ask first. There's a small unnamed *casa de cambio* at c/Primo de Rivera 9 (Mon–Thurs 9am–8pm or later, Fri 9am–1pm), which charges no commission, and black-market moneychangers who hang out on the stretch of Avenida de Juan Carlos I Rey nearest to Plaza de España, especially in the evenings, though the usual rules of caution about changing money on the street apply.

Accommodation

Prices are high in comparison with Morocco; however, you're unlikely to be staying more than a night. Price codes below are for high season.

Hotel Anfora, c/Pablo Vallesca 16 (☎952 683 340, fax 952 683 344). A two-star hotel, with air-conditioned rooms. Has a bar and café and a top-floor restaurant with great views. ⑤.

Hotel Avenida, Avda. Juan Carlos I Rey 26 (☎952 684 949, fax 952 683 226). An old-style hotel above the China Town bazaar. It hardly merits its three stars but the rooms are all en suite. ⑤.

Hostal-Residencia Cazaza, Avda. Primo de Rivera 6 (☎952 684 648). The rooms are a little sombre, but it's a friendly, well-maintained place, with TV and large bathroom in all rooms, and there's a small café on the ground floor for breakfast. ③.

Pensión El Puerto, c/Santiago 1 (☎952 681 270). Nothing fancy but cheap and friendly, indeed the only real cheapie in town, Moroccan-run. ②.

Pensión La Rosa Blanca c/Gran Capitan 7 (☎952 682 738). A charming, quiet little *pension* worth booking ahead as it is often full in summer. ③.

Parador de Melilla, Avda. de Candido Lobera – overlooking the Parque Lobera (☎952 684 940, fax 952 683 486, *parador@melilla.es*). The best upmarket choice: nothing much to look at, but with fine views over the town, and a swimming pool. ⑥.

Hotel Nacional, Avda. Primo de Rivera 10 (☎952 684 540 or 1, fax 952 684 481). Small but comfortable rooms with TV, a/c and newly refurbished bathrooms. ④.

Hostal-Residencia Parque, Avda. Generál Marina 15 (☎952 682 143). The location – opposite the park – is the best thing about this hotel. Rooms are very average. Nonetheless, it's a popular choice, invariably full. ③.

Hotel Rusadir, c/Pablo Vallesca 5 (☎952 681 240, fax 952 670 527). Melilla's top-range hotel is comfortable enough but lacks character or indeed anything much to justify its price – there's not even a pool. ⑥.

Hostal-Residencia Rioja, c/Ejército Español 10 (☎952 682 709). Simple and clean with shared bathrooms but hot water round the clock. ②.

Eating and drinking

Melilla has some great tapas bars, but not so much in the way of restaurants as such. Coming from Morocco, the easy availability of alcohol and open drinking culture are refreshing in more ways than one. The main concentration of restaurants and tapas bars lies in the area east of Avenida Juan Carlos I Rey, between the Plaza de España and the Municipal Market, but if you fancy trying your luck further afield, the area behind Los Carabos beach, 500m or so towards Nador from Plaza de España, is the up-and-coming restaurant area, with new eateries springing up on the Paseo Maritimo and on c/Marqués de Montemar, a block back from the beach. Places listed here are in the centre of town.

Anthony Pizza Factory, Avda de la Democracia 18, with a new branch at c/Candido Lobera 1. Excellent wood-oven pizzas, plus pasta dishes, steaks and saltimbocca. Daily except Mon 1–4.30pm & 8pm–12.30am (Sat till 1am). Moderate.

Bodega Madrid, c/Castelar 6. An excellent beer and tapas bar with huge rations of freshly cooked fish and seafood (you may want to go for a half-portion) eaten standing at wine-barrel tables; one of Melilla's livelier evening hangouts. Daily 11.15am–3pm & 7–10.45pm. Cheap to moderate.

London Park, c/Castelar 2. A lively bar, supposedly in the style of a British pub, with *platos combinados* (meat or fish with two veg), *bocadillos* (sandwiches) and cold lager, but no pies or ale. Daily 7am–2am, except Wed 6pm–2am. Cheap.

Casa El Marco (aka Meson de la Tortilla), c/San Miguel 2, Medina Sidonia. A good place for home-made tapas, and wine from the *porrón* (from which you attempt to pour it into your mouth without getting it on your clothes), though you can get it by the glass too – or drink beer instead. Daily except Mon 1.30–4.30pm & 8–11pm. Cheap to moderate.

La Pergola, Avda. Generál Macias, alongside the fishing port. Open air coffee, beer and cocktails. 3pm–2.30am (3am in summer), Sat & Sun 11.30am–3am. Meals available 8–11.30pm in winter, all opening hours in summer. Moderate.

Bar Piscis, c/Lopez Moreno 1. A fairly large bar serving cold beers and 450ptas/€2.70 *platos combinados*. Daily except Sun 10am–3pm & 6–11pm. Cheap.

Cafetería La Toga, Plaza Yamin Benarroch. A friendly café-bar, good for a breakfast of hot chocolate and *churros* (long dough fritters), or a *carajillo* (coffee with a slug of brandy) at any time of day. Daily except Sun 6.30am–10pm.

Restaurante Yasmina, c/Lopez Moreno 3. A classy fish restaurant where you can eat well for 2000ptas/€12, and very well indeed for 3000ptas/€18, with dishes including paella, of course, and also *zarzuela* (an assortment of fish and seafood stewed with saffron). Daily 2–4pm & 8pm–2am. Moderate to expensive.

Moving on
Ferries from Melilla (see p.172) run daily to **Málaga** and **Almería**, twice daily to Almería in summer. Making advance bookings is essential in August – with waits of up to three days possible if you just turn up for a boat – and the period at the end of Semana Santa (Easter week) is also best avoided

Alternatively, there are Iberia **flights** to **Málaga**, **Almería**, **Granada** and **Madrid**. Again, reserve ahead of time if possible, and be warned that flights don't leave in bad weather. The Iberia office is at the corner of Avenida Juan Carlos I Rey and c/Candido Lobera (☎952 682 434; Mon–Thurs mid-Sept–June 9am–1.30pm & 4.30–7.30pm; July–mid-Sept 9am–1.30pm & 5.30–8.30pm, Fri opening 10am

A helpful **travel agency** for information and reservations is Andalucía Travel, Avenida de la Democracia 13, facing the Parque Hernandez (☎952 670 730; Mon–Fri July–mid-Sept 9am–1pm & 4.30–8pm, mid-Sept–June 9am–1pm & 5–8.30pm, Sat 9am–1pm only).

Travelling into Morocco you can usually pick up collective grands taxis for **Nador** just over the border, but if there are none, or if they try to make you charter a whole taxi and you don't want to, then walk 100m to the roundabout and pick one up there. There are also city buses (#19) to Nador. CTM **buses** have direct connections from Beni Enzar once daily to Tetouan (currently at 9.30am Moroccan time), Oujda (9am), and Casablanca via Fes and Meknes (8.30pm).

The Zegzel Gorge, Berkane and Saïdia

The **route east from Nador to Oujda** is fast, efficient and well served by both buses and grands taxis. It holds little of interest along the way, but if you've got the time (or ideally a car), there's an attractive detour around Berkane into the **Zegzel Gorge**, a dark limestone fault in the Beni Snassen mountains – the last outcrops of the Rif. And on the coast there is the considerable attraction of **Saïdia**, one of the country's most pleasant and relaxed seaside resorts.

The gorge route

The **Oued Zegzel** is a tributary of the Moulouya, which as it runs south of Berkane has carved out a fertile shaft of mountain valleys. These for centuries marked the limits of the Shereefian empire.

The route through these valleys is easily accessible today but still forbiddingly steep: virtually all traffic goes anticlockwise (down) from Berkane to Taforalt, taking the P27 out of town and, after 10km, turning south onto the S403, climbing up to Taforalt, 10km from the turn-off. If you've got a car, this is the route to follow. If you're using public transport, stay on the bus to Berkane, where you can get a seat in a grand taxi to Taforalt and there negotiate another one back, this time via the gorge road. Neither is an expensive operation because the routes are used by local residents as well as tourists.

Taforalt, the Grotte du Chameau and the gorge
TAFORALT is a quiet mountain village, active (or as active as it ever gets) only for the **Wednesday souk**. It does, though, have a reliable supply of grands taxis, and you

should be able to move on rapidly towards the Zegzel Gorge; before settling on a price, get the driver to agree to stop en route at the Chameau cave.

This – the **Grotte du Chameau** – is 10km from Taforalt, a cavern of vast stalactites, one of which is remarkably camel-like in shape (hence the name). The cave, with various tunnels leading off, is completely uncommercialized and it is not always open (you will need to locate the *gardien* to unlock the entrance); a torch is also essential. Near the entrance to the cave is a hot stream, which locals use for bathing.

The Zegzel Gorge, or rather **gorges**, begin about a kilometre beyond the cave, scrupulously terraced and cultivated with all kinds of citrus and fruit trees. As the road crisscrosses the riverbed, they progressively narrow, drawing your eye to the cedars and dwarf oaks at the summit, until you eventually emerge (22km from Taforalt) on to the Berkane plain.

Berkane

BERKANE is a strategic little market town, French-built and prosperous, set amid an extensive region of orchards and vineyards. If you stay, you're likely to be the only Westerner in the town – in consequence there are no hustlers and people may even buy you a coffee.

The town is centred on a main square on the P27 road. Buses and Oujda grands taxis hang out in the street running south from here. Good eating places are to be found in the long, unpaved street running uphill from Boulevard Hassan II, along with lots of very dark, tented souks. Best of the cheap **hotels** is the *Ennajah* (☎05/661 2088; ①), on the corner of Boulevard Hassan II and Boulevard Moulay Youssef, 100m south of the main square; this also has a good restaurant, the owner having worked some time in Belgium. There is also a hotel, *Hôtel Zaki* (☎05/661 3743, fax 661 3460; ④), 500m east of the main square on the road towards Oujda, slick and comfortable, and mainly catering to businesspeople, with a/c, heating and satellite TV in all rooms, an in-house pizzeria, and a fitness room.

There isn't much to see in Berkane, but one thing worth a glance if you're in town is the now disused **church**, just north of the main road, 50m east of the main square, painted in red ochre, with a row of strange grimacing faces picked out in yellow along the top of its facade.

Moving on from Berkane is straightforward, with frequent buses and grands taxis to Nador, Oujda and Saïdia. Buses leave from just off the main square, as do grands taxis for Oujda. Grands taxis for Nador are to be found 200m west along the main road, while those for Saïdia leave from just north of the roundabout 300m east of the main square.

Saïdia

Sited almost on the Algerian border, **SAÏDIA** used to seem a good choice for staying put for a few days. A very low-key resort, rambling back from the sea in the shadow of a still-occupied nineteenth-century kasbah, it is fronted by one of the best beaches on the Mediterranean – an immense, sandy strand, stretching west to face the tiny Chafarinas islands at Ras El Ma (see p.158), and east, across the Oued Kiss, towards Algeria. In better times, it was a very relaxed place, Moroccans and Algerians mixing together by the seaside. These days, however, with what amounts to civil war in Algeria, there's a definite tension, signalled by a military presence guarding the beach and riverbank.

If you stay here, you're likely to be a rare foreign visitor, though you might find the occasional bird-watcher in residence, and a small number of European tourists in the know spend their summer holidays here. Saïdia has rewarding bird sites in the marshes and woodland stretching behind the beach towards the Oued Moulouya

A NOTE ON ALGERIA

It scarcely needs saying but Algeria is effectively off-limits to all foreign visitors. Since the nullified elections in 1993, over 40,000 people have been killed in attacks and reprisals by Islamic fundamentalists and the army. Foreigners, as well as Algerian intellectuals, journalists and musicians, have been particular targets. Although it is still possible to obtain entry visas for Algeria, and there is a consulate at Oujda (see below), entering the country at time of writing is still extremely unwise, though this may change if the peace process continues.

(see box on p.158). The town really only comes into its own in July and August, when many Moroccan families camp by the beach, and several hotels that are closed for the rest of the year open their doors – reservation is advisable at this time, wherever you intend to stay. The main square becomes pretty animated in summer when the town hosts an August **music festival**, centred on the square and the beach.

Practicalities

Buses and grands taxis will drop you by the northwest corner of the kasbah, from which the beach is a couple of blocks to the north. Turning left here along the seafront, Boulevard Mohammed V, you come after 300m to the main square, with three **hotels** close by. On the square itself is the summer-only *Hôtel Hannour* (☎05/662 5115; ④), a lively three-star establishment. Just beyond, Saïdia's only two year-round hotels face each other across Boulevard Hassan II (parallel with Boulevard Mohammed V, a block inland). They are the rather down-at-heel *Hotel Paco* (☎05/662 5110; ③), with cold-water showers, some en suite; and the *Hôtel Atlal* (☎05/662 5021, fax 662 5022; ④), a friendly and immaculate beach holiday hotel, with an assortment of rooms (all spacious and en suite) to suit couples, families or groups of friends. There are also no less than four **campsites**, the most central of which, *Camping Tennis*, a small municipal site with few facilities, is a block southwest of the *Hôtel Atlal*. A far better option, however, is *Camping al Mansour*, 500m east, past the new tourist complex and on the road to Ras El Ma and the Oued Moulouya (☎05/662 5165), a pleasant, shaded site, with a small row of self-catering bungalows (for up to five people each – and at bargain rates off-season; 250–600dh), tents to rent, and full facilities including permanent hot water.

The liveliest of the **café-restaurants** are by the market, past the kasbah, and there is also a trio around the main square. The best place in town to eat, however, has got to be the *Hôtel Atlal's* restaurant (daily 11am–3pm & 7pm–1am; moderate), a classy place for succulent fresh fish. The hotel also has a good **bar**, its walls covered with cockle shells.

Oujda and around

Open and easy-going, with a large and active university, **OUJDA** has that rare quality in Moroccan cities – nobody makes demands on your instinct for self-preservation. After the Rif, it is a surprise, too, to see women in public again, and to re-enter a Gallic atmosphere – as you move out of what used to be Spanish Morocco into the old French Protectorate zone. Morocco's easternmost town, Oujda was the capital of French Maroc Orient and an important trading centre. It remains today a lively and relatively prosperous place, strikingly modern by Moroccan standards, and with a population approaching three quarters of a million.

With its strategic location at the crossroads of eastern and southern routes across Morocco and Algeria, Oujda, like Taza, was always vulnerable to invasion and has

OUJDA

△ Grand Taxis & CTM
△ Nador & Melilla
▷ Sidi Yahia
▽ Taza
▽ Figuig

RESTAURANTS

Brasserie Restaurant de France B
Restaurant El Hana A
Iris Sandwich F
Restaurant Miami Inn D
Restaurant National E
Restaurant Wassila C

ACCOMMODATION

Hôtel Afrah 4
Hôtel Angad 6
Hôtel 16 Août 2
Chic Hôtel 3
Ibis Hôtel 7
Hôtel des Lilas 9
Hôtel Lutetia 11
Hôtel Al Manar 8
Hôtel Al Massira 14
Hôtel Oujda 12
Hôtel Raiss 1
Hôtel Riad 13
Royal Hôtel 10
Hôtel Simon 5

Train Station

Bus Station

Grands Taxis

Oued Nachef

frequently been the focus of territorial claims. Founded in the tenth century by Berber chieftain Ziri Ben Attia, it was occupied for parts of the thirteenth and fourteenth centuries by the Ziyanids, whose capital at Tlemcen is today just across the Algerian border. From 1727 until the early nineteenth century Oujda was under Turkish rule – the only town in present-day Morocco to have been part of the Ottoman Empire. Following the French defeat of the Ottomans in Algeria, France twice occupied the town, prior to its incorporation within the Moroccan Protectorate in 1912: an early and prolonged association, which remains tangible in the streets and attitudes.

In recent years, the town's proximity to the Algerian border and distance from the government in Rabat led to a reputation for dissidence and unrest. This was particularly evident during the Algerian border war in the early 1960s, and again, in the 1980s, in a series of student strikes. Just as important, however, was the restoration of Moroccan-Algerian relations in 1988, when for a time the city became truly pan-Maghrebi, with Algerians coming in to shop, and Moroccans sharing in some of the cultural dynamism of neighbouring Oran, the home of *Raï* music. Alas, this is all in the past now, following Algeria's descent into civil war, and the closure of the border.

The Town

Oujda consists of the usual **Medina** and **Ville Nouvelle**, the latter highly linear in its layout, having started out as a military camp.

The **Medina**, walled on three sides, lies right in the heart of town and is largely a French reconstruction – obvious by the ease with which you can find your way around. Unusually, though, it has retained much of the city's commercial functions and has an enjoyably active air with **Place du 16 Août**, the town's main square, at its northwest corner.

Entering from **Bab El Ouahab**, the principal gate, you'll be struck by the amazing variety of food – on both café and market stalls – and it's well worth a look for this alone. Olives are Oujda specialities, and especially wonderful if you're about after the September harvest. In the old days, more or less up until the French occupation, Bab El Ouahab was the gate where the heads of criminals were displayed.

Exploring the quarter, a good route to follow from the gate is straight down the main street towards **Place El Attarin**, flanked by a *kissaria* (covered market) and a grand fondouk. At the far end of the souks you come upon **Souk El Ma**, the irrigation souk, where the supply of water used to be regulated and sold by the hour. Walking on from here, you'll arrive back at Place du 16 Août.

Running along the outside of the Medina walls, the **Parc Lalla Aisha** is a pleasant area to seek midday shade. Following it round to the west takes you to the Bab Sidi Aisha, from which Rue El Ouahda runs north to the old French **Cathedrale Saint Louis**. This is an evocative place. Its present congregation (mass is held on Sat 6.30pm and Sun 9am) numbers about ten, the fonts are dry, and the statue niches empty, but there is a beautiful chapel; for admission, ring at the door of the presbytery at the back, on Rue d'Azila.

Practicalities

Arriving at the **train station** you are in easy walking distance of the centre. The new **bus station**, which handles most services, is more of a walk (or an inexpensive petit taxi ride), 500m southwest of the train station, across the Oued Nachef, but CTM services use their own terminal up Rue Ahfir, some 200m north of its junction with Boulevard Mohammed V. **Grands taxis** for Ahfir, Berkane and Al Hoceima leave nearby too (you'll probably have to change taxis at Berkane for Saïdia or Nador, but you may strike lucky and get one direct), but those for Taourirt and Taza leave by the main bus station – you'll have to change at Taza for Fes, and there for most points beyond but, amazingly, there are direct services all the way to Laayoune in the Western Sahara. The **airport**, Les Angads, is 15km north, off the P27 (☎05/668 3261); in town, RAM has an office alongside the *Hôtel Oujda* on Boulevard Mohammed V (☎05/668 3963 or 64), and operates daily flights to Casablanca, also served twice daily weekdays and once daily weekends by Regional Air Lines (☎05/670 4527).

There is still an **Algerian consulate** on Rue de Taza (☎05/668 3740 or 41), though they may tell you to go to Rabat for a visa. For **car repairs**, mechanics are to be found on Rue Ahfir, with a number of spares shops on Rue Madina El Mounaouara – the two streets meet at their junction with Boulevard Mohammed V. The Hôtel de Ville, the **post office**, several **banks**, and a **tourist office** (Mon–Thurs 8.30am–noon & 2.30–6.30pm, Fri 8.30–11.30am & 3–6.30pm) are all grouped around **Place du 16 Août**. **Internet** access is available at Arcosys Cyber, 8 Rue Tariq Ibn Ziad (daily 9am–11pm; 10dh/hr), and Espace Net Cybercafé, Boulevard Zerktounii at the corner of Boulevard Mohammed V, really more cyber than café, though you can get a coffee while you surf (Mon–Sat 8.30am–10pm, Sun 10am–12.15pm & 2.45–8.30pm; 20dh/hr).

Accommodation

There are a number of **hotels** in the **Medina**; many are poor value, but the better choices are detailed below. Around the **Ville Nouvelle** are a range of much better hotels, many of them built in the early 1990s. Booking ahead is a good idea during holiday periods, when many Moroccan migrant workers return home to their families. The closest **campsite** is in Saïdia (see p.166).

CHEAP

Hôtel Afrah, 15 Rue Tafna (☎05/668 6533, fax 668 8565). A modern hotel with neat decor (a great glass cupola over its patio, and some nice stucco work in the lobby), and a fine view across the Medina from its rooftop café. Comfortable en-suite rooms, heated in winter. ②.

Hôtel Angad, Bd. Ramdane El Gadi (☎05/669 1452). Another newish hotel, on a pedestrianized street just inside the Medina. En-suite rooms and a breakfast café. ②.

Hôtel 16 Août, 128 Rue de Marrakech (☎05/668 4197). Best of the cheap hotels, with clean rooms and hot showers available. ①.

Chic Hôtel, 34 Bd. Ramdane El Gadi (☎05/669 0566). The name's a bit optimistic but this is yet another early 90s hotel: clean, pleasant and well maintained. ①.

Hôtel des Lilas, Rue Jamal Eddine El Afghani (☎05/668 0840 to 42). A decent, modern hotel with a number of luxury suites, which are often offered at more or less normal room rates. ③.

Hôtel Lutetia, 44 Bd. Hassan Loukili (☎05/668 3365). An old hotel that looks its age, but respectable enough and conveniently positioned right by the train station. ③.

Royal Hôtel, 13 Bd. Zerktouni (☎05/668 2284). Another old hotel but a much better option with clean rooms, hot showers, and a secure garage. Next door, the *Café Les Pyramides* provides breakfast. ②.

Hôtel Simon, corner of Rue Tariq Ibn Ziad and Idriss Ben Bouchaib (☎05/668 6303). Located just inside the Medina, this was the first European-style hotel in Oujda – opened in 1910. It remains a nice, friendly place, with a restaurant and bar. All rooms have showers though hot water is occasional. ①.

MODERATE TO EXPENSIVE

Hôtel Al Manar, 50 Bd. Zerktouni (☎05/668 8855, fax 668 1670). A smart, modest establishment, opened in 1992 and wearing well. ④.

Hôtel Al Massira, Bd. Maghreb El Arabi (☎05/671 0798, fax 668 0477). A reasonable hotel, though getting a bit shabby, with a pool, tennis court and pleasant garden. ④.

Ibis Hôtel (aka *Moussafir*), Bd. Abdallah Chefchaouni/Place de la Gare (☎05/668 8201 to 05, fax 668 8208). One of the elegant "blue and white" chain of hotels, to be found by major train stations. It has a restaurant, bar, swimming pool, TVs in all rooms, and all in all is pretty good value. ⑤.

Hôtel Oujda, Bd. Mohammed V (☎05/668 4482, fax 668 5064). An old-established landmark hotel, undistinguished but with TV, a/c, heating and a bath in each room, plus a popular bar and a small swimming pool. ④.

Hôtel Raiss, Bd Mohammed V (☎05/670 3058, fax 668 8792). A friendly, clean and comfortable new hotel with TV and heating in all rooms – those at the back are quieter than those overlooking the street. Good breakfasts. ④.

Hôtel Riad, Av. Idriss Al Akbar (☎05/668 8353). Another 1991-vintage hotel. Good value, with clean, pleasant rooms, a restaurant, café and friendly bar. ④.

Eating and drinking

Oujda has a strong cultural life and is one of the most enjoyable Moroccan cities to while away an evening. Hustlers don't really feature here and the bars and restaurants are sociable and open places. Most of the town's bars are to be found in the **hotels**. Good bets include those in the *Ibis*, the *Riad*, and the *Simon*. A lively local place is *Bar Restaurant du Palais* on Boulevard Mohammed Derfoufi.

RESTAURANTS

The focus of evening activity is **Bab El Ouahab**, around which you can get all kinds of grilled food from stalls. On the other side of the Medina, too, there are plenty of good eating places on, or just off, **Boulevard Zerktouni**.

In the **Ville Nouvelle**, in addition to those found in the hotels mentioned opposite, recommended restaurants include:

Brasserie Restaurant de France, Bd. Mohammed V. One of the fancier places in town, upstairs from a café patisserie, with a nightclub attached. Offers a selection of mostly French fish and meat dishes, well prepared. Licensed. Daily 11am–11pm. Moderate.

Restaurant El Hana, 106 Bd. Mohammed Derfoufi. A cheap and cheerful place with tasty spit-roast chicken plus soups, tajines, salads and various meats. Daily 7am–2am. Cheap.

Iris Sandwich, Av. Idriss Al Akbar – near the *Al Massira* and *Riad* hotels. Sandwiches and snacks. Daily 11.30am–9.30pm. Cheap.

Restaurant Miami Inn, Bd. Mohammed V. The name is somewhat incongruous, but this is a handy spot for tajines and meat dishes, plus what they claim is a meat-free vegetable meal. Daily 10am–11pm. Cheap.

Restaurant National, Bd. Zerktouni, at the corner of Bd. Allal ben Abdallah. Seating upstairs. A good place for tajines and meat dishes, also claiming to offer a veg-only tajine, and *beldi* (country) chicken once weekly, but avoid the salads, which are left out uncovered on the counter by the cash till. Daily 7am–11pm. Cheap.

Restaurant Wassila, 19 Rue Tafna. One of several small café-restaurants on the pedestrianized streets south of Place du 16 Août. A friendly place with a small menu of staples (meat, chips, tajine), all well prepared. 7am–9pm. Cheap.

Sidi Yahia

SIDI YAHIA, 6km south of Oujda, is a rather unimpressive little oasis for most of the year, with a "cascade" that is switched on at weekends. However, it's a place of some veneration, housing as it does the tomb of the marabout **Sidi Yahia**, a holy man identified by local tradition with John the Baptist. Nobody is quite sure where the saint is buried – several of the cafés stake an optimistic claim – but at the **moussems** held here in August and September almost every shrub and tree in the oasis is festooned with little pieces of cloth, a ritual as lavish and extraordinary as anything in the Mediterranean church.

South to Figuig

In past years, before the eruption of civil war in Algeria, there was a well-established travel route from Oujda, south to the ancient **date palm oasis of Figuig**, and across from there into the Algerian Sahara. This is no longer a possibility. However, those into isolated journeys might still want to consider the route from **Oujda** to **Figuig** – and on from there to the southern Moroccan oasis town of **Er Rachidia** (see p.469).

If you're on for the trip, be warned it's a long, hot haul: 369km from Oujda to Figuig, and a further 393km to Er Rachidia. You can travel by bus (there is usually a 6am departure from Oujda, arriving at Figuig around 1pm; later departures will subject you to the full heat of the day), or, if you have transport, you can drive: the road is sealed all the way.

Whichever way you travel, expect to explain yourself at a number of military checkpoints: this is a sensitive border area.

The route

En route between Oujda and Figuig there are just a few roadside settlements and mining towns – for coal, copper, manganese and zinc. If you are driving, **AÏT BENI-MATHAR**, 83km from Oujda, is a good point to break the journey: the village has a group of kasbahs, an important (and ancient) **Monday souk**, and some grill-cafés. About 4km to its west is a small oasis, **Ras El Aïn**, with a (highly seasonal) waterfall.

Another possible stop could be **TENDRARA**, 198km from Oujda, a larger settlement with an important **Thursday souk**; it has a traditional marketplace in the centre and sheep and goats corralled on the outskirts. Again, there are grill-cafés.

At 241km, you reach **BOUARFA**, the region's administrative centre and transport hub, with buses to Er Rachidia (as well as Figuig and Oujda), and a couple of hotels. For details of **Bouarfa, Figuig and the route to Er Rachidia**, see p.469.

travel details

Trains

Oujda to: Casablanca (3 direct and 1 connecting daily; 10hr); Fes (4 daily; 5hr 15min); Guercif (4 daily; 2hr 20min); Kenitra (3 direct and 1 connecting daily; 8hr 30min); Marrakesh (3 connecting daily; 14hr–1/hr 45min); Meknes (4 daily; 6hr 30min); Rabat (3 direct and 1 connecting daily; 9hr); Tangier (1 direct and 2 connecting daily; 11hr); Taourirt (4 daily; 1hr 45min; connecting Supratours bus service to and from Nador), Taza (4 daily; 3hr 15min).

There are no longer any passenger services from Oujda to Bouarfa; nor currently across the border to Algeria.

Buses

Berkane to: Nador (19 daily; 1hr 30min); Oujda (20 daily; 1hr 30min); Saïdia (4 daily; 1hr).

Al Hoceima to: Aknoul (1 daily; 1hr 30min); Casablanca (2 CTM daily; 10hr 50min) via Rabat (9hr); Fes (2 CTM and 6 others daily; 5hr); Meknes (2 CTM and 1 other daily; 6hr); Nador (2 CTM and 6 others daily; 3hr); Oujda (1 CTM and 1 other daily; 4hr 30min); Tangier (1 CTM and 5 others daily; 6hr); Tetouan (1 CTM and 8 others daily; 5hr 30min) via Issaguen (2hr 30min) and Chaouen (4hr 30min).

Nador to: Aknoul (1 daily; 3hr 30min); Casablanca (2 CTM and 9 others daily; 12hr); Fes (2 CTM and 17 others daily; 5hr 30min); Figuig (1 daily; 9hr 30min); Guercif (3 daily; 3hr); Al Hoceima (2 CTM and 16 others daily; 3hr 30min); Meknes (2 CTM and 5 others daily; 6hr 30min); Midelt (2 daily; 6hr); Oujda (1 CTM and 16 others daily; 2hr 30min); Rabat (1 CTM and 16 others daily; 9hr 30min); Er Rachidia (2 daily; 14hr); Rissani (1 daily; 16hr); Saïdia (1 daily; 2hr); Tangier (1 CTM and 7 others daily; 12hr) via Tetouan (9hr 30min); Taourirt (1 ONCF/Supratours daily; 2hr 30min; connecting with train service to Fes, Meknes, Kenitra, Rabat and Casablanca); Taza (19 daily; 5hr).

Oujda to: Bouarfa (5 daily; 5hr); Casablanca (2 CTM and 14 others daily; 11hr) via Rabat (9hr 30min); Al Hoceima (1 CTM and 1 other daily; 4hr 30min); Fes (3 CTM and 18 others daily; 5hr 30min); Figuig (3 daily; 7hr); Meknes (3 CTM and 15 others daily; 6hr 30min); Nador (1 CTM and 16 others daily; 2hr 30min); Saïdia (5 daily; 1hr 30min); Taza (1 CTM and 23 others daily; 3hr 15min).

Taza to: Aknoul (2 daily; 1hr); Casablanca (2 CTM and 9 others daily; 7hr 30min) via Meknes (2hr 45min) and Rabat (6hr 15min); Fes (4 CTM daily and others roughly hourly; 2hr 30min); Al Hoceima

(1 CTM and 1 other daily; 3hr); Meknes (2 CTM and 3 others daily; 3hr 15min); Nador (17 daily; 3hr 30min); Oujda (1 CTM daily and others roughly hourly; 3hr 15min); Tangier (1 CTM daily; 8hr).

Grands taxis

Berkane to: Nador (1hr 30min); Saïdia (30min); Oujda (1hr 30min).

Al Hoceima to: Issaguen (2hr); Targuist (1hr 30min); Kalah Iris (1hr); Kassita (1hr); Nador (3hr); Oujda (5hr). Occasionally direct to Fes (4hr 30min); Taza (2hr 30min).

Bab Berred to: Issaguen (40min); Chaouen (50min).

Issaguen (Ketama) to: Bab Berred (40min); Al Hoceima (2hr); Taounate (1hr 20min); Targuist (30min).

Nador to: Beni Enzar (15min); Berkane (1hr 30min); Al Hoceima (3hr); occasionally direct to Oujda (2hr 30min).

Oujda to: Ahfir (45min); Berkane (1hr 30min); Al Hoceima (5hr); Laayoune (36hr); Taourirt (1hr 30min); Taza (3hr). Occasionally direct to Nador (2hr 30min).

Saïdia to: Ahfir (30min); Berkane (30min).

Taounate to: Fes (1hr 30min); Issaguen (1hr 20min).

Targuist to: Al Hoceima (1hr 30min); Issaguen (30min); Kalah Iris (45min).

Taza to: Aknoul (1hr); Fes (1hr 30min); Guercif (1hr); Kassita (1hr 30min); Oujda (3hr). Occasionally direct to Al Hoceima (2hr 30min).

Flights

Al Hoceima to: Casablanca (2 weekly; 1hr 15min); Fes (weekly summer; 40min); Tangier (weekly; 55min); Tetouan (weekly; 35min).

Oujda to: Casablanca (2–3 daily; 1hr 5min).

Ferries

Nador (Beni Enzar) to: Almería (13 weekly in winter, 3–4 daily in summer; 6–7hr); Sète (every four days in summer only; 36hr).

Melilla to: Málaga (1 daily; 7hr–8hr 30min); Almería (6 weekly in winter, 10 weekly in summer; 6hr–8hr 30min).

For further details on ferry services, see pp.11–14.

CHAPTER THREE

MEKNES, FES AND THE MIDDLE ATLAS

T he undoubted highlight of this chapter is **Fes**. The imperial capital for long periods under the Merenid, Wattasid and Alaouite dynasties, the city has for the past ten centuries stood at the heart of Moroccan history – and for five of these it was one of the major intellectual and cultural centres of the West, rivalling the great university cities of Europe. It is today unique in the Arab world, preserving the appearance and much of the life of a medieval Islamic city. In terms of monuments, it has as much as the other Moroccan imperial capitals together, while the city's souks, extending for over a mile, maintain the whole tradition of urban crafts.

In all of this – and equally in the everyday aspects of the city's life – there is enormous fascination and, for the outsider, a real feeling of privilege. But inevitably, it is at a cost. Declared a historical monument by its French colonizers, and subsequently deprived of its political and cultural significance, Fes today retains its beauty but is in evident decline. Its university faculties have been dispersed around the country, with the most important departments in Rabat; the Fassi business elite have mostly left for Casablanca; and, for survival, the city depends increasingly on the tourist trade. Nonetheless, two or three days here is an absolute must for any visit to Morocco.

Meknes, like Fes (and Rabat and Marrakesh) an imperial city, sees comparatively few visitors, despite being an easy and convenient stopover en route by train from Tangier or Rabat, or by bus from Chaouen. The megalomaniac creation of Moulay Ismail, the most tyrannical of all Moroccan sultans, it is once again a city of lost ages, its enduring impression being that of an endless series of walls. But Meknes is also an important modern market centre and its souks, though smaller and less secretive than those of Fes, are almost as varied and generally more authentic. There are, too, the

---

HOTEL PRICE CODES

The basis of our **hotel price codes**, set out below and keyed throughout the guide, is the price currently quoted for the cheapest double room in high season (June–September).

Note that cheaper prices in the lower categories are generally for rooms with just a washbasin – you always pay extra for **en-suite** shower and WC – and that double rooms can generally be converted into **triples/family rooms**, with extra beds, for a modest extra charge. Single occupancy usually costs about two thirds the price of a double, though in some places a single person will pay the same rate for a room as two people sharing, and in other places exactly half as much. Prices quoted are for bed only, without breakfast, but including local taxes.

① 40–100dh	③ 150–200dh	⑤ 400–800dh
② 100–150dh	④ 200–400dh	⑥ over 800dh

△ Tangier & Tetouan

△ Oujda

Sidi Kacem

Moulay Yacoub

Taza

◆ Volubilis

P3

FES

Friouato

P6

Moulay Idriss

Sidi Harazem

MEKNES

P20

Meghraoua

Bhalil

P24

Sefrou

P1

Imouzzer du Kandar

▲ Djebel Abad 1768m

4822

Djebel Bou Iblane ▲ 3190m

El-Hajeb

4620

4613

Talzemt

P21

Ifrane

S309

4653

Skoura

Azrou

Mischliffen

Boulemane

Djebel Bou Naceur ▲ 3340m

P24

M I D L E

A T L A S

3351

Timahdite

4656

Immouzer des Marmoucha

Cascades

Enjil des Ikhatarn

Aguelmouss

Mrirt

Sources de l'Oum er Rbia

Aguelmame Sidi Ali

Enjil

S330

Missour

S208

Aguelmame Azigza

Col du Zad

P20

S329

Khenifra

M O U N T A I N S

Zeida

P33

Midelt

△ Oujda

P24

Cirque de Jaffar

See 'Over the Atlas' map

Arhbala

D J E B E L   A Y A C H I

Ikassene

3425

PLATEAU DES LACS

Rich

P21

Imilchil

3443

M O U N T A I N S

Agoudal

6905

A T L A S

Er Rachidia

△ Figuig

DADES GORGE

3403

TODRA GORGE

P32

Msemrir

Tinerhir

Tamtatoucht

Tinejdad

local attractions of **Volubilis**, the most impressive of the country's Roman sites, and the hilltop town of **Moulay Idriss**, home to the most important Islamic shrine in Morocco.

South of the two imperial cities stretch the cedar-covered slopes of the **Middle Atlas**, which in turn gradually give way to the High Atlas. Across and around this region, often beautiful and for the most part remote, there are two main routes. The most popular, a day's journey by bus, skirts the range beyond the market town of **Azrou** to emerge via **Beni Mellal** at Marrakesh. The second climbs southeast from Azrou towards **Midelt**, an excellent carpet centre, before passing through great gorges to Er Rachidia and the vast date palm oasis of Tafilalt – the beginning of a tremendous southern circuit (see Chapter Seven). A third route leaves the main Azrou–Marrakesh highway at **El Ksiba** and makes its tortuous way **across the Atlas** via Imilchil and the Todra Gorge to Tinerhir (again, see Chapter Seven). Sections are being upgraded or replaced, but it remains a challenging route in the meantime, with the risk of flash flood damage. You can take this route if you have a 4x4 – or by getting lifts over the various stages in local Berber lorries or Landrover taxis.

If you're travelling one of the main highways, and you've got the time, the Middle Atlas has considerable attractions of its own. Close to Fes, **Immouzer** and **Ifrane** are popular summer resorts, their air and waters a cool escape from the city. The Berber market town of **Azrou** is host to a great **Tuesday souk** and surrounded by pine forests and mountain lakes. And off the Marrakesh road, near Beni Mellal, are the **Cascades d'Ouzoud** – waterfalls which crash down from the mountains, even in mid-summer, plunging from pool to pool into a gorge beside which you can swim, camp and hike.

Meknes

Cut in two by the wide river valley of the Oued Boufekrane, **MEKNES** is a sprawling, prosperous provincial city. Monuments from its past – dominated by the extraordinary creations of Moulay Ismail (for more on whom, see p.182) – justify a day's rambling exploration, as do the varied and busy souks of its Medina. In addition, the Ville Nouvelle is pleasant and easy to handle, and there is the appeal of Roman Volubilis, within easy short bus or taxi distance.

To get the most out of the city's monuments and the atmosphere of the Medina and souks, it's best to visit before heading to Fes. Getting a grasp of Meknes prepares you a little for the drama of Fes, and it certainly helps give an idea of quality (and prices) for crafts shopping; visited second, it is inevitably a little disappointing by comparison.

Orientation, arrival and information

Meknes is simpler than it looks on the map. Its **Ville Nouvelle** (aka in Arabic, *Hamriya*) stretches along a slope above the east bank of the river, radiating from an impressive public square, the **Place Administrative** – a stretch of garden and a fountain, flanked by the main post office, the Hôtel de Ville, a helpful Délégué du Tourisme, and a block of flats on stilts built in 1953 by Le Corbusier.

The **Medina** and its neighbouring **Mellah** (the old Jewish quarters) occupy the west bank, with the walls of Moulay Ismail's **Imperial City** edging away, seemingly forever, to their south. The focal point of the Medina is **Place el Hedim**, remodelled in the 1990s into a vast pedestrian plaza with fountains, decorated arcades and shops. This is a good place to fix your bearings: downhill, petits taxis, grands taxis and buses run to local destinations, while uphill buses #5, #7 and #9 head towards the Ville Nouvelle. If you are **driving**, it's worth noting that traffic on Avenue Mohammed V and Avenue Allal Ben Abdallah is one way, circulating anticlockwise.

The ramparts at Asilah

Larache: Spanish Mauresque buildings

Tangier beach and port

A view of Fes from the Merenid tombs

Fes tanneries

Meknes

Bou Inania medersa, Fes

Barbary apes near Azrou

Roman mosaic at Volubilis

Cascades d'Ouzoud

Royal palace gate, Fes

Mohammed V Mausoleum, Rabat

View of Rabat from Salé

The **tourist office** is at 27 Place Administrative (Mon–Thurs 8.30am–noon & 2.30–6.30pm, Fri 8.30–11.30am & 3–6.30pm; ☎05/552 4426), with unusually helpful staff, and useful information posted up on the noticeboard.

Arrival

Arriving by **bus** you will be dropped either at the main **bus station** on the north side of the New Mellah, just outside the Bab El Khemis, or (if coming by CTM) at the new **CTM bus station** on Avenue de Fes, east of the Ville Nouvelle.

Grands taxis from most destinations use a yard alongside the new bus station. Grands taxis from one or two local destinations use a yard across the road from the local bus stops below Place el Hedim in the Medina, and on Rue Omar el Moutahida in the Ville Nouvelle.

There are two **train stations**, both in the Ville Nouvelle on the east bank. The **main station** is a kilometre away from the central area; a smaller, more convenient one, the **Gare El Amir Abdelkader**, is a couple of blocks from the centre (behind the *Hôtel Majestic*); all trains stop at both.

Accommodation

Meknes's hotels are concentrated in the **Ville Nouvelle**, and if you want any comfort, or proximity to bars and restaurants, this is the place to stay. It's only a ten-minute walk from there to the **Medina**, monuments and souks.

Medina

These are all cheapies – and with pretty basic facilities.

Hôtel Agadir, Rue Dar Smen (☎05/553 0141). Clean and friendly, in an eccentric old building with small, basic rooms mostly tucked away in odd crannies. There are only cold showers available, but a hammam is nearby (see p.191). ①.

Maroc Hôtel, 7 Rue Rouamzine (☎05/553 0075). Cleanest and quietest of Medina hotels; most rooms look onto a patio garden full of orange trees. Cold showers, but a hammam nearby (see p.191). Cheaper rooftop sleeping in summer for 30dh. English spoken. ②.

Hôtel Meknes, 35 Rue Dar Smen (no phone). Undistinguished and not as friendly as most; it's between *Hôtel Nouveau* and *Hôtel Regina*, and possibly best as a fall-back if both are full. ①.

Hôtel Nouveau, 65 Rue Dar Smen (☎05/553 3139). Opposite the Banque Populaire. Helpful, warm reception, basic facilities, no external windows, and claims (despite name) to be the first hotel in the Medina. ①.

Hôtel de Paris, 58 Rue Rouamzine, (no phone). Up from the *Maroc Hôtel* and on the opposite side of the street; it's an older hotel, without showers, but there's a hammam nearby (see p.191). ①.

Hôtel Regina, 19 Rue Dar Smen (☎05/553 0280). A gloomy-looking place with public-lavatory-style tiling in the lobby, though the rooms aren't too bad. Hot showers available – at 5dh per quarter hour. ①.

Ville Nouvelle

Note that there are several prominent hotels in the Ville Nouvelle which are basically brothels – or unsuitable for one reason or another. Aim for those listed below and, even then, check tactfully before registering.

CHEAP

Auberge de Jeunesse (Youth Hostel), Av. Okba Ibn Nafi. (☎05/552 4698). Near the *Hôtel Transatlantique*, this is a well-maintained and friendly hostel with rooms around a courtyard. It's open all year: 8–11pm (open till midnight in summer – closed 10am–6pm on Sundays). ①.

Hôtel Bordeaux, 64 Av. de la Gare (☎05/552 2563). Near the main train station and CTM office. There is no obvious sign and it stands off the road, but it is well worth the search; it is alongside the

MEKNES

MEKNES: VILLE NOUVELLE

RESTAURANTS, BARS & CAFÉ'S

- Annexe Metropole
- Aubercyber
- Café-Restaurant Camprinus
- Bar Continental
- La Coupole
- Le Dauphin
- B Restaurant Diafa
- F Restaurant Pizza Fongue
- D Pizzeria Le Four
- R Café Français
- G Rotisserie Restaurant Karam
- A Restaurant Marhaba
- E Restaurant Mo-Dinero
- M Restaurant Montana
- I Restaurant Novelty
- Q Café Opéra
- L Cremerie du Palmier
- J Restaurant Zagora
- K
- H
- C
- P
- O

ACCOMMODATION

Hôtel Akouas	9
Hôtel Bab Mansour	11
Hôtel Bordeaux	13
Hôtel Majestic	4
Hôtel du Marché	3
Hôtel de Nice	5
Hôtel Ouslane	10
Hôtel Palace	6
Rif Hôtel	7
Hôtel Touring	8
Hôtel Transatlantique	1
Hôtel Volubilis	12
Youth Hostel	2

Volvo garage and a bar. Friendly with a good atmosphere and shady garden. Some rooms en suite but cold water only – hot public showers for men 100m east across the street, but nearest facilities for women at a hammam by the *Café l'Abeille*, 100m up Marhaj Yacoub el Mansour. ①.

Hôtel du Marché, 1 Rue Abou Hassan M'Rini, on the corner with Av. Hassan II (☎05/540 0133). This has seen better days but it's a better cheapie than the Medina places, with a handy petit taxi rank right outside the door, and real fireplaces in all rooms. ①.

Hôtel Touring, 34 Av. Allal Ben Abdallah (☎05/552 2351). Though the facilities are pretty average, this place is central and congenial, and has hot water 10pm–noon only. Some rooms en suite. ②.

MODERATE

Hôtel Majestic, 19 Av. Mohammed V (☎05/552 2035, fax 552 7427, *majestic.hotel@excite.fr*). An old, but comfortable hotel, with friendly management, clean rooms with heating and balconies (some en suite), and a terrace for alfresco breakfasts. All in all, probably the best mid-priced choice in the Ville Nouvelle – and convenient for the El Amir Abdelkader·train station. ③.

Hôtel de Nice, 10 Rue Accra (☎05/552 0318). A reasonable old hotel with helpful management; there's a bar, but the restaurant is now closed. Rooms en suite with heating. Good value for money. ③.

Hôtel Ouislane, 54 Av. Allal Ben Abdallah (☎05/552 1743). This is a failsafe if nothing else is available – a basic, old hotel, overpriced for the facilities on offer. Some rooms have a/c – at 100dh extra. ③.

Hôtel Palace, 11 Rue Ghana (☎05/551 1260). A better choice, with respectable rooms (en suite with 24hr hot water) and a reasonable bar. ③.

Hôtel Volubilis, 45 Av. des F.A.R. (☎05/552 5082). A lovely bit of faded 1930s grandeur complete with Art Deco lobby and facade. One of the oldest hotels in the quarter, and still good, but located on a noisy road junction. ③.

EXPENSIVE

Hôtel Akouas, 27 Rue Emir Abdelkader (☎05/551 5967 or 68, fax 551 5994). This new, central, hotel is a good choice. There's a lively nightlife hereabouts – and the *Akouas* has its own nightclub – but the rooms are quiet. ④.

Hôtel Bab Mansour, 38 Rue Emir Abdelkader (☎05/552 5239 or 40, fax 551 0741). A modern hotel opposite the *Akouas* which recommends itself as the choice *'pour hommes d'affaires'*. It has a garage, parking, a bar, a nightclub and a restaurant that is used to catering for vegetarians. ④.

Rif Hôtel, Rue Accra (☎05/552 2591 to 94, fax 552 4428). An upmarket 1950s tour group hotel, bang in the centre, with a bar, good restaurant and small swimming pool. ⑤.

Hôtel Transatlantique, Rue El Marinyen (☎05/552 5050 to 52, fax 552 0057). Meknes's luxury hotel has lovely gardens, stunning views and two swimming pools. Nevertheless, it's not in the *Palais Jamai* nor *La Mamounia* class. ⑤.

Camping

Camping Caravaning International, aka *Camping Aguedal* (☎05/555 5396). A twenty-minute walk from Place el Hedim (or a 10dh petit taxi ride), the city campsite is sited opposite the Heri es Souani. It's a pleasant, shaded site (*aguedal*, or *agdal*, means "garden"), with good facilities (hot water showers available), though not the cheapest campsite in Morocco.

Camping Belle-Vue, aka *Camping Zerhouane* on the road to Moulay Idriss, 14km from Meknes, 9km from Moulay Idriss (☎05/554 4168). A shaded site with a small café and a few rooms to let. Not as good as *Camping Aguedal* and not very convenient unless you have a car, though buses to and from Moulay Idriss will drop or pick you up here. Can also be found 11km along the direct road from Volubilis to Meknes, though roads in the area are somewhat confusing – for the campsite, it's easiest to ask directions to the nearby *Refuge Zerhouane*.

The Imperial City

More than any other Moroccan town, Meknes is associated with a single figure, the **Sultan Moulay Ismail** (see box overleaf) in whose 55-year reign (1672–1727) the city was built up from a provincial centre to a spectacular capital with twenty gates, over fifty palaces and some 45km of exterior walls.

THE SULTAN MOULAY ISMAIL (1672–1727)

"The Sultan Moulay Ismail," wrote his chronicler, Ezziani, "loved Mequinez, and he would have liked never to leave it." But leave it he did, ceaselessly campaigning against the rebel Berber chiefs of the south, and the Europeans entrenched in Tangier, Asilah and Larache, until the entire country – for the first time in five centuries – lay completely under government control. His reign saw the creation of Morocco's strongest ever – and most coherent – army, which included a crack Negro guard, the Abid regiment, and, it is reckoned, a garrison force of one in twenty of the male population. The period was really Morocco's last golden age, though the ruthless centralization of all decisions, and the fear with which the sultan reigned, led, perhaps inevitably, to a subsequent slide into anarchy and weak, inward-looking rule.

Ismail's achievements were matched by his tyrannies, which, even by the standards of the time – and contemporary Europeans were burning their enemies and torturing them on the rack – were judged extreme. His reign began with the display at Fes of 400 heads, most of them of captured chiefs, and over the next five decades, apart from battles, it is estimated that he was responsible for over 30,000 deaths. Many of these killings were quite arbitrary. Mounting a horse, Ismail might slash the head off the eunuch holding his stirrup; inspecting the work on his buildings, he would carry a weighted lance, with which to batter skulls in order to "encourage" the others. "My subjects are like rats in a basket," he used to say, "and if I do not keep shaking the basket they will gnaw their way through."

Throughout Morocco, the sultan was a tireless builder, constructing towns and ports, and a multitude of defensive kasbahs, palaces and bridges. By far his greatest efforts, however, were directed at Meknes, where he sustained an obsessive building programme, often acting as architect and sometimes even working alongside the slaves and labourers. Ironically, in Meknes itself, the passing of time has not been easy on his constructions. Built mainly of *tabia*, a mixture of earth and lime, they were severely damaged by a hurricane even in his lifetime, and thereafter, with subsequent Alaouite sultans shifting their capitals back to Fes and Marrakesh, were left to decay. Walter Harris, writing only 150 years after Ismail's death, found Meknes "a city of the dead ... strewn with marble columns, and surrounded by great masses of ruin". In recent years, however, the city authorities have set about restoring the main monuments with some energy.

The principal remains of Ismail's creation – the **Ville Imperiale** of palaces and gardens, barracks, granaries and stables – sprawl below the Medina, amid a confusing array of walled enclosures. If you intend to take in everything, it's a long morning's walk. Starting out from the Ville Nouvelle, make your way down to the main street at the southern edge of the Medina **(Rue Rouamzine/Rue Dar Smen)**, and along to **Place el Hedim** and its immense gateway, **Bab Mansour**. There are usually **guides** hanging around here if you want to use one; you don't need to, but if you can find someone entertaining, he'll probably elaborate on the story of the walls with some superbly convoluted local legend.

Bab Mansour and around

Place el Hedim ("square of demolition and renewal") immediately recalls the reign of Moulay Ismail. Originally, it formed the western corner of the Medina, but the sultan demolished the houses here in order to form a grand approach to his palace quarter, the *Dar Kebira*. He used it, too, as a depot for marble columns and other construction material he had gathered from sites and cities throughout Morocco, including Roman Volubilis.

The centrepiece of the city's whole ensemble of walls and gateways is the great **Bab Mansour**, startlingly rich in its ceremonial intent, and almost perfectly preserved. Its name comes from its architect – one of a number of Christian renegades who converted to Islam and rose to high position at Ismail's court; there is a tale that when the sultan inspected the gate, he asked El Mansour whether he could do better – a classic catch-22, whose response ("yes") led to immediate and enraged execution. The story may be apocryphal, however, for the gate was actually completed under Ismail's son, Moulay Abdallah.

Whatever, the gate is the finest in Meknes and an interesting adaptation of the classic Almohad design, flanked by unusual inset and fairly squat bastions, which are purely decorative, their marble columns having been brought here from Volubilis. The decorative patterns on both gate and bastions are basically elaborations of the *darj w ktarf* (a cheek-and-shoulder pattern, begun by the Almohads), the space between each motif filled out with a brilliant array of zellij created by a layer of cutaway black tiles, just like the ornamental inscription above, which extols the triumph of Ismail and, even more, that of Abdallah, adding that no gate in Damascus or Alexandria is its equal. Alongside Bab Mansour is a smaller gateway in the same style, **Bab Djemaa en Nouar**.

Nowadays, traffic passes through neither of these gates, and indeed the inside of Bab Mansour is now used as an arts and crafts gallery, sometimes displaying work from the Ensemble Artisanal (see p.187). Passing through the smaller gate to the left of Bab Mansour, as you face it, and then through a further gap beyond, you will find yourself in an open square, on the right of which is the green-tiled **Koubba El Khayatine** (daily 9am–noon & 3–6pm; 10dh). This was once a reception hall for ambassadors to the imperial court. Beyond it, a stairway descends into a vast series of subterranean vaults, known in popular tradition as the **Prison of Christian Slaves**. This was probably, in fact, a storehouse or granary, although there were certainly several thousand Christian captives at Ismail's court. Most were captured by the Sallee Rovers (see p.275) and brought here as slave labour for the interminable construction projects; supposedly, any of them who died while at work were simply buried in the walls they were building but, though most of the walls have since crumbled away, no remains of any such slaves have ever come to light to confirm the story.

Ahead of the *koubba*, set within the long wall and at right angles to it, are three modest **gates**. The one in the centre is generally closed and is at all times flanked by soldiers from the royal guard; within, landscaped across a lake and the sunken garden of Ismail's last and finest palace, are the **Royal Golf Gardens** – private and generally *interdit*. The gate on the left opens onto an apparently endless corridor of walls and, a few metres down, the entrance to the **Mausoleum of Moulay Ismail**.

The Mausoleum

Together with the tomb of Mohammed V in Rabat, and the Medersa Bou Inania in Fes, **Moulay Ismail's Mausoleum** (daily 9am–12.30pm & 3pm–sunset, except Friday open afternoons only for Muslims only; free) is the only active Moroccan shrine that non-Muslims may visit. Modest dress, for both women and men, is required.

The mausoleum has been a point of reverence since Ismail's death (it was constructed in his own lifetime) and continues in high esteem. This may be puzzling to Westerners, given the tales of the ruler's excesses, but in Morocco he is remembered for his achievements: bringing peace and prosperity after a period of anarchy, and driving out the Spanish from Larache and the British from Tangier. His extreme observance of orthodox Islamic form and ritual also conferred a kind of magic on him, as, of course, does his part in the foundation of the ruling Alaouite dynasty. Although technically the dynasty began with his brother, Moulay Rachid, Ismail is generally regarded as the founder.

Entering the mausoleum, you are allowed to approach the **sanctuary** in which the sultan is buried – though you cannot go beyond this annex. Decorated in bright zellij and spiralling stuccowork, it is a fine, if unspectacular, series of courts and chambers. But what is most interesting, perhaps, is that the shrine was thoroughly renovated in the 1950s at the expense of Mohammed V, and also that the sarcophagus is still the object of veneration. You will almost invariably see country people here, especially women, seeking *baraka* (charismatic blessing) and intercession from the saintly sultan's remains.

The Dar el Makhzen and Heri es Souani

Past the mausoleum, a gate to your left gives access to the dilapidated quarter of **Dar el Kebira**, Ismail's great palace complex. The imperial structures – there were originally twelve pavilions within the complex – can still be made out between and above the houses here: ogre-like creations, whose scale is hard to believe. They were completed in 1677 and dedicated at an astonishing midnight celebration, when, the chronicles record, the sultan personally slaughtered a wolf so that its head might be displayed at the centre of the gateway.

In the grandeur of the plan there is sometimes claimed a conscious echo of Versailles – its contemporary rival – though, in fact, it was another decade until the first reports of the French building reached the imperial court. When they did, Ismail was certainly interested, and in 1699 he even sent an ambassador to Paris with the task of negotiating the addition of Louis XIV's daughter, Princess Conti, to his harem. He returned without success.

On the opposite side of the long-walled corridor, beyond the Royal Golf Gardens, more immense buildings are spread out, making up Ismail's last great palace, the **Dar el Makhzen**. Unlike the Kebira, which was destroyed by the great earthquake of 1755 (the same one that levelled Lisbon), this is still a minor royal residence – though Hassan II rarely visits Meknes. The most you can get are a few brief glimpses over the heads of the guards posted by occasional gates in the crumbling, twenty-foot-high wall.

HORSES AND MULES

THE HARAS DE MEKNES

The **Haras de Meknes** is the largest national stud farm in Morocco. It is located in the Zitoun quarter on the southwest edge of town, near the military academy and the Rouah – the old imperial stables (see opposite). Take the road to Azrou or the bus #14 or #16 from the Ville Nouvelle and get off near the science and arts faculties of the university.

If you are interested, it's well worth an informal visit or, if you are knowledgeable and qualified, it is even possible to take out temporary membership of the club and help to exercise the horses (☎05/553 9753). On a short visit, you can see the *Première Ecurie,* the first stable to the left of the entrance. Here you will see valuable stallions of Arab and/or Berber stock. The cousins of such horses can be seen at riding stables around the world; and, in Morocco, they can, of course, be seen at any *fantasia* the length and breadth of the land.

SPANA

The British charity, **SPANA,** (Society for the Protection of Animals Abroad) is active in Meknes and you can visit their small centre on Rue de Laine, which runs from Bab El Qari (☎05/553 3294); you will recognize the street by the wool traders (*laine* is wool). SPANA is at no. 72 on the left. Visitors are welcome by arrangement, morning or afternoon.

In the morning, staff visit local markets and treat donkeys and mules on the spot; in the afternoon, the centre is open to treat all manner of animals brought by their owners. Mohamed Fafaite at the centre is keen on improving the footwear of the beasts of burden. Makeshift 'shoes' made of old car tyres are not good for the animals and he is encouraging blacksmiths through the Meknes Association of Blacksmiths, which is working nationally.

The corridor itself, which eventually turns a corner to bring you out by the campsite and the Heri es Souani, may perhaps be the **"strangee"** which eighteenth-century travellers recorded. A mile-long terrace wall, shaded with vines, it was a favourite drive of the sultan, who, according to several sources, was driven around in a bizarre chariot drawn by his women or eunuchs.

At the corridor's end is the chief sight of the Imperial City, the **Heri es Souani** (or Dar el Ma), which is often introduced by local guides as "Ismail's stables" (daily 9am–noon & 3–6pm; 10dh). The stables, in fact, are further south, and the startling series of high-vaulted chambers to be seen here were again a series of storerooms and granaries, filled with provisions for siege or drought. A twenty-minute walk from Bab Mansour, they give a powerful impression of the complexity of seventeenth-century Moroccan engineering. Ismail's palaces each had underground plumbing (well in advance of Europe), and here you find a remarkable system, with chain-bucket wells built between each of the storerooms. One on the right, near the back, has been restored; there are lights you can switch on for a closer look.

Equally worthwhile is the view from the **roof** of the as-Souani, approached through the second entrance on the right. From the roof garden, which in summer has a café, you can gaze out over the Dar El Makhzen and the wonderfully still **Agdal Basin** – built as an irrigation reservoir and pleasure lake, which now has a Geneva-style *jet d'eau* and beside which people picnic and wash their cars.

Over to the southwest, in the distance, you can make out another seventeenth-century royal palace, the **Dar el Baida** (the "White House"), now a military academy, and beyond it, the **Rouah**, or stables (see below).

The Rouah

The ramshackle ruins of Moulay Ismail's stables, the **Rouah**, are a thirty-minute walk from the Heri es Souani. They are officially closed to visitors – and unless you've a serious interest, not especially worthwhile. If you are committed, though, there is usually a *gardien* with keys, if you turn up and ask around. To find the site, follow the road diagonally behind *Camping Aguedal* and Heri es Souani for half a kilometre; when you reach a junction, turn right and you arrive at the **Djemaa Rouah** (Stable Mosque), a large, heavily restored building preceded by a well-kept gravel courtyard. Walk round behind the mosque and you will see the **stables** off to your right – a massive complex perhaps twice as large as the as-Souani.

In contemporary accounts the Rouah was often singled out as the greatest feature of all Ismail's building projects: some three miles in length, traversed by a long canal, with flooring built over vaults used for storing grain, and space for over 12,000 horses. Today, the province of a few scrambling goats, it's a conclusive ruin – piles of rubble and zellij tiles lining the walls and high arched aisles of crumbling pisé extending out in each direction. As such, it perhaps recalls more than anything else in Meknes the scale and madness of Moulay Ismail's vision.

The Medina

The Medina, although taking much of its present form and size under Moulay Ismail, bears less of his stamp. Its main sights, in addition to the extensive **souks**, are a Merenid medersa or "college" – the **Bou Inania** – and a nineteenth-century palace museum, the **Dar Jamai**; both are rewarding and easy to find.

The Dar Jamai

The **Dar Jamai** (daily 9am–noon & 3–6pm; closed Tues; 10dh) stands at the back of Place el Hedim, from which it is reached down a stairway. One of the best examples of a late nineteenth-century Moroccan palace, it was built in 1882 by the same family of viziers (high government officials) who put up the Palais Jamai in Fes. After 1912, it was used as a military hospital, becoming the Museum of Moroccan Art in 1920. The Andalucian Garden, with its cypress and fruit trees, and attendant birds, has been preserved.

The museum is one of the best in Morocco. Its exhibits, some of which have been incorporated to re-create reception rooms, are predominantly of the same age, though some of the pieces of **Fes** and **Meknes pottery** date back more or less to Ismail's reign. These ceramics, elaborate polychrome designs from Meknes and strong blue and white patterns from Fes, make for an interesting comparison, and the superiority of Fes's handicrafts tradition is evident. The best display, however, is of **Middle Atlas carpets**, and in particular the bold geometric designs of the Beni Mguild tribe.

The souks

To reach the souks from Place el Hedim, follow the lane immediately behind the Dar Jamai. You will come out in the middle of the Medina's major market street; on your right, leading to the Grand Mosque and Bou Inania Medersa, is **Souk es Sebbat**; on your left is **Souk en Nejjarin**.

Turning first to the left, you enter an area of textile stalls, which later give way to the carpenters' (*nejjarin*) workshops from which the souk takes its name. Shortly after this, you pass a mosque on your left, beyond which is an entrance to a parallel arcade. The **carpet market**, or **Souk Joutiya ez Zerabi**, is just off here to the left. Quality can be very high (and prices, too), though, without the constant stream of tourists of Fes or Marrakesh, dealers are much more willing to bargain. Don't be afraid to start low.

Out at the end of Souk en Nejjarin you come to another souk, the **Bezzarin**, which runs up at right angles to the Nejjarin, on either side of the city wall. This looks an unpromising, run-down neighbourhood, but if you follow the outer side of the wall, you'll come across an interesting assortment of craftsworkers, grouped together in their own trading guilds and often with an old fondouk or warehouse to the front of them. There are **basketmakers**, **ironsmiths** and **saddlers**, while near **Bab el Djedid**, at the top, you'll find **tent-makers** and a couple of **musical instrument workshops**.

Beyond the Dar Jamai, on **Souk es Sebbat**, the other option is a classier section of the market – starting off with the *babouche* vendors, and then moving on to the fancier goods aimed at tourists near the medersa, finally exiting into the covered **kissaria**, dominated by kaftan sellers. From here it's easy enough to find your way to the Bou Inania Medersa, whose imposing portal is visible on the left-hand side of the street. If you want a tea break, there's a nineteenth-century **fondouk** a short way back, which now doubles as a café and carpet/crafts emporium – look for its open courtyard. Meknes mint, incidentally, is reputed to be the best in Morocco.

Bou Inania Medersa

The **Bou Inania Medersa** (daily 9am–noon & 3–6pm; 10dh) was built around 1340–50, and is thus more or less contemporary with the great medersas of Fes. It takes its name from the notorious Sultan Abou Inan (see p.214), though it was actually founded by his predecessor, Abou El Hassan, the great Merenid builder of the Chellah in Rabat.

A modest and functional building, the medersa follows the plan of Hassan's other principal works in Rabat (the Chellah zaouia and Salé medersa), in that it has a single **courtyard** opening onto a narrow **prayer hall**, and is encircled on each floor by the

---

ARTS AND CRAFTS

The **Ensemble Artisanal** (Mon–Thurs 8.30am–noon & 2.30–6.30pm, Fri 8.30–11am & 3–6.30pm; ☎05/553 0808) is housed in a prominent, reddish building above and beyond the local bus and taxi park below Place el Hedim. It is large and trains apprentices, but despite the presence of a branch of the **Banque Populaire**, there is little to buy. There is a lot to be seen, however, including the work of the young people making **zellij** tiles. The building also houses several active co-operatives, including **La Cooperative Féminine de Céramique**.

The **Village des Potiers** is in the valley of the Oued Boufekrane which divides the Ville Nouvelle from the Medina. It's to the north, between Bab el Berdaïn and the *Hôtel Transatlantique*; if in doubt or taking a petit taxi, ask for Farharine. It's just about worth a visit but, if Safi is on your itinerary, you can give the Meknes potteries a miss.

The **Music Conservatoire** of Meknes is the impressive French-style building near Place Ifriquia, between Avenue Mohammed V and Avenue Allal Ben Abdallah. Here the students study and play classical Arab-Andalous music, together with *Milhum* and, less so, *Gharnati*. The Conservatoire gives occasional concerts. The **Institut Français**, Place Farhat Hachad (☎05/552 4071), also has a programme of music and other cultural activities and a popular student café.

students' **cells**, with exquisite screens in carved cedar. It has a much lighter feel to it than the Salé medersa, and in its balance of wood, stucco and zellij achieves a remarkable combination of intricacy – no area is left uncovered – and restraint. Architecturally, the most unusual feature is a ribbed dome over the **entrance hall**, an impressive piece of craftsmanship which extends right out into the souk.

From **the roof**, to which there's usually access, you can look out (and you feel as if you could climb across) to the tiled pyramids of the **Grand Mosque;** you can just catch a glimpse of the interior. The souk is mainly obscured from view, but you can get a good, general panorama of the town and the mosques of each quarter. Inlaid with bands of green tiles, the minarets of these distinctive mosques are unique to Meknes; those of Fes or Marrakesh tend to be more elaborate and multicoloured.

North from Bou Inania

North of the medersa and Grand Mosque, the Medina is for the most part residential, dotted with the occasional fruit and vegetable market, or (up past the mosque of Ben Khadra) a carpenters' souk, for the supply of wood. If you continue this way, you'll eventually come out in a long, open square which culminates in the monumental **Bab el Berdaïn** (The Gate of the Saddlers). This was another of Ismail's creations, and echoes, in a much more rugged and genuinely defensive structure, the central section of Bab Mansour.

Outside, the city walls continue to extend up along the main road to Rabat, and past – about 1500m out, near the new bus station – the **Bab el Khemis** (or Bab Lakhmis), another very fine gate with a frieze containing a monumental inscription etched in black tiles on the brickwork. Between the two gates, inside the wall on your left, you will catch occasional glimpses of an enormous **cemetery** – almost half the size of the Medina in extent. Non-Muslims are not permitted to enter the enclosure near the centre, in which lies the zaouia and shrine of one of the country's most famous and curious saints, **Sidi Ben Aissa**.

Reputedly a contemporary of Moulay Ismail, Ben Aissa conferred on his followers the power to eat anything, even poison or broken glass, without suffering any ill effects. His cult, the Aissaoua, became one of the most important in Morocco, and certainly the most violent and fanatical. Until prohibited by the French, some 50,000 devotees regularly attended the saint's annual moussem on the eve of Mouloud. Entering into a trance, they were known to pierce their tongues and cheeks with daggers, eat serpents and scorpions, or devour live sheep and goats. The only other confraternity to approach such frenzy was the Hamadcha of Moulay Idriss, whose rites included cutting each other's heads with hatchets and tossing heavy stones or cannonballs into the air, allowing them to fall down on their skulls. Both cults continue to hold moussems, though successive Moroccan governments have effectively outlawed their more extreme activities.

Restaurants, bars and nightlife

Meknes is a small town compared with Fes or even Tangier. In the Ville Nouvelle, most of the action is within a few blocks of the central Place Administrative. From here, a fifteen-minute walk or 10dh petit taxi will take you to the Medina, where all you need is on either side of the dog-leg Rue Rouamazine/Rue Dar Smen leading to the Bab Mansour and Place el Hedim.

Restaurants

In the **Ville Nouvelle** you'll find a dozen or so restaurants, mostly serving French-style menus. In the **Medina**, most places are basic café-grills – as well as those listed here, you'll find a group of very cheap hole-in-the-wall places doing fried fish and brochettes in Rue Rouamazine next to the *Maroc Hôtel*. However, there are also at least two excellent palatial restaurants – the *Collier de la Colombe* and the *Riad* – where you can tuck into excellent food in beautiful surroundings at a fraction of the price you'd pay in the touristy equivalent locales over in Fes, let alone back home.

MEDINA

Collier de la Colombe, 67 Rue Driba (☎05/555 5041). A smart but far from costly restaurant in the ornate mansion of "Sultan" Lakhal, a non-Alaouite pretender to the throne on the death of Moulay Youssef in 1927. Night and day, the views across the valley to the Ville Nouvelle are stunning. The à la carte menu is international, the cuisine is outstanding, and there are two very reasonable set menus. To find it, enter Place Lalla Aouda and walk diagonally across the square; follow the signs along the side street; the restaurant is 100m on the left. Daily 11.30am–3pm & 6.30–8.30pm, closed Fri lunchtime. Moderate.

Restaurant Economique, 123 Rue Dar Smen, opposite Bab Mansour and alongside *Restaurant Bab Mansour*, both are good café-restaurants, the *Economique* being marginally better. Daily 11am–9pm. Cheap.

Heri es Souani. There is a café in the rooftop garden of the Heri es Souani (see main map, pp.178–179) which looks down onto the campsite and the Agdal Basin – and beyond that to the Djebel Zerhoun. Perfect at sunset for courting couples and others, but closed for renovation at our last check.

Restaurant Riad, 79 Ksar Chaacha, Dar el Kebira (☎05/553 0542). A lovely little place in the only one of Moulay Ismail's original 12 pavilions to have survived the 1755 earthquake which largely destroyed the Dar el Kebira. It isn't easy to find (follow the green arrows from the entry to Dar el Kebira by Bab er Rih), but it's well worth the effort to sample traditional home cooking in the intimate atmosphere of its beautifully restored salons or by its patio garden. As well as very reasonable à la carte eating (*mechoui* needs to be ordered up to 3hr in advance), there are five set menus. Daily noon–3pm & 6.30–10pm. Moderate to expensive.

VILLE NOUVELLE

Café-Restaurant Camprinus, corner of Rue Charif Idrissi and Rue Omar Ibn El Ass and across the street from the Renault garage. Good traditional menu; you can eat well for 77dh. Daily noon–3.30pm & 6.30–8.30pm. Moderate.

La Coupole, corner of Av. Hassan II and Rue du Ghana. Popular with the locals. Reasonably priced Moroccan and European dishes. and a set menu. There's also a bar and a noisy nightclub. Daily noon–3pm & 6–11pm. Moderate.

Le Dauphin, 5 Av. Mohammed V, although the entrance is down the side street, Rue El Leanissa. Managed by the *Hôtel Bab Mansour*, this is an old-fashioned French place with reliable cooking and a reputation for seafood. Daily noon–3pm & 7–11pm. Expensive.

Restaurant Diafa, 12 Rue Badr El Kobra. This building looks like it's a private house and has extremely good and reasonably priced cooking, with two set menus though not a vast choice of dishes. Daily noon–3pm & 7pm–midnight. Moderate.

Restaurant Pizza Fongue, 8 Rue Accra, alongside the *Hôtel de Nice*. Limited menu, beyond the pizzas, but good value, and handy for out-of-hours snacks. Open 24hr. Cheap.

Pizzeria Le Four, 1 Rue Atlas – near the *Hôtel Majestic*, off Av. Mohammed V. The interior, mock Italian-Tudor, is a shade gloomy, but the food, vaguely Italian, is good value. Licensed. Daily noon–3pm & 7–10pm. Moderate.

Rotisserie Restaurant Karam, 2 Rue Ghana, off Av. Mohammed V. Small, intimate: grills and tajines. More a café than a rotisserie, which stays open for a late-night snack. Daily 11.30am–11pm. Cheap.

Restaurant Marhaba, 23 Av. Mohammed V, by the Empire cinema; not to be confused with the café *Glacier Marhaba* which fronts Av. Mohammed V. A functional eating place with soup, brochettes and lamb tajine – and popular with locals. Daily noon–8pm in winter, 9pm in summer. Cheap.

Annexe Metropole, 11 Rue Charif Idrissi, behind the *Metropole* proper which is at 12 Av. Hassan II. Excellent cooking and well worth the little extra. There are three set menus, one of which always offers either pastilla or *mechoui*. Licensed. Daily 10am–10pm. Moderate.

Restaurant Mo-Dinero, 16 Zenkat Antisrabe, one block east of the main post office in the Ville Nouvelle. Well-prepared chicken kebabs, pizzas and salads. Daily noon–3pm & 7–10.30pm. Cheap to moderate.

Restaurant Montana, 4 Rue Atlas – opposite *Le Four* (above). There is a bar on the ground floor; upstairs is a restaurant decorated to imitate a tent. Limited menu – and not so good as it used to be. Daily noon–3pm & 7–11pm. Moderate.

Restaurant Novelty 12 Rue de Paris. A restaurant alongside an all-day bar. Good value *plat du jour* 50dh, and menu at 60dh. Daily noon–3pm & 7–9pm. Cheap.

Restaurant Zagora, 34 Rue Emir Abdelkader. Excellent fresh fried fish, with chips and salad, in a friendly and unpretentious little café-restaurant. Daily 11am–2am. Cheap.

Cafés

Aubercyber, 6 Rue Badr el Kobra (*Aubercyber@bercyber.net.ma*). A very classy Internet café, with coffee and cakes upstairs and computers downstairs. Daily 9am–10.30pm.

Café Opéra, 7 Av. Mohammed V. A blend of café and patisserie which attracts a young crowd. and stays open daytime during Ramadan. Daily 6am–11pm.

Cremerie du Palmier, 53 Av. des F.A.R. Another excellent patisserie, with good *rayeb* (set yoghurt in a glass) located next door to the *Hôtel Excelsior*. Daily 3am–10pm.

Bars

There are bars in many of the Ville Nouvelle hotels, most of which are quite lively of an evening. For a sedate drink, the *Hôtel Transatlantique* would be your best bet. For something less sedate, male readers might care to try the following (several of which have female bar staff, though most women would find them rather intimidating nonetheless with their raucous, all-male clientele).

Café Français (aka *Club de Nuit*), by the *Hôtel Excelsior*, on Av. des F.A.R. A bar decorated with mirrors, with a nightclub attached. Bar open daily 6am–11pm, club nightly 9pm–3am.

Bar Continental, by the *Hôtel Continental*, on the opposite side of Av. des F.A.R. A nice bit of Art Deco ironwork on the doors to match the *Hôtel Volubilis* across the street; rather a seedy dive within, but fun if you're in that kind of mood. Daily 6am–10.30pm.

Cabaret Oriental, Av. Hassan II. Occasionally hosts bands into the small hours.

Volubilis Nightclub, part of the *Hôtel Volubilis* (entrance down an alley under the arch to the right of the hotel). Worth checking out. Nightly 9pm–3am.

Listings

Airlines Royal Air Maroc has an office at 7 Av. Mohammed V (☎05/552 0963); the nearest airport is at Saïs, south of Fes.

Banks are concentrated around Place Administrative, and along Av. Mohammed V (the Crédit du Maroc is at no. 33, Banque Populaire at no. 17, BMCE at no. 7) and Av. des F.A.R. (BMCE at no. 98). In the Medina, the Banque Populaire on Rue Dar Smen, near Bab Mansour, has exchange facilities, as does BMCE in Rue Rouamazine. BMCI by Dar Jamai in Place el Hedim has a bureau de change open Sundays 10am–noon & 3–5pm. The *Hôtel Rif* will exchange cash round the clock.

Bookshop Top Notch is an English bookshop, run by an American at 28 Rue Emir Abdelkader with a small selection of classics, second-hand books and African novels; worth browsing.

Car rental Try Bab Mansour Car, 3 Rue Safi (off Av. Hassan II at its western end; ☎05/552 6631). None of the major companies has offices in Meknes.

Car repairs Car mechanics and spare parts shops are concentrated around Bd. el Kods in the New Mellah, and the beginning of Zenkat Zalaka and Zenkat Nador at their junction with Av. des F.A.R. Renault garages are to be found on Rue Charif Idrissi (at the corner of Av. Mohammed V, just north of Place Ifriquia) and out on the Route de Fes.

Cinemas Central ones include the Camera on Place Ifriquia, the Regent next door to the *Hôtel Bab Mansour*, the Empire at 25 Av. Mohammed V, all of which show a mixture of Indian, American, French and Egyptian movies.

Festivals The city's Ben Aïssa Moussem (aka Moussem Cheikh El Kamal) is one of the country's most impressive. Also worth planning for are the Beni Rached Moussem (seven days after Mouloud; at the village of Beni Rached, out of town on the Moulay Idriss road) and the Moulay Idriss Moussem (at Moulay Idriss, second week of August).

Hammams In the Medina, there's one down the little street by the BMCE bank in Rue Rouamazine (women noon–8pm; men 6am–noon & 8pm–midnight); in the Ville Nouvelle, ask for Hammam Al Hadika, off the western end of Av. Hassan II, at 4 Rue Patrice Lumumba, with separate sections for women and men (both 7am–9pm).

Laundry Atlas Pressing, 26 Av. Allal Ben Abdallah, opposite Collège Allal Ben Abdallah; Pressing Marhaba, by the steps leading from Rue Rouamazine up to the *Collier de la Colombe* restaurant.

Medical services English-speaking doctors include Dr Mohammed Dbab at 4 Rue Accra (☎05/552 0187).

Post office The PTT is just off Place de France (Oct–mid-July Mon–Fri 8am–6.30pm; mid-July–Sept 8am–3.30pm; Ramadan 9am–3.30pm); the telephone section is open daily 8am–8.45pm and sells stamps, and there are public callboxes by the entrance and many *téléboutiques* on Av. Mohammed V and elsewhere. Branch post offices include one in the Medina at the corner of Re Dar Smen and Rue Rouamazine (Mon–Thurs 8am–12.15pm & 3–8.30pm, Fri 8am–11.30am & 3–8.30pm).

Pharmacies Pharmacie d'urgence de nuit, in the *Hôtel de Ville* on Place Administrative (☎05/552 3375) is open 8.30pm–8.30am, and there's another night pharmacy and dispensary behind the local bus stands just south of Place el Hedim.

Police The local HQ is Place Ferhat Hached, at the western end of Av. Hassan II (☎19). There's a smaller station next to Bab Djemaa en Nouar in the southwest corner of Place el Hedim.

Swimming pools There are two public pools down by the river Oued Boufekrane, reached along a lane from Bd. El Haboul or from the intersection of Av. Hassan II and Av. Moulay Ismail, both open June–Sept only. The first is very cheap at 5dh; just to its north is CODM Natation – classier, less crowded, and several times the price at 30dh.

Moving on

CTM has eight daily departures for **Fes** (the last at 11pm), and seven for **Casa** and **Rabat**. Other destinations covered at least once daily include Tangier, Nador, Oujda, Marrakesh, Agadir and Rissani. For most of these destinations it's a good idea to buy your ticket in advance. The same destinations are covered even more frequently from the main bus station – Fes and Moulay Idriss at least hourly for most of the day. One problem however is that the destination indicators here are in Arabic only, though you can ask for help at the small one-person information kiosk.

Grands taxis use a yard alongside the bus station, and destinations regularly include Moulay Idriss, Sidi Slimane, Ouezzane, Kenitra, Casablanca, Ifrane, Midelt, Er Rachidia and Khenifra (those for Fes leave just across the street). Some grands taxis for Fes and Oujda also leave from next to the CTM bus station (most grands taxis for Fes will set you down at the train station there, rather than the *gare routière*). Grands taxis for one or two local destinations use a yard across the road from the local bus stops below Place el Hedim in the Medina, and on Rue Omar el Moutahida in the Nouvelle Ville, though it is unlikely that you will need to use these. There's also a **taxi** rank (grands and petits taxis – but the former again for local destinations only, unless you charter one) at the junction of Avenue des F.A.R. and Avenue Mohammed V.

Volubilis and Moulay Idriss

An easy excursion from Meknes, **Volubilis** and **Moulay Idriss** embody much of Morocco's early history: Volubilis as its Roman provincial capital, Moulay Idriss in the creation of the country's first Arab dynasty. Their sites stand 4km apart, at either side of a deep and very fertile valley, about 30km north of Meknes.

Practicalities

You can take in both sites on a leisurely day-trip from Meknes. **Grands taxis** make regular runs to **Moulay Idriss** (10dh a place) from near the new bus station by Bab El

Khemis in the Medina and from near the French Cultural Centre just off Avenue Hassan II in the Ville Nouvelle. For **Volubilis**, you can take a Ouezzane bus and ask to be set down by the site (which is a 500m walk downhill from the P28 road), or you could charter a grand taxi. The whole taxi (*une course*) should cost 60dh (six times the price of a *place* to Moulay Idriss, for which it's on the way), which can be split between up to six passengers; if you pay a little more, the taxi driver will wait at Volubilis and take you on to Moulay Idriss, where you can look round at leisure and then get a regular place in a grand taxi back to Meknes. You could also walk between Volubilis and Moulay Idriss, which are only around 4km apart.

Non-Muslims are not permitted to stay overnight in the town of Moulay Idriss – the only place in Morocco to keep this religious prohibition. However, near Volubilis there is a **campsite**, *Camping Belle-Vue* 11km from Volubilis and 9km from Moulay Idriss (see p.196), and a **hotel**, the *Volubilis Inn* (☎05/554 4405, fax 554 4369; ⑥), 1km from Volubilis (which it overlooks), and 3km from Moulay Idriss – luxurious with dramatic views, but expensive and, without transport, inconvenient, although a minibus will pick you up in Meknes or Fes by prior arrangement. Food and drink are available from the Café Oualili, at the entrance to the site.

Volubilis

A striking sight, visible for miles from the various bends in the approach road, **VOLU-BILIS** occupies the ledge of a long, high plateau. Below its walls, towards Moulay Idriss, stretches a rich river valley; beyond lie dark, outlying ridges of the Zerhoun mountains. The drama of this scene – and the scope of the ruins – may well seem familiar. It was the key location for Martin Scorsese's film, *The Last Temptation of Christ*.

Some history

Except for a small trading post on the island off Essaouira, Volubilis was the Roman Empire's most remote and far-flung base. The imperial roads stopped here, having reached across France and Spain and then down from Tangier, and despite successive emperors' dreams of "penetrating the Atlas", the southern Berber tribes were never effectively subdued.

Direct Roman rule here, in fact, lasted little over two centuries – the garrison withdrew early, in 285 AD, to ease pressure elsewhere. But the town must have taken much of its present form well before the official annexation of North African Mauretania by Emperor Claudius in 45 AD. Tablets found on the site, inscribed in Punic, show a significant Carthaginian trading presence in the third century BC, and prior to colonization it was the western capital of a heavily Romanized, but semi-autonomous, Berber kingdom, which reached into northern Algeria and Tunisia. After the Romans left, Volubilis saw very gradual change. Latin was still spoken in the seventh century by the local population of Berbers, Greeks, Syrians and Jews; Christian churches survived until the coming of Islam; and the city itself remained alive and active well into the eighteenth century, when its marble was carried away by slaves for the building of Moulay Ismail's Meknes.

What you see today, well excavated and maintained, are largely the ruins of second- and third-century AD buildings – impressive and affluent creations from its period as a colonial provincial capital. The land around here is some of the most fertile in North Africa, and the city exported wheat and olives in considerable quantities to Rome, as it did wild animals from the surrounding hills. Roman games, memorable for the sheer scale of their slaughter (9000 beasts were killed for the dedication of Rome's Colosseum alone), could not have happened without the African provinces, and Volubilis was a chief source of their lions. Within just two hundred years, along with Barbary bears and elephants, they became virtually extinct.

The site

The entrance to the site (daily 9am–noon & 2.30–6pm; 15dh admission) is through a minor gate in the city wall, built along with a number of outer camps in 168 AD, following a prolonged series of Berber insurrections. Just inside are the **ticket office**, and the cool Café Oualili, named after the Arabic for Volubilis, which is a corruption of *oualili*, meaning oleander. Here there is a small, open-air **museum**, with remains of many altars and other sculptural fragments. From time to time, funds permitting, there are further excavations and discoveries – and attempts at the restoration of the fallen structures.

The best of the finds made here – which include a superb collection of bronzes – have all been taken to the Rabat museum which, for that alone, is worth a serious visit. Volubilis, however, has retained *in situ* the great majority of its **mosaics**, some thirty or so in a good state of preservation. You leave with a real sense of Roman city life and its provincial prosperity, while in the layout of the site it is not hard to recognize the essentials of a medieval Arab town.

Following the path up from the museum and across a bridge over the Fertassa stream, you come out on a mixed area of housing and industry, each of its buildings containing the clear remains of at least one **olive press**. The extent and number of these presses, built into even the grandest mansions, reflect the olive's absolute importance to the city and indicate perhaps why Volubilis remained unchanged for so long after the Romans' departure. A significant proportion of its 20,000 population must have been involved in some capacity in the oil's production and export.

Somewhat isolated in this suburban quarter is the **House of Orpheus**, an enormous complex of rooms just beside the start of a paved way. Although substantially in ruins, it offers a strong impression of its former luxury – an opulent mansion for perhaps one of the town's richest merchants. It is divided into two main sections – public and private – each with its separate entrance and interior court. The private rooms, which you come to first, are grouped around a small patio which is decorated with a more or less intact **dolphin mosaic**. You can also make out the furnace and heating system (just by the entrance), the kitchen with its niche for the household gods, and the **baths** – an extensive system of hot, cold and steam rooms.

The house's public apartments, a little further inside, are dominated by a large **atrium**, half reception hall, half central court, and again preserving a very fine mosaic, **The Chariot of Amphitrite Drawn by a Seahorse**. The best example here, however, and the mosaic from which the house takes its name, is that of the **Orpheus Myth**, located to the south in a room which was probably the *tablinium*, or archives.

Above the Orpheus House, a broad, paved street leads up towards the main group of public buildings – the Capitol and Basilica, whose sand-coloured ruins dominate the site. Taking the approach on the left, you pass first through the remains of the city's main **Public Baths**. Restored by the Emperor Gallienus in the second century AD, these are clearly monumental in their intent, though sadly the mosaics are only fragmentary. The arrangement of the **Forum** is typical of a major Roman town: built on the highest rise of the city and flanked by a triumphal arch, market, capitol and basilica.

The **Capitol**, the smaller and lower of the two main buildings, has been dated from inscriptions to 217 AD – a time at which this whole public nucleus seems to have been rebuilt by the African-born Severian emperors. Adjoined by small forum **baths**, it is an essentially simple building, with a porticoed court giving access to a small temple and altar. Its dedication – standard throughout the Roman world – was to the official state cult of Capitoline Jove, Juno and Minerva. The large five-aisled **Basilica** to its side served as the courthouse, while immediately across the forum were the small court and stalls of the central **market**.

The **Triumphal Arch**, right in the middle of the town, had no particular purpose other than creating a ceremonial function for the principal street, the Decumanus Maximus – on whose side it is more substantially ornamented. Erected in honour of the Severian emperor, Caracalla, its inscription records that it was originally surmounted by a bronze chariot. This and the nymphs, which once shot water into its basins below, are gone, though with its tall Corinthian columns (of imported marble), it is still an impressive monument. The medallions on either side, heavily eroded, presumably depict Caracalla and his mother, Julia Donna, who is also named in the inscription.

MANSIONS AND MOSAICS

The finest of Volubilis's mansions – and its mosaics – line the **Decumanus Maximus**, fronted in traditional Roman and Italian fashion by the shops built in tiny cubicles. Before you reach this point, however, take a look at the remains of an **aqueduct** and **fountains** across from the triumphal arch; these once supplied yet another complex of public baths. Opposite them is a small group of **houses**, mostly ruined but retaining an impressive **Mosaic of an Athlete** or "chariot jumper" – depicted receiving the winner's cup for a *desultor* race, a display of great skill which entailed leaping on and off a horse in full gallop.

First of the Decumanus Maximus mansions, the **House of the Ephebus** takes its name from the bronze of a youth found in its ruins (and today displayed in Rabat). In general plan it is very similar to the House of Orpheus, once again containing an olive press in its rear section, though this building is on a far grander scale – almost twice the size of the other – with pictorial mosaics in most of its public rooms and an ornamental pool in its central court. Finest of the mosaics is a representation of **Bacchus Being Drawn in a Chariot by Panthers** – a suitable scene for the *cenacula*, or banqueting hall, in which it is placed.

Separated from the Ephebus House by a narrow lane is a mosaic-less mansion, known after its facade as the **House of Columns**, and adjoining this, the **Knight's House** with an incomplete mosaic of **Dionysos Discovering Ariadne** asleep on the beach at Naxos; both houses are themselves largely ruined. More illuminating is the large mansion which begins the next block, similar again in its plan, but featuring a very complete mosaic of the **Labours of Hercules**. Almost comic caricatures, these give a good idea of typical provincial Roman mosaics – immediate contrasts to the stylish **Orpheus and Bacchus** and **Nymphs Bathing** of the second house down.

Beyond this area, approaching the partially reconstructed **Tangier Gate**, stands the **Palace of the Gordians**, former residence of the procurators who administered the city and the province. Despite its size, however, even with a huge **bath house** and pooled courtyards, it is an unmemorable ruin. Stripped of most of its columns, and lacking any mosaics, its grandeur and scale may have made it an all too obvious target for Ismail's building mania. Indeed, how much of Volubilis remained standing before his reign began is an open question; Walter Harris, writing at the turn of the twentieth century, found the road between here and Meknes littered with ancient marbles, left as they fell following the announcement of the sultan's death.

Back on the Decumanus, cross to the other side of the road and walk down a block to a smaller lane below the street. Here, in the third house you come to, is the most exceptional ensemble of mosaics of the entire site – the **Cortege of Venus**. You cannot enter the house but most of the fine mosaics can be seen by walking round the outside of the ruins. If you imagine walking into the main section of the house, a central court is preceded by a paved vestibule and opens onto another, smaller patio, around which are grouped the main reception halls (and mosaics). From the entrance, the **baths** are off to the left, flanked by the private quarters, while immediately around the central court is a small group of mosaics, including an odd, very worn representation of a **Chariot Race** – with birds instead of horses.

The villa's most outstanding mosaics lie beyond, in the "public" sections. On the left, in the corner, is a geometrical design, with medallions of **Bacchus Surrounded by the Four Seasons**; off to the right are **Diana Bathing** (and surprised by the huntsman Actaeon) and the **Abduction of Hylas by Nymphs**. Each of these scenes – especially the last two – is superbly handled in stylized but very fluid animation. They date, like that of the **Nereids** (two houses further down), from the late second or early third century AD, and were obviously a serious commission. It is not known for whom this house was built, but its owner must have been among the city's most successful patrons; here were found the bronze busts of Cato and Juba II which are now the centrepiece of Rabat's museum.

Leaving the site by a path below the forum, you pass close by the ruins of a **temple** on the opposite side of the stream. This was dedicated by the Romans to Saturn, but seems to have previously involved the worship of a Carthaginian god; several hundred votive offerings were discovered during its excavation.

Moulay Idriss

MOULAY IDRISS takes its name from its founder, Morocco's most venerated saint and the creator of its first Arab dynasty. His tomb and zaouia lie right at the heart of the town, the reason for its sacred status and the object of constant pilgrimage – and an important summer **moussem**, held in the second week of August. For non-Muslims, barred from the shrines, there is little specific that can be seen, and nothing that may be visited, but wandering the hilly lanes with their delightful window-views, or just sitting in a café absorbing the holiday-pilgrim atmosphere, is pleasant enough.

As you approach the town, locals will point out that the town looks like a Bactrian camel, with the shrine and zaouia as the saddle between the two humps.

The Town

Arriving in Moulay Idriss, you find yourself below an elongated square near the base of the town; above you, almost directly ahead, stand the green-tiled pyramids of the shrine and zaouia, on either side of which rise the two conical quarters of Khiber and Tasga.

The souks, such as they are, line the streets of the Khiber (the taller hill) above the zaouia. They offer a variety of religious artefacts for Muslim visitors, especially plain white candles for the shrines, together with excellent local nougat – which is produced and sold here in great quantities – and, in autumn, *arbutus* (strawberry tree) berries.

Moulay Idriss' shrine and zaouia, rebuilt by Moulay Ismail, stands cordoned off from the street by a low, wooden bar placed to keep out Christians and beasts of burden. To get a true sense of it, you have to climb up towards one of the vantage points near the pinnacle of each quarter – ideally, the **Terrasse Sidi Abdallah El Hajjam**

MOULAY IDRISS AND THE FOUNDATION OF MOROCCO

Moulay Idriss El Akhbar (The Elder) was a great-grandson of the Prophet Muhammad; his grandparents were Muhammad's daughter Fatima, and cousin and first follower, Ali. Heir to the Caliphate in Damascus, he fled to Morocco around 787, following the Ommayad victory in the great civil war which split the Muslim world into Shia and Sunni sects.

In Volubilis, then still the main centre of the north, Idriss seems to have been welcomed as an *imam* (a spiritual and political leader), and within five years had succeeded in carving out a considerable kingdom. At this new town site, more easily defended than Volubilis, he built his capital, and he also began the construction of Fes, later continued and considerably extended by his son Idriss II, that city's patron saint. News of his growing power, however, filtered back to the East, and in 792, the Ommayads had Idriss poisoned, doubtless assuming that his kingdom would likewise disappear.

In this they were mistaken. Idriss had instilled with the faith of Islam the region's previously pagan (and sometimes Christian or Jewish) Berber tribes and had been joined in this prototypical Moroccan state by increasing numbers of Arab Shiites loyal to the succession of his *Alid* line. After his assassination, Rashid, the servant who had travelled with Idriss to Morocco, took over as regent until 807, when the founder's son, Idriss II, was old enough to assume the throne.

right above the Khiber. It's not easy to find your way up through the winding streets (most end in abrupt blind alleys), and, unless you're into the challenge of it all, you'd do better to enlist the help of a young guide down in the *place*.

As you climb to the terrace, he will probably point out the unusual modern minaret of the **Idriss Medersa**, now a Koranic school. The Medersa was built with materials taken from Volubilis; the modern cylindrical minaret was built in 1939 by a *hadji* on his return from Mecca where he had seen one for the first time. A *surah* (chapter) from the Koran is inscribed in Kufic script in green mosaics.

There are several grill **cafés** on the elongated square. For more substantial fare, there is the *Restaurant Dar Diaf* (moderate), near the shrine, and the cheaper *Restaurant Baraka* (moderate), a small white building, near the *fantasia* ground on the way into the town.

Around Meknes

Heading **north** from Meknes, towards Larache, Tangier or Chaouen, Volubilis (see p.192) provides by far the most interesting excursion; heading **east to Fes**, there is little to delay you on the hour-long journey. Covered below are the routes **west to Rabat** and **south to Azrou**, both of which offer a few points of interest along the way. For details on the trains, buses and grands taxis from Meknes, see p.266.

West to Rabat: Khémisset and Lake Roumi

The road **west of Meknes** (P1) is a pleasant drive, running at first through a rich, cultivated landscape, then cutting across low, forested hills, with lavender (planted for perfume) on the lower slopes. Above a bend in the road, 30km from Meknes, is a model village (labelled "Village Pilote" on the *Michelin* map) built in 1965 as the first of a planned rehousing programme.

KHÉMISSET, 46km from Meknes, is a small market town, created by the French to encourage settlement of the scattered Zemmour Berbers of the region. It hosts a Tuesday souk which is known for its carpets and wood carvings, and has a pleasant **hotel**, the *Diouri* (☎/fax 03/755 2645; ③), on the eastern outskirts of town. Driving from Meknes to Rabat, the hotel is about midway, and its restaurant makes a good stop for lunch. If you want just a quick snack, try the *Café Yasmina* next door.

If you're in no hurry, a diversion to the **Dayet Er Roumi** – Lake Roumi – is highly recommended. This lies 15km southwest of Khémisset, just off the S106, and it's a gorgeous place: shimmering water, lots of birdsong, woodsmoke from the fires of shepherds – every inch the pastoral idyll. From April to October, a **campsite** (☎03/755 2977; 15dh per person and per tent) and **café** operate by the water's edge, and rent out pedalos to while away the afternoon. Swimming here is also fine, and you can fish, if you come equipped with a permit.

To reach the café and campsite, you need to turn left, off the S106, on a rough road by a cactus field with five trees; the signposted road to the lake, 1500m beyond, leads only to a group of lakeside houses. If you don't have a car, it's possible to charter a grand taxi at Khémisset.

South to Azrou: Agouraï, El Hajeb and the Paysage d'Ito

South of Meknes is one of Morocco's few remaining **wine-growing areas**. Under French rule, Morocco and Algeria produced up to a third of the table wine consumed in France – and had some respectable vintages. Since independence, inevitably, the profile and marketplace dropped, as, alas, has the quality, which is very hit-and-miss.

Nonetheless, some decent reds – marketed as *Toulal* – are produced at **AÏT-SOUALA,** on the minor S3065 road, west of the main Azrou road, and if you're curious, the vineyards can be visited. Continuing along the 3065 brings you out at the **kasbah** of **AGOURAÏ,** built by Moulay Ismail and now enclosing a small Berber village. It's an interesting spot, with water sluicing down the main street, and a buzzing Thursday **souk**. There is a café but no rooms or meals to be had, just drinks and cakes.

Back on the main road to Azrou, the P21, the cultivation changes to wheat, planted in the *poljes* or depressions of this classic *karst* countryside. The small town of **EL HAJEB** ("eyebrow" in Arabic) occupies a high, cliffside site, alongside a ruined nineteenth-century fort. It has a Monday **souk**, a bank and several cafés.

Just south of the town, the road divides, with a minor route, the S309, leading through cedar forests to Ifrane (see p.243). The P21 to Azrou, though, is the road to take, for after 18km (17km north of Azrou) you reach the remarkable **Paysage d'Ito** – a natural roadside balcony on the edge of a volcanic plateau, with a really stunning panorama, stretching for perhaps seventy kilometres. The landscape is wonderfully bizarre, with outcrops of extinct volcanoes, and was used as the backdrop for many of the early science fiction films of the 1950s and 1960s.

Nearby is the *Auberge d'Ito*. You can no longer sleep here, nor eat, unless you order in advance, but you can drink – and you won't be the only one. Be warned, however, that it's a little rough.

Fes (Fez)

The history of Fes is composed of wars and murders, triumphs of arts and sciences, and a good deal of imagination.

Walter Harris: *Land of an African Sultan*

The most ancient of the Imperial Capitals, and the most complete medieval city of the Arab world, **FES** is a place that stimulates your senses, with haunting and beautiful sounds, infinite visual details and unfiltered odours. More than any other city in Morocco, it seems to exist suspended in time somewhere between the Middle Ages and the modern world. As with other Moroccan cities, it has a French-built Ville Nouvelle – familiar and modern in appearance and urban life – but a quarter or so of Fes's 800,000 inhabitants continue to live in the extraordinary Medina-city of **Fes El Bali** – which owes little to the West besides its electricity and its tourists.

As a spectacle, this is unmissable, and it's difficult to imagine a city whose external forms (all you can really hope to penetrate) could be so constant a source of interest. But stay in Fes a few days and it's equally hard to avoid the paradox of the place. Like much of "traditional" Morocco, the city was "saved" and then re-created by the French – under the auspices of General Lyautey, the Protectorate's first Resident-General. Lyautey took the philanthropic and startling move of declaring the city a historical monument; philanthropic because he was certainly saving Fes El Bali from destruction (albeit from less benevolent Frenchmen), and startling because until then many Moroccans were under the impression that Fes was still a living city – the Imperial Capital of the Moroccan empire rather than a preservable part of the nation's heritage. In fact, this paternalistic protection conveniently helped to disguise the dismantling of the old culture. By building a new European city nearby – the Ville Nouvelle – and then transferring Fes's economic and political functions to Rabat and the west coast, Lyautey ensured the city's eclipse along with its preservation.

To appreciate the significance of this demise, you only have to look at the Arab chronicles or old histories of Morocco, every one of which takes Fes as its central focus. The city had dominated Moroccan trade, culture and religious life – and usually its politics, too – since the end of the tenth century. It was closely and symbolically linked with the birth of an "Arabic" Moroccan state due to their mutual foundation by Moulay Idriss I, and was regarded, after Mecca and Medina, as one of the holiest cities of the Islamic world. Medieval European travellers wrote of it with a mixture of awe and respect – as a "citadel of fanaticism" and yet the most advanced seat of learning in mathematics, philosophy and medicine.

The decline of the city notwithstanding, **Fassis** – the people of Fes – have a reputation throughout Morocco as successful and sophisticated. Just as the city is situated at the centre of the country, so are its inhabitants placed at the heart of government, and most government ministries are headed by Fassis. What is undeniable is that they have the most developed Moroccan city culture, with an intellectual tradition, and their own cuisine (sadly not at its best in the modern city restaurants), dress and way of life.

The development of Fes

When the city's founder, Moulay Idriss I, died in 792, Fes was little more than a village on the east bank of the river. It was his son, **Idriss II**, who really began the city's development, at the beginning of the ninth century, by making it his capital and allowing in refugees from Andalucian Córdoba and from Kairouan in Tunisia – at the time, the two most important cities of western Islam. The impact on Fes of these refugees was immediate and lasting: they established separate, walled towns (still distinct quarters today) on either riverbank, and provided the superior craftsmanship and mercantile experience for Fes's industrial and commercial growth. It was at this time, too, that the city gained its intellectual reputation. The tenth-century Pope Silvester II studied here at the Kairaouine University, and from this source he is said to have introduced Arabic mathematics to Europe.

The seat of government – and impetus of patronage – shifted south to Marrakesh under the Berber dynasties of the **Almoravides** (1068–1145) and **Almohads** (1145–1250). But with the conquest of Fes by the **Merenids** in 1248, and their subsequent consolidation of power across Morocco, the city regained its pre-eminence and moved into something of a "golden age". Alongside the old Medina, the Merenids built a massive royal city – **Fes El Djedid**, meaning "New Fes" – which reflected both the wealth and confidence of their rule. They enlarged and decorated the Kairaouine mosque, added a network of fondouks (inns) for the burgeoning commercial activity, and greatly developed the Kairaouine University – building the series of magnificent **medersas**, or colleges, to accommodate its students. Once again this expansion was based on an influx of refugees, this time from the Spanish reconquest of Andalucia, and it helped to establish the city's reputation as "the Baghdad of the West".

It is essentially Merenid Fes which you witness today in the form of the city and its monuments. From the fall of the dynasty in the mid-sixteenth century, there was decline as both Fes and Morocco itself became isolated from the main currents of Western culture. The new rulers – the **Saadians** – in any case preferred Marrakesh, and although Fes re-emerged as the capital under the **Alaouites**, it had begun to lose its international stature. Moulay Ismail, whose hatred of the Fassis was legendary, almost managed to tax the city out of existence, and the principal building concerns of his successors lay in restoring and enlarging the vast domains of the royal palace.

Under **French colonial rule**, there were positive achievements in the preservation of the old city and relative prosperity of the Ville Nouvelle, but little actual progress. As a thoroughly conservative and bourgeois city, Fes became merely provincial. Even so, it remained a symbol of Moroccan pride and aspirations, playing a crucial role in the **struggle for independence**. The nationalist factions came together in Fes in 1943 to form the unified independence party: **Istiqlal**; an event recorded in Arabic on a

△ Bab Ftouh (& Taza)

△ Merenid Tombs (& Chaouen)

FES EL BALI

Medersa
Bou Inania

Bab
Boujeloud

See 'Around Bab
Boujeloud map

Dar Batha

Bab
Mahrouk

Boujeloud
Gardens

Bab
Segma

FES EL
DJEDID

Bab
Semarine

American
Fondouk

GRANDE RUE DES MERENIDS

MELLAH
Synagogue

Kasbah Cherarda

MOULAY
ABDALLAH

GRANDE RUE DES MERENIDS

PLACE
DES
ALAOUITES

See 'Fes El
Djedid' map

GRAND MECHOUAR

Royal
Palace

MOULAY YOUSSEF

BD. DES ALAOUITES

BOULEVARD DES SAADIENS

Swimming
Pool

AVENUE DES MERENIDES

BOULEVARD DES SAADIENS

Oued Fes

FES VILLE NOUVELLE

ACCOMMODATION

Hôtel Amor	7
Hôtel Central	20
Hôtel CTM	22
Hôtel Errabie	25
Hôtel Excelsior	13
Grand Hôtel	15
Ibis Hôtel	1
Hôtel Kairouan	2
Hôtel Lamdaghri	14
Hôtel du Maghreb	19
Hôtel Menzeh Zalagh	5 & 6
Hôtel Mounia	21
Hôtel Nouzha	24
Hôtel Olympic	11
Hôtel du Pacha	9
Hôtel de la Paix	4
Hôtel Renaissance	16
Hôtel Rex	23
Hôtel Royal	3
Sheraton Fes Hôtel	8
Hôtel Sofia	17
Splendid Hotel	12
Hôtel Wassim	12
Youth Hostel	10

RESTAURANTS, BARS & CAFÉS

Pizzeria Assouan	Q
Bar Astor	L
Black Berry	B
Restaurant Chamonix	J
Restaurant La Cheminée	A
Café Chope	O
Café Cristal	I
Bar Dalila	E
Café Floria	F
Fish Friture	C
Gelattitalia	M
Al Khozma	P
Restaurant Marrakesh	H
Café Restaurant La	
Noblesse	J
Café Number One	O
Oued de la Bière	M
Cybercafé Peacock	K
Le Progres	L
Café de la Renaissance	S
Tivoli	G
Café Restaurant Tout	
Va Bien	D
Venisia Sandwich	N
Chez Vittoria	R
Zagora Restaurant	

tablet outside the *Hôtel Batha*, on Place de l'Istiqlal. And later, in 1955, the subsequent events in Fes were marvellously brought to life in Paul Bowles's novel *The Spider's House*.

Since **independence** in 1956, the city's position has been less than happy. The first sultan, Mohammed V, retained the French capital of Rabat, and with this signalled the final decline of the Fassi political and financial elites. In 1956, too, the city lost most of its Jewish community to France and Israel. In their place, the Medina population now has a predominance of first-generation rural migrants, often poorly housed in mansions designed for single families but now accommodating four or five, while the city as a whole is increasingly dependent on handicrafts and the tourist trade. If UNESCO had not moved in with its Cultural Heritage plan for the city's preservation, it seems likely that its physical collapse would have become even more widespread.

Socially, too, the city has had major problems. It was a focus of the riots of December 1990, in which the disaffected urban poor and the students vented their frustrations on government buildings, and burnt out the luxury *Hôtel des Merenides*, above the Medina, though without attacking any tourists.

Orientation, information, arrival and guides

Even if you'd felt you were getting accustomed to Moroccan cities, Fes is likely to prove bewildering. The basic layout is simple enough, with a Moroccan **Medina** and French-built **Ville Nouvelle**, but here the Medina comprises two separate cities: **Fes El Bali** (Old Fes), down in the pear-shaped bowl of the Sebou valley, and **Fes El Djedid** (New Fes), established on the edge of the valley during the thirteenth century.

Fes El Djedid, dominated by a vast enclosure of royal palaces and gardens, is relatively straightforward. **Fes El Bali**, however, where you'll want to spend most of your time, is an incredibly intricate web of lanes, blind alleys and souks. It takes two or three days before you even start to feel confident in where you're going, and on an initial visit you may well want to pay for a guide (see p.204) to show you the main sights and layout. The learning process is not helped, either, by the fact that most of the streetsigns are in Arabic only.

Fes's **tourist office**, the ONMT's *Délégation de Tourisme,* is in Immeuble Bennani at the corner of Avenue Moulay Youssef at Place de la Résistance aka La Fiat (☎05/562 3460; Mon–Fri 8.30am–noon & 2.30–6.30pm). There is also a *Syndicat d'Initiative* on the east side of Place Mohammed V, which is open the same hours plus Saturday mornings 9am–noon.

Arrival

BY TRAIN
The train station (☎05/562 5001) is in the Ville Nouvelle, ten minutes' walk from the concentration of hotels around Place Mohammed V. If you prefer to stay in Fes El Bali, either take a petit taxi, or bus #10 or #47 to Bab Boujeloud, where most of the old city's hotels are to be found; if you walk to Avenue Hassan II, you can pick up the #9 bus to nearby Dar Batha (pronounced *dar baat-ha*). From the train station, the #10 bus passes the main bus station and the #16 bus runs to the airport. Other buses from the train station run to outlying suburbs which are unlikely to interest you.

Beware of **unofficial taxi drivers** who wait at the station and charge very unofficial rates for the trip into town; the standard fare for Bab Boujeloud should be no more than 10dh per person. Be prepared, too, for hustlers: Fes rivals Marrakesh in this respect (though is not as bad as Tangier), and the station is, as everywhere, a prime target.

BY BUS

Coming in by bus can be confusing, since there are terminals in both the Ville Nouvelle and by the various gates to the Medina. However, coming from most destinations, you will probably arrive at the main **bus station** or *gare routière* just north of Bab Mahrouk, between Kasbah Cherada and Borj Nord (see Fes El Bali map pp.210–211). Buses run by CTM however will drop you at their office on the corner of Rue Tetouan and Avenue Mohammed V in the Ville Nouvelle (☎05/573 2992 – see Ville Nouvelle map pp.200–201), and generally depart from there also, although services to Marrakesh, Tangier and Tetouan call at the main bus station too. The other exception is if you're coming from **Taza and the east**: buses stop at the Medina's southeast gate, **Bab Ftouh**, before continuing to the main bus station. Leaving Fes by bus for the south, note that convenient **night buses** cover most routes – to Marrakesh and Rissani, for example.

BY GRANDS TAXIS

Like buses, grands taxis mostly operate from the *gare routière* outside Bab Mahrouk. Exceptions are those from **Immouzer**, **Ifrane** and **Azrou** (and sometimes Marrakesh), which use a rank opposite the CTM office, 100m west of Place de l'Atlas (see Ville Nouvelle map p.200–201) and those from/to **Sefrou** (and sometimes Immouzer), which use a rank 100m down southeast of Place de la Résistance (aka La

---

PETITS TAXIS AND CITY BUSES

Petits taxis in Fes generally use their meters, so they're very good value; after 9.30pm, there's a fifty percent surcharge on top of the meter price.

Useful petit taxi ranks include:

Place Mohammed V (Ville Nouvelle).
Main PTT on Av. Hassan II (Ville Nouvelle).
Place des Alaouites (Fes El Djedid).
Place Baghdadi (north of Bab Boujeloud, Fes El Bali).
Dar Batha (south of Bab Boujeloud, Fes El Bali).
Bab Guissa (north gate, by Palais Jamai, Fes El Bali).
Bab Er Rsif (central gate, south of the Kairaouine Mosque, Fes El Bali).
Bab Ftouh (southeast gate, Fes El Bali).

City buses Useful city bus routes are detailed, where relevant, in the text. As a general guide these are the ones you're most likely to want to use:

#2: Av. Mohammed V to Bab Semarine (by Av. Hassan II and Place des Alaouites).
#3: Place de la Résistance (aka La Fiat) via Bd. Allal el Fassi to Bab Ftouh.
#9: Route de Sefrou via Place Mohammed V to Dar Batha see opposite.
#10: Train station via *gare routière* (bus station) to Bab Ftouh.
#12: Bab Boujeloud to Bab Ftouh.
#16: Train station to the airport.
#17: Place Jbari (just west of Place de Florence) to Aïn Chkeff for the campsite (see p.209).
#19: Train Station to Place er Rsif, south of the Kairaouine Mosque.
#20 Place de Florence to the Arms Museum.
#27: Dar Batha to Place er Rsif, south of the Kairaouine Mosque.
#28: Place de la Résistance (aka La Fiat) via Bab Ftouh to Sidi Harazem.
#29: Place de l'Atlas to Place er Rsif, south of the Kairaouine Mosque.

Note: These **numbers are marked on the sides** of the buses; there are completely different numbers on the backs.

Fiat). **Meknes** grands taxis arrive outside the train station. Grands taxis from **Sidi Harazem, Taza, Taounate** arrive at **Bab Ftouh**.

BY AIR
Fes's tiny **airport** is 15km south of the city, at Saïs, off the P24 to Immouzer (☎05/562 4800), and is most easily reached by chartering a grand taxi from the *gare routière*, though you can also get to it on bus #16 from the train station. The only direct services at time of writing are to Casablanca (1–3 daily) and Paris (2 weekly). Details and tickets from the RAM office at 54 Avenue Hassan II (☎05/562 5516 or 17).

BY CAR
Be prepared for "motorbike guides" – Morocco's most annoying hustlers – who haunt the approach roads to Fes, attach themselves to tourist cars and insist on escorting you to a hotel. They can be deeply unpleasant and are not best countered by aggression; on the whole, it's easier just to tell them where you're going (book your hotel in advance) and give them a small tip on arrival. Make it clear you do not want a subsequent tour of the city.

Maps
The **maps** in this guide are as functional as any available. On pp.200–201 is a plan of the Ville Nouvelle, showing the outline of Fes El Djedid and edge of Fes El Bali; on pp.210–211 is a general plan of Fes El Bali (with enlargements of the Bab Boujeloud area on p.206 and the Kairaouine Mosque area on p.219). An additional map of Fes El Djedid is on p.279. Inevitably, all maps of Fes El Bali are heavily simplified: more than any other Medina in Morocco, the old city is composed of an impenetrable maze of lanes and blind alleys, whose precise orientation and localized names do not exactly lend themselves to cartography.

Guides
A half-day tour from an **official guide** is a useful introduction to Fes El Bali; the fee is 120dh for a half-day, no matter how many people are in your group. Official guides can identify themselves by round gold medallions and can be engaged at the Syndicat d'Initiative on the east side of Place Mohammed V, or outside the more upmarket hotels, or at the youth hostel.

Guides who tout their services are likely to be **unofficial** and technically illegal. This doesn't necessarily mean they're to be avoided – some who are genuine students (as most claim to be) can be excellent. But you have to choose carefully, ideally drinking a tea together before settling a rate or declaring interest. An unpleasant trick, employed by the more disreputable, is to take you into Fes El Bali and, once you're disorientated, maybe with dusk descending, demand rather more than the agreed fee to take you back to your hotel. Don't allow yourself to be intimidated – passers-by will be happy to direct you back to your hotel.

Whether you get an official or unofficial guide, it's essential to work out in advance the **main points you want to see**: a useful exercise would be to mark them on the map of Fes El Bali in this book and show this to your guide. At all events, make it clear that you're not interested in **shopping** (unless that's all you want to do). For some hints on shopping on your own see "Shopping for Crafts" on p.236. Remember if you enter a shop with a guide, official or otherwise, that they will take a commission from the shopkeeper on anything that you buy, which will be added to the price you pay (except in the case of new carpets with a price fixed by the state, in which case it will come out of the shopkeeper's profit); official guides are worse in this respect since they can command a much higher commission, often as much forty percent.

Accommodation

Staying in Fes, you have the usual choice between comfort (and reliable water supply) in the modern **Ville Nouvelle** hotels, or lack of facilities in the basic Medina hotels in **Fes El Bali** and **Fes El Djedid**. There is often a shortage of hotel space in all categories, so be prepared for higher than usual prices and – if possible – phone ahead to book a room.

If you are not overly concerned about the size and cleanliness of your room – or if you can afford one at the upmarket *Hôtel Batha* or *Hôtel Palais Jamai* – then **Fes El Bali/Fes El Djedid** is definitely the place to be. You will be at the heart of the city's souks and traditional life, well placed to explore the monuments, and witness to the amazing sounds of the early morning calls of muezzins from the hundreds of mosques.

Most visitors to Fes, however, are likely to be more comfortable in the **Ville Nouvelle**, where there is a wide choice of hotels – most of them adequate if unexciting – and a youth hostel. A few of the better hotels here have swimming pools, which can be worth a bit of a splurge in midsummer, when the heat of the plateau can be overwhelming. The Ville Nouvelle hotels also offer advantages in their proximity to restaurants and bars, and to the train station.

Fes El Bali

With two notable exceptions – the upmarket *Hôtel Batha* and *Palais Jamai* – all of the hotels in Fes El Bali are basic *pensions*, most of which could do with more regular cleaning and plumbing. Some are also overpriced, charging the equivalent of one-star prices when they can get away with it in the summer months. However, so long as your expectations are modest, they're adequate – and the group around Bab Boujeloud are in a great position, poised for exploration of the old city's sights and souks. The problem of water – or, rather, lack of it – in many of these cheap hotels can be overcome by taking a steam bath in one of the nearby hammams.

BAB BOUJELOUD

Bab Boujeloud is the western gateway to Fes El Bali and offers pedestrian access to Fes El Djedid. In the nearby **Place de l'Istiqlal** there are bus and petit taxi ranks for getting to and from the Ville Nouvelle. The hotels listed below are keyed on the map of the Bab Boujeloud area, overleaf. Most have only cold-water showers, though Boujeloud's water supply is in fact tepid year-round. There are also two hammams nearby (see p.236).

Hôtel de Jardin Public, signposted down a short lane by the Boujeloud Mosque (☎05/563 3086). A popular Boujeloud choice (though it gets mixed reports from readers). Friendly and quiet, with old-fashioned rooms, not all with external windows, and cold showers. ①.

Hôtel Cascade, 26 Rue Serajine (☎05/563 8442). Small, clean rooms – and most have windows. Hot showers. Helpful staff. ①.

Hôtel Lamrani, Talâa Seghira (☎05/563 4411). A friendly place with small but clean rooms – most with double beds. Opposite the Hammam Sidi Azouz. ①.

Hôtel Mauritania, 20 Rue Serajine (☎05/563 3518). A reasonable fall-back next door to the *Hôtel Cascade*. Washbasins in rooms; hot showers on corridor. ①.

Hôtel National, Place Boujeloud (☎05/563 3248). A basic but clean and friendly place with good views from its terrace. Cold showers. ①.

Pension Batha, 8 Sidi Lkhayat Batha (☎/fax 05/574 1150). A newly opened *pension* with pleasant old-fashioned decor in the rooms (including some nice stucco work on some of the ceilings) and en-suite hot showers in all of them. ②.

BAB FTOUH

An alternative group of cheap hotels – all pretty basic – is to be found by **Bab Ftouh** – a gate at the southeast corner of the Fes El Bali map (see pp.210–211); this is an untouristed area and all of the hotels listed are used more or less exclusively by Moroccans; it's also rather an underworld sort of area where even Moroccans watch their step. Grands taxis to Sidi Harazem, Taounate and other points east and north of Fes leave from Bab Ftouh – and buses to Taza and Al Hoceima often call here, though they start their journeys at the main bus station. Coming into Fes from those places, they will also drop passengers off here before continuing to the bus station. Although three of these places have only cold showers, and one has no showers at all, there is a hammam nearby with hot showers as well as a traditional steam bath – the Douche Andalous, behind the *Hôtel el Andalous* (from Bab Ftouh take a left immediately after the hotel and it's on the left), open for women 1–6pm, for men 6am–noon and 6.30–10pm.

Hôtel el Andalous, 31 Rue Kaid Khammer (☎05/576 1313). The best of the four hotels in the quarter, the same price as the others but cleaner and quieter with a roof terrace and rooms around a central patio. ①.

Hôtel el Hamra, Rue Bab el Hamra (no phone). Not good value, just as basic as the others in the area, but costing slightly more. ①.

Hôtel Bahia, Rue Sidi Ali Boughaleb (☎05/564 9201). Very basic indeed, with no showers. ①.

Hôtel Moulay Idriss, 2 Rue Kaid Khammer (no phone). Unused to tourists, with only Arabic spoken. ①.

UPMARKET OPTIONS IN FES EL BALI

Staying in style in Fes El Bali is the best of both worlds, but unfortunately it doesn't come cheap. The three places below are all keyed on the Fes El Bali map.

Hôtel Palais Jamai, Bab Guissa – the north gate. (☎05/563 4331, fax 563 5096). Along with Marrakesh's *Mamounia*, the most famous and historic hotel in Morocco. Its appeal is partly the building and gardens – the basis of which is a nineteenth-century vizier's palace (see p.225) – and partly its position, poised at the top of Fes El Bali, with panoramic views of the city below. It also has a rare literary fame, as one of the principal settings for Paul Bowles's novel, *The Spider's House*. You do have to pay a lot for the experience, and the service and maintenance aren't always what you might expect of a five-star palace. If you book independently expect to pay upwards of £130/$200 per night for a basic double and £14/$20 more for views over the Medina; it's a staggering £340/$550 for the cheapest of the original (and admittedly breathtaking) palace suites in the old part of the hotel. Rates may be a little lower as part of a package through one of the specialist travel agents (see "Getting There" in Basics). ⑥.

Hôtel Dar Batha, Place de l'Istiqlal (☎05/574 1077, fax 574 1078). This upmarket hotel, located near the Dar Batha museum, should be one to recommend highly. However, we've had several reports of individual reservations not being honoured (the hotel is much used by tour groups), so if you book, be sure to phone again and reconfirm. ④.

Hôtel Les Merenides, Bordj Nord – on the road above Fes El Bali, (☎05/564 5226, fax 564 5225, *meridien@extranet.net.ma*). This was one of the city's prestige hotels until the Fes riots of 1990, when it was left burnt out by the mobs. Restored to its former glory, it has all the comforts, and wonderful views. However, it is isolated from the city, a bit soulless, and for our money very much a second choice to the *Palais Jamai*. ⑥.

Fes El Djedid

Fes El Djedid's two hotels are in theory a good alternative to those around Bab Boujeloud: they are within a ten to fifteen-minute walk of Fes El Bali, and less frequented by tourists (and hustlers). See map on p.228 for locations.

Hôtel du Commerce, Place des Alaouites (☎05/562 2231). Old but comfortable and friendly, owned for decades by a Jewish family, with a lively café at street level. Its location on Place des Alaouites – facing the golden doors of the royal palace – is actually a little closer to the Ville Nouvelle than to Fes El Bali. ①.

Hôtel du Parc, off Grand Rue des Merenides (☎05/561 0564). Squalid toilets, grubby rooms and cold water showers make this very much a fall-back option, but it's friendly and it has a certain run-down charm, plus a terrace with views of the ramparts and the river. ①.

The Ville Nouvelle

As rooms can be tricky to obtain in Fes, we have listed most of the Ville Nouvelle hotels below – both the good and not so good.

YOUTH HOSTEL

Auberge de Jeunesse, 18 Rue Abdeslam Seghrini (☎05/562 4085). One of the best Moroccan youth hostels; easy-going, friendly and recently refurbished with small, spotless dorms from 45dh and double rooms. It's in a quiet backwater of the Ville Nouvelle, but near the Arabic Language Institute, if you want to learn colloquial Moroccan Arabic, and the *Hôtel Zalagh*, which will usually allow nonresidents to swim in their pool for a fee. Non-cardholders can stay here but pay very slightly more than HI cardholders. ②.

CHEAP

Hôtel Amor, 31 Rue Arabie Saoudite, previously Rue du Pakistan, (☎05/562 2724). One block from Av. Hassan II, behind the Bank al Maghrib. Attractive tiled frontage; restaurant and reasonable accommodation. ③.

Hôtel Central, 50 Rue du Nador, aka Brahim Roudani (☎05/562 2333). Good value, popular and often full. Rooms are clean and bright, heated in winter, some with small en-suite shower cubicles. ①.

Hôtel CTM, Rue Ksar El Kebir/Av. Mohammed V (☎05/562 2811). A pleasant 1930s building, with decent-sized rooms and a certain shabby charm. There are showers in most rooms, toilets on the corridor. Reasonable value and popular, so it's best to book in high season. ①.

Hôtel Excelsior, Av. Mohammed V /Rue Larbi El Kaghat (☎05/562 5602). This rather spartan fall-back cheapie was closed for refurbishment at our last check so with luck it will reopen a brighter, better place. ①.

Hôtel Errabie, 1 Rue de Tangier (☎05/564 0100, fax 565 9163). Just off the bottom, southern edge of the map – on the Route de Sefrou. A modern, well-built complex on the corner of a major junction, with three petrol stations. Café, patisserie, boulangerie, small swimming pool and hotel – simply but well finished, all rooms en suite, some with a/c. Easy parking. ③.

Hôtel Kairouan, 84 Rue de Soudan (☎05/562 3590). A simple, well-kept hotel with large rooms (all with showers) but in a rather no-man's-land site between the train station and town centre. ②.

Hôtel Lamdaghri, Rue Abbas Msaadi (☎05/562 0310). Big rooms with showers; restaurant on first floor and lively bar next door. Reasonable value, recently spruced up, and well placed at the centre of the Ville Nouvelle. ③.

Hôtel du Maghreb, 25 Av. Mohammed Es Slaoui (☎05/562 1567). One of the cheaper hotels in the Ville Nouvelle; basic but clean. Reception is up the stairs. ①.

Hôtel du Pacha, 32 Av. Hassan II (☎05/565 2290). An old-style downmarket hotel, catering mainly to Moroccans. The big minus here is that not all rooms have showers, and there are no shared ones. ①.

Hôtel Renaissance, 29 Rue Abdelkrim el Kattabi (☎05/562 2193). Despite a rather gloomy entrance, a friendly and clean billet in a central position – and pretty cheap. ①.

Hôtel Rex, 32 Place de l'Atlas (☎05/564 2133). Friendly, well maintained and very good value with a café on the ground floor. Handy for CTM departures (or late arrivals). ②.

Hôtel Royal, 36 Rue de Soudan (☎05/562 4656). Convenient for the train station, near the *Hôtel Kairouan* and rather better value for money. Rooms vary somewhat and it's worth making sure you get one of the better ones; all have showers and some dearer ones have toilets also. ②.

MODERATE

Grand Hôtel, Bd. Abdallah Chefchaouni (☎05/593 2026, fax 565 3847). Old colonial hotel with a great Art Deco facade, refurbished modern rooms with a/c and heating, some very large, all en suite and many with a bath. Facilities include a bar, restaurant, nightclub and garage. ④.

Ibis Hôtel, Place de la Gare/Av. des Almohades (☎05/565 1902, fax 565 1909). One of a chain of hotels (formerly called *Moussafir*) built beside train stations; rather impersonal with pleasant rooms, a not tremendously good restaurant, a bar and small swimming pool. ④.

Hôtel Mounia, 60 Rue Asilah (☎05/565 0771 or 72, fax 565 0773). Modern hotel (central heating, a/c, satellite TV in rooms) with friendly management. Restaurant and popular bar which can be noisy at times. ④.

Hôtel Nouzha, 7 Rue Hassan Dkhissi, just off Place d'Atlas (☎05/564 0002, fax 564 0084). A splendidly done-out hotel, with mosaic tilework and richly decorated cedarwood ceilings in the entrance lobby, comfortable, cosy rooms, all with a bath in the bathroom, two restaurants – the one for Moroccan food has great stucco work decoration – a bar and a basement restaurant/nightclub. ④.

Hôtel Olympic, Rue Houman el Fatouaki, off Av. Mohammed V, facing one side of the covered market (☎05/593 2682, fax 593 2665). Clean and reliable with a reasonable restaurant. Recently refurbished throughout – all rooms now have bathroom, TV, and heating in winter. ④.

Hôtel de la Paix, 44 Av. Hassan II (☎05/565 5072, fax 562 6880). An old-established tour group hotel, well worth a call. Recently refurbished, it has TV, a/c and heating in all rooms, a bar and a good seafood restaurant, *Le Nautilus*. ④.

Splendid Hotel, 9 Rue Abdelkrim el Kattabi (☎05/562 6770, fax 565 4892). An efficient modern hotel with newly refurbished and very pleasant rooms, a good restaurant, bar and small swimming pool; it attracts mainly tour groups and is not always interested in individual bookings. ④.

Hôtel Wassim, Rue du Liban – off Av. Hassan II, one block down from Av. des F.A.R. (☎05/565 4939, fax 593 0220). Quite a sophisticated hotel, built on local initiative and classy in an understated kind of way, with three restaurants, a bar, a nightclub (free for residents but open to all), and luxurious, fully equipped rooms. ④.

EXPENSIVE

Sheraton Fes Hôtel, Av. des F.A.R. (☎05/593 0909, fax 562 0486; toll-free booking from the US or Canada ☎1-800/325 3535; from the UK ☎0800/353535). The former *Hôtel de Fes* is now a link in the *Sheraton* chain. It is a large and not tremendously distinguished tour group hotel, on the fringe of the Ville Nouvelle. Useful features include a car rental firm, First Car, with a desk in the lobby. ⑥.

Hôtel Sofia, 3 Rue Arabie Saoudite, ex-Rue du Pakistan (☎05/562 4265 to 68, fax 562 6478). Modern chain hotel with pool and the works, frequented almost exclusively by tour groups; bar and nightclub open to nonresidents. ⑤.

Hôtel Menzeh Zalagh, 10 Rue Mohammed Diouri (☎05/562 5531, fax 565 1995, *menzeh.zalagh@ fesnet.net.ma*). A formerly state-owned hotel, now privatized, with quite a chic clientele (even the tour groups are select), and a new annexe on Rue Diyouri at the corner of Rue de Ravin (it is possible that either the original branch or the annexe may change its name). Facilities include the hotel's own hammam. The swimming pool is open to nonresidents, but expensive at 60dh. On the other hand, the fine views across to Fes El Djedid are anyone's for the cost of an orange juice. ⑤.

Camping

Camping International, Route de Sefrou (☎05/573 1439 or 40, fax 573 1554). A new site next to the (not yet open) new football stadium 4km from the city centre, accessible by bus #28 from Place de l'Atlas. A well-planned site popular with trans-Saharan overland tour groups, featuring a pool, a bar, tennis courts and horseriding. Well kept with plenty of greenery, shade and constant hot water, but pricey as campsites go.

Camping Diamant Vert (☎05/560 8367 or 69), Aïn Chkeff – 6km south of the city. Although well out of town, this is a pleasant and shady site, with its own swimming pool, restaurant, café, playground and Barbary apes. Staying here also gives easy access to the neighbouring **Reda leisure complex** which includes a swimming pool, sports facilities, peacocks, two restaurants (*Étoile de Fes* and *Pizzeria La Source*) and a disco/nightclub often with a live band, and the three-star *Hôtel Reda* (☎05/560 0978, fax 560 1078). It's really an option for those with transport, though bus #17 from Place Jbari just west of Place Florence in Fes Ville Nouvelle runs past the campsite.

Fes El Bali

With its mosques, medersas and fondouks, combined with a mile-long network of souks, there are enough "sights" in **Fes El Bali** to fill three or four days just trying to locate them. And even then, you'd still be unlikely to stumble across some of them except by chance or through the whim of a guide. In this – the apparently wilful secretiveness – lies part of the fascination, and there is much to be said for Paul Bowles's somewhat lofty advice to "lose oneself in the crowd – to be pulled along by it – not knowing where to and for how long . . . to see beauty where it is least likely to appear". If you do the same, be prepared to really get lost. However, despite what hustlers may tell you, the Medina is not a dangerous place, and you can always ask a boy to lead you out towards one of its landmarks: Bab Boujeloud, Talâa Kebira, the Kairaouine Mosque, Bab Er Rsif or Bab Ftouh.

Making your own way in purposeful quest for the souks and monuments, you should be able to find everything detailed in the following pages – with a little patience. If you want to avoid coinciding with tour groups, especially in summer, try visiting the main sights between noon and 2pm, while the groups stop for lunch. Before you start, it's not a bad idea to head up to the **Merenid tombs** on the rim of the valley (see box pp.212–213), where you can get a spectacular overview of the city and try to make out its shape. For a break or escape from the intensity of the Medina, head to the **Boujeloud Gardens** (officially retitled "Jardins de la Marche Verte"; open 9am–6pm), a real haven and with a pleasant open-air café, to the west of Bab Boujeloud.

There are four principal entrances and exits to Fes El Bali:

Bab Boujeloud. The western gate, easily identified by its bright polychrome decoration and the hotels and cafés grouped on either side.

Bab Er Rsif. A central gate, by the square (and car park) beside the Mosque Er Rsif, this is a convenient entrance, just a few blocks below the Kairaouine Mosque. Bus #19 and bus #29 run between the square and Avenue Mohammed V in the Ville Nouvelle, #19 continuing to the train station, #29 to Place de l'Atlas. Bus #27 runs between the square and Dar Batha.

Bab Ftouh. The southeast gate at the bottom of the Andalous quarter, with cemeteries extending to the south. Bus #18 runs between here and Place de l'Istiqlal (near Bab Boujeloud) and there is also a petit taxi rank.

Bab Guissa. The north gate, up at the top of the city by the *Hôtel Palais Jamai*: a convenient point to enter (or leave) the city from (or heading to) the Merenid tombs. Petits taxis are available by the gate.

FES EL BALI

ACCOMMODATION
Hôtel el Andalous	3
Hôtel Bahia	5
Hôtel Dar Batha	7
Hôtel el Hamra	6
Hôtel Les Merenides	1
Hôtel Moulay Idriss	4
Hôtel Palais Jamai	2

Merenid Tombs

Borj Nord (Arms Museum)

Bus Station
Grands Taxis

Kasbah Cherarda

Bab Mahrouk

Kasbah Cherarda

Fondouk

Hammam

Fountain

Cherabliyin Mosque

KASBAH EN NOUAR

Clock

Medersa Bou Inania

Bab Boujeloud

PLACE BAGHDADI

KASBAH BOUJELOUD

PTT

Dar Batha

PLACE DE L'ISTIQLAL

FES

See 'Around Bab Boujeloud' map

Petits Taxis

ROUTE DU TOUR DE FES

AVENUE DES MERINIDS

ROUTE DU TOUR DE DEFFES

Lycée

Bus #9

Boujeloud Gardens

Bab Es Seba

Bab Dakaken

Bab Djebala

Bab El Hedid

FEZ EL DJEDID

Bab Semarine

GRAND RUE DES MERNIS

AVENUE DE LA LIBERTE

Oued Fes

N

▽ *Ville Nouvelle*   ▽ *Ville Nouvelle*

THE MERENID TOMBS AND A VIEW OF FES

A crumbling and fairly obscure group of ruins, the **Merenid tombs** are not of great interest in themselves. People no longer know which of the dynasty's sultans had them erected and there is not a trace remaining of the "beautiful white marbles' vividly coloured epitaphs" which so struck Leo Africanus in his sixteenth-century description of Fes. Poised at the city's skyline, however, they are a picturesque focus and a superb vantage point. All round you are spread the Muslim cemeteries which ring the hills on each side of the city, while looking down you can delineate the more prominent among Fes's reputed 365 mosque minarets.

Getting up to the tombs is no problem. You can walk it in about twenty minutes from Bab Boujeloud, or take a taxi (around 10dh from the Ville Nouvelle). From the Boujeloud area, leave by **Bab El Mahrouk**, below the new bus station, and once outside the walls, turn immediately to the right. After a while you come to a network of paths worn into the hillside, which you can scramble up if sufficiently able-bodied to reach the stolid fortress of **Borj Nord** (a longer but more sedate route is to follow the road round from Bab Mahrouk). Despite its French garrison-like appearance, this and its southern counterpart across the valley were actually built in the late sixteenth century by the Saadians. The dynasty's only endowment to the city, they were used to control the Fassis rather than to defend them. Carefully maintained, the Borj now houses the country's **arms museum** (daily except Tues 8.30am–noon & 2.30–6pm; 10dh) – daggers encrusted with stones and an interminable display of row upon row of muskets, most of them confiscated from the Riffians in the 1958 rebellion. Pride of place is given to a cannon 5m long and weighing 12 tons, said to be used during the Battle of the Three Kings (see "History" in Contexts).

Clambering across the hillside from Borj Nord – or following (by road) Route du Tour du Fes past *Hôtel des Merenides* – you soon emerge at **the tombs** and an expectant clus-

Into the Medina: Bab Boujeloud and Dar Batha

The area around **Bab Boujeloud** is today the principal entrance to Fes El Bali: a place with a great concentration of cafés, stalls and activity where people come to talk and stare. Provincial buses leave throughout the day from **Place Baghdadi** (just west of the gate), while in the early evening there are occasional entertainers and a flea market spreading out towards the old Mechouar (the former assembly point and government square) and to **Bab El Mahrouk**, an exit onto the road to the Merenid tombs.

This focus and importance is all comparatively recent, since it was only at the end of the nineteenth century that the walls were joined up between Fes El Bali and Fes El Djedid and the subsequently enclosed area was developed. Nearly all the buildings here date from this period, including those of the elegant **Dar Batha** palace, designed for the reception of foreign ambassadors and now a **Museum of Moroccan Arts and Crafts**. Bab Boujeloud itself is comparatively modern, too, constructed only in 1913. Its tiled facades are blue (the traditional colour of Fes) on the outside, facing the ramparts, and green (the colour of Islam) on the interior, facing into the Medina.

DAR BATHA

The **Dar Batha** (closed for repairs on our last visit but in principle open daily except Tues 8.30am–noon & 2.30–6pm; 10dh) is worth a visit just for its courtyards and gardens, which offer useful respite from the general exhaustion of the Medina. The museum entrance is 30m up the narrow lane separating it from the *Hôtel Batha*.

The art and crafts collections concentrate on local artisan traditions. There are examples of **carved wood**, much of it rescued from the Misbahiya and other medersas; another room of **Middle Atlas carpets**; and examples of **zellij-work**, **calligraphy** and **embroidery**.

ter of guides. Wandering round here, you will probably be standing on the city's original foundations, before its rapid expansion under Moulay Idriss II. But it is **the view** across the deep pear-shaped bowl of the valley below which holds everyone's attention – Fes El Bali neatly wedged within it, white and diamond-shaped, and buzzing with activity.

Immediately below is Adourat El Kairaouine, or the Kairaouine quarter: the main stretch of the Medina, where Idriss settled the first Tunisian refugees. At its heart, towards the river, stands the green-tiled courtyard of the **Kairaouine Mosque**, the country's most important religious building, preceded and partially screened by its two minarets. The main one has a dome on top and is whitewashed, which is an unusual Moroccan (though characteristically Tunisian) design; the slightly lower one to its right (square, with a narrower upper floor) is Borj en Naffara (The Trumpeter's Tower), from which the beginning and end of Ramadan are proclaimed. Over to the right of this, and very easily recognized, are the tall pyramid-shaped roof and slender, decoratively faced minaret of the city's second great religious building, the **Zaouia of Moulay Idriss II**.

The **Andalous quarter**, the other area settled by ninth-century refugees, lies some way over to the left of this trio of minarets – divided from the Kairaouine by the appropriately named **Bou Khareb** (The River Carrying Garbage), whose path is marked out by a series of minarets. **Djemma El Andalous**, the principal mosque of this quarter, is distinguished by a massive, tile-porched, monumental gateway, behind which you can make out the roofs enclosing its great courtyard.

Orientation aside, there is a definite magic if you're up here in the early evening or, best of all, at dawn. The sounds of the city, the stillness and the contained disorder below all seem to make manifest the mystical significance which Islam places on urban life as the most perfect expression of culture and society.

From the tombs you can enter Fes El Bali either through **Bab Guissa** (which brings you out at the Souk El Attarin), or by returning to **Bab Boujeloud**. There is a petit taxi stand by Bab Guissa.

Above all, it is the **pottery** rooms which stand out. The pieces, dating from the sixteenth century to the 1930s, are beautiful and show the preservation of technique long after the end of any form of innovation. This timeless quality is constantly asserted as you wander around Fes. There is no concept here of the "antique" – something is either new or it is old, and if the latter, its age could be anything from thirty years to three centuries.

This same quality is occasionally reinforced at the museum itself when the work of local co-operatives is displayed for sale.

INTO THE MEDINA: THE TALÂA SEGHIRA AND TALÂA KEBIRA

Until you get a grasp of Fes El Bali, it's useful to stick with **Bab Boujeloud** as a point of entry and reference. With its polychrome tiled facades, it is a pretty unmistakeable landmark, and once inside, things are initially straightforward. You will find yourself in a small square (see map on p.206), flanked by the *Hôtel Cascade* (on your right) and with a couple of minarets almost directly ahead. Just beyond the *Hôtel Cascade*, an entrance straight ahead leads into the Kissaria Sejjarin, a small yard of craft shops, while the road itself twists round to the right, and then to the left again, passing a handful of small foodstalls (where you can buy chunks of pastilla, the great Fassi delicacy of pigeon pie), then the Boujeloud cinema, and under an arch just beyond to begin its descent into the Medina.

This is the **Talâa Seghira** (also known, in its French translation, as Rue du Petit Talâa), the lower of two main lanes into the Medina, traversed by dozens of alleys but running parallel for much of the Medina's length. Further down, the lane, renamed Rue Ben Safi, has little of specific interest until it loops up to rejoin the upper lane at the Souk El Attarin.

The upper lane, **Talâa Kebira** (aka Rue du Grand Talâa), reached through the Kissaria Sejjarin, or from an entrance opposite the *Hôtel Cascade*, is the major artery of the Medina and, with its continuations, runs right through to the Kairaouine Mosque, though in fact the section just next to Bab Boujeloud, suffused with the smoke of char-grilled kebabs and dappled with the slats of light that slip through its thatched cover, is among the most atmospheric parts of the Medina. For virtually its whole length the Talâa Kebira is lined with shops and stalls and, about a hundred metres down, it is host to the most brilliant of all the city's monuments, the **Medersa Bou Inania**. You can see the entrance to this medersa, down a step on your right, just before you come to a whitewashed arch-bridge over the road.

Bus #18 from the Ville Nouvelle has a stop more or less outside Dar Batha in Place de l'Istiqlal, two minutes' walk below Bab Boujeloud. Here, and around the gate, you'll be pestered with offers of a **guide**. If you don't want one, be firm and explain that you're only going down to Bou Inania – which will probably be your first move anyway. Most hustlers give up after about fifty metres or so. To get a **petit taxi** in the Bab Boujeloud area, walk up to Place Baghdad by the Boujeloud bus terminal.

THE BOU INANIA MEDERSA AND CLOCK

If there is just one building you actively seek out in Fes – or, not to put too fine a point on it, in Morocco – it should be the **Medersa Bou Inania**, even though parts of it are currently inaccessible due to repair work. The most elaborate, extravagant and beautiful of all Merenid monuments, it comes close to perfection in every aspect of its construction – its dark cedar is fabulously carved, the zellij tilework classic, and the stucco a revelation.

In addition, the medersa is the city's only building still in religious use that non-Muslims are permitted to enter. Nonbelievers cannot, of course, enter the prayer hall – which is divided from the main body of the medersa by a small canal – but are allowed to sit in a corner of the marble courtyard and gaze across to it. The **admission hours** are daily 8.30am–5.30pm (9am–4pm during Ramadan); occasionally tourists may be asked to leave at other times of prayer and, as with all the Fes medersas, there is a standard 10dh admission fee.

Set somewhat apart from the other medersas of Fes, the Bou Inania was the last and grandest built by a Merenid sultan. It shares its name with the one in Meknes, which was completed (though not initiated) by the same patron, **Sultan Abou Inan** (1351–1358). But the Fes version is infinitely more splendid. Its cost alone was legendary, and Abou Inan is said to have thrown the accounts into the river on its completion, claiming that "a thing of beauty is beyond reckoning".

At first glance, Abou Inan doesn't seem the kind of sultan to have wanted a medersa – his mania for building aside, he was most noted for having 325 sons in ten years, deposing his father, and committing unusually atrocious murders. The *Ulema*, the religious leaders of the Kairaouine Mosque, certainly thought him an unlikely candidate and advised him to build his medersa on the city's garbage dump, on the basis that piety and good works can cure anything. Whether it was this, or merely the desire for a lasting monument, which inspired him, he set up the medersa as a rival to the Kairaouine itself, and for a while it became the most important religious building in the city. A long campaign to have the announcement of the time of prayer transferred here failed in the face of the Kairaouine's powerful opposition; but the medersa was granted the status of a Grand Mosque – unique in Morocco – and retains the right to say the Friday *khotbeh* prayer.

THE MEDERSA

The basic **layout** of the medersa is quite simple – a single large courtyard flanked by two sizeable halls and opening onto an oratory – and is essentially the same design as that of the wealthier Fassi mansions. For its effect it relies on the mass of decoration and the light and space held within. You enter the **courtyard** – the medersa's outstanding feature – through a stalactite-domed entrance chamber, a feature adapted from Andalucian architecture.

Off to each side of the courtyard are stairs to the upper storey, lined with student cells, and to the roof. Depending on the progress of restoration work, you may or may not be able to go up; if you can, head straight for the roof to get an excellent (and very useful) overview of this part of the city. The cells, as is usual in medersas, are bare and monkish except for their windows and decorated ceilings.

In the courtyard, the **decoration**, startlingly well preserved, covers every possible surface. Perhaps most striking in terms of craftsmanship are the wood carving and joinery, an unrivalled example of the Moorish art of *laceria*, "the carpentry of knots". Cedar beams ring three sides of the courtyard and the elegant black Kufic script rings all four sides, dividing the zellij (ceramic tilework) from the stucco, thus adding a further dimension; unusually, it is largely a list of the properties whose incomes were given as an endowment, rather than the standard Koranic inscriptions. Abou Inan, too, is bountifully praised amid the inscriptions, and on the foundation stone he is credited with the title caliph, an emotive claim to leadership of the Islamic world pursued by none of his successors.

THE WATER CLOCK, LATRINES AND ABLUTIONS

More or less opposite the medersa, just across the Talâa Kebira, Bou Inania's property continued with an extraordinary **water clock**, built above the stalls in the road. In fact this was removed several years ago for research and possible restoration, and when it will be put back is anyone's guess. An enduring curiosity, it consisted of a row of thirteen windows and platforms, seven of which retained their original brass bowls. Nobody has yet been able to discover exactly how it functioned, though a contemporary account detailed how at every hour one of its windows would open, dropping a weight down into the respective bowl.

Clocks had great religious significance during the Middle Ages in establishing the time of prayer, and it seems probable that this one was bought by Abou Inan as part of his campaign to assert the medersa's pre-eminence; there are accounts of similar

THE FUNCTION OF MEDERSAS

Medersas – student colleges and residence halls – were by no means unique to Fes and, in fact, originated in Khorassan in eastern Iran, gradually spreading west through Baghdad and Cairo where the Al Azhar Medersa was founded in 972 and became the most important teaching institution in the Muslim world. They seem to have reached Morocco under the Almohads, though the earliest ones still surviving in Fes are Merenid, dating from the early fourteenth century.

The word medersa means "place of study", and there may have been lectures delivered in some of the prayer halls. In general, however, the medersas served as little more than dormitories, providing room and board to poor (male) students from the countryside and hence allowing them to attend lessons at the mosques. In Fes, where students might attend the Kairaouine University for ten years or more, rooms were always in great demand and "key money" was often paid by the new occupant. Although medersas had largely disappeared from most of the Islamic world by the late Middle Ages, the majority of those in Fes remained in use right up into the 1950s. Since then, restoration work, partly funded by UNESCO, has made them more accessible, though several, which have now been restored, are once again accommodating students. This means that visitors are sometimes welcome only at certain times; as restoration continues, accessibility is impossible to forecast.

constructions in Tlemcen, just across the border in Algeria. As to its destruction, Fassi conspiracy tales are classically involved – most of them revolve round the miscarriage of a Jewish woman passing below at the time of its striking and a Jewish sorcerer casting the evil eye on the whole device. The building to which the clock is fixed, which was, in fact, once owned by a rabbi, is popularly known as "The House of the Magician".

Completing the medersa complex, opposite the main entrance and immediately adjacent to the clock, are the original **latrines and ablutions** (*wudu*) built for Friday worshippers. These have recently been restored but remain, at time of writing, closed to the public. Predating their use in the West by some four centuries, the "Turkish-style" toilets here were at last look very functional, flushed by quantities of running water. If they reopen, or if you can persuade the *gardien* to let you in, take a look inside at the large central patio with its ablutions pool and unexpectedly rich stucco ceiling.

Further down Talâa Kebira

Making your way down the **Talâa Kebira** – a straightforward route to follow – you will eventually emerge at the labyrinth of lanes round the Kairaouine Mosque and Zaouia Moulay Idriss II. It's interesting less for any specific "sights" than for the general accumulated stimuli to your senses. The diarist Anaïs Nin expressed her reaction in terms of odours: ". . . of excrement, saffron, leather being cured, sandalwood, olive oil being fried, nut oil so strong at first that you cannot swallow". To which might be added sound – the shouts of muleteers (*balak!* means "look out!"), mantric cries from the beggars, the bells of water vendors – and, above all, the sight of the people, seen in shafts of light filtered through the rush roofings which cover much of the Talâa's length.

Along the first stretch, heading down from the Bou Inania Medersa, you pass a number of old **fondouks**. Before the advent in Morocco of French-style cafés, at the beginning of the twentieth century, the fondouks – or caravanserais as they're called in the East – formed the heart of social life outside the home. They provided rooms for traders and richer students, and frequently became centres of vice, intrigue and entertainment. There were once some two hundred in Fes El Bali, but although many still survive, often with beautiful fourteenth- and fifteenth-century decorations, they tend now to serve as small factories or warehouses.

The first fondouk that you pass, on your left at no. 49 Talâa el Kebira, has now become a workshop making drums, while just past it at no. 59 is one that has been turned into private residences. Much more interesting is the large fondouk 100m beyond at no. 89, which was originally a **Merenid prison**, fitted out with solid colonnades and arches; it is now home to people selling butter and honey out of large vats. No. 54, further down and across the street, has also been turned into private homes, while another fondouk, on the left after another 100m, is today used for curing animal skins (and smells awful).

RUE ECH CHERABLIYIN

A little way down from this latter fondouk, the street twists round to the right, past a small mosaic fountain, and changes name – to **Rue ech Cherabliyin**. Continuing past the oldest **hammam** still in use in Fes (men only), you find yourself in a district of **leather stalls and shoemakers**. The Fassi *babouches*, leather slippers, are reputed by Fassis to be the best in the country – although this is hotly disputed by Tafraoute in the south. Here, in Fes and unusually, you'll find sophisticated-looking grey and black pairs in addition to the classic yellow and white. If you want to buy a good pair, you'll have to spend some time examining the different qualities, and be prepared to bargain hard – prices will vary from 60dh to 600dh depending on quality (the very best are light in weight, made with *ziouani* leather – top-quality goatskin – and *metfoul* – with no stitching visible).

Passing through a gateway here, you will see ahead of you the green minaret of the **Cherabliyin** (Slippermakers') **mosque**, in the midst of the quarter. The mosque was endowed by the Merenid sultan, Abou El Hassan, builder of the Chellah complex in Rabat. It has been substantially restored, though the minaret is original. If you've gazed at the Koutoubia in Marrakesh, or the great Almohad monuments of Rabat, you'll recognize the familiar *darj w ktarf* motifs (see p.183) of its decoration.

SOUK EL ATTARIN

Beyond the Cherabliyin Mosque, the street again changes its name, to Rue de Tarafin and then Souk Tiyalin, flanked by a forgettable sequence of handicraft shops. Just past the *Palais des Merinides* (see p.235), Rue ben Safi, the continuation of Talâa Sghira, joins it from the right before reaching, at the bottom of the hill, an arched gateway marked **Souk El Attarin** – the "Souk of the Spice Vendors". This was the formal heart of the old city, and its richest and most sophisticated shopping district. It was traditionally around the grand mosque of a city that the most expensive commodities were sold and kept, and, approaching the Kairaouine, this pattern is more or less maintained. Spices themselves are still sold here, as well as Egyptian and Japanese imports, while in the web of little squares off to the left, you'll find all kinds of manufactured goods.

There are a few small cafés inside the spice souk, and on the main street is the **Dar Saada**, a nineteenth-century mansion now housing an expensive carpet shop and restaurant; you can look in or drink a cup of tea feeling only moderate pressure to buy something. Just beyond the Dar Saada, this time on the right of the street, is the principal **kissaria**, or covered market, again dominated by textiles and modern goods; totally rebuilt after a fire in the 1950s, it lacks any particular character.

Reaching the end of Souk El Attarin you come to a **crossroads of lanes** lying slightly askew from the direction of the street. On your right (and ahead of you) are the walls of the **Kairaouine Mosque**; to your left, and entered a few yards up the lane, is the magnificent **Attarin medersa** (see p.220). First, however, it seems logical to take a look at the area below the Souk El Attarin – dominated, as it has been for five centuries, by the **shrine and zaouia of Moulay Idriss II**, the city's patron saint.

The Zaouia of Moulay Idriss II and around

The principal landmark to the south of the Souk El Attarin is the **Zaouia Moulay Idriss II**, one of the holiest buildings in the city. Although enclosed by a highly confusing web of lanes, it is not difficult to find: take the first lane to the right – Rue Mjadliyin – as soon as you have passed through the arch into the Attarin and you will find yourself in front of a wooden bar which marks the beginning of its *horm*, or sanctuary precinct. Until the French occupation of the city in 1911, this was as far as Christians, Jews or mules, could go, and beyond it any Muslim had the right to claim asylum from prosecution or arrest. These days non-Muslims are allowed to walk round the outside of the zaouia, and although they are not permitted to enter, it is possible to get a glimpse inside the shrine and even see the saint's tomb.

Passing to the right of the bar, and making your way round a narrow alleyway, you emerge on the far side of the zaouia at the **women's entrance**. Looking in from the doorway, the **tomb** of Moulay Idriss II is over on the left, and a scene of intense and apparently high-baroque devotion is usually going on all round it. The women, who are Idriss's principal devotees, burn candles and incense here and then proceed around the corner of the precinct to touch, or make offerings at, a round brass grille which opens directly onto the tomb. A curious feature, common to many zaouias but rarely within view from outside, are the numerous European clocks – prestigious gifts and very popular in the nineteenth century, when many Fassi merchant families had them shipped over from Manchester (their main export base for the cotton trade). If you are Muslim, you can enter to check out the mosaics on the walls and the stucco work on the ceilings, as well as the beautifully carved, and original, wooden *minbar*. The zellij (tilework) motif repeated throughout the interior of the zaouia is based on a sixteen-pointed star, often doubled up to make thirty-two points.

There is no particular evidence that Moulay Idriss II was a very saintly marabout, but as the effective founder of Fes and the son of the founder of the Moroccan state, he obviously has considerable *baraka*, the magical blessing which Moroccans invoke. Originally it was assumed that Idriss, like his father, had been buried near Volubilis, but in 1308 an uncorrupted body was found on this spot and the cult was launched. Presumably, it was an immediate success, since in addition to his role as the city's patron saint, Idriss has an impressive roster of suppliants. This is the place to visit for poor strangers arriving in the city, for boys before being circumcised, and for women wanting to facilitate childbirth; also, for some unexplained reason, Idriss is a national protector of sweetmeat vendors. The shrine itself was rebuilt in the eighteenth century by Sultan Moulay Ismail – his only act of pious endowment in this city.

Round the other side of the zaouia is a tight network of lanes called the Kissaria, full of clothes shops. There is nothing especially exciting about it, but if you want a **fez** (hat, that is), this is the place to come. The red cylindrical hat with a black tassel, known as a fez, or more correctly a Fassi tarbouche, is worn, and indeed manufactured, not only in Fes, but as far afield as Egypt and Syria. The best shop to buy one is a small and not very special-looking place next to the Kissaria entrance by the southeast corner of Moulay Idriss's zaouia. In the eighteenth and nineteenth century the fez became associated with the Ottoman Empire, and in some places wearing it was a mark of support for the empire, as result of which it was actually banned by Kemal Atatürk when he took power in Turkey and abolished the empire for good. In its home town, sadly, the fez is going out of fashion, and tends only to be worn by older men – among the young it has given way to Western headwear, and to the Tunisian *chechia*.

PLACE EN NEJJARIN

Standing at the women's entrance to the zaouia, you'll see a lane off to the left – **Rue du Bab Moulay Ismail** – full of stalls selling candles and silverware for devotional offerings. If you follow this lane round to the wooden bar, go under the bar (turning to the right), and then, keeping to your left, you should come out in the picturesque square of **Place en Nejjarin** (Carpenters' Square).

Here is the **Nejjarin Fountain**, best known of several mosaic fountains in the Medina, and next to it the very imposing **Nejjarin Fondouk**, built in the early eighteenth century along with a beautiful canopied fountain on one side of the square. The fondouk was in pretty bad shape but still used until a few years ago as a hostel for students at the nearby Kairaouine university. It has now been restored. and opened to the public as a woodwork museum (daily 10am–5pm, Ramadan 10am–4.30pm; 10dh). The museum's exhibits are not of great interest to a nonprofessional, bar perhaps the fourteenth to eighteenth century cedarwood friezes exhibited on the middle floor and, on the top floor a *rbab* (string instrument – see p.584 beautifully inlaid with mother-of-pearl. It is worth entering however to see the interior of the building itself, wonderfully restored after six years of work – a small exhibit on the roof terrace covers the renovation.

In the alleys that lead off the square, you'll find the **Nejjarin souk**, most easily located by the sounds and smells (among Morocco's finest) of the carpenters chiselling away at sweet-smelling cedarwood. They produce mainly stools and tables – three-legged so they don't wobble on uneven ground – along with various implements for winding yarn, wooden boxes for storage and coffins. If there's a wedding coming up, you may see them making special ornamented tables, with edges, used for parading the bride and groom at shoulder level – a Fassi custom.

At the end of the Nejjarine souk, a passage leads off to the right; at the end of that, turn left to get back to Souk el Attarine.

SOUK EL HENNA

Just off Souk el Attarine, and accessible from the passage that leads to the Place en Nejjarine (first left off it), or 50m further down, opposite the Dar Saada restaurant, is the **Souk El Henna**, a quiet, tree-shaded square adjoining what was once the largest madhouse in the Merenid empire – an imposing building now in use as a storehouse. The stalls here continue to sell henna and other traditional cosmetics, such as *kohl* eyeliner (traditionally antimony but nowadays usually lead sulphide, which is cheaper but toxic), and lip reddener made from crushed poppy petals; on one side of the square there is a huge pair of scales used for weighing the larger deliveries. In addition several outlets here offer the more esoteric ingredients required for medical cures, aphrodisiacs and magical spells. If you get talking to the stallkeepers, you'll be shown an amazing collection of plant and animal (often insect) derivatives.

Pottery stalls are gradually encroaching on this traditional pharmacological business. Cheap but often striking in design, the pieces include Fassi pots, which are usually blue and white or very simple black on earthenware; and others from Safi, the pottery most commonly exported from Morocco, distinguished by heavy green or blue glazes; and Salé, often elaborate modern designs on a white glaze.

To get down to the square, take the lane to the right immediately in front of the entrance arch to Souk El Attarin.

The Kairaouine Mosque

The **Djemaa El Kairaouine** – the Kairaouine Mosque – was the largest mosque in Morocco until the construction of the new Hassan II Mosque in Casablanca – and vies with Cairo's Al-Azhar for the title of world's oldest university. It remains today the

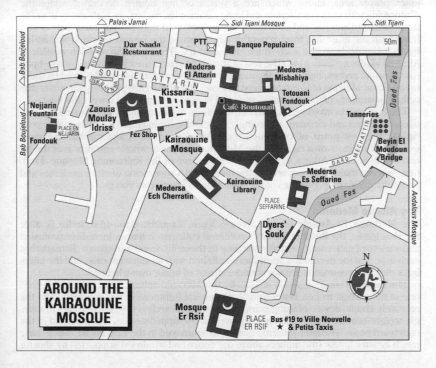

AROUND THE KAIRAOUINE MOSQUE

fountainhead of the country's religious life, governing, for example, the timings of Ramadan and the other Islamic festivals. There is an old Fassi saying that all roads in Fes lead to the Kairaouine – a claim which retains some truth.

The mosque was founded in 857 by the daughter of a wealthy refugee from the city of Kairouan in Tunisia, but its present dimensions, with sixteen aisles and room for 20,000 worshippers, are essentially the product of tenth- and twelfth-century reconstructions: first by the great Caliph of Cordoba, Abd Er Rahman III, and later under the Almoravids.

For non-Muslims, who cannot enter the mosque's courts and prayer halls, the Kairaouine is a rather elusive sight. The building is so thoroughly enmeshed in the surrounding houses and shops that it is impossible to get any clear sense of its shape, and at most you can get only partial views of it from the adjoining rooftops or through the four great entrances to its main courtyard. Nobody seems to object to tourists gaping through the gates, though inevitably the centrepieces that would give order to all the separate parts – the main aisle and the main mihrab – remain hidden from view if you are not Muslim. The overall layout of the mosque was much inspired by the Great Mosque of Cordoba in Spain. The courtyard is open to the sky with a large fountain at its centre, and two smaller ones under porticoes at each side, added in the seventeenth century and based on originals in the Alhambra at Granada. In the summer this area serves as the main prayer area, with its own mihrab directly opposite the main entrance, from which it is easily visible. It is backed by a cedarwood screen decorated with kufic inscriptions, and with the hexagrams and six-pointed stars that form the Karouian's dominant zellij motif.

Beyond the cedarwood screen, and invisible to non-Muslims, is the main aisle of the inner prayer area, above which are a series of five domes decorated under the Almoravids with stucco stalactites and kufic calligraphy, each more elaborately than the last, leading to another and even more richly decorated mihrab. The main aisle is also hung with the mosque's most venerable brass lamps, the largest of which was added by the Almohads in the early thirteenth century. The beautiful wooden *minbar* is Almoravid, dating from 1144. The rest of the inner prayer area is covered by row upon row of round arches, built when the mosque was enlarged in 956, and inspired by those in the Great Mosque of Córdoba. Here however the arches are painted plain white, the ceiling is similarly plain and unadorned, and simple rush matting covers the floor.

The best way to avoid getting lost in the vicinity of the mosque is to always keep it to one side of you and circulate accordingly (clockwise for example if you keep it to your right). The best **point of reference** round the Kairaouine – and the building most worth visiting in its own right – is the Medersa El Attarin, whose entrance is at the far end of the Souk El Attarin, at the northwest corner of the Kairaouine Mosque. From here you can make your way around the mosque to a succession of other medersas and fondouks, picking up glimpses of the Kairaouine's interior as you go.

The Attarin Medersa

The **Medersa El Attarin** (daily 8.30am–5.30pm, Ramadan 9am–4pm; 10dh) is, after the Bou Inania, the finest of the city's medieval colleges. It has an incredible profusion and variety of patterning – equally startling in the zellij, wood and stucco. Remarkably, each aspect of the decoration seems accomplished with an apparent ease, and the building's elegant proportions are never under threat of being overwhelmed.

The medersa was completed in 1325 by the Merenid sultan, Abou Said, and is thus one of the earliest in Fes. Interestingly, its general lightness of feel is achieved by the relatively simple device of using pairs of symmetrical arches to join the pillars to a single weight-bearing lintel – a design repeated in the upper storeys and mirrored in the courtyard basin. The later Merenid design, as employed in the Bou Inania, was to have much heavier lintels (the timbers above the doors and windows) supported by shorter projecting beams; this produces a more solid, step-like effect, losing the Attarin's fluid movement.

The basic ground plan, however, is more or less standard: an entrance hall opening onto a courtyard with a fountain, off which to the left are the latrines, and directly ahead the prayer hall. On your way in, stop a while in the **entrance hall**, whose zellij decoration is perhaps the most complex in Fes. A circular pattern, based on an interlace of pentagons and five-pointed stars, this perfectly demonstrates the intricate science – and the philosophy – employed by the craftsmen. As Titus Burckhardt explains (in his *Moorish Art in Spain*), this lies in direct opposition to the Western arts of pictorial representation:

> . . . *with its rhythmic repetitions, [it] does not seek to capture the eye to lead it into an imagined world, but, on the contrary, liberates it from all the pre-occupations of the mind. It does not transmit specific ideas, but a state of being, which is at once repose and inner rhythm.*

Burckhardt also notes that the way the patterns radiate from a single point serves as a pure simile for the belief in the oneness of God, manifested as the centre of every form or being.

In the **courtyard** you'll notice a change in the zellij base to a combination of eight- and ten-pointed stars. This probably signifies the hand of a different *maallem* (master craftsman), most of whom had a single mathematical base which they worked and reworked with infinite variation on all commissions. In comparison with these outer rooms, the actual **prayer hall** is very bare and meditative, focusing on its mihrab (or prayer niche) flanked by marble pillars and lit by a series of small zellij-glass windows.

If you are allowed to go up the stairs in the entrance hall, do so. Around the second floor are **cells** for over sixty students, and these operated as an annexe to the Kairaouine University until the 1950s. Budgett Meakin (in 1899) estimated that there were some 1500 students in the city's various medersas – a figure which may have been overestimated since it was based not on an actual count of the students themselves but on how many loaves of bread were prepared for them each day. Non-Muslims were not allowed into the medersas until the French undertook their repair at the beginning of the Protectorate, and were banned again (this time by the colonial authorities) when the Kairaouine students became active in the struggle for independence.

VIEWS OF THE KAIRAOUINE

If you can get onto it, one of the most complete possible **views of the Kairaouine Mosque** is available from the roof of the Attarin Medersa. Unfortunately, it rarely seems to be open to the public, but those blessed with the gift of the gab may be able to persuade the *gardien* to let them onto it.

Looking out across the mosque's green roof tiles three **minarets** are visible. The square one on the left belongs to the Zaouia Moulay Idriss. To its right are the Kairaouine's Burj an-Nattara (Trumpeter's Tower) and original minaret. The latter, slightly thinner in its silhouette than usual – most minarets are built to an exact 5:1 (height : width) ratio – is the oldest Islamic monument in the city, built in the year 956. Below it, you can also make out a considerable section of the central courtyard of the mosque – the **sahn**.

For a closer glimpse of the *sahn* at ground level, the best vantage point is the Bab El Wad gate: 20m down from the Attarin entrance (turn left as you step out, then immediately left again). At the end of the courtyard, a pair of magnificent pavilions are visible – the last additions to the structure of the mosque, added by the Saadians in the sixteenth century. They are modelled on the Court of the Lions in Granada's Alhambra palace, and were perhaps constructed by Spanish Muslim craftsmen.

Around the Kairaouine and Place Seffarine

There is a further new angle onto the *sahn* of the Kairaouine from the **Bab Medersa**, a gate near the end of this first stretch of the mosque wall. Opposite, as you'd expect, is another college – the semi-derelict **Misbahiya Medersa** which is currently closed for renovation. It has some fine details, though much of its best wood carving is now displayed at the Dar Batha museum. The elegant central basin was brought over by the Saadians from Almería in Spain; the marble floor in which it is set level came from Italy. Surprisingly large, with courtyards (and two latrines/ablutions) at each corner, it was built a couple of years before Bou Inania, again by the Merenid sultan, Abou El Hassan.

THE TETOUANI FONDOUK

Moving on around the corner of the Kairaouine, you pass the **Tetouani** (or *Istouanien*) **fondouk**, a well-preserved Merenid building where the traders from Tetouan used to stay. Now partially occupied by a carpet store, you can look inside without any obligation and you'll probably be shown the huge, ancient door lock which draws across its gateway.

A few doors down, past another, much smaller fondouk, is the original **Palais de Fes**, a grand nineteenth-century mansion that housed a fine carpet shop and a splendid restaurant, somewhat ambiguously said to be "dans un cadre du 14e siècle". The restaurant and carpet shop moved to Place er Rsif following a fire in 1999.

PLACE SEFFARINE AND THE KAIRAOUINE LIBRARY

Another gate to the Kairaouine, essentially of Almoravid construction, stands right opposite the Palais de Fes; it is one of the ten which are opened only for Friday prayers. Alongside, notice the cedar panelling, placed to guide the blind towards the mosque.

If you follow this round, through a tight-wedged alley, you soon emerge into a very distinctive open square, metalworkers hammering away on each of its sides, surrounded by immense iron and copper cauldrons and pans for weddings and festivals. This is **Place Seffarine** – almost wilfully picturesque, with its faience fountain and gnarled old fig trees.

On the near side of the square a tall and very simple entrance in the whitewashed walls leads into the **Kairaouine Library**, another building frustratingly denied to non-Muslims, and currently closed even to believers due to restoration work. Established by the Kairouan refugees in the ninth century, and bolstered by virtually the entire contents of Córdoba's medieval library, it once held the greatest collection of Islamic, mathematical and scholarly books outside Baghdad. Amazingly, and somewhat pointedly marking Fes's decline, much of the library was lost or dissipated in the seventeenth century. Now restored and in use, it is one of the most important in the Arab world.

The **university** here has had its function largely usurped by the modern departments established around Fes El Djedid and the Ville Nouvelle, and dispersed throughout Morocco. However, until recent decades it was the only source of Moroccan higher education. Entirely traditional in character, studies comprised courses on Koranic law, astrology, mathematics, logic, rhetoric and poetry – very much as the medieval universities of Europe. Teaching was informal, with professors gathering a group of students round them in a corner of the mosque, the students contriving to absorb and memorize the body of the professors' knowledge. It was, of course, an entirely male preserve.

A good spot to get your bearings, Place Seffarine offers a number of possible routes. You can continue round the mosque by taking the first lane to the right as you enter the square – **Sma't El Adoul** (The Street of the Notaries). The notaries, professional scribes, are sadly out of business, but before looping back to reach the Attarin medersa, you will be able to peek through a number of gates revealing the Kairaouine's rush-matted and round-arched interior. If you don't take this turning but continue straight ahead, you enter an area of souks specializing in **gold and silver jewellery** and used metal goods – a magnificent range of **pewter teapots** among them. As this road begins to veer left down the hill, a right turn will lead you up to the **Cherratin Medersa** (and eventually to Zaouia Moulay Idriss).

First, though, it is worth taking a look at the **Seffarine Medersa**, right on Place Seffarine.

THE MEDERSA ES SEFFARINE
The **Medersa Es Seffarine** is the earliest of these Fes colleges. Its entrance is fairly inconspicuous, and you might need it pointed out to you: leaving the Seffarine square at the bottom left-hand corner you follow a short lane down to the left and then briefly to the right – the door (studded and with an overhanging portico) is on your left. It is the only medersa still used as a hostel for students studying at the Kairaouine, and you can pop in for a look at any reasonable time with no charge.

Built around 1285 – twenty years before the Attarin, 42 before the Bou Inania – the Seffarine is unlike all the other medersas in that it takes the exact form of a traditional Fassi house, with an arched balcony above its courtyard and still with suggestions of former grandeur in the lofty prayer hall. Elsewhere, the wandering vine and delicate ablutions pool give it a domestic air; in the far left-hand corner are washbasins and latrines.

Next door are two newer medersas housing students from the Lycée.

THE MEDERSA ECH CHERRATIN
Very different from the Seffarin, and indeed all the previous medersas, the **Medersa Ech Cherratin** (see directions from Place Seffarine, see above) dates from 1670 and the reign of Moulay Rachid, founder of the Alaouite dynasty.

The whole design represents a shift in scope and wealth – to an essentially functional style, with student cells grouped round three corner courtyards and latrines/ablutions round the fourth.

The craftsmanship here represents a significant decline, though there is some impressive woodwork around the individual courtyards. It is interesting, too, in a general way as a rare surviving building from this period.

This medersa is being restored but is generally open to the public (daily 8.30am–5.30pm, Ramadan 9am–4pm; 10dh).

Continuing down the lane **beyond the entrance to the Medersa Es Seffarine**, swinging down the hill to the right, you reach **Rue des Teinturiers** (The Dyers' Souk: see the following section) and a **bridge** over the Oued Fes, below which you can leave the Medina by the square beside the **Mosque Er Rsif.**

South of the Kairaouine: the dyers' souk and tanneries
If you're beginning to find the medieval prettiness of the central souks and medersas slightly unreal, then this region, just below the Kairaouine, should provide the antidote. That's because the dyers' and tanners' souks – basis of the city's commercial wealth from the tenth to the nineteenth century – represent the nauseating underside of everything you've seen until now.

THE DYERS' SOUK
The **dyers' street – Souk Sabbighin** (or Rue des Teinturiers, in French) – is directly below the Seffarine Medersa. Continue down past the medersa to your left, and then turn right immediately before the bridge ahead.

The souk is short and very weird, draped with fantastically coloured yarn and cloth drying in the heat. Below, workers in grey, chimney-sweep-looking clothes toil over ancient cauldrons of multicoloured dyes. The atmosphere is thick and mysterious, and not a little disconcerting so close to one of the city's main entrances.

At the end of the dyers' souk you come to a second bridge, the humpbacked **Qantrat Sidi El Aouad** – almost disguised by the shops built on and around it. Walking across, you'll find yourself in the **Andalous quarter** (see p.226), and if you follow the main lane up to the left, Rue Sidi Youssef, you'll come out at the Andalous Mosque. Staying on the Kairaouine side of the river and taking the lane down to your right at the end of the souk, you should emerge at the open **square by the Rsif Mosque**; from here, if you want to return to the Ville Nouvelle, you can get a bus #19, #29 or #45 – or a petit taxi.

THE TANNERIES

For the tanneries quarter – the **Souk Dabbaghin** – return to Place Seffarine and take the right-hand lane at the top of the square (the second lane on your left if you're coming from the Palais de Fes). This lane is known as **Darb Mechattin** (Combmakers' Lane), and runs more or less parallel to the river for 150m or so, eventually reaching a fork. The right-hand branch goes down to the river and **Beyin El Moudoun Bridge** – another approach to the Andalous Mosque. The left branch winds up amid a maze of eighteenth-century streets for another 150 to 200m until you see the tanneries on your right; it sounds a convoluted route but is in fact a well-trodden one.

The most physically striking sight in Fes, the **tanneries** are constantly being visited by groups of tourists, with whom you could discreetly tag along for a while if you get lost. Otherwise, follow your nose or accept a guide up from the Place Seffarine. The best time to visit is in the morning, when there is most activity. You will be asked to pay a small fee – 10dh is usual – to one of the local *gardiens*. Shops with terraces overlooking the tanneries will often invite you in for a look, in return for the opportunity to show you what they have for sale (generally at high prices) – one such is the *Terrasse de la Tannerie*, a shop selling mostly leather goods at 10 Hay Lablida Choura, just past the main entrance to the tanneries themselves, where the pressure to buy is not usually too heavy (and remember: if they entice you in by telling you there's no obligation to buy, you are perfectly within your rights to hold them to that).

There is a compulsive fascination about the tanneries. Cascades of water pour through holes that were once the windows of houses; hundreds of skins lie spread out to dry on the rooftops; while amid the vats of dye and pigeon dung (used to treat the leather) an unbelievably gothic fantasy is enacted. The rotation of colours in the enormous honeycombed vats follows a traditional sequence – yellow (supposedly "saffron", in fact turmeric), red (poppy), blue (indigo), green (mint) and black (antimony) – though vegetable dyes have mostly been replaced by chemicals, with worrying effects on the health of the workers involved.

This innovation and the occasional rinsing machine aside, there can have been little change here since the sixteenth century, when Fes took over from Córdoba as the pre-eminent city of leather production. As befits such an ancient system, the ownership is also intricately feudal: the foremen run a hereditary guild and the workers pass down their specific jobs from generation to generation.

The processes can best be seen from surrounding terrace rooftops, where you'll be directed along with the other tourists. There is, oddly enough, a kind of sensuous beauty about it – for all the stench and voyeurism involved. Sniffing the mint that you are handed as you enter (to alleviate the nausea) and looking across at the others doing the same, however, there could hardly be a more pointed exercise in the nature of comparative wealth. Like it or not, this is tourism at its most extreme.

North to Bab Guissa and the Palais Jamai

This region – **north from Souk El Attarin** towards Bab Guissa and the Palais Jamai Hôtel – is something of a tailpiece to the Kairaouine quarter of Fes El Bali. It is not a route which many tourists take, scattered as it is with curiosities rather than monuments, but in this itself there's a distinct attraction. The only monument as such on the route is the **Mosque of Sidi Tijani**, the zaouia of an eighteenth-century marabout, and traditionally a stopover point for West African pilgrims en route to Mecca to do *hadj*. The interior is currently closed, even to Muslims, for repairs, but one feature worth checking out on the exterior is the hole to the right of the eastern doorway for placing donations, and more particularly the bronzework covering the mirror that surmounts it.

Continuing on to leave the city at Bab Guissa, you can walk out and round to the **Merenid Tombs**, a beautiful walk as the sun is going down on the city.

A ROUTE TO BAB GUISSA – AND THE JEWELLERS' SOUK

From **Souk El Attarin**, there are dozens of lanes climbing up in the general direction of Bab Guissa, many of them blind alleys which send you scuttling back to retrace your steps. One of the more interesting and unproblematic approaches is to take the first lane to your left just inside the entrance arch to the souk (that is, about 15m before you come to the *Dar Saada* palace restaurant). Following this as directly as you can, you will soon emerge at the **Joutia**, the ancient fish and salt market.

Spreading out above here is the **Sagha** – the **jewellers' quarter** – which curves round to the right into a small square flanked by the eighteenth-century **Fondouk Sagha** and a small fountain. The fondouk is now used as a warehouse for neighbouring shops, but you can wander in to take a look at the elegant cedar woodwork and (heavily restored) stucco if it's open.

Back at the main lane – Place Sagha and its fondouk are about 20m off to the right – you pass a series of small café-restaurants and a cinema near **Place Achabin**, the herbalists' square, where remedies and charms are still sold. The **café-restaurants** in this area are among the best value in Fes El Bali, serving good solid meals, and many double as patisseries, good for a mint tea or some fresh orange while rambling round the Attarin/Kairaouine area. Most of them are located in Rue Hormis.

Beyond Place Achabin, the road continues uphill, through an area filled with carpenters' workshops, towards Bab Guissa. On your way, look out for the **Fondouk Guissa** – or Fondouk El Ihoudi (The Jews' Fondouk) – on the left-hand side of the road. This dates back to the thirteenth century and was at the centre of the city's Jewish community until their removal to the Mellah in Fes El Djedid. It is used today for the sorting and storing of skins brought up from the tanneries: not a building for the queasy.

BAB GUISSA AND THE HÔTEL PALAIS JAMAI

The **Bab Guissa** and **Mosque Bab Guissa**, at the top of the hill, are of little interest, rebuilt in the nineteenth century to replace a string of predecessors which had occupied this site for 800 years. The fountain adjoining the mosque, on the other hand, is one of the city's most spectacular pieces of mosaic work, unfortunately now the object of neglect, used as an unofficial public toilet.

A quick right just before the gate, however, takes you up to the **Hôtel Palais Jamai** – a building whose luxury comes as quite a shock after a day's rambling through the Medina below. It was built towards the end of the nineteenth century by the Jamai brothers, viziers to Sultan Moulay Hassan and, in effect, the most powerful men in the country. Fabulously rapacious, the brothers eventually fell from power amid spectacular intrigues at the accession of Abdul Aziz in 1894. Walter Harris records the full story in *Morocco That Was*, dwelling in great detail on the brothers' ignominious fate – "perhaps the blackest page of Moulay Abdul Aziz's reign".

They were sent in fetters to Tetouan, and confined, chained and fettered, in a dungeon. In the course of time – and how long those ten years must have been – Hadj Amaati (The Elder) died. The governor of Tetouan was afraid to bury the body, lest he should be accused of having allowed his prisoner to escape. He wrote to the court for instructions.

It was summer, and even the dungeon was hot. The answer did not come for eleven days, and all that time Si Mohammed remained chained to his brother's corpse! The brother survived. In 1908 he was released after fourteen years of incarceration, a hopeless, broken, ruined man. Everything he had possessed had been confiscated, his wives and children had died; the result of want and persecution. He emerged from his dark dungeon nearly blind, and lame from the cruel fetters he had worn. In his days of power he had been cruel, it is said – but what a price he paid!

For an overt and dramatic contrast to this tale, wander into the hotel for a drink. Ask to do so on the terrace beside the old palace, now dwarfed by a huge modern extension. An hour in the gardens here, with their box-hedge courtyards and fountains, really does merit the bar prices (and there's an excellent Moroccan restaurant, in a beautiful old salon, if you can afford a splurge). The palace quarters themselves are used as special suites and conference rooms, but if they're unoccupied you may be able to look round one or two – ask at reception if a porter can show you the "Royal Suites"; a tip will be expected.

From **Bab Guissa** you can take a shortcut across through the hill cemetery to the Merenid tombs, or you can follow the road up and around. At **Bab Ferdaous**, just outside the *Palais Jamai,* there's a petit taxi stand, and from here **bus #10** runs to the train station in the Ville Nouvelle.

The Andalous Quarter

Coming across the **Bou Khareb** River from the Kairaouine to the **Andalous bank** is not quite the adventure it once was. For the first three centuries of their existence, the two quarters were entirely separate walled cities and the intense rivalry between them often resulted in factional strife. The rivalry still lingers enough to give each a distinct identity, though since the thirteenth century this has been a somewhat one-sided affair: as the Fassis tell it, the Andalousis are known for the beauty of their women and the bravery of their soldiers, while the Kairaouinis have always had the money.

Whatever the reasons, the most famous Andalucian scholars and craftsmen have nearly all lived and worked on the other side of the river and as a result the atmosphere has a somewhat provincial character. Monuments are few and comparatively modest, and the streets are quieter and predominantly residential. As such, it can be a pleasant quarter to spend the early evening – and to get caught up in the ordinary, daily life of Fes El Bali. Street trading here (and in the southern quarters of the Kairaouine side, too) tends to revolve round daily necessities, providing a link between the "medieval" town and continuing urban life. And your relationship with the city changes alongside, as you cease for a while to be a consuming tourist – a factor reflected also in the near-total absence of "guides" and hustlers.

There are four principal **approaches to the quarter**, all providing more or less direct access to the area round the Andalous Mosque.

Cross the river at the El Aouad Bridge. From here, take **Rue Sidi Youssef** up the hill to the right, and keep going straight to the top, where you'll come into line with the minaret of the Andalous Mosque. At this point, veer left, and you will see (on your right) the elaborate facade of the **Sahrija Medersa.**

Cross the river to the north, near the tanneries, on the Bein El Moudoun Bridge (The Bridge Between the Cities). Then follow the main street, **Rue Seftah**, all the way up the hill as it winds round to the Andalous Mosque.

Start at the square by Mosque Er Rsif. From here you can get to **Rue Sidi Youssef** by going through the gate opposite the mosque entrance, then taking a first left by the first mosque (Sidi Lemlili) you come to, followed by a right turn up the hill. The square can be reached (somewhat circuitously) from the area around the

Kairaouine Mosque, or you can get a **bus** to it (#19, #29 or #45) from the Ville Nouvelle, or (#27) from Dar Batha.

Start at Bab Ftouh, at the bottom of the quarter, and head north to the Andalous Mosque. Bus #3 runs to Bab Ftouh from Place de la Résistance (aka La Fiat) and **bus #12** connects Bab Boujeloud with Bab Ftouh. Bab Ftouh is connected by **bus #18** to the Place de l'Istiqlal, by the Dar Batha; a handy point from which to leave Fes El Bali.

THE SAHRIJA MEDERSA AND ANDALOUS MOSQUE

If you are seeking direction for your wanderings in the Andalous Quarter, the **Medersa Es Sahrija** is the quarter's most interesting monument and is generally rated the third finest medersa in the city, after the Attarin and Bou Inania. Anywhere else but Fes it would be a major sight, though here, perhaps because of the more accessible monuments, it fails to stand out as much as it should.

Still, it is currently undergoing restoration, and there's a considerable range and variety of original decoration. The zellij is among the oldest in the country, while the wood carving harks back to Almohad and Almoravid motifs with its palmettes and pine cones. Built around 1321 by Sultan Abou El Hassan, it is slightly earlier than the Attarin and a more or less exact contemporary of the medersa in Meknes – which it in many ways resembles. Some students live here, but access is welcomed.

There is little to be seen of the nearby **Andalous Mosque**, other than its monumental entrance gates, as it is built right at the highest point of the valley. Like the Kairaouine, it was founded in the late ninth century and saw considerable enlargements under the Almoravids and Merenids. The Sahrija Medersa originally served as a dormitory annexe for those studying at the mosque's library and under its individual professors.

A last Medersa, the **Sebhayin**, or **Medersa El Oued**, is located just southwest of the Sahrija. It, too, was once an Andalous Mosque student annexe, and it remains in use, as a residence for Lycée students.

TOWARDS BAB FTOUH AND THE POTTERS' QUARTER

South from the Andalous Mosque – out towards **Bab Ftouh** – you emerge into a kind of flea market: clothes sellers at first, then all variety of household and general goods and odds and ends. At the top of the hill, on the edge of a cemetery area, there are often entertainers – clowns, storytellers, the occasional musician, all performing to large audiences.

This region of the city, a strange no-man's-land of **cemeteries** and run-down houses, was once a leper colony, and traditionally a quarter of necromancers, thieves, madmen and saints. At its heart, close by Bab Ftouh, is the whitewashed **koubba of Sidi Harazem**, a twelfth-century mystic who has been adopted as the patron saint of students and the mentally ill. The saint's moussem, held in the spring, is one of the city's most colourful; in past centuries it was often the cue for riots and popular insurrections. The **potters' quarter** used to be located by Bab Ftouh, though they have recently been moved out to Aïn Nokbi, some two kilometres along the Taza road. You will see the columns of black smoke and the buildings of the *Complexe Céramique du Maroc* down to the left of the road. If you're interested in the techniques – the moulding, drying and decorating of the pots and tiles – it's possible to look around the workshops. Although the quarter is new, the designs and workmanship remain traditional.

At **Bab Ftouh** you can pick up a petit taxi to any part of town (the route up to the Merenid tombs is good for its views), or you can catch bus #18 back to the Ville Nouvelle.

Fes El Djedid

Unlike Fes El Bali, whose development and growth seems to have been almost organic, **Fes El Djedid** – "Fes the New"– was an entirely planned city, built by the Merenids at the beginning of their rule, as both a practical and symbolic seat of government. The work was begun around 1273 by the dynasty's second ruling sultan, Abou Youssef, and in a manic feat of building was completed within three years. The capital for much of its construction came from taxes levied on the Meknes olive presses; the Jews were also taxed to build a new grand mosque; and the labour, at least in part, was supplied by Spanish Christian slaves.

The site which the Merenids chose for their city lies some distance from Fes El Bali. In the chronicles this is presented as a strategic move for the defence of the city, though it is hard to escape the conclusion that its main function was as a defence of the new dynasty against the Fassis themselves. It was not an extension for the people, in any real sense, being occupied largely by the **Dar el Makhzen**, a vast royal palace, and by a series of army garrisons. With the addition of the **Mellah** – the Jewish ghetto – at the beginning of the fourteenth century, this process was continued. Forced out of Fes El Bali following one of the periodic pogroms, the Jews could provide an extra barrier (and scapegoat) between the sultan and his Muslim faithful, as well as a useful and close-to-hand source of income.

Over the centuries, Fes El Djedid's fortunes have generally followed those of the city as a whole. It was extremely prosperous under the Merenids and Wattasids, fell into decline under the Saadians, lapsed into virtual ruin during Moulay Ismail's long reign in Meknes, but revived with the commercial expansion of the nineteenth century – at which point the walls between the old and new cities were finally joined.

At the close of the nineteenth century, the *Encyclopedia Britannica* noted of Fes that: "The Jews suffer great persecutions and many indignities, but many of them continue to amass money."

Events last century, largely generated by the French Protectorate, have left Fes El Djedid greatly changed and somewhat moribund. As a "government city", it had no obvious role after the transfer of power to Rabat – a vacuum which the French filled by establishing a huge *quartier reservé* (red-light district) in the area around the Grand Mosque. This can have done little for the city's identity, but it was not so radical or disastrous as the immediate aftermath of independence in 1956. Concerned about their future status, and with their position made untenable by the Arab-Israeli war, virtually all of the Mellah's 17,000 **Jewish population** emigrated to Israel, Paris or Casablanca; today only a few Jewish families remain in the Mellah, though there is still a small community in the Ville Nouvelle.

The Jewish Community Centre (☎05/562 2446) is at 24 Rue Zerktouni, opposite the copse which faces the *Splendid Hôtel*; the current president of the community is Dr Guigui (☎05/562 3039). With his help, or that of others at the centre, you could learn more about the community – or about the old synagogues in Fes El Djedid (see pp.231–232).

Generally speaking, Moroccan Jews are well thought of and, at any one time, several hold high office in the government. Similarly, Moroccan Jews who play leading roles in Israel are noted with pride. At the same time, however, it was reported that recently a Fes hotel turned Israeli tourists away; we have omitted it from our list.

You can reach Fes El Djedid in a ten-minute walk from **Bab Boujeloud** (the route outlined below), or from the Ville Nouvelle by walking up or taking a **bus** (#2 from Place de la Résistance, aka La Fiat)) to **Place des Alaouites** and **Bab Semarine** beside the Mellah.

West from Boujeloud

Walking down to Fes El Djedid from **Bab Boujeloud** involves a shift in scale. Gone are the labyrinthine alleyways and souks of the Medina, to be replaced by a massive expanse of walls. Within them, to your left, are a series of gardens: the private **Jardins Beida**, behind the Lycée, and then the public **Jardins de Boujeloud** with their pools diverted from the Oued Fes. The latter have an entrance towards the end of the long Avenue des Français, and are a vital lung for the old city. If everything gets too much, wander in, lounge about on the grass, and spend an hour or two at the tranquil **café**, by an old waterwheel, at their west corner.

THE PETIT MECHOUAR

Continuing westward along Avenue des Français, you pass through a twin-arched gate to reach an enclosed square, the **Petit Mechouar**, which was once the focus of city life and used until the mid-1970s by the same sort of acts (snake charmers, jugglers and story-tellers) that are still found in Marrakesh's Djema el Fna. Such performers were cleared away when the Mechouar was closed for repairs, and have not been allowed back since.

The Petit Mechouar has five exits. On its eastern side are two, the one leading onto Avenue des Français and, just south of that another double archway, **Bab Baghdadi**, through which begins the main street of Fes El Djedid proper – the **Grande Rue**. Across the square on the west side, Bab Moulay Abdallah leads to the eponymous Moulay Abdallah quarter (see p.230), while to the south **Bab Mechouar** opens onto the grounds of the Royal Palace. It was at this gate that ordinary citizens would approach the palace to petition the king, and the mechouar was the place where they would wait for admission.

To the right is the monumental **Bab Dekakin** (Gate of the Benches), more correctly known as **Bab es Seba**, a Merenid structure which was, until King Hassan realigned the site in 1967–71, the main approach to the Royal Palace and Fes El Bali. It was on this gate that the Infante Ferdinand of Portugal was hanged, head down, for four days in 1443. He had been captured in an unsuccessful raid on Tangier and his country had failed to raise the ransom required. As a further, salutary warning, when his corpse was taken down from the Bab, it was stuffed and displayed beside the gate, where it remained for the next three decades.

THE VIEUX MECHOUAR

Through the three great arches you will find yourself in another, much larger courtyard, the **Vieux Mechouar**. Laid out in the eighteenth century, this is flanked along the whole of one side by the Makina, an Italian-built arms factory built in 1886, which is today partially occupied by a rug factory and various local clubs.

A smaller gate, the nineteenth-century **Bab Segma**, stands at the far end of the court, forcing you into an immediate turn as you leave the city through the Merenid outer gateway, whose twin octagonal towers slightly resemble the contemporary Chellah in Rabat.

If you are walking to the **Merenid tombs** from here, you can either turn sharp right and scramble up the hillside after the Borj Nord, or go straight ahead along the longer Route du Tour de Fes. The latter route takes you past the huge **Kasbah Cherada**, a fort built by Sultan Moulay Rashid in 1670 to house – and keep at a distance – the Berber tribes of his garrison. The partially walled compound is now the site of a hospital, a school and an annexe of the Kairaouine University.

QUARTIER MOULAY ABDALLAH AND THE SOUKS

Back at the Petit Mechouar – and before turning through the double arch onto the Grande Rue de Fes El Djedid – a smaller gateway leads off to the right at the bottom of the square. This gives entrance to the old *quartier reservé* of **Moulay Abdallah**, where the French built cafés, dance halls and brothels. The prostitutes were mostly young Berber girls, drawn by a rare chance of quick money, and usually returning to their villages when they had earned enough to marry or keep their families. The quarter today has a slightly solemn, empty feel about it, with the main street twisting down to Fes El Djedid's 1276 **Grand Mosque**. At the western end of the quarter, Bab Bou Jat leads on to the **Grand Mechouar**, a large open space that can also be entered from the main road to its north.

Through the main gateway, the **Grand Rue** zigzags slightly before leading straight down to the Mellah. There are **souks**, mainly for textiles and produce, along the way but nothing very much to detain you too long. Just by the entrance, though, immediately to the left after you go through the arch, a narrow **lane** curves off into an attrac-

---

THE EVENING ROOST AT FES

For bird-watchers, the evening roost at Fes makes a spectacular sight. The performance begins with the frenzied activities of the resident starlings (including spotless starlings) but these are soon eclipsed by the overhead passage of dozens of little egrets, gracefully returning to their roost sites in the Middle Atlas and environs. The skies soon appear to swarm with literally thousands of alpine swifts, wheeling on crescent-shaped wings in search of insects for their young in nests in the city walls. To complete the spectacle, it is worth casting an eye along the rooftop silhouette as the light begins to fade. With a little perseverance it is possible to locate the characteristic body profiles of white storks on their rooftop nests along the perimeter walls which line Fes El Djedid.

tive little area on the periphery of the Boujeloud gardens. There's an old **water wheel** here which used to supply the gardens, and the *Café Noria* (see p.235) in the gardens nearby. On the way down, you pass a handful of stalls; among them are, traditionally, the *kif* and *sebsi* (*kif* pipe) vendors – though only the latter now remain.

The Mellah and Royal Palace

With fewer than a dozen Jewish families still remaining, the **Mellah** is a rather melancholic place, largely resettled by poor Muslim emigrants from the countryside. The quarter's name – *mellah*, "salt" in Arabic – came to be used for Jewish ghettos throughout Morocco, though it was originally applied only to this one in Fes. In derivation it seems to be a reference to the job given to the Fassi Jews of salting the heads of criminals before they were hung on the gates.

The enclosed and partly protected position of the Mellah represents fairly accurately the Moroccan Jews' historically ambivalent position. Arriving for the most part with compatriot Muslim refugees from Spain and Portugal, they were never fully accepted into the nation's life. Nor, however, were they quite the rejected people of other Arab countries. Inside the Mellah they were under the direct protection of the sultan (or the local *caid*) and maintained their own laws and governors.

Whether the creation of a ghetto ensured the actual need for one is, of course, debatable. Certainly, it was greatly to the benefit of the reigning sultan, who could both depend on Jewish loyalties and manipulate the international trade and finance which came increasingly to be dominated by them in the nineteenth century. For all this importance to the sultan, however, even the richest Jews had to lead extremely circumscribed lives. In Fes before the French Protectorate, no Jew was allowed to ride or even to wear shoes outside the Mellah, and they were severely restricted in their travels elsewhere.

HOUSES, SYNAGOGUES AND CEMETERIES

Since the end of the Protectorate, when many of the poorer Jews here left to take up an equally ambivalent place at the bottom of Israeli society (though this time above the Arabs), memories of their presence have faded rapidly. What still remain are their eighteenth- and nineteenth-century **houses** – immediately and conspicuously un-Arabic, with their tiny windows and elaborate ironwork. Cramped even closer together than the houses in Fes El Bali, they are interestingly designed if you are offered a look inside.

The **Hebrew Cemetery** is easy to find; it lies to the east of the Place des Alaouites, on the edge of the Mellah overlooking the valley of the Oued Zitoun (see Fes El Djedid map). It is open every day, except Saturday, from 7am to sunset, closing slightly earlier on Fridays in time for the Jewish Sabbath. The small iron gate faces the car park, between the *Garage Sahar* and the start of the flea market on the side street.

The neat, white, rounded gravestones extend to the horizon. 12,000 of them have names, while another 600 are unnamed, mostly victims of a typhus epidemic which hit the Mellah in 1924. Also among the graves are the small, pitiful tombs of those who died young. Visitors leave a pebble on the gravestone to mark their visit, or burn a candle in the recess provided. The most visited tombs are those of former chief rabbis, notably that of the eighteenth-century Rabbi Yehuda ben Attar, prominently covered in green and black mosaic tiles, and that of Lalla Solika Hatchouel, surmounted by three vase-like turrets. Lalla Solika caught the eye of the king's son, Prince Moulay Abderrahman, who asked her to convert to Islam so that he could marry her. When she refused, he had her imprisoned and executed, and she has since been venerated as a martyr.

At the far end, with an entrance from the cemetery and another from the Mellah, is the **Habanim Synagogue**, built in 1928 and in regular use for services and as a religious school until quite recently. It has now, with help from American Jewry, been opened as a museum, containing a massive clutter of bric-a-brac, much of it only very tangentially related to Fes's Jewish community. The centrepiece is a *huppa* (wedding canopy) and two bridal costumes, and the ark in the eastern wall, which marks the direction of prayer and contains a three-hundred-year-old Torah scroll, is surmounted with some beautiful stucco work. There's also a room full of photographs, the most interesting of which are a series of postcards of Fes, including the Mellah, dating back to 1912.

During opening hours, there is always someone to show you round the cemetery and museum. There is no charge but a donation is expected. The *gardien* of the cemetery, Aziz Youmni, is an excellent person to ask for directions to the other synagogues on, or just off, the Grande Rue des Merenides. At one time there were thirty-eight, of which most are now shops or private residences. The oldest is the seventeenth-century **Ibn Danan Synagogue** (down the side street off Grande Rue des Merenides by no. 86), reopened following restoration in 1999. The most striking thing about the otherwise unremarkable interior is the collection of brass and glass lamps, but just as many mosques are adjoined by a hammam, so this synagogue has a *mikve* (ritual bath) in its basement. Other synagogues in the quarter, nearly as old, but smaller, include the **El Fassayine Synagogue**, now a martial arts club, and the **Synagogue Mansiano**, now a private residence.

THE ROYAL PALACE

At the far end of the Mellah's main street – Grand Rue des Merenides (or Grand Rue de Mellah) – you come into **Place des Alaouites**, fronted by the new ceremonial gateway to the **Royal Palace**. The palace, which has been constantly rebuilt and expanded over the centuries, is one of the most sumptuous complexes in Morocco, set amid vast gardens, with numerous pavilions and guest wings.

In the 1970s, it was sometimes possible to gain a permit to visit part of the palace grounds, which were described in Christopher Kininmonth's *Traveller's Guide* as "the finest single sight Morocco has to offer . . . many acres in size and of a beauty to take the breath away". Today, the palace complex is strictly off limits to all except official guests, though it was reputedly little used by Hassan II, the last king, who divided most of his time between his palaces in Ifrane, Rabat and Marrakesh.

Eating and drinking

By day at least, there's little to keep you in the **Ville Nouvelle**, the new city established by Lyautey at the beginning of the Protectorate. Unlike Casa or Rabat, where the French adapted Moroccan forms to create their own showplaces, this is a pretty lacklustre European grid. The Ville Nouvelle is, however, home to most of the faculties of the city's university, and is very much the city's business and commercial centre. If you want to talk with Fassis on a basis other than that of guide to tourist, you'll stand the most chance in the cafés here, and it's more likely that the students you meet are exactly that. The quarter is also the centre for most of the city's restaurants, cafés, bars, bookshops and other facilities.

Fes El Bali and **Fes El Djedid** are quieter at night, except during Ramadan (when shops and stalls stay open till two or three in the morning). They have, as with all Medina quarters throughout Morocco, no bars, and with the exception of a few "Palace-Restaurants", many of which are open for lunch only and cater mainly for tour groups, their eating places are on the basic side.

Ville Nouvelle

The Ville Nouvelle has quite a selection of restaurants, though few go any way towards justifying the city's reputation as home of the country's finest cuisine. Cafés, at least, are plentiful – and there are a few bars.

RESTAURANTS

The better possibilities include:

Pizzeria Assouan, 4 Av. Allal Ben Abdallah. A pizzeria that also serves pasta and tajines among a very wide repertoire of dishes, with a Chinese and Vietnamese menu if you fancy a change from European and North African food. Adjoining it is an upmarket café and patisserie, also called Assouan. Daily 11am–3pm & 5pm–midnight. Moderate.

Restaurant Chamonix, 5 Rue Moukhtar Soussi, off Av. Mohammed V, behind the *Grand Hôtel*. A reliable restaurant serving Moroccan and European dishes, notably pizza and pasta; set menu for 52dh. Attracts a younger crowd and, in summer, stays open later than its standard hours of 9am–10pm daily. Cheap.

Restaurant La Cheminée, 6 Av Lalla Asma (aka Rue Chenguit) on the right on the way to the train station. Small and friendly licensed restaurant. Daily noon–2.30pm & 6–10pm. Moderate.

Fish Friture, 138 Bd. Mohammed V, at the far end of a short passageway off the main street. Fish dishes are the mainstay, and they're good – the paella must be one of the best you'll get this side of the Straits of Gibraltar. Service is courteous and quick, and there are meat dishes and omelettes as well as fish. Daily 10am–9pm. Moderate.

Al Khozma, 25 Av. Mohammed Slaoui. A small place offering savoury crepes, a small but good choice of fish dishes, brochettes or a 60dh set menu. Daily 10am–11pm. Cheap to moderate.

Restaurant Marrakesh, 11 Rue Abes Tazi (between Hotels *Mounia* and *CTM*). Small, with a limited menu, but the food is well cooked and well tasty. Daily noon–10pm. Cheap.

Le Nautilus, in the basement of the *Hôtel de la Paix*, 44 Av. Hassan II. A rather classy restaurant renowned for its fish and seafood. Mon–Sat noon–3pm & 7pm–midnight. Moderate.

Café Restaurant La Noblesse, 16 Place 16 Novembre, across the car park at the back of the covered market. New, it started Chinese as *Le Mandarin*, but quickly reverted to local cuisine – as yet untested, but it's a useful place for a restaurant. Daily 10.30am–midnight. Moderate.

Oued de la Bière (aka *Restaurant Ten Years*), Av. Mohammed V. A reasonable but not tremendously exciting restaurant whose set menu includes the option of couscous, lamb tajine with prunes or chicken tajine with lemon and olives. Daily 11am–3pm & 6–11pm. Moderate.

Café Restaurant Tout Va Bien, 51 Rue Tetouan. One of a group of cheap eateries just off Place de l'Atlas. The food (tajine, spit-roast chicken, brochettes and kefta) is not great but it's open round the clock and it's cheap.

Café 24/24, Place 16 Novembre at the corner of Rue Hamoun el Fetouaki (by *Hôtel Olympique*). A café-restaurant worthy of note for its claim to supply a meal (burgers, steak, brochettes) at any time of the day or night, so handy if you get the munchies in the wee hours. Open 24hr. Cheap.

Venisia Sandwich, 7 Av. El Houria, formerly Av. de France, round the corner from the *Hôtel Amor*. A superior fast-food joint with grilled sausages, fish and kefta, plus a range of salads. Daily 11am–midnight. Cheap.

Chez Vittoria, 21 Rue du Nador, aka Brahim Roudani, almost opposite the *Hôtel Central*; reliable and value for money, with a small variety of pizzas and pasta dishes – but not very exciting. Daily noon–3pm & 6.30–11.30pm. Expensive.

Zagora Restaurant, 5 Bd. Mohammed V. French dishes à la carte, or a set menu of Moroccan dishes; large portions are value for money; service cheerful and helpful. Daily 12.30–3pm & 7–11pm. Moderate.

CAFÉS AND BARS

Cafés and **patisseries** are scattered throughout the Ville Nouvelle, with some of the most popular around Place Mohammed V – the *Café de la Renaissance* here was an old Foreign Legion hangout, now popular with gay Moroccan men – and along Avenue Mohammed Es Slaoui, Avenue Hassan II and Boulevard Mohammed V. One of the most popular of these, boasting excellent croissants (and very clean toilets), is the *Café Floria*, a block north of the PTT on Avenue Hassan II. Other notable cafés include the *Cristal* across the square from the *Renaissance*, heavy with 1930s atmosphere and known for doing a good espresso, and the *Number One* in Avenue Lalla Asma, with mirror-tile decor dating from the disco era. The *Bistro Pub Barbecue Le Progres* at 21 Avenue Mohammed Es Slaoui, is rather like a pub without alcohol, but it has a pool table and a young crowd of regulars. The rather elegant *Peacock*, two doors down at no.

25, is not only a top-class patisserie, but a cybercafé to boot, with Internet access upstairs. Good **ice creams** are to be had at *Black Berry*, 59 Boulevard Abdallah Chefchaouni, or *Gelatitalia* on Rue Libya, just off Rue el Houria.

For **bars**, you have to look a little harder. Some might enjoy the seedy but cheap *Dalilla* at 17 Boulevard Mohammed V, whose upstairs bar is a place for serious Moroccan drinking. The *Astor*, by the cinema of the same name at 18 Avenue Mohammed Slaoui, has a cellar bar that doubles up as the city's only kosher restaurant, while at the *Tivoli* just 50m to its east at no. 46, the back bar is more relaxed than the loud front bar. Around the corner on Boulevard Mohammed V, two doors up from the *Oued de la Bière*, the *Café Chope*, with its 1930s mock-classical interior, does some of the best bar snacks in town. Beyond these places (none of them likely to feel very comfortable for women – though the downstairs bar at the *Astor* should be all right since it's a restaurant as well), you're down to the handful of **hotel bars**: in the *Ibis, de la Paix, Mounia, Nouzha, Lamdaghri, Splendid* and *Grand,* and the upmarket and rather dull *Sheraton Fes* and *Sofia.*

Fes El Bali

Fes El Bali has possibilities for budget meals and, at greater cost, for sampling (relatively) traditional cuisine in some splendid old palaces. **Fes El Djedid** also has some basic café-restaurants, though none worth specially recommending.

CAFÉ-RESTAURANTS AND SNACKS

There are two main areas for **budget eating** in Fes El Bali; just inside Bab Boujeloud – try the *Restaurant des Jeunes* below the *Hôtel Mauritania* (daily 8am–9pm; cheap) – and along Rue Hormis, (which runs up from Souk El Attarin towards Bab Guissa in the north and has some good hole-in-the-wall places), as well as the larger and very popular but unsignposted *Restaurant Basalah* almost opposite the *Cine Hillal* (Sat–Thurs noon–7pm; cheap). Other cheap café-restaurants are to be found near Bab Ftouh.

If your money doesn't allow a full meal, you can get a range of **snacks** around Bab Boujeloud, including delicious chunks of pastilla from the stalls near the beginning of Talâa Seghira, kefta or brochettes around the corner on Talâa Kebira, and freshly made crisps (potato chips) from the corner opposite the Hammam Mernisi.

RESTAURANTS

For a Fassi banquet, in an appropriate palace setting, most restaurants charge around 150–200dh a head. Some places, particularly those in the heart of Fes El Bali, serve lunch only because, even in daylight, they are difficult to find. If you're interested, phone ahead for a table at one or other of the following:

Restaurant Al Fassia, in the *Hôtel Palais Jamai*, Bab Guissa (☎05/563 4331). A distinguished Moroccan cuisine restaurant, with a terrace overlooking the Medina, open evenings only, with a belly dancing floorshow. There are few more stylish ways to spend an evening, but count on at least 390dh each, more if you order (24hr in advance) one of the specials such as *mechoui* or stuffed sea bass. Daily 7.30–11pm. Expensive. The hotel also has a fine French restaurant, *Al Jounaina*.

Restaurant Al Firdaous, 10 Rue Jenjifour, Bab Guissa – just down from the *Hôtel Palais Jamai* (☎05/563 4343). A rich merchant's house of the 1920s. Meals, with music and a floorshow (featuring mock weddings, fire dancing and belly dancing) in the evenings. There's a choice here of five set menus costing from 270dh to 500dh. Daily 3pm & 8.30–11.30pm. Expensive.

Palais de Fes, 15 Makhfia er Rsif, off Place er Rsif behind the Cinema el Amal (☎05/576 1590). A magnificent restaurant and carpet shop, with excellent food and a panoramic terrace, moved from its former location opposite the Kairaouine Mosque following a fire in 1999. There is a choice of set menus, and reservation is compulsory. They will pick you up from your hotel by car on request. Daily 10am–midnight. Expensive.

Restaurant Palais Tijani, east of Sidi Ahmed Tijani Mosque (☎05/574 1071). Less grandiose than the other palace-style eateries, and without the floorshow, but arguably better value for money. The emphasis here is on the food ("Fes seen through its cuisine", it advertises), but the atmosphere is also rather more intimate than the other *palais*, the diners as likely to be Moroccan as foreign, and the prices more akin to those of a normal restaurant. Daily 6am–midnight. Moderate.

Palais des Merinides (☎05/563 4028), near the Cherabliyin Mosque, 650m from Bab Boujeloud. Beautifully restored palatial decor, with good views from the terrace should you fancy a climb before dining. There's a choice of set menus (130–190dh) or à la carte eating, and there's also a special Fassi menu featuring chicken pastilla (pigeon if ordered 24hr in advance). Daily 8am–11pm or the last customer. Expensive.

Dar Saada, 21 Souk El Attarin (☎05/563 7370). Wonderful pastilla or (ordered a day in advance) *mechoui*. Portions are vast and two people can do well by ordering one main dish and a plate of vegetables. Located in the Souk El Attarin, in another century-old palace (see p.217), and labelled on our map on p.211. The fine decor was renewed after a disastrous fire in 1972. Lunches only. Daily 8am–5.45pm. Expensive.

CAFÉS

There are plenty of small **cafés** all over the Medina, but few worthy of special mention. At the very heart of the Old City, at the northwest corner of the Kairaouine Mosque and opposite the Attarin Medersa, the *Café Boutouail* (Sat–Thurs 6am–10pm, Fri 6am–12.30pm & 7–9.30pm) does a good line in coffee and pastries – seating is hidden away upstairs – but its speciality is *panachi*, a mixture of milk, almond milk, and raisins, with a blob of ice cream on top for good measure. The *Café Restaurant la Noria* by the waterwheel off the Boujoud Gardens and accessible from Avenue des Français and Grande Rue des Merenides (daily 8am–9pm) is a good spot to have breakfast or stop for a coffee, but not particularly good for meals (though it serves tajines).

Listings

Airlines Royal Air Maroc has an office at 54 Av. Hassan II in the Ville Nouvelle (☎05/562 5516).

Arabic Language Institute in Fes (ALIF) is at 2 Rue Ahmed Hiba (☎05/562 4850, *www.azure.net/alif*) near the Youth Hostel and the *Hôtel Menzeh Zalagh*. This American initiative offers a range of courses and the possibility of private/specialized lessons. There are three-week (60hr) and six-week (120hr) courses in Colloquial Moroccan Arabic or Modern Standard Arabic at all levels. ALIF also has its own residence for students, or the option of a homestay with a Moroccan family. Since ALIF doubles up as an English school, the American Language Center, it is also a good place to meet up with young Moroccans.

Banks Most of the banks are grouped along Bd. Mohammed V. As always, the BMCE (branches at Place Mohammed V, Place Florence and Place de l'Atlas) is best for exchange and handles VISA/Access transactions, as well as travellers' cheques. Others include: Banque Populaire (Av. Mohammed V; quick service for currency and travellers' cheques), Crédit du Maroc (Av. Mohammed V) and SGMB (at the intersection of Rue el Houria and Rue Soudan). Banque Populaire also has three branches in Fes El Bali: halfway down Talâa Sghira, north of the Medersa el Attarin, and on Rue Kaid Khammar by Bab Ftouh. SGMB by Bab Boujeloud is closed Friday afternoon but open Saturday morning. One place that will change money outside banking hours (or within them) is Karima Voyages at 106 Bd. Mohammed V (Mon–Sat 8.30am–12.30pm & 2.30–8pm, Sun 8.30am–12.30pm only). Most of the four- or five-star hotels will change money and cheques at a pinch.

Bookshops The Librairie du Centre, 134 Bd. Mohammed V (near the post office), has a small shelf of books in English, mostly classic novels.

Car rental Fes has quite a number of rental companies, though none are as cheap as the best deals in Casa. Call around the following, which all allow return delivery to a different centre: First Car, Av. des F.A.R, (☎05/593 0909), also at the *Sheraton* hotel; Avis, 50 Bd. Abdallah Chefchouni (☎05/562 6746); Budget, 6 Rue Chenguit aka Av. Lalla Asma (☎05/594 0092); Europcar, 45 Av. Hassan II (☎05/562 6545); Hertz, Bd. Lalla Maryem, 1 Kissariat de la Foire (☎05/562 2812); Tourvilles, 15 Rue Houman el Fetouaki, off Bd. Mohammed V (☎05/562 6635). Avis, Europcar and Hertz have desks at the airport.

Car repairs Mechanics can be found in the vicinity of the train station. The garage on Rue Soudan (☎05/562 2232) is good for Renault repairs.

SHOPPING FOR CRAFTS

Fes has a rightful reputation as the centre of Moroccan traditional crafts but if you're buying rather than looking, bear in mind that it also sees more tourists than any of its rivals, except perhaps Marrakesh. Rugs and carpets, however much you bargain, will probably be cheaper in Meknes, Midelt or Azrou; and although the brass, leather and cloth here are the best you'll find, you will need plenty of energy, a good sense of humour and a lot of patience to get them at a reasonable price. Fassi dealers are expert hagglers – making you feel like an idiot for suggesting a ludicrously low price, jumping up out of their seats to make to push you out of the shop, or lulling you with mint tea and elaborate displays.

All of this can be fun, but you do need a certain confidence and to have some idea of what you're buying and how much you should be paying for it. For some guidelines on **quality**, take a look at the historic pieces in the **Dar Batha** museum – keeping in mind, of course, that exhibits here are the best available. If you want to check on the prices of more modest and modern artefacts, have a browse through the various shops along Av. Mohammed V in the **Ville Nouvelle**, which tend to have fairly fixed prices (and are easy to leave!), and, especially, at the government-run and strictly fixed-price Centre Artisanal, out past the *Sheraton Fes Hôtel* and on the left-hand side of Av. Allal Ben Abdallah (Mon–Sat 10.30am–6.30pm, partly open Sun same hours). It's not the best in the country – the one in Marrakesh leaves it standing – but it's worth a visit, time permitting.

Cinemas Several in the Ville Nouvelle, show foreign films – mainly dubbed into French. The one inside Bab Boujeloud is entertaining, showing an Indian and a Kung Fu film ("the history and the geography", as they call it) each day, as does the one at Bab Ftouh.

Festivals and cultural events Since 1995, Fes has hosted a **Festival of World Sacred Music** (held in June), which has developed into the country's most interesting and inspiring cultural festival. Recent years have seen Sufi chanters from Azerbaijan, dervishes from Kurdistan, a Javanese gamelan, a Byzantine choir from Greece, and a Jewish cantor. Concerts take place at Place Moulay Hassan north of the Mechouar, at the Batha Museum, and sometimes further afield, such as amid the ruins of Volubilis. Details are available from the secretariat (☎05/563 6201 or 99; *fesfestival@ fesnet.net.ma*), or on the festival's Web site at *www.fezfestival.com*. Major local festivals are the students' Moussem of Sidi Harazem (held outside the city in Sidi Harazem at the end of April) and the Moulay Idriss II Moussem (held in the city, in September). There are other moussems held locally – ask at the tourist office for details – and some good events a little further out, like the Fête des Cerises at Sefrou (see p.239) in June, and the Fête du Cheval at Tissa (see p.143) in September.

Cultural events in the city are relatively frequent, both Moroccan- and French-sponsored. Again, ask for details at the tourist office, or at the Institut Français (☎05/562 3921) on Rue des Etats-Unis, at the corner of Rue Loukili. A *Son et Lumiére* show is presented from March to October; daily except Sun, 9.30pm; the show lasts 45min and costs 100dh. The show is in Arabic, English, French or Spanish – check that it will be in a language you understand on the night you intend to go. The audience views the show from the Borj Sud, which is south of Bd. Allal El Fassi, the broad avenue which links the Ville Nouvelle with Bab El Djedid and Bab Ftouh, between which a track leads uphill alongside the Bab Ftouh cemetery (see Fes El Bali map). Information and reservations from Immeuble la Mamda, Apt 65, Place de Florence (☎/fax 05/593 1893).

Petrol stations Several are to be found around Place de l'Atlas, near the beginning of the road to Sefrou and Midelt.

Hammams Two are located through Bab Boujeloud, on the Talâa Seghira; if you are unfamiliar with the routine, and since the staff may well speak Arabic and Berber only, it is best, especially for women, to ask someone at your hotel to escort you. At Hammam Mernisi, on the bend in the road just before you reach the cinema, and the cleaner and better of the two options, the hours are: women noon–6pm, men 6am–noon & 6pm–10pm. At Hammam Sidi Azouz, opposite *Hôtel Lamrani*, hours are: women noon–10pm, men 10pm–noon. The oldest hammam in Fes (Hammam Kantarte Bourous – for men only) is on Rue ech Cherabliyin. Don't forget to take your towel, soap, shampoo and swimsuit (or change of underwear).

Internet access Internet clubs include *Cyber Internet* at 42 Rue des Etats Unis, currently one of the best-value places in Morocco for email and Internet access (daily 8.30am–midnight; 10dh/hr). Other options include *F@ssinet* two floors up at 12 Av. Hassan II (Mon–Sat 9am–9pm, Sun 10am–1pm & 3–8pm; 25dh/hr), and the *Peacock* cybercafé at 25 Rue Mohammed Slaoui (daily 9.30am–9pm; 15dh/hr).

Laundry In the Nouvelle Ville, try Pressing Dallas, 44 Rue Asilah near *Hôtel Mounia* (☎05/565 0739); near Bab Boujeloud, there's a laundry at the northern end of Place Istiqlal by the local post office.

Newspapers In summer you may find some British dailies on sale at stalls on Av. Mohammed V (for example on the corner of Rue Abdelkrim El Khattabi), otherwise try the newsagent at 16 Place 16 Novembre for the *USA Today* and the British *Guardian Weekly*, as well as *Time*, *Newsweek* and *The Economist*; the *International Herald Tribune* is sometimes sold at 34 Av. Hassan II.

Pharmacies There are numerous pharmacies throughout the Ville Nouvelle, and there's also one just outside Bab Boujeloud, and one on Grande Rue des Merenides in the Mellah. The Pharmacie du Municipalité, just up from Place de la Résistance, on Av. Abdelkrim El Kattabi, stays open all night.

Police There are *commissariats* by the post office on Av. Mohammed V, and off Place de l'Istiqlal on the road to the right of the post office that leads to Cinema Boujeloud. The police emergency number is ☎19.

TWO NEARBY SPAS: MOULAY YACOUB AND SIDI HARAZEM

The spa villages of **Moulay Yacoub** and **Sidi Harazem**, respectively 20km northwest and 15km southeast of Fes, are largely medicinal centres, offering – as for many centuries past – cures for the afflicted. They are local rather than tourist attractions, but Moulay Yacoub, in particular, makes a pleasant day-trip for a swim and hot bath. Either site can be reached by grand taxi from the *gare routière* to Moulay Yacoub (7dh) and from Bab Ftouh to Sidi Harazem (5dh). Bus #28 runs from Place de la Résistance (aka La Fiat) to Sidi Harazem.

MOULAY YACOUB

The trip to **MOULAY YACOUB** takes you across pleasant, rolling countryside, with wonderful views south across the plain of Saïss, with the Middle Atlas beyond. The village itself tumbles down a steep hillside, with baths, a swimming pool and large hammam (separate sections for women and men) around midway down (open daily 6am–10pm; a bath costs 10dh). At the foot of the hill, in the "basin", are new and more scientific thermal baths used for serious medical treatment. Cars and taxis park at the top of the village, leaving you to descend flights of steps, flanked with some attractive little restaurants and cafés.

The spa has three basic **hotels** – the best of which is the *Hôtel Lamrani* (☎05/569 4021; ②); it's open year round and has recently been renovated. Recently, two bright new hotels have opened: the *Hôtel Fadoua* (☎05/569 4050 or 57, fax 569 4098; ④) and the *Hôtel Moulay Yacoub* (☎05/569 4070 or 71, fax 569 4012; ⑤). There are also numerous rooms to let in private houses – and you won't lack for offers.

SIDI HARAZEM

The eucalyptus-covered shrine of **SIDI HARAZEM** was established by Sultan Moulay Er-Rachid in the seventeenth century, though the centre owes its current fame to its best-selling mineral water. The oasis is today heavily orientated towards its health industry; the old thermal baths tend to be crowded and the swimming pool is only full in summer (15dh). The main point of a visit, for those not seeking a cure, would be for the April moussem – one of the Fes region's biggest.

There is a state-run **hotel**, the *Sidi Harazem* (☎05/569 0057 or 72; ③), near the thermal baths and swimming pool; both its accommodation and restaurant are pricey and, for a worthwhile snack, you would be better advised to walk the 600m to the grill complex beyond the hotel; look for the charcoal smoke and smell the brochettes.

Post office The main PTT is on the corner of Bd. Mohammed V/Av. Hassan II in the Ville Nouvelle (open July–Sept Mon–Fri 8am–3.30pm, Sat 8am–noon; Oct–June Mon–Fri 8.30am–6.45pm, Sat 8am–noon); the **poste restante** section is inside the main building; the **phones section** (daily 8.30am–9pm) has a separate side entrance when the rest is closed. There are branch post offices on Place des Alouites on the edge of the Mellah, and in the Medina just north of Medersa el Attarin.

Swimming pools There is a Municipal Pool (open mid-June to mid-Sept) on Av. des Sports, just west of the train station. The upmarket *Hôtel Menzeh Zalagh* (see p.208) has an open air pool, but at 60dh for nonresidents, this is a little pricey.

Moving on

Buses for most destinations leave from the main **bus station** or *gare routière* just north of Bab Mahrouk, between Kasbah Cherada and Borj Nord. CTM however leave from their office on the corner of Rue Tetouan and Avenue Mohammed V in the Ville Nouvelle. For buses for Nador/Melilla, ONCF/Supratours run connecting buses from Taorirt on the Oujda line; you can buy tickets straight through.

Like buses, **grands taxis** mostly operate from the *gare routière*. Exceptions are those for **Immouzer, Ifrane** and **Azrou** (and sometimes Marrakesh), which use a rank opposite the CTM office, 100m west of Place de l'Atlas and those to **Sefrou** (and sometimes Immouzer), which use a rank 100m down southeast of Place de la Résistance (aka La Fiat). **Meknes** grands taxis depart from outside the train station. Grands taxis based at Bab Ftouh run to **Sidi Harazem, Taza, Taounate** and other points east and north of Fes.

THE MIDDLE ATLAS

Heading south from Fes, most people take a bus straight to either **Marrakesh** or to **Er Rachidia**, the start of the great desert and *ksour* routes. Both journeys, however, involve at least ten to twelve hours of continuous travel, which, in the summer at least, is reason enough to stop off along the way.

The second, stronger reason, if you have the time (or, ideally, a car), is to get off the main routes and up into the mountains. Covered in forests of oak, cork and giant cedar, the **Middle Atlas** is a beautiful and relatively little-visited region. The brown-black tents of nomadic Berber encampments immediately establish a shift from the European north, the plateaux are pockmarked by dark volcanic lakes, and, at **Ouzoud** and **Oum Er Rbia**, there are some magnificent waterfalls. If you just want a day-trip from Fes, the Middle Atlas is most easily accessible at **Sefrou**, a relaxed market town, 28km southeast of Fes.

On the practical front, **bus** travellers may find a few problems stopping en route between Fes and Marrakesh, as many of the buses arrive and depart full. However, by taking the occasional grand taxi, or stopping for a night to catch a dawn bus, you shouldn't find yourself stuck for long. Along the Fes–Azrou–Midelt–Er Rachidia route, buses are no problem. This is the old *Trek es Sultan*, or Royal Road, an ancient trading route that once carried salt, slaves and other commodities with caravans of camels across the desert from West Africa.

Sefrou and around

SEFROU, 28km south of Fes, is a very ancient walled town at the foothills of the Middle Atlas. The first stop on the caravan routes to the Tafilalet, it marked, until the Protectorate, the mountain limits of the *Bled El Makhzen* – the governed lands. It actually predates Fes as a city and might well have grown into a regional or Imperial Capital, if Moulay Idriss I and II had not acted differently. Into the 1950s, at least a third of the then 18,000 population were Jews; there seems to have been a Jewish-Berber population here long before the coming of Islam and, although most of them subsequently converted, a large number of Jews from the south again settled in the town under the Merenids. Today, sadly, only a handful of Jews remain.

From Fes, the town can be reached in an hour by **bus** or **grand taxi**; the latter leave from just below Place de la Résistance (aka La Fiat) in the Ville Nouvelle. In summer it makes a cool day-trip, as it is situated some 2900ft above sea level; in winter, it can often be covered in snow; it is a relaxed place which sees few tourists (or hustlers). The only times that the town draws crowds are during the annual **Fête des Cerises**, a cherry festival in June, usually the last weekend, with the crowning of the Cherry Queen on Saturday evening and, before and after, various music, folklore and sports events; and during the August **Moussem of Sidi Lahcen El Youssi**, a seventeenth-century saint from neighbouring Azzaba, 13km to the east of Sefrou – his zaouia and tomb are to be found in the Medina on the north bank of the Oued Aggaï.

The Town

Although Sefrou is not a large place – the population today is only 40,000 – its layout is a little confusing. If you are coming in by bus or grand taxi, you are usually dropped in the recently landscaped **Place Moulay Hassan**, off which is **Bab M'kam**, the main entrance to the Medina. Beyond the square, the road and some of the buses continue round a loop above the town and valley, crossing the **Oued Aggaï** and straightening out onto **Boulevard Mohammed V**, the principal street of the modest Ville Nouvelle.

The Medina

In many ways it's a pity that Sefrou is so close to Fes, in comparison with which its Medina inevitably feels rather low-key. It is, however, on its own modest scale, equally well preserved, and the untouristy atmosphere makes it a very pleasant place to explore. The **Thursday souk**, for example, remains very much a local affair, drawing Berbers from neighbouring villages to sell their garden produce and buy basic goods.

Enclosed by its nineteenth-century ramparts and split in two by the river, the Medina isn't difficult to find your way around. Coming from the PTT on Boulevard Mohammed V, you can take a shortcut down on the right of the road by way of **Bab Merba**, straight into the Mellah; if you were then to turn to the left, this would eventually lead you to Place Moulay Hassan by way of the small **Mosque Adloun** and the nearby **Hammam Adloun** with its unique chimney. You would arrive on the *place* through the new, small **Bab Taksebt**. The most straightforward approach, though, is through **Bab M'Kram**, the old main gate on the *place* – on your left as you face the walls.

Entering at Bab M'Kram, you find yourself on the main street of the old Arab town, which winds clockwise down to the river, passing through a region of **souks**, to emerge at the **Grand Mosque**. The souks include some impressive ironwork stalls and, reflecting the traditional Jewish heritage, a number of silversmiths.

The Mellah

The **Mellah**, a dark, cramped conglomeration of tall, shuttered houses and tunnel-like streets, lies across the river from the Grand Mosque. It is today occupied largely by Muslims, though many of Sefrou's Jews only left for Israel after the June 1967 Six-Day War, and the quarter still seems distinct.

Over the years of the French Protectorate, the Sefrou Jewish community had become quite well off, owning good agricultural land in the environs. But when most of the houses here were built, in the mid-nineteenth century, the people's living conditions must have been pretty miserable. Edith Wharton, visiting in 1917, found "ragged figures . . . in black gabardines and skull-caps" living one family to a room in most of the mansions, and the alleys were lit even at midday by oil lamps. "No wonder," she concluded rather sanctimoniously, "[that] the babies of the Moroccan ghettos are nursed on date-brandy, and their elders doze away to death under its consoling spell."

From the Mellah, you can return, still clockwise, to the *place* by way of the Mosque Adloun (see above).

Into the hills

High enough into the Middle Atlas to avoid the dry summer heat, Sefrou is a place where you might actually want to do some walking. There are dozens of **springs** in the hills above the town and, for part of the year, active waterfalls.

For a relatively easy target, take the road up behind the post office, which will divide into a fork after about a kilometre. The right branch goes up past the campsite; the left leads to a small, deserted, French military post, known as the **Prioux**, and to the **koubba** of one Sidi Bou Ali Serghin. The views from around here are exciting: in winter, the snow-capped Mischliffen; in summer, the cedars and holm oaks cresting the ridges to infinity.

Another good walk is to go up in the hills above the **Oued Aggaï**, a path followed by **Rue de la Kelâa** (just before the bridge, approaching from the post office direction). There are gorges, coves and waterfalls in this direction (for which you may want to engage a local guide).

Practicalities

Following the closure of the old *Hôtel des Cerises*, which stands empty on the bend of Boulevard Mohammed V, the choice is between two **hotels**. The *Hôtel Sidi Lahcen El*

Youssi (☎05/568 3428; ④)) has an alpine chalet feel, a restaurant (no liquor licence at present), and a swimming pool – sometimes full of water. Its rival, *Hôtel La Frenaie* (☎05/566 1027; ②), is on the left as you enter Sefrou from Fes. It was originally run by a Frenchman, but is now in Moroccan hands; recently renovated to a good standard, it has a snack bar and pool table on the ground floor which attracts a young crowd. Alternatively, a couple of kilometres to the west of town, there is a **campsite** (☎05/566 0001 or 03), a well-maintained site, with plenty of shade and friendly staff, but only cold-water showers.

For **food and drink**, in addition to the hotels, you could try the *Café-Restaurant Oumnia*, on Boulevard Mohammed V at the corner of Rue Tarik Ibn Ziad (daily 8am–8pm; cheap), for inexpensive meals.

Note that the town's two **banks** are not very wised up to cashing cheques, though they have no problems with cash exchange.

Between the *Hôtel La Frenaie* and Place Moulay Hassan (see below), the **Centre Artisanal** is worth a visit for its wood carvings and carpets which you can usually see being created by hand.

Around Sefrou

Signposted off the Fes road, 7km northwest of Sefrou, **Bhalil** claims pre-Islamic Christian origins and, more visibly, retains a number of troglodyte (cave) dwellings. If you have a car, this is worth a brief detour on your way from Fes; it is signposted to the right 5km before Sefrou. The **cave houses** are to the rear of the village, reached by a dirt road; ask directions to Mohammed Chraibi (BP 42, Bhalil), the official guide, who will show you his own cave home.

The village itself – or at least the old part of it – is charming, its whitewashed houses tumbling down a hillside, and connected by innumerable bridges.

South and east of Sefrou are some of the most attractive swathes of the Middle Atlas: dense, wooded mountains, with great scope for hiking or piste driving, and not a hint of tourism. Immediately south of the town is the Massif du Kandar, which loops round to Imouzzer du Kandar. To the east, further afield, are the Bou Iblane mountains – an exploration of which could be combined by drivers with the Djebel Tazzeka circuit, near Taza (see p.147).

If you are simply intending to head south from Sefrou, there is a daily bus to **Midelt**, via the quiet roadside town of **Boulemane**, but none to Ifrane or Azrou on the Fes–Marrakesh road. To cross over to this route on local transport, it would be simplest to return to Fes. Boulemane itself can be worth a stop for its Sunday souk which serves a wide and diverse area.

The Massif du Kandar

The 4620 route over the Massif du Kandar leaves the P20 Sefrou–Midelt road 14km south of Sefrou. It has some rough stretches of track but is passable in summer with a Renault 4; in winter, you need to check conditions locally. For those without transport, it would be possible to charter a grand taxi in Sefrou (or, travelling west–east, in Immouzer du Kandar) for the 34km route.

Shortly after the piste turns off from the Sefrou–Midelt road, it begins to climb up into the hills around the **Djebel Abad** (1768m). If you reckon your car can make it – or you feel like walking – you can follow a rocky 4km track almost to the summit of the mountain; this leads off, to the right of the road, 10km down the 4620, coming from the Sefrou direction.

The Djebel Bou Iblane

East of Sefrou – and southeast of Fes – is a huge area of high country, culminating in the two mountains of **Djebel Bou Iblane** (3190m) and **Djebel Bou Naceur** (3340m).

It is an extraordinarily varied landscape: the northern aspects rise from the cedar forests, while the south is stark and waterless, although demarcated by the great Oued Moulouya. The whole area is sparsely populated, and trekkers are almost unknown, yet it's rewarding and has relatively easy access. From either Sefrou or Fes, you could arrange a grand taxi to take you to the centre of the range – dropping you either at the forestry hut of **Tafferte** or at the largely abandoned ski resort under Djebel Bou Iblane where the local *caid* has an office; he is responsible for this great empty quarter.

From here, a web of *pistes* radiate throughout the area, and a circular trek with a mule would be memorable.

Grands taxis run to **Skoura** (on route 4653) and **Immouzer des Marmoucha** (on route 4656) giving access from the east. As with so many lesser-known ranges, the best sources of information are the Peyron Guides (see p.33) and AMIS (see p.5).

Imouzzer du Kandar, Ifrane and Mischliffen

The first hills you see of the Middle Atlas, heading directly south from the plains around Fes, seem strangely un-Moroccan. At the "hill station" resort of **Ifrane**, where the French colonial chiefs retreated from the heat, the king now has an important summer palace, and at **Mischliffen** there's a ski centre. En route, and a little more mundane, is another small French-built hill station, **Immouzer du Kandar**, and, in the wet season, a gorgeous freshwater lake, the **Dayet Aaoua**.

Imouzzer du Kandar

IMOUZZER DU KANDAR, 36km south of Fes, is a one-road, one-square kind of place, where Fassis come up to swim, picnic and spend a few days. There are a handful of hotels if you feel like doing the same, and some good restaurants, too: it's a relaxed place, with a pleasant atmosphere.

A small Monday **souk** is held within the ruined kasbah, and a **festival**, the *Fête des Pommes*, takes place in August, with a number of music and dance events. The municipal **swimming pool**, near the centre, is open from mid-June to mid-September and filled, like everything here, with natural spa water. **Grands taxis** for Azrou and Ifrane leave by the market; for Fes and Sefrou they leave from a station on the left 100m up the Fes road. **Buses** pass regularly en route between Fes and Azrou.

Around the town centre, there are several decent **restaurants** with near-identical menus; as ever, the busiest are the best.

Hotels

Immouzer has a good choice of **hotels**, except at the very bottom of the scale, where the two most basic choices – the *du Centre* and the *Kandar* – are not cheap enough to be worth using.

Hôtel Chaharazed, 2 Place du Marché (☎05/566 3012, fax 566 3445). On the main road, opposite the square – reservations advisable in summer. Comfortable rooms with heating, a/c, TV and a balcony, plus a reasonable restaurant, two bars, and friendly, efficient staff. ④.

Hôtel La Chambotte (☎/fax 05/566 3374). A small French-style *auberge* with a good restaurant, across the road from the *Hôtel Royal*. The showers are hot and there's central heating when called for; previously seasonal, it is now open year-round. ③.

Hôtel du Rif, 500m south of the main square on the Ifrane road (☎05/566 3392). Sombre but decent rooms in a quiet location. Cold showers. ①.

Hôtel Royal, Bd. Mohammed V (☎05/566 3080). Central hotel with a reliable restaurant, but facing a small lake now permanently devoid of water and waterfowl. ④.

Hôtel Smara, on the main square, opposite the *Chaharazed* (☎05/566 3464). Basic but clean and friendly, with a lively café-restaurant attached. Hot common showers. ①.

Hôtel des Truites, 200m north of the main square on the Fes road (☎/fax 05/566 3002). The best choice: a delightful place with a bar, (unpredictable) restaurant, and great views northwards towards Fes. Rooms in the annexe are en suite. ③.

Dayet Aaoua

A good excursion from Immouzer, or an alternative place to break the journey south, is the lake of **Dayet Aaoua**; it is sited just to the east of the P24, 9km south of Immouzer. You can camp round the lakeside, but note that like other lakes in the Ifrane area, Aaoua is often dry – due to the prevalence of limestone and sometimes to climatic changes. On the other hand, when it is full of water, it has a rewarding **birdlife habitat** – see box overleaf.

The P24 continues past the lake to Ifrane, climbing through ever more dense shafts of forest. If you are driving, it's possible to reach Ifrane by a longer and more scenic route, following a piste (4627) up behind the Dayet Aaoua, then looping to the right, past another (often dry) lake, **Dayet Hachlef**, on piste 3325, before joining the last section of the road in from Boulemane (P21).

Ifrane

IFRANE was created in 1929 as a self-conscious *"poche de France"*, and its pseudo-Alpine villas and broad suburban streets have a distinctly peculiar feel in their Moroccan setting. After independence, they were absorbed by Moroccan government ministries and the wealthier bourgeoisie, and in recent years they have been granted additional prestige by the addition of a **Royal Palace**, whose characteristic green tiles (a royal prerogative) can be seen high above the trees on the descent into the valley.

Ifrane is also the site of another royal initiative. On January 16, 1995, King Hassan II inaugurated the **Al Akhawayn** University, to the west of the Fes road on the northern edge of town, just beyond the *Hôtel Mischliffen*. The name of this institute of higher education, Al Akhawayn ('brothers' in Arabic), registers it as being the brainchild and beneficiary of the Moroccan king and his 'brother' King Fahd of Saudi Arabia; it has also been funded by the United States and, to a lesser extent, by the British Council. The undergraduate and postgraduate curricula are modelled on the American system of higher education and the language of instruction is English. Inevitably, many of the staff are, as yet, American, but it is impolitic to refer to it, as some do, as an American university.

King Hassan was keen to underpin this novel creation with the religious and cultural values of Christianity and Judaism as well as of Islam; it is dedicated to 'practical tolerance between faiths'; there are a mosque, church and synagogue on the campus to provide, as the king put it, "a meeting place for the sons of Abraham" – a concept endorsed by the Prince of Wales when he visited Ifrane on February 28, 1996.

You can visit the university campus, preferably on a weekday afternoon when the students are about. Dominated by chalet-style buildings, with cream walls and russet-tiled roofs, mirroring those in Ifrane, its architect was Michel Pinseau, who designed the great showpiece *Mosquée Hassan II* in Casablanca. Inevitably, there have been criticisms of the new university. The car park, crowded with expensive models, confirms the view that it is an elite initiative – restricted to those who can pay. There is also something of an anti-French feel; Moroccan academics are trying to escape the French educational strait-jacket and have begun to 'arabize' science teaching in the established universities.

As befits a royal resort and aspiring academia, **Ifrane town** is quite impressive in itself – squeaky clean, brilliantly lit by streetlamps and illuminated globes, and with a steady growth of new, costly houses. Not surprisingly, it is expensive (for accommodation, meals

BIRDLIFE IN THE DAYET AAOUA AND MIDDLE ATLAS LAKES

Like other freshwater lakes in the Middle Atlas, **Dayet Aaoua**, has, when it's full, a good mosaic of habitat types and supports a wide variety of animals. Green frogs take refuge from the summer drought within the lake's protective shallows, and a multitude of dragonflies and damselflies patrol the water's surface in their resplendent reds blues and greens.

The **birdlife** is similarly diverse, attracting all kinds of waders and wildfowl. Waders include black-winged stilt, green sandpiper, redshank and **avocet** (one of Morocco's most elegant birds), and the deeper waters provide food for flocks of grebes (great-crested, black-necked and little varieties), and in the spring the magnificent **crested coot** (which has spectacular bright red knobs on either side of its white facial shield, when in breeding condition). The reedbeds provide cover for **grey heron** and **cattle egret** and ring out with the sound of hidden **reed-** and **fan-tailed warbler**.

The water's edge is traced by passage grey and yellow wagtails and in the summer the skies are filled with migrating swallows and martins – the sand martin especially. This abundance of life proves an irresistible draw for resident and migrant birds of prey and Aaoua offers regular sightings of the acrobatic **red kite** circling overhead. You may also see flocks of collared pratincole, whose darting flight is spectacular, and quartering overhead, the characteristic form of **Montagu's harrier**, ever alert for any unsuspecting duck on the lake below.

If the lake is dry, you will find, in the words of John Keats, that 'the sedge has withered from the lake and no birds sing'. But remember that there are still birds to be seen alongside – or close to – the 17km stretch of the P24 between Ifrane and Azrou. Here you will find the endemic Levaillant's green **woodpecker, firecrest,** short-toed **tree creeper** and local variants of the **jay** and **blue tit.**

White storks, ravens and a colony of **lesser kestrels** have been recorded in the low hills behind the *Hôtel Panorama* in Azrou (see p.247).

GOURAUD'S CEDAR

Eight kilometres from Azrou, and marked on the Michelin map, is the legendary **Cèdre Gouraud**. This is well signposted from the main road and your arrival at the Gouraud cedar, amongst others of much the same calibre, is confirmed by a sign nailed to the tree. It's reputed to be at least 800 years old, 130ft high and its girth around 25ft. Its history is a mystery. Colonel Gouraud was Lyautey's second in command from 1912 to 1914 and, indeed, some say that Lyautey's cedar is nearby. Why two soldiers should lend their names to trees is not clear, "confusion worse confounded" by a recent authority which says that Gouraud's cedar was felled at the turn of the century, when it was at least 980 years old. Maybe the sign is moved from tree to tree, possibly by the **Barbary apes** which you will see hereabouts (see box p.248). They are no friend of the cedar; they hungrily gnaw the buds or tear off strips of the bark.

Another enemy is the **processionary caterpillar** which eats the foliage. In spring, they live in a colony – in a white shroud-like 'tent' – to protect themselves from daytime feathered predators. At night, they come out and eat the neighbouring foliage. When that is gone, one of their number is sent to find more foliage elsewhere. On its return, the colony sets off in a procession, head-to-tail, and spins a new "tent" for daytime security. Naturally, they are highly televisual, as in David Attenborough's BBC series, *The Private Life of Plants*.

A local qualified guide, who could help with the trip to the Gouraud Cedar, and elsewhere, is Kallal Mohamed, 27 Rue Sidi Rachid, Sabbab, Azrou (☎05/556 1949).

and even provisions in the shops) and somewhat lacking in the human touch. A policeman is on permanent duty to stop anyone posing for photographs on the resort's landmark **stone lion** – carved apparently by an Italian prisoner of war – and when the court is in residence in summer, security is very tight.

Nonetheless, a walk by the river, below the royal palace, is pleasant, as is the cool summer air, and the excellent municipal swimming pool.

Practicalities

Ifrane has a *Syndicat d'Initiative* **tourist office** in Place du Syndicat, on the corner of Avenue Mohammed V and Avenue Prince Moulay Abdallah (☎05/556 6821). The **bus station** is behind the municipal market off the Meknes road, 300m from the town centre, with plenty of buses to Fez and Azrou, fewer to Meknes, Rabat, Casablanca, Marrakesh and even Agadir and Nador. **Grands taxis** are based just beside the bus station, and reach Fes, Azrou and Immouzer on a regular basis, Meknes less frequently.

Accommodation is expensive and not always easy to obtain at the four hotels. However, there is a municipal **campsite** (☎05/556 6156) on Boulevard Mohammed V (the Meknes road), near the market, open all year, with a little shop open in summer.

Hôtel Chamonix, Rue du Marche Verte (☎05/556 6825, fax 556 6826). A new and good-value hotel in the centre of town, with light, airy rooms done out in pastel green, and heating, a/c and TV in each. There's also a nightclub open Friday and Saturday nights. ④.

Hôtel Mischliffen, Route de Fes (☎05/556 6607, fax 556 6622 or 23). 800m from the town centre, overlooking the lake, with superb views and facilities. ⑤.

Hôtel Perce-Neige, Rue des Asphodelles (☎05/556 6350, fax 556 7116). A friendly and efficiently run place with small but comfortable carpeted rooms, some with a large terrace, and all with satellite TV, heating and a/c. There's also a restaurant, a cosy bar, and day-care facilities for children. ④.

Hôtel les Tilleuls, Rue des Cascades (☎05/556 6658, fax 556 7079). A pleasant, modern town-centre hotel with en-suite facilities throughout, a restaurant and, it is claimed, three bars. ④.

The Mischliffen

The Mischliffen is simply a shallow bowl in the mountains – the crater of an extinct volcano – enclosed on all sides by cedar forests. There's no village here and few buildings, and it's of interest, really, mainly for the skiing.

In the skiing season (Jan–March: but snow cover is often patchy) there are taxis from Ifrane up to its **refuge-club** (restaurant and bar, but no accommodation) and to the rather ancient **ski lifts**. You can **rent ski equipment** in Ifrane at the *Hôtel Chamonix*.

Azrou

AZROU, the first real town of the Middle Atlas, stands at a major junction of routes – north to Meknes and Fes, south to Khenifra and Midelt. As might be expected, it's an important market centre (the main souk is held on Tuesday), and it has long held a strategic role in controlling the mountain Berbers. Moulay Ismail built a kasbah here, the remains of which still survive, while more recently the French established the prestigious **Collège Berbère** – part of their attempt to split the country's Berbers from the urban Arabs.

The collège, now the Lycée Tarik Ibn Ziad, and still a dominant building in the town, provided many of the Protectorate's interpreters, local administrators and military officers, but in spite of its ban on using Arabic and any manifestation of Islam, the policy was a failure. Azrou graduates played a significant role in the nationalist movement – and were uniquely placed to do so, as a new French-created elite. Since independence, however, their influence has been slight outside of the army, many Berber student activists of the 1950s and 1960s having followed Mehdi Ben Barka's ill-fated socialist UNEP party (see p.560).

The Town and its souk

Arriving in the town, you immediately notice a massive outcrop of rock – the *azrou* ("rock" in Berber) from which the town takes its name. Adjoining it is the main square, **Place Mohammed V**, with an impressive new Grand Mosque, as yet unfinished. On the other side of the rock is a public swimming pool, which in summer is almost reason enough to stop over in town.

The most compelling reason for a visit to Azrou, however, is provided by its **Tuesday souk**, which draws Berbers from all the surrounding mountain villages. It is held a little above the main part of town – just follow the crowds up to the quarter across the valley. The fruit and vegetable stalls sprinkled all over this area seem at first to be all there is; look further, though, and you'll see a stretch of wasteland – often with a few musicians and storytellers performing – beyond which is a smaller section for carpets, textiles and general goods. The **carpet stalls**, not particularly geared towards tourists, can turn up some beautiful items; reasonably priced if not exactly bargains.

For a further selection of rugs and carpets take a look at the **Coopérative Artisanale** (Mon–Fri 8.30am–noon & 2.30–6pm), on the Khenifra road; this has seen better days – it's a bit sleepy compared with other co-operatives – but some decent modern rugs, plus stone and cedar carvings, are still produced. Also worth an hour or so are some of the permanent stalls near the new bus station and in the old quarter of town off **Place Saouika** (aka Place Moulay Hachem Ben Salah). Most of the rugs you are shown have bright, geometric designs, based on the traditional patterns of the Beni M'Guild tribe.

There is little else to do in the town, though you can spend most of the day climbing through the hills roundabout – there are many seasonal springs – or wandering down to the river, which is reputedly well stocked with trout. Further afield – see the box feature on p.248 – there are also extensive cedar forests.

Practicalities

Just north of the new Grand Mosque is the **bus station**, with the **grand taxi** station just behind, and downstairs from it.

Two **banks** (BMCE and Banque Populaire) are located in Place Mohammed V. The **PTT** is just east of the square, behind the Banque Populaire.

Bear in mind that, in winter particularly, the nights are cold and that central heating is to be found only in the dearer (and more distant) **hotels**.

Accommodation

Hôtel Amros, 6km out on the Meknes road (☎05/556 3663, fax 556 3680). An upmarket hotel for which you will need a petit taxi. According to season, there is a nightclub, a swimming pool and tennis courts, as well as a restaurant and bar. ⑤.

Hôtel Azrou, Route du Khenifra (☎05/556 2116, fax 556 4273). 300m downhill to the southwest of Place Mohammed V. A good-value place, with pleasant rooms, some en suite, a good restaurant and bar, and English spoken. Hamid who works here is the local representative of a firm called *Sochalat* (☎/fax 05/556 0427), which organizes treks and hunting expeditions in the region. ②.

Hôtel Beauséjour, 45 Place Saouika (☎05/556 3272). One of the cheapest hotels in town; central with a fine roof terrace, and hot showers available. The next door café, with the same management, is good for breakfast and snacks. ①.

Hôtel des Cèdres, Place Mohammed V (☎05/556 2326). A good-value place with clean and comfortable rooms, and a long balcony overlooking the square. Common bathrooms, but hot water. ②.

Hôtel Panorama, Rue El Hansali (☎05/556 2010, fax 556 1804). A short walk from the town centre; good views and birdlife in woods behind. But ownership has changed and standards fallen. Some rooms en suite; hot water, central heating, a restaurant and a bar. ④.

Hôtel Salam, off Place Saouika (☎05/556 2562). Central and best of the downmarket accommodation, but cold showers. *Café Salam* is next door and good. ①.

Hôtel Ziz, 83 Place Saouika (☎05/556 2362). Not too impressive – and cold showers. Best as a reserve if other cheapies are full and better than the nearby *Hôtel Atlas*. ①.

Auberge de Jeunesse (Youth Hostel), Route de Midelt-Ifrane (☎05/556 3733). On the outskirts of town, about 1km from the centre and before the road forks to Midelt/Er Rachidia (P21) and to Ifrane/Fes (P24). Friendly and well run, with good views too. ①.

Eating

The best place to **eat** in town – though it tends to be colonized by drinkers in the evening – is the restaurant of the *Hôtel Azrou* (daily 11.30am–3pm & 6–11pm; cheap to moderate), where the trout in particular is recommended. The *Hôtel des Cèdres* also has a reasonable restaurant (daily 11.30am–3pm & 7–9pm; cheap to moderate) – though reports on it have been mixed. For some reason it is cheaper in both of these to eat *à la carte* than to order the set menu. For cheaper eating, you'll find several places facing the Grand Mosque on the roads leading out from the main square, with brochettes, tajines and spit-roast chicken among the foods on offer, though if you opt for the latter at lunchtime, make sure you're not eating the birds that were left on the spit from the night before. The stalls towards the *azrou* rock tend to be better than those towards the bus station.

Moving On

There are several daily bus services to Fes, Meknes, Khenifra, Beni Mellal, Midelt and Er Rachidia, with fewer to destinations like Marrakesh, Casablanca and Rabat, and only one to Aïn Leuh. If you want to get to Er Rachidia and Rissani, and there is no direct bus, take the Midelt bus and change there. Similarly, to reach Marrakesh, you may have to change at Beni Mellal. One possible problem is that most bus services are just passing through, and tickets may only go on sale when the bus arrives and the conductor tells the people in the ticket office how many places are available – following which, if seats are scarce, there will be a mad scramble for tickets. By arriving early and establishing a place by the ticket window, you may be able to ensure that you are at the front of the queue if that happens.

There are also regular grand taxi runs to Midelt, Meknes, Ifrane and Fes, and sporadic (but possible) ones to Khenifra and Beni Mellal. Grands taxis for Aïn Leuh have their own station at the beginning of the Khenifra road opposite the Grand Mosque and the *azrou*.

Aïn Leuh and the waterfalls of Oum Er Rbia

South of Azrou lies some of the most remote and beautiful country of the Middle Atlas: a region of cedar forests, limestone plateaus and polje lakes, that is home to some superb wildlife (see box below), including Barbary apes.

It makes rewarding countryside for a few days' exploration, either by car or on foot. At the heart of the region – an obvious focus for a trip – are the **waterfalls of Oum Er Rbia**, the source of Morocco's largest river. If you don't have transport, you can get a daily **bus** from Azrou to **Aïn Leuh**, 30km along the route (and with some minor falls of its own), or, if you have the money, or get a group together, you could always charter a **grand taxi** from Azrou.

Aïn Leuh

AÏN LEUH (17km from Azrou along the main Khenifra road, then 13km up the S303) is a large Berber village, typical of the Middle Atlas, with its flat-roofed houses tiered above the valley. As at Azrou, there are ruins of a kasbah built by Moulay Ismail; and in the hills behind the town there are **springs** and a more or less year-round waterfall.

Aïn Leuh's **souk** is held on Wednesday (a good day to hitch), though it can extend a day in either direction. It is the weekly gathering point of the **Beni M'Guild** tribe – still semi-nomadic in this region, and to be seen camping out beside their flocks in heavy, dark tents. As a colonial *zone d'insécurité*, this part of the Atlas was relatively undisturbed by French settlers, and the traditional balance between pasture and forest has remained largely intact.

BARBARY APES AND OTHER CEDAR FOREST WILDLIFE

The **cedar forests** which lie to the **south of Azrou** are a unique habitat in Morocco, their verdant atmosphere contrasting starkly with the surrounding aridity and barrenness of the Middle Atlas range. They shelter several troupes of **Barbary apes**, a glimpse of which is one of the wildlife highlights of a visit to Morocco. They can be found feeding along the forest margins – sometimes on the outskirts of Azrou itself – but they are shy animals and any excessive intrusion is likely to be met with a retreat to the lofty sanctuary of the treetops.

Almost as interesting is the forest **birdlife**, whose possibilities include the two species of Moroccan woodpecker, the pied and red great spotted and green and yellow Levaillant's varieties. Other overhead highlights include the splendid **booted eagle**, often seen soaring on outstretched wings in an attempt to evade the unwanted attentions of resident ravens. Kestrels nest in the Oum Er Rbia gorge, near the falls (see opposite) in spring.

The cedars also provide shelter for a vibrant carpet of flowers – pink peonies, scarlet dianthus, blue germander, golden compositae and a variety of orchids – which makes an ideal haven for a host of **butterflies** (from April onwards), among them the brilliant sulphur cleopatra, large tortoiseshell and cardinal.

The Oum Er Rbia sources and Aguelmane Azigza

The road to the **Oum Er Rbia waterfalls** begins just south of Aïn Leuh and is sign-posted "Aguelmane Azigza/Khenifra". Though it is now paved along its entire course, with several new bridges over the Rbia, it can still become waterlogged and impassable in winter, so ask about conditions in Azrou or Khenifra before setting out. For the most part it runs through mountain forest, where you're almost certain to come across apes.

About 20km south of Aïn Leuh, to the left of the road, there's a small lake, **Lac Ouiouane**, adjoining a couple of farms and a large *maison forestière*. A stretch of more open country, with grazing sheep and odd pitched-roof farmsteads, leads to the descent to the Oum Er Rbia valley. The road twists down, bends through a side valley and round to a concrete bridge over the Rbia, with a small parking area by the river. (Coming from the south, the descent to the Oum Er Rbia is unmistakeable – around 45km from Khenifra.)

Guides will offer their services here for the **walk to the falls** but they are unneces-sary as a clear path leads up to the gorge – a ten- to fifteen-minute walk. At the end of the path is a small waterfall, down petrified limestone deposits. All the water comes out in forty or more springs (*sources*), a little further down the gorge. Many have rough café-shelters built beside them, along the river edge.

The natural basin below the falls seems like a tempting place to swim, though beware that the currents here are extremely strong; there are smaller pools nearby. The water, full of salts, is not drinkable.

Aguelmane Azigza and beyond

On past the bridges, the main road heads off to the west, crossed by a confusing array of *pistes*. After 18km, a turnoff on the left leads to the **Aguelmane Azigza**, a dark and very deep lake, secluded among the cedar trees. You can camp and swim here, as many Moroccans do. There's also a **lodge-café**, relatively new, though closed up, for some reason, recently.

Azigza has terrific **wildlife**. The wooded slopes of the lake throng with insect life, including the brilliant red and black grasshopper and the beautiful small Amanda's blue butterfly, while the forest provides nesting and feeding areas for woodland finches and titmice, including the elusive hawfinch with its diagnostic heavy bill. There's more birdlife in the waters, too, including diving duck (mainly grebes and coot) and marbled teal in autumn and winter.

From the Azigza turnoff, it's a further 24km to Khenifra. Alternatively, for the exploration-minded, the P3404 piste (poor but being improved) leads off east into the Djebel Irhoud mountains to Itzer and, finally, Zeïda on the P21 (see below). A rather better road, the P3485, which is being surfaced, runs off from this to join the P21 at Kia Aït Outfella, just south of the Col du Zad.

South to Midelt and Er Rachidia

If you're travelling the southern circuits of the *ksour* and kasbahs of the south, you're almost certain to take this route in one direction or the other. It's 125km from **Azrou to Midelt** and a further 154km to **Er Rachidia** – quite feasible distances for a single bus trip or a day's driving, but more satisfying taken in a couple of stages. You cross passes over both Middle and High Atlas ranges, catch a first glimpse of the south's fab-ulous *pisé* architecture and end up in the desert.

Azrou to Midelt

Climbing up from Azrou, the Midelt road (P21) follows a magnificent stretch of the Middle Atlas, winding through the forests to emerge at the **valley of the Oued Gigou**,

---

BIRDLIFE AROUND ZEÏDA

Thirty kilometres north of Midelt and within 15km of Zeïda is a stony desert area renowned for the elusive **Dupont's Lark**. Other species to be found on the vast, open scrubby plain are the **Red-rumped Wheatear, Thick-brilled Lark, Lesser Short-toed Lark** and **Trumpeter Finch**. East and west of the P21 between kilometre posts 27 and 28 are recommended.

North of Zeïda, the aqueduct, parallel with the road, has **Rock Sparrows** and **Spotless Starlings**.

---

the view ahead taking in some of the range's highest peaks. By bus you have little alternative but to head straight to Midelt, reached in around two hours, via the market village of Timadhite (large **Thursday souk**). With a car, there are two very brief and worthwhile detours.

The first of these comes 52km from Azrou, as the road levels out on a strange volcanic plateau littered with dark pumice rock. A turnoff here, to the left, (and where persistent 'guides' hang out) is signposted to **Aguelmane Sidi Ali**, the largest of many mountain lakes formed in the extinct craters of this region. It's only a kilometre from the road: long, still and eerily beautiful. Besides an occasional shepherd's tent and flock, there is unlikely to be anything or anyone in sight; if you can improvise a fishing rod, there are reputed to be plenty of trout, pike and perch.

The other point where you might want to leave the road is 24km further down, past the Col du Zad, a 2178m pass across the Middle Atlas. Superb trekking country lies west of the col, leading to the Oued Sefrou (a north-south piste goes via Kerrouchen and its marvellous cedar forests, another haunt of Barbary apes). South of the col, a road leads right in for 6km to the small village of **ITZER**, whose **market** is one of the most important in the region. Held on Mondays and Thursdays, it can be a good source of Berber rugs and carpets.

Back on the main road, you pass road junctions near Boulôjul (with the P20 from Boulemane) and Zeïda (with the P33 from Khenifra). A few kilometres south of Zeïda is a small, but good tourist complex, the *Centre Timnay* (☎/fax 05/558 3434), including a shop, café-restaurant, swimming pool (in summer) and a clean **campsite**, with shared accommodation available for those without tents. The centre has been developed by its owner, Aït Lemkaden Driss, as a base for **Landrover, mountain bike and walking expeditions** in the region.

Midelt

At **MIDELT**, approached through a bleak plain of scrub and desert, you have left the Middle Atlas behind. Suddenly, through the haze, appear the much greater peaks of the High Atlas, which rise sheer behind the town to a massive range, the **Djebel Ayachi**, at over 3700m. The drama of this site, tremendous in the clear, cool evenings, is the most compelling reason to stop over, for the town itself initially looks very drab – one street with a couple of cafés and hotels and a small souk. In fact, it's a pleasant place to stay – partly because so few people do, partly because it's the first place where you become aware of the more relaxed (and predominantly Berber) atmosphere of the south. Indeed, there is the hint of a frontier town, a sense reinforced by the derelict mines at Mibladene and Aouli, northeast of Midelt, in the nearby gorge of Oued Moulouya (see box on p.252).

Midelt is so far inland that the microclimate is one of extremes: bitterly cold in winter and oppressively hot in summer. One of the best times to visit is in the autumn, particularly at the start of October when there is a modest apple festival – and, year round,

△ ❶ & Azrou   △ Mibladene (S317)

MIDELT

N

Oued Outat

Cirque de Jaffar (3424)

ACCOMMODATION
Hôtel Atlas	4
Hôtel El Ayachi	7
Hôtel Boughafar	2
Hôtel Kasbah	6
Hôtel El Massira	3
Hôtel Mimlal	1
Hôtel Roi de la Bière	5

Bus Station

Souk El Djedid
Carpet Souk

Kasbah
Myriem

Etoile du Sud

Grands Taxis

AVENUE MOHAMMED V

MOULAY ABDALLAH

AVENUE DE LA MARCHE VERTE

AVENUE HASSAN II

AVENUE DES FAR

P21

△ ❻ & El Rachidia

PTT   ❼ **Municipal**
△ **Campsite**

RESTAURANTS
Café-Restaurant Fès	A
Restaurant Le Pin	B

0   100m

the best time to be here is for the huge **Sunday souk**, which spreads back along the road towards Azrou.

The Town

The most interesting section of town, meriting at least a stop between buses, is the area around the old souk – **Souk Djedid**, behind the stalls facing the bus station. Just to the south of the main souk, which is a daily fruit and vegetable market, is an arcaded **carpet souk**, its wares slung out in rotation in the sunlight (for natural bleaching) and piled up in bewildering layers of pattern and colour in the various shops to the rear. This is a relaxed place for shopping and the rugs are superb – mostly local, geometric designs from tribes of the Middle Atlas. Ask to see the "antique" ones, few of which will be more than ten or twenty years old, but they are usually the most idiosyncratic and inventive. Good examples can also be seen at the *Etoile du Sud* carpet shop, just south of the souk, behind the *Hôtel Occidental*, or the *Maison Berbère* at 15 Rue Mohammed Amraoui, a few doors up from the *Hôtel Atlas*, but in either case you will have to bargain hard to get a decent price and, it goes without saying, don't turn up with a guide.

A better place to buy carpets – and traditional-styled blankets and textiles – is at the **Atelier de Tissage**, part of a convent run by a group of Franciscan nuns, where you can also see them being made. The Atelier is a workshop where local women can learn, practise and pass on traditional carpet-making skills, and earn a decent living by using them. It is located just off to the left on the road to **Tattiouine** (signposted Cirque Jaffar from the town centre and over the Oued Outat to the west). Many of the nuns have been living here for years, and will quite happily talk about their time in Morocco.

MIBLADENE AND AOULI: MOROCCAN KLONDIKE

Less than an hour's drive from Midelt, on the banks of the **Oued Moulouya** where it emerges from its spectacular gorge, is the deserted mining settlement of **Aouli**. You can reach it by car from Midelt, first along the S317, past **Mibladene** (11km from Midelt) and then, by the 3419, to Aouli (25 km).

Once past Mibladene (appropriately "our mother earth" in Berber) where there are modest excavations still being worked, the road deteriorates and drops into the gorge which is exciting enough in itself. Soon, you reach the apocalyptic mining ruins on both sides of the river. Here, from the turn of the twentieth century, and long before then on a more modest scale, the locals mined **lead**, which contained **silver**. In 1979, around 3000 still worked here but, by the mid-1980s, all had gone.

You don't have to be an industrial archeologist to be impressed by the tunnels, aqueducts, aerial ropeways, barrack-like living quarters and, above all, buildings pressed high against the cliff face resembling a Tibetan monastery. There are tracks cut into the sides of the gorge, first used by mules and then a mineral-line railway passing through tunnels. Everywhere there is rusting ironmongery.

Beyond Aouli, a rough track continues downstream to **Ksabi** and from there you can complete the circuit, by the S329 and P21 to Midelt. But this calls for a Renault 4 or 4 x 4, particularly in bad weather. Otherwise you must return the way you came.

At the outset, the exit from Midelt is not easy to find because it is not signposted. Leave by the straight, narrow road opposite the *Hôtel Zohors*, and alongside the Banque Populaire, on Avenue Mohammed V.

At the moment, there are seven nuns (four French, two Spanish and one Polish) and they also run a clinic and a small hospital, as part of the convent. The complex is known, locally, and inevitably, as *Kasbah Myriem* (☎05/558 2443); the atelier is open every day, except Fridays and Sundays. The nuns welcome visitors who wish to join them in celebrating Mass on Saturday evenings and Sunday mornings.

If you follow the Tattiouine road a few kilometres further, you find yourself in countryside very different from that around Midelt, with eagles soaring above the hills and mule tracks leading down to the valleys, and an occasional kasbah. For more on this area – and the Cirque du Jaffar beyond – see opposite.

Practicalities

Midelt's **bus station**, in the centre of town, has regular departures to Azrou, Meknes, Fes, Er Rachidia and Rissani, with fewer services to Casablanca and Rabat. The **grand taxi** stand, behind it on Avenue Moulay Abdallah, has regular runs to Azrou, Fes, Meknes, Zeida, Khenifra and Er Rachidia.

ACCOMMODATION

Midelt has a reasonable spread of accommodation but many of the **hotels** are often full by mid-afternoon at busy tourist times of year, so arrive early or make a reservation by phone the day before. There is a **Municipal Campsite** behind the *Hôtel El Ayachi*, bare and shadeless, on stony ground and with cold showers only. A better place to camp (if you have, or can arrange transport) is at the *Centre Timnay*, 30km northwest of Midelt on the road P21 to Azrou.

There are small **hammams** in the town for men and women – ask directions.

Hôtel Atlas, 3 Rue Mohammed Amraoui (☎05/558 2938). A spotless, cosy *pension*; family run and very friendly. Small, so arrive early or book in advance. Showers cost extra. ①.

Hôtel el Ayachi, Rue Agadir: follow the signs (☎05/558 2161, fax 558 3307). The town's main upmarket hotel, favoured by tour groups and often block booked. Despite a 1990 *International*

Gastronomy Award, still on proud display, the restaurant and service are not terribly brilliant but, with captive diners, the management doesn't appear too troubled. ④.

Hôtel Boughafar, 7 Av. Mohammed V (☎05/558 3099). A reasonable little place opened in 1995; rooms are okay, with toilets and hot showers on the landing; there are great views from the roof terrace; and a restaurant. It's also handy for the bus station, but locks its doors at 11pm. ③.

Hôtel Kasbah, 2km out on Er Rachidia road (☎05/558 0405, fax 558 3945). A three-star hotel, part of the Kasbah Asmaa chain – the Kasbah being the hotel, and the Asmaa its attached restaurant. For those who need to keep cool, facilities include air conditioning and pool. ④.

Hôtel el Massira, 11 Rue des Ancients Combattants (☎05/558 1134). A new place with clean, though rather austere rooms, and cold showers in the hotel itself but a hammam with hot showers adjoining (women 8am–7pm, men 7pm–midnight). ③.

Hôtel Mimlal, Route de Meknes, 1km out of town (☎05/558 2266). Simple hotel with sombre rooms, en-suite hot showers but shared toilets on the corridor. Also has a reasonable restaurant. ③.

Hôtel Roi de la Bière, corner of Av. Hassan II and Av. des F.A.R. (☎05/558 2675). A pleasant and comfortable place, clean and well kept, founded in 1938, when it lived up to its name, though it doesn't serve beer nowadays. Some rooms have showers, albeit cold – but the welcome is warm. ②.

EATING

For **meals**, the best place to try is the *Café-Restaurant Fes* on Rue des Esserghin (off Avenue Mohammed V; daily noon–3pm & 6–9pm; cheap), which does a very generous *menu du jour* (they like advance warning if possible), with vegetarian tajine for those who don't eat meat, and quince stewed in sugar and cinnamon for afters. Other decent places include the *Restaurant Le Pin*, part of a tourist complex on Avenue Moulay Abdallah (daily 10am–3pm & 7–10pm; moderate), whose offerings include tajines, brochettes and omelettes.

The Cirque Jaffar, Djebel Ayachi and beyond

The classic route around Midelt is the **Cirque Jaffar**, a good piste which leaves the Midelt–Tattiouine road to edge its way through a kind of hollow in the foothills of the **Djebel Ayachi** (see box overleaf). This runs round the *cirque*, then loops back to the Midelt–Azrou road after 34km (turn right, onto the 3426, near the *Maison Forestière de Mitkane*); it is only 79km in all back to Midelt, though it takes a good half-day to get around.

Across the Atlas

Renault 4s make it over the Atlas from Midelt to Tinerhir in summer, though it's a lot easier with four-wheel-drive vehicles; everyone needs a pick and spade for the occasional very rough detour (beware of scorpions, by the way, when shifting rocks), as well as some warm clothes and a tent for sleeping out at night (Atlas nights are cold). If you don't have a vehicle, you can use Berber lorries over the various stages, which provide a kind of bus service most days. Travelling this way, you should reckon on up to three days for the journey to Imilchil (though you might make it in one), and a similar number from there down to the Todra Gorge and Tinerhir (see p.446).

South towards Er Rachidia

There's less adventure in continuing **south from Midelt to Er Rachidia**, though the route is a striking one, marking the transition to the south and the desert. The area was long notorious for raids upon caravans and travellers carried out by the Aït Haddidou, a nomadic Berber tribe, fear of whom led the main spring along this route to be known as *Aïn Khrob ou Hrob* – "Drink and Flee". The tribe were pacified with great difficulty by the French, as late as the 1930s, and in consequence, the traditional *ksour* (fortified villages) are often shadowed by old Foreign Legion posts.

DJEBEL AYACHI AND TOUNFITE

Djebel Ayachi can be climbed from Midelt, either returning to the town, or as part of a through-trek to Tounfite. From Midelt, a taxi or pick-up can be arranged to the springs 2km beyond Tattiouine, and the long **Ikkis valley** followed, with a bivouac at its head (the col at the end leads to the Cirque du Jaffar). An easy ascent leads to the many summits of this huge range, which was long thought to be the highest in Morocco (it is 3700m – compared to Toubkal at 4167m). A descent south to the Oued Taarart valley brings you to several villages and a Wednesday truck out to Tounfite.

At **Tounfite**, rooms are available and buses and taxis link it with **Boumia** (with a Thursday souk), Zeïda and Midelt. The village also gives access to the Djebel Masker (3265m), – a long day's climb, rising from cedar forests. Ayachi and Masker are long wave-crests, seen from a distance they appear to curve over the horizon such is the scale.

SERIOUS EXPEDITIONS

From Tounfite, an interesting piste runs west, between the Toujjet and Oujoud peaks to the head of the Melwiya plains and Arghbala, beyond which lies the main piste across the Central Atlas via Imilchil. South of Djebel Masker lies a chaos of spectacular peaks, little visited. The only information in English at present is in Michael Peyron's *Grand Atlas Traverse* guide, which details the whole zone between Midelt and the Toubkal massif.

The Tizi n'Talrhmeht and Rich

Around 30km south of Midelt, you cross one of the lower passes of the High Atlas, the **Tizi n'Talrhmeht** (Pass of the She-Camel), before descending to what is essentially a desert plain. At Aït Messaoud, just beyond the pass, there's a distinctly *Beau Geste*-like Foreign Legion fort, and a few kilometres further down, you come across the first southern *ksar*, Aït Kherrou, a river oasis at the entrance to a small gorge. After this, the *ksour* begin to dot the landscape as the road follows the path of the great Ziz river.

The main settlement in these parts is **RICH**, a market town and administrative centre, approached from the main road (P21) along a rather bizarre red-washed esplanade. Enclosed by palms watered by a *seguia* or *khettara* (irrigation channel) from the Oued Ziz, the town developed around a *ksar* and was an important fort during the Protectorate. It still has shades of *Beau Geste* about it, as well as a lively Monday **souk**. Several **hotels** lie just off the main square, including the *Salama* (☎05/558 9343; ①) which has a small café, and the marginally preferable *Al Massira* (☎05/558 9340; ①) which has hot showers, a restaurant and views from its roof terrace.

Over the Atlas from Rich

West of Rich, the Atlas mountains stretch into the distance, skirted by a road up behind the town which trails the last section of the Oued Ziz. The 3443 road west from Rich begins as the 3442 and is surfaced as far as the junction with the Imilchil–Todra trans-Atlas route (3445/3483), with further work in progress. Minibus taxis run up this impressive route daily – a wonderful trip through great gorges, valleys and passes – and lorries will head for the Imilchil souk on Fridays.

The route is passable (just) in a Renault 4, though only in the dry summer months, and it can also be travelled in stages by **Berber lorries** (*camionettes*), paying as you go. Landrover taxis also cover the route and, if there are enough customers, you will be able to pay for a *place* rather than chartering the whole vehicle. The most promising day to set out from Rich by *camionette* or Landrover is Friday (or early Saturday morning), when you might get a shared vehicle all the way to Imilchil for its Saturday souk; make enquiries at the Rich hotels.

The Ziz Gorge

The scenic highlight of the regular Midelt–Er Rachidia route is the dramatic **Ziz Gorges**, tremendous erosions of rock which carve a passage through the Atlas. The route follows the Ziz valley from AÏT KROJMANE (7km from Rich) onwards, just past the *Ziz* ("gazelle" in Berber) filling station. About 20km from Rich, you will see, down on the right between the road and the river, a cluster of modern buildings, signposted **Hammat Moulay Ali Cherif**. This is a small, but well-known, spa with outdoor hot springs (over 36°C), rich in magnesium and sulphates, and said to cure rheumatic disorders. You will see the afflicted hopefuls in the nearby thickets from which steam rises. Men and women bathe on alternate days. There is a café and some primitive rooms to rent.

A further 5km on, you enter the gorges proper, around 25km from Rich, shortly after the **Tunnel du Légionnaire**, built by the French in 1930 to open up the route to the south, and still guarded by drowsy soldiers. The gorges are truly majestic, especially in late afternoon, cut by great swathes of sunlight, and the incredible mountain landscape is accompanied by sudden vistas of brilliant green oasis and red-brown *ksour*.

You emerge from the gorges near the vast **Barrage Hassan Addakhil**, built in 1971 to irrigate the valley of the Tafilalt beyond, and to supply electricity for Er Rachidia. The dam also regulates the flow of the Oued Ziz, preventing the serious flooding which occurred frequently before it was built, as witnessed by the deserted *ksour* in the gorges above and below the lake.

Azrou to Kasba Tadla

The **main route from Azrou to Marrakesh** – the P24 – skirts well clear of the Atlas ranges, its interest lying in the subtle changes of land, cultivation and architecture on the plains as you move into the south. The towns along the way are hot, dusty, functional market centres, unlikely to tempt you to linger. However, once again, contact with the Middle Atlas is close at hand, if you leave the main road and take to the *pistes*. A great network of them spreads out behind the small town of **El Ksiba**, itself 8km off the P24 but easily hitched to from the turnoff or reached by bus from Kasba Tadla.

Khenifra

With long-distance buses regularly passing through **KHENIFRA**, you're unlikely to get stranded here, but if you're following this chapter in reverse (from Marrakesh), note that you can approach the Cascades of Oum Er Rbia (see p.249) from Khenifra, so you may want to stay. An old market town, and now a provincial centre, it stands on **Oued Oum Rbia**. Moulay Ismail built a kasbah here, replaced by local ruler Moha ou Hammou at the close of the nineteenth century, the walls of which still stand alongside the humpback bridge built by Moulay Ismail. But the once clear, fast flowing river is filthy, and the modern quarters, bisected by the main road (P24) from Fes to Marrakesh, not much more enticing. Wide avenues and dull buildings come to life, from an outsider's perspective, only at the weekly Sunday souk or the Saturday afternoon rug auction put on by Berber women just across the new bridge near the bus station.

Historically, the town's chief claim to fame is as a focus of resistance under Moha ou Hammou, in the early years of the Protectorate. The French suffered a costly victory here, losing 600 men when they took the town in 1914. There's an impressive **monument** recording this event – 7km south of Khenifra on the left-hand side of the P24 going towards Marrakesh. The town also played an important part in the struggle for independence which climaxed on August 20, 1955. Gavin Maxwell in his book *Lords of the Atlas* (see p.609) records that Gilbert Grandval, Resident General, returned from Paris to Rabat "at 2am on the 20th, and at 7am the Director of the Interior, General Leblanc, telephoned to him with the opening words, 'It is war.' Massive rioting had broken out at Khenifra, and the General asked authorisation to use aircraft. The Medina was surrounded by troops, but mounted tribesmen were visible on all the ridges that could be seen from the town. Grandval gave his authorisation, but on the condition that use of aircraft should be limited to low flying dispersal of tribal cavalry, and that no shot be fired or bomb dropped. This was only the beginning; during the next few hours, the situation was repeated at Boujad, Safi, Ouezzane, Petit Jean, Casablanca and Rabat." These demonstrations would soon lead to Moroccan independence.

Practicalities

Heading north into town on Avenue Zerktouni, the main road in from the P24 Fes–Marrakesh road, you pass the **bus station** on your left with dozens of daily services to Marrakesh, Meknes, Fes, Kasbah Tadla, Beni Mellal and Azrou, seven a day to Midelt, and plenty more to destinations nationwide. There are often direct services to Midelt and even Er Rachidia, but if not, you can take one to "Trente Trois", the junction of the P24 Fes–Marrakesh road with the P33 road towards Midelt, and pick up onward transport there. Grands taxis for Fes and Meknes leave from a different station in the Medina.

Turning left 200m beyond the bus station, at the junction with Khenifra's main thoroughfare, Avenue Mohammed V, you cross the oued, and pass the **PTT** and BMCE **bank**, which face each other across the street. On your right, just past the PTT, is the **municipal market**, which marks the beginning of the **Medina**, with lively narrow streets, but nothing of special interest.

ACCOMMODATION AND EATING

The best place to **eat** is the restaurant of the *Hôtel de France* (daily 11am–4pm & 6–11pm; moderate), offering the likes of steak, tajine and couscous. More conveniently located eating places can be found along Avenue Zerktouni between the bus station and the junction of Avenue Mohammed V.

If you've just visited the Cascades of Oum Rbia from Khenifra, or if you plan to do so, you might want to use the town's **hotels**, the better among which are:

Hôtel Arego, 9 Av. Zerktouni, 200m north of the bus station (☎05/558 6487). Simple but clean and friendly, with shared bathrooms. It's on the main road so the rear rooms are quieter than the front ones. ②.

Hôtel de France, Quartier des F.A.R., 800m north of the bus station (☎05/558 6114). Large, clean, en-suite rooms, and service with a smile from cheery receptionist Ahmed. The restaurant is excellent – better than the hotel in fact. ②.

Hôtel Hammou Zayani, Cité el Amal, 500m uphill east from the junction of Av. Zerkatouni and Av. Mohammed V (☎05/558 6020, fax 558 6532). On a hill overlooking the 'new' town, and top choice for comfort though a bit run-down, with tennis courts, a swimming pool and a nightclub. ④.

Hôtel Melilla, off Av. Zerktouni, next to the bus station. (☎05/538 4609). Opened in 1995, with comfortable though slightly chintzy en-suite rooms, each with a TV and armchair. ②.

Hôtel Najah, Av. Zerktouni, just north of the junction with Av. Mohammed V (☎05/558 8331 or 32, fax 558 7874). Central, older, businessperson's hotel with comfortable en-suite rooms – and satellite TV in every room. Café, restaurant and patisserie. ④.

Hôtel Atlas (formerly Hôtel Rif), Av. Zerktouni, just north of the bus station (☎05/558 8030). Comfortable and clean with hot water round the clock. ②.

Hôtel Sahara, 3 Av. Bir Anzarane (☎05/538 5318). Just behind the municipal market; cheap, but clean and friendly. ①.

Oulmès

Northwest of Khenifra, a road leads through the Djebel Mouchchene, a forested outcrop of the Middle Atlas, towards Rabat. This is an attractive route through countryside cut by rivers and ravines, and with wild boar in the hills. There is a major **souk** at the crossroads settlement of Aguelmouss each Saturday.

Midway along the route is the small town of **OULMÈS** and – some 4km distant – the spa-hamlet of **OULMÈS-TARMILATE**, home of Morocco's most popular fizzy mineral water. The spa makes a good stop, if you can afford the *Hôtel les Thermes* (☎03/755 2293; ③; closed July and Aug). Below the hotel you can walk down to a spring known as **Lalla Haya**, where Oulmès water cascades out from the rocks.

El Ksiba, Aghbala and across the Atlas

EL KSIBA is a sizeable and busy Berber village lying 6km south of the P24 Fes–Marrakesh road, with a **Sunday souk**, and enclosed by apricot, olive and orange groves. It has one **bank**, Crédit Agricole, and one small, pleasant **hotel**, the *Henri IV* (☎/fax 02/341 5002; ①), in the *Quartier Administrative* (from the centre of the village, take the road that leads uphill opposite the *Petrom* station and bear left after about 300m – coming in by car from the P24, you can reach it by taking a left before you come into the village). This is still a pleasant place, in a pleasant setting, but not as welcoming as it used to be. The **PTT** is next door. A little beyond here, the road divides, with the left fork leading after 800m to the *Auberge des Artistes* (☎/fax 02/341 5490), opened by a local French resident in 1999, a pleasant spot in the middle of the countryside with at present **camping** facilities only, though there are rooms in the pipeline, and a restaurant that claims to be open all hours (moderate). The right fork leads after 2km to another campsite, *Camping Taghbalout*, cheaper but more rustic, with cold water showers, hidden in the wooded Atlas slopes, along the Aghbala road.

South of El Ksiba, the road crosses the Atlas by way of Imilchil and the Todra gorge to Tinerhir (see map, p.452). Once a challenging piste, this is being upgraded steadily with tarmac in many places. The Todra gorge and the Tassent–Ikkassene stretch are regularly washed out by flash floods, and can be in an appalling state, with the result that the route should only be tackled in a 4x4 vehicle.

From El Ksiba, the 1901 road twists through forest to a panoramic col, then descends to a river and a junction with the 1805 road to Ouaouizaght and Azilal via the Bin el Ouidane reservoir (see p.262), a fine panoramic drive. **Ouaouizaght** has a busy Wednesday souk, and one hotel, the *Hôtel Atlas* (☎02/344 2042; ①) at the top end of town.

OLIVE OIL

On the main road (P24) near El Ksiba, and particularly either side of **Tirhboula** (45km from Beni Mellal), you will see plastic bottles hanging from roadside trees to advertise the availability of **olive oil** crushed from local olives in the adjacent domestic presses. Whether or not you have a passion for cooking, or drenching your salads, with olive oil, it's well worth a stop in early autumn to see the presses at work. You'll be welcome to visit – and to buy.

When **ripe**, the black olives can contain up to 60 percent oil. Some of them are harvested **unripe** or green and then pickled in salt. Both ripe and unripe olives are normally bitter; this can be corrected by soaking them first in an alkaline solution.

The 1901 road meanwhile turns upwards by a gorge and continues through varied forest to cross the **Tizi n'Isli** pass (a village of the same name lies just off the road). From the pass, it snakes down to a junction where the trans-Atlas road (1903) heads south, while route 1901 continues eastward to **Arhbala**, a busy market town with a Wednesday souk, and cafés that have rooms to rent. The road continues to meet the P33 Beni Mellal–Midelt road, an attractive circuit.

Heading south from its junction with 1901, route 1903 crosses a girder bridge and continues (under construction for part of the way) to **Ikassene**, which has become something of a staging post, with several cafés, and rooms available. Beyond Ikkassane, the going is hazardous. Floods have largely destroyed the piste (a new line is being developed), and driving is frequently up the river-bed itself, and only suitable for four-wheel-drive vehicles. At Tassent, the piste hauls upwards on many bends (periodic landslides may block it) to a high valley and a col, giving a view to the Tislit lake, beyond which lies **Imilchil** (see p.454).

Kasba Tadla

KASBA TADLA was created by Moulay Ismail, and takes its name from a fortress he built here, strategically positioned beside the Oum Er Rbia river. It remains a military town, and is scarcely a place to linger. However, if you have a car, or are between buses, you might as well take the odd hour to look round. The town is centred around a main street, Avenue Mohammed V. At its southern end is the walled **kasbah**, featuring an impressive though derelict Grand Mosque, with a crumbling brick minaret, and an interesting smaller mosque, whose minaret features the same protruding perches as that of the Great Mosque in Tiznit (see p.510). The rest of the area inside the walls is taken up with the poor makeshift homes typical of Morocco's *bidonvilles*. The most remarkable feature in town is the four tall, square pillars over the oued at the Kasbah Tadla turn-off on the P24 Fes–Marrakesh road (about 1km from the town centre). This is a **memorial** to the French soldiers killed hereabouts from 1912 to 1933. Understandably, it is not as well preserved as the monument outside Khenifra which celebrates Moroccan resistance to the French in 1914, but it affords a fine view of the *bidonville* by the river and the town beyond. The town's other main feature of interest is a sizeable **souk** held on Mondays.

For anyone stranded, there are two cheap and very basic **hotels** off Avenue Mohammed V, a few blocks north of the kasbah. The better of the two is the almost charmingly ramshackle *Hôtel des Alliés* at 38 Avenue Mohammed V (☎02/341 8587; ①), complete with iron bedsteads and a bar that could have been transported from 1930s France, lacking only the odd Gauloise-smoking peasant and bottle of *Pastis* behind the counter (alcohol is no longer served here). The only other option is the even cheaper and more basic *Hôtel Atlas*, round the block at 46 Rue Majjati Obad (no phone; ①).

Your best bet in town for **eating** is the *Restaurant Kordouba*, a couple of blocks south at the corner of Avenue Mohammed V and Rue Tarik Ibn Ziad (daily 10am–10pm; cheap), serving chicken, brochettes and steak. The *Salem* opposite the *Hôtel des Alliés* (daily 8am–11pm; cheap) is characterful in its own way, but the food isn't great and the place is a bit too spit-and-sawdust for comfort. For those who do need a bar with a bottle of *Pastis* behind it or, more to the point, a cold beer, the *Café de la Place* opposite the *Restaurant Kordouba* (daily 10am–2pm & 4–10pm) has a liquor licence, though you'd have to be pretty brave if female to march in there alone and demand a drink.

Besides pinball and pool, the only other **entertainment** is the *Cinéma Chantecler*, on Avenue Mohammed V, by the *Hôtel des Alliés*. The town's three banks are on Rue Mejjati Obad near the *Hôtel Atlas*. The PTT is on Avenue des F.A.R. (which runs parallel with Avenue Mohammed V, two blocks east) heading out of town towards the P24 Fes–Marrakesh road. On the same road in the other direction, 500m north of the town centre, the **bus** station has departures for Beni Mellal and Khenifra, and further afield to Marrakesh, Fez, Meknes, Midelt and Casablanca, with even one daily departure each for Tangier and Agadir. Facing it across the street, the **grand taxi** yard offers regular runs to Beni Mellal, El Ksiba and Zaouiet ech Cheikh, where you can get an onward vehicle to Khenifra.

Beni Mellal

BENI MELLAL is one of Morocco's fastest-growing towns, with a population of some 400,000. It has few specific sights – and few tourists – and makes an easy, restful stop en route to Marrakesh. As a market centre for the broad, prosperous flatlands to the north, it hosts a large **Tuesday souk** – good for woollen blankets, which feature unusual Berber designs. Olives are grown on the lower slopes of the Djebel Tassemit and the plain is well known for its oranges. It is also important for its transport links (for details of which, see p.267).

As far as sights go, the town's **kasbah** in the old Medina, yet another of Moulay Ismail's endowments, has often been restored and is of no great interest. Time would be better spent walking up to the smaller, ruined **Kasbah de Ras El Aïn**, set above gardens and from which local jokers say you can see the sea on a clear day, and to the spring of **Aïn Asserdoun**, to the south of town. The latter (signposted on a Circuit Touristique from town which peters out thereafter) is especially pleasant, feeding a series of artificial falls (Moroccans love waterfalls) amid well-tended gardens.

If you're in Beni Mellal on a Saturday, it's worth a trip to what is traditionally the Middle Atlas's largest weekly **market**, held 35km southwest of the town at **SOUK SEBT DES OULAD NEMÂA**. There are regular buses.

Practicalities

The main road from Fes to Marrakesh (once the P24) now skirts the northern suburbs of Beni Mellal as the P24a and, as so often, the **bus station** has been built here; to reach the centre from here you may want to get a petit taxi to save a longish uphill walk. The old Fes–Marrakesh road still runs through the core of the town, as the **Avenue Mohammed V**, and midway along there are brief views of the plain to the north and glimpses to the south of the cream-and-white arcaded **Place de la Libération**, focus of the old **Medina** quarter, which climbs up the lower slopes of the Djebel Tassemit. The **Ville Nouvelle** sprawls down onto the plain to the south, towards, and now beyond, the ring road.

There are plenty of **banks** in town, but when they are closed (or simply to avoid the whole bank rigmarole), you can change money at *Imilchil Voyages*, 333 Avenue Mohammed V, 8.30am–10pm seven days a week. **Internet** and email access are available for very low rates at Iconet at 57 Rue #9, by 404 Avenue Mohammed V [open daily 9am–midnight; 10dh/hr]. The helpful **tourist office** is on the first floor of the **Immeuble Chichaoui** on Avenue Hassan II (☎02/348 7829; open Mon–Fri 8.30am–noon and 2.30–6.30 pm; in summer, 7am–2pm). For details of local guides – and adventure tours – into the Atlas from Beni Mellal, see the box on p.261.

Accommodation

There are twenty or so **hotels** scattered in and around the town, many built in the 1990s. The pick of them are:

Hôtel Aïn Asserdoun, Av. des F.A.R. (☎/fax 02/348 3493). A friendly place, with a small restaurant, comfortable accommodation and en-suite bathrooms; popular with Moroccans passing through or visiting for sports fixtures. ③.

△ El Ksiba

△ Kasba Tadla

Ain Asserdoun

Kasbah Ras El Ain

N

RUE IBN SINA
NEW MEDINA

Ensemble Artesanal

CTM

RUE TARIK IBN ZIAD

RUE MOHAMED HANSALI

AVENUE MOHAMED V

P24a

OLD MEDINA

PLACE DE LA LIBERATION

Souk

AVENUE DES F.A.R.

Bus Station

PTT

AVENUE MOHAMED V

Stadium

AVENUE HASSAN II

AVENUE HASSAN II

AVENUE MOHAMED V

△ Casablanca

△ Marrakesh

P24a

1 km

0

BENI MELLAL

RESTAURANTS
Café-Restaurant Tawda   C
Sandwich Noumidia   B
Chez Ben Souda   A

ACCOMMODATION
Hôtel Ain Asserdoun   2
Hôtel Al Bassatine   3
Hôtel Chems   9
Hôtel Ouzoud   10
Hôtel de Paris   5
Hôtel Es Saada   7
Hôtel Tassamet   8
Auberge Vieux Moulin   4
Hôtel des Voyageurs   6
Hôtel Zidania   1

Hôtel al Bassatine, Ouled Hamdane, Route de Fkih Ben Salah (☎02/348 6805, fax 348 6806). On the northwest edge of town, alongside the orange and olive groves. Comfortable rooms and the best restaurant in the neighbourhood (but no alcohol). ④.

Hôtel Chems, (☎02/348 3460, fax 348 3987). One of two hotels out on the original Marrakesh road built for groups on escorted seven-day Imperial Cities tours, and the poshest place in town; facilities include a swimming pool, tennis courts and a nightclub. ⑤.

Hôtel Ouzoud, (☎02/348 3752, fax 348 8530). This looks indistinguishable from the nearby *Hôtel Chems*, but the welcome is warmer and the service better; good restaurant, bar and swimming pool. ④.

Hôtel de Paris, Hay Ibn Sina, New Medina (☎02/348 2245). A 1950s-style place, fifteen minutes from the town centre; the accommodation is rather drab (though getting a facelift on our last visit), but the restaurant is good. ②.

SOUTH OF BENI MELLAL: ATLAS HIKES AND PISTES

The mountains south and southeast of Beni Mellal and the Bin el Ouidane reservoir are ideal trekking and Landrover country. In the foothills, **Djebel Tassemit** (2248m) – which towers like a high wall behind Beni Mellal – offers a challenge and fine views; reached by Aïn Asserdoun and the Kasbah de Ras el Aïn. **Djebel R'Nim** (2411m) can be climbed from the pass to **Ouaouizaght**. The road from Marrakesh to Aghbala via Azilal, Bin el Ouidane and Ouaouizaght (S508, then 1805, then 1901) is surfaced all the way and offers grand scenery, far more interesting than the P24 across the plain through Beni Mellal.

The real mountains lie to the south. A road crosses the east end of the reservoir to wend its way through to Tillouggite (which has a Saturday souk), becoming a jeepable piste at the col. It continues spectacularly to reach the Oued Ahansal (bridge washed out in 1999), from where one branch goes up the Oued Mellal to Anergui, access for **Mouriq** (3223m), Laqroun (3117m) and the **Mellal Gorges**. The other branch goes to Tamga, facing the soaring limestone walls of the peak nicknamed "*La Cathédrale*" (a spectacular goat path actually leads to the summit dome). The piste then makes a high and tortuous ascent to **Zaouia Ahancal**, a marabout's shrine at the village of **Agoudim** in what are known as "the Dolomites of Morocco" (70km from Tillouguit).

Zaouia Ahancal is also reached by a piste from Aït Mohammed and Azilal, descending under Aroudane's massive cliffs. Agoudim's tower architecture is unique north of the Atlas, and it has long been a religious centre, besides being strong enough to stop the Glaoui chieftains (see p.408) from expanding their fiefdom further east. The Taghia gorges upstream from the village, and the plateau country beyond, offer some of the best trekking in the Atlas, and can be combined with a start/finish in the more popular Bou Guemez.

PRACTICALITIES

It would be possible to cover this route in stages, using irregular local Berber lorries or jeeps. Mohammed Achari (Iskataffen, Bureau Jabant, Aït Bou Guemez, Azilal, ☎02/345 9327) is one of several local **guides** who know the area well, and can organize means of transport such as mules or Landrovers too. For maps, contact Atlas Maps (see p.31), the same firm as AMIS (see p.5), which also regularly treks this area. Landrover expeditions are also arranged by **Imilchil Voyages**, 333 Av. Mohammed V, Beni Mellal (☎/fax 02/348 7259).

For **accommodation**, Agoudim has several gîtes, and there is another at Amezraï, by the perched *agadir* a kilometre to Agoudim's north.

A topographical guide, *Randonnées Péderstres dans le Massif du Mgoun*, is published in Morocco (and unobtainable anywhere else). While useful, the gorge explorations mentioned in it are highly dangerous scrambles rather than sedate walks, and the text should be treated with caution.

Hôtel es Saada, 129 Rue Tarik Ibn Ziad (☎02/348 2991). A cheap but clean place with helpful management; recently renovated; hot showers – and a hammam on the ground floor. With a laundry next door. ①.

Hôtel Tassamet, 186 Rue Ahmed El Hansali, in a recess of the street (☎02/342 1313). A modern hotel in the Old Medina, clean and welcoming with en-suite bathrooms and balconies in some rooms, and good views from front-facing rooms and from the roof terrace. ①.

Auberge Vieux Moulin, Av. Mohammed V (☎02/348 2788). This old-style French hotel, with rooms off a wide central corridor is still under French management, but has lost much of its charm of late. A reasonable fall-back, nonetheless. ②.

Hôtel des Voyageurs, Av. Mohammed V (☎02/348 2472). Along with the *Es Saada*, this was the best of the cheapies, backing on to the old Medina with stunning views from the rooftop terrace. At last check it was closed for renovation, but hopes to reopen soon. ①.

Hôtel Zidania, Av. des F.A.R. (☎/fax 02/348 1898, fax 348 1898). The best – and cheapest – of a trio of hotels facing the bus station. All rooms en suite. ①.

Eating

For **meals**, high-class options include the French-style restaurants of the *Auberge Vieux Moulin* (daily noon–2.30pm & 7.30–10pm; moderate), specializing in steak and brochettes, with cold cuts for starters, and the *Hôtel de Paris* (daily10.30am–3pm & 6pm–midnight; moderate), which is popular with tour groups and offers self-service buffet as well as à la carte. Excellent Moroccan food at rather lower prices in the town centre can be had at the *Café Restaurant Tawda* on Avenue Mohammed V, opposite the kasbah (daily 5.30am–midnight; cheap), whose rabbit tajine with raisins and cinnamon takes some beating. Cheaper eats are to be had, as ever, in the Old Medina, where *Sandwich Noumidia* at 141 Rue Ahmed el Hansali (daily 10am–11pm; cheap) is the best of a trio of popular eateries doing roast chicken, brochettes and kefta kebabs. Another popular place offering more exotic fare such as liver and brain kebabs (as well as ordinary lamb and kefta ones, or chicken and chips) is *Chez Ben Souda* at 136 Avenue Mohammed V (daily noon–11pm; cheap).

The Cascades d'Ouzoud

The **Cascades d'Ouzoud** are the most spectacular in Morocco, with an unusual series of plunges from wide to narrow (usually it's the reverse), and magnificent pools for swimming in, all set in a lush valley invisible till the last moment. Cafés offering camping spots abound off good paths and, high summer apart, are never too busy. The atmosphere is laid-back and relaxing, and the site is at its best from March until mid-June, hot in summer. To maximize your visit, an overnight stop is recommended. To swim below or in the cascades by the light of the full moon is something special, and in late afternoon there are often arching rainbows to be seen.

Ouzoud lies 18km down a surfaced road off the S508 Marrakesh–Azilal road, 21km before Azilal. You could try your chances hitching from the turn-off, but you are safer going into Azilal, where there are regular grands taxis to the falls (12.50dh a place or 75dh for the whole taxi). Getting back to Azilal is generally no problem, with grands taxis regularly shuttling from the falls. From Beni Mellal, a grand taxi to the falls should cost around 360dh (60dh per person if you can fill it).

Bin El Ouidane and Azilal

On the way from Beni Mellal to Azilal, the road climbs almost straight up from the plain, zigzagging through the hills and crossing the immense **Bin el Ouidane reservoir**. This was one of the earliest (1948–55) and most ambitious of the country's irrigation schemes and has changed much of the land around Beni Mellal – formerly as dry and barren as the phosphate plains to the northwest. It also supplies much of central Morocco's electricity.

There's a small **hotel** beside the barrage, the *Hôtel du Lac* (☎02/344 2465, fax 344 2430; ③), which offers the choice of rooms in its main building, or camping by the river downstream of the dam. It has a bar, a restaurant, boats for hire, and fishing; swimming is prohibited. In winter, be warned, it is very cold up here – and, although the hotel has hot water, it has no room heating.

AZILAL, 27km further on, has the feel of a small village, with a garrison, banks, a Thursday souk and transport links; but it is now a provincial capital which explains a lot of new housing. It also explains why there is a **tourist office** on the main road (Rue Tarik Ibn Ziad), just west of the yard where buses and grands taxis drop you (☎02/345 8334), which will help you to contact mountain guides. One such is Rachid Boutafala, B.P. 58, Azilal (☎02/345 8784), who speaks French, Spanish and a little Dutch (his wife is Flemish). He knows best the Bou Guemez Valley, Oued Tessaout and Ighil Mgoun (see p.264).

If by any chance you need a **hotel** here, your best choice is the friendly and comfortable *Hôtel Tanoute,* a kilometre out of town on the Beni Mellal road (☎02/345 8778, fax 345 8281; ①–③), where the older, downstairs rooms without en-suite showers cost exactly the same as those in the cheap grotty places in town. Of the latter, there are three, all east of the bus yard: the *Tissa* (☎02/345 8589; ①), the *Ouzoud* (☎02/345 8482; ①) and the *Souss* (☎02/345 8114; ①), whose manager, Mustapha, has a degree in English. The brand new *Hôtel Assoufrou*, just west of the bus yard, (☎/fax 02/345 8442; ③) should also be open by the time you read this. Good places to eat are thin on the ground – the *Hôtel Tanoute* has a good restaurant, but only open in summer. There are two banks in town: the Banque Populaire, 100m east of the bus yard, and the Crédit Agricole, 200m west of it. Just beyond the Crédit Agricole, the PTT and Complexe Artesanal face each other across the main road.

Buses from Azilal serve Marrakesh three times daily, including a 5am departure to Agadir. There are also two buses to Casablanca, five to Beni Mellal (including CTM's at 10am, and two others via Afourer, with the remaining two skirting the north of the Bin el Ouidane reservoir via Ouaouizate). Only two daily buses serve Demnate. **Grands taxis**, from the same yard as the buses, mostly serve Beni Mellal, with some to the Cascades d'Ouzoud, though you may also be able to get one 45km westward to Tanant, and one from there to Demnate. The Bou Guemez is now reached by a new road with an irregular minibus service, usually leaving Azilal on Sunday, Tuesday and Thursday.

The Cascades

The **Cascades d'Ouzoud** are a popular place to camp in the summer, with both Moroccan and foreign tourists attracted by the falls and their unique ambience, though they are, as yet, refreshingly uncommercialized. At the head of the road, there is a small, friendly **hotel**, variously called *Mohammed's* or *Dar Essalam* (☎02/345 9657; ①), built around a courtyard with lime trees; you can rent rooms or sleep on the roof. A second hotel, the *Hôtel des Cascades* (☎02/345 9607; ①) has now opened a few minutes away along the row of cafés and stalls running off to the left – a path which, followed to its end, gives the most extensive view of the falls. Several further **cafés** are located on terraces along the way down to the falls, and most offer camping for a few tents, either for a small fee, or free if you eat at them during your stay. They tend to have a youthful, international clientele.

From the campsites, paths wind down to the valley and the great basins below the **cascades**. You can swim in one of these – a fabulous natural pool – and might spot the occasional Barbary ape under the oak and pomegranate trees. Your best chance of a sighting is at daybreak or an hour or so before dusk, when they come out to drink in the river. On the lip of the falls, there are some little sheds containing small, ancient **watermills**, some of which are still in use. The river is diverted through them, before plunging over the edge; worn grindstones litter the edge of the abyss.

A memorable short hike is to go beyond the lower pools to the so-called "Mexican village" (although some local guides prefer "Berber village"), a fascinating place connected by semi-underground passages. To get there, follow the path down to the lower pools and you will see a path climbing up on the left, past a farmhouse and up to the top of the plain. Follow this path west. The village is sited on the slopes of the wooded hills, about 1km along the path, which drops to a stream before climbing up to the houses.

On from Ouzoud

Continuing to Marrakesh from Ouzoud on local transport, it's easiest to backtrack to Azilal, picking up a bus there to Beni Mellal or (if you time it right) direct to Marrakesh. If you are driving, however, you could head down to KHEMIS-DES-OULAD on the Beni Mellal–Marrakesh road (P24); 17km of this 51km route is poor piste, passable only in dry weather.

Bou Guemez valley and Ighil Mgoun

The **Bou Guemez valley** ("*La Vallée Heureux*") is second only to Djebel Toubkal in popularity among mountain-lovers, not only for its own unique beauty, but also as a base

---

IGHIL MGOUN

Ighil Mgoun, at 4068m, is Morocco's only summit above four thousand metres outside the Toubkal massif, and a popular target for hillgoers, giving an easy but long ascent from a base on the Tessaout Sources/Tarkeddit plateau, itself most easily reached from the Bou Guemez valley. This remote spot is the start of the Oued Tessaout, which descends the spectacular Wandras gorge (climbing involved) and also the Arouss gorge (climbing) to the Bou Guemez and, eastwards then south, Mgoun drains out to Imi n'Wakka and Kelaal de Mgouna, 3–4 days including many hours of wading gorges (flash flood risk), easy but dramatic. **Tarkeddit** (3565m) gives excellent climbing on its traverse. West of 'Mgoun, two rarely-visited peaks of 3883m and 3877m, are the highest between 'Mgoun and the Toubkal area. Other peaks too make this a deservedly popular area. Several gîtes make walking in the Bou Guemez itself worthwhile, while east, between **Azurki** (3677m) and **Ouaougoulzat** (3763m), both skiers' objectives in winter, is the seasonal **Lac Izoughar** (Izourar), beyond which lies the vast nomad plateaux and gorges between Zaouia Ahancal and the Dadès (see p.264).

THE TESSAOUT VALLEY
Demnate is the gateway into the **Tessaout valley**, and to **Imi n'Waka** and **Tarbat n'Tirsal**, below vast Djebel Rhat and near Tizi n'Tighist, with the finest area of **rock carvings** in Morocco (and the continuation to the Bou Willi/Bou Guemez valleys). From the Tuesday souk at **Aït Tamlil**, the **Oued Tessaout** gives high-class trekking to its source under Mgoun. **Djebel Rhat** (3781m) and **Djebel Tignousti** (3891m) to the north, and a whole crest of peaks to the south, are all worth climbing. Passes south from **Toufghine/Aït Tamlil** (accessible by piste), **Magdaz** (the most beautiful village in the Atlas, now also accessible by piste) and **Amezri** (reached by piste from the south) allow exits to the south, piste routes covered by a daily truck except from Magdaz (mule pass only). From Aït Tamlil, trekking links can also be made to Telouet (see p.407), either north or south of Djebel Anghomar (3610m).

for **Ighil Mgoun** (4068m), the highest summit in Morocco outside the Toubkal massif (see box opposite). There are also some astonishing gorges and passes on the southward trek through the mountains to exit via Kelaal de Mgouna.

A new road, turning off near Aït Mhammed and tarmacked for half its length, gives access to the lower end of the Bou Guemez and Bou Willi valleys. Most visitors arrive by Landrover from Marrakesh, but an irregular minibus service operates from Azilal (see opposite), and more infrequently from Aït Mhammed via the old piste, which enters over an eastern pass that is often blocked in winter. Recommended for trekkers is the two-day walk in from Aït Mhammed via the pretty hamlet of **SREMPT** (with a gîte, run by Sabre Brahim), and the **Tizi n'Aït Ouriat** (2606m) with its great views of the mountain ranges. Another possible approach is via Demnate (see overleaf) from where trucks go on to the road-end at **Imi n'Wakka** (Tabat n'Tirsal) under the bulk of Djebel Rhat. There is a spectacular trek of several days down the Bou Willi valley to connect with the Bou Guemez. On the **Tizi n'Tirghyst** (2390m) are prehistoric rock-carved pictures.

A longer circuit goes round the west flank of **Djebel Rhab** (3797m) and **Djebel Tignousti** (3820m) to reach the **Oued Tessaout** which is followed to its head under Ighil Mgoun whence the Bou Guemez can be regained. East from the Bou Guemez is the seasonal lake of **Izoughar**, dominated by Djebel Azourki and other big hills. A *tizi* leads to Arouadane and the Zaouia Ahanesal area of spectacular gorges. **Agoudim**, a village of remarkable architecture has several gîtes (1km south of Zaouia Ahanesal) as has **Taghia** which faces the finest gorge and cliff scenery in the country, a rock-climbers' playground of Dolomitic scope. There are many other treks, peaks, climbs and gorges of note, well covered in Peyron (see p.33), and making use of local experts is highly recommended.

Several of the Bou Guemez valley villages have gîte accommodation, meals and mule hire (see lists in the ONMT Atlas guide). Mohammed Achari (Donar Iskattefen, Aït Bou Guemez, Bureau Tabant, par Azilal, ☎02/345 9327) is a mountain guide of wide experience who has helped many British parties, and offers a full range of services, including Landrover rental.

Azilal to Marrakesh: Demnate

Having come as far as Azilal and the cascades, it is easier to continue along the S508 road to Marrakesh rather than try and cut back onto the main road from Beni Mellal. It is in any case the more interesting route.

Demnate

You may have to change buses along the way at **DEMNATE**, a walled market town, with a Glaoui-era kasbah, an old Mellah (half the population were Jews until the 1950s), and a **Sunday souk**. The souk is by far the largest in the region and an interesting, unaffected event worth trying to coincide with. It is held just outside the ramparts, the stalls spreading out into the town streets with their used clothes and other goods, together with enormous stacks of fresh produce.

The surrounding area is well known for its **olives** and attractive glazed **pottery** which is made at out-of-town Bougrhat – also worth a visit. Another trip, if you have time and transport, is to follow the road up above the town to a curious-looking natural bridge – **Imi n'Ifri** (around 6.5km from Demnate). It spans a yawning gorge, the result of the partial collapse of an underground cave system. Those of a vertiginous disposition should stay away from the edge. There's a seasonal restaurant and you can sit outside and watch the iridescent choughs and little swifts, with their white rumps and square tails, ever-wheeling in pursuit of insects; it's also a good spot to look for *sibsib* (ground squirrels – see p.514) playing on the roadside walls above the gorge. Close by is a series of springs, which account for the Demnate valley's prosperous and intense cultivation, this is the site of a large moussem held two weeks after the Aïd El Kebir.

Demnate sees few tourists and makes for a relaxed stopover. Buses will drop you just inside Bab el 'Arabi (the Gate of the Arabs). The PTT is just by the gate, with a Banque Populaire close at hand. For **accommodation**, you can choose between three basic but extremely cheap (and identically priced) establishments: the *Hôtel Iminifri*, just inside the gate (no phone; ①), the *Hôtel-Café Ettaoufik* across the street and next to the PTT (no phone; ①), and the friendly and slightly better *Hôtel Ouzoud* (☎04/445 6087; ①), which is outside the gate and 150m further down the street on the left. Mountain **guides** can be contacted through the Iminifri, or via the Bureau des Guides (out of the gate and 2km further down the main road on the right; ☎04/445 6084).

Demnate to Marrakesh

The land between Demnate and Marrakesh is generally poor and rocky, distinguished only by sporadic clusters of farmhouses or shepherds' huts. If you take the bus, it might follow either of the routes to Marrakesh – the S508 via Tamelelt (where you rejoin the P24) or the well-paved 6206 road via Tazzerte and Sidi Rahhal.

Given the choice, go for the latter. An old Glaoui village, **TAZZERTE** has four crumbling kasbahs, off the road, from which the clan (see Telouet, p.408) used to control the region and the caravan routes to the north. There is a small Monday market held here, and a larger one on Fridays at Sidi Rahhal, 7km further down.

SIDI RAHHAL, named after a fifteenth-century marabout, is also a point of significant local pilgrimage and host to a small, but important, moussem held at the time of Aïd El Kebir. The saint in whose honour the festivities take place has an unusual Judeo-Muslim tradition, and a multitude of stories told about him. All are timeless in their evocations of magic and legend. The most popular ones recount how he had the power to conduct himself and other creatures through the air – a "talent" which led to a minor incident involving the Koutoubia minaret in Marrakesh, whose upper storey one of his followers is supposed to have knocked down with his knee. His favours are sought by the mentally ill and their families.

Coming into Marrakesh from either Demnate or Beni Mellal, you skirt part of the huge **palmery** which encloses the northern walls of the city. Arriving by bus, you will almost certainly find yourself at the main **bus station** by Bab Doukkala – a ten-minute walk from the centre of Gueliz (or the Ville Nouvelle), or twenty minutes (or an 8–10dh taxi ride) from Place Djemaa El Fna and the Medina.

Trains

travel details

Fes to: Casablanca (8 daily; 4hr 10min); Kenitra (8 daily; 2hr 50min); Marrakesh (5 direct and 1 connecting daily; 10hr); Meknes (9 daily; 50min); Oujda (4 daily; 5hr 15min); Rabat (8 daily; 3hr 30min); Tangier (1 direct and 3 connecting daily; 5hr 10min); Taza (4 daily; 2hr).

Meknes to: Casablanca (8 daily; 3hr 20min); Fes (9 daily; 55min); Kenitra (8 daily; 2hr); Marrakesh (5 direct and 1 connecting daily; 9hr 10min); Oujda (4 daily; 6hr 30min); Rabat (8 daily; 2hr 40min); Tangier (1 direct and 3 connecting daily; 4hr 20min); Taza (4 daily; 3hr 10min).

Buses

Azilal to: Afourer (3 daily; 40min); Agadir (1 daily; 7hr); Beni Mellal (5 daily; 1hr 30min); Casablanca (2 daily; 5hr); Demnate (2 daily; 1hr); Marrakesh (3 daily; 3hr); Ouaouizate (2 daily; 1hr).

Azrou to: Agadir (1 daily; 13hr); Aïn Leuh (1 daily; 40min); Beni Mellal (8 daily; 5hr); Casablanca (3 daily; 5hr 30min); Fes (16 daily; 1hr 30min) via Ifrane (20min) and Immouzer (45min); Khenifra (25 daily; 1hr 40min); Marrakesh (3 daily; 9hr); Meknes (18 daily; 1hr); Midelt (18 daily; 3hr); Rabat (5 daily; 4hr); Er Rachidia (14 daily; 6hr);

Rissani (1 daily; 9hr); Tangier (1 daily; 8hr); Tetouan (2 daily; 7hr).

Beni Mellal to: Agadir (1 CTM and 6 others daily; 8hr); Azilal (1 CTM and 4 others daily; 1hr 30min); Azrou (8 daily; 5hr); Casablanca (3 CTM and over 40 others daily; 3hr 30min); Demnate (4 daily; 3hr); Essaouira (1 daily; 6hr); Marrakesh (2 CTM and some 30 others daily; 4hr); Fes (3 CTM and 9 others daily; 6hr); El Jadida (2 daily; 5hr 30min); Midelt (2 CTM and 3 others daily; 4hr 30min); Rabat (1 CTM and 9 others daily; 2hr 30min); Er Rachidia (1 CTM and 1 other daily; 6hr); Safi (2 daily; 6hr).

Demnate to: Azilal (2 daily; 1hr); Marrakesh (9 daily; 1hr 30min).

Fes to: Agadir (1 CTM and 4 others daily; 12hr); Azrou (16 daily; 1hr 30min); Beni Mellal (3 CTM and 9 others daily; 6hr); Casablanca (10 CTM and 24 others daily; 5hr 30min) via Rabat (4hr); Chaouen (2 CTM and 8 others daily; 5hr); Al Hoceima (2 CTM and 6 others daily; 5hr); Ifrane (16 daily; 1hr 30min); Immouzer (hourly; 45min); Khenifra (3 CTM and 12 others daily; 4hr); Marrakesh (3 CTM and 12 others daily; 10hr) via Beni Mellal (7hr); Meknes (8 CTM daily and others hourly 7am–7pm; 50min); Midelt (7 daily; 5hr 30min); Moulay Yacoub (roughly hourly; 30min); Nador (2 CTM and 17 others daily; 5hr 30min); Oujda (2 CTM and 18 others daily; 5hr 30min); Er Rachidia (2 CTM and 7 others daily; 8hr 30min); Rissani (2 CTM and 5 others daily; 10hr 30min); Sefrou (17 daily; 30min); Tangier (3 CTM and 7 others daily; 5hr 45min); Taza (4 CTM daily and others roughly hourly; 2hr 30min); Tetouan (3 CTM and 12 others daily; 5hr 20min).

Kasbah Tadla to: Beni Mellal (4 daily; 1hr); El Ksiba (3 daily; 20min); Fes (13 daily; 5hr 30min); Midelt (3 daily; 4hr).

Meknes to: Agadir (1 CTM and 2 others daily; 12hr); Azrou (18 daily; 1hr) Beni Mellal (6 daily; 6hr); Casablanca (10 CTM and 7 others daily; 4hr 30min); Azrou (2 CTM and 16 others daily; 1hr 30min); Chaouen (5 daily; 5hr 30min); Fes (8 CTM daily and others hourly 7am–7pm; 50min); Al Hoceima (2 CTM and 1 other daily; 6hr); Larache (12 daily; 5hr 30min); Marrakesh (8 daily; 9hr); Midelt (2 CTM and 12 others daily; 5hr 30min); Nador (2 CTM and 5 others daily; 6hr 30min); Ouezzane (7 daily; 4hr); Oujda (3 CTM and 15 others daily; 6hr 30min); Rabat (7 CTM and 15 others

daily; 3hr); Er Rachidia (1 CTM and 4 others daily; 8hr 30min); Rissani (1 CTM and 1 other daily; 10hr 30min); Tangier (3 CTM and 7 others daily; 7hr); Tan Tan (1 daily; 21hr 30min); Taza (2 CTM and 9 others daily; 3hr 15min); Tetouan (2 CTM and 7 others daily; 7hr).

Midelt to: Azrou (18 daily; 3hr); Beni Mellal (5 daily; 4hr 30min); Casablanca (4 daily; 8hr); Khenifra (2 daily; 3hr); Meknes (14 daily; 5hr 30min); Nador (2 daily; 6hr); Oujda (1 daily; 13hr); Rabat (5 daily; 7hr); Er Rachidia (18 daily; 3hr); Rissani (7 daily; 6hr).

Grands Taxis

Azilal to: Beni Mellal (1hr) and the Cascades d'Ouzoud (40min).

Azrou to: Aïn Leuh (20min); Midelt (2hr 30min); Meknes (45min); Ifrane (20min); Fes (1hr 30min); and occasionally Khenifra (1hr 30min) and Beni Mellal (3hr 30min).

Beni Mellal to: Azrou (3hr 30min); Azilal (1hr); Kasbah Tadla (40min) and Khenifra (2hr).

Fes to: Azrou (1hr 30min); Casablanca (3hr 30min); Ifrane (1hr); Immouzer (40min); Meknes (40min); Moulay Yacoub (30min); Rabat (2hr 30min); Sefrou (30min); Sidi Harazem (30min); Taounate (1hr); and Taza (1hr 15min).

Ifrane to: Fes (1hr); Azrou (20min); Immouzer (30min); and occasionally Meknes (1hr).

Imouzzer du Kandar to: Azrou (45min); Ifrane (30min); Fes (40min) and Sefrou (40min).

Kasbah Tadla to: Beni Mellal (40min); El Ksiba (30min); and Zaouiet ech Cheikh (40min).

Khenifra to: Beni Mellal (2hr); Zaouiet ech Cheikh (40min); "Trente Trois" (15min); Midelt (2hr 30min); and occasionally Er Rachidia (4hr 30min).

Meknes to: Azrou (45min); Fes (40min); Ouezzane (2hr 30min); Kenitra (1hr 30min); Khenifra (1hr 30min); Moulay Idriss (35min); and Sidi Slimane (1hr).

Midelt to: Azrou (2hr 30min); Fes (4hr); Meknes (4hr); Zeida (20min); "Trente Trois" (2hr 15min); Khenifra (2hr 30min); and Er Rachidia (2hr).

Zaouiet ech Cheikh to: Khenifra (40min); El Ksiba (20min); and Kasbah Tadla (40min).

Flights

Fes to: Al Hoceima (weekly summer; 40min); Casablanca (1–3 daily; 45min).

CHAPTER FOUR

THE WEST COAST: FROM RABAT TO ESSAOUIRA

This chapter takes in almost five hundred kilometres of Atlantic coastline, from Kenitra in the north to the popular resort of Essaouira in the south, and ranges through long stretches of scarcely developed lagoons and sands to Morocco's urban heartland. This latter comprises the cities of Rabat and Casablanca – the respective seats of government and of industry and commerce – and the neighbouring towns of Kenitra, Salé (alongside Rabat) and Mohammedia (alongside Casablanca). Together, these have a population of around five million – close on a fifth of the country's total. It's an astonishingly recent growth along what was, until the French Protectorate, a neglected strip of coast. At the turn of the last century, Rabat was a straggling port with a population of 30,000 (today it's 900,000), while Casablanca (modern population 3,500,000), had just 20,000 inhabitants. In Morocco now, the bulk of new investment is in the Casablanca and Kenitra areas – and around Settat, 68km from Casablanca, on the road to Marrakesh.

Inevitably, it is French and post-colonial influences that are dominant in the main coastal cities. Don't go to **Casa** – as Casablanca is popularly known – expecting some exotic movie location; it's a modern city that looks very much like Marseilles. **Rabat**, too, which the French developed as a capital in place of the old imperial centres of Fes and Marrakesh, looks markedly European, with its cafés and boulevards, though it also has some of Morocco's finest and oldest monuments, dating from the Almohad and Merenid dynasties. If you're on a first trip to Morocco, Rabat is an ideal place to get to grips with the country. Its westernized streets make an easy cultural shift and it's an excellent transport hub, well connected by train with Tangier, Fes and Marrakesh. Casa is maybe more interesting after you've spent a while in the country, when you'll appreciate both its differences and its fundamentally Moroccan character.

South along the coast, populations and towns thin out, as the road skirts a series of beaches and dunes, with the odd detour inland when cliffs take hold. **El Jadida**, established as a beach resort by the French, now fulfils the same function for middle-class Casablanca. **Oualidia**, to its south, has a similar, though rather more relaxed and small-scale style. **Safi**, between Oualidia and Essaouira, is a predominantly industrial town, but a friendly place, with some excellent beaches nearby.

Finally, there is **Essaouira**, which is also easily accessible from Marrakesh, and is, to put it simply, Morocco's most enjoyable resort. A beautiful walled town, with an active fishing port, long sandy beaches and a very relaxed feel, its only drawback is the wind, which can blow incessantly in spring and early summer (September to November is the best time to visit). However, even this wind has been used to help promote the town as Morocco's chief windsurfing resort.

Kenitra and the coast to Rabat

Travelling to Rabat from Tangier or Fes, you will bypass the stretch of coast around **Kenitra** – which for the most part is no great loss. Kenitra is a dull little town, and its waterfront at **Mehdiya** is scruffy and unattractive. Further south, however, there are pleasant detours (if you have transport) to the **Plage des Nations** – Rabat's local beach resort – and to the botanical extravagance of the **Jardins Exotiques**; if you're dependent on buses, these can be visited as a day-trip from the capital. **Bird-watchers** may also want to explore the **Lac de Sidi Bourhaba**, near Mehdiya, which has protected status due to its notable birds of prey.

Kenitra and Mehdiya

KENITRA was established by the French as Port Lyautey – named after the Resident General – with the intention of channelling trade from Fes and Meknes. It never quite took off, however, losing out in industry and port activities to Casablanca, despite the rich farming areas of its hinterland. It has a population today of around 300,000, employed mainly in paper mills and a fish cannery. Until recently, additional income was provided by a large naval and military base, shared with the US, but the Americans left after the Gulf War, and the Moroccans have scaled down their own operations. A rather sad array of bars, pizza joints and discos struggle along in their wake.

Orientation is straightforward, with a long main street, **Avenue Mohammed V/Avenue Mohammed Diouri** – running from the main train station (at one end of town) to the bus station (at the other) by way of the central **Place Administrative**. It's about a fifteen-minute walk from the square to either bus or main train station, known as Gare de Ville or simply as Kenitra to differentiate it from the smaller station known as Kenitra Medina which, coming from Tangier or Fes/Meknes, is always the first stop.

The town has a dozen or so **hotels** and a good campsite. For **food**, besides the hotel restaurants noted below, there are two other good ones; *Restaurant Chez Ouidad*, 52 Rue de la Mamora, is owned by someone who spent fourteen years in Belgium learning his trade and serves traditional dishes; and the more upmarket *Champs Elysée*, 48 Rue Moulay Abdellah, serving generous portions of paella.

If you're looking for **nightlife**, try the area around the triangular garden, at the junction of Avenue Mohammed V, Avenue Mohammed Diouri and the pedestrianized Rue Reine Elizabeth. Look for *Mama's Club, Le Village* nightclub/discotheque, and *007*. Don't expect too much.

Accommodation

Hôtel Ambassy, 20 Av. Hassan II (☎03/737 9978, fax 03/737 7420). Comfortable and central; there is a bar and billiards. The restaurant, *Le Turbot*, is not as good as the accommodation; better to eat elsewhere. The *Café Restaurant Ouazzani* next door is recommended. ④.

Hôtel de Commerce, 12 Rue Amira Aïcha (☎03/737 1503). A small hotel near the Hôtel de Ville. Simple, but adequate rooms with separate facilities on the corridor. Clean and well kept. ②.

Hôtel d'Europe, 63 Av. Mohammed Diouri (☎03/737 1450). An older hotel, opposite the *Hôtel La Rotonde*. En-suite rooms are dearer than those with separate facilities. Value for money, and the ground-floor café is good too. ④.

Hôtel Mamora, top end of Av. Hassan II, across the Place Administrative from the Hôtel de Ville (☎03/737 1310, fax 03/737 1446). Comfortable, with en-suite facilities, swimming pool and reasonable restaurant, albeit with limited menu. ④.

Hôtel de la Poste, 307 Av. Mohammed V (☎03/737 9982). Basic and cheap – but with hot showers in most rooms. Good value. ③.

Hôtel La Rotonde, 60 Av. Mohammed Diouri (☎ & fax 03/737 1401). Friendly, with recently restored decor and a good restaurant. Well placed for the remaining nightlife. ③.

Hôtel Safir, on the Place Administrative (☎03/737 1921, fax 03/737 1926). Top of the market, with swimming pool, but business types prefer the *Hôtel Mamora* across the way. Ask for a room at the back, overlooking the pool. ⑤.

Camping La Chenaie, on the edge of town (☎03/736 3001). As you approach from Rabat look for signs to the left to the *Complexe Touristique*. There's tennis, swimming pool and a new football stadium. The campsite is good, inexpensive and secure.

Mehdiya

MEHDIYA PLAGE, Kenitra's beach, 11km to the west, is a dull, greyish strip with a few houses and chalets, intermittent beach cafés and plenty of day visitors in summer. It's easily reached by grand taxi (these leave Kenitra from Avenue Mohammed Diouri), but if you're after a spot to break a journey and swim, you'd be better off at the more relaxed Plage des Nations, to the south.

The road from Kenitra to Mehdiya Plage runs along the left bank of the estuary of the Oued Sebou, passing first the large **fish cannery** and then continuing along below

---

BIRD-WATCHING AT LAC DU SIDI BOURHABA

Lac du Sidi Bourhaba, just inland from Mehdiya, is a long, narrow freshwater lake, divided by a central causeway. The best viewing points for its rich birdlife are on the causeway, where the ever-present damselflies and dragonflies provide a spectacular display of flight and colour. Marsh frogs and Berber toad also make their vocal contribution from the sanctuary of the northern reedbeds.

The **birdlife** of Sidi Bourhaba is outstanding. The reedbeds throng with the calls of flitting reed and melodious warbler and the open stretches of water hold good numbers of crested coot (in spring) and marbled teal (in autumn and winter). It is, however, for its birds of prey that the site is best known. Circling almost constantly overhead are **marsh harriers**, with their characteristic low quartering flight, and these are joined on occasion by the smaller and whiter black-shouldered **kite** with its diagnostic black shoulders (and red eyes if you get close enough). In winter, look for the **European hobby**, **greater flamingo** and, at any time, **wading godwits**. At sunset you may also see the **African marsh owl**.

In early spring, you will find wild crocuses, marigolds and white broom.

Mehdiya's ruined **kasbah**. Overlooking the estuary, this was built by the Portuguese, extended by the Spanish, demolished and then restored by Moulay Ismail and, finally, knocked about in the course of US troop landings in World War II (see box on p.307); it shelters the remains of a seventeenth-century governor's palace.

The only year-round accommodation is the *Complexe Belle Vue* (☎03/738 8366) on the corniche road below the fort, which has a fish restaurant, bar and Khaima nightclub. The other option, if you decide to stay, is to take up the offers of a room with a family; otherwise stay in Kenitra and travel out daily.

A couple of kilometres inland is the birdlife-rich **Lac du Sidi Bourhaba** (see opposite), flanked by a koubba that is the site of an August **moussem**.

The Plage des Nations and Jardins Exotiques

The Plage des Nations (22km from Kenitra) and Jardins Exotiques (6km further on) are easily visited if you are driving the coast road between Kenitra and Rabat. If you don't have transport, they could be taken in as a day-trip from Rabat. In summer, there are regular grands taxis to the beach from Rabat's satellite town of Salé, as well as a local bus (#28; every 20min from the Bab Khemis terminal in Salé), which runs past the gardens and on to the turn-off to the beach. Alternatively, you could charter a taxi from Rabat (or Kenitra) to take you out to the gardens and/or beach, and back.

Plage des Nations
The **Plage des Nations**, or Sidi Bouknadel as it's sometimes known, was named after the foreign diplomats and their families who started swimming there – and continue to do so. Unlike the capital's Kasbah or Salé beaches, it has a very relaxed, friendly and cosmopolitan feel about it and is unusual in that young Moroccan women feel able to come out here for the day. The beach itself is excellent, with big, exciting waves – but dangerous currents, and is patrolled by lifeguards along the central strip. It's flanked by a couple of beach cafés and the modern *Hôtel Firdaous* (☎03/782 2131, fax 03/782 2143; ⑤), which has a swimming pool open to all for a small charge, plus a snack bar and two restaurants.

The beach lies 2km off the P2 coast road, reached along a surfaced track. On the main road, directly opposite the turn-off, is an old villa recently opened as the **Museé Dar Beghazi**, named after its enterprising Fassi owner (☎03/782 2178; daily 8am–5pm; 50dh). It has a fine collection of Andalucian and Islamic art, carpets, woodwork, armour, jewellery – and a coach, and, as one of the few private collections on display in Morocco, merits a diversion.

If you take the #28 bus from Salé to Plage des Nations, be aware that it turns round a couple of kilometres before the beach turn-off, just after the village of Bouknadel. Most passengers get out here and head left for the beach: a forty-minute walk along a path that heads off diagonally towards the sea, past market gardens, round some woods and then joins the final stretch of the road.

Jardins Exotiques
The **Jardins Exotiques** were laid out by one M. François in the early 1950s, in what contemporary French guidebooks called "une manière remarquable". They fell into something of a decline in the 1980s but have recently been taken over by the Ministry of the Interior, whose gardeners have been assiduously renovating the various original creations. If you can visit the gardens in spring or early summer, they are a delight.

Entering the gardens (daily 9am–6pm; 10dh admission), you find yourself directed across a series of precarious bamboo bridges and dot-directed routes through a sequence of regional creations. There is a **Brazilian rain forest**, dense with water and orchids; a formal **Japanese garden**; and then suddenly a great shaft of **French**

Polynesia, with rickety summerhouses set amid long pools, turtles paddling past, palm trees all round and flashes of bright-red flowers. The last of the series, returning to a more local level, is an **Andalucian garden** with a fine collection of Moroccan plants. There is, as yet, no café nor leaflet/booklet; a missed opportunity.

Rabat

Capital of the nation since independence – and, before that, from 1912 to 1956, of the French Protectorate – **RABAT** is in many ways the city you'd expect: elegant in its spacious European grid, slightly self-conscious in its civilized modern ways, and, as an administrative centre, a little bit dull. If you arrive during Ramadan, you'll find the main avenues and boulevards an astonishing night-long promenade – at other times, it's hard to find a café open past ten at night. Rabat, as they tell you in Casa, is provincial.

None of this makes any difference to the considerable historic and architectural interest in the city – and across the estuary in **Salé**– which includes some of the finest and oldest Arab monuments in the country, dating from the Almohad and Merenid dynasties. You can spend an enjoyable few days looking round these, and out on the local beaches, and there is a major plus in that, unlike Fes or Marrakesh, you can get round the place quite happily without a guide, and talk in cafés with people who do not depend on tourist money.

Some history

Rabat's **monuments** punctuate the span of Moroccan history. The plains inland, designated *Maroc Utile* by the French, have been occupied and cultivated since Paleolithic times, and there were Neolithic settlements on the coast south of Rabat, notably at present-day Temara and Skhirat.

Both Phoenicians and Carthaginians established trading posts on modern-day Rabat's estuary site. The earliest known settlement, Sala, occupied the citadel known today as **Chellah**. Here, after the demise of the Carthaginians, the **Romans** created their southernmost colony. It lasted well beyond the break up of the empire in Africa and eventually formed the basis of an independent Berber state, which reached its peak of influence in the eighth century, developing a code of government inspired by the Koran but adapted to Berber customs and needs. It represented a challenge to the Islamic orthodoxy of the **Arab** rulers of the interior, however, and to stamp out the heresy, a *ribat* – the fortified monastery from which the city takes its name – was founded on the site of the present-day kasbah.

The *ribat's* activities led to Chellah's decline – a process hastened in the eleventh century by the founding of a new town, **Salé**, across the estuary. But with the arrival of the **Almohads** in the twelfth century, the Rabat Kasbah was rebuilt and a city again took shape around it. The Almohad fort, renamed **Ribat El Fathi** (Stronghold of Victory), served as a launching point for the dynasty's campaigns in Spain, which by 1170 had returned virtually all of Andalucia to Muslim rule.

Under the Almohad Caliph **Yacoub El Mansour**, a new Imperial Capital was created. Its legacy includes the superb **Oudaïa Gate** of the kasbah, **Bab Er Rouah** at the southwest edge of town, and the early stages of the **Hassan Mosque**. Until recent years, this was the largest ever undertaken in Morocco and its minaret, standing high above the river, is still the city's great landmark. Mansour also erected over five kilometres of fortifications – but neither his vision nor his success in maintaining a Spanish empire was to be lasting. He left the Hassan Mosque unfinished, and only in the last sixty years has the city expanded to fill his dark circuit of *pisé* walls.

After Mansour's death, Rabat's significance was dwarfed by the imperial cities of Fes, Meknes and Marrakesh, and the city fell into neglect. Sacked by the Portuguese, it was little more than a village when, as New Salé, it was resettled by seventeenth-century Andalucian refugees. In this revived form, however, it entered into an extraordinary period of international piracy and local autonomy. Its corsair fleets, the **Sallee Rovers**, specialized in the plunder of merchant ships returning to Europe from West Africa and the Spanish Americas, but on occasion raided as far afield as Plymouth and the Irish coast – Daniel Defoe's Robinson Crusoe began his captivity "carry'd prisoner into Sallee, a Moorish port".

The Andalucians, owing no loyalty to the Moorish sultans and practically impregnable within their kasbah perched high on a rocky bluff above the river, established their own pirate state, the **Republic of the Bou Regreg**. They rebuilt the Medina below the kasbah in a style reminiscent of their homes in Spanish Badajoz, dealt in arms with the English and French, and even accepted European consuls, before the town finally reverted to government control under Moulay Rashid, and his successor, Moulay Ismail. Unofficial piracy continued until 1829 when Austria took revenge for the loss of a ship by shelling Rabat and other coastal towns. From then until the French creation of a capital, Rabat-Salé was very much a backwater.

Arrival

Arriving by **train**, **Rabat Ville** station is at the heart of the Ville Nouvelle, with many hotels within a few minutes' walk. All trains stop here and its new escalators make access to and from the platforms hassle-free, while on the concourse there is a BMCE branch, a Budget car rental desk (☎03/770 5789) and a Tourisme kiosk which can help with train times but little else. **Rabat Agdal** station serves the southern suburbs and the Royal Palace; the royal train is occasionally seen here in a siding. **Salé** station serves Salé to the north of the estuary, with a relatively new station, **Salé Tabriquet**, serving the northern quarters of the town, but unlikely to attract many visitors.

The main **bus terminal** is located in Place Zerktouni – 3km out from the centre by the road junction for Casa and Beni Mellal. To get into town from here (or vice versa), you'll have to take a local bus (#30 and others stop along Boulevard Hassan II by the *Hôtel Majestic*) or compete for a petit taxi (6dh or so – usually metered – for up to three people). Easier, if you are coming by bus from the north, is to get off in **Salé** (see p.292) and take a grand taxi from there into Rabat; the distance is no greater than staying on the bus until the main bus terminal and then returning to the town centre by local bus or petit taxi. Experienced travellers, with little or no luggage, advocate splitting the difference by asking the bus driver to stop on the dual carriageway between the Kasbah des Oudaïas and the Medina, and then walking through the latter to Boulevard Hassan II and the Ville Nouvelle.

Grands taxis from non-local destinations operate from outside the main bus station (see above).

Mohammed V Airport is out beyond Casablanca and a dozen trains a day run to and from the airport and **Casablanca Voyageurs** station. From there, it's best to take another train to Rabat; the full fare from the airport to Rabat is 52dh. See "Travel Details", p.340 for further information.

Orientation, information and city transport

With its **Medina** and **Ville Nouvelle** bounded by the river and Almohad walls, central Rabat never feels like a big city, and indeed all the city's points of interest are within easy walking distance.

The most helpful **tourist office** is in Agdal, on the corner of Avenue Al Abtal and Rue Oued Fes (☎03/777 5171); bus #3 drops you opposite the tourist office, which has had a crashed car sitting on its front lawn for some years. The receptionist at the side

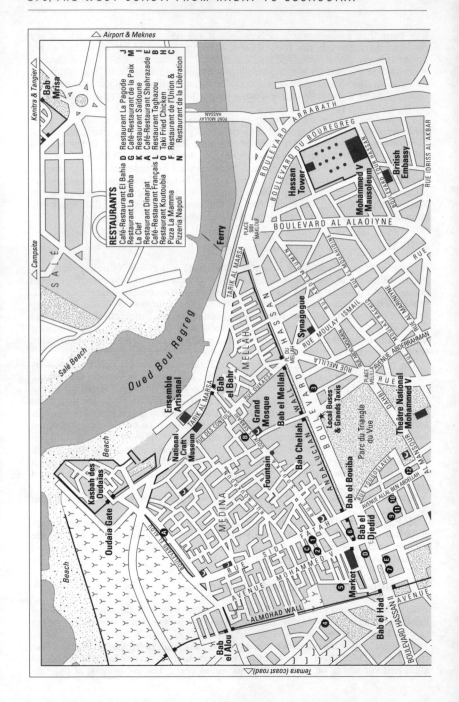

△ Airport & Meknes

RESTAURANTS

Café-Restaurant El Bahia | D
Restaurant La Bamba | G
La Clef | K
Restaurant Dinarjat | I
Café-Restaurant Français | A
Restaurant Koutoubia | O
Pizza La Mamma | L
Pizzeria Napoli | F

Restaurant La Pagode | J
Café-Restaurant de la Paix | M
Restaurant Saïdoune | I
Café-Restaurant Shahrazade | E
Restaurant Taghazou | B
Taki Fried Chicken | H
Restaurant de l'Union & | C
Restaurant de la Libération | N

△ Airport & Meknes

RABAT

Chellah

American Embassy

Algerian Embassy

French Embassy

Bab Zaer

American Bookstore

British Council

Division de la Cartographie

Archeological Museum

Grand Mosque

Cathedral

Flower Market

RAM

MECHOUAR

Rabat Ville Train Station

English Bookshop

Bab er Rouah

Royal Palace

PTT

ALMOHAD WALL

ACCOMMODATION

Auberge de Jeunesse (Youth Hostel)	4
Hôtel Balima	14
Hôtel Bélère	19
Hôtel Berlin	9
Hôtel Bouregreg	3
Hôtel Central	13
Hôtel Chellah	20
Hôtel Dorhmi	6
France Hôtel	5
Hôtel Gaulois	8
Ibis Moussafir	21
Hôtel Al Maghrib Al Jadid	2
Hôtel Ma estic	7
Hôtel Ma liss	16
Hôtel Ma rakesh	1
Hôtel d'O say	18
Hôtel la Paix	10
Royal Hôtel	12
Splendid Hôtel	11
Hôtel Terminus	17
Hôtel Velleda	15

0   200m

entrance has brochures and maps; outside and to the right is the underground car park; ask at the office on the left about free posters to take home; a mixture of charm and perseverance often works.

Local bus services radiate out from Boulevard Hassan II. Buses #1, #2 and #4 run from here (via Avenue Allal Ben Abdallah) to Bab Zaer and close to Chellah; #6 and #12 cross the bridge to Salé; and #17 heads south to Temara Beach.

Petits and **grands taxis** can be found on Boulevard Hassan II and by the train station. Note that petits taxis are not allowed to run between Rabat and Salé.

Accommodation

Hotel space can be tight in midsummer, and especially in July, when budget-priced rooms in particular are at a premium. It's best, if at all possible, to make an advance reservation by phone. A couple of cheapies aside, all of the better hotels are to be found in the Ville Nouvelle and there's little to gain here from staying in the Medina, which is in any case only a stroll across the boulevard. The nearest **campsite** is across the river at **Salé**; see p.292.

Ville Nouvelle Hotels

Most of the Ville Nouvelle hotels are modest, French-built places. If your budget is limited, go for one of these as the four- and five-star hotels are mostly standard chain efforts, and there are better splurges elsewhere.

CHEAP

Auberge de Jeunesse (Youth Hostel), 43 Rue Marrassa (☎ & fax, 03/772 5769). Conveniently sited, just west of the Almohad walls of the Medina and to the north of Bd. Hassan II. It's pleasant, clean and well furnished, with a redecorated courtyard. IYHF card preferred and strict opening hours: 8–10am, noon–3pm and 6–10.30pm. Despite the 'cook pot' symbol in the IYHF guide, there are no self-catering facilities. ①.

Hôtel Berlin, 261 Av. Mohammed V (☎03/770 3435). A small nine-room establishment, with hot showers; located above the Chinese *Restaurant Hong Kong*. Central, and value for money. ①.

Hôtel Central, 2 Rue Al Basra (☎03/770 7356). Not to be confused with the *Hôtel du Centre* in the Medina (which is not recommended), this is one of the best cheapies in the city, located alongside the (prominent) *Hôtel Balima* on Av. Mohammed V – and thus convenient for restaurants, banks, the train station, and a nightcap at the *Balima* bar. There's also a pleasant café for breakfast, right next door. ②.

Hôtel Gaulois, corner of Rue Hims and Av. Mohammed V (☎03/772 3022, fax 773 8848). One of a cluster of budget hotels around the bottom end of Av. Mohammed V. The rooms do not live up to the spacious grand entrance, but are value for money, and you can pay a little more for a shower en suite. ②.

Hôtel Velleda, 106 Av. Allal Ben Abdallah (☎03/776 9531). A decent hotel near the train station, though not very easy to find, being tucked away on the fourth floor (there is a lift) above a dry cleaners/laundry. All rooms have showers and some have toilets as well. ②.

MODERATE

Hôtel Majestic, 121 Av. Hassan II (☎03/772 2997, fax 770 8856). This is a friendly old hotel with a faded charm, facing the Medina; it's often full, though, and you'll be lucky to find a room much after midday. There are good eating places nearby, including the next door *Café Restaurant Shahrazade*. ④.

Hôtel d'Orsay, 11 Av. Moulay Youssef, on Place de la Gare (☎03/770 1319, fax 770 8208). A change of owner signalled by a change of decor (and a sign which can be read from the nearby station), but it's still friendly, helpful and efficient, and convenient for the train station and numerous café-restaurants. It's very popular with Moroccan (and overseas) businessmen, so book ahead. ④.

Hôtel la Paix, 2 Rue Ghazza, on corner with Av. Allal Ben Abdallah (☎03/772 2926). A reasonably pleasant downtown standby; en-suite showers; breakfasts extra. ④.

Royal Hôtel, 1 Rue Amman, on corner with Av. Allal Ben Abdallah (☎03/772 1171, fax 772 5491). Across the road from the Royal Cinema; comfortable and reasonable rooms, the best of which overlook the attractive Parc du Triangle de Vue. ④.

Splendid Hôtel, 8 Rue Ghazza (☎03/772 3283, fax 772 3283). This nice old hotel has a sense of better days; the best rooms overlook a courtyard which the owner plans to landscape. Opposite, the *Café-Restaurant Ghazza* is good for breakfast and snacks. ③.

Hôtel Terminus, 384, Av. Mohammed V (☎03/770 0616, fax 770 1926). Round the corner from the *Hôtel d'Orsay* and a possible alternative if it's full. It's a large, featureless block, but the interior has been recently updated and it's now reasonable ④.

EXPENSIVE

Hôtel Balima, corner of Rue Jakarta and Av. Mohammed V (☎03/770 8625). This was once Rabat's top hotel but has been long overtaken by the competition. It has been refurbished recently and still has quite reasonable prices, not least for its suites. Thami El Glaoui, Pasha of Marrakesh, (see p.360) stayed in one of these on his visits to the city in the early 1950s. The open-air café between the hotel and the avenue is shaded and popular, and the bar is equally so. ④.

Hôtel Bélère, 33 Av. Moulay Youssef (☎ & fax 03/770 9801). Comfortable, air-conditioned tour-group hotel, well positioned for the train station. Rooms are OK but somewhat overpriced. ⑤.

Hôtel Bouregreg, corner of Rue Nador and Bd. Hassan II (☎03/772 4110, fax 773 4002). This centrally placed hotel, where the *Hôtel Rex* once stood, attracts tour groups and car rental visitors who appreciate the secure parking available. ⑤.

Hôtel Chellah, 2 Rue d'Ifni (☎03/770 1051, fax 770 6354). An upmarket tour-group hotel with comfortable rooms in a rather characterless block, some way out from the centre and sights. On the plus side, it has a good grill-restaurant, *Le Kanoun*. ⑤.

Ibis Moussafir, 32–34 Rue Abderrahmane El Ghafki/Place de la Gare Rabat Agdal (☎03/777 4919, fax 777 4903). Like all the Moussafir chain, this hotel is by a train station, which unfortunately means that everything of interest is a taxi ride away. ⑤.

Hôtel Majliss, 6 Rue Zahla (☎07/773 3726, fax 773 3731). A new de luxe hotel, overlooking the platforms of the Rabat Ville station. The more expensive rooms at the back have views over the roof of the parliament building to the Atlantic. ⑤.

Medina hotels

Hôtel Dorhmi, 313 Av. Mohammed V (☎03/772 3898). The best Medina choice – refurbished to a decent standard, and nicely positioned, just inside Bab El Djedid and above the pleasant *Café Essalam*. Competitive prices, though hot showers are extra. ②.

France Hôtel, 46 Souk Semarine (☎03/772 3457). At the far western end of the street by the market, this hotel has a bit of character, with a banana tree patio and terrace. Basic facilities, but friendly staff – and there are excellent public showers in the next street. ①.

Hôtel Al Maghrib Al Jadid, 2 Rue Sebbahi (☎03/773 2207, fax 720 2583). Corner hotel on a side road off Av. Mohammed V. A reasonable place, with hot showers extra. ①.

Hôtel Marrakesh, 10 Rue Sebbahi (☎03/772 7703, fax 720 2583). Another decent if basic pension, with cold showers, but good-sized rooms, and friendly staff. ①.

The Medina and souks

Rabat's **Medina** – all that there was of the city until the French arrived in 1912 – is a compact quarter, wedged on two sides by the sea and the river, on the others by the twelfth-century Almohad and seventeenth-century Andalucian walls. It's not the most interesting Medina in the country – open and orderly in comparison to those of Fes or Marrakesh, for example – but coming here from the adjacent avenues of the modern capital it remains a surprise. In appearance, the quarter is still essentially the town created by Andalucian Muslim refugees from Badajoz in Spain, and with these external features intact, its way of life seems remarkably at odds with the government business and cosmopolitanism of the Ville Nouvelle.

That this is possible – here and throughout the old cities of Morocco – is largely due to **Marshal Lyautey**, the first, and certainly the most sympathetic to the indigenous culture, of France's Resident Generals. Colonizing Algeria over the previous century, the French had destroyed most of the Arab towns, replacing their traditional structures (evolved through the needs of Islamic customs) with completely European plans. In Rabat, Lyautey found this system already under way, the builders tearing down parts of the Medina for the construction of a new town and administrative quarters. Realizing the aesthetic loss – and the inappropriateness of wholesale Europeanization – he ordered work to be halted and the Ville Nouvelle built outside the walls.

It was a precedent accepted throughout the French and Spanish zones of the colony, a policy which inevitably created "native quarters", but one which also preserved continuity, maintained the nation's past and, at least so Lyautey believed, showed the special relationship of the Protectorate. Lyautey himself resigned and left Morocco in 1925 but when he died in 1934 he was returned to Morocco and buried in a Moorish monument in Rabat. Symbolism was reversed when, in 1961, his body was "repatriated" and entombed in Les Invalides, the soldiers' church, in Paris.

Into the Medina

The basic grid-like regularity of its Medina, cut by a number of long main streets, makes Rabat a good place to get to grips with the feel and lay-out of a Moroccan city. Its plan is typical, with a main market street – **Rue Souika** and its continuation **Souk Es Sebbat** – running beside the Grand Mosque, and behind it a residential area scattered with smaller souks and "parish" mosques. The buildings, characteristically Andalucian, in the style of Tetouan or Chaouen, are part stone and part whitewash, with splashes of yellow and turquoise and great, dark-wood studded doors.

From **Boulevard Hassan II**, half a dozen gates and a series of streets give access to the Medina, all leading more or less directly through the quarter, to emerge near the kasbah and the hillside cemetery. On the west side, the two main streets – **Avenue Mohammed V** and **Rue Sidi Fatah** – are really continuations of Ville Nouvelle avenues, though, flanked by working-class café-restaurants and cell-like hotels, their character is immediately different. Entering along either street, past a lively, modern food market and a handful of stalls selling fruit, juice and snacks, you can turn very shortly to the right and come out at the cubicle shops on **Rue Souika**. Dominated by textiles and silverware along the initial stretch, these give way to a concentration of *babouche* and other shoe stalls as you approach the Grand Mosque. They are all fairly everyday – though quite high quality – shops, not for the most part geared to tourists.

Stalls selling cheaper goods, and the *joutia* (flea market), are off towards the river, round the old Jewish quarter of the Mellah (see below). Along the way are few buildings of particular interest, as most of the medieval city – which predated that of the Andalucians on this site – was destroyed by Portuguese raids in the sixteenth century.

The **Grand Mosque**, founded by the Merenids in the fourteenth century, is a partial exception, though it has been considerably rebuilt – its minaret, for example, was only completed in 1939. Entry to the mosque is forbidden to non-Muslims. Opposite, there is a small example of Merenid decoration in the stone facade of a public **fountain**, which now forms the front of an Arabic bookshop.

The Mellah and Joutia

The most direct approach from Boulevard Hassan II to the Grand Mosque section of the Medina is through **Bab Chellah**, which gives way onto a broad, tree-lined, pedestrian way. Alternatively, continuing a couple of blocks past the *Hôtel Bouregreg*, you can go in by the **Bab El Mellah**, which gives onto Rue Oukassa.

To the east of this street is the **Mellah**, the old Jewish quarter, and still the poorest and most run-down area of the city. It was designated as a Jewish quarter only in 1808

– Jews previously owned several properties on Rue des Consuls, to the north – and no longer has a significant Jewish population. If you can find a local guide, you may be able to look into some of its seventeen former **synagogues**. None of these function: the only active synagogue in the city is a modern building, one block from here, at the bottom end of Rue Moulay Ismail.

With its meat and produce markets, the Mellah looks a somewhat uninviting and impenetrable area, but it is worth a wander through towards the river. A **Joutia**, or **flea market**, spreads out along the streets below Souk Es Sebbat, down to Bab El Bahr. There are clothes, pieces of machinery, and vendors touting wonderful old movie posters, garishly illustrating titles like *Police Militaire* and *La Fille du Désert*.

Towards the kasbah: Rue des Consuls

Beyond the Mellah, heading towards the kasbah, you can walk out by **Bab El Bahr** and follow an avenue near the riverside up to the Oudaïa Gate; to the left of this busy main road is the Musée National de l'Artisanat (National Craft Museum) currently closed, but due to reopen soon; directly opposite is a lively, above-average **Ensemble Artisanal** (Mon–Sat 9am–6pm). Here you can watch, and buy, a range of crafts: embroidery, silk belts, small carpets, leather, copper and wood.

Rue des Consuls, a block inland is not so busy and is a more interesting approach to the kasbah; like the Mellah, this, too, used to be a reserved quarter – the only street of the nineteenth-century city where European consuls were permitted to live. Many of the residency buildings survive, as do a number of impressive merchants' fondouks – most in the alleys off to the left. The main street, particularly at its upper end, is largely a centre for **rug and carpet shops** and on Monday and Thursday mornings becomes a **souk**, with locals bringing carpets – new and old – to sell.

Rabat carpets, woven with very bright dyes (which, if vegetable-based, will fade), are a traditional cottage industry in the Medina, though they're now often made in workshops, one of which you can see on the kasbah's *plateforme* (see p.283). Some of the traditional carpets on sale, particularly in the shops, will have come from further afield. They are officially graded (superior, extra superior, etc) at a special centre just off Rue des Consuls – to the right as you climb towards the kasbah.

The Kasbah des Oudaïas

The site of the original *ribat* and citadel of the Almohad, Merenid and Andalucian towns, the **Kasbah des Oudaïas** is a striking and evocative quarter. Its principal gateway, the **Bab Oudaïa**, is perhaps the most beautiful in the Moorish world, and within the kasbah walls is the **Museum of Moroccan Arts**, housed in a seventeenth-century palace, and a perfect **Andalucian garden**.

The Bab Oudaïa

The **Bab Oudaïa**, like so many of the great external monuments of Morocco, is of Almohad foundation. Built around 1195, concurrent with the Hassan Tower, it was inserted by Yacoub El Mansour within a line of walls already built by his grandfather, Abd El Moumen. The walls in fact extended well to its west, leading down to the sea at the edge of the Medina, and the gate cannot have been designed for any real defensive purpose – its function and importance must have been purely ceremonial. It was to be the heart of the kasbah, its chambers acting as a courthouse and staterooms, with everything of importance taking place nearby. The **Souk El Ghezel** – the main commercial centre of the medieval town, including its wool and slave markets – was located just outside the gate, while the original sultanate's palace stood immediately inside.

KASBAH DES OUDAÏAS

N

0   50m

Oued Bou Regreg

Beach - swimming

Carpet Workshop

PLATEFORME

△ Cafés

RUE ZIRARA

RUE DJEMAA

Tower

RUE BAZZO

△ Beach & Cafés

RUE BAZZO

Beach

RUE BAZZO

Oudaïa Gate

RUE BAZZO

Café Maure

Palace Museum

Andalucian Gardens

PLACE SOUK EL GHEZEL

RUE DES CONSULS

The gate itself doesn't impress so much by its size, which is not unusual for an Almohad structure, as by the visual strength and simplicity of its decoration. This is based on a typically Islamic rhythm, establishing a tension between the exuberant, outward expansion of the arches and the heavy, enclosing rectangle of the gate itself. Looking at the two for a few minutes, you begin to sense a kind of optical illusion – the shapes appear suspended by the great rush of movement from the centre of the arch. The basic feature is, of course, the arch, which here is a sequence of three, progressively more elaborate: first, the basic horseshoe; then, two "filled" or decorated ones, the latter with the distinctive Almohad *darj w ktarf* patterning, a cheek-and-shoulder design somewhat like a fleur-de-lys. At the top, framing the design, is a band of geometric ornamentation, cut off in what seems to be an arbitrary manner but which again creates the impression of movement and continuation outside the gate.

The dominant motifs – scallop-shell-looking palm fronds – are also characteristically Almohad, though without any symbolic importance; in fact, there's very little that's symbolic in the European sense in any Islamic decoration, the object being merely to distract the eye sufficiently to allow contemplation.

Around the kasbah

You can enter the **kasbah** proper through the Oudaïa Gate (or, if it's closed, through the small gateway on its right), or by a lower, horseshoe arch at the base of the ceremonial stairway. This latter approach leads directly to the **Andalucian gardens** and **palace museum**, which can also be reached fairly easily after a short loop through the kasbah, along Rue Djemaa and, then right, down Rue Bazzo.

An airy, village-like part of the city, the kasbah is a pleasant quarter in which to wander – and not remotely dangerous or "closed to visitors" as the hustlers round the gate may try to suggest. Hardly more than 150m from one end to the other, it's not a place where you really need a guide; but if you're approached, talk to the hustlers, be easygoing and explain you're only wandering down to *la plateforme*.

Once inside the Oudaïa Gate, it would actually be hard not to find the way down to the *plateforme* since the single main street, **Rue Djemaa** (Street of the Mosque), runs straight down to a broad belvedere/terrace commanding views of the river and sea. Along the way, you pass by the **Kasbah Mosque**, the city's oldest, founded in 1050, though rebuilt in the eighteenth century by an English renegade known as Ahmed El Inglisi – one of a number of European pirates who joined up with the Sallee Rovers.

El Inglisi was also responsible for several of the forts built below and round the seventeenth-century **plateforme**, originally a semaphore station, on which was built an eighteenth-century warehouse, now housing a carpet co-operative workshop. The guns of the forts and the *plateforme* regularly echoed across the estuary in Salé. The Bou Regreg ("Father of Reflection") River is quite open at this point and it would appear to have left the corsair fleets vulnerable, harboured a little downstream, where the fishing boats today ferry people across to Salé. In fact, a long sandbank lies submerged across the mouth of the estuary – a feature much exploited by the shallow-keeled pirate ships, which would draw the merchant ships in pursuit, only to leave them stranded within the sights of the city's cannon. This is action which you can imagine, up here amid the lowlying alleys and the sea towers, though as so often in Morocco, it's hard to come to terms with just how recent a past it is.

At the same time, the long sandbank, which contributed to the prosperity of Rabat/Salé until the mid-nineteenth century, proved a handicap in the early twentieth century and diverted commercial trade to the better-endowed Casablanca.

From the *plateforme*, it's possible to climb down towards the *Restaurant Caravelle* – a good lunch stop – and the **beach**, crowded with locals throughout the summer, as is the Salé strip across the water. Neither of these beaches is very inviting, in fact, and if you're more interested in swimming than in keeping your head above the polluted water, you'd be better off at the more relaxed (and less exclusively male) sands at the Plage des Nations or Temara Plage (see pp.273 and 295).

The Palace Museum and Gardens

Getting down to the **Palace Museum** and gardens is fairly straightforward: from Rue Djemaa, the main kasbah street, Rue Bazzo zigzags down towards them.

Depending on which fork you take, you'll come out either by the entrance to the palace or at the **Café Maure** – beside the gardens. Oddly enough, the café is not at all "Moorish" but it's a fine place to retreat; high on a terrace overlooking the river, serving mint tea, brewed up on an ancient brazier, and trays of pastries. It's used as much by Moroccans as tourists, and is therefore reasonably priced.

The **Palace** itself is seventeenth century, one of many built by Moulay Ismail, the first sultan since Almohad times to force a unified control over the country. Ismail, whose base was at Meknes, gave Rabat – or New Salé, as it was then known – a relatively high priority. Having subdued the pirates' republic, he took over the kasbah as a garrison for the Oudaïas – Saharan tribesmen who accepted military service in return for tax exemption, and who formed an important part of his mercenary army. This move was in part because they proved uncontrollable in Fes or Meknes, but it was also an effective way of ensuring that the pirates kept up their tribute with a constant supply of slaves and booty.

An interesting building in its own right, the palace and adjacent buildings now house the fine **Museum of Moroccan Arts** (daily except Tues 9am–noon & 3–5.30pm; 10dh admits to all buildings). At any specific time, some exhibits are being restored or loaned elsewhere, thus some collections, described in current publicity, are sometimes – and often inexplicably – missing. The lack of explanation, and occasional disinterest, from those on duty can be frustrating.

However, in this case, the buildings themselves compensate for any disappointment about the contents. The design of the main building is classic: a series of reception rooms grouped round a central court, giving access to the private quarters where you can take a look at the small hammam – a feature of all noble mansions. Within the main building, there are usually displays of Berber and Arab jewellery from most of the regions of Morocco, while the main reception hall has been furnished in the styles of nineteenth-century Rabat and Fes. A room just off to the left as you leave is often shut, though opened on request; once the palace mosque, it usually houses a display of local carpets.

In a nearby building, against the kasbah wall, there is a display of traditional Berber costumes from the Rif to the Tafilalt, with some of the best examples coming from the Zemmour region around Khémisset. Back in the main building, you should ask about the display of Berber musical instruments. These particular items, together with the carpets and costumes, again reveal the startling closeness of a medieval Andalucian past.

The beautiful **Andalucian Gardens** occupy the old palace grounds. What you see today was actually constructed by the French in the twentieth century – though true to Spanish-Andalucian tradition, with deep, sunken beds of shrubs and flowering annuals. If you're familiar with Granada, it's illuminating to compare the authentic Moorish concept here with the neat box hedges with which the Alhambra has been restored. But historical authenticity aside, it's a delightful place, full of the scent of datura, bougainvillea and a multitude of herbs and flowers. It has a definite modern role, too, as a meeting place for women, who gather here in dozens of small groups on a Friday or Sunday afternoon.

The Hassan Mosque and Mohammed V Mausoleum

The most ambitious of all Almohad buildings, the **Hassan Mosque** and its vast minaret dominates almost every view of the capital – a majestic sight from the kasbah, from Salé, or glimpsed as you arrive across the river by train. If it had been completed, it would (in its time) have been the second largest mosque in the Islamic world, outflanked only by the one in Smarra, Iraq. Even today its size seems a novelty.

There is also the poignancy of its ruin. Designed by El Mansour as the centrepiece of the new capital and as a celebration of his great victory over the Spanish kings at Alarcos, the mosque's construction seems to have been more or less abandoned on his death in 1199. The tower was probably left much as it appears today; the mosque's hall, roofed in cedar, was used until the Great Earthquake of 1755 (which destroyed central Lisbon) brought down its central columns. Its extent, however, must always have seemed an elaborate folly. Morocco's most important mosque, the Kairaouine in Fes, is less than half the Hassan's size, but served a much greater population, with adequate space for 20,000 worshippers. Bearing in mind that it is only men who gather for the weekly Friday prayer – when a town traditionally comes together in its Grand Mosque – Rabat would have needed a population of well over 100,000 to make adequate use of the Hassan's capacity. As it was, the city never really took off under the later Almohads and Merenids, and when Leo Africanus came here in 1600, he found no more than a hundred households, gathered for security within the kasbah.

The **tower**, or minaret, was begun by Yacoub El Mansour in 1195 – at the same time as the Koutoubia in Marrakesh and the Giralda in Seville – and it's one of the few Moroccan buildings to approach the European idea of monumentality. This is due in part to its site, on a level above the river and most of the city, but perhaps equally to its unfinished solidity. The other great Moroccan minarets, perfectly balanced by their platform decoration and lanterns, are left "hanging" as if with no particular weight or height. The Hassan Tower, with no such movement, stands firmly rooted in the ground.

The minaret is unusually positioned at the centre rather than the northern corner of the rear of the mosque. Some 50m tall in its present state, it would probably have been around 80m if finished to normal proportions – a third again the height of Marrakesh's Koutoubia. Despite its apparent simplicity, it is perhaps the most complex of all Almohad structures. Each facade is different, with a distinct combination of patterning, yet the whole intricacy of blind arcades and interlacing curves is based on just two formal designs. On the south and west faces these are the *darj w ktarf* of the Oudaïa Gate; on the north and east is the *shabka* (net) motif, an extremely popular form adapted by the Almohads from the lobed arches of the Córdoba Grand Mosque – and still in contemporary use.

The Mohammed V Mausoleum

Facing the tower – in an assertion of Morocco's historical independence and continuity – are the **Mosque and Mausoleum of Mohammed V**, begun on the king's death in 1961 and inaugurated six years later. Now Hassan II and his brother, Moulay Abdellah, are buried here too, alongside their father. The **Mosque**, extending between a stark pair of pavilions, gives a somewhat foreshortened idea of how the Hassan Mosque must once have appeared, roofed in its traditional green tiles.

The **Mausoleum**, designed by a Vietnamese architect, Vo Toan, was one of the great prestige projects of modern Morocco. Its brilliantly surfaced marbles and spiralling designs, however, seem to pay homage to traditional Moroccan techniques, while failing to capture their rhythms and unity. It is, nevertheless, an important shrine for Moroccans – and one which, unusually, non-Muslims are permitted to visit. You file past fabulously costumed royal guards to an interior balcony; the tomb of Mohammed V, carved from white onyx, lies below, an old man squatting beside it, reading from the Koran.

Around the Ville Nouvelle

French in construction, style and feel, the **Ville Nouvelle** provides the main focus of Rabat's life, above all in the cafés and promenades of the broad, tree-lined Avenue Mohammed V, and in the pleasant **Parc du Triangle de Vue** (closes 6pm), opposite the south wall of the Medina – both popular afternoon meeting places. Another attractive and colourful spot is the **Flower Market**, held in a sunken garden just to the north of Avenue Moulay Hassan.

There's a certain grandeur in some of the old, *Mauresque* public buildings around the main boulevards, too, which were built with as much desire to impress as any earlier epoch. However, it's the **Almohad walls and gates**, the **citadel of Chellah** (see the next section) and the excellent **Archeological Museum** which hold most of interest in the quarter.

The walls and gates

More-or-less complete sections of the **Almohad walls** run right down from the kasbah to the Royal Palace and beyond – an extraordinary monument to Yacoub El Mansour's vision. Along their course four of the original **gates** survive. Three – **Bab El Alou, Bab El Had** and **Bab Zaer** – are very modest. The fourth, **Bab Er Rouah** (Gate of the Wind), is on an entirely different scale, recalling and in many ways rivalling the Oudaïa.

Contained within a massive stone bastion, **Bab Er Rouah** again achieves the tension of movement – with its sunlike arches contained within a square of Koranic inscription – and a similar balance between simplicity and ornament. The east side, approached from outside the walls, is the main facade, and must have been designed as a monumental approach to the city; the shallow-cut, floral relief between arch and square is arguably the finest anywhere in Morocco. Inside, you can appreciate the gate's archetypal defensive structure – the three domed chambers aligned to force a sharp double turn. They're used for exhibitions and are usually open.

From Bab Er Rouah, it's a fifteen-minute walk down towards the last Almohad gate, the much-restored **Bab Zaer**, and the entrance to the **Chellah**. On the way, you pass a series of modern gates leading off to the vast enclosures of the **Royal Palace** – which is really more a collection of palaces, built mainly in the nineteenth century and decidedly off-limits to casual visitors – and, off to the left (opposite the *Hôtel Chellah*), the Archeological Museum.

The Archeological Museum

Rabat's Archeological Museum on Rue Brihi (daily except Tues 9–11.30am & 2.30–5.30pm; 10dh) is the most important in Morocco. Although small – surprisingly so in a country which saw substantial Phoenician and Carthaginian settlement and three centuries of Roman rule – it houses an exceptional collection of Roman-era bronzes.

The bronzes are displayed in a special annexe with a separate entrance; if it's closed, seek entry (at no extra cost). They date from the first and second centuries AD and were found mainly at the provincial capital of Volubilis (near Meknes), together with a few pieces from Chellah and the colonies of Banasa and Thamusida. Highlights include superb figures of a guard dog and a rider, and two magnificent portrait heads, reputedly those of Cato the Younger (Caton d'Utique) and Juba II – the last significant ruler of the Romanized Berber kingdoms of Mauretania and Numidia before the assertion of direct imperial rule. Both of these busts were found in the House of Venus at Volubilis.

Back in the main building, there are showcases on two floors; each contains finds from different digs, of little interest unless you have already visited the area – or plan to do so. Captions are in French and, if you ask, you may be provided with a guide to the museum – also in French.

Citadel of Chellah

The most beautiful of Moroccan ruins, **Chellah** (daily 8am–6pm; 10dh) is a startling sight as you emerge from the long avenues of the Ville Nouvelle. Walled and towered, it seems a much larger enclosure than the map suggests, and it feels for a moment as if you've come upon a second Medina. The site is, in fact, long uninhabited – since 1154, when it was abandoned in favour of Salé across the Bou Regreg. But for almost a thousand years prior to that, Chellah (or *Sala Colonia*, as it was known) had been a thriving city and port, one of the last to sever links with the Roman Empire and the first to proclaim Moulay Idriss founder of Morocco's original Arab dynasty. An apocryphal local tradition maintains that the Prophet himself also prayed at a shrine here.

CHELLAH: THE SANCTUARY

Mihrab
Oratory
Cells
Tomb of Shams ed Douna
Basin
Zaouia of Abou El Hassan
Ablutions
Tomb of Abou El Hassan
Ruined Minaret
Pool
Mosque of Abou Youssef

0   5m

▽ *Chellah Gate & main entrance to site*

Under the Almohads, the site was already a royal burial ground, but most of what you see today, including the gates and enclosing wall, is the legacy of the Merenid sultan, **Abou El Hassan** (1331–51). The greatest of Merenid rulers, conquering and controlling the Maghreb as far east as Tunis, Abou El Hassan, "The Black Sultan", was also their most prolific builder. In addition to Chellah, he was responsible for important mosques in Fes and Tlemcen, as well as the beautiful medersas of Salé and Meknes.

The **main gate** here is the most surprising of Merenid monuments, its turreted bastions creating an almost Gothic appearance. Its base is recognizably Almohad, but each element has become inflated, and the combination of simplicity and solidity has gone. In its original state, with bright-coloured marble and tile decoration, the effect must have been incredibly gaudy – a bit like the nineteenth-century palaces you see today in Fes and Marrakesh. An interesting technical innovation, however, the stalactite (or "honeycomb") corbels which form the transition from the bastion's semi-octagonal towers to their square platforms; these were to become a feature of Merenid building. The Kufic inscription above the gate is from the Koran and begins with the invocation: "I take refuge in Allah, against Satan."

To your left, as you enter, are the main **Roman ruins**, now open to the public after many years of closure (same times and admission as the Chellah). They are small in scale; similar to other river and seaside sites such as Banasa and Thamusidia, and little grander than Cotta, near Tangier (see p.101) and Tamuda, near Tetouan. None of these, including Chellah, was more than a trading post and all are overshadowed by Volubilis (see p.192). Nevertheless, the ruins which can now be seen are from 200 BC onwards; they're well signposted and include a forum, a temple and a craftsmen's quarter.

The Sanctuary

From the main gate, the **Islamic ruins** are down to the right, within a second inner sanctuary approached along a broad path through half-wild gardens of banana, orange and ancient fig trees, sunflowers, dahlias and poisonous datura plants.

Their most prominent and picturesque feature is a tall stone-and-tile **minaret**, a ludicrously oversized stork's nest perched invariably – and photogenically – on its summit. Storks, along with swallows and crows, have a certain sanctity in Morocco, and their presence on minarets is a sign of good fortune.

The sanctuary itself appears as a confusing cluster of tombs and ruins, but it's essentially just two buildings: a mosque, built by the second Merenid sultan, Abou Youssef (1258–86), and a zaouia, or mosque-monastery, added along with the enclosure walls by Abou El Hassan. You enter directly into the *sahn*, or courtyard, of **Abou Youssef's Mosque**, a small and presumably private structure built as a funerary dedication. It is now very much in ruins, though you can make out the colonnades of the inner prayer hall with its mihrab to indicate the direction of prayer. To the right is its minaret, now reduced to the level of the mosque's roof.

Behind, both in and outside the sanctuary enclosure, are scattered **royal tombs** – each aligned so that the dead, dressed in white and lying on their right sides, may face Mecca to await the Call of Judgement. Abou Youssef's tomb has not been identified, but you can find those of both **Abou El Hassan** and his wife **Shams ed Douna**. Hassan's is contained within a kind of pavilion whose external wall retains its decoration, the *darj w ktarf* motif set above three small arches in a design very similar to that of the Hassan Tower. Shams ed Douna (Morning Sun) has only a tombstone – a long, pointed rectangle covered in a mass of verses from the Koran. A convert from Christianity, Shams was the mother of Abou El Hassan's rebel son, Abou Inan, whose uprising led to the sultan's death as a fugitive in the High Atlas during the winter of 1352.

The **Zaouia** is in a much better state of preservation, its structure, like Abou El Hassan's medersas, that of a long, central court enclosed by cells, with a smaller oratory or prayer hall at the end. Each of these features is quite recognizable, along with those of the ablutions, preceding the main court, for the worshippers' purification. There are fragments of zellij tilework on some of the colonnades and on the minaret, which again give an idea of its original brightness, and there are traces, too, of the mihrab's elaborate stucco decoration. Five-sided, the **mihrab** has a narrow passageway (now blocked with brambles) leading to the rear – built so that pilgrims might make seven circuits round it. This was once believed to give the equivalent merit of the *hadj*, the trip to Mecca: a tradition, with that of Muhammad's visit, probably invented and propagated by the zaouia's keepers to increase their revenue.

Off to the right and above the sanctuary enclosure are a group of **koubbas** – the domed tombs of local saints or marabouts – and beyond them a **spring pool**, enclosed by low, vaulted buildings. This is held sacred, along with the eels which swim in its waters, and women bring hard-boiled eggs for the fish to invoke assistance in fertility and childbirth. If you're here in spring, you'll get additional wildlife, with the storks nesting and the herons roosting.

At the far end of the sanctuary, you can look down a side-valley to the Bou Regreg estuary. From here, you can appreciate that this site was destined, from early times, to be settled and fortified. It was hidden from the sea by low hills and a bend in the Bou Regreg river. At the same time, once navigated, access from the river was easy and safe. The fertile lowland by the river was ideal for crops and grazing animals. Pliny said that the meadows were invaded by herds of elephants, which were slaughtered for their ivory, and that nomad tribes, intent on pillage, fared no better. The site itself was easy to defend and the springs provided water in times of siege.

Nowadays, you can also appreciate from here the steady expansion inland of Salé – with its sprawling suburb, Betana. Salé is also expanding, ribbon-like, either side of the main road north towards Kenitra, the main reason for the additional train station, Salé Tabriquet.

Eating, drinking and nightlife

For a capital city, Rabat is pretty quiet. By 9.30 at night, the restaurants are closing up and most of the population are at home. Nonetheless, the city's café-life is pleasant, and it has one of the country's best collections of restaurants – many of them inexpensive.

Medina café-restaurants

As ever, the cheapest places to eat are to be found in the **Medina**. Just on the edge of the quarter, down Avenue Mohammed V and along Rue Souika, there are a string of good, everyday **café-restaurants** – clean enough and serving regular Moroccan fare. They are excellent value, especially at lunchtime, when many have fixed-price meals for the office and shop workers. Alternatively, for only a few dirhams, you can pick up a range of snacks and juices just inside the Medina walls, by the market shown on our main city map. Elsewhere, facing the *Hôtel Al Maghrib Al Jadid*, there are the popular and cheap *Restaurant de l'Union* and *Restaurant de la Libération* on Avenue Mohammed V. Alternatively in the Medina, is the upmarket *Restaurant Dinarjat*, 6 Rue Belgnaoui, with a reputation for fine Moroccan dishes, or the popular *Restaurant Taghazout*, 7 Rue Sebbahi, which has simple fare and offers a good breakfast.

Ville Nouvelle restaurants

In the **Ville Nouvelle** you can pick from a fine selection of Moroccan and French restaurants, plus a few Oriental places for a change of cuisine.

Café-Restaurant El Bahia, Bd. Hassan II, built into the Andalucian wall, near the junction with Av. Mohammed V. Reasonably priced tajines, kebabs and salads, served in a pleasant courtyard, upstairs or on the pavement outside. Service can be slow and helpings modest, but ambience compensates. Cheap to moderate.

Hôtel Balima, Av. Mohammed V. Inexpensive dishes in the snack bar all day; pricier ones in the main restaurant, but they're nothing special – the indoor bar and outdoor café under the trees are the thing here. Open evenings only. Moderate.

Restaurant La Bamba, 3 Rue Tanta – a small sidestreet behind the *Hôtel Balima*. Mainly Moroccan dishes, but there's paella to promote the Spanish theme. There are several other eating places on this street so there are alternatives if *La Bamba* doesn't suit, including *La Mammu* opposite (see below). Moderate.

La Clef, Rue Hatim – a narrow sidestreet just off Av. Moulay Youssef, and near the *Hôtel d'Orsay*. There's serious drinking in the bar downstairs, but the restaurant upstairs is quiet and serves good French and Moroccan dishes. Try tajines, brochettes and the excellent pastilla. Moderate.

Restaurant Entrecôte, 74 Av. Fal Ould Ouemir, Agdal. A petit taxi ride from the town centre, this place has a French menu and excellent fish dishes. Moderate.

Café-Restaurant Français, 3 Av. Moulay Youssef, just off Place de la Gare and alongside the *Hôtel d'Orsay*. Another downstairs bar with upstairs restaurant like *La Clef* nearby. Arguably the best and most consistent around the train station. Moderate.

Restaurant Hong Kong, 261 Av. Mohammed V on the first floor. Good Chinese cuisine and value for money. Closed Mondays. Moderate.

Restaurant Koutoubia, 10 Rue Pierre Pavent (☎03/772 0125). Off Rue Moulay Abdelaziz, facing RTM (radio and TV station) and near the *Hôtel Chellah*. There's an upmarket bar and, with a separate entrance through a quaint wood and glass extension, an old-style restaurant. It claims the late King Hassan among past clientele, and an elderly patron who knew his father, Mohammed V. Excellent cooking. Expensive.

Pizza La Mamma, 6 Rue Tanta. It's opposite *La Bamba* and is its Italian-style rival, providing an excuse for pizza and pasta. *La Dolce Vita*, next door to *La Mamma*, is owned by the same patron and so takes care of the sweet course. Moderate.

Le Mandarin, 100 Av. Abdel Krim Al Kattabi (☎03/772 4699; closed Wed). Popular business restaurant in L'Océan quarter, southwest of the Bab Oudaïa. The best Oriental food in the city. Moderate to expensive.

Pizzeria Napoli, 8 Rue Moulay Abdelaziz, between the *Hôtel Chellah* and *Restaurant Koutoubia* – and facing RTM (Radio Television Morocco). Pizzas cooked over a wood fire – to eat in or take away.

Restaurant La Pagode, 13 Rue Baghdad – parallel to (and south of) the train station. Small restaurant serving Vietnamese and Chinese dishes. Moderate.

Café-Restaurant de la Paix, 1 Av. Moulay Youssef, just off Place de la Gare. Again, as with the nearby *La Clef* and *Français*, there's some heavy drinking in the ground-floor bar, but you can eat well outside (in an old French-style glass corridor) or upstairs. Moderate.

Restaurant Saïdoune, in the mall at 267 Av. Mohammed V, opposite the *Hôtel Terminus*. A good Lebanese restaurant run by an Iraqi; also a bar. Closed Fri. Moderate

Café-Restaurant Shahrazade, 119 Bd. Hassan II, next to the *Hôtel Majestic*. Quick, friendly service, in or out of doors. Cheap to moderate.

Taki Fried Chicken, in an arcade on Av. Mohammed V across from the Parliament building. Reports have been mixed so if in doubt try the *McDonald's* across from the train station or the *Pizza Hut* on Rue Tanta instead.

Cafés, bars and nightlife

Avenues Mohammed V and Allal Ben Abdallah have some excellent **cafés**, for coffee, soft drinks and pastries. Particularly pleasant spots include the **Hôtel Balima** outdoor café (very popular with locals – and a bit cruisy), the **Café Maure** in the kasbah, and the café in the shady **Parc du Triangle de Vue**, just south of Boulevard Hassan II, which is usually full of students working or arguing over a mint tea.

Bars – outside the main hotels – are few and far between. The one inside the *Hôtel Balima* is as good as any; it tends to stay open as late as there are customers and attracts an interesting crowd of Moroccan drinkers. Other bars are to be found at the restaurants *La Clef, de la Paix* and *Koutoubia* (see above). There is also the *Baghdad Bar* on Rue Tanta, behind the *Hôtel Balima,* and the *Bar Le Grillon*, at the bottom end of Avenue Allal Ben Abdallah.

After these have closed, the city's **late-night options** are a handful of **disco-bars** around Place de Melilla (east of the Parc du Triangle de Vue), and on Rue Patrice Lumumba – where you'll find the *Biba* and *Jefferson* discos. Another popular dance-club is *5th Avenue*, near the Moulay Youssef Sport complex, in the Agdal quarter, south of the centre, easiest reached by petit taxi. If you went early, you could eat first at the *Pizza Reggio* in the complex; the prices are reasonable and there's a good atmosphere.

Finally, and back in the Ville Nouvelle, the *Jour et Nuit* nightclub, at the junction of Avenue Abderrahman Neggay and Rue Moulay Rachid, attracts a young crowd until the early hours.

Listings

In addition to listings below, you may want to consult *Telecontact*, an annual directory with Yellow Pages-style listings for businesses and services in the Rabat/Casablanca/Kenitra region. It is available from newsstands.

Airlines Royal Air Maroc is just across from the train station on Av. Mohammed V (☎03/770 9766) and Air France (☎03/770 7066) is on the same avenue just below the *Hôtel Balima* at no. 281. Neither British Airways nor Iberia has an office in Rabat; the nearest are in Casablanca (☎02/230 7607 and ☎02/229 4003 respectively).

Banks Most are along Av. Allal Ben Abdallah and Av. Mohammed V. The BMCE exchange counter at 260 Av. Mohammed V is open Mon–Fri 8am–noon & 2–7pm, Sat & Sun 10am–2pm & 4–7pm, and at the train station Mon–Fri 8am–noon & 3–7pm, Sat–Sun 9am–noon & 3–6pm; they handle VISA/Mastercard, travellers' cheques and cash.

Beaches Nearest options are the Kasbah and Salé beaches, with the latter best reached by one of the ferryboats which cross from below the Mellah. For clearer waters, head by bus to either Plage des Nations (see p.273) or Temara Plage (see p.295).

Books The American Bookstore, Rue Tangier (marked on our map) has a good selection of Penguin novels along with an enterprising shelf on Moroccan architecture, Islam and some of Paul Bowles's translations of Moroccan fiction. The English Bookshop, 7 Rue Alyamama (again marked on our map), stocks new titles; it also has a wide selection of secondhand paperbacks (Mon–Sat 9am–noon & 3–7pm). You can get coffee-table books on Morocco and phrasebooks from several of the bookshops along Av. Mohammed V – look for Kalila Wa Dimna at no. 334.

Car rental Cheaper deals tend to be available in Casablanca, but if you want a car in Rabat, there are twenty or so rental agencies to choose from. Main companies include: Avis, 7 Zankat Abou Faris Al Mairini (☎03/776 9759); Budget, Rabat Ville train station (☎03/770 5789, fax 770 1477); Europcar InterRent, 25 bis Rue Patrice Lumumba (☎03/772 4141, fax 720 0241); Hertz, 467 Av. Mohammed V (☎03/770 9227); National Car Rental, corner of Rue de Caire/Rue Ghandi (☎03/772 2731, fax 772 2526); Visa Car, Av. Moulay Youssef (☎ & fax 03/770 9513).

Car repairs Try Concorde, 6 Av. Allal Ben Abdallah or, particularly for Renaults, the garage at 14 Av. Misr.

Cinemas There are several cinemas on or near Av. Mohammed V; Cinema Martignan has the latest US and French films. Near the *Hotel Royal*, is the Cinema Royal, more given to Kung Fu and Asian romances. More of an arts cinema is the smaller Salle de 7ème Art on Av. Allal Ben Abdallah; advance booking advisable.

Culture The Théâtre National Mohammed V on Rue Cairo (south of Bd. Hassan II – see map) puts on a range of concerts (Arabic and Western classical music) and films. There are a number of cultural centres: American, 41 Av. Allal Ben Abdallah; British, 6 Av. Moulay Youssef; German, 10 Rue Jebli; and French, 2 Rue Gandhi.

Embassies include: Britain, 17 Bd. Tour Hassan (☎03/772 9696, fax 707 4531); Canada, 13 bis Rue Jaâfar As-Saddik (☎03/767 2880); Denmark, 4 Rue Khémisset (☎03/773 9293); Netherlands, 40 Rue Tunis (☎03/773 3512); Sweden, 159 Av. John Kennedy (☎03/775 9313); USA, 2 Av. Marrakesh – near the far end of Av. Allal Ben Abdallah (☎03/776 2265). Standard hours are Mon–Fri 8.30–11.30am, though you can phone at any time in an emergency. Irish citizens are represented by the British Embassy; Australians by the Canadians; Israelis by the Bureau de Liaison d'Israel, 52 Bd. Mehdi Ben Barka Souissi (☎03/765 7681).

Galleries Unusually for Morocco, Rabat has a number of worthwhile art galleries, showing works by contemporary artists. L'Atelier, 16 Rue Annaba, is the major dealer; try also Galerie Marsam, 6 Rue Osquofiah (opposite *Restaurant l'Oasis*); and Galerie Le Mamoir, 7 Rue Baït Lahm (near *Hôtel Bélère* and *Visa Car*).

Golf The Dar Es Salaam Royal Golf Club, 7km out of Rabat on Zaers Road (☎03/775 5864, fax 775 7571), is one of the country's finest, with two 18-hole and one 9-hole courses designed by Robert Trent-Jones.

Hiking maps Division de la Cartographie, Ministère de l'Agriculture et de la Réforme Agraire (MARA), 31 Av. Moulay Hassan; Mon–Thurs 8.30–11am & 2.30–5.30pm. Hiking maps to the Toubkal area are sold over the counter; other topographic maps of the main hiking areas in the High and Middle Atlas, which can be selected from the official index, have to be ordered and collected 48hr later, discounting Sat and Sun, but only if officially sanctioned. There's no postal service. These are good maps, at up to 1:50,000, but the policy and the service make it virtually impossible to buy them.

Internet access *Student Cyber*, 83 Av. Hassan II (daily 8.30am–11.30pm; 10dh per hour).

Libraries The British Council, 36 Rue Tangier (☎03/776 0836; marked on our map) operates a small library, with UK papers available for browsing, and puts on various films and events in English. It's also a possible source of information if you want to stay on in Morocco and teach English; open Mon–Fri 9.30am–noon & 2.30–5.45pm; closed Mon am. The George Washington Library, 35 Av. de Fes, has American newspapers. The American Women's Association Library, 22 bis Al Jazair (Mon and Wed 10am–noon, Thurs 5.30–7.30pm, Fri 2–4pm, Sat 10am–noon; (liable to change, check beforehand) has a one-for-one paperback exchange, open to all. These libraries can also put you in touch with people if you want to take lessons in Moroccan Arabic.

Police The main office is in Rue Soekarno, a couple of blocks from Av. Mohammed V; a central police post is manned at Bab El Jdid. In emergency ☎19.

Post office The central PTT (open 24hr for phones and there are call boxes outside) is halfway down Av. Mohammed V; its *poste restante* section is across the road from the main building. The PTT also has a small Postal Museum, with displays of Moroccan stamps; pride of place is given to Morocco's first official stamp, dated May 12, 1912, showing the Grand Mosque in Tangier.

Supermarkets There are two supermarkets facing the Cathedral (see above). Or, if you have transport, there is the Centre Commercial Marjane, between Rabat and Salé.

Salé

Although it's now essentially a suburb of Rabat, **SALÉ** was the pre-eminent of the two right through the Middle Ages, from the decline of the Almohads to the uneasy alliance in the pirate republic of Bou Regreg (see p.275). Under the Merenids, in particular, it was a port of some stature, and endowed as such, the most notable survival of these times being its superb **Medersa Bou Inan** – a monument to rival the best of those of Rabat.

In the last century, following the French creation of a capital in Rabat, and the emergence of Casablanca as Morocco's great port, Salé passed into a backwater role. The original Ville Nouvelle, as developed during the Protectorate, was restricted to a small area around the bus station and the northern gates. But, more recently, Salé has spread inland and alongside the main road north towards Kenitra. The increased Salé-Rabat traffic has called for an additional road bridge over the Bou Regreg and new train station (see p.275). Nevertheless, Salé still looks and feels very distinct from Rabat, particularly within its medieval walls where the souks and life remain surprisingly traditional.

From Rabat you can cross the river to Salé by **rowing boat** (see the map), or take a **bus** (#6 or #12) from Boulevard Hassan II. The boats charge 5dh per person and drop you close to the Salé beach; from here it's a steep walk up to **Bab Bou Haja**, one of the main town gates. Both buses drop you at an open terminal just outside the town's principal gate, **Bab Mrisa**.

Salé has a basic but well-managed **campsite**: *Camping de la Plage* (☎03/784 4566; open all year), near the beach, but the only **hotel**, the *Saadiens*, has closed. Unless you want to use the campsite as a base for Rabat, there seems little reason to stay. In the evenings, you can eat reasonably at one of the many **cafés** along Rue Kechachin, but the streets empty even earlier than those in Rabat.

OULJA: THE COMPLEXE DES POTIERS

On the Salé side of the estuary, 3km out from the town, the suburb of **Oulja** houses one of Morocco's finest **potteries**. It has been open only since 1989, established around a rich vein of clay, so its techniques and kilns are modern. For instance, while just three out of the 180 kilns at Safi (Morocco's largest potting town) are fired by gas or electricity, here the ratio is almost exactly the reverse, with just a few specialist kilns using tamarisk wood fuel. Nevertheless, despite different techniques, lovely and wonderfully imaginative objects are produced at both Oulja and Salé.

The complex also has a major craft/exhibition centre, an area specializing in basketwork and a friendly café. Visitors are made welcome at the twenty-odd potteries on the complex and you could pick interesting potteries at random. Good ones, however, include:

#12 **Poterie Demnate** (☎ & fax 03/781 3629). The patron, Bennami Abdelaziz came here after working in Demnate. Wares are enhanced by striking hand-painted flowers.

#10 **Poterie Hariky** (☎03/781 1319, fax 780 9890). Superb Islamic designs, by family-named business.

#9 **Poterie Tarfaya** (☎03/781 0091). Traditional tea sets and mugs – some of their work can be seen in the Hassan II Mosque in Casablanca.

Oulja can be reached by grand taxi from Rabat or Salé. If you want a taxi back, arrange for it to return; otherwise you'll have to walk. If so, head east to cross the first bridge; you can then cut up to the high ground towards the Tour Hassan.

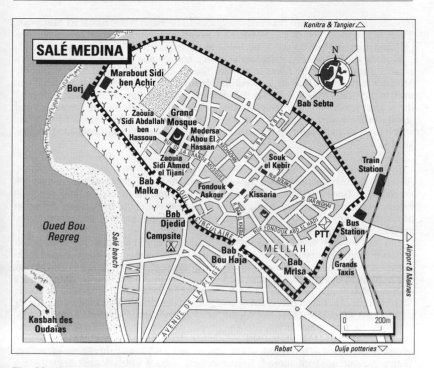

The Medina

The most interesting point to enter Salé's Medina is through **Bab Mrisa**, near the grand taxi terminal. Its name – "of the small harbour" – recalls the marine arsenal which used to be sited within the walls, and explains the gate's unusual height. A channel running here from the Bou Regreg has long silted up, but in medieval times it allowed merchant ships to sail right into town, a device that must have been useful during the years of the pirate republic. Robinson Crusoe was brought into captivity through this gate in Daniel Defoe's novel. The gate itself is a very early Merenid structure of the 1270s, its design and motifs (palmettes enclosed by floral decoration, bands of Kufic inscription and *darj w ktarf*) still inherently Almohad in tone.

THE SOUKS

Inside Bab Mrisa you'll find yourself in a small square, at the bottom of the old **Mellah** (Jewish) quarter. Turning to the left and continuing close to the walls, you come out after around 350m at another gate, **Bab Bou Haja**, beside a small park. If you want to explore the souks – the route outlined below – take the road along the left-hand side of the park. If not, continue on just inside the walls to a long open area; as this starts to narrow into a lane (about 40m further down) veer to your right into the town. This should bring you out more or less at the **Grand Mosque**, opposite which is the **Medersa of Abou El Hassan**.

The park-side street from Bab Bou Haja is **Rue Bab El Khebaz** (Street of the Bakers' Gate), a busy little lane which emerges at the heart of the **souks** by a small **kissaria** (covered market) devoted mainly to textiles. Most of the alleys here are grouped round specific crafts, a particular speciality being the pattern-weave mats produced for the sides and floors of mosques – to be found in the **Souk El Merzouk**. There is also a wool souk, the **Souk El Ghezel**, while wood, leather, ironware, carpets and household items are to be found in the **Souk El Kebir** – the grand souk.

Close by the kissaria is a fourteenth-century hospice, the **Fondouk Askour**, with a notable gateway (built by Abou Inan – see the Medersa below), and beyond this the Medina's main street, **Rue de la Grande Mosque** leads uphill through the middle of town to the Grand Mosque. This is the simplest approach, but you can take in more of the souks by following **Rue Kechachin**, parallel. Along here are the carpenters and stone-carvers, as well as other craftsmen. In **Rue Haddadin**, a fairly major intersection which leads off to its right up towards Bab Sebta, you'll come upon gold - and coppersmiths.

THE GRAND MOSQUE AND MEDERSA

As far as buildings go, the **Grand Mosque** marks the most interesting part of town, its surrounding lanes fronting a concentration of aristocratic mansions and religious zaouia foundations. Almohad in origin, the mosque is one of the largest and earliest in Morocco, though what you can see as a non-Muslim (the gateway and minaret) are recent additions.

You can, however, visit its **Medersa** (10dh admission; you will probably need to ask in shops nearby for the *gardien*), opposite the mosque's monumental, stepped main entrance. Salé's main monument and recently restored, it was founded in 1341 by Sultan Abou El Hassan (see Chellah, in Rabat), and is thus more or less contemporary with the Bou Inania medersas in Meknes and Fes. Like them, it follows the basic Merenid plan of a central courtyard opening onto a prayer hall, with a series of cells for the students – for whom these "university halls" were endowed – round its upper floors. If this is the first example you've seen, it will come as a surprise after the sparse Almohad economy of the monuments in Rabat. The great Merenid medersas are all intensely decorated – in carved wood, stucco and zellij – and this is no exception. Within the entrance gate, there is hardly an inch of space which doesn't draw the eye away into a web of intricacy.

What is remarkable, despite a certain heaviness which the great Merenid medersas manage to avoid, is the way in which each aspect of the workmanship succeeds in forging a unity with the others, echoing and repeating the standard patterns in endless variations. The patterns, for the most part, derive from Almohad models, with their stylized geometric and floral motifs, but in the latter there is a much more naturalistic, less abstracted approach. There is also a new stress on calligraphy, with monumental inscriptions carved in great bands on the dark cedarwood and incorporated within the stucco and zellij. Almost invariably these are in the elaborate cursive script, and they are generally passages from the Koran. There are occasional poems, however, such as the beautiful foundation inscription, set in marble against a green background, on the rear wall of the court, which begins:

> *Look at my admirable portal!*
> *Rejoice in my chosen company,*
> *In the remarkable style of my construction*
> *And my marvellous interior!*
> *The workers here have accomplished an artful*
> *Creation with the beauty of youth . . .*

(Translation from Richard B. Parker, *Islamic Monuments in Morocco*).

The medersa is only sporadically visited and you'll probably have it to yourself (except for the sparrows and the caretaker) – a quiet, meditative place. Close to its entrance there is a stairway up to the old, windowless cells of the students and to the **roof**, where, looking out across the river to Rabat, you sense the enormity of the Hassan Tower.

ZAOUIAS, MOUSSEMS AND MARABOUTS
Round the Grand Mosque, and over to the northwest, you can view (but not enter, unless you are Muslim) a trio of interesting buildings.

The first of these is the **Zaouia Sidi Ahmed El Tijani**, whose elaborate portal faces the Grand Mosque and Medersa. Zaouias are a mix of shrine and charitable establishment, maintained by their followers, who once or more each year hold a moussem, a pilgrimage-festival, in the saint-founder's honour.

The most important of Salé's moussems is that of its patron saint, **Sidi Abdallah Ben Hassoun**, whose **zaouia** stands at the end of the Rue de la Grande Mosquée, a few steps before the cemetery. The saint, who for Muslim travellers plays a role similar to St Christopher, lived in Salé during the sixteenth century, though the origins and significance of his moussem are unclear. Taking place each year on the eve of Mouloud – the Prophet's birthday – it involves a spectacular procession through the streets of the town with local boatmen, dressed in corsair costumes, carrying huge and elaborate wax lanterns mounted on giant poles. It is by all accounts a lively occasion, much of which can be witnessed away from the forbidden precincts.

At the far end of a cemetery (again forbidden to non-Muslims), which spreads down to the river, is a third revered site, the white koubba and associated buildings of the **Marabout of Sidi Ben Achir**. Sometimes known as "Al Tabib" (The Doctor), Ben Achir was a fourteenth-century ascetic from Andalucia. His shrine, said to have the ability to attract shipwrecks and quell storms – good pirate virtues – reputedly effects cures for blindness, paralysis and madness. Enclosed by nineteenth-century pilgrim lodgings, it, too, has a considerable annual moussem on the eve of Mouloud.

South towards Casablanca

It's a little over an hour by grand taxi from Rabat to Casa (under an hour by express train) and, if you're making a quick tour of Morocco, there's little to delay your progress. The landscape, wooded in parts, is a low, flat plain, punctuated inland by a series of scruffy light-industrial towns.

On the coast, things are slightly more promising: **Mohammedia** has a fine beach and good restaurants, and is, with the smaller resorts of **Temara** and **Skhirat**, a popular seaside escape for the affluent of Rabat and Casablanca. For visitors, however, there's a lot more to get excited about on the coast south from Casa towards Agadir.

Rabat to Mohammedia

Temara Plage, some 14km to the south of Rabat, is (along with Plage des Nations, see p.273), the capital's closest beach resort. If you are planning a day-trip, you could take a grand taxi direct to the beach from Rabat (around 20min), or local bus #17 to **Temara Ville** (4km inland); both leave Rabat from Avenue Hassan II.

If you're driving, the **coast road** is preferable. Leaving Rabat, take Boulevard Misr alongside the Medina wall, then bear left onto Avenue Al Moukaouma and its continuation Avenue Sidi Mohammed Ben Abdallah. The route is built up almost the whole way from Rabat to Temara. Along the way, you pass by the **National Zoo**; a vast **Complexe Olympique**, built for the 1983 Mediterranean games.

Temara Zoo
Temara Zoo (Mon–Fri 10am–6pm; Sat & Sun: 9.30am–6pm; 7dh) is an unexpected delight. Most "zoos" in Morocco are scrubby little enclosures with a few sad-looking Barbary apes. This one, however, is positively palatial, as you might expect from what was formerly King Hassan's private menagerie. Amid the imaginatively laid-out

grounds there are lions, elephants, gazelles, jackals, desert foxes, giraffes and monkeys; there is a lake, too, with pelicans and wading birds.

Temara Ville and Plage

TEMARA VILLE has an old **kasbah**, dating from Moulay Ismail's reign. Other than that, there's little else to delay you, unless you want to stock up for picnics on the beach or the campsites further south. TEMARA PLAGE consists of several sandy strips, plus a cluster of discos that provide a summer alternative to the lack of action in Rabat. Few people stay here overnight, other than the well-heeled of Rabat, who maintain summer villas. However, if you want a beach base for Rabat, there are three **hotels**. The *Hôtel La Felouque* (☎03/774 4388, fax 774 4565; ⑤), by the main beach, known locally as Plage Les Sables d'Or, has a swimming pool, tennis courts and a well-regarded **restaurant**, *Les Sables d'Or*. Better value for money is the *Hôtel Panorama* (☎03/774 4289, fax 774 4819; ④), whose terrace overlooks the beach; the staff are friendly, and there is some attempt to maintain lawns and gardens. A third option is the *Hôtel St Germain en Laye* (☎03/774 4230, fax 774 4850; ④); it's cheaper than *La Felouque*, and there are discounts out of season.

Back on the coastal road, there is a good **restaurant**, the *San Francisco*, built by a Moroccan returned from thirty years in California, and decorated with a full-size Ford Mustang bursting through the bar mirror.

Ech Chiana

ECH CHIANA, also known as Rose Marie Plage, is 9km south from Temara and a slightly plusher resort, with a luxury beachside **hotel**, *La Kasbah* (☎03/774 9116, fax 774 9198; ⑤), popular with French package tourists. A little back from the beach there is also the cheaper *Hôtel Les Gambusias* (☎03/774 9008, fax 774 9198; ④), which does good meals, especially fish dishes, and has a swimming pool and a seasonal **campsite**. A second campsite (July–Sept) is attached to the restaurant-bar, *Plage Johara* (☎03/774 9251).

Skhirat Plage

The **Royal Palace** at SKHIRAT PLAGE was the site of a notorious coup attempt by senior Moroccan generals during King Hassan's birthday celebrations in July 1971. The coup was mounted using a force of Berber cadets, who took over the palace, imprisoned the king and massacred a number of his guests. It came within hours of being successful, being thwarted by the apparently accidental shooting of the cadets' leader, General Mohammed Medbuh, and by the strength of personality of Hassan, who reasserted control over his captors. Among the guests who survived was Malcolm Forbes (see p.91).

The palace still stands, though it has understandably fallen from royal favour, and there are a good many luxurious French-style villas in the vicinity – some old, some new, many unfinished. On the beach to the south of the main resort is *La Potinière* (☎03/774 2204; ②), a French-style *auberge*, run by a French couple; it's open in July and August only. The nearby *Hôtel Amphitrite* has been demolished, and the future of the site was unknown on our last visit.

Getting to the resort by public transport, take any of the slow **trains** on the Rabat–Casa line to Skhirat Ville, a small (and uninteresting) farming town, on the hillside, a couple of kilometres up from the beach.

Bouznika and Mansouria

If you have transport, there are further turn-offs to beaches, prior to Mohammedia. The coastal plain here is increasingly barren and the beaches are less developed, indeed isolated, and in places reached only by sandy tracks from the main road. At **BOUZNIKA**

PLAGE and **DAHOMEY PLAGE**, around 20km before Mohammedia, there are primitive summer **campsites**. Further south, 6km before Mohammedia, **MANSOURIA** has
two more campsites, the *Oubaha* (June–Sept) and the rather better *Mimosa* (☎02/332
3325; open all year).

Bouznika is famous for its two *haras* (stud farms). The most prestigious is the **Haras
Royal de Bouznika**, with its extensive stables, grassy acres and a pool or two.
Unfortunately, but not surprisingly, visitors lacking blue blood are not likely to gain
access. The other is one of the national stud farms, of which the largest is at Meknes
(see p.184), and if you are a hippophile and show interest, you could probably visit on
an open day or for an event.

The last place of note before Mohammedia is **PORT BLONDIN**, at the mouth of the
Oued Nefifikh and the beginning of the Mohammedia sands. It's flanked by a couple of
seasonal campsites and the *Hôtel La Madrague* (☎ & fax 02/332 2020; ④), a rambling
building, but well maintained by friendly staff.

From here, it's a straight run into Mohammedia, its approach heralded by bright new
villas either side of the road (now S222).

Mohammedia

The port of **MOHAMMEDIA** has a dual identity. As the site of Morocco's main oil
refineries, and the base of its petrochemical industry, it's an important industrial and
commercial city, with a population of some 130,000. Yet it's also a big-name resort – a
holiday playground for Casablanca – with one of the best beaches on the Atlantic, a
racecourse, the Ibn Batouta yacht marina and the Mohammedia Royal Golf Club
(☎02/332 4656, fax 332 1102) where the game was originally played in the sand in the
1920s, before a Frenchman, Pierre Uruguayen, shaped the present eighteen holes.

These two faces of the city – tourism and industry – are kept quite distinct, with the
latter contained in a zone to the southwest of the city centre and beach. In summer,
the city's population is given a huge boost by Moroccan tourists, mainly from Casa,
who camp by the beach in what is called *Mohammedia-Est*: a sequence of tented villages that stretch northeast towards Port Blondin and Mansouria. For foreign visitors,
there is perhaps less to tempt a stay. Despite a longish history as a trading port, this
was still a small village at the turn of the twentieth century and the city has little in the
way of monuments of "old Morocco". The only sight to speak of is a modern building,
the **Erradouane Mosque**, which with its elegant minaret has become a landmark of
Mohammedia since it was inaugurated in March, 1991.

Still, Mohammedia makes a very pleasant stopover, with its friendly, easy-going
atmosphere, and a fine selection of restaurants. If you are flying in or out of Casablanca,
you could do a lot worse than spend a first or last night here; it's only 20 minutes by train
from Casa and there are a dozen or so trains a day each way. In July, it may be worth a
special trip, too, for the week-long **Mohammedia Festival**, which encompasses all
kinds of cultural activities, craft exhibitions, a *fantasia*, cycling races and a marathon.

Practicalities

Orientation is not difficult as "downtown" Mohammedia covers quite a small area.
Between the **rail station** and the **Ville Nouvelle**, there is a small **kasbah/Medina**
area, built in a period of Portuguese occupation and still preserving their gateways. To
the west of the kasbah, a sequence of boulevards leads down to the beach. **Buses** and
grands taxis operate beside a small park on Rue de Baghdad, just in front of the train
station; local bus #1 runs from here, too, down to the beach.

Mohammedia has most facilities you'll need. There is a branch of the BMCI **bank** at
the top end of Avenue des F.A.R., facing the small roundabout in front of the main entrance
to the kasbah, and a branch of the BMCE on Rue Rachidi, one block to the west of Rue de

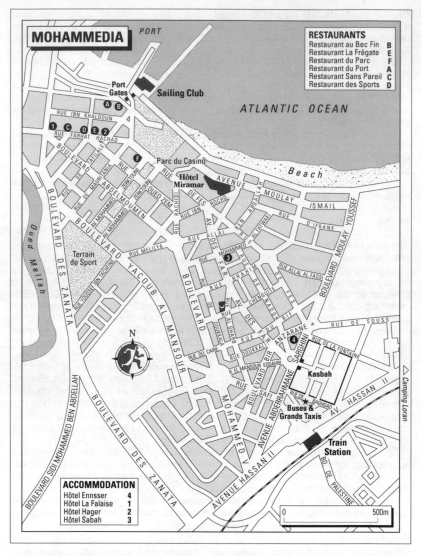

MOHAMMEDIA

PORT

RESTAURANTS
Restaurant au Bec Fin	B
Restaurant La Frégate	E
Restaurant du Parc	F
Restaurant du Port	A
Restaurant Sans Pareil	C
Restaurant des Sports	D

Port Gates

Sailing Club

ATLANTIC OCEAN

RUE IBN KHALDOUN

RUE FARHAT HACHAD

Parc du Casino

Beach

Hôtel Miramar

AVENUE MOULAY

BOULEVARD DE MAURITANIA

RUE DE FES

RUE RACHIDI

BOULEVARD YACOUB AL MANSOUR

RUE MELILYA

Terrain de Sport

RUE ALLAL

MOULAY

D'IFRANE

ISMAIL

MOULAY YOUSSEF

BOULEVARD

RUE ALLAL AL FASSI

Oued Meliah

BOULEVARD DES ZANATA

N

RUE DE SOUSS

RUE DE LA FONTAINE

Kasbah

Buses & Grands Taxis

AV. HASSAN II

Camping Loran

Train Station

BOULEVARD SIDI MOHAMMED BEN ABDELLAH

BOULEVARD DES ZANATA

AVENUE HASSAN II

BD. DE PALESTINE

0   500m

ACCOMMODATION
Hôtel Ennsser	4
Hôtel La Falaise	1
Hôtel Hager	2
Hôtel Sabah	3

Fes. The **PTT** is on Avenue Mohammed Zerktouni, also one block to the west of Rue de Fes – and facing the Parc du Casino. The **travel agency** Fedala Voyages at 35 Avenue des F.A.R. (☎02/332 7390) is helpful for confirming flights, arranging car rental, etc.

ACCOMMODATION
There are, at time of writing, four open **hotels**, and three closed ones; the *Miramar* (which has been picketed for over a year by its redundant staff), the *Samir* (which stands empty) and the *Castel*. The **campsite** too, *Camping Loran*, 2km north of Mohammedia

on the Rabat road, has an uncertain future, and has been closed even in summer, making sites up the coast, and with better reputations, more attractive alternatives.

Hôtel Ennsser, Bd. Moulay Youssef (no phone). This simple hotel with cubicles off a first floor corridor has undergone a facelift, but the facilities are limited and the ground-floor café lively or noisy, depending on your point of view. ③.

Hôtel La Falaise, Rue Farhat Hachad (☎02/332 4828). Run by an energetic French lady and closer to the beach than the *Ennsser*. Ten reasonable rooms, but only one en suite. Located off a central courtyard, behind a café/snack bar. ②.

Hôtel Sabah, 42 Av. des F.A.R. (☎02/332 1451, fax 332 1456). A modern hotel, halfway between the kasbah and the port. Expensive and catering more for businessmen than tourists. ⑤.

Hôtel Hager, Rue Farhat Hachad (☎02/332 5921, fax 332 5929). Only opened in 2000 this is a modest but modern hotel. ④.

EATING AND DRINKING

For its size, Mohammedia's choice of **restaurants** is impressive. **Breakfast and snacks** can be had at several pavement cafés facing the main entrance to the kasbah: the *Tiznit* and *Tarfaya* both serve grills and brochettes. Just inside the main gate of the kasbah, on the right, there are a number of similar café-restaurants worth a try.

Mohammedia has a few **bars** additional to the restaurants and hotels: the *Ranch Club*, for instance, on Rue de Fes, facing the Parc du Casino (the old Casino itself is now permanently closed). If it's nightlife you crave, it would be better to stay in Casa and explore the Aïn Diab corniche (see p.312).

Restaurant au Bec Fin, Rue Cheikh Chouaib Doukali, near the port gates. A small, but highly recommended restaurant with a truly Spanish flavour. Moderate.

Restaurant La Frégate, Rue Oued Zem, near the *Hôtel La Falaise*. Lobster, prawns, shrimps and all manner of seafish. Generous helpings, particularly of shellfish paella. And there's a takeaway and delivery service. Moderate to expensive.

Restaurant du Parc, Rue de Fes, facing the Parc du Casino and next to the Ranch Club. Excellent, with fish specialities. Moderate.

Restaurant du Port, 1 Rue du Port, next to the port gates. Previously known as *Chez Irène,* this is possibly the town's best-known restaurant, renowned for its charcoal grills, served in a flower-strewn garden. Indoors, there's strongly nautical decor. Same patron as *La Brasserie Bavaroise*, 133/139 Rue Allal Ben Abdallah, Casablanca. Moderate to expensive.

Restaurant Sans Pareil, Rue Farhat Hachad – near the *Hôtel La Falaise*. French cuisine, seafood and paella. Moderate.

Restaurant des Sports, Rue Farhat Hachad. Large and classy, with 'folkloric spectacles' at weekends in the season. The owners trained at Cornell University – and it shows. Excellent seafood. Moderate to expensive.

Casablanca (Casa, Dar El Baida)

The principal city of Morocco, and capital in all but administration, **CASABLANCA** (*Dar El Baida* in its literal Arabic form) is now the largest port of the Maghreb – and busier even than Marseilles, the city on which it was modelled by the French. Its development, from a town of 20,000 in 1906, has been astonishing but it was ruthlessly deliberate. When the French landed their forces here in 1907, and established their Protectorate five years later, Fes was Morocco's commercial centre and Tangier its main port. Had Tangier not been in international hands, this probably would have remained the case. However, the demands of an independent colonial administration forced the French to seek an entirely new base. Casa, at the heart of *Maroc Utile*, the country's most fertile zone and centre of its mineral deposits, was a natural choice.

Superficially, with a population of over three and a half million, Casa is today much like any other large southern European city: a familiarity which makes it fairly easy to

ACCOMMODATION

Auberge de Jeunesse	1	Hôtel Kon-Tiki	9	Hôtel Plaza	3
(Youth Hostel)		Hôtel Lausanne	15	Hôtel Rialto	14
Hôtel Aviatic	24	Hôtel du Louvre	16	Hôtel Terminus	23
Hôtel Basma	13	Hôtel Metropole	18	Hôtel Toubkal	2
Hôtel Colbert	12	Hôtel Miramar	7	Hôtel Touring	5
Hôtel Excelsior	4	Hôtel Mon Rêve	6	Hôtel Volubilis	20
Hôtel Guynemer	17	Hôtel des Negociants	8	Hôtel Windsor	11
Hôtel Ibis Moussafir	22	Hotel de Noailles	21		
Hôtel Kenzi Al Mounia	10	Hôtel de Paris	19		

Mosquée Hassan II

Minaret

El Hank, Ain Diab & Anfa

BOULEVARD SOUR DJEDID

BD. SIDI MOHAMMED BEN ABDALLAH

BOULEVARD ZIRAOUI

RUE JULES MAURAN

RUE DE GOULMINA

BOULEVARD MOULAY YOUSSEF

RUE DE GOULMINA

RUE SMARACH CHLEUH

OLD MEDINA

Chleuh Mosque

Grand Mosque

Koubba Sidi Belyout

RUE DES ANGLAIS

Bab Marraksh

Clocktower

BD. FELIX HOUPHOUET

Bus to Ain Diab

AVENUE DES F.A.R.

PLACE OUED EL MAKHAZINE

RUE ET M. GUEDJ

AVENUE

PLACE DES NATIONS UNIES

Synagogue

LUSITANIA

PLACE DE LA FRATERNITÉ

BOULEVARD D'ANFA

BOULEVARD MOULAY YOUSSEF

RUE DE PARIS

RUE IDRISS LAHRIZI

RUE ALLAL BEN

AV. HOUMAN

RUE ALLAL

RUE ABDALLAH

PTT

PLACE MOHAMMED V

Cathédrale du Sacré Coeur

Tribunal

Prefecture

French Consul

BOUL MOULAY YOUSSEF

Parc de la Ligue Arabe

BD. A. REITZER

BD. RAHAL EL

MAARIF

ONMT

BOULEVARD MOHAMMED ZERKTOUNI

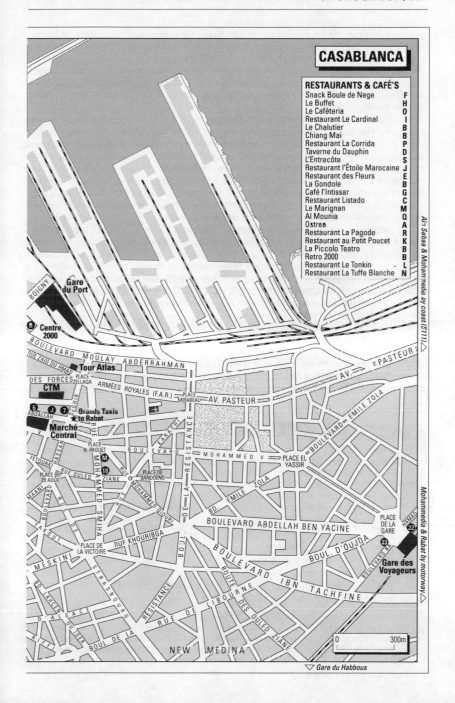

CASABLANCA

RESTAURANTS & CAFÉ'S

Snack Boule de Nege	F
Le Buffet	H
Le Caféteria	O
Restaurant Le Cardinal	I
Le Chalutier	B
Chiang Mai	B
Restaurant La Corrida	P
Taverne du Dauphin	D
L'Entrecôte	S
Restaurant l'Étoile Marocaine	J
Restaurant des Fleurs	E
La Gondole	B
Café l'Intissar	G
Restaurant Listado	C
Le Marignan	M
Al Mounia	Q
Ostrea	A
Restaurant La Pagode	R
Restaurant au Petit Poucet	K
La Piccolo Teatro	B
Retro 2000	B
Restaurant Le Tonkin	L
Restaurant La Tuffe Blanche	N

get your bearings and a revelation as you begin to understand something of its life. Arriving here from the south, or even from Fes or Tangier, most of the preconceptions you've been travelling round with will be happily shattered by the city's cosmopolitan beach clubs or by the almost total absence of the veil. But these "European" images shield what is substantially a first-generation city – and one still attracting considerable immigration from the countryside – and perhaps inevitably some of Morocco's most intense social problems.

Alongside its show of wealth and its prestige developments – most notably the vast **Mosquée Hassan II**, on a promontory looking out to the Atlantic – the city has had since its formation a reputation for extreme poverty, prostitution, crime, social unrest and the *bidonvilles* (shanty towns) which you will see both sides of the rail track as you approach Casablanca. The *bidonville* problem resulted partly from the sheer extent of population increases – which exceeded one million in the 1960s – and partly because few of the earlier migrants intended to stay permanently. Most of them sent back their earnings to their families in the country, intending to rejoin them permanently as soon as they had raised sufficient funds for a business at home.

The pattern is now much more towards permanent settlement, and this, together with a strict control of migration and a limited number of self-help programmes, has eased and cleared many of the worst slums. Also, *bidonville* dwellers have been accorded increasing respect during recent years. They cannot be evicted if they have lived in a property over two years, and after ten years they acquire title to the land and building, which can be used as collateral at the bank for loans. The dread of every *bidonville* family is to be evicted and put in a high-rise block, which is regarded as the lowest of the low on the housing ladder.

The problem of a concentrated urban poor, however, is more enduring and represents, as it did for the French, an intermittent threat to government stability. Casa, through the 1940s and 1950s, was the main centre of anti-French rioting, and post-independence it was the city's working class which formed the base of Ben Barka's Socialist Party. There have been strikes here sporadically in subsequent decades, and on several occasions, most violently in the food strikes of 1982, they have precipitated rioting.

NEW NAMES AND NEW AVENUES

The names of Casa's chief squares – **Place Mohammed V** and **Place des Nations Unies** - are a source of enduring confusion. In 1991, Hassan II declared that the old Place des Nations Unies (around which are grouped the city's main public buildings) be known as Place Mohammed V, while the old Place Mohammed V (the square beside the Medina) became renamed Place des Nations Unies.

Note also that, as elsewhere in Morocco, many of the **old French street names** have been revised to bear Moroccan names; older people and many petit taxi drivers still use the old names – as do some street maps still on sale. Significant conversions include:

Rue Branly – Rue Sharif Amziane
Rue Claude – Rue Mohammed El Qorri
Rue Colbert – Rue Chaouia
Rue Foucauld – Rue Araibi Jilali
Rue de l'Horloge – Rue Allal Ben Abdallah

Further map confusion is likely to be caused by the proposed remodelling of avenues to create a ceremonial approach from the (new)Place des Nations Unies to the Mosquée Hassan II. The planned route – the so-called **Mosquée–Théâtre axis** – will mean a fair amount of demolition southwest of the Old Medina, though, at time of writing, work was yet to begin.

Whether Casa's development can be sustained, and the lot of its new migrants improved, must decide much of Morocco's future.

Arrival

Trains from Marrakesh run to the **Gare des Voyageurs**, 2km from the centre at the far end of Boulevard Mohammed V. From Rabat (and Fes/Tangier), trains for Marrakesh pass through Gare des Voyageurs or, if Casablanca is their final destination, terminate at the central Gard du Port, 150m from Place des Nations Unies. If dropped at Voyageurs you can wait for a train from the airport (see below) which passes through the station and terminates at the Gare du Port.

If you don't want to wait for a train from the airport you might just get a place on bus #30 which runs into town from the square in front of the **Gare des Voyageurs**; otherwise, reckon on a twenty-minute walk or a petit taxi ride. Boulevard Mohammed V runs straight ahead from the square in front of the station, curving slightly to the left as you come to the next main square, Place El Yassir.

Bus stations are more central and straightforward. All the CTM buses arrive at the CTM *gare routière* on Rue Léon l'Africain (off Avenue des F.A.R. and behind the *Hôtel Safir*). Private line buses use a terminal south of the Place de la Victoire.

Grands taxis usually stop just behind the CTM *gare routière* (see buses, above), near the *Hôtel Safir* and the Complex Culturel Sidi Belyout at 28 Rue Léon l'Africain.

Coming from the **Aéroport Mohammed V**, used by all international and most domestic flights, there is a train service to Casablanca, calling at both the Voyageurs (20 min) and Port (30 min) stations; it runs roughly every hour from 6.15am to 10.45pm and costs 25dh. There is also a shuttle bus between the airport and the CTM *gare routière*.

For flights at odd hours you would need to charter a grand taxi to get from/to Casa and the airport, costing around 200dh.

Orientation, information and city transport

Casa is a large city by any standards and it can be a bewildering place in which to arrive, especially if you come in on one of the trains that terminate at the main **Gare des Voyageurs** rather than continuing on to the better-situated **Gare du Port** (see above).

Once you're in the city centre, however, orientation is relatively straightforward. It's focused on a large public square, **Place Mohammed V** (but note box opposite), and most of the places to stay, eat, or (in a rather limited way) see, are located in and around the avenues that radiate from it. A few blocks to the north, still partially walled, is the **Old Medina**, which was all there was of Casablanca until around 1907. Much further out to the south is the **Habous** quarter – the **New Medina**, created by the French, while to the west, along the corniche past the Mosquée Hassan II, lies the beach suburb of **Aïn Diab**.

Our map covers the city centre, but not Habous and Aïn Diab; to see how these relate, take a look at the map in the Casablanca **tourist office** pamphlet. Along with other information, this is available at the city's Délégation du Tourisme (formerly ONMT) office at 55 Rue Omar Slaoui (☎02/227 1177; Mon–Fri 8.30am–noon & 2.30–6.30pm), or the **Syndicat d'Initiative** at 98 Boulevard Mohammed V (☎02/222 1524; Mon–Fri 8.30am–noon & 3–6.30pm: Sat 8.30am–noon), which is more helpful and has regular exhibitions of local artists' work.

City transport

Getting around the city, **petits taxis** are easy to find along the main avenues and are invariably metered – as long as the meter is switched on you will rarely pay more than

6dh per taxi for a trip round town. For Aïn Diab the fare is currently 18dh (4dh extra if you get the driver to detour en route round the Mosquée Hassan II). There is a 20 percent surcharge at night.

You are unlikely to need to make use of **city bus** services, other than those from the airport or Gare des Voyageurs (see "Arrival"), and, if headed for the seaside, the #9 service from Boulevard de Paris to Aïn Diab. They get very crowded at rush hours.

Traffic is a nightmare in Casa: if you can avoid **driving**, try to do so. If you have a car, the larger hotels at Aïn Diab offer more security than those in the city centre.

Accommodation

Although there are a large number of hotels in Casa, they operate at near capacity for much of the year and can fill up at short notice for conferences. If possible, phone ahead for a room, or at least arrive fairly early in the day. Even if you have a reservation, it's wise to phone ahead the day before to confirm. If there is a royal-patronage event on, your hotel may well be commandeered.

City centre

The recommendations listed below are in the main, central area of the city. No hotels in the Old Medina have been included, as most overcharge for miserable rooms; in the "new city", by contrast, many of the cheaper places are quite stylish Art Deco buildings.

CHEAP

Auberge de Jeunesse (Youth Hostel), 6 Place Ahmed El Biolaoui, previously Amiral Philibert (☎02/229 5587, fax 222 7677). A friendly, airy place, nicely sited just inside the Medina, and well maintained. Neither IYHF nor national YHA cards are required. Despite being more expensive than most (45dh in dormitory, 120dh double room, including breakfast and shower), it's value for money – and popular; reservations are advisable June–Sept. Open 8–10am & noon–11pm. On the leafy square, there's a good café, small PTT and a hammam.

Hôtel Colbert, 38 Rue Chaouia (☎02/231 4241). Useful location if you arrive by bus; it's one block from the CTM. The hotel sign is difficult to see, but it's across the street from the daily flower stalls against the outer wall of the Marché Central. A bit gloomy, but clean and friendly. Rooms with showers cost more. There are several grill-cafés alongside for a quick snack or meal. ①.

Hôtel Kon-Tiki, 88 Rue Allal Ben Abdallah (☎02/231 4927). Ordinary but satisfactory. There are a couple of good breakfast cafés nearby, and the *Cintra* bar next door might (or might not) appeal. ①.

Hôtel du Louvre, 36 Rue Nationale (☎02/227 3747). Central and pleasant, but some rooms are better than others, so check before deciding. ②.

Hôtel Miramar, 22 Rue León l'Africain (☎02/231 0308). New on the scene, with a café next door and only 50m from the CTM. ①.

Hôtel Mon Rêve, 7 Rue Chaouia (☎02/231 1439). One of the best in a cluster of cheap hotels in this area. Showers on the corridor. ①.

Hôtel des Negociants, 116 Rue Allal Ben Abdallah (☎02/231 4023, fax 254 3589). Opposite *Hôtel Touring* (see below). Recently renovated and popular with Moroccan families. ②.

Hôtel Rialto, 9 Rue Salah Ben Bouchaib (☎02/227 5122). Opposite the Cinema Rialto and just of Bd. Mohammed V. Popular and worth making a reservation for in high season. ②.

Hôtel Terminus, 184 Bd. Ba Hamad (☎02/224 0025). Close to the Gare des Voyageurs, so quite convenient: clean, decent rooms with hot showers on the corridor. It's not in the same league as the nearby *Hôtel Ibis* (see "Expensive") but then it's less than one third of the cost. ②.

Hôtel Touring, 87 Rue Allal Ben Abdallah (☎02/231 0216). Another old French hotel that gets rather mixed reports from readers, but is popular with Moroccan visitors. A fall-back, really. ①.

Hôtel Volubilis, 20 Rue Abdelkrim Diouri (☎02/220 7789). Another fall-back choice – nothing special, nothing terrible. ①.

MODERATE

Hôtel Aviatic, 197 Bd. Brahim Roudani (☎02/225 7855). Well maintained and popular, but a little way out, by the Parc de la Ligue Arabe. Rooms on the courtyard are quieter. ④.

Hôtel Excelsior, 2 Rue El Amraoui Brahim, off Place des Nations Unies (☎02/220 0263, fax 226 2281). Another once-grand hotel, opened in 1915 and thus Casa's oldest surviving hotel, although outclassed these days by the big chain hotels on Av. des F.A.R. It's central and retains an elegance and very convenient location, near the Gare du Port. ④.

Hôtel Guynemer, 2 Rue Mohammed Belloul (☎02/227 5764, fax 247 3999). Refurbished recently and now very comfortable. Good restaurant, occasionally with music. It's not that easy to find so it might be worth investing in a petit taxi. ④.

Hôtel Lausanne, 24 Rue Tata – aka Rue Poincaré (☎02/226 8690, fax 226 8083). Not easy to find; it's opposite the Cinema Lutetia which most locals know well. The owner has lived in Switzerland where, according to Bernard Shaw, they know all about hotels. The *Hôtel Lausanne* illustrates his point; it's comfortable and well managed – and there is to be a *salon de thé* next door. ④.

Hôtel Metropole, 89 Rue Mohammed Smiha (☎02/230 1213, fax 230 5801). Off Bd. Mohammed V, this is a smart hotel with a bar and restaurant. ④.

Hotel de Noailles, 22 Bd. du 11 Janvier (☎02/226 0583, fax 222 0589) just off Av. Lalla Yacout. Immaculate and tasteful with a *salon de thé* and a touch of class, but friendly with it. ④.

Hôtel de Paris, 2 Rue Sharif Amzian (☎02/227 3871, fax 229 8069), on the corner with the pedestrianized length of Rue Prince Moulay Abdallah. In the centre of town and highly recommended; it's often full, so book or arrive early. ④.

Hôtel Plaza, 18 Bd. Felix Houphouct Boigny (☎02/229 7822, fax 298 7741). A short walk up from the Gare du Port. Another old hotel with big gloomy rooms, some en suite. However, it's been in the throes of refurbishment and is still reasonable value. ④.

Hôtel Windsor, 93 Place Oued El Makhazine (☎02/220 0352, fax 220 0387). Another nice hotel; large rooms with showers or bathrooms. The long-term plans for the area include a metro system with a station, and proposed new theatre, on Place Oued El Makhazine. ④.

EXPENSIVE

Hôtel Basma, 35 Av. Moulay Hassan I, just off Place des Nations Unies (☎02/222 3323, fax 226 8936). A newish business hotel, with a first floor restaurant. Views over the Medina and towards the Mosquée Hassan II. ⑥.

Hôtel Ibis Moussafir, Bd. Ba Hamad, Place de la Gare (☎02/240 1984, fax 240 0799). As with all hotels in this popular chain, the site is by the train station; in this case Casa-Voyageurs, so it's hardly central, though convenient for a late arrival (book in advance) or early departure. Restaurant, (sometimes noisy) bar, and small swimming pool. ⑤.

Hôtel Kenzi Al Mounia, 24 bis Bd. de Paris (☎02/223 0403, fax 223 0411). One of a luxury chain (represented in Marrakesh by the *Hotel Kenzi Semiramis*), situated behind the PTT, with "international" facilities including satellite television and presidential suites. ⑥.

Hôtel Toubkal, 9 Rue Sidi Belyout – off Av. des F.A.R. (☎02/231 1414, fax 231 1146). An upmarket location, near the chic shops on Bd. Mohammed V, and with luxurious, air-conditioned rooms. Nonetheless, it's nothing very special for the price. ⑤.

Aïn Diab

The seaside suburb of Aïn Diab (12dh by petit taxi) provides an alternative base if you can afford any of the trio of hotels below; all are comfortable business/tourist places, close to the beach. The few cheaper hotels in the area cater exclusively for Moroccan guests, and tourists are unlikely to find rooms on offer.

Azur Hôtel, 41 Bd. de la Corniche (☎02/239 1364, fax 231 1146). Previously the *Hôtel Tarik*, there's been a change of name but not of owner, and the hotel is much the same as before. It's on the landward side of the coast road, so does not have ready access to the beach, but it has a swimming pool. The rooms are simple, but elegantly finished. ⑤.

Hôtel Bellerive, 38 Bd. de la Corniche (☎02/239 1409, fax 239 3493). Overlooks the beach so the absence of a swimming pool is no great drawback, and the restaurant, albeit a touch expensive, compensates. ⑤.

Hôtel de la Corniche, Bd. de la Corniche (☎02/236 2782, fax 239 1110). Old, well-established hotel on the beach and with a swimming pool. A little careworn but still comfortable. ⑤.

Hôtel de la Côte, Bd. de la Corniche (☎02/294 2808, fax 236 0413). Formerly the *Hôtel Karam* it's barely recognisable now, with a glitzy facade which would not look out of place in Las Vegas, and an evening cabaret with Oriental dancers. ⑥.

Camping

Camping Oasis, Av. Omar El Khayam, Beausejour (☎02/225 3367). This is the nearest site, 8km out on the P8 road to Azemmour and El Jadida. It's frequented mainly by camper vans. If driving, follow Bd. Brahim Roudani out from the centre; this eventually becomes Av. Omar El Khayam. Hereabouts, ask for Marché Beausejour; the campsite, which is poorly signposted, is on the left at the end of this street market. There's no camp shop, but the local street market is more than sufficient. Bus #31 and #35 run past the site.

For details of **other accessible campsites**, see the Rabat to Mohammedia coast (pp.295–297), or the coast southwest to El Jadida (pp.315–317).

The City

Guidebooks used to declare, with some amazement, that Casa had not a single "real" monument. Given the scale and success of the 1930s **Art Deco** landmarks of the city centre – including the ensemble of public buildings on **Place Mohammed V** designed by the French architect d'Henri Prost – this was never quite true. However, the city did undoubtedly lack any one single, great building: a situation that, in part, prompted King Hassan II's decision to construct the **Mosquée Hassan II** on a truly epic scale.

The King first spoke of the Mosque on July 9, 1980 (his birthday and Youth Day) saying: "I wish Casablanca to be endowed with a large, fine building of which it can be proud until the end of time . . . I want to build this mosque on the water, because God's throne was on the water. Therefore, the faithful who go there to pray, to praise the creator on firm soil, can contemplate God's sky and ocean." Thus the Mosque now stands beside the sea on the road to Aïn Diab – and, if curiosity leads no further in this city, it must be seen – indeed, it cannot be missed.

The Mosquée Hassan II

Work on the huge complex of the **Mosquée Hassan II** was launched in 1980 and the mosque was inaugurated on August 30, 1993. The whole complex, however, and the proposed remodelling of the avenues leading towards it from Place des Nations Unies, is unlikely to be completed in the next decade. Raised on a rocky platform reclaimed from the ocean, it represents the late monarch's most ambitious building project, and his legacy to Moroccan architecture. Despite the Moroccan tradition of refusing non-Muslims access to religious sites and buildings, the mosque is open to all, on accompanied one-hour visits (9am, 10am, 11am & 2pm; closed Fridays; adults 100dh, students 50dh, children 25dh).

Designed by the French architect, Michel Pinseau, the mosque-complex is a phenomenal undertaking. Looking out towards it from the city centre, its huge size tricks you into thinking it's far nearer than it is. Its minaret is actually two hundred metres high, making it by far the tallest structure in the country – as well as the tallest minaret in the world; a laser on its summit projects a beam towards Mecca – to 'point out the way to Allah'. The mosque itself provides space for 25,000 worshippers within, where a glass floor reveals the ocean below, and a further 80,000 in its courtyard. Statisticians note that it is thus second only to Mecca in the mosque-size league – and that St Peter's in Rome could fit comfortably inside. In order that the faithful can "contemplate God's sky", the enormous roof of the Mosque rolls open on occasions. Eventually, the complex will include a medersa, museum and a library. The medersa has been completed;

YOU MUST REMEMBER THIS . . .

Probably the best-known fact about Casablanca is that it wasn't the location for the movie – all of which was shot in Hollywood. In fact, Warner Bros, upset by the Marx Brothers filming *A Night in Casablanca*, attempted to copyright the very name Casablanca – which could have been inconvenient for the city.

The film of course owes its enduring success to Humphrey Bogart, Ingrid Bergman and Sam's songs, but at the time of its release it received a major publicity boost by the appearance of Casablanca and Morocco in the news. As the film was being completed, in November 1942, the Allies launched **Operation Torch**, landing 25,000 troops on the coast north and south of Casablanca, at Kenitra, Mohammedia and Safi. The troops were commanded by General Eisenhower and consisted principally of Americans, whom Roosevelt believed were less likely than the British to be fired on by the Vichy French government in Morocco. An even more fortunate coincidence, however, took place in the week of the film's première in Los Angeles in January 1943. Churchill and Roosevelt had arranged an Allied leaders' summit, and the newsreels revealed its location: the **Casablanca Conference**, held in a hotel (long since gone) in the affluent suburb of Anfa, out beyond Aïn Diab.

Such events – and the movie – are not, it has to be said, evoked by modern-day Casa. Film buffs with a strong sense of irony, however, might check out **Rick's Bar** (open from 10pm) in the *Hôtel Hyatt Regency* on Place des Nations Unies, where the waiters take your (very expensive) drinks orders dressed in trenchcoats and fedoras. And for a glimpse of True Brit Expat life, as it used to be lived, there is always the **Churchill Club** on Rue Pessac in Aïn Diab. Established in 1922, as the "British Bank Club", its one condition of membership is that "the English language only should be spoken on the premises". One of the social highlights of the week is still the post-church and pre-Sunday lunch drinks.

the other two were started in 1987, and due for completion in August 1993, but are not yet finished. It's not possible for non-Muslims to visit the medersa, but it's assumed that, when completed, visitors will be welcome in the museum, if not the library.

The facts of the mosque's construction are almost as startling as its size. During the early 1990s, when it was being readied for opening, 1400 men worked by day and a further 1100 by night. Most were master-craftsmen, working marble from Agadir, cedar from the Middle Atlas, granite from Tafraoute, and (the only import) glass from Murano near Venice. Equally extraordinary was its cost – which is reckoned to have exceeded £500m/$750m – and the fact that this was raised entirely by public subscription. Press reports outside Morocco have alleged resentment of an overenthusiastic sponsoring operation which generated donations through non-voluntary deductions from wages, as well as door-to-door collections – including approaches to expatriate Moroccan workers everywhere from Germany to Saudi Arabia. However, in Morocco there is a genuine pride in the project, and pictures of the mosque are displayed in homes and cafés throughout the land. The mosque had a knock-on effect on the economy, too; at one stage the level of donations was so high that it temporarily reduced Morocco's money supply and brought down inflation.

The fact that the mosque bears the late king's name inspired rumours that it was designed in part as his mausoleum, along the lines of that of his father, Mohammed V, in Rabat. However, as we now know, he wished in fact to rest alongside his father, and that is where his tomb is to be found. It's important to add that in addition to his secular position, Hassan was also "Commander of the Faithful", the spiritual leader of Moroccan Muslims, and the building's site, in addition to reflecting his wish to give the city a heart and a memorable symbol, is designed to represent God's creation of earth, sea and sky.

Mauresque: Place Mohammed V and around

The French city centre and its formal, colonial buildings already seem to belong to a different and distant age. Grouped round **Place Mohammed V** (the former Place des Nations Unies), they served as models for administrative architecture throughout Morocco, and to an extent still do. Their style, heavily influenced by Art Deco, is known as *Mauresque* – a French idealization and "improvement" on Moorish design. The effect of the central ensemble is actually very impressive, the only feature out of place being a clocktower in the préfecture – an irresistible French colonial addition. Three times a week the fountain is lit from within by changing coloured lights, to taped music.

Other fine Mauresque and Art Deco buildings are to be seen along Boulevard Mohammed V, including a couple of the older hotels. They are beginning to be appreciated by the local authorities and there are, apparently, plans to establish an Art Deco historic district. Trademarks of the style on these private buildings are wrought-iron windows, staircases and balconies, and floral, animal and geometric designs on stuccoed pediments and friezes.

The Cathedral and Quartier Habous

More European in style, though again adopting traditional Moroccan forms, is the old **Cathedral of Sacré Cœur** at the far end of the **Parc de la Ligue Arabe**. It was built to a wonderfully balanced and airy design, paying genuine homage to its Moroccan setting, but it has fallen on hard times. After independence, it was used as a school and then as a theatre and cultural centre; now it's empty and, although the exterior is still magnificent, the interior is desecrated by neglect. Its future is uncertain; entry is forbidden – and may even be dangerous.

About a kilometre to the southwest, at the end of Avenue Mers Sultan, is the **New Medina** – or **Quartier Habous** – which displays a somewhat more bizarre extension of *Mauresque*. Built in the 1930s as a response to the first *bidonville* crisis, it was intended as a model quarter, and after half a century it still has a kind of Lego-land look, with its neat little rows of streets. What's most unreal, perhaps, is the neighbourhood mosque, flanked by a tidy stretch of green just as if it were a provincial French church.

South again from the New Medina, at the junction of Avenue Mers Sultan and Avenue 2 mars, alongside the Rond-point de l'Europe, is a last sight in these parts – the **Church of Notre-Dame de Lourdes**. Completed in the 1950s, it's smaller than the cathedral and still in use. Its beautiful stained-glass windows, the work of Gabriel Loire, a master craftsman from Chartres, are its pride and joy.

The Jewish Community

Today, more than 60 percent of Morocco's 6000 to 7000 Jews live in Casablanca, mainly in the **Lusitania district** – on and around Rue Ibn Rochd, formerly Rue Lusitania. The city's principal synagogue, **Benarroch**, stands at the junction of Rue Ibn Rochd and Rue J.J. Rousseau; another, **Em Habanime**, is to be found on Rue Ibn Rochd. In the same area, there are two Jewish **schools**, one primary and the other secondary, on Bd. Moulay Youssef near its intersection with Boulevard d'Anfa at Place de la Fraternité; up to 350 children attend these schools, though other Jewish children attend Moroccan state schools. A Jewish museum will open shortly in a nearby building that served as a *yeshiva* (rabbinical college for Orthodox students) until 1990. For more information and to arrange a visit, contact the nearby **Foundation**, 51 Rue Abou Dhabi (☎02/299 4940, fax 299 4941).

For further information on Jewish affairs in Casablanca, visit the ICF business school at 73 Boulevard Mohammed V and ask to speak with the director, M. Abergel (☎02/222 1759 or ☎02/236 2268).

The Old Medina and the port

The **Old Medina**, lapsing into dilapidation above the port, is largely the product of the late nineteenth century, when Casa began its modest growth as a commercial centre. Before that, it was little more than a group of village huts, half-heartedly settled by local tribes after the site was abandoned by the Portuguese in 1755. *Casa Branca*, the town the Portuguese founded here in the fifteenth century after the expulsion of the pirates, had been virtually levelled by the great earthquake of that year. Only its name ("The White House"; *Casablanca* in Spanish; *Dar El Baida* in Arabic) survives.

Now relatively underpopulated, the Medina has a slightly disreputable, if also fairly affluent, air. It is said to be the place to go to look for any stolen goods you might want to buy back – a character well in keeping with many of the stalls. There's nothing sinister though, and it can be a good source for cheap snacks and general goods. A single main street, which starts from the top end of Boulevard Felix Houphouet Boigny by a restored clocktower as **Rue Chakib Arsalane**, becomes **Rue Jemaa Ach Chleuh** halfway along. This street edges its way right through the quarter, past most of the market stalls and the principal mosque from which it takes its second name. At the far end, a small eighteenth-century bastion, the **Skala**, has been restored, with some old cannons. The walls on the west side of the Medina, starting with the restored Ottoman-style clock tower, have also been renovated.

While in the Medina area, you might also take the time to wander down to the **Centre 2000** complex, by the Gare du Port. Built in the mid-1980s, it encompasses twenty or so shops and five restaurants (see p.311), and all in all is quite an eye-opener into modern Casa life.

The one other building of interest hereabouts is the **Koubba of Sidi Belyout**, on the left as you walk up Boulevard Felix Houphouet Boigny from the Gare du Port and Centre 2000. There's a high wall round a small enclosure (which is forbidden to non-Muslims) but through the open door you can see the white domed tomb. Sidi Belyout is the patron saint of Casablanca and he has lent his name to the district southeast of the port. Legend has it that he despaired of mankind, blinded himself and went to live with animals who took care of him.

Aïn Diab: the beach

You can get out to the beach suburb of **Aïn Diab** by bus (#9 from Boulevard de Paris; see our map), by petit taxi (easily engaged around Place des Nations Unies) or on foot. The beach starts around 3km out from the port and Old Medina, past the Mosquée Hassan II, and continues for about the same distance.

A beach right within Casa may not sound alluring – and it's certainly not the cleanest and clearest stretch of the country's waters – but Aïn Diab's big attraction is not so much the sea, in whose shallow waters Moroccans gather in phalanx formations, as the **beach clubs** along its front. Each of these has one or more pools, usually filled with filtered seawater, a restaurant and a couple of snack bars; in the fancier ones there'll also be additional sports facilities like tennis or volleyball and perhaps even a disco. The novelty of coming upon this in a Moroccan city is quite amazing, and it's a strange sight to see women veiled from head to toe looking down onto the cosmopolitan intensity unfolding beneath them.

The prices and quality of the **beach clubs** vary enormously and it's worth wandering round a while to check out what's available. Most locals have annual membership and for outsiders a day or weekend ticket can work out surprisingly expensive (80–160dh), but there's quite often one place which has thrown its doors open for free in an attempt to boost its café business. If you are taking a petit taxi from the Mosquée Hassan II or the city centre, ask to be set down at any one of *Le Tonga, Miami, Tahiti* or *Plage Anfa;* then reconnoitre and make your choice.

CHURCH OF ST JOHN THE EVANGELIST

The **Church of St John the Evangelist**, on Rue Felix and Max Guedj, stood in open fields when it was built in 1906. It now stands, partially hidden by a high wall and the tall trees surrounding it, in the centre of modern Casablanca – testimony to the phenomenal growth of the city.

Within twelve months of its consecration, the church was involved in events which led to the **first French landings** here. Some Europeans working on the port were murdered as Shaweea tribesmen from the interior invaded the town. They sacked the church, destroying the organ and ripping up the lectern Bible. Peace of a sort was restored by a French bombardment and subsequent occupation of the town.

In 1942, during **World War II**, the church was filled with troops involved in Operation Torch, when American troops landed at Casablanca and elsewhere on the Atlantic coast (see p.307). An early member of the congregation at this time was General George Patton, who had led his troops ashore at Safi. He presented the oak pulpit, which still stands in the church, "in memory of the men of all nations who fell in the fighting around Casablanca".

Currently, Rev John Gooch (☎02/225 7120) is the chaplain and many Americans still attend his services, details of which are displayed on the door in the high wall.

Out beyond Aïn Diab, along the corniche and inland from it, is the suburb of **Anfa**, where the city's wealthy have their villas, and companies their corporate headquarters – including the striking **OCP** (*Office Chérifien des Phosphates*) shiny black block alongside the Old Casablanca airport, now known as Aeroport Casa Anfa and used for private and business internal flights. Here, too, are the villas of rich Saudis, and overlooking the corniche, the wealthy **Ibn Saud Foundation** and its beautiful mosque.

Restaurants, bars and nightlife

Casa has the reputation of being the best place to eat in Morocco, and if you can afford the fancier restaurant prices, this is certainly true. There are fine seafood restaurants along the corniche at Aïn Diab and the bays beyond, and some stylish old French colonial ones round the central boulevards. On a budget, too, there's little problem in finding good-value meals or snacks.

The city is equally well known for its **ice cream parlours** and **pâtisseries**; three of the best are **Oliver's**, Av. Hassan II; **L'Igloo**, Bd. du Janvier (south of Place Mohammed V); and **Gâteaux Bennis**, 2 Rue Fkih El Gabbas in the Quartier Habous.

Restaurants

Good restaurants in three areas – **downtown Casa**, inside the **Centre 2000** (the shopping complex by the port) and around the **Corniche/Aïn Diab** – are suggested below. In addition, there are inexpensive hole-in-the-wall eateries in the **Old Medina**, and if you're putting together a picnic, the **Marché Central** (daily 6am–2pm) on Rue Chaouia groans under the weight of the freshest and best produce in Morocco.

DOWNTOWN: AROUND THE MAIN BOULEVARDS

Snack Boule de Neige, 72 Rue Araibi Jilali. Open all hours, serving tasty and cheap snacks.

Le Buffet, 99 Bd. Mohammed V. Quick and bright, and very popular. Good value *menu du jour*. Unlicensed. Cheap to moderate.

Le Caféteria, corner of Rue Abdelkrim Diouri and Rue Chaouia, near *Hôtel Volubilis*. Casa's answer to the American drugstore; popular with the city's youth. Unlicensed. Cheap to moderate.

Restaurant Le Cardinal, 11 Bd. Mohammed V. Traditional French restaurant on the first floor. Moderate.

Restaurant La Corrida, 35 Rue El Avaar – parallel to Rue Mustata Al Maani. Informal tapas-style Spanish restaurant run by a Spanish-French couple. In summer, you can eat in the garden. Closed Sundays and for the month of September. Moderate.

Taverne du Dauphin, 115 Bd. Felix Houphouet Boigny (☎02/222 1200). Long-established and very popular fish restaurant. You may need to queue, or you might try making a reservation. Moderate to expensive.

L'Entrecôte, 78 Av. Mers Sultan, next to a RAM office. French cuisine in a relaxed setting. Moderate to expensive.

Restaurant l'Etoile Marocaine, 107 Rue Allal Ben Abdallah. Ambitious, with specialities like pastilla and mechoui. A good atmosphere and convenient for the CTM bus station and Marché Central. Unlicensed. Open for lunch and dinner. Cheap to moderate.

Restaurant des Fleurs, 42 Av. des F.A.R. The snack bar downstairs is good for breakfast; upstairs, there is a more formal restaurant serving French and Moroccan dishes. Cheap to moderate.

Café l'Intissar, 14 Rue Chaouia, corner with Rue Allal Ben Abdallah. Excellent-value dishes – with a reliable *plat du jour* – served up by a young enthusiastic team. Unlicensed. Cheap to moderate.

Restaurant Listado, 133 Bd Felix Houphouet Boigny. A new fish restaurant with an imaginative menu. Open for lunch and dinner. Moderate.

Le Marignan, 69 Bd. Mohammed V, corner with Rue Mohammed Smiha. Basement restaurant with excellent Korean food, some cooked at the tables. Moderate to expensive.

Al Mounia, 95 Rue du Prince Moulay Abdallah. Traditional Moroccan cuisine served in a salon or out in the garden. You can eat well for 150dh. Closed Sundays.

Ostrea, Port de Pêche de Casablanca. This place, tucked away in the port area, deserves to be better known, especially for its oysters from Oualidia. Moderate to expensive.

Restaurant La Pagode, 95 Rue Ferhat Hachad. A good Chinese restaurant, a little out from the city centre, near *Hôtel du Palais*. Moderate.

Restaurant au Petit Poucet, 86 Bd. Mohammed V. A slice of old Casablanca style, this French restaurant is dressed up like a 1920s Parisian salon (which is really what it was). It was here that the French aviator and writer Saint-Exupéry used to recuperate between his mail-flights south to the Sahara; a couple of framed sketches by him grace the walls. You come for the decor rather than the food – which is OK but nothing more. Prices are moderate and there is a (much cheaper) snack bar next door.

Restaurant Le Tonkin, 34 Rue Prince Moulay Abdallah. On the pedestrianized length of the street and on the first floor Chinese and Vietnamese dishes served in an "exotic setting". Moderate.

Restaurant La Tuffe Blanche, 57 Tahar Sebti. One of the few remaining Jewish eating places and serving halal dishes. Convenient for the *Hôtel Guynemer* and *Hôtel de Paris*. Cheap to moderate.

CENTRE 2000

There are four restaurants in this shopping centre, of which we would recommend three, and two more nearby.

Le Chalutier A busy Spanish-run fish restaurant. Closed Sun Moderate.

La Gondole Despite the name, it's French-run – Toulousian to be precise. But it serves a range of European dishes. Leave the centre by the exit alongside *La Cage* nightclub. Moderate.

La Piccolo Teatro The latest restaurant on the block, serving Franco-Italian dishes in a relaxed setting. Moderate to expensive.

Retro 2000 The most upmarket Centre 2000 choice, serving French cuisine with flair, supervised by chef Jacky Rolling. Popular with businessmen for lunch and *bon viveurs* for dinner. Closed Sun Expensive.

Chiang Mai Outside the centre, opposite *La Gondole*, with a Vietnamese menu and range of prices, making it the cheapest of all for a lunchtime snack. Cheap to moderate.

ON THE COAST

Listings below are from east to west along the Corniche to Aïn Diab and beyond. It's often best to phone in advance to make reservations and check opening hours.

Le Cabestan, El Hank (☎02/239 1190; closed Sun). French cuisine, overseen by a highly competent patronne. Nice views of the El Hank lighthouse. Moderate to expensive.

La Mer, El Hank (☎02/236 3315). Almost next door to *Le Cabestan*, it specializes in seafood and fish. Expensive.

Orient Express, 41 Bd. de la Corniche (☎02/236 7073). An eccentric bar-restaurant, alongside the *Azur Hôtel*, in a coach from the Orient Express. Now more drinking than eating, but still fun.

Notre Alsace, 59 Bd. de la Corniche (☎02/236 7191). A very pleasant bar-restaurant-brasserie; also has a few rooms to let. Moderate.

Restaurant La Mamma, corner of Bd. de la Corniche and Bd. de Biarritz (☎02/239 1558). A wide range of pasta and standard Italian dishes. Moderate.

Restaurant Sijilmassa, Bd. de Biarritz (☎02/236 1350). Classic Moroccan dishes, including pastilla, served in gardens overlooking the sea. Fantastic view, but you may be discouraged by the restrictions. Women and children must be accompanied; cheques and credit cards are not accepted; and photography is forbidden. Moderate.

A Ma Bretagne, Sidi Abderrahmane, 2km west of Aïn Diab (☎02/236 2112; closed Sun and throughout Aug). French gastronomes visit Casablanca purely to eat at this restaurant, which is run by André Halbert, one of just three *Maître Cuisiniers de France* working in Africa and recipient of an award for the best French cooking in the continent. All the certificates and awards are displayed in the foyer. Specialities include *huîtres au Champagne* and *salade de l'océan au foie gras*; the site is delightful, close to the little island marabout of Sidi Abderrahmane (see p.315). Naturally, it's not cheap and you should anticipate upwards of 300dh a head.

Bars and nightclubs

Casa has a surprisingly elusive **nightlife**, at least in the centre, where the clubs tend to be 1960s-themepark-stripjoints. More happens out at Aïn Diab, though none are much recommended to Western women out for a hassle-free drink. Hotel bars provide a fall-back – see the hotel listings for suggestions. **Nightclubs** generally open around 11pm, close about 3am, and charge 100dh.

CENTRAL CASA

Au Petit Poucet, 86 Bd. Mohammed V. A bar attached to the famous restaurant; one of the more pleasant downtown serious drinking holes.

American Bar, 49 Bd. Felix Houphouet Boigny. Similar, if perhaps noisier.

La Cage, Centre 2000. Attracts a young crowd.

Club 84, Bd. El Mouahadine, near Gare du Port. Much the same as *La Cage* – and they are near enough to try both.

Don Quichotte, 6 Bd. Felix Houphouet Boigny at the junction with Av. des F.A.R. A real late-night dive, where you'll likely meet some Casa low-life.

La Arizona, across Av. des F.A.R. from the *Don Quichotte* on Rue El Amraoui Brahim, near the *Hôtel Excelsior*. Dancing of all sorts, a lot of noise and occasional shows.

Hôtel Safir, Av. des F.A.R in front of the CTM bus station. The hotel has an expensive, very swish (and pretty tasteful) bar – as well as a disco. Relaxed – especially by comparison with all the above.

Hôtel Hyatt Regency, Place des Nations Unies. The hotel houses *Rick's Bar* (see boxed feature "You must remember this . . . " on p.307), another expensive bar, and a nightclub, the *Black House*.

ON THE COAST

Le Balcon 33, 33 Bd. de la Corniche. Lively regular disco.

Le Tube, Bd. de la Corniche. Another popular disco.

Palm Beach Club, Aïn Diab. If you want to live a little more dangerously, try this beer hall, with its belly dancers, heavy-drinking crowd and police on the door to prevent trouble.

Metropolis, in the *Hôtel Suisse*; **La Notte** and **Calypso** are also on the Corniche and can be fun. Or maybe the driver of your petit taxi will tell you which bars and nightclubs are suited to your taste.

Listings

In addition to listings below, you may want to consult *Telecontact*, an annual directory with Yellow Pages-style listings for businesses and services in the Rabat/Casablanca/ Kenitra region. It's available from newsstands.

Airlines Air France, 15 Av. des F.A.R. (☎02/229 3030); British Airways/GB Airways, c/o Menara Tours, Tour Atlas (6th floor), 57 Place Zellaqa (☎02/230 7629); Iberia, 17 Av. des F.A.R. (☎02/229 4003); Regional Air Lines, 41 Av. des F.A.R. (☎02/253 8080); Royal Air Maroc, 44 Av. des F.A.R. (☎02/231 1122).

Banks SGMB, 84 Bd. Mohammed V; Crédit du Maroc, 48–58 Bd. Mohammed V; BMCE, 140 Av. Hassan II, has ATM. Most of the larger hotels will change money outside banking hours. Central ones include the *Royal El Mansour* at 27 Av. des F.A.R., *Hôtel Safir* at 160 Av. des F.A.R. and the *Hyatt Regency* on Place des Nations Unies.

Books/Newspapers For English-language books try English Forum, 27 Rue Mouftaker Abdelkader, or the American Language Centre Bookstore, 1 Place de la Fraternité (just off Bd. Moulay Youssef), both of which have a good range of paperbacks and fair sections on Morocco. Librairie Farairie, 43 Rue Araibi Jilali, and Librairie Nationale, 2 Av. de Mers Sultan, are also good for a browse. British newspapers and the *International Herald Tribune* are available from stands around Place des Nations Unies (and in the *Hyatt Regency* on the square) and at the Gare du Port.

Car rental *Telecontact* lists 65 car rental firms in Casa. Competition is stiff and deals are generally the best in the country, if you spend a while phoning around, or call in at the offices grouped along the Av. des F.A.R. Afric Cars, 33 Rue Mohammed Radi Slaoui (☎02/224 2187); Avis, 19 Av. des F.A.R. (☎02/231 2424); Budget, Tour des Habous, Av. des F.A.R. (☎02/231 2424); Ennass Car, 18 Bd. Anfa (☎02/222 0813); Europ-Car/InterRent, Tour des Habous, Av. des F.A.R. (☎02/231 3737); First Car, 157 Bd. Hassan Seghir (☎02/231 8788); Goldcar, 5 Av. des F.A.R. (☎02/220 2509); Hertz, 30 Av. des F.A.R. (☎02/248 4710); National Car Rental, 5 Av. des F.A.R.(☎02/247 2540); VISA Car, 17 Av. des F.A.R. (☎02/222 3075); and Weekend Cars, 39 Rue Omar Slaoui (☎02/247 2558).

Car repairs Garages include Renault: Place de Bandoeng (☎02/230 0591); Leyland and Fiat: Afric Auto, 147 Rue Mustapha El Maoui (☎02/227 9285); Ford: AutoHall, 44 Av. Lalla Yacout (☎02/231 9056); Peugeot: Siara, 193 Av. des F.A.R. (☎02/230 1762); and Volvo: Saidia StarAuto, 88 Av. Lalla Yacout (☎02/231 9003).

Consulates USA, 8 Bd. Moulay Youssef (☎02/226 4550); Denmark, 30 Rue Sidi Belyout (☎02/222 0752). France, 1 Rue Prince Moulay Abdallah (☎02/226 5355). Norwegians are represented by the Norwegian Consul in Casablanca (10am–noon; ☎02/230 5961). There is no longer a British Consulate.

Cultural events The Complex Cultural Sidi Belyout, 28 Rue Léon l'Africain (☎02/230 3760), behind the CTM bus station, has a programme of music, drama and dance. The older communal theatre is nearby on Av. des F.A.R. and hosts visiting groups. The Centre Culturel Français, 121/3 Bd. Mohammed Zerktouni (☎02/225 9077) has an extensive programme, particularly in winter: films, concerts, recitals, exhibitions, and library. Details of these, and other events are to be found in the local press, occasionally in the fortnightly *La Quinzaine du Maroc,* from the venues, from the tourist offices and in the major hotels.

Ferry agent COMANAV Voyages, 30 Av. des F.A.R. (☎02/248 4841, fax 248 4843), will give details and sell tickets for most ferry departures from Morocco.

Cinemas Casa is well served by cinemas. The Dawliz chain has two cinemas: Dawliz Habous (two screens) in the city near the *Restaurant des Fleurs* (and the Cinema Rif) and Dawliz Corniche (three screens) near *McDonald's* on the Corniche. Besides the Cinema Rif on Av. des F.A.R. (see above), there are the Empire on Av. Mohammed V, the Lusitania opposite the *Hôtel Lausanne* on Rue Tata and, said to be the best, the Lynx on Av Mers Sultan.

Hammams Every neighbourhood has several; one of the best is said to be the new 'Turkish' hammam, Rue Gerra in the Maarif area – ask a petit taxi to take you there.

Laundry La Vomatic International, 34 Rue Salah Ben Bouchaib.

Medical aid Dial ☎15 for emergency services or call SOS Médecins (☎02/220 2020). Addresses of doctors can be got from the larger hotels. Details of pharmacies open out of hours are to be found in the local press, or on lists displayed by all pharmacies.

Police Phone ☎19. Main station is on Bd. Brahim Roudani.

Post office The main PTT (for phones/*poste restante*) is on Place Mohammed V (Mon–Fri 8.00am–6.30pm & Sat 8am–noon). Use separate entrance (open 24hr a day) for international calls and *poste restante*.

Shopping Alpha 55, Av. de Mers Sultan, is a useful department store, with a good, 7th-floor restaurant. For Moroccan crafts, there are many shops on both sides of Bd. Felix Houphouet Boigny; here you might gain extra by bargaining but, at the upmarket boutiques at the Centre 2000, you can expect to pay more. Supermarkets are mainly out of the town centre; there are two on Route Bouskara, in L'Oasis district: Macro and, with a *Pizza Hut* as an added attraction, Marjane. There is another Macro in Aïn Sebaa.

Sports Casa is the best place in Morocco to see football; the city's rivals, RAJA and WYDAD both have grounds in the Beausejour district; check the local press for fixtures. The city also boasts a racecourse, the Hippodrome, at Anfa (active some Sundays) and, beside it, a 9-hole golf course (☎02/236 5355, fax 239 3374); there is another golf course with 18 holes at Mohammedia to the northeast (☎02/332 4656, fax 232 1102). As well as the beach clubs on the Corniche, you can swim in the open-air Piscine Oceanic in Aïn Sebaa. In the Maarif district, there is the Stade d'Honneur, a sports complex (☎02/236 2372) with a lot to offer. Finally, and not strictly sport, if you have children to entertain, there is the Sindibad amusement park beyond the hotels on the Corniche, with a huge cut-out of Sinbad, plus pedalos, dodgems, roundabouts and slides.

Tours If you want to book onto a tour of Morocco, KTI Voyages, based in Casa, are a very reliable operator, used by British companies like Hayes & Jarvis and Kuoni; their head office is at 161 Av. Hassan II (☎02/227 6244). If you want to see a lot in a short time, and are rich, you could fly from Casa Anfa with Privair (☎02/213 8639) to the destination of your choice.

Moving on

CTM run **buses** to just about everywhere, including Safi, Essaouira, Agadir, Tiznit and various European destinations; tickets and times from the terminal on Rue Léon l'Africain. If you are heading south for Essaouira, the best service is the "Mumtaz Express", which leaves at 5.00pm, arriving 9.30pm at Essaouira; most other services run via El Jadida and/or Safi. **Grands taxis** also run to Rabat, from the main stand.

You'll probably prefer to go by **train** to Rabat, Tangier, Meknes, Fes or Marrakesh. These departures are mainly (but not exclusively) from the Gare des Voyageurs but every train from Gare du Port to the airport passes through Gare des Voyageurs so it's not hard to make a connection.

Regional Air Lines runs a domestic service from Casablanca to Essaouira, Laayoune, Oujda and Tangier, see "Travel Details" for further information.

Casa to Marrakesh: Settat

The road and railway run side by side, south across the plains from **Casa** to **Marrakesh**. To the east lies the desolate and dusty phosphate-mining region, the Plateau des Phosphates. To the west, the land is more fertile and watered by Morocco's greatest river, the Oum Er Rbia, and its tributaries, inevitably dammed wherever convenient for irrigation and hydroelectricity.

SETTAT, 60km south of Casablanca, is the major city on the way to Marrakesh – a sizeable town and still growing. Though the bulk of new investment is in the Casablanca area, Kenitra and Settat are joint second, with the Rabat-Salé area representing only a small percentage of new investment. Already, Settat is the centre of the Moroccan **cotton industry**: spinning, weaving and ready-made clothes. In 1992, the Spanish company Tavex, a leading European producer of denim cloth, built a factory here and it now produces half the denim needed for Morocco's clothing industry.

The wealth of Settat is to be seen in its civic architecture and commercial edifices, mostly banks. The entry to the town follows a wall-watered valley; green lawns and trees on both sides and you'll pass the university and the nine-hole Settat University

Golf Club (☎02/340 2131, fax 340 2099). There's also the luxurious *Hôtel du Parc* (☎02/340 3941, fax 340 4208; ⑥). In the town itself there are two adequate hotels, both on Place Mohammed V; *Hôtel de la Place* (☎02/340 3062; ①) and *Hôtel Al Massira* (☎02/340 4072, fax 340 1092; ③).

Boulaouane: kasbah and wine

Fifty kilometres west of Settat, and halfway to El Jadida on the coast, is the impressive **Kasbah de Boulaoune** and the revitalized vineyards famous for **Gris de Boulaoune**, Morocco's best-known rosé. Despite these attractions, the area is rarely visited, mostly due to a lack of public transport and the necessity of a car, but, if it's possible, a detour en route from Settat to El Jadida can be most rewarding. If you fancy a visit and don't have your own transport, local advice in Settat is to arrange a taxi for a half or full day-trip, rather than searching for car rental outlets.

The **kasbah** stands high on a rocky outcrop above a great loop of the Oum Er Rbia, a natural site for a stronghold. It was built by Moulay Ismail in 1710 as a control post on the inland route from the Sahara to the Mediterranean, and to stand astride the rival regions of Doukkala, the hinterland of Safi and El Jadida, and Chaouia, the hinterland of what is now Casablanca.

Though strategically important, the kasbah rarely saw any action, and it appears today very much as it did in the eighteenth century. It has a well-preserved gateway, bearing the details of its construction. The high crenellated walls are complete with seven bastions, and the square minaret still stands; the mosque below however is not in such good shape. Alongside is the Koubba of Sidi Mansana. A *gardien* will no doubt greet you at the gateway and gladly show you round.

The future of the kasbah is uncertain. The French made it a historic monument in 1924 but took no steps to restore it. In the last ten years, there have been discussions about restoration, but lack of finance and a quarrel between present-day Doukkla and Chaouia have postponed a start.

The **Gris de Boulaoune** has a history too, but it's only in the last few years that it's come into its own. Nowadays, as you drive through the area, the impressive rolling countryside is dotted with copses of eucalyptus and conifers, between which are the large vineyards producing the wine. The efforts of this Moroccan-French enterprise over the last ten years, including the construction of new irrigation channels, has resulted in a wine which is, according to one Moroccan monthly magazine, "*le plus célèbre du Maroc*".

South to El Jadida

Buses and trains cover the ninety-odd kilometres from **Casablanca to El Jadida** on swift inland routes, of no great interest save for the town of **Azemmour**, an old Portuguese fortress town at the estuary of the Oum Er Rbia. Using public transport, Azemmour is easiest visited as an excursion from El Jadida, which is only 16km further southwest.

If you have transport of your own, the old **S130 road** is an enjoyable alternative, trailing the coast the whole way from **Casa to Azzemmour**. As you clear the urban area, the beaches are increasingly enticing and, as yet, virtually undeveloped.

Sidi Abderrahmane and beyond

En route to Azemmour, the most attractive spot is the beach facing the picturesque little island **Marabout of Sidi Abderrahmane**, 10km from central Casa, in the first bay that you come to after passing through Aïn Diab. The island itself is a tiny outcrop of rock, under fifty metres from the rock shore, from which it's possible to walk across at low tide. Non-Muslims, however, may not enter the shrine, which is entirely occupied by the marabout – or pilgrim centre – laid out around the shrine of Sidi Abderrahmane, a Muslim Sufi from Baghdad. The pilgrims are, for the most part, the mentally ill, for whom the saint has supposedly curative powers, and their families.

Nearby, overlooking the beach, is *A Ma Bretagne* (see p.312), the finest – and most expensive – **restaurant** in the Casablanca area. If you can afford it, and read this in time to make an advance booking, this is likely to be the best meal you ever have in Morocco, or anywhere else come to that.

Further along towards Azzemour, there's little beyond a couple of **campsites**, fronting onto stretches of beach. First of these, 16km from Casa, is *Camping Desserte des Plages*, reached by turning right off the S130, 5km before Dar Bouzza. It's a modest family affair, with no phone and a summer-only café. The other site, *Camping des Tamaris* (☎02/233 0060), is at Hajra Khala; 19km from Casablanca turn right and it's then a further 5km to the coast and campsite. This takes its name from the surrounding tamarisk bushes whose combustible branches fuel the pottery kilns of Safi.

Azemmour

AZEMMOUR has an oddly remote feel – and history, considering its strategic site on the great Oum Er Rbia river. It has long been outside the mainstream of events. When the Portuguese controlled El Jadida, Safi and Essaouira, they stayed here for under thirty years; later, when the European traders moved in on this coast, the town remained a "closed" port. Little bothered by the French, it remains today very much a backwater and sees possibly fewer tourists than any other Moroccan coastal town.

A short visit, nonetheless, is worthwhile, and the town is easily reached by **bus** or **grand taxi** from El Jadida. It's also on a branch line which runs from the Casablanca–Marrakesh main line but there is only one **train** a day and the station is 2km out of town, on the far side of the P8.

Once in town, getting your bearings is pretty straightforward. Buses and grands taxis stop on **Avenue Mohammed V**, the main thoroughfare of the new town, where drivers will also emerge. At the street's end is a garden square, the **Place du Souk**, with the **Medina** straight ahead. If you want to stay, there are two hotels, both on Avenue Mohammed V: at no. 38 is the sparse but clean *Hôtel la Victoire* (☎02/334 7157; ①), and at no. 78 the *Hôtel de la Poste* (☎02/335 7702; ②) has recently been renovated. The town also has several café-restaurants, best of which is the *Café El Manzah* on Place du Souk, with an active card school upstairs. There's another café-restaurant down at the beach (see opposite).

THE EMBROIDERY OF AZEMMOUR

The **embroidery** of Azemmour is distinctive and attractive, but it's more likely to be seen on display in Tangier's Kasbah Museum, or in Rabat's Oudaïas Museum than locally.

Its appeal lies in its design and technique. The designs reflect Renaissance Italy, filtered through Iberia. They depict stylized women, possibly goddesses, with upraised arms and full, triangular skirts. There are mythological animals – dragons, griffins and other fabulous beasts. The trees are stylized like a Jewish menorah, the candlestick with seven branches and the ancient symbol of Judaism. The technique is often to fill the background with small cross-stitches, revealing the subject in silhouette, reminiscent of embroidery from Assisi.

The Medina

The Portuguese remained in Azemmour long enough to build a circuit of walls, which are stacked directly above the banks of the river and dramatically extended by the white, cubist line of the **Medina**. The best view of all this – and it is impressive – is from across the river, on the way out of town towards Casablanca.

To look round the Medina, make your way to the Place du Souk, on the landward side of the ramparts, where you will see a sixteenth-century **gate** with an unusual, European-style, semicircular arch. Through it extends the old **kasbah** – largely in ruins but safe enough to visit. If you wait around, the local *gardien* will probably arrive, open things up and show you round; if he doesn't turn up, you might find him by asking at the cafés. Once inside the ruins, you can follow the parapet wall round the ramparts, with views of the river and the gardens, including henna orchards, along its edge. You'll also be shown **Dar El Baroud** (The House of Powder), a large tower built over the ruins of an old gunpowder store; note also the ruined Gothic window.

The old **Mellah** – Azzemour had a substantial Jewish population until the 1960s – lies beyond the kasbah at the northern end of the Medina. Here, beside ramparts overlooking the Oum Er Rbia, you will be shown the old town synagogue which is still well maintained and visited occasionally by practising Jews from Casablanca and El Jadida. It's cared for by a local family and you can – for an additional tip – see inside, where rests the tomb of Rabbi Abrahim Moul Niss – still a shrine for Jewish pilgrims and the focus of an August *moussem*.

These sights might not sound like much on paper, and you'll have to negotiate the final tip with the *gardien*, but all in all it's an interesting and enjoyable break from El Jadida, or a stop en route to the town, and easily combined with a swim.

Haouzia beach – and birds

The river currents at Azemmour are notoriously dangerous, but there's a nice stretch of **beach** half an hour's walk through the eucalyptus trees beyond the town. If you go by road, it's signposted to the "Balneaire du Haouzia", a small, cabins and camping complex occupying part of the sands. There is a **restaurant** here, *La Perle* (☎02/334 7905), which is fairly expensive but good (around 125dh per person), serving paella and other fish dishes; it's open all year. In summer, you can camp in the private complex; and, in winter, you can safely camp alongside the restaurant.

For **bird-watchers**, the scrub dunes around the mouth of the river should prove rewarding territory.

Golf and Mehioula

The coast between Azemmour and El Jadida is showing signs of development, the most ambitious of which is the **El Jadida Royal Golf Club** (☎02/335 2251, fax 335 4150), beside the sea, 10km from Azemmour and 7km from El Jadida. The eighteen-hole golf course was designed by the American Cabell B. Robinson and is one of the most attractive in Morocco, with mimosa, sand dunes, a large lake and, across the bay, the skyline of El Jadida. Alongside is the *Royal Golf Hotel* (☎02/335 4141, fax 335 3473; ⑥) managed by Club Med but open to nonmembers and with a swimming pool.

El Jadida (Mazagan)

EL JADIDA is a stylish and beautiful town, retaining the lanes and ramparts of an old Portuguese Medina. It was known as *Mazagan* under the Portuguese who held it from 1506 until 1769, when it was taken by Sultan Sidi Mohammed Ben Abdallah. Moroccan *Mazagan* was renamed *El Jadida* – "The New" – after being resettled, partly with Jews

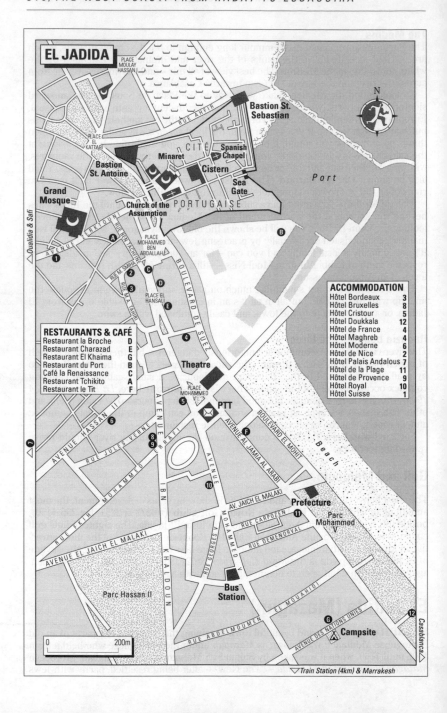

EL JADIDA

PLACE MOULAY HASSAN

RUE AHFIR

Bastion St. Sebastian

PLACE EL KATTABI

CITÉ

Spanish Chapel

Minaret

Bastion St. Antoine

Cistern

Grand Mosque

Sea Gate

Port

Church of the Assumption

PORTUGAISE

PLACE MOHAMMED BEN ABDALLAH

⊳ Oualidia & Safi

AVENUE ZERKTOUNI

RUE M SMIHA

RUE MA TAHIRI

PLACE EL HANSALI

BOULEVARD DE SUEZ

Theatre

PLACE MOHAMMED

PTT

AVENUE HASSAN II

RUE JULES VERNE

AVENUE MOHAMMED

RUE FKIH MOHAMMED

RUE ERRAFI

AVENUE

BOULEVARD EL MOHIT

AVENUE AL JAMIA AL ARABI

Beach

Prefecture

Parc Mohammed V

AV. JAICH EL MALAKI

RUE CARPOZEN

RUE DEMENORVAL

MOHAMMED V

RUE GEORGES

IBN KHALDOUN

AVENUE EL JAICH EL MALAKI

Parc Hassan II

Bus Station

EL MOUAHIDI

RUE ABDELMOUMEN

AVENUE DES NATIONS UNIES

Campsite

⊳ Casablanca

RESTAURANTS & CAFÉ

Restaurant la Broche	D
Restaurant Charazad	E
Restaurant El Khaima	G
Restaurant du Port	B
Café la Renaissance	C
Restaurant Tchikito	A
Restaurant le Tit	F

ACCOMMODATION

Hôtel Bordeaux	3
Hôtel Bruxelles	8
Hôtel Cristour	5
Hôtel Doukkala	12
Hôtel de France	4
Hôtel Maghreb	4
Hôtel Moderne	6
Hôtel de Nice	2
Hôtel Palais Andalous	7
Hôtel de la Plage	11
Hôtel de Provence	9
Hôtel Royal	10
Hôtel Suisse	1

0   200m

N

⊳ Train Station (4km) & Marrakesh

from Azemmour, by the nineteenth-century Sultan Abd Er Rahman. Under the French, it grew into a quite sizeable administrative centre and a popular beach resort.

Today it's the beach that is undeniably the focal point. Moroccans from Casablanca and Marrakesh, even Tangier or Fes, come here in droves in summer, and, alongside this mix, there's an unusual feeling of openness. The bars are crowded (a rare feature in itself), there's an almost frenetic evening promenade and – as in Casa – Moroccan women are visible and active participants.

Arrival, orientation, information and accommodation

By **bus**, you will almost certainly arrive at the bus station at the southern end of town, from where it's a twenty-minute walk to the Medina or to most hotels. Coming by **train** (there is one daily service to and from Rabat/Casa) you arrive at a station 1.5km out of town along the Marrakesh road (P8); petits taxis are usually available.

Once you realize that the beach faces northeast, not southwest as you would expect, orientation is straightforward, with the old **Portuguese Medina**, walled and looking out over the port, and the **Ville Nouvelle** spreading to its south along the seafront.

In summer you'd also be well advised to make a **hotel** booking – rooms can be very hard to find. In fact, at all times you may prefer to make some phone calls before pacing the streets, as the town extends for some distance along the seafront. Bear in mind also that, in summer, prices get hiked up to match demand.

If you have problems, the helpful **Délégation de Tourisme**, Avenue des F.A.R. (☎02/334 4788) or the more accessible **Syndicat d'Initiative**, 33 Place Mohammed V (☎02/337 0656), may have some ideas; there are flats and villas for rent, if you are staying for a week or more.

The **campsite**, *Camping Caravaning International*, Avenue des Nations Unies (☎02/334 2755), offers moderate facilities with lots of shade and is a popular site; the only disadvantage is its distance: 15min to the bus station and another 20min to town.

Hotels

Hôtel Bordeaux, 47 Rue Moulay Ahmed Tahiri (☎02/337 3921). Not easy to find; it's off Rue Ben Tachfine and beyond the signposted *Restaurant Tchikito*. An old hotel – the oldest in town, so the patron claims. Attractively refurbished and well maintained. Hot showers on the corridor. This is the best value for money in town. ①.

Hôtel Bruxelles, 40 Av. Ibn Khaldoun (☎02/334 2072). Bright and cheerful, with pleasant, clean rooms – and balconies at the front; despite the address, it's next to the *Hôtel Royal*. ②.

Hôtel Cristour, 7 Av. Mohammed V (☎02/334 2643) opposite the theatre and behind the prominent *Café Français*. Small rooms off a courtyard. Adequate, but noisy. A useful fall-back at the bottom end of the market. ①.

Hôtel Doukkala, Av. Al Jamia Al Arabi (☎02/334 3737, fax 334 0501). This modern package hotel, on the beach south of town, was privatized in 1995 but has seen little improvement. However, it can boast tennis courts and a swimming pool. A moderately expensive fall-back. ④.

Hôtel de France/Hôtel Maghreb, 12/16 Rue Lescoul (☎02/334 2181). This is in reality one hotel – though with two entrances, stairways and names. It's old and roomy, with great views of the sea, hot showers on the landing, and a ground floor café. Highly recommended. ①.

Hôtel Moderne, 21 Av. Hassan II (☎02/334 3133). Very much a family hotel, with a small garden. Hot showers on the corridor. ①.

Hôtel de Nice, 15 Rue Mohammed Smiha (☎02/335 2272). Off Rue Ben Tachfine and on the same street as the *Restaurant Tchikito*, which is well signposted. An OK fallback. ①.

Hôtel Palais Andalous [off map], Rue de la Nouie aka Bd. Docteur de Lanouy – it's opposite Hôpital Mohammed V (☎02/334 3745, fax 335 1690). Built in the 1930s for a local pasha and converted into a hotel in 1980, this remains quite an attractive place – and, out of season, reasonably priced. However, there have been mixed reports, and its cost and distance may make it a less appealing option. ④.

Hôtel de la Plage, 3 Av. Al Jamia Al Arabi (☎02/334 2648). Despite the rather grim bar on the ground floor, this is friendly, with clean, perfectly adequate rooms and separate facilities on the corridor. Convenient for the bus station and the *patron* also owns the campsite. ①.

Hôtel de Provence, 42 Av. Fqih Mohammed Errafi (☎02/334 2347, fax 335 2115). When the English owner of this popular hotel died, his Moroccan partner pledged to maintain standards and this central place is still the best mid-range choice, with a good restaurant, a garden for breakfast, and covered parking nearby. Be sure to reserve ahead, particularly in the high season. ④.

Hôtel Royal, 108 Av. Mohammed V (☎02/334 2839). Refurbished, large, airy rooms with erratic plumbing, a garden and lively bar. Convenient for the bus station. ②.

Hôtel Suisse, 145 Av. Zerktouni (☎02/334 2816). Small, friendly, with a garden and patio; en-suite facilities and pleasant café next door (same owner) for breakfast. Good value. ②.

The **Hôtel Agudeal**, **Hôtel du Port**, **Hôtel El Jadida**, and (once upmarket) **Marrahôtel** are at time of writing not recommended except as last resorts.

The town and beaches

El Jadida's **Medina** is the most European-looking in Morocco: a quiet, walled and bastioned seaside village, with a handful of churches scattered on its lanes. It was founded by the Portuguese in 1513 – and retained by them until 1769 – and it is still popularly known as the **Cité Portugaise**. As they withdrew, the Portuguese blew up several of the churches and other important buildings. The Moors who settled here after the Portuguese withdrawal tended to live outside the walls. Budgett Meakin, writing in the 1890s (see p.599), found an "extensive native settlement of beehive huts, or *nouallahs*" spreading back from the harbour, while European merchants had re-established themselves in the "clean, prosperous and well-lighted streets" of the Medina. As in all the open ports on this coast, there was also an important Jewish community handling the trade with Marrakesh; uniquely, old Mazagan had no separate Jewish mellah.

The Cité Portugaise

The **Cité Portugaise** is steadily being restored, and a walk round its newly spruced-up ramparts is not to be missed. Nor, above all, is a visit to the beautiful old **Portuguese Cistern** (Mon–Fri 9am–noon & 2–6pm, June–Sept 7pm; 10dh which also entitles you to visit the ramparts), a subterranean vault that mirrors its roof and pillars in a shallow film of water covering the floor. It's entered midway along the Medina's main street, on the left walking down, opposite a small souvenir shop.

The cistern was used to startling effect in Orson Welles's great film of *Othello*; he staged a riot here, provoked by Iago to discredit Cassio, and filmed it from within and above. It currently features in a Moroccan TV ad for *Samar* coffee and locals associate it with that, rather than Orson Welles. If the idea of competing with either appeals, you'll need a fast film for the refracted light.

At the entrance to the cistern there is a useful model of the Cité Portugaise, and if you continue up the street you'll come to its most prominent feature – the **Porte de la Mer**, the original sea gate which opened onto the port. The churches and chapels, long converted to secular use, are generally closed; but, if you have time, you can look for the small Spanish chapel (see map p.318) and the even smaller synagogue nearby, closed and bricked-up. More impressive is the seventeenth-century Portuguese Church of the Assumption by the entrance to the Cité Portugaise; it's now a cultural centre and is being restored. The minaret of the **Grand Mosque** here was once a five-sided watchtower or lighthouse, and is said to be the only pentagonal minaret in Islam.

The beaches

El Jadida's town **beach** spreads southeast from the *cité* and port, well beyond the length of the town. It's a popular strip, though from time to time polluted by the ships

Mosquée Hassan II, Casablanca

The walls, Essaouira

Camels near Essaouira

Essaouira

Safi pottery

Thuya workshop, Essaouira

Cité Portugaise, El Jadida

Marrakesh souk

Locksmith, Marrakesh

Dyers' souk, Marrakesh

Djemaa El Fna, Marrakesh

Craft school, Marrakesh

Djebel Oujdad, High Atlas

Lakes below Anhroner, High Atlas

Imlil, High Atlas

in port. If it doesn't look too good, or you feel like a change, take a petit taxi 3km northwest along the coastal road past the **Phare Sidi Ouafi** (lighthouse), a broader strip of sand where dozens of Moroccan families set up tents for the summer. Good swimming is to be had and there are makeshift beach cafés.

Plage Sidi Bouzid, 2km further southwest, is more developed, flanked by some fancy villas, a chic restaurant-bar, *Le Requin Bleu*, renowned for its fish, the less expensive *Restaurant Beausejour* and makeshift summer camping. The beach can be reached on bus #2 from alongside Place Mohammed Ben Abdallah, or by grand taxi.

Eating and drinking

For its size, El Jadida is well served by **restaurants**, and has most other facilities you might want to make use of. **Bars** are to be found mainly in the hotels – try the *Hôtel de la Plage* (lively), *de Provence* (pleasant) and *Palais Andalous* (more upmarket).

Restaurants

Restaurant La Broche, 46 Place El Hansali. In keen competition with the neighbouring *Restaurant Charazad*. Open 11.30am–3.30pm & 6.30–11pm; menu of the day 45dh. Cheap to moderate.

Restaurant Charazad, 38 Place El Hansali. Separated from *La Broche*, its nearest competitor, by the Cinema de Paris; the menu is similar, and includes vegetarian couscous, but sometimes dishes are not available. Nevertheless, marginally cheaper. Cheap to moderate.

Restaurant El Khaima, Av. des Nations Unies, opposite the campsite. Good-value Moroccan and Italian dishes. Well worth the walk. Moderate.

Restaurant du Port, at the northern end of the port, in an unprepossessing building, this first floor restaurant has a great view of the sea and serves good and plentiful seafood. Moderate to expensive.

Hôtel-Restaurant de Provence, 42 Av. Fqih Mohammed Errafi. Well-prepared, French-inspired meals, open to nonresidents, and licensed. Worth making a reservation (☎02/334 2347).

Café La Renaissance, Place El Hansali. One of the more popular places for an evening coffee and cake – and to watch the world go by. Cheap.

Restaurant Tchikito, Rue Mohammed Smiha. A memorable fish restaurant, with generous helpings and Koranic decorations. Unlicensed but the atmosphere is intoxicating. Moderate.

Restaurant Le Tit, 2 Av. Al Jamia El Arabi, by the PTT. Classy cooking and good service. Moderate.

In high season, there are many more eateries. Before deciding where to eat, stroll through Place El Hansali and Place Mohammed Ben Abdallah or along Boulevard El Mohit towards Parc Mohammed V until somewhere catches your eye.

Listings

Banks include Credit du Maroc, BMCI and WAFA on Av. Al Jamia El Arabi, and BMCE, with ATM, on the corner of Av. Ibn Khaldoun and Av. Fqih Mohammed Errafi.

Car rental There are two possibilities: Fedala, 4 Av. Ibn Khaldoun (☎02/334 3426) and Narjis, near the central market (☎02/335 1482).

Cinemas The Cinema de Paris and Cinema Rif are both on Place El Hansali.

Post office The main PTT is on Place Mohammed V (Mon–Fri 8.30am–noon & 2.30–6.30pm).

Souk A Wednesday souk takes place by the lighthouse northwest of town.

Theatre El Jadida is the only Moroccan town to boast a pre-independence theatre still in use – a fine building facing the town hall in the centre of town.

El Jadida to Safi

Once again, the main road (and express buses) south, from **El Jadida to Safi**, take an inland road, across the plains. The coast road, however, is almost as direct, and a very pleasant drive, with little development, lovely stretches of beach, and major **bird habitats** around the low-key resort of **Oualidia**. It's not much frequented by tourists, who seem to visit either El Jadida from Casa or Essaouira from Marrakesh – rarely both.

El Jadida to Oualidia

The main sights along this strip of coast come from **bird-watching**, though there is a minor ancient ruin at **Moulay Abdallah** and fine beaches once you are beyond Cap Blanc and the industrial **Port de Jorf-Lasar** (17km from El Jadida), the terminal for the OCP phosphate plants on the plains inland.

Moulay Abdallah and the ruins of Tit

MOULAY ABDALLAH, 11km from El Jadida, is a tiny fishing village, dominated by a large zaouia complex and partially enclosed by a circuit of walls in ruins. At the zaouia an important **moussem** is held towards the end of August, attracting tens of thousands of devotees – and almost as many horses in the parades and *fantasias*.

The village walls span the site of a twelfth-century **ribat**, or fortified monastery, known as **Tit** ("eyes" or "spring" in the local Berber dialect) and built, so it's thought, in preparation for a Norman invasion: a real threat at the time – the Normans having launched attacks on Tunisia – but one which never materialized. Today, there is little to see, though the minaret of the modern **zaouia** (prominent and whitewashed) is Almohad in origin; behind it, up through the graveyard, you can walk to a second, isolated minaret, which is thought to be even older. If it is, then it is perhaps the only one surviving from the Almoravid era – a claim considerably more impressive than its simple, block-like appearance might suggest.

Sidi Abed and Sidi Moussa

The first good beach beyond Cap Blanc is at **SIDI ABED**, a small village with a café-restaurant and a scattering of villas, 27km from El Jadida. A couple of kilometres before the village, and on the right travelling towards it, is *Le Relais* (☎02/334 5498, fax 334 5063; ④), with showers in the rooms and toilets on the corridor, and year-round, except for Ramadan, it's a restaurant: worth a stopover if you have time.

The coast hereabouts is an alternation of sandy beach and rocky outcrops, and past **SIDI MOUSSA**, 37km from El Jadida, it's backed by huge dunes, then, towards Oualidia, cut off by a long expanse of salt marshland. From here on south, for the next 70km or so, bird-watchers are in for a treat (see box opposite) but Sidi Moussa is attractive to non-twitchers, too, with its estuary-like lagoon, its beach, and a very pleasant **hotel**, the *Villa la Brise* (☎02/334 6917, fax 334 6933; ③), with French cooking, a bar, and a swimming pool that's full in summer. It's a popular base for fishing parties.

South of Sidi Moussa, the roadside is flanked by saltpans and by extensive plastic hothouses, for intensive cultivation of tomatoes and other vegetables; 63km from El Jadida, there's a Friday souk at **SOUK EL DJEMAA**, as the name suggests.

Oualidia

OUALIDIA, 78km from El Jadida, is a stunningly picturesque little resort – a fishing port and lagoon beach, flanked by a kasbah and a royal villa. The **kasbah** is seventeenth century, built by the Saadian Sultan El Oualid (after whom the village is named) as a counterweight and alternative to El Jadida, then held by the Portuguese. Until Sultan Sidi Mohammed took El Jadida, the extensive lagoon made an excellent harbour and, as late as 1875, a French geographer thought that "by a little dredging the place would again become the safest shipping station on the whole Moroccan seaboard". The **royal villa**, which now stands empty, was built by Mohammed V, who celebrated many birthdays and other family events here.

Today, most Moroccans know Oualidia for its **Japanese oysters**; Morocco's first oyster farm was launched here in 1957 and nowadays it harvests some 200 tons a year, most of which are sold locally. But the town really deserves to be better known as a resort: its beach is excellent for surfing and windsurfing, the atmosphere is relaxed, and swimming is safe and easy.

Practicalities

Oualidia is on the El Jadida/Safi CTM and local **bus routes**; services stop near the petrol station.

Most visitors to Oualidia are Moroccan families, who settle into tent colonies in and around the **campsite**, *Camping Oualidia* (☎02/336 6556; open July–Sept), which is pleasantly laid out in a garden behind the sand dunes. The **hotels** are all very good, too, and offer seafood meals to residents and nonresidents alike. Besides the hotels, there are a number of other **restaurants**; two to look out for on the top road are *Restaurant Thalassa*, which has set menus for around 50dh, and, on the right as you enter El Jadida, *Le Parc à Huitres No7*, which serves and sells oysters.

Motel-Restaurant à l'Araignée Gourmande (☎02/336 6447, fax 336 6144). This stands alongside the lagoon beach, and offers good-value rooms and a wide range of fixed-price menus, starting at 65dh, though recent reports suggest a decline in standards. ④.

Complexe Touristique Chems (☎02/336 6940). Also alongside the beach – and under the same management as nearby *L'Araignée Gourmande*. There are cabins of various sizes, from singles to fully equipped bungalows for up to five people; all with hot showers. It offers half-board for around 300dh a head, which is not bad value as the restaurant is pretty good. ④.

Hôtel Hippocampe (☎02/336 6108, fax 336 6499). A delightful place, halfway up the slope from the lagoon up to the village on the top. Rooms off a flower-filled courtyard and steps down to a "private" beach; also has a pool. Once again, half-board is preferred – at around 500dh. ⑤.

L'Initiale Hotel Restaurant, Oualidia Plage (☎02/336 6246). Situated next to the lagoon, this newly opened, family-run place is close to the beach, with a mixture of food on offer in the restaurant, including vegetarian options. Most of the nine rooms have a sea view. Booking advisable. ⑤.

Inland from Oualidia: Kasbah Gharbia

The Doukkala plains, inland from the El Jadida–Safi coast have long been a fertile and fought-over region, and there are scattered forts and kasbahs at several villages. One of the most interesting and accessible is at **GHARBIA**, 20km from Oualidia on the S1336 across an undulating limestone plateau. The **kasbah** here is a vast enclosure, four kilometres long on each side, bastioned at intervals, and with a gate at each point of the compass, giving onto roads to Oualidia, Safi, El Jadida and Marrakesh: a strategic site. Within, a few houses remain in use and there's a large white house in the

---

BIRD HABITATS AROUND OUALIDIA

The 70km of coast between Sidi Moussa (36km south of El Jadida) and Cap Beddouza (34km south of Oualidia) is one of the richest **birdlife habitats** in Morocco. The coastal wetlands, sands and saltpans, the jagged reefs, and the lagoons of Sidi Moussa and Oualidia shelter a huge range of species – flamingos, avocets, stilts, godwits, storks, waders, terns, egrets, warblers and many small waders. Numerous countryside species come in, too; golden oriole and hoopoe have been recorded, and flocks of shearwaters are often to be seen not far offshore.

The best watching locations are the two **lagoons** and the rocky headland at **Cap Beddouza**.

centre, occupied by the *caid* in the days of the Protectorate. If you visit – the trip is only really feasible if you have transport – you will be shown round by a charming bunch of locals, intent on pointing out the various features.

Cap Beddouza and Lalla Fatna

Continuing south from Oualidia, the road climbs a little inland and above the sea, which is hidden from view by sand dunes. It's a pretty stretch and the more so as you approach **Cap Beddouza**, where the rocky headland gives way intermittently to sandy beaches, sheltered by cliffs. At the cape there is a lighthouse and the *Auberge Cap Beddouza* (☎04/462 5843; ③), with a restaurant, bar and basic, rather overpriced cabins on the cliff top.

The best of the cliff-sheltered beaches is known as **Lalla Fatna**, 51km from Oualidia and just 15km short of Safi (with which it's connected by local bus #10 or #15). It's totally undeveloped, with nothing more than a **koubba** and in summer a few Moroccan tents, sometimes a café. If you are intending to stay, you'll need your own transport and to take provisions. The beach is a steep two-kilometre descent from the road; camping on the beach, make sure you've pitched your tent far enough back from the tides. There is a **moussem** at the koubba on the thirteenth day of Chaâbane (the month before Ramadan).

Finally, beyond Cap Safi, you pass the marabout of Sidi Bouzid, overlooking Safi with its Medina, port and industry. Down below is **Sidi Bouzid beach** – Safi's local strand – where on November 8, 1942, American troops under General Patton landed as the southernmost thrust of *Operation Torch* (see box on p.307), the Vichy French position offering little resistance. The cliff top is a good vantage point and capped by a couple of nice **restaurants**: *La Corniche* (☎04/446 3584) and *Le Refuge* (☎04/446 4354; closed Mon). It's said that on a clear day and with your back to the sea, you can see the foothills of the High Atlas from here.

Safi

Flanked by a strip of fertilizer factories, a vast grain silo and sardine-canning plants, **SAFI** is not the prettiest of Moroccan towns. It does, however, provide a glimpse of an active, modern and working community and the old **Medina** in its centre, walled and turreted by the Portuguese, holds a certain interest. The city – it merits the name with a population of over 300,000 – also has a strong industrial-artisan tradition, with a whole quarter devoted to **pottery workshops**. These have a virtual monopoly on the green, heavily glazed roof tiles used on palaces and mosques, as well as providing Morocco's main pottery exports, in the form of bowls, plates and garden pots.

The main interest in Safi is in its **Medina**, the adjoining **Dar El Bahar** fort, and the **Colline des Potiers**, the potters' quarter on the hill northeast of the Medina. Further out, on the Oualidia road, is the main industrial quarter and the new port.

South of Safi, the **coast** is heavily polluted and industrialized, and for a beach escape you'll want to head north. Local buses #10 and #15 run to **Lalla Fatna** and **Cap Beddouza** (see above) from the Place de l'Indépendance. In summer there are also local buses to **Souira Kedima** (see p.328).

Dar El Bahar, Kechla and the Medina

The **Dar El Bahar**, or Château de la Mer (Mon–Fri 8.30am–noon & 2.30–6.30pm; 10dh), is the main remnant of Safi's brief Portuguese occupation (1508–41). Sited on the waterfront, above the old port, it was built – in the Manueline style of the day – as the governor's residence, and saw subsequent use as a fortress and prison. Within, you

Sidi Bouzid / Town Beach △   △ Campsite, Marabout of Sidi Bouzid, Oualidia & El Jadida

Port

COLLINE DÊS POTIERS

Bab El Khouass

MEDINA

R. DES FORGERONS

Sidi Bou Dheb

Pottery Souk

Bab Chaaba

Kechla

RUE DU SOCCO

Zaouia Hamidouch

Grand Mosque

Portuguese Chapel

MOULAY

YOUSSEF

△ El Jadida & Marrakesh

Dar El Bahar

PLACE DE L'INDEPENDANCE

AVENUE

PTT

Jardins Publiques

RUE IBNOU BADIS

Swimming Pool

PLATEAU

AVENUE DE LA LIBERTE

MOHAMMED V

PLACE MOHAMMED

RUE DU RBAT

RUE ALLAL BEN ABDALLAH

RUE BEN NACEUR

RUE DHIS

RUE IBNOU BADIS

R. CHAWI

AVENUE

AVENUE MOHAMMED

PTT

ZERKTOUN

AVENUE DE LA LIBERTE

RUE EL AIBOUB

RUE DU CAID SIDI ABDERRAHMAN

AVENUE MOHAMMED V

PLACE IBNOU SINA

AVENUE MEDINA MOUNOUARA

AVENUE

ALLAL LLAN

PLACE IDRISS

RUE EL KHADIR RHAILANE

RUE EL KHADIR RHAILANE

△ Essaouira

Bus Station

Train Station

RESTAURANTS & CAFÉ'S

Café-Restaurant El Bahia	E
Restaurant Gégéne	F
Restaurant de la Poste	B
Restaurant de Safi	C
Restaurant La Trattoria	A
Café M'Zoughan	D

ACCOMMODATION

Hôtel Anis	7
Hôtel Assif	8
Hôtel Atlantide	6
Hôtel de l'Avenir	1
Hôtel Majestic	2
Hôtel Les Mimosas I & II	9
Hôtel l'Océan	4
Hôtel Safir	5
Hôtel Sevillana	3

SAFI

can see the old prison cells at the foot of a spiral staircase to the ramparts, where a line of Dutch and Spanish cannon is ranged pointing out to sea.

The old Medina walls climb north, enclosing the Medina, to link with another and larger fortress known as the **Kechla** – again, Portuguese in origin, and housing the town's modern prison until 1990. It's now the National Ceramics Museum (8.30am–noon & 2–6pm, closed Tues; 10dh) with a not too exciting collection of local ceramics, marginally better than that in the Dar Batha Museum in Fes. Of rather more interest are further cannon (British this time), garden courtyards and Portuguese coats-of-arms.

In the **Medina** proper, there is one further relic of the Portuguese, the **Chapelle Portugaise**. This was the choir of their cathedral – left uncompleted on their withdrawal – and again has Manueline motifs. It's most easily found if you enter the quarter from Avenue Moulay Youssef. Moving round from here, you reach the Rue du Socco – the main street – which leads uphill past a series of **souks**, food and domestic-goods markets, to the old city gate of **Bab Chaaba** and, through it, to the Colline des Potiers. En route, and just before the city gate, you pass through the **Souk de Poterie**. If you are looking to buy goods, you are likely to find better pieces here than in the showrooms at the foot of the Colline des Potiers itself.

Although non-Muslims are forbidden entry, it's worth mentioning two important Sufi shrines in the Medina: the **Marabout Sidi Bou Dheb** (at the bottom end of Rue du Socco) and the **Zaouia of Hamidouch** (near the Kechla). Sidi Bou Dheb is perhaps the best-known Sufi saint in Morocco and both his marabout and the Hamdouchia zaouia host **moussems** (held in May in recent years) attended by their respective brotherhoods; these feature music, dervish-type dancing and, often, trance self-mutilation with hatchets and knives. Heady stuff.

A more recent religious building is the **Jewish meeting place** and **synagogue** on Avenue Zerktouni. Built on the site of an ancient holy spot, it was opened in July 1993 under the patronage of the governor of Safi.

Colline des Potiers

The **Colline des Potiers** (potters' quarter) sprawls above the Medina and is impossible to miss, with its dozens of whitewashed beehive-kilns and chimneys, merging into the cemeteries beyond. The processes here remain traditional – electricity and gas have made scarcely an inroad on the tamarisk-fired kilns – and the quarter is worth at least the time it takes to wander up the new concrete steps and pathways. At the foot of the hillside is a street of showrooms. The products on display are of interest, but the colour dyes and garish designs are hardly comparable to the beautiful old pieces that can be seen around the country's crafts museums. Indeed, you are as likely to see U-bends for toilets being fired, as anything else.

And the sardines?

Safi's famed sardines are caught in the deeper waters of the Atlantic from Boujdour in the south to Safi in the north. There are around five hundred 18–20m wooden trawlers in the town fleet and you can still see them being made in the boatyards at Safi, Essaouira and Agadir. The fleet lands 350,000 tons of sardines annually and most of

---

THOR HEYERDAHL AND SAFI

Thor Heyerdahl, of Kon Tiki fame, had a theory that ancient Mediterranean people could have crossed the Atlantic to Central America long before Columbus made the same voyage in 1492. To test his theory he built *Ra*, a reed ship (see p.109), in 1969 in Safi, and prepared to sail across the Atlantic from the town. When asked why he had chosen Safi, Heyerdahl replied:

> *Safi is one of the oldest African ports beyond Gibraltar. Casablanca is a modern port, but Safi has been known from ancient times. Safi lies just where a coastal sailor coming from the Mediterranean world would be most likely to be swept out to sea by the elements. Just beyond Safi, the Canary current and the trade wind seize anything that floats, and sends it to America.*

His first attempt in *Ra* failed, but a year later, in 1970, *Ra II* successfully crossed the Atlantic and reached Barbados, proving Heyerdahl's theory correct.

them are canned in Safi. Increasingly, those caught further south are landed at the nearest port and brought to Safi in refrigerated trucks. Most of the tins get sold abroad – Morocco being the world's largest exporter of sardines.

Practicalities

Arriving by **bus**, you should find yourself at the bus station, around 1.5km south of the Medina. The **train station** (Safi has one train a day to and from the Casa–Marrakesh line at Benguerir) is a similar distance.

From either, it's easiest to hire a petit taxi or get on a city bus into one of the main squares, **Place de l'Indépendance**, just south of the Medina, or **Place Mohammed V** on the higher ground (known by the French as the *Plateau*); recently it's been spruced up with gardens, and is flanked by most of the city's major public buildings, including the PTT and the Municipalité. Most of the **banks** can be found around Place Ibnou Sina.

For a town which is not well endowed with historic monuments, beaches or memorable vistas, Safi also has an unusually helpful **tourist office**, located near the bus station at 26 Ruc Imam Malik (☎04/462 2496; Mon–Fri 8.30am–noon & 2.30–6.30pm) and there's an additional information kiosk behind the PTT and near the *Hôtel Assif* (no phone, same hours).

ACCOMMODATION

Safi has a reasonable range of hotels, catering more for Moroccan business travellers than tourists. Nonetheless, you should find a room without great difficulty.

The **campsite**, *Camping International Safi*, is 2km north of town, signposted to the right of the road to Oualidia. Spacious and well shaded, with a shop, pool and usual facilities; it has some great views over the town and towards the sea. Open summer only, it's 1km from here to the beach at Sidi Bouzid.

Hôtel Anis, on corner of Rue du R'bat and Rue de la Falaise (☎04/436 3078). Rooms with en-suite facilities and a few apartments, good for families and/or long stays. Also has car parking. ③.

Hôtel Assif, Av. de la Liberté (☎04/462 2940, fax 404 1862). Doubled in size and now with an underground car park, it's the best mid-range hotel. Light, airy rooms and a good restaurant. ④.

Hôtel Atlantide, Rue Chawki (☎04/446 2160). A pleasant old hotel, with views over the town from the balconies, a swimming pool and good restaurant. ④.

Hôtel de l'Avenir, 1 Impasse de la Mer (☎04/446 2657). The best of a trio of cheap hotels tucked just inside the Medina (the *Essaouira* and *Paris* are tolerable fall-backs). Cold showers in the rooms; hot showers (5dh) on the corridor. Grand views of the sea and a busy café downstairs. ①

Hôtel Majestic, Place de l'Indépendance (☎04/446 4011, fax 446 2490). Fine views of the Dar El Behar and the sea. Clean and pleasant rooms; hot showers 5dh. The recommended cheapie. ①.

Hôtel Les Mimosas I and II, Rue Ibn Zaidoun (☎04/462 6312, fax 462 5955). Built in the 1970s and now a little careworn. The hotel is one side of the road, with the *Golden Fish* disco/nightclub (10pm–1am) and apartments opposite. Underground car park and value for money, but not central. ③.

Hôtel l'Océan, 5 Rue du R'bat (☎04/446 4207). A decent fall-back if the *Majestic* is full. ①.

Hôtel Safir, Av. Zerktouni (☎04/446 4299, fax 446 4573). Good modern hotel with a swimming pool, tennis court, restaurant and bar, and commanding views over the city. ⑤.

Hôtel Sevillana, 1 Rue Ben Hassan (☎04/446 2391). Not easy to find; look hard for the sign. Recently redecorated rooms are OK, if a bit cramped, and there's a pleasant terrace. ①.

EATING

Café-Restaurant El Bahia, Place de l'Indépendance. Café downstairs and restaurant above, with fancy Moroccan dishes. Moderate.

Restaurant Gégéne, 8 Rue de la Marine, just off Place de l'Indépendance. A lively restaurant and recently extended, with limited but satisfying menu. Moderate.

Restaurant de la Poste, 40 Place de l'Indépendance. The upstairs restaurant is good: French cuisine and seafood. Moderate.

Restaurant de Safi, 3 Rue de la Marine, next to Gégéne. Grills. Cheap to moderate.
Restaurant La Trattoria, 2 Route de l'Aouinate (☎04/462 0959). Near the Délégation des Pêches Maritime de Safi, follow the signs to *La Trattoria*. Upmarket and very pleasant Italian restaurant. Live music: Thurs–Sat evenings. Moderate to expensive.
Café M'Zoughan, Place de l'Indépendance. Café-pâtisserie, good for breakfast.

Safi to Essaouria: Kasbah Hamidouch

Travelling by bus, you usually have no option but to take the inland P8, if heading southwest from **Safi to Essaouria**. With your own transport, you could follow the minor road S6531/6537, which runs past the canning plants towards **Souira Kedima**, around 30km south of Safi. This is a fine beach fronted by a rather bleak holiday-bungalow complex, used by people from Safi and Marrakesh on their summer holidays; nearby, on a windswept headland, there is an old Portuguese fortress known as **Agouz**.

A little beyond Souria Kedima, a new bridge allows you to cross the Oued Tensift to reach, along a stretch of good but sandy piste, the large and isolated fortress of **Kasbah Hamidouch**. This was built by the ever-industrious Moulay Ismail to control the mouth of the Tensift – one of the most active Moroccan rivers, which here finishes its course from Marrakesh. You can reach its ramparts across the fields.

South of the kasbah, a **new road** – still marked tentatively on some current maps – heads off along the coast towards Essaouira via **Cap Hadid**; it joins the Marrakesh-Essaouira road (P10) 4km outside Essaouira.

Djebel Hadid was once mined for iron ore and, indeed, in the nineteenth century, this coast was known as the Iron Coast.

Essaouira (Mogador)

ESSAOUIRA is by popular acclaim Morocco's most likeable resort: an eighteenth-century town, enclosed by medieval-looking battlements, facing a cluster of rocky off-shore islands, and trailed by a vast expanse of empty sands and dunes. Its whitewashed and blue-shuttered houses and colonnades, its wood workshops and art galleries, its boat-builders and sardine fishermen, its feathery Norfolk Island pines which only thrive in a pollution-free atmosphere: all provide a colourful and very pleasant backdrop to the beach. Many of the foreign tourists making their own way to Essaouira, are drawn by the wind, known locally as the *alizee*, which in spring and summer can be a bit remorseless for sunbathing but creates much-sought-after waves for **surfing** and **windsurfing**. In recent years, the town has gained quite a reputation in this respect, promoting itself as "Wind City, Afrika" and hosting national and international surfing contests.

The life of the resort, too, is easy and uncomplicated, and very much in the image of the youthful Europeans and Marrakchis who come here on holiday. Not that Essaouira is exclusively a backpackers' resort – these days it attracts all kinds of independent travellers, and increasing numbers of packages, with new chain hotels and villas springing up along the corniche. But, as yet, it's very far from spoilt, and remains a thoroughly enjoyable base to rest up after being in the cities, the Atlas or the desert.

Some history

Fronted by dramatic sea bastions and fortifications, Essaouira seems a lot older than it is. Although a series of forts had been built here from the fifteenth century on, it was only in the 1760s that the town was established and the present circuit of walls constructed. It was known to European sailors and then traders – as **Mogador**, said to be a reference to the prominent *koubba* of Sidi Mgdoul, used for navigating entry to the

ORSON WELLES' OTHELLO

Orson Welles filmed much of his **Othello** in Essaouira, returning the Moor (played by Welles himself) to his homeland. The film opens with a tremendous panning shot of the Essaouira ramparts, where Welles placed a scene-setting "punishment" of Iago, suspended above the sea and rocks in a metal cage. Later locations included a local hammam for the murder of Rodrigo – the costumes Welles had ordered from Jewish tailors in the Mellah were not ready, so he had to shoot a scene with minimal clothing – and the Portuguese cistern in El Jadida (see p.320).

The film was something of a personal crusade for Welles, who financed it himself, leaving the cast at intervals to try and borrow money off friends in Italy and France. During the course of the filming, he got through at least four – and perhaps six – Desdemonas, beginning with his fiancée Lea Padovani, until he soured relations by beginning an affair with one of the crew. In the end they were all dubbed, as indeed were many other of the characters – Welles performing most himself.

On its release in 1952, *Othello* was panned by the critics, and at Welles's death it was the only one of his dozen films to which he owned the rights. Forty years on, however, it was restored by his daughter for its anniversary, and shown at film festivals worldwide, and to huge acclaim. Even Essaouira had an open-air showing, in the presence of King Mohammed VI (Prince Héritier at the time); this event was accompanied by the official naming of a park area on the front **Orson Welles' Square**, complete with a thuja wood memorial made by Samir Mustapha, one of the town's most talented young craftsmen.

bay. Less likely is the legend that the town's patron saint was a Scotsman named McDougal who was shipwrecked here in the fourteenth century. To the Moroccans it was known as *Seurah,* from the Berber "little picture".

The work on the town's walls, which was completed in 1770, was ordered by the Sultan **Sidi Mohammed Ben Abdallah**, and carried out by a French captive architect, Theodore Cornut, which explains the town's unique blend of Moroccan Medina and French grid layout. The sultan's original intention was to provide a military port, as Agadir was in revolt at the time and Sultan Mohammed Ben Abdallah needed a local base. It lent itself superbly to the purpose, as its series of forts ensured complete protection for the bay. Soon, however, commercial concerns gained pre-eminence. During the nineteenth century, Mogador was the only Moroccan port south of Tangier that was open to European trade, and it prospered greatly from the privilege. Drawn by protected trade status, and a harbour free from customs duties, British merchants settled in the kasbah quarter, and a large Jewish community in the Mellah, within the northeast ramparts.

Decline set in during the French Protectorate, with Marshal Lyautey's promotion of Casablanca. Anecdote has it that he arrived in Essaouira on a Saturday when the Jewish community was at prayer; he cast a single glance at the deserted streets and decided to shift to the port of Casablanca further up the coast. The decline was accelerated after independence, by the exodus of the Jewish community. These days, however, the town is very much back on its feet, as a fishing port, market town and ever more popular resort.

Orientation and information

Though having long outgrown its ramparts, Essaouira is a simple place to get to grips with. At the north end of town is the **Bab Doukkala**; at the south is the town's pedestrianized main square, **Place Prince Moulay El Hassan**, and the fishing **harbour**. Between them run two main parallel streets, **Avenue de l'Istiqlal/Avenue Mohammed Zerktouni** and **Rue Sidi Mohammed Ben Abdallah**.

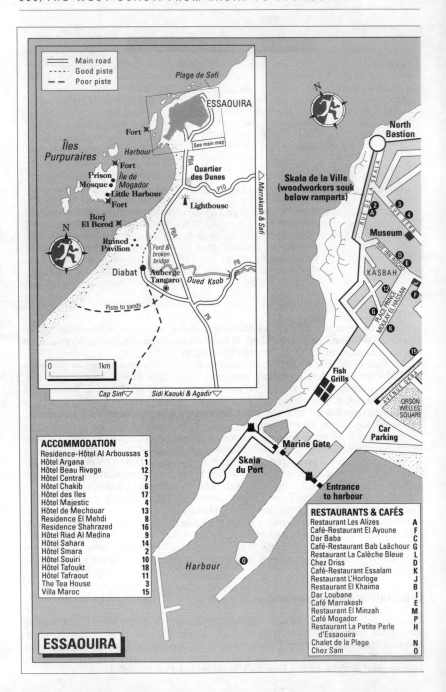

Main road
Good piste
Poor piste

Plage de Safi

ESSAOUIRA

Fort

See main map

Îles Purpuraires

Harbour

Fort

Prison
Mosque · *Île de Mogador*

· Little Harbour

Fort

Borj El Berod

Ruined Pavilion

Diabat · Auberge Tangaro

Ford & broken bridge

Oued Ksob

Piste to sands

Quartier des Dunes

P8A

P10

△ *Marrakesh & Safi*

Lighthouse

P8A

P8

P8

0   1km

Cap Sim ▽   *Sidi Kaouki & Agadir* ▽

North Bastion

Skala de la Ville
(woodworkers souk below ramparts)

RUE DE LA SKALA

RUE D'EFB

2
A
3
4

Museum

RUE IBN ROCHD

D
E

KASBAH

12

PLACE PRINCE MOULAY EL HASSAN

J
F

G

K

15

AVENUE OQBA

ORSON WELLES SQUARE

Car Parking

Fish Grills

Marine Gate

Skala du Port

◆ **Entrance to harbour**

Harbour

O

ESSAOUIRA

ACCOMMODATION
Residence-Hôtel Al Aboussas	5
Hôtel Argana	1
Hôtel Beau Rivage	12
Hôtel Central	7
Hôtel Chakib	6
Hôtel des Iles	17
Hôtel Majestic	4
Hôtel de Mechouar	13
Residence El Mehdi	8
Residence Shahrazed	16
Hôtel Riad Al Medina	9
Hôtel Sahara	14
Hôtel Smara	2
Hôtel Souiri	10
Hôtel Tafoukt	18
Hôtel Tafraout	11
The Tea House	3
Villa Maroc	15

RESTAURANTS & CAFÉS
Restaurant Les Alizes	A
Café-Restaurant El Ayoune	F
Dar Baba	C
Café-Restaurant Bab Laâchour	G
Restaurant La Calèche Bleue	L
Chez Driss	D
Café-Restaurant Essalam	K
Restaurant L'Horloge	J
Restaurant El Khaima	B
Dar Loubane	I
Café Marrakesh	E
Restaurant El Minzah	M
Café Mogador	P
Restaurant La Petite Perle d'Essaouira	H
Chalet de la Plage	N
Chez Sam	O

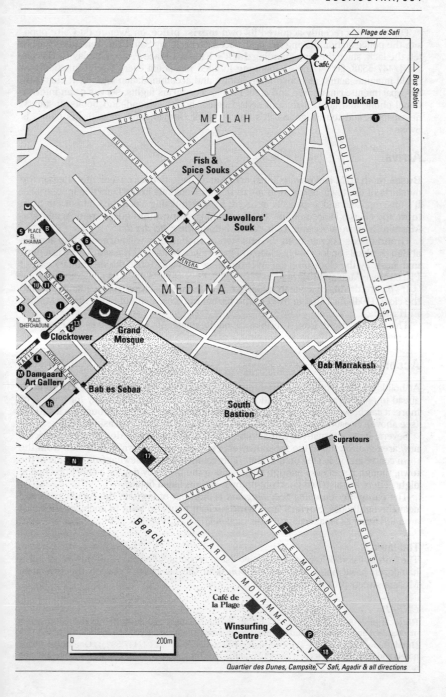

△ Plage de Safi

Café

Bab Doukkala

△ Bus Station

BOULEVARD MOULAY YOUSSEF

RUE EL MELLAH

MELLAH

RUE DE KUWAIT

RUE OUIDA

RUE DJI MOHAMMED BEN ABDALLAH

Fish & Spice Souks

AVE MOHAMMED ZERKTOUNI

Jewellers' Souk

5 PLACE EL KHAIMA
B
6
C
7 8

RUE DE LA SKALA

RUE MOHAMMED EL QORY

AVENUE DE L'ISTIQLAL

RUE MENSRA

MEDINA

9

RUE ATTARIN

10 11

H
J I
14 13
Clocktower

Grand Mosque

Bab Marrakesh

PLACE CHEFCHAOUNI

AVENUE MERS I.CARE

L
M Damgaard Art Gallery
1h

Bab es Sebaa

South Bastion

Supratours

17

N

AVENUE LALLA AICHA

RUE LAGGUASS

BOULEVARD MOHAMMED

Beach

AVENUE EL MOUKAOUAMA

Café de la Plage

Winsurfing Centre

P
18

0   200m

Quartier des Dunes, Campsite,▽ *Safi, Agadir & all directions*

The town has recently acquired its own **tourist office**, on Avenue du Caire opposite the police station, having for years been "served" by Safi. However, it has hardly felt the lack, since the long-standing **Jack's Kiosk**, 1 Place Prince Moulay El Hassan (☎04/447 5538, fax 447 6901) has long fulfilled just about every useful function you could imagine, acting as information booth, and accommodation agency. It currently lets apartments, runs horse and camel trips, reconfirms flights, serves as an international phone and fax centre, and sells English books (secondhand books upstairs), newspapers and tourist goods. It's run by Jack Oswald, who, despite his name, is Swiss.

Arrival

Buses (both CTM and private lines) arrive at a bus station, inconveniently sited on the outskirts of the town, about 1km north of Bab Doukkala in the Quartier Industrielle. It's unsignposted and, especially at night, it's worth taking a petit taxi into or out from town; the charge is around 7dh (10dh at night). **Supratours** buses from Agadir and Marrakesh arrive at Avenue Lalla Aicha, behind the *Hôtel des Iles*.

Grands taxis operate from the bus station, though they will normally drop arrivals at Bab Doukkala or, less likely, close to Place Prince Moulay El Hassan. There is a **petit taxi rank** by the clocktower on Avenue Oqba Ibn Nafia (once the mechouar) east of Place Prince Moulay El Hassan.

If you are driving, it's worth making use of the **car parking** space, manned round the clock (10dh for 24hr) in front of the harbour offices, south of Place Prince Moulay El Hassan.

The weekly **flight** from Casablanca on Regional Air Lines arrives at Essaouira Mogador airport on Saturday morning.

Accommodation

At holiday times (summer, Christmas/New Year), you need to arrive early or book ahead to ensure the accommodation of your choice; if you plan to stay for a week or more, it can be worth renting an apartment or a villa, for example, through Jack's Kiosk (see above). Season by season, more apartments are available, so ask around.

Several hotel alternatives can also be found in the **Quartier des Dunes** district, a new area growing up at the far southwest extremity of the town beach, 3km from the town centre and indicated on our map. This removes you somewhat from the life of the town, though it's an easy enough walk – along the beach by day, or a short taxi hop at night. There are also two good out-of-town options listed below.

The **campsite**, *Camping Sidi Magdoul* is 3km out of town on the Agadir road and near the lighthouse. **Surfers and windsurfers** may also want to consider the coast around Diabat as an alternative base (see p.337).

The town

The **hotels** listed below are a selective list of recommended places. If they're all full, a half-dozen basic hotels (eg *Agadir, Amis*) in the alleyways between the two main Medina streets provide last resorts.

CHEAP

Hôtel Argana, Av. 2 Mars (☎04/447 5975). Facing the noisy and dusty Bab Doukkala square, a marketplace and occasional funfair, this is a reasonable hotel; some rooms have showers. ①.

Hôtel Beau Rivage, Place Prince Moulay El Hassan (☎ & fax 04/447 5925). One of the oldest hotels and now showing its age, but still popular with backpackers. Rooms at the front overlook the noisy square. ②.

Hôtel Central, 5 Rue Dar Dheb, off Av. Mohammed Ben Abdallah (☎04/416 2802). Near the *Agadir* and not too attractive, but useful if everywhere else is full. ①.

Hôtel Chakib, 2 Rue Sidi Abdesmih (☎04/447 5291). Midway between the two main Medina streets. Fairly modern, with cold showers on the corridor; another useful fall-back. ①.

Hôtel Smara, 26 Rue Skala (☎04/447 5655). A small hotel with small rooms, but the sea view from the terrace and the front rooms is a bonus ②.

Hôtel Tafraout, 7 Rue de Marrakesh (☎04/447 6276). Modernish hotel in the heart of the Medina; comfortable rooms, some with showers, and a roof terrace. ①.

MODERATE

Hôtel Majestic, 40 Rue Derb Laâlouj (☎04/447 4909). Central, near Place El Khaima, and after a bleak period it seems to have put its house in order. ④.

Hôtel de Mechouar, Av. Okba Ibn Nafia (☎04/447 5828, fax 478 4827). Recently renovated, this is a rather stylish hotel, with a café-gallery downstairs, and a nice position facing the ramparts. If you can get one of the rooms at the front, it's good value for money. ④.

Residence El Mehdi, 15 Rue Sidi Abdesmih(☎04/447 6465, fax 447 5943). A converted *riad* (courtyard), comfortable rooms and a reliable kitchen, along with many local artefacts and old photos of Essaouira on show. ④.

Hôtel Sahara, Av. Okba Ibn Nafia (☎04/447 5292, fax 447 6198). Big rooms around a central well, and hot showers most of the time. ④.

Residence Shahrazed, 1 Rue Youssef El Fassi (☎04/447 2977). Opposite the police station and alongside the *Syndicat d'Initiative*. Recently converted and well equipped. ④.

Hôtel Souiri, 37 Rue Attarine (☎04/447 5399, fax 447 5339). Very central and very popular, with rooms at the front are better. ④.

Hôtel Tafoukt, 58 Bd. Mohammed V (☎04/478 4504, fax 478 4505). One kilometre south of the old town, facing the beach, this is a comfortable modern block, much nicer than it looks and with a good restaurant, *La Petite Algue*, and a bar, both open to nonresidents. Half board available but not obligatory. Book early for peak periods. ④.

The Tea House, 74 Rue Derb Laâlouj (☎04/478 3543). Two self-contained and well-equipped apartments (sleeping up to five in each) in an old house off the street. It's not easy to find – look for the sign "Maison du Bois" or call ahead and arrange to be met. It's run by a Scottish woman, Alison Macdonald, who lives there with her husband. ④.

EXPENSIVE

Residence-Hôtel Al Arboussas, 24 Rue Derb Laâlouj, opposite the museum (☎04/447 2610, fax 447 2633). A large house, nicely converted into apartments. ⑤.

Hôtel des Iles, Bd. Mohammed V (☎04/447 2329, fax 447 2472). Outside, but close to, the Medina. Comfortable, but a bit dull with rooms in a main block and chalet rooms round the swimming pool. Nonresidents can use the pool for 35dh a day. Overpriced, but discounts out of season. ⑤.

Hôtel Riad Al Medina, 3 Rue Attarine (☎04/447 2727, fax 447 5227). Opened in 1996, this is a stylish conversion of a substantial town house, with thirty pleasant (if somewhat overpriced) en-suite rooms off the three-storey central courtyard, and a sauna. The old house has a local notoriety from the 1960s hippies who lived here – Jimi Hendrix slept in the place, so it's said. ⑤.

Villa Maroc, 10 Rue Abdallah Ben Yassin near the clocktower (☎04/447 6147, fax 447 5806). This unique hotel, straight out of a *World of Interiors* magazine, features two old houses converted into a dozen or so rooms and suites – heated in winter and decorated with the finest Moroccan materials. Most of the year you will need to book several months ahead, though it's always worth a call on the off chance. If you can't get a room, nonresidents can dine here if they reserve before 4pm. It's accessible on foot only, along a newly paved passage just inside the Medina wall, though the hotel will carry your luggage from its car park. ⑤.

Quartier des Dunes

Al Jasira Hôtel, 18 Rue Moulay Ali Cherif, Quartier des Dunes (☎04/447 5956, fax 447 6047). Opened in 1998 and already popular, particularly with families in the holiday season. There are 39 rooms and a restaurant. ⑤.

Hôtel Ryad Mogador, where Bd. Mohammed V leaves the seafront and turns inland to become the P10 (☎04/478 3555, fax 478 3556). A severe building with little exterior charm, but a much more restful and subdued interior. ⑥.

Residence Vent des Dunes, Villa 20 (☎ & fax 04/447 5391). Leave the seafront at the *Villa Quieta* and this place is beyond the *Al Jasira*. There are fourteen rooms, with communal showers and toilets, and a small restaurant. ③.

Hôtel Villa Quieta, 86 Bd. Mohammed V (☎04/478 3281, fax 478 5032). Though a fifteen-minute walk along Bd. Mohammed V, this is a really charming place, with delightful owners and staff. A luxurious mansion built in semi-traditional style by the current owner's father in the 1950s, the rooms are all very tasteful and comfortable, retaining an upscale guesthouse rather than hotel feel. There is a swimming pool planned. Drinks and breakfast only. ⑤.

Out of town

Hôtel Jasmine, 8km out on the Agadir road (☎04/447 4440). Decent family-run possibility when everywhere in town is full, offering half-board. ③.

Auberge d'Ounara, 24km out on the Marrakesh road (☎04/478 5140). More of a complex, with cabin-style accommodation round a swimming pool, and a restaurant and bar. ④.

The Town

There are few formal "sights" in Essaouira, but it's a great place just to walk around, exploring the **ramparts**, the **harbour** and the **souks** – above all the **thuja wood workshops** – or wandering along the immense windswept **beach**.

The Skala de la Ville, thuja wood workshops and galleries

The ramparts are the obvious place to start a tour of Essaouira. If you head north along the lane at the end of Place Prince Moulay El Hassan, you can gain access to the **Skala de la Ville**, the great sea bastion which runs along the northern cliffs. Along the top of it are a collection of European cannon, presented to Sultan Sidi Mohammed Ben

---

CRAFTS IN ESSAOUIRA

The quality of the marquetry and carving in Essaouira is so high that it seems invidious to pick out individual workshops from the forty or so along the Skala. However, there are certain outlets elsewhere in the town that are worth visiting; some of them also display the work of local artists, many of whom are well known in Morocco and in Europe. These include:

Afalkay Art, 9 Place Prince Moulay El Hassan. A vast and somewhat impersonal emporium, but useful for gauging quality and prices elsewhere.

Jiska, 11 Rue Derb Laâlouj, near the museum. A popular boutique which includes Alain Delon among its regular customers: old and new carpets, ceramics from Fes and Safi, original thuja sculptures and many leather jackets.

Galerie La Kasbah, 4 Rue Tetouan. There is usually a good show of arts and crafts in the open-air courtyard.

Galerie d'Art Frederic Damgaard on Av. Oqba Ibn Nafia (daily 10am–1pm & 3–7pm). It's more a gallery for paintings than thuja creations, regularly exhibiting twenty or so locally based artists. However, it's run by a Danish furniture designer, who uses the traditional thuja techniques in a highly imaginative, modern context – and these pieces are well worth seeing.

Espace Othello, 9 Rue Mohammed Layachi, behind the *Hôtel Sahara*. This art gallery was opened in 1993 and displays the work of local artists; most of which is for sale. The owner is the *patron* of the nearby *Restaurant El Minzah*.

Abdallah by ambitious nineteenth-century merchants, and at its end is the circular **North Bastion**, with panoramic views across the Medina, kasbah and Mellah quarters, and out to sea.

Along the Rue de Skala, built into the ramparts, are a group of **marquetry and wood-carving workshops**, long established in Essaouira. These artisans produce amazingly painstaking and beautiful marquetry work from the local **thuya** (or *thuja*, or *arar* in Arabic), a mahogany-like hardwood from a local coniferous tree, from which they adapt both the trunk and the roots (or *loupe*). With total justice, they claim that their produce is the best in the country. If you see good examples elsewhere they've probably come from here, and if you're thinking of buying – boxes and chess sets are for sale, as well as traditional furniture – this is the best place to do it.

Also of interest for the local craft content is the **Musée Sidi Mohammed Ben Abdallah** (8.30am–6.30pm; closed Tues) on Rue Derb Laâlouj. It displays carpets, costumes and musical instruments decorated with marquetry, which are still used by the gnaoua musicians locally and on overseas tours. One feature of the collection is the display of interrelated artefacts associated with the different brotherhoods. And don't miss the gallery of pictures of old Essaouira, recently exhibited in the Pompidou Centre in Paris. The museum is housed in a nineteenth-century mansion which served as the town hall during the Protectorate; it's been restored recently and the central courtyard is now glassed over.

Spice and jewellery souks and the Mellah

The town's **other souks** spread around and to the south of two arcades, on either side of Rue Mohammed Zerktouni, and up towards the Mellah. Worth particular attention are the **Marché d'Epices** (spice market) and **Souk des Bijoutiers** (jewellers' market). Stallholders in the spice souk will extol the virtues of their wares, including exotic remedies for baldness, infertility and so on.

The jewellery business was one of the traditional trades of Essaouira's Jewish community, who have long since deserted the **Mellah**, in the northwest corner of the ramparts. A gloomy-looking part of the town, it was locked at night up until the end of the nineteenth century.

There have been various estimates as to the size of the **Jewish community** in the last quarter of the nineteenth century, ranging from 4000 to 9000 – the likelihood being at the top end of the scale. It is also probable that they comprised around half of the total population. Trade was carried out mainly with Marseilles and London, but there were never more than 300 Europeans living in the Mellah, engaged primarily in trade. The principal exports were almonds, goatskins, olive oil and ostrich feathers; and the principal imports were cotton goods (half the total value) and tea. The philanthropist **Moses Montefiore** was born here.

Today, the old Jewish quarter is noticeably in decline, with many of its houses deserted and in a dangerous condition. A dozen or so Jews currently live in Essaouira, but not necessarily in the old and fetid Mellah.

At the northeast corner of the Medina, **Bab Doukkala** leads to a small Christian cemetery (the entrance is on the left), and the area around the gate also houses an embryonic artists' centre, the most notable feature of which is the *Mogador Café* displaying psychedelic pictures. Some 400m beyond Bab Doukkala there is further evidence of the former Jewish community in the extensive Jewish cemetery – two vast grey lanes of tombstones, carefully tended and well ordered, in a site on both sides of the road. The principal entrance is on the right.

The port

At some point, it's worth making your way down to the **harbour** via the Marine Gate. Essaouira is the country's third fishing port after Agadir and Safi, and the port area bustles with life for most of the day, with the local wooden fishing boats being built or repaired, and the fishing fleet bringing in the day's catch.

Just outside the port area, on the road to the main square, is a line of wonderful **fish grill-cafés**, with wooden tables and benches laid out overlooking the sea. These are an absolute must for a stay in Essaouira (and some would say a must for every day of a stay), with a feast of sardines and other fish, freshly caught and grilled in front of you. Despite the initial hustle for custom, the atmosphere is relaxed and standards high.

The beach

Essaouira has beaches to the north and south. The main town beach, to the **south**, extends for miles from the town, often backed by dunes, out towards Cap Sim. On its early reaches, the main activity, as ever in Morocco, is football. There's virtually always a game in progress and at weekends a full-scale local league, with a dozen matches side by side and kick-offs timed by the tides. If you're a player, you'll be encouraged to join in, but the weekend games are fun just to watch, and on occasions half the town seems to turn out.

The southern beach also has a dozen or so **camel** men, offering rides on their beats up and down the sands, or out to the dunes. Most of them operate in pairs and they can be fiercely competitive for custom (they're not beyond galloping off as soon as they've enticed you to ride). So, if you have young kids, watch the scene for a while and be sure to pick someone you feel confident about – it's a long way to fall. You'll need to bargain for rates.

The beach to the north of town, known as the **Plage de Safi**, is good in hot weather and with a calm sea, but the water can be dangerous if the wind is up. It's reached from

---

THE ILE DE MOGADOR AND ELEONORA'S FALCON

Out across the bay from Essaouira lie the **Iles Purpuraires**, named from the dyes for purple imperial cloth that the Romans once produced on the islands. Here also, Sir Francis Drake ate his Christmas lunch in 1577, commenting on the "verie ugly fish". The largest of the islands, known as the **Ile de Mogador**, is flanked on each side by a fort which, together with the fort on the islet just off the town harbour and the Borj El Berod on the beach, covers all possible approaches to the bay. It also has a small harbour, a mosque, a few rusting cannons and a nineteenth-century prison used for political exiles, but long closed.

It is of most interest these days, however, as a nature reserve, for this is the only non-Mediterranean breeding site of **Eleonora's falcon** – Morocco's most dramatic bird. They are not hard to see, with binoculars, from the beach. The best time is the early evening half-light, when you might spot as many as two or three dozen of these magnificent birds, gliding in low over the sea to hawk for insects. The falcons are summer visitors to Morocco, staying between May and October before making the long return journey south to Madagascar for the winter. The nearby river course also has many **waders** and **egrets** and occasional rarities such as gull-billed tern and Mediterranean gull.

The island has no inhabitants, save for a *gardien* who keeps an eye on the falcons. If you want to visit – and this is strongly discouraged when the birds are resident – you'll first have to get a *permit d'autorisation* from the *Province*, signposted inland from Boulevard Mohammed V after the *Hôtel Tafkout*, and then the approval of the harbour-master in his office before the Marine Gate; the latter's say-so depends on the state of the tide and the weather forecast. Then, and only then, can you negotiate for a boat ride. Don't pay for the ride until you've been collected and returned to the town.

A visit such as this is problematic, time-consuming and calls for perseverance – but it is possible. Allow a couple of days at least for due processes.

the north end of town by skirting left through a malodorous area, the reward being miles of often delightfully empty sand.

Bordj El Berod and Diabat

Walking further along the beach, past the football and the crowds, you pass the riverbed of the Oued Ksob (note that you can't cross this at high tide) and come upon the ruins of an old fort, the **Bordj El Berod**. Inland you can see the ruins of a royal summer pavilion and a broken bridge. The fort is an excellent viewing spot for the Iles Purpuraires, offshore, and their birdlife (see box opposite).

A little further south, inland through the scrub, is the small Berber village of **Diabat**. This was once a legendary hippy hangout, and local mythology has it that both Cat Stevens and Jimi Hendrix spent time in the colony (though it seems that Hendrix only ever stayed a few days in Essaouira). These days, the village has reverted to an ordinary Berber farming village.

Few venture beyond the Oued Ksob, from which an aqueduct once carried water to Essaouira, but a walk to Cap Sim and back is an all-day challenge. Take plenty of water, take care with the tides and visit the *Auberge Tangaro* on the way back. (see p.339)

Eating and drinking

With its fishing fleet and market, Essaouira offers a good range of cafés and restaurants – a few of the upmarket ones being licensed to sell alcohol. However, for an informal lunch, or early evening meal, you can do no better than eat at the line of **grills** down at the port, an Essaouira institution, and cooking fish as fresh as it is possible to be.

Essaouira doesn't have much by way of **nightlife** – it's a café more than a bar scene – but you can get a beer or a bottle of wine at the *Chalet de la Plage*, (though it prefers customers to eat as well) and at the *Café Mogador* on the seafront. Alternatives are basically down to the hotels *Mechouar*, *Tafoukt* and *des Iles*; at the latter, Moroccans gather to drink beer and play chess and draughts.

If you want to buy your own beer or wine, at very much lower prices, there are a number of small supermarkets.

Restaurants

Restaurant Les Alizes, 26 Rue Skala. Next to the *Hôtel Smara* and away from the mainstream, this restaurant has built up a good reputation for dining well on Moroccan dishes. Cheap.

Café-Restaurant El Ayoune, Rue Hajjali. A new eatery just off the *place*, serving breakfast, lunch and dinner. Swift service, but you're not rushed. Cheap.

Dar Baba, 2 Rue de Marrakesh, on corner with Rue Sidi Mohammed Ben Abdallah. Italian dishes: spaghetti, pasta, pizza. Cheap.

Café-Restaurant Bab Laâchour, on the *place*. A café favoured by locals downstairs, with a more tourist-oriented restaurant on the floor above. The menu includes fish dishes and rivals *Chez Sam*. Cheap.

Restaurant La Calèche Bleue, Av. Okba Ibn Nafia, to one side of Galerie d'Art Frederic Damgaard; the *Restaurant El Minzah* is on the other side of the gallery. The two restaurants have much in common, but if you are looking for something simpler and cheaper, the *La Calèche Bleue* is better. There are a few *calèches* in Essaouira which operate from Bab Doukkala, but they aren't blue. Cheap.

Chez Driss, 10 Rue Hajjali, just off the *place*. Well established and one of the town's most popular meeting places. Delicious fresh pastries and coffee in a quiet leafy courtyard. Ideal for a leisurely breakfast. Cheap.

Café-Restaurant Essalam, on the *place*. Mohammed El Ouajibi is still in charge but slack supervision endangers standards. The set meals are value for money, though choices are limited, and there is growing competition from newcomers in the area. On the walls, you will see small watercolours by Charles Kérival who visits and paints Essaouira often. Born in Brittany, he discovered Morocco when the oil-tanker on which he was working visited Casablanca in 1956. Cheap.

Restaurant L'Horloge, Place Chefchaouni. Moderately priced Moroccan meals, standard and lacking imagination, but value for money. Housed in one-time synagogue. Moderate.

Restaurant El Khaima, Rue Derb Laâlouj/Place El Khaima. Rather overpriced meals in a modern building, surrounded by a traditional tent (hence *Khaima*) and far back from the street, almost opposite the museum and on a square which it shares with lock-up workshops. On the plus side, it's licensed, takes cards, and stays open late. Moderate to expensive.

Dar Loubane, 24 Rue du Rif, a stone's throw from Place Chefchaouni. A new upmarket restaurant on the ground floor patio of an attractive eighteenth-century mansion. Moroccan and French cuisine; friendly service, interesting semi-kitsch decor and exhibits which are of interest. Live gnaoua music takes place on Saturday evenings when it's advisable to make a booking. Cheap to moderate.

Café Marrakesh, on the *place*. Open all day, but especially good for breakfast. Popular with locals who will want to chat. Cheap.

Restaurant El Minzah, Av. Okba Ibn Nafia, alongside the Galerie d'Art Frederic Damgaard, and housed in a converted almond store. Pleasant atmosphere; set menus and à la carte. Moderate.

Restaurant La Petite Perle d'Essaouira, 2 Rue El Hajalli. This central restaurant has had a new lease of life. It's small and dark but the food is traditional and good, the servings generous and the prices moderate.

Chalet de la Plage, Bd. Mohammed V – on the seafront, just above the high-tide mark. Built entirely of wood by the Ferraud family in 1893, the building is now a little gloomy and barnacled with marine mementos, but the seafood and sea views are truly memorable. Avoid lunchtime when day-trippers overwhelm the kitchen. Licensed. Moderate to expensive.

Chez Sam, in the harbour. This is another Essaouira institution – a wooden shack, built like a boat, set seductively right by the waterfront in the harbour. Service can be a bit hit-and-miss but the portions are generous, the fish is usually cooked pretty well, there's beer and wine available, and fishingboats to watch through the portholes. Moderate to expensive.

Listings

Banks There are four banks in or near Place Prince Moulay El Hassan: a BMCE, BCM, Banque Populaire and Credit du Maroc.

Festivals A dozen or so local moussems, fairs and festivals are held between March and October. The main event is the Festival d'Essaouira in June, the main focus of which is Gnaoua music, with groups from Tangier, Marrakesh and, of course, Essaouira. In October, the air rally commemorating the Aéropostale Service of the 1920s passes through Essaouira.

Post office The PTT is just outside the ramparts on Av. Lalla Aicha; it's open 8am–6pm daily; the phone section is a lot less reliable than Jack's Kiosk (see p.332), or the recently installed *téléboutiques*.

Shopping Despite its size, Essaouira rivals Marrakesh and Fes as a centre for attractive items of lasting value, and it's relatively hassle-free. For a worthy cause, you may choose to look for the little exhibition of the *Association des Parents et Amis des Handicapés* at 11 Rue El Fatouaki, open every afternoon; there are home-made items for sale.

Moving on

Leaving Essaouira for **Marrakesh**, there is a nonstop Supratours bus which leaves from Avenue Lalla Aicha and arrives in Marrakesh at the train station; tickets for this should be bought from the nearby kiosk the day before. They also run a daily service to Agadir.

The best buses direct to **Casablanca** are the CTM "Mumtaz Express" (leaves Essaouira bus station daily at midnight, arriving Casa at 5am) and the night "Pullman du Sud"; they cost around 10dh more than other departures – money that you will, in any case, save on baggage loading. A SATAS bus also leaves Essaouira bus station travelling to Casa via Safi and El Jadida.

There's also one weekly **flight** on Regional Air Lines to Agadir and Casablanca. See "Travel Details" for more information.

WINDSURFING AROUND ESSAOUIRA

Essaouira and its nearby beaches are Morocco's prime windsurfing centre, drawing enthusiasts almost year-round. There is a windsurfing centre in Essaouira, and the hotels south of Essaouira at Diabat and Sidi Kaouiki (see below) have become major gathering points. The trade wind at Essaouira is northwesterly and blows year-round; it's stronger in summer but the swell is bigger in winter. The winds are strong (sails required are 5.03.5) and the water is cool enough at any time of year to make a wetsuit essential.

South to Agadir

The main road south from Essaouira to Agadir (P8) runs inland for the first 100km or so, with just the occasional *piste* leading down to a beach or fishing hamlet scattered along the rugged, cliff-lined coast. Along this stretch there is just one resort, **Sidi Kaouki**, which has the reputation of being Morocco's best windsurfing beach.

The region **inland** is known as the **Haha**, populated by Tashelhaït-speaking Berbers, and actually the westernmost range of the High Atlas. Its slopes are covered in **argan trees** (see p.487) which are often to be seen with a goat halfway up, nibbling away at the fruit. A handful of very rough *pistes* head into the hills, struggling over the mountains to meet the Tizi Maachou road from Marrakesh to Agadir.

Sidi Kaouki and Cap Sim

The old road south from Essaouira used to go via **Diabat**, but since the bridge over the Oued Ksob was broken and replaced by a tricky ford, the main road (P8A leading to P8) crosses the river upstream before joining the P8 to Agadir. A turning to the right just before this junction takes you to Diabat by a metalled side road (see inset map on p.330).

En route to Diabat and signposted from the main road is the *Auberge Tangaro* (☎04/478 5735 or 478 4784; ⑥), a rather chic, Italian-owned place that provides a tempting alternative to staying in Essaouira, if you have transport of your own. Little used except at weekends, when groups of French and German windsurfers arrive from Casablanca and Marrakesh, the *auberge* has a number of **chalet rooms**, and it serves excellent meals. Half-board is obligatory. Next door is a small **campsite** with hot showers and youth hostel prices (20dh per person). The beach is a half-hour hike.

Back on the P8, a further 7km brings you to a sideroad signposted to **SIDI KAOU-KI**. The beach here attracts **windsurfers** virtually year-round, and looks set for mainstream development. Currently, the choice of accommodation is limited to three possibilities. The *Residence Kaouki Beach* has ten comfortable rooms; it's run by the *Villa Maroc* in Essaouira (bookings through it: ☎04/447 3147; ②). Half-board is available and much cheaper than the *Auberge Tangaro;* the restaurant is fine and open – by reservation – to nonresidents in the evening. The newer *Auberge de la Plage* (☎04/447 6600, fax 447 3383; ④) is managed by a German/Italian couple who have a small stable and horses to hire for trekking along the beach. There's also the mildly eccentric *Villa Bougies* (☎04/447 2411; ④), with four rooms, nine beds, solar energy and lots of candles. To supplement the hotel restaurants, there is one beach café, *Chez Omar.*

Near the beach is the original **Marabout of Sidi Kaouki**, which has a reputation for curing sterility in women, and beyond that is **Cap Sim**, backed by long expanses of dunes.

On towards Agadir

The piste south of Sidi Kaouki, marked on the Michelin map, requires a four-wheel-drive vehicle, but back on the inland P8 there is little of interest. **SMIMOU** is a tiny roadside stop with a petrol station and a couple of café-restaurants; to the east, one of the better roads leads into the hills to Souk Tnine Imi N'Tilt, where a large **Monday souk** takes place. **TAMANAR** has a petrol station but the roadside **hotel-restaurant**, *Etoile du Sud* has closed.

Fifteen kilometres south of Tamanar, a metalled road cuts down to the coast at **POINTE IMESSOUANE**, which used to be a picturesque little harbour with a few fishermen's cottages, but has now changed beyond recognition; with the help of the Japanese government there are now living areas and storerooms for the fishermen, and the architecture, with two floors of doors, looks more new-millennium medersa than traditional fishermen's quarters. Just as intriguing are the reasons behind Japan's contribution to the scheme, with cynics suggesting it's an attempt to secure support for their position on whaling when the issue is next discussed. The little harbour and impressive coast remain and you can stay overnight at the *Auberge Kahina* (☎04/882 6032; ③), which offers six double rooms, a restaurant and glorious sea views. Just to the east is a bay and beach known as **Imoucha**, which, like Sidi Kaouki, is popular with **windsurfers** – and, to a lesser degree, surfers.

A few kilometres beyond the roadside settlement of **TAMRI** (117km), the road rejoins the coast, passing a lagoon, which might detain bird-watchers, and the fishing village of Taghazoute (see Chapter Eight) before the final run to Agadir. Honey and bananas are on sale by the roadside, the latter to boost your sense of arrival in the south.

travel details

Trains

Casablanca Port to: Mohammed V airport (9–12 daily; 45min); Rabat (15–22 daily; 1hr); Kenitra (12–17 daily; 1hr 45min).

Casablanca Voyageurs to: Mohammed V airport (9–12 daily; 35min); Marrakesh (8 daily; 3hr 30min); Rabat (13 daily; 1hr); Kenitra (12–17 daily; 1hr 30min); Meknes (8 daily; 3hr 45min); Fes (8 daily; 4hr 45min); Oujda (3 direct and 1 connecting daily; 10hr); Asilah (3 direct and 1 connecting daily; 4hr 50min); Tangier (3 direct and 1 connecting daily; 5hr 40min).

Kenitra to: Rabat (12–17 daily; 30min); Casablanca (13 daily; 1hr 30min); Mohammed V airport (9–12 daily; 2hr 5min); Marrakesh (8 daily; 5hr); Meknes (8 daily; 2hr 15min); Fes (8 daily; 3hr 15min); Oujda (3 direct and 1 connecting daily; 8hr 30min); Asilah (3 direct and 1 connecting daily; 3hr 20min); Tangier (3 direct and 1 connecting daily; 4hr 20min).

Rabat Ville to: Casablanca (13 daily; 1hr); Mohammed V airport (9–12 daily; 1hr 35min); Marrakesh (8 daily; 4hr 30min); Kenitra (12–17 daily; 30min); Meknes (8 daily; 2hr 45min); Fes (8 daily; 3hr 45min); Oujda (3 direct and 1 connecting daily; 9hr); Asilah (3 direct and 1 connecting daily; 3hr 50min); Tangier (3 direct and 1 connecting daily; 4hr 40min).

Buses

Casablanca to: Agadir (10 CTM and 14 others daily; 9hr); Beni Mellal (3 CTM and over 40 others daily; 3hr 30min); Er Rachidia (1 CTM daily; 10hr 15min); Essaouira (3 CTM and 10 others daily; 5hr); Fes (10 CTM and 24 others daily; 5hr 30min); Kenitra (4 CTM daily; 2hr); Laayoune (2 CTM and 1 other daily; 19hr); Marrakesh (8 CTM and 24 others daily; 4hr); Meknes (10 CTM and 7 others daily; 4hr 30min); Nador (2 CTM and 9 others daily; 12hr); Ouarzazate (3 CTM daily; 8hr 20min); Oujda (2 CTM and 14 others daily; 11hr); Rabat (19 CTM daily and very frequent private services; 1hr 20min); Safi (8 CTM and 12 others daily; 4hr 45min); Tangier (5 CTM and 32 others daily; 6hr 30min); Tetouan (3 CTM and 16 others daily; 6hr); Tiznit (8 CTM and 7 others daily; 11hr).

Essaouira to: Agadir (16 daily; 3hr 30min); Casablanca (3 CTM and 10 others daily; 5hr); Rabat (1 CTM and 2 others daily; 6hr 30min);

Marrakesh (1 CTM and 11 others daily; 3hr 30min); Safi (1 CTM and 13 others daily; 3hr 30min); Taroudannt (3 daily; 10hr).

Rabat to: Agadir (8 daily; 11hr); Casablanca (19 CTM daily and very frequent private services; 1hr 20min); Fes (10 CTM and 24 others daily; 4hr); Marrakesh (1 CTM and 12 others daily; 5hr 30min); Meknes (7 CTM and 15 others daily; 3hr); Nador (1 CTM and 16 others daily; 9hr 30min); Safi (9 daily; 6hr); Salé (frequent; 15min); Tangier (6 CTM and 28 others daily; 5hr); Tetouan (4 CTM and 28 others daily; 5hr).

Safi to: Agadir (1 CTM and 16 others daily; 5hr); Casablanca (8 CTM and 12 others daily; 4hr 45min); El Jadida (3 CTM and 8 others daily; 2hr 30min); Essaouira (1 CTM and 13 others daily; 3hr 30min); Fes (1 daily; 10hr 30min); Meknes (1 daily; 9hr 30min); Rabat (9 daily; 6hr); Oualidia (3 CTM and 8 others daily; 1hr 25min).

El Jadida to: Casablanca (3 daily; 2hr 30min); Oualidia (2 daily; 1hr 30min); Rabat (2 daily; 4hr).

Grands Taxis

Casablanca to: Rabat (1hr 20min); Safi (3hr 30min

Rabat to: Casablanca (1hr 20min); Fes (2hr 20min); Salé (15min).

Safi to: Casablanca (3hr 30min), El Jadida (2hr), Marrakesh (2hr 30min).

Flights

Essaouira to: Casablanca (2 weekly; 1hr).

Casa Mohammed V to: Agadir (4 daily; 55min); Al Hoceima (2 weekly; 1hr 15min); Dakhla (3 weekly; 3hr 15min); Essaouira (2 weekly; 1hr); Fes (daily; 40min); Laayoune (daily; 1hr 30min); Marrakhesh (4 daily; 40min); Ouarzazate (3 weekly; 1hr 5min); Oujda (2–3 daily; 1hr 5min); Tangier (6 weekly; 50min); Tetouan (4 weekly; 1hr 5min).

CHAPTER FIVE

MARRAKESH

M arrakesh – "Morocco City", as early travellers called it – has always been something of a pleasure city, a marketplace where the southern tribesmen and Berber villagers bring in their goods, spend their money and find entertainment. For visitors it's an enduring fantasy – a city of immense beauty, low, red and tentlike before a great shaft of mountains – and immediately exciting. At the heart of it all is a square, Djemaa El Fna, really no more than an open space in the centre of the city, but the stage for a long-established ritual in which shifting circles of onlookers gather round groups of acrobats, drummers, pipe musicians, dancers, storytellers, comedians and fairground acts. However many times you return there, it remains compelling. So, too, do the city's architectural attractions: the immense, still basins of the Agdal and Menara gardens, the delicate Granada-style carving of the Saadian Tombs and, above all, the Koutoubia Minaret, the most perfect Islamic monument in North Africa.

Unlike Fes, for so long its rival as the nation's capital, the city seems much more rooted in the present than the past. After Casablanca, Marrakesh is Morocco's second largest city and its population continues to rise. It has a thriving industrial area and is the most important market and administrative centre of southern Morocco. This is not to suggest an easy prosperity – there is heavy unemployment and poverty here, as throughout the country – but a stay in Marrakesh leaves you with a vivid impression of life and activity. And for once this doesn't apply exclusively to the new city, **Gueliz**; the **Medina**, substantially in ruins at the beginning of the twentieth century, was rebuilt and expanded during the years of French rule and retains no less significant a role in the modern city.

The Koutoubia and Saadian Tombs excepted, Marrakesh is not a place of great monuments. Its beauty and attraction lie in the general atmosphere and spectacular location – with the magnificent peaks of the Atlas rising right up behind the city, hazy in the heat of summer and shimmering white with the winter snow.

Marrakesh has **Berber** rather than Arab origins, having developed as the metropolis of Atlas tribes – Maghrebis from the plains, Saharan nomads and former slaves from

---

HOTEL PRICE CODES

The basis of our **hotel price codes**, set out below and keyed throughout the guide, is the price currently quoted for the cheapest double room in high season (June–September).

Note that cheaper prices in the lower categories are generally for rooms with just a washbasin – you always pay extra for **en-suite** shower and WC – and that double rooms can generally be converted into **triples/family rooms**, with extra beds, for a modest extra charge. Single occupancy usually costs about two-thirds the price of a double, though in some places a single person will pay the same rate for a room as two people sharing, and in other places exactly half as much. Prices quoted are for bed only, without breakfast, but including local taxes.

① 40–100dh	③ 150–200dh	⑤ 400–800dh
② 100–150dh	④ 200–400dh	⑥ over 800dh

Africa beyond the desert, Sudan, Senegal and the ancient kingdom of Timbuktu. All of these strands shaped the city's souks and its way of life, and in the crowds and per-formers in Djemaa El Fna, they can still occasionally seem distinct.

For most travellers, Marrakesh is the first experience of the south and its generally more laid-back atmosphere and attitudes. **Marrakchis** are renowned for their warmth and sociability, their humour and directness and there seems a greater openness too, with women enjoying a more public presence, often riding mopeds around on the streets. And even at its heart, Marrakesh feels more like a conglomeration of villages than an urban community, with quarters formed and maintained by successive genera-tions of migrants from the countryside.

Some history

The original date of Marrakesh's **foundation** is disputed, though it was certainly close to the onset of **Almoravid** rule – around 1062–70 – and must have taken the initial form of a camp and market with a *ksour*, or fortified town gradually developing round it.

The city's founder (as that of the Almoravid dynasty) was **Youssef Ben Tachfine**, a restless military leader who conquered northern Morocco within two years and then, turning his attention towards Spain, defeated the Christian kings, to bring Andalucia under Moroccan rule. Tachfine maintained both Fes and Marrakesh as bases for his empire, but under his son, the pious **Ali Ben Youssef**, Marrakesh became very much the dominant centre. Craftsmen and architects from Córdoba worked on the new city: palaces, baths and mosques were built; underground chan-nels, known as *khettara*, were built to provide water for the town and the growing palmery; and, in 1126–27, the first seven-kilometre **circuit of walls** was raised, replac-ing an earlier stockade of thorn bushes. These, many times rebuilt, are essentially the city's present walls – made of *tabia*, the red mud of the plains, mixed and strengthened with lime.

Of the rest of the Almoravid's building works, there remains hardly a trace. The dynasty that replaced them – the orthodox and reforming **Almohads** – sacked the city for three days after taking possession of it in 1147. Once again, though, Marrakesh was adopted as the empire's pre-eminent capital, its domain stretching as far as Tripolitania (modern Libya) in the wake of phenomenal early conquests.

With the accession to the throne in 1184 of **Yacoub El Mansour**, the third Almohad sultan, the city entered its greatest period. Under this prolific builder, *kissarias* were constructed for the sale and storage of Italian and oriental cloth, a new kasbah was begun, and a succession of poets and scholars arrived at the court – among them Ibn Rochd, aka *Averroes*, the most distinguished of Arabic medieval philosophers, who was born in Córdoba (1126) and died in Marrakesh (1198). Mansour's reign also saw the construction of the great **Koutoubia Mosque** and minaret.

It is astonishing to think that this whole period of Almoravid and Almohad rule – so crucial to the rise of both the city and the nation – lasted barely two centuries. By the 1220s, the empire was beginning to fragment amid a series of factional civil wars, and Marrakesh fell into the familiar pattern of pillage, ruination and rebuilding. It revived for a time to form the basis of an independent **Merenid** kingdom (1374–86) but overall it gave way to Fes until the emergence of the Saadians in the early sixteenth century.

Taking Marrakesh, then devastated by famine, in 1521, and Fes in 1546, the **Saadians** provided a last burst of imperial splendour. Their first sultans regained the Atlantic coast, which had been extensively colonized by the Portuguese; **Ahmed El Mansour**, the great figure of the dynasty, defeated the Portuguese at the Battle of the Three Kings and led a conquest of Timbuktu, seizing control of the most lucrative car-avan routes in Africa. The **El Badi Palace** – Marrakesh's largest and greatest build-ing project – was constructed from the proceeds of this new wealth, though it again fell

Semlalia Hotels & Casablanca △   Safi & El Jadida △   Palmery △

Institut Français

AVENUE MOHAMMED

Ibn Tafail
Hospital

Majorelle
Garden

AVENUE YACOUB EL MANSOUR

RUE IBN AICHA

Bethel
Synagogue

American
Library

BOULEVARD MOHAMMED ZERKTOUNI

Bus
Station

CTM
Office

PLACE
ABDELMOUMEN
BEN ALI

BMCE

ONMT

RUE SOURIYA

RUE DE LA LIBERTE

Crédit
du Maroc

PLACE
MOURABITON

Bab
Doukkala

GUELIZ

Market

AVENUE

BOULEVARD MOHAMMED ZERKTOUNI

AVENUE DES NATIONS - UNIES

AVENUE MOHAMMED V

PLACE
DU 16
NOVEMBRE

Bab Er
Raha

BOULEVARD MOULAY RACHID

PTT

Train Station

PLACE EL
MASSIRA

AVENUE HASSAN II

AVENUE HASSAN II

Supratours

PARC DES
SPORTS

PLACE
DE LA LIBERTE,
EL HOURIA

Bab
Nkob

HIVERNAGE

Swimming
Pool

AVENUE M. EL HANSALI

Bab El
Makhzen

Bab El
Djedid

AVE HOUMAN

ACCOMMODATION
Hôtel Agdal	8
Hôtel Amalay	3
La Maison Arabe	9
Hôtel Atlas	16
Hôtel Farouk	10
Hôtel Le Grand Imilchil	13
Residence El Hamra	1
Ibis Moussafir Hôtel	11
Hôtel Islane	15
Kenza Hôtel	2
Hôtel La Mamounia	17
Hôtel Oudaya	5
Hôtel du Pacha	6
Hôtel Toulousain	7
Hôtel des Voyageurs	4
Hôtel Yasmine	12
Youth Hostel	14

Menara
Gardens

Basin

Olivery

Olivery

RESTAURANTS & CAFÉ'S
Café Agdal	A	Cafeteria Le Jet d'Eau	T
Bagatelle Restaurant	N	Dar Marjana	M
Boule de Neige	D	Rotisserie de la Paix	L
Le Cantanzaro	H	Le Pavillon	R
Le Dragon d'Or	B	Restaurant Puerto Banus	S
Restaurant L'Entrecôte	F	Café Snack Le Sindibad	J
Al Fassia	P	Café Le Siroua	G
Le Jacaranda	E	La Trattoria	K
Chez Jack'Line	C	Villa Rosa	O
Restaurant Le Jardin	Q	Restaurant Yacout	I

0 —————— 500m

MARRAKESH

Souk El Khemis

Bab El Khemis

ROUTE DES REMPARTS

Oued Issil

Zaouia Sidi Bel Abbes

Bab Taghzout

RUE BAB TAGHZOUT

RUE ASSOUEL

RUE DE BAB KHEMIS

Zaouia Sidi Mohammed Ben Slimane

RUE EL GZA

Chrob ou Chouf Fountain

Dab Debbagh

Tanneries

See 'Souks' map

Ben Youssef Mosque

PLACE EL MOUKEF

RUE BAB DOUKKALA

Bab Doukkala Mosque

Dar El Glaoui

PLACE BEN SALAH

N

Bab Aylen

ROUTE DES REMPARTS

Oued Issil

Mouassin Mosque

Zaouia Sidi Ben Salah

RUE AL YAMANE

MEDINA

DERB DEBBACHI

See 'Lower Medina' map

Ensemble Artisanal

See 'Medina Hotels' map

PL. DJEMAA EL FNA

Dar Si Said

Bab Aghmat

Koutoubia

EL FETOUAKI

PL. YOUSSEF BEN TACHFINE

AVENUE HOUMAN EL FETOUAKI

Bahia Palace

Kasbah Mosque

El Badi Palace

Bab Er Robb

Bab Agnaou

Saadian Tombs

Royal Palace

ROUTE DES REMPARTS

Bab Ahmar

Bab Ksiba

Agdal Gardens

▽ Asni   ▽ Ourika

victim to dynastic rivalry and, apart from its mausoleum (the **Saadian Tombs**), was reduced to ruins by **Moulay Ismail**, the second, but first effective, sultan of the Alaouite dynasty, who preferred Meknes to Marrakesh.

Subsequent history under the **Alaouites** – the dynasty perpetuated today by King Mohammed VI – is largely undistinguished. Marrakesh remained an imperial capital, and the need to maintain a southern base against the tribes ensured the regular, alternating residence of its sultans. But from the seventeenth to the nineteenth century, it shrank back from its medieval walls and lost much of its former trade. The *Encyclopaedia Britannica* recorded in 1875 that "the wall, 25 or 30 feet high and relieved by square towers at intervals of 360 feet, is so dilapidated that foot-passengers, and in places even horsemen, can find their way in and out through the breaches. Open spaces of great extent are numerous enough within the walls, but for the most part they are defaced by mounds of rubbish and putrid refuse."

During the last decades prior to the Protectorate, the city's fortunes revived somewhat as it enjoyed a return to favour with the Shereefian court. **Moulay Hassan** (1873–94) and **Moulay Abd El Aziz** (1894–1908) both ran their governments from here in a bizarre closing epoch of the old ways, accompanied by a final bout of frantic palace building. On the arrival of **the French**, Marrakesh gave rise to a short-lived pretender, the religious leader El Hiba, and for most of the colonial period it was run as a virtual fiefdom of its pasha, **T'hami El Glaoui** – the most powerful, autocratic and extraordinary character of his age (see p.360).

Since **independence**, the city has undergone considerable change, with rural emigration from the Atlas and beyond, new methods of cultivation on the Haouz plain and the development of a sizeable tourist industry. The impressive **Palais des Congrès**, opened in 1989, has given Marrakesh international prestige, hosting national and international events. All of these factors combine to make Marrakesh Morocco's best-known city and, after Casablanca, the country's largest trading base and population centre – over 1,425,000 at the last estimate.

Arrival, orientation, information and city transport

Arriving at the **train station**, on the edge of the new town Gueliz, keep your wits about you as you emerge, or you'll immediately find yourself engaged with a guide or taxi driver. A regular petit taxi (beware unofficial taxis without meters) is a good idea in general, since it's quite a walk to hotels in Gueliz – and a long way to the Medina; the taxi fare should be no more than 10dh to the Medina, less to hotels in Gueliz. The #3 and #8 buses run from the station to the Place de Foucauld, alongside Place Djemaa El Fna. However, if you plan to stay at the youth hostel, you should, luggage permitting, be able to walk there from the train station in five minutes or so.

The **gare routière** (for most long-distance bus services) is just outside the walls of the Medina by Bab Doukkala. You can walk into the centre of Gueliz from here in around ten minutes by following Avenue des Nations Unies; to the Place Djemaa El Fna it's around 25 minutes, most easily accomplished by following the Medina walls down to Avenue Mohammed V. Alternatively, catch the #3 or #8 bus, which run in one direction to the Koutoubia, in the other to Gueliz; or save yourself trouble by taking a petit taxi (about 10dh).

Supratours arriving from Essaouira, Agadir, Laayoune and Dakhla pull into the new bus station next to the train station.

The city's **airport** is 5km to the southwest. The #11 bus is supposed to run every half hour to the Place Djemaa El Fna, but it is very erratic. Petits taxis or grands taxis are a better option, though you will have to watch that you pay a reasonable fare. The grands taxis currently display a price of 50dh (day) and 60dh (night) for the trip from the airport to Gueliz.

Arriving at the airport before 8am or after about 6pm any day of the week, you won't always find the BMCE or Banque Populaire kiosk open to change money or traveller's cheques; taxis, however, will accept pounds or dollars, at more or less the equivalent dirham rate.

Orientation and information

Once in the city, and despite its size and the maze of its souks, Marrakesh is not too hard to navigate. The broad, open space of **Djemaa El Fna** lies right at the heart of the **Medina**, and almost everything of interest is concentrated in the web of alleyways north and south of the square. Just to the west of the Djemaa El Fna is the unmistakeable landmark of the **Koutoubia** minaret – in the shadow of which begins **Avenue Mohammed V**, leading out through the Medina walls at Bab Nkob and up the length of the French-built new city, **Gueliz**. Only in the **souks** might you want to consider taking a guide, and you'll have plenty of offers.

The ONMT **tourist office**, now referred to as the Délégué Régional du Tourisme, is on Place Abdelmoumen Ben Ali (☎04/443 6239) and the Syndicat d'Initiative, now referred to as APOTM (Association Provinciale des Opérateurs de Tourisme de Marrakech) is at 170 Av. Mohammed V (no phone). Both are open Mon–Fri 9am–noon & 3–6.30pm, Sat 9am–noon. The ONMT occasionally houses an exhibition of local art, otherwise both offices offer little information of any use.

City transport

It is a fairly long walk between Gueliz and the Medina, but there are plenty of **petits taxis** and **grands taxis**, which will take you between the two for around 10dh. There are taxi ranks at most intersections in Gueliz and in the Medina at the Place Djemaa El Fna, outside the *Grand Hôtel Tazi* and at the Place des Ferblantiers end of Avenue Houman El Fetouaki. **Bus** #1 also runs between the main Gueliz squares and the Koutoubia/Place de Foucauld in the Medina. (For more bus routes, see the box).

Note that very few of the petits taxis are **metered** (or admit to a functioning meter); you either have to fix a price in advance, haggle on arrival, or just decide on what you're paying and hand it over at the end of the trip; most trips should cost around 10dh, or

---

LOCAL BUS ROUTES

The following buses leave from Av. El Mouahidine alongside Place de Foucauld, opposite *Hôtel de Foucauld*:

#1 to Gueliz, along Av. Mohammed V.

#2 to Riad El Arous and Bab Doukkala (for the bus station).

#3 to Douar Laskar by Av. Mohammed V/Av. Hassan II, via the train station and passing close to the youth hostel.

#4 to Daoudiat (a northern suburb), by Av. Mohammed V/Av. d'El Jadida, passing close to the Jardin Majorelle.

#8 to Douar Laskar by Av. Mohammed V/Av. Moulay El Hassan, via the train station and close to the youth hostel.

#10 to Bd. de Safi, by Bab Doukkala, via the bus station.

#11 to the airport by Av. Menara.

#14 to the train station.

15dh in the evening. Grands taxis have by law to display prices for specified trips; these prices are per trip and not per person, as drivers often claim.

In addition to taxis, there are **calèches**, horse-drawn cabs which line up near the Koutoubia, the Badi Palace and some of the fancier hotels. These can take up to five people and are not much more expensive than petits taxis – though be sure to fix the price in advance, particularly if you want a tour of the town.

An alternative for exploring the more scattered city sights, such as the Agdal and Menara gardens or the palmery, is a **bike** or **moped**. You can rent them from the outlets detailed in "Listings" at the end of the chapter (see p.376); they will cost up to 100dh a day. **Grands taxis** can also be chartered by the day for around 150dh, which works out very reasonable if you split it between four people (the taxis take a maximum six passengers – but four is comfortable). Negotiate at the ranks in Djemaa El Fna or by the PTT in Gueliz.

Accommodation

There's a choice between staying in the Medina or the Ville Nouvelle (Gueliz), and further options in the hotel-dominated quarters of Hivernage or Semlalia, out on the Casablanca road.

The **Medina** has the main concentration of cheap hotels, most of which are quite pleasant (though they can be cold in winter), along with a few more expensive places on its periphery. Given the attractions of Place Djemaa El Fna and the souks, these have to be the first choice.

The main advantages of **Gueliz** hotels are their convenience if you are arriving late at night, particularly at the train station, and, in the more upmarket ones, the presence of a swimming pool. Hotels in **Hivernage** and **Semlalia** are all upmarket, modern buildings, consistently comfortable and sometimes with wonderful pools and design. Semlalia, however, is a bit remote, and Hivernage, while not too far from Djemaa El Fna, lacks any city life of its own.

Advance bookings for hotels are a wise idea, especially for the cheaper places in the Medina. The worst times are the **Easter** and **Christmas/New Year** holiday periods, when you may arrive and find virtually every decent place full to capacity.

Camping and youth hostel

There is no city **campsite**; the municipal site (still on many maps) closed in 1995, but there are two campsites to the north of the city.

Camping Caravanning Ferdaous, (☎02/331 3167 or ☎04/443 6584). The site is 13km from the city centre on the Casablanca road(P7). It's fine for an overnight stay if using a car, but as a base for exploring Marrakesh on foot, you'd be better off in a Medina *pension*.

Camping Caravanning Internationale, (☎04/443 6785). The site is at Sidi Rahal. Take the Casablanca road(P7) and turn left onto the Safi/El Jadida road(P9). The campsite is 9.5km after leaving the P7. The facilities are, as yet, minimal.

Youth Hostel, Rue El Jahid, Gueliz (☎04/444 7713). Quiet, clean, family-run hostel, with small garden. Useful first-night standby if you arrive late by train, just five minutes' walk from the station (8–9am & 2–10pm: IYHF cardholders given priority).

Medina hotels and pensions

Most of the accommodation in the Medina is grouped around a compact, easily walkable area just south of the Place Djemaa El Fna (see map opposite). The **cheaper** hotels and *pensions* detailed below are the best of those available; there are many others in the same grid of streets, some of which are keyed on our map for reference and finding your way around, but are not recommendations. At time of writing, most *pensions* charge between 80–120dh for a double room.

**MARRAKESH:
MEDINA HOTELS
& RESTAURANTS**

DJEMAA EL FNA

Banque Populaire
Bureau de Change

Banque
du Maroc

Hammam
(men & women)

Crédit
du Maroc

PTT

Wafa
Bank

Horse & Carriage Stand

Place de
Foucauld

Local Buses

BMCE

Cinema
Mabrouka

RUE DE LA RECETTE

Hammam
(men only)

Banque
Populaire

AVENUE EL MOUAHIDINE

BMCI

Banque
Populaire

AVENUE HOUMAN EL FETOUAKI

0   100m

ACCOMMODATION

Hôtel Afriquia	5	Hôtel Gallia	13
Hôtel Ali	4	Hôtel la Gazelle	14
Hôtel El Amal	9	Hôtel Ichbilia	6
Hôtel Arset El Bilk	12	Hôtel Medina	11
Hôtel Central Palace	3	Hôtel Sherazade	8
Hôtel CTM	1	Hôtel Smara	7
Hôtel Essaouira	10	Hôtel Souria	15
Hôtel de Foucauld	17	Grand Hôtel Tazi	16
Hôtel de France	2		

RESTAURANTS & CAFÉ'S

El Bahja	F
Restaurant Diamant Rouge	E
Café Etoile de Marrakesh	B
Café Restaurant Iceberg	G
Mik Mak	C
Pâtisserie des Princes	D
Laiterie et Pâtisserie Toubkal	A

CHEAP

Hôtel Afriquia, 45 Derb Sidi Bouloukat (☎04/444 2403). Decent rooms off a pleasant courtyard with orange trees. Clean, well maintained and excellent value. ②.

Hôtel Ali, Rue Moulay Ismail (☎04/444 4979, fax 444 0522). A deservedly popular small hotel with reliable showers in most rooms, heating in winter, air-conditioning in summer – and a rooftop terrace for sunbathing. The restaurant serves à la carte lunch and, in the evening, an excellent (and modest-priced) buffet with ten or more dishes, steaming tajine-style. The hotel is used as an assembly point for various groups heading to the High Atlas and so is a good source of trekking (and other) information. It also changes money and rents bikes. Reservations are advisable. ②.

Hôtel Central Palace, 59 Derb Sidi Bouloukat (☎04/444 0235, fax 444 2884). Previously known as *Hôtel Central* and with fading charm, but it has now been smartened up and extra rooms are provided by a new annexe. ②.

Hôtel CTM, Place Djemaa El Fna (☎04/444 2325). Decent-sized, clean rooms. Doubles with showers, albeit cold, are a little more expensive. The hotel is above the old bus station (hence its name) and has a useful underground garage, if you have a car to look after. ②.

Hôtel El Amal, 93 Derb Sidi Bouloukat (☎04/444 5043). Converted house with eleven rooms on two floors. Clean, modern facilities which work. ②.

Hôtel Essaouira, 3 Derb Sidi Bouloukat (☎04/444 3805). One of the most popular cheapies in Marrakesh – and with good reason. It's a well-run, safe place, with 30 rooms, hot showers for 5dh, a laundry service and rooftop café. ①.

Hôtel de France, 197 Rue Zitoun El Kadem (☎04/444 3067). Not to be confused with the dire *Hôtel du Café de France* on the Djemaa El Fna, this is one of the oldest and best of the cheapies, attracting a wide age range. Cash and traveller's cheques changed. ①.

Hôtel la Gazelle, 12 Rue Bani Marine (☎04/444 1112). Well-kept hotel with bright, airy rooms, and free hot showers, on a street with a row of outdoor foodstalls and small grill cafés; price-wise it's above average, but well worth it. ②.

Hôtel Ichbilia, 1 Rue Bani Marine (☎04/432 0486). Near the Mabrouk cinema, and well placed for shops, banks and cafés, with comfortable rooms off a courtyard and gallery, but separate toilet and showers. Don't be confused if locals refer to it as *Hôtel Sevilla;* Ichbilia is the Arabic for Seville. ②.

Hôtel Medina, 1 Derb Sidi Bouloukat (☎04/444 2997). Marvellous; a real gem – small, clean, laid-back and friendly. Showers extra (5dh hot) and breakfast (9dh each) on the terrace. ①.

Hôtel Smara, 77 Derb Sidi Bouloukat (☎04/433 5568). Small and not easy to find, but useful as a fallback. ①.

Hôtel Souria, 17 Rue de la Recette (☎04/442 6757). Deservedly popular hotel which rivals the *Medina* as the best in these listings. The grand old *patronnne* has died, but her heirs are maintaining a fine tradition: small, clean and family run. ②.

MODERATE

Hôtel Arset El Bilk, Rue Bani Marine (☎04/442 6448, fax 439 0980). A relatively new hotel, almost opposite the well-established *Hôtel la Gazelle*. With showers and toilets en suite in all rooms, it is an attractive alternative to the *Gazelle* and nearby *Ichbilia* (see above). ③.

Hôtel de Foucauld, Av. El Mouahidine – facing Place de Foucauld (☎04/444 5499, fax 444 1344). Rooms are on the small side, but this is a generally reliable choice, with friendly staff, bicycles for rent and tours arranged, help with local information and a restaurant. Like the *Ali* opposite, some High Atlas guides hang out here. ④.

Hôtel Gallia, 30 Rue de la Recette (☎04/444 5913, fax 444 4853). A pleasant building in a quiet cul-de-sac. Airy and spotless rooms off two tiled courtyards, one with fountain, palm tree and caged birds. Central heating in winter, air-conditioning in summer and good breakfasts. A long-term favourite and highly recommended. Booking is advisable. ③.

Hôtel Sherazade, 3 Derb Djama, Riad Zitoun Kadem (☎ & fax 04/442 9305). Old merchant's house transformed into a comfortable, beautifully furnished and popular hotel. Booking advisable. ④.

Grand Hôtel Tazi, corner of pedestrianized Rue Bab Agnaou/Rue El Mouahidine (☎04/444 2787, fax 444 2152). A once quite grand hotel that has seen better days. Managed by an extended family, the rooms are generally comfortable and most have TV, en-suite toilet and bath/shower. There's a bar open to nonresidents and a restaurant (with 20 percent discount for residents, but you would be better advised to eat elsewhere). The swimming pool, however, is a real plus – and can be used by nonresidents. ④.

Medina/Hivernage periphery

The hotels below are located on the periphery of the Medina, over towards the Hivernage quarter. They are more upmarket (and the *Mamounia* is as pricey as Morocco gets) but, if you can afford them, all offer excellent locations.

MODERATE TO EXPENSIVE

Hôtel Islane, 279 Av. Mohammed V (☎04/444 0081, fax 444 0085). A very central location, only a short walk from the Djemaa El Fna, facing the Koutoubia. The views compensate for the traffic noise from rooms at the front – and there is a rooftop restaurant. ④.

La Maison Arabe, 1 Derb Assebbe Bab Doukkala – opposite the Doukkala mosque (☎04/438 7010, fax 438 7072). A classy addition to the hotel scene, this is a gorgeous nineteenth-century mansion, newly restored as a series of luxurious suites, each with its own private terrace. At 1900dh and up, the prices rival the Mamounia, but if money's no object . . . ⑥.

Hôtel La Mamounia, Av. Bab Jdid (☎04/444 4409, fax 444 4940; *www.mamounia.com*). Set within its own palace grounds, this is – alongside the *Palais Jamai* in Fes – the most beautiful hotel in Morocco. It is also the most expensive, with doubles from 2500dh if you book independently. Room prices drop a bit during the low season, or if you book as part of a holiday package. For a description of the gardens and some history of the hotel, see p.372. ⑥.

Hôtel Yasmine, Bd. El Yarmouk (☎04/444 6200, fax 444 6386). A small hotel that does not look too attractive, but the staff are helpful, the rooms are adequate and it has a swimming pool. ④.

Gueliz

This is a selection of the better-value and best hotels in these areas – and a review of a few others that are used by package tour operators.

Hôtel Agdal, 1 Bd. Mohammed Zerktouni (☎04/443 3670, fax 443 1239). One of the best hotels in Gueliz, with a pool, bar and restaurant; it is also well placed for the other restaurants around Place Abdelmoumen Ben Ali. ⑤.

Hôtel Amalay, 87 Av. Mohammed V (☎04/443 1367, fax 443 1408). Replacing the lamented *Hôtel Renaissance*, the *Amalay* has had a few teething problems, but offers air-conditioning and a good restaurant in a central location. ⑥.

Residence Ezzahia, Av. Mohammed Abdelkrim El Kattabi (☎04/444 6244, fax 443 0028). Built in the late 1980s, well furnished and with a pool and restaurant. It's a little way out on the Casablanca road, but bicycles, mopeds and motorbikes can be rented opposite. ③.

Hôtel Farouk, 66 Av. Hassan II (☎04/443 1989, fax 444 0522). This is highly recommended, being owned by the same family as the *Ali* in the Medina. Warm welcome, hot showers in all rooms, excellent restaurant – and convenient for the train station. ②.

Residence El Hamra, 26 Av. Mohammed V (☎04/444 8423, fax 444 6986). Self-catering apartments which are not terribly exciting, but would suit a family or a group of three or four. ⑤.

Ibis Moussafir Hôtel, Av. Hassan II/Place de la Gare (☎04/443 5929, fax 443 5936). Tasteful chain hotel by the train station, with a swimming pool, bar and restaurant. ④.

Kenza Hôtel, Av. Yacoub El Mansour (☎04/444 8330, fax 443 5386). A fine hotel with tastefully luxurious rooms and furnishings, an enticing pool, two bars and two restaurants. Not very central, but close to the Jardin Majorelle. ⑤.

Hôtel Oudaya, 147 Rue Mohammed El Bekal (☎04/444 8512, fax 443 5400). A friendly hotel in a quiet backstreet, popular with the clients of package tours. Rooms are a little small, but public areas are spacious and tastefully decorated in traditional style. ④.

Hôtel du Pacha, 33 Rue de la Liberté (☎04/443 1326, fax 443 1326). An old-style hotel with a courtyard, but with some modern rooms as well – and a good restaurant. ③.

Hôtel Toulousain, 44 Rue Tariq Ben Ziad (☎04/443 0033, fax 443 1239). Behind the municipal market; set back off the street. Friendly and known locally as the Peace Corps hotel after its regular clientele over the years. Some rooms have showers; breakfast extra. ③.

Hôtel des Voyageurs, 40 Bd. Mohammed Zerktouni (☎04/444 7218). Old, respectable hotel; unexciting, but inexpensive. Rooms with showers extra. ②.

Hivernage

Hivernage has a concentration of upmarket hotels and if you're on a package, you're likely to find yourself here. The two below are the pick of the bunch if you are looking to book independently.

Hôtel Atlas, Av. de France (☎04/433 9900, fax 443 3308). One of the largest and best known of the Hivernage hotels. Outwardly bleak and barrack-like, but reportedly friendly and helpful with good restaurant. ⑤.

Hôtel Le Grand Imilchil, Av. Echouhada (☎04/444 7653, fax 444 6165). On a fine avenue, near to Place de la Liberté and not too far from the Medina. The swimming pool may be small but the hotel is good value for the price. ⑤.

Semlalia

Semlalia might suit you if you have a car, or if you want to spend a good part of your time in Marrakesh lazing by the pool, with trips into the Medina by taxi (15dh).

Hôtel Kenzi Semiramis, B.P 525, 3km out of town on the Route de Casablanca(☎04/443 1377, fax 444 7127). Part of the Kenzi chain which specializes in sports, this hotel specializes in golf, running a shuttle service to the Amelkis golf course (see "Listings"). Expensive, but there are promotional rates. ⑥.

Hôtel Tichka, Triangle d'Or, B.P. 894, 3km out of town on the Route de Casablanca (☎04/444 8710, fax 444 8710). State-of-the-art hotel, with fine architecture and internal decor by Bill Willis, an American designer. On Saturday evenings, there's a pool-side Moroccan buffet. ⑥.

Hôtel Tropicana, alongside *Hôtel Tichka,* but no B.P. (☎04/444 7450, fax 444 7458). Lively and, at two-thirds the cost of the *Tichka,* good value for money. It's currently managed by Nouvelles Frontières; hence, its competitive pricing. ⑤.

The Djemaa El Fna

There's nowhere in Morocco like the **Djemaa El Fna** – no place that so effortlessly involves you and keeps you coming back. By day it's basically a market, with a few snake charmers, storytellers and an occasional troupe of acrobats. In the evening it becomes a whole carnival of musicians, clowns and street entertainers. When you arrive in Marrakesh, and after you've found a room, come out here and you'll soon be immersed in the ritual: wandering round, squatting amid the circles of onlookers, giving a dirham or two as your contribution. If you want a respite, you can move over to the rooftop terraces of the *Café de France* or the *Restaurant Argana* to gaze over the square and admire the frame of the Koutoubia.

As a foreigner in the Djemaa El Fna, you can feel something of an interloper. Sometimes the storyteller or musician will pick on you to take part or contribute generously to the end-of-show collection and, entering into the spectacle, it's best to go denuded of the usual tourist trappings – watches, belt-wallets, etc; **pickpockets** do very well out of the square. Beware, also, of being duped by women selling "silver" jewellery; if you decline to buy, they may give you a "present" – and as you move on, large male friends will arrive to accuse you of stealing the trinket.

Some say that the same tourists preyed upon by petty criminals are now vital to the Djemaa's survival, though apart from the snake charmers, monkey handlers and water vendors (all of whom live by posing for photographs), there's little that has compromised itself for outsiders. In many ways it actually seems the opposite. Most of the

THE DEVELOPMENT OF THE DJEMAA EL FNA

Nobody is entirely sure when or how Djemaa El Fna came into being – nor even what its name means. The usual translation is "assembly of the dead", a suitably epic title that seems to refer to the public display here of the heads of rebels and criminals. This is certainly possible, since the Djemaa was a place of execution well into the nineteenth century; the phrase, though, might only mean "the mosque of nothing" (djemaa means both "mosque" and "assembly" – interchangeable terms in Islamic society, as is synagogue in Jewry), recalling an abandoned Saadian plan to build a new grand mosque on this site.

Whichever is the case, as an open area between the original kasbah and the souks, the square has probably played its present role since the city's earliest days. It has often been the focal point for rioting and every few years there are plans to close it down and to move its activities outside the city walls. This, in fact, happened briefly after independence in 1956, when the new "modernist" government built a corn market on part of the square and tried to turn the rest into a car park. The plan, however, lasted for only a year. Tourism was falling off and it was clearly an unpopular move – taking away an important social focal point as well as eliminating a perhaps necessary expression of the past. As Paul Bowles has said, without the Djemaa El Fna, Marrakesh would become just another Moroccan city.

people gathered into circles round the performers are Moroccans – Berbers from the villages and lots of kids. There is no way that any tourist is going to have a tooth pulled by one of the dentists here, no matter how neat the piles of molars displayed on their square of carpet. Nor are you likely to use the scribes or street barbers or, above all, understand the convoluted tales of the storytellers, round whom are gathered perhaps the most animated, all-male crowds in the square.

Nothing of this, though, matters very much, and should certainly not deter you from visiting. There is a fascination in the remedies of the herb doctors, with their bizarre concoctions spread out before them. There are **performers**, too, whose appeal is universal. The square's acrobats, itinerants from Tazeroualt, have for years supplied the European circuses – though they are perhaps never so spectacular as here, thrust forward into multiple somersaults and contortions in the late afternoon heat. There are child boxers and sad-looking trained monkeys, clowns and Chleuh boy dancers – their routines, to the climactic jarring of cymbals, totally sexual (and traditionally an invitation to clients).

And finally, the Djemaa's enduring sound – the dozens of **musicians** playing all kinds of instruments. Late at night, when only a few people are left in the square, you encounter individual players, plucking away at their *ginbris,* the skin-covered two- or three-string guitars. Earlier in the evening, there are full groups: the *Aissaoua,* playing oboe-like *ghaitahs* next to the snake charmers; the Andalous-style groups, with their *ouds* and violins; and the black Gnaoua, trance-healers who beat out hour-long hypnotic rhythms with iron clanging hammers and pound tall drums with long curved sticks.

If you get interested in the music there are two small sections on opposite sides of the square where stalls sell recorded **cassettes**: one is near the entrance to the souks and the other is on the corner with the recently pedestrianized Rue Bab Agnaou. Most of these are by Egyptian or Algerian Raï bands, the pop music that dominates Moroccan radio, but if you ask they'll play you Berber music from the Atlas, classic Fassi pieces, or even Gnaoua music – which sounds even stranger on tape, cut off only by the end of the one side and starting off almost identically on the other. These stalls apart, and those of the nut roasters, whose massive braziers line the immediate entrance to the potters' souk, the **market** activities of the Djemaa are mostly pretty mundane.

The Koutoubia

The absence of any architectural feature on Djemaa El Fna – which even today seems like a haphazard clearing – serves to emphasize the drama of the **Koutoubia Minaret**, the focus of any approach to the city. Nearly seventy metres high and visible for miles on a clear morning, this is the oldest of the three great Almohad towers (the others are the Hassan Tower in Rabat and the Giralda in Seville) and the most complete. Its proportions – a 1:5 ratio of width to height – established the classic Moroccan design. Its scale, rising from the low city buildings and the plains to the north, is extraordinary, the more so the longer you stay and the more familiar its sight becomes.

Completed by Sultan Yacoub El Mansour (1184–99), work on the minaret probably began shortly after the Almohad conquest of the city, around 1150. It displays many of the features that were to become widespread in Moroccan architecture – the wide band of ceramic inlay near the top, the pyramid-shaped, castellated *merlons* (battlements) rising above it, the use of *darj w ktarf* (cheek and shoulder motif) and other motifs – and it also established the alternation of patterning on different faces. Here, the top floor is similar on each of the sides but the lower two are almost eccentric in their variety; the most interesting is perhaps the middle niche on the southeast face, a semicircle of small lobed arches, which was to become the dominant decorative feature of Almohad gates. At the summit are three great balls made of copper – the subject of numerous legends, mostly of supernatural interventions to keep away the thieves. They are thought to originally have been made of gold and were possibly the gift of the wife of Yacoub El Mansour, presented as penance for breaking her fast for three hours during Ramadan.

If you look hard at the tower, you will notice that, close to the arches, the stones of the main body of the tower become slightly smaller. This seems odd today but originally the whole minaret would have been covered with plaster and its tiers of decoration painted. To see just how much this can change the whole effect – and, to most tastes, lessen much of its beauty – take a look at the kasbah mosque (by the Saadian Tombs) which has been carefully but completely restored in this manner.

There has been talk over the years about doing the same with the Koutoubia but in the end the authorities settled for a cleaning-up and restoration of the structure, completed just before the Millennium to stunning effect – especially when floodlit at night. At the same time as the restoration work, archeologists excavated the precincts of the mosque confirming that the original mosque, which predates the tower, had to be rebuilt to correct its alignment with Mecca.

Alongside the mosque, and close to Avenue Mohammed V, is the tomb of Fatima Zohra, now in a white koubba. She was the daughter of a seventeenth-century religious leader and tradition has it that she was a woman by day and a white dove by night, with many women dedicating their children to her.

The souks and northern Medina

It is spicy in the souks, and cool and colourful. The smell, always pleasant, changes gradually with the nature of the merchandise. There are no names or signs; there is no glass . . . You find everything – but you always find it many times over.

Elias Canetti: *The Voices of Marrakesh*

The **souks** of Marrakesh sprawl immediately north of Djemaa El Fna. They seem vast the first time you venture in, and almost impossible to navigate, though, in fact, the area that they cover is pretty compact. A long, covered street, **Rue Souk Smarine**, runs for half their length and then splits into two lanes – **Souk El Attarin** and **Souk El Kebir**. Off these are virtually all the individual souks: alleys and small squares devoted to specific crafts, where you can often watch part of the production process. At the top of the main area of souks, too, you can visit the Saadian **Ben Youssef Medersa** – the most important monument in the northern half of the Medina and arguably the finest building in the city after the Koutoubia Minaret.

If you are staying for some days, you'll probably return often to the souks – and this is a good way of taking them in, singling out a couple of specific crafts or products to see, rather than being swamped by the whole. To come to grips with the general layout, though, you might find it useful to walk round the whole area once with a **guide** (see below). Despite the pressure of offers on Djemaa El Fna, don't feel that one is essential, but until the hustlers begin to recognize you (seeing that you've been in the souks before), they'll probably follow you in; if and when this happens, try to be easygoing, polite and confident – the qualities that force most hustlers to look elsewhere.

The most interesting **times** to visit are in the early morning (between 6.30 and 8am) and late afternoon, at around 4 to 5pm, when some of the souks auction off goods to local traders. Later in the evening, most of the stalls are closed, but you can wander unharassed to take a look at the elaborate decoration of their doorways and arches; those stalls that stay open, until 7 or 8pm, are often more amenable to bargaining at the end of the day.

THE SOUKS

△ Zaouia Sidi Bel Abbes

RUE AMESFAH

COVERED PASSAGEWAY

RUE BAROUDIENNE

△ Bab Dukkala

RUE MOUASSIN

RUE BAB DOUKKALA

Ben Youssef Mosque

Fondouk

Ben Youssef Medersa

△ Bab Debbagh (Tanneries)

Almoravid Koubba

Marrakesh Museum

SOUK CHAARIA

Hammam

SOUK TALAA

Souk Haddadine (Blacksmiths)

Souk Cherratin (Leather)

Souk Chouari (Carpenters)

Souk des Babouches (Slipper Makers)

Kissarias

SOUK EL KEBIR

Souk Teinturiers (Dyers)

RUE MOUASSIN

Souk des Bijoutiers (Jewellery)

Fountain

SOUK EL ATARIN

Mouassin Mosque

La Criée Berbère (Carpets)

Souk des Chaudronniers (Coppersmiths)

RAHBA KEDIMA

Apothecary Stalls

RUE MOUASSIN

Souk Btana (Sheepskins)

Souk Larzal (Wool)

RUE SOUK SMARINE

RUE EL KSOUR

Souk Marine (Textiles)

PLACE DE BAB FTOUH

Qessabin Mosque

△ Koutoubia

Potters' Souk

Restaurant Dar Hadj Idder

N

PLACE DJEMAA EL FNA

Café de France

0   100m

Towards Ben Youssef: the main souks

On the corner of Djemaa El Fna itself there is a small potters' souk, but the main market area begins a little further beyond this. Its **entrance** is initially confusing. Standing at the *Café de France* (and facing the mosque opposite), look across the street and you'll see the *Café El Fath* and, beside it, a building with the sign "Tailleur de la Place" – the lane sandwiched in between them will bring you out at the beginning of Rue Souk Smarine.

Souk Smarine and the Rahba Kedima

Busy and crowded, **Rue Souk Smarine** is an important thoroughfare, traditionally dominated by the sale of textiles and clothing. Today, classier tourist "bazaars" are moving in, with American Express signs displayed in the windows, but there are still dozens of shops in the arcades selling and tailoring traditional shirts and caftans. Along its whole course, the street is covered by a broad, iron trellis that restricts the sun to shafts of light; it replaces the old rush (*smar*) roofing, which along with many of the souks' more beautiful features was destroyed by a fire in the 1960s.

Just before the fork at its end, Souk Smarine narrows and you can get a glimpse through the passageways to its right of the **Rahba Kedima**, a small ramshackle square with a few vegetable stalls set up in the middle of it. Immediately to the right, as you go in, is **Souk Larzal**, a wool market feverishly active in the dawn hours, but closed most of the rest of the day. Alongside it, easily distinguished by smell alone, is **Souk Btana**, which deals with whole sheepskins – the pelts laid out to dry and then displayed on the roof. You can walk up here and take a look at how the skins are treated.

The most interesting aspect of Rahba Kedima, however, is the **apothecary stalls** grouped round the near corner of the square. These sell all the standard traditional cosmetics – earthenware saucers of cochineal (*kashiniah*) for rouge, powdered *kohl* or antimony for darkening the edges of the eyes, *henna* (the only cosmetic unmarried

---

CRAFTS, "GUIDES", THE SOUKS AND SHOPS

Like Fes, Marrakesh can be an **expensive** place to buy craft goods – though if you have anything to barter (designer T-shirts, trainers, rock music cassettes, etc), you'll find people eager enough to arrange an exchange. Before setting out into the souks in search of rugs, blankets, or whatever, check out the classic designs in the **Dar Si Said** museum and take a look at the more-or-less fixed prices in the well-run **Ensemble Artisanal** (daily 9am–1pm & 3–7pm), on Avenue Mohammed V, midway between the Koutoubia and the ramparts at Bab Nkob.

Behind the Ensemble Artisanal, but part of the same complex, there are a dozen or so active workshops with young people learning a range of crafts.

Official **guides** (50dh for a half day) can be arranged at the ONMT or large hotels; unofficial ones can be found in Djemaa El Fna and almost anywhere you're seen looking perplexed. Some of the latter can be fine, others a struggle, as you are escorted into shop after shop; fix a price in advance. A favourite recommendation of the hustlers is the so-called Berber market – "only today", they'll tell you, with great urgency. In fact, all the main **souks** are open every day, though they're quiet on Friday mornings. Even the big Souk El Khemis (the Thursday Market, held outside Bab Debbagh) now operates most days of the week.

If you prefer to buy from a more **conventional shop**, there are many in Gueliz and, possibly cheaper, in the Medina. Try, for example, two shops next to the *Stylia* restaurant in the Medina: Artisanal Dar Essalam, 26 Rue Ksour (☎04/444 3865) sells pottery, leather goods, marquetry and wood-carving – some of it from Essaouira. The shop is housed in an old mansion, and the ceiling is worth a free look. Dar El Ksour, 28 Rue Ksour (☎04/444 2813) sells old and modern carpets and rugs. Both take cash or cards.

women are supposed to use) and the sticks of *suak* (walnut root or bark) with which you see Moroccans cleaning their teeth.

In addition to such essentials, the stalls also sell the herbal and animal ingredients that are still in widespread use for manipulation, or spellbinding. Magic, white and black, has always been very much a part of Moroccan life, and there are dozens of stories relating to its effects. The stalls hold roots and tablets used as aphrodisiacs, and there are stranger and more specialized goods – dried pieces of lizard and stork, fragments of beaks, talons and gazelle horns.

La Criée Berbère

At the end of Rahba Kedima, a passageway to the left gives access to another, smaller square – a bustling, carpet-draped area known as **La Criée Berbère** (the Berber auction) aka **Souk Zrabia**.

It was here that the old **slave auctions** were held, just before sunset every Wednesday, Thursday and Friday, until the French occupied the city in 1912. They were conducted, according to Budgett Meakin's account in 1900, "precisely as those of cows and mules, often on the same spot by the same men . . . with the human chattels being personally examined in the most disgusting manner, and paraded in lots by the auctioneers, who shout their attractions and the bids". Most had been kidnapped and brought in by the caravans from Guinea and Sudan; Meakin saw two small boys sold for £5 apiece, an eight-year-old girl for £3 and 10 shillings and a "stalwart negro" went for £14; a beauty, he was told, might exceptionally fetch £130 to £150.

These days, **rugs and carpets** are about the only things sold in the square, and if you have a good deal of time and willpower you could spend the best part of a day here while endless (and often identical) stacks are unfolded and displayed before you. Some of the most interesting are the Berber rugs from the High Atlas – bright, geometric designs that look very different after being laid out on the roof and bleached by the sun. The dark, often black, backgrounds usually signify rugs from the Glaoui country, up towards Telouet; the reddish-backed carpets are from Chichaoua, a small village nearly halfway to Essaouira, and are also pretty common. There is usually a small **auction** in the *criée* at around 4pm – an interesting sight with the auctioneers wandering round the square shouting out the latest bids, but it's not the best place to buy a rug – it's devoted mainly to heavy, brown woollen *djellabas*.

Around the kissarias

Cutting back to **Souk El Kebir**, which by now has taken over from the Smarine, you emerge at the **kissarias**, the covered markets at the heart of the souks. The goods here, apart from the many and sometimes imaginative *couvertures* (blankets), aren't that interesting; the kissarias traditionally sell the more expensive products, which today means a sad predominance of Western designs and imports. Off to their right, at the southern end of the kissarias, is **Souk des Bijoutiers**, a modest jewellers' lane, which is much less varied than the one established in the Mellah (see p.367) by Jewish craftsmen. At the northern end is a convoluted web of alleys that comprise the **Souk Cherratin**, essentially a leather workers' souk (with dozens of purse-makers and sandal cobblers), though it's interspersed with smaller alleys and souks of carpenters, sieve-makers and even a few tourist shops. If you bear left through this area and then turn right, you should arrive at the open space in front of the Ben Youssef Mosque; the medersa (see p.358) is off to its right.

The Dyers' Souk and a loop back to the Djemaa El Fna

Taking the earlier left fork along **Souk El Attarin** – the spice and perfume souk – brings you out on the other side of the **kissarias** and the long lane of the **Souk des Babouches** (slipper-makers) aka **Souk Smata**.

The main attraction in this area is the little **Souk des Teinturiers** – the dyers' souk. To reach it, turn left along the first alley you come to after the Souk des Babouches. Working your way down this lane (which comes out in a square by the Mouassin Mosque), look to your right and you'll see the entrance to the souk about halfway down – its lanes rhythmically flash with bright skeins of wool, hung from above. If you have trouble finding it, just follow the first tour group you see.

There is a reasonably straightforward alternative route back to Djemaa El Fna from here, following the main street down to the **Mouassin Mosque** (which is almost entirely concealed from public view, built at an angle to the square beside it) and then turning left on to Rue Mouassin. As you approach the mosque, the street widens very slightly opposite an elaborate triple-bayed **fountain**. Built in the mid-sixteenth century by the prolific Saadian builder, Abdallah El Ghalib, this is one of many such fountains in Marrakesh with a basin for humans set next to two larger troughs for animals; its installation was a pious act, directly sanctioned by the Koran in its charitable provision of water for men and beasts.

Below the Mouassin Mosque is an area of coppersmiths, **Souk des Chaudronniers**. Above it sprawls the main section of **carpenters'** workshops, **Souk Chouari** – with their beautiful smell of cedar – and beyond them the **Souk Haddadine** of blacksmiths – whose sounds you'll hear long before arriving.

The Ben Youssef Medersa

One of the largest buildings in the Medina, and preceded by a rare open space, the recently restored **Ben Youssef Mosque** is quite easy to locate. Its **medersa** (daily 9am–6pm; 10dh) – the old student annexe, and their home until they had learnt the Koran by rote – stands off a side street just to the east, distinguishable by a series of small, grilled windows. The entrance porch is a short way down the side street, covering the whole lane at this point.

Like most of the Fes medersas (see p.215 for a description of their development and function), the Ben Youssef was a Merenid foundation, established by Sultan Abou El Hassan in the fourteenth century. It was, however, almost completely rebuilt under the Saadians, and it is this dynasty's intricate, Andalucian-influenced art that has left its mark. As with the slightly later Saadian Tombs, no surface is left undecorated, and the overall quality of its craftsmanship, whether in carved wood, stuccowork or zellij, is startling. That this was possible in sixteenth-century Marrakesh, after a period in which the city was reduced to near ruin and the country to tribal anarchy, is remarkable. Revealingly, parts have exact parallels in the Alhambra Palace in Granada, and it seems likely that Muslim Spanish architects were employed in its construction.

Inside the medersa, you reach the main court by means of a long outer **corridor** and a small entry **vestibule**. To the side of this are stairs to **student cells**, arranged round smaller internal courtyards on the upper floors, an **ablutions hall** and **latrine**, still in evil-smelling use. Until very recently, a remarkable tenth-century Ommayad marble basin – decorated with eagles and griffins – completed the ensemble, though it has now been removed to the Dar Si Said museum.

The **central courtyard**, weathered almost flat on its most exposed side, is unusually large. Along two sides run wide, sturdy, columned arcades, which were probably used to supplement the space for teaching in the neighbouring mosque. Above them are some of the windows of the **dormitory quarters**, from which you can get an interesting perspective – and attempt to fathom how over eight hundred students were once housed in the building.

At its far end, the court opens onto a **prayer hall**, where the decoration, mellowed on the outside with the city's familiar pink tone, is at its best preserved and most elaborate. Notable here, as in the court's cedar carving, is a predominance of pine cone and palm motifs; around the mihrab (the horseshoe-arched prayer niche) they've been applied so as to give the frieze a highly three-dimensional appearance. This is rare in Moorish stuccowork, though the inscriptions themselves, picked out in the curling, vegetative arabesques, are from familiar Koranic texts. The most common, as in all Moroccan stucco and zellij decoration, is the ceremonial *bismillah* invocation: "In the name of Allah, the Compassionate, the Merciful . . . ".

The Almoravid Koubba

Even though it is signposted opposite the entrance to the Ben Youssef medersa, the **Almoravid Koubba** (aka **Koubba Ba'adiyn**) is easy to pass by – a small, two-storey kiosk, which at first seems little more than a grey dome and a handful of variously shaped doors and windows. Look closer, though, and you may begin to understand its significance and even fascination. For this is the only intact surviving Almoravid building, and it is at the root of all Moroccan architecture. The motifs you've just seen in the medersa – the pine cones, palms and acanthus leaves – were all carved here for the first time. The windows on each of the different sides became the classic shapes of Almohad and Merenid design – as did the merlons, the Christmas tree-like battlements; the complex "ribs" on the outside of the dome; and the dome's interior support, a sophisticated device of a square and star-shaped octagon, which is itself repeated at each of its corners. Once you see all this, you're only a step away from the eulogies of Islamic art historians who sense in this building, which was probably a small ablutions annexe to the original Ben Youssef Mosque, a powerful and novel expression of form.

Excavated only in 1952 – having been covered over amid the many rebuildings of the Ben Youssef medersa – the koubba lies just to the south of the present (mainly nineteenth-century) Ben Youssef Mosque. It is mostly below today's ground level, though standing with your back to the mosque you can make out the top of its dome behind the long, low brick wall. There is an entrance gate down a few steps, opposite the Ben Youssef Mosque, where a *gardien* will emerge to escort you round and sell you a ticket (10dh), and may also show you the huge, old water conduits nearby, which brought water from the Atlas.

If the koubba is closed, you can get almost as good a view from the roof of a very ancient (but still active) hammam down to the right; the attendants will give you access for a small tip.

The Marrakesh Museum

The latest attraction in this area is the magnificent **Marrakesh Museum** on Place Ben Youssef (daily 9am–1pm & 2–6.30pm; 20dh), housed in a late-nineteenth-century palace, **Dar Mnebbi**. The palace was built for Mehdi Mnebbi, defence minister of Moulay Abdelziz (1894–1908), who later became Moroccan ambassador in London, before returning to live in Tangier, and selling his palace to T'hami El Glaoui, Pasha of Marrakesh. With independence in 1956, the palace was taken over by the state but left in an increasing state of neglect for many years.

In 1995, Omar Benjoullan, a patron of the arts, bought and restored the derelict building, and in March 1997 it opened as the Marrakesh Museum. The museum has permanent displays of jewellery, Arabic calligraphy (including several early Korans) and contemporary Moroccan art and sculpture, with works by artists such as Fatima Hassan and Hassan El Glaoui.

Above all, it is the restoration itself which is most memorable. In the entrance courtyard, the statue of the Djemaa El Fna waterseller is both quixotic and photogenic, while the inner courtyard now has a glass roof and a grand chandelier hanging above a central fountain. There's also a small café and bookshop.

EL GLAOUI: THE PASHA OF MARRAKESH

T'hami El Glaoui, the famous pasha of Marrakesh during the French Protectorate, was the last of the great southern tribal leaders, an active and shrewd supporter of colonial rule and a personal friend of Winston Churchill. Cruel and magnificent in equal measure (see p.408), he was also one of the most spectacular partygivers around – in an age where rivals were not lacking. At the extraordinary *difas* or banquets held at the Dar El Glaoui, his Marrakesh palace, "nothing", as Gavin Maxwell wrote, "was impossible" – hashish and opium were freely available for the Europeans and Americans to experiment with, and "to his guests T'hami gave whatever they wanted, whether it might be a diamond ring, a present of money in gold, or a Berber girl or boy from the High Atlas".

Not surprisingly, there was little enthusiasm for showing off the palace since El Glaoui's death in 1956, an event that led to a mob looting the palace, destroying its fittings and even the cars in the garages, and then lynching any of Glaoui's henchmen to be found.

However, passions have burnt out over the years, and the family has been rehabilitated – one of T'hami's sons, Glaoui Abdelssadak, is high up in the Moroccan civil service and vice president of Gulf Oil.

The tanneries and northern gates

The main souks – and the tourist route – stop abruptly at the Ben Youssef medersa. Beyond them, in all directions, you'll find yourself in the ordinary **residential quarters** of the Medina. There are few particular "sights" to be found here, but if you've got the time, there's an interest of its own in following the crowds, and a relief in getting away from the central shopping district of Marrakesh, where you are expected to come in, look round and buy.

Probably the most interesting targets are **Bab Debbagh** and **Souk El Khemis**. From Ben Youssef you can reach these quite easily: it's about a fifteen-minute walk to the first, another fifteen to twenty minutes round the ramparts to the second. As you pass the entrance porch to the medersa, you quickly reach a fork in the side street. To the left, a covered passageway leads around behind the mosque to join Rue Amesfah (see below). Head instead to the right, and then keep going as straight as possible until you emerge at the ramparts by Bab Debbagh; on the way you'll cross a small square and intersection, **Place El Moukef**, where a busy and sizeable lane goes off to the left – a more direct approach to Bab El Khemis.

Turning right instead of left from Place El Moukef, you arrive within ten minutes at Place Ben Salah and the **Zaouia of Sidi Ben Salah** with a very fine, and prominent minaret built by a fourteenth-century Merenid sultan.

Bab Debbagh and the tanneries

Bab Debbagh is supposedly Almoravid in design, though over the years it must have been almost totally rebuilt. Passing through the gate, you become aware of its very real defensive purpose: three internal rooms are placed in such a manner as to force anyone attempting to storm it to make several turns. The leather goods shop, to the right of Bab Debbagh, gives good views from its roof (for a small fee) over the quarter.

Looking down, you have an excellent view over the **tanneries**, built here at the edge of the city for access to water (the summer-dry Oued Issil runs just outside the walls) and for the obvious reason of the smell. If you want to take a closer look at the processes, come in the morning, when the co-operatives are at work; any of the kids standing around will take you in. As at Fes, a tour is an ambivalent experience; there's certainly a beauty about the proceedings, but the traditional, natural dyes have been in large part replaced by modern chemicals, which can cause cancer in the workers.

Bab El Khemis

Following the road from Bab Debbagh, outside the ramparts, is the simplest approach to **Bab El Khemis** (Gate of the Thursday Market) another reconstructed Almoravid gate, built at an angle in the walls. The Thursday market now seems to take place more or less daily, around 400m to the north, above a cemetery and marabout's tomb. It is really a local produce market, though odd handicraft items do occasionally surface.

North of the Ben Youssef Mosque

The area immediately **north of the Ben Youssef Mosque** is cut by two main streets: Rue Assouel (which leads up to Bab El Khemis) and Rue Bab Taghzout, which runs up to the gate of the same name and to the Zaouia of Sidi Bel Abbes. These were, with Bab Doukkala, the principal approaches to the city until the last century and along them you find many of the old **fondouks** used for storage and lodging by merchants visiting the souks.

One of these fondouks is sited just south of the mosque and a whole series can be found along Rue Amesfah – the continuation of Baroudienne – to the north and west. Most are still used in some commercial capacity, as workshops or warehouses, and the doors to their courtyards often stand open. Some date from Saadian times and have fine details of wood carving or stuccowork. If you are interested, nobody seems to mind if you wander in.

The Zaouia of Sidi Bel Abbes

Rue Amesfah runs for around 150m north of the intersection with Rue Baroudienne before reaching the junction of Rue Assouel (to the east) and **Rue Bab Taghzout** (to the west). Following Rue Bab Taghzout, you pass another fondouk, opposite a small recessed fountain known as **Chrob ou Chouf** ("drink and admire"), and around 500m further down, the old city gate of **Bab Taghzout**. This marked the limits of the original Almoravid Medina, and continued to do so into the eighteenth century, when Sultan Mohammed Abdallah extended the walls to enclose the quarter and the **Zaouia of Sidi Bel Abbes**.

Sidi Bel Abbes was born in Ceuta in 1130. As a marabout and a prolific performer of miracles, particularly giving sight to the blind, he is the most important of Marrakesh's seven saints, and his **zaouia**, a kind of monastic cult centre, has traditionally wielded very great influence and power, often at odds with that of the sultan and providing a refuge for political dissidents.

The present buildings, entry to which is strictly forbidden to non-Muslims, date largely from a reconstruction by Moulay Ismail, an act that was probably inspired more by political motivation than piety. You can see something of the complex and its activities from outside the official boundary – do not, however, try to pass through the long central corridor. The zaouia has always prospered and still owns much of the quarter to the north and continues its educational and charitable work, distributing food each evening to the blind.

The tomb of Sidi Bel Abbes is in the nearby Sidi Marouk cemetery and can, for a small fee, be visited by non-Muslims; look for the white koubba with the light green dome. A couple of blocks to the southwest, there is a smaller, though again significant **zaouia** dedicated to **Sidi Mohammed Ben Slimane**, a Saadian marabout and another of Marrakesh's seven saints.

West to Bab Doukkala: Dar El Glaoui

A third alternative from Ben Youssef is to head west **towards Bab Doukkala.** This route, once you've found your way down through Souk Haddadine to **Rue Bab**

Doukkala, is a sizeable thoroughfare and very straightforward to follow. Midway, you pass the **Dar El Glaoui**, the old palace of the pasha of Marrakesh (see p.360) and a place of legendary exoticism throughout the first half of the twentieth century. Part of it is nowadays occupied by the Ministry of Culture; visitors are allowed in at the discretion of the caretaker, but there's little to see. The main section of the palace remains private.

The Lower Medina: the Royal Palace, Saadian Tombs and Mellah

Staying in Marrakesh even for a few days, you begin to sense the different appearance and life of its various Medina quarters, and nowhere more so than in the shift from north to south, from the area to the north of Djemaa El Fna and that to the south of it. At the southern extremity (a kind of stem to the mushroom shape of the city walls) is **Dar El Makhzen**, the royal palace. To its west stretches the old inner citadel of the **kasbah**; to the east, the **Mellah**, once the largest Jewish ghetto in Morocco; while rambling to the north of it is a series of mansions and palaces built for the nineteenth-century elite.

All in all, it's an interesting area to wander round, though you inevitably spend time trying to figure out the sudden and apparently arbitrary appearance of ramparts and enclosures. And there are two obvious focal points, not to be missed: the **Saadian Tombs**, preserved in the shadow of the kasbah mosque, and **El Badi**, the ruined palace of Ahmed El Mansour.

The Saadian Tombs

Sealed up by Moulay Ismail after he had destroyed the adjoining Badi Palace, the **Saadian Tombs** (daily 9am–5pm; 10dh) lay half-ruined and half-forgotten at the beginning of the last century. In 1917, however, they were rediscovered on a French aerial map and a passageway was built to give access from the side of the kasbah mosque. Restored, they are today the city's main "sight" – over-lavish, maybe, in their exhaustive decoration, but dazzling nonetheless. Now there is no longer a compulsory guided tour, you are left to look round on your own or even just to sit and gaze; best time to go is late afternoon when the crowds and heat have largely gone. A quiet, high-walled enclosure, shaded with shrubs and palms and dotted with bright zellij-covered tombs, it seems as much a pleasure garden as a cemetery.

Some form of burial ground behind the royal palace probably predated the Saadian period, though the earliest of the tombs here dates from 1557, and all the principal structures were built by Sultan Ahmed El Mansour. This makes them virtual contemporaries of the Ben Youssef Medersa – with which there are obvious parallels – and allows a revealing insight into just how rich and extravagant the El Badi must once have been. Their escape from Moulay Ismail's systematic plundering was probably due to superstition – Ismail had to content himself with blocking all but an obscure entrance from the kasbah mosque. Despite this, a few prominent *Marrakchis* continued to be buried in the mausoleums; the last, in 1792, was the "mad sultan", Moulay Yazid, whose 22-month reign was one of the most violent and sadistic in the nation's history. Named as the successor to Sidi Mohammed, Moulay Yazid threw himself into a series of revolts against his father, waged an inconclusive war with Spain, and brutally suppressed a rebellion which was supporting his brother in Marrakesh. A massacre followed his capture of the city, though he had little time to celebrate his victory – a bullet in the head during a rebel counterattack killed him soon after.

△ Zaouia Sidi Bel Abbes

Ⓐ
Ⓑ
PLACE DJEMAA EL FNA
See 'Medina Hotels' map

Ⓒ

MARRAKESH: LOWER MEDINA

RUE EL KOUTOUBIA

◁ Bab Doukkala

Fatima Zohra Koubba

PLACE DE FOUCAULD

AV. EL MOUAHIDINE

RUE MOULAY ISMAIL

RUE BANI MARINE

RUE BAB AGNAOU

RIAD ZITOUN KADEM

RIAD ZITOUN DJEDID

N

Dar Si Said (Museum)

Ⓒ
Ⓓ
Ⓔ

P

Maison Tiskiwln

Bahia Palace

PTT ✉

Ⓕ

RUE IBN ROCHD

AVENUE HOUMAN EL FETUUAKI

Market

ARSET EL MAACH

PLACE DES FERBLANTIERS

Ⓖ

Ⓗ

El Badi Palace

MELLAH (HAY ESSALAM)

PTT ✉

Kasbah Mosque

Bab er Robb

Bab Agnaou

Saadian Tombs

Grands Taxis

RUE DE LA KASBAH

Berrima Mosque

RUE BERRIMA

Dar el Makhzen (Royal Palace)

RESTAURANTS
Restaurant Argana   A
Café-Restaurant El Badi   H
Restaurant El Bahia   F
Restaurant Al Baraka   C
Restaurant Doüirya   G
Café Restaurant El Fatha   B
Palais Gharnatta   D
Dar Mima   E

KASBAH

Mechouar

Bab Ksiba

RUE DE BAB LAHRI

Bab Lahri

Agdal Gardens

0   200m

▽ Basin (2 km)

The mausoleums

There are two main **mausoleums** in the enclosure. The finest is on the left as you come in – a beautiful group of three rooms, built to house El Mansour's own tomb and completed within his lifetime. Continuing round from the courtyard entrance, the first hall is a **prayer oratory**, a room probably not intended for burial, though now almost littered with the thin marble stones of Saadian princes. It is here that Moulay Yazid was laid out, perhaps in purposeful obscurity, certainly in ironic contrast to the cursive inscription round the band of black and white zellij: "And the works of peace they have accomplished", it reads amid the interlocking circles, "will make them enter the holy gardens."

Architecturally, the most important feature of this mausoleum is the mihrab, its pointed horseshoe arch supported by an incredibly delicate arrangement of columns. Opposite this is another elaborate arch, leading to the domed **central chamber** and **El Mansour's tomb**, which you can glimpse through the next door in the court. The tomb, slightly larger than those surrounding it, lies right in the middle, flanked on either side by those of the sultan's sons and successors. The room itself is spectacular, faint light filtering onto the tombs from an interior lantern in a tremendous vaulted roof, the zellij full of colour and motion and the undefined richness of a third chamber almost hidden from view. Throughout, there are echoes of the Alhambra in Granada, built two centuries previously, and from which its style is clearly derived.

The **other mausoleum**, older and less impressive, was built by Ahmed in place of an existing pavilion above the tombs of his mother, Lalla Messaouda, and of Mohammed ech Sheikh, the founder of the Saadian dynasty. It is again a series of three rooms, though two are hardly more than loggias. Messaouda's tomb is the niche below the dome in the outer chamber. Mohammed ech Sheikh is buried in the inner one – or at least his torso is, since he was murdered in the Atlas by Turkish mercenaries, who salted his head and took it back for public display on the walls of Istanbul.

Outside, **round the garden and courtyard**, are scattered the tombs of over a hundred more Saadian princes and members of the royal household. Like the privileged 66 given space within the mausoleums, their gravestones are brilliantly tiled and often elaborately inscribed. The most usual inscription reads quite simply:

> There is no God but God.
> Muhammad is God's envoy.
> Praise Be to God.
> The occupant of this tomb died on . . .

But there are others – epitaphs and extracts from the Koran – that seem to express the turbulence of the age to a greater degree, which, with Ahmed's death in 1603, was to disintegrate into nearly seventy years of constant civil war. "Every soul shall know death", reads one tombstone; "Death will find you wherever you are, even in fortified towers", reads another. And, carved in gypsum on the walls, there is a poem:

> O mausoleum, built out of mercy, thou whose
> walls are the shadow of heaven.
> The breath of asceticism is wafted from thy tombs
> like a fragrance.
> Through thy death
> the light of faith has been dimmed,
> the seven spheres are fraught with darkness
> and the columns of glory
> broken with pain.

Getting to the Saadian Tombs, the simplest route from Djemaa El Fna is to follow **Rue Bab Agnaou** outside the ramparts. At its end you come to a small square flanked by two gates. Directly ahead is **Bab Er Robb** – outside of which the grands taxis and private-line buses leave for Ourika and other local destinations. To the left, somewhat battered and eroded, is the city's only surviving Almohad gateway, **Bab Agnaou** (Gate of the Gnaoua [the blacks]). This is an impressive structure, smaller than the monumental gates of Rabat, but sharing much of their force and apparent simplicity. Notice how the semicircular frieze above its arch creates a strong, three-dimensional effect without any actual depth of carving. At the time of its construction, it was the only stone building in Marrakesh apart from the Koutoubia Minaret.

Passing through the gate, the **kasbah mosque** is in front of you: its minaret looks gaudy and modern but is, in fact, contemporary with both the Koutoubia and Hassan towers – it was restored to its exact original state in the 1960s. Work is still going on to clear and make good the space alongside the mosque. The narrow passageway to the Saadian Tombs is well signposted, at the near right-hand corner of the mosque.

El Badi Palace

To reach the ruins of the **El Badi Palace** (daily 9am–5pm; 10dh) – which seems originally to have sprawled across the whole area east of the kasbah mosque – you have to backtrack slightly from the Saadian Tombs. At Bab Agnaou, follow the ramparts up again, this time taking the road just inside them, until you come to a reasonably sized street on your right (just before the walls temporarily give out). Turn into this street, keep more or less straight, and in about 550m, you'll emerge at **Place des Ferblantiers** – a major intersection. On the south side of the square is a gate known as **Bab Berrima**, which opens onto a long rectangular enclosure, flanked on either side by walls; go through it, and on your right you'll come to the Badi's entrance.

The Incomparable Palace

Though substantially in ruins, and reduced throughout to its red *pisé* walls, enough remains of El Badi to suggest that its name – "The Incomparable" – was not entirely immodest. It took the sultan Moulay Ismail over ten years of systematic work to strip the palace of everything moveable or of value, but even so, there's a lingering sense of luxury and grandeur. The scale, with its sunken gardens and vast, ninety-metre-long

---

AHMED EL MANSOUR

The El Badi Palace was begun shortly after Ahmed El Mansour's accession, its initial finance coming from the enormous ransom paid out by the Portuguese after the Battle of the Three Kings at Ksar El Kebir. Fought in the summer of 1578, this was one of the most disastrous battles in Christian medieval history; ostensibly in support of a rival Saadian claimant, but to all intents a Portuguese crusade, it was led by the young king, Dom Sebastião, and supported by almost his entire nobility. Few escaped death or Moorish capture. Sebastião himself was killed, as were both the Saadian claimant and the ruling sultan.

As a result, Ahmed – dubbed *El Mansour* (The Victorious) – came to the throne, undisputed and commanding immediate wealth from the ransoms paid for the captured Portuguese nobles. He reigned for 25 years, trading in sugar and slaves with Britain, Spain and Italy; seized the gold route across the Sahara with the resultant capture of Timbuktu, which earned him the additional epithet *El Eddahbi* (The Golden); and maintained peace in Morocco through a loose confederation of tribes. It was the most prosperous period in the country's history since the time of the Almohads – a cultural and political renaissance reflected in the coining of a new title, the Shereefian Empire, the country's official name until independence in 1956.

THE MARRAKESH FESTIVAL

Marrakesh utilizes the Badi Palace – and other venues in the city – for an annual two-week **Festival National des Art Populaires**. This is the country's biggest and best folklore and music festival, and is currently held in June. If you are interested in Moroccan music, it would be worth planning your trip around it – were you to be able to establish the precise dates, which vary year by year and which the ONMT themselves often don't know.

The festival comprises a series of totally authentic and unusual performances, with groups of musicians and dancers coming in from all regions of Morocco. A typical programme will span the range of Moroccan music – from the Gnaoua drummers and the panpipers of Jajouka, to Berber *ahouaches* from the Atlas and southern oases, to classical Andalous music from Fes.

The shows are held each evening from around 9pm to midnight (tickets are 50dh); before they start, towards sunset, there is a **fantasia** at Bab El Djedid – a spectacle by any standard, with dozens of Berber horsemen firing their guns in the air at full gallop.

pool, is certainly unrivalled, and the odd traces of zellij and plaster still left evoke a decor that was probably as rich as that of the Saadian Tombs.

What you see today is essentially the ceremonial part of the **palace complex**, planned on a grand scale for the reception of ambassadors, and not meant for everyday living. It seems likely that El Mansour and the multiple members of his court each had private palaces – smaller, though built to a similar ground plan – to the west and south, covering much of the area occupied by the Dar El Makhzen, the present Royal Palace.

The **entrance** in current use was probably not the main approach. Going through, you find yourself at the side of a **mosque**, like everything else within this complex, of enormous height. To the rear extends the great **central court**, over 130m long and nearly as wide, and constructed on a substructure of vaults in order to allow the circulation of water through the pools and gardens. When the pools are filled – as during the June folklore festival which takes place here – they are an incredibly majestic sight, especially the main one, with an island that was originally surmounted by an elaborate double fountain.

On each side of the pools were summer pavilions, traces of which survive. The most prominent is at the far end, a monumental hall that was used by the sultan on occasions of state and known as the **Koubba El Hamsiniya** (The Fifty Pavilion), after the number of its columns. Strangely enough, their size and splendour were documented by an observer far removed from the Arab chroniclers who extolled their beauty. The French philosopher Montaigne, while travelling through Italy, saw craftsmen preparing the columns – "each of an extreme height . . . for the king of Fes and Barbary".

South of the courtyard are ruins of the palace **stables**, and beyond them, leading towards the intriguing walls of the present royal palace, a series of **dungeons**, used into the last century as a state prison. You can explore part of these and could easily spend a whole afternoon wandering round the various inner courts above, with their fragments of marble and zellij and their water conduits for the fountains and hammams. Like the Saadian Tombs, the Badi inspired contemporary poets, and there is an account, too, by the chronicler El Ifrani, of its construction:

El Mansour made workmen come from all the different countries . . . He paid for the marble sent from Italy in sugar, pound for pound awarded his workers very generously . . . and paid attention even to the entertainment of their children, so that the artisans might devote themselves entirely to their work without being distracted by any other preoccupation.

If this is even half true, there could be no greater contrast with the next great Moroccan builder, and dismantler of the El Badi Palace, Moulay Ismail, whose palace workmen in Meknes were beaten up, starved and abused, and then buried in the walls where they fell. But sixteenth-century crèches aside, the most enduring account of the palace concerns its state opening, a fabulous occasion attended by ambassadors from several European powers and by all the sheikhs and *caids* of the kingdom. Surveying the effect, Ahmed turned to his court jester for an opinion on the new palace. "Sidi," the man replied, "this will make a magnificent ruin."

The Mellah

It was in 1558 – five years before Ahmed's accession – that the Marrakesh **Mellah**, the separate Jewish quarter in Morocco, was created. There is no exact record of why this was done at this particular time. Possibly it was the result of a pogrom, with the sultan moving the Jews to his protected kasbah – and they, in turn, forming a useful buffer zone (and scapegoat) between his palace and the populace in times of social unrest. But, as likely as not, it was simply brought about to make taxation easier. The Jews of Marrakesh were an important financial resource – they controlled most of the Saadian sugar trade, and comprised practically all of the city's bankers, metalworkers, jewellers and tailors. In the sixteenth century, at least, their quarter was almost a town in itself, supervised by rabbis, and with its own souks, gardens, fountains and synagogues.

The present Mellah, which is now known officially as the **Hay Essalam** quarter and is much smaller in extent, is now almost entirely Muslim – most of the *Marrakchi* Jews left long ago for Casablanca (where some 6000 still live) or emigrated to France or Israel. The few who remain, outwardly distinguishable only by the men's small black skullcaps, are mostly poor or old or both. Their quarter, however, is immediately distinct: its houses are taller than elsewhere, the streets are more enclosed, and even the shop cubicles are smaller. Until the Protectorate, Jews were not permitted to own land or property – nor even to ride or walk, except barefoot – outside the Mellah; a situation that was greatly exploited by their landlords, who resisted all attempts to expand the walls. Today, although this is not a prized neighbourhood in which to live, its air of neglect and poverty is probably less than at any time during the past three centuries.

Around the quarter

The main entrance to the Mellah, which is still a largely walled district, is at **Place des Ferblantiers** – the tinsmiths' square. Formerly called Place du Mellah, this was itself part of the old Jewish souk, and an archway (to your right, standing at Bab Berrima) leads into it. Near the upper end is a **jewellers' souk**, one of the traditional Jewish trades now more or less taken over by Muslim craftsmen; further down are some good spice and textile souks. Right at the centre – and situated very much as the goal of a maze – is a small square with a fountain in the middle, **Place Souweka**. You will almost certainly find yourself back here if you wander round for a short while and manage to avoid the blind alleys.

To the east, some 200m away, is the **Jewish cemetery**, the **Miâara**, reckoned to date from the early seventeenth century. It is well tended and boasts eleven Jewish marabout (*tsadikim* in Hebrew) shrines. Nearby are two **synagogues**. The **Lazama**, on Rue Talmud Torah is still in use. The smaller **El Fassiines** may, with American help, become a museum. Neither is easy to find, but a local guide could show you.

Just outside the Mellah, on Arset El Maach, are two further synagogues. The **Bitoun** has a leaking roof and is being restored. The **Rabbi Pinhas** is smaller and still in use – to find it, walk from Place des Ferblantiers eastwards along Arset El Maach and after 100m look for a brown wooden door on the left (it's the only wooden door of this length). If you have a problem finding it, or want to know when it might be open, ask at 4 Arset El Maach, which is further along and on the right, facing the municipal compound for trucks. Alternatively, you could contact the Communauté Israélite de Marrakech (see p.378) or telephone the Bitoun Synagogue office on ☎04/444 8266.

You may well be directed to other synagogues (*s'noga*) which look more like lived-in houses (and indeed often are lived-in houses). This should not surprise you because, even when in active use, many of the Moroccan synagogues were as much private houses as temples – " . . . serving also as places in which to eat, sleep and to kill chickens", according to Budgett Meakin (see "Contexts", p.599).

North of the Mellah: the Bahia Palace

Heading north from the Mellah – back towards Djemaa El Fna – there are three direct and fairly simple routes. To the left of Place des Ferblantiers, **Avenue Houman El Fetouaki** will bring you out by the Koutoubia. North of the square, two parallel streets, **Riad Zitoun Kadem** and **Riad Zitoun Djedid** lead up to the Djemaa El Fna.

Zitoun Kadem is basically a shopping street, lined with grocers, barbershops and, at the far end, a couple of hammams (open all day; one each for men and women). Zitoun Djedid is more residential, and it is here that you find the concentration of **palaces and mansions** built in those strange, closing decades of the nineteenth and the first few years of the twentieth century, when the sultans Moulay Hassan and Moulay Abd El Aziz held court in the city. Several of these are now upmarket restaurants, notably *Restaurant Douirya* and *Palais Gharnatta*. You may not want to pay for a meal and the "tourist spectacle" in these (see p.374) but it's worth looking into one or two of them on your way just to see the turn-of-the-century decor.

The Bahia

By far the most ambitious and costly of these mansions was the **Bahia Palace** (daily 8.30–11.45am & 2.30–5.45pm; 10dh, plus at least 10dh tip for obligatory guided tour), built by the grand vizier, Si Ahmed Ben Moussa. Shrewd, wilful and cruel, as was the tradition of his age, **Bou Ahmed** (as he was better known) was a black slave who rose to hold massive power in the Shereefian kingdom and, for the last six years of his life, exercised virtually autocratic control. He was first chamberlain to Moulay Hassan, whose death while returning home from a *harka* he managed to conceal until the proclamation of Abd El Aziz in Rabat (see "Writers on Morocco", in "Contexts", for the dramatic account). Under Abd El Aziz (who was just 12 when he acceded to the throne), Bou Ahmed usurped the position of vizier from the ill-fated Jamai brothers (see p.225), and then proceeded to rule.

He began building the Bahia in 1894, later enlarging it by acquiring the surrounding land and property. He died in 1900. The name of the building means "The Effulgence" or "Brilliance", but after the **guided tour** round various sections of the rambling palace courts and apartments you might feel this to be a somewhat tall claim. There is reasonable craftsmanship in the main **reception halls**, and a pleasant arrangement of rooms in the **harem quarter**, but for the most part it is all fabulously vulgar and hasn't aged too well. Perhaps this is the main reason for a visit: you come away realizing just how much mastery and sophistication went into the Saadian medersa and tombs, and how corrupted and dull these traditions had become.

But there is also a certain pathos to the empty, echoing chambers – and the inevitable passing of Bou Ahmed's influence and glory. Walter Harris, who knew the vizier, described his demise and the clearing of his palace in *Morocco That Was*, published just twenty years after the events, by which time Bou Ahmed's name had already become "only a memory of the past":

For several days as the Vizier lay expiring, guards were stationed outside his palace waiting in silence for the end. And then one morning the wail of the women within the house told that death had come. Every gateway of the great building was seized, and no one was allowed to enter or come out, while within there was pandemonium. His slaves pillaged wherever they could lay their hands. His women fought and stole to get possession of the jewels. Safes were broken open, documents and title-deeds were extracted, precious stones were torn from their settings, the more easily to be concealed, and even murder took place . . . A few days later nothing remained but the great building – all the rest had disappeared into space. His family were driven out to starvation and ruin, and his vast properties passed into the possession of the State. It was the custom of the country.

For some years during the Protectorate, the palace was used to house the resident-general, and it is still called into use when the royal family is in the city. This is usually during the winter months, at which times there is no public admission.

Finding your way to the palace is easy enough: from Rue Zitoun follow the signs to the *Palais Gharnatta* restaurant, keeping straight when they suddenly direct you to the right under an arch.

The Dar Si Said Museum

Also worth your while in this area is the **Dar Si Said** (daily except Tues 9–11.45am & 2.30–5.45 pm; Fri 9–11.30am & 3–5.45pm; 10dh admission), a smaller version of the Bahia, built by a brother of Bou Ahmed, who, being something of a simpleton, nonetheless gained the post of royal chamberlain. It's a pleasurable building, with beautiful pooled courtyards, scented with lemons, palms and flowers, and it houses an impressive **Museum of Moroccan Arts**.

The museum is particularly strong on its collection of **Berber jewellery** and daggers, swords and other weapons – boldly designed objects of great beauty. There are also fine displays of eighteenth- and nineteenth-century **woodwork**, some of it from the Glaoui kasbahs and most of it in cedar wood. Besides the furniture, there are Berber doors, window frames and wonderful painted ceilings. There are also a number of traditional **wedding chairs** – once widely used for carrying the bride, veiled and hidden, to her new home. Today, such chairs are still made in the souks and used, albeit symbolically, to carry the bride from her womenfolk in one room to the groom's menfolk in the next room. Indeed, the video of the marriage of the late King Hassan's eldest daughter shows this ceremony in full.

Near the entrance is the museum's most important exhibit, recently brought here from the Ben Youssef medersa. It is a marble **basin**, rectangular in shape and decorated along one side with what seem to be heraldic eagles and griffins. An inscription amid the floral decorations records its origin in tenth-century Córdoba, then the centre of the western Muslim world; the Ommayad caliphs, for whom it was constructed, had few reservations about representational art. What is surprising is that it was brought over to Morocco by the highly puritan Almoravid sultan Ali Ben Youssef and, placed in his mosque, was left untouched by the dynasty's equally iconoclastic successors, the Almohads.

Also near the entrance, do not miss the **fairground swings**, shaped like a wooden Ferris wheel, and used at moussems until the early 1960s.

Dar Si Said is on a block to the west of Riad Zitoun Djedid. You can either turn right opposite a mosque, midway along Riad Zitoun Djedid walking from Place des Ferblantiers; or you can turn right 100m before the mosque and, from the car park there, take the gate to the right of the Prefecture de Marrakesh Medina as you face it with your back to the car park. This latter route passes the **Maison Tiskiwin** (see below), which is 30m inside the gate.

Maison Tiskiwin

A further, superb collection of Moroccan art and artefacts is housed in the **Maison Tiskiwin**, which lies between the Bahia and Dar Si Said palaces at 8 Rue de la Bahia. It is easy to find from either the Bahia or Dar Si Said car park; look for the yellow sign with white lettering. It's open every day 9.30am–12.30pm & 3–6pm.

Behind the wooden door is a beautiful town house, built at the turn of the twentieth century in Spanish-Moroccan style, and furnished from the collection of a Dutch anthropologist, Bert Flint, who has been resident in Morocco since the 1950s. Each of the rooms features carpets, fabrics, clothes and jewellery from a different town or region, including the south and sub-Sahara, and backed by informative notes (in French).

For some years Dr Flint had a second museum in Agadir, housing the exhibits from the south and sub-Sahara, but this has now closed, hence the presence of these items in Marrakesh. He hopes to reopen an Agadir outpost soon.

The gardens

With summer temperatures of 34 to 38°C – and peaks well above that – it seems best to devote at least the middle of a Marrakesh day to total inactivity. A good place to do so is one of the city's gardens. There are two – the **Agdal** and **Menara** – designed for just this purpose. Each begins near the edge of the Medina, rambles through acres of orchards and olive groves and has, near its centre, an immense, lake-size pool of water. This is all – they are not flower gardens, but, cool and completely still, they seem both satisfying and luxurious, and in perfect contrast to the close city streets. Other, smaller gardens of note include the gorgeous **Jardin Majorelle**, which should on no account be missed, and those of the fabled **Hôtel La Mamounia**.

With the exception of *La Mamounia*, you will want **transport** to get to any of these gardens – either a petit taxi or calèche. If you are considering a calèche trip at any stage, the Agdal or Menara are the perfect destinations. Alternatively, to take in both gardens and tour the ramparts and palmery, you could rent a **bike** or charter a grand taxi for the day.

Jardin Agdal

The **Agdal** is a confusingly large expanse – some 3km in extent and with half a dozen smaller irrigation pools in addition to its *grand bassin*. Beginning just south of the Mellah and Royal Palace, it is a logical continuation of a tour of the Lower Medina. Take the road outside the ramparts below Bab Agnaou/Bab Er Robb, and then turn left as you are about to leave the city at Bab Irhli; this route will take you through a mechouar (parade ground) by the Royal Palace and to the corner gate of the garden. The garden is often closed during the winter months, if the king is in residence in Marrakesh.

The garden is watered by an incredible system of wells and underground channels, known as *khettera,* that go as far as the base of the Atlas in the Ourika Valley and that date, in part, from the earliest founding of the city. Over the centuries, the channels have at times fallen into disrepair and the gardens been abandoned, but the present nineteenth-century layout probably differs little from any of its predecessors. It is surrounded by walls, with gates at each of the near corners, while inside, the orange, fig, lemon, apricot and pomegranate orchards are divided into square, irrigated plots by endless raised walkways and broad avenues of olive trees.

If you walk out here, it is around 4km from Djemaa El Fna, and a further 2km of unsignposted paths to the main series of pools at its heart. The largest of these is the

Sahraj El Hana (Tank of Health), which was probably dug by the Almohads and is flanked by a ramshackle old *minzah*, or summer pavilion, where the last few precolonial sultans held picnics and boating parties. You can climb up on its roof for a fabulous view over the park and across to the Koutoubia and Atlas, and if the caretaker's around, you'll be shown the steam-powered launch which capsized in 1873, bringing Sultan Sidi Mohammed to his death – or, as his epitaph rather more elegantly put it, he "departed this life, in a water tank, in the hope of something better to come". The launch is in a wooden shed and, failing the caretaker, you could peep between the warped planks.

Nowadays, probably the most dangerous thing you could do here would be to swim in the algae-ridden waters, though the kids do it and it does look unbelievably tempting. It's perhaps better just to pick up some food beforehand – and perhaps a bottle of wine from the Gueliz – and spread out a picnic in local fashion on the paved, shaded pathway round the water's edge.

Jardin Menara

The **Menara** is in a similar vein to the Agdal, though it has just the one central basin, and it is more olive grove than orchard, with lines of trees rather than groves and walks. It is also much more visited: a popular picnic spot for local families, as well as tourists drawn by its postcard image *bassin* and *minzah*, with its backdrop of the High Atlas mountains. If you just want to gaze upon one of these still sheets of water, then come out here; it's a lot easier to get to than the Agdal (and a cheaper ride too). The garden couldn't be simpler to find: just follow Avenue de la Menara from Bab Djedid, by the *Hôtel La Mamounia*. In summer, it has several drinks stalls.

Like the Agdal, the Menara was restored and its pavilions rebuilt in the mid-nineteenth century. The poolside *minzah* (10dh admission) is said to have replaced an original Saadian structure.

Jardin Majorelle

The subtropical **Jardin Majorelle** (or Jardin Bou Saf) is one of the most delightful spots in Marrakesh: a small, meticulously planned botanical garden, created from the 1920s on by the French painter, Jacques Majorelle (1886–1962). Now superbly mature, it is owned and splendidly maintained by fashion designer Yves Saint Laurent, and is open daily to visitors (8am–noon & 2–5pm winter; 8am–noon & 3–7pm summer; garden 15dh, museum 15dh; no unaccompanied children or animals allowed). The entrance is on a small side street off the jacaranda-lined Avenue Yacoub El Mansour.

The garden – twelve acres in extent – has an amazing feeling of tranquillity, an atmosphere enhanced by the verdant groves of bamboo, dwarf palm and agave, and the various lily-covered pools. Its keynote colour, used as a wash on the walls, is a striking cobalt blue – the colour of French workmen's overalls, so Majorelle claimed, though it seems to have improved in the Moroccan light. This brilliantly offsets both the plants – multicoloured bougainvillea, rows of bright orange nasturtiums and pink geraniums – and also the strong colours of the pergolas and concrete paths – pinks, lemon yellows and apple greens. The garden's enduring sound is the chatter of the common bulbuls, flitting among the leaves of the date palms, and the pools also attract bird residents such as turtle doves and house buntings. The garden became better known abroad when it was featured by Yves Saint Laurent in a brilliant reproduction at the 1997 Chelsea Flower Show in London. Recently the trees, plants and grasses have been cropped, presumably on the advice of a horticulturalist, so as to improve the garden in the long term.

In Majorelle's former **studio**, a **Museum of Islamic Arts** exhibits Saint Laurent's fine personal collection of North African carpets, pottery, furniture and doors; Saint

Laurent was himself born in Algeria. It also has one room devoted to Jacques Majorelle's engravings and paintings – mainly of interest for the local scenes (fifty years ago), which include the fortified village of Anemiter and the Kasbah of Aït Benhaddou, near Ouarzazate.

Hôtel La Mamounia

You might consider spending an hour or two looking round the gardens of the luxurious **Hôtel La Mamounia**. Walled from the outside world, laid out only five minutes' walk from the Djemaa El Fna, these were once royal grounds, laid out by the Saadians with a succession of pavilions. Today they're slightly Europeanized in style but have retained the traditional elements of shrubs and walkways.

For the cost of a drink or some tea on the terrace – the latter not cripplingly exorbitant – you can sit and admire the surroundings. The swimming pool is strictly reserved for residents, and you need to dress up just to get in the place: visitors are not allowed in wearing shorts or jeans, and there have been reports of well-dressed nonresidents being turned away, though this may be more to do with recent redecoration. Whatever, it's worth a try.

If you ask at the desk, and the staff aren't too busy, someone may be prepared to give you a quick tour of the old part of the hotel – where the **Winston Churchill suite** is preserved as visited by its namesake. There are editions of Churchill's books on the shelves, a truly sultan-like bed (and smaller sleeping quarters for his manservant) and photographs of him painting in the gardens. Churchill was a frequent visitor to Marrakesh from the 1930s to the 1950s, and the Mamounia gardens were, as he remarked when he was there with Franklin D. Roosevelt in 1943, the loveliest spot in the whole world. Significantly, it was here that Churchill painted his only picture during World War II.

Even though the hotel has been rebuilt and enlarged since Churchill's day, it's not hard to understand the lasting appeal. Decoratively, it is of most interest for the 1920s Art Deco touches of **Jacques Majorelle** (see previous page), and their enhancements, in 1986, by King Hassan's then-favourite designer, **André Paccard**. The collective result is a splendid fantasy of **public rooms** – including a **casino**, where you might want to gamble your all on the prospect of a stay.

Eating, drinking and nightlife

Marrakesh **eating and entertainment options** break down less rigidly than usual between the Ville Nouvelle, in this case Gueliz, and the Medina. **Gueliz**, naturally enough, is where you'll find most of the city's French-style cafés, bistros and restaurants, and virtually all the bars. In the **Medina**, however, there's plenty of choice for meals, including the spectacle of the Djemaa El Fna food stalls, many inexpensive café-restaurants, and a number of upmarket palace-restaurants (a couple of which offer Morocco's traditional cuisine at its very best).

Medina cafés and restaurants

Recommendations for the Medina span the range: from 30dh to 550dh a head; from a bench in the Djemaa El Fna to the most sumptuous palace decor. Only the places listed under "Moderate" or "Expensive" are licensed to sell alcohol.

Note that many of the **palace-restaurants** are well hidden in the Medina and often difficult to find, especially at night; if in doubt, phone in advance and ask for directions – sometimes the restaurant will send someone to meet you. Be wary of palace-restaurants that aren't listed below; they tend to be geared towards tour groups, with kitsch belly-dancing entertainment, and uninteresting food.

Recommendations are shown on the main Marrakesh map on pp.344–345, the Medina Hotels and Restaurants map on p.349 and the Lower Medina map on p.363.

Cheap café-restaurants

Café-Restaurant El Badi, by Bab Berrima, on a rooftop overlooking Place des Ferblantiers and towards the Mellah. This is a fine viewpoint, level with nesting storks on the palace walls; the café serves a limited range of hot and soft drinks, and a modest set menu. On the far side of the square, the tinsmiths still work and the entrance to the Mellah is lined with gold and jewellery boutiques.

Rue Bani Marine. This narrow street which runs south from the PTT and Bank al Maghrib on Djemaa El Fna, between and parallel to Rue Bab Agnaou and Rue Moulay Ismail, has about ten excellent-value café-restaurants and several mobile grill-bars. Look for *Casse-Croûte des Amis* and, alongside the *Hôtel Gazelle*, *El Bahja*, with its *hadj* patron. It's popular with locals and knowing tourists.

Restaurant Diamant Rouge, just off Djemaa El Fna, opposite *Hôtel Panorama*. A small, bright, lively café serving salads, sandwiches, cakes and fruit juices.

Café Restaurant El Fatha. Another small café, with balcony terrace, on the northern side of the square. It's quiet and doesn't get too crowded; usual range of snacks and drinks.

Mik Mak, Place de Foucauld, by *Hôtel Ali*. A well-established pâtisserie, for pastries and a range of breads; useful for takeaway breakfasts and picnics, but it doesn't have tables and chairs.

Pâtisserie des Princes, 32 Rue Bab Agnaou. A sparkling new pâtisserie which rivals *Mik Mak* – and has a back room for breakfast, morning coffee, afternoon tea and ice cream at all hours.

Laiterie et Pâtisserie Toubkal, in the far corner of Djemaa El Fna, beyond *Hôtel CTM* and best recognized by its backdrop of a dozen colourful carpets for sale. As well as fruit juices, yoghurts and pâtisseries, there's soup and brochettes.

Moderate restaurants

Hôtel Ali, Rue Moulay Ismail. Justifiably popular restaurant in this highly recommended hotel, with à la carte lunches from 60dh, and a marvellous buffet every evening, featuring, harira, salads, couscous and ten or more tajine-style dishes – you can eat what you like, and as much as you wish, for a bargain 60dh (50dh for residents).

Restaurant Argana, Place Djemaa El Fna. This is possibly the best Djemaa El Fna vantage point – opposite the Bank al Maghrib. There's a limited choice of French-Moroccan dishes and the service can be slow – better to time your visit for sunset. Allow 70dh per person.

Café Etoile de Marrakesh, on Rue Bab Agnaou (not to be confused with the simpler *Café Etoile* nearer Djemaa El Fna). Very popular with the locals, especially at midday; you can eat upstairs on the balcony for around 50dh.

Hôtel de Foucauld, Av. El Mouahidine. The restaurant is attached to the hotel; it may be small, but the welcome is warm, the food is good and the helpings generous – second helpings of fine harira soup are the order of the day; menu 100 to 125dh.

DJEMAA EL FNA FOODSTALLS

Even if you don't eat at one of them, at some stage you should at least wander down the makeshift lane of food stalls at the north end of the Djemaa El Fna. They look great in the evening, lit by lanterns, and have boundless variety. To partake, just take a seat on one of the benches, ask the price of a plate of food and order all you like; if you want a soft drink or mineral water, the owners will send a boy to get it for you. Guides often suggest that the stalls aren't very healthy, but, as the cooking is so visible, standards of cleanliness are doubtless higher than in many hidden kitchens. If you're still wary, head for the orange vendors on the far side of the *Hôtel CTM*, or go for a handful of cactus fruit, peeled in a couple of seconds at the stalls nearby.

Hôtel du Café de France, Place Djemaa El Fna. Another superb viewpoint. The hotel itself is wretched but the restaurant and café are acceptable; nothing special, but reliable.

Café Restaurant Iceberg, Av. El Mouahidine. Although it's central and popular with the locals, this pleasant eating place is largely ignored by tourists. At street level, it's usually crowded with full-time coffee drinkers, but upstairs there's a comfortable restaurant and you can eat well for around 90dh. The present owner has been in charge for 35 years – before that it was an ice-cream parlour – hence its name.

Hôtel Islane, 279 Av. Mohammed V. The rooftop restaurant was originally known as *Pizzeria Venetia*, but poor management gave it a bad name. Changes have improved things and traditional Moroccan dishes are now good and well served at around 120dh a head. And the view of the Koutoubia remains unparalleled.

Dar Mima, 9 Derb Zaouia El Khadiria, off Riad Zitoun Djedid (☎04/438 5252). A modest nineteenth-century town house converted into a simple, but comfortable restaurant. The à la carte menu represents what you would be served if you visited a Marrakeshi family. Expect to pay 250dh per person – and ring in advance to arrange a guide to get you there.

Expensive: palace restaurants

Restaurant Al Baraka, 1 Place Djemaa El Fna, by the Commissariat de Police (☎04/444 2341). French-Moroccan restaurant open for lunch (11.30am–2pm) and dinner (8pm–late) in a beautiful fountain courtyard. Around 350dh a head.

Restaurant El Bahia, 1 Riad Zitoun Djedid (☎04/438 5831). Relatively easy to find, between the Place des Ferblantiers and the post office, this beautifully restored palace offers a set menu, music and dancing – all in a hassle-free atmosphere.

Restaurant Doüirya, 14 Derb Djedid, Hay Essalam/Mellah, near Place des Ferblantiers (☎04/440 3030). *Doüirya* may mean small house, but this is on a grand scale with a remarkable ceiling. Open daily for lunch (150dh–200dh) and dinner with Andalous music (350dh). Easy to find.

Palais Gharnatta, 5/6 Derb El Arsa, off Riad Zitoun Djedid (☎04/444 0615). From the car park of the Dar Si Said Museum, take the gate to the right of the Prefecture de Marrakesh Medina and, after passing the Maison Tiskiwin on your right, look for signs to the restaurant. The sixteenth-century decor is magnificent, the central alabaster fountain is also sixteenth century and from Italy. The food and music are also fine. According to the visitors' book, Jacqueline Kennedy and the Aga Khan have eaten here and, according to the publicity, some of *The Return of the Pink Panther* was filmed here. Cost 350dh per head.

Dar Hadj Idder, 1 Derb El Hajra, (☎04/444 5375). Leave Place Djemaa El Fna by Derb Debbachi, between the Pharmacie Menara and the Qessabin Mosque; the restaurant is on a side street to the right (with a sports shop on the corner). The original building and garden were a gift from El Glaoui, Pasha of Marrakesh, to Hadj Idder, his chamberlain. Thus, the building is in the grand style, but not very old. Traditional feasts at midday and in the evenings; 200dh to 350dh.

Dar Marjana, 15 Derb Ettir, off Rue Bab Doukkala (☎04/444 5773). Look for the sign above the entrance to a passageway diagonally across the street from the corner of the Dar El Glaoui; take the passage and look for the green door facing you before a right turn. This is an early nineteenth-century palace, said by some to be the most beautiful palace in the Medina, while the food is rightly praised by Michelin. Open evenings only, but closed on Tuesdays; it will cost you about 550dh.

Le Pavillon, 47 Derb Zaouia (☎04/439 1240). Despite signs at Bab Doukkala, which lead to 9 Derb Hanah (the back entrance to Le Pavillon's kitchen), this is best approached from the Bab Doukkala Mosque alongside the defunct cinema, El Fath. The restaurant is owned by a star professional decorator, Gerrard, who has beautifully restored this middle-class house, (there are tasteful brass plates labelling both doors), which is best seen in evening light. The restaurant is open every evening, except Tuesday. The menu is always value for money: 250dh–300dh.

Restaurant Yacout, 79 Sidi Ahmed Soussi (☎04/438 2900). Another gorgeous old palace in the heart of the Medina, and another restaurant that gets Michelin plaudits. You must book ahead (it opens every evening, save Monday, from 8pm onwards) and take a petit taxi – the driver will usually walk with you to the plain door – there's no sign. Five-course meals are served round an Andalucian courtyard with pool, and there's a terrace with views over the Medina for coffee: 500dh a head.

Gueliz restaurants

Although Gueliz is not so picturesque a setting for a meal, it would be a mistake to dismiss it entirely as modern and French. It is, after all, the city's main centre and its restaurants are generally good value, while the pricier ones are licensed. If you want to menu-browse, the main concentration of places is around Place Abdelmoumen Ben Ali.

Cheap

Café Agdal, 86 Av. Mohammed V, facing *Hôtel Amalay*. Good for breakfast and snacks; open 'til late.

Boule de Neige, 20 Rue de Yougoslavie, close to Place Abdelmoumen Ben Ali. A lively pâtisserie which serves breakfast and all-day snacks.

Cafeteria Le Jet d'Eau, Place de la Liberté. Open all day: breakfast from 20dh and menu of the day for 60dh.

Café Snack Le Sindibad. A new ground floor and pavement café in front of the new *Résidence Elite* and shopping mall on Av. Mohammed V. Harira soup with hard-boiled eggs and dates followed by a tajine kefta for 32dh.

Café Le Siroua, 20 Bd. Mohammed Zerktouni, next to the cinema, Colisée. A small, friendly café, open long hours. Good for breakfast, orange juice and coffee.

Moderate

Bagatelle Restaurant, 101 Rue de Yougoslavie (☎04/443 0274). A pleasant place run by a French couple – and in summer meals are served outside in the shady garden. You can eat well for under 100dh. Closed Wed and Sept.

Le Cantanzaro, Rue Tarik Ibn Ziad (☎04/443 3731). Behind the municipal market, near the *Hôtel Toulousain*. One of the city's most popular Italian restaurants, crowded at lunchtime with locals, expats and tourists. The low ceiling with beams may be *ersatz*, but the Italian dishes are genuine and generous, and there's a takeaway service as well. Closed Sun.

Le Dragon d'Or, 10 bis Bd. Mohammed Zerktouni (☎04/443 0617). Vietnamese and Chinese cuisine, with bright and cheerful decor; it's popular with local families and there's a takeaway service. Prices are reasonable if a group pick and mix. Open lunchtime and evenings.

Restaurant L'Entrecôte, 55 Bd. Mohammed Zerktouni (☎04/444 9428). On the ground floor of a new speculative block. The menu is truly international: pizzas, paella and hamburgers; but the speciality is 'Wild West' steaks. The express menu of two courses and coffee is 70dh and there's a children's menu at 50dh. Closed Sundays.

Hôtel Farouk, 66 Av. Hassan II (☎04/443 1989). The restaurant, and hotel, may not be as well known as the *Ali*, which is its better half in the Medina, but it is equally good, and value for money.

Chez Jack'Line, 63 Av. Mohammed V, near Place Abdelmoumen Ben Ali (☎04/444 7547). French, Italian and Moroccan dishes, directed by the indefatigable Jack'Line Pinguet and supervised by Ulysses, her silent and elderly green parrot. You can eat splendidly for 75dh to 100dh.

Restaurant Le Jardin, Rue Oum Rabia, on a side road off Av. Mohammed V; look for the *Pizza Hut* on the opposite side of the avenue (☎04/444 8210). Modern decor, with pink walls and little lamps on each table. The speciality is crêpes, both savoury and sweet – and there's always a choice of good grills. Up to 150dh per head.

Rotisserie de la Paix, 68 Rue Yougoslavie, alongside the former cinema Lux-Palace (☎04/443 3118). Established in 1949, this continues to offer fine French and Moroccan dishes, served in a salon with a roaring fire in winter, in a shaded garden in summer. Specialities include boeuf bourguignon on Wednesdays and couscous on Thursdays.

Restaurant Puerto Banus, Rue Ibn Hanbal, opposite the Police Headquarters on the Royal Tennis Club (☎04/444 6534). French management and Spanish dishes: gazpacho soup and a generous paella cost 120dh.

Expensive

Al Fassia, 232 Av. Mohammed V (☎04/443 1060). At the junction with Rue Sebou, this restaurant is truly Moroccan, both in decor and cuisine. Lunch is around 120dh but, in the evening, dinner will cost twice that. The ambience and service are superb.

Le Jacaranda, 32 Bd. Mohammed Zerktouni – on Place Abdelmoumen Ben Ali, (☎04/444 7215). French auberge with beams and a fireplace. The menu is extensive and tempting; with self-discipline and modest bottle of wine, it will cost around 250dh a head. Closed all day Tues and lunchtime Wed. There is usually an interesting exhibition of work by local artists.

La Trattoria, 179 Rue Mohammed El Bekal (☎04/443 2611). Decor by the acclaimed Bill Willis (as in the *Hôtel Tichka*) while the owner and cuisine are Italian. The service is friendly and the cooking excellent. Open evenings, Tues–Sun. Cost 275dh to 325dh.

Villa Rosa, 64 Av. Hassan II, next to the *Hôtel Farouk* (☎04/443 0832). Once managed by an Italian, the restaurant is now in French hands. Light wood, pastel shades and silk drapes decor; French menu and faultless dishes. There's also a jazz bar and a courtyard of citrus trees. You can eat well for 250dh a head.

Bars and nightlife

Entertainment and nightlife in the **Medina** revolve around Djemaa El Fna and its cafés, though sometimes there might be a music group playing in an enclosure behind the Koutoubia on Avenue Mohammed V. The only bars in easy reach are in the hotels *Tazi* and *Foucauld* (on the roof), or, for those on expense accounts, the *Mamounia*; see hotel listings for addresses. In **Gueliz**, there's more variety. Some of the hotels have **discos** (you could try the *N'Fis*, the *Tropicana*, *Le Marrakech* or the *Mansour Eddahbi*), and many have **bars**, in which you are more likely to have Moroccans for company.

Gueliz bars

Hôtel Amalay, 87 Av. Mohammed V. Next to the Shell petrol station close to Place Abdelmoumen Ben Ali. Fairly relaxed.

Café-Bar de l'Escale, Rue Mauretania, just off Av. Mohammed V.

Hôtel Oasis, 50 Av. Mohammed V. Beyond Place Abdelmoumen Ben Ali, going towards Route de Casablanca. Enter by a door beside the hotel.

Brasserie du Petit Poucet, corner of Av. Mohammed V/Rue Mohammed El Bequal. This drinkers' bar is along a corridor by the restaurant (which itself is long past its 'sell-by' date).

Hôtel La Renaissance, on Place Abdelmoumen Ben Ali. The hotel is closed but the café on the ground floor and pavement still functions, as does the rooftop terrace bar, known as the *Mirador,* which offers beers and great views up Av. Mohammed V to the Koutoubia and the High Atlas beyond. Take the lift from the café to the terrace.

Café Oued El Had, 100 Av. Casablanca – a petit taxi ride to the outskirts of town. A complex of three bars – the best of them upstairs. Open until 2am.

Casino

Grand Casino, in the *Hôtel La Mamounia*, Av. Bab Djedid. This feels pretty unreal, walking in from the Medina. Roulette, craps and blackjack, and lots of slots. Entrance is free, but men need a tie and jacket. Opens 8pm 'and stays open until you run out of money'.

Listings

Airlines Sole agents for British Airways and GB Airways are Menara Tours (see Travel Agencies, below). RAM, 197 Av. Mohammed V (☎04/443 6205; Reservations ☎04/444 6444). RAM and Air France have desks at the *Hôtel Atlas* (see main map). For **airport information** ☎04/444 7862.

American Language Center 3 Impasse des Moulins, off Bd. Mohammed Zerktouni, Gueliz (☎04/444 7259). The center is mainly for locals to learn English – there are no Arabic classes – but you can study in the library or become a subscriber and borrow books.

Banks Most banks have branches in both Gueliz and the Medina; many have a *bureau de change* alongside and these stay open longer in the late afternoon/early evening; an increasing number also have cash points/ATMs. As elsewhere, the BMCE is the best bet for exchange – accepting VISA/Mastercard, traveller's cheques and most currencies; it has branches in Gueliz (144 Av.

Mohammed V) and in the Medina (Place Foucauld/Rue Moulay Ismail – back entrance for exchange), open 10am–2pm and 4–8pm every day and both have ATMs. Banque Populaire has a useful *bureau de change* just off Place Djemaa El Fna, on Rue Bab Agnaou (Mon–Sat 9am–noon & 4–7pm). Crédit du Maroc has a counter for exchange at 215/217 Av. Mohammed V and another new one on Rue Bab Agnaon (in both cases Mon–Sat 9.30am–2pm & 3.30–7pm); both branches have ATMs. There is a new BCM *bureau de change* next to the *Hôtel Imperial Borj*, on Av. Echouhada in the Hivernage quarter (Tues–Fri 9am–noon & 2–4pm, closed Sat afternoon and all day Sun). Most three- and four-star hotels will change traveller's cheques and most currencies.

Bicycles, mopeds and motorbikes Bikes can be rented from *Hôtel de Foucauld* and *Hôtel Ali* in the Medina; and there's a small repair shop near *Hôtel Atlas*, Rue de la Recette, from which you can also rent bikes. Elsewhere, bikes can be rented from *Hôtel Imperial Borj*, Av. Echouhada, Hivernage, and from 76 Av. Mohammed Abdelkrim El Kattabi opposite *Résidence Ezzahia*. Mopeds and motorbikes can be rented from Marrakesh Motos, aka Chez Jamal Boucetta, at 31 Av. Mohammed Abdelkrim El Kattabi (☎04/444 8359), near the Goodyear garage. Rates are up to 100dh a day.

Bookshops Two good bookshops (stocking mainly French titles) face each other across Av. Mohammed V in Gueliz: Librairie Chatr at no. 19 and Librairie Gilot at no. 44. In the new *Résidence Taib*, 55 Bd. Mohammed Zerktouni, Gueliz, there is Librairie d'Art which stocks the beautiful ACR range of French art and coffee-table books, including *La Vie et l'Oeuvre de Jacques Majorelle and Marrakech: Demeures et Jardins secrets*. In the Medina, there's a small bookshop which sells French books and a range of stationery, Librairie Ghazali, 51 Rue Bab Agnaou.

Car rental Marrakesh rates are generally the most competitive after Casablanca. The best-value deals are usually from local agencies, with whom you can bargain for discounts; try Concorde Cars, 154 Av. Mohammed V (☎04/443 9973); Fathi Cars, 183 Av. Mohammed V (☎04/443 1763); Najm Car, 21 Rue Loubnane (☎04/443 7891) or *Hôtel du Pacha*; Nomade Car, 112 Av. Mohammed V (☎04/444 7126), or Tansift Car, 72 Av. Mohammed Abdelkrim El Kattabi (☎04/444 9145). National/international agencies include Avis, 137 Av. Mohammed V (☎04/443 3727, fax 443 3169); Budget, *Hôtel La Mamounia* (☎04/444 0720, fax 443 7483); Citer, 1 Rue de la Liberté (☎04/443 0683); Europcar/InterRent, 63 Bd. Mohammed Zerktouni (☎04/443 1228, fax 443 8749); First Car, 234 Av. Mohammed V (☎04/443 8764, fax 443 8749); Hertz, 154 Av. Mohammed V (☎04/443 9984, fax 443 9993) and Tourist Cars, 64 Bd. Mohammed Zerktouni (☎04/444 8457). All have desks at the airport, or will meet arrivals by arrangement.

Car repairs Garage Ourika, 66 Av. Mohammed V (☎04/444 8266), deals with Hondas, Fiats, Toyotas and BMWs (look for the large Honda sign). Garage Renault, Route de Casablanca, after the Safi crossroads (☎04/444 8082) deals with Renaults; and Thomiel, 68 Rue Tarik Ibn Ziad (☎04/443 1359) deals with Peugeots, Citroëns, Talbots and Mercedes. For spare parts, try the following which are close to one another: Sud Transmission, 8/10 Bd. Moulay Rachid (☎04/443 3434); Société-Jihad Pièces Autos, 18 Bd. Moulay Rachid (☎04/443 4098); and Union Pièces Autos, 18 Av. El Mansour Eddahbi (☎04/443 1790).

Cinemas In Gueliz, the Colisée, alongside the *Café Le Siroua* on Bd. Mohammed Zerktouni, is one of the best. It shows general releases and has enjoyed a recent face-lift. In the Medina, the Cinéma Mabrouka on Rue Bab Agnaou and the Cinéma Eden, off Derb Dabbachi, have a certain curiosity value, but watch your wallet.

Consulates The only consulate in Marrakesh is the Consulat de France, on Rue Ibn Khaldoun in the shadow of the Koutoubia (☎04/444 4006). The British Honorary Consul can be contacted at Residence Jaib, 55 Bd. Zerktouni (☎04/443 6078); emergencies only.

Dentist Dr Bennani, 112 Av. Mohammed V (first floor), opposite the ONMT office, Gueliz, is recommended (☎04/443 1145). He speaks some English.

Doctor Dr Abdelmajid Bentbib, 171 Av. Mohammed V, Gueliz (☎04/443 1030), is recommended and speaks English.

Ferry tickets COMANAV Voyages, Kawkab Centre, 16–17 Rue Imam Chafi (☎04/443 6602).

Food shopping Putting together a picnic lunch, or supplies for the Atlas, the municipal market on Av. Mohammed V, in Gueliz, is convenient, as is the covered market between Av. Houmane El Fetouaki and Arset El Maach in the Medina.

French Culture The Institut Français (Djebel Gueliz, BP566) is to be found on the edge of Gueliz alongside the Lycée Français Victor Hugo and the Ecole Française Renoir with which it shares beautiful grounds (☎04/444 6930, fax 444 7497). The monthly programme includes theatre, cinema, lectures and exhibitions, and there is a good library. Bus #7 from the Medina or Gueliz.

Golf There are three golf courses: the Marrakesh Royal Golf Club (☎04/440 4705, fax 440 0084), 5km out on the road to Ouarzazate, built for T'Hami El Glaoui after a visit to England and played on by Churchill and Eisenhower; the Palmeraie Golf Club (☎04/430 1010, fax 430 2020), 9km out on the road to Tizi n'Tichka, built, as the name suggests, in Youssef Ben Tachfine's palmery; and the Amelkis Golf Club, Bd. Mohammed Zerktouni (☎04/440 4414), the least-known course but the closest to the city centre. All courses are open to nonmembers: green fees around 150dh.

Internet access In the Medina, *Cyber Behja*, 27 Rue Bani Marine (daily 9am–11pm; 15dh per hour), others nearby, including *Hôtel Ali*. In Gueliz, *Cybercafé Hivernage*, 106bis Rue Yougoslavie (Mon–Fri 9am–9pm, Sat & Sun 10am–8pm; 20dh per hour).

Jewish community The Communauté Israélite de Marrakech (☎04/444 8754) is on Impasse des Moulins, opposite the American Language Center. Here there is the Synagogue Beth Habad. For other synagogues and the Jewish community in general, see pp.367–368.

Laundry In Gueliz, Blanchisserie Oasis, 44 Rue Tarik Ibn Zaid, behind the municipal market (☎04/443 4578); in the Medina, Blanchisserie du Sud, 10 Rue Bab Agnaou (☎04/444 3331).

Newspapers The most reliable newsagent for American and British newspapers is outside the ONMT office on Av. Mohammed V; you can buy *The International Herald Tribune*, *Time*, *Newsweek*, plus British publications *The Guardian*, *Independent*, *Times*, *Weekly Telegraph* and *Economist*.

Pharmacies There are several along Av. Mohammed V, including a good one, the Pharmacie de la Liberté, just off Place de la Liberté, which will call a doctor for you. In the Medina, try Pharmacie Menara on Place Djemaa El Fna. There's an all-night pharmacy by the Commissariat de Police on Djemaa El Fna and another on Rue Khalid Ben Oualid near the fire station in Gueliz. Other all-night and weekend outlets are listed in pharmacy windows and the local press, for example, *Le Message de Marrakech*.

Photography Photographic equipment, film and batteries can be obtained from Wrédé, 142 Av. Mohammed V (☎04/443 5739).

Post office The main PTT, which receives all *poste restante* mail, is on Place 16 Novembre, midway down Av. Mohammed V in Gueliz (Mon–Sat 8am–2pm). There is also a separate office, round the side, for sending parcels. The Medina PTT in Place Djemaa El Fna stays open until 7pm.

Swimming pools There's a large municipal pool on Rue Abou El Abbes Sebti – the first main road to the left off Av. Mohammed V as you walk past the Koutoubia towards Gueliz; it's very popular and 99 percent male. Many hotels (but, alas, not the *Mamounia*) allow nonresidents to use their pools if you have a meal, or for a fee. A useful one, if you're staying in the Medina, is the pool at the *Grand Hôtel Tazi*, a short walk from the Place Djemaa El Fna. The municipal pool in the Daoudiaf quarter is very popular with the locals.

Telephones The post office has a telephone section, with its own entrance, which stays open until 9pm; operators will place a call for you. However, with so many *téléboutiques* around town, including one opposite the main PTT, the telephone section is not much use – except for reversed-charge (collect) calls.

Travel agencies Menara Tours, 41 Rue de Yougoslavie (☎04/444 6654), near the ONMT office in Gueliz, are agents for British Airways and run good tours of the south. The Best of Morocco (see "Basics", p.5), 3rd floor, Apartment 15, 92 Bd. Mohammed Zerktouni (☎04/443 9842) offers a comparable service – Landrover desert safaris of the south.

Weather ☎04/443 0409; Telex 04/443 0566.

Moving on

Trains are the most comfortable way of getting to Casablanca and Rabat. If you're heading to **Tangier** it's possible to do the trip in one go, most easily by booking (in advance) a couchette on the night train (10–12hrs); this must be done on the morning of the day of travel.

Buses to most **long-distance destinations** leave from the main terminal at **Bab Doukkala**. Buy tickets a day in advance – or turn up early – for the more popular destinations such as Fes, El Jadida, Taroudannt or Zagora, and note that **CTM** and all the private companies have their own individual ticket windows – choices can be more extensive than at first appears. CTM also has an office on Boulevard Mohammed

Zerktouni in Gueliz, near the ONMT office, where you can buy tickets, and where some of the buses make a secondary call.

Supratours express buses for Essaouira, Agadir and Laayoune leave from the new bus station by the train station in Gueliz, though they only sell tickets if there is space after the allocation for train passengers from Casablanca/Rabat. Grands taxis are generally on hand to pick up the overflow at these times and are good value, a place to Agadir costing around 80dh.

Grands taxis can also be useful for other destinations and run from Bab Doukkala and Bab Er Robb. For further information see "Travel Details" below.

Taxis run less frequently to other destinations but you could try asking some of the drivers at the stands in Djemaa El Fna and by Bab Er Raha (between Avenue Mohammed V and Bab Doukkala). Essaouira and Agadir are both possible.

Buses to **local destinations**, including Ourika, Asni (the trailhead for Djebel Toubkal) and Moulay Brahim, leave from just outside **Bab Er Robb**. (Some buses also run to Asni from the Bab Doukkala bus station).

There are flights from Marrakesh airport to Geneva, London and Paris plus Agadir and Casablanca within Morocco. For more information see "Travel Details" below.

travel details

Trains

Marrakesh to: Casablanca Voyageurs (8 daily; 3hr 10min); Fes (5 direct and 2 connecting daily; 9hr 40min); Kenitra (8 daily; 4hr 45min); Meknes (5 direct and 2 connecting daily; 8hr 45min); Oujda (4 daily changing at Casa or Fes; 14hr 10min); Rabat (8 daily; 4hr 10min); Settat (8 daily; 2hr); Tangier (1 direct and 3 connecting daily; 9hr).

Buses

Marrakesh to: Agadir (5 CTM and 23 others daily; 4hr); Asni (10 daily; 1hr 30min); Azilal (1 CTM and 2 others daily; 3hr); Beni Mellal (2 CTM and some 30 others daily; 4hr); Casablanca (8 CTM and 24 others daily, at least one hourly 4am–8pm; 4hr); Dakhla (1 CTM daily; 24hr); Demnate (9 daily; 1hr 30min); El Jadida (9 daily; 6hr); Essaouira (1 CTM and 11 others daily; 3hr 30min); Fes (3 CTM and 12 others daily; 10hr); Goulimine (3 CTM and 14 others daily; 9hr 30min);

Laayoune (2 CTM and 3 others daily; 15hr); Meknes (8 daily; 9hr); Ouarzazate (4 CTM and 2 others daily; 5hr); Rabat (1 CTM and 12 others daily; 5hr 30min); Safi (11 daily; 2hr); Smara (1 CTM and 2 others daily; 13hr 15min); Taroudannt (1 CTM and 3 others daily; 6hr 30min); Tafraoute (3 daily; 10hr); Tangier (2 CTM and 3 others daily; 10hr); Tata (4 daily; 10hr); Tiznit (2 CTM and 7 others; 7hr); Zagora (1 CTM and 1 other daily; 9hr 30min).

Grands Taxis

Bab Doukkala to: Agadir (3hr; if no direct service is available, change at Inezgane); Casablanca (2hr 30min); Inezgane (3hr); Ouarzazate (3hr); Taroudannt (4hr).

Bab er Robb to: Asni (1hr); Setti Fatma (2hr).

Flights

Marrakesh to: Agadir (weekly; 35min); Casablanca (daily; 40min).

CHAPTER SIX

THE HIGH ATLAS

The High Atlas, North Africa's greatest mountain range, contains some of the most intriguing and most beautiful regions of Morocco. A historical and physical barrier between the northern plains and the pre-Sahara, its Berber-populated valleys feel – and indeed are – very remote from the country's mainstream or urban life. For visitors, it is, above all, trekking country, with walks to suit all levels of ability and commitment, from casual day-hikes to weeks of serious expedition routes combining a series of peaks (djebels) and passes (tizis or, in French, cols). Rock-climbing and ski mountaineering are also on offer, and mountain-biking, too, is increasingly popular on the dirt tracks (pistes) and mule paths. You could also ride. There are horses for hire at Ouirgane for organized local treks while the adventurous might consider buying (and reselling) a mule at one of the local souks; those who have done it claim there is no better way to experience the mountain culture.

Despite the forbidding appearance of its peaks, these are surprisingly populated mountains; their slopes drop away to valleys and streams, with Berber villages terraced into their sides. At many of the **villages** – particularly in the two main hiking centres around Morocco's highest peak **Djebel Toubkal** (4167m) and the **Bou Goumez Valley** – *gîte*-style accommodation is offered in local houses, and there is an established infrastructure of guides and mules for trekking. It must be stressed, though, that part of the attraction of Atlas trekking is that it remains so undeveloped in comparison with, say, the Pyrenees or Alps. The network of *pistes* and paths is there because it remains in everyday local use, and you enter a mountain life which has hardly altered in centuries.

This chapter – although entitled "The High Atlas" actually covers only the **Western part of the range**; for more on **easterly peaks and routes**, which offer four-wheel drive or travel on local Berber trucks, as well as trekking, see Chapter Seven.

Seasons

The High Atlas are subject to **snow** from **November to April**, and even the major Tizi n'Tichka and lesser Tizi n'Test passes can be closed for periods of a day or more. The

---

HOTEL PRICE CODES

The basis of our **hotel price codes**, set out below and keyed throughout the guide, is the price currently quoted for the cheapest double room in high season (June–September).

Note that cheaper prices in the lower categories are generally for rooms with just a washbasin – you always pay extra for **en-suite** shower and WC – and that double rooms can generally be converted into **triples/family rooms**, with extra beds, for a modest extra charge. Single occupancy usually costs about two-thirds the price of a double, though in some places a single person will pay the same rate for a room as two people sharing, and in other places exactly half as much. Prices quoted are for bed only, without breakfast, but including local taxes.

① 40–100dh	③ 150–200dh	⑤ 400–800dh
② 100–150dh	④ 200–400dh	⑥ over 800dh

HIGH ATLAS BERBERS

Until recent decades, the High Atlas region – and its **Berber inhabitants** – was almost completely isolated. When the French began their "pacification" in the 1920s, the way of life here was essentially feudal, based upon the control of the three main passes (*tizis*) by a trio of "clan" families, "the Lords of the Atlas". Even after the French negotiated the co-operation of these warrior chiefs, it was not until the spring of 1933 – 21 years after the establishment of the Protectorate – that they were able to subdue them and control their tribal land, and only then with the co-operation of the main feudal chief, **T'hami El Glaoui**, who continued to control the region as pasha of Marrakesh (see p.360).

These days, the region is under official government control through a system of local *caids*, but in many villages the role of the state remains largely irrelevant, and if you go trekking you soon become aware of the mountains' highly distinctive culture and traditions. The longest established inhabitants of Morocco, the Atlas Berbers, never adopted a totally orthodox version of Islam (see Contexts) and the Arabic language has, even today, made little impression on their indigenous **Tachelhaït** dialects. Their **music** and **ahouache** dances (in which women and men join together in broad circles) are unique, too, as is the village **architecture**, with stone or clay houses tiered on the rocky slopes, craggy fortified **agadirs** (collective granaries), and **kasbahs**, which continued to serve as feudal castles for the community's defence right into the twentieth century.

Berber women in the Atlas go about unveiled and have a much higher profile than their rural counterparts in the plains and the north. They perform much of the heavy labour – working in the fields, herding and grazing cattle and goats and carrying vast loads of brushwood and provisions. Whether they have any greater status or power within the family and village, however, is questionable. The men retain the "important" tasks of buying and selling goods and the evening/night-time irrigation of the crops, ploughing and doing all the building and craftwork.

As an outsider, you'll be constantly surprised by the friendliness and openness of the Berbers, and by their amazing capacity for languages – there's scarcely a village where you won't find someone who speaks French or English, or both. The only areas where you may feel exploited – and pestered by kids – are the main trekking circuits around Djebel Toubkal, where tourism has become an all-important source of income. Even the hustling, however, is gentler than in the cities – and, given the harshness of life up here, its presence is hardly surprising.

thaw can present problems, too, when the snows melt in spring causing flash floods (see box opposite). If you are driving across the Atlas, and get caught by the snow, the easiest route from Marrakesh to the south is road 6543 to Agadir, then the P32 through Taroudannt and Taliouine, but the passes are seldom blocked for long and notices outside Marrakesh on the roads inform if they are open or closed.

For more on trekking seasons – and be aware that winter routes above the snow line are a serious endeavour here – see the "Trekking Practicalities" box, on pp.388–389.

Routes and passes

The **Djebel Toubkal** massif provides the focus for most trekking expeditions. It can be reached easily from Marrakesh by taking a bus or taxi to **Asni** – just over an hour's journey – and a truck or taxi from there on to the trailhead at **Imlil**. The region can also be approached from **Ourirgane** or **Ijoukak**, a little further west, or, more energetically, from the **Ourika Valley** – a summer playground for Marrakesh – or the ski resort of **Oukaïmeden**.

Asni, Ourirgane and Ijoukak all lie on the dramatic **Tizi n'Test road**, which runs over the highest Atlas pass to connect Marrakesh with Taroudannt: a switchback of almost continuous hairpin curves to be driven with care. As well as its scenic appeal and trekking possibilities, the route has an easily accessible historic attraction in the ruins

---

FLASH FLOODS

The possibility of flash floods must be taken seriously, as they can erupt suddenly and violently and are extremely dangerous. In August 1995, summer storms caused devastating flooding in the Atlas, destroying much of the trailhead villages of Imlil and Setti Fatma – the latter with its annual festival in full swing. Dozens of buildings and bridges were washed away in the valley and over 300 lives lost, mainly young visitors camping for the festivities.

It's wise, at almost any time of year, to **camp on high ground**, avoiding any spot where water can lie or that might become a course for the torrents when they descend. This includes, most obviously (although it's hard to believe in summer), dried up and apparently terminally inactive river beds.

---

of the twelfth-century mosque of **Tin Mal**, the base from which the Almohads swept down to conquer Morocco and Spain.

Further west, and only opened in the 1970s, the **Tizi Maachou** has less drama, unless you leave the main road behind to get into the hills for some trekking in the Western Atlas, the least-known part of the range. For most travellers it simply offers a fast and convenient route between Marrakesh and Agadir.

Southeast of Marrakesh is the **Tizi n'Tichka**, a more substantial road pass, which cuts across to Ouarzazate and today bears most of the traffic across the Atlas. It was built to replace the old caravan route to Tafilalt, which was controlled during the nineteenth century and for much of the twentieth by the legendary **Glaoui family**, "the Lords of the Atlas" (see p.408). Their kasbah, a bizarre cluster of crumbling towers and kitschy-looking 1930s reception halls, is still to be seen at **Telouet**, just an hour from the main road.

The Ourika Valley and Oukaïmeden

The **Ourika Valley** is a pleasant prelude to the Atlas, an enjoyable escape from the summer heat of Marrakesh, with the village of **Setti Fatma** a popular weekend resort for young *Marrakchis*, who ride out here on their mopeds to lie around beside the streams and waterfalls.

The valley has seen many floods, the worst in 1995 (see box above) since when there has been a huge reconstruction programme and efforts to make Setti Fatma safe. The village lies at the end of the road, but a small mule track continues up the valley to passes to Tachdirt and Oukaïmeden, which has the best skiing in Morocco and amazing prehistoric rock carvings, and through to Imlil and Toubkal, making it an important starting/finishing point for trekking. A high pass leads to the Oued Zat Valley, dominated by Taska n'Zat, a peak and valley offering demanding routes and best left to the experienced. Setti Fatma has many pleasant spots, including waterfalls to visit and streamside cafés, and one of the country's biggest moussems takes place here in mid-August.

Getting to the Ourika Valley

There is a regular service of **buses**, **minibuses** and **grands taxis** leaving from Marrakesh's Bab er Robb terminus, with increased services outwards in the morning and back to the city in the evening. In the event of no services from Bab er Robb, buses leave from further out on the Ourika road. **Setti Fatma** (67km from Marrakesh) is about a two-hour journey by bus or taxi and it's best to get transport headed there (or at least to **Asgaour** (63km), the last village before Setti Fatma) and not just to the near end of the valley at **Dar Caid Ouriki** (33km) or **Arhbalou** (50km). Returning from Setti Fatma, you might have to walk to Asgaour to pick up a bus or taxi.

Into the valley

The Ourika Valley really begins at **SOUK TNINE DE L'OURIKA** (30km from Marrakesh), a small roadside village, which, as its name proclaims, hosts a Monday **souk** – an excursion offered by many of the tour hotels in Marrakesh. Just beyond it, across the river, is **DAR CAID OURIKI**, with a picturesque zaouia set back in the rocks, near the ruins of an old caidal **kasbah**.

Beyond here, scattered at intervals over the next forty kilometres, are a series of tiny hamlets, interspersed with a few summer homes and the occasional hotel or café-restaurant. The one sizeable settlement is **ARHBALOU** (50km from Marrakesh), where most of the local people on the buses get off. The village has a "palace-restaurant", *Le Lion d'Ourika* (☎04/444 5322), which has plans to open as a hotel, as well as basic rooms to let in the village. There is good walking in the surrounding hills; as well as the possibility of some serious trekking in Djebel Yagour (see "Treks from Setti Fetma"). A road west into the mountains leads to the trekking trailhead and ski resort of Oukaïmeden.

Moving on through the valley **towards Setti Fatma**, those with transport might want to stop at the **antiques/crafts shop**, *Le Musée d'Arhbalou*, 4km south of Arhbalou, which often has interesting stock. A further 2km on, there are pleasant **rooms** at the *Hôtel Amnougar* (☎04/444 5328; ④).

Setti Fatma

SETTI FATMA, a straggly riverside village largely rebuilt after the 1995 devastation, is the most compelling Ourika destination. The setting, with grassy terraces and High Atlas peaks rising on three sides to over 3600m, feels like a real oasis after the dry plains around Marrakesh.

In the rocky foothills above the village are a series of six (at times, seven) **waterfalls**. To reach them, and at certain times of year they can be completely inaccessible, you first have to cross the stream by whatever bridge has been thrown up after the last floods; near the beginning of the climb are several cafés, where you can order a tajine for your return. The first waterfall is a fairly straightforward clamber over the rocks, flanked by another café, the *Immouzer*. The higher ones are a lot more strenuous, and quite tricky when descending, requiring a head for heights and solid footwear. Returning, from the first of the falls you can loop back to Setti Fatma via the village's twin, Zaouia Mohammed, a few hundred metres further down the valley.

Setti Fatma Moussem

The Setti Fatma Moussem – one of the three most important festivals in the country – takes place for four days around the middle of August, centred on the **Koubba of Setti Fatma**, a little upstream from the *Café des Cascades*. Entry to the *koubba* is forbidden to non-Muslims, but the festival itself is as much a fair and market as religious festival and well worth trying to coincide with on your travels.

Treks from Setti Fatma

Ourika cuts right into the **High Atlas**, whose peaks begin to dominate as soon as you leave Marrakesh. At Setti Fatma these same mountains provide a startling backdrop which, to the southwest, takes in the main **trekking/climbing zone of Toubkal**. The usual approach to this is from Asni – see p.387 – but it is possible to set out from Setti Fatma, or from Oukaïmeden (see below).

If you are thinking of approaching Toubkal from Setti Fatma, one route is to trek via **Timichi** and **Oukaïmeden** and take the trail from there to Tachdirt. It is around six hours' walk from Setti Fatma to Timichi (see p.397), and a similar figure on to Oukaïmeden (see below), including a steep ascent to the Tizi n'Ouhattar. The ridge connecting this *tizi* with the Tizi n'Itbir, under Argour, gives pleasant rock scrambling (3100m). The two-to-three-day trek direct from **Timichi to Tachdirt** is perhaps best done in the opposite direction – and is so described on p.397.

Other adventurous treks from Setti Fatma include the **Djebel Yagour**, with its many prehistoric rock carvings; **Adrat Meltzen**, via **Tourcht** (one bivouac) or the secluded **Oued Zat** region reached by the demanding Tizi n'Tilst. The **Taska n'Zat–Arjoût peaks** require scrambling (up gorges and on the crests) while the way down the Oued Zat offers some days of gorges to reach the *piste* out. An ancient route climbs to the **Tizi Tazarzit** and reachs the P31 at **Agouim** south of the range. These are some of the hardest options in the range which may partly account for their neglect. One of the guides from Imlil would be useful, or you could ask for Hosain Izahan at the *Café Azapza* in Setti Fatma.

Practicalities

Setti Fatma has several **accommodation** options. Best are those at the modern *Hôtel Tafoukt* (with en-suite shower and toilet; ②), at the beginning of the village, or the rooms at the *Café-Restaurant Asgaour* (①) in the village proper, which are a little more basic but spotless and overlooking the river; the *Asgaour* patron, Chebob Lahcen, also cooks excellent meals. The *Café des Cascades* (the first on the route to the falls) also has decent if basic rooms, and the *Café Atlas*, at the north end of the village, has roof space. The *Hotel Gare* (①) is next to the boulangerie/shop and beyond the taxi turning area, lining the sweep of concrete road built after the 1995 floods, there are several hotels/restaurants: the *Zohour, Toubkal, Atlas* and *Bella*. None is very appealing so the *Café-Restaurant Asgaour* is the best bet. *Le Noyer* is an attractive restaurant. The *Hôtel Azrou* (①) is a bit of a last resort.

Alternatively, try the excellent *Auberge Bella* (②), a little way back up the valley towards Arhbalou. This is excellent, provides good food and has a shop.

Asgaour, on the edge of Setti Fatma, has two of the region's better hotels; *La Perle d'Ourika* (①) perhaps the friendliest, and the *Auberge Tafoukt* (①)with some rooms en suite.

Oukaïmeden

The village and ski centre of **OUKAÏMEDEN** is a much easier trekking base from which to set out towards Toubkal – and a good target in its own right, even if you don't have anything that ambitious in mind. "Ouka", as it's known, is reached via a good modern road which veers off from Ourika just before Arhbalou. **Grands taxis** sometimes go up from Marrakesh in the winter for the skiers or you have to charter a whole taxi for yourself. The resort has a 10dh entrance fee. A snowplough keeps the road open in the ski season.

Details on the fascinating **prehistoric rock carvings** showing animals, weapons, battle scenes and puzzling symbols can be found in an indispensable guidebook (on sale in the CAF chalet and in Marrakesh bookshops), *Gravures Rupestres du Haut Atlas*. For a few dirhams a local will guide you to the better sites.

Skiing

Ouka has, on the slopes of **Djebel Oukaïmeden**, the best **skiing** in Morocco, and up until the war could boast the highest ski lift in the world, which still remains impressive today at 3273m. It gives access to good piste and off-piste skiing, too, with several nursery and intermediate runs on the lower slopes.

HIGH ATLAS WILDLIFE

The High Atlas has unique flora and fauna, which are accessible even to the most reluctant rambler if you base yourself at **Oukaïmeden**, **Imlil** or **Ouirgane**.

The spring bloom on the lower slopes comprises aromatic thyme and thorny caper, mingling with golden spreads of broom. Higher slopes are covered by more resilient species, such as the blue tussocks of hedgehog broom. The passes ring to the chorus of the painted frog and the North African race of the green toad during their spring breeding seasons, while some species of reptile have become adapted to the specific environment of the stony walls that form the towns and villages of the Atlas mountains, such as the **Moorish gecko**. **Butterflies** which brave these heights include the Moroccan copper and desert orange tip. Other inhabitants range from the almost-invisible praying mantis to the scampering ground squirrel and rare elephant shrew.

Birds to be found among the sparse vegetation include Moussier's redstart and the crimson-winged finch, which prefers the grassy slopes where it feeds in flocks; both birds are unique to North African mountains. The rocky outcrops provide shelter for both chough and alpine chough, the mountain rivers are frequented by dippers who swim underwater in their search for food. Overhead, darting Lanner falcon or flocks of brilliantly coloured bee-eaters add to the feeling of abundance which permeates the slopes of the High Atlas. In the cultivated valleys look out for the magpie which, uniquely, has a sky-blue eye mark; there are, too, storks galore. Other High Atlas birds, as the snow melts, include shore larks, rock bunting, alpine accentor, redstarts and wheatears.

Flora is impressive, too. The wet meadows produce a fantastic spread of hooped-petticoat daffodils, *romulea* and other bulbs. Oukaïmeden in May/June has acres of orchids.

Snowfall and snow cover can be erratic but February to April is fairly reliable. Slopes are sometimes icy early and wet by afternoon, but not having to queue in the mornings lets you get in plenty of skiing. Equipment can be hired from several shops next to *Chez Juju* (one offers gear at a reasonable 100dh a day), ski-passes cost just 30dh, and lessons are available from local instructors. The lifts close at the end of April (even if there are perfect conditions for skiing).

Several other summits are accessible for **ski-mountaineering** sorties, and cross-country enthusiasts often ski across to Tachdirt.

Trekking: Oukaïmeden to Tachdirt

For casual walkers, the trails from Oukaïmeden are strictly summer only: routes can be heavily snow-covered even late into spring. However, weather conditions allowing, the **trail to Tachdirt** (3hr) is pretty clear and easy-going. It begins a short distance beyond the ski lift, veering off to the right of the dirt road that continues for a while beyond this point. The pass, **Tizi n'Eddi**, is reached in about two hours; on the descent, the trail divides in two, either of which branch will lead you down into Tachdirt. For more details of this route, described in reverse, and routes on from Tachdirt, see pp.396–398.

Practicalities

There are several **hotels**, including the excellent *Chalet-Hôtel Chez Juju* (☎04/445 9005; ③), which has solid French food and a bar (also open in summer). The *Kenzi Louka* (☎04/431 9080 or 431 9086; ⑤) is a vast, luxury establishment in a huge old building in the village.

The *Club Alpine Chalet* (☎04/431 9036; 20dh per night for members, 40dh non-members) is well equipped, with a bar and restaurant and is cheaper, especially for members of Alpine Clubs. They sell Atlas guidebooks and camping is also possible.

The Djebel Toubkal Massif

The **Toubkal Massif**, a more or less roadless area enclosing the High Atlas's highest peaks, is the goal of almost everyone who goes trekking in Morocco. It is easy to get to from Marrakesh – Asni, the "first base", is just over an hour by bus or, simpler, by grand taxi (from Bab Er Robb) – and its main routes are reasonably well charted. Walking even fairly short distances, you feel very much a visitor in a rigidly individual world. The villages look amazing, their houses stacked one on top of another in apparently organic growth from the rocks, and, even while working in the fields, the women dress in brilliantly coloured costumes.

From late spring to late autumn (see note on "Seasons" on p.388), the region's trails are accessible for anyone reasonably fit. Mule tracks round the mountain valleys are well contoured and kept in excellent condition, and there's a network of village *gîtes*, unofficial houses and refuge huts for accommodation.

In summer, **Djebel Toubkal**, at 4167m the highest peak in North Africa, is walkable right up to the summit; if you're pushed for time, you could trek it, and be back in Marrakesh, in three days – though at the risk of altitude sickness. Further away, over a demanding pass, and much less visited, is **Lac d'Ifni**, tucked in a hollow in the mountains, while infinite variations on **longer treks** could lead you into the mountains for a week, two weeks, or more. For anyone really short on time, or who feels unable to tackle an ascent of Toubkal, it's possible to get a genuine taste of the mountains by spending time exploring the beautiful valleys and lower passes of the range. Options head east and west over *tizis* to neighbouring villages and valleys which can be followed down to the Tizi n'Test road or you can go over passes to Ijoukak or down valleys such as the Ourika or Agoundis, all areas free of organized trekking groups. If heading on over the Tizi n' Test afterwards, there is a splendid view to the Toubhad range from the final bends of the ascent.

Moulay Brahim

MOULAY BRAHIM is a picturesque village, just off the main Marrakesh–Asni road and dominating the gorges leading up from the plains. The **Kik Plateau** and its escarpment, which runs above the main road towards Ouirgane, is botanically rich and offers perhaps the best panorama of the Atlas mountains. It can be reached from the top end of the town, on a *piste* past marble quarries (see p.390).

The village is a popular weekend spot for *Marrakchis* and an alternative base for a first night in the Atlas, with several **hotels** – mostly cheapies such as the central *Alfouki* and the *Talfoukt* at the entrance to the town (both ①) plus the better-equipped and larger *Star's Hôtel* and the uninspiring *Haut Rocher* (both ②) above the town. There are plenty of good eating places, and regular **buses** and **taxis** to/from Asni/Marrakesh. It hosts a large **moussem** two weeks after the Mouloud.

Asni

The end of the line for the Toubkal bus and Marrakesh grands taxis, **ASNI** is little more than a roadside village and marketplace, from where you can head straight on to Imlil, though a night here is quite pleasant - once the touts have left off their excessive importuning.

The basin is a big fruit-growing area, earmarked for development, and the most interesting time to be here before heading on to Toubkal is for the **Saturday souk**, when the enclosure behind the row of shop cubicles is filled with local produce and livestock stalls, plus the odd storyteller or entertainer. An advantage of arriving on Saturday

TOUBKAL TREKKING PRACTICALITIES

EQUIPMENT AND EXPERIENCE

Unless you're undertaking a particularly long or ambitious trek – or are here in winter conditions – there are no technical problems to hold anyone back from trekking in the Toubkal area, or climbing the peak itself. However, the mountain needs to be taken seriously and taken slowly until you are acclimatized. You must have decent **footwear and clothing** – it's possible to be caught out by summer storms as well as bad winter conditions – and must also be prepared to camp out if necessary, as the Toubkal refuge is often full.

The main physical problems are the high altitudes (3000–4000m throughout the Toubkal region), the midday heat and the tiring process of walking over long sections of rough boulders or loose scree. All of these can combine to make casual ascents by the inexperienced an unhappy and perhaps foolhardy experience.

SEASONS

Toubkal is usually under **snow** from November until mid-June. If you have some experience of winter trekking and conditions, it is feasible to climb the peak, and trek the low-level routes, year round, though for Toubkal you may need to wait around a couple of days for clear weather, and carry and know how to use an ice axe and crampons (which can usually be rented in Imlil). For beginners, trekking is better limited to below the snow line. And only those with winter climbing experience should try going much beyond hut level, from November to May; ice axe, crampons, good rain gear and winter competence are required, as several fatalities have recently shown. Full rivers and flash floods in spring and high summer can pose additional problems.

ALTITUDE

Toubkal is 4167m above sea level and much of the surrounding region is above 3000m, so it's possible that you might get **acute mountain sickness (AMS)** aka altitude sickness. Aspirins can help, but just sucking on a sweet or swallowing often is as good as anything. Most people experience some symptoms of AMS but serious cases are rare. Hurrying is a major cause of altitude sickness so pace your ascent, allowing your body time to acclimatize. If you do develop more than slight breathlessness and really feel like vomiting, going down straight away is the best, and almost immediate, cure.

ACCOMMODATION

At most Atlas villages, it is usually possible to arrange a room in a local house; just turn up and ask. At some of the villages on more established routes, there are official *gîtes*, often the homes of mountain guides, who can provide mules and assistance – as well as food, showers, toilets and sometimes hammams. All *gîtes* have to be of recognized quality for inclusion in the ONMT *GTAM* pamphlet (see "Guidebooks", opposite). Most charge around 30–40dh per person for a night and can provide meals.

There are also three refuge **huts**, Toubkal (formerly known as Neltner), Tazaghart (formerly known as Lepiney) and Tachdirt, run by the *Club Alpin*; they charge 30dh per person for a bed on average (less for members of Alpine Clubs, more for casual visitors); Toubkal is often fully booked – especially at Easter – and is always crowded in March/April and July–September.

If you are doing anything remotely ambitious, however, you'll need to be prepared to **camp**, for which you will need a tent and warm sleeping bag – nights can be cold, even in summer.

GUIDES AND MULES

Guides can be engaged at Imlil and at a number of the larger villages in the Toubkal region; **mules**, too, can be hired, usually in association with a guide or porter. Rates are around 150dh a day for a guide, 80dh for a mule. One mule can usually be shared among several people – and if you're setting out from Imlil, say, for Lac d'Ifni, or the Toubkal or Tazaghart refuges, it can be a worthwhile investment. Two extras are to be added to the price – a fee to the car park supervisor in Imlil and a tip to the porter at the end. (Payment to all parties, incidentally, is best made at the end of a trip.)

Note that guides are more reluctant – and reasonably so – to work during the month of **Ramadan** (see p.6).

WATER
A quart bottle of **water** is enough because you can refill it regularly. However, with Giardiasis **bacteria** being present in many of the streams and rivers downriver from human habitation – including the Toubkal trailhead, Imlil – purification tablets are highly advisable, as, of course, is boiling the water.

CLOTHES
Even in the summer months you'll need a warm sweater or jacket and preferably a windbreaker, but tents at this time aren't necessary if you're just ascending Toubkal, so long as you have a good sleeping bag and bivibag/groundsheet. Hiking boots are ideal though you can get by with a decent pair of trainers or jogging shoes. Some kind of hat is essential and sunglasses are helpful.

OTHER THINGS TO BRING
You can buy **food** in Asni, Imlil and some of the other villages – or negotiate meals – though it gets increasingly expensive the higher and the more remote you get. Taking along a variety of canned food, plus tea or coffee, is a good idea. Water purification tablets are worthwhile on longer trips, as are stomach pills and insect repellent.

Children constantly ask you for cigarettes, bonbons and cadeaux – but it's perhaps better for everyone if you don't give in, and limit **gifts** to those who offer genuine assistance. A worthwhile contribution trekkers can make to the local economy is to trade or give away some of your gear – always welcomed by the guides, who need it.

GUIDEBOOKS/INFORMATION
There are almost limitless Atlas trekking routes, only a selection of which are detailed in these pages. For other ideas, either engage a guide at Imlil, or invest in the Atlas Mountain trekking guidebooks by **Michael Peyron** (West Col) – pick of the bunch, **Robin Collomb** (West Col), or **Karl Smith** (Cicerone Press); you may well find one or other of these books on sale at Imlil or the CAF at Oukaïmeden. The booklet *La Grande Traversée des Atlas Marocains*, published by the ONMT, is also useful, listing all the qualified guides, *muletiers* and *gîtes*, along with their tarifs. This can be obtained from Morocco Tourist Offices and the English-language guidebooks are available from specialist bookshops (see p.31).

MAPS
Large scale maps (most are 1:100,000; Toubkal also 1:50,000) are best obtained in advance – see p.32. Occasionally guides or shops at Imlil (or *Hôtel Ali* in Marrakesh, see p.349) may have maps to sell. Refuges have maps on display.

SKI-TOURING
The Toubkal Massif is popular with **ski-mountaineering** groups from February to April. Most of the *tizis* (cols), and Djebel Toubkal and other peaks, can be ascended, and a *Haute Route* linking the huts is possible. Toubkal summit to Sidi Chamarouch must rank as fine a descent on ski as you'll ever find.

The Toubkal refuge can get pretty crowded at these times, and the Tachdirt refuge (or, for a serious approach in winter, Tazarart refuge) can make better bases.

morning (or Friday night) is that you can stock up with cheap supplies before heading into the mountains.

Practicalities
Transport from Asni **to Imlil** is pretty straightforward, with minibuses, pick-ups (*camionettes*) and taxis shuttling back and forth along the 17km of road, along with larger lorries on Saturdays for the souk. All normally wait until they fill their passenger quota, though the latter can be chartered; a place is currently 15dh for tourists.

Buses from Asni run to Marrakesh, Moulay Brahim or Ijoukak and – at around 6am – over the Tizi n'Test for Taroudannt (see p.404), but check in advance as the service changes regularly. A place in a **grand taxi** can be negotiated to Marrakesh (12.5dh), Moulay Brahim (3dh) or Ouirgane (12dh). Buses and taxis leave from the souk entrance area.

Asni has a **youth hostel** which will store luggage if you want to go off trekking unencumbered. It's at the south end of the village, and is open all year and to all comers, with slightly higher charges for non-IYHF members. There are no cooking facilities and you'll need your own sleeping bag, though blankets can be rented; the location by the river can be very cold in winter. Nonetheless, a friendly place and good meeting point.

Touts may also offer rooms but you should be wary of accepting, especially if alone, or female.

For **meals**, most of the café-stalls will fix you a tajine or harira.

Walks around Asni and Moulay Brahim

With time to spare, there are many local walks in the fruit-growing areas around Asni and Moulay Brahim, which will get you acclimatized for the higher peaks. They are not much explored and so have a charm of their own.

The Kik Plateau
The forested slopes above Asni and Moulay Brahim are dominated by a rocky scarp which is the edge of the hidden limestone **Kik Plateau**. In spring a walk up here is a delight, with a marvellous spread of alpine flowers and incomparable views. To get the best from it, set off early in the day and carry water; six to eight hours walking will bring you over the plateau and onto Moulay Brahim or Ouirgane.

Leaving Asni, walk up the Test road to where it swings out of sight (past the red conical hill). Just past a souvenir stall a mule track breaks off and can be seen rising up the hillside. Take this, then fork right to gain the first pass. Turn right again, through fields, and you eventually join the plateau edge, which you can follow to **Moulay Brahim**; leave the crest to join a *piste* down to the left, which passes big marble quarries just before the village. You can also cut down to Asni by a path leaving the route midway along.

An alternative day's trek on the plateau is to make for **Ouirgane**, further south on the Tizi n'Test road (see p.401). On the rise to the plateau keep on, forking left, to the pass/village of Tizi Ouadou and then follow the dip to where it's crossed by a rough *piste*. Take this down to the road at Tizi Ouzla and follow the road down, with salt mines apparent below. Turn off right to work through paths to join the Nfis River and follow this to Ouirgane.

Valley approaches
The valleys between Asni/Ouirgane and Imlil (Mizane), Tachdirt (Imenane) and Tizi Oussem (Azzadene) offer fine walks, which you might do to acclimatize yourself prior

to tackling Toubkal or other mountains. They are all much easier-going if you walk them downhill – back to Asni/Ouirgane, from which it is easy enough to return to Imlil.

Imlil to Asni. This is a pleasant half-day walk. From Imlil, walk back down the road, then, after about an hour, swap over to the old mule track on the east side of the valley. Take this path up, arriving eventually at a pass going along the trackless crest to the prow that looks to Asni and back to the hills. Descend from here and continue down along the east side of the valley to Asni.

Tachdirt to Asni. There is a long but straightforward trail from Tachdirt down-valley to Asni, taking seven to nine hours. It's an enjoyable route, through a fine valley with no road or electricity – a good (and neglected) exit from the mountains. You could also do this route from Imlil, heading off towards the trail at the Tizi n'Tamatert (1hr from Imlil), then dropping down to the bottom of the valley at Tinhourine. If you want to camp out a night, en route, there are possible places to pitch a tent below Ikiss or Arg. There are also rooms and soft drinks available at Ikiss and Amsakrou. A fine pass rises opposite Ikiss to cross a *tizi* to Aguersioual and so back to Imlil, an excellent round trip.

Imlil

The trip from Asni to **IMLIL** is a startling transition. Almost as soon as it leaves Asni, the road begins to climb, while below it the valley of the Oued Rhirhaia unfolds before you, heaped with boulders from the terrible flash flood of 1995 (the worst on record). Small villages crowd onto the rocky slopes above.

At Imlil the air feels quite different – silent and rarefied at 1740m – and paths and streams head off in all directions. If you want to make an early start for the Toubkal (Neltner) hut and the ascent of Toubkal, the village – now more or less rebuilt after the flash flood – is a better trailhead than Asni, as is Aroumd (the next village on towards Toubkal – see p.394). It is not advisable to try and reach the Toubkal Refuge from Asni in one day.

Practicalities

Imlil has many provisions shops and a fair choice of accommodation comprising a CAF refuge, several hôtel-cafés, and a small cluster of houses offering *gîtes*. Among the best of the latter are those offered by the guide Aït Idir Mohammed (contact him at the shop behind the concrete route indicator) or at the *gîte* near the school (☎&fax 04/448 5616). Baggage can be stored while trekking.

CAF Refuge. Old-established French Alpine Club refuge, rebuilt after the flash flood. It provides bunk beds, camping mattresses and blankets, as well as kitchen and washing facilities and luggage storage; rates vary according to membership of Alpine Club, YHA, etc but are still cheap. The *gardien* can provide meals.

Hôtel-Café Soleil (☎04/448 5622) On the square by the river, this place offers decent rooms and does superb tajines. ①.

Hôtel-Café Aksoual (☎04/448 5612) Facing the *Refuge* and with similarly decent accommodation as the *Soleil*. ①.

Hôtel Etoile de Toubkal (☎04/448 5618). As fancy as Imlil gets – and expensive. ③.

Kasbah du Toubkal. This tastefully restored kasbah above Imlil is essentially a field study centre but offers traditional accommodation to individuals – and it can be used by campers. It was used as the setting for *Kundun*, the Martin Scorsese film about the life of the Buddha. Rooms can be booked through the *Hôtel Foucauld* in Marrakesh (☎04/444 5499) or through the British company *Discover Ltd* (☎01883/744 392). ③.

Trekking resources and guides

A good source of **information** is the *CAF Refuge*, with its noticeboard, book and *gardiens* (wardens). Lahcen Askary, based at the Shopping Centre facing the *CAF Refuge*,

△ Marrakesh   Ourika Valley & Marrakesh △

TOUBKAL MASSIF

N

△ Setti Fatma & Ourika Valley

△ Difficult route to Ourika Valley (Kissaria Gorge)

Oukaïmeden
(Hotels/refuge)

Ski Lift

Oukaïmeden
3273m

Tizi n'Eddi

Timguist   Timichi

Agouns

Angour
3616m

Adrar
n'Ineghmar
3892m

Tamadout

INEMANE VALLEY

AÏT MIZANE VALLEY

Amsakrou

Ikiss

Tizi n'Tachdirt

Tachdirt
(Rooms)

Bou
Iguenouane
3882m

Aguersioual

Matat

Tizi n'Likemt

Aksoual
3842m

Azib Likemt

Imlil
(Refuge/rooms)

Id Aissa

Aroumd
(Rooms)

Azib Tifni

Tizi
Oussem
(Rooms)

Tizi Mzic

Aguelzim

Sidi
Chamarouch
(Rooms)

Tizi n'Tagharat

Tizi n'Terhaline
3247m

Azib
Tamsoult

Tazaghart
Refuge

Tadat

Afekoï

Tissaldai

Tazaghart
3845m

Tizi Melloul

Toubkal
4167m

Toubkal
Refuge

Ras
n'Ouanoukrim

Tizi n'Ouanoums

Tizi n'Ouagane

Timzakane

Amsouzart
(Rooms)

Lac d'Ifni
2312m

Imhilene

Imlil

Taliouine ▽

is a guide who speaks English. Also helpful is the *Hôtel-Café Soleil* owner, Aziam Brahim, who works for part of the year for a French trekking company, and his brother Ibelaid Brahim.

All the above are among the most experienced of the **qualified guides** listed in the guides office in the corner of the car park near the *CAF Refuge*. They can arrange treks, ascents, mules, camping, guides, *gardiens* for your baggage and food.

Imlil to Djebel Toubkal

Most trekkers leaving Imlil are en route for the **ascent of Djebel Toubkal** – a walk rather than a climb, after the snows have cleared, but a serious business nonetheless (see box on p.388). The route to the ascent trailhead, however, is fairly straightforward – and enjoyable in its own right, following the Mizane Valley to the village of **Aroumd** (4km from Imlil; 1hr–1hr 30min) and from there through the pilgrim hamlet of **Sidi Chamarouch** to the **Toubkal (Neltner) Refuge** (3200m; 12km from Imlil – 5–6hr in all), at the foot of Toubkal.

If you start out late in the day, Aroumd can be a useful first base, though most trekkers set out early to mid-morning from Imlil to stay the night at the Toubkal refuge, starting out at first light the next morning for Toubkal in order to get the clearest possible panorama from its heights. Afternoons can be cloudy.

Imlil to Aroumd

To **walk from Imlil to Aroumd**, you basically follow the course of the Mizane river. On the west side there's a well-defined mule track that zigzags above the river for about 2km before dropping to the floor of the valley, just before a crossing point to Aroumd; there is also a more circuitous *piste*, driveable in a reasonably hardy vehicle. On the east bank, there's a rough path – much the same distance but slightly harder to follow.

AROUMD (aka AROUND, AREMD) is the largest village of the Mizane Valley, an extraordinary-looking place, built on a huge moraine spur above the valley at 1840m. Terraced fields of corn, potatoes, onions, barley and various kinds of fruit line the valley sides and there is some grazing, too; the village streets are often blocked by goats or cattle – and permanently covered in animal excrement and flies.

This notwithstanding, Aroumd is used as a base or overnight stop by trekking companies. Several houses are well-equipped *gîtes* and Omar le Rouge (☎04/448 5613) also offers camping by the west bank of the river. Meals can be provided, otherwise supplies are best brought along; there is only one small shop. A second *gîte*, *Restaurant Residence Aremd* sits overlooking the school.

Aroumd to Sidi Chamarouch and Toubkal Refuge

From Aroumd, the **Toubkal trail** goes up the flood plain then follows the east (ie the Aroumd) side of the Mizane, climbing and zigzagging round the hard, grey rocks, high above the river. If you have been following the main mule trail on the west side of the valley from Imlil to Aroumd, you can join the Toubkal trail without going round into Aroumd.

The river is crossed once more, 1hr 30min to 2hr further from Aroumd, just before you arrive at the village of **SIDI CHAMAROUCH**. Set beside a small waterfall, this is an anarchic cluster of houses, all built one into another. Its seasonal population of ten or twelve run soft drinks/grocery shops for tourist trekkers and for Moroccan pilgrims, who come to the village's marabout shrine – sited across the gorge from the village and reached by a modern concrete bridge which non-Muslims are strictly forbidden to cross. The shrine is probably a survival of a very ancient nature cult – in these parts often thinly veiled by the trappings of Islam. (On the approach to the village you may notice a tree, sacred to local tradition, where the Berbers hang strips of cloth and make piles of stones.) **Camping** below the village, beside the stream, is possible. **Rooms** are also available.

Beyond Sidi Chamarouch, the Toubkal trail climbs steeply in zigzags and then traverses the flank of the valley well above the Mizane (the water from the river is not safe to drink untreated until you get above the Toubkal Refuge). The trail is pretty clear the whole way to the **Toubkal Refuge,** which, at 3207m, marks the spring snow line. In winter the snow line can drop to Sidi Chamarouch and mules have to be replaced by porters if you want assistance to the Toubkal Refuge.

The Toubkal Refuge

Even in mid-August it gets pretty cold up at the **Toubkal Refuge** (formerly *Refuge Neltner*) once the sun has disappeared behind the ridge. You will probably, therefore, want to take advantage of its shelter. The refuge is open all year and charges 30dh per person for a bed (22.50dh with IYHF card; 10dh with Alpine Club membership). The *gardien* is usually prepared to cook meat or vegetable tajine for guests (about 25dh per person), though beware that the refuge can be very busy – and crowded. There are plans to completely rebuild it, offering double the capacity and greater comfort – and charging up to 100dh a night.

Another reason for staying at the refuge is that the area around is covered in rubbish (human waste, too), so if you plan on **camping** nearby, you'll want to go some way upstream or use the meadows a bit down from the hut.

Climbing Toubkal

At the Toubkal Refuge you're almost bound to meet people who have just come down from **Djebel Toubkal** – and you should certainly take advantage of talking to them (and/or the refuge *gardien*) for an up-to-the-minute description of the routes and the state of the South Cirque trail to the summit. If you don't feel too confident about going it alone, take a guide – they are usually available at the refuge – but don't let them try and rush you up the mountain (see Toubkal Trekking box for further details).

THE SOUTH CIRQUE

The **South Cirque** (*Ikkibi Sud*) is the most popular and straightforward ascent of Toubkal and, depending on your fitness, should take between 2hr 30min and 3hr 30min (2–2hr 30min coming down). It is now a well-worn route and with reasonable instructions on the spot is easy enough to follow without a guide. More of a problem – and something you should be careful about at any time of the year – is finding the right track down. It is easy to find yourself in fields of loose scree.

The **trail** begins above the Toubkal Refuge, dropping down to cross the stream and then climbing over a short stretch of grass and rock to reach the first of Toubkal's innumerable fields of boulders and scree. These – often needing three steps to gain one – are the most tiring (and memorable) feature of the trek up, and gruelling for inexperienced walkers. The summit, a sloping plateau of stones marked by a tripod, is eventually reached after a lot of zigzagging up out of the cirque.

It should be reiterated that **in winter even this ascent is a snow climb** and not for walkers.

THE NORTH CIRQUE

An alternative – though longer (4hr 30min) and more ambitious – ascent is the **North Cirque** (*Ikkibi Nord*). En route you will pass the remains of an aircraft (it crashed while flying arms to Biafra) and the small peak of Tibherine has its engine as a cairn. The final ridge to the summit area calls for some scrambling and in general the route calls for experience.

The Toubkal Refuge to Lac d'Ifni and beyond

Lac d'Ifni is one of the largest mountain lakes in the Atlas – and the only one of any size in the Toubkal region. From the refuge it's about a 4–5hr trek, again involving long, tedious stretches over loose rock and scree, and with odd stretches of snow remaining into July. On the way back, the scree scrambling is even more pronounced. To make the trip worthwhile, take along enough food for a couple of days' camping; there are no facilities of any kind en route.

Toubkal to Lac d'Ifni

The Lac d'Ifni trail begins at the Toubkal Refuge, climbing up a rough, stony slope and then winding round to the head of the Mizane Valley towards the imposing Tizi n'Ouanoums. The pass is reached in about an hour and the path is reasonably easy to follow. The trail up the pass itself is a good, gravel path, zigzagging continually until you reach the summit (3664m), a narrow platform between two shafts of rock.

The views from the *tizi* are superb, taking in the whole route that you've covered and, in the distance to the south, the hazy green outline of the lake (which disappears from view as you descend). At this point the hard work seems over – but this is a totally false impression. The path down the valley to Lac d'Ifni is slow, steep progress, the scree slopes are apparently endless, and the lake doesn't come back into sight until you are almost there. It is, in fact, virtually enclosed by the mountains, and by what look like demolished hills – great heaps of rubble and boulders.

Lac d'Ifni is a fine sight, its only human habitations a few shepherds' huts, and the only sound that of water idly lapping on the shore; it is exceptionally deep – up to 50m over much of its area. It makes a poor campsite, however, with scrubby terraces, somewhat fly-ridden by day, and no drinking water source (the lake waters are polluted). You can camp much more enjoyably by carrying on for another hour until you reach the first patches of irrigated valley, high above the village of Imhilene.

On from Lac d'Ifni: a loop to Tachdirt or Imlil

Most people return from Lac d'Ifni to the Toubkal refuge by the same route but it's quite feasible to make a longer, anticlockwise, loop towards Tachdirt or Imlil.

LAC D'IFNI TO SIDI CHAMAROUCH

From the lake, you can strike east to the valley above Imhilene, and beyond it to the kasbah-like village of Amsouzart, reached in around three hours. There is a café/campsite here and *gîte* accommodation and meals at Omar's house; ask for him at the café or shop, which is your last chance of supplies on this route.

At Amsouzart, the path to the north follows the west bank of the river, reaching the village of Tissaldaï in about four hours; camping is possible in the valley above. From here, it's at least four hours of strenuous trekking to get up the Tizi n'Terhaline (3247m). It's worth all the effort, as you descend into a beautiful valley. After about two hours' walking from the pass, you will reach Azib Tifni, a collection of shepherds' huts, none more than a metre high.

You can then follow the valley west over another high pass, Tizi n'Tagharat to descend steeply to Sidi Chamarouch.

THE LOOP TO TACHDIRT

An alternative route from Azib Tifni (see opposite) is to follow the valley to the east, into one of the magnificent gorges of this region. Crossing the first pass, you can camp easily near Azib Likemt (2hr from Azib Tifni), beyond which another more demanding pass, the high Tizi n'Likemt (3555m) leads to Tachdirt CAF refuge; there is also good camping on the Tizi n'Likemt side of the valley by springs. From the beginning of October, these *azibs* are empty as the valley becomes completely cut off in winter.

The country east of Azib Likemt, the Kissaria Gorges, is wild in the extreme (too hard even for mules), so it is inadvisable to try and reach the Ourika Valley that way.

If making this loop and including Toubkal it is strongly advisable to go in the other direction to gain acclimatization and fitness before climbing the mountain.

Tachdirt and beyond

Tachdirt (3000m), 8km east of Imlil, is an alternative and in many ways more attractive base for trekking expeditions. As at Imlil, there is a CAF refuge, and a fine range of local treks and onward routes. But despite its comparatively easy access – a pleasant mule track up the valley over Tizi n'Tamatert (more direct than the tortuously winding *piste*) – the village sees only a handful of the trekkers who make it up to Toubkal.

You can walk the **mulepath from Imlil** in three to four hours, or on Saturdays there is a Berber **lorry** (for the Asni souk) along the *piste*. There is only one small shop in the village (soft drinks are sold at the refuge), so take along your own food. The **CAF refuge** (20dh a bed; cooking facilities and some supplies available through the *gardien*) is just above the trail on the left-hand side as you enter the village; it's kept locked, but the *gardien* should soon appear. He can arrange a guide and mules. There is also a gîte in the village.

Tachdirt to Setti Fatma

This is one of the more obvious routes for anyone contemplating anything beyond a simple day-trip into the hills. Taken at a reasonable pace, the route can be accomplished in two days' walking from Tachdirt. There is a well-defined trail all the way, used by locals (who take mules along the whole length), so no particular skills are demanded beyond general fitness and a head for heights. Several sections of the trail are quite exposed and steep.

You'll probably want to carry some food supplies with you. However, meals are offered at the village of Timichi, so cooking gear and provisions are not essential. If you are carrying gear, you might want to hire mules at Tachdirt.

TACHDIRT TO TIMICHI

Tachdirt to Timichi is a superb day's walk. The first three hours or so are spent climbing up to the Tizi n'Tachdirt (3616m), with ever more spectacular views. The character of the valley changes abruptly after the pass, green terraced fields giving way to rough and craggy mountain slopes. The path down is one of the more exposed sections of the route. As you approach Timichi the valley again becomes more green and vegetated.

TIMICHI has several *gîtes* and makes a good overnight stop. A hard but impressive pass leads to Oukaïmeden and it is possible to follow the valley up and out under the peak of Angour. The normal three-day recommended route is Oukaïmeden–Tachdirt–Timichi–Oukaïmeden.

TIMICHI TO SETTI FATMA

Timichi to Setti Fatma is another beautiful trek, taking about half a day. At first you follow the river fairly closely but soon the track climbs upward, to about 300m above the riverbed. There is little water available for several miles, and the track is perched on the side of the extremely steep valley. You finally join up with a *piste* that zigzags down into the Ourika Valley about 2km north of Setti Fatma.

Tachdirt to Oukaïmeden

This is a fairly straightforward route – a three- to four-hour walk over a reasonable mule track by way of the 2960m **Tizi n'Eddi**.

The Angour Traverse

Hiking along the ridge of Angour is pretty demanding, taking a full day from Tachdirt and (if the weather turns on you) demanding a night's bivouac. It requires basic climbing skills.

From Tachdirt, the trail zigzags up the left-hand side of the **Imenane Valley** up towards **Tizi n'Tachdirt** (which remains visible the whole way). At the pass (a three-and-a-half-hour steep walk), head north up a rough, grassy slope, to break through crags onto the sloping **plateau**, which can be followed to the **summit of Angour** (3616m). This plateau is an unusual feature on a peak with such dramatic cliffs. It is split by a valley. With care, you can follow a ridge down from here to **Tizi n'Eddi** (to pick up the Oukaïmeden trail), or break away straight down to Tachdirt. A guide would be useful.

Tachdirt to Imlil via Tizi n'Aguersioual

An alternative route back from **Tachdirt to Imlil** is by way of **Tizi n'Aguersioual**. This takes you down-valley to the hamlets of Tinerhourhine (1hr) and Ikiss (15min further down; soft drinks/rooms). From Ikiss a good path on the other side of the valley (ask someone to point it out) leads up to the Aguersioual pass and then zigzags down to the village of Aguersioual, from where you can follow the Asni road back up to Imlil.

West of Imlil: Tizi Oussem and the Tazaghart Refuge

The area west of Imlil and the Djebel Toubkal trail offers a good acclimatization trek to **Tizi Oussem**, harder treks to the south to the **Tazaghart Refuge** (accessible also from the Toubkal Refuge), and the possibility of one- or two-day treks **out to Ouirgane or Ijoukak** on the Tizi n'Test road, or back to the Asni–Imlil road at **Tamadout**.

Tizi Oussem and on to Ouirgane

The village of **TIZI OUSSEM** is in the next valley west of Imlil and is reached in about four hours over the Tizi Mzic; the track is not that easy to find and suffered badly in the 1995 flood, so ask for initial directions. The most interesting section is the path down from the pass to the village. If you are heading for the Tazaghart Refuge, another path from the pass follows round the hillside to Azib Tamsoult, and then to the gorge for the Tazaghart hut. The valley itself offers a long day's trek **down to Ouirgane** on the Tizi n'Test road. At its foot it becomes a *piste*, but this wanders off to the right and you should abandon it in order to go left and, with luck, arrive at the *Au Sanglier Qui Fume* in Ouirgane (see p.401). Experienced walkers can make a three-day expedition to reach **Ijoukak**, with two camps en route, one just below the Tizi Ouarhou (2672m) and the second before the Tizi n' Iguidi.

The **route to Ouirgane** has been made more difficult because of the flood damage (the valley bed is utterly destroyed). From Tizi Oussem you need to keep to the east bank initially and then drop onto the flood plain to ensure facing the west bank at a narrowing. The path keeps high then zigzags down to cross the river to gain height on the east side, passing the walled farm of Azerfsane. The path swings west and drops to the river where the *piste* used to end. A mule track on the left bank helps you cross to pull up to a spur with a commanding view to the rich Ouirgane (Wirgane) Valley. When the *piste* veers off, cut down and follow cultivation paths on the left bank (or use the bare valley bottom) to reach the main road and the accommodation options.

You can also reach Asni by keeping to the east bank and a rising path, then *piste*, over the **Tizi n'Tacht** to reach the Asni-Imlil *piste* at Tamadout.

The Tazaghart Refuge and around
The **Tazaghart Refuge** (formerly known as the *Refuge Lepiney*) is some 6hr 30min to 7hr 30min from Imlil and essentially a rock-climbing base for the fine cliffs of **Tazaghart**. To get access, you (or a porter) may have to go down to the village of Tizi Oussem to get the hut *gardien*, Omar Abdallah, who is also a very good (and extremely pleasant) guide; he can arrange a room in the village, too. Details of a number of climbs from the refuge are given in the Collomb guide, but be warned that in winter they require crampons and ice axes – and climbing experience; there was a fatal accident here in 1989, involving an organized trekking party.

Tizi Melloul (3–4hr from the Tazaghart refuge) allows trekking access to Tazaghart (3843m), an extraordinary plateau and fine vantage point. You can also cross Tizi Melloul and, with one camp or bivouac, walk **down the Agoundis Valley to Ijoukak**. The Agoundis Valley can also be reached over the Tizi n'Ouaganc at the head of the Neltner Valley.

Tizi n'Test: Ouirgane, Ijoukak and Tin Mal

The **Tizi n'Test**, the road that extends beyond Asni to Taroudannt or Taliouine, is unbelievably impressive. Cutting right through the heart of the Atlas, it was blasted out of the mountains by the French from 1926 to 1932 – the first modern route to link Marrakesh with the Souss plain and the desert, and an extraordinary feat of pioneer-spirit engineering. Until then, it had been considered impracticable without local protection and knowledge: an important pass for trade and for the control and subjugation of the south, but one that few sultans were able to make their own.

Through much of the nineteenth century – and the beginning of the twentieth – the pass was the personal fief of the **Goundafi** clan, whose huge kasbahs still dominate many of the crags and strategic turns along the way. Much earlier it had served as the refuge and power base of the Almohads, and it was from the holy city of **Tin Mal**, standing above the Oued Nfis, that they launched their attack on the Almoravid dynasty. As remote and evocative a mountain stronghold as could be imagined, Tin Mal is an excursion well worth making for the chance to see the carefully restored ruins of the twelfth-century mosque, a building close in spirit to the Koutoubia, and for once accessible to non-Muslims, except on Fridays.

Practicalities
If you are setting out by **bus from Marrakesh**, you should have three choices, leaving at either 5am (sometimes 6am), 2pm or 6pm. The 5am/6am bus is the only direct one to Taroudannt (7hr 30min), but the others go as far as Ijoukak (4hr); the 2pm bus stops there, and the 6pm one goes on to Taliouine (arriving, after a scary night descent, at around 1–2am). It's important to turn up at least 30min before departure if you want tickets on the morning bus. If you're **coming from Asni**, you can pick up any of these buses a little over an hour after they leave Marrakesh.

For anyone **driving**, some experience of mountain roads is essential. The route is well contoured and paved, but between the pass and the intersection with the P32, the Taliouine–Taroudannt road, it is extremely narrow (one and half times a car's width) with almost continuous hairpin bends and blind corners. Since you can actually see for some distance ahead, this isn't as dangerous as it sounds – but you still need a lot of confidence and have to watch out for suicidal local drivers bearing down on you without any intention of stopping or slowing down. Bus and lorry drivers are, fortunately,

MOUNTAIN BIKING IN THE HIGH ATLAS

Mountain biking in Morocco offers some of the best adventure riding in the world and there are routes suitable for all abilities. The High Atlas has an awesome number of jeep and single donkey tracks that cover the countryside and numerous **adventure companies** offer mountain biking as a pursuit in Morocco (for details see Basics, p.5). Travelling independently it's important to be aware of local sensibilities; ride slowly through villages, giving way to people where necessary, especially those on donkeys and children tending livestock; pick your way carefully through cropped fields and palmeries, or take a detour if possible; and try not to pass through inhabited areas in large groups – be discreet and the rewards will be wonderful. If **renting a bike**, negotiate essential extras like a pump, puncture repair kit and/or spare inner tube. A helmet isn't absolutely necessary but probably recommendable, as is carrying plenty of water. Filling up from village wells is possible, but always ask permission first. For general information on planning and problems see Basics, pp.46–48.

Of the **two routes** detailed below, the first can be done by a novice with a rented bike, whilst the second is best left to the proficient, preferably on their own bike. Both routes begin and end at *Restaurant Le Source Bleu* (see p.402) in Amizmiz; the first is possible as a day-trip from Marrakesh, the second, more taxing route, requires a stopover at *Le Source Bleu*. As few roads are signposted, the Amizmiz 1:100,000 **topographical map** is highly recommended, available from specialist map shops before you leave home (see p.31) and, increasingly, in Marrakesh and Imlil. Times given for completing routes are guides only; allow yourself plenty of time to take photos, enjoy the hospitality offered en route, and fix the odd puncture.

ROUTE 1 THE OUED AMIZMIZ

This ride follows the **Oued Amizmiz** along undulating jeep track, crossing the river at the natural point where track meets valley bottom, and passing by picturesque villages, crop terraces and bizarre rock formations. It is essentialy flat, with only **two notable hills**, and ends with a **dramatic descent** back into Amizmiz. The track is good quality *piste* and **the route**, though easy enough for anyone to tackle, is still interesting enough for the serious biker to appreciate too. The 38km should take about three to four hours.

From *Le Source Bleu* take the jeep track down until it meets the *piste* road running from Amizmiz to Azegour and then head on uphill, through the **Tizi Ghourane** and past the *Maison Forestière* (Ranger's Station). About 1.5km past the *Maison Forestière* a narrow jeep track branches off left, taking you down the west side of the valley to pass through the village of **Aït Ouskri**, from where there are tremendous views up the valley, its arid slopes contrasting with the lush terraces below, to Djebel Gourza and Djebel

more considerate. Try to avoid driving the route at midday in the summer months when cars are liable to overheat.

From November to the end of April, the pass is occasionally blocked with **snow**. When this occurs, a sign is put up on the roadside at the point where the Asni–Test road leaves Marrakesh and on the roadside past Tahanoute.

The road to the pass

Heading out on the dawn bus from Marrakesh, you have the least interesting part of the Taroudannt journey to catch up on lost sleep. The landscape over the first hour of the Haouz plain to **TAHANAOUTE** (Tuesday souk) is fairly monotonous up until the gorges of the Moulay Brahim up to Asni. There is some "Badlands" scenery (forested to stop erosion) and you can see salt leaking from the soil before a rich basin and a second watershed leads to the bigger Ouirgane basin. If you are driving, the road off

Imlit. The *piste* continues, passing the villages of Tizgui, Toug al Kheyr and, after 10km, Imi-n-Isli and Imi-n-Tala, before crossing the river at **Addouz** and bringing you to the eastern side of the Amizmiz Valley. Care should be taken if **crossing the river in spring**, when it can become swollen from melted snow. Following the *piste* through Imzayn, and sticking to the lower track, leads to Igourdan and, after about 12km, **Aït Hmad**, with the earlier part of the route and the villages on the western edge of the valley clearly visible. Enthusiasm to greet you on the part of local schoolchildren in Aït Hmad can cause a few wobbles as you make your way through the village.

Leaving this excitement behind, the road widens to become a full-width *piste* jeep track allowing a fast but safe downhill back into Amizmiz town.

ROUTE 2 AZEGOUR AND TOULKINE

This ride is a great test of stamina, technical skills and route finding, taking in some of the best views and villages in the area; with strenuous uphills and a very technical final descent, it is really only for the fit and experienced. Good brakes and seven to eight hours are needed to cover the 42km.

The route starts as for Route 1; uphill through the Tizi Ghourane to the *Maison Forestière* then, 1.5km on, keep going straight (instead of taking the left-hand track), skirting the impressive **Djebel Timerghit** and rising higher up the Oued Amizmiz Valley, with increasingly stunning views. About 10km along, the *piste* flattens and remains relatively easy-going until you reach **Azegour**, where the route crosses the seasonal Assif Wadaker at the ford and leads right, bringing you to the village of **Toulkine**. This stretch of track becomes quite sandy in sections and can make things harder going, but from here the **scenery** becomes even more stunning – verdant fields ringed by jagged mountains.

On the other side of the village the right-hand donkey track, lined with cairns, heads north, up and over the hill, leading to the hamlet of **Adghous**. From here the trail can be difficult to follow and you'll need to **ask locals** for directions to Amizmiz; common sense and your map are the best ways to keep on the right track. A path leads down through the houses of Adghous, the hamlet starting to spread out over another valley, where an improbable left turn, just past some beautiful stone and mud houses, takes you through a dip (you'll have to carry your bike) and picks up a donkey track on the far side. It's worth pausing for the **spectacular view** of Adghous, sitting on a spur overhanging the valley, before continuing on the upper track, along a highly technical section – single track, rutted, stony and eroded – until the pre-Atlas plains to the north become visible. There is an obvious single-track leading down the valley towards these plains, and at the village of **Tiqlit**, this track widens to become a fast jeep track. Follow this until you leave the valley and are on the plains, where a jeep track to the right will lead you through the village of Wadaker and back to Amizmiz.

to the right to the *Residence Ouirgane* (see below) is worth following for the view alone.

Ouirgane and the Nfis gorges

OUIRGANE is a tiny place, long touted by French guidebooks as a beautiful valley and *étape gastronomique*. In the early hours of an Atlas morning, coming from Marrakesh, this might not be much of an attraction, but after trekking around Toubkal, it is a wonderful place – with a dash of luxury – to lie around and recover. It is also a very pleasant base in itself for day walks, mountain-bike forays or horse riding. It hosts a Thursday souk.

There are three **hotels**. The *Résidence de la Roseraie* (☎4 through the operator; ⑤), is a grand four-star place, with a swimming pool, sauna, tennis and prices to match. It offers horse riding: 250dh for a half day, 3500dh for a week's package, including two nights at the hotel. You should bring your own helmet. Much cheaper is *Au Sanglier*

Qui Fume (☎04/448 5707; ④), across the river. French run, the food is good and the garden setting and pool a delight. Popular in the summer, when booking is advisable. Evidence of the 1995 floods is still to be seen, with the garden piled with huge boulders. There are also simple, pleasant rooms at the *Café Badaoui*. Lastly, high on a viewpoint hill is the *Residence Ouirgane* (☎04/411 7447; ④), built in traditional style in superb gardens.

Trekking up behind Ouirgane, one rewarding route is to head for **Tizi Ouadou** and the **Kik Plateau** – and then down to Asni and back by taxi. Rather more ambitiously, you could strike northwest to Amizmiz, by way of the Nfis gorges.

OUIRGANE TO AMIZMIZ: THE NFIS GORGES
From Ouirgane, a seven-hour walk by the **Nfis gorges** leads to **AMIZMIZ**, which has regular bus and grand taxi connections with Marrakesh along the S507 (to/from the Bab Er Robb). It is also the site of a long-established **Tuesday souk**, one of the largest Berber markets of the Atlas, and not on the tourist trail. The town itself comprises several quite distinct quarters – including a zaouia, kasbah and former Mellah – separated by a small ravine. **Accommodation** is available 4km out of town (ask for directions) at the pleasant *Restaurant Le Source Bleu* (☎04/445 4595; ③). The *Hôtel de France* in town has now closed.

Ijoukak
IJOUKAK is an important shopping centre where the Agoundis Valley joins the Nfis; buses stop at its many cafés and there is limited accommodation. The last café at the Tizi n'Test end has pleasant rooms behind and cheap spaces on the roof.

Walking out from Ijoukak, you can easily explore Tin Mal and Talâat n'Yacoub (see pp.404–406) or try some more prolonged **trekking in the Nfis and Agoundis valleys** – see below. The Agoundis can also be enjoyable just as a day's wandering, if you have nothing more ambitious in mind, or you can take the winding forestry road up the hill dominating the village for its commanding view.

Trekking around Ijoukak

Ijoukak gives access to some of the most enjoyable trekking in the High Atlas – all much less developed than the main Toubkal area. Starting from the village, you can trek east up the **Agoundis Valley towards Toubkal**, or west up the long **Ogdemt Valley**. The region to the **west of the Tizi n'Test road** is wilder still; for details – in reverse – of the trek to Afensou and Imi n'Tanoute (on the Marrakesh–Agadir road), see the "Tichka Plateau treks", p.410.

The **survey map** for the area (if you can get hold of it) is *Tizi n'Test* (1:100,000).

Agoundis Valley
East from Ijoukak winds the **Agoundis River Valley**. It offers alternative access to Toubkal, but is seldom used. To reach the Toubkal Refuge would take two days of serious trekking. However, if "peak bagging" is not part of your plan, you could still enjoy a day's trek or an overnight trip up this way.

From Ijoukak walk back down the road towards Marrakesh until you cross the river (200m). A dirt road leads off to your right. A small sign there warns you not to fish for trout in the river. This road continues along the valley for about 10km. It's used by lorries hauling ore from the mines. If you're in a hurry, you could hitch a lift; otherwise, the walk is a pleasant one. There are several villages strung out along the valley making use of the year-round water to farm small patches in the river bottom and on the terraced hillsides. About 2km down the road there is a small square hut below the road on the right. It's a **watermill** which is fascinating to watch if you happen to catch someone inside. Another 3km further and you'll pass an abandoned **rock-crushing factory**, its huge tin and timber structure half falling down. In the house just beyond it, to the west, Ibrahim and Abdallah Jhouliyine offer **rooms** and **meals**. Just beyond is the village of **TAGHBART**.

The road splits after 8km, the right fork descending to the river, crossing and continuing on into the mountains to the south. Take the left fork (get off the lorry if you've hitched this far) and follow it as it curves round to the left, to the northeast. At the curve is another village, **EL MAKHZEN**. The road has now been extended a couple of kilometres to **TIJRHICHT**. Along this last section is an ingeniously constructed irrigation ditch hugging the cliffside beneath the road. Here the road ends and a mule trail begins. If you've hitched up here, it probably will have taken you no more than half an hour; on foot it's about two to three hours.

The **trail towards Toubkal Refuge** begins to climb into a narrowing limestone gorge with the river a great distance below. Tiny Berber villages are perched on rocky outcrops every 2–3km giving good views in both directions, until Toubkal finally appears, rising above the upper reaches of the valley.

At **AÏT YOUB** (8km from the end of the road), you will have reached the last and highest cultivated areas (1900m), taking around 3hr 30min to arrive this far, with the help of the occasional lift. Figure on six to eight hours' walking, depending on your fitness.

Toubkal refuge and **Djebel Toubkal** are another long day's trek from here. It's possible to hire a mule and a muleteer, who acts as a guide simply because he knows the way. However, this is not as straightforward and organized as in more frequented places like Imlil. This far into the mountains it's unlikely that you will find anyone who speaks English, but with simple French or Arabic phrases you should be understood.

If you wish to continue on foot alone, *Guide Collomb* is helpful from here. Keep in mind that snow can impede your crossing the pass until midsummer. In any case, you'll need to stay overnight in Aït Youb. Camping should be no problem. It's usually best to ask permission for politeness' sake. When you ask, be prepared for an offer of hospitality and a night's stay in the village. You're in no way imposing by accepting it, but it is understood in all but a few cases that you'll offer something in return when you leave. It will customarily be turned down at least once but usually accepted with persistence on your part. In winter/spring it is perhaps best to descend the Agoundis. It's easier to retreat from the Neltuer side if the Tizi n'Ouagane is deemed impassable.

Ougdemt Valley

West from Ijoukak and the Agoundis Valley lies the **Ougdemt**, a long, pleasant valley filled with Berber villages surrounded by walnut groves.

A dirt road for lorries now stretches for several kilometres up the valley from **MZOUZITE** (3km beyond Tin Mal and 8km from Ijoukak). Beyond this, a trail continues winding up along the river to **ARG** at the head of the valley (6–7hr walking). From Arg you could aim for **Djebel Erdouz** (3579m) to the north of Tizi n'Tighfist (2895m), or the higher **Djebel Igdat** to the south (3616m), by way of Tizi n'Oumslama. Both are fairly straightforward when following the mule paths to the passes and can be reached in five to six hours from Arg. Be sure to take your own water in summer as the lower elevations can be dry. A two to three-day traverse of these peaks on to Djebel Gourza (3280m) and down to Tin Mal is a challenging adventure. The east ridge of Erdouz gives serious scrambling.

For the very adventurous, a further expedition could be undertaken **all the way to the Tichka plateau** – summer grazing pastures at the headwaters of the Nfis River – and across the other side to the Marrakesh–Agadir road. This would take at least six days from the Tizi n'Test road and require you to carry provisions for several days at a time.

For a detailed route description, see Peyron's *Great Atlas Traverse*. A brief summary of this trail, taken from the opposite direction, follows in the "Tichka Plateau treks" section on p.410.

Idni and the pass

At **IDNI**, well up on the pass, the small *Café Igdet* has very basic rooms (with bed mats), hot meals and tea. From the hamlet, a path zigzags down to the Nfis which can then be followed out to the main road again.

The **Tizi n'Test** (2092m) lies 18km up from Idni. There's a small café on the *col* and one or two down on the south side; buses will stop on request. From the summit of the pass a *piste* rises up towards a platform mounted by a TV relay station. The views down to the Souss Valley and back towards Toubkal can be stunning and experienced climbers can backpack along the crest west from here to descend into the Nfis Valley later with the massive cliffs of Flillis dominating the view. There is also a *piste* (path direct from the *tizi* to join it) leading down to Souk Sebt Tanammert on the Nfis. Descending this and following the Nfis east is a good trip; one bivouac.

Over the pass, the **descent towards Taroudannt/Taliouine** is hideously dramatic: a drop of some 1600m in little over 30km. Throughout, there are stark, fabulous vistas of the peaks, and occasionally, hundreds of feet below, a mountain valley and cluster of villages. Taroudannt is reached in around 2hr 30min to 3hr, Taliouine in a little more; coming up, needless to say, it all takes a good deal longer. For details on Taroudannt and Taliouine, see Chapter Eight.

Tin Mal Mosque

The **Tin Mal Mosque**, quite apart from its historic and architectural importance, is a beautiful ruin – isolated above a lush reach of river valley, harsh mountains backing its buff-coloured walls. It has recently been restored and reopened and is a highly worthwhile stop if you're driving the Tizi n'Test. If you're staying at Ijoukak, it's an easy eight-kilometre walk, passing en route the old Goundafi kasbah in Talâat n'Yacoub (see below). You can return on the opposite side of the Nfis.

The mosque is set a little way above the modern village of Tin Mal (or Ifouriren) and reached by wandering uphill, across a road bridge. It is kept locked, but the *gardien* will soon spot you, open it up and let you look round undisturbed (10dh admission – and a tip is expected by the *gardien*). It is used by villages for the Friday service and closed to non-Muslims on that day.

The mosque
The **Tin Mal Mosque** was built by Abd El Moumen around 1153–54, partly as a memorial and cult centre for Ibn Toumert and partly as his own family mausoleum. Obviously fortified, it probably served also as a section of the town's defences, since in the early period of Almohad rule, Tin Mal was entrusted with the state treasury. Today, it is the only part of the fortifications – indeed, of the entire Almohad city – that you can make out with any clarity. The rest was sacked and largely destroyed in the Merenid conquest of 1276 – a curiously late event, since all of the main Moroccan cities had already been in the new dynasty's hands for some thirty years.

That Tin Mal remained standing for that long, and that its mosque was maintained, says a lot about the power Toumert's teaching must have continued to exercise over the local Berbers. Even two centuries later the historian Ibn Khaldun found Koranic readers employed at the tombs, and when the French began restoration in the 1930s they found the site littered with the shrines of marabouts.

IBN TOUMERT AND THE ALMOHADS

Tin Mal's site seems now so remote that it is difficult to imagine a town ever existing in this valley. In some form, though, it did. It was here that **Ibn Toumert** and his lieutenant, **Abd El Moumen**, preached to the Berber tribes and welded them into the **Almohad** ("unitarian") movement; here that they set out on the campaigns which culminated in the conquest of all Morocco and southern Spain; and here, too, a century and a half later, that they made their last stand against the incoming Merenid dynasty.

This history – so decisive in the development of the medieval Shereefian empire – is outlined in "The Historical Framework" in "Contexts". More particular to Tin Mal are the circumstances of Ibn Toumert's arrival and the appeal of his puritan, reforming teaching to the local tribes. Known to his followers as the *Mahdi* – "The Chosen One", whose coming is prophesied in the Koran – Toumert was himself born in the High Atlas, a member of the Berber-speaking Masmouda tribe, who held the desert-born Almoravids, the ruling dynasty, in traditional contempt. He was an accomplished theologian and studied at the centres of eastern Islam, a period in which he formulated the strict Almohad doctrines, based on the assertion of the unity of God and on a verse of the Koran in which Muhammad set out the role of religious reform: "to reprove what is disapproved and enjoy what is good". For Toumert, Almoravid Morocco contained much to disapprove of and, returning from the East with a small group of disciples, he began to preach against all manifestations of luxury – above all, wine and performance of music – and against women mixing in male society.

In 1121, Toumert and his group arrived in Marrakesh, the Almoravid capital, where they began to provoke the sultan. Ironically, this was not an easy task – Ali Ben Youssef, one of the most pious rulers in Moroccan history, accepted many of Toumert's charges and forgave his insults. It was only in 1124, when the reformer struck Ali's sister from her horse for riding unveiled (as was desert tradition), that the Almohads were finally banished from the city and took refuge in the mountain stronghold of Tin Mal.

From the beginning in this exiled residence, Ibn Toumert and Abd El Moumen set out to mould the Atlas Berbers into a religious and military force. They taught prayers in Arabic by giving each follower as his name a word from the Koran and then lining them all up to recite it. They also stressed the significance of the "second coming" and Toumert's role as *Mahdi*. More significant, perhaps, was the savage military emphasis of the new order. Hesitant tribes were branded "hypocrites" and massacred – most notoriously in the Forty-Day Purge of the mountains – and within eight years none remained outside Almohad control. In the 1130s, after Ibn Toumert had died, Abd El Moumen began to attack and "convert" the plains. In 1145, he was able to take Fes and, in 1149, just 25 years after the march of exile, his armies entered and sacked Marrakesh.

Architecturally, Tin Mal presents a unique opportunity for non-Muslims to take a look at the interior of a traditional Almohad mosque. It is roofless, for the most part, and two of the corner pavilion towers have disappeared, but the mihrab (or prayer niche) and the complex pattern of internal arches are substantially intact.

The arrangement is in a classic Almohad design – the T-shaped plan with a central aisle leading towards the mihrab – and is virtually identical to that of the Koutoubia in Marrakesh, more or less its contemporary. The one element of eccentricity is in the placing of the **minaret** (which you can climb for a view of the general layout) over the mihrab: a weakness of engineering design that meant it could never have been much taller than it is today.

In terms of decoration, the most striking feature is the variety and intricacy of the **arches** – above all those leading into the mihrab, which have been sculpted with a stalactite vaulting. In the **corner domes** and the **mihrab vault** this technique is extended with impressive effect. Elsewhere, and on the face of the mihrab, it is the slightly austere geometric patterns and familiar motifs (the palmette, rosette, scallop, etc), of Almohad decorative gates that are predominant.

The Goundafi kasbahs

The **Goundafi kasbahs** don't really compare with Tin Mal – nor with the Glaoui kasbah in Telouet (detailed in the following Tizi n'Tichka section). But, as so often in Morocco, they provide an extraordinary assertion of just how recent is the country's feudal past. Despite their medieval appearance, the buildings are all nineteenth- or even twentieth-century creations.

Talâat n'Yacoub and other kasbahs

The more important of the kasbahs is the former Goundafi stronghold and headquarters near the village of **TALÂAT N'YACOUB**. Coming from Ijoukak, this is reached off to the right of the main road, down a very French-looking, tree-lined country lane; it is 6km south of Ijoukak, 3km north of Tin Mal and has an interesting mountain **souk** on Wednesdays.

The **kasbah**, decaying, partially ruined and probably pretty unsafe, lies at the far end of the village. Nobody seems to mind if you take a look inside, though you need to avoid the dogs near its entrance. The inner part of the palace-fortress, though blackened from a fire, is reasonably complete and retains traces of its decoration.

It is difficult to establish the exact facts with these old tribal kasbahs, but it seems that it was constructed late in the nineteenth century for the next-to-last Goundafi chieftain. A feudal warrior in the old tradition, he was constantly at war with the sultan during the 1860s and 1870s, and a bitter rival of the neighbouring Glaoui clan. His son, Tayeb El Goundafi, also spent most of his life in tribal campaigning, though he finally threw in his lot with Sultan Moulay Hassan, and later with the French. At the turn of the century, he could still raise some 5000 armed tribesmen with a day or two's notice, but his power and fief eventually collapsed in 1924. The writer, Cunninghame Graham, was detained here by the Goundafi, and his book (see "Contexts", p.608) describes the medieval scene well.

Agadir n'Gouj and Tagoundaft

Another dramatic-looking Goundafi kasbah stands to the left of the road, a couple of kilometres south of Tin Mal. This one, **Agadir n'Gouj** is set on a hilltop, and is now privately owned. It is well preserved – as indeed it should be, having been constructed only in 1907.

When the road begins to turn up and away from the river, another stark ruin looms up on the left. This is the **Tagoundaft**, the most imposing but seldom visited of the Goundafi kasbahs.

Telouet and the Tizi n'Tichka

The **Tizi n'Tichka** – the direct route from Marrakesh to Ouarzazate – is not so remote or spectacular as the Tizi n'Test pass. As an important military (and tourist) approach to the south, the road is modern, well constructed and relatively fast. At **Telouet**, however, only a short distance off the modern highway, such mundane current roles are underpinned by an earlier political history, scarcely three decades old and unimaginably bizarre. For this pass and the mountains to the east of it were the stamping ground of the extraordinary **Glaoui** brothers, the greatest and the most ambitious of all the Berber tribal leaders. Their kasbah-headquarters, a vast complex of buildings abandoned only in 1956, are a rewarding detour (21km from the main road).

For trekkers, bikers or four-wheel-drivers, Telouet has an additional and powerful attraction, offering an alternative and superb *piste* to the south, following the old tribal **route to Aït Benhaddou**.

Telouet: the Glaoui kasbah

The **Glaoui kasbah** at **TELOUET** is one of the most extraordinary sights of the Atlas – fast crumbling into the dark red earth, but visitable, and offering a peculiar glimpse of the style and melodrama of recent Moroccan political government and power. There's little of aesthetic value – many of the rooms have fallen into complete ruin – but nevertheless, even after over forty years of decay, there's still vast drama in this weird and remote eyrie, and in the painted salon walls, often roofless and open to the wind. The sumptuous heart of the building has however been made safe.

The kasbah

Driving through Telouet village you bear off to the right, on a signposted track, to the **kasbah**. The road twists round some ruins to a roughly paved courtyard facing massive double doors. Wait a while and you'll be joined by a caretaker-guide (tours 20dh per group), necessary in this case since the building is an unbelievable labyrinth of locked doors and connecting passages; it is said that no single person ever fully knew their way around the complex. Sadly, these days you're shown only the main halls and reception rooms. You can ask to see more – the harem, the kitchens, the cinema – but the usual reply is "*dangereux*", and so it most likely is: if you climb up to the roof (this is generally allowed) you can look down upon some of the courts and chambers, the bright zellij and stucco enclosing great gaping holes in the stone and plaster.

The **reception rooms** – "the outward and visible signs of ultimate physical ambition", in Maxwell's phrase – at least give a sense of the quantity and style of the decoration, still in progress when the Glaouis died and the old regime came to a sudden halt. They have delicate iron window grilles and fine carved ceilings, though the overall result is once again the late nineteenth- and early twentieth-century combination of sensitive imitation of the past and out-and-out vulgarity. There is a tremendous scale of affectation, too, perfectly demonstrated by the use of green Salé tiles for the roof – usually reserved for mosques and royal palaces.

The really enduring impression, though, is the wonder of how and why it ever came to be built at all.

Practicalities

Getting to Telouet is easy enough if you have transport: it is a straightforward 21km drive from the Tizi n'Tichka (P31) road, along the paved 6802. Using **public transport**, there is a daily **bus** from Marrakesh, departing from Bab Rhemat (daily – at around 2–3pm), to Telouet and on to Anemiter (see below); it returns from Anemiter at 6.30am (7am from Telouet). Alternatively, there are shared **grands taxis** from Marrakesh to Anemiter, via Aït Ourir and Telouet.

Telouet itself is tiny, though there are two small **hotels**, the *Auberge Telouet* at the *kasbah* turnoff, which also has two houses in the village (☎04/489 0717) and *Chez Bennouri*, run by Mohammed Benouri (a trekking guide) and his father, in part of an old ksar. There are several **cafés**, which serve meals and a small **souk** takes place on Thursdays.

Irherm and Taddert

IRHERM, 10km beyond the Tichka mountain pass, has a small basic **hotel** and bar, *Chez Mimi* – a reasonable place to stay if you get stuck. **TADDERT**, on the Marrakesh side of the pass, has a dishevelled, rather gloomy and overpriced old **auberge**, *Les Noyers* (☎3 through operator; ➀), though with some compensation in its views and the region's beautiful mountain stream, holm oaks and walnut trees. There's a pleasant half-hour walk to the village of Tamguememt, above the stream.

THE GLAOUI

The extent and speed of **Madani** (1866–1918) and **T'Hami** (1879–1956) **El Glaoui's** rise to power is remarkable enough. In the mid-nineteenth century, their family were simply local clan leaders, controlling an important Atlas pass – a long-established trade route from Marrakesh to the Drâa and Dades valleys – but lacking influence outside of it. Their entrance into national politics began dramatically in 1893. In that year's terrible winter, **Sultan Moulay Hassan**, on returning from a disastrous *harka* (subjugation/burning raid) of the Tafilalt region, found himself at the mercy of the brothers for food, shelter and safe passage. With shrewd political judgement, they rode out to meet the sultan, feting him with every detail of protocol and, miraculously, producing enough food to feed the entire 3000-strong force for the duration of their stay.

The extravagance was well rewarded. By the time Moulay Hassan began his return to Marrakesh, he had given *caid*-ship of all the lands between the High Atlas and the Sahara to the Glaouis and, most important of all, saw fit to abandon vast amounts of the royal armoury (including the first cannon to be seen in the Atlas) in Telouet. By 1901, the brothers had eliminated all opposition in the region, and when **the French** arrived in Morocco in 1912, the Glaouis were able to dictate the form of government for virtually all the south, putting down the attempted nationalist rebellion of El Hiba, pledging loyalty throughout World War I, and having themselves appointed **pashas of Marrakesh**, with their family becoming *caids* in all the main Atlas and desert cities. The French were content to concur, arming them, as Gavin Maxwell wrote, "to rule as despots, [and] perpetuating the corruption and oppression that the Europeans had nominally come to purge".

The strange events of this age – and the legendary personal style of T'Hami El Glaoui – are beautifully evoked in Gavin Maxwell's *Lords of the Atlas*, the brooding romanticism of which almost compels a visit to Telouet:

> *At an altitude of more than 8,000 feet in the High Atlas, [the castle] and its scattered predecessors occupy the corner of a desert plateau, circled by the giant peaks of the Central Massif . . . When in the spring the snows begin to thaw and the river below the castle, the Oued Mellah, becomes a torrent of ice-grey and white, the mountains reveal their fantastic colours, each distinct and contrasting with its neighbour. The hues are for the most part the range of colours to be found upon fan shells – reds, vivid pinks, violets, yellows, but among these are peaks of cold mineral green or of dull blue. Nearer at hand, where the Oued Mellah turns to flow though the Valley of Salt, a cluster of ghostly spires, hundreds of feet high and needle-pointed at their summits, cluster below the face of a precipice; vultures wheel and turn upon the air currents between them . . .*
>
> *Even in this setting the castle does not seem insignificant. It is neither beautiful nor gracious, but its sheer size, as if in competition with the scale of the mountains, compels attention as much as the fact that its pretension somehow falls short of the ridiculous. The castle, or kasbah, of Telouet is a tower of tragedy that leaves no room for laughter.*

The *tizi* at the head of this valley offers green meadows for camping and a route through to the old Glaoui pass via Titoula and the Tizi n' Telouet; a three-day trek.

An **alternative** stopping point, if you are following the Tichka north from Ouarzazate and don't want to carry on to Marrakesh, is **AÏT OURIR**. On the main road, just outside the village, is an attractive **hotel**, *Le Coq Hardi* (☎156 through operator; ②), with a bar, restaurant, swimming pool (not always filled) and garden; it's used by tour groups, so book ahead for a room.

Telouet to Aït Benhaddou

Before the construction of the Tichka road, the **pass from Telouet to Aït Benhaddou** was the main route over the Atlas. It was the presence in the Telouet kasbah of T'Hami's xenophobic and intransigent cousin, Hammou ("The Vulture"), that caused the French to construct a road along the more difficult route to the west.

If you have four-wheel drive (or a mountain bike), or want a good two-day walk, it is possible to follow the old pass, heading south from Telouet along the 6803 *piste*. This is surfaced as far as Anemiter but pretty rough beyond there, and requires fording at several points – most precariously just north of Aït Benhaddou, where a bridge collapsed in floods in 1989.

All in all, it is 35km from Telouet to Aït Benhaddou. If you are walking or biking, the route offers tranquillity and unparalleled views of green valleys, a river that splashes down the whole course and remarkable coloured scree slopes amid the high, parched hillsides. Despite the absence of settlements on most of the maps, much of the **valley** has scattered communities, all making abundant use of the narrow but fertile valley. This unveils a wealth of dark red and crumbling **kasbahs**, collections of homes grouped among patchworks of wheatfields, terraced orchards, olive trees, date palms and figs – and everywhere children calling to each other from the fields, the river or the roadside. You will need to take provisions for the trip but mules can be hired at Anemiter and Telouet. From Telouet trails southwards take trekkers on an alternative route to that given below, though this should not be tackled in high summer.

Telouet to Anemiter

There are shared taxis (and the daily bus) between Telouet and **ANEMITER** (12km), one of the largest and best-preserved fortified villages in Morocco. It has a basic *auberge* (☎04/489 0780). Elyazid Mohammed and his brother offer village accommodation, and the brothers Bouchahoud, both mountain guides, have a fine *gîte* at Tighza near the end of the Oued Ounila *piste* (☎04/444 5499).

At the head of the Oued Ounila on which Anemiter stands lies the huge sprawl of Anrhomer (3607m) and the smaller Zarzamt. Between them lie the turquoise **Tamda lakes**. Beyond here, crossing the Tizi n'Fedrahate, a *piste* from the south breaks over to the splendid **Tessaout valley** and, from Aït Timlil, climbs north to Demnate. North of this area lies a magnificent and almost unknown trekking area, surprising when it has such notable entry routes. The **Bou Goumez/Mgoun** area further east (see p.264) is second only to Toubkal in popularity. Trekking right through on long west–east links is highly recommended (and detailed in Peyron's guide).

Anemiter to Aït Benhaddou

There are occasional truck-taxis (*camionettes*) south of Anemiter, along the *piste*, but if you're setting out without transport it would be best to accept that you'll walk most of the way to Tamdaght, where the road resumes; it takes around ten hours.

Leaving Anemiter, the main mule track clings to the valley side, alternately climbing and descending, but with a general downhill trend as you make your way south. After three kilometres you cross a sturdy bridge. Beyond here the *piste* follows the left bank of the river to the hamlet of Assako (2hr 30min walk from Anemiter), where it climbs to the left round some spectacular gorges and then drops steeply.

Walkers should aim to get beyond this exposed high ground before camping. At Tourhat, around six or seven hours from Anemiter, you might be able to find a room in a village home. Another three hours south of Tourhat, the trail brings you to **TAMDAGHT**, a scattered collection of buildings with a classic **kasbah**. This was used as a setting for an MGM epic, and retains some of its authentic Hollywood decor, along with ancient and rickety storks' nests on the battlements.

From **Tamdaght to Aït Benhaddou** the road is again paved to Aït Benhaddou (see p.423), where there are cafés and three simple hotels where you can pick up a taxi (or usually hitch a lift) on to Ouarzazate.

Marrakesh to Agadir: the Tizi Maachou

The direct route from **Marrakesh to Agadir** – the **Imi n'Tanoute**, or **Tizi Maachou**, pass – is, in itself, the least spectacular of the Atlas roads but if you are in a hurry to get south it is a reasonably fast trip (4hr drive to Agadir) and when the Test and Tichka passes are closed through snow, it normally remains open. Its hinterland also offers some exciting trekking, well off the beaten track, for more on which see the section below ("Tichka Plateau treks").

Chichaoua, Imi n'Tanoute and the pass

Leaving Marrakesh, most of the buses follow the Essaouira road (P10) as far as **CHICHAOUA**, a small village and administrative centre with several cafés and **hotels**, and a makeshift campsite, with no facilities or security. The village is set at the entrance to the mountains, and is famed in a small way for its carpets. Brightly coloured and often using stylized animal forms, they are sold at the local **Centre Coopératif** and also at the **Thursday market**. The village is the most pleasant stop along the road to break your journey. Beyond Chichaoua, the **road to Essaouira** continues across the drab Chiadma plains. Sidi Mokhtar, 25km on from Chichaoua, has a **Wednesday souk** with an attractive array of carpets.

For **Agadir**, you begin a slow climb towards **IMI N'TANOUTE**, another administrative centre, with a **Monday souk**, and then cut through the last outlying peaks of the High Atlas. Imi n'Tanoute is of little interest, though if you need to stay before setting out on a trek (see below), there are **rooms** at a couple of the cafés, and provisions. There is a minor tarred road, the 6403, which breaks off the Marrakesh–Essaouira road just west of the Pont du Nfis and goes direct to Imi n'Tanoute. It's no faster but pleasantly unbusy.

A few kilometres further along from Imi n'Tanoute on the Agadir road, the phrase "Allah – Nation – King" (Alla–al-Watan–al-Malik) is picked out in painted stone letters, over 15m high, on the hillside. Beyond it is the pass, **Tizi Maachou**, at 1700m. The road, often lined with locals selling bottles of golden argan oil (see p.487) passes the **dams of Tanizaourt** before descending to the fertile **Souss Valley**, with its intensive greenhouse cultivation. If you are planning to trek into the Atlas from Timesgadiouine or Argana (see pp.411–413), make sure you get dropped at the appropriate turnoff.

Western High Atlas: Tichka Plateau treks

Exploring the **Tichka Plateau** and the **western fringes of the Atlas**, you move well away from the tourist routes, miles away from any organized refuge, and pass through Berber villages which see scarcely a foreigner from one year to the next. You'll need to carry provisions, and be prepared to camp or possibly stay in a Berber village home if you get the invitation – as you almost certainly will. Sanitation is poor in the villages and it's not a bad idea to bring water purification tablets if you plan to take water from mountain streams – unless you're higher than all habitation (see also box on Trekking, pp.388–389). Eating and drinking in mountain village homes, though, is surprisingly safe as the food (mainly tajines) is cooked slowly and the drink is invariably mint tea.

Getting into these mountains, there are approaches from both north and south: **Imi n'Tanoute**, **Timesgadiouine** and **Argana**, on the main Marrakesh–Agadir bus route (north), and **Taroudannt–Oualed Behril** (south). From the north approaches, rides on trucks bound for mines or markets at trailheads have to be used; from the south, *camionettes* ply up daily to Imoulas, the Medlawa Valley and Tigouga.

The *IGN* 1:100,000 maps for the area are *Tizi n'Test* and *Igli*, available from Atlas Maps (see p.31).

Imi n'Tanoute to the Tichka Plateau

A dirt road leads up into the mountains from Imi n'Tanoute to **Afensou**, nearby where a Thursday market (Al Khemis) is held, making your best chance of a lift up on Wednesday with one of the lorries. This trip takes several hours, so don't arrive late in Imi n'Tanoute or you might get stranded. The road (not really suitable for ordinary passenger cars) crosses the **Tizi n'Tabghourt** at 2666m, from where you can ascend Djebel Tabghourt offering a magnificent panorama of the Western Atlas, often white with snow until early summer.

At Afensou you are in the **Haut Seksawa** with some of the highest mountain walks in the Atlas lying to the south and holding the romantic **Tichka Plateau** in their midst. **Moulay Ali** (3349m) dominates and the ridge from it to the main chain remains unclimbed. The **Tizi Asdim** gives the easiest access to the Tichka Plateau, passing under **Djebel Ikkis** (3183m) and other climbing peaks. A few other *tizis* offer routes across the range and the traversing of the main ridge provides an exceptionally good multi-day trip with plenty of scrambling.

Afensou can also be reached on a new, better *piste* from **Timesgadiouine** (serving the mines above the village) which makes a spectacular crest-route into the Seksawa (see below).

Timesgadiouine and the Aït Driss

The second access point to the mountains along the Marrakesh–Agadir road is **TIMESGADIOUINE**, about 50km south of Imi n'Tanoute. A signposted road leads off beside a café/petrol station. The actual village is 3–4km along the dirt road.

Souk Sebt Talmakent

SOUK SEBT TALMAKENT is most easily arrived at by using the lorries which drive up on Friday afternoons for the Saturday souks, or which go up during the week to the mines above Afensou. passing through Souk Sebt Talmakent on the way. Be prepared for a wait and a long dusty ride. If you ride up on Friday afternoon, you can camp overnight. Basic food items can be bought here. There are one or two cafés but no rooms, although the government workers posted to this nowhere place might offer you a room in their offices.

The Aït Driss

The **Aït Driss River** winds its way just below Souk Sebt Talmakent. It's a pretty valley that narrows to a gorge for a kilometre or two before spreading out and filling up with walnut trees and Berber villages. As you trek up, several other tributaries come down on your right from the main ridge. The two most conspicuous peaks, **Tinerghwet** (3551m) and **Awlim** (3482m), are the same two you can see from Taroudannt, which lies in the Souss plain on their far side. Turn up any of these tributaries for an interesting day's trek. For camping, you're better off in the Aït Driss Valley, where the ground is flatter.

In September you'll see entire families out for the **walnut harvest**. The men climb high into the trees to beat the branches with long poles. Underneath, the women and children gather the nuts, staining their hands black for weeks from the outer shells. In this part of the Atlas, the women often wear their hair in bunches that hang down the sides of their faces.

To the head of the Aït Driss

You can reach the **head of the Aït Driss** at Tamjlocht in a day's trekking from Souk Sebt Talmakent. From there a steep climb over the **Tizi n'Wannas** pass (2367m) takes you to Tizza, a small village at the head of the parallel valley, the Warguiwn. From Tizza trek east up a small valley 2–3km, then climb up **Tizi n'Timirout** (2280m) – which is not named on the survey map. There's a dramatic view of the main ridge from this pass, its rugged peaks stretching to the northeast. The most prominent one is Moulay Ali at 3349m. Afensou (see p.411) awaits you after a long descent, from where you can hitch back out to Souk Sebt Talmakent or Imi n'Tanoute or continue trekking to the Tizi n'Test road.

The Aït Driss Valley can be followed to its head (mule track) and the Tizi n'Tizzert crossed to southern villages (see below). This also gives access to Mtadene (3366m) and the main crest westwards.

Argana to Djebel Tichka

ARGANA, the third access point, lies off on a signposted road to the left some kilome-tres on down the Agadir road, a large town but virtually abandoned since the new road bypassed it, and with something of the appearance of a frontier town in the Wild West. An old kasbah above points to its one-time importance.

Careful questioning and a long walk will lead you to **Tafilatt** and **Arg**, villages under the high wall of **Djebel Tichka**, gained by brutally steep tracks. A little below the crest on the other side lies the Oued Tichka, which breaks out to the south (a notable water channel leads its waters to the north side). Following this river to reach the peaks of **Tinerghwet** and **Awlim** is one of the most rewarding ventures of its kind. Both peaks demand some scrambling and route-finding abilities and Awlim has acres of unclimbed

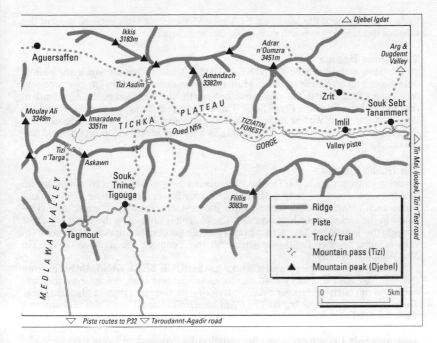

△ *Djebel Igdat*

Ikkis 3183m

Adrar n'Oumzra 3451m

Aguersaffen

Arg & Ougdemt Valley

Amendach 3382m

Tizi Asdim

Zrit

Souk Sebt Tanammert

Moulay Ali 3349m

PLATEAU

Imaradene 3351m TICHKA

Oued Nfis

TIZIATIN FOREST

Imlil

GORGE

Valley piste

Tizi n'Targa

Askawn

Souk Tnine, Tigouga

Flilis 3083m

△ *Tin Mal, Ijoukak, Tizi n'Test road*

Tagmout

	Ridge
	Piste
-----	Track / trail
⌇	Mountain pass (Tizi)
▲	Mountain peak (Djebel)

MEDLAWA VALLEY

0   5km

▽ *Piste routes to P32* ▽ *Taroudannt-Agadir road*

cliffs. Passes southwards to Tasguint and Imoulas can round off a visit to this little-visited area.

Southern approach to the Tichka Plateau

In the last few years the potential for mountain exploration in the Western High Atlas and "lost world" of the Tichka Plateau (and the beautiful valleys leading up to the heights) has been realized. Going it your own way, *camionettes* from Taroudannt (see p.491) and Ould Behril ply up to **Tasguint, Imoulas, Tagmout** and **Souk Tnine Tigouga**, from where mule trails lead over the crests. The main routes are outlined below.

Imoulas

IMOULAS is the main town of the foothills, with a Sunday souk. From here a *piste* extends for about 6km northwest to Tinighas, from where there is a dramatic route through a gorge to high *azibs* and a hard ascent to **Djebel Tinerghwet** (3551m), the highest peak in the area, and **Awlim** (3482m). East of Awlim extends the "**Ridge of a Hundred Peaks**", running on to the distant Tichka Plateau. Awlim's east face has climbing potential; a branch *piste* goes to Tasguint and the Tizi n'Ifguig which gives access to the route.

Tagmout

Houses may offer accommodation here or at the end of the *piste*, up the beautiful Medlawa Valley. A long zigzag mule track reaches the Tizi n'Targa, at the head of the Tichka Plateau. Tagmout/Tigouga *camionettes* leave from east of Taroudannt so from there Imoulas is the easiest access point. A superb two-day trek (three if from Tasguint) leads to Alekjane and the Medlawa. El Aouad Ali (see p.495) has inspired most of the western trekking and is worth contacting in Taroudannt.

Souk Tnine Tigouga

As the name suggests, **SOUK TNINE TIGOUGA** has a **Monday souk**, the easiest time to get a lift up (or out of) here. Mule tracks west and east of Awlim give access to the Tichka Plateau and the only pass out north, the Tizi Asdim, to Aguersaffen, Afensou and the Seksawa. From Souk Tnine Tigouga a *piste* curls east to several villages and the Tizi n'Waddir mule track onto the lower Tichka Plateau. Djebel Flillis (3083m) in the ridges jutting to the south, is a worthy objective for experienced hillgoers.

The Tichka Plateau

However you approach it, the **Tichka Plateau** is a delight. Grazing is controlled so the meadows are a mass of early daffodils and spring flowers. **Imaradene** (3351m) and **Amendach** (3382m) are the highest summits, west and east, and are superlative viewpoints in the secluded northeast corner. The plateau is drained by the Oued Nfis, first through the Tiziatin oak forest, using or bypassing gorges, then undergoing a series of villages, one, another Imlil, is a shrine to the Toumert, the founder of the Tin Mal/Almohad dynasty.

A two-day trek from the plateau will take you to **SOUK SEBT TANAMMERT**. From this Saturday market, a lorry road climbs up to the Test road, not far from the pass itself. You can hitch out here or continue trekking for two more days to Mzouzite, near Tin Mal: one day north to Arg via Tizi n'Aghbar (2653m) and Tizi n'Tiddi (2744m), and the second day east along the long Ougdemt Valley to Mzouzite, as described under the Tizi n'Test section (see p.403). An excellent trail also descends the Oued Nfis Valley from Souk Sebt Tanammert, going through beautiful gorges and forested countryside. An exceptional walk linking the Tichka Plateau to Djebel Toubkal using guides/mules from Taroudannt and Imlil for successive sections, is available from the trekking company, AMIS (see p.5).

travel details

Buses

Marrakesh (**Bab Doukkala** terminal) to: Agadir (20 daily; 4hr); Ouarzazate (6 daily; 4–5hr); Taroudannt (4 daily; 6hr 30min)

Buses to **Ourika**, **Asni** (the trailhead for Djebel Toubkal; 1hr 30min), and **Moulay Brahim**, leave from just outside **Bab Er Robb**. (Some buses also run to Asni from the Bab Doukkala bus station). At times Ourika and Asni departures may be from further out on the appropriate roads. The bus/taxi station is closed during royal visits.

Grands taxis

Grands taxis run from Marrakesh to **Ourika** and **Asni** – negotiate for these by Bab Er Robb (12.5dh is the local rate for a place to Asni).

CHAPTER SEVEN

THE GREAT SOUTHERN OASIS ROUTES

Immediately when you arrive in the Sahara, for the first or the tenth time, you notice the stillness. An incredible, absolute silence prevails outside the towns; and within, even in busy places like the markets, there is a hushed quality in the air, as if the quiet were a constant force which, resenting the intrusion of sound, minimizes and disperses it straightaway. Then there is the sky, compared to which all other skies seem faint-hearted efforts. Solid and luminous, it is always the focal point of the landscape. At sunset, the precise, curved shadow of the earth rises into it swiftly from the horizon, cutting it into light section and dark section. When all daylight has gone, and the space is thick with stars, it is still of an intense and burning blue, darkest directly overhead and paling toward the earth, so that the night never really grows dark.

Paul Bowles: *The Baptism of Solitude*

The Moroccan pre-Sahara begins as soon as you cross the Atlas to the south. It is not sand for the most part – more a wasteland of rock and scrub – but it is powerfully impressive. The quote from Paul Bowles may sound over the top, but staying at M'hamid or Merzouga, or just stopping a car on a desert road between towns, somehow has this effect.

There is, too, an irresistible sense of wonder as you catch a first glimpse of the great southern river valleys – the **Drâa**, **Dadès**, **Todra**, **Ziz** and **Tafilalt**. Long belts of date palm oases, scattered with the fabulous mud architecture of kasbahs and fortified *ksour* villages, these are the old caravan routes that reached back to Marrakesh and Fes and out across the Sahara to Timbuktu, Niger and old Sudan, carrying gold, slaves and salt well into the nineteenth century. They are beautiful routes, even today, tamed by modern roads and with the oases in decline, and if you're travelling in Morocco for any length of time, they are a must. The simplest circuits – **Marrakesh–Zagora–Marrakesh**, or **Marrakesh–Tinerhir–Midelt** – can be covered in around five days, though to do them any degree of justice you need a lot longer.

The **southern oases** were long a mainstay of the precolonial economy. Their wealth, and the arrival of tribes from the desert, provided the impetus for two of the great royal dynasties: the Saadians (1154–1669) from the Drâa Valley, and the present ruling family, the Alaouites (1669–) from the Tafilalt. By the nineteenth century, however, the advance of the Sahara and the uncertain upkeep of the water channels had reduced life to bare subsistence even in the most fertile strips. Under the French, with the creation of modern industry in the north and the exploitation of phosphates and minerals, they became less and less significant, while the old caravan routes were dealt a final death blow by the closure of the Algerian border after independence. The pattern of the last twenty-five years has been one of steady emigration to the northern cities.

Today, there are a few urban centres in the south; **Ouarzazate** and **Er Rachidia** are the largest and both were created by the French to "pacify" the south; they seem only to underline the end of an age. Although the date harvests in October, centred on

Erfoud can still give employment to the *ksour* communities, the rest of the year sees only the modest production of a handful of crops – henna, barley, citrus fruits and uniquely roses – the latter developed by the French around **El Kelâa des Mgouna** for the production of rose-water and perfume in May. And to make matters worse, in recent years the seasonal rains have frequently failed. Perhaps as much as half the male population of the *ksour* now seeks work in the north for at least part of the year.

Tourism brings in a little money, particularly to Ouarzazate and Zagora – once the Gate of the Desert (52 days to Timbuktu) – but it too declined in the 1990s, leaving many hotels empty or, in the case of Ouarzazate, unfinished.

OUARZAZATE AND THE DRÂA

Ouarzazate – easily reached from Marrakesh (6hr by bus) – is the main access point and crossroads of the south. East of the town stretches the Dadès River, the "Valley of the Thousand Kasbahs", as promoted by the Ministry of Tourism. South, on the other side of a tremendous ridge of the Anti-Atlas, begins the **Drâa Valley** – 125km of date palm oases, which eventually merge into the Sahara near the village of M'hamid.

▽ *Tanezrouft route to Mali*

It is possible to complete a circuit through and out from the Drâa, heading from the valley's main town, **Zagora**, across *piste* roads west through Foum Zguid and Tata to the Anti-Atlas, or north into the Djebel Sarhro (an October to April trekking area – see pp.440–444 for details), or east across to Rissani in the Tafilalt. However, most visitors content themselves with a return trip along the main **P31** between Ouarzazate and Zagora: a great route, taking you well south of anywhere in the Tafilalt, and flanked by an amazing series of turreted and cream-pink-coloured *ksour*.

Ouarzazate

At some stage, you're almost bound to spend a night in **OUARZAZATE** and it can be a useful base from which to visit the *ksour* and kasbahs of Aït Benhaddou or Skoura. It is not exactly compelling in itself, however. Like most of the new Saharan towns, it was created as a garrison and administrative centre by the French in the late 1920s and remains pretty much the same today: a deliberate line of functional buildings, together with an array of modern hotels, set along the main highway and lent an odd sort of permanence by the use of concrete in place of the *pisé* of the *ksour*.

TRANSPORT

All the main road routes in this chapter are covered by regular **buses**, and often grands taxis. On many of the others, local **Berber trucks** (*camionettes*) or **Landrover and transit taxis** (detailed in the text) run a bus-type service, charging standard fares for their trips, which are usually timed to coincide with the network of souks or markets in villages en route. The trucks cover a number of adventurous desert *pistes* – such as the direct routes from Zagora to Foum Zguid and Tata or to Rissani – and some very rough roads over the Atlas behind the Dadès or Todra gorges. If you plan to **drive** on these, you'll need to have a decent vehicle (4x4s are essential for some routes) and be able to do basic mechanical repairs.

Travelling by bus in the desert, in summer, the main disadvantage is the sheer physical exhaustion involved: most trips tend to begin at dawn to avoid the worst of the heat and, for the rest of the day, it can be difficult to summon up the energy to do anything. If you can afford to **rent a car** – even for just two or three days – you'll be able to take in a lot more, with a lot less frustration, in a reasonably short period of time. There are numerous rental outlets in Ouarzazate, most of which allow you to return their vehicles to Agadir, Marrakesh, Fes, or even Casablanca.

Petrol stations can be found along all the main routes, but they're not exactly plentiful. Fill the tank whenever and wherever you have the opportunity. It's wise to carry **water**, too, in case of overheating, and, above all, be sure you've got a good **spare tyre** – punctures tend to be frequent on all southern roads. As throughout the country, however, local **mechanics** are excellent (Er Rachidia has an especially good reputation) and most minor – and routine – problems can be quickly dealt with.

CLIMATE AND SEASONS

Temperatures can climb well above 50°C in midsummer and you'll find the middle of the day is best spent being totally inactive. If you have the option, spring is by far the most enjoyable time to travel – particularly if you're heading for Zagora (reckoned to be the hottest town in the country), or Rissani-Merzouga. Autumn, with the date harvests, is also good. In winter, the days remain hot, though it can get fairly cool at night, and further south into the desert, it can actually freeze. Some kind of light hat or cap, and sunglasses, are pretty much essential.

Be aware, too, that the Drâa, in particular, is subject to **flash floods** in spring, as the snow melts in the Atlas and forges the river currents. Passes across the Atlas at this time, and even trips such as Ouarzazate to Aït Benhaddou or Skoura, can be difficult or impossible.

HEALTH

Rivers in the south are reputed to contain **bilharzia**, a parasite that can enter your skin, including the soles of your feet, so, even when walking by streams in the oases, take care to avoid contact.

During the 1980s, Ouarzazate was a bit of a boom town. The tourist industry embarked on a wildly optimistic building programme of luxury hotels, based on Ouarzazate's marketability as a staging point for the "Saharan Adventure", and the town was given an additional boost from the attentions of movie-makers. The region first came to prominence in the film world forty years ago, when David Lean shot *Lawrence of Arabia* (1962) at nearby Aït Benhaddou and in the Tafilalt, and in the 1990s numerous directors – most famously Bernardo Bertolucci, filming Paul Bowles's novel, *The Sheltering Sky* (1990) – used the town as a base. The town even spawned its own film studios, the Atlas Corporation, 6km northwest on the main road (P31) towards Marrakesh. The Gulf War interruption to tourism, however, and the recessionary 1990s

HOTEL PRICE CODES

The basis of our **hotel price codes**, set out below and keyed throughout the guide, is the price currently quoted for the cheapest double room in high season (June–September).

Note that cheaper prices in the lower categories are generally for rooms with just a washbasin – you always pay extra for **en-suite** shower and WC – and that double rooms can generally be converted into **triples/family rooms**, with extra beds, for a modest extra charge. Single occupancy usually costs about two-thirds the price of a double, though in some places a single person will pay the same rate for a room as two people sharing, and in other places exactly half as much. Prices quoted are for bed only, without breakfast, but including local taxes.

① 40–100dh	③ 150–200dh	⑤ 400–800dh
② 100–150dh	④ 200–400dh	⑥ over 800dh

have left Ouarzazate with a rather depressed air and many of its hotels unfinished or vacant. In anticipation of more traffic, the authorities built a new bypass to the north of the town, but the traffic, at present, isn't here.

Despite these developments and disappointments, Ouarzazate still has a mystic attraction for Moroccans – similar to the resonance of Timbuktu for Europeans. Indeed, many urban Moroccans respond to any mention of Ouarzazate with the odd rejoinder: "see Ouarzazate and die". Maybe this dates from the adventures of the Foreign Legion in the 1930s. If so, the only echo today is the early morning bugle sounding reveille behind the walls of the barracks.

Orientation, arrival and information

Orientation is simply a matter of getting your bearings along the old highway and main road, **Avenue Mohammed V**, at the east end of which is the town's main sight, Kasbah Taorirt. The **CTM bus station** more or less marks the centre, with the **PTT** alongside. Private line long-distance **buses** now operate from a new bus station on the bypass to the north of town. To reach the centre from here, you'll need to take a petit taxi. **Grands taxis** operate from alongside both the CTM and new bus stations. Ouarzazate's **airport** is just 2km north of town and served by local taxis.

The helpful **tourist office** (☎04/488 2458; Mon–Fri, 8.15–11.30am & 2.15–4.30pm) is on Avenue Mohammed V, just across from the PTT.

Accommodation

Finding a hotel room should present few problems. Most of the cheaper and unclassified places are grouped in the centre of town; the more upmarket ones are mainly set back on the plateau to the north. More romantic alternatives would be to stay at Kasbah Tifoultoutte (see p.422) or Aït Benhaddou (see p.423).

The campsite, **Camping Restaurant Ouarzazate** (☎04/488 4636), is 4km east of the centre, just past the Kasbah Taorirt. It's a well-maintained site, with clean toilets and showers, but limited shade. Meals are available and alongside it is the municipal swimming pool, now incorporated in the Complex Touristique Le Ouarzazate (see p.423).

Cheap

Hôtel Amlal, 24 Rue du Marché, near junction with Av. Prince Heritier Sidi Mohammed (☎04/488 4030, fax 488 4600). A newish hotel which is reasonably comfortable and decent value for money, though the restaurant functions only for breakfast, and the area is a bit desolate – but safe enough and with a *gardien* to look after parked cars. ②.

Hôtel Atlas, 13 Rue du Marché (☎04/488 2307, fax 488 6400). Some rooms have showers, others use showers on the corridor; in both cases hot water in the evenings. A possible fall-back if the nearby *Hôtel Royal* is full. ①.

Hôtel Bab Sahara, Place Mouahidine (☎04/488 4722, fax 488 4465). A 1990s-built hotel, convenient for the CTM bus station, grands taxis and shops. The café serves breakfast, and there's a restaurant upstairs. The only drawback is that it's in the noisiest quarter of town. ②.

Hôtel Royal, 24 Av. Mohammed V (☎04/488 2258). This is the best of the real cheapies, with a variety of rooms, priced accordingly; it's central and can be noisy. ①.

Moderate

Hôtel La Gazelle, Av. Mohammed V (☎04/488 2151, fax 488 4727). This old hotel, with its attractive garden courtyard full of birdlife, is being improved with a new wing. In the meantime its restaurant and noisy bar continue as before. Useful for late arrivals or early departures, particularly if you have your own transport; otherwise you might be better off in the town centre. ③.

Hôtel Saghro, 1km south of the town in the Tabount district and on the Zagora road (☎04/485 4135, fax 485 4145). A modern hotel and a bargain, although it's some distance from the centre. There are a few shops and a petrol station nearby. ③.

Kasbah Tifoultoutte (☎ & fax 04/488 5899). A converted kasbah, 7km out of town, offering half-board. See p.422 for details. ④.

Hôtel La Vallée, also in the Tabount district (☎04/485 4035, fax 485 5043). Arguably the best value around; the only drawback is the distance from the town centre, compensated by meals by the pool and dawn from the terrace. Used for overnights by trekking groups, including Exodus and Explore. ③.

Hôtel Residence Al Warda, Av. Mohammed V on corner with Place du 3 Mars (☎04/488 2154). On first sight these well-equipped apartments are an attractive option, but they have not been well maintained. A fall-back option. ③.

Expensive

Hôtel Kenzi Azghor, Av. Prince Moulay Rachid (☎04/488 6501, fax 488 6353). This established hotel has fabulous views to the south and a good-sized swimming pool. It joined the Kenzi chain in 1995, and is probably the best in Ouarzazate. ⑤.

Hôtel Bélère, Av. Prince Moulay Rachid (☎04/488 2203, fax 488 3145). A little more fancy than the *Hôtel Azghor* and more expensive; once again it has a fine swimming pool. ⑤.

Hôtel Le Meridien Berber Palace, Av. Prince Moulay Rachid (☎04/488 3105, fax 488 3071). A state-of-the-art hotel that looks like a film set for *The Arabian Nights*. ⑥.

The Town and Kasbahs

Aside from the local Glaoui Kasbah of **Taorirt**, and that of **Tifoultoutte**, 10km out on the old southern bypass, Ouarzazate has little in the way of sights. If it's not too hot, a good walk is to the **El Mansour Eddahbi Barrage** (east of the town), quite a sight in spring after heavy rains. If you follow the bank round to the east of the lake you come to the semi-ruined **kasbah**, a romantic spot for a picnic or photocall.

There is little else in – or to – Ouarzazate, and really the most interesting option is to get out for the day, either to Aït Benhaddou (see p.423) or a little along the Dadès to Skoura – a beautiful and rambling oasis (see p.435), easily accessible as a day-trip using the Boumalne/Tinerhir buses.

Kasbah Taorirt

The **Kasbah Taorirt** (8am–6.30pm) stands to the right of Avenue Mohammed V, at the east (Tinerhir direction) end of town. It's a dusty, twenty-minute walk from the bus stations.

Although built by the Glaoui, the kasbah was never an actual residence of its chiefs. However, located at this strategic junction of the southern trading routes, it was always controlled by a close relative. In the 1930s, when the Glaoui were the undisputed masters of the south, it was perhaps the largest of all Moroccan kasbahs – an enormous family domain housing numerous sons and cousins of the dynasty, along with several hundred of their servants and labourers, builders and craftsmen, even semi-itinerant Jewish tailors and moneylenders.

Since then, and especially since being taken over by the government after independence, the kasbah has fallen into drastic decline. In 1994, the government announced plans to "rehabilitate" the kasbah – and also those at Aït Benhaddou (see opposite) but currently the work has still not started and parts of the structure have disappeared, washed away by heavy rains; others are completely unsafe, and it is only a small section of the original, a kind of village within the kasbah, that remains occupied today. That part is towards the rear of the rambling complex of rooms, courtyards and alleyways. What you are shown is just the main reception courtyard and a handful of principal rooms, lavishly decorated but not especially significant or representative of the old order of things. With an eye, perhaps, to tourism, they are known as "the harem".

Crafts
Opposite the Kasbah Taorirt is the **Centre Artisanal** (Mon–Fri 8.30am–noon & 3–6.30pm, Sat 8.30am–noon, Sun 10am–noon), a complex of half a dozen or so little shops with good quality items at fixed (but not cheap) prices. Besides stone carvings and pottery, look for two local specialities: the geometrically patterned, silky woollen carpets of the region's Ouzguita Berbers, and the silver jewellery – necklaces and earrings incorporating *tazras* (chunky orange copal beads). There are also musical instruments used for the *ahouach*, a dance usually performed in the light of great fires until the first rays of daylight. Finally, there's Rachid Maatallah's minerals shop at no. 6, and Mohammed Ouirghare, next door at no. 7, has stone carvings and pottery.

There are many shops on Avenue Mohammed V and, after studying the items at the **Centre Artisanal**, you may choose to try your bargaining skills there. Better still, but more difficult to find, is the **Maison Berbère** in the Tabount district, the other side of the river on the road to Zagora; this is a branch of the Alaoui family chain selling high quality carpets and rugs in towns south of Ouarzazate: Zagora, Tinerhir and Rissani.

Kasbah Tifoultoutte
Around seven kilometres from Ouarzazate is the **Kasbah of Tifoultoutte** (8am–7pm), originally owned by the Glaoui clan. It stands majestically on the banks of the Oued Tifoultoutte, though it's rather more impressive from a distance than on entry. To reach it, cross the river to the Tabount district and turn right as if going to the Maison Berbère and then continue along the road to Marrakesh.

In the 1960s, the kasbah was converted into a hotel for the cast of *Lawrence of Arabia*. Today it offers half board and a restaurant specializing in tour groups (daily noon–11pm). It's also open for **visits** which include panoramic views from the roof.

Eating

There are reasonable but pricey **restaurants** at all the large hotels and the two tourist complexes (see listings), cheap **café-grills** grouped round Place Mouahidine and along the nearby Rue du Marché.

Cafés and restaurants
Restaurant Chez Dimitri, 22 Av. Mohammed V (next to *Hôtel Royal*). Founded in 1928 to serve the Foreign Legion, this bar-brasserie is licensed and has a wide-ranging menu (80dh). Patronized by film stars, tourists and occasional locals. The photographs of the early days contribute to the mystique of Ouarzazate.

Etoile du Sud, facing the Kasbah Taorirt. A reliable, friendly restaurant, open all hours and serving traditional Moroccan meals starting at 40dh.

Glacier 3 Mars, 7 Place du 3 Mars. Cheap café-brasserie, popular with locals.

Chez Nabil, Rue de la Poste (near the Cinéma Atlas). Good for breakfasts and snacks.

Restaurant Royal (aka *Chez Boussalem*), 24 Av. Mohammed V. A small, not terribly imaginative place, but value-for-money meals at around 65dh.

Restaurant Es Salam, (aka *Chez Moulay*) Av. Prince Heritier Sidi Mohammed. An excellent, inexpensive restaurant, unconnected with the (not very good) hotel next door: *menu du jour* 60dh.
Café Restaurant des Voyageurs, Av. Mohammed V, near the post office. More café than restaurant – the breakfasts are good and convenient for the bus stations.

Tourist complexes

Complexe Touristique Le Ouarzazate (☎04/488 3110, 488 4406) in the Sidi Daoud district (alongside the campsite) has a restaurant seating 600 and most evenings there are displays of song, music and dance. The complex incorporates the municipal swimming pool and entry and use of all its facilities costs 30dh.
Ksar El Farrah (aka *Fantasia*), also in the Sidi Daoud district. This specializes in *fantasias* and serves lunches in the shade of tents (☎04/488 5555).

Listings

Airport The Aeroport Taorirt is 2km north of town, and served by petits taxis. There are daily RAM flights to Casablanca and less frequently to Al Hoceima, Fes, Oujda, Tangier and Tetouan. RAM has an office at 1 Av. Mohammed V (☎04/488 5102, fax 488 6893).
Banks All the banks are on the north side of Av. Mohammed V. They include (moving west to east): Crédit du Maroc, Wafabank, BMCE, BCM and Banque Populaire.
Bikes – including mountain bikes – can be rented from Ksour Voyages, 11 Place du 3 Mars.
Car rental Avis, Place du Mars (☎04/488 7870, fax 488 4310); Budget, Av. Mohammed V, next to the *Hôtel Residence Al Warda* (☎04/488 4202, fax 488 4212); Europcar/InterRent, Place du Mars (☎04/488 2035, fax 488 4027); Hertz, 33 Av. Mohammed V (☎04/488 2084, fax 488 3485); National Car Rental, Place du Mars (☎04/488 5244, fax 488 5260).
Car repairs Garage Raquiq El Habib, Quartier Industriel No. 99 (☎04/488 4933) is recommended.
Cinema Cinéma Atlas, Rue de la Poste, next to the *Hôtel Es Saada*.
Post office The PTT on Av. Mohammed V has *poste restante* facilities, plus a direct-dialling international phone section; it's open Mon–Sat 8.30am–noon & 2.30–6pm.
Shopping The Super Marché, 73 Av. Mohammed V, opposite *Chez Dimitri* is well stocked, including beer and wine, and is open until 10pm; just the place to stock up for picnics.
Tours If you're passing through Ouarzazate and have an urge to explore around M'Hamid and further south, try Iriqui Excursions, Place du Mars (☎04/488 5799, fax 488 4991) which has tours on *Le Circuit St Exupéry* and visits to places associated with the Paris-Dakar Rally.

Moving on

There are **CTM services**, leaving from their station near the PTT, to Agadir (via Taliouine, Taroudannt and Inezgane), Casablanca, Er Rachidia, Marrakesh, M'Hamid and Zagora. SATAS and other long-distance buses go from the new *gare routière* on the bypass by the *Hôtel Habil;* they're cheaper, but take longer. Between them they run as – or more – frequently than CTM, but timings often change.

Grands taxis leave from alongside the CTM bus station on regular runs along the Dadès to Boumalne (30dh a place; connections on towards Tinerhir and Er Rachidia), and can be negotiated for Marrakesh or Zagora.

Aït Benhaddou

The first thing you hear from the guides on arrival at **AÏT BENHADDOU**, 32km from Ouarzazate, is a list of its movie credits. This is a feature of much of the Moroccan south – where landscapes are routinely fantastic and cheap, exotic-looking extras are in plentiful supply – but, even so, the Benhaddou kasbahs have a definite edge over the competition. *Lawrence of Arabia* was filmed here, of course; Orson Welles used it as a location for *Sodom and Gomorrah*; and for *Jesus of Nazareth* the whole lower part of the village was rebuilt. In recent years, more controlled restoration has been carried out under UNESCO auspices and, in 1994 the government announced plans to "rehabilitate" Aït Benhaddou in order to conserve the national and cultural heritage.

Aït Benhaddou is not really the place to catch a glimpse of fading kasbah life but it is one of the most spectacular sights of the Atlas, piled upon a dark shaft of rock above a shallow, reed-strewn river. Its collection of kasbahs are among the most elaborately decorated and best preserved; they are less fortified than is usually the case along the Drâa or the Dadès, but, towered and crenellated, and with high, sheer walls of dark red *pisé*, they must have been near impregnable in this remote, hillside site.

As ever, it's impossible to determine exactly how old the kasbahs are, though there seem to have been buildings here since at least the sixteenth century. The importance of the site, which commands the area for miles around, was its position on the route from Marrakesh through Telouet to Ouarzazate and the south: the caravans passing through it carried salt across the Sahara and returned with gold, ivory and slaves. In time, this trade diminished, largely because the coast of West Africa was opened up: hence the colonial Ivory Coast and Gold Coast and the trans-Atlantic slave trade.

In the twentieth century, the significance of this route disappeared with the creation of the new French road over the Tichka pass, which has led to severe depopulation over the last thirty years. There are now only half a dozen families living in the kasbahs, earning a sparse living from the valley's agriculture and rather more from the steady trickle of tourists.

Practicalities

Getting to Aït Benhaddou is simple enough by car. Leaving Ouarzazate on the P31 (Tizi n'Tichka) road, you turn right after 18km – along a new, surfaced road (the old *piste* road runs 4km north). Without a car, the best solution is to get together with others and charter a grand taxi from Ouarzazate. Otherwise, you'll need to get a bus to the turn-off and walk from there. Arriving in the town is somewhat confusing. When you reach the "new village", on the west bank of the river, the road comes to an end. There's a **café** here and usually a few guides around, who will escort you across the river (in winter you have to wade across, though it is usually only knee-deep) up to the **kasbahs**. They are bisected by an incredibly confusing network of lanes, so a guide is useful – and if you ask, it should be possible to see one or two kasbah interiors. At the top of the hill are the ruins of a vast and imposing **agadir**, or fortified granary.

Leaving town, if you don't have your own transport, you'll have to try and flag down one of the Marrakesh–Ouarzazate buses (which may not be inclined to stop).

If you're into trekking, mountain biking, or very rough *piste*-driving, the **jeep track** beyond Aït Benhaddou continues to **Tamdaght**, and from there mule paths climb over the old pass to **Telouet** (see p.407).

Accommodation and eating
For many years there have been three rival establishments catering mainly for tour group lunches, but also offering meals in the evening and reasonable overnight accommodation.

Auberge Al Baraka (☎04/489 0305, fax 488 6273) Still the cheapest of the three, it has nine en-suite rooms, all with hot showers, and a good salon restaurant. ②.

Hôtel Restaurant La Kasbah (☎04/489 0302, fax 488 3787). Recently enlarged and improved, this place is poised on a terrace overlooking the village. ④.

Auberge El Ouidane (☎04/489 0312). This has been bought by the owner of the *Hôtel Restaurant La Kasbah* and is now being refurbished. Good views of the village. ③.

KSOUR AND KASBAHS

Ksour (*ksar* in the singular), or kasbahs, are to be found throughout the southern valleys and, to an extent, in the Atlas. They are essentially fortified tribal villages, massive but transitory structures, built in the absence of other available materials out of the mudclay *pisé* of the riverbanks and lasting only as long as the seasonal rains allow. A unique and probably indigenous development of the Berber populations, they are often monumental in design and fabulously decorated, with bold geometric patterns incised or painted on the exterior walls and slanted towers.

The **kasbah**, in its southern form, is similar to the *ksar*, though instead of sheltering a mixed village community, it is traditionally the domain of a single family and its dependants. **Agadirs** and **tighremts**, also variants of the *ksar* structure, used to serve as a combination of tribal fortress and communal granary or storehouse in the villages.

THE DADÈS KASBAHS

Ksour line the route more or less continuously from Agdz to Zagora; most of the larger and older ones are grouped a little way from the road, up above the terraces of date palms. Few that are still in use can be more than a hundred years old, though you frequently see the ruins and walls of earlier *ksour* abandoned just a short distance from their modern counterparts. Most are populated by **Berbers**, but there are also Arab villages here, and even a few scattered communities of **Jews**, still living in their mellahs. All of the southern valleys, too, have groups of **Haratin**, Blacks descended from the west Sudanese slaves brought into Morocco along these caravan routes. Inevitably, these populations have mixed to some extent – and the Jews here are almost certainly converted Berbers – though it is interesting to see just how distinct many of the *ksour* still appear, both in their architecture and customs. There is, for example, a great difference from one village to the next as regards women's costumes, above all in the wearing and extent of veils.

Visiting the region, bear in mind that all of the Drâa *ksour* and kasbahs tend to be further from the road than they look: it's possible to walk for several hours without reaching the edge of the oasis and the upper terraced levels.

South to Zagora: the Drâa oases

The road from **Ouarzazate to Zagora** is wide and well maintained, though it does take its toll on tyres. As in the rest of the south, if you're driving make sure you have a good spare and the tools to change it with. If you're on the bus, get yourself a seat on the left-hand side for the most spectacular views.

Although Zagora is the ostensible goal and destination, the valley is the real attraction. Driving the route, try to resist the impulse to burn down to the desert, and take the opportunity to walk out to one or another of the *ksour* or kasbahs. Using local transport, you might consider hiring a grand taxi for the day – or half-day – from Ouarzazate, stopping to explore some of the kasbahs en route; if you intend to do this, however, be very clear to the driver about your plans.

The lake and over the Tizi n'Tinififft

The route begins unpromisingly: the course of the Drâa lies initially some way to the east and the road runs across bleak, stony flatlands of semi-desert. After 15km a side road, the P31F, leads 11km down to the **El Mansour Eddahbi barrage and reservoir**. In 1989 freak rains flooded the reservoir, and the Drâa, for the first time in recent memory, ran its course to the sea beyond Tan Tan.

BIRDS AND THE EL MANSOUR EDDAHBI BARRAGE

For bird-watchers, the shore line of the El Mansour Eddahbi Barrage is likely to attract migrants at the appropriate times of the year; ruddy shellduck, other waterfowl and waders are possible. Hereabouts, there have also been sightings of mourning wheatear, trumpeter finch, blackbellied sandgrouse, thick-billed lark (and other larks) and raptors, including lanner falcon.

On the main road, the first interest comes just beyond Aït Saoun, one of the few roadside villages along this stretch, where a dramatic change takes place. Leaving the plains behind, the road climbs, twists and turns its way up into the mountains, before breaking through the scarp at the pass of **Tizi n'Tinififft** (1660m). From the summit of the pass there are fine views to the north, with the main Atlas mountains framing the horizon.

The pass is just 4km beyond Aït Saoun. Beyond it the road swings down through a landscape of layered strata, until finally, some 20km from the pass, you catch a first glimpse of the valley and the oases – a thick line of palms reaching out into the haze – and the first sign of the Drâa Kasbahs, rising as if from the land where the green gives way to desert.

Agdz

You descend into the Drâa Valley at **AGDZ** (pronounced Ag–a–dèz), 68km from Ouarzazate, a stopping point for many of the buses and a minor administrative centre for the region. The village consists of just one long street, blood-red coloured, save for the columns of its arcade of shops, picked out in flashes of white and blue. Many of these sell carpets and pottery – and in the few minutes before the bus leaves, prices can drop surprisingly. If you stop here – travelling in either direction – it is unlikely that you'll get a place back on the Zagora/Ouarzazate bus; however, there are **grands taxis** (to either destination), which, like the buses, leave from the Grande Place, and it's possible to stay, too.

It's certainly worth a stop, for just to the north of the village begins a beautiful **palmery**. If the river here is low enough (take care to avoid the bilharzia-infested water) you can get across to view a few **kasbahs** on the far side, in the shadow of **Djebel Kissane** which, as you approach Agdz from the north – and in certain lights – looks more like Djebel Tajine. Geologically speaking, however, it's an outcrop of the **Djebel Sarhro** (see p.440).

Accommodation and eating

The village has a trio of **hotels** which provide an attractive and low-key introduction to the valley. The *Hôtel Drâa* (☎04/484 3024; ①) and *Hôtel des Palmiers* (☎04/484 3127; ①) are clean and adequate, and both are on the Grande Place; the former, given advance warning, will arrange excursions and picnics. By the ceremonial archway at the northern entry to the town is the pricier *Hôtel Kissane* (☎04/484 3044; ④), a very pleasant place with obliging staff, a new pool and a good salon **restaurant**. The *Hôtel Drâa* also has a restaurant (lunch or dinner 55dh) and the *Restaurant En Nahda*, next to the *Hôtel des Palmiers*, does inexpensive grills.

There is also a **campsite**, *Camping Kasbah Palmerie* (☎ & fax 04/484 3640) alongside the Kasbah Asslim; to get to it, turn left off the main street just after the Grande Place on the right. The signpost says 2km to the campsite, but it's possibly twice that. The site has plenty of shade, a swimming pool and clean and simple sanitation, and you can also have a room in the kasbah (①).

Tamnougalt, Timiderte and Tinzouline

The *ksour* at **TAMNOUGALT** – off to the left of the road, about 6km past Agdz – are perhaps the most dramatic and extravagant of any in the Drâa. A wild cluster of buildings, each is fabulously decorated with pockmarked walls and tapering towers. The village was once the capital of the region, and its assembly of families (the djemaa) administered what was virtually an independent republic. It is populated by a Berber tribe, the Mezguita.

A further 8km south is the more palace-like Glaoui kasbah of **TIMIDERTE**, built by Brahim, the eldest son of the one-time pasha of Marrakesh, T'hami El Glaoui. A kilometre to the south, across stepping stones in the river, is another superb kasbah, the **Aït Hammousaid**. There are also rock carvings to be seen 7km to the west of Timiderte, signposted from the main road.

Another striking group of *ksour*, dominated by a beautiful and imposing *caid's* kasbah, stands back from the road at **TINZOULINE**, 57km beyond Timiderte (37km north of Zagora). There is a large and very worthwhile **Monday souk** held here and, if you're travelling by bus, the village is one of the better places to break the journey for a while.

Zagora

ZAGORA seems unpromising at first sight: a street-village with a few modern hotels and government buildings. Two things, however, redeem it. The first is its location: this is the most productive stretch of the Drâa – indeed, of all the southern valleys – and you only have to walk a mile or so out of the town to find yourself amid the palms and oasis cultivation. The second is a distinct air of unreality. Directly behind the town rises a bizarre Hollywood-sunset mountain, and at the end of the main street is a mock-serious roadsign to Timbuktu ("*52 jours*" – by camel – if the border were open).

Another draw for Zagora is its festivals. The Drâa's big event, the **Moussem of Moulay Abdelkader Jilali**, is celebrated here during the Mouloud, and like other national festivals here, such as the **Fête du Trône**, is always entertaining.

Orientation

Though it can seem a bit of a hassle on arrival, and in summer the oven-dry heat is staggering (as are the *frigidaire* nights in winter), Zagora is an easy place to get oriented. Almost everything of note is on the main street, **Boulevard Mohammed V**, or the lower – and lesser – **Avenue Hassan II**. Across the river, to the southeast, is the palmery and hamlet of **Amazrou**, a good alternative base, with a couple of hotels and two campsites.

Accommodation

There is a good choice of hotels – in Zagora and Amazrou – and some nicely located campsites, especially for those with transport.

HOTELS

Hôtel des Amis, Bd. Mohammed V (☎04/484 7924). The cheapest rooms in Zagora: some are en suite and some have a balcony overlooking the street; showers are sometimes hot, and the Hammam Naceur is nearby. In summer the hotel rents out (slightly cooler) space on its *terrasse*. There's a reasonable restaurant (*menu du jour* 50dh) on the ground floor. ①.

Hôtel La Fibule du Drâa (☎04/484 7318, fax 484 7271), towards Amazrou – see p.429. Much the same facilities and price as the *Kasbah Asmâa*. There's a swimming pool and reasonable, if limited, restaurant. It's often used by tour groups. ④.

Hôtel Kasbah Asmâa (☎04/484 7241, fax 484 7527), 150m beyond the bridge (over the Oued Drâa) at Amazrou. A kasbah-style hotel, set in a beautiful garden, with a swimming pool and excellent restaurant. It's smaller, has better decor and a warmer welcome than its rival *Hôtel La Fibule du Drâa*. The Alaoui family also own the new *Hôtel Kasbah Asmâa* outside Rissani (see p.434), and are building a third hotel at Tinerhir. ④.

Hôtel de la Palmeraie, Bd. Mohammed V (☎04/484 7008, fax 484 7878). At the far end of the main street, this is a popular hotel, recently expanded from a dozen to close on sixty rooms. Consequently, there is a range of prices: the most expensive are en suite with showers. It caters for budget groups and offers good half-board prices. The restaurant does a 75dh *menu du jour* and there's a bar open to nonresidents. Occasionally a little frenzied, but a good choice. ③.

Hôtel Riad Salam Bd. Mohammed V (☎04/484 7418, fax 484 7551). This 4-star hotel is on the left as you enter the town and just before the entrance gateway. From outside, it's featureless, but inside it's better – albeit the reception is a little off-hand. It has two swimming pools, three tennis courts, two restaurants and a hotel bar; the 150 spacious rooms are the height of luxury. ⑤.

Hôtel Pullman Reda (☎04/484 7079, fax 484 7012), on the road from Zagora down to the Oued Drâa. Another relatively new tour-group hotel which has the edge on the *Hôtel Tinsouline* and possibly the *Hôtel Riad Salem* but, costing at least 40 percent more than the *Tinsouline* and 20 percent more than the *Riad Salem*, it's not such a bargain. ⑤.

Hôtel Tinsouline, Av. Hassan II (☎04/484 7252, fax 484 7042). Zagora's original "grand hotel" is now privatized. It's showing its age, but the rooms are OK, service is reasonable, and there's a pool. The restaurant is not up to much, however. ④.

Hôtel Vallée Drâa, Bd. Mohammed V (☎04/484 7210). Very welcoming and clean, with hot showers. The restaurant has a menu du jour at 60dh. ①.

CAMPING

Camping Sindibad, Av. Hassan II – five minutes' walk from the town centre (☎04/484 7553). A small, pleasant site, with lots of shade and a swimming pool. Hot showers and a few rooms for rent.

There's a café with traditional meals for 50dh. Dedicated campers still report this as the best site in town.

Camping d'Amazrou (☎04/484 7419). The entrance is alongside the *Hôtel La Fibule du Drâa* (see p.427) in the Amazrou palmery. It's better suited to those with transport and more of a family site – with its own camels available for rides over towards the mountain.

Camping de la Montagne (☎ & fax 04/484 7558). This site is alongside the irrigation canal, upstream of the bridge over the Oued Drâa, and 2km from the main Zagora–Tamegroute road (6958). It's older and cheaper than the *Sindibad* and *Amazrou* sites, but it's bleak and not too clean. Given the other two sites, it offers no advantages.

Amazrou

Amazrou is a hamlet and palmery just to the south of Zagora, across the Drâa, and a great place to spend the afternoon, wandering (or biking – you can rent mountain bikes from the *Hôtel La Fibule du Drâa*) amid the shade of its gardens and *ksour*. The village is, inevitably, wise to the ways of tourism – children try to drag you into their houses for tea and will hassle you to adopt them as guides – but for all that, the oasis life and cultivation are still fairly unaffected.

The local sight, which any of the kids will lead you towards, is the old Jewish kasbah, **La Kasbah des Juifs**. The Jewish community here were active in the silver jewellery trade – a craft continued by Muslim Berbers after their exodus. It's possible to visit some of the workshops.

Djebel Zagora

Across the valley from Zagora are two **mountains**. Djebel Zagora is strictly speaking the bulky one, with a military post on top, but the name is also used for the smaller, sugarloaf hill above *Camping de la Montagne*.

Watching the sunset from the slopes of the mountain is something of a tradition. Take the road out to the *Hôtel La Fibule du Drâa/Hôtel Kasbah Asmâa*, then turn left almost at once at the river to follow the track/irrigation channel to *Camping de la Montagne*. Here, swing right on the rough track which leads to a pass between the two peaks, then bends back, rising across the hillside to make an elbow bend on a spur. This is the popular viewpoint – and just feasible by a Fiat Uno or, preferably, a 4x4. The views are startling: you look out across the palmery to further *ksour*, to the Djebel Sarhro (see pp.440–444), and even to a stretch of sand dunes to the south.

There are ruins a little downhill of an eleventh-century Almoravid fort, built as an outpost against the powerful rulers of Tafilalt; later it was used to protect the caravans passing below, to and from Timbuktu. The road subsequently goes on to the military fort on the summit (entry forbidden) but the view gains little; from the spur a footpath runs across and down the hillside and can be followed back down to the road just opposite *La Fibule du Drâa*.

On foot you can climb the mountain more directly on an old zigzag footpath up from near the *Hôtel Kasbah Asmâa*.

Eating

There are **meals** to be had at most of the Zagora/Amazrou hotels; *La Fibule du Drâa* and *Kasbah Asmâa* are especially good. In addition, the *Restaurant Timbouctou* and *Restaurant Es Saada*, both on Avenue Mohammed V, do inexpensive Moroccan staples, and are as popular with locals as tourists. Finally, it's worth checking out the *Restaurant La Rose des Sables*, next to the Maison Berbère carpet/crafts shop on Avenue Hassan II.

The **dates** of the Zagora oasis are some of the finest in Morocco and stallholders at the market sell dozens of varieties: among them, the sweet *boufeggou*, which will last for up to four years if stored properly; the small, black *bousthami*; and the light, olive-coloured *bouzekri*.

Listings

Banks There are two banks: BMCE is opposite the *gare routière*/grand taxi park and the Banque Populaire is on the same side, but midway down Bd. Mohammed V.

Bikes New mountain ones are available to rent at the *Hôtel La Fibule du Drâa*; they are a good way to explore the palmery and kasbahs of Amazrou; rates are negotiable.

Camel trips There are three camel owners in Zagora, based at the *Kasbah Asmâa, Camping d'Amazrou* (which can be arranged through *Hôtel La Fibule du Drâa*) and *Camping de la Montagne* (see p.429). All offer standard trips at the same prices: for an hour, an afternoon or morning (including lunch), or a full day (with three meals). They are open to negotiation for longer trips.

Petrol There is an Agip station by the Banque Populaire, and others by the exit from town on the Agdz/Ouarzazate road.

Post office The PTT on Bd. Mohammed V offers *poste restante* and phones.

Shopping There is a branch of the Maison Berbère carpet/crafts shop on Av. Hassan II. This is one of the best-quality outlets in the south, with other Alaoui family branches at Ouarzazate, Tinerhir and Rissani.

Souk Markets take place on Wednesdays and Sundays; with dates in autumn. There are daily stalls at the entrance for fresh vegetables and fruit.

Swimming pool There is no public pool but the *Hôtel Tinsouline* allows nonresidents to swim for a steep 50dh a day.

Tours Most of the hotels offer tours or expeditions to kasbahs in the Drâa Valley and/or into the desert: it's worth shopping around, and comparing prices.

Moving on

CTM **buses** for Ouarzazate, Marrakesh and, in the other direction, M'Hamid depart from the company's office on Boulevard Mohammed V; private lines leave from the *gare routière*/grand taxi park further along the street.

Grands taxis have regular runs to Ouarzazate, from the rank by the *gare routière*. Grands taxis can also be negotiated for a trip south to Tamegroute and M'hamid (see below).

South to M'hamid

The **Zagora oasis** stretches for some 30km south of the town, when the Drâa dries up for a while, to resurface in a final fertile belt before the desert. You can follow this route all the way down: the road is now sealed over the full 98km from **Zagora to M'hamid**, and with a car it's a fine trip with the option of a night's stop near the dunes at Tinfou, or beyond.

If you don't have transport, it's a bit of an effort; there are buses to Tamegroute and further south to M'hamid, but times are inconvenient: the CTM leaves Zagora at 4pm, and arrives at M'hamid at 7pm, and there are local buses which leave Zagora later for Tamegroute only. It is possible to charter a grand taxi for an early morning departure, however, which would not be too expensive if you can find a group to share costs, and limit your sights to a day visit to **Tamegroute** and the **sand dunes** near Tinfou.

Tamegroute and Tinfou

Tamegroute (19km from Zagora) is reached by a good road (6958) down the left/east bank of the Drâa, just past the *Hôtel La Fibule du Drâa*. Take care that you get onto this one; the old road to the south (6965 and still marked on some maps) to **Anagam**, on the right/west bank, is now out of use. **Tinfou** lies 10km on from Tamegroute at a point marked on the Michelin map as "Dunes".

Tamegroute

TAMEGROUTE is an interesting and unusual village. At first sight, it is basically a group of *ksour* and kasbahs, wedged tightly together and divided by low, covered passageways with an unremarkable Saturday souk and small potters' co-operative. Despite appearances, it was once the most important settlement in the Drâa valley; it appears on nineteenth-century maps – produced in Europe – as *Tamgrat* or *Tamagrut*, surrounded by lesser places whose names have little or no resonance today.

It owes its importance to its ancient and highly prestigious zaouia, which was a seat of learning from the eleventh century and, from the seventeenth century, the base of the Naciri Brotherhood. Founded by Abou Abdallah Mohammed Ben Naceur (an inveterate traveller and revered scholar), this exercised great influence over the Drâa tribes until recent decades. Its sheikhs (or holy leaders) were known as the "peacemakers of the desert" and it was they who settled disputes among the *ksour* and among the caravan traders converging on Zagora from the Sudan. They were missionaries, too, and as late as the 1750s sent envoys to preach to and convert the wilder, animist-minded Berber tribes of the Atlas and Rif.

Arriving in the village, you'll likely be "adopted" by a guide and taken off to see the **Zaouia Naciri** (daily 8am–12.30pm & 2–6pm; donations expected), the entrance to which is on a side-street to the left of the main road (coming from Zagora). If you prefer to explore unaided, look for the tall white minaret to the left of the main road.

The zaouia consists of a marabout (the tomb of Naceur, closed to non-Muslims), a medersa (theological college – still used by up to 80 students, preparing for university) and a small library, which welcomes non-Muslim visitors and where you can see illuminated Korans, some on animal hides, as well as twelfth-century works on mathematics, medicine and history. The sanctuary, as for centuries past, is a refuge for the sick and mentally ill, whom you'll see sitting round in the courtyard; they come in the hope of miraculous cures and/or to be supported by the charity of the brotherhood and other benevolent visitors.

The **library** was once the richest in Morocco, containing 40,000 volumes. Most have been dispersed to Koranic schools round the country, but Tamegroute preserves a number of very early editions of the Koran printed on gazelle hide, and some interesting books, including a thirteenth-century algebra primer featuring Western Arabic numerals, which, although subsequently dropped in the Arab world, formed the basis of the West's numbers, through the influence of the universities of Moorish Spain.

The **potters' co-operative** is on the left as you leave Tamegroute travelling towards Tinfou. Visitors are welcome (Mon–Fri 7am–7pm) and if you want to see the production of pottery in its simplest form, you'll find this an ideal opportunity. Don't be surprised to find the green glaze, on finished items, reminiscent of Fes pottery. This is no accident; the founders of the Naciri Brotherhood wanted to develop Tamegroute – to city status, they hoped. They invited merchants and craftsmen from Fes to settle in Tamegroute and two families, still working in the pottery, claim Fes forebears.

More recently, in 1995, the pottery enjoyed further patronage, in the form of a state grant to purchase two gas-fired kilns. This is part of a project to revive the fortunes of the Drâa valley. You will see bowls thrown from the local clay on a foot-operated wheel and then the sun-dried "biscuit" stacked in seven traditional kilns built into the slope. Spinifex (known locally as jujube) and sagebrush raise the temperature to 1000°C, producing the green-glazed ware in a single firing. The minerals for the glaze colour are found locally (copper) and near Tata (manganese).

Inevitably, you will be pressed to visit the shop of the co-operative, though whether you decide to buy or not, will depend on your taste and pocket.

The village **hotel**, the *Riad Dar Naciri* is no longer reliable. The newly opened *Jnane Dar* (☎04/484 8522; ①) is good. There's a pavilion, nomad tents and a small *auberge*, with seven rooms; meals are available and the entrance is opposite that of the zaouia.

Tinfou

The tiny hamlet of **TINFOU** stands at the edge of an impressive line of sand dunes – a good substitute for Merzouga if you want to see a real Moroccan sand desert. It is home to an idiosyncratic **auberge**, *Le Repos du Sable* (☎ & fax 04/484 8566; ②), an old kasbah building, with a medieval room key system, a wonderfully ramshackle pool, a private hammam, and a restaurant. The *auberge* has long been a favourite of readers of this book. What makes it special is the Farouj family who run it. The parents, Hassan and Fatima, are both artists, who have exhibited widely in Morocco and Europe. One of their sons, Mourad, manages the *auberge*, while a second son, Majid, is a camel driver, and arranges trips out to the sand dunes. After some mixed reports the *auberge* seems to be back on track.

Competition, in the form of *Porte au Sahara*, aka *Bivouac Sahara* (☎04/484 8562, fax 484 7002; ⑤), may well spur the Farouj family into action. This venture, set up by a German in 1991, is to be found just before the *auberge* (coming from Zagora), also on the left. It has ten comfortable and well-equipped rooms, and also offers camping in a tent, or on the roof terrace (mattresses provided). It has a rather pricey restaurant and, again, offers camel trips to the dunes, through Abdallah Aabi, who will be touting custom before you have downed your first cool drink on the veranda.

Besides the local dunes, the best **camel expeditions** will take you east to the Djebel Tadrant or south towards the Djebel Bani.

Tinfou to M'hamid

About 4km south of Tinfou, you cross the Oued Drâa, and shortly after that are joined by the old road from Zagora to M'hamid (6965). Ahead, apparently blocking the route, rises the great mass of the **Djebel Bani** (1095m), through which the road winds up and over a high-level pass. Once across, you enter a picturesque stretch of palmery; 6km before Tagounite, signs to the left will direct you to the *Kasbah Aït Isfoul* (☎04/484 8302, fax 484 7608; ②), which has **rooms and camping**; the view from the kasbah looking towards the dunes, palm trees and a distant village is memorable.

Moving on, **TAGOUNITE** (74km from Zagora) has a **Thursday souk** and two hotels: *Hôtel Essada* (☎04/484 8128; ④) with eight rooms and further space on its terrace; and the new *Hôtel L'Oasis* (☎04/484 8127; ②) at the other end of the village. A *piste* to the west – suitable for 4x4 vehicles only – leads off to Foum Zguid (see p.434).

MARATHON DES SABLES

A Frenchman, Patrick Bauer, founded the Marathon des Sables in 1986. This annual six-day event is run over 229km and is generally acknowledged as "the toughest foot race in the world". The race, which in 1999 attracted 580 runners from 26 countries, takes place in March/April and the constantly changing route has recently included places such as Tagounite, Foum Zguid and Merzouga.

The best-known British runner to complete the course is probably Chris Moon, who lost his right arm and leg clearing mines in Mozambique in 1995, but went on to run several long-distance races, including the London Marathon and the Marathon des Sables. The fastest time for the course is held, suitably enough, by a Moroccan, Lahcen Ahansal, who ran the route in 17hr 19min in 1997.

For further information on the race contact Chris Lawrence at Best of Morocco, a company based in the UK (see "Basics", p.5).

Continuing south, the road crosses another pass of the Djebel Bani, the **Tizi Beni Slimane**, to reach the last fertile belt of the Drâa, the **M'hamid El Gouzlane** – Plain of the Gazelles. A few kilometres on, at the palmery/village of **OULAD DRISS**, the Drâa turns sharply towards the west and the Atlantic; there are some well-preserved *ksour* to explore here. There's a small **campsite**, *Carrefour des Caravanes* (☎ & fax 04/484 8665; ①) with some indoor accommodation, and the new *Auberge Kasbah Touareg* (☎04/484 8678; ①) with ten rooms.

A signpost, echoing that of Zagora, tells you that it is *"50 jours à Timbuktu"*; the two days' camel ride thus far from Zagora takes around an hour and a half by car – though only a little further south of here, a camel would come into its own. On the final approach to M'hamid, sand has often drifted across the road, despite being lined with woven palm-leaf shields.

M'hamid

M'HAMID El DJEDID (new M'hamid) is just a small administrative centre, the end rather than climax of this trip. It was once an important market place for nomadic and trans-Saharan trade, but of this role only a rather mundane **Monday souk** remains; there is no sign of any camel traders or Blue Men, as the tourist literature suggests. Of rather more interest, however, are the **sand dunes** about 4km away from the village, and the *ksour* of **M'hamid El Bali** (old M'hamid), the village across the Drâa that existed prior to a Polisario attack in the 1970s.

The best **place to stay** in new M'hamid is undoubtedly the *Hôtel Sahara* (☎04/484 8009; ①). This was once a primitive place, but now the village has electricity and piped water and its rooms are clean and cheap; a café behind serves decent meals. It has a rival in the *Hôtel Iriqui* (☎04/484 8023; ①–②) across the village square, with rooms, space on the roof terrace and showers.

M'Barek Naâmani, the *patron* of the *Hôtel Sahara*, a tall Touareg, will be delighted to arrange for overnight, or longer, **expeditions**. If you have the time and get this far it would be a pity not to taste the real Sahara.

The **bus** back from M'hamid leaves at 6am, passes Tinfou around 7.15am and arrives in Zagora at 9am. A second bus usually leaves M'hamid at 3.30pm.

Desert pistes east and west from Zagora

Most people return from Zagora to Ouarzazate, which is the only road covered by bus, and in some ways the most interesting route, allowing you to continue east along the Dadès Valley towards Boumalne and the Dadès Gorge and then to Tinerhir and the Todra Gorge. For the adventurous, however, there are *pistes* **east to Rissani** or **west to Foum Zguid** (and beyond to Tata). The Rissani route is possible by Landrover taxi, or the occasional grand taxi and the Foum Zguid route by lorry or Landrover taxi if you coincide with the markets. With your own vehicle, you'll generally have no difficulty, except for the stretch of *piste* between Zagora and Foum Zguid, as long as you keep to the recently surfaced roads. Bear in mind, however, that sudden storms cause flooding which can wash the road away particularly where the road runs close to mountain streams or, indeed, crosses them by ford or bridge. Such hazards are more dangerous at night – and driving in the dark is best avoided.

East: Zagora to Rissani

The long route east from **Zagora to Rissani**, in the Tafilalt, is covered by **taxi** (Landrover and occasionally grand) regularly, but particularly on Wednesdays, and sometimes on

Saturdays, to serve weekly souks. Ask your hotel for information and help in booking a place if that's thought advisable. The usual route is to backtrack 66km along the Drâa to **Tansikht**, before heading 233km east to Rissani, via **Nkob, Tazzarine** and **Alnif**. The more direct route from Zagora, over the **Tizi n'Tafilalt**, has partially disappeared and is very hard to follow.

Conveniently sited midway between Zagora and Rissani is **TAZZARINE**, set in a grassy oasis surrounded by bare mountains. The modern *Hôtel Restaurant Bougafer* (☎04/483 9169, fax 483 9086; ③) has simple, but handsome **rooms** with constant hot water and showers (electricity is available from 6pm–6am only). The licensed restaurant is good; *menu du jour* 50dh. The hotel has developed a campsite which, despite the enthusiasm of the owner, remains more of a shadeless compound than a proper site. Better is the well-established and friendly **campsite**, the *Amastton*, a small, shady, well-maintained site, watered by a natural spring. It has a couple of rooms for rent (①) or you can sleep in a Berber tent.

At the entrance to the campsite is a **prehistoric rock carving** (*gravure rupestre*) transported from elsewhere; you can see them *in situ* at Nkob (30km distant), Tiouririne (7km) and Aït Ouazik (26km) and one of the camp staff will gladly act as a guide to these or other local sights.

The **rest of the journey** holds less interest. The road crosses a bare plain with distant mountains on both sides. The only other accommodation en route is at **Alnif**, 70km further towards Rissani, where there are two hotels; the *Bougafer* (☎05/578 8309, fax 588 4289; ①), the older and quieter of the two; and *La Gazelle du Sud* (☎ & fax 05/578 3813; ①) which is being updated and expanded. You join the Erfoud/Rissani road alongside the new *Hôtel Kasbah Asmâa* and turn right to reach Rissani in 3km.

Besides its interest as a "new" route, the road from Zagora to Rissani completes a circuit: from Ouarzazate to Zagora and then anticlockwise to Rissani, Erfoud, Tinerhir for the Todra Gorge, and Boumalne for the Dadès Gorge. Previously visiting them all on one trip called for considerable backtracking. Our **map of the Djebel Sarhro** on p.441 shows these routes, and the accompanying section gives a few details on **trekking possibilities** in the region.

The improved surface of this west/east route should not trick you into assuming that the south/north routes (Nkob to Boumalne Dadès or Tinerhir and Alnif to the Tinerhir/Tinejdad road) are now surfaced throughout; they are not and a 4x4 vehicle, with sound navigation, is essential.

West to Foum Zguid

West from Zagora the maps indicate a road **direct to Foum Zguid**: a route which extends beyond to Tata and from there on towards Tiznit or Taroudannt. After almost two decades of military restriction, this route has recently been opened to tourists; the first section, from Zagora to Foum Zguid, is still poor *piste*, only advisable for a 4x4. Without a car, you can travel by *camionette* (lorry) taxi which runs regularly, but particularly on Sundays and Wednesdays; the *camionette* taxi costs 50dh. Ask for details from your hotel in Zagora and try to book in advance.

In **FOUM ZGUID**, which has a Thursday souk and a small **hotel** and café, you can pick up a daily bus or *camionette* taxi most days to Tata (see p.503); there are also buses (Tues, Thurs & Sat) to Tazenakht (change for Taroudannt/Agadir) and Ouarzazate – thus completing another unusual circuit.

Agdz to the Taliouine road

Finally, and again to the west, there is a *piste* from **Agdz to Tazenakht**, on the road to Taliouine. This is a route for *piste* enthusiasts – it won't save any time over driving to Tazenakht via Ouarzazate – but it is fairly practicable by car (Fiat Uno and certainly 4x4 will be okay), if at times difficult to follow, particularly west of **Tasla** where you should take the track on the southern side of the valley. It is completed by a sealed section, from the cobalt mines at Arhbar to the S510 Foum Zguid road.

Settlements along the way include **Aït Smegane-N-El Grara** which has a café; **Bou Azzer**, which is just a mine and some workers' accommodation, and **Tazenakht**, at the junction of the Agadir, Ouarzazate and Foum Zguid roads, which is quite a transport hub, with regular buses and grands taxis to Ouarzazate, plus buses to Foum Zguid, Tissint and Tata. The village also offers decent rooms and meals at the *Hôtel Zenata* (☎04/484 1032; ②), or less enticing ones (despite the en-suite showers, and even a swimming pool) at the *Café-Restaurant Etoile* (☎04/484 1159; ①). There's also a Banque Populaire and petrol station. Alongside the *Café-Restaurant Etoile* is a large courtyard with a magnificent display of carpets, blankets and clothes, including many of the bold geometric designs of the Ouzguita tribe. If you have time on your hands, you could also visit the carpet co-operative. Souk days in Tazenakht are Friday and Saturday.

THE DADÈS AND TODRA

The **Dadès**, rambling east from Ouarzazate, is the harshest and most desolate of the southern valleys. Along much of its length, the river is barely visible above ground, and the road and plain are hemmed in between the parallel ranges of the High Atlas and Djebel Sarhro – broken, black-red volcanic rock and limestone pinnacles. This makes the oases, when they appear, all the more astonishing, and there are two here – Skoura and **Tinerhir** – among the most beautiful in the country. Each lies along the main bus route from Ouarzazate to Er Rachidia and to Erfoud, offering an easy and excellent opportunity for a close look at a working oasis and, in Skoura, a startling range of kasbahs.

Impressive though these are, however, it is the two gorges that cut out from the valley into the High Atlas that steal the show. The **Dadès** itself forms the first gorge, carving up a fertile strip of land behind **Boumalne du Dadès**. To its east is the **Todra Gorge**, a classic, narrowing shaft of high rock walls, which you can trail by car or transit lorry from Tinerhir right into the heart of the Atlas. If you're happy with the isolation and uncertainties of the **pistes beyond**, it is possible, too, to continue across the mountains – a wonderful trip which emerges in the Middle Atlas, near Beni Mellal on the road from Marrakesh to Fes.

To the south of the Dadès, the **Djebel Sarhro** also offers exciting options from October to April, either trekking on foot, or exploring its network of rough *piste* roads in a 4x4 vehicle. Tours and treks can be arranged through British trekking companies (see "Basics", p.5) or in the trailhead towns of El Kelâa des Mgouna, Boumalne du Dadès and Tinerhir.

The Skoura oasis

The **Skoura oasis** begins quite suddenly, around 30km east of Ouarzazate, along a tributary of the Drâa, the **Oued Amerhidl**. It's an extraordinary sight even from the road, which for the most part follows along its edge – a very extensive, very dense palmery, with an incredibly confusing network of tracks winding across fords and through the trees to scattered groups of *ksour* and kasbahs.

Skoura village

SKOURA village, which lies off the main road, at the east end of the oasis, consists of little more than a souk and a small group of administrative buildings, where buses stop.

You'll probably want the services of a guide to explore some of the kasbahs, and possibly visit one or two that are still inhabited.

Don't plan to stay here as the only beds were at the *Hôtel Nikhil* which has now closed. Food, however, is available at a couple of café-restaurants, *Atlas* and *La Casbah*. There is a **Monday souk**.

Kasbahs in the Skoura oasis

The Skoura oasis comprises a thin line of irrigated, fertile palmery, with dry rocky slopes to either side. Animals are not permitted to graze in the precious, cultivated area and so are kept just on the dry side of the line; to feed them, women constantly struggle up from the valley with huge loads of greenery – a characteristic sight here and throughout the southern valleys.

Southwest of Skoura

The best point to stop and explore the Skoura oasis is 2.5km before you arrive at the village proper, coming from Ouarzazate (see sketch-map). Seasoned travellers will remember that here, by the roadside, there was a ruined kasbah, with a recent, single-storey building alongside. This was the **Kasbah de Ben Moro**, dating from the seventeenth century and said to have been built by a Spanish sheikh expelled from Andalucia. Today, the kasbah has been turned into a fine hotel (☎ & fax 04/485 2116; ④–⑤) by a modern Spanish expat, Juan Romero from Cádiz, with thirteen rooms and displays of some of the old equipment from the mills, kitchens and animal quarters.

The palmery hereabouts is one of the lushest in Morocco, full of almond, olive and fig trees, vines and date palms, with alfalfa grass planted below for animal feed. Following the paths behind the Kasbah de Ben Moro, you pass the half-hidden **Marabout of Sidi Aïssa** (Jesus in his Arabized form), and then the (usually dry) riverbed of the Oued Amerhidl. Straight across is the **Kasbah Amerhidl**, the grandest and most extravagantly decorated in the oasis, and again seventeenth century in origin. The owner's family lives there from time to time and so it is maintained properly. It may well look familiar; it's eminently photogenic and features in travel brochures and coffee table books – and on the back of the current 50 dirham note.

KASBAH MAINTENANCE AND DESTRUCTION

Several of the Skoura kasbahs date, at least in part, from the seventeenth and eighteenth centuries, though the majority here – and throughout the Dadès oases – are relatively modern. Most of the older fortifications were destroyed in a vicious tribal war in 1893, and many that survived were pulled down in the French "pacification" of the 1920s and 1930s. Once a kasbah has been left unmaintained, it declines very fast – twenty years is enough to produce a ruinous state, if the *pisé* walls are not renewed.

The kasbah walls in the Dadès – higher and flatter than in the Drâa – often seem unscaleable, but in the course of a siege or war there were always other methods of conquest. A favourite means of attack in the 1890s, according to Walter Harris, who journeyed here in disguise, was to divert the water channels of the oasis round a kasbah and simply wait for its foundations to dissolve.

Kasbah Amerhidl can also be reached by car, from a turning further along the Skoura road. If you come this way, you'll be surrounded by any number of boys as soon as you stop, and you really have no option but to pay one to watch your car or be your guide. The kasbah is open to small groups year round, with informal arrangements as to exact times – show up and someone will be around to let you in.

Beyond Kasbah Amerhidl, a track heads off southwest, past a couple of tumbledown buildings to another impressive-looking kasbah, the **Dar Aït Sidi El Mati**, and from here it's possible to complete a circuit on foot back to the P32, emerging by the ruinous **Kasbah El Kabbaba**.

Whilst you're here, if you have transport – or a lot of energy – you could search out another kasbah, the isolated **Kasbah Ben Amar**. This is still lived in and well maintained. To find it, backtrack along the P32 towards Ouarzazate, and before the bridge over the Oued Amerhidl, look for a track off to the left/southeast; follow the track for a couple of kilometres and you will see the kasbah ahead. It commands magnificent views of the course of the Oued Dadès.

North of Skoura

There are further impressive kasbahs to the north of Skoura village, but they are harder to find, and taking a guide along would be invaluable (Mohammed from the kasbah Ben Moro would be a good choice). To find them, drive through Skoura village and leave it just beyond the closed *Hôtel Nikhil*, crossing the dry river bed which is quite wide at this point.

After about 4km, and still well within the palmery, you should come to a pair of kasbahs, **Dar Aït Sous** and **Dar Lahsoune**; the former, small but once very grand, is in a ruinous state, used only for animals; the latter, once a Glaoui residence, is state-owned, and private. A further 2km drive – and directions from locals – takes you to the magnificent **Kasbah Aït Ben Abou**, which is second in Skoura only to kasbah Amerhidl. It lies on well-farmed land and is still inhabited.

Finally, on the edge of the palmery, you might follow the trail to the imposing **Marabout Sidi M'Barek ou Ali**. A high wall, broken only by a door, encloses the marabout, which doubles as a grain store – a powerful twofold protection on both spiritual and military levels.

Skoura to El Kelâa des Mgouna

From **Skoura**, eastwards towards **El Kelâa des Mgouna**, the road runs parallel to the Oued Drâa which flows, out of sight, across this semi-desert plateau. Seven kilometres before El Kelâa des Mgouna, is a small hamlet **Amejgag**, with the riverside *Hôtel Rosadamaskina* (☎04/483 4913, fax 483 6969; ③), a small but brightly furnished place, with great charm and frequented by the artist, Charles Kerival, whose watercolours successfully capture the feel of southern Morocco. Note that the hotel was once called *Auberge Pont d'Almou* and is still referred to as such on some road signs.

El Kelâa des Mgouna

Travelling through the Dadès in spring, you'll find Skoura's fields divided by the bloom of thousands of small, pink Persian roses – cultivated as hedgerows dividing the plots. At **EL KELÂA DES MGOUNA** (also spelt Qalat Mgouna), 50km east across another shaft of semi-desert plateau, there are still more, along with an immense kasbah-style **rose-water factory** with two prominent chimneys. Here, the Capp et Florale company distil the *eau de rose*. In late May (sometimes early June), a **rose festival** is held in the village to celebrate the new year's crops: a good time to visit, with villagers coming down from the mountains for the market, music and dancing.

The rest of the year, El Kelâa's single, rambling street is less impressive. There's a **Wednesday souk**, worth breaking your journey for, but little else of interest beyond the locked and deserted ruins of a **Glaoui kasbah**, on a spur above the river. The local shops are always full of *eau de rose*, though, and the factory can be visited too, for a look at – and an overpowering smell of – the distillation process. A second factory, Aromag, alongside the Mobil petrol station, 13km out along the Tinerhir road, can also be visited; it is run by a French company, based – of course – at Grasse.

One of a hundred varieties, *Rosa Centifolio* has, as the name implies, hundreds of small leaves on each small bush. Folklore has it that they were brought from Persepolis by the Phoenicians. Aerial photographs testify to there being 4200km of low hedges; each metre yields up to one kilo of petals and it takes ten tons of petals to produce two to three litres of rose oil. The petals are picked by women who start very early in the morning before the heat dries the bloom.

Practicalities

The town has three **banks** (Banque Populaire, as usual in the south; Crédit Agricole; and Wafabank) and two **hotels**. The cheap option, inconspicuously signposted on the main street, is the *Hôtel du Grand Atlas* (☎04/483 6838; ①), a pleasant little place, with a hammam and a simple restaurant. It is run by Lahcen Aaddi and his son, Hassan, who can put you in touch, if you wish, with guides for trekking in the Djebel Sarhro (see p.440) and Djebel Mgoun.

The other hotel, up by the kasbah, is *Les Roses de Dadès* (☎ & fax 04/488 3807; ④), an old "Grand Hôtel du Sud", owned by ONMT, with a swimming pool, but little motivation as it awaits privatization.

Vallée des Roses

If you have transport, this "secret valley" of the **Asif Mgoun**, north of El Kelâa, would make a good one-day excursion, or a detour en route to Boumalne. The valley begins due north of the town and is trailed by the minor road 6903 to Tourbist and Bou Tharar, where the 6904 leads south back to El Goumt on the main P32 road; both should be practicable with a Fiat Uno. In spring, the route is lined by thousands of roses, and there are some notable kasbahs at **Bou Tharar**.

Boumalne du Dadès

BOUMALNE DU DADÈS is a more interesting stop than El Kelâa. It is again well poised for exploration of the Djebel Sarhro and for the bird-rich Vallée des Oiseaux

BOUMALNE DU DADÈS (schematic)

RESTAURANTS
Restaurant Ossikis **B**
Restaurant Place **A**
de la Mosquée

ACCOMMODATION
Hôtel Adrar 4
Hôtel Almander 6
Hôtel Bougafer 3
Hôtel Chems 7
Kasbah Tizzarouine 8
Hôtel Madayeq 2
Hôtel Soleil Bleu 1
Hôtel Vallée des Oiseaux 5

Artisanal de Boumalne & Maison Aït Atta

PTT

CTM Office

Covered Market

MARKET SQUARE

Shell petrol station

MILITARY BARRACKS

Total petrol station

0   200m

△ Dadès Gorge & Msemrir

Oued Dadès

Scarp

Scarp

▽ Ouarzazate

△ Tinerhir

(guides can be arranged for both through the hotels), and is the gateway to the Dadès Gorge. In addition, it has some charm of its own, with the old town on the eastern bank of the Dadès climbing up the slope to the plateau where a military barracks and trio of hotels command the valley and the entry to the gorge.

Practicalities

Approaching the town from the Ouarzazate road, you reach a small market square (the souk takes place on Wednesday) and the old *Hôtel Adrar*, above which is a mosque and a covered market open daily. **Grands taxis** and local buses go from the market square or from the front of the covered market; the CTM office is downhill from the market square. Uphill from here, on the plateau, are several hotels, a Shell petrol station, a PTT, a Banque Populairc and two **shops**. Both of the shops – the Artisanale de Boumalne and Maison Aït Atta – are worth looking round for a range of carpets and carvings, on sale without great pressure.

Grands taxis make regular runs to Ouarzazate and Tinerhir. For Msemrir and the Dadès Gorge, you can usually get a Landrover taxi, transit or lorry; a transit/minibus leaves for Msemrir daily between noon and 2pm, returning at dawn the next morning.

For details of **guides for trekking and bird-watching**, see the listings below for the hotels *Soleil Bleu* and *Kasbah Tizzarouine*.

Accommodation and eating

There is a decent selection of **hotels**, all of which have **restaurants** – though a few hours' notice may be required for meals. In addition, for simple Moroccan fare, try the *Restaurant Ossikis* on the market square or the *Restaurant Place de la Mosquée*, halfway up the hill by the grand mosque.

HAMMADA BIRDS AND THE VALLÉE DES OISEAUX

Boumalne offers some exceptional bird-watching and wildlife possibilities – as can be seen from the logbook at the *Hôtel Soleil Bleu* (see hotel listings). To the south of the town are abundant and accessible areas of **hammada** or desert fringe, and a grassy valley. The hammada provides an austere environment, whose dry, sunny conditions are ideal for cold-blooded reptiles and are frequented by Montpelier snake, Atlas agama and fringe-toed lizard. The **grassy plains** provide food for small herds of Edmi gazelle and Addax antelope and shelter for a variety of specialist bird species such as **cream-coloured courser, red-rumped wheatear** and **thick-billed lark**. Predatory **lanner falcon** patrol the skies and the rare and elusive **Houbara bustard** makes an occasional appearance.

The most rewarding birding trip in the region is to the so-called **Vallée des Oiseaux**, which heads off the 6907 from Boumalne to Iknioun in the Djebel Sarhro. This is the "Tagdilt track" and well known to birdwatchers; it's marked by a line of green (picturesque) shading on the Michelin map. Here, you'll find **Temmink's horned lark, bar-tailed desert lark, eagle owl** and several **sandgrouse**: pin-tailed, crowned and black-bellied. And, for extra measure, they make traditional pottery at Tagdilt.

Hôtel Adrar (☎04/483 0355). An adequate hotel with 26 rooms on three floors; it's handy for the buses, taxis and market square, and there's a reasonable restaurant and terrace café from which to watch the day go by. ①.

Hôtel Almander (☎04/483 0172). A new hotel, just below the *Chems* and sharing the same spectacular views. It's already doubled its number of rooms so must be good. ②.

Hôtel Bougafer (☎ & fax 04/483 0768). Behind the *Hôtel Adrar*, this was once only a restaurant/café, but now has six rooms which are, considering that the tariff is half that of the *Adrar*, good value. Like the *Adrar*, it has hot showers separate from the rooms. ②.

Hôtel Chems (☎04/483 0041, fax 483 1308). An attractive hotel, with a good restaurant and a new Moroccan salon. Built on the hillside, the rooms overlooking the valley have spectacular views; and all the rooms are en suite. ②.

Kasbah Tizzarouine (☎04/483 0690). More of a compound than a kasbah, but with an impressive gatehouse, this relatively new venture is half a kilometre beyond the *Hôtel Chems*, along a side road and with some impressive views from the scarp edge. Within the compound, you can camp or park a campervan, sleep in a Berber tent, rent well-equipped rooms or (the *pièce de résistance*) occupy a *chambre troglodytique*. There are five caves on the cliff edge; two of them were originally occupied by nomads twice a year as they moved their animals from the valleys to the Djebel Sarhro and back. In addition, Dahni Mohammed Lamnaouar, who works at the *Tizzarouine*, is a qualified mountain guide and can be contracted here for a range of trips. ②.

Hôtel Madayeq (☎04/483 0763). A chain hotel owned by ONMT and awaiting privatization; from the outside it looks like a drunken kasbah, made up of huge up-ended bricks. Indoors, the decor and service evoke memories of Intourist hotels. ④.

Hôtel Soleil Bleu (☎ & fax 04/483 0163). Reached along a *piste*, 300m beyond the *Hôtel Madayeq*, this has stunning views of the valley. Recently a second storey has been added and there are now sixteen rooms, all with showers. It's run by the Najim brothers, who specialize in tours and treks, particularly for bird-watchers; day visits to the Vallée des Oiseaux and other promising locations (see box feature) are possible, and the hotel maintains an excellent bird-watching log. ②.

Hôtel Vallée des Oiseaux (☎ & fax 04/483 0764). A motel-style place with a pleasant garden but, away from the edge of the plateau, no views; some en-suite rooms. ②.

The Djebel Sarhro

The **Djebel Sarhro** (or Saghro) lies south of the road from Ouarzazate to Tinerhir and east of that from Ouarzazate to Zagora. It's a starkly beautiful jumble of volcanic peaks,

DJEBEL SARHRO

Major road
Minor road
Piste
Trail
Battlefield
Dunes

N

Erfoud
Rissani
P21
Touroug
Goulmima
P32
Tinejdad
Tinerhir
Todra Gorge
Mecissi
DJEBEL OUGNAT
Oum Jrane
Alnif
Tarhbalt
Djebel Bou Gafer (1398m)
Kadam
Moudou
Amalou n'Mansour (2712m)
Imi n'Ouzguz Waterfalls
Imi n'Site
Tizlit
Iknioun
Msemrir
Dadès Gorge
Vallée des Oiseaux
Tagdiit
Tizi n'Tazazert (2283m)
Djebel Amlal (2447m)
Bab n'Ali
Nkob
Boumalne Du Dadès
Vallée des Roses
El Kelâa des Mgouna
Djebel Afougal (2196m)
DJEBEL SARHRO
Oued Dadès
Rock Carvings
Mellal
Tazzarine
Ait Ouzik
Rock Carvings
Rock Carvings
DJEBEL RHART
Djebel Zagora
Zagora
Tamegroute
Tinfou
Tizi n'Tafilalt
M'hamid
Oued Drâa
Djebel Kissane
Tansikht
Agdz
Skoura
P32
Ouarzazate
P31

50km

0

quite unlike the High Atlas or Anti-Atlas, and punctuated by gorges, ruined kasbahs, occasional villages, and the black tents of the semi-nomadic **Aït Atta** tribe. Fiercely independent through the centuries, and never subdued by any sultan, the Aït Atta were the last bulwark of resistance against the French, making their final stand on the slopes of Djebel Bou Gafer in 1933 (see box opposite).

Until recently, the Djebel Sarhro saw few visitors but it's becoming better known and more accessible through **trekking** operators like Explore and Sherpa Expeditions (see "Basics", p.5). They operate here from October to April, when the High Atlas is too cold and snow-covered for walking; in the summer, Sarhro itself is impracticable, being too hot and exposed, and with water, always scarce, quite impossible to find. In fact, Djebel Sarhro means "dry mountain" in Berber.

Independent exploration of the range is possible by **car** (all roads on our map are passable by Renault 4L in reasonable weather). However, bear in mind that road signs are rare and that flash floods often lead to diversions or worse; navigation is not easy and taking along a local guide would be useful.

A **guide** is certainly recommended for trekking. They can be contacted through the *Hôtel Soleil Bleu* and the *Kasbah Tizzarouine* in Boumalne Dadès and the *Hôtel Tomboctou* in Tinerhir. Alternatively, if you are approaching the Djebel Sarhro from the southwest, you could discuss your plans and hire a guide at the campsite at Agdz; qualified guides are also based at Nkob. The bureau for guides, based at El Kelâa des Mgouna, no longer functions – despite its inclusion in current ONMT literature.

Treks and routes

When planning a trek in the Sarhro, bear in mind the harshness of the terrain and the considerable distances involved. With the exception of the **Vallée des Oiseaux**, off the Boumalne–Iknioun road (see wildlife box on p.440), this is not an area for short treks, and nor does it have much infrastructure; you will need to be prepared to camp.

Given ten days, you could set out from El Kelâa des Mgouna, explore the area west of the **Tizi n'Tazazert** and loop back to El Kelâa or Boumalne. Alternatively, with about five days free, you could travel by local taxi from Boumalne du Dadès or Tinerhir to **Iknioun** and then walk south, by **Djebel Bou Gafer**, to **Imi n'Site** and **Nkob**, taking local transport from there either back to Boumalne or Tinerhir or across to Tansikht on the Ouarzazate–Zagora road.

You could also do the latter trip in the opposite direction from the Drâa Valley, arranging a guide at **Nkob**.

Iknioun to Nkob

The easiest access to the range for **trekkers** is a transit taxi from Boumalne to **IKNIOUN**; this runs most days, but Wednesday, after the Boumalne souk, is the most reliable. There are **rooms** in Iknioun, if you wish to stay. Alternatively, you can ask to be dropped at the junction of the *piste* 7km before Iknioun (there is a large sign here, so you shouldn't miss it), which you could follow in two or three days' **walk to Nkob** (35km). The people at the village 1km along the Nkob road will provide rooms for a first night's stop, though walkers should be prepared to camp beyond here. The Nkob souk is on a Sunday, so if you walk slowly, you can pick up a ride on the Saturday.

Following this route – which is also practicable with a four-wheel-drive vehicle – it takes about an hour's walk to reach a junction (at 2014m) to Tioutf: turn left here and climb steadily for an hour to a faux col, and then across an easy plateau for half an hour to the true col, **Tizi n'Tazazert** (2283m). From here, it's downhill, through rocky scenery, with table-top mesas and volcanic cones visible to the west; there are traces of underground water, with palm trees in gullies, and camels grazing almost to the winter

THE BATTLE FOR BOU GAFER

For three centuries or more, the **Aït Atta** tribe were the great warriors of the south, dominating the Djebel Sarhro and its eastern extension, the Djebel Ougnat. At the beginning of the twentieth century, the British journalist Walter Harris reported seeing the young men at Touroug, one of their tribal strongholds (see map on p.441), practising running with galloping horses, holding onto their tails – a breakneck skill which enabled those on foot to travel as fast as the riders.

As guerrilla fighters, the Aït Atta resisted the French occupation from the outset. Led by **Hassou Ba Salem**, they finally retreated, at the beginning of 1933, to the rocky stronghold of the **Djebel Bou Gafer**, a chaos of gorges and pinnacles. Estimates vary, but the Aït Atta had at least a thousand fighting men, who, together with their families, totalled around 7000 people, accompanied by their flocks. They faced vastly superior French forces. Ali, the son of Hassou Ba Salem, says that, according to his father, these included 83,000 troops and four aircraft squadrons.

David Hart in the *Aït Atta of Southern Morocco* (1984) concluded that this was "the hardest single battle which the French had ever had to fight in the course of their 'pacification' of Morocco". The French first attacked the stronghold on 21 February and, after that, there were almost daily attacks on the ground and from the air. Many died on both sides but the Aït Atta did not surrender for over a month, by which time they were reduced to half their strength and had run short of ammunition. The victors, moving in on March 25, occupied, according to one of them, "an indescribable charnel house".

Hassou Ba Salem's conditions on surrender included a promise that the Aït Atta could maintain their tribal structures and customs, particularly insofar as law and order were concerned, and that they would not be "ruled" by the infamous T'Hami El Glaoui, the pasha of Marrakesh, whom they regarded as a traitor to their homeland. The French were content to accept, the battle meaning that their "pacification" was virtually complete, and giving them access to the valuable silver and copper mines at Moudou.

Hassou Ba Salem died in 1960 and was buried at Tagia, his birthplace, 5km from Tinerhir. Ali, his son, succeeded him as leader of the tribe, and took part in the 1975 Green March into the Western Sahara. He died in 1992 and is also buried at Tagia. As for the battlefield itself, local guides will show you the sites, including ruins of the fortress. It is still littered with spent bullets, which are covered in spring by colourful clumps of thyme, rockroses and broom.

---

snow line. The *piste* zigzags down in two hours' walking (there are a lot of shortcuts for walkers), running due south down the main valley to Nkob. If you have the energy, there's an interesting excursion off to the west, up a side valley, to the striking **mountain "gate" of Bab n'Ali**.

At **NKOB** there is some accommodation and nearby rock carvings. Transits run from here to the main road at **TANSIKHT**, on the Drâa.

Other driving routes

In addition to the **north–south route** over the **Tizi n'Tazazert** to Tansikht, it is possible to drive over a much lower pass, the **Tizi n'Tafilalt**, to Zagora. There are also **east–west routes** between **Tansikht** and **Rissani** (in Tafilalt), which are much better established and are described at the end of the Drâa section (see p.433).

From these roads, there are astonishing views of the surrounding mountains, of which the most notable are **Djebel Afougal** (2196m), **Djebel Amlal** (2447m) and, the highest, **Amalou n'Mansour** (2712m). All of them are climbed by one or other of the trek operators. **Djebel Bou Gafer** (1598m) is lower and less remarkable but its history (see box) adds interest; it can be approached on foot from Moudou or Kadem, though either way a guide is again advisable and you may need to camp overnight to make the most of a visit to the battlefield.

Other less demanding attractions include the **Imi n'Ougoulz waterfalls** and **prehistoric rock carvings** near Nkob, Mellal and Tazzarine (local guides are essential for all of these).

The Dadès Gorge

The **Dadès Gorge**, with its high cliffs of limestone and weirdly shaped erosions, begins almost immediately north of Boumalne. Leaving the P32, you follow the 6901 road, signposted "Mserhir" (Msemrir). Most travellers cover the first 25km or so by car or taxi, then turn back, which makes for a fine day's trip. If you have a 4x4, however, you could **loop over to the Todra Gorge** or continue **up and across the High Atlas** to the Beni Mellal–Marrakesh road. Alternatively, a couple of days' walking along the gorge from Boumalne will reward you with superb scenery, and plenty of kasbahs and *pisé* architecture to admire; there are rooms in several of the villages en route to Msemrir.

The gorge is accessible by local transport from Boumalne, with Peugeot taxis, transit vans and Berber pick-ups (*camionettes*) and lorries (*camions*) leaving regularly from the market square for Aït Ali (25km) and less often to Msemrir (63km). Pick-ups run occasionally to Atlas villages beyond but they do so more often on the Todra gorge (see p.449) route, which would make an easier access point if you plan to cross the Atlas on local transport. Returning to Boumalne, a transit/minibus leaves Msemrir daily at 4am.

See our **map** "Over the Atlas: Beyond Todra and Dadès" on p.452 for routes.

Into the gorge: Boumalne to Msemrir

For the first 15–20km, the **Dadès Gorge** is pretty wide and the valley carved out of it is green and well populated. There are *ksour* and kasbahs clustered all along this stretch, many of them flanked by more modern houses, though even these usually retain some feature of the decorative traditional architecture.

Boumalne to Aït Oufi

About three kilometres along the road (6901) into the gorge from Boumalne, you pass the fine old **Glaoui kasbah** of Aït Youl, strategically sited as always to control all passage. Four kilometres further in, where the road begins to turn into a hairpin corniche, there is a superb group of **ksour** at **AÏT ARBI**, built against a fabulous volcanic twist of the rocks. The kasbahs seem like natural extensions of their setting – tinged with the colour of the earth and fabulously varied, ranging from bleak lime-white to dark reds and greenish blacks.

Four kilometres on from here is a region known as **Tamnalt**, which is also known by the locals as the "Hills of Human Bodies" after its strange formations which, in fact, look mostly like feet. Geologically the rock is a weathered conglomerate of pebbles which probably lay where a great river entered a primordial sea. Hereabouts, you climb over a little pass, flanked by the *Café-Restaurant Meguirne,* 13km from Boumalne. The views make this a fine place to stop for lunch (as tour groups do) and it also has seven basic **rooms** for rent (no phone; ①). Nearby there is a hidden side-valley, entered by a narrow gorge: the owners of the *Meguirne* take a proprietary interest in this patch of nature and will try to involve you in *le camping sauvage*. A kilometre north of the *Meguirne* there are further rooms – clean and quite reasonable – at the *Hôtel-Restaurant Kasba* (no phone; ②), which again caters for tour groups by day, laying on "Berber Weddings" in its courtyard.

On from here, the valley floor is less fertile and the hills gentler. The road continues through the hamlet of Aït Ali (25km from Boumalne) to a spot known as **Aït Oufi**, where a bridge spans the river, and the gorge narrows quite dramatically. There is a little **hotel**, the *Auberge des Gorges du Dadès* (☎ & fax 04/483 1710; ②), by the bridge, an attractive place to stay, offering a choice between cheap, basic **rooms** or pricier ones with en-suite hot showers, **bivouac tents** on the terrace, or **camping** alongside the river where the few poplar trees provide some shade. The *auberge* serves meals, and arranges **mule** and **4x4 trips** into the gorge and Atlas. It has a tie-up with the *Hôtel de Foucauld* in Marrakesh.

There is further accommodation 2km further along the road (which deteriorates into a poor *piste*) from the bridge, on the east bank of the river. This consists of a row of small, fairly basic **hotels**, hemmed in by slabs of cliff; they are, in order of appearance: the *Auberge du Peuplier* (☎ & fax 04/483 1748; ①), *Hôtel La Gazelle du Dadès* (☎04/483 1753; ①), *Hôtel La Kasbah de la Vallée* (☎ & fax 04/483 1753; ②), and *Auberge Tisadrine* (☎04/483 1745; ①), beyond which a more upmarket hotel is being built. The best rooms, with en-suite showers, are at *La Gazelle* and *La Kasbah*. All of them offer riverside camping.

The gorge at this point has narrowed to a canyon, and there are some good walks to be had, stream hopping and wading; the hotels will help with advice and, if you want, fix you up with a guide.

Aït Oufi to Msemrir

The road north of Aït Oufi is a bone-shaking *piste*, and in a rental car you may decide to go no further than the canyon mouth described above – and even then you may decide to walk the last 2km from the bridge. After passing the cluster of hotels, the road climbs by a coil of hairpin bends above the gorge, before squeezing through a tight, narrow gap to reach **Taghia n'Dadès** where there is the small and basic *Café-Hôtel Taghia* (①: no electricity and limited toilet facilities). Walking from here, you can scramble up the hill east to a cave with stalactites, or go north to a small but impressive gorge, with views down over the Dadès Gorge.

Spring floods permitting, it is usually possible to drive on to Msemrir (63km in all from Boumalne). For a distance, the east side of the gorge is dominated by the **Isk n'Isladene** cliffs and then the road follows a canyon to **Tidrit** where it snakes up and crosses the face of one of the huge canyon loops before the final run to Msemrir. Two kilometres before Msemrir, the **Oussikis** valley, to the left, can be visited by an even rougher *piste*.

On from Msemrir

At **MSEMRIR** there is **accommodation** and meals to be had at the *Café Agdal* and the newer *Hôtel Aït Atta* (both ①). Beyond here, is a choice of *piste* routes: east to join the Todra Gorge at Tamtatoucht (6–8hr by Landrover), or north across the High Atlas. People drive Renault 4Ls across both these routes in summer but they are not really suitable transport – and will break rental conditions. There are frequent wash-outs, bare slabs to cross and other hazards, and really best left for lorries or Landrovers with four-wheel drive.

Over the Atlas

Heading over the High Atlas, the most direct route is to join the road from Todra at Agoudal: 60km or so of very rough driving, over the **Tizi n'Ouano**. Some details of the route beyond is included in the Todra Gorge section (see p.449).

If you are looking for local transport, you may strike lucky with a lorry from Msemrir to Agoudal, but the route isn't driven nearly as regularly as that from Todra, so be prepared for a long wait at Msemrir – and winter often closes this road completely.

Across to Tamtatoucht

If you are intent on **crossing the Todra Gorge** to Tamtatoucht, there is virtually no chance of a local lorry, though you might just find a lift with fellow tourists. It should be added, too, that, if you are driving, you'd find it considerably easier to go in the other direction. Coming from the Dadès it's a long, uphill haul, and the seventy-odd kilometres of *piste*, often in a shocking state, can take a full day to travel.

About a kilometre out from Msemrir, the **Imilchil** *piste* swings off across the valley; the Tamtatoucht track (not always worthy of the name) keeps on up the valley to reach **Tizi n'Uguent Zegsaoun** (2639m). The *piste* then sweeps down to follow the **Tizgui n'Ouaddou** valley and next climbs to a smaller pass where the view opens out to the plains stretching to Aït Hani. A very rough descent over limestone joins the plain and crosses it to hit the Tamtatoucht/Aït Hani *piste* (see pp.451–453 including map).

Tinerhir (Tinghir)

TINERHIR is largely a base for the trip up into the **Todra Gorge** – but it's also a much more interesting place than other administrative centres along this route. It's overlooked by a ruinous but ornamental Glaoui kasbah, and just east of the modern town is an extensive palmery, which feels a world apart, with its groups of *ksour* built at intervals into the rocky hills above. Don't be in too much of a hurry to catch the first lorry up to the Todra Gorge – the Tinerhir and, to the northeast, Todra **palmeries** are major attractions in themselves.

The palmeries seem all the more special after the **journey from Boumalne**: a bleak drive across desolate plains, interrupted by the sudden oases of **Imiter** (with several fine kasbahs) and Timadriouine. The **Djebel Sarhro** (see p.440) looms to the south for the latter part of the trip, dry barren outlines of mountains, like something from the Central Asia steppes; the drama of this part of the range was another big backdrop in David Lean's *Lawrence of Arabia*.

If you're interested in buying **crafts**, Tinerhir has a branch of the excellent **Maison Berbère** chain (run by the Alaoui family like those in Ouarzazate, Zagora and Rissani), which usually has high-quality rugs, carpets and especially silver; there are now two shops, both near the Place Principale: one by the mosque and the other by the *Café de la Gazelle* – find one and they'll take you to the other so you can buy at both.

South of Imiter, in the foothills of the Djebel Sarhro, you will see – from the Boumalne-Tinerhir road (P32) – the spoil and silver mines of the Société Métallurgique d'Imiter (SMI). Outside interest is not encouraged and rumours abound locally about other mining enterprises, possibly including gold mining; as you enter Tinerhir, you pass alongside the SMI company houses, signposted *Cité de Personnel*.

Practicalities

Orientation is straightforward. The centre of Tinerhir is a long **garden square**, flanked by hotels, café-restaurants and the **PTT**; here are to be found the **grands taxis** for standard runs to Boumalne, Er Rachidia and Erfoud and the **lorries** which go up the Todra Gorge to Tamtatoucht and Imilchil. In the **Place Principale** to the southwest of the garden square are the local **buses** and **CTM** office; long-distance buses, passing through Tinerhir en route for Agadir and Rabat, call here or stop on Avenue Mohammed V facing the central garden.

Four **banks** (Banque Populaire, Crédit du Maroc, Wafabank and BMCE) are on the northwest side of Avenue Mohammed V as it leaves the Place Principale towards Boumalne; BCM is on the Place Principale, alongside the CTM office.

Accommodation

Most of the cheaper **hotels** line Avenue Hassan II, facing the central garden; the most expensive ones are a bit more scattered, but all walkable from the set-down points of taxis and buses – with the possible exception of the *Hôtel Kenzi Bougafer* out on the Boumalne road opposite the souk.

There's a campsite, **Camping Ourti**, on Avenue Mohammed V (☎04/483 3205), on the Boumalne road, beyond the souk. It's a new site, enthusiastically managed by a young crowd, open year-round and with a good range of facilities – including hot showers and a swimming pool (April–October) There's a restaurant (50dh) and a few bungalows, which sleep up to three people (35dh per head). The site can also arrange 4x4 transport, driver and guide for the gorge, or other expeditions.

HOTELS

Hôtel l'Avenir, near the central market (☎ & fax 04/483 4599). This excellent budget hotel was set up by a Spaniard, Roger Mimó (see below). Standards remain high and it's often used by groups. ②.

Hôtel Houda, 11 Rue Moulay Ismail (☎04/483 4613). On a side street, off Av. Hassan II, close to the CTM office and the *Hôtel Raha* and *Hôtel Salam* (neither of which is recommended), this small hotel opened in 1995 and is a good cheap choice. ②.

Hôtel Kenzi Bougafer, Av. Mohammed V (☎04/483 3280, fax 483 3282). A modern hotel (opened 1993), located opposite the Monday souk. It's a luxurious place, already promoted from three to four stars, with very comfortable suites, rooms, a restaurant, bar and swimming pool. ⑤.

Hôtel L'Oasis, Av. Mohammed V (☎ & fax 04/483 3670). Another promising, central choice, recently remodelled to include ten en-suite rooms. ②.

Hôtel Al Qods, 8 Av. Hassan II (☎04/483 4605). A small, clean and very reasonable hotel with hot showers, and a restaurant. ①.

Hôtel Saghro, on a hill to the north of the town centre (☎04/483 4181). Another of the "Grands Hôtels du Sud", owned by ONMT, and rather drifting along awaiting privatization. Still, it has a swimming pool, restaurant and bar (residents only), and the views of the palmeries are stunning. ⑤.

Hôtel du Todra, Av. Hassan II (☎04/483 2071, fax 483 4565). Though open since the 80s, this place has been recently renovated and now has over 50 rooms with bath, a new bar and restaurant. ④.

Hôtel Tomboctou, Av. Bir Anzarane (☎04/483 4604, fax 483 3505; tomboctu@iam.net.ma). On a side road, opposite BMCE and to the left of Av. Mohammed V (direction Boumalne). A kasbah built for Sheikh Bassou in 1944, this hotel was tastefully converted by Roger Mimó, who established the *Hôtel L'Avenir*. The place is a delight – one of the memorable small hotels of Morocco – and Roger (who is author of an excellent Spanish trekking guide on Morocco) is a great source of knowledge. He can help with your plans and hire guides and vehicles for you. ④.

Eating

There are **restaurants** at the hotels *L'Avenir, Kenzi Bougafer, Al Qods, Saghro* and *Tomboctou*: the *Kenzi Bougafer* and *Saghro* are expensive and the latter is overpriced; otherwise all are recommended. The restaurants *Central* and *L'Avenir*, in the centre, and *Kasbah* and *La Palmeraie*, on the road out to Er Rachidia, are all good, too – the (relatively upmarket) *Kasbah*, especially.

Moving on

There are regular **buses** from Tinerhir to Ouarzazate (the 6am goes on to Marrakesh), to Fes and Meknes (leaving at 7pm), and to Er Rachidia, and **grands taxis** in both directions (places available for Ouarzazate/Boumalne/Er Rachidia/occasionally Erfoud).

The Berber lorries (*camionettes*) make regular runs to villages in the **Todra Gorge and beyond**; on Mondays, from around noon (following the souk), numerous lorries set out for Atlas villages, including one that goes right over the mountains to Arhbala, driving through the night. Note that you can also arrange transport (and/or trips) for the **Todra Gorge** (or beyond) through the *Hôtel Tombouctou* or *Camping Ourti* (see above).

The Tinerhir and Todra palmeries

There are **palmeries** to the southeast and northeast of Tinerhir, lining both sides of the Todra River. For an overview, the *Hôtel Saghro* has the town's best viewing point. To explore, you're best off renting a **bike** from Roger Mimó at the *Hôtel Tomboctou*, and discussing a route with him; our map was based upon his sketches. Alternatively, you could hire a mule – and arrange a guide – in one of the oasis villages.

The palmeries follow the usual pattern in these valleys: date palms at the edge, terraces of olive, pomegranate, almond and fruit trees further in, with grain and vegetable crops planted beneath them. The **ksour** each originally controlled one section of the oasis, and there were frequent disputes over territory and, above all, over access to the mountain streams for each *ksour*'s network of water channels. Even in the twentieth century, their fortifications were built in earnest, and, as Walter Harris wrote (melodramatically, but probably with little exaggeration): "The whole life was one of warfare and gloom. Every tribe had its enemies, every family had its blood feuds, and every man his would-be murderer."

Our map indicates several good viewing points, or **miradors**; don't miss the length of road between Taorirt and Ichmarirne – which is breathtaking in the hour before sunset. The map also names the most picturesque villages – many of which have **ksour and kasbahs** with extraordinarily complex patterns incised on the walls. Some include former Jewish quarters – mellahs – though today the populations are almost entirely Berber and Muslim, mainly from the Aït Todra tribe north of Tinerhir and the Aït Atta tribe to the south.

Southeast of Tinerhir there are potteries at **El Harat**, while at nearby **Tagia** are the tombs of the Aït Atta's chiefs, Hassou Ba Salam, and his son, Ali Ba Salam (see p.443). There's a marabout near El Harat which is the focus of a June/July moussem; this area was originally settled by black slaves who were known as Haratin. For more on the **Todra palmery** – and the approach to the gorge – see p.449.

Berber women collecting wood, near Tata

Aït Benhaddou kasbahs

Argan trees near Taroudannt

Rock carvings near Souk el Hadd

Dadès valley hairpins

Sidi Ifni: Spanish Art Deco

Tata

Ameln valley, Tafraoute

The famous sign at Zagora

The dunes at Merzouga

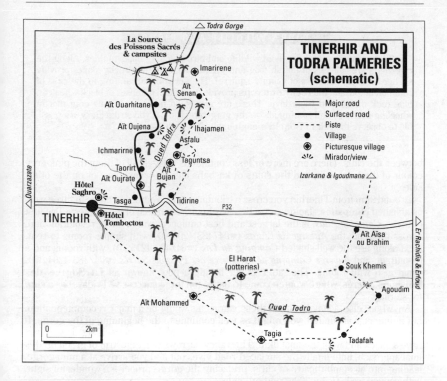

The Todra Gorge

Whatever else you do in the south, spend at least a night in the **Todra Gorge**. You don't need your own transport, nor any great expeditionary zeal to get up there, and yet it seems remote from the routes through the main valleys – still and splendid in the fading evening light when the day visitors have gone.

The deepest, narrowest and most spectacular part of the gorge is only 15km from Tinerhir, and there are three hotels where you can get a meal and stay the night. These can be reached by grand taxi or minibus from Tinerhir; they leave frequently and charge 6–8dh a place. Returning to Tinerhir, you stand a better chance of a taxi if you walk back to the **Zaouia Sidi Abdelâli**, 3km before the gorge, or hitch a lift with day visitors or other tourists.

Beyond the cluster of hotels, the road turns into a *piste*, providing an adventurous route right **over the Atlas** via the village of Imilchil (famed for its wedding market), as well as a possible loop over to the Dadès gorge. You can arrange transport along the Imilchil route, either by chartering it at Tinerhir, or by paying for a place on a series of Berber lorries, which shuttle across for village souks. If you plan to drive the route, you will need a suitable (preferably 4x4) vehicle.

Tinerhir to the gorge

En route to the gorge proper, the road climbs along the Todra palmery (see palmery map above), a last, fertile shaft of land, narrowing at points to a ribbon of palms

TODRA WILDLIFE AND BIRDS

The **Todra Gorge** offers excellent wildlife and bird-watching opportunities. Along the **riverbeds** are colonies of marsh frog and green toad, while the rocky slopes provide shelter for small numbers of ground squirrel. The **scrubby areas** ring to the calls of common bulbul and the **rocky outcrops** provide occasional glimpses of black wheatear, blue rock thrush and rock dove. There are also good numbers of pale crag martin **wheeling** overhead and soaring above the gorge crest and, if you strike lucky, it's possible to observe the pair of **Bonelli's eagles** which nest in the gorge.

between the cliffs. There are more or less continuous villages, all of them the pink-grey colour of the local rock, and the ruins of kasbahs and *ksour* up above or on the other side.

Around 9km from Tinerhir, you cross a tributary of the Todra, and come to three well-established **campsites**, flanking a particularly luxuriant stretch of the palmery. The first of these, *Camping Atlas*, is the largest and best equipped, with a shop, restaurant and, across the road, the *Auberge de l'Atlas* (☎04/483 4209; ①) with simple rooms to rent. Next along are the well-shaded *Camping du Lac* (☎04/483 4215; ①), with rooms and a restaurant, and *Auberge Camping de la Source des Poissons Sacrés* (☎04/483 4204; ①), again also with rooms. The latter is set beside a pool known as **La Source des Poissons Sacrés**, where women come to bathe (on three successive Fridays) as a cure for sterility.

Anywhere else, a stay in one of these campsites would be a major recommendation, but if time is at all limited, you might as well continue to the beginning of the gorge. If you're on local transport, and it's not too hot, you could get yourself set down here, have a snack and walk the final 6km. The valley narrows to a thin strip of green on this final approach, until finally the surfaced road gives out and you arrive at a mini-gorge, leading into an amphitheatre of cliffs, prefacing the **gorge** proper – a wonderful sight, with canyon walls rising 300m on both sides.

The mouth of the gorge

The really enclosed section of **the gorge** extends for just a few hundred metres; it should certainly be walked, even if you're not going any further, for the drama of the scenery. If you're interested in **birds**, this is also one of the best bird-watching locations in the south (see box above).

If at all possible, take the time to stay the night here, as the beauty of the place unfolds in the evening light. Just at the end of the surfaced road, and before the ford into the gorge proper, is the *Hôtel El Mansour* (☎04/483 4213; ①), an attractively ramshackle place with a pair of palm trees growing out through the roof, excellent and copious meals, and a choice of sleeping in one of four rooms, on the roof (the best option in summer), or on mattresses in the downstairs salon. Alongside is the *Auberge Etoiles des Gorges* (☎04/483 5158; ①); with only six rooms you should arrive early or phone ahead – the *auberge* restaurant serves traditional dishes in generous portions. The latest arrival here is the *Hôtel La Vallée* (☎04/483 5580; ①), where, once again, it's worth making reservations.

Through the mini-gorge in the amphitheatre of cliffs are two slightly fancier hotels, *Les Roches* (☎04/483 4814, fax 483 3611; ③) and *Yasmina* (☎04/483 4207, fax 483 3013; ③). These each have restaurants, sometimes under pressure from tour groups, but the food is good and the set lunches are a bargain. Again, they offer a choice of accommodation, including en-suite rooms, or cheaper beds in the salon or tent dining rooms, or out on the terrace. Prices fluctuate according to season and thus demand.

All these hotels are very friendly and relaxed – and all are very cold in winter, when the sun leaves the gorge early in the afternoon. If you wanted to camp, you would do better walking four or five kilometres up the gorge, to reach a more open section, though be sure to pitch your tent on reasonably high ground, in case of flash floods.

Climbing

The Todra Gorge is increasingly being recognized for its climbing potential. There are now many bolted routes, French Grade 5 and above. The *Hôtel El Mansour* keeps an excellent French topo-guide for reference which includes 150 such routes.

Beyond Todra: over the Atlas

It is possible to continue on *piste* routes beyond the Todra Gorge to **Tamtatoucht**, and from there across the High and Middle Atlas ranges, to emerge on either the P24 (Azrou–Beni Mellal), or the P21 (Midelt–Er Rachidia). In between, you are travelling on isolated and at times very rough tracks, for which four-wheel-drive vehicles (or mountain bikes) are highly desirable, though people make it across in Renaults or Citroëns in summer. If you don't have transport, you can travel on a succession of **Berber lorry-taxis** (*camionettes*), timed to coincide with local village souks. The attractions of this journey are considerable, offering a real experience of Berber mountain life – the villagers are generally very open and friendly – and some of the most exciting scenery in Morocco, in a succession of passes, mountains, rivers and gorges.

It's also possible to cross from the Todra Gorge to the **Dadès Gorge**, on a rough *piste* from Tamtatoucht (see p.452).

Practicalities

There are no **banks** between Tinerhir and Khenifra/Kasba Tadla/Rich, so you'll need to have enough cash for the journey. Don't underestimate the expense of buying **food** in the mountains (30–100 percent above normal rates), nor the prices charged for rides in the **Berber lorries**; as a very general guideline, reckon on about 20dh for every 50km. There are police stations at Aït Hani and Imilchil if you need serious help or advice on the state of the *pistes*.

Setting out on the **lorries** from Todra, the managers of the hotels at the mouth of the gorge usually have an idea of when the next *camionette* will pass through – and will help arrange your first ride. Promising days to start out are **Wednesday** (to coincide with Aït Hani's Thursday souk) and **Friday** (for Imilchil's Saturday souk), but it is all a bit pot luck, and you should be prepared for the odd day's wait in a village for a ride, or to walk one or other of the stages of the route. Eventually, everyone seems to get across to **Arhbala** or **Naour** (where there are buses down to Kasba Tadla/Khenifra) or to **Rich** (on the Midelt–Er Rachidia road and bus route); heading for Rich, the most used route is the 3443 from Bouzmou.

Travelling from the **north or east**, the same pattern applies, with lorries up from Arhbala/Rich for the Imilchil souk, and down to Todra/Tinerhir after it.

Driving, it would be unwise to attempt the route, without a four-wheel-drive vehicle, outside the midsummer period of June to September.

Tamtatoucht and beyond

The road up the Todra Gorge (from the hotels) is the worst section of the route; the track crosses or uses the river beds, or jolts along rough embankments. A marabout marks the top end of the gorge and a delightful shady walk; and then, 17km from the entrance to the gorge, you reach **TAMTATOUCHT**: a sizeable sprawl with a few basic

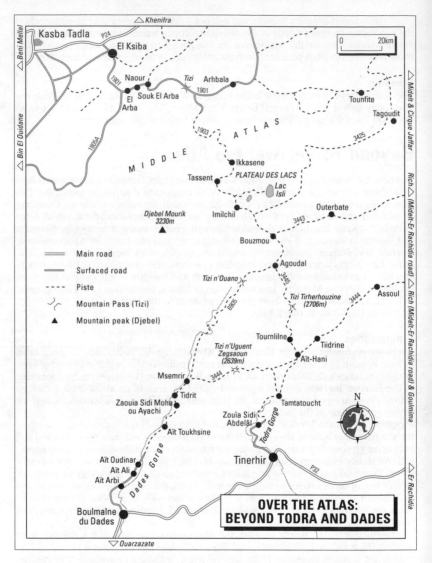

Main road

Surfaced road

- - - Piste

Mountain Pass (Tizi)

▲ Mountain peak (Djebel)

OVER THE ATLAS: BEYOND TODRA AND DADES

hotels and cafés. At the entrance is the new and friendly *Auberge Baddou* (①), with clean rooms, hot showers, good food and *terrasse panoramique*. You can also camp alongside. Beyond this point, the road improves considerably, though it is still un-surfaced and slow, difficult mountain driving.

Across to the Dadès Gorge

It's at Tamtatoucht that anyone intent on **crossing over to the Dadès Gorge** (see p.446) should turn off to the west, on the very rough *piste* 3444 to Msemrir; lifts are most unlikely, so it's basically an option for Landrover-type vehicles. The start of this route has been altered by storms and you should seek local advice on whether to cut across, or go via Aït Hani.

Whichever route is advised, you will eventually join the Aït Hani–Msemrir *piste* before a tough ascent across limestone pavements. The track goes over a small pass and then up the long **Tizgui n'Ouadda** valley towards a huge scarp before the final sweeping bends to the **Tizi n'Uguent Zegsaoun** (2639m). The difficulties then increase; the road is in a bad state with wash-outs and diversions. Only when you edge the final plain and join the Msemrir-Agoudal *piste* does it improve – by which stage Msemrir is just around the corner.

Aït Hani and on to Imilchil

Continuing north from Tamtatoucht into the High Atlas, you head towards **AÏT HANI**, another large village, almost the size of Tamtatoucht. It's just off the main route, and if you're driving you can keep going, turning after the town, rather than into it. On the outskirts, as you approach from the south, there is a police/military post, café and store; there's no hotel or rooms. This region is generally high and barren landscape – the locals travel amazing distances each day to collect wood for fuel. A poor and little-used *piste* leads east from Aït Hani towards Goulmima/Rich.

North of Aït Hani there is a stiff climb up to 2700m at **Tizi Tirherhouzine**, then down to **AGOUDAL**. This is a friendly village, and though again there is no official hotel, you'll probably be offered a room. It is in a less harsh setting, too, better irrigated, and the people seem more relaxed than at Aït Hani. There is the chance of a

---

ROCKS, FOSSILS AND MINERALS

Along roadsides in the High and Anti-Atlas and down into the southeast, boys bound into the paths of oncoming cars to offer crystalline mementos of Morocco, and rocks, fossils and minerals are staples of most tourist shops in the south. Before purchasing, you might want to read these notes:

Geode Tennis-ball-sized specimens of crystals in a hollow geode cost around £12/$20 in Britain or the US; on the Moroccan hard-shoulder, they may cost more. Brilliant orange and red geodes and slices of rock crystal (quartz) look attractive but are unknown to natural science, as are the quartz geodes given an iridescent metal coating by vendors.

Ammonites Attractive spirals of ammonites (from Carboniferous to Jurassic) are common in the limestone areas of Britain but in Morocco they can be bought sliced and polished as well as "raw". Do not rely on the species name you are given by the shopkeeper – look at the centre of the spiral of the ammonite and at the ridge around its shell to check how far natural features have been "enhanced" by a chisel.

Trilobites Slightly older than ammonites, trilobites often appear in shops as identical beige-coloured fossils on grey slate. In nature, they are rarely so perfect – beware plaster casts. The early trilobite *paradoxides* is about the size of a hand, with long whisker-like spines. A deep-sea inhabitant, it is often found looking rather squashed sideways, where the silts on which it lived have been sheared by pressure. The *Calymene* and *Phacops* types of trilobites are about 200 million years younger than *Paradoxides*. They measure about two inches long, with a crab-like outer skeleton. The half-rounded shield-like skull, often found separated from the exo-skeleton, can appear in a shop with the rest of the skeleton carved around it as a tribute to modern Moroccan craftsmanship.

In the black limestone regions near Erfoud, the white crystalline shapes of **belemnoids**, **ammonites** and **nautilus** are cross-sectioned and polished to emphasize the internal structure before being formed into ash-trays and even coffee tables, which can of course be transported for you at a cost. They don't always look so good back home.

room at **BOUZMOU**, the next village on, where you might also pick up a *camionette* along *piste* 3443 to Rich on the Midelt–Er Rachidia road. This is the most commonly used (and best condition) route east from the Imilchil road and sees a lot more traffic than *pistes* 3444 or 3445.

The road north improves greatly from Agoudal on, passing beyond Bouzmou through a fertile region to reach **IMILCHIL** (45km from Agoudal). This beautiful village, with a fine caidal kasbah, is for most people the highlight of the route. It's famed for its September moussem – the so-called **Marriage Market of Aït Haddidou**. The moussem, once a genuine tribal function, is now somewhat corrupted by tourism (groups are shuttled up from Marrakesh), but it's a lively, extravagant occasion all the same. Imilchil has a couple of small **hotels** and café-restaurants. It also has several resident trekking guides; Bassou Chabout (postal address: 51930 Imilchil Centre, Province d'Er Rachidia) is reliable and qualified.

To the east of Imilchil is the **Plateau des Lacs** – flanked by the twin mountain lakes of **Isli** and **Tislit**, named after a couple from Berber folklore, whose love was thwarted and whose tears fell to form the two lakes. Some groups go up here to camp, but it's not especially compelling. The route north of Imilchil to Arhbala, by contrast, runs through spectacular scenery, with steep drops off the road side, constant climbs and descents, and a slow move into forestation. This section has few settlements – and certainly nowhere the size of Imilchil.

A paved road starts a few miles after **CHERKET**. At **ARHBALA** (see p.258), there is a very basic hotel near the marketplace (Wednesday souk), and a daily bus on to El Ksiba, where you can pick up connections to Khenifra and Beni Mellal. Another surfaced road heads off to join the Khenifra–Midelt road (P33).

Tinerhir to Er Rachidia and Erfoud

East from Tinerhir, there is little to delay your progress to **Erfoud/Er Rachidia** and the Tafilalt. The more attractive route is the minor road (3451) from **Tinejdad to Erfoud**; the **Er Rachidia road** (P32) is a fast but dull highway. Neither presents any problems for drivers.

Using local transport, you can get buses or grands taxis along the P32 to Er Rachidia; the taxis involve changes at **Tinejdad** (buses and taxis leave from the east end of the town) and **Goulmima**. Alternatively, a private-line bus leaves Tinejdad (from the square used by the grands taxis, on the main road) daily at 9.30am along the 3451 **to Erfoud and Rissani**, arriving at Rissani about four hours later; to make the connection, get a grand taxi from Tinerhir to Tinejdad.

Er Rachidia via Goulmima

This is a straightforward and largely barren route, broken only by the oases of Tinejdad and Goulmima.

GOULMIMA, a long, straggling palmery, is made up of some twenty or so scattered **ksour**. If you have transport, and are interested in exploring, ask directions along the complex network of tracks to the *ksour* known as **Gheris de Charis**, the grandest in the palmery. Modern Goulmima, beside the highway, is signalled by the usual "triumphal" entrance and exit arches of the south, and has little more within. There is, however, a Banque Populaire, and a small **hotel**, the *Gheris*, 2 Rue Saadian, off Boulevard Hassan II (☎05/578 3167; ②); despite the address it actually faces the main road. One highlight of the hotel is a unique collection and display of herbs. For **meals**, the *Restaurant Elle et Lui* is recommended. There's also a **campsite** to the east of the town, *Les Palmiers* (☎ and fax 05/578 4004), which is difficult to find (follow the signs)

and inaccessible to camper vans, but has a restaurant and six en-suite rooms (②).
Buses leave from the street to the left of the eastern archway exit (coming from
Tinerhir), **grands taxis** from further up this street.

Erfoud via Tinejdad

This alternative route – **direct to Erfoud** – is, in parts, eerily impressive. It's well-
surfaced all the way to Erfoud, though sections are sometimes covered over with sand,
the result of small, spiralling sandstorms that can suddenly blow across the region and,
for twenty or thirty seconds, cut visibility to zero.

The road branches off from the P32 to Er Rachidia at **TINEJDAD**; at the junction
itself, there is the useful and welcoming *Café Restaurant Oued Ed-Dahab*. Tinejdad itself
is one long street, either side of which are the usual services: petrol station, post office,
bank and cafés. If you want – or have – to spend the night, the only accommodation is
the *Hôtel Tizgue* (☎05/578 6774; ①). From here the road follows a course of lush oases
– populated by the Aït Atta tribe, traditional warriors of the south who used to control
land and exact tribute as far afield as the Drâa, 175 km to the southwest and on the far
edge of the Djebel Sarhro (see p.440). There are some impressive kasbahs – ask directions to the **Kasbah Asrir**.

You leave the oasis at **MELLAB**, which has another fine **ksar**, and from then on it's
more or less continuous desert *hammada* until the beginning of the vast palmery of **EL
JORF** – the Tafilalt's largest *ksar* (population 6000) – on the approach to Erfoud. There
are a few cafés in the modern village, a post office and a petrol station, but no hotel.
Beside the road, over much of the distance from Mellab to Erfoud, the land is pockmarked by parallel lines of strange, volcanic-shaped humps – actually man-made entries
to the old underground **irrigation channels** or *khettara*. Another curiosity, notable
here and elsewhere along the oasis routes, are the Berber **cemeteries** walled off from
the desert at the edge of the *ksour*. These consist of long fields of pointed stones thrust
into the ground and the occasional cactus and thorn bush, but otherwise unidentified:
a wholly practical measure to prevent jackals from unearthing bodies – and in so doing,
frustrating their entry to paradise.

ER RACHIDIA, THE ZIZ VALLEY AND THE TAFILALT

The great date-palm oases of the **Oued Ziz** and **Tafilalt** come as near as anywhere in
Morocco to fulfilling Western fantasies about the Sahara. They do so by occupying
the last desert stretches of the **Ziz** Valley: a route shot through with lush and amazingly cinematic scenes, from its fertile beginnings at the *Source Bleue* (springwater
pool) oasis meeting point of **Meski**, to a climax amid the rolling sand dunes of
Merzouga. Along the way, once again, are an impressive succession of *ksour*, and an
extraordinarily rich palmery – historically the most important territory this side of
the Atlas.

Strictly speaking, the Tafilalt (or Tafilalet) comprises the oases south of **Erfoud**, its
principal town and gateway. Nowadays, however, the provincial capital is the French-
built garrison town and administrative centre of **Er Rachidia**. If you're making a circuit of the south, you will pass through here, from or en route to Midelt – a journey
through the great canyon of the **Ziz Gorges** (see p.459). Er Rachidia is also a crossroads for the route east to Figuig – which used to be an important crossing point into
Algeria when the frontier was open.

THE TAFILALT: PAST AND PRESENT

The Tafilalt was for centuries the Moroccan terminus of the **caravan routes** – the famous **Salt Road** to the south across the Sahara to West Africa, by way of Timbuktu. Merchants travelling south carried with them weapons, cloth and spices, part of which they traded en route at Taghaza (in modern-day Mali) for local **salt**, the most-sought after commodity in West Africa. They would continue south and then make the return trip from the old Kingdom of Ghana, to the west of Timbuktu, loaded with **gold** (one ounce of gold was exchanged for one pound of salt at the beginning of the nineteenth century) and, until European colonists brought an end to the trade, with **slaves**.

These were long journeys: Taghaza was twenty days by camel from Tafilalt, Timbuktu sixty, and merchants might be away for up to a year if they made a circuit via southern Libya (where slaves were still sold until the Italian occupation in 1911). They also, of course, brought an unusual degree of contact with other cultures, which ensured the Tafilalt a reputation as one of the most unstable parts of the Moroccan empire, frequently riven by religious dissent and separatism.

The separatism had a long history, dating back to the eighth century, when the region prospered as the independent kingdom of **Sijilmassa** (see p.466); the dissent began when the *Filalis* – as Tafilalt's predominantly Berber population is known – adopted the **Kharijisite heresy**, a movement which used a Berber version of the Koran (orthodox Islam forbids any translation of God's direct Arabic revelation to Muhammad). Then in the fifteenth century it again emerged as a source of trouble, fostering the Marabout uprising that toppled the Saadian dynasty.

It is with the establishment of the **Alaouite** (or, after their birthplace, *Filali*) dynasty that the Tafilalt is most closely associated. Mounted from a zaouia in Rissani by Moulay

Er Rachidia

ER RACHIDIA was established by the French as a regional capital – when it was known as Ksar Es Souk, after their Foreign Legion fort. Today, it represents more than anywhere else the new face of the Moroccan south: a shift away from the old desert markets and trading routes to a modern urban centre. The town's role as a military outpost, originally against tribal dissidence, particularly from the Aït Atta (see p.443), was maintained after independence by the threat of territorial claims from Algeria, and there is still a significant garrison here, even though Morocco's military focus has long been hundreds of miles distant, in the Western Sahara.

The town is, in fact, quite a pleasant and relaxed place to stay, with an air of relative prosperity, and a large student population, at the lycée and university. In the evenings, the streets come alive, with groups strolling along the main street and packing into the café-restaurants.

Practicalities

Er Rachidia has a functional grid layout, with most facilities – banks, cafés and restaurants, a covered market and tourist office – strung along the highway/main street, **Avenue Moulay Ali Cherif**. This runs all the way through town, between the familiar southern ceremonial roadside arches, turning into **Avenue El Massira** after crossing the bridge over the Oued Ziz.

All **buses** arrive at the main bus station, on the Place Principale, just south of Avenue Moulay Ali Cherif.

Rachid, and secured by his successor Moulay Ismail, this is the dynasty which still holds power in Morocco, through Mohammed VI, the fifteenth sultan in the line. The Alaouites were also the source of the wealth of many of the old kasbahs and *ksour*, from the time of Moulay Ismail, through to the last century, the sultans exiled princes and unruly relatives out here to the edge of the desert.

The Tafilalt was a major centre of resistance to the French, who were limited to their garrison at Erfoud and an outpost of the Foreign Legion at Ouled Zohra until 1931.

THE TAFILALT TODAY – AND BAYOUD DISEASE

The Tafilalt today, deprived of its contacts to the south, is something of a backwater, with a population estimated at around 80,000 and declining, as the effects of drought and Bayoud disease have taken hold on the palms. Most of the population are smallhold farmers, with thirty or so palms for each family, from which they could hope to produce around a thousand kilos of dates in a reasonable year. With the market price of dates around 6dh a kilo there are no fortunes to be made.

It is reckoned that two-thirds of Moroccan palmeries are infected with **Bayoud disease**. First detected in the Drâa at the beginning of the twentieth century, this is a kind of fungus, which is spread from root to root and possibly by transmission of spores. Palms die within a year of an attack, creating a secondary problem by leaving a gap in the wedge of trees, which allows the winds to blow through. The disease cannot be treated economically – the most that farmers can do is to isolate trees by digging a ditch round them and the only real hope seems to lie in the development of resistant species of palms. Moroccan and French scientists, in collaboration with the Total oil company, are at present working on new methods of propagation and cross-breeding. A resistant species has already, in fact, been developed in France, but there's one problem: the dates, so far, taste awful.

Accommodation, eating and drinking

Despite its size, Er Rachidia has a limited choice of decent **hotels** and if you want to **camp**, the position is no better: the municipal site, still signposted just across the bridge, is closed and the *Source Bleue* at Meski, 18km south of Er Rachidia (see p.459), is the nearest possibility. Fortunately, the tourist complex at Meski has now improved beyond measure and it's a recommended alternative.

You can **eat** well at the hotels *Kenzi Rissani, M'Daghra, Oasis* and *Renaissance*. Alternatively, there are any number of cafés and restaurants, of which the *Restaurant Imilchil*, serving excellent food in an attractive setting opposite the covered market, and *Café Terminus*, on Avenue Moulay Ali Cherif, are recommended.

There's also a nameless place by the entrance to the bus station which serves good *harira* soup and there's a reasonable **bar**, cheaper than that in the *Hôtel L'Oasis*, facing the PTT.

HOTELS

Hôtel M'Daghra, 92 Rue Madaghra (☎05/557 4087, fax 579 0864). Opened in 1994, this is an OK place, a block south of the bus station. En-suite rooms and a reasonable restaurant. ③.

Hôtel Meski, Av. Moulay Ali Cherif (☎05/557 2065). 400m out of town, on the right as you come in from Midelt or Goulmima. Car parking is assured, but it's not convenient for public transport. There are rooms with and without showers; the restaurant is alcohol-free. All in all, best kept in reserve in case other hotels are full. ②.

Hôtel de l'Oasis, 4 Rue Sidi Bou Abdallah (☎05/557 2519). Previously this was barely value for money, but it's been revitalized and has good en-suite rooms and a flourishing restaurant in the cellar. It's also conveniently central. ②.

Hôtel Renaissance, 19 Rue Moulay Youssef (☎05/557 2633). This is very much the best budget choice, offering cheap, simple rooms, some with showers, and a decent restaurant; again, close to the bus station. ①.

Hôtel Royal, 8 Rue Mohammed Zerktouni (☎05/557 3068). This is the best of the three hotels near Place Hassan II, convenient for grands taxis, 100m uphill from the bus station. The nearby *Hôtel Marhaba* and *Hôtel Oliviers* (aka *Zitoun*) are both cheaper, but not recommended. ①.

Hôtel Kenzi Rissani, Av. Al Massira (☎05/557 2186, fax 557 2585). Just across the bridge, on the right-hand side travelling towards Meski. This was privatized in 1994, and is now one of the Kenzi chain. It's considerably improved and has some sparkle and energy; the rooms have been refurbished and TV installed – and the restaurant functions; evening meal 140dh. ⑤.

Listings

Banks There are four banks – Banque Populaire, BMC, BMCE and BMCI – all shown on the map.

Car repairs There is a Renault agent on Place Hassan II, which carries a large supply of parts and will order others efficiently from Fes.

Petrol stations There is a Ziz station on the Midelt road, and a Somepi station on the Erfoud road.

Petits taxis leave from outside the covered market on Av. Moulay Ali Cherif.

Post office The PTT on Av. Mohammed V has all usual services.

Shopping The covered market is a reliable source of fresh food. There's a good craft shop, 6 Rue Sidi Ben Abdellah, by the *Hôtel de l'Oasis*; for once, the invitation to "just look" is sincere and there's no hassle. The Ensemble Artisanal (8.30am–noon & 2.30–6.30pm) is on Av. Moulay Ali Cherif, opposite the Banque Populaire, on the way out of town towards the *Hôtel Kenzi Rissani*; it has a good display of local goods: pottery, brass, wood and, truly indigenous, basketware made of palm leaves. Once again, there's no hassle and the staff are knowledgeable and helpful.

Tourist office There's a helpful Délégation du Tourisme (☎05/557 0944; Mon–Fri: summer 7am–2pm; winter 8.30am–noon & 2.30–6.30pm) at 44 Av. Prince Moulay Abdallah, found by leaving town on the Tinerhir road and turning right opposite the new PTT.

Tours The *Hôtel Renaissance* offers Landrover expeditions.

Moving on

Buses leave at least four times a day for Erfoud/Rissani, and a similar number head north to Midelt and Fes or Meknes, via the dramatic Ziz Gorges. The CTM bus to Ouarzazate goes on to Marrakesh.

It's usually no problem to get a seat in a **grand taxi** to Erfoud or, paying the same price, to the Meski turning; these leave from opposite the bus station, as do grands taxis to Tinerhir. Grands taxis from Place Hassan II run to other destinations: check on your destination before setting out with baggage.

Meski and the Ziz valley

The small palm grove of **MESKI** is watered by a natural spring-water pool – the famous **Source Bleue**, extended by the French Foreign Legion and long a postcard image and favourite campsite for travellers. It's set on the riverbank, below a huge ruined *ksar* on the opposite bank and, with several of the springs channelled into a **swimming pool**, it's as romantic a spot as any in the south. Outside midsummer, you might also consider walking part of the way downstream in the valley bottom, southeast of Meski. The superb four-hour **trek** along the Oued Ziz will bring you to **Oulad Aïssa**, a *ksar* with fabulous views over the upper Tafilalt.

In recent years, the **campsite** was poorly maintained but it has now been taken over by the local commune of M'Daghra which seems to have got a grip on the place, though there are reports of hustlers on site. The pool is enticing; and as it's moving spring water it's said to be safe from bilharzia. The toilets are also flushed by spring water; and the camping areas are shaded by bamboo, palms and tamarisks. The **café** is modest, but meals are usually available, given a little notice.

The *source* is somewhat insignificantly signposted, to the south of the Erfoud road, 18km south of Er Rachidia. Coming by bus, ask to get out by the turn-off: from here it's only 400m down to the pool and campsite. **Going on** to Erfoud or back to Er Rachidia from Meski can be tricky, since most of the buses pass by full and don't stop. However, this is an easy place to hitch a lift from other tourists.

South from Meski: the Ziz palmery

Heading south from Er Rachidia and Meski, **towards Erfoud**, the P21 trails the final section of the **Oued Ziz**. Make sure you travel this in daylight, as it's one of the most pleasing of all the southern routes: a dry red belt of desert just beyond Meski, and then, suddenly, a drop into the valley and the great **Tizimi palmery** – a prelude of the Tafilalt, leading into Erfoud. Away from the road, **ksour** are almost continuous – glimpsed through the trees and high walls enclosing gardens and plots of farming land.

If you want to stop and take a closer look at the *ksour*, **AOUFOUSS**, midway to Erfoud, and the site of a **Thursday souk**, is perhaps the most accessible. **MAADID**, too, off to the left of the road as you approach Erfoud, is interesting – a really massive **ksar**, which is considered to be the start of the Tafilalt proper.

Between Aoufouss and Maadid, 15km from Erfoud and to the west of the road near the one remaining tower of Borj Yerdi, you will see a couple of spectacular **chalybeate geysers** shooting aerated iron-bearing water up to five metres into the air: a photo-opportunity, if nothing else – and not a hustler in sight.

Erfoud

ERFOUD, like Er Rachidia, is largely a French-built administrative centre, and its desultory frontier-town atmosphere fulfils little of the promise of the Tafilalt. Arriving from Er Rachidia, however, you get a first, powerful sense of proximity to the desert, with frequent sandblasts ripping through the streets, and total darkness in the event of a (not uncommon) electrical black-out. This desert position is best appreciated from the vantage point of the **Borj Est**, the hill-fort 3km across the river, from where you can get a glimpse of the sands to the south; the fort itself is still used by the military, but

△ ❶ *Tinerhir (3451)*

ERFOUD

Usine de Marmar

Hospital

PTT

H. Fossile Export

AVENUE MOULAY ISMAIL

AVENUE MOULAY ISMAIL

Ⓐ **Banque Populaire**

Total petrol station

Ziz petrol station

CTM buses

Rissani (P21) ◁

Er Rachidia (P21) ▷

RESTAURANTS & CAFÉ'S
Café des Dunes	B
Restaurant les Fleurs	C
Restaurant de la Jeunesse	E
Restaurant l'Oasis	D
Restaurant Sijilmassa	A
Café du Sud	F

ACCOMMODATION
Hôtel Esaada	6
Hôtel Farah Zouar	3
Hôtel La Gazelle	2
Hôtel Kasbah Tizmi	1
Hôtel Lahmada	4
Hôtel Merzouga	9
Hôtel Les Palmiers	10
Hôtel Sable d'Or	8
Hôtel Salam	5
Hôtel Tafilalet	7
Hôtel Ziz	11

Oued Ziz

PLACE DES FAR

Souk

N

0   100m

Ford/weir

▽ *Borj Est & Merzouga (3461)*

you can drive up to the public car park, by petit taxi or rental car, and then walk the last 200 metres for the all-round views.

Views apart, for most travellers Erfoud functions very much as a staging post for the sand dunes near **Merzouga**, and/or the last oasis village of **Rissani**. Its only other point of interest, aside from its **date festival** (see box opposite), is the local **marble industry**, which produces a unique, high-quality black marble which, like all marbles, is metamorphosed limestone, in this case containing fascinating fossils. When polished, it's attractive and can be seen locally on every bar top and reception desk.

You can visit the marble works on the Tinerhir road; ask – or look for – the Usine de Marmar (see map). A German sculptor, Fred Jansen, and his Arts Natura group, pioneered carving the marble so that the fossils are revealed in 3D and, at its best, this is most impressive. But the process has been developed locally without taste so that the contrived artifacts are pure kitsch. The better-class work can be seen in the showroom at the marble works (Mon–Sat 8am–noon & 2–4pm) or the more central H. Fossile Export opposite the *Hôtel Esaada* on Avenue Moulay Ismail.

Accommodation and eating

Erfoud has an impressive range of **hotels**, at all price levels, although its finest – the old kasbah-like four-star *Hotel Sijilmassa* – has departed from the lists of late and was converted into a residence for the late King Hassan II (his first palace in the province). In picking a hotel, you may want to go for one that offers transport to the dunes at Merzouga in order to see the desert dawn. Or you may prefer to stay en route to Merzouga; the *Hôtel Erfati* (☎05/557 7372; ⑤), 1.5km from Erfoud on the road to Rissani, is the latest

THE FESTIVAL OF THE DATES

Erfoud's **Festival of Dates** is held over three days in October and you will be richly rewarded if you can visit at that time. As with all such events, it's a mixture of symbolism, sacred rites and entertainment. Traditionally, dates bring good luck: tied to a baby's arm they ensure a sweet nature, thrown at a bride they encourage fertility, and offered to strangers they signify friendship.

On the first morning of the festival, prayers are said at the mausoleum of Moulay Ali Shereef at Rissani and, the same evening, there is a fashion show of traditional costumes: a pride of embroidered silk, silver and gold headdresses, sequins and elaborate jewellery. Then there are processions, athletics and, on the last night, traditional music and spiritual songs.

and grandest development in the area with ample en-suite rooms, bar and restaurant; the *Hôtel Kasbah Asmâa* on the same road is not recommended.

Most of the hotels have **restaurants**. In addition, the *Restaurant les Fleurs, Restaurant de la Jeunesse, Restaurant l'Oasis* and *Café du Sud*, all on Avenue Mohammed V, serve modestly priced meals, as do the *Café des Dunes*, near the *Hôtel Tafilalet*, the *Restaurant Sijilmassa*, opposite the hospital on Avenue Moulay Ismail, and the *Café-Restaurant de Clap*, near the CTM.

CHEAP

Hôtel Esaada, 50 Av. Moulay Ismail (☎05/557 6317). It changes too often for its financial well-being: noisy and near the Total petrol station. A fall-back. ①.

Hôtel La Gazelle, Av. Mohammed V (☎05/557 6028). By the *Gendarmerie Royale* and opposite the PTT. Pleasant and cheerful nine-room hotel with en-suite rooms and constant hot water. There's a good restaurant in the basement; *menu du jour* 75dh. ①.

Hôtel Lahmada, Av. Mohammed V (☎05/557 6980). A modern hotel, opened in 1994. En-suite rooms with quality furniture and the corridors are tiled. Value for money. ②.

Hôtel Merzouga, 114 Av. Mohammed V (☎05/557 6532). Spotless en-suite rooms with hot showers; or you can sleep on the terrace for 25dh a head. ①.

Hôtel Les Palmiers, 36 Av. Mohammed V (☎05/557 5086, fax 557 8039). There are showers in the rooms, and toilets along the corridors; and redecoration, including the downstairs café, is promising. ①.

MODERATE TO EXPENSIVE

Hôtel Farah Zouar, Av. Moulay Ismail (☎ & fax 05/557 6230). On the roundabout where roads to Rissani and to Tinerhir part. An elegant hotel, whose *terrasse panoramique* looks over the palmery and towards Borj Est. It's a friendly place and caters for individuals rather than groups. Restaurant, but no bar. ④.

Hôtel Kasbah Tizmi (☎05/557 6179, fax 557 7375). One kilometre from the town centre on the Tinerhir road, this hotel is built in traditional style with *pisé* walls and is worth a visit, even if you can't afford to stay. ⑨.

Hôtel Sable d'Or, 179 Av. Mohammed V (☎05/557 6348), near the junction with Av. Moulay Ismail and the Banque Populaire. Good on most counts: clean, comfortable, en suite, hot showers, views from terrace. ③.

Hôtel Salam, Av. Moulay Ismail (☎05/557 6665, fax 557 6426). A pricey tour group hotel with an old and (more expensive) new wing. Swimming pool and restaurant. ⑤.

Hôtel Tafilalet, Av. Moulay Ismail (☎05/557 6535, fax 557 6036). The top choice if you have a little money to spare. It rivals the much more expensive *Hôtel Salam* (see above), with a swimming pool, attractive decor and friendly staff. The hotel also runs a useful shuttle to Merzouga and owns the *Hôtel Merzouga* there. ④.

Hôtel Ziz, 3 Av. Mohammed V (☎05/557 6154, fax 557 6811), at the bottom end of the main street and nearest to the Sunday souk. Well-furnished en-suite rooms, air-conditioned and around a small courtyard. The owner, quite an entrepreneur, runs the wholesale warehouse next door, and again has a couple of Landrovers available for the sunrise shuttle to Merzouga. ③.

Moving on

CTM **buses** leave from Avenue Mohammed V; others from the Place des F.A.R. There is a daily private-line service to Tinejdad, which allows you to make a connection to Tinerhir, avoiding the need to backtrack via Er Rachidia.

The dunes of Merzouga

The **Erg Chebbi** – the sand dunes at **Merzouga** – are one of the great sights of Morocco. They are reached most directly along the 3461 road south of Erfoud, which is surfaced for the first 16km, then gives way to 35km of *piste*. It is along this road that the Landrover tours are offered by the *Hôtel Ziz* and *Hôtel Tafilalet*, to catch sunrise at the dunes. If you can't afford these, it may be possible to join up with other tourists doing the trip – try asking round at the *Hôtel Salam* or *Hôtel Tafilalet*, either the night before or at dawn. Your presence may be welcome as an extra shoulder to push the car if it gets trapped in the sand.

You can, alternatively, reach Merzouga by way of **Rissani** – or complete a circuit by travelling back this way. The Merzouga–Rissani route is covered in a southeast to northwest direction on p.465; it's served by local transit and Landrover taxis.

Erfoud to Merzouga

The road from Erfoud to Merzouga is practicable by Renault 4L. It takes around an hour and a quarter, and is reasonably easy to follow, with a line of telephone poles running parallel almost the whole way. A guide isn't necessary, though, if you're travelling alone, an extra person to push, when you get stuck in the sandy tracks, would be wise.

Leaving Erfoud, you cross the Oued Ziz by a ford-cum-weir and drive past the road which goes up to the Borj Est (3km). At around the 15km mark, the surfaced road gives

---

DESERT WILDLIFE AND THE LAKE

Merzouga makes an excellent centre for the exploration of Morocco's sandy (or "true") desert, whose flora and fauna show ingenious adaptations to these least hospitable of living conditions. Bird-watchers will find most of interest. In early spring a lake, **Dayet Srji**, usually forms just to the west of Merzouga village, and it regularly attracts scores of pink flamingos – a wonderful sight out here in the wilds.

During the spring migration, the lake and the bushes thereabouts attract many birds which have just crossed the desert; look particularly for the ruddy sheldrake and note that the first Moroccan sighting of Kittllitz's plover was recorded here. More unusual sightings, if you strike lucky, might include the desert sparrow, Tristram's desert warbler, Egyptian nightjar and Arabian bustard.

The desert is also an ideal environment for **reptiles**, including the Algerian sand lizard and Berber skink, and typical **desert mammals** – more often located by their giveaway tracks in the morning sand than by nocturnal sightings – include the jerboa, desert hedgehog and fennec (desert fox).

Plant life is limited because of the extreme scarcity of water; the only survivors include the lichens and algae which can take up sufficient water from the condensation of dew which forms on the undersurfaces of rocks and stones, although even the desert has an all-too-brief **spring bloom** when the rains do come – dominated by pink asphodels and mauve statice.

TAFILALT AND THE ROADS TO MERZOUGA

△ Er Rachidia

Erfoud

Borj Est

Ouled Zohra

E R G   C H E B B I

Oued Amerbouh

P21

Oued Ziz

El Mansouriya

Haroun

N

Sijilmassa
Rissani

Ksar d'Akbar
Zaouia of Moulay Ali Shereef

Oulad Abdelhalim

Ouirhlane

Asserchine

Tinrheras

Tabassant

Zaouiet El Maati

Irara

Gaouz

Hassi Bedi

Legend

——	Surfaced road
- - -	Piste
⌂	Ksar
🛆	Fort
⌒	Dune

Oued Ziz

Merzouga

ACCOMMODATION

Auberge Kasbah Derkaoua	1
Auberge Café du Sud	4
Auberge La Caravanne	3
Auberge Les Dunes d'Or	5
Auberge Er Chebbi	6
Auberge Kasbah des Dunes	7
Hôtel Merzouga	9
Auberge l'Oasis	8
Auberge Yasmina	2

Dayet Sriji
(seasonal salt lakes)

0   5km

▽ Taouz

way to *piste*. Not far beyond is the little *Auberge Kasbah Derkaoua* (aka *Chez Michel*; ☎05/557 7140; half board ④), an attractive, French-run **hotel**, which offers charming rooms and superb meals; it closes January and June to late August and booking is advisable in March and April when groups of ornithologists fly in – hotel transport will meet RAM flights at Er Rachidia and there's now a helipad at the hotel.

From this point on, the line of telephone poles becomes useful, as the road splays into numerous parallel tracks carved out by cars, Landrovers and motorbikes, in the sandy crust. The dunes, clearly visible by this stage, provide further orientation, aligned almost perfectly north–south. On the *hammada*/dune line is a twenty-kilometre string of little **auberges**, offering rooms, meals and camping. They are listed in the order in which you would find them, following a north–south route on the *hammada*/ dune line. At the end of the route, just before Merzouga itself, there's also a hotel.

Accommodation

Auberge Yasmina (☎05/557 6783, fax 577 4071). A small, basic place but the setting is fabulous; you can camp amongst a few trees and, in winter/spring there's sometimes a small lake nearby, with flamingos. ②.

Auberge La Caravanne (☎06/135 1654, fax 05/557 5219). New, with en-suite rooms and a swimming pool. ②.

Auberge Café du Sud (☎05/557 5606). Small place, with just ten rooms but cheap. ①.

Auberge Les Dunes d'Or (☎05/557 7146). A larger place with rooms around a courtyard, hot showers, good cooking, pleasant staff. Parked outside is the rusting fuselage of a plane used in a film of Antoine de Saint-Exupéry's fable, *Le Petit Prince*. ②.

Auberge Erg Chebbi (☎05/557 7320). One of the more comfortable places with good rooms. ②.

Auberge Kasbah des Dunes Another small, basic hotel near the hamlet of Hassi Bedi ("white well"). Not as good as *L'Oasis*, but an acceptable alternative if the latter is full. There's the opportunity to meet the locals; quite an experience. ①.

Auberge L'Oasis (☎ & fax 05/557 7321). A cheerful place with twelve rooms around a courtyard and the possibility of camping and camel rides; it's also near Hassi Bedi. ①.

Hôtel Merzouga One kilometre before you arrive at Merzouga village, and overlooked by the highest of the sand dunes, this is an outpost of the *Hôtel Tafilalet* in Erfoud and can be booked through them (☎05/557 6535). It's well managed and has now taken over the next-door *Hôtel Salam*: together they offer a range of accommodation and, as in most of the auberges, you can choose to sleep in a tent or on the terrace/roof if you prefer. ②.

Merzouga village – and camel trips

Merzouga village is no great shakes, but if you want to stay, there are half a dozen **café-hotels** scattered in and round the village, most of them pretty basic, with no electricity and outside toilets and showers. The best of these cheapies is the *Café des Amis* but, having come this distance, it's a shame not to stay alongside the dunes (in one or other of the options above).

Any visitor to Merzouga will receive no end of offers of **camel trips** – anything from a couple of hours' climb up the dunes to two or three days' trekking. It's best to seek the advice of the staff at one of the auberges recommended above if you want to be assured of your money's worth. For the uncommitted, two hours at sunset should be sufficient to get a taste of the dunes and avoid getting saddle-sore. The prices are highly negotiable: 75dh per person is perhaps about right for a two-hour ride.

The dunes

The **dune** beside the *Hôtel Merzouga* is said to be the highest in Morocco – and, so locals would have it, the world. It is undeniably impressive and it may look familiar, for it was used in a Renault advert, with a car driving down its slope. Cars, incidentally, seem to have an uncontrollable passion for dunes, for Merzouga is a post in the **North African Rally** (held in January); the drivers' stickers add a slightly surreal tone to the village. A more appropriate transport on the dunes is demonstrated by local kids, who sandsurf on plastic bags down the slopes of an evening.

The desert of dunes fascinates Moroccans and foreigners alike. Mention Merzouga anywhere in Morocco and people will tell you of the power of the sands to cure rheumatics who come here to be buried up to the neck in the sand; the patient is only under the sand for a minute or two – otherwise it can be fatal. The dunes also have a wide-ranging aesthetic appeal; witness the film directors, writers, artists and photographers who struggle to convey their beauty. An extraordinary book of photographs by Michel Teuler illustrates this and one critic, Gérard Lanux, visiting the dunes has put into words their dramatic appeal: "Here there isn't a single trace of man's presence, of his appetite for conquest or destruction. The real master is invisible. The wind shapes the landscape as it likes. It is an unchanging landscape which is constantly changing. There is something both derisory and magnificent to want to grasp something imperceptible, to want to fix for eternity lights and shapes which no longer exist. This is perhaps the real mystery and real lesson of the desert: to make us believe that death is possible while telling us that there is only life and perpetual transformation".

Merzouga to Rissani

Landrover taxis leave Merzouga for Rissani at around 7am; passenger **lorries** at a similar time on the morning after a souk. The *piste* route is not that easy to follow, and if you are driving, it would be wise to join a party with one of these vehicles, or arrange a local guide; as with the Erfoud route, you will certainly need two or more people to push the car when you get stuck in the sand. More seriously, if you were caught in high winds you could easily get lost in a sandstorm, and recent rains would present problems to all but four-wheel-drive vehicles. Assuming you're not stuck or lost too often, or too long, the trip should take around two hours.

The route (or a route) is essentially this: leave Merzouga past the post office (on your left); keep the telephone poles on your right for a while; follow the *pistes* off to the left; skirt the (dry) salt lake and you'll eventually hit a sealed road somewhere in Rissani's palmery. You then bear left to reach Rissani.

Rissani and around

RISSANI stands at the last visible point of the Ziz River; beyond it, steadily encroaching on the present town and its ancient *ksour* ruins, begins the desert. From the eighth to the fourteenth centuries, this was the site of the first independent kingdom of the south, Sijilmassa (see box overleaf). It was the first capital of the Tafilalt, and served as the last stop on the great caravan routes south. The British journalist Walter Harris reported thriving gold and slave auctions in Rissani as late as the 1890s.

Rissani has a special place in modern Moroccan lore. It was from the zaouia here – which is still an important national shrine – that the ruling **Alaouite dynasty** launched its bid for power, conquering first the oases of the south, then the vital Taza Gap, before triumphing finally in Fes and Marrakesh. Its main interest lies in the scenic approaches to the village, from Erfoud or Merzouga; in its surrounding **ksour**; and its three-times weekly **souks**.

The village

A quarter of Rissani's population still live in a large seventeenth-century **ksar**, in addition to which there is just the Place al Massira and one street, lined by the usual administrative buildings. It's a quiet place, which comes to life three times a week for the **souk** – held on Sunday, Tuesday and Thursday. This is more for locals than tourists but often turns up a good selection of Berber jewellery – including the crude, almost iconographic designs of the desert. Some of the basic products (dried fruits, farming implements and so on) are interestingly distinct from those of the richer north. Don't expect camels, as some guides promise: apart from the caravans, these were never very common in Tafilalt, the Berbers preferring more economical mules. They are still very much in evidence.

The souk aside, you might care to visit the modest **museum** in the central *ksar*; it is signposted the *Centre d'Etudes et de Recherches Alaouites* (Mon–Fri 8.30am–noon &

SIJILMASSA: THE BERBER KINGDOM

Sijilmassa was founded in 757 by Berber dissidents, who had broken away from orthodox Islam, and for five centuries, until its collapse under civil unrest in 1393, it dominated southern Morocco. The early dominance and wealth of Sijilmassa was due to the fertility of the **oases** south of Erfoud. These are watered by parallel rivers, the Oued Rheris
and Oued Ziz, which led to Sijilmassa's description as the "Mesopotamia of Morocco".
Harvests were further improved by diverting the Ziz, just south of modern Erfoud, to
the west of its natural channel, thus bringing it closer to the Rheris and raising the water
table. Such natural wealth was reinforced by Sijilmassa's trading role on the **Salt Road**
to West Africa (see box on pp.456–457), which persisted until the west coast of Africa
was opened up to sea trade, particularly by the Portuguese, in the fifteenth century.
Coins from Sijilmassa, in this period, have been found as far as Aqaba in Jordan.

Historians disagree about the extent and pattern of Sijilmassa at its height. Some see
it as a divided city, comprising several dispersed *ksour*, much as it was after the civil war
at the end of the fourteenth century. Others view it as a single, elongated city, spread
along the banks of the rivers: 14km from end to end, or half a day's walk.

There is still a gate to be seen on the east side of the Oued Ziz, at the ancient city's
northern extremity, just south of El Mansouriya. This is known locally as the **Bab Errih**
and may date from the Merenid period (1248–1465), although it has certainly undergone restoration since then. The Alaouites, who brought Sijilmassa to renewed prominence as the provincial capital of the Tafilalt in the seventeenth century, did a major
restoration of the garrison. The southernmost point of the ancient city was near the *ksar*
of Gaouz, on the "Circuit Touristique".

The (mainly Alaouite) central area is under excavation by a joint team from the
Moroccan Institute of Archeology and the Middle Tennessee State University, under the
direction of Dr Ronald Messier. The most accessible and visible remains are to be found
a little to the west of Rissani, on the east bank of the Oued Ziz, and within the right angle
formed by the north–south main road (P21) as it turns east into Rissani. Here can be
traced the walls of a mosque with an early mihrab facing south, an adjoining medersa
and the walls of the citadel with towers on the length by the river. In Rissani, there is a
small museum and study centre where you may get help to explore the site.

With thanks to Dr Ron Messier.

2.30–6.30pm; free). There's interesting material about the Alaouite dynasty, but not
much on Sijilmassa nor the excavations there, and most of the captions are in Arabic.
Nevertheless, the staff are enthusiastic and will let you browse in the library where, as
you would expect, the texts are mainly in French. Here, for example, there's a catalogue of rock carvings in southern Morocco. There are plans to move the museum and
library to the nineteenth-century Ksar Al Fida; if it's moved, you would need to take a
petit taxi from the town centre to find it.

Two permanent **craft shops** might also draw you into an hour or two's browsing: the
Maison Touareg (☎05/557 5493), on the left of the road out to Merzouga, and **Maison
Berbère** (☎05/557 5054), more difficult to find – across the open area alongside the
Centre de la Jeunesse (not to be confused with the new youth hostel, see below). The
Maison Berbère is part of the Alaoui family chain which has a reputation for quality
rugs – and no hassle.

Practicalities

The village has a **bank** (Banque Populaire), **post office**, several **petrol stations** and a
men's **hammam**. Rissani also offers a choice of three **hotels**, all of which have restaurants. In the village, you'll find the *Hôtel El Filalia* (☎05/557 5103, fax 577 4071; ①)
with cheap rooms, and space on its roof terrace, the smaller *Hôtel Panorama* (no phone; ①)
and the *Hôtel Sijilmassa* (☎05/557 5042; ②), which is much better quality and value.

The town's latest acquisition is an official *Youth Hostel* (☎05/557 5389, fax 577 4071; ①), run by Abdellah Ouchatti, who can arrange visits to Merzouga and elsewhere. The hostel is not easy to find; if in difficulty ask for the "donkey parking".

Moving on

Leaving Rissani, you can get Landrover or transit **taxis** to **Merzouga** (see p.465 for the route), or, on market days, lorries (*camionettes*) laden to the hilt with Berbers; travelling by taxi, it's best to specify a particular hotel in or around Merzouga. To secure a ride in one of the *camionettes*, head down the main street, past the bank and taxi stand, to the petrol station and *Hôtel Panorama*.

Heading **west** from Rissani, the 10am **bus** to **Er Rachidia** connects with the 1pm bus to Tinerhir (arriving around 4.30pm) and Ouarzazate. Grands taxis also run direct from Rissani to **Tinerhir** (45dh).

An alternative route out from Rissani is the **road west to Zagora**, via Alnif. This is detailed in reverse on p.433 and is possible by car or, if you can coincide with the market days, by a local Landrover taxi. The taxi usually leaves the *Hôtel El Filalia* on Thursdays and Sundays, after the Rissani market, arriving in Zagora around ten hours later; it's possible to arrange a place through the hotel.

Ksour around Rissani

Rissani's older monuments are well into the process of erosion – both through crumbling material and the slow progress of the sands. **Sijilmassa**, whose ruins were clearly visible at the beginning of the last century, has more or less vanished (though see the box feature). The various kasbahs and reminders of the Alaouite presence are also mostly in an advanced stage of decay, though there is just enough remaining to warrant a battle with the morning heat.

From the village's administrative street/bus terminal you can head towards a collection of *ksour* on the signposted "Circuit Touristique". The first you encounter, about 2.5km to the southeast, houses the **Zaouia of Moulay Ali Shereef**, the original Alaouite stronghold and mausoleum of the dynasty's founder. Many times rebuilt – the last following floods in 1955 – the shrine is forbidden to non-Muslims.

Beside it, dominating this group of buildings, is the nineteenth-century **Ksar d'Akbar**, an awesomely grandiose ruin which was once a palace in exile, housing the unwanted members of the Alaouite family and the wives of the dead sultans. Most of the structure, which still bears considerable traces of its former decoration, dates from the beginning of the nineteenth century. A third royal *ksar*, the **Ksar Oualad Abdelhalim**, stands around 1.5km further down the road. Notable for its huge ramparts and the elaborate decorative effects of its blind arches and unplastered brick patterning, this is one of the few really impressive imperial buildings completed in the twentieth century. It was constructed around 1900 for Sultan Moulay Hassan's elder brother, whom he had appointed governor of the Tafilalt.

You can complete the circuit by passing a further group of *ksour* – **Asserehine, Zaouiet El Maati, Irara, Gaouz, Tabassant, Tinrheras** and **Ouirhlane** – and then looping back into town past a section of **Sijilmassa**. Tinrheras, a ruined *ksar* on a knoll, has fine views over Tafilalt.

EAST TO BOUARFA AND FIGUIG

The six- to eight-hour desert journey from **Er Rachidia to Figuig** (pronounced F'geeg) is spectacular in its isolation and scenically extraordinary: the real outlands of Morocco, dominated by huge empty landscapes and blank red mountains. It used to be quite a common route for travellers intent on entering Algeria, in the south, but the civil war there has ended such traffic and the border is closed. It is thus a somewhat perverse route to take – a lot of travelling in order to complete a loop via Bouarfa to northern Morocco at Oujda. You can, however, make the journey easily enough by car, the only diversion being the roadside *gendarmerie* who pass the time collecting car numbers and your mother's maiden name. Their concern makes more sense when you note the proximity of the "undefined boundary" with Algeria, shown on some maps and running parallel to the road.

It's 400km from **Er Rachidia** to **Figuig** via **Boudnib** and **Bouarfa**, and a further 360km from **Figuig** to **Oujda** via **Bouarfa**, with few sights along the way. If you do want to stop en route, you have the choice of the *Hôtel Le Jardin* (no phone; ①) in Boudnib, the *Hôtel Tamalte* (☎05/679 8799; ②), on Rue de la Marche Verte in Bouarfa, or, of course, one of the two hotels in Figuig itself (see below).

Figuig

The southern oases are traditionally measured by the number of their palms, rather than in terms of area or population. FIGUIG, with something like 200,000 trees, has long been one of the largest – an importance enhanced by its strategic border position. The oasis has even less of an administrative town than usual, still basically consisting of its seven distinct villages which in the past feuded almost continuously over water and grazing rights.

At least twice Figuig has been lost by Morocco – in the seventeenth-century wars, and again at the end of Moulay Ismail's reign – and as recently as 1975 there was fighting in the streets here between Moroccan and Algerian troops. In recent decades the settlement reverted to a quiet existence, with a modest trade from its frontier position – including a trickle of tourists crossing into southern Algeria. Since the **Algerian civil war** erupted in the mid-1990s, however, the border has been effectively sealed and Figuig's economy has virtually collapsed.

Practicalities

Orientation is relatively simple, with almost everything on the road by which you enter the town. The *Hôtel El Meliasse* (☎05/689 9062; ①), is on the first floor of the building next to the Shell petrol station. Further on, the recently reopened *Hôtel Figuig* (☎05/689 9309; ①) has five double rooms and a small dorm sleeping eight; the restaurant is good with generous servings and the view down the valley to the closed border, and Algeria beyond, is stunning. There is a branch of the Banque Populaire in town and, opposite, try the *Café de la Paix* for **snacks**, or the *Café Oasis* in the little park. Beyond that, there is nowhere else to eat.

Buses tend to arrive, and leave from, the central *Salon de thé: Les Palmiers*, with services to Oujda leaving early in the morning. Tickets are sold in advance but, as each bus is owned by a different company, you'll need to ask around to find out where to buy the ticket for the bus of your choice. Heading for **Er Rachidia,** there are just two buses a day from Bouarfa (at 8am and 2pm); you will need to catch the 5am bus from Figuig if you want to avoid a long wait at Bouarfa.

Exploring the ksour

Figuig's **ksour** are signposted off the main road and are spread out round the base of the hill – each enclosing its own palmery within high turreted walls. Although sporadically organized into a loose confederation, they were until last century fiercely independent – and their relations with each other were peppered with long and bitter blood feuds and, above all, disputes over the limited water supply. Their strange, archaic shape – with watchtowers rising above the snaking *feggaguir* (or irrigation channels) – evolved as much from this internal tension as from any need to protect themselves from the nomadic tribes of the desert. Likewise, within each of the *ksour*, the elaborate tunnel-like networks of alleys are deliberate (and successful) attempts to prevent any sudden or easy progress.

Your best chance of getting an overview of it all is to head for the *platforme*, a man-made lookout poised above the *ksar* of **Zenaga**. The view from here spans a large part of the palmery and its pink-tinged *ksour*, and you can gaze at the weird, multicoloured layers of the enclosing mountains. If you can find the energy – Figuig in summer feels a little like sitting inside a fan-heater – head down into Zenaga, the largest and richest of the seven villages. Going to your left, you should reach its centre, more developed than most in this area, with a couple of shops and a café in addition to a mosque. For a look at the other *ksour*, you would be well advised to hire someone local, preferably through your hotel, to guide you.

El Maiz is the prettiest village, with small vaulted lanes and houses with broad verandas. In **El Hammam**, as the name suggests, there is a hot spring, used by the people for their ablutions. Anyone offering their services as a guide will take you to it. Back on the other side of the administrative road is the **Ksar El-Oudarhir**, which also has some natural springs (one hot, one salty), and terraces similar to the ones in El Maiz.

All of the *ksour* have exclusively Berber populations, though up until the 1950s and 1960s there was also a considerable Jewish population. Until the beginning of the twentieth century, Figuig was also the final Moroccan staging point on the overland journey to Mecca.

Figuig to Oujda

Unless you have a strange fascination for very small town life, there is really nowhere else on this eastern plateau between Figuig and Oujda which offers much temptation. **TENDRARA** (Tuesday market) and **AÏT BENIMATHAR** both have basic café-hotels, if you need to stay overnight. Aït Benimathar is the better choice – a quiet little **hot water oasis**, full of tortoises and snakes. Even if you don't want to stay, it's not a bad place to spend the middle of an afternoon, which you can do by taking the early morning bus from Figuig, then catching a later one for the final 50km to Oujda.

travel details

Buses

Ouarzazate to: Agadir (1 CTM daily; 8hr 30min); Casablanca (1 daily; 8hr 20min); Marrakesh (1 CTM and 4 others daily; 3hr 30min); Taliouine/Taroudannt (2 daily; 3hr 30 min/5hr); Tinerhir (3 daily; 5hr); Zagora (3 daily; 5hr 30min).

Zagora to: Marrakesh (2 daily; 9–11hr); Ouarzazate (4 daily; 4–5hr).

Tazenakht to: Agadir (1 CTM and 4 others daily; 6hr) via Taliouine (1hr 30min) and Taroudannt (3hr 30min); Er Rachidia (1 daily; 6hr) via Tinerhir (3hr); Foum Zguid (3 daily; 1hr 30min); Goulimine (2 daily; 10hr 30min) via Tiznit (8hr); Marrakesh (1

CTM and 2 others daily; 6hr 30min); Ouarzazate (2 CTM and 8 others daily; 1hr 30min); Tan Tan (1 daily; 16hr 30min); Tata (3 daily; 4hr), Zagora (1 daily; 4hr 30min).

Tinerhir to: Er Rachidia (2 daily; 3hr); Ouarzazate (3 daily; 5hr).

Er Rachidia to: Casablanca (1 CTM daily; 10hr 15min); Erfoud/Rissani (4 daily; 1hr 30 min/3hr); Fes (3 daily; 8hr 30min); Figuig (1 daily via Bouarfa; 10hr); Marrakesh (1 CTM daily; 9hr 45min); Meknes (1 daily; 8hr); Midelt (5 daily; 3hr 30 min); Tinerhir (2 daily; 3hr).

Erfoud to: Er Rachidia (4 daily; 1hr 30min); Fes (1 daily; 11hr); Rissani (4 daily; 1hr 30min).

Rissani to: Meknes (1 CTM daily: 8hr 30min); Tinejdad/Goulmima (1 daily; 3hr 30 min/4hr).

Figuig to: Er Rachidia (via Bouarfa; 1 daily; 10hr); Oujda (4 daily; 7hr).

Grands Taxis

From Ouarzazate Regularly to Zagora (3hr). Negotiable for Skoura (1hr) and Aït Benhaddou (1hr 45min, but expensive private trip).

From Zagora Regularly to Ouarzazate (3hr); lorries to Rissani (10hr) and Foum Zguid (8hr).

From Boumalne Landrover taxi at least daily to Msemrir (3hr). Regular run to Tinerhir (50min).

From Tinerhir Regular runs to Boumalne (50 min) and Tinejdad (1hr; from there on to Er Rachidia).

From Er Rachidia Fairly frequent runs to Erfoud (along the route you can negotiate a ticket to Meski) and to Tinejdad (2hr).

From Erfoud Fairly frequent runs to Rissani (1hr 30min) and Erfoud (2hr). Landrover trips direct to Merzouga (1hr; relatively expensive).

Flights

Ouarzazate to: Casablanca (I daily; 45min).

CHAPTER EIGHT

AGADIR, THE SOUSS AND ANTI-ATLAS

S outhern Morocco's major tourist destination is **Agadir**, a city that was rebuilt specifically as a resort following its destruction by an earthquake in 1960. It became something of a showpiece for the "new nation", and these days is an established beach city, with some fine hotels around its great sweep of sand. If you are travelling around Morocco, however, you are unlikely to want to stay for long, for Agadir is very deliberately developed – mainly as a winter resort for Europeans – and feels rather sanitized of local, Moroccan culture.

You don't have to travel far to find a very different country. Just north of Agadir is a series of small fishing villages and cove-beaches without a hotel in sight, while a short way inland is **Paradise Valley**, a beautiful and exotic palm gorge, from which a mountain road trails up to the seasonal waterfalls of **Immouzer des Ida Outanane** – a superb one- or two-day trip. To the south of Agadir, too, the beaches are scarcely developed, ranging from solitary campsites at **Sidi Rbat** – one of Morocco's best locations for bird-watching – and **Sidi Moussa d'Aglou**, down to the old port of **Sidi Ifni** – only relinquished by Spain in 1969 and full of splendid Art Deco colonial architecture.

Inland and to the south of Agadir are the **Souss** and the **Anti-Atlas**, easy-going regions whose Chleuh Berber populations share the distinction of having together cornered the country's grocery trade. **Taroudannt**, capital of the wide and fertile Souss valley, has massive walls, animated souks and good hotels – a natural place to stay on your way to Marrakesh (which can be reached over the spectacular **Tizi n'Test** pass) or Ouarzazate. Further south, into the Anti-Atlas mountains, **Tafraoute** and its valley are even more compelling – the stone-built villages and villas set amid a stunning landscape of pink granite and vast rock formations.

For those with more time, a number of adventurous *piste* and desert trips can be made in the region. One of the best is the **Tata loop**, a surfaced but little-travelled road across

---

HOTEL PRICE CODES

The basis for our **hotel price codes**, set out below and keyed throughout the guide, is the price currently quoted for the cheapest double room in high season (June–September).

Note that cheaper prices in the lower categories are generally for rooms with just a washbasin – you always pay extra for **en-suite** shower and WC – and that double rooms can generally be converted into **triples/family rooms**, with extra beds, for a modest extra charge. Prices quoted are for bed only, without breakfast, but including local taxes. See p.49 for more details on accommodation in Morocco.

① 40–100dh	③ 150–200dh	⑤ 400–800dh
② 100–150dh	④ 200–400dh	⑥ over 800dh

the southern Anti-Atlas to the pre-Sahara, comprising a string of true desert **oases**. The route is most easily covered from Tiznit, but it is feasible to do it east to west from Taroudannt. It's well off the usual (or even unusual) tourist trails and is highly recommended.

A more well-trodden route is down to **Goulimine**, the most accessible "desert town" in this part of Morocco, and promoted by the tourist trade for its camel market – the traditional meeting place of the "Blue Men" (Touareg tribesmen, whose faces are tinged blue by their masks and robes). Alas, it is now more frequented by tourists than anyone else. Nonetheless, it is quite a drive, and with your own vehicle you can explore several oases nearby. Going further, you begin to need real commitment to reach towns in the deep south, like Tan Tan or Laayoune, which are covered in the following chapter.

Agadir

AGADIR was, by all accounts, a characterful port, prior to the terrible earthquake of February 29, 1960: a tremor that killed 15,000 and left most of the remaining 50,000 population homeless. Just four years into independence, it was an especially traumatic event, which created a great will to re-create a city that showed Morocco in its best, modern face. Four decades on, the result is quite impressive, with swathes of park and garden breaking up the hotel and residential zones. The beach, too, is magnificent and untrammelled by Spanish Costa-style high-rise building. However, it's hard to escape the feeling that the city lacks soul, and though the lack of bustle has novelty value coming from any other Moroccan town, it doesn't exactly merit a stay unless you just want to hang out on the beach.

Perhaps the city is best treated as a staging post – or a place to rest up – before moving on to Marrakesh, Essaouira, Taroudannt or Tafraoute. If you are booked on an Agadir package, you should certainly look at making a number of excursions, through your holiday company or going it alone. Renting a car for two or three days, the towns above are all in striking distance, while **Paradise Valley** and the waterfalls of **Immouzer des Ida Outanane** (see p.489), up in the mountains, are easy local trips.

Some history

Agadir's history closely parallels that of the other Atlantic ports. It was colonized first by the Portuguese in the fifteenth century, then, recaptured by the Saadians in the sixteenth, carried on its trading with intermittent prosperity, overshadowed, more often than not, by the activities of Mogador (Essaouira) and Mazagan (El Jadida).

Abroad, up until the earthquake, Agadir's name was known mainly for a crisis in colonial squabbling in 1911. The Germans, protesting against French and British plans to carve up North Africa, sent a gunboat to Agadir, which let loose a few rounds across the bay. Like the Fashoda crisis in Egypt, the event very nearly lead to a larger conflict.

Orientation, information, arrival and city transport

"Downtown" Agadir is centred on the junction of **Boulevard Hassan II** and **Avenue Prince Moulay Abdallah** with **Avenue du Prince Sidi Mohammed**. Rebuilt in 1960s "modernist" style, it has all the trappings of a town centre, with office blocks, a tourist office, post office (PTT), Hôtel de Ville (town hall), municipal market and banks. Just to the northeast is an area known as **Nouvelle Talborjt**, where there is a concentration of budget hotels, local café-restaurants and, until the opening of the new bus station, most of the long-distance bus company offices. The fancier hotels are grouped along the avenues parallel to the beach: **Boulevard Mohammed V**, **Boulevard Hassan II** and **Boulevard du 20 Août**.

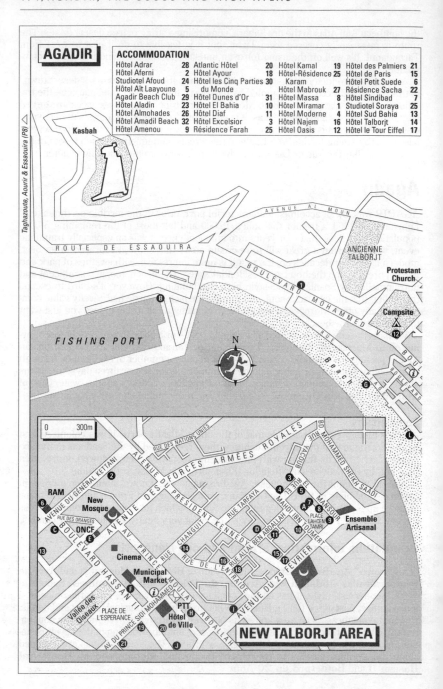

AGADIR

ACCOMMODATION

Hôtel Adrar	28	Atlantic Hôtel	20	Hôtel Kamal	19
Hôtel Aferni	2	Hôtel Ayour	18	Hôtel-Résidence	25
Studiotel Afoud	24	Hôtel les Cinq Parties	30	Karam	
Hôtel Aït Laayoune	5	du Monde		Hôtel Mabrouk	27
Agadir Beach Club	29	Hôtel Dunes d'Or	31	Hôtel Massa	8
Hôtel Aladin	23	Hôtel El Bahia	10	Hôtel Miramar	1
Hôtel Almohades	26	Hôtel Diaf	11	Hôtel Moderne	4
Hôtel Amadil Beach	32	Hôtel Excelsior	3	Hôtel Najem	16
Hôtel Amenou	9	Résidence Farah	25	Hôtel Oasis	12

Hôtel des Palmiers	21
Hôtel de Paris	15
Hôtel Petit Suede	6
Résidence Sacha	22
Hôtel Sindibad	7
Studiotel Soraya	25
Hôtel Sud Bahia	13
Hôtel Talborjt	14
Hôtel le Tour Eiffel	17

Taghazoute, Aourir & Essaouira (P8)

Kasbah

AVENUE AL MOUN

ROUTE DE ESSAOUIRA

ANCIENNE TALBORJT

Protestant Church

BOULEVARD MOHAMMED

Campsite

FISHING PORT

N

Beach

0   300m

RUE DES NATIONS UNIES

AVENUE DES FORCES ARMÉES ROYALES

BD MOHAMMED SHEIKH SAADI

RUE YACOUB EL MANSOUR

RAM

AVENUE DU GÉNÉRAL KETTANI

New Mosque

RUE DES ORANGES

ONCF

BOULEVARD HASSAN II

AVENUE DU PRESIDENT KENNEDY

AVENUE PRINCE

RUE CHANGUIT

RUE TARFAYA

RUE ALLAL BEN ABDALLAH

MAHDI IBN TOUMERT

PLACE LAHCEN TAMRI

Ensemble Artisanal

Cinema

Municipal Market

Vallée des Oiseaux

PLACE DE L'ESPERANCE

RUE DE L'ENTRAIDE

AVENUE MOULAY

RUE PRINCE SIDI MOHAMMED

MOULAY ABDALLAH

PTT

Hôtel de Ville

AVENUE DU 29 FEVRIER

AV DU PRINCE SIDI MOHAMMED

NEW TALBORJT AREA

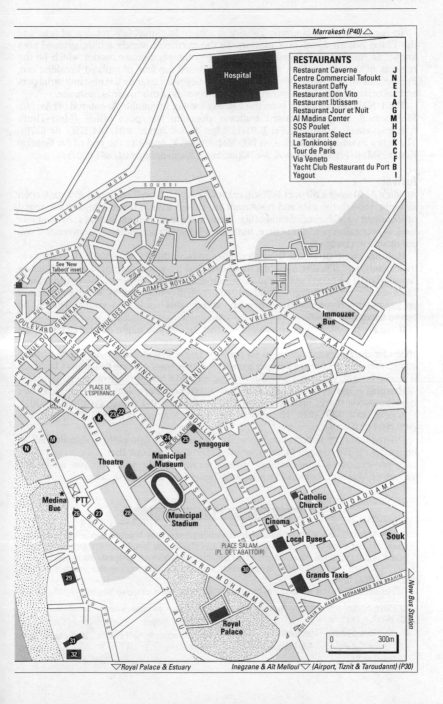

△ Marrakesh (P40)

Hospital

RESTAURANTS
Restaurant Caverne	J
Centre Commercial Tafoukt	N
Restaurant Daffy	E
Restaurant Don Vito	L
Restaurant Ibtissam	A
Restaurant Jour et Nuit	G
Al Madina Center	M
SOS Poulet	H
Restaurant Select	D
La Tonkinoise	K
Tour de Paris	C
Via Veneto	F
Yacht Club Restaurant du Port	B
Yagout	I

BOULEVARD MOHAMMED CHEIKH SAADI

AVENUE AL MOUN SOUSSI

AVENUE MOKHTAR SOUSSI

RUE CAIRE

CHOURADA

AVENUE DES FORCES ARMÉES ROYALES (FAR)

RUE DES NATIONS UNIES

AV. DU 29 FEVRIER

See 'New Talborjt' inset

BOULEVARD DU HASSAN

BOULEVARD DU MADRID

AVENUE GÉNÉRAL KETTANI

AVENUE PRINCE MOULAY ABDALLAH

AVENUE DU 29 FEVRIER

RUE DU PRÉSIDENT KENNEDY

RUE 18 NOVEMBRE

Immouzer Bus ★

PLACE DE L'ESPERANCE

BOULEVARD DU 20 AOUT

BOULEVARD MOHAMMED

Ⓚ ㉓㉒

㉔ Ⓜ RUE DE L'ESPRIT ㉕ **Synagogue**

Ⓝ

Theatre

Municipal Museum

HASSAN II

Catholic Church

AVENUE MOUQAOUAMA

Medina ★ Bus

PTT

㉖ ㉗ ㉘

Municipal Stadium

Cinoma

Local Buses

Souk

PLACE SALAM (PL. DE L'ABATTOIR)

㉚

Grands Taxis

㉙

BOULEVARD MOHAMMED V

BOULEVARD DU 20 AOUT

ROUTE DE L'OUED SOUSS

RUE CHAIR AL HAMRA MOHAMMED BEN BRAHIM

▷ New Bus Station

㉛
㉜

Royal Palace

0 ——— 300m

▽ Royal Palace & Estuary   Inegzane & Aït Melloul ▽ (Airport, Tiznit & Taroudannt) (P30)

To the southeast of Nouvelle Talborjt is a more working-class residential area and the **Place Salam local bus station**. To the northeast stands a hilly, grassed area known as **Ancienne Talborjt** – a memorial to the earthquake, under which lie the remains of the old Medina, which were bulldozed for fear of typhoid breaking out. Further north, still, round the old **kasbah**, and beyond it, stands the new industrial port and suburb of **Anza**. Another industrial zone spreads south towards Inezgane.

The **ONMT** tourist office is on the balcony level of Immeuble A, entered off Av. Sidi Mohammed along the raised walkway opposite the post office (Mon–Thurs 8.30am–noon & 2.30–6pm, Fri 8.30–11.30am & 3–6.30pm; ☎04/884 6377 or 6379). There is a Syndicat d'Initiative on Bd. Mohammed V, opposite the end of Av. Général Kettani (Mon–Fri 9am–noon & 3–6.30pm, Sat 9.30am–noon; ☎04/884 0307).

Arrival

Agadir's **Al Massira airport** is 25km east of the city. It is well equipped and stays open all night, though the café and restaurant are closed from around 7pm, and car rental offices open only during normal office hours and are closed on Sundays. At least one bank is generally open all the time, but taxis will usually accept foreign currency if you are unable to change it.

Holiday companies run their own buses to meet flights and shuttle passengers to their hotels, and if you've bought a flight-only deal it's worth tagging along with fellow passengers. If you don't get one of these, airport officials will direct you to the **grands taxis** outside, which charge a standard 150dh fare to central Agadir, which covers up to six passengers. If you plan to share a fare, arrange this inside the terminal. There is no bus to downtown Agadir.

If you are planning to move straight on from Agadir, you might do best to take a taxi or bus to Inezgane (13km southeast of Agadir; see p.485). Grands taxis charge around 100dh for the run (again for up to six people). The blue and white GAB #22 bus (every 40min; 6am–7pm) charges 3dh per person. It leaves from outside the airport building. If money is tight, you could take this to Inezgane and a bus or taxi from there to Agadir.

Renting a car at the airport on arrival should be no problem, as several agencies have branches there, including First Car (☎04/883 9297), Budget (☎04/883 9101), Europcar (☎04/883 9066), Hertz (☎04/883 9071), National (☎04/883 9121) and Avis (☎04/884 0345).

Driving from the airport, you are well positioned for a first night at Agadir (half an hour's drive), Taroudannt (45min), or even Marrakesh (about 4hr).

At present, most **long-distance buses** serving Agadir will drop you off at Rue Yacoub el Mansour, behind Place Lahcen Tamri (see map inset), which is where the

CITY TRANSPORT

Agadir is for the most part a **walkable** city, though you may want to use petits taxis for transport between the Talborjt bus station and the beach hotels, or for getting to the grand taxi terminal at Place Salam. Alternatively, you can rent **mopeds** or **motorbikes** (see "Listings" on pp.483–485), which would also allow you to explore the beaches north and south of town.

There are also a few useful local bus routes: fares for most of these bus trips are 3.50dh:

#1 Place Salam – Av. Prince Moulay Abdallah – Port Anza

#5, #6 Place Salam – Inezgane

#12 Place Salam – Av. Mohammed V – Taghazoute

#13 Place Salam – Aourir – Imi Miki

#14 Place Salam – Taghazoute – Tamri

#17 Inezgane – Sidi Bibi – Tifnite turn-off – Massa

#22 Inezgane – Agadir Airport

old *gare routière* stood. Exceptions are buses run by the train company ONCF, in conjunction with Supratours, which leave passengers outside their office in Rue des Oranges, off Boulevard Hassan II. This will change when Agadir's new bus station is completed, probably within the lifetime of this edition of the *Rough Guide*. The new terminus will be southeast of the centre on Rue Chair al Hamra Mohammed ben Brahim, just beyond the Souk, and all long-distance buses will arrive at and leave from there.

In any case, if you're coming in by bus from the south, you might find yourself dropped at Inezgane, 13km southeast (see p.485). Even buses continuing to Agadir may stop for an hour at Inezgane, so it's probably best to continue by local bus or grand taxi; either local buses #5 or #6, or a grand taxi (3dh a place) will drop you at the local bus terminal in Place Salam (aka Place de l'Abattoir).

Accommodation

Agadir has a vast number of hotels, tourist apartments and "holiday villages", though in high-season periods – Christmas/New Year, Easter, July and August – it is still worth booking ahead. Out of season, you can often get discounts at the large, four-star hotels. If you plan to move out of Agadir more or less immediately, you might be better off staying at **Inezgane** (see p.485), where long-distance buses leave for the south.

Nouvelle Talborjt/City Centre

Most of the budget-priced hotels are to be found in Nouvelle Talborjt, in the grid of streets around the bus station. They are all small, independently run places, frequented to an extent by Moroccans on holiday, as well as tourists. Down towards the city centre are a few more upmarket places.

CHEAP

Hôtel Aït Laayoune, Rue Yacoub El Mansour (☎04/882 4375). The former *Hôtel Tifawt*, handy for bus departures, and a reasonable fall-back option if the other cheapies are full. ①.

Hôtel Amenou, 1 Rue Yacoub El Mansour (☎04/884 1556). A plain and simple hotel with showers in some of the rooms, hot water round the clock, and a roof terrace in case you fancy a bit of sunbathing. ①.

Hôtel Diaf, Rue Allal Ben Abdallah (☎04/882 5852). One of the best cheapies around – reliable, welcoming and comfortable. Some rooms have en-suite bathrooms, but hot water is available 7.30–11am & 7–9pm only. ②.

Hôtel Excelsior, 20 Rue Yacoub El Mansour (☎04/882 1028). Basic but clean rooms set around two small patios, each with a tree growing through the roof. ①.

Hôtel Massa, Place Lahcen Tamri (☎04/882 2409). One of the very cheapest hotels in town, with clean, simple rooms around two upstairs courtyards, and shared hot-water showers. ①.

Hôtel Najem, 23 Rue de l'Entraide (☎04/882 5466). Friendly, quiet and generally a good deal for the price. Some rooms have en-suite if rather grubby bathrooms, and there are also common showers, and a roof terrace. ②.

Hôtel le Tour Eiffel, 25 Rue 29 Février (☎04/882 3712). A pleasant place with a café-restaurant downstairs, handy for breakfast. ①.

MODERATE TO EXPENSIVE

Hôtel Aferni, Av. Général Kettani (☎04/884 0730, fax 884 0330). An ugly-looking building, but comfortable and tasteful within, with friendly staff, a pool and terrace, and TVs and fridges in each room. ④.

Atlantic Hôtel, Bd. Hassan II (☎04/884 3661 or 62, fax 884 3660). A good-value, comfortable hotel with a small garden, near the city centre. ④.

Hôtel Ayour, 4 Rue de l'Entraide (☎04/882 4976, fax 884 2474). Another decent mid-budget choice; friendly and offering a bit more privacy than usual. ④.

Hôtel El Bahia, Rue el Mahdi Ibn Toumert (☎04/882 2724, fax 882 4515). A fine little hotel – beautifully modernized and with friendly, English-speaking staff, cosy, en-suite rooms, all with satellite TV, but not all with outside windows. ④.

Hôtel Kamal, Bd. Hassan II (☎04/884 2817, fax 884 3940). Quite large, cool, comfortable rooms set round a small swimming pool. ⑤.

Hôtel Moderne, Rue El Mahdi Ibn Toumert (☎04/882 3373). Tucked away in a quiet location. Rooms with and without showers en suite. Some may consider the pink and blue decor in the rooms a minus point. ③.

Hôtel des Palmiers, Av. Prince Sidi Mohammed (☎04/884 3719, fax 882 2580). Clean, quite large, well-kept rooms, a bar and an excellent restaurant. ④.

Hôtel de Paris, Av. Kennedy (☎04/882 2694, fax [c/o El Bahia] 882 4515). A well-kept place, whose rooms are built around a courtyard with trees. ④.

Hôtel Petit Suede, Bd. Hassan II (☎04/884 0779, fax 884 0057). A very pleasant, small hotel – one of the first built after the earthquake, so with a bit of character. It also does car rental (with a 10 percent discount to *Rough Guide* readers). ③.

Hôtel Sindibad, Place Lahcen Tamri (☎04/882 3477, fax 884 2474). Comfortable and popular hotel with a restaurant and bar, and TV in all rooms. ④.

Hôtel Sud Bahia, Rue des Administrations Publiques (☎04/884 0782, fax 884 6386). Large but welcoming 1960s-style package-tour hotel, with a good-sized swimming pool, restaurant, bar and nightclub; also exchange and car rental. ④.

Hôtel Talborjt, Rue de l'Entraide (☎04/884 0386, fax 884 0396). A popular modern hotel with large rooms and pleasant touches of traditional decor such as stucco panels and carpets, as well as a cosy though rather smoky bar. ④.

Main boulevards – towards the beach

The hotels along the main boulevards, and particularly towards the beach, are rather fancy places.

Hôtel Adrar, Bd. Mohammed V (☎04/884 0417, fax 884 0545). Not a very imposing building but it has a good reputation for service, and a full range of facilities including pool, sauna and restaurants. ⑤.

Agadir Beach Club, Route de l'Oued Souss (☎04/884 4343, fax 884 0863; *abcmaroc@ marocnet.net.ma*). A very grand hotel at the southern end of the beach, with no less than seven restaurants, and loads of sports facilities. It has ramps and claims to be wheelchair friendly. ⑥.

Hôtel Aladin, Rue de la Jeunesse (☎04/884 3228, fax 884 6071). Small hotel in a quiet back street, with a small pool, a coffee bar and restaurant. ④.

Hôtel Amadil Beach, Route de l'Oued Souss, south of the *Agadir Beach Club* (☎04/884 0620, fax 884 2248; *amadil@agadirnet.net.ma*). A huge complex, with a trio of pools and everything from sauna to pétanque; beach-trikes are rented nearby, too. It has ramps, like the *Agadir Beach*, and also claims to be wheelchair friendly. ④.

Hôtel les Cinq Parties du Monde, Bd. Hassan II (☎04/884 5481). Handy for Place Salam bus and grand taxi station, with clean rooms off a tiled courtyard, plus a decent restaurant. ④.

Hôtel Mabrouk, Bd. du 20 Août (☎04/884 0606, fax 884 5286). A small, friendly hotel, with an attractive garden and large pool. ④.

Hôtel Miramar, Bd. Mohammed V (☎04/884 0770). This was the only hotel that survived the earthquake. It's a homely, twelve-room place, elegantly redesigned by André Paccard, doyen of the *Hôtel La Mamounia* in Marrakesh and several of King Hassan's palaces. It's value for money, with a bar and Italian restaurant, but no pool. ④.

Hôtel Oasis, Bd. Mohammed V (☎04/884 3313 or 15, fax 884 4260). Efficient Swiss-run package hotel with a large pool, a fitness club and all the conveniences you'd expect, including satellite TV and room safes, but, on the minus side, small rooms, bland food and Muzak in public areas. ⑤.

Studios and apartments

At the mid-range of the price scale, **studios and apartments** (résidences) are as popular as hotels in Agadir. All of those listed below are in the city centre/main avenue-beach area and have self-catering facilities and in some cases good restaurants, too; many of them discount prices by 40 percent out of season.

Résidence Farah, (☎04/884 3933, fax 884 3364; ④); **Hôtel-Résidence Karam**, (☎04/884 4255 or 56, fax 884 1234; ⑤); **Studiotel Soraya**, (☎04/882 7809, fax 882 7808; ⑤); **Studiotel Afoud** (☎04/884 3999, fax 884 3709; ⑤, all on or off Rue de la Foire. The *Farah* and *Afoud* have highly regarded Moroccan restaurants. All except the *Farah* have (small) swimming pools.

Résidence Sacha, Place de la Jeunesse (☎04/882 5568, fax 884 1982). Just off the town centre in a quiet square. French-managed, good-sized studios (some with private gardens), and a small swimming pool.⑤.

Towards Inezgane

There are several hotels (and a new youth hostel) off the road south of town towards Inezgane and the airport, with access to stretches of the beach. The recommendations below are, for convenience, listed in order of appearance driving from Agadir on the Inezgane road, and detailed as being on the left or right of the road.

Auberge de Jeunesse/Youth hostel, off Route de Inezgane, 5km from Agadir, right (☎04/823 2754). Tricky to find and often apparently closed (keep on ringing the doorbell), but clean and quiet if you do manage to stay here. IYHF cards compulsory, and not available here.

Hôtel Jacaranda, off Route de Inezgane, 5km from Agadir, right (☎04/823 2717, fax 823 2716; *jacaranda_hotel@futurenet.net.ma*). A new and very suave establishment, using ecologically sound thick walls, rather than air-conditioning, to keep out the heat, but otherwise offering the usual four-star luxuries, with a solar-heated pool, original artworks in the rooms and some beautiful stuccowork in the lobby. ⑥.

Hôtel Pyramid, Chemin de l'Oued Souss, off Route de Inezgane, 6km from Agadir, right (☎ & fax 04/883 4705). An attractive hotel with a swimming pool and stable, where you can rent horses or camels to go trekking along the dunes and over to the bird-rich estuary. ④.

Hôtel-Club Hacienda, Chemin de l'Oued Souss, off Route de Inezgane, 6km from Agadir, right (☎04/833 3627, fax 833 3621). A top-category *Village de Vacances* rather closer to the beach, offering tennis, swimming, stables and all the facilities, with a nine-hole golf course across the street. ⑤.

Hôtel-Restaurante La Pergola, Route de Inezgane, 8km from Agadir, left (☎04/884 4705, fax 883 7269). Characterful French-run hotel with a restaurant which, when on form, is memorable. ④.

Hôtel Provençal, Route de Inezgane, 9km from Agadir, right (☎04/883 2612, fax 883 3431). Another French-style auberge, with a decent restaurant, plus a bar, a swimming pool and a well-kept garden with flowers and banana trees. ④.

Camping

Camping Agadir, Bd. Mohammed V (☎04/884 6683, fax 884 6684). This is reasonably well located, within easy walking distance of the centre and beach, and is fairly secure, but there's limited shade and camper vans dominate. It has a snack bar and other facilities. Open all year.

THE SOUSS ESTUARY: BIRDS AND THE PALACE

For anyone with an interest in **bird-watching**, the **Oued Souss estuary** should prove rewarding. The northern banks of the river have good views of a variety of waders and wildfowl including greater flamingo (most evident in August and September), spoonbill, ruddy shelduck, avocet, greenshank and curlew, while the surrounding scrubby banks also have large numbers of migrant warblers and Barbary partridge.

An additional sight, of a rather different nature, is the **Royal Palace**, built in the 1980s in an imaginative blend of traditional and modern forms, which can be glimpsed from the riverbank. It cannot, of course, be visited.

To reach the estuary by road, take the Inezgane road out of town and turn right at the signpost to the **Hôtel Pyramid** (see Agadir hotels – "Out of Town beach hotels"). You could also walk along the beach – if you're energetic – from Agadir, but be warned that there have been reports of robberies at knifepoint along the way, so leave your valuables behind. Alternatively, if your main interest is wildlife, you might want to stay out here, as the hotel rents out horses, with which you can trek through the woods, and along the dunes to the estuary.

The Town and beach

More than most resorts, Agadir's life revolves round its beach. The town itself, being modern and very much a resort, has few sights of any note. If you have kids to amuse, you might consider a ride on the "tourist real train", which does a thirty-minute run (10dh) around town every hour or two (listen for the whistle and bell), starting out from Boulevard 20 Août opposite the end of Rue de la Plage.

Along the beach

Agadir's **beach** is as good as they come: a wide expanse of fine sand which extends an impressive distance to the south of the town, is swept each morning and, being patrolled by mounted police, is almost devoid of hustlers. Along its course are a number of cafés which sell drinks and rent out sunbeds and umbrellas – the *Oasis Bar* is one of the nicest, very clean and with good service. The ocean – it should be stressed – has a **very strong Atlantic undertow** and is definitely not suitable for children unless closely supervised.

At the south end of the beach, **wet-biking** (200dh for 20min) is available near the *Hôtel Amadil*. Beyond it, a firm called Locafun (☎04/882 4595 – ask for Martine) rent out beach-trikes and buggies, and some of their employees do a sideline in horse and camel rides. All of these can be rented for a ride along the sands, up on the dunes, and over to the estuary (see box on previous page). This is reached past an area known as **Founty**, quite a pleasant place, where a hundred or so villas are scattered behind the sand dunes and eucalyptus forest.

The fishing port

To the north of the beach, the **fishing port** is worth a stroll. You can haggle for fish yourself, at very low prices, if you're doing your own cooking, or have it cooked for you at grills in the Marché du Port by the entrance. Most of these operate until 11pm in summer, 7pm in winter, and prices are very reasonable.

The Valley of the Birds

As a break from the beach, you might wander into the **Valley of the Birds** (Wed–Sun 9.30am–12.30pm, & Tues–Sun 3–6pm winter, 3–7pm summer; 5dh), a dry river valley which runs down from Boulevard Hassan II, under Boulevard Mohammed V, to Boulevard du 20 Août. It's basically a narrow strip of parkland, with a little aviary and zoo, a waterfall and a children's playground: all very pleasant, and the lush vegetation draws a rich variety of birds throughout the year.

A few blocks to the south is an outdoor theatre – built along Roman odeon lines –and a pedestrian precinct of tourist shops and restaurants where a new **Municipal Museum** is under construction.

Markets

Agadir has two main markets, both containing stalls selling normal Moroccan goods, as well as tourist souvenirs. There's also a new "traditional" medina, where crafts are made and sold.

The **Marché Municipal**, a two-storey concrete block, stands in the centre of town between Avenue des F.A.R. and Avenue Prince Sidi Mohammed, with a display of wet fish downstairs cheek by jowl with fossils and handicrafts. Upstairs, it's almost all tourist shops selling goods from around the region, and indeed the country. Starting prices are very high, and you can certainly get some of the same things cheaper elsewhere, but there are some interesting goods here and it's worth a look around.

Much more Moroccan in style is the **souk**, in a massive walled enclosure on Rue Chair al Hamra Mohammed Ben Brahim, selling fruit, vegetables and household goods; here the tourist stalls are in a minority, albeit a significant one.

Off the Inezgane road, 4km out of town, the new **"Medina d'Agadir"** (daily 8am–6pm; 20dh) is a traditional-style artisans' village, where crafts are made and sold to tourists. The whole place was constructed using time-honoured techniques, as are the items sold within it. Nonetheless, no matter how carefully authentic they may have been, there really is very little authenticity about the atmosphere of the place, and obviously an enclosure selling handicrafts to tourists is nothing like a real living medina. The *Medina d'Agadir* can be reached by free minibus six times daily from the kiosk at the junction of Boulevard 20 Août and Chemin de Oued Souss, and is signposted from the Agadir–Inezgane road.

Ancienne Talborjt and the old kasbah

The raised plateau of Ancienne Talborjt, which entombs the town demolished in the 1960 earthquake, stands to the west of the city centre. It is marked by a small mosque and unfinished memorial garden. Relatives of the 15,000 dead come to this park area to walk, remember and pray: a moving sight, even after so many years.

For visitors, a more tangible sight of old Agadir is the kasbah, on the hill to the north of the port. This is an eight-kilometre trip, worth making if you have transport, or by petit taxi, for a marvellous view of Agadir and the coast. You can see the kasbah quite clearly from central Agadir – and more particularly a vast "Allah–Nation–King" slogan, picked out in Arabic, in white stones, on the slopes below.

Athough it survived the quake, the kasbah is little more than a bare outline of walls and an entrance arch – the latter with an inscription in Dutch and Arabic recording that the Netherlands began trading here in 1746 (capitalizing on the rich sugar plantations of the Souss plain). It's not much, but it is one of the few reminders that the city has any past at all, so complete was the destruction of the 1960 earthquake.

Eating, drinking and nightlife

For an international resort, Agadir is a bit staid, with little in the way of bars, clubs or discos, outside of the large hotels. However, there are plenty of cafés and restaurants, for all budgets, including a few "ethnic" choices if you feel like a break from Moroccan or French-style food.

Restaurants

As with hotels, there's a concentration of inexpensive café-restaurants in **Nouvelle Talborjt**, where you can get regular Moroccan meals (including some bargain set menus) at pretty much regular Moroccan prices. There's also a scattering of cafés and mid-price restaurants on or near the **beach**, including two that stay open 24 hours, along with a fair range of more sophisticated places – a few of which almost justify a stopover in themselves. If your hotel doesn't provide **breakfast**, several places in Nouvelle Talborjt will do so (the *Ibtissam* and the *Select* for example), while many of the cafés around Place Salam bus station have stalls outside selling *harsha* and *msimmen* (Moroccan breads) to eat with a coffee and croissant.

NOUVELLE TALBORJT/CITY CENTRE

Restaurant Caverne, Bd. Hassan II, near the *Atlantic Hotel*. Good food at reasonable prices, with a bargain set menu (changed daily), and Moroccan specialities for two – such as pastilla or rabbit tajine – if ordered a day in advance. Daily noon–3pm & 6–10pm. Moderate.

Restaurant Daffy, Rue des Oranges. A tourist trap, but a pleasant one, with couches around the inside tables, and serving reasonable set menus, or dishes like pastilla or mechoui for two if ordered in advance. Daily noon–10.30pm. Cheap to moderate.

L'Etoile de Marrakech, on the ground floor of the *Studiotel Afoud*, Rue de la Foire (☎04/884 3999). Renowned for its traditional Moroccan dishes, the restaurant at the front of the hotel (serving the same food) is open daily 7.30–10.30am for breakfast, noon–3pm for lunch, 7–11pm for dinner, with snacks served in between times, while the Etoile du Marrakech itself, at the back of the hotel, gets going with live music at 11pm and continues until 2 or 3am. Moderate.

Restaurant Ibtissam, Place Lahcen Tamri. The best of a trio of cheapies all next to each other, handy for breakfast as well as for lunch and dinner. Serves Moroccan and international staples, with a set menu available, and vegetarian options if requested. Daily 8am–11pm. Cheap.

Restaurant Select, 38 Rue Allal Ben Abdallah. Food varies from mediocre to delicious, but always good for the price. Set menu available. Daily 7.30am–10pm. Cheap.

SOS Poulet, Av. Moulay Abdallah, near the PTT. Chicken meals (brochettes, sandwiches, or quarter, half or whole roast chickens with rice or chips) to eat in or take away. Daily noon–midnight. Cheap.

La Tonkinoise, ground floor of *Résidence Tislit*, Av. Prince Sidi Mohammed (☎04/884 2527). Chinese and Vietnamese cooking, some of the latter very good. The Soupe Tonkinoise is highly recommended. Daily noon–2pm & 6pm–midnight. Moderate.

Tour de Paris, Av. Hassan II (☎04/884 0901 or 06). A pricey but high-quality place, with classic dishes like pastilla, couscous and several tasty tajines, along with live light music. Daily noon–3pm & 7–11pm. Expensive.

Via Veneto, Bd. Hassan II (☎04/884 1467). The best Italian food in town, with wood-oven pizzas, *osso bucco* and paella among a fine selection of meat and fish dishes. Daily noon–11pm. Moderate.

MAIN BOULEVARDS/TOWARDS THE BEACH

Restaurant Don Vito, on the beach. Good for pizza and pasta, snacks and soft drinks, though the wall-to-wall Roger Whittaker is a bit much to take. Daily 10am–midnight. Moderate.

Restaurant Jour et Nuit, on the beach off Rue de la Plage (☎04/884 0610). French-style dishes and snacks. Daily 24hr. Moderate.

Le Miramar, in the *Hôtel Miramar*, Bd. Mohammed V (☎04/884 0770). This is the city's most chic restaurant – a beautifully decorated place overlooking the fishing port. Fine Italian cooking, particularly fish and seafood. Daily noon–2pm & 7–10.30pm. Expensive.

Centre Commercial Tafoukt, Bd. du 20 Août. This tourist complex has a number of moderate to expensive restaurants, with French, Moroccan, Italian and seafood menus. Also tucked away inside is the *Eis Pub* (see below). Across the street, in the **Al Madina Center**, you'll find moderately priced Lebanese food, and even a Tex-Mex.

Yacht Club Restaurant du Port, Port d'Agadir (☎04/884 3708) – near the campsite. An excellent place for fresh fish and seafood – as you'd expect from the location inside the fishing port. Take your passport, as you have to go through customs. Daily noon–3pm & 7–11pm. Moderate.

PÂTISSERIE AND ICE CREAM

Yagout, Av. 20 Février between Rue de l'Entraide and Prince Moulay Abdallah. Agadir's best pâtisserie produces Lebanese specialities such as *baklava* as well as excellent versions of Moroccan favourites. Daily 7am–11pm.

Eis Pub, Centre Commercial Tafoukt, Bd. du 20 Août. The best ice creams in Agadir – served up in waffle cones – and cakes to die for. Daily 9am–11pm.

Bars and nightlife

The *Jour et Nuit* restaurant (see above) has a bar open 24 hours, while clubs and hotel discos tend to stay open as long as there are people upright on the dance floor – as late as 4 or 5am in summer, but often only till 2am off season. Promising options include:

Disco Tan Tan, in the *Hôtel Almohades* (☎04/884 0233). Generally the best of the hotel discos, certainly the liveliest and most popular with both locals and tourists.

Byblos Disco, in the *Hôtel Les Dunes d'Or* (☎04/882 3362). This can be lively, too, though admission and drinks are expensive.

Moving on

Agadir is a reasonable transport terminal, with efficient buses to a range of destinations, and regular grands taxis run to Taroudannt and Tiznit. If you are going somewhere out of the way, you may need to connect with a bus or grand taxi at Inezgane. This can be reached most easily by grand taxi; they leave throughout the day from Place Salam, charging 3dh a place.

Driving to the airport from Agadir, you have a choice of routes. The easiest is to leave Agadir by way of Aït Melloul and the Taroudannt (P32) road, turning right at the signposted junction. Alternatively, you can approach from the north, leaving Agadir on the Marrakesh (P40) road, then turning off (left) just after Tikiouine. For details of car rental companies, see "Listings" below.

By bus

Leaving Agadir by **bus**, the best services are operated by ONCF/Supratours (ticket office at 10 Rue des Oranges; ☎04/884 1207), CTM and SATAS, though you may need to use other private lines for a few minor destinations, or travel via Inezgane. All the services leave from Rue Yacoub el Mansour, except those of ONCF/Supratours, which depart from Rue des Oranges (off Boulevard Hassan II near the junction with Avenue Gen Kettani). That will change soon however, since all long-distance bus services will arrive and depart at the new *gare routière* on Rue Chair al Hamra Mohammed ben Brahim just past the souk, as soon as it is completed. For more information see "Travel Details", p.527.

By grand taxi

Agadir's **grands taxis** gather at a rank a block south of the local bus station at **Place Salam**. They run to Inezgane and Aourir (those for Anza run from right next to the local bus station itself), as well as direct to Tiznit, Taroudannt and sometimes to other southern destinations, but it is often easier to take one to Inezgane and get a connection there.

Listings

Airlines Royal Air Maroc has an office on Av. du Général Kettani, opposite the junction with Bd. Hassan II (☎04/884 0793). They fly from Agadir to Casablanca (4 or 5 daily), Layounne (3 weekly), Dakhla (weekly) and Marrakesh (weekly). Also twice weekly to Las Palmas in the Canary Islands, and direct scheduled flights to major European cities. Regional Air Lines (04/883 9339) also flies to Casa (1 or 2 daily), Laayoune (5 weekly) and Las Palmas (daily).

Banks There are over a dozen banks in the downtown area; regular summer hours are Mon–Fri 8am–noon & 2.30–5pm; in winter Mon–Thurs 8.15–11.30am & 2.15–4.30pm, Fri 8.15–11.15am & 2.45–4.45pm. Banque Populaire on Bd. Hassan II is helpful; they also have a little bureau de change, next to Hôtel Kamal on Bd. Hassan II. ABM on Av. Prince Sidi Mohammed (opposite the PTT), BMCE on Av. du Général Kettani and Crédit du Maroc on Av. des F.A.R. are useful for VISA/Access transactions. BMCE's bureau de change, right next to the bank, is open daily 8am–noon & 2–7pm, and there's a bureau de change at Tarik Reisen travel agency, 20 Marché Cité Charaf, on the road connecting Bd. 20 Août to Chemin de Oued Souss near the *Hôtel Amadil*, daily 9am–9pm. There is now a proliferation of ATMs that accept VISA cards. Most large hotels also change money.

Books and newspapers The Crown English Bookshop by the ONMT tourist office in Immeuble A, off Av. Prince Sidi Mohammed has a selection of secondhand books in English, as well as a few new ones by Moroccan writers or about Morocco. A small selection of paperbacks and coffee table books on Morocco are sold at Al Mouggar on Av. Prince Moulay Abdallah opposite the end of Av. 29 Février, and the odd one or two at Atlas Bureau, 16/18 Av. Prince Moulay Abdallah, and Debit Pilote, 65 Bd. Hassan II near the junction of Av. des F.A.R. British daily papers, as well as *OK!* magazine, *Time*, *Newsweek*, *The Economist*, *USA Today* and the *International Herald Tribune* can be found at Debit Pilote as well as at stands on Bd. Hassan II between Av. des F.A.R. and Av. Prince Sidi Mohammed, and at the foot of the latter, as well as at larger hotels.

Car rental If you're heading for the Anti-Atlas or southern oases, renting a car in Agadir makes a lot of sense. It's also very competitive, with fifty or so companies competing for your custom. Shopping around, check that you are being offered an all-inclusive price (insurance, etc), and whether you can return the car to another city, or to Agadir airport. A good place to start looking is the Bungalow Marhaba on Bd. Mohammed (see map), where you'll find Afric Cars (☎04/884 0922; highly recommended by our resident Agadir correspondent), Hertz (☎04/884 0939), Budget (☎04/884 4600), Europcar (☎04/884 0337), Avis (☎04/884 1755) and Tourist Cars (☎04/884 0200), together with the local operators Weekend Cars (☎04/884 0667) and Lotus Cars (☎04/884 0588). The main agencies also have branches at the airport (see p.476). Other companies with offices in Agadir include First Car in Immeuble Oumlil on Av. Hassan II (☎04/882 6796 to 98), National in Immeuble Sud Bahia on Ave. Hassan II (☎04/884 0026), and recommended local firm Amoudou Cars on Bd. Hassan II at the corner of Av. Mouqaouama (☎04/882 5010).

Car repairs Past recommendations include: for Renaults, Castano, Rue Kadi Aïad; for Citroëns/Peugeots, Garage Citroën, Bd. 2 Mars, corner of Av. Mouqaouama (☎04/882 0619); for Fiats, Auto-Hall, Rue de la Foire (☎04/884 3973). There are many others, doubtless equally good, mostly around the junction of Av. Mouqaouama with Bd. Hassan II.

Cinemas The town has three: the Sahara on Pl. Lahcen Tamri in Talborjt; the Salam, on Av. Mouqaouama opposite the city bus station; and Rialto, the newest, off Av. des F.A.R., behind the municipal market.

Consulates An honorary British consul is based at Complet Tours, 1 Immeuble Beausouss, opposite the campsite entrance (☎04/882 3401 or 02). Norway has an honorary consul based at the *Hôtel Kamal* in Bd. Hassan II (☎04/884 2817), and Sweden has one based at the *Hôtel Adrar* in Bd. Mohammed V (☎04/884 0417). Other consulates include Belgium, France, Finland, Italy, Peru and Spain. There is no US, Canadian, Australian or Dutch consular representation.

Craft shops Good first stops are Adrar, on Av. Prince Moulay Abdallah, through the passageway behind the Crown English Bookshop, and the Uniprix shop at the corner of Bd. Hassan II and Av. Prince Sidi Mohammed and Sud Galeries, further along Bd. Hassan II in front of the *Hotel Atlantic*, as they sell goods at fixed prices. So, too, does the chaotic Ensemble Artisanal (Mon–Thurs 8.30am–noon & 2.30–6pm, Fri 8.30–11.30am & 3–6.30pm) on Rue 29 Février, just north of Place Lahcen Tamri. There is also the Medina d'Agadir off the Inezgane road (see p.481). If you buy anything elsewhere in Agadir – rugs, carpets, babouches, etc – you will have to do some very heavy bargaining indeed. You would do better (and have more fun) visiting the souks at Taroudannt for the day.

Food and drink shops The Uniprix shop (see above) also sells the cheapest spirits, beer and wine (along with general provisions). The best supermarket is Sawma Supermarket, 1 Rue Hôtel de Ville, just off Bd. Hassan II near Rue de la Foire. The honey shop at 129 Rue Marrakech, near the junction with Av. Mouqaouama, sells various kinds of honey and, more interestingly, argan oil.

Ferries For Tangier ferries, book at COMANAV, Bd Mohammed V, opposite the campsite (☎04/884 0453). The ferry from Agadir to Las Palmas (Canary Islands) has been discontinued.

Internet access Internet clubs are springing up all over town. Current addresses include: AgadirNet, 33–34 Immeuble Oumlil, Av. Hassan II (☎04/882 1180 or 90; *PostMaster@ Agadirnet.net.ma*); Naviganet 2000, 1 Av. Hyber Girode, opposite the *Hôtel Marhaba* (daily 8am–8pm; ☎04/882 8252; *navnet@iam.net.ma*); Intellegentsia, Rue d'Alger, Cité Suisse (☎04/882 8413; *intellig@iam.net.ma*).

Medical care Most of the big hotels can provide addresses for English-speaking doctors. Current recommendations include a doctor – Dr Martinez Espinoza (☎04/882 0631); and a dentist – Dr Noureddine Touhami, Immeuble MZ, Apt. 4 (near the PTT), Av. Prince Moulay Abdallah (☎04/884 2648). Alternatively, take a taxi to the Polyclinique (☎04/882 4956) or the Clinique Massira, on Av. Prince Moulay Abdallah at the junction of Av. 29 Février (☎04/884 3238).

Moped/motorbike/bike rental Various operators rent out Yamaha 125s (useful for day-trips to Immouzer and beyond) at around 250dh a day, with lower rates for the week, and also cheaper mopeds (200dh a day) which are intended for local use but handy for shuttling to Banana Village and the beach at Taghazoute. They can be found along Bd. 20 Août, on the stretch between *Résidence Tafoulet* and a little way beyond the *Hôtel Mabroule*, as well as just off there on Route de l'Oued Souss. It pays to deal with a decent firm, since a number of cowboy outfits operate, renting unserviced bikes with inadequate insurance cover and no redress in the event of a breakdown. A reliable firm will have several, usually identical vehicles on display, will rent for 24hr rather than just until nightfall (when they'll need their bike back to get home), and will be able to show you full paperwork (rather than just a receipt) proving that the insurance, minimal though it might be, covers you (and passenger if necessary) and detailing help in the event of a breakdown.

Post offices The main PTT is right in the middle of town at the top of Av. Sidi Mohammed, Mon–Fri 8.30am–6.45pm, Sat 8.30am–noon; the efficient telephone section is open 8am–9pm daily. There's a smaller post office on Av. 29 Février in Nouvelle Talborjt, opposite the Ensemble Artisanal, and an even smaller one on Bd. 20 Août near the junction of Chemin de Oued Souss.

Travel agents Menara Tours on the 4th floor of the blue fronted building just south of the *Hôtel Miramar* on Bd. Mohammed V (☎04/884 2732) offers all usual services, including car rental.

Inezgane

INEZGANE, on the north bank of the Oued Souss, is almost a suburb of Agadir, just 13km distant. The two could hardly be more different, though, for Inezgane is wholly Moroccan, and is a major transport hub for the region – much more so than Agadir – with buses and grands taxis going to most southern destinations.

It's connected with Agadir by local bus #5 and #6 (very frequent) and by frequent grands taxis (3dh a place, arriving/leaving Agadir at Place Salam). These, along with intercity buses, each have their own section of the *gare routière*, which is on Avenue Mokhtar Soussi, a wide street with arcades on both sides, running from the central Place Al Massira to the main Agadir road. Across Avenue Mokhtar Soussi, through the arcades, is a wonderful city **market**, full of fruit, veg, spices, knick-knacks and traditional cosmetics, and a hundred times more authentic than anything you'll find in Agadir. From Place Al Massira, the road makes a ninety-degree turn, and crosses Boulevard Mohammed V, Inezgane's main street, where you'll find the PTT and most of the shops.

Useful **bus and grand taxi departures** from Inezgane include Taroudannt, Essaouira and Marrakesh (for a fuller list of destinations and journey times, see p.528). Note that grands taxis from Inezgane to Taroudannt sometimes cover the route in two stages: the first taxi takes you to **Ouled Teima** (or "44" as it's known after the kilometre-marker from Agadir), where your driver will arrange a connection on to Taroudannt.

Accommodation

If you arrive late at Agadir airport, and want to head straight on south, you could do a lot worse than stay here, rather than Agadir; you may be able to negotiate a slightly cheaper taxi from the airport, too (around 100dh). Rooms are usually no problem, with dozens of hotels on and around the central Place Al Massira, and near the bus station, and prices at around half what they would be in equivalent Agadir hotels.

Hôtel de Paris, 30 Bd. Mohammed V (☎04/833 0571). Cheap and basic, with an inexpensive restaurant. Some rooms have en-suite shower, with hot water in the evening. ①.

Hôtel al Qods, 50 Place Al Massira (☎04/883 6322, fax 883 7724). Clean and friendly. Some rooms have an en-suite shower, but no toilet, and there's hot water round the clock. ①.

North of Agadir: the coast to Cap Rhir

Along the coast north of Agadir, tourist development rapidly begins to fade, and the beach at Taghazoute (19km from Agadir) belongs to a different world, with entirely local accommodation and not a "proper" hotel in sight. This – and the coast towards Cap Rhir – is popular surfing territory, and Essaouira (see p.328) is of course a major surfing resort. The route is also a good one for bird-watchers – as is the coastline south of Agadir.

Public transport is pretty straightforward. From Agadir, city buses #12 and #14 run regularly up the coast to Taghazoute, #14 continuing to Tamra, while Essaouira buses take the route beyond, via Cap Rhir. The coast is a good target, too, if you rent mopeds or motorbikes in Agadir.

Agadir to Taghazoute

The coast road north of Agadir begins unpromisingly, passing through the city's industrial sector, a strip known as **Cité Anza**. You can see and smell the petrol, butane, cement and fish, and may wonder why you left Agadir bay.

At 11km from Agadir, however, things improve, as you reach **AOURIR**, where a road heads inland to Paradise Valley and Immouzer des Ida Outanane (see overleaf). Aourir and its sister village of **TAMRAGHT**, a kilometre beyond, are jointly known as "Banana Village" after the thriving banana groves that divide them, and the roadside stalls selling bananas in season. Both Aourir and Tamraght have new **hotels**: Aourir's is the *Hôtel Littoral* (☎04/831 4726, fax 831 4357; *hotellittoral@casanet-a.net.ma*; ④), just past the Immouzer turn-off, on your right if heading north, with spotless rooms, tiled floors, self-catering suites and a terrace, an amazing bargain compared to Agadir's hostelries. Even more of a bargain, however, is the *Auberge Immorane*, just north of Tamraght (☎04/831 4345, fax 884 7633; ③), with immaculate rooms, beautiful tiled floors, carpets and tasteful traditional decor throughout.

You can **eat** extremely well at the roadside café-restaurants in Aourir, which are a weekend favourite of the wealthier Agadiris; the ones to look for are on the left heading north, 200m after the Immouzer turn-off, opposite the Afriquia petrol station. The best of them is the *Baraka* (daily noon–3pm, summer noon–9pm; moderate), which offers delicious chicken or lamb tajines, or mechoui, but no other options. Otherwise, the *Banana Village* restaurant (daily 24hr; moderate) at the *Hôtel Littoral* does a variety of fish and pasta dishes (including pesto or Napolitana for vegetarians), and claims to be open 24hr.

Aourir and Tamraght share "Banana Beach", a sandy strip, broken by the Oued Tamraght, the dividing line between the two villages.

Around 2km north of Tamraght, a prominent rocky headland, **Les Roches du Diable**, is flanked by further good beaches on either side. The southern one is used by fishermen who stay in bamboo huts here in the summer. Shortly beyond here (16km from Agadir but opposite a beach which calls itself "Km 17"), a signposted *piste* leads to Ranch R.E.H.A., where you can go **horse trekking** into the mountains; you can book by phone (☎04/884 7549) or through many of the larger Agadir hotels.

Taghazoute

Eighteen kilometres from Agadir is the fishing village of **TAGHAZOUTE** (also spelt Tarhazoute, and marked on some maps as Taghagant), a ramshackle cluster of compact, colourwashed houses. It is flanked on either side – indeed, from way north of Cap Rhir down to Agadir – by a great swathe of **beach**, interrupted here and there by headlands and for the most part deserted. Many places in the village have no running water, and it inevitably attracts a rather different clientele from Agadir. Up until ten years ago, it was Morocco's hippy resort par excellence, and things haven't changed all that much. International hippydom has been replaced by surfers, many of them Moroccan (a surf shop just off the main square rents out boards and sells most surfing accoutrements), and there's an added camper-van community of elderly Europeans in the winter, while in summer the café-managers still belt out nonstop rock music.

Accommodation is mainly in private rooms, all pretty basic, which give you buckets to fetch water for washing from the spring beside the mosque (there are hammams

ARGAN TREES

One of the stranger sights of the Souss is goats clambering about the trunks of spiny, knotted **argan** trees – a tree, similar to the olive, that is found only in this region. The argan **nuts** are harvested from late May onwards, depending on the height above sea level, and often have to be recovered from the goat dung (having passed through their gut).

Unappetizing though that might sound, argan **oil** has a sweet and rich taste, and is used in many Moroccan dishes and salads, or for dunking bread. It is quite a delicacy, and not easily extracted: whilst one olive tree provides around five litres of olive oil, it takes the nuts from thirty argan trees to make just one litre of argan oil. Plastic **bottles** of argan oil are occasionally sold at the roadside in the Oued Souss area, but are often adulterated with cheaper oils. A good place to buy argan oil is the honey shop in Agadir (see p.484).

for both sexes in Tamraght/Banana Village). Most people rent rooms by the week and rates are therefore highly negotiable – try 250dh a week for two people. It has a hotel on the beach, the *Auberge Taghazoute* (☎04/820 0046 or 06/138 2617; ②), with small but pleasant rooms, hot-water showers, and a roof terrace with great views over the beach, perfect to relax on in the evening. There's also a campsite, *Camping Taghazoute*, set just back from the best beach, which is south of the village (☎04/820 0153).

For **meals**, *Restaurant Les Sables d'Or* (☎04/820 0010; daily 8.30am–8.30pm or later; moderate), on the cliff top at the south end of the village, is highly recommended, specializing in seafood and not as pricey as it looks. They'll do lobster if ordered 48 hours in advance, and it's a café and bar as well, with steps down to the beach. Otherwise, small restaurants in the village serve up grilled fresh fish at very reasonable prices indeed. The *Panorama* at the south end of the village beach (daily 7.30am–10pm; cheap) in particular does some excellent fish dishes.

Taghazoute can be reached from Agadir by local bus #12 or #14 (from Place Salam or Boulevard Mohammed V). There are also sixteen daily bus services in each direction between Agadir and Essaouira that will stop at Taghazoute.

On to Cap Rhir: beaches and bird-watching

North of Taghazoute is a beach known as **25km–Plage** (its distance from Agadir). This is an attractive spot, defined by a rocky headland, and offering good surfing. A further 5km brings you to – yes, **30km–Plage**, flanked by smart summer villas, and the little village of Aghout. From here on to Cap Rhir, there are many little beaches, with caves on the rocky outcrops. The stretch is also known as **Paradis Plage**, and so marked on some maps. At the spot known as Amesnaz (not a village as such), 33km from Agadir, there's a really superb strand.

Cap Rhir (41km from Agadir) is distinguished by its lighthouse, one of the country's first, built by the French in 1926; the keepers welcome visits – and tips. This area, together with **TAMRI** village and **lagoon**, 3km north (at the end of local bus route #14 from Agadir), is particularly good for **bird-watching**. A report in *Bird Watching* magazine claimed some notable seabird sightings at the cape in recent years, among them Madeiran and Bulwer's petrels, "though you are more likely to see Cory's or Manx Shearwaters, Gannet and Common Scoter". At the lagoon, Audouin's gulls come in to bathe. This is the most reliable site to see the **bald ibis** (see box below) which roosts on the cliffs north of Tamri and feeds in the lagoon and on the surrounding hillsides. Passing motorists stop here to buy Tamri's excellent bananas from roadside stalls, and there are several **cafés** for other sorts of sustenance.

THE BALD IBIS

The scruffy-looking but highly distinctive **bald ibis** is one of the world's **rarest** birds. A large wader with shimmering dark green plumage, it is named after its white head, featherless on the crown, with a ducktail-like tuft behind. Once common across central and eastern Europe, the Mediterranean and the Middle Eastern Levant, the bald ibis had already disappeared from a lot of its traditional haunts by the beginning of the twentieth century and been hunted out of many Mediterranean habitats by the 1950s, when agricultural use of chemical pesticides killed it off in many more. Its last Middle Eastern colony, at Birecik in Turkey, disappeared in 1989. Now the colony at **Tamri**, plus three in the Souss Valley (notably at the Aoulouz Gorge – see p.499), are the bald ibis's last remaining hold-outs in the world, with a population totalling just 250 birds, or sixty breeding pairs. In 1993, Britain's Royal Society for the Protection of Birds began assisting the Moroccan government with a conservation programme for the bald ibis, and recent developments include the planting in early 2000 of plastic dummy birds on newly cleared out clifftop ledges in an effort to attract the slaphead wader to new, safer sites. How successful the scheme will be remains to be seen.

For the continuation of this route along the P8, see pp.339–340, where it is covered in a north–south direction from Essaouira. For much of the distance the road runs some way inland, with just the occasional *piste* leading down to the sea.

Inland to Paradise Valley and Immouzer

The trip up to **Immouzer des Ida Outanane** and its waterfalls – via **Paradise Valley**, a beautiful palm-lined gorge – is a superb excursion from Agadir. It is feasible in a day (Immouzer is 62km from Agadir) but much more enjoyable if you stay the night at one or other of the superb auberges (35km up the valley or at Immouzer) or take time to explore and camp in the valley.

The 7002 road to Immouzer is surfaced the whole way; it leaves the P8 coast road at Aourir, 12km north of Agadir (make sure you take the right-hand fork in the village – the left-hand one is a dead-end, up a palmery). A daily bus leaves Agadir at 2pm (from a small parking area on Boulevard Mohammed Cheikh Saâdi, 200m southeast of its junction with Avenue du 29 Février), arriving in Immouzer at 6pm (except Thurs, arrives 8am); it returns Saturday to Wednesday mornings at 8am, Wednesday evening at 5pm and Thursday afternoon at 2pm. Alternatively, take a grand taxi or city bus to Aourir, from where there are minibuses to Immouzer, though mostly on Thursday for the weekly souk.

A new surfaced road now connects Immouzer with Amsekroud and Taroudannt, so motorists with their own vehicle no longer need to go back to Agadir before moving on.

Paradise Valley

Paradise Valley begins around 10km east of Aourir, as the road sweeps down into a deep, palm-lined gorge, with a river snaking along the base. The best stretch starts just after the turn-off for Immouzer. You can hire a mule to explore the valley's numerous Berber villages, and it's a glorious place to camp, though pitch your tent well away from the riverbed in case of flash floods.

For those not camping, there's an excellent place to stay 5km further along the "main road" (7002), at around the 35km mark from Aourir, in the form of a small **auberge**, the *Hôtel Tifrit* offering half board (☎04/882 6044; ④). Set among palms and olives, with a river winding through, this is a rival for Immouzer's famous *Hôtel des Cascades* – and less than half the price. It is run by a charming family, has simple, cool rooms (with solar-powered electric lights) and a swimming pool, and provides fine Moroccan meals on its scenic terrace.

A further 20km of winding mountain road takes you up a steep ascent past a quiet corner with several pleasant café-restaurants before winding on to the village of **Immouzer des Ida Outanane**, tucked away in a westerly outcrop of the Atlas.

Immouzer des Ida Outanane and beyond

IMMOUZER DES IDA OUTANANE is a minor regional and market centre (of the Ida Outanane, as its full name suggests). The **waterfalls**, for which the village is renowned, roll down from the hills 4km to the northwest: follow the road down through the main square and off to the left. They can be spectacular in spring, when the waters reach flood levels and almond blossoms are everywhere, but tight control of irrigation reduces the cascade on most occasions to a trickle, with the villagers "turning on" the falls for special events only. However, the petrified canopy of the falls is of interest in its own right, and there's a full **plunge pool**, and also a second waterfall, nearby, which is still allowed to flow its natural course (ask directions to "Le Deuxième Cascade").

However, what is really appealing here is the overall feel of things. There's a hamlet just across the stream from the falls, and a **café** (*Café de Miel*) with basic food, near which you can camp out in the olive groves. The whole area is perfect for walkers. You can follow any of the paths with enjoyment – a good one, near the village, cuts up across the cliffs to the *Hôtel des Cascades* – or even trek off to the Marrakesh road (see below). The birdlife adds an exciting dimension, with birds of prey commonplace; Bonelli's eagle is a good bet, and you might well spot golden eagles or crag martins.

In Immouzer village, there's a **souk** every Thursday. The local speciality is honey, made by bees that browse on wild thyme, lavender and other mountain herbs. There's also a honey moussem every August for a week starting in the middle of the month.

Accommodation

Hôtel des Cascades (☎04/882 6016 or 23, fax 882 6024; ⑤) is on the edge of Immouzer and signposted from its main square. It's a really delightful place, set amid gardens of vines, apple and olive trees, roses and hollyhocks, with a panorama of the mountains rolling down to the coast (all rooms have a balcony and a share of the view), and a spectacular path down to the foot of the falls. The food, too, is memorable and there's a swimming pool (full in summer) and tennis court, and the hotel can organize trekking on foot or by donkey, and maintains a couple of *gîtes* to overnight in, as well as having arrangements with families further afield to put up guests.

If at all possible, book ahead. The only alternative accommodation is in the café on your right as you enter the village, the *Amalou*, below the falls, or the *Hôtel Tifrit*, 16km distant on the road up from Paradise Valley.

East from Immouzer: treks and pistes

A newly surfaced road breaks off from the Immouzer–Agadir road, 5km south of Immouzer, and leads to the Agadir–Marrakesh road (P40): it makes for a varied and interesting full day's hike and you can catch a bus or taxi back on the P40 to Agadir. The *Hôtel des Cascades* will run walkers to the end of the initial valley (or you could walk there the night before and sleep out on the pass beyond; carry water), from which the road winds up to cross a high limestone plateau. It then drops to circuit a huge hollow in the hills and descends to a (seasonal) river before climbing up to a pass through to the P40.

The road on through Immouzer is also being surfaced and gives a grand motor circuit through hilly country with tempting off-road camping and walks possible. This is a high route – often snowbound in winter and perilous in spring after the thaw – and quite spectacular in parts, blasted out of sheer rock face, before descending amid Martian-red hills to meet the P40 at Argana, by way of Isk. Routes northwards are well worth exploring if you have four-wheel drive, bringing you out on the P8 at Smimou (see p.340), or the P40 near the Tizi Maachou pass (see p.339).

The Coast South of Agadir

The stretch of coast south of Agadir is virtually undeveloped, once you clear the sprawl at the edge of Inezgane. It is accessible at a couple of points from the P30, but there is little to go out of the way for until you reach the Massa lagoon.

On the main road, the hamlet of **Sidi Bibi**, (20km south of Agadir, and marked on the Michelin map), has a wonderful open-air tajine restaurant, where those with their own transport might be tempted to take a break. A short way beyond Sidi Bibi, signposts point the way to **Tifnite**, a little collection of fishing huts, strange to come upon so close to "international" Agadir. Tifnite attracts a few camper-van travellers in summer, and taxis wait at the turn-off to take local residents there from the main road. The turn-off can be reached from Inezgane on local bus #17.

The Massa lagoon

The **Massa lagoon**, around 40km south of Agadir, is possibly Morocco's most important **bird habitat** (see box below), attracting unusual desert visitors and often packed with flamingos, avocets and ducks. The immediate area of the lagoon is a protected zone, closed to visitors, but you can get in some rewarding bird-watching on the long, wild beach and rolling sand dunes at Sidi Rbat. The best times to visit are March to April or October to November.

Transport of your own is a considerable advantage for exploring the lagoon area. The best approach from Agadir is to turn west off the P30 Tiznit road at Aït Belfa; from the south you can turn west along the 7053 towards Tassila, shortly after reaching the Oued Massa. Either route will bring you to a T-junction in the centre of **Massa**, a long,

---

THE MASSA LAGOON: BIRD-WATCHING

The protected reserve of **Oued Massa** has perhaps the richest habitat mix in Morocco, drawing in a fabulous array of birds. The **sandbars** are visited in the early morning by flocks of sandgrouse (black-bellied and spotted species) and often shelter large numbers of cranes; the **ponds** and **reedbed** margins conceal various waders, such as black-tailed godwit, turnstone, dunlin, snipe, as well as the black-headed bush shrike (tschagra) and little crake; the deeper **open waters** provide feeding grounds for greater flamingo, spoonbill, white stork and black-winged stilt; and overhead the skies are patrolled by marsh harrier and osprey.

The surrounding **scrubby areas** also hold black-headed bush shrike and a variety of nocturnal mammals such as Egyptian mongoose, cape hare and jackal, while the Sidi Rbat complex offers its own wildlife highlights – a local population of Mauritanian toad in the shower block at night and a café terrace.

Enthusiasts with transport might also like to follow the Oued Massa inland, 20km to the east, to the **Barrage Youssef Ben Tachfine**, an enormous freshwater reservoir, edged by the Anti-Atlas. Possible sightings include black wheatear and rock dove. By the lake is a car park, where camper vans sometimes overnight.

straggling village, where a left turn will lead you to a **hotel**, the *Kasbah Tassila* (☎04/826 0047, fax 826 0046; ②). The hotel, behind a distinctive yellow and white doorway, was originally a market compound built in 1851, and is popular with tour groups from Agadir who come down by the busload to eat a meal here. In the opposite direction from the T-junction, 8km of sandy road lead alongside the coast and north of the lagoon to a marabout's tomb, **Sidi Rbat**. There was a campsite here, but it was closed down in 1996 after a firm of Brits, Spaniards and Moroccans were caught bringing down consignments of hash from Ketama and using the site's remote location to load it onto boats for export. Pitching your tent where you can is still possible, however, and local fishermen sometimes let foreign visitors stay in their lock-up caves on the beach.

If you don't have transport, you could charter a taxi in Agadir or Inezgane for the day. Alternatively, you could take a local bus or grand taxi from Agadir to Inezgane, and local bus #17 (every half-hour till 7pm) or a grand taxi from there to Massa. Bus #17 continues to Arbalo, halfway to Sidi Rbat, from where you can walk to the beach along the Oued, an area rich in birdlife. The beach itself is often misty and overcast – even when Agadir is basking in the sun – but on a clear day, it's as good as anywhere else and the walks, at any rate, are enjoyable.

Taroudannt and around

With its majestic, red-ochre circuit of walls, **TAROUDANNT** is one of the most elegant towns in Morocco and an excellent "first base" if you arrive in the country at Agadir. The walls, the souks and the stark, often heat-hazed backdrop of the High Atlas to the north, are the town's chief attractions – though none of them is powerful enough to bring in the Agadir tour groups in any great number. It's a very friendly, laid-back sort of place, with all the good-natured bustle of a Berber market town. In addition, the town forms a useful base for trekking into the Western High Atlas or on to the Djebel Sirwa to the east, while for anyone into great road journeys, it stands at the beginning of two superb road routes – north over the **Tizi n'Test** to Marrakesh (see p.399), and south to the oases of **Tata** and Foum El Hassan (see p.502).

Taroudannt's position at the heart of the fertile Souss Valley has always given it a commercial and political importance – it was often the first major conquest of new imperial dynasties. It never became a "great city", however. Even the Saadians, who made Taroudannt their capital in the sixteenth century (and built most of its circuit of walls), moved on to Marrakesh. The town's present status, as a major market centre, but with a population of only around 30,000, is probably much as it always has been.

Arrival, orientation and accommodation

On arrival, the town can seem highly confusing, with ramparts heading off for miles in every direction and large tracks of open space and derelict building areas – some due to flash flooding, others under cultivation.

In fact, the central town, with its souks and workshops, is quite compact, and within the walled "inner city" there are just two main squares – **Place Assarag** (officially renamed Place Alaouyine) and **Place Talmoklate** (officially Place en Nasr) – with the **souk** area between them to the north. Place Assarag, with its low arcaded front and its many cafés, is very much the centre of activity. Over to the east is a further walled enclosure, the old **kasbah** area, in one corner of which is the *Hôtel Palais Salam*. **Buses and grands taxis** operate to and from the new **gare routière** outside the walls by Bab Zorgane (see pp.527–528 for details of departures).

TAROUDANNT

Getting round town, there are **petits taxis** (usually to be found in Place Talmoklate) and, with similar tariffs, a few horse-drawn **calèches**. You can also rent **bicycles** (see "Listings" on p.497 for details).

Hotels

All the cheaper **hotels** are on or around Place Assarag or Place Talmoklate, while dotted round town are a few fancier places, including a fine splurge, the Hôtel Palais Salam.

CHEAP

Hôtel les Arcades, Place Assarag (☎04/885 2373). Better known for its restaurant, but it has three decent enough rooms and very friendly staff. ①.

Hôtel Mentaga, Place Talmoklate (☎04/885 2383). Four rooms round each of the six landings; unusually for Morocco, it is run by a woman, who was widowed but has kept the hotel going. ③.

Hôtel les Oliviers, Av. du Prince Heritier Sidi Mohammed (☎04/885 2021). Small, pretty basic rooms – but cheap, clean and friendly with a rather better "salon" for up to five people. ①.

Hôtel El Warda, 8 Place Talmoklate (☎04/885 2763). A basic place with small rooms; those at the front have balconies overlooking the square. ①.

Hôtel de la Place, Place Assarag (☎04/885 2623). Slightly grubby and rather basic rooms, but okay for the price with friendly staff and a roof terrace. ①.

Hôtel Roudani, overlooking Place Assarag (☎04/885 2219). Slightly better rooms, some with bathroom, hot water round the clock, a relaxed and welcoming atmosphere, meals on the square, and a fine rooftop terrace for breakfast. ①.

Hôtel Soleil, Av. Mohammed V (☎04/855 1707). A new and very homely little place. Most rooms have en-suite showers, and there's a pleasant garden and a roof terrace with views of the Atlas mountains. ①.

Hôtel Taroudannt, Place Assarag (☎04/885 2416, fax 885 1553). A Taroudannt institution and the oldest hotel in town, this was run by a grand old French *patronne* up until her death in 1988, and retains her influence (and amazing poster collection). Very good value with a patio garden, cool air and bar. The cooking is variable, but good if you strike lucky. ①.

MODERATE TO EXPENSIVE

Hôtel Gazelle d'Or, 1km out of town to the southwest (☎04/885 2039). This is an extraordinary place, worth seeing even if you have no possibility of staying: a hunting lodge created by a French baron in the 1920s, in a Morocco-meets-Provence style. It was converted to a hotel after the war and guests (mostly well-heeled Brits) stay in bungalows in the lush gardens. Rates are astronomical, starting at around 4000dh – quite possibly the highest in North Africa. Facilities include horse riding and croquet. ⑥.

Hôtel Palais Salam, (☎04/885 2501, fax 885 2654; *palsalam@agadirnet.net.ma*). Located in a nineteenth-century palace, just inside the ramparts of the kasbah (entrance outside the walls), this is a bit of a gem – probably one of the best splurges in the country. It's worth paying more (you may not need to in winter) to get the rooms or suites in the towers or garden pavilions, rather than on the new modern floor. There is a small swimming pool, cocktail bar, tennis court, and three excellent restaurants. ⑤.

Hôtel Saadiens, Bordj Oumansour (☎04/885 2473, fax 885 2118). A pleasant modern hotel, north of the squares, very clean, with a rooftop restaurant, a pâtisserie, hot showers and swimming pool. ④.

Hôtel Tiout, Av. Prince Heritier Sidi Mohammed (☎04/885 0341). Recently refurbished, with spotless, airy and prettily decorated rooms (all with en-suite showers, some with baths, and most with a balcony), plus a restaurant, and a pleasant roof terrace with a fountain. ④.

The Town

Taroudannt's twin attractions are its **ramparts** – best toured by bike – and its **souks**. The latter are not large by Moroccan city standards, but are varied and authentic and much of the work you find here is of outstanding quality. On Thursdays and Sundays there is a **regional souk**, which brings in Chleuh Berbers from the villages to sell farm

TREKKING FROM TAROUDANNT

The Western High Atlas – routes across which are covered on pp.410–414 – are easily accessible from Taroudannt, the peaks of Tinerghwet (3551m) and Awlim (3482m) west of the Tichka Plateau looking temptingly close as you look out to the mountains from a roof terrace at dawn or dusk. One of the very best trekking routes in Morocco – "The Wonder Walk" as it is called by some trekking companies – is a two-week trip up to the plateau and on to Djebel Toubkal (see p.387), Morocco's highest peak. The Djebel Sirwa (see p.500) is also within easy reach of the town.

If you are interested in a guided trek, contact El Aouad Ali (BP127, Taroudannt, Souss, Morocco; fax 04/885 3644; or through the *Hôtel Roudani* or *Hôtel Taroudannt*). He is a highly knowledgeable, English-speaking mountain guide, and possible itineraries include the "Wonder Walk" above, though he is happy to take you on one- or two-day treks if you prefer, providing a real experience of Berber life. Independent trekkers can also use his services to get established before going on to trek, climb or (increasingly popular on the Tichka Plateau) ski-tour.

produce and a few odd pieces of craftwork; this takes place out by the northeast gate, **Bab El Khemis**.

The souks

There are two principal souks: the **Souk Arab Artisanal**, immediately east of Place Assarag (and north of Place Talmoklate), and the **Marché Berbère**, south of Place Talmoklate.

The **"Arab" souk** – easiest approached along the lane by the BMCE bank (you will probably emerge in Place Talmoklate – it's a tiny area) – is good for rugs, carpets, leather goods and other traditional crafts, but most especially jewellery. This comes mainly from the Anti-Atlas villages nowadays (little of it is as "antique" as the sellers would have you believe), though until the 1960s there was an active artisan quarter here of predominantly Jewish craftsmen. Some stalls also sell striking limestone sculptures, similar to the ones found in the north at Chaouen and an obvious oddity – often figurative in design and more African than Islamic. For good-quality wares, the Antiquaire Haut Atlas, run by Licher El Houcine at 36 Souk Smara, is recommended, while the shop at no. 120 does superb hand-embroidered kaftans for women, and *gandoura* (short-sleeve) and *foukia* (long-sleeve) robes for men.

The **Marché Berbère** is a more everyday souk, with spices and vegetables, as well as clothing and pottery, and again jewellery and carpets. It is most easily entered alongside the *Hôtel Mentaga* in Place Talmoklate. Interesting shops include the Cadeaux de Taroudannt, 35 Avenue Nasr (next door to the *Hôtel Mentaga*), run by Benjeddi Ahmed.

The tanneries

The leather **tanneries**, as ever, are located some distance from the main souks – placed outside the town walls on account of their smell – leather is cured in cattle urine and pigeon droppings – and for the proximity to a ready supply of water. In comparison to Marrakesh, or particularly Fes, the tanneries here are small, but have recently been tidied up and are quite an attraction. Sheep, cow and goat leather articles are all on sale, but sadly, various skins of rarer or endangered species may be on display and should not be bought, for legal as much as ethical reasons: their importation is banned in most Western countries. If you want to visit the tanneries, follow the continuation of the main street past the *Hôtel Taroudannt* to the ramparts; turn left there and, after 100m, take the first turning to the right.

The walls and kasbah

The town's various **walls and bastions** can hardly be ignored, and, outside the height of summer, they make an enjoyable circuit to explore. They total around five kilometres in extent and there are stairs up onto them in a couple of places. Some people walk round the outside, but it's easier to rent a bicycle (see "Listings" opposite) and cycle round instead.

On your way round, take a good look at the old kasbah quarter round the *Hôtel Palais Salam*. Now a kind of village within the town, this was once a winter palace complex for the Saadians and contains the ruins of a fortress built by Moulay Ismail. Outside the walls here are a couple of palm-shaded parks popular for an evening stroll – and keep in mind that nonresidents can use the swimming pool at the Palais Salam for a daily fee of 40dh.

Beyond the walls to the south, signs point to the *Hôtel Gazelle d'Or* (see below), a pleasant cycle ride. A mint tea on its terrace is just about affordable and worthwhile for a look at the gardens, especially in spring, but it's best to call in advance as they usually refuse admittance to nonresidents without a reservation.

Eating and drinking

Basic and inexpensive **café-restaurants** can be found along the street between the two main squares – you could pick from any one of these hole-in-the-wall stalls, most of which have just a couple of tables outside. Listed below are some of the places large enough to have a name, along with the better hotel restaurants.

Hôtel les Arcades, Place Assarag. A restaurant on the square serving good-value tajines and sometimes couscous. Daily 8am–11pm. Cheap.

Snack El Baraka (Chez Fouad), Av. Sidi Mohammed – between the two squares. A small restaurant serving a variety of kebabs (lamb, chicken, liver, kefta) and sandwiches. Daily 9am–11pm. Cheap.

Hôtel Gazelle d'Or, 1km out of town (☎04/885 2039). The tented dining room here is quite a sight – and a major extravagance for dinner, when men are required to wear jackets and ties. Lunch by the pool is less costly – and nobody would be likely to object to your swimming afterwards. Reservation is compulsory. Daily 1–3pm & 8–9.30pm. Expensive.

Chez Nada, Av. Moulay Rachid. Excellent tajines, and also pastilla if ordered three hours in advance. Daily noon–3.30pm & 7–9.30pm (functions as a café between times). Moderate.

Hôtel Palais Salam, kasbah. French and Moroccan restaurants – both superb in the evening (lunches cater for groups). There is also a pleasant terrace bar. The French restaurant has a set menu, while Moroccan meals must be ordered in advance – before 10am for lunch, before 6pm for dinner. Both operate daily noon–3pm & 7.30–10.30pm. Expensive.

Hôtel Roudani, Place Assarag. Tasty tajines and couscous, including vegetarian options. Excellent value. Daily 9am–10.30pm. Cheap.

Hôtel Saadiens, Bordj Oumansour. Top-floor set-menu terrace restaurant, with a view of the High Atlas. Daily noon–3pm & 7–10pm. Cheap.

THE TIZI N'TEST

The Tizi n'Test route from Taroudannt to Marrakesh (S501) is one of the most exciting mountain roads in Morocco: a series of hairpin bends cutting across the High Atlas. It is described, in the opposite direction, on p.399–406. There are no regular grands taxis, and the bus from Taroudannt no longer runs, though there are buses from Taliouine and Ouled Berhil. The bus from Ouled Berhil departs at 6am, so you'd need to get a grand taxi from Taroudannt by around 5am to make the connection, or overnight in Ouled Berhil itself (see p.499) to be on the safe side. If driving, be aware that the road is pretty hairy going – see p.399 for further details.

Hôtel Taroudannt, Place Assarag. Fine French and Moroccan meals (daily noon–2.30pm & 7–9pm) – and a bar (daily 5–10pm). Moderate.

Listings

Banks There are six within the city walls: the BMCE, SGMB and Banque Populaire on Place Assarag, Crédit du Maroc and BCM just off it on Av. Mohammed V, and the BCMI just off Place Talmoklate in Av. Bir Zaran. All have exchange facilities.

Bicycles can be rented by the hour, half- or full-day from a little shop on Av. Mohammed V just off Place Assarag between Crédit du Maroc and BCM (5–10dh an hour, 40–60dh a day).

Car repairs There are garages and spares shops just inside Bab Zorgane and Bab Targhount, including a shop for Peugeot spares just inside the latter (☎04/885 2522).

Hammam There is a hammam located on Av. Mohammed V 30m along from the *Hôtel Taroudannt* – it is signposted only in Arabic (a green tiled entrance, no. 30, next to a butcher's), so you may need to ask someone. Women can steam from noon to 6pm; men 4–11am and 6pm–midnight; 5dh admission (massage extra).

Trekking See box on p.495.

Moving on

The most reliable **bus services** are those operated by CTM (whose office is in the Hôtel les Arcades in Place Assarag) and SATAS (on the south side of Place Assarag), both of which have departures from the **gare routière** by Bab Zorgane. However, the CTM and SATAS buses do not originate in Taroudannt and may already be full on arrival, sometimes even bypassing the town completely as a result. For more information see "Travel Details", p.527.

There are no longer any bus services from Taroudannt to Marrakesh via Tizi n'Test – go to Ouled Berhil or Taliouine and pick the bus up there.

Grands taxis operate from a rank outside Bab Zorgane on regular runs to and from Inezgane/Agadir, (often with a change of cars midway at Ouled Teima – see p.485), with less frequent departures for Marrakesh, Ouled Berhil and Aoulouz (on the road to Taliouine), and Igherm (on the way to Tata). They can also be chartered for Taliouine, or at considerable expense, Asni or Marrakesh (over the Tizi n'Test road). For Amsekroud, they leave from just outside Bab Targhount.

Around Taroudannt: Freija and Tioute

East of Taroudannt, the oases and kasbahs of **Freija** and **Tioute** are close enough to explore in a half-day's trip by car (or an energetic day by rented bike). Freija lies 11km east of Taroudannt, on the south bank of the Oued Souss; Tioute is a further 26km.

Bird-watchers may find they don't actually reach either site, due to the attractions of the **Oued Souss** itself (see overleaf).

Freija

The shortest **route to Freija** is to turn south from the Ouarzazate road (P32) at Aït Iazza, 8km out from Taroudannt. After a further kilometre, ford the riverbed (this may be impossible in spring if the river is in flood) and follow an abandoned causeway.

Freija is interesting for two features. First, it is an ancient, fortified village, standing on a low hill above (and safe from flooding by) the Souss. In the past it was easy to defend; today, it affords sweeping views of the river, the fertile plains beyond, and the High Atlas. Second are the remains of an old kasbah, a little further to the south, alongside the road in from the 7027. Built of *pisé* (mud and gravel), this is now crumbling in parts but the guest section (fronting the road) remains in good condition, and families

---

THE OUED SOUSS: BIRD-WATCHING

The **Oued Souss** is another key Moroccan bird habitat, with a rich array of winter residents, and a huge range of migrants in the spring.

Using Taroudannt as your base, the bridge or causeway north of **Freija** (see previous page) would be good points to spend a day bird-watching. Hoopoe, woodchat shrike, orphean, sub-Alpine and Bonelli's warbler, bee-eater and nightingale are all likely sightings in the spring, while stone curlew, great grey shrike and serin are common in winter. Raptors are also likely to be evident: black and black-shouldered kite, griffon vulture and tawny eagle among them. In the evening, you might spot black-bellied sandgrouse and red-necked nightjar.

Another site, more scenic and likely to be even more rewarding for birds, is the **Aoulouz Gorge**, 90km east of Taroudannt (just off the P32 Taroudannt–Taliouine road). The gorge is home to a small colony of bald ibis (see box p.488); spring migrants include everything from booted eagle and black kite to white stork; and Barbary falcon, Moussier's and black redstart, blue rock thrush and rock bunting all winter here.

Over **Taroudannt** itself, you can usually see little and pallid swift in the evenings, while serin and Spanish swallow are common in scrubby areas.

---

still occupy the resident wings, along with their domestic animals. If you enter the courtyard and show an interest, you are likely to be invited in to look round.

Tioute

TIOUTE can be reached directly from Freija on the minor 7024 road, or – more easily – by turning right off the 7025 Igherm road 16km beyond Aït Iazza. Either way, you should arrive at one of the seven straggling villages which form Tioute palmery, with a hill before you, capped by a large, stone-built Glaoui kasbah.

A rough track leads up to the kasbah, which is one of the grandest in the south and still owned by the local *caid*. It has been renovated and operates as a restaurant (☎04/885 1048), catering mainly for tour groups. If you just turn up, you may be able to see part of the interior – including water tanks, a vault for valuables, a prison for hostages, and an open space for festivities. Profiled against the first foothills of the Anti-Atlas, it is a highly romantic sight – a location for *Ali Baba and the Forty Thieves*, starring Fernandel and Yul Brynner. Equally impressive are its fabulous views over the luxuriant palmery, with the High Atlas peaks beyond. If you want to avoid sharing it with the tour groups (who arrive around lunchtime), be sure to get here early.

Taliouine and the Djebel Sirwa

The roads east from **Taroudannt to Taliouine** lack the drama of Tizi n'Test – the great route from Taroudannt to Marrakesh – but they are efficient approaches to the southern oases. There are some scenic stretches, too, particularly the Taliouine–Ouarzazate section, which changes gradually to semi-desert and offers views of the weirdly shaped mountains of the Anti-Atlas.

For trekkers, the **Djebel Sirwa** (or Siroua), north of Taliouine, is one of the finest mountain sections of the Anti-Atlas. It is scarcely less impressive than the more established High Atlas trekking areas, and a great deal less frequented.

Taroudannt to Taliouine – and an approach to Toubkal

The new 7027 road follows the **Oued Souss** from Taroudannt, shortening the approach to Taliouine for drivers but it's a narrow tarmac strip, with horrendous verges. Better to stick to the old P32, which the new road meets just south of the village of **Aoulouz**.

Buses and grands taxis run along the P32, with a major halt (and taxi stage) at **OULED BERHIL**, 43km east of Taroudannt. Grands taxis from here serve three destinations: Taroudannt, Aoulouz, and Tajingont (15km on the road to Tizi n'Test – but no onward connections). An old kasbah 800m south of the main road (signposted from the centre of the village) has been turned into a sumptuous **hotel-restaurant**, the *Riad Hida* (claims to be open 24hr, but food must be ordered 1hr in advance; moderate),with rooms, suites and spacious grounds (☎04/853 1044, fax 853 1226; ⑤). The house formerly belonged to a Dane, who scrupulously restored its traditional and highly ornate ceilings and architecture. The garden is magnificent, and both the rooms and the meals are very good value indeed. The only other place to stay is the *Hôtel Nasr* (no phone; ①), very basic but very cheap, just off the main road on the way to the *Riad Hida*.

Aoulouz gives onto a **gorge**, rich in bird-watching opportunities (see box opposite). If you decide to stay, there is a small **hotel**, the *Vallée de Souss* (no phone; ①) on the main road, with a restaurant, and the *Café Restaurant Sa'ada* by the grand taxi station, which has a few rooms (①). The village hosts souks on Wednesdays and Sundays. Aoulouz is a regular **grand taxi** stage, with runs to Ouled Berhil (and sometimes direct to Taroudannt) and Taliouine.

Towards Toubkal; the Assif n'Tifnout

To the east of Aoulouz, *piste* P32b leads to Taïssa, at the southern end of the **Assif n'Tifnout** valley, which is trailed north by a rough *piste* to Amsouzart, just east of **Lac d'Ifni** and **Djebel Toubkal** (see map on p.392). It is possible to drive this in a sturdy vehicle and you can make a two-day tour, returning to Taliouine (or doing it in the opposite direction – see overpage). Alternatively, you could walk it. From Aoulouz there are minibuses to Assarag, where you'll find rooms, and from where a few hours' walk north will take you to Amsouzart where you can find rooms; from there you can reach Lac d'Ifni and Djebel Toubkal.

Taliouine and around

TALIOUINE lies at a pass, its land gathered into a bowl, with a scattering of buildings on and above the roadside. More village than town, its dominant feature is a magnificent **kasbah** (east of the village) built by the Glaoui, though in a much-decayed state. It is nowadays used mainly to house farm animals, though the best-preserved section is still inhabited by a few families, who might offer to show you round. The kasbah's decoration is intricately patterned, its windows moulded with palm fronds (some still showing their original paint), and the towers (climb very much at your own risk) are built round squat, downward-tapering pillars.

With your own vehicle, you can set out from Taroudannt, visit the kasbah and move on easily enough to Ouarzazate the same day. Relying on public transport, you should reckon on staying, which, in any case, is an attractive proposition. Few tourists do, despite the presence of **hotels** in all price ranges, and there are other kasbahs in the hills round the village, if you have time to explore them.

Practicalities

Taliouine has a choice of five **hotels**, with a clear winner, the *Souktana*. Travelling by bus, ask to be dropped outside it, if possible.

The village also has several **hammams** (your hotel can give you directions), and a Monday **souk** is held across the valley behind the kasbah. It's also a centre for **saffron**, which is grown in the hill country around it and harvested in September and October.

It can be bought from the Cooperative Souktana de Safran at their office on the eastern edge of town. If heading for Tazenakht, look out for the small *Café Tinfat*, some 15km out of Taliouine, whose proprietor weighs out handfuls on antique brass scales at bargain prices.

Heading on by **bus** from Taliouine can occasionally be tricky as buses can arrive – and leave – full for Taroudannt or Ouarzazate; it might pay to go to the main bus stop, as buses can pass the *Souktana* full and then leave half empty from the bus stop.

Grands taxis from Taliouine make the run west to Aoulouz (change for Ouled Berhil and Taroudannt), and less frequently east to Tazenakht. See "Travel Details", p.528 for further information.

Hotels

Auberge Souktana, opposite the kasbah 2km east of town (☎04/853 4075, fax 823 1411). A wonderful little place, run by Ahmed Jadid (an experienced mountain guide – see opposite) and his French wife Michelle. It's best to book ahead or turn up early in the day as they have only four rooms (plus a cheaper "château room" in the old water tower), though there's space for camping, and you can sleep on the roof terrace (if it isn't too cold). ②.

Grand Hôtel Ibn Toumert, right next to the kasbah (☎04/885 1231). A comfortable place but nothing very special for the price, though it has a pool and some rooms have views of the kasbah. ⑤.

Hôtel Renaissance, by the grand taxi stop (no phone). A simple Moroccan hotel, low in price and handy for onward transport, but not top of the league for comfort. ①.

Auberge Askaoun, just east of town (☎04/853 4017). A reasonable fall-back choice if you can't get a room at the *Souktana*. The *Askaoun* is a friendly little place with space for campers. ①.

Motel Camping Siroua, town centre (☎04/853 4304, fax 853 4089). A new place with small but prettily decorated rooms, a good restaurant, and a camping ground. ②.

Another approach to Djebel Toubkal

A classic *piste* route north of Taliouine (*piste* 6386) skirts the edge of the Djebel Sirwa to reach **Amsouzart**, just east of Lac d'Ifni and Djebel Toubkal. There, you could trek in the Toubkal area, or alternatively make a loop back down to Aoulouz via the Assif n'Tifnout (see previous page). This route is shown on the "Région de Marrakech" inset on the Michelin map (Amsouzart is unmarked but is just north of Mezguemnat), and Ahmed Jadid at the *Souktana* has a detailed route map, and usually offers it as a **two-day Landrover expedition**, though at last check his Landrover was out of commission. In summer it is just about practicable in an ordinary car; from Taliouine the road is surfaced halfway to Askaoun, and worth an evening's drive for the scenery.

Djebel Iguiguil

South of Taliouine, **Djebel Iguiguil** is an isolated peak reaching 2323 metres in height and offering a good day's excursion in a 4x4. Four-wheel drive is essential for the 43km 6837 *piste* that leaves the P32 once it has hauled up the first pass east from Taliouine, turning off at a sign for Agadir Melloul. The first pass along the track gives a fine view of the peak across the plain. Just before a souk outside Agadir Melloul, turn off right and pass the village of **Aït Hamed**, whose old agadir is worth a visit, before curling up to the lower slopes of the highest peak between Djebel Aklim (the highest peak in the Atlas, reaching 2531m) and the Sarhro. Detailed information on this area can be obtained from Atlas Maps in Scotland (see p.31).

The Djebel Sirwa (Siroua)

The **Djebel Sirwa** (or Siroua) is an isolated volcanic peak, rising from a high area (3000m-plus, so take it easy) to the south of the High Atlas. It offers trekking as good

DJEBEL SIRWA (SIROUA) TREK

— Surfaced road
- - - - Piste
· · · · · · · Trail
1,2,etc Overnight stops

Djebel Sirwa 3305m

Plateau

Azibs **3**

4 Gorge camp

Gueliz 2905m

⊲ Taroudannt & Agadir (P32)

Askaoun & Lac d'Ifni

Atougha ● Gorges

Ti-n-Iddr ● **2**

Tisgui Cliff village

Tagouyamt main town of area

Agadirs ● Akhfame ● **1**

Taliouine

Zagmouzine Valley

Tamgout ●

Ouamrane Valley

Piste ⊿

5

Tislit Gorge/rock towers

Souk ◆
Grand Hotel ● ● Auberge Souktana
Old Kasbah

N

● Ihoukarn

0   5km

Day 6 Walk to Ifrane ⊿ (car out)

Day 6 ⊿ Out to P32 Taliouine-Ouarzazate road

▽ *Tazenakht & Ouarzazate (P32)*

as you can find anywhere – rewarded by magnificent views, a cliff village and dramatic gorges. It is best in spring; winter is extremely cold.

A week-long circuit, taking in Sirwa, is outlined on our map, the numbers being the overnight halts. Mules to carry gear, as well as tent rental, can be arranged by **Ahmed Jadid** at the *Auberge Souktana* or by **El Aouad Ali** in Taroudannt (see box on p.495), though neither operate in the Sirwa in winter. Mules would be a worthwhile investment to ensure enjoyment – and accurate navigation. Having Ali or Ahmed along, however, is the best guarantee of success. Both are great characters – and cooks, and both speak fluent French and English.

If you are going it alone, the relevant survey maps are the 1:100,000 Taliwine and 1:50,000 Sirwa. Ahmed Jadid can show you these, and he dispenses advice whether or not you engage his guiding services.

The circuit

The initial day is a gentle valley ascent along a *piste* to **AKHFAME** where there are rooms and a kasbah. The *piste* actually reaches west of here as far as Atougha but, souk days apart, transport is nonexistent and the walk is a pleasant introduction. Beyond Akhfame the *piste* climbs over a pass to another valley at **TAMGOUT** and up it to **ATOUGHA**, before contouring round into the upper valley, where you can stay at azibs (goat shelters) or bivouac.

Djebel Sirwa (3304m) can be climbed from **Atougha** in five to six hours: a pull up from the southern cirque onto a plateau, crowned with rock towers; the nervous may want to be roped for one section of the final scramble. The sub-peak of **Guliz** is worth ascending, too, and a bivouac in the gorge below is recommended.

Beyond Guliz, you should keep to the lower paths to reach **TISGUI** – and don't fail to visit the unique **cliff village** just outside: its houses, ranked like swallows' nests on a 1000ft precipice, are now used as grain stores. Continuing the circuit, past fields of saffron, you reach **TAGOUYAMT**, the biggest village of the Sirwa area and connected by *piste* to the Taliouine road. Trails, however, leave it to pass through a couple of villages before reaching the river, which is followed to the extraordinary conglomerate features of the **Tislit gorges**. This natural sculpture park is amazing; you can camp or get rooms at the village.

On the last day, you can follow the valley to **IHOUKARN** and then to **IFRANE**, where it's possible to get a vehicle out; alternatively, a three-hour trek to the southeast leads to the Taliouine–Ouarzazate road, near its highest point, from where transport back to Taliouine is easier. Ahmed can arrange transport at either point to meet unaccompanied parties.

The Tata circuit

Heading **south** across the **Anti-Atlas** from Taroudannt, or east from Tiznit, you can drive, or travel by bus, or a combination of grands taxis and trucks, to the desert oases of **Tata**, **Akka** and **Foum El Hassan**. This is one of the great Moroccan routes, increasingly popular since it was surfaced, though still very much a world apart, with its camel herds and lonely, weatherbeaten villages. As throughout southern Morocco, **bilharzia** is prevalent in the oases, so avoid contact with pool and river water.

Roads and transport

The paved roads along the Taroudannt–Tata–Tiznit circuit are not clearly marked on all maps (the Michelin has them right), so are worth setting out here. They are: the 7027/7025 from Taroudannt to Igherm; then the 7085 to Imitek; and finally the 7111, which joins the Akka–Tata road (7084) 5km south of Tata.

The route can be covered in either direction, but transport is sparse, which means you'll have to think ahead if you want to stop off at various places en route and be somewhere with a reasonable hotel by the time transport dries up. The other problem with buses from Tiznit to Tata is that they all leave in the morning, so there are only **grands taxis** after that. These run from Tiznit to Bou Izakarn, and from there to Foum el Hassan, Tata and sometimes Akka. From Foum El Hassan, you can get grands taxis direct to Tata which will drop you off at the next main stop, Akka, and from there you should be able to get a grand taxi on to Tata. But don't leave it too late – grands taxis stop running around 6pm and the last one from Akka to Tata may be well before that. The other problem is that smaller places like Oum El Alek and Aït Herbil have nowhere to stay and are not served by grands taxis – they'll drop you off, but are unlikely to be passing with a free space and picking you up. One way to solve these problems if you have the money is to rent a car.

Taroudannt to Tata

Leaving the P32 Taroudannt–Taliouine road after 8km at Aït Iazza, the Tata road skirts through the edge of the oasis of **Freija**, and past the turning to **Tioute** (for both of which, see pp.497–498), before winding its way up into the stark Anti-Atlas mountains.

At **IGHERM** (also spelt IRHERM, 93km from Taroudannt), where there's a **Wednesday souk**, the bus will stop for a long break. The region is said to be known for its silver daggers and inlaid rifle butts, though more than likely you'll just find an assortment of hand-made copper pots and water urns. Igherm itself, now an administrative centre and with some new buildings to prove it, was a copper town for centuries, carrying on trade with the Saharan caravans. The souk apart, it is today a drab, sluggish town – not a place to get stranded – which you may well do if you take a grand taxi from Taroudannt to Igherm, since you will not find one on to Tata. You may get something on market day, but on other days, if travelling by grand taxi, get one direct from Taroudannt to Tata and give Igherm a miss. If you do find yourself stranded here, there are a couple of rooms at the *Restaurant Atlas* on the way into the village from Taroudannt.

Routes from Igherm to **Taliouine** and **Tafraoute** are currently being upgraded – the former should now be surfaced all the way; the latter was surfaced for all but the first

15km of its length at our last check, and may well be completed by the time you read this, though you should ask locally before risking non-4WD vehicles along it.

The very rough *piste* 7086 heads south to Tata, though it has seen little traffic since the surfacing of the 7085. Just down the old *piste* lies the oasis of **Anammer**, a blaze of almond blossom in March and dominated by one of the best-preserved agadirs in Morocco: a huge walled courtyard surrounded by layers of minute store-rooms, which are reached by tree-trunk ladders. A petrified water channel plunges down from the plateau to reach the agadir.

Not much **transport** is to be had out of Igherm, though there are grands taxis to Taroudannt. If you want to enquire about trucks (or road conditions) to Taliouine or Tafraoute, try asking around the main square (where there's a petrol station), or in the café-restaurant just off it, where the truck drivers hang out and play cards.

The paved 7085 road south from Igherm crosses the **Tizi Touzlimt** and then descends to Issafen, also called Khemis Issafen for its Thursday souk. You may need to change vehicles here; again, if stranded, there's *Café-Restaurant Atlas*, on the main road, with two rooms available. The fine trekking route from Tafraoute (see p.513) comes out here, as you enter the **Akka Valley**, lined by a palmery over the next thirty kilometres. It's a wonderful trip, with the amazing contours of the Anti-Atlas mountains to the east, which twirl and twist from pink to grey-green, their sharply defined bands of rock varying from horizontal to vertical.

At Imitek, the last oasis before Tata, the surfaced road becomes the 7111 for Tata (35km). The 7085 deteriorates to *piste* for a 34km stretch to Akka.

Tata

TATA is a small administrative and garrison town, flanking a large oasis. Its tiled and colonnaded streets are laid out in a rigid grid below a steep-sided hill – known as **La Montagne** (largely occupied by the military) – and flanked by the predictable duo of **Avenue des F.A.R.** and **Avenue Mohammed V**. Just off the latter, in the centre of town, is the main square, **Place Marche Verte**, which **buses** run in and out of.

The town is a leisurely place with a friendly (if early-to-bed) air, and distinct desert influences in the darker complexion of the people, the black turbans of the men and the

TATA (schematic)

ACCOMMODATION
Hôtel Essalam 3
Hôtel Marche Verte 1
Les Relais des Sables 5
Hôtel de la Renaissance 4
Hôtel Sahara 2

EAST TO THE DRÂA: FOUM ZGUID

The route from **Tata** to **Foum Zguid** and, for the intrepid, beyond to Zagora is a much more remote journey than the "Tata loop", and the second leg at least is strictly for the committed. In the past, the Foum Zguid to Zagora section was closed to foreigners without a permit, though it has been open for some time now.

From **Tata**, there is now a sealed road, two daily buses, and regular grands taxis. The route runs through a wide valley, following the course of a seasonal river, amid some extremely bleak landscape, which is now and then punctuated by the occasional oasis and ksar. There are passport controls at Tissint (halfway) and again as you approach **FOUM ZGUID**, a tiny town with one small hotel and a few cafés opposite a welcome palmery and some ksour. There are also campsites at both Foum Zguid and Tissint.

From **Foum Zguid**, there are three **buses** a day to Tazenakht and Ouarzazate, two continuing to Marrakesh. In the other direction, all three run to Tissint, two continuing to Tata, of which one goes on to reach Bou Izakarn, Goulimine and Tan Tan. Heading west, a ride with a lorry along more *very rough piste* will get you to **Zagora** in seven or eight hours (Sunday and Tuesday, being local souks, offer your best chance of finding one). Transport on this road is a bit haphazard; it also lacks most of the redeeming features of Tata to Foum, with no oases or villages to break the tedium.

colourful sari-like coverings of the women (who wear black in the Anti-Atlas). It makes for a good overnight stop along this circuit.

Practicalities

Tata has a Banque Populaire, a post office, two petrol stations and a good souvenir shop, Maison des Nomades. There's a Sunday market in town and very lively Thursday souk held at an enclosure – or, more accurately, a series of *pisé* courtyards – known as El Khemis, 6km out on the Akka road (7084); the mainstay is dates.

ACCOMMODATION AND EATING

Tata's hotels range from rock-bottom to basic, but since the *Renaissance* has a cheap wing with reasonable rooms at low prices, it shouldn't be necessary to use the cheap options at all unless you really need to find the lowest possible price. The *Hôtel Marche Verte*, by the bus station, and *Hôtel Bir Inzran*, off Av. Mohammed V by the hospital (both ①), are very basic, and not particularly recommended.

There is a small **campsite**, *Camping Municipal*, Avenue Mohammed V (☎04/880 2626), overlooking the oued, with a small patch of shade but little else (20dh per person incl. tent).

For meals, you'll find several **grill-cafés** under the colonnades on Avenue Mohammed V and on Place de la Marche Verte. For something more fancy (and/or a drink), your only choices are the restaurants in the *Relais des Sables* and *Renaissance* hotels – at the latter it's best to order meals a few hours in advance, if possible.

Hôtel Essalam, 41 Av. Mohammed V (☎04/880 2124). The staff are friendly but rooms are basic and not very clean. ①.

Les Relais des Sables, Av. des F.A.R. (☎04/880 2301 or 02, fax 880 2300). A smart hotel with comfortable rooms built round a succession of little gardens – and a swimming pool, bar and restaurant. ④.

Hôtel de la Renaissance, 9 Av. des F.A.R. (☎04/880 2225 or 29, fax 880 2042). On both sides of the road – an older cheaper section on one side and a new, more comfortable block on the other. The restaurant is good – and licensed, and there's a pool too. A double room in the old block costs very little more than in the cheaper hotels, and is well worth the small difference. ①–③.

Hôtel Sahara, 81 Av. Mohammed V (☎04/880 2161). The rooms here are a bit better than those in the Essalam, and grouped around a covered courtyard, but the hotel is still pretty basic, with no decent washing facilities for example. ①.

MOVING ON
A number of **buses** start their journeys in Tata with destinations including Agadir, Bou Izakarn and Casablanca, via Igherm, Taroudannt and Marrakesh. For full details see "Travel Details", p.527.

Waiting for **grands taxis** to get together enough passengers and set off can take quite a time, but there are reasonably regular departures to Akka, Foum el Hassan, Bou Izakarn, Taroudannt, Tissint and Foum Zguid, as well as taxi-trucks to Foum Zguid (especially on Sunday night and Monday morning for Foum Zguid's Monday souk).

Akka and its oasis

Continuing along the circuit towards Tiznit, the 7084 passes through **AKKA**, a roadside town with a large palmery extending to the north. It is said to have been one of the northern depots of the ancient caravan routes and still hosts an important weekly **souk**, on Thursdays, where the oasis dates (Akka means "dates" in the local Berber language) are much in evidence. There is also a smaller souk on Sundays, and the palmery rewards a visit, with its traditional oasis life.

At present, unfortunately, the town has just one **café-hotel**, the *Tamdoult* (☎04/880 8030; ①), an unwelcoming place with poor rooms, though decent food, and a rough and ill-equipped **campsite** on the main road – it may look closed and abandoned, but someone should eventually turn up and open it for you if you ask around; otherwise (and probably better), you can pitch a tent in the municipal garden next door, under the shade of its date palms.

As well as three **buses** a day to Tata (one continuing to Ouarzazate), and three the other way to Bou Izakarn (one continuing to Goulimine and Tan Tan, the others to Agadir, Marrakesh and Casa), there are **grands taxis** to Tata and Bou Izakarn, though not usually to Foum el Hassan.

Around the palmery

It's worth taking a morning to explore Akka's palmery. You will probably need to do so on foot, as most of the oasis *pistes* are impossible in a two-wheel drive vehicle. Its local sights include a **kasbah** and an **agadir**, southeast of the village of Aït Rahal, and **Les Cascades** – a series of shallow, dammed irrigation pools, enclosed by palms. Local people bathe in these pools, but they are reputed to harbour bilharzia, so be careful to avoid contact with the water – both here and in the irrigation canals. To reach them on foot, you leave Akka by crossing the dry riverbed by a concrete barrage and then follow a path through the almost continuous palmery villages of Aït Aäntar, Tagadiret and Taouriret.

A three-hour trek to the northwest of Aït Rahal is the **Targannt Gorge**, in which a cluster of oases are tucked between the cliffs. There are ruins of houses, though the place is deserted nowadays, save for the occasional nomadic camel herder. The route is across desert, passable to Landrover-type vehicles, though the track is poorly defined. En route (and an aid to navigation) is a small hill on which the French built a barracks. There are **rock engravings** of oxen at the eastern end of the hill – some modern, others perhaps up to two thousand years old. Approaching the gorge, a lone palm tempts you to its mouth. A guide from the village would be helpful, while bringing food and a tent would reward you with a gorgeous camping spot.

Oum El Alek

There are more **rock carvings**, said to be prehistoric, near the village of **OUM EL ALEK** (or Oum El Aälague), 7km southeast of Akka, off the Tata road. Anyone with a particular interest is best advised to get in touch with the official *gardien*, Mouloud Taârabet who lives in Oum El Alek and can be contacted in the village, or through the *Café-Hôtel Tamdoult* in Akka. Mouloud knows all the rock carvings in the region, and should be able to take you to any of them you want to see, if you have a car or are prepared to charter a taxi. (See also Aït Herbil, below).

West to Foum El Hassan and Aït Herbil: rock carvings

The next major oasis beyond Akka is **FOUM EL HASSAN** (also spelt Fam El Hisn), 90km to the west – and 6km off the main road. This is basically a military post on the edge of an oasis. Some fighting with Polisario took place here several years ago, but everything's quiet now; there is, however, passport control. Buses between Tata and Bou Izakarn make the 6km detour to stop here, and there are grands taxis to Bou Izakarn and Tata. If you need a room, the only possibility is at the rather basic *Hôtel-Café Assahra* (no phone; ①) on the right-hand side of the square. Besides a couple more cafés and a few shops, there's very little else.

Tircht

There are countless **prehistoric rock carvings** in this region, and engaging a guide you will probably be shown the local favourites. Those at **Tircht** can be reached by foot from Foum El Hassan by following the oued through the "V" in the mountains behind the town (bear right after 2km where it splits). Tircht is a peaked mountain to the left about 5km from town, but neither it nor the carvings are easy to find: you are best advised to employ someone from town as a guide. The best require a little climbing to get to, but they are among the finest in Morocco – elephants and rhinoceros, 15–30cm high, dating roughly from 2000–500 BC, a time when the Sahara was full of lakes and swamps. Camping is possible here in the valley and preferable to staying in the town.

Aït Herbil

Less renowned are the rock carvings at the village of **AÏT HERBIL**, 2km off the P30, around 15km west of Foum El Hassan. The junction is easy to recognize, as it's right opposite a Ziz filling station. You can get there by grand taxi from Foum El Hassan, Akka, Tata or Bou Izakarn. For onward travel, however, you'll be lucky to find a passing grand taxi with places free, so short of hitching, you'll have to depend on buses, of which the last eastbound passes at around 11am. There are two series of rock carvings, marked as "A" and "B" on our sketch map opposite, both easily accessible on foot. To get to them take the right-hand *piste* of the two opposite the Ziz station, driveable for 2km as far as Aït Herbil, a village worth seeing for its many patterned, colourful doors.

To reach **"A"**, when nearly through the village, turn right down a street that takes you across the dry riverbed. On the opposite bank is a steep rock fall, and to the right of a patch of distinctively lighter grey rocks (indicating several deep and dangerous wells) are perhaps as many as a hundred small carvings, depicting gazelles, bison, a giraffe and a bird or two. The rock fall looks recent but clearly, with the carvings all in the same place, it has not shifted for centuries, even millennia. The old ruined kasbah, which should be to your north (your left as you leave the village), is a useful landmark.

For **"B"** leave the village to the southeast, walking through the palmery, and again across the dry riverbed, to find a concrete irrigation channel which at this point runs high above the level of the river. Before reaching the partly deserted village of Eghir, high on the left, look for carvings on the rocks to the left. Alternatively, follow the irrigation channel for 800m from the main road. There are fewer examples here but they are larger.

West to Bou Izakarn

Beyond Aït Herbil, the P30 continues across a barren patch of hammada to the oasis and roadside village of **TAGHJICHT** (or Tarhjijt), where a road heads off north to Amtoudi (see below). If you need to stay the night, en route, Taghjicht has a good **hotel**, the *Taghjijt* (☎04/887 3053; ③). The village also has regular grand taxi runs to Bou Izakarn; in the other direction you might be lucky and pick one up on its way to Foum El Hassan. At **TIMOULAY**, 26km further west, it is usually possible to get a grand taxi to Ifrane de l'Anti-Atlas (see overleaf). You should also be able to get a taxi for the final 14km stretch to Bou Izakarn, on the main Tiznit–Goulimine road.

BOU IZAKARN is a larger village with a Friday **souk**, a PTT, Banque Populaire, municipal swimming pool (summer only), and a basic **hotel**, the *Anti-Atlas*, (☎04/878 8134; ①). A place across the street and about fifty metres towards Goulimine does very good, and cheap, fried fish. There are regular buses and grands taxis. Taxi runs include Goulimine (these leave from a rank on the Goulimine road at the south end of the village), and Tiznit (for Tafraoute), Ifrane, Inezgane (for Agadir), and Foum El Hassan (all these leave from the main taxi rank in the town centre).

Amtoudi (Id Aïssa)

If you have transport, it's worth making an excursion from the Bou Izakarn/Tiznit road to visit **AMTOUDI** (or Id Aïssa, as it appears on most maps). This can be reached by either of two roads north of the P30 (at around 55km and 70km from Foum El Hassan); they join at **Souk Tnine D'Adaï** where the last 10km of road to Amtoudi become rougher and less distinct. Using local transport, you might be able to negotiate a grand taxi at **Taghjijt**, the second junction, especially on a Monday, when there is a market at Souk Tnine D'Adaï. If you intend to stay, be sure to have enough provisions, since Amtoudi has just one small shop and a lunch-only restaurant for visiting tour groups.

The sight that brings tour groups to Amtoudi is its **agadir**, which is one of the most spectacular and best preserved in North Africa. Agadirs are collective, fortified storehouses, where grain, dates, gunpowder and other valuables were kept safe from marauding tribes. This one is built impressively on a pinnacle of rock. You can climb (or ride a mule) up a winding track and walk around the site, providing the *gardien* is there. If by chance you find the place overrun by visitors, you can escape the crowds with a walk down the palm-filled **gorge**; here another imposing but decaying agadir is perched on top of the cliff and, after about 3km, you'll come to a spring and waterfall. It is possible to **camp** near the river.

Ifrane de l'Anti-Atlas

IFRANE DE L'ANTI-ATLAS is one of the most rewarding oasis detours on the Tata loop. A small Berber settlement, it comprises three surrounding *douar* (each with its own kasbah and endless walls), together with **Souk Ifrane**, an administrative and market centre (Sunday souk), with a pink, fort-like barracks. The place is particularly out of the way and visitors can expect to be the object of attention and followed everywhere by kids, but it's worth braving them: there are beautiful walks among the douar, springs, and ingenious water channels.

If you have a car, you may want to just stop a few hours, but there are cheap, basic rooms available at the *Café de la Paix* with a roof terrace looking out across the valley and distant oasis; this is also the best place to eat.

The Oasis and Mellah

The Ifrane oasis is the centre of one of the oldest settled regions in Morocco – and was one of the last places in the south to convert to Islam. Across the dry riverbed stand the ruins of the old **Jewish kasbah**, or **Mellah**. Legend holds that Ifrane's Jews settled here in the sixth century BC, fleeing persecution from King Nebuchadnezzar of Babylon; this has yet to be substantiated but it is certain that the Jewish community goes back to pre-Islamic days. It endured up until the 1950s, when, as elsewhere in the south, there was a mass exodus to Israel and, to an extent, Casablanca and Rabat. A Berber family has since moved into one of the inhabitable kasbahs, and a few of the other buildings remain partially intact; the rest is a mass of crumbling walls. Locals recall their former Jewish neighbours as "good people" who kept mainly to themselves.

Around the next bend in the stony riverbed, and up the hill on the right, lies the Jewish **cemetery**. Broken tombstones, inscribed in Hebrew, lie strewn about. It's said that relatives still come here to visit the graves and burn candles in memory of the deceased. The Muslim past of Ifrane is evident as well, with white-domed tombs of saints and marabouts dotting the surrounding countryside.

Tiznit and around

Despite its solid circuit of walls, **TIZNIT** was founded as late as 1882, when Sultan Moulay Hassan (Hassan I) was undertaking a *harka* – a subjugation or (literally) "burning" raid – in the Souss and Anti-Atlas. It still seems to signal a shift towards a desert, frontier-town mentality and past: to the west the Chleuh Berbers of the Anti-Atlas suffered their first true occupation only with the bitter French "pacification" of the early 1930s, and Tiznit itself was the base of **El Hiba**, who declared himself sultan here in 1912 after learning of Moulay Hafid's surrender to the French under the Treaty of Fes. The so-called "Blue Sultan" – a name given on account of his blue desert robes – El Hiba led a considerable force of Berbers to Marrakesh, which acknowledged his authority, before advancing on Fes in the spring of 1913. Here they were defeated, though El Hiba's resistance continued, first in Taroudannt, later into the Anti-Atlas, until his death, near Tafraoute, in 1919.

The town bears the stamp of its military history – huge *pisé* walls, neat administrative streets and a considerable garrison – but it's not a bad staging point en route to Tafraoute, Sidi Ifni or Tata. It is easily reached by bus from Agadir or grand taxi from Inezgane and has an exhilarating beach at **Sidi Moussa d'Aglou**, 17km distant, where the surf and the fierce Atlantic currents have warded off development.

The Town

Tiznit has five kilometres of walls and eight major gates, the most important of which are **Bab Ouled Jarrar** and **Les Trois Portes**. Most of the traffic in and out of the walls passes through these gates – the latter of which (as its name suggests) was a French addition. Quite why it is called Les Trois Portes ('the three gates') is not clear, since there are in fact four.

The promise of Tiznit's walls turns out to be a little empty, with large areas, as at Taroudannt, occupied by gardens or nothingness. There is, however, a certain fascination in realizing just how recent the place is – a traditional walled town built little more than a century ago – and in seeing how the builders simply enclosed a number of

TIZNIT

Bab Khemis
Hammam
Bab Targua
Bab Aglou
PASSAGE IDAOUM KNOUN
Aglou Grands Taxis
Sidi Moussa d'Aglou (7060)
Bab el Mader
PLACE AL KOUFA
Empire Cinema
PTT
Source Bleu
Grand Mosque
Agadir (P30)
Hammam
Bab el Aouina
SATAS
Ifni and Mirhleft Grands Taxis
Sidi Ifni (7064)
AVENUE HASSAN I
MECHOUAR
SOUK
RUE DU BAIN MAURE
Douche Atlas
CTM
El Bahia Cinema
Banks
RUE DE L'HÔPITAL
Les Trois Portes
Open-air market
AV. DU 20 AOÛT
Centre Artisanal
PTT
Souk
Banque Populaire
Bab Oulad Jarrar
Campsite
AVENUE HASSAN II
Banks
BMCE Bank
AV. MOHAMMED V
Agadir and Tafraoute Grands Taxis
Tafraoute (P7074)
Thursday Souk
RUE BIR ANZARANE
Bou Izakarn Grands Taxis
Goulimine (P30)

ACCOMMODATION

Hôtel El Amal	11
Hôtel des Amis	2
Hôtel Atlas	4
Hôtel Belle Vue	1
Hôtel CTM	6
Hôtel Mauretanie	10
Hôtel Al Mourabatine	3
Hôtel de Paris	8
Hôtel Sahara	5
Hôtel du Soleil	7
Hôtel de Tiznit	9

RESTAURANT

Bon Acceuil	A

0   100m

existing ksour within their new grid. These are the large angled enclosures, clearly visible on our map.

Taking a brief loop through the town, start out at the **jewellery souk** (*Souk des
Bijoutiers*), still an active crafts industry despite the loss to Israel of the town's large
number of Jewish craftsmen. The jewellers occupy the northern part of the **main
souk**, which can be entered from the Mechouar. Over to the south, across Avenue du
20 Août, is a larger **open-air market**, mainly selling food and produce, and there's a
more workaday **municipal market** selling meat, fruit, veg and household goods, just
off Avenue du 20 Août. The town's main weekly souk (Thursdays) is held out on the
Tafraoute road.

North of the Mechouar, Rue de l'Hôpital winds round, past the hospital, to join the
main road from Bab Ouled Jarrar which then heads towards an arcade of shops and a
mosque (at the top of Rue du Bain Maure). Taking a left just before the arcade of shops,
bearing left at the T-junction and right at the next fork, brings you to the **Great**

Mosque, which has an unusual minaret, punctuated by a series of perches. These are said to be an aid to the dead in climbing up to paradise, and are more commonly found south of the Sahara in Mali and Niger. Alongside the mosque is the **Source Bleue**, dedicated to the town's patroness, Lalla Tiznit, a saint and former prostitute martyred on this spot (whereupon water miraculously appeared). These days, more or less devoid of water, the spring is profoundly unflattering to her.

Following the street north of the *source*, you reach the north gate, **Bab Targua**, formerly an entry point for animals. The next gate round is **Bab El Mader**, beside a large Muslim cemetery with a picturesque white marabout's tomb, its corners picked out in green. To the north of the city wall is an area of rather mournful olive groves and an abandoned palmery.

Practicalities

Arriving by **bus** you'll find yourself set down in the **Mechouar** – the old parade ground, now the main square – just inside the town walls. Coming by **grand taxi**, you will probably be dropped outside the walls, at one of the locations detailed on our map.

Around the Mechouar and along the adjacent **Avenue 20 Aôut** you'll find banks, the post office, bus offices, a market area and a Centre Artisanal – and all of the cheap **hotels**. A few more upmarket hotels are outside the walls on the Goulimine road. Email and Internet access are available at Rozanet, 83 Rue du Bain Maure (*rozanet@iam.net.ma*) for 12dh per hour.

There are traditional **hammams** just inside the walls at Bab El Khemis and between Bab El Aouina and the nameless pedestrian-only gate at the Medina's southwestern corner.

Accommodation and eating

There are a dozen or more cheap **hotels** in the walled city, the best of which are listed below; none can guarantee hot water, but in a cul-de-sac off Rue du Bain Maure there is a public showerhouse, *Douche Atlas* (men and women 5am–9pm; 5dh; sign in Arabic only).

The **campsite**, *Camping Municipal*, just outside Bab Ouled Jarrar, is a secure but unshaded site.

There are numerous **café-restaurants** in and around the Mechouar, the best of which is the *Bon Accueil*, directly opposite the *Atlas* (daily noon–9pm; cheap). The *Hôtel el Amal*'s restaurant (daily noon–midnight; cheap) serves up excellent tajines, with soup and snacks available, while the *Hôtel du Soleil*'s restaurant is open 24hr for meals (cheap). For a more upmarket meal, or a drink, your best bets are the restaurant of the *Hôtel de Paris* (daily 5am–1am; moderate), with a good selection of chicken, steak or brochette dishes, or the *restaurant gastronomique* at the *Hôtel Tiznit* (daily 7am–11pm; moderate).

HOTELS

Hôtel el Amal, Rue Bir Anzarane (☎04/886 2462). A small new hotel with bright, airy rooms, some with shower and toilet en suite, and friendly, efficient staff. ①.

Hôtel des Amis, Mechouar (☎04/886 2129). Spartan but clean and good value, with friendly staff and a terrace overlooking the square. ①.

Hôtel Atlas, Mechouar (☎04/886 2060). A popular hotel with quite a decent restaurant. Some rooms are slightly nicer (and dearer) than others, and there's access from the official roof terrace to a bit of the roof where you can sit undisturbed and watch the square. ①.

Hôtel Belle Vue, Rue du Bain Maure (☎04/886 2109). Best of the cheapies, though marginally dearer than the others – bright, clean and inviting, and quiet too. ①.

Hôtel CTM, opposite the former grand taxi rank (☎04/886 2211). A friendly place with clean rooms and showers, and a café-restaurant on the first floor, though no direct outside windows. ①.

Hôtel Mauretanie, Rue Bir Anzarane (☎04/886 2072). A reasonable choice, but nothing special, with decent rooms, easy parking, a restaurant, and several cafés and shops nearby. ①.

Hôtel al Mourabatine, Rue du Bain Maure (☎04/886 2755). A fall-back option really – basic but decent, and very cheap indeed. ①.

Hôtel de Paris, Av. Hassan II (☎04/886 2865). A friendly and modestly priced hotel, with cosy rooms and a deservedly popular local restaurant. ①.

Hôtel Sahara, Rue de l'Hôpital (☎04/886 2498). Another fall-back option, similar to the *al Mourabatine*, but friendlier. ①.

Hôtel du Soleil, Rue Bir Anzarane (☎04/860 0289, fax 886 2259). A very good deal, with fresh, pleasant rooms with en-suite shower or bath. ①.

Hôtel de Tiznit, Rue Bir Anzarane (☎04/886 2411, fax 886 2119). The poshest hotel in town, with a bar, a swimming pool (25dh for nonresidents) and, in summer, a nightclub. ④.

Cinemas

Tiznit has a couple of **cinemas** – the El Bahià just off Avenue Hassan II opposite Bab El Aouina, and the Empire inside the Medina off Place al Koufa near the southwestern corner.

Moving on

All **buses** leave from the Mechouar, with regular services to Agadir, Bou Izakarn, Goulimine, Marrakesh, Tafraoute, and Tan Tan. The CTM office is to the right of the exit to Rue du Bain Maure as you look at it. SATAS have their office diagonally across the Mechouar and there are also various private firms offering similar destinations, plus services to Sidi Ifni, Ouarzazate (via Akka, Tata and Foun Zguid) and Demnate.

Grands taxis operate from four different places. For Agadir, Inezgane and Tafraoute, they run from the Tafraoute road, just east of the roundabout where it meets Avenue Hassan II and Rue Bir Anzarane. Grands taxis for Bou Izakarn, Goulimine, Mihrleft and, less frequently, Tan Tan and Laayoune start opposite the *Hôtel Mauretanie* on Rue Bir Anzarane just south of the roundabout. For Sidi Ifni and Mirhleft, they set off behind the mosque at the junction of the Ifni road with Avenue Hassan II near Bab el Aouina, while for Sidi Moussa d'Aglou, they leave from Avenue Hassan II near the southwestern corner of the Medina.

For more information see "Travel Details" on p.527.

Sidi Moussa d'Aglou

The beach at **SIDI MOUSSA D'AGLOU** is 17km from Tiznit, along a barren, scrub-lined road. **Grands taxis** make routine runs from Tiznit (leaving from Avenue Hassan II by the southwestern corner of the Medina), though some only go to Aglou village, 3km short of the beach. What awaits you is an isolated expanse of sand, with a wild, body-breaking Atlantic surf. It has a dangerous undertow, and the beach is watched over in summer by military police coastguards, who only allow swimming if conditions are safe – if in doubt, ask them. **Surfing** can be good but you have to pick the right spots.

Quite a few Moroccans (many of them migrant workers from France) come down here in the middle of summer, and there's a trickle of Europeans in winter. Between times, however, the place is very quiet. If you want to stay, you'll find a municipal **campsite** (*Camping Plage Aglou*) about 500m before you get to the beach, on the right if coming from Tiznit. A smaller site (*Camping Azrou Zougane*) with a few rooms can be found 2km south along the beach. Alternatively, by the beach, at the end of the road, is the *Café-Restaurant Ameragh* (☎04/886 6196; daily 11am–3pm & 6.30–11pm; cheap), which offers fish tajines and other tasty grub.

There are a couple of marabout tombs on the beach and, about 1.5km to the north, a tiny (and rather pretty) **troglodyte fishing village**, with a hundred or so primitive cave huts dug into the rocks.

Tafraoute

Approached by beautiful scenic roads through the Anti-Atlas – either from Tiznit (the best approach) or Agadir, with new surfaced roads being constructed from Igherm and Tata too – **Tafraoute** is worth all the effort and time it takes to reach. The town is the centre for villages built among a wind-eroded, jagged panorama of granite tors – "like the badlands of South Dakota", as Paul Bowles put it, "writ on a grand scale". To the north lies the **Ameln Valley**, with its many villages built below – or high among – the quartz range of the **Djebel el Kest**. A striking feature on it is the lion's face – a rock formation so called because it really does look like the face of a lion in the afternoon light.

The best time for a visit to Tafraoute is early spring, in order to see the almond trees in full blossom, or in autumn, after the intense heat has subdued. In midsummer, it can be stunningly hot here, destroying almost all incentive to wander round the villages.

The routes from Tiznit and Agadir

Both approaches to Tafraoute are rewarding and, if you're driving, you may well want to take advantage of this by coming in from Tiznit and leaving for Agadir, or vice versa. If you're doing just one, the Tiznit approach has a distinct edge, winding through a succession of gorges and a grand mountain valley. The road connecting Tafraoute with Igherm (and from there either Taroudannt or Tata) is now surfaced for all but 15km of its length, and will probably be finished by the time you read this, while asphalt is also snaking its way southward towards Akka via the gold mines of Bou Zarif (which it is being laid to serve), though it will probably be a couple of years yet before there is a through route surfaced all the way.

Buses and **grands taxis** cover the route from Tiznit several times daily, but there is only one bus a day along the road from Agadir via Aït Baha.

Tiznit to Tafraoute

The Tiznit–Tafraoute road (7074) passes a succession of oasis-like villages, almost all of them named after the souk that they are host to (see p.68 for the Arabic day names). In winter and spring the road is sometimes crossed by streams but it is generally passable enough; the drive takes around two hours, but leave plenty of time to see (and navigate) the mountains before dusk.

At **ASSAKA** (20km from Tiznit), a substantial bridge has been built over the Oued Tazeroualt – the river that causes most difficulty in winter and spring. Around 19km further on, just before Tighmi, a road heads south into the Anti-Atlas to the **Zaouia of Sidi Ahmed ou Moussa** (10km), which for a while in the seventeenth century controlled its own local state, the Tazeroualt, whose capital was at nearby (and now deserted) **Illigh**. The zaouia remains active and hosts a **moussem** during the second or third week of August, which would be worth trying to attend. Sidi Ahmed is the patron of Morocco's acrobats – most of whom come from this region of Morocco – and return to perform.

Just beyond **TIGHMI** (aka Tirhmi; 42km from Tiznit), the road begins its ascent of the **Col du Kerdous** (1100m). At the top of the pass, the *Hôtel Kerdous* (☎04/886 2063; ④), created from an old fortress, is worth at least a stop for a tea and breathtaking views. This area is also a hot spot for paragliding – Ibrahim at the *Hôtel Tafraout* in Tafraoute has details.

GROUND SQUIRRELS

Along the road from Tiznit to Tafraoute, you may notice children holding little furry animals for sale – live, on a piece of string – by the roadside. These are **ground squirrels**, which are known locally as *anzid* or *sibsib*, and are destined for the **tajine** dish, in which they are considered quite a delicacy, their flesh being sweet since they subsist mainly on a diet of almonds and argan nuts. Recognizable by the prominent stripes down their backs, and by their long tails, ground squirrels are common in the tropics, and have long been ascribed medicinal properties in Morocco. You will not get *anzid* tajine in any restaurant however, unless perhaps you provide the squirrels yourself.

At the end of the descent is the village of **JEMAA IDA OUSSEMLAL** (64km from Tiznit), which offers basic rooms at the *Hôtel de la Victoire* (①), and the last petrol station before Tafraoute. The road **divides** as you enter the village. The left fork, which runs downhill through the village (and past the hotel), is the **"old road"**, which continues to Tafraoute as the 7074 – a picturesque route that drops into the Ameln Valley via Had Tahala (once a Jewish village). The right fork (7146), skirting the village, is a **"new road"** to Tafraoute, via Aït Ouafka and **IZERBI**, where the minister of housing has a Disney-style chateau. It is a longer route but well surfaced, flatter and faster going, arriving in Tafraoute through a grand spectacle of mountains and the lunar landscape around Agard Oudad (see p. 519). There's even a third possibility now, avoiding Izerbi by taking a left where the road forks just after Aït Ouafka.

Agadir/Inezgane to Tafraoute via Aït Baha

The S509 road runs from Agadir to Tafraoute via Aït Baha. It is a bit drab between Agadir and Aït Baha, but the section from there on to Tafraoute is a highly scenic (and slow and winding) mountain ride past a series of fortified kasbah-villages. There's one daily bus along this route, plus another from Agadir to Aït Baha only.

AÏT BAHA is the largest village on the route, a characterless roadside halt with two basic **hotels**, the *Tafraoute* (①) and the *El Massira* (☎04/824 4050; ①), and a newer, better one, the *Al Adarissa* (☎04/825 4461; ④), two cafés and very little shade. The village hosts a **Wednesday souk**.

Beyond, the most spectacular kasbah to be seen is **TIOULIT** off to the left of the road, around 35km from Aït Baha. Another 25km brings you to a junction of roads, with the left fork heading off to Irherm on the Tata loop (a very rough *piste* once you pass the village of **AÏT ABDALLAH**), the right to Tafraoute. Around 5km beyond this junction is the village of **SIDI ABDALLAH EL JABAR**, scene of a small, but lively moussem around its zaouia, celebrated annually October 20–22.

Tafraoute

TAFRAOUTE stands at the edge of a rambling palmery – quite unexpected after a rather barren approach over the last few kilometres from both Tiznit and Agadir. It is a small place, created as an administrative centre by the French, and little expanded since, as Tafraoutis prefer to stick to their villages, or at least return to them after working elsewhere or abroad (see box p.516). It is a pleasant place and most visitors – women as well as men – find it one of the most relaxed destinations in Morocco, despite the fact that touts from other regions have recently been making a nuisance of themselves, claiming to be the guides mentioned in this and other books, and spinning all sorts of yarns to coax the unwary into carpet shops where they can be subjected to the old hard-sell routine.

RESTAURANTS & CAFÉ'S
Café-Restaurant Étoile d'Agadir	D
Restaurant l'Étoile du Sud	C
Restaurant Marrakesh	B
Boulangerie-Café Olivier d'Or	A

ACCOMMODATION
Hôtel les Amandiers	5
Hôtel Redouane	3
Hôtel Salama	2
Hôtel Tafraout	4
Hôtel Tanger	1

Getting around the Ameln villages, you can use a combination of taxis and walking, or rent mountain bikes from an outlet opposite the PTT.

Accommodation

The town has just five hotels, so it's wise to arrive early or book ahead to be sure of a room. The **campsite**, *Camping Etoile du Sud*, is ten minutes' walk from the centre (☎ c/o *Etoile du Sud* restaurant 04/880 0038; ①). A small, secure enclosure, with hot showers. It also has four rooms for rent.

Hôtel Les Amandiers, on the hill above the town – ten minutes' walk (☎04/880 0008 or 88, fax 880 0343). Kasbah-style building offering comfortable rooms with a choice of shower or bath, a dull restaurant (cheaper for residents), but great views from the terrace, and the town's only swimming pool (very pleasant) and bar. ⑤.

Hôtel Redouane, by the bridge (☎ & fax 04/880 0066). A bit seedy with basic and not very clean rooms at erratic prices. Has a terrace restaurant on the first floor. ①.

Hôtel Salama (☎04/880 0026, fax 880 0448), across the river from the *Redouane*. A good-value hotel with comfortable rooms, en-suite bathrooms and a roof terrace, plus solar-powered hot water. ②.

Hôtel Tafraout, Place Moulay Rachid – by the petrol station (☎04/880 0060). Much better than the *Redouane* and *Tanger*, with clean and pleasant rooms, a warm welcome and very helpful staff. This hotel is often used as a base by paragliding groups, and Ibrahim who works here keeps details of local paragliding spots. ①.

Hôtel Tanger, across the road from the *Redouane* (☎04/880 0033). Slightly better rooms, cheaper for singles, with friendly staff and quite a good restaurant where you can eat outside. ①.

Eating

In addition to the hotels (of which the *Tanger* has a reasonable restaurant, offering a vegetarian tajine among other dishes), there are three restaurants in the town:

Café-Restaurant Etoile d'Agadir A great little place, serving classic tajines (lamb with prunes and almonds, chicken with lemon and olives) and other Moroccan dishes, all delicious and beautifully presented. Daily 8am–6pm. Cheap.

Restaurant l'Etoile du Sud. A set-menu restaurant serving delicious Moroccan food, either indoors or outside in a Bedouin-style tent, with an occasional cabaret and floor show for tour groups. Daily 8.30am–10pm. Moderate.

TAFRAOUTE: VILLAGE ECONOMICS

Among Tafraoute villagers, **emigration** to work in the grocery and hotel trade – all over Morocco and France – is a determining aspect of life. The men always return home to retire, however, building European-looking villas amid the rocks, and most of the younger ones manage to come back for a month's holiday each year – whether it be from Casablanca, Tangier, Paris or Marseilles.

But for much of the year, it is the women who run things in the valley, and the only men to be found are the old, the family-supported or the affluent. It is a system that seems to work well enough: enormously industrious, and very community-minded, the Tafraoutis have managed to maintain their villages in spite of adverse economic conditions, importing all their foodstuffs except for a little barley, the famed Tafraoute almonds and the sweet oil of the argan tree.

Oddly enough, this way of life has exact parallels in Tunisia, with the people of Djerba; less surprisingly, both social structures developed through crisis and necessity. Between 1880 and 1882, this whole region was devastated by famine.

Restaurant Marrakesh A family-run place with excellent-value meals and friendly service. The couscous here is particularly good. Daily 8am–10pm. Cheap.

Listings

Banks The Banque Populaire is open only on Wednesdays for the town's souk, but there's an inconspicuous BMCE behind the PTT, with standard opening hours.

Guides One guide highly recommended for trekking or four-wheel-driving around the region is Mohammed Ouhammou Sahnoun, who lives in the village of Tiouada and can be contacted by phone or fax (☎ & fax 04/880 0547) or via either the *Hôtel Tafraout* or Houssine Laroussi, who runs the Coin des Nomades shop. Another recommended guide is Mohammed Ouakrim, who can be contacted through the *Restaurant l'Etoile du Sud*. Beware however of touts falsely claiming to know or to be these people – if necessary, ask to see their state-issued ID cards.

Hammam The old hammam is down a side street by the central mosque. There's another near the bend in the main street (behind the bakery, turn left and it's 100m further, under the arch), and a new one, off Place Moulay Rachid (50m down the Ameln Valley road, then right and right again after another 50m). All the hammams have entrances for men and women, open from around 5am, but the women's side closes at around 5pm, the men's stays open till about 7.30pm.

Henna tattoos Najat el 'Adam, who works at the *Etoile du Sud* restaurant, paints henna designs on hands or feet, and can be contacted via the restaurant.

Shopping There's a Wednesday souk, held in the centre of town. Worthwhile permanent crafts shops include the Coin des Nomades (aka Meeting Place of Nomads) and Artisanat du Coin, both unpressurized. Tafraoute is well known for its *babouches*, and a narrow street of *cordonniers* sell quality slipperwear just below the Coin des Nomades.

Post office The PTT is open Mon–Fri 8.30am–noon & 2–6.30pm. There are a trio of *téléboutiques* in town, but no phones taking I.A.M. phonecards.

Sports For information on paragliding sites, ask Ibrahim at the *Hôtel Tafraoute*. For information on rock-climbing sites, ask Houssine Laroussi at the Coin des Nomades shop.

Moving On

Buses leave from the main street where CTM and a firm called El Hilal have their offices. There are departures for Tiznit, Agadir, and Casa via Izerbi and Marrakesh. Departure points and times change frequently, however, so always check them in advance.

Grands taxis leave from the same street, opposite the CTM office. The only regular destination for collective taxis is Tiznit. For full details see "Travel Details", p.527.

The Ameln Valley and around

You could spend days, if not weeks, wandering round the 26 villages of the **Ameln Valley**. Set against the backdrop of the rocks, they are all beautiful both from afar and close up – with springs, irrigation systems, brightly painted houses, and mosques. On no account, either, should you miss out on a walk to see the **painted rocks** in their albeit faded glory.

Starting out from Tafraoute, **Oumesnat**, 6km to the northeast, is a good first objective, as you can usually get a lift there, or charter a taxi at modest cost; taxis could also be arranged to pick you up from a village at the end of the day. From Oumesnat, you could walk the length of the valley from village to village: the walk to **Anemeur**, for example, is around 10–12km. More serious walkers might consider making an ascent of the **Djebel El Kest** (2359m) or, best of all, **Adrar Mkorn** (2344m), an isolated peak to the southeast with spectacular twin tops (this involves some hard scrambling). The area of the **lion's face** at Asgaour (and many other areas scattered on both the southern and northern slopes of the Djebel el Kest) offers excellent rock climbing on sound quartzite. The *Hôtel les Amandiers* keeps a book with full details.

The **Ameln villages** are built on the lower slopes of the Djebel El Kest, between the "spring line" and the valley floor, allowing gravity to take the water through the village and on to the arable land below. Tracks link the villages, following the contour lines – and frequently the irrigation channels – and most are accessible from the road only by crossing an intricate network of these irrigation canals, orchards and allotments. Many of the villages have basic shops where you can buy drinks, if little else.

Oumesnat to Anameur – and a loop back to Tafraoute

OUMESNAT, like most Ameln settlements, emerges out of a startling green and purple rockscape, crouched against the steep rock walls of the valley – on which locals point out the face of a lion. From a distance, its houses, perched on the rocks, seem to have a solidity to them – sensible blocks of stone, often three storeys high, with parallel sets of windows. Close up, they reveal themselves as bizarre constructions, often built on top of older houses deserted when they had become too small or decrepit; a few of them, with rooms jutting out over the cliffs, are held up by enormous stilts and have raised doorways entered by short (and retractable) ladders.

One of the houses, known as **La Maison Traditionelle**, is owned by a blind Berber and his son, who will show visitors round (tip expected). They give an interesting tour, explaining the domestic equipment – grindstones, water-holders, cooking equipment – and the layout of the house with its guest room with separate entrance, animals' quarters, and summer terrace for sleeping out. To get the most from a visit, you may need to engage an interpreter; the guides in the "Listings" section for Tafraoute will interpret for you if you engage them.

From Oumesnat, you can walk through or above a series of villages to **ANAMEUR**, where there is a *source bleue*, or natural springwater pool, a meandering hike of around three hours. Along the way is **Tazoulte**, one of four local villages with Jewish cemeteries, remnants of a community now completely departed, though Jewish symbols are still inscribed on the region's silverware, which was traditionally made by Jews.

The Ameln's highest village, **TAGOUDICHE** (Tagdichte on the road sign), where the trail up the **Djebel El Kest** (or Lekst) begins, is accessible by Landrover along a rough *piste*. There is a shop, and a floor can usually be found if you want to stay overnight, for an early morning ascent. The Djebel El Kest is a rough and rocky scramble – there's no actual climbing involved – over a mountain of amethyst quartzite. There is a black igneous dyke below the summit pyramid, the summit being a pilgrimage site, with shelters on the top.

Returning to Tafraoute from the Ameln Valley, you can walk over a pass back from the 7148 road near Ighalene in around three hours. The path isn't particularly easy to find but it's a lovely walk, taking you past flocks of sheep and goats tended by their child-shepherds. The route begins as a *piste* (east of the one to Tagoudiche), then you follow a dry riverbed off to the right, up a side-valley, where the zigzags of an old track can be seen. Cross to go up here – not straight on – and, once over the pass, keep circling left till you can see Tafraoute below.

Tirnmatmat

To the west of Tafraoute, the road (7148) along the Ameln Valley crosses an almost imperceptible watershed into a valley. At Aït Omar (see map), a *piste* heads north to **TIRNMATMAT**, a welcoming village. Around 200m beyond it, on the north bank of the river, are numerous **carvings** in the rocks, depicting hunters and animals (some of these may be prehistoric), along with more modern graffiti (including a VW Beetle of clearly recent vintage).

The **ridge walk** to the south of this village is taken by some trekking parties and is really special, with Bonelli's eagles circling below, goats climbing the argan trees, and wild boar snuffling round the bushes.

Agard Oudad and the painted rocks

A short but enjoyable walk from Tafraoute is to head south to **AGARD OUDAD** (3km from Tafraoute), a dramatic-looking village built under a particularly bizarre outcrop of granite. Like many of the rocks in this region, this has been given a name. Most of the others are named after animals – people will point out their shapes to you – but this one is known (in good French-colonial tradition) as **Le Chapeau de Napoléon** (Napoleon's hat).

A stranger sight, however, awaits you in the form of "Les Pierres Bleues" – the **Painted Rocks**– 1.5km to the southwest of the village. The painting was executed in 1984 by a Belgian artist, **Jean Verame**, together with a team of Moroccan firemen, who hosed some 18 tons of paint over a large area of rocks; Verame had previously executed a similar project in Sinai. The rocks have lost some of their sharpness of colour over the years but they remain weird and wonderful: blue and red hills, clusters of black and purple boulders, mesmerizing in effect. To reach them on foot, walk through the village and follow the flat *piste* round to the right, behind the Chapeau de Napoléon, then walk parallel to the oued for 1.5km – if you're in doubt a young guide will take you. In a car, you can go partway along a signposted *piste* off the new road to Tiznit – a longer 5km route with a ten-minute walk at the end. But, unless you prefer a longer route, don't follow the road sign if you are on foot.

Tazka

Another easy walk from Tafraoute is to **TAZKA**, about 2km southwest, where there is a prehistoric carving of a gazelle. To get there, follow a path through the palmery, as shown on our Tafraoute map (p.515). When you emerge, past the remains of an old kasbah, you will see on your left the houses of Tazka at the foot of a high granite bluff. Take the lesser path to the right of the bluff and the carvings – a modern one on the rockface and an old one on the tilted surface of a fallen rock – are on your left after around 200m.

A southern circuit from Tafraoute

A beautiful day-trip from Tafraoute is to drive southeast towards Souk El Hadd Issi, a route that takes in some of the most beautiful country of the Anti-Atlas, including a fabulous gorge and palmery. If you have a sturdy vehicle and a taste for bone-shaking *pistes*, you can make a loop of it, returning to Tafraoute on the "new road" from Tiznit via Izerbi. The route is also offered as a **Landrover trip** by local guide Mohammed Ouhammou Sahnoun (see Tafraoute "Listings", p.516), who lives in Tiouada. He also offers **accommodation** in his house, where he is setting up an *Auberge Sahnoun* (☎ & fax 04/880 0547; ①) for anyone interested in using it as a base to explore the local area, though space is limited so it's best to call ahead.

Leaving Tafraoute, follow the "new road" out past Agard Oudad, turning left around 3km south of the village. This road climbs over the hills, with superb panoramas back across Tafraoute and the Ameln Valley, to reach **TLETA TAZRITE** (15km from Tafraoute), which has a souk on Friday – not Tuesday as its name implies.

From here, a new surfaced road leads south to the massive palmery at **Aït Mansour**, and will eventually continue all the way to Akka. Heading east from Tleta, the road is also surfaced, but quite broken up. Following it past the modern village of **TARHAT** (Taghaout) you enter a canyon, which the *piste* follows for the next 46km, and just a little beyond here, high on your left, are the twelfth-century remains of **ancient Tarhat**, a fortified village and agadir perched on the lip of a sheer rock wall. A footpath leads up to it from the modern village.

At **TIZERKINE**, a lovely oasis snaking along the canyon, all semblance of paved road comes to an end. A passable *piste* continues (be sure to take the right fork, 5km from Tizerkine) to the village of **TEMGUILCHT**, dominated by the very large and impressive **Zaouia Sidi Ahmed ou Mohammed** (no entrance to non-Muslims), where there is a moussem in honour of the saint every August. The road continues past **Tiouada** and on to SOUK EL HADD ISSI (Souk El Had Arfallah Ihrir on the Michelin map), with a Sunday souk; then past a fine agadir (5km on); and finally north to meet the road from Aït Mansour.

Four kilometres west of Souk el Hadd Issi, a rougher *piste* heads southwards, and continues all the way to Aït Herbil (see p.506). Off this *piste* are a number of ancient **rock carvings**, though they are not easy to find and a guide would be advisable. The first and least difficult group of carvings to find are some 700m east of the *piste*, about 6.4km south of the junction. They feature long-horned cattle, and also elephants, which lived in this part of Africa when the carvings were made.

From Aït Bounouh, a *piste* climbs over the hills to bring you out on the "new road" from Tiznit to Tafraoute near Izerbi. At Izerbi, *pistes* also continue south towards Amtoudi and the Bou Izakarn–Tata road.

Tiznit to Goulimine – and Sidi Ifni

Heading **south from Tiznit to Goulimine**, you have a choice of routes: a fast inland road across scrubby desert via **Bou Izakarn**, where the road to Ifrane de l'Anti-Atlas and the Tata oasis (see p.503) heads off east into the Anti-Atlas; or a more circuitous journey along the coast, by way of the splendid old Spanish colonial port of **Sidi Ifni**. Most people will probably choose to do one route down and the other back, which is a good idea, especially as Sidi Ifni often turns out to be an unexpected highlight for many visitors.

Tiznit to Sidi Ifni: Mirhleft

The route down the coast from Tiznit to Sidi Ifni passes, around the midway point, the roadside village of **MIRHLEFT**, a friendly, bustling little place, overlooked by a ruined French fort and set back a kilometre from a good beach. Buses and grands taxis from Tiznit could drop you here – or you could use Sidi Ifni as a base. The beach itself is a beautiful, totally undeveloped curve of sand, with crashing waves and strong currents; it attracts surfers and camper vans.

The village has several cafés and five basic **hotels**. Four of them are on the village's main street, the best being the *Hôtel Farah* (☎06/212 0681; ③) with a friendly, English-speaking proprietor. The *Hôtel du Sud* (☎04/871 9024; ③) and the *Hôtel Tafoukt* (☎04/871 9077; ③) are also clean and bright. Prices vary with demand. For camper vans there is an accepted parking area, along a track leading from the waterstand to the beach. The village also hosts a Monday souk, devoted mainly to secondhand items.

To the south are further **beaches**, of which the best are **Plage du Marabout** (3km from Mirhleft, by a prominent marabout tomb) and **Plage Aftas**.

Sidi Ifni

SIDI IFNI is uniquely interesting: a town that was relinquished by Spain only in 1969, after the Moroccan government closed off landward access to the colonial enclave.

Mirhleft & Tiznit (7064)

Abbainou & Goulimine (7129)

RESTAURANTS
Restaurant Lanzarote A
Chez Mustapha B

Former Spanish
Naval Secretariat

Camping
el Barco

Women's
Hammam

Jardin
Houria

**Grands Taxis
(Mirhleft, Tiznit,
Inezgane)**
★

Men's
Hammam

**Grands Taxis
(Tan Tan
Goulimine)**
★

Spanish
Consulate

Law Courts

ACCOMMODATION
Hôtel Aire Nouvelle 6
Hôtel Aït Ba Hamram 1
Hôtel Bellevue 5
Hôtel Houria 4
Hôtel Ifni 7
Hôtel Suerte Loca 2
Hôtel Wejan 3

PLACE
HASSAN II
(PLAZA
ESPANA)

Banque
Populaire

★ Local Buses

AVENUE SIDI MOHAMMED ABDALLAH

Town
Hall

Cinema

PTT

Royal
Palace

Filling
Station

Municipal
Market

Lighthouse

HASSAN II

AVENUE

Former Airfield

SIDI IFNI

Camping
Sidi Ifni

Old Port

Weekly Souk & New Port (7014)

More than thirty years on, it still preserves an outpost air and can seem rather wonderful. Built in the 1930s, on a cliff-top site, it is full of sweeping architectural lines and elaborate ironwork: all in all, a bizarre memorial to colonialist purpose (or perhaps the lack of it), and surely the finest and most romantic Art Deco military town ever built. It is a very relaxed place with a decaying film-set atmosphere, but unfortunately much of it really is decaying, and many of its fine 1930s buildings are sadly becoming the victims of neglect. On Sundays a large **souk** takes place just east of the abandoned airfield. On June 30 every year there is a **festival** to celebrate Ifni's 1969 reincorporation into Morocco.

The town, or more accurately the site then known as Santa Cruz del Mar Pequeño, "Holy Cross of the Small Sea", was Spanish from 1476 to 1524, when the Saadians threw them out. In 1860, the Treaty of Tetouan – the culmination of Morocco's first military defeat by a European power in 200 years – gave it back to them, though they didn't reoccupy it until 1934, after they (and the French) had "pacified" the interior.

Approaching Sidi Ifni from Tiznit, you pass through a modern and nondescript suburb called Colomina. Then the road swings down, across the Oued Ifni, and into Sidi Ifni proper. Once you've arrived in town, you should have no orientation problems: it's a straightforward grid, with steps leading down to the sea.

The Town

It is the Spanish feel – and the **Art Deco architecture** – that is most attractive about Sidi Ifni. The town beach, with a marabout tomb at its northern end, is not that great (Mirhleft, see p.520, is better) and is prone to long sea mists.

The obvious place to start out is the **Place Hassan II**, still commonly known by its original name, **Plaza de España**. It stands at the heart of the town and immediately sets a tone for the place. Its centrepiece is an Andalucian garden with Spanish tiled benches and a Moroccan tiled fountain, flanking a plinth which once bore the statue of General Capaz, who took Ifni for Spain in 1934. At one end of this square stands a **Spanish consulate** – a building straight out of García Márquez, now, it seems, terminally closed. Next to it, a **church** in Moorish-Art Deco style has now been adopted for use as the law courts. At the other end of the plaza, by a **town hall** complete with town clock, the former governor-general's residence is now the **royal palace**. Many of these buildings are in immaculate condition, with their stunning pastel shades picked out. The square is also used as the site of an annual **art exhibition** every February, featuring paintings and sculpture by local, Moroccan and international artists.

More Art Deco splendour is to be seen off the square and along Avenue Hassan II, as well as around the **post office** which was also rather splendid before the top storey was demolished, and from where the town issued its own stamps under Spanish rule, featuring wildlife, traditional costumes and even the town's buildings, as stamp collectors may recall. Next to the *Hôtel Suerte Loca* and alas sadly dilapidated nowadays, a building in the shape of a ship once housed the **naval secretariat** – its two forward portholes being windows of cells where miscreant sailors were held. And there are a whole sequence of monumental **stairways**, rambling down towards the port and beach, and a magnificent Art Deco **lighthouse**. There is also a small **maze** (perhaps the only one in Morocco) in the Jardin Houria on Avenue El Houria, but it has been totally neglected and is nowadays used as a public toilet.

To the south of the town is the **old port**, built by the Spanish, and out to sea is an odd little concrete island, where ships used to dock. It was connected to the mainland by a unique cable car, which hauled goods as well as passengers. There's a **new port** further south, with big new sardine- and anchovy-processing factories. On the way to the latter is the former Spanish prison, now disused, and an airfield, also disused, whose last landing was an American locust-spraying plane, forced down here on one engine after being shot at by Polisario guerrillas in 1988. The airport building is now a meteorological station.

If you have a special interest in Ifni's past, you may care to call in on the barber's shop at 25 Avenue Mohammed V, where Hassan Aznag, the barber, will be glad to show you his collection of old photos of the town and to chat about its history.

Accommodation and eating

Finding **accommodation** is easy enough, with seven hotels, all moderately priced. The hotels *Aire Nouvelle*, Avenue Sidi Mohammed Abdallah (☎04/887 5298; ①), *Houria* (aka *Hôtel Liberté*; ①), off Avenue Mohammed V, *Ifni*, Avenue Mohammed V (☎04/887 5807; ①) and *Wejan* (①), off Avenue Mohammed V, all have small, clean rooms catering mainly for a Moroccan clientele; all are very cheap, but the *Houria* and the *Wejan* are even cheaper than the other two.

Of the two **campsites**, *Camping Sidi Ifni*, Avenue Sidi Mohammed, is rather spartan with little shade (5dh per person), and *Camping el Barco*, Rue de la Plage (☎04/878 0707), while similarly shadeless is, at least, right on the beach (10dh per person).

HOTELS

Hôtel Aït Ba Hamram, Rue de la Plage – at the bottom of the steps (☎04/887 5267). This rather grand building was under renovation at our last check, and due to reopen as a three-star hotel in the near future. ④.

Hôtel Bellevue, Place Hassan II (☎04/887 5072, fax 878 0499). Another fine building, also good value, with a new wing, sweeping views over the beach, a noisy bar and a decent restaurant.②.

Hôtel Suerte Loca, Rue Moulay Youssef (☎04/887 5350, fax 878 0003). A characterful place – the name ("Crazy Luck") and a bodega-style bar (not licensed) reveals its small-town Spanish origins – which has been renovated and is run by a very welcoming (and English-speaking) family. It has cheap rooms in the old Spanish wing, slightly pricier en-suite ones in a new wing, and is deservedly popular. It also has a good café-restaurant and a terrace overlooking the town and sea. ①.

EATING

Apart from the hotels mentioned above, there is not a vast choice of places to eat, though you'll find a few cheap **restaurants** around the souk and post office, notably the *Restaurant Lanzarote* off Avenue Mohammed V (daily 8am–2.30am; cheap), which serves fish or chicken tajines, fried fish and brochettes, and is named in memory of ten local people, many of them regulars, who died trying to smuggle themselves into the Canary Islands on a small boat that was overwhelmed by the weather in December 1999. Another hole-in-the-wall place worth trying is *Chez Mustapha* (no sign but last in the block) behind the municipal market on the corner of Avenue Hassan II and Avenue el Houria (daily 9.30am–11pm; cheap).

Surfing and paragliding

Sidi Ifni has become something of a base for **surfing and paragliding**. Favourite spots for the former are on the main beach, just in front of the tennis courts, and another beach 100m south of the new port. Favourite paragliding spots are **Legzira**, a beach 11km north of Ifni overlooked by a Spanish fort, where there's a basic hotel (no phone; ①), though without electricity, and the hills behind Ifni. Ahmed at the *Hôtel Suerte Loca* can provide details for those interested.

Moving on

Sidi Ifni has easy connections with Tiznit and Goulimine by bus and grand taxi. There are three daily **bus** departures for Tiznit, Inezgane and Marrakesh leaving from Avenue Mohammed V, opposite the Banque Populaire; morning departures for Tiznit and Inezgane leave from across the street outside no. 24 Avenue Mohammed V; afternoon departures for Tiznit and Inezgane leave from Avenue al Adarissa. **Grands taxis** run to Mirhleft, Tiznit, Inezgane, Goulimine and sometimes Tan Tan, leaving four blocks east of Avenue Mohammed V (see map). For more information see "Travel Details", p.527.

There is little of note on the route south from Sidi Ifni to Goulimine, though the route itself is a pleasant one, especially in spring, when the slopes are green with a mass of euphorbia.

Tiznit to Goulimine via Bou Izakarn

Moussems apart, it is the **route down** to Goulimine that is the main attraction. It is best taken, at least in one direction, with a detour to Sidi Ifni (see above).

Travelling on the inland route, the only place of any size that you pass is the palmery and village of **BOU IZAKARN**. Grands taxis can be negotiated here for Ifrane de l'Anti-Atlas and Amtoudi (see pp.507–508).

Goulimine

GOULIMINE (also spelt Guelmim or Gulimime) sounds pretty exciting in the brochures: "The Gateway to the Sahara", with its nomadic "blue men" and traditional

camel market. The truth, sadly, is considerably more mundane. Goulimine is actually a fairly standard administrative town with a distinctly frontier feel to it, and a couple of small, fairly animated souks.

Though the scenery is indeed impressively bleak, you're still a long way short of seeing any Saharan dunes, and Goulimine's Saturday souk, known as the camel market, is a rather depressing sham, maintained largely for tour groups bussed in from Agadir. The market has all the usual Moroccan goods on sale: grain, vegetables, meat, clothes, silver, jewellery, sheep and goats. What it doesn't have in very great numbers are camels, as the beasts have steadily fallen from favour over the years in the wake of lorries and transit vehicles, and the caravan routes are more or less extinct. The few you do see here have been brought in either just for show or to be sold off for meat. If you are interested, the market is held a kilometre out of town on the road to Tan Tan; it starts around 6am and a couple of hours later the first tour buses arrive. A second market, just off Avenue des F.A.R., sells mainly food and is open evenings only.

The locals have recently begun to indulge in theatrical cons, ferrying people out to see "genuine *hommes bleus*" in tents outside town, but for a more convincing and exciting sense of the desert, you would do a lot better to make for M'hamid in the Drâa (see p.430) or Merzouga in the Tafilalt (see p.462).

The one time that a visit to Goulimine would be worthwhile in itself is if you could coincide with one of the region's annual moussems – when you really are likely to see Touareg nomads. It's difficult to get information about the exact dates of the **moussems** – they vary considerably from year to year – but there is usually a large one held in June at Asrir, 10km southeast of Goulimine.

Moussems and markets aside, the nearest thing Goulimine has to a tourist sight is the remains of **Caid Dahman Takni's palace**, in the back streets behind the *Hôtel la Jeunesse*, ruined now, but barely a hundred years old.

Practicalities

Arriving by bus or grand taxi, you'll probably be dropped at the *gare routière*, though night CTM services and some grands taxis may drop you elsewhere. At the heart of the town is the **Place Bir Anzarane**, with the main cluster of hotels and café-restaurants to its north.

There is a **tourist office** at 3 Residence Sahara out on the Agadir road (☎04/887 2911; Mon–Fri 8.30am–noon & 2.30–6.30pm). In addition, the town has five **banks** and numerous **shops**, several of which specialize in Saharan "antiques" – mainly carpets and jewellery, but also leather goods, silverware, knives, stones and old money. The town **hammam**, with showers as well as steam, is open for both sexes 6am–midnight. It is right in the centre of town, by the **post office**. If you prefer full immersion, there is a municipal **swimming pool** (open summer only) out on the new Asrir road. You can access the **Internet** at Internet World on Avenue Youssef ibn Tachfine, by the *Hôtel Salam* (*anakhla@iam.net.ma*).

Accommodation and eating

Accommodation is somewhat limited. A trio of more interesting alternatives to a night in Goulimine are detailed in the "Around Goulimine" section, overleaf.

The *Hôtel Salam* has the best **meals**, as well as rooms. Other places worth considering for eating include *Café Marche Verte* on the Agadir road and the *Café de la Poste* and *Café Jour et Nuit*, up near the PTT (all open 24hr; cheap). The *Hôtel Salam* has a **bar**, but its customers are nearly all male.

Several of the hotels and cafés put on shows of **Guedra dancing** on Friday and Saturday nights and Saturday lunchtimes. Much has been written about this traditional, seductive women's dance of the desert – performed, from a kneeling position (developed for the low tents) to a slow, repetitive rhythm. The shows here, however, are a bit of a travesty.

Hôtel Bahich, 31 Av. Abaynou (☎04/877 2178). A bright new hotel with comfortable though sparsely furnished rooms, some of which have en-suite showers. ③.

Hôtel l'Ere Nouvelle, Bd. Mohammed V (☎04/887 2118). Plain but clean, with friendly staff and hot showers on request. ①.

Hôtel la Jeunesse, Bd. Mohammed V – opposite (no phone). A tolerable second choice, if the above is full. Located up a steep flight of steps. ①.

Hôtel Oued Ed Dahab, Place Bir Anzarene (☎04/887 2807). Upstairs rooms around the terrace are cheaper than the downstairs rooms, which have recently been renovated. ①.

Hôtel Place Bir Anzarane, Place Bir Anzarane (☎04/887 2602). Not bad, although few rooms have outside windows. There are no showers but the hammam is nearby (diagonally across the square, between the mosque and PTT).①.

Hôtel Salam, Route de Tan Tan (☎04/887 2057, fax 877 0912). You might decide it's worth paying the extra money for a room here at the town's finest hotel. It offers reasonably large rooms round an open patio, a decent restaurant and Goulimine's only bar. The hotel displays 3-D paintings by an excellent local artist, Hamid Kahlaoui. ③.

Moving on

Daytime **bus departures** are from the *gare routière* on the Bou Izakarn road. These include **SATAS** services to Agadir, Assa-Zag, Ouarzazate, Tiznit, and Tan Tan. There are also numerous departures with smaller companies for Agadir, Marrakesh and Tan Tan, a few to Essaouira and Casablanca, a couple to Rabat, one to Meknes, and one to Ouarzazate via Tata. Only one **CTM** bus leaves from the *gare routière* (8pm to Casa): all later CTM departures leave from outside the CTM office at the *Café Marche Verte* on the Agadir road. **ONCF/Supratours** services leave from their office, just past CTM.

Grands taxis can be found around the *Café Marche Verte* at night (between around 10pm and 6am); in the daytime they leave from the *gare routière* for Ifni, Bou Izakarn, Tiznit, Inezgane, Agadir, Tan Tan, Laayoune and Smara, from a station on Avenue Hassan II, 100m north of the *Hôtel Salam* for Assaka (Landrover taxis can also be found there), and from stations on the new Asrir road for Asrir, Aït Bekkou and Assa-Zag.

For further information see "Travel Details", opposite.

Around Goulimine: springs, oases and Plage Blanche

There are good little trips out from Goulimine to the hot springs of **Abbainou**, 15km northeast, and to the oasis of **Aït Boukha**, 17km southeast; both offer pleasant alternative **accommodation** to a night in Goulimine. So, too, does the recently established auberge-campsite at **Fort Bou-Jerif**, an old French Foreign Legion post, inland from **Plage Blanche** – the "White Beach" that stretches for sixty or so kilometres along the coast southwest of Goulimine.

Abbainou

ABBAINOU is a tiny oasis, with a koubba and hot springs, channelled into two bath enclosures – divided according to sex – where you can soak the afternoon away. The women's enclosure (28°C) is very welcoming, though the men's is 10°C hotter! There is mixed bathing in the evenings.

Located 15km northeast of Goulimine, the oasis is an easy excursion if you have transport; if you don't, you could negotiate a grand taxi (from the main rank by the souk). The French-run *Auberge Abainou* at the oasis has **rooms** round a courtyard, cold showers, a restaurant and a bar. There is also a **campsite**, *Camping Abainou* (also with rooms), and several café-restaurants.

Aït Bekkou

The largest and most spectacular oasis in the Goulimine area is **AÏT BEKKOU** (or Aït Boukka), 10km southeast along the road to Asrir, then a further 7km on *piste*. It can be reached by grand taxi from Goulimine (station on the Asrir road). Alongside the palmery is an impressive new **hotel**, the *Tighmert* (☎04/877 1989; ③), built in mock-kasbah style and decorated, like the *Hôtel Salam* in Goulimine, with paintings by Hamid Kahlaoui.

Aït Bekkou is a thriving agricultural community, with an especially lush strip of cultivation along a canal, irrigated from the old riverbed and emerging from a flat expanse of sand. You might even see the odd herd of camels being grazed out here. To reach the canal, head for the thicket of palms about 2km behind the oasis (or pick up a guide on the way).

Fort Bou-Jerif and Plage Blanche

Fort Bou-Jerif is a truly romantic spot, set beside the Oued Assaka, 13km from the sea. It is marked on the Michelin map by a little fort symbol (with the words *O. Noun* to the left). The **auberge-campsite** here is run by a French couple, Guy and Evy Dreumont. If the attractions of staying at an old French Foreign Legion camp in the middle of nowhere are not enough to entice you, consider that there is also excellent food (camel tajine, no less), and that the Dreumonts offer some superb **four-wheel-drive excursions** in the area, including, of course, trips to the Plage Blanche. They offer rooms in a "motel" (③) and a "hotel" (④) as well as camping (20dh per person), or a nomadic tent to sleep in if you don't have your own (30dh per person), plus power points for caravans, and rows of very clean showers (hot water) and toilets. To book ahead, write to them at: Fort Bou Jerif, BP 504 *piste* Goulimine, Morocco (fax 04/887 3039).

The easiest route to the fort from Goulimine is via the new sealed road to Assaka (grands taxis do the run from a station on the new Sidi Ifni road), then 6km of *piste*, which you could probably persuade your grand taxi driver to take you along for a small fee. The fort can, alternatively be approached by car or campervan over 18km of easy *piste* from Tisséguemane or by Landrover along the coast from Sidi Ifni. Failing that, you might be able to get a lift from Guy, who comes into town twice a week to pick up groceries from a store at the end of Avenue Hassan II (over the oued from the town, it's the next grocery store on the left, with a *tabac* sign), or hire a Landrover taxi from the station on Avenue Hassan II, about 100m north of the *Hôtel Salam*.

travel details

Buses

Agadir to: Beni Mellal (1 CTM and 6 others daily; 8hr); Casablanca (10 CTM and 14 others daily; 9hr); Dakhla (4 daily; 19hr 30min); Essaouira (2 CTM and 16 others daily; 3hr 30min); Fes (1 CTM and 4 others daily; 12hr); Goulimine (2 CTM and 7 others daily, 4hr 30min); Immouzer (1 daily; 2hr 30min); Laayoune (6 daily; 11hr); Marrakesh (5 CTM and 23 others daily; 4hr); Meknes (1 CTM and 2 others daily; 12hr); Ouarzazate (1 CTM and 3 others daily; 7hr 30min); Rabat (8 daily; 11hr); Er Rachidia (1 daily; 11hr); Safi (1 CTM and 12 others daily; 5hr 30min); Smara (3 daily; 9hr); Tafraoute (5 daily; 5hr); Tangier (3 CTM and 1 other daily; 16hr); Tan Tan (4 CTM and 10 others daily; 6hr); Taroudannt (1 CTM and 8 others daily; 2hr 30min); Tata (2 daily; 9hr); Tiznit (3 CTM and 8 others daily; 2hr).

Goulimine to: Agadir (2 CTM and 7 others daily; 4hr 30min), via Tiznit (2hr 30min); Assa-Zag (2 daily; 3hr); Casablanca (1 CTM and 7 others daily; 14hr); Dakhla (4 daily; 15hr 30min); Laayoune (4 CTM and 2 others daily; 7hr); Marrakesh (3 CTM and 14 others daily; 9hr 30min); Ouarzazate (1 daily; 15hr) via Tata (9hr 30min), Foum el Hassan (6hr) and Akka (8hr); Rabat (2 daily; 16hr); Smara (3 daily; 6hr); Tan Tan (4 CTM and 10 others daily; 3hr).

Sidi Ifni to: Inezgane (3 daily; 3hr 30min); Marrakesh (1 daily; 8hr 30min); Tiznit (3 daily; 2hr 30min).

Tafraoute to: Agadir (5 daily; 5hr); Aït Baha (1 daily; 2hr); Casablanca (4 daily; 14hr); Marrakesh (3 daily; 10hr); Rabat (1 daily; 16hr); Tiznit (5 daily; 3hr); Essaouira (2 daily; 9hr 30min).

Taliouine to: Agadir (8 daily; 4hr 30min) via Taroudannt (2hr); Ouarzazate (5 daily; 3hr) via Tazenakht (1hr 30 min); Er Rachidia (1 daily; 11hr) via Tinerhir (8hr); Goulimine (1 daily; 9hr) via Tiznit

(6hr 30min); Marrakesh (2 daily; 9hr); Rabat (1 daily; 15hr 30min) via Casablanca (13hr 30min); Zagora (1 daily; 6hr).

Taroudannt to: Agadir (1 CTM and 8 others daily; 2hr 30min); Casablanca (1 CTM and 5 others daily; 10hr); Essaouira (3 daily; 10hr); Marrakesh (1 CTM and 3 others daily; 6hr 30min); Ouarzazate (1 CTM and 5 others daily; 5hr) via Taliouine (2hr) and Tazenakht (3hr); Rabat (3 daily; 13hr); Tata (2 daily; 5hr).

Tata to: Agadir (4 daily; 9hr); Bou Izakarn (4 daily; 6hr) via Akka (1hr 30min) and Foum el Hassan (3hr 30min); Casablanca (4 daily; 15hr); Goulimine (1 daily; 9hr 30min); Ouarzazate (3 daily; 5hr) via Foum Zguid (2hr 30min); Marrakesh (4 daily; 10hr); Rabat (1 daily; 17hr); Tan Tan (12 hr 30min); Taroudannt (2 daily; 5hr) via Igherm (2hr 30min); Tiznit (3 daily; 7hr).

Tiznit to: Agadir (3 CTM and 8 others daily; 2hr); Bou Izakarn (11 daily; 1hr); Casablanca (8 CTM and 7 others daily; 11hr); Dakhla (1 daily; 17hr 30min); Goulimine (2 CTM and 7 others daily; 2hr 30min); Laayoune (2 daily; 9hr); Marrakesh (2 CTM and 6 others daily; 7hr); Ouarzazate (1 daily; 9hr 30min); Rabat (2 daily; 13hr); Sidi Ifni (1 daily; 2hr 30min); Smara (1 daily; 7hr); Tafraoute (5 daily; 3hr); Tata (3 daily; 7hr); Tan Tan (1 CTM and 7 others daily; 5hr 30min).

Grands taxis

Agadir to: Aourir (15min); Inezgane (15min); Tiznit (1hr 15min) and Taroudannt (1hr 30min). Change at Inezgane for most southern destinations.

Aoulouz to: Ouled Berhil (30min); Taliouine (40min) and Taroudannt (1hr).

Bou Izakarn to: Goulimine (1hr); Tata (3hr 30min); Tiznit (1hr 30min); Inezgane (3hr 30min);

Ifrane de l'Anti-Atlas (20min) and Foum El Hassan (1hr 30min).

Goulimine to: Agadir (4hr 45min); Aït Bekou (30min); Asrir (15min); Assaka (1hr); Assa-Zag (2hr); Bou Izakarn (1hr); Inezgane (4hr 30min); Laayoune (5hr); Sidi Ifni (1hr); Smara (4hr 30min); Tiznit (2hr 30min) and Tan Tan (2hr 30min).

Inezgane to: Agadir (15min); Dakhla (15hr); Essaouira (2hr 30min); Goulimine (4hr 30min); Laayoune (9hr); Marrakesh (3hr); Massa (45min); Ouled Teima (40min); Sidi Ifni (3hr 30min); Smara (8hr); Tan Tan (6hr 15min); Taroudannt (1hr 15min) and Tiznit (2hr).

Ouled Berhil to: Aoulouz (30min) and Taroudannt (40min).

Sidi Ifni to: Goulimine (1hr); Inezgane (3hr 30min); Mirhleft (45min); Tiznit (1hr 30min) and occasionally Tan Tan (3hr 30min).

Taliouine to: Aoulouz (40min) and Tazenakht (1hr).

Taroudannt to: Agadir (1hr 30min); Amsekroud (1hr); Aoulouz (1hr); Igherm (1hr); Inezgane (1hr 15min); Marrakesh (4hr); Ouled Berhil (40min); Ouled Teima (45min) and Tata (3hr).

Tata to: Akka (1hr); Bou Izakarn (3hr 30min); Foum el Hassan (2hr); Foum Zguid (2hr 30min); Taroudannt (3hr) and Tissint (1hr).

Tiznit to: Agadir (1hr 15min); Bou Izakarn (1hr 30min); Goulimine (2hr 30min); Inezgane (1hr); Mirhleft (45min); Sidi Ifri (1hr 30min); Sidi Moussa d'Aglou (15min) and Tafraoute (2hr).

Flights

Agadir to: Casablanca (4 daily; 55min); Dakhla (weekly; 2hr 10min); Laayoune (2 weekly; 1hr 5min); Marrakesh (weekly; 35min).

THE DEEP SOUTH AND WESTERN SAHARA

Few travellers venture south of Goulimine – and on the face of it there is little enough to commend the trip. The towns – **Tan Tan**, **Tarfaya**, **Laayoune** and **Dakhla** – are modern administrative centres, with no great intrinsic interest. The route, however, across vast tracts of *hammada* – bleak, stony desert – is another matter. The odd line of dunes unfolds on the horizon to the east, the ocean parallels much of the road to the west, and there is no mistaking that you have reached the **Sahara** proper. Returning, if you don't fancy a repeat of the journey, there are flights from Dakhla and Laayoune to Agadir, or from Laayoune to the **Canary Islands** (also accessible from Agadir).

An additional point of interest, now that the war with Polisario seems to be at an end, is the attention being lavished on the region by the Moroccan authorities. The **Saharan Provinces** (including – controversially – the former Spanish Sahara, claimed by Morocco with the 1975 Green March) begin just to the south of Tan Tan. **Laayoune**, never greatly regarded by the Spanish, has been transformed into a showcase capital for the new provinces; there are industrial plans for **Tarfaya**; and, with an eye to the traditional nomadic dwellers, the Moroccan authorities have also been assisting in building up the local camel herds.

The region's economic importance was long thought to centre on the phosphate mines at **Boukra**, southeast of Laayoune. However, these have not been very productive in recent years, and the deposits are not especially rich by the standards of the Plateau des Phosphates east of Casablanca. In the long term, the rich

---

HOTEL PRICE CODES

The basis of our **hotel price codes**, set out below and keyed throughout the guide, is the price currently quoted for the cheapest double room in high season (June–September).

Note that cheaper prices in the lower categories are generally for rooms with just a washbasin – you always pay extra for **en-suite** shower and WC – and that double rooms can generally be converted into **triples/family rooms**, with extra beds, for a modest extra charge. Single occupancy usually costs about two-thirds the price of a double, though in some places a single person will pay the same rate for a room as two people sharing, and in other places exactly half as much. Prices quoted are for bed only, without breakfast, but including local taxes.

① 40–100dh	③ 150–200dh	⑤ 400–800dh
② 100–150dh	④ 200–400dh	⑥ over 800dh

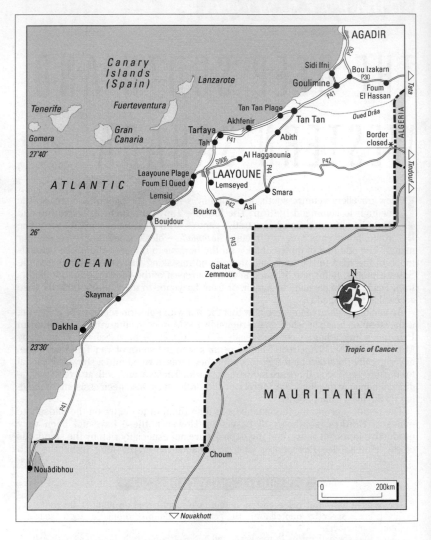

deep-water fishing grounds offshore are likely to prove a much better earner. This potential is gradually being realized with the development of fishing ports at Laayoune, Dakhla and Boujdour, together with industrial plants for fish storage and processing.

Throughout the Western Sahara and the former Spanish Protectorate nowadays, Spanish is fast being replaced by French as the dominant second language. Some older residents still speak Spanish, but officials, administrators, and other migrants into the Western Sahara from Morocco proper, as well as younger people in general, are much more likely to understand French.

Goulimine to Tan Tan

The approach from **Goulimine to Tan Tan** runs along 125km of straight desert road, across a bleak area of scrub and hammada. There are few features to speak of en route: a café and petrol station (55km from Goulimine); a small pass (85km); and finally a crossing of the **Oued Drâa** (109km), invariably dry at this point.

In colonial times, the Drâa was the border between the French and Spanish protectorates and a *piste* heads west to a last French **fort** at its mouth. Somewhat confusingly, although this was the border of the Protectorate, the land to the south was not actually part of the Spanish Saharan colonies: the northernmost of these, Seguiat El Hamra, began at the 27°40' N line just south of Tarfaya, and the southern one at the 26th parallel, just south of Boujdour. After independence in 1958, the Spanish gave back to Morocco the strip of territory north of 27°40', keeping the two Saharan colonies until November 1975 (see box on p.535).

Tan Tan

Arriving at **TAN TAN**, under an archway of kissing camels, you might just find yourself wondering why. A drab administrative centre, it survives in a low-key way through its status as a duty-free zone (the shops are full of radios and electric razors) and rather more so by its fishing port (25km distant), which is responsible for a large percentage of Morocco's sardine exports. Its one claim to fame is that it was a departure point for the famous **Green March** (La Marche Verte, or el Massira el Khadra – see p.535), an event commemorated on postcards throughout the south.

The town has around 50,000 inhabitants, many of them former nomads, who retain their distinctive pale blue robes. This clothing is much in evidence in the **souks** – the most animated part of a hot, sleepy town – as are a variety of *shesh*, strips of cotton that are wrapped round the head. The latter are a wise investment as sun protection if you're heading further south.

Orientation

Tan Tan's main artery is the inevitable **Avenue Mohammed V**, and most of the town is spread out along it. Although the avenue is lined with buildings for the whole of its length, you can still catch glimpses down side streets of a parallel ridge, and to the west the riverbed of Oued Ben Khlil, overgrown in parts with castor oil plants and poisonous thorn apples, which "flows" north to join Oued Drâa.

Just off the bottom end of Avenue Mohammed V is the **Place de la Marche Verte**, with the **bus** and **grand taxi** rank, and several hotels. At the other end, a smaller square with several cafés and an arcade of shops down one side is referred to locally as **La Poste de la Police** because of the small police post in the middle of it. **Petits taxis** can be found here, along with more cheap hotels, and **grands taxis** for Tan Tan Plage. Beyond the square, the street continues up to meet **Boulevard Hassan II**, the main road in and out of town, which enters from Goulimine through the kissing camel archway and heads out, across the riverbed, towards Tan Tan Plage, the airport and Laayoune.

Most of the administrative buildings are at this (north) end of town. The main **PTT** is on Boulevard Hassan II, with branch offices off the Laayoune road and in Place de la Marche Verte. There are three **banks**: BMCE on Boulevard Hassan II at the junction with Avenue Mohammed V, Crédit Agricole across the street, and Banque Populaire down near La Poste de la Police. **Internet** and email access are available at *Micronet*,

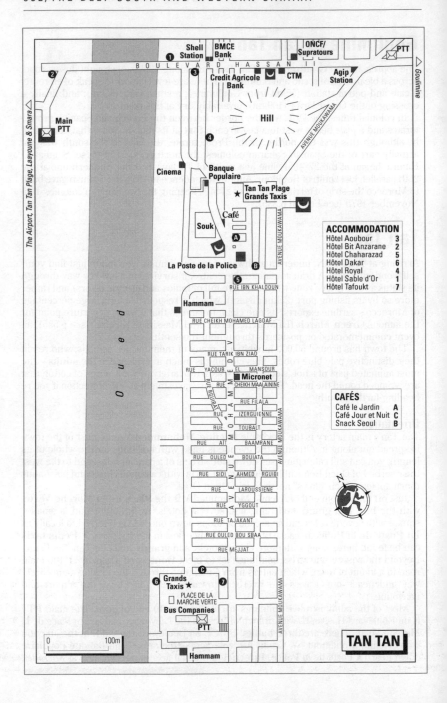

TAN TAN

BOULEVARD HASSAN II

Shell Station
BMCE Bank
ONCF/Supratours
PTT
Credit Agricole Bank
CTM
Agip Station
Main PTT
Hill
Cinema
Banque Populaire
Tan Tan Plage Grands Taxis
Café
Souk
La Poste de la Police
RUE IBN KHALDOUN
Hammam
RUE CHEIKH MOHAMED LAGDAF
RUE TARIK IBN ZIAD
RUE YACOUB EL MANSOUR
RUE CHEIKH MAALAININE
Micronet
RUE FILALA
RUE IZERGUIENNE
RUE TOUBALT
RUE AIT BAAMRANE
RUE OULED BOUIATA
RUE SIDI AHMED RGUIBI
RUE LAROUSSIENE
RUE YGGOUT
RUE TAJAKANT
RUE OULED BOU SBAA
RUE MEJJAT
Grands Taxis
PLACE DE LA MARCHE VERTE
Bus Companies
PTT
Hammam

RUE RGUIBAT
AVENUE MOHAMMED V
AVENUE MOUKAWAMA

The Airport, Tan Tan Plage, Laayoune & Smara
Goulimine

ACCOMMODATION

Hôtel Aoubour	3
Hôtel Bit Anzarane	2
Hôtel Chaharazad	5
Hôtel Dakar	6
Hôtel Royal	4
Hôtel Sable d'Or	1
Hôtel Tafoukt	7

CAFÉS

Café le Jardin	A
Café Jour et Nuit	C
Snack Seoul	B

Oued

0   100m

N

237 Avenue Mohammed V (daily 10am–1pm & 3pm–midnight; 40dh/hr before 6pm, 20dh/hr after; *micronet@iam.net.ma*). Should you need a **hammam**, there's one for both sexes just behind the southern end of Place de la Marche Verte, and another at the far end of the street that leads north from the square.

Accommodation

There are a number of unclassified hotels on and around Place de la Marche Verte and La Poste de la Police, most of them grotty if very cheap. Better choices include:

Hôtel Aoubour, junction of Av. Mohammed V and Bd. Hassan II (☎04/887 7594). Clean and cheap. Its appeal is that it's handy for CTM and ONCF bus departures. Upstairs rooms are better than downstairs ones. ①.

Hôtel Bit Anzarane, 154 Bd. Hassan II (☎04/887 7834; fax 887 7417). Across the oued on the edge of town, this is a good-value place, with decent rooms (shared bathrooms, but should have some en suite in the near future), and reasonable prices. Its main drawback is its distance from the centre. ②.

Hôtel Chaharazad, La Poste de la Police (☎04/876 0405). Rather basic but friendly and cheap – a reasonable fall-back option. ①.

Hôtel Dakar, Place Marche Verte (☎04/887 7245). Pricier than the *Tafoukt* (see below) with en-suite showers in some rooms, but nothing else to justify the price difference. ②.

Hôtel Royal, Av. Mohammed V – up past La Poste de la Police (☎04/887 7186). A comfortable place, with carpeted rooms and en-suite bathrooms throughout. It is in fact a military officers' mess, but they'll take tourists if they have room. ③.

Hôtel Sable d'Or, Av. Hassan II (☎04/887 8069). The best hotel in town, new with immaculate large rooms, some with balcony, and very reasonable prices. ③.

Hôtel Tafoukt, 98 Pl. Marche Verte (☎04/887 7031). The best value in Place Marche Verte hotels, clean, with shared showers. ①.

Eating and drinking

For a **meal**, there are cafés around Place de la Marche Verte, best of which is the *Jour et Nuit* (24hr; cheap) which, true to its name, can produce you a tajine at any hour of the day or night. The best place to sip a mint tea and watch the world go by is in one of the cafés at La Poste de la Police, in particular, the *Café le Jardin* with its big open shelter, and slightly dilapidated garden behind (daily 7am–9pm). The *Snack Seoul* on the same square (daily 10am–4am; cheap) offers sandwiches and roast chicken, but nothing Korean despite the name.

There is no licensed bar in town, and entertainment is limited to the Renaissance **cinema** between La Poste de la Police and the oued. It has a café, *Le Glacier*, attached.

Moving on

Most **buses** leave from Place de la Marche Verte, the south side of which has a row of ticket offices. There are several daily services to Agadir, Marrakesh and Casablanca, a couple to Rabat and Laayoune, and one each to Essaouira, Tata, Ouarzazate and Meknes.

CTM and ONCF/Supratours buses stop outside their offices on Boulevard Hassan II near the main post office. CTM operate four night services to Agadir, Marrakesh and Casablanca (8pm, 10pm, 11pm and midnight, the last continuing to Rabat). They also run services southwards: one to Smara at 2am, the other to Laayoune and Dakhla at 10pm. ONCF/Supratours buses leave for Agadir at 10.30pm, midnight and 1.30am, either continuing to, or connecting for Marrakesh. Heading south, there are departures for Laayonne at 9pm and 2.30am (the latter continuing to Dakhla), and one at 2.30am for Smara.

Grand taxi runs include Goulimine, Inezgane, Agadir, Smara and Laayoune; if you strike lucky, you may also find direct taxis for Tarfaya and Tiznit (especially early mornings). They leave from Place de la Marche Verte except for taxis to Tan Tan Plage, which run from just north of La Poste de la Police.

Tan Tan Plage

TAN TAN PLAGE, 28km from town on the coastal route to Laayoune, has been theoretically earmarked for development as a resort. The ambitious four-star *Hôtel Ayoub*, long planned, hopes to open shortly. Tan Tan Plage already has one hotel, the *Marin* (☎04/887 9507; ③). There are also several fish restaurants, the best of which is the *Etoile de l'Océan*, opposite the *Hôtel Marin*.

The **beach** itself is unenticing – littered with broken glass, not too clean due to the proximity of a large sardine port nearby, and often swamped in seaweed.

A loop through Smara

It's possible to make a **loop** from Tan Tan along the new road, the P44, to Smara, returning by way of the P42 to Laayoune, and from there across to Tan Tan via Tarfaya – a circuit of some 800km. There are **buses** along each section (though not very frequent). If you're driving, you will find **petrol stations** in Tan Tan, Smara and Laayoune – petrol and diesel, incidentally, are subsidized throughout the Saharan provinces (including the former Spanish Sahara), and cost little more than half what you pay in Morocco proper – so if you embark on the trip be sure to fill up, and to carry good water supplies.

Tan Tan to Smara

The ONMT literature on the Deep South extols the P44 between Tan Tan and Smara as "the new Saharan road". It is indeed impressive, in the sheer absence of habitation and features: there are grand vistas of hills and valleys to the east for the first 20km, then, for the next 200km to Smara, it's perfectly flat.

At 75km from Tan Tan is the route's single roadside hamlet, **ABITH** (or Abbatih), where there are a couple of flyblown cafés and a flagpole. Another 36km and you cross into the Western Saharan provinces, with a petrol station where you enter, so that you can take advantage of the lower fuel prices immediately. There is nothing else of interest before Smara, although the desert does get perceptibly darker in colour, due to the presence of black basalt.

Smara

SMARA (Es Semara) developed as an important caravan route across the Sahara, but today it is basically a military garrison town. The only link with its past is the remains of the Palace and Great Mosque of **Ma El Aïnin**, the "Blue Sultan", who controlled the region at the turn of the twentieth century. If you do come to the town you should certainly see them.

The military presence in Smara includes both the Moroccan army and the UN, here to supervise the ceasefire and referendum. The difficulties of this are apparent even from a cursory look at the town, for there is a huge tented city outside of former residents of Western Sahara returned from the north; Polisario, inevitably, contest their origins and right to vote. Nonetheless, Smara manages quite an ambience, in spite of itself. The area around the souk in particular gets very lively of an evening, with grills in action along the street, traders selling their wares, and even the odd medicine man and snake charmer in attendance.

THE SAHARAN PROVINCES

Until 1988 any trip **south of Tan Tan**, into the **Saharan Provinces** (newly created to include the **former Spanish Sahara**, while not coinciding with its boundaries), involved getting permission from the military authorities. The routes are today open quite routinely – indeed the Moroccan authorities are actively encouraging tourists to explore the region.

THE GREEN MARCH, WAR AND POLITICAL CLAIMS

The politics of the former Spanish Sahara are a highly sensitive matter in Morocco: so much so, that all maps and guides of the country must have the territory included and labelled as part of the Moroccan kingdom. Some background to this is included in "Contexts" (p.562). The essential facts are that the old Spanish colonies of **Rio de Oro** and **Seguiat El Hamra**, sometimes referred to as the **Western Sahara**, were occupied by Morocco on Spanish withdrawal in 1975. These claims were based on historic Moroccan control of the area, including the presence of a fort said to have been built by Moulay Ismail in the 1670s near Laayoune, and the activities here of Hassan I.

Whatever their legitimacy, King Hassan II enjoyed enormous acclaim with his tactical occupation of the territory – the so-called **Green March** (*La Marche Verte*) of November 1975, when 350,000 unarmed civilians walked across the old frontier and "returned" the territories to the Alaouite Kingdom of Morocco. Territorial counterclaims, however, came almost immediately from Mauritania and from various groups among the indigenous Saharawis.

Through the next two decades, a war raged on and off in the desert between the Moroccan military (who administer the entire former Spanish colony) and Algerian-backed **Polisario** guerrilla fighters, operating from bases round Tindouf, across the border in Algeria. The war, which for a time affected areas within Morocco's "former" boundaries, was, by the end of the 1980s, largely contained by the creation of an extraordinary "**desert wall**" (see p.563). In the meantime Polisario increasingly turned to diplomacy to gather support.

In 1988 a UN-sponsored ceasefire, with a **referendum** on "incorporation" or independence, was accepted in principle by both sides, and it seemed a settlement was at last in sight. However, the years since have seen frustration of the UN aims, with arguments over the voting list leading to repeated postponement of the referendum. In theory, it will still take place, but observers are sceptical. Having invested so much in the territory not only in military terms, as subsidies, tax concessions and infrastructure building have all been a heavy drain on the economy – it seems inconceivable that Morocco would relinquish its claims. Polisario have threatened renewed military action if the referendum fails to take place, but at time of writing the stalemate and truce seem entrenched.

VISITING THE PROVINCES

Given the factors above, travellers are advised to get **up-to-date information** before attempting anything too ambitious in the region. Visiting **Laayoune** and **Smara** is nowadays pretty routine, though it does involve answering a series of questions (name, age, profession, parents' names, passport number and date of issue, etc) at numerous police checkpoints along the way. This is all usually very amicable, but time-consuming, and taxi drivers may, as a result, be unwilling to carry foreigners. Apart from this, the only obstacle here would be for visitors who admit to being a writer or journalist: a profession not welcome in the region, unless under the aegis of an official press tour.

A more practical problem, however, is **accommodation**, with UN supervisors occupying many of the better hotels in Laayoune and Smara. It would be wise to phone a few places in these towns in advance of a visit if you want a good hotel (the problem does not apply to cheap places).

As for continuing south, the **border with Mauritania** is, at present, open and functional, although all traffic must form part of a convoy. If this forms part of your planning, however, you would be wise to get reports from recent travellers. The regulations and procedures have been getting easier over the last ten years, but that could change.

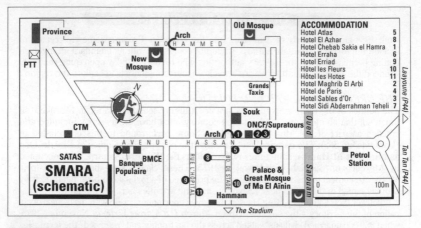

Accommodation

None of Smara's dozen **hotels** offer much in the way of luxury, and the best of them is largely occupied by UN personnel at present, so book ahead if you want more than a basic room. No hotels have en-suite bathrooms: some of the cheaper places now have hot shared showers, but usually ask a small extra fee for using them.

Hotel Atlas, Av. Hassan II, entrance round the side (no phone). Managed, unusually, by a woman. Basic, with a jarring mixture of floor tiles. ①.

Hotel El Azhar, Rue de Figuig (no phone). Basic and cheap, paint-splattered floors give the rooms an unfinished look, though the entrance and corridors have been retiled. Hot showers available. ①.

Hotel des Jeunes de Sakia el Hamra (aka Hôtel Chebab Sakia el Hamra), Av. Hassan II (☎04/889 9524). Larger, cleaner rooms than most of the cheapies. Hot showers available. The reception is on the first floor, above the ONCF/Supratours office. ①.

Hotel Erraha, 16 Av. Hassan II (no phone). Not the best choice: a basic place with cold showers only. There are cafés on either side. ①.

Hotel Erriad, Rue l'Hôpital (☎04/888 8104). Clean, quiet and basic, with hot water, but quoting rather higher prices than the other cheapies. ②.

Hôtel les Fleurs (aka Hôtel Zouhaur), 70 Bd. de Stade (☎04/889 9558). A friendly place with clean rooms and toilets. Cold showers only but right opposite the hammam. ①.

Hôtel Café-Restaurant les Hôtes, Rue l'Hôpital, by the hospital (☎04/889 9772). The upstairs single rooms here are rather better than the dark downstairs doubles. ①.

Hotel Maghrib El Arbi, Av. Hassan II (☎04/889 5191 or 889 9151). Smara's top offering, sometimes block-booked by the UN, though it keeps a few rooms free. Two single rooms here are cheaper than a double. ③.

Hôtel de Paris, 152 Av. Hassan II (☎04/889 9986). A new place with clean but bare rooms and hot water showers. ①.

Hotel Sables d'Or, 1 Av. Hassan II (☎04/889 9452). Another basic but adequate place, though with no hot water. ①.

Hotel Sidi Abderrahman Teheli, 2 Av. Hassan II, entrance round the side (no phone). A new, friendly place with small, clean rooms and great views of town from the roof terrace. Hot showers available. ①.

The Town

Ma El Aïnin's Palace is fairly well preserved. It stands near the oued and comprises the distinct residences of Ma El Aïnin's four main wives, one of which is now occupied by the *gardien* and his family. If you knock on the door, someone will open up and show you around, usually for a fee. Inside you can see the domed zaouia. Though plastered over, it is, like the rest of the palace, built of black basalt from the local hills. You can also see the palace's original armoured doors. What's left of the **Great Mosque**, a separate building further away from the river, is less well preserved, but you can still see the mihrab, and rows of basalt arches.

The **old mosque** marked on our map is also made of local basalt, with a rather pretty stone minaret. This stands in the part of town built under Spanish rule, roughly bounded by the two arches and the *Hôtel Sables d'Or*. A distinctive aspect of the houses here (and elsewhere in the region) is the eggshell-like domes which serve as roofs, a device said to keep the interior cooler. Behind the mosque, you'll also find some of the strange tubular barracks put up by the Spanish to house their troops, now private homes. Like most buildings in Smara, they are painted a deep red ochre.

Practicalities

There isn't much in the way of **restaurants** in town, though there are open-air grills and fried fish stalls around the souk and on Boulevard de Stade. Avenue Hassan II has a lot of cafés – few of them do food, though some may do sporadically: your best bets are the cafés of the hotels *Sables d'Or* and *Atlas*.

The town **hammam** is near the *Hôtel les Fleurs*. Coming up Boulevard de Stade from Avenue Hassan II, take the next right after the hotel and it's on the left. The first entrance is for women, the third for men, as illustrated above them (the second is for wood to heat the water).

International phone calls can now be made from *téléboutiques*, but not yet by direct dialling: you have to give the number you want, they call the post office and get a connection, and then you pay after the call. The prettiest, or at least kitschest *téléboutique* in town is at 258 Avenue Hassan II, where the booths are decorated like phone keypads, and the walls hung with artificial flowers and plastic bunches of grapes. The **post office** is by the local administration Province at the western end of Avenue Mohammed V. The town also has a couple of **banks** (BMCE and Banque Populaire), a **petrol station**, and several garage-workshops for **car repairs**.

Moving on

Buses are operated by ONCF/Supratours, SATAS and CTM, who each have an office on Avenue Hassan II, and each have a departure to Marrakesh via Tan Tan, Goulimine, Tiznit and Agadir. ONCF/Supratours run the only daily service to Laayoune. **Grands taxis** leave from a square near the *Hôtel Sables d'Or*. Runs are to Laayonne, Tan Tan, Agadir and Marrakesh.

Note that the **road east from the town**, towards the Algerian town of Tindouf (where the Polisario have their main base), is firmly closed.

Smara to Laayoune

West from Smara, heading towards Laayoune, you pass through slightly more featured landscape than the route from Tan Tan to Smara. For the first 5km the desert remains black-ish from the basalt, before resuming its customary lighter hue for the rest of the route.

A new road has now been laid covering parts of the route. The old road cuts from time to time across the pre-existing *piste*, which is still marked by lines of cairns and poles. South of the new road, 30km from Smara stands a large brown flat-topped hill called **Gor El Bered** (Hill of the Wind). At the foot of its west side, just north of the old road is a small brown cupola-domed building resembling a marabout but it is in fact a structure built by the Spanish in the 1930s to extract chalk from the calcium-rich rock of the hill. A genuine marabout is to be found at **Sidi Khatari**, south of the new road some 90km from Smara. A couple of kilometres beyond, a water-processing plant desalinates the brackish water of the local well, before pumping it through recently laid pipes to Smara. Opposite is a **petrol station** and **café**. More intrepid travellers might try to locate the prehistoric rock carvings nearby at Asli; ask the petrol station owner for directions.

There is little of any note to be seen for the next 70-odd kilometres before the **turn-off to Boukra**, a mining town with a large garrison 25km to the southeast. Thereafter, however, you become aware of the **Boukra-Laayoune conveyor belt** snaking its way south of the road, bearing phosphates seaward for export. The vast region south of Boukra is a restricted military zone, and inaccessible to casual visitors.

As the road swings west for the last 50km before Laayoune its surface markedly improves and the canyon of the **Seguiat El Hamra** comes into view on the northern side. Seguiat El Hamra means "Red River" and, though there is no water in it for most of the year, the local clay turns it red when it does flow. The canyon is pretty impressive, but if you stop to take a snapshot be sure you are out of range of anything military. Meanwhile, signs along the road warn of animals crossing; the animal depicted, naturally, is a camel.

The oasis of **LEMSEYED**, 12km before Laayoune, is a local beauty spot offering fine views over the canyon. Across the Oued, the **Fort of Dchira** was built by the Spanish in the very early days of their rule. It's currently occupied by the Moroccan army.

Tan Tan to Laayoune

The route between **Tan Tan Plage and Laayoune** cuts dramatically between desert and ocean. The coast, somewhat defying expectations, is mainly cliff – the desert dropping directly away to the sea, with only the occasional stretch of beach.

Tan Tan to Tarfaya

Between Tan Tan and Tarfaya there is little more than the roadside settlement of **AKHFENIR** (about 150km south of Tan Tan) with its 24–hour petrol station and six cafés, of which the *Café Paris* serves the best fresh fish in the area, while the *Café Puerto Cansado*, with its brightly painted cartoon characters and English-speaking owner, has the only pool table in town. The *Puerto Cansado* can also arrange accommodation, as well as trips to **Puerto Cansado**, 27km south (permit required) where you can see flamingos. Just beyond here is a rare stretch of accessible beach, with reputedly wonderful fishing.

Tarfaya

TARFAYA is a small town (population 7000) with a fishing port and a large monument to the Green March. It may be in line for greater things if an oil shale development, currently under consideration by Shell, goes ahead, but for the moment it's a quiet place, probably not far different from its years as a staging post for the Aéropostale Service – when aviators such as **Antoine de Saint-Exupéry** (author of *Night Flight* and *The Little Prince*) used to rest up on their way down to West Africa.

The air service is commemorated annually in October by a "**Rallye Aérien**", with small planes flying south from Toulouse to Dakar in Senegal; Tarfaya is a night's stop. A monument to Saint-Exupéry in the form of a plane stands at the northern end of the beach. Oddly enough, Tarfaya was actually founded, at the end of the last century, by a Scottish trader, named Donald Mackenzie, and was originally known as Port Victoria.

Mackenzie's original fort, now known as **Casa Mar** lies just offshore – a few metres' swim at low tide. During the Spanish occupation, the town was called Villa Bens and served as a very low-key capital for the "Southern Protectorate"; they abandoned it in 1958, leaving a church and a handful of villas.

These days Tarfaya has been overshadowed by Laayoune, though it has two **hotels**, the *Tarfaya* (no phone; ①), and the *Elmassira Elkhadra* (☎04/889 5045; ①), which are both pretty basic but can get quite busy during the fishing season (Dec–Mar). For **meals** try the *Embiric Restaurant*, with fish and tajine, or one of the cafés on the main street to the harbour.

South to Laayoune

South of Tarfaya you cross the old border of Spanish Sahara at Tah, and traverse real sand desert – the **Erg Lakhbayta**. The effect, however, is lighter than that implies, for along the way are a series of enormous **lagoons**, their water prevented from reaching the sea by long spits of sand, and **salt pans**, still being worked. These are important migratory sites, which should provide rewards for **bird-watchers**.

Laayoune

With a population of 100,000, **LAAYOUNE** (AL AYOUN) is the largest and the most interesting town in the Western Sahara. Its development as a provincial capital is almost immediately obvious – and impressive, as you survey its building programmes such as the 30,000-seat stadium, with real grass, maintained for the area's handful of football teams. The city has the highest per capita government spending in Morocco and soldiers, billeted here for the conflict with Polisario, have been employed in many of the projects.

The population growth – from little more than a village when the Moroccans took over – has been aided by massive subsidies, which apply throughout Western Sahara, and by an agreement that settlers should initially pay no taxes. They are a mix of Saharawis, many of them driven here by the drought of the last few years, and Moroccan immigrants from the north in search of work. The fact that almost everyone in town is here by choice – few current residents were actually born here – gives the place a dynamism and pioneering feel that contrasts quite sharply with the weight of tradition that hangs heavy on cities like Fes and Marrakesh. The result is that, although Laayoune has little in the way of obvious sights, its atmosphere is quite a change from that of Moroccan towns further north.

Orientation, information and accommodation

The first sight of Laayoune, coming from Tarfaya, is across the steep-sided valley of the **Seguiat El Hamra**, which has been dammed to make another, shallow lagoon. The old **lower town**, built by the Spanish, lies on the southern slope of the valley, with the new **upper town**, developed since the Green March, on the high plateau beyond. Our map opposite is somewhat diagrammatic. Note that the main street uptown, Avenue Mecka al Mokarrama on street signs, is also called Avenue de la Mecque or Avenue Mekka.

There may be no tourists in town but there's a tourist delegation and information office on Avenue de l'Islam, opposite the *Parador* (Mon–Fri 8.30am–noon & 2.30–6.30pm; ☎04/889 1694 or 95).

Laayoune's **hotels** have done good business over the past few years with the UN, who block-book the best, and often spread into others. It is therefore wise to phone ahead, unless you're happy with a basic room at an unclassified hotel, of which there are maybe a score, mostly in the Souk Djaj and Souk Djemal districts.

LAAYOUNE (schematic)

RESTAURANTS
E Chez Claudio
B La Mama
D La Perla
C La Poissonnier
A Café-Restaurant Sefrou

ACCOMMODATION
Hôtel El Alya   6
Hôtel Assahel   11
Hôtel Jodesa   9
Hôtel Lakouara   5
Hôtel Marhaba   3
Hôtel Al Massira   8
Hôtel Nagjir   10
Hôtel Parador   7
Hôtel Rif   1
Hôtel Sidi Ifni   2
Hôtel Smara   4

CHEAP

Hotel Assahel, Av. Moulay Idriss I (☎04/889 0170). A good-value choice among the small group of cheapies off Place Dchira, not very central but well placed for the Tan Tan and Dakhla grand taxi stations, and popular with visitors from Francophone West Africa. Hot showers available. ①.

Hôtel Marhaba, Av. de la Marine – opposite the defunct Cinema Adgrad (☎04/889 3249). A reasonable, inexpensive hotel, a cut above most of the others in this category. Hot showers available. ①.

Hôtel Rif, just off Bd. 28 Février, overlooking the Seguiat El Hamra (☎04/889 4369). The same price but much better value than most of Laayoune's cheap hotels – clean and friendly, though without hot water. ①.

Hôtel Sidi Ifni, Souk Djaj, off Av. de la Marine (☎04/889 3488). Top choice among the Souk Djaj cheapies – clean, pleasant and quiet. No hot water but hot showers available at the Douche Sakia el Hamra across the street. ①.

Hôtel Smara, 130 Av. Salem Bila, Souk Djemal (off to the left of our map; no phone). One of the better choices among the various cheap hotels in the Souk Djemal quarter, cleaner and more pleasant than most of the others, though still pretty basic. ①.

MODERATE TO EXPENSIVE

Hôtel Al Massira, 12 Av. Mecka al Mokarrama (☎04/889 4225; fax 889 0962). A smart and efficient modern hotel, UN block-booked but with fifteen rooms free. ⑤.

Hôtel El Alya, 1 Rue Kadi El Ghalaoui, just behind the Goulimine grand taxi station (☎04/889 0246). Very run-down with large rooms, all with en-suite bathrooms complete with bath, friendly staff, and interesting hand-painted (but peeling) decor on the corridor walls and ceilings. ③.

Hotel Jodesa, 223 Av. Mecka al Mokarrama (☎04/899 2063 or 64; fax 889 3784). The best choice in this category, new with cosy carpeted rooms, some en suite, and a roof terrace. ④.

Hôtel Lakouara, Av. Hassan II (☎04/889 3378). A comfortable place with en-suite bathrooms and 24hr hot water, block-booked by the UN, but with three spare rooms. ④.

Hôtel Nagjir, 6 Place Bir Anzarane (☎04/889 4168; fax 889 3911). New and very comfortable, with a restaurant, and, when open (which they weren't at our last check), a bar and disco. Largely occupied by the UN, but with twelve spare rooms. ⑥.

Hôtel Parador, Av. de l'Islam (☎04/889 4500; fax 889 0962). The old Spanish grand hotel, run by the same management as the *Al Massira*, but rather more traditional in style. Again, largely but not completely occupied by the UN. ⑥.

The Town

Most of the new building is in the upper town; the bulk of the old Spanish settlement, more dishevelled, lies down below, stretching eastwards from the old **cathedral**, which is now closed (rusting notices proclaim it "property of the Spanish government"). If you head east across the square in front, where parents bring their kids to play in the evening, you pass a pair of fort-like buildings painted in yellow ochre and used by the military as HQs, and come into the district of **Souk Djaj** (Chicken Market), spread out along the northern side of Avenue de la Marine. Pleasantly run-down, with a smattering of cheap hotels, its houses are typified by the eggshell-domed roofs said to cool the interior. A few tiled Spanish street signs are still in evidence, though most have been replaced by blue metal plaques painted in Arabic and French.

East of Souk Djaj, the district of **Ejercito** (Spanish for army) houses Moroccan troops as it did their Spanish predecessors. South of Avenue de la Marine, some of the tubular barracks are now private houses, hemmed in by more modern, box-like, blocks of flats. The other district left from Spanish days is **Colomina**, to the south of Avenue Mecka al Mokarrama. It's referred to popularly as Colomina Tarduss (Kick) because, when the Spanish left, local people kicked in the doors to squat their houses. Nowadays, most of the quarter has been rebuilt.

A more workaday, working-class area is **Souk Djemal**, west of the Goulimine grand taxi station. This is where the **main market** is located and it's the most animated part of town, especially around dusk. It also shows perhaps a truer face of the new Laayoune than the grandiose monuments in the centre, with people milling round and buildings in which people live and work, rather than just administrative centres.

Most striking of the modern developments is the **Place Mechouar**, which is flanked by the new **Great Mosque**. Lining one side of the square is a series of tent-like canopies for shade and at each corner are towers to floodlight the square at night. There is also an ambitious **Palais des Congrès**, designed by one of the late King Hassan's favourite architects, French-born André Paccard. Across the way is the new **stadium**, which, if the Moroccans have their way, and FIFA decide to go for Africa, will be a venue for World Cup football before very long.

In addition to such public statements, there are a few pleasant corners, like the landscaped gardens of the **Colline des Oiseaux**, with their cages of exotic birds – with blinds to be drawn down over the cages in the event of sandstorms. To get in, go to the entrance on Avenue Ockba ben Nafaa, and ask the *gardien* to open up. Of some interest, too, is the **Complexe Artisanal**, behind the New Mosque, where twenty little workshops, capped with cupolas, provide space for metal, wood and jewellery craftsmen.

Eating

The hotels *Al Massira*, *Nagjir* and *Parador* have **restaurants**, but those at the *Parador* and *Al Massira* are not always open to non-UN personnel. *La Perla* at 185 Avenue Mecka al Mokarrama (daily noon–3pm & 6.30–11pm; cheap) offers classy eating – prawn bisque, gazpacho and a fine selection of fabulous fresh fish dishes – at prices you'd be lucky to pay in a greasy spoon back home. The service is good too. The more expensive *La Poissonnier* next door at no. 183 (daily noon–3pm & 6.30–11pm; moderate) has similar food with a slightly more chic ambience. For genuine wood-oven pizzas, try *Chez Claudio*, a small but pleasant pizzeria behind the *Hôtel Nagjir* (daily 9am–10pm; cheap). Pizzas are also available at *La Mama* at the western end of Avenue Hassan II near the *Hôtel Lakouara* (daily 11am–3pm & 6pm–midnight; cheap), which also claims to offer Spanish paella.

Several of the cafés along Avenue Hassan II also do good tajines at low prices, but the liveliest place to hang out in the evenings is **Souk Djemal**, and this is also a good place for cheap evening meals and for breakfast, with *melaoui* and *harsha* available at the café to the left of the market among others. The *Café-Restaurant Sefrou* on the other side of the market (daily 24hr; cheap) has tasty stews, fried fish and sardine balls in the evening, as well as tajines.

Listings

Airlines RAM's office is next to the *Hôtel Nagjir* in Place Bir Anzarane (☎04/889 4071 or 77). Regional Air Lines and Atlantic Airways are represented by Baida Travel at 52 Av. Mecka al Mokarrama (☎04/889 0969).

Banks Mostly located at the foot of Bd. Mohammed V, near Place Hassan II. They include: BMCE, Banque Populaire, BCM, Wafabank and Banque Al Maghrib. BMCE, Banque Populaire and BCM also have branches in Place Dchira.

Car rental No major firms are represented and there is a rapid turnover of small operators due to shortage of punters, so it's best to phone ahead if you intend to rent a car. Companies operating at present include: Mobil Car at 110 Av. Mecka al Mokarrama (☎04/899 4570) and Nadir Car at 233 Av. Mecka al Mokarrama (☎04/890 3054).

Hammams There's one just off Av. de la Marine (southside) between Pl. Hassan II and *Hôtel Marhaba*, and another near the *Hôtel Nagjir*.

Internet access Two companies currently offer Internet access and email facilities: Lintel at 216 Av. Mecka al Mokarrama, and W@dernet, also on Av. Mecka al Mokarrama, next to the water towers.

Post office The main office is on Pl. Hassan II, complete with its original weighing machine marked 'Correos' in Spanish. Opening hours are 8.30am–noon & 2.30–6.30pm except Fridays when lunch break is 11.30am–3pm. Only the phone section is open Saturday afternoons and Sundays. There's a branch office on Place Dchir.

Moving On

Bus services are operated by four companies. CTM departures are from outside their office at 198 Avenue Mecka al Mokarrama, and run to Boujdour and Dakhla, and Agadir, Marrakesh and Casablanca (the last departure continues to Rabat). SATAS's office is nearby on Place Bir Anzarane, where their buses leave for Boujdour and Dakhla and for Agadir (at 7.30am, continuing to Casablanca, and at 7.30pm, continuing to Marrakesh). ONCF/Supratours run services from their office on Avenue Oum Saad at the southern end of Avenue Moulay Ismail. They leave for Boujdour and Dakhla at 7.30am, for Smara at 6pm, and for Tan Tan, Goulimine and Agadir 5.15pm (continuing to Marrakesh) and 9pm (connecting for Marrakesh). The only other bus service from Laayoune is Etoile du Sahara's noon departure for Tan Tan leaving from Place Bir Anzarane in front of the *Hôtel Nagjir*.

There are four **grand taxi** stations: for Goulimine, Agadir, Inezgane and occasionally Marrakesh, they leave from Souk Lamkhaleh at the western end of Avenue Hassan II; for Boujdour and Dakhla they leave from a rank south of Colomina (cross the football ground from Avenue Oum Saad, continue to the wall marking the airport perimeter, turn left alongside it, and it's off on your left – or take a petit taxi); for Smara and Tan Tan, and sometimes Goulimine, they leave from the Tan Tan Station (Mahatat Tan Tan) off Avenue Mezouar, parallel with the Smara road about a kilometre beyond Place Bir Anzarane (again, easiest to reach by petit taxi); while for Laayoune Plage, the rank is in Colomina behind the Complexe Artisanal. Landrover taxis can be chartered in Rhaiba, near the Dakhla grand taxi station.

The **airport** (☎04/889 3346 or 47) is about a kilometre out of town, beyond Place Mechouar and there are scheduled flights on RAM to Casablanca, Dakhla and Las Palmas in the Canary Islands, and by Regional Air Lines to Casablanca via Agadir. There is also currently a twice-weekly charter with Atlantic Airways to Las Palmas, costing a bit less than RAM's scheduled flight. For further information see "Travel Details", p.546.

Laayoune Plage

LAAYOUNE PLAGE is 20km distant: leave town on the P41 towards Boujdour, then, past the airport, turn right off the main road and quickly left at a sign to Camping Touristique. At the beach – which is very windy, year-round, with big Atlantic breakers – there is a sporadically open café-restaurant. Places to stay include the *Hôtel Josefine* (☎04/899 8478; ②) and the *Bungalows le Champignon* campsite (☎04/899 8229). Nearby at **Foum el Oued**, the *Hôtel Nagjir* in Laayoune has a four-star *Nagjir II* under construction, which should be open by the time you read this – for more details call them on ☎04/889 4168.

South from Laayoune to Dakhla

Continuing **south of Laayoune** down to Dakhla is pretty routine now, and you no longer need special permission. There are four daily buses along this route from Agadir, as well as grand taxi runs; the buses are often full, so you may have to push your way on if you want to pick them up en route. The road is reasonably good, though drivers should beware of occasional sand-drifts, and camels grazing by or on the road.

Foreigners will need to form-fill at checkpoints along the way (more easily avoided in a grand taxi, where the police or gendarmes may not notice there's a tourist aboard).

Laayoune to Dakhla

The first habitation along the road is **LEMSID**, 110km from Laayoune, where a small **café-shop** provides basic meals for the route's lorry drivers.

South of Lemsid, the sea is guarded by cliffs most of the way to the newly developed fishing port of **BOUJDOUR**. The landscape here is a little more mellow, with a long beach to the north. Rocks, however, make the sea dangerous for swimming and surfing. Boujdour has a petrol station, various cafés and a pleasant, friendly **hotel**, the *Al Qods* (☎04/889 6572 or 73; ②). The street from the grand taxi stand down to the sea comes alive in the evening with restaurants serving up freshly fried, freshly caught fish, and stalls selling charcoal-grilled brochettes and sausages. The nearest thing to a sight in town is the lighthouse, though it's not open to the public. If you need a bank, the BMCE and Banque Populaire both have branches here. No alcohol is available in town, so supplies brought in from elsewhere are likely to be appreciated.

South again from Boujdour the road runs inland, rejoining the coast at the tiny settlement of Skaymat – less of an oasis than it looks on the map.

Dakhla

Some 544km from Laayoune, you reach the town of **DAKHLA** (or Ad Dakhla) on a long spit of land, just 20km north of the Tropic of Cancer. Until 1975, this was a Spanish outpost, known as Villa Cisneros, and capital of the Rio de Oro colony. In those days, only the colonists and people working for them were allowed into town – the Saharawi nomads who lived in the desert were excluded. In 1975, the Spanish left and the Mauritanians moved in, to be replaced by the Moroccans four years later. Since then, Dakhla has grown somewhat, though it retains a lazy, sun-bleached atmosphere, with whitewashed, low-rise buildings and an easy-going feel. Increasing numbers of Europeans in camper vans are coming down this way in winter, drawn by the deserted beaches and year-round sunshine – even in January it's hot, and this is the furthest south you can get by land without needing a visa. The main industry is fishing, and there is also a strong military presence.

Coming into town, you pass a **police checkpoint**, where you will have to show your passport and answer the full set of questions about your profession, parents' names and purpose of visit. The town proper starts 3km further down the road. As you enter the town centre, you cross Avenue Hassan II, which runs from east to west across the spit, and beyond which the main road becomes Avenue Mohammed V.

Practicalities

Though the town has spread itself out in recent years, most of the things that you will need lie within a small area. North of the town centre, and opposite the grand taxi station, is a group of three **hotels**, including Dakhla's top address, the *Hôtel Doumss* (☎04/889 8047, fax 889 8045; ④). Next door is the basic but adequate *Hôtel Wahda* (☎04/889 7485; ①), and behind these, overlooking a rocky and rather rubbish-strewn shore, the quiet and rather pleasant *Hôtel Miramar* (☎04/889 7548; ①). The remaining hotels are across Avenue Hassan II in the town centre, and you may have to try a few (or call ahead) before you find a room as they are often full. First choice is the *Hôtel al Moukouama* a block south of Avenue Hassan II, just west of Avenue Mohammed V (☎04/893 0720 or 21; fax 893 0722; ①). A little to the south, on Avenue Mohammed V, is Dakhla's oldest hotel, the *Bahia* (①). If those are full, try the *Hôtel Riad*, a block west and a couple south (☎04/883 0924; ①), or the *Hôtel Sahara*, just around the corner on Avenue Sidi Ahmed Laroussi (☎04/889 7773; ①). The **campsite**, *Camping Mousafir* (☎04/889 8279) is 5km out of town, 1km north of the police checkpoint, in a pink-walled enclosure next to its own beach, and currently being upgraded. It offers a small number of rooms as well as camping space but is rather inconveniently located for town amenities – the only way into town without your own transport is either to hitch, or walk to the police checkpoint and take a taxi from there (13dh), since town taxis are not allowed beyond it.

For **eating**, various places in the same area as the town-centre hotels serve very cheap tajines or freshly fried fish – take a wander and follow your nose. If you fancy something a little classier, try the *Samarkand*, just to the south on Avenue Mohammed V (daily 8am–10pm; cheap) which offers some very pleasant open-air eating on a terrace overlooking the sea. There is one **bar** in town, the *Bar Restaurant Casa Juan* next to the *Hôtel Bahia* on Avenue Mohammed V (daily 9am–2pm & 3.30–9pm), full with sailors of an evening, but it refuses to serve local people except for off-sales.

Should you need it, there is a **tourist office** behind the CTM office at 1 Rue Tiris (☎04/889 8389; Mon–Fri 8.30am–2pm & 3–6.30pm). Dakhla has two **banks**: the BMCE is on Avenue Hassan II at the junction with Avenue Mohammed V, while the Banque Populaire is a block to the southwest of the *Hôtel Moukouama*. The main **post office** is just west of the *Hôtel Moukouama* – the area to its west, up to Avenue Hassan II, is the **red-light district**, but not as sleazy as you might expect, with bunches of rather innocent-looking girls smiling rather disarmingly at their potential customers, mostly sailors, from the windows and doorways of their one-storey houses.

The Garage Mécanique Général on Avenue Mohammed V just south of the *Hôtel Bahia* is the oldest **garage** in town, and its mechanics are **Landrover experts** who you may wish to visit for a last minute pit stop before the long journey south – or north. If taking a **bus**, ONCF/Supratours has an office right next door, CTM has an office round the corner (to the northwest), and the SATAS office is next to the *Hôtel Doumss*. The **grand taxi** station, which is opposite, has regular runs to Boujdour, Laayoune, Agadir and sometimes Marrakesh. Dakhla also has an **airport**, to the west of town, with flights to Casablanca, Agadir and Laayoune. RAM's office in town is directly behind the PTT.

The road to Mauritania

If you are travelling south from **Dakhla to the Mauritanian border** you will have to obtain a *laisser-passer* from the Suretée (a little to the southwest of the Post Office), for which you should apply at least a day in advance (though you may be lucky and get one if you apply early enough – before 10am – on the day of departure). These are becoming little more than a formality, but you will need a **Mauritanian visa** and two passport photos, plus all the relevant documents for your vehicle if you have one. After the Suretée, you'll need to visit the Gendarmerie and, if you have a vehicle, you'll need to clear it with customs.

Armed with your *laisser-passer*, you exit Morocco from Dakhla (where there are immigration, customs and police checks) in one of the twice-weekly **convoys** (Tuesday and Friday). If you're without a vehicle, you'll first have to find one to take you – ask around hotels and the campsite for fellow travellers willing to give you a lift. As a last resort, turn up at the police checkpoint north of town, where the convoy assembles, and see if you can persuade someone to take you.

A Moroccan official collects everybody's passports and accompanies the convoy, although the last Moroccan checkpoint is at the Dakhla turn-off from the main road. The convoy continues to the end of the surfaced road, where you spend a night in the desert before being given back your passport and waved off into the sands. From here, it's a day-long, 56-kilometre drive through the desert, with a succession of checks by Mauritanian officials at small stone huts, and long queues to complete border formalities. The last checkpoint is at **La Gouèra** on the west side of the Nouadhibou peninsula, which, though part of the Western Sahara, is under Mauritanian control. From here it's on to Mauritania proper in the shape of **Nouadhibou**.

The route, it scarcely needs to be said, is quite an adventure: 464km of mixed *piste* and tarmac down to Nouadibhou, crossing the tropic just south of Dakhla. **Tsetse fly** are said to be a problem in La Gouèra, so be sure to carry some repellant. Moroccan sugar is frequently smuggled across the border into Mauritania, where it's more expensive. Coming the other way, cigarettes are the main item of contraband (usually American, complete with Surgeon General's warning).

Coming up from Mauritania, your big problem is that the Mauritanian authorities do not in principle allow exit by land via Nouadibhou—La Gouèra, on the grounds that the border area is mined and dangerous. It would be unwise to try and dodge the Mauritanian border post, as there genuinely are minefields, but they usually allow vehicles through in practice, so long as you go with a guide who can help you to negotiate a safe path. Once in Moroccan-held territory, the Moroccan authorities should not give you any problems on entry, and you can travel up to Dakhla with the next convoy.

travel details

Buses

Laayoune to: Dakhla (4 daily; 9hr) via Boujdour (3hr 30min); Agadir (6 daily; 10hr 30min) via Goulimine (7hr) and Tiznit (8hr 30min); Casablanca (3 daily; 19hr); Marrakesh (5 daily; 15hr); Smara (1 daily; 3hr); Tan Tan (7 daily; 4hr 30min) via Tarfaya (1hr 30min).

Smara to: Laayoune (1 daily; 3hr); Marrakesh (3 daily; 13hr 15min) via Tan Tan (3hr), Tiznit (7hr) and Agadir (9hr).

Dakhla to: Agadir (4 daily; 19hr 30min) via Boujdour (5hr 30min), Laayoune (9hr), Tan Tan (13hr 30min) and Goulimine (16hr); Marrakesh (1 daily; 24hr); Casablanca (1 daily; 28hr).

Tan Tan to: Laayoune (7 daily; 4hr 30min) via Tarfaya (3hr); Smara (3 daily; 3hr); Dakhla (4 daily; 13hr 30min); Agadir (14 daily; 6hr) via Goulimine (3hr); Essaouira (1 daily; 11hr); Marrakesh (15 daily; 12hr); Casablanca (14 daily; 16hr); Rabat (3 daily; 17hr 30min); Beni Mellal (1 daily; 18hr); Meknes (1 daily; 21hr 30min); Ouarzazate (1 daily; 17hr 30min) via Tata (12hr 30 min).

Grands Taxis

Laayoune to: Smara (3hr); Tan Tan (3hr 30min); Dakhla (6hr); Goulimine (5hr); Agadir or Inezgane (9hr); Laayoune Plage (20min).

Smara to: Laayoune (3hr); Tan Tan (2hr); Agadir or Inezgane (8hr); Marrakesh (12hr); Goulimine (4hr 30min).

Dakhla to: Boujdour (3hr 30min); Laayoune (6hr); Agadir or Inezgane (15hr); Marrakesh (18hr).

Tan Tan to: Goulimine (2hr 30 min); Inezgane (6hr); Agadir or Inezgane (6hr 15min); Smara (3hr); Laayoune (3hr 30min); Tan Tan Plage (20min).

Flights

Laayoune to: Agadir (2 weekly; 1hr 5min); Casablanca (daily; 1hr 30min); Dakhla (2 weekly; 1hr 5min).

Dakhla to: Agadir (weekly; 2hr 10min); Casablanca (3 weekly; 3hr 15min); Laayoune (2 weekly; 1hr 5min).

PART THREE

THE

CONTEXTS

HISTORY

Morocco's emergence as a nation-state is astonishingly recent, dating from the occupation of the country by the French and Spanish at the turn of the twentieth century, and its independence in 1956. Prior to this, it is best seen as a kind of patchwork of tribal groups, whose shifting alliances and sporadic bids for power defined the nature of government.

With a handful of exceptions, the country's ruling sultans controlled only the plains, the coastal ports and the regions around the imperial capitals of Fes, Marrakesh, Rabat and Meknes. These were known as *Bled El Makhzen* – the governed lands, or, more literally, "Lands of the Storehouse". The rest of the Moroccan territories – the Rif, the three Atlas ranges and the outlying deserts – comprised *Bled es Siba*, "Lands of the Dissidents". Populated almost exclusively by Berbers, the region's original (pre-Arab) inhabitants, they were rarely recognized as being under anything more than local tribal authority.

The balance between government control and tribal independence is one of the two enduring themes of Moroccan history. The other is the emergence, expansion and eventual replacement of the various **sultanate dynasties**. These at first seem dauntingly complicated – a succession of short-lived tribal movements and confusingly similar-named sultans – but there are actually just seven main groups.

The first of them, the **Idrissids**, became the model by founding the city of Fes towards the end of the eighth century and bringing a coalition of Berber and Arab forces under a central *makhzen* (government) authority. The last, the **Alaouites**, emerged in the mid-seventeenth century from the great palm oasis of Tafilalt and, continuing with the current king, Mohammed VI, still hold constitutional power. It is around these groups – together with the medieval dynasties of the **Almoravids, Almohads, Merenids, Wattasids** and **Saadians** – that the bulk of the following sections are organized.

PREHISTORY

The first inhabitants of the **Maghreb** – the Arab term for the countries of North Africa – probably occupied the **Sahara**, for thousands of years a great savannah, fertile enough to support elephants, zebras and a whole range of other game and wildlife. Little is known about these ancestors of the human species, although it seems likely that there were groups of hunter-and-gatherer hominids here as early as 1,000,000 BC.

Around 15,000 BC there seem to have been **Paleolithic** settlements, and before the Sahara went into decline (from 3000 BC), primitive pastoral and agricultural systems had begun to develop. It is possible also to trace the arrival of two independent Stone-Age cultures in the Maghreb: the Neolithic **Capsian Man** (circa 10,000–5000 BC), probably emerging from Egypt, and, slightly later, **Mouillian Man**. From these people, fair-skinned and speaking a remote "Libyan" language, stem the cave and rock drawings of the pre-Sahara and High Atlas, the earliest archeological sites in Morocco.

PHOENICIANS AND CARTHAGINIANS

The recorded history of the area begins about 1100 BC with a series of trading settlements established by the **Phoenicians**. These were small, isolated colonies, most of them built on defensible headlands round the coast, and there was probably little initial contact between them and the inhabitants of the interior, whom they knew as Libyans and Ethiopians – or collectively as *Barbaroi*, or **Berbers**.

As the emphasis shifted away from the Phoenicians, and their African trading routes were taken over by the former colony of **Carthage** (modern Tunis), some of the ports grew into considerable cities, exporting grain and grapes, and minting their own coinage. On the "Moroccan" coast, the most important colonies were at **Lixus** (near Larache), **Tingis** (Tangier) and **Chellah** (near Rabat), but they spread as far east as Melilla; in the south a flourishing dye factory was also maintained on an island off Essaouira.

Officially, the Carthaginian Empire collapsed with its defeat in the **Punic Wars** (196 BC) against Rome, but in these provincial outposts, life seems to have been little affected. If anything, the colonies grew in stature and prosperity, absorbing hundreds of Punic refugees after the Roman sacking of Carthage. It was a first sign of Morocco's intrinsic historic and geographic isolation in what was to become known as *Maghreb El-Aska* (Land of the Farthest West). Even after the Romans had annexed and then abandoned the country, Punic was still widely spoken along the coast.

BERBER KINGDOMS AND ROMAN RULE

Prior to total Roman annexation, and the imposition of direct imperial rule in 24 AD, the "civilized" Moroccan territories for a while formed the **Berber kingdom of Mauretania**. This was probably little more than a confederation of local tribes, centred round **Volubilis** (near Meknes) and **Tangier**, but it gained a certain influence through alliance and occasional joint rule with the adjoining Berber state of **Numidia** (essentially modern Algeria).

The most important of the Berber rulers, and the only ones of which any substantial records survive, were **Juba II** (25 BC–23 AD) and his son **Ptolemy**. Both were heavily Romanized: Juba, an Algerian Berber by birth, was brought up and educated in Rome, where he married the daughter of Antony and Cleopatra. His reign, if limited in its extent, seems to have been orderly and prosperous, and under his son the pattern might well have continued. In 42 AD, however, Emperor Caligula summoned Ptolemy to an audience in Lyons and had him assassinated – so the story goes, for appearing in a more brilliant cloak than his own. Whatever the truth, and Rome may just have been eager for direct rule, it proved an inauspicious beginning.

ROMAN RULE

The early years of Rome's new imperial province were taken up with near-constant **rebellions** – the first one alone needing three years and over 20,000 troops to subdue.

Perhaps discouraged by this unexpected resistance, the **Romans** never attempted to colonize Morocco-Mauretania beyond its old limits. The Rif and Atlas mountains were left unpenetrated, and, of the interior, it was only **Volubilis** – already a city of sorts, and at the heart of the north's fertile vineyards and grain fields – that was in any way exploited. In this the Romans were establishing an enduring precedent: not just in their failure to subdue *Bled Es Siba*, which also defied the later sultans, but also in their treatment of Morocco as a useful "corridor" to the greater agricultural wealth of Algeria, Tunisia and Spain.

When the Roman legions were withdrawn in 253 AD, and the **Vandals** took power in southern Spain, the latter were interested only in taking Tangier and Ceuta for use as staging posts en route to northern Tunisia. Similarly, the **Byzantine General Belisarius**, who defeated the Vandals and laid claim to the Maghreb for Justinian's Eastern Empire, did little more than replace the Ceuta garrison.

It was understandable, of course. Any attempt to control Morocco would need manpower far in excess of these armies, and the only overland route through the country – across the Taza gap – was scarcely practicable even in peacetime. Not until the tenth century, and the great northward expansion of the desert nomads, was Morocco to become a land worthy of substantial exploitation in its own right, and even then only through the unifying and evangelizing impetus of Islam.

THE COMING OF ISLAM

The irruption of **Islam** into the world began in 622 AD, when the Prophet Muhammad moved with his followers from Mecca to Medina. Within thirty years they had reached the borders of India, to the east; were threatening Byzantine Constantinople, to the north; and had established themselves in the Maghreb at Kairouan in present-day Tunisia.

After this initial thrust, however, sweeping across the old provinces of the Roman world, the progress of the new religion was temporarily slowed. The Berbers of Algeria – mainly pagans but including communities of Christians and Jews – put up a strong and unusually unified resistance to Arab control. It was only in 680 that the governor of Kairouan, **Oqba Ibn Nafi**, made an initial foray into Morocco, taking in the process the territory's last Byzantine stronghold at Ceuta.

What happened afterwards is unclear. There is a story, perhaps apocryphal, that Oqba embarked on a 5000-kilometre **march through Morocco**, raiding and subjugating all in his path, and preaching Islam all the way to the west – the Atlantic Ocean. But whether this expedition had any real Islamicizing influence on the Moroccan Berbers is questionable. Oqba left no garrison forces and was himself killed in Algeria on his way back to Kairouan.

Islam may, however, have taken root among some of the tribes. In the early part of the eighth century the new Arab governor of the west, **Moussa Ibn Nasr**, returned to Morocco and managed to establish Arab control (and carry out mass conversions to Islam) in both the northern plains and the pre-Sahara. However, like the Romans and Byzantines before him, his main thrust was towards **Spain**. In 711, the first Muslim forces crossed over from Tangier to Tarifa and defeated the Visigoths in a single battle; within a decade the Moors had taken control of all but the remote Spanish mountains in northern Asturias; and their advance into Europe was only halted at the Pyrenees by the victory of Charles Martel at Poitiers in 732.

The bulk of this invading and occupying force were almost certainly **Berber converts** to Islam, and the sheer scale of their military success must have had enormous influence in turning Morocco itself into a largely Muslim nation. It was not at this stage, however, in any way an Arab one. The extent of the Islamic Empire – from Persia to Morocco, and ancient Ghana to Spain – was simply too great for Arab numbers. Early attempts to impose taxes on the Moroccan Berbers led to a rebellion and, once again outside the political mainstream, the Maghreb fragmented into a series of small, independent **principalities**.

THE IDRISSIDS (8TH–11TH CENTURIES)

The Maghreb's fragmentation found an echo in the wider events of the Muslim world, which was undergoing its first – and most drastic – dissension, with the split into **Sunni** and **Shia** sects. In Damascus the Sunni Ummayad dynasty took power, the Shi'ites dispersing and seeking refuge to both the east and west.

One of them, arriving in Morocco around 787, was **Moulay Idriss**, an evidently charismatic leader and a direct descendant (great-grandson, in fact) of the Prophet Muhammad. He seems to have been adopted almost at once by the citizens of Volubilis – then still a vaguely Romanized city – and by the Aouraba Berber tribe. He was to survive for three more years, before being poisoned by order of the Sunni caliph, but in this time he managed to set up the infrastructure of an essentially Arab court and kingdom – the basis of what was to become the Moroccan nation. Its most important feature, enduring to the present with Mohammed VI, was his being recognized as *imam*. To the Moroccans this meant that he was both spiritual and political leader, "commander of the faithful" in every aspect of their lives.

Despite the brevity of Moulay Idriss's reign, and his sudden death in 791 or 792, his successors, the **Idrissids**, were to become the first recognizable Moroccan dynasty. Moulay Idriss himself left a son, born posthumously to a Berber woman, and in 807, after a period of an apparently orderly regency, **Moulay Idriss II** was declared sultan and *imam*. He ruled for a little over twenty years – something of a golden age for the emerging Moroccan state, with the extension of a central, Arabized authority throughout the north and even to the oases beyond the Atlas.

Idriss's most important achievement, however, was the establishment (if perhaps not the foundation) of the city of **Fes**. Here, he set up the apparatus of court government, and here he also welcomed large contingents of Shi'ite **refugees**. Most prominent among these were groups from Córdoba and Kairouan, then the two great cities of Western Islam. In incorporating them, Fes (and, by extension, Morocco) became increasingly Arabized, and was suddenly transformed into a major Arab centre in its own right. The **Kairaouine University** was established, becoming one of the three most important in Islam (and far ahead of those in Europe); a strong crafts tradition took root; and Fes became a vital link in the trade between Spain and the East, and between the Maghreb and Africa south of the Sahara.

Fes was to remain the major Moroccan city, and the country's Arab spiritual heart, right up until the twentieth century. The Idrissid state, however, split once more into **principalities**, most of which returned to their old isolation, until, at the turn of the tenth century, the context began to change. In Al-Andalus – the Muslim territories of Spain – the Western Caliphate collapsed and itself splintered into small rival states. Meanwhile in Tunisia, the well-established Fatimid dynasty moved their capital to Egypt, clashed with their nominated governors, the Zirids, and unleashed upon them the hostile nomadic tribe of the Banu Hilal.

It was a move which was to have devastating effects on the Maghreb's entire lifestyle and ecological balance, as the **Hilali** nomads swept westwards, destroying all in their path, laying to ruin the irrigation systems and devastating the agricultural lands with their goats and other flocks. The medieval Maghrebi historian, **Ibn Khaldun**, described their progress as being like a swarm of locusts: "the very earth seems to have changed its nature", he wrote, "all the lands that the Arabs have conquered in the last few centuries, civilization and population have departed from them".

THE ALMORAVIDS (1062–1145)

Morocco was to some extent cushioned from the Hilali, and by the time they reached its southern oases (where they settled), the worst was probably over. But with the shattered social order of the Maghreb, and complex power struggles in Moorish Spain, came an obvious vacuum of authority.

It was this which created the opportunity for the two great Berber dynasties of the Middle Ages – the **Almoravids** and the **Almohads**. Both were to emerge from the south, and in each case their motivating force was religious: a purifying zeal to **reform** or destroy the decadent ways which had reached Morocco from the wealthy Andalucian Muslims of Spain. The two dynasties together lasted only a century and a half, but in this period Morocco was the pre-eminent power of western Islam, maintaining an **empire** that at its peak stretched right across the Maghreb to Libya, south to Senegal and ancient Ghana and north into Spain. Subsequent history and achievements never matched up to this imperial dream, though even today its memories are part of the Moroccan concept of nation.

"**Greater Morocco**", the nationalist goal of the late 1950s, sketched out areas that took in Mauritania, Algeria, Tunisia and Libya, while even the present war in the Sahara looks back to the reality of the medieval empires.

The **Almoravids** began as a reforming movement among the Sanhaja Berbers in Koumbi Saleh, capital of ancient Ghana, in what is now Mauritania. A nomadic desert tribe – similar to the Touaregs who occupy the area today – they had been converted to Islam in the ninth century, but perhaps only to nominal effect. The founders of the Almoravid movement, a local sheikh who had returned from the pilgrimage to Mecca and a *fakir* from the Souss plain, found widespread abuse of orthodox practice. In particular, they preached against drinking palm wine, playing licentious music and taking more than four wives. It held an appeal for this already ascetic, tent-dwelling people, and rapidly took hold.

Founding a *ribat* – a kind of warrior monastery similar to the Templar castles of Europe – the Almoravids soon became a considerable military force. In 1054, they set out from the *ribat* (from which the movement derived its name) to spread the message through a *jihad* (holy war), and within four years they had captured and destroyed the ancient empire of Ghana to the south. Turning towards Morocco, they established themselves in Marrakesh by 1062, and under the leadership of **Youssef Ben Tachfine** went on to extend their rule throughout the north of Morocco and, to the east, as far as Algiers.

At no time before had any one leader exercised such strong control over these territories; nor had the tribes before been united under a single religious doctrine – a simple, rigorous and puritanical form of Sunni orthodoxy. And so it remained, at least as long as the impetus of *jihad* was sustained. In 1085, Youssef undertook his first, and possibly reluctant, expedition to **Spain**, invited by the Muslim princes of **Al-Andalus** after the fall of Toledo to the Christians. He crossed over the straits again in 1090, this time to take control of Spain himself. In this he was successful, and before his death in 1107, he had restored Muslim control to Valencia and other territories lost in the first wave of the Christian Reconquest.

The new Spanish territories had two decisive effects. The first was to reorientate

Moroccan culture towards the far more sophisticated and affluent Andalucian civilization; the second, to stretch the Almoravid forces too thin. Both were to contribute to the dynasty's decline. Youssef, disgusted by Andalucian decadence, had ruled largely from **Marrakesh**, leaving governors in Seville and other cities. After his death, the Andalucians proved disinclined to accept these foreign overlords, while the Moroccans themselves became vulnerable to charges of being corrupt and departing from their puritan ideals.

Youssef's son **Ali** was himself, in fact, extraordinarily pious, but he was unprepared for (nor interested in) ceaseless military activity; in Spain he turned to Christian mercenaries to maintain control. His reign, and that of the Almoravids, was effectively finished by the early 1140s, as a new movement, the Almohads, seized control of the main Moroccan cities one after another.

THE ALMOHADS (1145–1248)

Ironically, the **Almohads** shared much in common with their predecessors. Again, they were forged from the Berber tribes – this time in the High Atlas – and again, they based their bid for power on an intense puritanism. Their founder **Ibn Toumert**, attacked the Almoravids for allowing their women to ride horses (a tradition in the desert), for wearing extravagant clothes, and for being subject to what may have been Andalucian corruptions – the revived use of music and wine.

He also provoked a **theological crisis**, claiming that the Almoravids did not recognize the essential unitary and unknowable nature of God: the basis of Almohad belief, and the source of their name – the "unitarians". Banished from Marrakesh by Ali, Ibn Toumert set up a *ribat* in the Atlas at **Tin Mal**. Here he waged war on local tribes until they accepted his authority, and he eventually revealed himself to them as the Mahdi – "the chosen one" and the final prophet promised in the Koran.

Charismatic and brutal in his methods, Toumert was aided by a shrewd assistant and brilliant military leader, **Abd El Moumen**, who took over the movement after Toumert's death and extended the radius of their raids. In 1145, he was strong enough to displace the Almoravids from Fes, and two years later he drove them from their stronghold in Marrakesh.

With the two cities subdued, he was now effectively sultan.

Resistance subsided and once again a Moroccan dynasty moved **towards Spain** – this time finally secured by the third Almohad sultan, **Yacoub El Mansour** (The Victorious), who in 1195 defeated the Christians at Alarcos. El Mansour also pushed the frontiers of the empire east to Tripoli, and for the first time, there was one single rule across the entire **Maghreb**, although it did not stretch as far south as under the Almoravids. With the ensuing wealth and prestige, Yacoub launched a great building programme – the first and most ambitious in Moroccan history – which included a new capital in **Rabat** and the magnificent (and in large part still surviving) gateways and minarets of Marrakesh and Seville.

Once more, though, imperial expansion precipitated disintegration. In 1212, Yacoub's successor, **Mohammed en Nasr**, attempted to drive the Spanish Christians as far back as the Pyrenees and met with decisive defeat at the battle of **Las Navas de Tolosa**. The balance of power in Spain was changing, and within four decades only the Kingdom of Granada remained in Muslim hands. In the Maghreb, meanwhile, the eastern provinces had declared independence from Almohad rule and Morocco itself was returning to the authority of local tribes. In 1248, one of these, the **Merenids** (or Beni Merin), took the northern capital of Fes and turned towards Marrakesh.

THE MERENIDS AND WATTASIDS (1248–1554)

This last (300-year) period of Berber rule in Morocco is very much a tailpiece to the Almoravid and Almohad empires – marked by increasing domestic **instability** and economic stagnation, and signalling also the beginning of Morocco's **isolation** from both the European and Muslim worlds. Under the Merenids, the Spanish territories were not regained, and Granada, the last Moorish city, fell to Ferdinand and Isabella in 1492. Portuguese sea power saw to it that foreign seaports were established on the Atlantic and Mediterranean coasts. To the east, the rest of the Maghreb fell under Turkish domination, as part of the Ottoman Empire. The Portuguese ability to navigate beyond Mauritania also meant the eventual end of the trans-Sahara caravan route.

In Morocco itself, the main development was a centralized administrative system – the **Makhzen** – which was maintained without tribal support by standing armies of Arab and Christian mercenaries. It is to this age that the real distinction of *Bled El Makhzen* and *Bled Es Siba* belongs – the latter coming to mean everything outside the immediate vicinities of the imperial cities.

THE MERENIDS

Perhaps with this background it is not surprising that few of the twenty-one **Merenid sultans** – or their cousins and successors, the Wattasids – made any great impression. The early sultans were occupied mainly with Spain, at first in trying to regain a foothold on the coast, later with shoring up the Kingdom of Granada. There were minor successes in the fourteenth century under the "Black Sultan", **Abou El Hassan**, who for a time occupied Tunis, but he was to die before being able to launch a planned major invasion of Al-Andalus, and his son, **Abou Inan**, himself fell victim to the power struggles within the mercenary army.

The thirteenth and fourteenth centuries, however, did leave a considerable **legacy of building**, perhaps in defiance of the lack of political progress (and certainly a product of the move towards government by forced taxation). In 1279, the garrison town of **Fes El Djedid** was established, to be followed by a series of brilliantly endowed colleges, or **medersas**, which are among the finest surviving Moorish monuments. Culture, too, saw a final flourish. The historians **Ibn Khaldun** and **Leo Africanus**, and the travelling chronicler **Ibn Battuta**, all studied in Fes under Merenid patronage.

THE WATTASIDS

The **Wattasids**, who usurped Merenid power in 1465, had ruled in effect for 45 years previously as a line of hereditary viziers. After their coup, they maintained a semblance of control for a little under a century, though the extent of the *Makhzen* lands was by now minimal.

The **Portuguese** had annexed and colonized the seaports of Tetouan, Ceuta, Tangier, Asilah, Agadir and Safi, while large tracts of the interior lay in the hands of religious warrior brotherhoods, or **marabouts**, on whose alliances the sultans had increasingly to depend.

THE SAADIANS AND CIVIL WAR (1554–1669)

The rise and fall of the **Saadians** was in some respects a replay of all of the dynasties that had come before them. They were the most important of the *marabouts* to emerge in the early years of the sixteenth century, rising to power on the strength of their religious positions (they were *Shereefs* – descendants of the Prophet), climaxing in a single, particularly distinguished reign, and declining amid a chaos of political assassinations, bitter factional strife and, in the end, civil war.

As the first **Arab dynasty** since the Idrissids, they marked the end of Moroccan Berber rule, though this was probably less significant at the time than the fact that theirs was a government with no tribal basis. The *Makhzen* had to be even further extended than under the Merenids, and Turkish guards – a new point of intrigue – were added to the imperial armies.

Slower to establish themselves than the preceding dynasties, the Saadians began by setting up a small principality in the **Souss**, where they established their first capital in **Taroudannt**. Normally, this would have formed a regular part of *Bled El Makhzen*, but the absence of government in the south allowed them to extend their power to **Marrakesh** around 1520, with the Wattasids for a time retaining Fes and ruling the north.

In the following decades the Saadians made breakthroughs along the coast, capturing Agadir in 1540 and driving the Portuguese from Safi and Essaouira. When the Wattasids fell into bankruptcy and invited the Turks into Fes, the Saadians were ready to consolidate their power. This proved harder, and more confusing, than anyone might have expected. **Mohammed esh Sheikh**, the first Saadian sultan to control both the southern and northern kingdoms, was himself soon using Turkish troops, and was subsequently assassinated by a group of them in 1557. His death unleashed an incredibly convoluted sequence of factional murder and power politics, which was only resolved, somewhat fortuitously, by a battle with the Portuguese twenty years later.

THE BATTLE OF THE THREE KINGS

This event, **The Battle of the Three Kings**, was essentially a Portuguese crusade, led by the youthful King Sebastião on the nominal behalf of a deposed Saadian king against his uncle and rival. At the end of the day all three were to perish on the battlefield, the Portuguese having suffered a crushing defeat, and a little-known Saadian prince emerged as the sole acknowledged ruler of Morocco.

His name was **Ahmed** "**El Mansour**" (The Victorious, following this momentous victory), and he was easily the most impressive sultan of the dynasty. Not only did he begin his reign clear of the intrigue and rivalry that had dogged his predecessors, but he was immensely wealthy as well. Portuguese ransoms paid for the remnants of their nobility after the battle had been enormous, causing Portugal to go bankrupt – the country, with its remaining Moroccan enclaves, then passed into the control of Habsburg Spain.

Breaking with tradition, Ahmed himself became actively involved in European politics, generally supporting the Protestant north against the Spanish and encouraging Dutch and British trade. Within Morocco he was able to maintain a reasonable level of order and peace, and diverted criticism of his use of Turkish troops (and his own Turkish-educated ways) by embarking on an **invasion of Timbuktu** and the south. This secured control of the Saharan salt mines and the gold and slave routes from Senegal, each sources of phenomenal wealth, which won him the additional epithet of *El Dhahabi* (The Golden One). It also reduced his need to tax Moroccans, which made him a popular man.

CIVIL WAR AND PIRACY

Ahmed's death in 1603 caused abrupt and lasting chaos. He left three sons, none of whom could gain authority, and, split by **civil war**, the country once again broke into a number of principalities. A succession of **Saadian rulers** retained power in the Souss and in Marrakesh (where their tombs remain testimony to the opulence and turbulence of the age); another *marabout* force, the **Djila**, gained control of Fes; while around Salé and Rabat arose the bizarre **Republic of the Bou Regreg**.

The Bou Regreg depended almost entirely on **piracy**, a new development in Morocco, though well established along the Mediterranean coasts of Algeria and Tunisia. Its practitioners were the last Moors to be expelled from Spain

– mainly from Granada and Badajoz – and they conducted a looting war primarily against Spanish ships. For a time they had astounding success, raiding as far away as the Irish coast, dealing in arms with the British and the French, and even accrediting foreign consuls.

MOULAY ISMAIL AND THE EARLY ALAOUITES (1665–1822)

Like the Saadians, the **Alaouites** were *Shereefs*, first establishing themselves as religious leaders – this time in Rissani in the **Tafilalt**. Their struggle to establish power also followed a similar pattern, spreading first to Taza and Fes and finally, under Sultan **Moulay Rashid**, reaching Marrakesh in 1669. Rashid, however, was unable to enjoy the fruits of his labour, since he was assassinated in a particularly bloody palace coup in 1672. It was only with Moulay Ismail, the ablest of his rival sons, that an Alaouite leader gained real control over the country.

MOULAY ISMAIL

The reign of **Moulay Ismail**, perhaps the most notorious in all of Morocco's history, stretched over 55 years (1672–1727) and was to be the country's last stab at imperial glory. In Morocco, where his shrine in Meknes is still a place of pilgrimage, he is remembered as a great and just, if unusually ruthless, ruler; to contemporary Europeans – and in subsequent historical accounts – he is noted for extravagant cruelty. His rule certainly was tyrannical, with arbitrary killings and an appalling treatment of his slaves, but it was not much worse than that of the European nations of the day; the seventeenth century was the age of the witch trials in Protestant Europe, and of the Catholic Inquisition.

Nevertheless, Moulay Ismail stands out among the Alaouites because of the grandness of the scale on which he acted. At **Meknes**, which he made his new imperial capital, he garrisoned a permanent army of some 140,000 black troops, a legendary guard he had built up personally through slaving expeditions in Mauritania and the south, as well as by starting a human breeding programme. The army kept order throughout the kingdom – Morocco is today still littered with their kasbah garrisons – and were able to raise taxes as required. The

Bou Regreg pirates, too (the so-called Sallee Rovers), were brought under the control of the state, along with their increasingly lucrative revenues.

With all this, Ismail was able to build a palace in Meknes that was the rival of its contemporary, Versailles, and he negotiated on equal terms with the **Europeans**. Indeed, it was probably the reputation he established for Morocco that allowed the country to remain free for another century and a half before the European colonial powers began carving it up.

SIDI MOHAMMED AND MOULAY SLIMANE

Like all the great, long-reigning Moroccan sultans, Moulay Ismail left innumerable sons and a terminal dispute for the throne, with the powerful standing army supporting and dropping heirs at will.

Remarkably, a capable ruler emerged fairly soon – Sultan **Sidi Mohammed** – and for a while it appeared that the Shereefian empire was moving back into the mainstream of European and world events. Mohammed recaptured the port of El Jadida from the Portuguese, founded the port of Essaouira, traded and conducted treaties with the Europeans, and even recognized the **United States of America** – the first ruler to do so.

At his death in 1790, however, the state collapsed once more into civil war, the two capitals of Fes and Marrakesh in turn promoting claimants to the throne. When this period drew to some kind of a close, with **Moulay Slimane** (1792–1822) asserting his authority in both cities, there was little left to govern. The army had dispersed; the *Bled Es Siba* reasserted its old limits; and in Europe, with the ending of the Napoleonic wars, Britain, France, Spain and Germany were all looking to establish themselves in Africa.

Moulay Slimane's rule was increasingly isolated from the new realities outside Morocco. An intensely orthodox Muslim, he concentrated the efforts of government on eliminating the power and influence of the **Sufi brotherhoods** – a power he underestimated. In 1818 Berber tribes loyal to the Derakaoui brotherhood rebelled and, temporarily, captured the Sultan. Subsequently, the sultans had no choice but to govern with the co-operation of local sheikhs and brotherhood leaders.

Even more serious, at least in its long-term effects, was Moulay Slimane's isolationist attitude towards **Europe**, and in particular to Napoleonic France. Exports were banned; European consuls banished to Tangier; and contacts which might have helped maintain Moroccan independence were lost.

MOULAY HASSAN AND EUROPEAN DOMINATION

Once started, the European domination of Moroccan affairs took an inevitable course – with an outdated, medieval form of government, virtual bankruptcy and armies press-ganged from the tribes to secure taxes, there was little that could be done to resist it.

The first pressures came from the **French**, who defeated the Ottomans in 1830 and occupied Algiers. Called to defend his fellow Muslims, Sultan **Abd Er Rahman** (1822–59) mustered a force but was severely defeated at Isly. In the following reign of **Mohammed III** (1859–73), **Spanish** aspirations were also realized with the occupation of Tetouan – regained by the Moroccans only after the offer to pay Spain massive indemnities and provide them with an Atlantic port (which the Spanish later claimed in Sidi Ifni).

MOULAY HASSAN

Outright occupation and colonization were by the end of the nineteenth century proving more difficult to justify, but both the French and the Spanish had learned to use every opportunity to step in and "protect" their own nationals. Complaints by **Moulay Hassan**, the last precolonial sultan to have any real power, actually led to a debate on this issue at the 1880 **Madrid Conference**, but the effect was only to regularize the practice on a wider scale, beginning with the setting up of an "international administration" in Tangier.

Moulay Hassan could, in other circumstances, have proved an effective and possibly inspired sultan. Acceding to the throne in 1873, he embarked on an ambitious series of modernizing **reforms**, including attempts to stabilize the currency by minting the *rial* in Paris, to bring in more rational forms of taxation, and to retrain the army under the instruction of Turkish and Egyptian officers. The times, however, were against him. He found the social and monetary reforms obstructed by foreign merchants and local *caids*, while the European powers forced him to abandon plans for other Muslim states' involvement in the army.

Moulay Hassan played off the Europeans as best he could, employing a British military chief of staff, **Caid MacClean**, a French military mission and German arms manufacturers. On the frontiers, he built kasbahs to strengthen the defences at Tiznit, Saïdia and Selouane. But the government had few modern means of raising money to pay for these developments. Moulay Hassan was thrown back on the traditional means of taxation, the *harka*, setting out across the country to subdue the tribes and to collect tribute. In 1894, returning across the Atlas on just such a campaign, he died.

SULTANS

The last years of independence under Moulay Hassan's sons, Moulay Abd El Aziz and Moulay Hafid, were increasingly dominated by Europe.

The reign of **Abd El Aziz** (1894–1907), in particular, signalled an end to the possibilities of a modern, independent state raised by his reforming father. The sultan was just a boy of ten at his accession, but for the first six years of his rule the country was kept in at least a semblance of order by his father's vizier, **Bou Ahmed**. In 1900, however, Bou Ahmed died, and Abd El Aziz was left to govern alone – surrounded by an assembly of Europeans, preying on the remaining wealth of the court.

The first years of the twentieth century in Morocco were marked by a return to the old ways. In the Atlas mountains, the tribal chiefs established ever-increasing powers, outside the government domain. In the Rif, a pretender to the throne, **Bou Hamra**, led a five-year revolt, coming close to taking control of Fes and the northern seat of government.

European manipulation during this period was remorselessly cynical. In 1904, the French negotiated agreements on "spheres of influence" with the British (who were to hold Egypt and Cyprus), and with the Italians (who got Tripolitana, or Libya). The following year saw the German Kaiser Wilhelm visiting Tangier and swearing to protect Morocco's integrity, but he was later bought off with the chance to "develop" the Congo. France and Spain, meanwhile, had reached a secret arrangement on how they

were going to divide Morocco and were simply waiting for the critical moment.

In 1907, the French moved troops into **Oujda**, on the Algerian border and, after a mob attack on French construction workers, into Casablanca. Abd El Aziz was eventually deposed by his brother, **Moulay Hafid** (1907–12), in a last attempt to resist the European advance. His reign began with a coalition with the principal Atlas chieftain, **Madani El Glaoui**, and intentions to take military action against the French. The new sultan, however, was at first preoccupied with putting down the revolt of Bou Hamra – whom he succeeded in capturing in 1909. By this time the moment for defence against European entrenchment, if indeed it had ever been possible, had passed. Claiming to protect their nationals – this time in the mineral mines of the Rif – the Spanish brought over 90,000 men to garrison their established port in Melilla. Colonial occupation, in effect, had begun.

THE TREATY OF FES

Finally, in 1910, the two strands of Moroccan dissidence and European aggression came together. Moulay Hafid was driven into the hands of the French by the appearance of a new pretender in Meknes – one of a number during that period – and, with Berber tribesmen under the walls of his capital in Fes, was forced to accept their terms.

These were ratified and signed as the **Treaty of Fes** in 1912, and gave the French the right to defend Morocco, represent it abroad and conquer the *Bled Es Siba*. A similar document was also signed with the Spanish, who were to take control of a strip of territory along the northern coast, with its capital in Tetouan and another thinner strip of land in the south, running eastwards from Tarfaya. In between, with the exception of a small Spanish enclave in Sidi Ifni, was to be French Morocco. A separate agreement gave Spain colonial rights to the Sahara, stretching south from Tarfaya to the borders of French Mauritania.

The arbitrary way in which these boundaries were drawn was to have a profound effect on modern Moroccan history. When Moroccan nationalists laid claim to the Sahara in the 1950s – and to large stretches of Mauritania, Algeria and even Mali – they based their case on the obvious artificiality of colonial divisions.

THE FRENCH AND SPANISH PROTECTORATES (1912-56)

The fates of **Spanish and French Morocco** under colonial rule were to be very different. When **France** signed its Protectorate agreement with the sultan in 1912, its sense of **colonial mission** was running high. The colonial lobby in France argued that the colonies were vital not only as markets for French goods but because they fulfilled France's "*mission civilisatrice*" – to bring the benefits of French culture and language to all corners of the globe.

There may have been Spaniards who had similar conceptions of their role in North Africa, but reality was very different. **Spain** showed no interest in developing the Sahara until the 1960s; in the north the Spanish saw themselves more as conquerors than colonists. Its government there, described by one contemporary as a mixture of "battlefield, tavern and brothel", did much to provoke the Rif rebellions of the 1920s.

LYAUTEY AND "PACIFICATION"

France's first resident-general in Morocco was **General Hubert Lyautey**, often held up as the ideal of French colonialism with his stated policy: "Do not offend a single tradition, do not change a single habit." Lyautey recommended respect for the terms of the Protectorate agreement, which placed strict limits on French interference in Moroccan affairs. He recognized the existence of a functioning Moroccan bureaucracy based on the sultan's court with which the French could co-operate – a hierarchy of officials, with diplomatic representation abroad, and with its own social institutions.

But there were other forces at work: French soldiers were busy unifying the country, ending tribal rebellion; in their wake came a system of roads and railways that opened the country to further colonial exploitation. For the first time in Moroccan history, the central government exerted permanent control over the mountain regions. The "**pacification**" of the country brought a flood of French settlers and administrators.

In France these developments were presented as echoing the history of the opening up of the American Wild West. Innumerable articles celebrated "the transformation taking place, the stupendous development of Casablanca port, the birth of new towns, the construction of roads and dams . . . The image of the virgin lands in Morocco is contrasted often with metropolitan France, wrapped up in its history and its routines . . . ".

Naturally, the interests of the natives were submerged in this rapid economic development, and the restrictions of the Protectorate agreement were increasingly ignored.

SPAIN AND REVOLT IN THE RIF

The early history of the **Spanish zone** was strikingly different. Before 1920 Spanish influence outside the main cities of Ceuta, Melilla and Tetouan was minimal. When the Spanish tried to extend their control into the Rif mountains of the interior, they ran into the fiercely independent Berber tribes of the region.

Normally, the various tribes remained divided, but faced with the Spanish troops they united under the leadership of **Abd El Krim**, later to become a hero of the Moroccan nationalists. In the summer of 1921, he inflicted a series of crushing defeats on the Spanish army, culminating in the massacre of at least 13,000 soldiers at **Annoual**. The scale of the defeat, at the hands of tribal fighters armed only with rifles, outraged the Spanish public and worried the French, who had Berber tribes of their own to deal with in the Atlas mountains. As the war began to spread into the French zone, the two colonial powers combined to crush the rebellion. It took a combined force of around 360,000 colonial troops to do so.

It was the last of the great tribal rebellions. Abd El-Krim had fought for an independent **Rifian state**. An educated man, he had seen the potential wealth that could result from exploiting the mineral deposits of the Rif. After the rebellion was crushed, the route to Moroccan independence changed from armed revolt to the evolving middle-class resistance to the colonial rulers.

NATIONALISM AND INDEPENDENCE

The French had hoped that by educating a middle-class elite they would find native allies in the task of binding Morocco permanently to France. It had the opposite effect. The educated classes of Rabat and Fes were the first to demand reforms from the French that would give greater rights to the Moroccans. When the government failed to respond, the demand for reforms escalated into demands for total independence.

Religion also played an important part in the development of a nationalist movement. France's first inkling of the depth of nationalist feeling came in 1930, when the colonial government tried to bring in a **Berber dahir** – a law setting up a separate legal system for the Berber areas. This was an obvious breach of the Protectorate agreement, which prevented the French from changing the Islamic nature of government. Popular agitation forced the French to back down.

It was a classic attempt to "divide and rule", and as the nationalists gained strength, the French resorted more and more to threatening to "unleash" the Berber hill tribes against the Arab city dwellers. They hoped that by spreading Christianity and setting up French schools in Berber areas, the tribes would become more "Europeanized" and, as such, useful allies against the Muslim Arabs.

Up until World War II, Morocco's **nationalists** were weak and their demands aimed at reforming the existing system, not independence. After riots in 1937, the government was able to round up the entire executive committee of the small nationalist party. But with French capitulation in the war, the climate changed. In 1943, the party took the name of **Istiqlal** (Independence); the call for complete separation from France grew more insistent.

The loyal performance of Moroccan troops during the war had raised hopes of a fairer treatment for nationalist demands, but postwar France continued to ignore Istiqlal, exiling its leaders and banning its publications. During the postwar period, it steadily developed into a mass party – growing from 10,000 members in 1947 to 100,000 by 1951.

To some extent, the developments of the 1950s, culminating in Moroccan independence in 1956, resemble events in Algeria and Tunisia. The French first underestimated the strength of local independence movements, then tried to resist them and finally had to concede defeat. In Algeria and Tunisia, the independence parties gained power and consolidated their positions once the French had left. But in Morocco, Istiqlal was never uncontested after 1956 and the party soon began to fragment – becoming by the 1970s a marginal force in politics.

The decline and fall of Istiqlal was due mainly to the astute way in which Sultan (later King) **Mohammed V** associated himself with the independence movement. Despite threats from the French government, Mohammed became more and more outspoken in his support for independence, paralysing government operations by refusing to sign legislation. Serious rioting in 1951 persuaded the French to act: after a period of house arrest, the sultan was sent into exile in 1953.

This only increased his popularity. After a brief attempt to rule in alliance with **Thami El Glaoui**, the Berber pasha of Marrakesh who saw the sultan's absence as an opportunity to expand his power base in the south, the French capitulated in 1955, allowing the sultan to return. The government in Paris could see no way out of the spiralling violence of the nationalist guerrillas and the counterviolence of the French settlers. Perhaps equally significant, they could not sustain a simultaneous defence of three North African colonies – and economic interests dictated that they concentrate on holding Algeria. In 1956, Morocco was given full **independence** by France and Spain.

On independence, Sultan Mohammed V changed his title to that of king, foreshadowing a move towards a **constitutional monarchy**.

MOHAMMED V

Unlike his ancestor sultans, **Mohammed V** had inherited a united country with a well-developed industrial sector, an extensive system of irrigation and a network of roads and railways. But years of French administration had left little legacy of trained Moroccan administrators. Nor was there an obvious party base or bureaucracy for the king to operate within.

In 1956, Istiqlal party members held key posts in the first **government**. The regime instituted a series of reforms across the range of social issues. Schools and universities were created, a level of regional government was introduced and ambitious public works schemes launched. There were moves, also, against European "decadence", with a wholesale cleanup of Tangier, and against the unorthodox religious brotherhoods – both long-time targets of the Istiqlal.

Mohammed V, as **leader of the Muslim faith** in Morocco and the figurehead of independence, commanded huge support and influence in Morocco as a whole. In government, however, he did not perceive the Istiqlal as natural allies. The king bided his time, building links with the army – with the help of Crown Prince Hassan, whose period as commander-in-chief was a defining moment in his political development – and with the police.

Mohammed's influence on the army would prove a decisive factor in the Moroccan state withstanding a series of **rebellions** against its authority. The most serious of these were in the Rif, in 1958–59, but there were challenges, too, in the Middle Atlas and Sahara. The king's standing and the army's efficiency stood the test. Crown Prince Hassan, meanwhile, as the army commander, helped to translate internal pressures into renewed nationalism. The army began a quasi-siege in the south, exerting pressure on the Spanish to give up their claims to the port of **Sidi Ifni**.

In party politics, Mohammed's principal act was to lend his support to the **Mouvement Populaire** (MP), a moderate party set up to represent the Berbers, and for the king a useful counterweight to Istiqlal. In 1959, the strategy paid its first dividend. Istiqlal was seriously weakened by a split which hived off the more left-wing members into a separate party, the **Union Nationale des Forces Populaires** (UNFP) under Mehdi Ben Barka. There had always been a certain tension within Istiqlal between the moderates and those favouring a more radical policy, in association with the unions. A tendency towards parties dividing within and among themselves has been apparent in Moroccan politics ever since, helping to maintain the primal role of the Palace in the political arena.

MODERN MOROCCO: HASSAN II (1961–99)

The death of Mohammed V in 1961 led to the accession of **King Hassan II**, who was to dominate the kingdom for nearly four decades. For much of this reign Hassan ruled as an **autocrat**, albeit with a veneer of parliamentary party politics. But by the time that he died, in July 1999, the monarchy, although still by far the most powerful political institution in Morocco, was an institution that had begun to engage with other political and social forces – and had established the roots of a more open political culture.

The hand over to Hassan's son **Sidi Mohammed Ben Hassan** – now reigning as **Mohammed VI** – was achieved peacefully after Hassan was buried with full national and international honours. Hassan's legacy included leaving a government led by a long-time opponent, Socialist leader **Abderrahmane El Youssoufi**, and a more rounded civil society than had seemed possible only a few years before. Thus while the late king's legacy was widely glorified, the local media was by then sufficiently independent also to consider some of his failings as well in their analyses of Morocco's path **after Hassan**.

Hassan had presided over a period of **dramatic change**, forged upon a deeply **uneven** legacy of colonial rule. The French had built an administrative capital in Rabat and a relatively sophisticated infrastructure in Casablanca and other economically useful zones, but most other regions were left without adequate roads, health and education facilities or other trappings of a modernizing state. In the kingdom's northern and southern extremities, Spanish colonial rule left even less on which the new state could base its policy of creating viable development. At independence, there was an almost total absence of doctors or graduates in the Spanish zones.

Despite the poverty still apparent in large areas of the country, much was done during Hassan's reign to bring the kingdom into the modern world. It was an achievement in the face of a huge **population explosion** in the 1970s and 1980s, which saw the population rise from 8 million at Independence to perhaps more than 30 million today. It's a predominantly youthful population – more than 40 percent are aged under 14 – and is clamouring for the sort of education and jobs of which their parents and grandparents were routinely deprived.

VALUES AND TRADITIONAL ROLES

While the quest for modernization has been one theme running through post-independence Morocco, **traditional values** – as perceived by the Palace and a network of local religious and customary authorities – are another important factor in understanding the contemporary kingdom.

In many respects Hassan was a very modern monarch, regularly pictured playing golf, flying a jet fighter, or meeting fellow heads of state.

As a power politician he had few peers. But he was also careful to maintain his status as a traditional ruler – one of the very few who remained in the Afro-Arab world. When in his flowing robes at a state occasion or religious festival, Hassan was very much the Amir Al-Muminin (commander of the faithful), **Morocco's religious leader** as well as its temporal ruler.

This role is of great political significance to the monarchy, giving the ruler the sort of deep-rooted legitimacy so lacking in other developing countries – a fact not lost on young King Mohammed VI. Presiding over a complex system of traditional loyalties, ethnic and regional divisions, Hassan used traditions based in the days of the Sultanate to underpin his modern monarchy – maintaining the Palace at the centre of the Moroccan political universe. Indeed, according to his view of democracy, it would have been an abnegation of the king's religious role if he were not to play a central role in government.

Achieving the balance between continuity and change was not easy, as whatever formula the king chose would have to involve the genuine devolution of power. This only really happened right at the end of Hassan's reign, when multiparty politics became a reality with the 1998 elections resulting in a coalition government led by opposition. However, in the 1990s, the promotion of more responsive local authorities (*collectivités locales*) had also set a form of **devolution** under way. Hassan even talked of dividing the country along federal lines, with the German *länder* as a model. A third pointer to the emergence of a new Morocco in the decade was the emergence of literally thousands of **nongovernmental organisations** (NGOs) and other associations.

All of this was encouraging, especially given the continued postponement of general elections in the period 1989–97 – an impasse caused in large part by the political system's inability to develop a new configuration in which the Throne would remain dominant yet with genuine input from a wider **body of opinion**. Those pushing to be heard include a growing younger generation of professionals who feel alienated from the traditional political parties, which are mostly still run by men who emerged during the independence struggle and Hassan's first years as monarch.

Riots in Fes in December 1990 showed that there was a large urban underclass whose voice had to be heard, but perhaps surprisingly, such incidents have been rare in recent years. Far more common – and underlining tensions within the kingdom – have been strikes by workers for improved living conditions, protests by unemployed graduates (graduate unemployment may be as high as 80 percent), and sometimes violent incidents in the kingdom's universities.

On campus, the student movement linked to Morocco's biggest opposition party, the **Union Socialiste des Forces Populaires** (USFP) – in government since 1998 – went into retreat as a growing Islamist movement took control of student unions. This is one sign that the **rise of radical Islam** across the Arab world – and notably in neighbouring Algeria after civil conflict erupted in 1991–92 – has not left Morocco unaffected, for all that Hassan felt confident about his unique blend of religious authority and the efficiency of his security forces.

CONSTITUTION AND ELECTIONS

Domestic politics since independence have centred on a battle of wills between the dominant political forces in the kingdom: the Palace and its allies; a legalized opposition which has at times formed a part of the government; and underground movements such as the Marxist-Leninist Ilal Amam (which has all but disappeared) and, more recently, groups of Islamist radicals.

Even before independence, in a 1955 speech, Mohammed V had promised to set up "democratic institutions resulting from the holding of free elections". The country's first constitution was not ready until after his death, and it was only in 1962, under Hassan II, that it was put to, and approved by, a popular referendum. The constitution was drafted in such a way as to favour the pro-monarchy parties of the centre – setting the pattern that was to prevail up until the 1998 elections.

The 1960s were marked by the fragility of Morocco's political party structure and the authorities' greater enthusiasm for using the bullet and torture chamber than the ballot box to handle opposition. This mood was reflected in the **Ben Barka affair**, a notorious incident whose political ramifications endured for the next two decades, when Mehdi Ben Barka, leader of the opposition UNFP party, was assassinated in Paris, with apparent connivance from the governments of Morocco and France.

The opposition subsequently split, with the largest element of the UNFP going on to form the USFP, led by Abderrahim Bouabid until his death in 1992. These parties were largely ineffectual, especially after Hassan announced a new constitution in 1970, following a period of emergency rule. However, the events of 1971–72 showed the real nature of the threat to the monarchy.

In July 1971, a group of soldiers broke into the royal palace in Skhirat in an attempt to stage a **coup**; more than 100 people were killed, but in the confusion Hassan escaped. The following year another attempt was launched, as the king's private jet was attacked by fighters of the Moroccan Air Force. Again, Hassan had a very narrow escape – his pilot was able to convince the attacking aircraft by radio that the king had already died. The former interior minister, General Mohamed Oufkir disappeared (apparently murdered in custody) soon after and the armed forces were restructured. Typical of the younger Hassan's style, Oufkir's family remained imprisoned and incommunicado until 1991.

THE SAHARAN CONFLICT

Hassan's great challenge was to give a sense of destiny to the country, a cause similar to the struggle for independence that had brought such prestige to his father. That cause was provided in 1975, when the Spanish finally decided to pull out of their colony in the **Western Sahara** and launch a referendum on its future status.

In the 1950s the nationalist party of Istiqlal had laid claim to the Sahara, as well as parts of Mauritania, Algeria and Mali, as part of its quest for a "greater Morocco". But by 1975, Hassan had patched up the border dispute with Algeria and recognized the independent government in Mauritania. It turned out this was only a prelude to a more realistic design – Moroccan control of the Western Sahara.

The discovery of **phosphate reserves** in the Sahara during the 1960s brought about Spain's first real attempt to develop its Saharan colony. Before then it had been content merely to garrison the small coastal forts in Dakhla (then known as Villa Cisneros) and La Gouera, with occasional forays into the interior to pacify the tribes. With increased investment in the region during the 1960s, the nomads began to settle in the newly created towns along the coast, particularly the new capital in Laayoune. As education became more widespread, the Spanish were confronted with the same problem the French had faced in Morocco thirty years earlier – the **rise of nationalism**. International pressure began to mount on General Franco's government to decolonize one of the last colonies in Africa. Meanwhile, the Saharans began to press for independence themselves; in 1973, a group of radicals formed the *Frente Popular para la Liberación de Saguia El Hamra y Rio de Oro*, or **Polisario**, which began guerrilla operations against the Spanish.

Spanish withdrawal from the Western Sahara in 1975 coincided with General Franco's final illness. King Hassan timed his move perfectly, sending some 350,000 Moroccan civilians southwards on **Al Massira** – the "**Green March**" – to the Sahara. Spain could either go to war with Morocco by attacking the advancing Moroccans or withdraw without holding the promised referendum. Hassan's bluff worked, and the popular unrest of the 1960s and the coup attempts of 1971–72 were forgotten under a wave of patriotism. Without shedding any blood, Morocco had "recaptured" part of its former empire. In November 1975 a secret agreement was reached in Madrid to divide the Spanish Sahara between Morocco and Mauritania as soon as Spanish troops had withdrawn.

Both parties, however, had underestimated the native Saharawis' determination to fight for an independent Sahara, their Saharan Arab Democratic Republic (SADR). Nearly 40,000 of them fled the Moroccan advance, taking refuge in Mauritania and Algeria. In an unprecedented move, Algeria ceded an area of its territory in the desolate Hamada region southeast of **Tindouf** to Polisario. Saharawi refugees settled in camps run by Polisario. (According to the best estimates there are now about 170,000 people living in five tented and increasingly unhygienic camps.) A classic guerrilla campaign ensued against Morocco and Mauritania, until Saharawi pressure proved too much for Mauritania and it withdrew from its alliance with Morocco in 1979. By the early 1980s Polisario had succeeded in closing the territory's mines and had pinned the Moroccan Forces Armées Royales (FAR) into an area round the capital, Laayoune, and Dakhla in the south.

The early success of Polisario's campaign said much for the Saharawis' prowess as desert guerrilla fighters, as well as to the high level of military support offered by Algeria, which used Polisario as a stick with which to beat Morocco, its perceived rival for regional dominance. But beginning in 1981, the Moroccans built a series of heavily defended **desert walls** that excluded the Polisario from successively larger areas of the desert. By 1987 the sixth wall had effectively blocked off Polisario from Mauritania and left only 15 percent of the land area outside Moroccan control.

Meanwhile the Moroccan government was making concerted attempts to win the approval of the Saharan residents, injecting vast sums into creating a model city and capital in Laayoune. Under United Nations auspices, a **ceasefire** was agreed in the spring of 1989 – and there has been no major military conflict since. Protracted negotiations have continued for a **referendum** on the territory's future to be held among the Saharawis. However, arranging this referendum has proved highly problematic, even for such committed diplomatists as UN Secretary General **Kofi Annan** and his special envoy, former US secretary of state **James Baker III**.

A resolution to the dispute is essential if **North Africa is to have lasting peace**. The Saharan dispute remains a potential point of conflict in a volatile region, and a lasting settlement would also help efforts to promote regional unity. These had seemed promising when in February 1989 Algerian, Libyan, Mauritanian, Moroccan and Tunisian leaders met in Marrakesh and agreed to form the long-awaited regional grouping, the **Arab Maghreb Union**. This is known by its evocative acronym UMA, from the French Union de Maghreb Arabe but sounding like the Arabic word 'umma, or community. However, the UMA has been stalled in recent years by disputes, hinging on the rivalries which have long divided North African states – leading to the closure of the Algerian-Moroccan border for several years.

ECONOMIC AND SOCIAL PROBLEMS

The attention and budget demanded by the Saharan war compounded economic problems. By 1981, an estimated 60 percent of the population were living below the poverty level, unemployment ran at approximately 20 percent (40 percent among the young) and perhaps 20 percent of the urban population lived in shantytowns, or *bidonvilles*. This situation has improved markedly but **poverty remains a pressing issue** for policy-makers and swathes of the population alike.

Official figures for **unemployment** and even gross domestic product (GDP) are often approximate. The young "student" operating as a guide in Fes or Marrakesh may well not appear in national employment figures. The shopkeeper he leads you to could also be in the informal economy, outside the tax net and compass of official data. And despite sometimes strenuous efforts to modernize and rationalize economic behaviour in the 1970s and 1980s, the "**informal sector**" remains enormous – perhaps equal in size to GDP, fuelled by farmers and traders who exist outside the tax net, and by the cannabis trade in northern Morocco.

Informal economic activity and the family network (for many still the only effective system of social services they know) have acted as a safety-valve for a hard-pressed population. The informal economy also finances some of Morocco's richest citizens, whose huge wealth – reflected in the opulent villas, discreetly hidden in the most upmarket quarters of major cities, such as Casablanca's "California" suburb – may also not appear in official data.

The most dramatic manifestation of the potential for popular unrest that poverty engendered were the 1984 "**bread riots**". This violent episode was triggered when a government under intense pressures to repay its **burgeoning debt** and cope with the problems of depressed phosphate prices and one of Morocco's regular **droughts** conceded to International Monetary Fund (IMF) demands and raised the prices of staple foods. King Hassan had to intervene personally to reverse the decision – and, in the opinion of many analysts, save his monarchy from a populist rising.

But despite the pessimistic assessments of many analysts, the 1984 bread riots were not repeated later in the decade and since then, like many developing countries, Morocco has been involved in a process of almost perpetual economic reform. This was marked in the 1990s by one of Africa's biggest **privatization** drives as King Hassan firmly nailed his colours to the mast of economic liberalization. New efforts were made to encourage foreign investment in technologically advanced manufacturing industries, **textiles** and, an increasingly important earner, **tourism**. Modern management skills have begun to take hold with the emergence of a new managerial class independent of the old social loyalties. The decade ended with the Medi Telecom consortium bidding over US$1 billion for a licence to install a GSM mobile telephone system, and privately financed power plants helping to raise energy capacity.

Morocco's controversial application to join the **European Union**, made in the 1980s, was rejected. But Brussels has pushed European governments to develop closer relations with the kingdom and in 1996 Morocco's became only the second Arab government (after Tunisia) to sign one of the European Union's **Euro-Mediterranean Partnership** agreements. This accord opens the way for the kingdom to join a free trade zone planned for the region in the next decade – which is seen as a lifeline to Arab economic planners looking to create jobs and other opportunities for young and under-employed populations on Europe's southern flank.

CHANGE AND ELECTIONS

The opposition, which had been quiet through much of the 1980s, started to reassert itself in the 1990s, as traditional opposition parties showed revived enthusiasm for challenging the government – though not the king. They did this in the knowledge that if their opposition failed, younger Moroccans may be tempted to follow Islamist and other illegal political trends.

The mid-1990s saw Morocco cleaning up its previously appalling **human rights** record. It was finally understood that a bad press abroad could damage international relations. In 1992, a leading dissident, Abraham Serfaty, was one of many well-known figures in a **release of political prisoners** that included many soldiers held since the 1972 failed coup in a dungeon prison at Tazmamart in the High Atlas.

Many of the former student radicals who survived imprisonment and torture in the 1960s, '70s and '80s now hold positions of responsibility in the local press, universities and even government departments. As a new **civil society** has begun to emerge – especially in the liberalized commercial capital of Casablanca – serious newspapers such as the Casablanca-based daily *L'Economiste* have taken root, as have women's magazines which challenge social taboos.

In 1996 Hassan judged there to be sufficient consensus on the direction of Moroccan politics to hold a referendum on constitutional reforms, opening the way for a new bicameral parliamentary system. Local and national elections were held in 1997 and for the first time there seemed the prospect of bringing the opposition into government, with genuine power.

Disappointingly, the elections produced a lacklustre campaign and much voter apathy, as a three-way split gave right-wing, centrist and left-wing/nationalist groupings a similar number of seats in the lower house of parliament. This meant that, once again, the nation's dominant figures, Hassan and his powerful interior minister **Driss Basri**, would act as arbiters between rival groups. After a long period of power-broking, Hassan appointed the USFP (Socialist) leader **Abderrahmane Youssoufi** prime minister. He, in turn, appointed Morocco's first government of "alternance", including USFP and rightist Istiqlal ministers.

ISLAMIST POLITICS

While leftists dominated the opposition in the first three decades of independence, **radical Islam** posed the greatest challenge in the 1990s – and potentially this decade.

One notable factor in the 1997 general election was that Islamist deputies were voted into parliament for the first time, under the *Mouvement Populaire Constitutionnel et Démocratique* **(MPCD)** banner.

This parliamentary debut for the Islamists came at a time when their calls for a change in views on public morality and private sector development were gaining appeal among those most alienated by increasing social tensions and allegations of corruption. A growing number of Moroccans wear modern urban Islamist fashions, and small neighbourhood mosques and Islamic charitable organizations are extremely popular. Whether this leads to greater public support for more radical parties remains a key question.

THE NEW KING: MOHAMMED VI (1999–)

Even as he suffered his final illnesses, King Hassan II bestrode the Moroccan scene, and the possibility that he might depart leaving a political vacuum alarmed many Moroccans, as well as many of the king's allies abroad. This dread about the future was fuelled by concerns that the kingdom could be divided by ethnic and regional rivalries – a fear the Palace, ever schooled in Moroccan traditions of divide-and-rule, did nothing to play down. Concern about the future as well as the loss of a historic leader was reflected in the outpourings of grief at the July 1999 funeral of a king who was hugely respected, but was perhaps less widely loved by his subjects.

However, the hand over to **King Mohammed VI** went smoothly, and ushered in a **new style** of rule. Indeed, after years when the 35-year-old crown prince's ability to lead such a large and complex country had been widely questioned, Sidi Mohammed emerged from his father's shadow to make an impressive start. He won considerable popular support by visiting the **troubled north** (long ignored by Hassan), restoring **civil rights** to those remaining political prisoners not covered by previous amnesties (with over 10,000 released in first year amnesties), and promising a more **relaxed and consensual** form of rule.

In what seemed like a North African version of Robert Graves' novel of Roman political life, *I Claudius*, Mohammed VI quickly showed he could wield his own **authority** by sacking Hassan's powerful but unpopular right-hand man, Minister of State for the Interior **Driss Basri**. He has thus emerged from the shadows as very much his own king. Whether being photographed by paparazzi in jeans, leather jacket and shades chilling out in Paris, or wooing the potentially fractious population of Morocco's impoverished, cannabis-producing north, he has won widespread popular support. This has been especially the case among **younger Moroccans**, whose alienation from political parties dominated by an ageing nomenklatura and a society whose benefits have gone to a small and gilded middle class threatened to feed into support for illegal Islamist groups.

But Mohammed was anointed king with **much still to be done** if Morocco's social and economic liberalization, belatedly sponsored by an older, more mellow Hassan, was to take root – and there are signs that, for some Moroccans at least, the honeymoon period is coming to a close. The young monarch has got on well with the ageing prime minister, but Youssoufi and many of his younger supporters are looking for more **political reforms** which may not be forthcoming.

For all the talk of reform, King Mohammed's Morocco is still very much dominated by the Palace – where a younger generation of advisers is settling in, many drawn from the **royal school** created by King Hassan to educate his sons with the brightest and best the kingdom could offer. These are an impressive body of men (and a few women now reaching top jobs), but while they talk the language of globalization, their political mandate remains essentially feudal. The king himself, meantime, fresh thinking and more tolerant of old rivals though he may be, remains rooted in his father's political traditions, as both monarch and Al Amir Al Muminin (commander of the faithful).

With the king playing a hands-on role in overhauling the political environment, a major question is what role, if any, **radical Islamists** are to play in a changing political system. In May 2000, Mohammed made headlines by freeing his father's most implacable critic, **Abdessalam Yassine**, leader of the banned **Al-Adl wal Ihsane** (Justice and Charity) movement. Until then, Al-Adl wal Ihsane had been considered politically beyond the pale. Basri, the arch political player of the 1980s and 1990s, toyed with the Islamist movement, allowing the more pliable **MPCD** to enter parliament in 1998 in a classic piece of Moroccan divide-and-rule. Should Al-Adl wal Ihsane be allowed to compete in the formal political arena, its opposition would be much more resolute, as is apparent from the behaviour of Al Adl wal Ihsane students who dominate politics on many campuses, and the state would be unlikely to display great tolerance.

Nonetheless, to date, the young king has proved surprisingly successful in rejuvenating the monarchical and political system. He has needed to do so, if he is now to address the **crucial issues** facing Morocco: unemployment, poverty, a huge young population, the need for a resolution in the Western Sahara, and the spectre of radical Islam that has torn apart neighbouring Algeria. The hope is that the West, and in particular the European Union (by whom Morocco is seen as a buffer against a wave of African immigration and its daily tragedy of boat people attempting to cross the straits to Spain) will provide support for both the king and system to prosper.

CHRONOLOGY:
EVENTS AND MONUMENTS

10,000– 5000 BC	**Capsian** and **Mouillian Man** spread across the Maghreb Neolithic cultures	**Rock carvings** in Oukaïmeden, Foum El Hassan and other less accessible sites
1100 BC	**Phoenician** settlements	Bronze Age. First trading port in **Lixus** (near Larache)
500 BC	**Carthaginians** take over Phoenician settlements and greatly expand them	Remains in Lixus, and in Rabat Archaeological Museum
146 BC	Fall of Carthage at end of the Third Punic War; Roman influence spreads into **Berber kingdoms** of Mauretania-Numidia	Bust of Juba II (Rabat)
27 BC	Direct **Roman** rule under Emperor Caligula	**Volubilis** developed as provincial capital; other minor sites at Lixus and Tangier
253 AD	Roman legions withdrawn	Mosaics in Tetouan and Rabat museums
429	**Vandals** pass through	
535	**Byzantines** occupy Ceuta	

ISLAM

622	Muhammad and followers move from Mecca to Medina and start spread of Islam	
ca. 705	**Moussa Ibn Nasr** establishes Arab rule in north and pre-Sahara, and in 711 leads Berber invasion of Spain	

IDRISSID DYNASTY (788–923)

788	**Moulay Idriss** establishes first Moroccan Arab dynasty	Founding of Moulay Idriss and Fes
807	Moulay Idriss II (807–836)	**Fes** developed with Kairouan and Andalucian refugee quarters, and establishment of Kairaouine Mosque
10th–11th c.	Hilali tribes wreak havoc on Maghrebi infrastructure	

ALMORAVID DYNASTY (1062–1145)

1062	**Youssef bin Tachfine** establishes capital in Marrakesh; first great Berber dynasty	**Koubba** in **Marrakesh** is only surviving monument, except for walls and possibly a minaret in **Tit** (near El Jadida)
1090	Almoravid invasion of **Spain**	

ALMOHAD DYNASTY (1147–1248)

1120s	**Ibn Toumert** sets up a ribat in Tin Mal in the High Atlas	Ruined mosque of **Tin Mal**

1145– 1147	**Abd El Moumen** takes first Fes and then Marrakesh	Extensive building of walls, gates and **minarets**, including the Koutoubia in **Marrakesh**

1195   **Yacoub El Mansour** (1184–99) extends rule to Spain, and east to Tripoli

New capital begun in **Rabat**: Hassan Tower, Oudaia Gate

1212   Defeat in Spain at Las Navas de Tolosa

MERENID DYNASTY (1248–1465)

Abou Youssef Yacoub (1258–86) establishes effective power

Zaouia and mausoleum in **Chellah** (Rabat); new city (El Djedid) built in **Fes**
Medersas in Fes (Bou Inania, Attarin, etc), Meknes and Salé

Abou El Hassan (1331–51) and **Abou Inan** (1351–58), two of the most successful Merenids, extend rule briefly to Tunis

Portuguese begin attacks on Moroccan coast, taking Ceuta and later other cities

Portuguese cistern in El Jadida; walls and remains in Azzemour, Asilah and Safi

WATTASID DYNASTY (1465–1554)

Wattasids – Merenid viziers – usurp power

Chaouen built and **Tetouan** founded again by refugees

Fall of **Granada**, last Muslim kingdom in Spain; Jewish and Muslim refugees settle in Morocco over next 100 years or so

Marabouts establish zaouias, controlling parts of the country

SAADIAN DYNASTY (1554–1669)

Mohammed esh Sheikh (d. 1557) founds dynasty in Marrakesh

Saadian Tombs and **Ben Youssef medersa** (Marrakesh); pavilion extensions to **Kairaouine Mosque** (Fes)

Battle of Three Kings leads to accession of **Ahmed El Mansour** (1578–1603), who goes on to conquer Timbuktu and the gold and slave routes to the south

El Badi palace (Marrakesh)

Pirate **Republic of Bou Regreg** set up by Andalucian refugees

Rabat Medina

ALAOUITE DYNASTY (1669–)

Moulay Ismail imposes the Alaouite dynasty on Morocco

New imperial capital in **Meknes** (Ismail's mausoleum, etc); **kasbahs** and **forts** built; **palaces** in Tangier and Rabat

Sidi Mohammed (1757–90)

Moulay Suleiman (1792–1822)

Ismail and his successors rebuild **grand mosques**, etc, especially in **Marrakesh**, where many later Alaouites make their capital – many of the city's **pavilions** and **gardens** date from the early eighteenth century

Final burst of **palace** building – El Badi (Marrakesh), Palais Jamai (Fes)

Treaty of Fes brings into being French and Spanish **"Protectorates" (1912–56)**

European **Villes Nouvelles** built outside the Moroccan Medinas; **"Mauresque"** architecture developed for administrative buildings

T'Hami El Glaoui becomes pasha of Marrakesh **(1907)**. French use T'Hami El Glaoui to conquer the southern tribes **(1912)**

Glaoui palaces in Telouet and Marrakesh; **kasbah** fortresses throughout the south

Riffian revolt under Abd El Krim **(1921)**

Nationalist **Istiqlal** party formed in Fes **(1943)**

Independence (1956)

Accession of **Hassan II (1961)**

Green March into Western Sahara (1975)

Democratic elections (1997)

New royal **palaces** in all major cities – most recently and spectacularly in Agadir. **Hassan II Mosque** in Casablanca

Accession of **Mohammed VI (1999)**

ISLAM IN MOROCCO

It's difficult to get any grasp of Morocco, and even more so of Moroccan history, without first knowing something of Islam. What follows is a very basic background: some theory, some history and an idea of Morocco's place in the modern Islamic world. For more depth on each of these subjects, see the book listings on p.607.

BEGINNINGS: PRACTICE AND BELIEF

Islam was a new religion born of the wreckage of the Greco-Roman world beyond the Mediterranean. Its founder, a merchant named **Muhammad** (this is the standard spelling today of the Prophet's name – and a more accurate transcription from the Arabic) from the wealthy city of Mecca (now in Saudi Arabia), was chosen as God's Prophet: in about 609 AD, he began to receive divine messages which he transcribed directly into the **Koran** (*Qu'ran*), Islam's Bible. This was the same God worshipped by Jews and Christians – Jesus (*Aïssa* in Arabic) is one of the major prophets in Islam – but Muslims claim that he had been misunderstood by both earlier religions.

The distinctive feature of this new faith was directness – a reaction to the increasing complexity of established religions and an obvious attraction. In Islam there is no intermediary between man and God in the form of an institutionalized priesthood or complicated liturgy, as in Christianity; and worship, in the form of prayer, is a direct and personal communication with God. Believers face five essential requirements, the so-called **"Pillars of faith"**: prayer five times daily (*salat*); the pilgrimage (*hadj*) to Mecca; the Ramadan fast (*sanm*); almsgiving (*zakat*); and, most fundamental of all, the acceptance that "There is no God but God and Muhammad is His Prophet" (*shahada*).

THE PILLARS OF FAITH

The Pillars of Faith are still central to Muslim life, articulating and informing daily existence. Ritual **prayers** are the most visible. Bearing in mind that the Islamic day begins at sunset, the five daily times are sunset, after dark, dawn, noon and afternoon. Prayers can be performed anywhere, but preferably in a mosque, or in Arabic, a *djemaa*. In the past, and even today in some places, a *muezzin* would climb his minaret each time and summon the faithful.

Nowadays, the call is likely to be less frequent, and prerecorded; even so, this most distinctive of Islamic sounds has a beauty all its own, especially when neighbouring *muezzins* are audible simultaneously. Their message is simplicity itself: "God is most great (*Allah Akhbar*). I testify that there is no God but Allah. I testify that Muhammad is His Prophet. Come to prayer, come to security. God is great." Another phrase is added in the morning: "Prayer is better than sleep".

Prayers are preceded by ritual washing and are recited with the feet bare. Facing Mecca (the direction indicated in a mosque by the *mihrab*), the worshipper recites the Fatina, the first chapter of the Koran: "Praise be to God, Lord of the worlds, the Compassionate, the Merciful, King of the Day of Judgement. We worship you and seek your aid. Guide us on the straight path, the path of those on whom you have bestowed your Grace, not the path of those who incur your anger nor of those who go astray." The same words are then repeated twice in the prostrate position, with some interjections of *Allah Akhbar*. It is a highly ritualized procedure, the prostrate position symbolic of the worshipper's role as servant (Islam literally means "obedience"), and the sight of thousands of people going through the same motions simultaneously in a mosque is a powerful one. On Islam's holy day, Friday, all believers are expected to attend prayers in their local grand mosque. Here the whole community comes together in worship led by an *imam*, who may also deliver the *khutba*, or sermon.

Ramadan is the name of the ninth month in the lunar Islamic calendar, the month in which the Koran was revealed to Muhammad. For the whole of the month, believers must obey a rigorous fast (the custom was originally modelled on Jewish and Christian practice), forsaking all forms of consumption between sunrise and sundown; this includes food, drink, cigarettes and any form of sexual contact. Only a few categories of people are exempted: travellers, children, pregnant women and warriors engaged in a *jihad*, or holy war. Given the climates in which many Muslims live, the fast is a formidable undertaking, but in practice it becomes a time of intense celebration.

The pilgrimage, or **hadj**, to Mecca is an annual event, with millions flocking to Muhammad's birthplace from all over the world. Here they go through several days of rituals, the central one being a sevenfold circumambulation of the Kaba, before kissing a black stone set in its wall. Islam requires that all believers go on a *hadj* as often as is practically possible, but for the poor it may well be a once-in-a-lifetime occasion, and is sometimes replaced by a series of visits to lesser, local shrines – in Morocco, for instance, to Fes and Moulay Idriss.

Based on these central articles, the new Islamic faith proved to be inspirational. Muhammad's own Arab nation was soon converted, and the Arabs then proceeded to carry their religion far and wide in an extraordinarily rapid territorial expansion. Many peoples of the Middle East and North Africa, who for centuries had only grudgingly accepted Roman paganism or Christianity, embraced Islam almost immediately.

DEVELOPMENT IN MOROCCO

Islam made a particularly spectacular arrival in Morocco. **Oqba Ibn Nafi**, the crusading general who had already expelled the Byzantines from Tunisia, marked his subjugation of the far west by riding fully armed into the waves of the Atlantic. "O God," he is said to have exclaimed, "I call you to witness that there is no ford here. If there was, I would cross it."

This compulsory appreciation of Morocco's remoteness was prophetic in a way, because over the succeeding centuries Moroccan Islam was to acquire and retain a highly distinctive character. Where mainstream Islamic history is concerned, its development has been relatively straightforward – it was virtually untouched, for instance, by the Sunni–Shia conflict that split the Muslim world – but the country's unusual geographical and social circumstances have conspired to tip the balance away from official orthodoxy.

Orthodoxy, by its very nature, has to be an urban-based tradition. Learned men – lawyers, Koranic scholars and others – could only congregate in the cities where, gathered together and known collectively as the *ulema*, they regulated the faith. In Islam, this included both law

and education. Teaching was at first based entirely in the mosques; later, it was conducted through a system of colleges, or medersas, in which students would live while studying at the often adjoining mosque. In most parts of the Islamic world, this very learned and sophisticated urban hierarchy was dominant. But Morocco also developed a powerful tradition of **popular religion**, first manifested in the eighth-century Kharijite rebellion – which effectively divided the country into separate Berber kingdoms – and endures to this day in the mountains and countryside.

MARABOUTS

There are three main strands of this popular religion, all of them deriving from the worship of saints. Everywhere in Morocco, as well as elsewhere in North Africa, the countryside is dotted with small domed **marabouts**: the tombs of holy men, which became centres of worship and pilgrimage. This elevation of individuals goes against strict Islamic teaching, but probably derives from the Berbers' pre-Islamic tendency to focus worship round individual holy men. At its simplest local level, these saint cults attracted the loyalty of the Moroccan villages and the more remote regions.

More prosperous cults would also endow educational institutions attached to the marabout, known as **zaouias**, which provided an alternative to the official education given in urban medersas. These inevitably posed a threat to the authority of the urban hierarchy, and as rural cults extended their influence, some became so popular that they endowed their saints with genealogies traced back to the Prophet. The title accorded to these men and their descendants was Shereef, and many grew into strong political forces. The classic example in Morocco is the tomb of Moulay Idriss – in the eighth century just a local marabout, but eventually, the base of the Idrissid clan, a centre of enormous influence that reached far beyond its rural origins.

Loyalty to a particular family – religiously sanctified, but essentially political – was at the centre of the shereefian movements. In the third strand of popular devotion, the focus was more narrowly religious. Again, the origins lay in small, localized cults of individuals, but these were individuals worshipped for their magical and mystical powers. Taken up and developed by subsequent followers, their rituals became the focal point of **brotherhoods** of initiates.

THE AISSAOUA

Perhaps the most famous Moroccan brotherhood is that of Sidi Mohammed Bin Aissa. Born in Souss in the fifteenth century, he travelled in northern Morocco before settling down as a teacher in Meknes and founding a zaouia. His powers of mystical healing became famous there, and he provoked enough official suspicion to be exiled briefly to the desert – where he again revealed his exceptional powers by proving himself immune to scorpions, snakes, live flames and other hostile manifestations. His followers tried to achieve the same state of grace. Six hundred were said to have attained perfection – and during the saint's lifetime, zaouias devoted to his teachings were founded in Figuig and elsewhere in the Maghreb.

Bound by its practice of a common source of ritual, the Aissaoua brotherhood made itself notorious with displays of eating scorpions, walking on hot coals and other ecstatic practices designed to bring union with God. It was perhaps the most flamboyant of these brotherhoods, but most at any rate used some kind of dancing or music, and indeed continued to do so well into this century. The more extreme and fanatical of these rites are now outlawed, though the attainment of trance is still an important part of the moussems, or festivals, of the various confraternities.

TOWARDS CRISIS

With all its different forms, Islam permeated every aspect of the country's pre-twentieth-century life. Unlike Christianity, at least Protestant Christianity, which to some extent has accepted the separation of church and state, Islam sees no such distinction. **Civil law** was provided by the *sharia*, the religious law contained in the Koran, and **intellectual life** by the *msids* (Koranic primary schools where the 6200 verses were learned by heart) and by the great medieval mosque universities, of which the Kairaouine in Fes (together with the Zitoura in Tunis and the Al Azhar in Cairo) was the most important in the Arab world.

The religious basis of Arab study and intellectual life did not prevent its scholars and scientists from producing work that was hundreds of years ahead of contemporary "Dark Age" Europe. The remains of a monumental water clock in Fes and the work of the historian Ibn Khaldun, are just two Moroccan examples. Arab work in developing and transmitting multicultural influences (Greco-Roman, Persian, Indian and Chinese) was also vital to the whole development of the European Renaissance. By this time, however, the Islamic world – and isolated Morocco in particular – was beginning to move away from the West. The Crusades had been one enduring influence promoting division. Another was the Islamic authorities themselves, increasingly suspicious (like the Western Church) of any challenge and actively discouraging of innovation. At first it did not matter in political terms that Islamic culture became static. But by the end of the eighteenth century, Europe was ready to take advantage. Napoleon's expedition to Egypt in 1798 marked the beginning of a century in which virtually every Islamic country came under the control of a **European power**.

Islam cannot, of course, be held solely responsible for the Muslim world's material decline. But because it influences every part of its believers' lives, and because East–West rivalry had always been viewed in primarily religious terms, the nineteenth and twentieth centuries saw something of a **crisis in religious confidence**. Why had Islam's former power now passed to infidel foreigners?

REACTIONS

Reactions and answers veered between two extremes. There were those who felt that Islam should try to incorporate some of the West's materialism; on the other side, there were movements holding that Islam should turn its back on the West, purify itself of all corrupt additions and thus rediscover its former power. While they were colonies of European powers, however, Muslim nations had little chance of putting any such ideas into effective practice. These could only emerge in the form of co-operation with, or rebellion against, the ruling power. But the postwar era of **decolonization**, and the simultaneous acquisition through oil of relative economic independence, brought the Islamic world suddenly face to face with the question of its own spiritual identity. How should it deal with Western values and influence, now that it could afford – both politically and economically – almost total rejection? A return to the totality of Islam – **fundamentalism** – is a conscious choice of one consistent spiritual identity, one that is deeply embedded in the consciousness of a culture already unusually aware of tradition. It is also a rejection of the West and its colonial and exploitative values. Traditional Islam, at least in some interpretations, offers a positivist brand of freedom that is clearly opposed to the negative freedoms of Western materialism. The most vehement Islamic fundamentalists, in Morocco as elsewhere, are not passive reactionaries dwelling in the past, but young radicals – often students – eager to assert their "anti-imperialist" religion.

MODERN MOROCCO

There are two basic reasons why only a few Islamic countries have embraced a rigidly traditional or fundamentalist stance. The first is an ethical one: however undesirable Western materialism may appear, the rejection of all Western values involves rejecting also what the West sees as the "benefits" of development. Perhaps it is begging the question in strictly Islamic terms to say that the emancipation of women, for example, is a "benefit". But the leaders of many countries feel that such steps are both desirable and reconcilable with a more liberal brand of Islam, which will retain its place in the national identity. The other argument against militant Islam is a more pragmatic, economic one. Morocco is only one of many countries which would suffer severe economic hardship if they cut themselves off from the West: they have to tread a narrow line that allows them to maintain good relations both with the West and with the Islamic world.

ISLAM AND THE STATE

In Morocco today, Islam is the official state religion, and King Mohammed's secular status is interwoven with his role as "commander of the faithful". Internationally, too, he plays a leading role. Meetings of the Islamic Conference Organisation are frequently held in Morocco and, in one of the most unlikely exchanges, students from Tashkent in Uzbekistan came to study at Fes University. For all these indications of Islamic solidarity, though, **state policy** remains distinctly moderate – sometimes in the face of extremist pressure.

RURAL RELIGION

Not surprisingly, all of this has had more effect on urban than on rural life – a difference accentuated by the gap between them that has always existed in Morocco. Polarization in religious attitudes is far greater in the **cities**, where there is tension between those for and against secularization, as well as a large body of urban poor, for whom Islamic fundamentalism can seem to offer solutions.

Away from the cities, religious attitudes have changed less over the past two generations. Religious brotherhoods such as the Aissaoua have declined since the beginning of the century, when they were still very powerful, and the influence of mystics generally has fallen. As the official histories put it, popular credulity in Morocco provided an ideal setting for charlatans as well as saviours, and much of this has now passed. All the same, the rhythms of **rural life** still revolve around local marabouts, and the annual moussems, or festivals-cum-pilgrimages, are still vital and impressive displays.

WILDLIFE

Few countries in the Mediterranean region can match the variety and quality of the wildlife habitats to be found in Morocco. Whether you are an expert botanist, a dedicated bird-watcher or simply a visitor with an interest in a totally different environment, the wildlife experience of your travels should be extremely rewarding.

HABITATS

There are three main **vegetation zones** which can be distinguished as you travel through the country.

The most northerly and westerly zone – the **Mediterranean** and **northern Atlantic coastal strips** – is typical of the European Med region, encompassing semi-arid pastoral lands of olive groves and cultivated fields.

Further inland lie the barren **Rif mountains** (the home of *kif* or marijuana plants) and the more fertile **Middle Atlas range**, where the montane flora is dominated by cedar forest which, despite its reduction in more recent times, provides a unique mosaic of forest and grassland. The **High Atlas**, beyond, is more arid but has its own montane flora.

Finally, there is the most southerly zone of the desert fringe or **Sahel**, a harsh environment characterized by pebbly *hammada*, tussock grass, the occasional acacia tree and a number of sand dunes, or *ergs*.

These zones provide a wide variety of **habitat types**, from coastal cliffs, sand dunes and estuarine marshlands to subalpine forests and grasslands, to the semi-arid and true desert areas of the south. The **climate** is similarly diverse, being warm and humid along the coastal zones, relatively cooler at altitude within the Atlas ranges and distinctly hotter and drier south of the High Atlas, where midday temperatures will often climb higher than 40°C during the summer months. Not surprisingly, the plant and animal life in Morocco is accordingly parochial, species distributions being closely related to the habitat and climate types to which they are specifically adapted.

Many of these habitats are currently under threat from land reclamation, tourist development and the inevitable process of **desertification**, and the resulting habitat loss is endangering the existence of several of the more sensitive species of plants and animals to be found in Morocco. Human persecution of wildlife, however, is limited, as the tribes are largely disarmed and hunting is more the pre serve of French tourists.

On the positive side, the *International Committee for Bird Preservation* (I.C.B.P.) and the *Eaux de Forêt* of the Moroccan Agriculture Ministry have been involved in the designation of protected status to several **wetland sites** along the Atlantic coast; at Merdja Zerga and Lac de Sidi Bourhaba, education centres have been set up with resident wardens and interpretative materials. The government has also done some good work on the problems of erosion and desertification and has implemented extensive and impressive schemes of **afforestation and reclamation**.

BIRDS

In addition to a unique range of **resident bird species**, distributed throughout the country on the basis of vegetation and climatic zonation, the periods of late March/April and September/ October provide the additional sight of vast **bird migrations**.

Large numbers of birds which have overwintered south of the Sahara migrate northwards in the spring to breed in Europe, completing their return passage through Morocco in the autumn. Similarly, some of the more familiar north European species choose Morocco for their overwintering grounds to avoid the harshness of the northern winter. These movements can form a dramatic spectacle in the skies, dense flocks of birds moving in procession through bottleneck areas such as Tangier and Ceuta where sea crossings are at their shortest.

RESIDENT SPECIES

The **resident species** can be subdivided on the basis of their preferred habitat type:

Coastal/marine species. These include the familiar moorhen and less familiar **crested coot**, an incongruous bird which, when breeding, resembles its northern European relation but with an additional pair of bright red knobs on either side of its white facial shield. Other species include the diminutive **little ringed plover** and **rock dove**.

South of the High Atlas. Among these are some of the true desert specialities, such as the **sandgrouse** (spotted, crowned, pin-tailed and black-bellied varieties), **stone curlew, cream-coloured courser** and **Houbara bustard** – the latter standing over two feet in height. Other well-represented groups include **wheatears** (4 varieties), **larks** (7 varieties) and **finches**, **buntings, warblers, corvids, jays, magpies, choughs** and **ravens** (crow family), **tits** (primarily blue, great and coal) and **owls** (barn, eagle, tawny and little). Although many of these species can be found in northern Europe, subtle variations in colour and pattern can be misleading and a closer look is often worthwhile.

Raptors (birds of prey) provide an enticing roll call of resident species, including **red-** and **black-shouldered kite, long-legged buzzard, Bonelli's, golden** and **tawny eagles, Barbary, lanner** and **peregrine falcons** and more familiar **kestrel**.

MIGRANT SPECIES

Migrant species can be subdivided into three categories: summer visitors, winter visitors and passage migrants.

Summer visitors. The number of species visiting Morocco during the summer months may be low but includes some particularly interesting varieties. Among the **marine/coastal types** are the **manx shearwater, Eleonora's falcon** and **bald ibis** – in one of its few remaining breeding colonies in the world.

The **mountain species** include the small **Egyptian vulture** and several of the **hirundines** (swallows and martins) and their close relatives, the **swifts**, such as **little swift**, **red-rumped swallow** and the more familiar **house martin**.

A particularly colourful addition at this time of year in the **Sahel regions** is the **blue-cheeked bee-eater**, a vibrant blend of red, yellow, blue and green, unmistakeable if seen close up.

Winter visitors. The list of winter visitors is more extensive but composed primarily of the marine or coastal/estuarine varieties. The most common of the truly marine (*pelagic*) flocks include **Cory's shearwater, storm petrel, gannet, razorbill** and **puffin**. These are often found congregated on the sea surface, along with any combination of **skuas** (great, arctic and pomarine varieties), **terns** (predominantly sandwich) and **gulls** (including black-headed, Mediterranean, little, herring and the rarer Audouin's) flying overhead.

A variety of coastal/estuarine species also arrive during this period, forming large mixed flocks of **grebes** (great-crested, little and black-necked), **avocet, cattle egret, spoonbill, greater flamingo**, and wildfowl such as **shelduck, wigeon, teal, pintail, shoveler, tufted duck, pochard** and **coot**.

Migrant **birds of prey** during the winter months include the **common buzzard** (actually a rarity in Morocco), **dashing merlin** and both **marsh** and **hen harriers**.

Passage migrants. There are many birds which simply pass through Morocco en route to other areas, and are thus known as passage migrants. Well-represented groups include **petrels** (5 varieties) and **terns** (6 varieties) along coastal areas, and **herons** (4 varieties), **bitterns, cranes, white** and **black stork** and **crake** (spotted, little, Baillon's and corncrake) in the marshland/estuarine habitats.

Further inland, flocks of multicoloured **roller**, **bee-eater** and **hoopoe** mix with various **larks**, **wagtails** and **warblers** (13 varieties), forming large "windfall" flocks when climatic conditions worsen abruptly. Individual species of note include the aptly named **black-winged stilt**, an elegant black and white wader, with long, vibrant red legs, often found among the disused saltpans; and the nocturnal **nightjars** (both common and red-necked), which are most easily seen by the reflection of their eyes in the headlamps of passing cars.

Birds of prey can also form dense passage flocks, often mixed and including large numbers of **black kite, short-toed eagle** and **honey buzzard**. Over open water spaces, the majestic

THE SHAPE OF MOROCCO

For geologists, Morocco is a place of pilgrimage, a country where the structure of the land lies exposed to view, quite unlike other more temperate parts of Europe where it is hidden by grass, soil and cities.

Long after the layers of rock forming Morocco were laid down at the bottom of some early sea or river estuary, an ocean formed between Europe and Africa at a time when Africa was still attached to Brazil. The rocks forming the Anti-Atlas and Tafilalt region are therefore very old indeed (in places Precambrian) whilst the High Atlas on the other side of a long fault-line are quite young (Jurassic). It was not until quite recent geological times that the whole of Africa swung round anticlockwise, more or less, to its present position. About the time the chalk Downs of southern England were being laid down, Spain was moving westwards along the Moroccan coast.

When you travel through the landscape of Morocco, bear in mind that these rocks were formed when Europe and America were in a different position to where they are now and that the dry rock surfaces you will encounter were not caused by the tiny streams, flash floods and winds of the present, but by climates many millenia past.

osprey may be seen demonstrating its mastery of the art of fishing.

"Vagrant" species. Finally, Morocco has its share of occasional or "vagrant" species, so classified on the unusual or rare nature of their appearances. These include such exotic varieties as **glossy ibis**, **pale-chanting goshawk**, **Arabian bustard** and **lappet-faced vulture**. Inevitably, they provide few, if any, opportunities for viewing.

FLORA

In the light of its climatic harshness and unreliable rains, the flora of Morocco is remarkably diverse. Plant species have adapted strategies to cope with the Moroccan climate, becoming either specifically adapted to one particular part of the environment (a habitat type), or evolving multiple structural and/or biochemical means of surviving the more demanding seasons. Others have adopted the proverbial "ostrich" philosophy of burying their heads (or rather their seeds in this case) in the sand and waiting for climatic conditions to become favourable – often an extremely patient process.

The type of flowers that you see will obviously depend entirely on where and when you decide to visit. Some parts of the country have very short flowering seasons because of high temperatures or lack of available water, but generally the best times of year for flowering plants are either just before or just after the main temperature extremes of the North African summer.

The very best time to visit is **spring** (late March to mid May), when most flowers are in bloom. Typical spring flowers include purple

barbary nut iris, deep blue **germander** and the aromatic **claret thyme**, all of which frequent the slopes of the Atlas ranges. Among the **woodland flora** at this time of year are the red **pheasant's eye**, pink **virburnum**, violet **calamint** and purple **campanula**, which form a resplendent carpet beneath the cedar forests. By late spring, huge tracts of the High Atlas slopes are aglow with the golden hues of **broom** and, secluded among the lowland cereal crops, splashes of magenta reveal the presence of **wild gladioli**.

By **midsummer** the climate is at its most extreme and the main concern of plants is to avoid desiccation in the hot, arid conditions. Two areas of exception to these conditions are the **Atlantic coastal zones**, where sea mists produce a slightly more humid environment, and the upper reaches of the **Atlas ranges** which remain cool and moist at altitude throughout the year. Spring comes later in these loftier places and one can find many of the more familiar garden rock plants, such as the **saxifrages** and **anemones** in flower well into late July and August.

Once the hottest part of the summer is past (September onwards), then a second, **autumn** bloom begins with later varieties such as **cyclamens** and **autumn crocus**.

HABITAT VARIETIES

The range of plants you are likely to encounter is similarly influenced by specific habitats:

Seashores. These include a variety of sand-tolerant species, with their adaptations for coping with water loss, such as **sea holly** and **sea stocks**. The dune areas contrast starkly with the Salicornia-dominated salt marshes – monotonous landscapes broken only by the occasional dead **tamarisk** tree.

Arable land. Often dominated by cereal crops – particularly in the more humid Atlantic and Mediterranean coastal belts – or **olive and eucalyptus groves**, which extend over large areas. The general lack of use of herbicides allows the coexistence of many **"wild flowers"**, especially in the fallow hay meadows which are ablaze with the colours of **wild poppy**, **ox-eye daisy**, **muscali** (borage) and various yellow composites.

Lowland hills. These form a fascinating mosaic of dense, shrubby species, known as *maquis*, lower-lying, more grazed areas, known as *garrigue*, and more open areas with abundant aromatic herbs and shrubs.

Maquis vegetation is dominated by **cistaceae (rockroses)** and the endemic **argan** tree. The lower-lying *garrigue* is more typically composed of aromatic herbs such as **rosemary**, **thyme** and **golden milfoil**. Among these shrubs, within the more open areas, you may find an abundance of other species such as **anemones, grape hyacinths** and **orchids**.

The orchids are particularly outstanding, including several of the *Ophrys* group, which use the strategy of insect imitation to entice pollinators and as such have an intricate arrangement of flowers.

Mountain slopes. Flowering later in the year, the slopes of the **Atlas ranges** are dominated by the blue-mauve **pitch trefoil** and golden drifts of **broom**. As you travel south through the Middle Atlas, the verdant **ash, oak, atlantic cedar** and **juniper forest** dominates the landscape. Watered by the depressions that sweep across from the Atlantic, these slopes form a luxurious spectacle, ablaze with colour in spring.

Among the glades beneath the **giant cedars** of the Middle Atlas, a unique flora may be found, dominated by the vibrant **pink peony**. Other plants which form this spectacular carpet include **geranium, anchusa, pink verburnum, saffron mulleins, mauve cupidanes, violet calamint, purple campanula**, the diminutive **scarlet dianthus** and a wealth of **golden composites** and **orchids**.

Further south, the **Toubkal National Park** boasts its own varieties and spring bloom; the thyme and thorny caper are interspersed with the blue-mauve **pit trefoil**, **pink convulvulus**, the silver-blue and pinks of everlasting flowers of **cupidane** and **phagnalon** and golden spreads of **broom**. At the highest altitudes, the limestone Atlas slopes form a bleak environment, either covered by winter snows or scorched by the summer sun. However, some species are capable of surviving even under these conditions, the most conspicuous of these being the widespread purple tussocks of the **hedgehog broom**.

Steppeland. South of the Atlas, temperatures rise sharply and the effect on flora is dramatic; the extensive cedar forests and their multicoloured carpets are replaced by sparse grass plains where the horizon is broken only by the occasional stunted **holm oak, juniper** or **acacia**. Commonly known as wattle trees, the acacia were introduced into North Africa from Australia and their large yellow flowers add a welcome splash of colour to this barren landscape. One of the few crop plants grown in this area is the **date palm**, which is particularly resistant to drought. The steppeland is characterized by the presence of **esparto grass**, which exudes toxins to prevent the growth of competing species. These halfa grass plains are only broken by the flowering of **broom** in May. Within rocky outcrops, this spring bloom can become a mini-explosion of colour, blending the hues of **cistus** and **chrysanthemum** with the pink of **rockrose**, yellow of **milfoil** and mauve of **rosemary**.

Desert fringe (*hammada*). Even the desert areas provide short-lived blooms of colour during the infrequent spring showers; dwarf varieties such as pink **asphodels**, yellow **daisies** and mauve **statice** thrive briefly while conditions are favourable. Under the flat stones of the hammada, colonies of lichens and microscopic algae eke out an existence; their shade tolerance and ability to obtain sufficient water from the occasional condensation which takes place under these stones allows them to survive in this harshest of environments. No matter how inhospitable the environment or extreme the climate, somewhere, somehow, there are plants surviving – if you take time to look for them.

AMPHIBIANS

There are very few remaining amphibians in Morocco – relics of a bygone, more fertile era, now restricted to scarce watery havens. They are more apparent by sound than sight, forming a resonant chorus during the night and early morning. One of the more common varieties is the **green frog**, typically immersed up to its eyes in water, releasing the odd giveaway croak. Another widespread individual, most abundant in the regions round Marrakesh, is the **western marsh frog**.

The toads are represented by the **Berber toad**, another nocturnal baritone, and the **Mauritanian toad** whose large size and characteristic yellow and brown-spotted coloration make it quite unmistakeable.

Some Moroccan amphibians are capable of survival at surprisingly **high altitudes**. The **painted frog** is a common participant in the chorus that emanates from the *oueds* (riverbeds) of the High Atlas, while the wide-ranging whistle of the North African race of the **green toad**, famed for its ability to change its colour with the surrounding environment, can be heard at altitudes in excess of 2000m.

REPTILES

Reptiles are far more widespread in their distribution than their amphibious cousins. Their range extends from the Mediterranean coastal strip – where the few remaining **tortoises** (sadly depleted through "craft items" sold to the tourist trade) are to be seen – to the *hammada* itself.

The forested slopes of the Middle Atlas are frequented by the **blue and green-eyed lizard** and the **chameleon**; the former uses its size and agility to capture its prey, whereas the latter relies on the more subtle strategy of colour co-ordination, stealth and a quicksilver tongue.

Several species have adapted to the specific environment of the stony **walls** that form the towns and villages. The **Spanish wall lizard** is a common basker on domestic walls, as is the **Moorish gecko**.

Further south, the drier, scrub-covered slopes form an ideal habitat for two of Morocco's largest **snakes**. The **horseshoe snake** (which can exceed 2m in length) and **Montpelier snake** hunt by day, feeding on birds and rats. Also found in this harsh environment are the **Atlas agama** and **fringe-toed lizard**.

Finally, there are the **desert "specialists"**, such as the **Algerian sand lizard** and **Berber skink**. The skinks make a fascinating spectacle; commonly known as "sand fish", they inhabit the ergs and appear to "swim" through the sand, where their yellow-brown coloration provides the perfect camouflage. Of numerous species of lizard that live in the *hammada*, the more obvious include the many colours and varieties of the **spiny-tailed lizard** (*dhub* in Arabic), an omnivore feeding on a mixed diet of insects, fruit and young shoots. The one really poisonous species is the **horned viper**, only half a metre in length, which spends the days buried just below the surface of the sand and feeds by night on jerboas and lizards.

MAMMALS

Larger animal life in Morocco is dominated by the extensive nomadic herds of goats, sheep and camel which use the most inaccessible and barren patches of wilderness as seasonal grazing areas.

One of the most impressive of the wild mammals, however, is the **Barbary ape** – in fact not a true ape but a Macaque monkey. These frequent the cedar forests south of Azrou in the Middle Atlas and can be seen on the ground foraging for food in the glades. Other inhabitants of the cedar forest include **wild boar** and **red fox**.

A speciality of the Oued Souss, outside Agadir, is the **common otter**; this is now a rare species in Morocco and can only be seen with considerable patience and some fortune.

The majority of the smaller mammals in Morocco live south of the Atlas ranges in the *hammada*, where the ever-present problem of water conservation plays a major role in the lifestyle of its inhabitants. Larger herbivores include the **Edmi gazelle** and the smaller, and rarer, **Addax antelope,** which graze the thorn bushes and dried grasses to obtain their moisture.

Many of the desert varieties reduce the problems of body temperature regulation by adopting a nocturnal lifestyle. Typical exponents of this strategy are the **desert hedgehog** and numerous small rodents such as the **jerboa**. A common predator of the jerboa is the **fennec** (desert fox), whose characteristic large ears are used for both directional hearing (invaluable as a nocturnal hunter) and heat radiation to aid body cooling.

An oddity, found in the Djebel Toubkal area of the High Atlas, is the African **elephant shrew** – a fascinating creature, like a little mouse, with an elephantine trunk.

INSECTS

Insect life is widespread throughout Morocco, its variety of form occupying unique, overlapping roles.

BUTTERFLIES

Most colourful are the butterflies, of which over a hundred species have been recorded, predominantly in the Middle and High Atlas ranges. The most obvious, which can be seen from April onwards, are generally the largest and most colourful, such as the brilliant sulphur **Cleopatra**, **large tortoiseshell** and **cardinal**. Located on the grassy slopes within the ranges are less conspicuous varieties: the **hermit**, **Spanish marbled white**, **fritillaries**, **graylings**, **hairstreaks** and **blues** – such as the small **larquin's** and **false baton**.

Later in the year, from about June onwards, the glades and woodland edges of the Middle Atlas cedar forests provide the perfect habitat for **dark green fritillaries**, while in the higher flowery fields, at altitudes of up to 2000m, **knapweed fritillaries**, **large grizzled** and **Barbary skippers** abound. Particularly attractive is the **Amanda's blue**, found at altitudes in excess of 600m through till midsummer if nectar remains available.

On the rocky slopes of Toubkal National Park, south of Marrakesh, the **Moroccan copper butterfly** may be seen flitting through the thyme. In the higher Atlas gorges (1700m or more), the **desert orange tip** is more prevalent, being found on its larval food plant, the thorny caper. The Atlas also sees one of the world's most extraordinary butterfly migrations, when waves of painted ladies and Bath whites pass through, having crossed the Sahara from West Africa, en route across the Bay of Biscay to the west of England.

OTHER INSECTS

Other common groups include **grasshoppers**, **crickets** and **locusts**. In the High Atlas, **praying mantis** may be seen, such as **eremiaphila**, whose brown coloration provides excellent camouflage.

Beetles are another common group, though they tend to avoid the heat of the day, remaining in their burrows and emerging at night to feed. The **darkling beetles** are particularly abundant and voracious scavengers.

Finally there are **arachnids**, of which there are three major groups in Morocco – scorpions, camel spiders and spiders. **Scorpions** are nocturnal, hiding under suitable covered depressions during the day such as rocks and boulders (or rucksacks and shoes). Some of the six or so species which may be found in Morocco are poisonous but most are harmless and unlikely to sting unless provoked. The **camel spiders** (or wind-scorpions) are unique. They lack a poisonous tail but possess huge jaws with which they catch their main source of prey, scorpions.

Spiders are not common in Morocco, only being found in large numbers within the Atlas ranges. Here, it is possible to see several small species of **tarantula** (not the hairy South American variety) and the white **orb-web spider** *Argiope lobata*, whose coloration acts as a disruptive pattern against pale backgrounds.

A CHECKLIST OF THE MAIN SITES

Features on key Moroccan wildlife, and especially bird, habitats are to be found throughout the guide; the main entries are boxed. They include:

● **AGADIR/OUED SOUSS** Riverbank attracts waders and wildfowl, migrant warblers and Barbary partridge. p.479.

● **AGUELMAME AZIGZA** Middle Atlas occasional inland lake and forest: hawfinch, diving duck and marbled teal in autumn/winter. p.249.

● **BOUMALNE: DESERT HAMMADA** Atlas agama and fringe-toed lizard; specialist bird species such as cream-coloured courser, red-rumped wheatear and thick-billed lark. **Houbara bustard**. p.440.

● **CEDAR FORESTS SOUTH OF AZROU** Species include green-eyed lizard and chameleon; **butterflies** from April onwards; **Barbary apes**. Moroccan woodpecker and **booted eagle**. p.248.

● **DAYET AAOUA** Another Middle Atlas occasional lake: flocks of grebes, **crested coot**, grey heron and cattle egret; migrant birds of prey include **red kite**. p.244.

● **DJEBEL TAZZEKA NATIONAL PARK** Where the Rif merges with the Middle Atlas: slopes covered in cork oak and woodland; **butterflies** from late May/early June, and **birds** such as the hoopoe. p.148.

FIELD GUIDES

There are few publications specifically about Moroccan wildlife, but some field guides to Mediterranean Europe extend coverage to North Africa, and most are in any case reasonably practicable for the area.

Butterflies
Lionel Higgins and Norman Riley *A Field Guide to the Butterflies of Britain and Europe* (Collins, UK/Stephen Green Press, US).

Flowers
Oleg Polunin and Anthony Huxley *Flowers of the Mediterranean* (Oxford UP, UK/US).

Mammals
Theodor Haltenorth and Helmut Diller *A Field Guide to the Mammals of Africa* (Collins, UK/Stephen Green Press, US).

Birds
P and F Bergier *A Birdwatcher's Guide to Morocco* (Prion Press, UK). An excellent practical guidebook which includes site-maps and species lists.
Heinzel, Fitter and Parslow *The Birds of Britain and Europe with North Africa and the Middle East* (Collins, UK/Stephen Green Press, US).

● **DJEBEL TOUBKAL NATIONAL PARK** High Atlas mountains: sights include Moorish gecko, rare butterflies; Moussier's redstart and crimson winged finch, both unique to North African mountains; hooped-petticoat daffodils, *romulea* and various other bulbs in spring. p.386.

● **ESSAOUIRA** Coastal dunes, river and offshore islands attract **waders** and **egrets**; also **Eleanora's falcon** between May and October. p.336.

● **FES** Evening roost of egret and alpine swift; **white stork** on rooftop nests of walls. p.230.

● **LAC DU SIDI BOURHABA** Freshwater lake, with outstanding **birds of prey**. p.272.

● **MARRAKESH: JARDIN MAJORELLE**. Lush garden with turtle doves, house buntings and common bulbuls. p.371.

● **MERDJA ZERGA** Large wetland area guarantees good **bird** numbers at all times of year, especially **gulls and terns** (including the **Caspian tern**). p.111.

● **MERZOUGA** Sandy (or "true") desert: all-too-brief **spring bloom** of pink asphodels and mauve statice; Algerian sand lizard and Berber skink; **birds** include fulvous babbler, blue-cheeked bee-eater, the rare desert sparrow and even Arabian bustard. p.462.

● **NADOR/KARIET ARKMANE/RAS EL MA** Salt marshes and coastal sand dunes, good for waders and gulls. p.158.

● **OUALIDIA** Mix of ragged, rocky coast, sands, lagoon, marshes and salt pans. Good for small waders. p.323.

● **OUED MASSA** Important inland lagoon and reserve that is perhaps the country's number one bird habitat. p.490.

● **OUED MOULOUYA**. Lagoons and sand spits, with outstanding birds. p.158.

● **TODRA GORGE** Marsh frog and green toad; ground squirrel; common bulbul, black wheatear, blue rock thrush and rock dove. **Bonelli's eagles** nest in the gorge. p.450.

MUSIC

Wherever you go in Morocco you are likely to hear music. It is the basic expression of the country's folk culture – indeed to many of the illiterate country people it is the sole expression – and in its traditions it covers the whole history of the country. There are long and ancient pieces designed for participation by the entire communities of Berber villages; songs and instrumental music brought by the Arabs from the east and Andalucian Spain; and in more recent times, the struggle for independence, too, found celebration in song.

Although the most common musical phenomenon that you will hear is the **muezzin** calling the faithful to prayer, amplified from minarets, most Moroccan music is performed for the sake of entertainment rather than religion. At every weekly **souk,** or market, you will find a band playing in a patch of shade, or a stall blasting out cassettes they have on sale. In the evenings many **cafés** feature musicians, particularly during the long nights of Ramadan. **Television** also plays its part, with two weekly programmes devoted to music, and the **radio stations**, too, broadcast a variety of sounds.

Festivals are perhaps the most rewarding. Every popular or religious festival involves musicians, and the larger **moussems** (p.62) are always rewarding. Keep an eye out for cultural festivals, too, in particular the summer **Asilah Festival** (p.102), and the **Festival of Sacred Music** held at the end of May in **Fes** (p.236).

Below, David Muddyman reviews the breadth and depth of Moroccan music, from the formal repertoire of classical **andalous** to the innovations of electric *chaabi*.

BERBER MUSIC

Berber music is quite distinct from Arab-influenced forms in its rhythms, tunings, instruments and sounds. It is an extremely ancient tradition, probably long predating even the arrival of Arabs in Morocco, and has been passed on orally from generation to generation. There are three main categories: village music, ritual music and the music of professional musicians.

Village music is essentially a collective performance. Men and women of the entire village will assemble on festive occasions to dance and sing together. The best-known dances are the **ahouach**, in the western High Atlas, and the **ahidus**, performed by Chleuh Berbers in the eastern High Atlas. In each, drums (*bendirs*) and flutes (*neys*) are the only instruments used. The dance begins with a chanted prayer, to which the dancers respond in chorus, the men and women gathered in a large ring in the open air, round the musicians. The *ahouach* is normally performed at night in the patio of the kasbah; the dance is so complicated that the musicians meet to prepare for it in a group called a *laamt* set up specially for the purpose. In the *bumzdi*, a variation on the *ahouach*, one or more soloists perform a series of poetic improvisations.

Ritual music is rarely absent from any rites connected with the agricultural calendar – such as moussems – or major events in the life of individuals, such as marriage. It may also be called upon to help deal with *djinn*, or evil spirits, or to encourage rainfall. Flutes and drums are usually the sole instruments, along with much rhythmic hand-clapping, although a community may have engaged professional musicians for certain events.

The **professional musicians**, or *imdyazn*, of the Atlas mountains are itinerant, travelling during the summer, usually in groups of four. The leader of the group is called the *amydaz* or poet. He presents his poems, which are usually improvised and give news of national or world affairs, in the village square. The poet may be accompanied by one or two members of the group on drums and *rabab*, a single-string fiddle, and by a fourth player, known as the *bou* *oughanim.* This latter is the reed player, throwing out melodies on a double clarinet, and also acting as the group's clown. *Imdyazn* are found in many weekly souks in the Atlas.

RWAIS

Groups of **Chleuh Berber** musicians, from the Souss Valley, are known as **rwais**; again they are professional musicians. A *rwai* worthy of the name will not only know all the music for any particular celebration, but have its own repertoire of songs – again commenting on current events – and be able to improvise. A *rwai* ensemble can be made up of a single-string *rabab,* one or two *lotars* (lutes) and sometimes *nakous* (cymbals), together with a number of singers. The leader of the group, the *rayes,* is in charge of the poetry, music and choreography of the performance.

A **rwai performance** will start with the *astara,* an instrumental prelude, played on *rabab,* giving the basic notes of the melodies that follow (this also makes it possible for the other instruments to tune to the *rabab*). The astara is not in any particular rhythm. Then comes the *amarg,* the sung poetry which forms the heart of the piece. This is followed by the *ammussu,* which is a sort of choreographed overture; the *tamssust,* a lively song; the *aberdag,* or dance; and finally the *tabbayt,* a finale characterized by an acceleration in rhythm and an abrupt end. Apart from the *astara* and *tabbayt,* the elements of a performance may appear in a different order. The arrangement and duration of the various parts are decided upon freely by the *rwais.*

ANDALOUS MUSIC

Morocco's classical music comes from the **Arab-Andalucian tradition**, and is to be found, with variations, throughout North Africa. It is thought to have evolved, around a thousand years ago, in Córdoba, Spain (then ruled by the Moors), and its invention is usually credited to an outstanding musician from Baghdad called Zyriab). One of his greatest innovations was the founding of the classical suite called **nuba**, which forms what is now known as **andalous music**, or **al-âla**. There are, in addition, two other classical traditions, **milhûn** and **gharnati**, each with a distinctive style and form.

Andalous music, far from being the scholastic relic you might expect, is very much alive, popular and greatly loved. Television, which plays an important part in the Moroccan music scene, broadcasts nightly programmes of andalous classics during Ramadan, and people who don't have their own TVs congregate at local cafés to watch the shows.

Originally there were twenty-four **nuba** linked with the hours in the day. Only four full and seven fragmentary *nuba* have been preserved in the Moroccan tradition. Complete *nuba* would last between six and seven hours, are rarely performed in one sitting and are usually chosen to fit the time of day or occasion. Each *nuba* is divided into five main parts, or *mizan,* of differing durations. These five parts correspond to the five different rhythms used within a suite. If a whole *nuba* were being performed then these five rhythms would be used in order: the *basît* rhythm (6/4); *qaum wa nusf* rhythm (8/4); *darj* rhythm (4/4); *btâyhi* rhythm (8/4); and *quddâm* rhythm (3/4 or 6/8).

Traditionally each *mizan* begins with instrumental preludes – *bughya, m'shaliya* and *tuashia* – followed by a number of songs, the *sana'a.* There can be as many as twenty *sana'a* within a given *mizan* although for shorter performances an orchestra may only play three or four before going on to the next rhythm.

The words to many *sana'a* deal, though often obliquely, with subjects generally considered taboo in Islamic society like alcohol and sex – perhaps signifying archaic, pre-Islamic and nomadic roots – although others are religious, glorifying the Prophet and divine laws. The fourteenth *sana'a* of the *basît mizan* in **Al-'Ushshâq** tells of the desire for clarity following an active night entirely given over to the pleasures of sex and wine:

Obscure night steals away
Chased by the light
that sweeps up shadows
The candle wax runs
as if weeping tears of farewell
And then, suddenly and behold,
the birds are singing
and the flowers smile at us.

When the Arabs were driven out of Spain, which they had known as Al-Andalus, the different musical schools were dispersed across Morocco. The school of Valencia was re-established in Fes, that of Granada in Toua and

Chaouen. The most famous **orchestras** are those of Fes, led by **Abdelkrim Rais**; Tetouan, led by **Abdesadak Chekara**; and Rabat, which was led by the great Moulay Ahmed Loukili until his death in 1988 and is now under **Haj Mohamed Toud**.

Other cities, however, such as **Tangier** and **Meknes**, have their own andalous orchestras and are just as fanatical about the music as the major cities. The **Orchestra of Tangier** have their own clubhouse, in the old city kasbah, where musicians sit with enthusiasts and play most evenings, in between sucking on their mint tea.

A typical andalous orchestra uses the following instruments: *rabab* (fiddle), *oud* (lute), *kamenjah* (violin-style instrument played vertically on the knee), *kanun* (zither), *darabouka* (metal or pottery goblet drums), and *taarija* (tambourine). Each orchestra has featured unusual instruments from time to time. Clarinets, flutes, banjos and pianos have all been used with varying degrees of success.

MILHÛN AND GHARNATI

Milhûn is a semiclassical form of sung poetry – a definition which sounds a lot drier than it is. Musically it has many links with andalous music, having adopted the same modes as *al-âla* orchestras and, like them, uses string instruments and percussion. But the result can be quite wild and danceable.

The *milhûn* suite comprises two parts: the *taqsim* (overture) and the *qassida* (sung poems). The *taqsim* is played on the *oud* or violin in free rhythm, and introduces the mode in which the piece is set. The *qassida* is divided into three parts: the *al-aqsâm*, being verses sung solo; the *al-harba*, the refrains sung by the chorus; and the *al-drîdka*, a chorus where the rhythm gathers speed and eventually announces the end of the piece. The words of the *qassida* can be taken from anywhere – folk poetry, mystical poems or nonsense lines used for rhythm.

Al-Thami Lamdaghri, who died in 1856, was one of the greatest *milhûn* composers. He is credited with many well-known songs including *Al-Gnawi* (*The Black Slave*), *Aliq Al-Masrûh* (*The Radiant Beauty*) and *Al-'Arsa* (*The Garden of Delight*):

Open your eyes
Taste the delights and the generous nature
Of this heavenly garden

The branches of the wonderful
    trees intertwine
Like two lovers meeting again
And totter about, heady with happiness
The smile of flowers,
Mingled with the tears of the dew
Recall the melancholic exchange
Of a sad lover and his joyous beloved
Birds sing in the branches
Like as many lutes and rababs.

The **milhûn orchestra** generally consists of *oud*, *kamenjah*, *swisen* (a small, high-pitched folk lute related to the *gimbri*), the *hadjouj* (a bass version of the *swisen*), *taarija*, *darabouka* and *handqa* (small brass cymbals). As well as musicians, an orchestra will normally feature a number of **singers**. Some of the best known are **Abdelkrim and Saïd Guennoun** of Fes, **Haj Husseïn** and **Abdallah Ramdani** of Meknes, and **Muhammad Berrahal** and **Muhammad Bensaïd** of Salé.

Gharnati, the third music of Arab-Andalucian tradition, is mainly played in Algeria but there are two important centres in Morocco – the capital, Rabat, and Oujda, near the Algerian border. As with *al-âla*, *gharnati* music is arranged in suites or *nuba*, of which there are twelve complete and four unfinished suites.

The *gharnati* orchestra consists of plucked and bowed instruments together with percussion: the usual *ouds* and *kamenjahs* supplemented by the addition of banjo, mandolin and Algerian lute, the *kwîtra*.

SUFI BROTHERHOODS

Music in orthodox Islam is frowned upon unless it is singing God's praises. As well as the chants of the Koran, which are improvised on a uniform beat, the *adhan*, or call to prayer, and the songs about the life of the prophet Muhammad, there is another entire range of prayers and ceremonies belonging to the **Sufi brotherhoods**, or *tarikas*, in which music is seen as a means of getting closer to Allah. These include the music used in processions to the tombs of saints during moussems.

The aim is for those present to reach a state of mystical ecstasy, often through **trance**. In a private nocturnal ceremony called the *hadra*, the Sufi brothers attain a trance by chanting the name of Allah or dancing in a ring holding hands. The songs and music are irregular in

THE MASTER MUSICIANS OF JAJOUKA

During the late 1950s and early 1960s Tangier was as bohemian a city as any, attracting beats and, in their wake, rock stars. In 1968 the Rolling Stones paid the first of several visits and their then guitarist, **Brian Jones** was introduced to the Berber **Master Musicians of Jajouka** in the foothills of the Rif Mountains.

The Master Musicians are essentially trance musicians, producing an awesome sound through a multitude of double-headed drums and the dark drones and melodies of the ghaita, or rhaita, a double-reed pipe or shawm similar in sound to the oboe. They are a kind of brotherhood, and the leadership of the group is passed down from father to son. The present chief, **Bachir Attar**, inherited the post when his father died in the late 1980s.

Jones recorded the Master Musicians with the aid of psychedelic sound trickery and produced his strange *Pipes of Jajouka* album. Its heady concoction of hypnotic rhythms, wailing pipes and Jones' heavy sound treatments gave what for many was close to a mystical experience – especially when stoned immobile on *kif*. For many years this was the only record available of Moroccan music.

Although the Rolling Stones returned to Morocco in the mid-1980s to use Jajouka on their *Steel Wheels* album, the Master Musicians' next solo recording didn't emerge until 1990 when American bassist and composer Bill Laswell travelled to Morocco. Using the latest digital technology, he produced an album of purity and power. Since then, they have experienced a revival of interest, spurred by the burgeoning World Music scene, appearing at festivals around the world. They have recorded a further CD, and the original Brian Jones album has also been re-released.

rhythm, and quicken to an abrupt end. Some brotherhoods play for alms in households that want to gain the favour of their patron saint.

The **Gnaoua brotherhood** (see "Islam in Morocco") is a religious confraternity whose members are descendants of slaves brought from across the Sahara by the Arabs. They have devotees all over Morocco, though the strongest concentrations are in the south, particularly in Marrakesh.

The brotherhood claim spiritual descent from **Sidi Bilal**, an Ethiopian who was the Prophet's first *muezzin*. Most Gnaoua ceremonies, or *deiceba*, are held to placate spirits, good and evil, who are inhabiting a person or place. They are often called in cases of mental disturbance or to help treat someone stung by a scorpion. These rites have their origins in sub Saharan Africa, and an African influence is evident in the music itself. The principal instrument, the *gimbri* or *sentir*, is a long-necked lute almost identical to instruments found in West Africa. The other characteristic sound of Gnaoua music is the *garagab*, a pair of metal castanets, which beat out a trance-like rhythm.

Jilala are another brotherhood who are devotees of **Moulay Abdelkader Jilal**. Their music is even more hypnotic and mysterious than that of the Gnaoua and seems to come from a different plane of existence. The plaintive cycling flute (the *qsbah*) and the mesmeric beats of the *bendir* (frame drums) carry you forward unconsciously. While in a trance Jilala devotees can withstand the touch of burning coals or the deep slashes of a Moroccan dagger, afterwards showing no injury or pain.

Nowadays, Gnaoua music can be heard at festivals and in the entertainment squares of Marrakesh and elsewhere. Gnaoua music, featuring the wonderful **Mustapha Baqbou**, has been superbly recorded by Bill Laswell and issued on Axiom.

CHAABI

All of the musical forms mentioned above have had their impact on the most popular music of Morocco – **chaabi**, which means simply "popular" and covers a bewildering mix of styles. The music that takes this name started out as street music performed in the squares and souks, but it can now be heard in cafés, at festivals and at weddings. Many towns have café-meeting places where the locals sing songs in the evenings (some cafés keep their own instruments for musicians who can't afford their own) and, at its more basic level, *chaabi* is played by itinerant musicians, who turn up at a café and bang out a few songs. These songs are usually finished with a *leseb*, which is often twice the speed of the song itself and forms a background for syncopated clapping, shouting and dancing. Early evening during Ramadan is

FOLK INSTRUMENTS

Folk instruments are very rudimentary and fairly easy to make, and this, combined with the fact that many music cafés keep their own, allows for a genuinely amateur development. Many of the instruments mentioned below are also to be found under the same or similar names (and with slight variations) in Algeria, Tunisia, Libya and even Egypt.

Morocco has a great many stringed and percussion instruments, mostly fairly basic in design. There are also a few **wind instruments**. The **Arab flute**, known by different tribes as the *nai, talawat, nira* or *gasba*, is made of a straight piece of cane open at both ends, with no mouthpiece and between five and seven holes, one at the back. It requires a great deal of skill to play it properly, by blowing at a slight angle. The **ghaita** or *rhita*, a type of oboe popular under various names throughout the Muslim world, is a conical pipe made of hardwood, ending in a bell often made of metal. Its double-reeded mouthpiece is encircled by a broad ring on which the player rests his lips in order to produce the circular breathing needed to obtain a continuous note. It has between seven and nine holes, one at the back. The **aghanin** is a double clarinet, identical to the Arab *arghoul*. It consists of two parallel pipes of wood or cane, each with a single-reed mouthpiece, five holes and a horn at the end for amplification. One pipe provides the tune while the other is used for adornments.

The most common **stringed instrument** is the **gimbri**. This is an African lute whose soundbox is covered in front by a piece of hide. The rounded, fretless stem has two or three strings. The body of the smaller treble *gimbri* is pear-shaped, that of the bass *gimbri* (*hadjuj* or *sentir*) rectangular. The Gnaouas often put a resonator at the end of the stem to produce the buzz typical of Black African music. The **lotar** is another type of lute, used exclusively by the Chleuh Berbers. It has a circular body, also closed with a piece of skin, and three or four strings which are plucked with a plectrum.

The classic Arab lute, the **oud**, is used in classical orchestras and the traditional Arab orchestras known as *takhts*. Its pear-shaped body is covered by a piece of wood with two or three rosette-shaped openings. It has a short, fretless stem and six strings, five double and one single. The most popular stringed instruments played with a bow are the **kamanjeh** and the **rabab**. The former is an Iranian violin which was adopted by the Arabs. Its present Moroccan character owes a lot to the Western violin, though it is held vertically, supported on the knees. The *rabab* is a spike fiddle, rather like a viol. The bottom half of its long, curved body is covered in hide, the top in wood with a rosette-shaped opening. It has two strings.

The Chleuh Berbers use an archaic single-stringed *rabab* with a square stem and soundbox covered entirely in skin. Lastly, there is the **kanum**, a trapezoidal Arab zither with over seventy strings, grouped in threes and plucked with plectra attached to the fingernails. It is used almost exclusively in classical music.

Rapid hand-clapping and the clashes of bells and cymbals are only part of the vast repertoire of Moroccan **percussion**. Like most Moroccan drums the **darbuka** is made of clay, shaped into a cylinder swelling out slightly at the top. The single skin is beaten with both hands. It is used in both folk and classical music. The **taarija**, a smaller version of the *darbuka*, is held in one hand and beaten with the other. Then there are treble and bass **tan-tan** bongos, and the Moorish **guedra**, a large drum which rests on the ground. There is also a round wooden drum with skins on both sides called a **tabl**, which is beaten with a stick on one side and by hand on the other. This is used only in folk music.

As for **tambourines**, the ever-popular **bendir** is round and wooden, 40 or 50cm across, with two strings stretched under its single skin to produce a buzzing sound. The **tar** is smaller, with two rings of metal discs round the frame and no strings under its skin. The **duff** is a double-sided tambourine, often square in shape, which has to be supported so that it can be beaten with both hands.

Only two percussion instruments are made of metal: **karkabat**, double castanets used by the Gnaouas, and the **nakous**, a small cymbal played with two rods.

the best time to find music cafés of this kind in full swing.

During the 1970s a more sophisticated version of *chaabi* began to emerge, with groups setting themselves up in competition with the commercial Egyptian and Lebanese music which dominated the market (and the radio) at the time. These groups were usually made up of two stringed instruments – a *hadjuj* (bass *gimbri*) and a lute – and a *bendir* and *darabouka* or *tam-tam* as percussion. As soon as they could afford it, they updated their sound and image with the addition of congas, buzuks, banjos and even electric guitars. The *hadjuj* and *bendir*, however, remain indispensable.

Their music is a fusion of Arab, African and modern Western influences, combining Berber music with elements taken from the Arab *milhûn* and Sufi rituals, Gnaoua rhythms and the image of European groups. Voices play an important part, with the whole group singing, either in chorus or backing a lead soloist. Lyrics deal with love as well as social issues, and occasionally carry messages which have got their authors into trouble with the authorities – even jailed.

CHAABI GROUPS

The three most popular groups of this kind are Jil Jilala, Lem Chaheb and Nass El Ghiwane, all from Casablanca.

Jil Jilala, which means "Generation of Jilali", was formed in 1972 as a Sufi theatre group devoted to their leader, Jilali. Their music is based on the *milhûn* style, using poetry as a reference (and starting) point. More recently they have worked with Gnaoua rhythms and they occasionally use a *ghaita* in their line-up. The group's central figures are the conga-player and lyricist **Mohammed Darhem**, and **Hassan Mista**, who plays an amplified, fretless *buzuk*. They are rhythmically accompanied by two bendir players – Moulai Tahar and Abdel Krim Al-Kasbaji – and have recorded with a variety of *hadjuj* players, including **Mustapha Baqbou**.

Nass El-Ghiwane, the most politicized of the three *chaabi*-fusion groups, lays great emphasis on the words of its recitatives and verses and chorus. The band's music, again, combines Sufi and Gnaoua influences while the

words may lambast a lazy government official or talk of social injustices. Originally a five-piece band of banjo, *hadjuj*, *bendir*, *tam-tam* and *darabouka*, the band was fronted by lead singer **Boujmia**, a man with a soaring, powerfully melodic voice. He was killed in a car crash in the early 1980s and the rest of the group have continued as a four-piece since. There has been a retrospective cassette from Boujmia's time released in Morocco on the Hassania label, which includes *The Table*, the song that made them famous:

Where are they now?
The friends who sat at my table
Where are they now?
All the friends that I loved
Where are the glasses?
Where are the glasses we drank from?
Friendship can be bitter
But it was also sweet to sit at my table

The third major *chaabi* group, **Lem Chaheb** is probably the Moroccan group best known abroad, through its work with the German band **Dissidenten** (two of whose members play and record with them). Featuring the virtuoso figure of guitarist and *buzuk* player Lamrani Moulay Cherif, they are also the most Westernized of the three big names in electric *chaabi*.

In the 1980s another generation of groups emerged, combining traditional and modern influences, this time based in Marrakesh but concentrating on Gnaoua rhythms. The most successful of these has been **Muluk El Hwa** (*The Demon of Love*), a group of Berbers who used to play in the Djemaa El Fna in Marrakesh. Their line-up is totally acoustic: *bendir*, *tam-tam*, *sentir*, *buzuk*, *garagab* and hand claps. The only album available in Europe is *Xara*

WHERE TO BUY INSTRUMENTS

FES
Both Talâa Kebira and Talâa Seghira, close to Bab Boujeloud, have stores at intervals. Nearby here, ask for Abdillah Alami in the Kasbah Boujeloud, who sells excellent hand-made drums.

MEKNES
A musical instrument souk is under the archway connecting Souk Bezzarin and Rue des Sarraria, on the edge of the Medina – just past Bab El Djedid, if coming from Place El Hedim. Stalls are good value and there is much choice in a small area.

TETOUAN
A couple of good shops to browse and bargain in are to be found in and around the Rue Terrafin and Rue Ahmed Torres area.

AVERAGE PRICES
Oud (£50–100/$80–160); Ghaïta (£10–25/$16–40); Naï (£5–10/$8–16); Bendir (£5–10/$8–16); Tara (£5–10/$8–16); Hadjuj (£40–60/$65–95); Darabouka (£10–15/$16–24); Qasba (£10–15/$16–24); Garageb (£3–4/$5–7); Tan-Tan (£8–20/$13–32); Gimbri (£20–40/$32–65).

DISCOGRAPHY

There has been quite a boom in CDs of Moroccan music in recent years. Most record stores in Britain or the US with a decent World Music section should yield at least a few discs of ethnic, folk and Andalous music, or fusion with European groups. In Morocco itself (see overleaf), cassettes are the medium.

COMPILATIONS

Ⓒ **Various** *Morocco: Crossroads of Time* (Ellipsis Arts, US). An excellent introduction to Moroccan music that comes with a well-designed and informative book. The disc includes everything from ambient sounds in the Fes Medina, to powerful *Jilala* and *Gnaoua* music, *Andalous*, *Rwai*, *Berber*, and some good contemporary pop from Nouamane Lahlou.

CLASSICAL/ANDALOUS

Ⓒ **Juan Peña Lebrijano and the Orquesta Andalusi de Tanger** *Encuentros* (GlobeStyle, UK) and *Casablanca* (Hemisphere, UK). A stunning cross-cultural blend that combines the passion of flamenco with the beauty and grace of andalous music.

Ⓒ **Orchestre Moulay Ahmed Loukili de Rabat** *Nuba Al-'Ushshâq* (Maison des Cultures du Monde, France). Six-CD set. The only problem with this is the price (£75/$120). It's quite an experience, finely presented and with informative notes.

Ⓒ **Ustad Massano Tazi** *Musique Classique Andalouse de Fès* (Ocora, France). Again, beautifully recorded and presented. Includes *Nuba Hijaz Al-Kabir* and *Nuba Istihilal*.

Ⓒ **Various** *Maroc: Anthologie d'Al-Melhûn* (Maison des Cultures du Monde, France). A three-CD set containing performances from many of Morocco's finest *milhûn* singers. A good introduction.

CHAABI AND CONTEMPORARY

Ⓒ **Najat Aatabou** *The Voice of the Atlas* (GlobeStyle, UK). A superb collection of some of Najat's best-loved songs, including *Shouffi Rhirou* which has been covered brilliantly by the 3 Mustaphas 3.

Ⓒ **Ahlam** *Revolt Against Reason* (Barbarity, Switzerland). A close second to Aisha Kandisha (see below) in the 1990s Moroccan-meets-hip hop stakes, featuring some wonderfully expressive singing.

Ⓒ **Aisha Kandisha's Jarring Effects** *El Buya* (Barbarity, Switzerland). This intoxicating mix of Moroccan melodies and traditional string instruments with scratching reverb and rushes of industrial noise is a great, still largely unheralded, early 1990s classic.

Ⓒ **Hassan Erraji** *Nikriz, La Dounia and Marhaba* (Riverboat, UK). Erraji is an *oud*-player, who fuses his classical training with accessible jazz. *Nikriz* is a real showcase for his talents; *La Dounia* has a starker, and more Arabic content; *Marhaba*, the latest, is more song-based, upbeat and very listenable.

Ⓒ **Lem Chaheb** *Lem Chaheb* (Club du Disques Arabe, France). A compilation from the late 1980s. The band's usual line-up of guitar, *buzuk*, percussion is augmented by trumpets and synthesizers provided by two members of Dissidenten.

Ⓒ **Sidi Seddiki** *Shouf!* (GlobeStyle, UK). A fine debut album of *chaabi* meets pop from a London-based musician.

Ⓒ **Yosefa Dahari** *Yosefa* (Worldly Dance, UK). Just what the label says: dance music with English and Maghrebi songs. A bit of an exotica product but one with promise.

Ⓒ **Hassan Hakmoun and Zahar** *Trance* (Real World, UK). Gnaoua rhythms meet jazz dance psychedelia.

GNAOUA AND JILALA

Ⓒ **Various** *Gnawa Night – Music of the Marrakesh Spirit Masters* (Axiom, UK). Gnaoua music at its evocative best, recorded by Bill Laswell.

Al-Andalus (Erde Records, Germany), a collaboration with the Spanish group **Al Tall**. The album features medieval Valencian music and Arabic poetry from Andalucia, which deals with subjects still relevant today – the whims of rulers, exile, love and wine.

Another of their contemporaries, **Nass El Hal**, formed in 1986, offer two shows – one using a

CD **Various** *Moroccan Trance Music* (Sub Rosa, Belgium). Not for the faint-hearted, this is intense Gnaoua and Jilala music, combined on the disc with some of Paul Bowles' personal recordings.

CD **Various** *Moroccan Trance 2* (Sub Rosa, Belgium). Good atmospheric selections featuring a Gnaoua brotherhood from Marrakesh, alongside three tracks of the Master Musicians of Jajouka.

CD **Various** *Music of Islam Vol 6: Gnawa* (Celestial Harmonies, US). Clear studio recordings of a Gnaoua group from Marrakesh, with fierce *gimbri* from Ahmed Baqbou, brother of Jil Jilala's Mustapha Baqbou.

CD **Maleem Mahmoud Ghania with Pharoah Sanders** *The Trance of the Seven Colours* (Axiom/Island, US). Gnaoua-jazz crossover, featuring the great sax player from Coltrane's band.

INSTRUMENTALISTS

CD **The Master Musicians of Jajouka** *Apocalypse Across the Sky* (Axiom, UK). Without the electronic trickery of Brian Jones' seminal album, the power and clarity of these remarkable performers stands out all the more on Bill Laswell's outing.

CD **Hmaoui Abd El-Hamid** *La Flûte de l'Atlas* (Arion, France). Hypnotic and haunting flute-like *ney*, backed by percussion, *oud* and zither.

TOP TEN MOROCCAN CASSETTES

In Morocco, cassettes of all kinds are readily available in any market – and you can buy videos of many artists, too. The following are a personal top ten to ask for (in order of priority).

1. **Nass El-Ghiwane** *Nass El-Ghiwane* (Hassania, Morocco). The only remaining recordings with singer Boujmia. Powerful and hypnotic.

2. **Najat Aatabou** *Najat Aatabou* (Hassania, Morocco). A traditional line-up of *oud*, violin and drums accompany Najat's magnificent voice.

3. **Jil Jilala** *The Candle* (Disques Gam, Morocco). Poetic introductions to a set of atmospheric songs.

4. **Abdelkrim Rais and the Orchestra of Fez** *Vol 5* (Fassi Disques, Morocco). *Nuba Maya*, which is featured on this cassette, has some of the most beautiful melodies in the Andalous tradition.

5. **Hamid Zahir** *Hamid Zahir* (Tichkaphone, Morocco). From the old school of *chaabi* singers. A rich textural orchestra of traditional instruments and vibrant drumming carry Hamid through an uplifting selection of songs and fiery *lesebs*.

6. **Lem Chaheb** *Lem Chaheb* (Nissim, Morocco). This early tape includes the wonderfully infectious *Nari Nari* which was later covered by Dissidenten as *Radio Arab* – the Moroccan equivalent of the Byrds' jangling guitar sound.

7. **L'Haj L'Houcine Toulali** *L'Haj L'Houcine Toulali* (Tichkaphone, Morocco). Popular *milhûn* at its best. His orchestration is some of the most accomplished, and the melodies stay with you for a long time.

8. **Orchestra Faysel** *Orchestra Faysel* (Forkafane, Morocco). A very odd mixture. Synthesizer, drum machine, *buzuk* and *bendir* lead the trance dance Berber beats. If the Velvet Underground had been Moroccan, they might have sounded like this.

9. **Mohamed Bajaddoub** *L'Age d'Or de la Musique Andalouse Vol 2* (Disques Gam, Morocco). Beautiful arrangement of Andalous suites. Very inspiring stuff.

10. **Nass El Ghiwane** *Chants d'espoir* (Hassania, Morocco). From the late 1980s, a haunting collection of long narratives that draw you in even though you may not understand the lyrics.

traditional acoustic line-up with *buzuk* and violin, the other with drum kit and electric guitar. Their repertoire includes peasant harvest and hunting songs, and religious dances.

Other groups with recordings to their name include **Izanzaren**, of the Casablanca school, and **Shuka**, who do everything from andalous to Gnaoua.

NAJAT AATABOU

Other *chaabi* artists have remained firmly traditional in their use of instruments, but forward-looking in their musical approach. One such is the sensational singer **Najat Aatabou**. She is proud of her Berber heritage and uses traditional Berber rhythms (though she now sings in Arabic or French) and is very outspoken in her lyrics, which address the inequality between men and women and the injustice of traditional family rules. She is equally capable of writing beautiful love songs. When her ensemble use electric instruments they blend beautifully with more traditional *oud* and *bendir*.

Aatabou's first release, the eye-opening *J'en ai marre* (*I am sick of it*), sold 450,000 copies. Her second release, *Shouffi Rhirou* (*Look for Another Lover*), and every subsequent release have sold more than half a million copies, and she is now a huge star throughout the Maghreb and can fill large venues in Europe. A wonderful compilation CD, *The Voice of the Atlas* (which includes *Shouffi Rhirou*), is available on GlobeStyle records.

FUSION AND DANCE

Morocco is an ideal starting point for all kinds of fusion experiments. From the 1960s on, such disparate figures as Brian Jones (see box on p.583), Robin Williamson, John Renbourn and Pharaoh Sanders have been attracted by its rhythms, and in the 1980s and 1990s collaborations have come thick and fast.

The most successful, perhaps, has been that of the Berlin-based **Dissidenten**. Before their collaboration with Lem Chaheb (see p.585), they had worked with **Mohammed Zain**, a star player of the *nai* (flute) from Tangier who belongs to a Sufi sect, and Gnaoua *gimbri* players Abdellah El Gourd, Abderkader Zefzaf and Abdalla Haroch. Their albums with Lem Chaheb have placed a genuine Moroccan element into a rock context.

A number of Moroccan singers and musicians have also crossed over into 1990s dance music. **Yosefa Dahari** is a name to look out for in this respect, with her work (sung in Maghrebi and English) on the Worldly Dance Music label with David Rosenthal and Gil Freeman. **Hassan Hakmoun** is another – a New York-based Gnaoua musician who mixes it in the city with

all manner of ideas and musicians. Also resident in New York these days is **Bachir Attar**, leader of the **Jajouka** troupe (see box, p.583), who has recorded with jazz saxophonist Maceo Parker under the direction of avant-garde funk producer Bill Laswell.

Laswell has also been involved in production work with the group **Aisha Kandisha's Jarring Effects** (or AKJE), who mix Moroccan trance sounds with rock, hip hop and techno. They released an amazing debut CD, *Buya*, in 1991 on the Swiss Barbarity label, and followed up with a techno-driven, Laswell production, *Shabeesation*. They are only known on a subterranean level in Morocco and are yet to perform or release a cassette at home. They have an attitude as radical as their music – akin to, say, Cypress Hill or Ice Cube. Their name refers to a female spirit, whose very mention is taboo, and their lyrics question Moroccan social and religious norms.

The **Barbarity label** has now released about a dozen titles by Aisha Kandisha and other like-minded Moroccan bands seeking to fuse Moroccan music with Western electronic and dance influences. Their catalogue includes CDs by the AKJE side project Amira Saqati, and the bands **Ahlam** and **Argan**, both of which feature AKJE musicians.

Elsewhere, expatriate Moroccans have been active in various new treatments. In Britain, **Sidi Seddiki**, Rabat-born but a Londoner since childhood, produced a seductive blend of Moroccan music and Western pop: strong, catchy songs, drawing on *chaabi*, and using a superb classical flautist. Belgium, meanwhile, has provided a base for the blind multi-instrumentalist **Hassan Erraji**, who has released a trio of jazz-flavoured discs with his multicultural groups Belcikal (now disbanded) and Arabesque. He is well worth seeing live, too, with his startling juggling with the *bendir*.

In **Spain** there have been a couple of notable collaborations between flamenco musicians and Andalucian orchestras, such as that of **José Heredia Maya and Enrique Morente** with the **Tetouan Orchestra** (Ariola, Spain), and **Juan Peña Lebrijano** with the **Tangier Orchestra** (GlobeStyle, UK).

The Tetouan orchestra have also collaborated in concert with the British composer **Michael Nyman**.

MOROCCAN RAÏ

Raï – the word means "opinion" – originated in the western Algerian region around the port of Oran. It has traditional roots in Bedouin music, with its distinctive refrain (*ha-ya-raï*), but as a modern phenomenon has more in common with Western music. The backing is now solidly electric, with rhythm guitars, synthesizers and usually a rock drum kit as well as traditional drums. Its lyrics reflect highly contemporary concerns – cars, sex, sometimes alcohol – which have created some friction with the authorities.

Moroccans have taken easily to the music. Algerian *raï* stars such as **Cheb Khaled, Cheb Mami** and **Chaba Fadhela** are to be heard on cassettes in most souks, while home-grown *raï* stars include **Cheb Khader, Cheb Mimoun** and the mysterious **Chaba Zahouania**. The latter is said to be forbidden by her family from being photographed for her recordings.

Raï influence is also to be heard in the folk music of the **Oujda** area, the closest Moroccan town to Oran, in artists like **Rachid Briha** and **Hamid M'Rabati**.

SEPHARDIC MUSIC

Moroccan Jews, many of whom have now emigrated to Israel, left an important legacy in the north of the country, where their songs and ballads continued to be sung in the medieval Spanish spoken at the time of their expulsion from Spain five centuries ago. Apart from the narrative ballads, these were mainly songs of courtly love, as well as lullabies and biblical songs, usually accompanied on a *tar*.

Moroccan Sephardic traditions and music continue to thrive in Israel. One of the stars of the 1998 Fes Festival of Sacred Music was the Moroccan Jewish singer, **Albert Bouhadanna**, who performed with Mohammed Briouels's Orchestra. Meantime, a rising star in World Music circles is **Emil Zrihan**, now resident in Israel but born in Rabat, whose music mixes Arab and Andalucian influences with the Hebrew liturgy.

MOROCCAN STORYTELLING

Storytelling is an age-old Moroccan tradition – and an active one, as any visit to a weekly souk will reveal. The American novelist Paul Bowles, a resident in Tangier more or less since the war, became interested in such tales in the early 1950s and began tape-recording and transcribing examples told by various Moroccan friends – Ahmed Yacoubi, Larbi Layachi, Abdeslam Boulaich and, in particular, Mohammed Mrabet, with whom he continues to collaborate.

Mrabet's work now amounts to a dozen collections of stories, novels and novellas. The piece included here is in some ways atypical – Mrabet's interests are rooted more in his experience of city life – but it shows his showmanship and masterful handling of a deeply traditional theme of Moroccan storytelling, the casting of spells. Abdeslam Boulaich, better known as a painter, reveals a similar interest in folk humour. Mohamed Choukri, by contrast, is a more literary figure, with a novel and books on Tennessee Williams and Jean Genet to his name. Alone among the three authors here, he wrote his text (in Classical Arabic), with Bowles translating from an oral reading in Maghrebi.

For details of books by these various authors, see the bibliography on pp.607–615.

MOHAMMED MRABET: *THE LUTE*

A young man named Omar got onto his mare one day and rode over his father's land for many miles, looking for the right place to build a small house of his own. He came to a hill between the forest and the olive groves. This is the spot, he said, here I can play my lute all day.

Little by little he built a cottage, bringing the materials from his father's house, and doing all the work himself. When it was done he furnished it with everything he needed for the pleasant life he intended to lead. His most important possession was his lute, which he had trained so that when anyone was coming it sounded its strings in warning. Then Omar would look into the opening under the strings and watch the person as he approached.

Outside the house he built an arbor of canes where he could lie back and drink his tea. And he would sit out there in the shade of the arbor with the green trees all around him, smoking *kif* and drinking tea. At length he would take down his lute and begin to play.

Farther down the valley lived two sisters whose father and mother had died, leaving them alone in a big house. The younger sister was still only a girl, and there was a handsome village lad with whom she was friendly. The older sister, who desired the boy for herself, caught sight of him talking to the girl under a tree. Later she questioned her.

Who was that you were talking to?

The boy from the village.

What did he say to you?

The girl smiled and looked very happy. He said beautiful words and wonderful things. Because I love him and he loves me.

What? cried the woman. And you're not ashamed to say such a thing?

Why should I be? We're going to be married.

The older sister jumped up and rushed out. She began to burn powders and to chant, and it was not long before she burst into the room with a scream and flung a handful of black powder over the girl. At that instant her sister no longer stood in front of her – only a camel, which she chained outside.

A few days later the village boy came to see the younger sister. The woman greeted him from the doorway and invited him into the house. He sat down and looked around, and then through the window he saw the camel.

Why have you got that camel chained to the ground with its legs tied together? he asked her.

She's a bad animal, the woman said. I have to keep her chained up so she won't get into trouble.

Let the poor thing loose so it can graze, he told her. It has no life at all this way. Unfasten the chain and untie the ropes.

No, no. I can't do that.

The boy waited a moment. Then he said: The girl who lives here. Where is she?

That girl? She's getting married tomorrow.

What? he cried. But she was going to marry me!

No. She never mentioned anything about that to me, she told him. Anyway, that's the way it is.

Then she laughed. And what about me? Don't you like me?

Yes, he said. Of course I like you.

Why don't you and I get married, then?

The boy looked at her, and then he looked out at the camel. All right, he said at length. I'll marry you. But only if you set that camel free.

Without saying anything the woman went outside and undid the chain and ropes, and the camel walked away. Then she came in and said she would see him that evening.

As the boy went along the path to the village he came upon the camel waiting for him. He was horrified to hear it speak with the voice of the girl.

Don't trust my sister, it said. You see what she's done to me. I'm the one you were going to marry. Go as far away from here as you can, and stay away. I've got to try and get back my body somehow.

Then the camel walked away, and the boy was too downcast to call after it. He left the village the same afternoon.

One day not long afterward as Omar lay under his arbor on a mat drinking tea, the cords of his lute suddenly sounded. When he peered inside it he saw a camel. He watched it come nearer, and then he hung up the lute and went out into the orchard. The camel walked straight to him and said: Good afternoon.

Omar was startled. You can speak?

I said good afternoon. Yes, I can speak.

I've never seen a talking camel, he said.

But I'm not a camel. That's the trouble. And she told him what her sister had done to her. Then she said: I have a favor to ask of you. Let me stay here with you for a while.

Omar looked thoughtfully at the animal, and said: Ouakha. You can stay with me.

The camel lay down beside the arbor, and Omar began to play the lute. It was the hour when the birds sang and flew from tree to tree. When the birds became quiet, he glanced at the camel and saw that tears were falling from its eyes. He put the lute aside.

The next day as Omar sat in the arbor talking with the camel, he heard the strings of the lute. When he looked inside, he saw a woman walking through the wilderness, over the rocks and between the trees. He watched for a while, but she did not come any closer. Finally she disappeared. He sat down.

Tell me, he said to the camel. What was your sister doing at the moment you felt yourself becoming a camel?

The camel thought for a while. Then it said: She sprinkled some powder over my head, and she had a piece of green cloth in her hand. I saw her fold it three times and then throw it on top of a chest.

I have a friend who might be able to help, Omar told her. He often comes by around this hour.

As they sat there a large crow came flying over the trees, and alighted on the ground beside the arbor. After they had greeted each other, Omar said: You're an expert thief, aren't you?

The crow was embarrassed. It's true I've stolen things. But all that is in the past.

Omar smiled. Good, he said. But you've still got to steal one more time. Do you know Tchar Flanflani?

Yes.

You've got to get into that big house there and look around until you find a green cloth. Don't unfold it. Bring it to me.

Ouakha, said the crow, and it flew off.

They did not have to wait long for it to return, carrying the green cloth in its claws. As Omar took the cloth in his hands and let it unfold, instead of a camel lying on the ground beside the arbor, it was a girl.

He stared at her first in amazement and then with delight, for she was beautiful. Then she jumped up and threw her arms around him, and he embraced her. Together they went into the house.

The following day when the sister looked to see if the green cloth was safe in its place, she did not find it. She searched for it inside the house and out, but without success. As Omar and the girl sat in the shade of the arbor, the strings of the lute began to vibrate. He peered into it and saw the woman walking in the forest.

Here, he said to the girl. Look in here and see if you know who that is.

She looked inside the lute and drew back. It's my sister! she whispered. She's looking for me.

Omar hung up the lute and walked out to the orchard to meet the woman. When he came up to her she looked at him and said: Who are you?

That's what I want to ask you, he said. Who are you and where have you come from and what do you want here? This is my land you're on, and the edge of it is a long way from here.

I'm looking for a camel, she said. A camel I've lost.

I have your camel, he told her.

What! Where is it? What have you done with it?

It's over there, he said, pointing to the arbor where the girl stood. And she came out and walked toward them.

The woman looked at Omar. You won't win! she cried. Then she turned and went back the way she had come.

A few days after this, Omar put the girl onto the mare and rode with her to his father's house, where they celebrated their marriage with a wedding feast that lasted for three days. Then the married couple rode back to the little house. The two were very happy together, and the days passed swiftly.

But one moonlit night as they lay asleep in bed, the lute hanging on the wall twanged its strings. Omar sprang up and put his eye to the hole. A woman dressed all in white walked in the brilliant moonlight. He pulled the lute down and played softly for a while. The next time he looked in, a dense white cloud had formed around the figure of the woman in the orchard, and the cloud was so thick that she could not move one way or the other. Omar hung the lute on the wall and got back into bed.

What was it?

It was your sister. She's down there in the orchard now, dressed all in white. I've got her shut in. She can't go forward or backward.

Let her go! the girl begged him. We mustn't be cruel to her. I can't bear to think of her suffering.

Omar paid no attention to her pleas, but turned over and went to sleep. In the morning after he had bathed and had his breakfast, he sat down under the arbor, smoked a few pipes of *kif*, and said to the girl: Come here and look.

Inside the lute she saw the swirling cloud among the olive trees. Omar took the lute and played on it for a moment. Then he handed it back, and she looked again. The cloud had disappeared, and the woman stood there shouting up at them from the orchard.

I'll be back! she screamed.

Another night as they slept, the lute again sounded a warning, and Omar seized it and put his eye to the hole. Seeing the woman, he played a loud fast melody for a while. When he peered in the next time, he saw that once again a cloud had formed around the woman, but this time it had risen high into the air with her,

where it remained, as still as a rock. He got into bed and said nothing about it.

But the next morning when the girl looked outside she called to Omar. There's something hanging in the air above the orchard!

It's your sister, he said.

Forgive her this time, and she'll never come back to bother us any more, his wife said, and she went on pleading with him.

Your sister will never change, Omar told her. She ought not to be pardoned and turned loose to do harm in the world.

But the girl sobbed and begged him to let her sister down, and finally he got up and plucked on the lute. The cloud slowly settled onto the ground and blew away. This time the woman did not stay to say anything, but ran off as soon as she felt the earth beneath her feet.

When she got back to her house, she shut herself in and fasted for four days. At the end of this time she had a vision of two trees whose trunks stood very close one to the other. She forced herself between them and knew that something great had happened. When she turned, she saw eight strings of gut stretched from a crosspiece between the tree trunks, and she knew that this was the way to get into Omar's house without alerting the lute. From then on she spent all her time preparing the strips of gut and the other things she would need when she found the two trees. When she had everything ready, she began to go regularly to the forest below the little house, in search of the place she had seen in her vision. She found it one night. It was in a dense part of the woods, just below the house. Quickly she squeezed in between the two tree trunks.

The moment she had pushed through, a wall formed around her body and over her head, so that she was encased in a shell of rock between the two trees. The lute by Omar's bed made a loud sound as though it had been hurled to the floor, and then it began to play a strange, halting melody, a thing Omar had never heard it do before. He waited until it had stopped, and then he took it down and looked into it.

Your sister! he cried. There's nothing I can do! She's dying. The lute did it by itself. I didn't touch it.

The girl seized the lute and held it close to her face. Beyond the strings she saw the two trees and the boulder between them. And then through the casing of the stone she saw her sister's face. Her mouth was open and her eyes rolled from side to side as she gasped.

Then the wall of stone around her body became smoke and blew away through the trees, and she fell forward onto the ground.

The next morning Omar and his wife went to the spot and found her body lying there between the two arar trees.

We must bury her, said the girl.

Not on my land, Omar told her. On her own land, if you like, but not here.

And each afternoon when he sat with his wife under the arbor playing the lute, the crow came and sat with them, and listened.

1977

ABDESLAM BOULAICH: *THREE HEKAYAS*

COWARDICE

A Moslem, a Jew, and a Christian were sitting in a cafe talking about Heaven. They agreed that it was a difficult place to get into, but each one thought he would have a better chance than the others.

You have to have the right clothes, the Christian told them. I always wear a jacket and a tie.

Let's go and see, said the other two.

They started out, and when they got close to Heaven, the Moslem and the Jew stopped walking, and the Christian kept going until he reached the door of Heaven.

Our Lord Solomon, who guards the door, said to him: Where are you going?

Inside, the Nazarene answered.

Who are you?

My name is John.

Stand back, said Our Lord Solomon.

Then the Jew and the Moslem spoke together. The Moslem said: He didn't get in. But we will.

I'll go first, said the Jew.

That's right. You go, the Moslem told him.

So the Jew walked up to the door of Heaven. And Our Lord Solomon said to him: Where are you going?

Inside.

Who are you?

Yaqoub, said the Jew.

Stand back!

The Moslem saw this and said to himself:

That's that. Neither one of them got in. Now I'll try.

He walked until he got to the door of Heaven. Then he pulled the hood of his djellaba down over his face. And Our Lord Solomon said to him: Where are you going?

Inside.

Who are you? Our Lord Solomon asked him.

I am the Prophet Mohammed, he said. And he went in. The Jew was watching. He said to himself: If he can get in there, so can I.

And he took a sack and filled it with sticks of wood and slung it over his shoulder. Then he walked up to the door.

Where are you going? asked Our Lord Solomon.

The Jew stuck his foot in the door.

Who are you?

The Prophet Mohammed's manservant, he said. And the Jew went in.

The Christian had been watching. He was afraid to try to get in by lying, and so he went back to his country and told everyone that Heaven did not exist.

STUPIDITY

In a small mountain village lived a man who could not talk very well because he had no roof to his mouth. When it came time for him to marry, his family chose him a girl who had the same trouble. But since the man had never seen her, nor had the girl seen him, neither one knew how the other one spoke.

The day of the wedding, the man went into the girl's room. The servant brought in the taifor with a pot of couscous on it, and then she went home, leaving the front door unlatched.

The man sat with his hands folded in front of him, and so did the girl. Each one was looking at the other, waiting for the other to speak. She was waiting for the man to say: Eat. And he was waiting for her to say: Eat. He was afraid to speak for fear she would hear his voice and not be able to love him. And the girl was afraid he would hear hers and not want her for a wife. Each one looked at the other, and the door of the house was unlatched.

A beggar was passing through the street, crying: For the love of Allah, a little bread! And no one paid him any attention. When he came to the house of the bridegroom he saw the door ajar, and he pushed it open and walked in. He went through the courtyard and came to the room where the two were sitting. Then he saw the man and the girl looking at one another, with the food in front of them on the taifor, and neither one saying anything. The bridegroom saw the beggar standing there. He wanted to tell him to get out. But he would not speak, and so he shook his head up and down at him. But the beggar thought he meant: Go on and eat. He sat down and began to eat the couscous, and he went on eating until there was only a little left. Then he ate the meat, and when he had finished, he took the bone and hung it around the man's neck on a string, because he thought the man was simple-minded. And he went out.

A dog was running through the street. When it came to the house of the bridegroom it caught the smell of food coming through the open door, and it went into the courtyard. It ran to the door of the room where they were sitting, and went in. The man and the girl sat still and said nothing. The dog put its feet up on the taifor and licked up the rest of the couscous. It was still hungry. Then it saw the bone that hung around the bridegroom's neck, and it seized it between its jaws and tried to run. The man fell over onto the floor, and the dog dragged him to the door. The dog kept pulling, and the man's head hit the wall.

Then the man cried out: Help me untie the string!

The girl heard his words, and she was no longer afraid to speak.

The beggar was right! she said. I can't live with such a man!

But you speak the same way! he cried.

I'm the only one who wouldn't have minded that, she told him. And she went out of the house, and left the man on the floor with the dog pulling at the bone.

GREED

A sickly man who lived in the city married a girl from the country. He was never very hungry, but the girl was healthy and ate a great deal. One day the man went to the market and bought many vegetables and four cow's feet. When he took the food home to his wife, he told her: Make me a stew so I can have it when I come home for lunch.

Yes, she said.

But wait for me, he said. Don't eat anything until I get back.

I won't, she said.

When he had gone she made the stew. And then she waited. He ought to be here soon, she said to herself. He'll be here any minute.

After he had finished working, the man went to a café and began to play cards. He stayed there in the café a long time, and his wife went on waiting. Soon she was very hungry. She took one of the cow's feet out of the stew and ate it. And she said to herself: It doesn't matter. When he comes I'll make up something to tell him.

The man came home and sat down. Where's the stew? he said. You haven't eaten anything, have you?

Not yet, she told him. She brought the stew and began to ladle it out. Then the man noticed that there were only three feet in the pot. He began to shout: And the other foot? Where is it?

I haven't got it, she said. You brought three and I cooked three. I hate cow's feet anyway.

The man was very unhappy. Do you want to kill me? he cried. Bring me the other foot, or I may die right here.

Die, if that's what you want, she told him. Why are you waiting?

The man rolled over onto the floor and began to moan.

Get up! said his wife. But he only told her to fetch the *fqih* and make him wash him so he could be buried.

When she came in with the *fqih*, the girl said to her husband again: Get up off the floor!

Have you got the cow's foot? he asked her.

The *fqih* began to wash him.

Get up! she said. Don't you want to have your burial clothes put on you?

Have you brought the cow's foot?

She did not answer. The people came in and dressed the man in his *kfin*, ready to be buried. And then they laid him on the litter.

You're off to the cemetery, his wife told him. They carried him through the doorway into the street.

Where's the cow's foot? he cried. His wife shut the door.

The people walked through the streets carrying him on the litter. When they passed in front of the market, the butcher saw the procession. Who's that who has died? he asked. They told him.

And to think that only this morning he was here in my shop, the poor man, and he bought four cow's feet!

When the dead man heard this, he sat up on

his litter. How many did you say? he called to the butcher.

Four!

Ah, you see? he said. And my wife told me I'd bought only three.

No. It was four, said the butcher.

The man lay down again. And the men carrying him were talking and did not notice anything. They went on their way to the cemetery. When they got there they lifted him off the litter and started to lower him into the ground. But at that moment he sat up again.

Wait! he told the fqih. I've got three cow's feet at home that I still haven't eaten. It's not good to be hungry when you arrive in Heaven. I'm going to run back and eat them now. If I do get to Heaven then, at least I'll have some food inside me.

The people let go of him, and he ran home. When he went into the house his wife said: You came back? You're still alive?

Give me the three cow's feet, he told her. She gave them to him. He ate one. But then he was no longer hungry, and his wife ate the other two.

1961

MOHAMED CHOUKRI: THE PROPHET'S SLIPPERS

More pleasure and fantasy. More money, more ways of getting hold of it. I was tired of enjoying myself, and yet I was not satisfied. Fatin walked toward me, white as snow in the blood-red light of the bar. She took one of my notebooks, looked at it, and grinned.

She muttered something unintelligible and moved away again, disappearing among those who were kicking the air. It was three o'clock in the morning, and I was bored and nervous. Om Kalsoum was singing: "Sleep never made life seem too long, nor long waiting shortened life."

A black man appeared, white on black. He took one of my books and began to read aloud: "This total liberty has its tragic and pessimistic side." He put it down. "What's that book about?" he demanded.

"It's about a man who doesn't understand this world," I said. "He hurts himself and everybody who comes near him."

He nodded, lifted his glass, and drank. When he had finished, he said: "You're crazy."

I saw Fatin writing in a notebook. Meanwhile I smoked, drank, and thought about the matter

of the slippers. The lights went off. Women cried out. When they came on again, both men and women murmured. I bought another drink for Khemou, and she gave me a kiss that left a sweet taste in my mouth. Her brown tongue tickled. She was eating chocolate, and her laugh was red in the light from the bar. Khemou walked off and Fatin came up to me. She handed me a slip of blue paper. On it she had written: Rachid. What do you know about love? You spend more time writing about love than you do making love. The one who has never studied love enjoys it more than the one who knows all about it. Love is not a science. Love is feeling, feeling, feeling.

Miriam Makeba went into "Malaysia." She has a white voice. I began to write on the same piece of blue paper. Fatin, you are my red bed, and I'm your black blanket. I'm beginning to see it that way.

I looked around for Fatin. Her mouth was a wound in her face, and a foreign sailor was sucking on it. She had her right arm around him and was pouring her drink onto the floor with her left hand. Khemou came by and offered me her lips, like a mulberry. I bought her another drink. I was so pleased with the effect of her kiss that I began to think once more about selling the slippers. How much ought I to ask for them? A million francs, the Englishman ought to pay, if he wants the Prophet's slippers. He's an idiot in any case, or he couldn't be taken in by such a tale. But how can I tell just how stupid he is? It was he who first brought it up, the black-market story.

Fatin appeared, black, blonde, white. I handed her the slip of blue paper. She looked at me and smiled. I was thinking that girls like her only made trouble. Her little mouth now looked like a scar that had healed. I thought of the Indian poet Mirzah Asad Allah Ghalef:

> For those who are thirsty
> I am the dry lip.

She wants a kind of love that will make her unhappy. What I like about her is that she still believes the world ought to be changed.

Khemou and Latifa began to scream at each other like two cats fighting, while Miriam Makeba's white voice continued to sing. Khemou pulled Latifa's black hair, knocked her down, and kicked her face. Latifa screamed and the blood ran from her nose. The colors all came together in my head. Leaving the blue paper with me, Fatin ran to separate the two. I read on it: *You're right. I serve them my flesh, but I don't feel it when they eat me.*

Vigon is singing in his white voice. "Outside the Window." Vigon is singing, and I think of the almond trees in flower, and of snow, which I love.

Khemou and Latifa came out of the rest room. They had made up, like two little girls. They began to laugh and dance as if nothing had happened. I sat there smoking, while in my imagination I attacked each man in the bar whose face I didn't like. A kick for this one. a slap in the face for that one, a punch in the jaw for that one over there. Watching myself do as I pleased with them put me into a better frame of mind.

Tomorrow I'll sell the slippers. Fatin came past again, and I asked her why Khemou and Latifa had been quarrelling. She said it was because Khemou had told the man Latifa was drinking with that she had tuberculosis.

Is it true? I asked her.

Yes, she said. But she says she's cured now.

The Englishman and I were at my house, eating couscous. He turned to me and said: "This is the best couscous I've ever tasted."

From time to time he looked toward the corner where my grandmother sat, her head bent over. I told him the couscous had been sent from Mecca. "My aunt sends a lot of it each month."

He looked at me with amazement. "It's fantastic!"

So that he would get the idea, I added: "Everything in the house was brought from Mecca. Even that incense burning is sent each month."

We finished the couscous and started on another dish of meat baked with raisins and hot spices. "It's called mrozeya," I told him.

He muttered a few words, and then said: "Ah, nice. Very nice." My grandmother's head was still bent over. I saw that the Englishman was looking at her, sitting there in her white robes. The incense and the silence in the room made her seem more impressive. She was playing her part very well. Our demure little servant brought the tea in a silver teapot. She too was dressed in immaculate white, and she too kept

her face hidden. Her fingers were painted with elaborate designs in henna, and her black hair shone above her enormous earrings. She made no false moves. She greeted the Englishman without smiling, as I had instructed her to do. It became her to look grave. I had never seen her so pretty.

The mint tea with ambergris in it seemed to please the Englishman. "Do you like the tea?" I asked him.

"Oh, yes! It's very good!"

There was silence for a while. I thought: The time has come to rub Aladdin's lamp. I got up and went to whisper in my grandmother's ear. I did not even form words; I merely made sounds. She nodded her head slowly, without looking up. Then I lifted the white cushion and removed the piece of gold-embroidered green silk that covered it.

The Englishman looked at the slippers, made colourless by age. His hand slowly advanced to touch the leather. Then he glanced at me, and understood that I did not want him to touch them.

"My God! They're marvellous!"

I covered the slippers as I stood there, in order to let him observe them through the veil of green silk. Slowly and with great care I turned and put the cushion back into its place, as if I were applying a bandage to an injury. He glanced at me, and then stared for a long time in the direction of the slippers. Understanding that it was time to leave, he stood up.

We were sitting at the Café Central. For the third time since we had left the house, he said: "Then it's impossible?"

"A thing like that is so difficult," I said. "I wouldn't know how to do it. It was hard enough to get her to let you even look at them. You can be sure you're the only Christian ever to have seen them. And no other is going to, either."

"I understand," he said. "But perhaps we can come to an agreement."

"I understand too. But what can I do? Those slippers are my grandmother's very life. If she should find them missing, she might lose her mind, or have a heart attack. I'm very fond of her, naturally, and I respect her feelings about the slippers."

"I'll give you time to think about it," he said. "But try and persuade her."

"Yes. But when you think of how hard it was to get her to allow you to look at them, you can see how much harder it would be to persuade her."

"Do what you can," he said.

I said I would. but that I thought it was out of the question. Then I said: "Listen. I have an idea. But only on one condition."

"What's that?"

I hesitated for an instant.

"Tell me. Perhaps we can find a way."

"You'd have to leave Tangier the minute you got the slippers."

"That would be all right," he said, understanding. "It's an excellent tactic."

"And I'd have to get out of Tangier myself and stay somewhere else. And I couldn't come back as long as my grandmother was still alive."

"No."

"I couldn't stay on here once they were gone."

"I quite understand."

"It's those slippers that keep her alive, you might say."

"Yes, yes. How much do you want for them?"

I stared at him, and my voice said: "A million francs."

"Oh !" he cried. "No! That's very high!"

"But you'll have something extremely rare. No museum has anything like them. And I'll regret what I've done for the rest of my life."

"I know, I know. But that's a great deal of money. I'll give you half a million. I can't pay any more than that."

"You'd have to pay more than that," I told him.

"No, no. I can't. I haven't got it."

"You give me your address, and I'll write you from wherever I go, and you can send me the rest later."

We looked at each other for a few seconds. In my mind I was thinking: Go on, say the word, Mister Stewart.

"Very well," he finally said.

Wonderful, Mister Stewart, I thought.

"Where shall we meet tomorrow?" I asked him.

He reflected for a moment, and said: "I'll wait for you in the lobby at the Hotel Minzah."

"No," I said. "Outside the hotel. In the street. And you must have your ticket with you, so you can leave the minute I give you the slippers."

"Of course."

"What time will that be?"

While he hesitated I was thinking: Come on, Mister Stewart. Make up your mind.

"At three o'clock in the afternoon."

I got up, shook hands with him, and said: "Keep it to yourself."

"I shan't breathe a word."

"It's not only my grandmother who's going to be upset, but everybody who knows she has the slippers."

I walked away. A moment later I turned and saw him leaving the café.

I found him waiting for me in front of the hotel. He seemed nervous, and he looked wide-eyed at the bag I was carrying. I saw that he had a packet in his hand. Half a million, I thought. More pleasure, more time to think of other such tricks later. The colors in the bar.

I motioned to him to follow me, and stopped walking only when we were a good distance from the entrance to the hotel. We stood facing one another, and shook hands. He looked down at my bag, and I glanced at the packet he held in his hand.

I opened the bag, and he touched the slippers for a second. Then he took it out of my hands, and I took the packet from him. Pointing to a parked car, he said: "There's the car that's going to take me to the airport."

I thought to myself: And tonight I'll be at the Messalina Bar.

I sat down in the corner the same as always. I smoked, drank, and bought kisses without haggling over their price. I'm fed up with pleasure. Fed up, but not satisfied. One woman is not enough.

"Khemou's in the hospital," Fatin told me. "And Latifa's at the police station. She got drunk and hit Khemou on the head with a bottle."

I asked Fatin who the girls were who were sitting in the corner opposite me. She said they were both from Dar El Beida. She picked up one of my notebooks and walked away with it. I waved at the younger of the two. She spoke for a while with her friend. And I drank and smoked and waited for the first kiss of a girl I had never yet touched.

She got up and came over, and I saw the small face relax. Her mouth was like a strawberry. She began to sip the drink I bought her. Her lips shone. Her mouth opened inside mine. A strawberry soaked in gin and tonic. Eve eating mulberries. Adam approaches her, but she puts the last berry into her mouth before he can get to her. Then he seizes the last berry from between her teeth. The mulberry showed Eve how to kiss. Adam knows all the names of things, but Eve had to teach him how to kiss.

Two men had begun to fight over one of the girls. The shorter of the two lost his balance. The other kicked until someone seized him from behind.

Fatin put a piece of blue paper in front of me. I was drinking, smoking, and eating mulberries from the new small mouth. I read what was written on the piece of blue paper. I'm not the same person I was yesterday. I know it but I can't say it clearly. You must try and understand me.

The new face held up her empty glass. I looked again at the mulberries. The barman was busy drawing squares on a small piece of white paper. "Give her another drink," I told him. The friend who had been sitting with her came over. "Give her a drink too," I said.

I thought: More mulberries and human flesh. More tricks and money. I began to write on Fatin's slip of blue paper: I must not try to understand you.

1973

WRITERS ON MOROCCO

As any glimpse at the book listings on p.607 will show, there's a long tradition of writing on Morocco. The pieces here – from Budgett Meakin, Walter Harris, Elias Canetti and Paul Bowles – represent the best of the genre and much of its range.

BUDGETT MEAKIN: *IN MOORISH GUISE*

To those who have not themselves experienced what the attempt to see an eastern country in native guise entails, a few stray notes of what it has been my lot to encounter in seeking for knowledge in this style, will no doubt be of interest. Such an undertaking, like every other style of adventure, has both its advantages and disadvantages. To the student of the people the former are immense, and if he can put up with whatever comes, he will be well repaid for all the trials by the way. In no other manner can a European mix with any freedom with the natives of this country. When once he has discarded the outward distinguishing features of what they consider a hostile infidelity, and has as far as possible adopted their dress and their mode of life, he has spanned one of the great gulfs which have hitherto yawned between them.

Squatted on the floor, one of a circle round a low table on which is a steaming dish into which each plunges his fist in search of dainty morsels, the once distant Moor thaws to an astonishing extent, becoming really friendly and communicative, in a manner totally impossible towards the starchy European who sits uneasily on a chair, conversing with his host at ease on the floor. And when the third cup of tea syrup comes, and each lolls contentedly on the cushions, there is manifested a brotherly feeling not unknown in Western circles under analogous circumstances, here fortunately without a suggestion of anything stronger than "gunpowder".

Yes, this style of thing decidedly has its delights – of which the above must not be taken as the most elevating specimen and many are the pleasant memories which come before me as I mentally review my life "as a Moor". In doing so I seem to be again transported to another world, to live another life, as was my continual feeling at the time. Everything around me was so different, my very actions and thoughts so complete a change from what they were under civilisation, that when the courier brought the periodical budget of letters and papers I felt as one in a dream, even my mother tongue sounding strange after not having heard it so long.

Often I have had to "put up" in strange quarters; sometimes without any quarters at all. I have slept in the mansions of Moorish merchants, and rolled up in my cloak in the street. I have occupied the guest chambers of country governors and sheikhs, and I have passed the night on the wheat in a granary, wondering whether fleas or grains were more numerous. I have been accommodated in the house of a Jewish Rabbi, making a somewhat similar observation and I have been the guest of a Jewish Consular Agent of a foreign Power, where the awful stench from the drains was not exceeded by that of the worst hovel I ever entered. I have even succeeded in wooing Morpheus out on the sea-shore, under the lea of a rock, and I have found the debris by the side of a straw rick an excellent couch till it came on to rain. Yet again, I have been one of half a dozen on the floor of a windowless and doorless summer-house in the middle of the rainy season. The tent of the wandering Arab has afforded me shelter, along with calves and chickens and legions of fleas, and I have actually passed the night in a village mosque.

When I set out on my travels in Moorish guise, it was with no thought of penetrating spots so venerated by the Moors that all non-Muslims are excluded, but the idea grew upon me as I journeyed, and the Moors themselves were the cause. This is how it came about. Having become acquainted to some extent with the language and customs of the people during a residence of several years among them as a European, when I travelled – with the view of rendering myself less conspicuous, and mixing more easily with the natives – I adopted their dress and followed their style of life, making, however, no attempt to conceal my nationality. After a while I found that when I went where I was not known, all took me for a Moor till they heard my speech, and recognised the foreign accent and the blunders which no native could make. My Moorish friends would often remark that were it not for this I could enter mosques and saint-houses with impunity.

For convenience' sake I had instructed the one faithful attendant who accompanied me to call me by a Muslim name resembling my own, and I afterwards added a corruption of my surname which sounded well, and soon began to seem quite natural. This prevented the attention of the bystanders being arrested when I was addressed by my man, who was careful also always to refer to me as "Seyyid", Master, a term never applied to Europeans or Jews.

Having got so far, a plan occurred to me to account for my way of speaking. I had seen a lad from Manchester, born there of an English mother, but the son of a Moor, who knew not a word of Arabic when sent to Morocco by his father. Why could I not pass as such a one, who had not yet perfected himself in the Arabic tongue? Happy thought! Was I not born in Europe, and educated there? Of course I was, and here was the whole affair complete. I remember, too, that on one or two occasions I had had quite a difficulty to persuade natives that I was not similarly situated to this lad. On the first occasion I was taken by surprise, as one among a party of English people, the only one dressed in Moorish costume, which I thought under those circumstances would deceive no one. When asked whence I came, I replied "England", and was then asked, "Is there a mosque there?" I answered that I was not aware that there was one, but that I knew a project had been set on foot to build one near London. Other questions followed, as to my family and what my father's occupation was, till I was astonished at the enquiry, "Has your father been to Mekka yet?"

"Why, no", I answered, as it dawned upon me what had been my interrogator's idea – "he's not a Muslim!"

"Don't say that!" said the man.

"But we are not", I reiterated, "we are Christians".

It was not as difficult to persuade him that I was not at least a convert to Christianity from Islam, as I should have thought it would have been to persuade him that I was a Muslim. Bearing this in mind, I had no doubt that by simply telling the strict truth about myself, and allowing them to draw their own conclusions, I should generally pass for the son of a Moorish merchant settled in England, and thus it proved. Once, during a day's ride in Moorish dress, I counted the number of people who saluted by the way, and was gratified to find that although on a European saddle this suggested to the thoughtful that my mother must have been a European, and I heard one or two ask my man whether she was a legal wife or a slave! In conversation, however, I was proud and grateful to proclaim myself a Christian and an Englishman. My native dress meant after all no more than European dress does on an Oriental in England: it brought me in touch with the Moors, and it enabled me to pass among them unobserved.

Another striking instance of this occurred in Fez, where, before entering any house, I paid an unintentional visit to the very shrine I wished to see. Outside the gates I had stopped to change my costume, and passing in apart from my faithful Mohammed, after a stroll to about the centre of the city, I asked at a shop the way to a certain house. The owner called a lad who knew the neighbourhood, to whom I explained what I wanted, and off we started. In a few minutes I paused on the threshold of a finely ornamented building, different from any other I had seen. All unsuspicious, I enquired what it was, and learned that we were in a street as sacred as a mosque, and that my guide was taking me a short cut through the sanctuary of Mulai Idrees!

Some days later, lantern and slippers in one hand, and rosary in the other, I entered with the crowd for sunset prayers. Perspiring freely within, but outwardly with the calmest appearance I could muster, I spread my prayer-cloth and went through the motions prescribed by law, making my observations in the pauses, and concluding by a guarded survey of the place. I need hardly say that I breathed with a feeling of relief when I found myself in the pure air again, and felt better after I had had my supper and sat down to commit my notes to paper. In the Karûeeïn I once caught a suspicious stare at my glasses, so, pausing, I returned the stare with a contemptuous indignation that made my critic slink off abashed. There was nothing to do but to "face it out".

From *The Land of the Moors: A Comprehensive Description*, by Budgett Meakin (London, 1901).

WALTER HARRIS:
THE DEATH OF A SULTAN

In 1893 Mulai Hassen determined to visit the desert regions of Morocco, including far-off Tafilet, the great oasis from which his dynasty had originally sprung, and where, before becoming the ruling branch of the royal family, they had resided ever since their founder, the great-grandson of the Prophet, had settled there, an exile from the East.

Leaving Fez in the summer, the Sultan proceeded south, crossing the Atlas above Kasba-El-Maghzen, and descended to the upper waters of the Wad Ziz. An expedition such as this would have required a system of organisation far in excess of the capabilities of the Moors, great though their resources were. Food was lacking; the desert regions could provide little. The water was bad, the heat very great. Every kind of delay, including rebellion and the consequent punishment of the tribes, hampered the Sultan's movements; and it was only toward winter that he arrived in Tafilet with a fever-stricken army and greatly diminished transport.

Mulai Hassen returned from Tafilet a dying man. The internal complaint from which he was suffering had become acute from the hardships he had undergone, and he was unable to obtain the rest that his state of health required, nor would he place himself under a regimen. For a few months he remained in the southern capital, and in the late spring 1894 set out to suppress a rebellion that had broken out in the Tadla region.

While camping in the enemy country he died. Now, the death of the Sultan under such circumstances was fraught with danger to the State. He was an absolute monarch, and with his disappearance all authority and government lapsed until his successor should have taken up the reins. Again, the expedition was in hostile country, and any inkling of the Sultan's death would have brought the tribes down to pillage and loot the Imperial camp. As long as the Sultan lived, and was present with his expedition, his prestige was sufficient to prevent an attack of the tribes, though even this was not unknown on one or two occasions, and to hold his forces together as a sort of concrete body. But his death, if known, would have meant speedy disorganisation, nor could the troops themselves be trusted not to seize this opportunity to murder and loot.

It was therefore necessary that the Sultan's demise should be kept an absolute secret. He had died in the recesses of his tents, themselves enclosed in a great canvas wall, inside which, except on very special occasions, no one was permitted to penetrate. The knowledge of his death was therefore limited to the personal slaves and to his Chamberlain, Bou Ahmed.

Orders were given that the Sultan would start on his journey at dawn, and before daylight the State palanquin was carried into the Imperial enclosure, the corpse laid within it, and its doors closed and the curtains drawn. At the first pale break of dawn the palanquin was brought out, supported by sturdy mules. Bugles were blown, the band played, and the bowing courtiers and officials poured forth their stentorian cry, "May God protect the life of our Lord". The procession formed up, and, led by flying banners, the dead Sultan set out on his march.

A great distance was covered that day. Only once did the procession stop, when the palanquin was carried into a tent by the roadside, that the Sultan might breakfast. Food was borne in and out; tea, with all the paraphernalia of its brewing, was served: but none but the slaves who knew the secret were permitted to enter. The Chamberlain remained with the corpse, and when a certain time had passed, he emerged to state that His Majesty was rested and had breakfasted, and would proceed on his journey – and once more the procession moved on. Another long march was made to where the great camp was pitched for the night.

The Sultan was tired, the Chamberlain said. He would not come out of his enclosure to transact business as usual in the "Diwan" tent, where he granted audiences. Documents were taken in to the royal quarters by the Chamberlain himself, and, when necessary, they emerged bearing the seal of State and verbal replies were given to a host of questions.

Then another day of forced marches, for the expedition was still in dangerous country; but Mulai Hassen's death could no longer be concealed. It was summer, and the state of the Sultan's body told its own secret.

Bou Ahmed announced that His Majesty had died two days before, and that by this time his young son, Mulai Abdul Aziz, chosen and nominated by his father, had been proclaimed at Rabat, whither the fleetest of runners had been sent with the news immediately after the death had occurred.

It was a fait accompli. The army was now free of the danger of being attacked by the tribes; and the knowledge that the new Sultan was already reigning, and that tranquillity existed elsewhere, deterred the troops from any excesses. Many took the occasion of a certain disorganisation to desert, but so customary was this practice that it attracted little or no attention.

Two days later the body of the dead Sultan, now in a terrible state of decomposition, arrived at Rabat. It must have been a gruesome procession from the description his son Mulai Abdul Aziz gave me: the hurried arrival of the swaying palanquin bearing its terrible burden, five days dead in the great heat of summer; the escort, who had bound scarves over their faces – but even this precaution could not keep them from constant sickness – and even the mules that bore the palanquin seemed affected by the horrible atmosphere, and tried from time to time to break loose.

No corpse is, by tradition, allowed to enter through the gates into a Moorish city, and even in the case of the Sovereign no exception was made. A hole was excavated in the town wall, through which the procession passed direct into the precincts of the palace, where the burial took place. Immediately after, the wall was restored.

From *Morocco That Was*, by Walter Harris (1921). Reprinted in a paperback edition by Eland Books, London.

ELIAS CANETTI: *THE UNSEEN*

At twilight I went to the great square in the middle of the city, and what I sought there were not its colour and bustle, those I was familiar with, I sought a small, brown bundle on the ground consisting not even of a voice but of a single sound. This was a deep, long-drawn-out, buzzing "e-e-e-e-e-e-e-e". It did not diminish, it did not increase, it just went on and on; beneath all the thousands of calls and cries in the square it was always audible. It was the most unchanging sound in the Djemaa El Fna, remaining the same all evening and from evening to evening.

While still a long way off I was already listening for it. A restlessness drove me there that

I cannot satisfactorily explain. I would have gone to the square in any case, there was so much there to attract me; nor did I ever doubt I would find it each time, with all that went with it. Only for this voice, reduced to a single sound, did I feel something akin to fear. It was at the very edge of the living; the life that engendered it consisted of nothing but that sound. Listening greedily, anxiously, I invariably reached a point in my walk, in exactly the same place, where I suddenly became aware of it like the buzzing of an insect: "e-e-e-e-e-e-e-e".

I felt a mysterious calm spread through my body, and whereas my steps had been hesitant and uncertain hitherto I now, all of a sudden, made determinedly for the sound. I knew where it came from. I knew the small, brown bundle on the ground, of which I had never seen anything more than a piece of dark, coarse cloth. I had never seen the mouth from which the "e-e-e-e-e" issued; nor the eye; nor the cheek; nor any part of the face. I could not have said whether it was the face of a blind man or whether it could see. The brown, soiled cloth was pulled right down over the head like a hood, concealing everything. The creature – as it must have been – squatted on the ground, its back arched under the material. There was not much of the creature there, it seemed slight and feeble, that was all one could conjecture. I had no idea how tall it was because I had never seen it standing. What there was of it on the ground kept so low that one would have stumbled over it quite unsuspectingly, had the sound ever stopped. I never saw it come, I never saw it go; I do not know whether it was brought and put down there or whether it walked there by itself.

The place it had chosen was by no means sheltered. It was the most open part of the square and there was an incessant coming and going on all sides of the little brown heap. On busy evenings it disappeared completely behind people's legs, and although I knew exactly where it was and could always hear the voice I had difficulty in finding it. But then the people dispersed, and it was still in its place when all around it, far and wide, the square was empty. Then it lay there in the darkness like an old and very dirty garment that someone had wanted to get rid of and had surreptitiously dropped in the midst of all the people where no one would notice. Now, however, the people had dispersed and only the bundle lay there. I never waited until it got up or was fetched. I slunk away in the darkness with a choking feeling of helplessness and pride.

The helplessness was in regard to myself. I sensed that I would never do anything to discover the bundle's secret. I had a dread of its shape; and since I could give it no other I left it lying there on the ground. When I was getting close I took care not to bump into it, as if I might hurt or endanger it. It was there every evening, and every evening my heart stood still when I first distinguished the sound, and it stood still again when I caught sight of the bundle. How it got there and how it got away again were matters more sacred to me than my own movements. I never spied on it and I do not know where it disappeared to for the rest of the night and the following day. It was something apart, and perhaps it saw itself as such. I was sometimes tempted to touch the brown hood very lightly with one finger – the creature was bound to notice, and perhaps it had a second sound with which it would have responded. But this temptation always succumbed swiftly to my helplessness.

I have said that another feeling choked me as I slunk away: pride. I was proud of the bundle because it was alive. What it thought to itself as it breathed down there, far below other people, I shall never know. The meaning of its call remained as obscure to me as its whole existence: but it was alive, and every day at the same time, there it was. I never saw it pick up the coins that people threw it; they did not throw many, there were never more than two or three coins lying there. Perhaps it had no arms with which to reach for the coins. Perhaps it had no tongue with which to form the "I" of "Allah" and to it the name of God was abbreviated to "e-e-e-e-e". But it was alive, and with a diligence and persistence that were unparalleled it uttered its one sound, uttered it hour after hour, until it was the only sound in the whole enormous square, the sound that outlived all others.

From *The Voices of Marrakesh*, by Elias Canetti (© Marion Boyars, London, 1978); first published in German in 1967.

PAUL BOWLES: POINTS IN TIME, X

The country of the Anjra is almost devoid of paved roads. It is a region of high jagged mountains and wooded valleys, and does not contain a town of any size. During the rainy season there are landslides. Then, until the government sends men to repair the damage, the roads cannot be used. All this is very much on the minds of the people who live in the Anjra, particularly when they are waiting for the highways to be rebuilt so that lorries can move again between the villages. Four or five soldiers had been sent several months earlier to repair the potholes along the road between Ksar Es Seghir and Melloussa. Their tent was beside the road, near a curve in the river.

A peasant named Hattash, whose village lay a few miles up the valley, constantly passed by the place on his way to and from Ksar Es Seghir. Hattash had no fixed work of any sort, but he kept very busy looking for a chance to pick up a little money one way or another in the market and the cafés. He was the kind of man who prided himself on his cleverness in swindling foreigners, by which he meant men from outside the Anjra. Since his friends shared his dislike of outsiders, they found his exploits amusing, although they were careful to have no dealings with him.

Over the months Hattash had become friendly with the soldiers living in the tent, often stopping to smoke a pipe of kif with them, perhaps squatting down to play a few games of ronda. Thus, when one day the soldiers decided to give a party, it was natural that they should mention it to Hattash, who knew everyone for miles around, and therefore might be able to help them. The soldiers came from the south, and their isolation there by the river kept them from meeting anyone who did not regularly pass their tent.

I can get you whatever you want, Hattash told them. The hens, the vegetables, oil, spices, salad, whatever.

Fine. And we want some girls or boys, they added.

Don't worry about that. You'll have plenty to choose from. What you don't want you can send back.

They discussed the cost of the party for an hour or so, after which the soldiers handed Hattash twenty-five thousand francs. He set off, ostensibly for the market.

Instead of going there, he went to the house of a nearby farmer and bought five of his best hens, with the understanding that if the person for whom he was buying them should not want them, he could return the hens and get his money back.

Soon Hattash was outside the soldiers' tent with the hens. How are they? he said. The men squeezed them and examined them, and pronounced them excellent. Good, said Hattash. I'll take them home now and cook them.

He went back to the farmer with the hens and told him that the buyer had refused them. The farmer shrugged and gave Hattash his money.

This seemed to be the moment to leave Ksar Es Seghir, Hattash decided. He stopped at a café and invited everyone there to the soldiers' tent that evening, telling them there would be food, wine and girls. Then he bought bread, cheese and fruit, and began to walk along the trails that would lead him over the mountains to Khemiss El Anjra.

With the twenty-five thousand francs he was able to live for several weeks there in Khemiss El Anjra. When he had come to the end of them, he began to think of leaving.

In the market one morning he met Hadj Abdallah, a rich farmer from Farsioua, which was a village only a few miles from his own. Hadj Abdallah, a burly, truculent man, always had eyed Hattash with distrust.

Ah, Hattash! What are you doing up here? It's a while since I've seen you.

And you? said Hattash.

Me? I'm on my way to Tetuan. I'm leaving my mule here and taking the bus.

That's where I'm going, said Hattash.

Well, see you in Tetuan, said Hadj Abdallah, and he turned, unhitched his mule, and rode off.

Khemiss El Anjra is a very small town, so that it was not difficult for Hattash to follow along at some distance, and see the house where Hadj Abdallah tethered his mule and into which he then disappeared. He walked to the bus station and sat under a tree.

An hour or so later, when the bus was filling up with people, Hadj Abdallah arrived and bought his ticket. Hattash approached him.

Can you lend me a thousand francs? I haven't got enough to buy the ticket.

Hadj Abdallah looked at him. No. I can't, he said. Why don't you stay here? And he went and got into the bus.

Hattash, his eyes very narrow, sat down again under the tree. When the bus had left,

and the cloud of smoke and dust had drifted off over the meadows, he walked back to the house where the Hadj had left his mule. She still stood there, so he quietly unhitched her, got astride her, and rode her in the direction of Mgas Tleta. He was still smarting under Hadj Abdallah's insult, and he vowed to give him as much trouble as he could.

Mgas Tleta was a small tchar. He took the mule to the fondaq and left it in charge of the guardian. Being ravenously hungry, he searched in his clothing for a coin or two to buy a piece of bread, and found nothing.

In the road outside the fondaq he caught sight of a peasant carrying a loaf in the hood of his djellaba. Unable to take his eyes from the bread, he walked towards the man and greeted him. Then he asked him if he had work, and was not surprised when the man answered no. He went on, still looking at the bread: If you want to earn a thousand francs, you can take my mule to Mdiq. My father's waiting for her and he'll pay you. Just ask for Si Mohammed Tsuli. Everybody in Mdiq knows him. He always has a lot of men working for him. He'll give you work there too if you want it.

The peasant's eyes lit up. He agreed immediately.

Hattash sighed. It's a long time since I've seen good country bread like that, he said, pointing at the loaf that emerged from the hood of the djellaba. The man took it out and handed it to him. Here. Take it.

In return Hattash presented him with the receipt for the mule. You'll have to pay a hundred francs to get her out of the fondaq, he told him. My father will give it back to you.

That's all right. The man was eager to start out for Mdiq.

Si Mohammed Tsuli. Don't forget.

No, no! Bslemah.

Hattash, well satisfied, watched the man ride off. Then he sat down on a rock and ate the whole loaf of bread. He had no intention of returning home to risk meeting the soldiers or Hadj Abdallah, so he decided to hide himself for a while in Tetuan, where he had friends.

When the peasant arrived at Mdiq the following day, he found that no one could tell him where Si Mohammed Tsuli lived. He wandered back and forth through every street in the town, searching and enquiring. When evening came, he went to the gendarmerie and asked if he might leave the mule there. But they questioned him and accused him of having stolen the animal. His story was ridiculous, they said, and they locked him into a cell.

Not many days later Hadj Abdallah, having finished his business in Tetuan, went back to Khemiss El Anjra to get his mule and ride her home. When he heard that she had disappeared directly after he had taken the bus, he remembered Hattash, and was certain that he was the culprit. The theft had to be reported in Tetuan, and much against his will he returned there.

Your mule is in Mdiq, the police told him.

Hadj Abdallah took another bus up to Mdiq.

Papers, said the gendarmes. Proof of ownership.

The Hadj had no documents of that sort. They told him to go to Tetouan and apply for the forms.

During the days while he waited for the papers to be drawn up, signed and stamped, Hadj Abdallah grew constantly angrier. He went twice a day to talk with the police. I know who took her! he would shout. I know the son of a whore.

If you ever catch sight of him, hold on to him, they told him. We'll take care of him.

Although Tetuan is a big place with many crowded quarters, the unlikely occurred. In a narrow passageway near the Souq El Fouqi late one evening Hadj Abdallah and Hattash came face to face.

The surprise was so great that Hattash remained frozen to the spot, merely staring into Hadj Abdallah's eyes. Then he heard a grunt of rage, and felt himself seized by the other man's strong arm.

Police! Police! roared Hadj Abdallah. Hattash squirmed, but was unable to free himself.

One policeman arrived, and then another. Hadj Abdallah did not release his grip of Hattash for an instant while he delivered his denunciation. Then with an oath he struck his prisoner, knocking him flat on the sidewalk. Hattash lay there in the dark without moving.

Why did you do that? the policemen cried. Now you're the one who's going to be in trouble.

Hadj Abdallah was already frightened. I know. I ought not to have hit him.

It's very bad, said one policeman, bending over Hattash, who lay completely still. You see, there's blood coming out of his head.

A small crowd was collecting in the passageway.

There were only a few drops of blood, but the policeman had seen Hattash open one eye and had heard him whisper: Listen.

He bent over still further, so that his ear was close to Hattash's lips.

He's got money, Hattash whispered.

The policeman rose and went over to Hadj Abdallah. We'll have to call an ambulance, he said, and you'll have to come to the police station. You had no right to hit him.

At that moment Hattash began to groan.

He's alive, at least! cried Hadj Abdallah. Hamdul'lah!

Then the policemen began to speak with him in low tones, advising him to settle the affair immediately by paying cash to the injured man.

Hadj Abdallah was willing. How much do you think? he whispered.

It's a bad cut he has on his head, the same policeman said, going back to Hattash. Come and look.

Hadj Abdallah remained where he was, and Hattash groaned as the man bent over him again. Then he murmured: Twenty thousand. Five for each of you.

When the policeman rejoined Hadj Abdallah, he told him the amount. You're lucky to be out of it.

Hadj Abdallah gave the money to the policeman, who took it over to Hattash and prodded him. Can you hear me? he shouted.

Ouakha, groaned Hattash.

Here. Take this. He held out the banknotes in such a way that Hadj Abdallah and the crowd watching could see them clearly. Hattash stretched up his hand and took them, slipping them into his pocket.

Hadj Abdallah glared at the crowd and pushed his way through, eager to get away from the spot.

After he had gone, Hattash slowly sat up and rubbed his head. The onlookers still stood there watching. This bothered the two policemen, who were intent on getting their share of the money. The recent disclosures of corruption, however, had made the public all too attentive at such moments. The crowd was waiting to see them speak to Hattash or, if he should move, follow him.

Hattash saw the situation and understood. He rose to his feet and quickly walked up the alley.

The policemen looked at each other, waited for a few seconds, and then began to saunter casually in the same direction. Once they were out of sight of the group of onlookers they hurried along, flashing their lights up each alley in their search. But Hattash knew the quarter as well as they, and got safely to the house of his friends.

He decided, however, that with the two policemen on the lookout for him, Tetuan was no longer the right place for him, and that his own tchar in the Anjra would be preferable.

Once he was back there, he made discreet enquiries about the state of the road to Ksar Es Seghir. The repairs were finished, his neighbours told him, and the soldiers had been sent to some other part of the country.

From *Points in Time*, by Paul Bowles (Peter Owen, London, 1982).

BOOKS

There is a real wealth of books about Morocco, set in Morocco, or (increasingly) by Moroccans – and you won't regret having one or two along on a trip. Personal favourites include Paul Bowles's Fes novel, *The Spider's House*, Esther Freud's magic evocation of a childhood hippy trip to Marrakesh, *Hideous Kinky*, Walter Harris's evocation of the last days of feudal Morocco in the 1920s, *Morocco That Was*, and the various story collections of Mohammed Mrabet, impeccably rendered by Paul Bowles.

The main Internet bookstores – **Amazon** in particular (try both its .com and .co.uk sites) – are likely to yield the highest returns on the more esoteric books recommended below, while Internet bookseller search sites such as **abebooks.com** and **bibliofind.com** are good for those out of print (o/p in the listings below). You might also want to try a couple of specialist booksellers based in the UK, who will ship books worldwide: the **Maghreb Bookshop**, 45 Bruton Street, London WC1 (☎020 7388 1840) supplies rare and out-of-print books on all aspects of North Africa, while **Keith Harris Books**, PO Box 207, Twickenham, TW2 (☎020 8898 7789) is an excellent mail order specialist for books on Morocco.

GENERAL/TRAVEL

GENERAL INTRODUCTIONS

Orin Hargraves, *Culture Shock! Morocco* (Kuperard, UK/Graphi Arts Center, US). Hargraves worked in Morocco in the 1980s as a Peace Corps volunteer and this invaluable paperback, published in 1995, is a distillation of his experience, supported by an impressive range of research and, clearly, a lot of conversations throughout the country. He offers perceptive accounts of almost every aspect of contemporary Moroccan life, along with a good overview of history and religion, and an instructive section of do's and don'ts. Highly recommended.

CLASSIC TRAVEL BOOKS

Paul Bowles, *Points in Time* (Peter Owen, UK/Ecco Press, US; o/p), *Their Heads Are Green* (Peter Owen, UK). Novelist, poet and composer Paul Bowles (1910–1999) lived in Tangier for half a century and, more or less singlehandedly, brought translations of local writers (see "Moroccan Storytelling" on pp.590–598) to Western attention (see below). These two books of his own are superb. *Points* is a series of tales and short pieces inspired by episodes and sources from earliest times to the present day; the final piece is excerpted in our "Writers on Morocco" section. *Heads* includes a couple of travel essays on Morocco and a terrific piece on the psychology of desert travel.

Elias Canetti, *The Voices of Marrakesh* (Marion Boyars, UK). A small, compelling volume of impressions of Marrakesh in the last years of French rule, by the Nobel prize-winning author. The atmosphere of many pieces still holds – see the excerpt printed under "Writers on Morocco".

Walter Harris, *Morocco That Was* (Eland Books, UK). Harris, *Times* correspondent in Tangier from the 1890s until his death in 1933, saw the country at probably the strangest ever stage in its history – the last years of "Old Morocco" in its feudal isolation and the first of French occupation. *Morocco That Was*, first published in 1921, is a masterpiece – alternately sharp, melodramatic and very funny. It incorporates, to some extent, the anecdotes in his earlier *Land of an African Sultan* (1889, o/p) and *Tafilet* (1895, o/p).

Peter Mayne, *A Year in Marrakesh* (Eland Books, UK). Mayne went to Marrakesh in the early 1950s, found a house in an ordinary district of the medina, and tried to live like a Moroccan. He couldn't, but wrote an unusually perceptive account explaining why.

Budgett Meakin, *The Land of the Moors* (1900; reprinted by Darf Publishers, UK), *The Moors: A Comprehensive Description* (1902, o/p). These wonderful encyclopedic volumes were the first really detailed books on Morocco and Moroccan life. Many of Meakin's "Comprehensive Descriptions" remain accurate and the sheer breadth of his knowledge – from "Berber Feuds" to "Specimen Recipes" and musical notations of "Calls to Prayer" – is fascinating in itself. Highly recommended library browsing.

PRE-20TH CENTURY TRAVELS

Leo Africanus, *History and Description of Africa* (no recent edition but available in major libraries). Written in the mid-sixteenth century, this was the book Budgett Meakin followed, "astounded at the confirmation [of its accuracy] received from natives of remote and almost inaccessible districts". Leo, who was Moroccan by birth, was captured as a young man by Christian pirates. He subsequently converted and lived in Italy; the book was suggested to him by the pope, and so there's more than a hint of propaganda about his accounts. (See also Amin Malouf, under "Western Fiction".)

Margaret and Robin Bidwell (eds), *Morocco: The Traveller's Companion* (IB Tauris, UK, o/p). A good if rather traditional anthology from the mid-1990s, with excerpts from key writers of the past five centuries, including many translated by the editors from the French.

Edmondo de Amicis, *Morocco: Its People and Places* (1882, reprinted by Darf Publishers, UK). Intrepid journeying through Morocco in eras when few Europeans travelled beyond Tangier or the coast. Illustrated with copious line drawings.

R. B. Cunninghame Graham, *Mogreb-El-Acksa: A Journey in Morocco* (1898; reprinted by Northwestern UP, US). And yet more adventuring and anecdotes, most interesting of which is an enforced stay in a caidal kasbah in the High Atlas (his host did not understand the motive of "curiosity").

John Drummond Hay, *Western Barbary: its Wild Tribes and Savage Animals* (1846, o/p). The account is more sympathetic (and less wild) than the title suggests: a fine narrative of a journey from Tangier to Larache, during which Hay (the future British consul in Tangier) is told fabulous tales of local life.

20TH CENTURY TRAVELS

Nina Epton, *Saints and Sorcerers* (1958, o/p). A very readable – and inquiring – travelogue, concentrating on folk customs and religious sects and confraternities in the 1950s.

Thor Heyerdahl, *The Ra Expeditions* (1971, o/p). Heyerdahl is best known for his Kon-Tiki raft voyage from Peru to the South Pacific. He launched his later raft, Ra, built of papyrus reeds, from Safi, Morocco, and reached Barbados, in 1970 – "proving" that Egyptians had reached the Atlantic and crossed to the West Indies. He also found that within living memory similar boats were used for fishing off the Moroccan coast.

John Hopkins, *Tangier Journals 1962–79* (1997; Arcadia, UK/Cadmus Editions, US). Entertaining journals of Tangier life – and travels across Morocco – from an American novelist, resident in Tangier during the Beat years. Bowles, Burroughs, and the like, figure large in the diary entries.

Sylvia Kennedy, *See Ouarzazate and Die* (1992; o/p). An account of visits to Morocco in 1990–91, both before and during the Gulf War. The narrative is hyperbolic and highly critical – Moroccan officials would not be impressed to find the book in your luggage – but it has interesting observations nonetheless.

Rom Landau, *Morocco: Marrakesh, Fez, Rabat* (1967, o/p). Landau wrote numerous books on Morocco in the 1950s and '60s, few of them particularly inspiring. This one's redeeming feature is an excellent series of photographs – including rare pictures of mosque interiors.

Wyndham Lewis, *Journey into Barbary* (1932; Black Sparrow Press, US). You'll learn more about Lewis than Morocco from this obscure, eccentric and rambling text – but the drawings are wonderful.

Antoine de Saint-Exupéry, *Wind, Sand and Stars* and *Southern Mail* (Penguin UK/Harcourt Brace, US). Accounts by the French aviator (and author of the children's classic, *The Little Prince*) of his postal flights down to West Africa, by way of Cap Juby in the then Spanish Sahara. **Stacy Shiff**'s biography, *Saint-Exupéry* (Pimlico, UK) is, if anything, even more gripping, taking the story through to Saint-Exupéry's disappearance flying for the Free French in 1944.

Gordon West, *By Bus to the Sahara* (1932; Black Swan, UK; o/p). This fascinating travelogue, reprinted in the 1990s but again out of print, describes a journey from Tangier to Rissani, as undertaken by the author and his wife, an amateur artist, coyly referred to as "the spirit". As a touristic insight into prewar Morocco, it is unique.

Edith Wharton, *In Morocco* (1920; Ecco Press, US). Wharton dedicated her book of travels in Morocco to General Lyautey, Resident-General of the Protectorate, whose modernizing efforts she greatly admired. By no means a classic, it is nonetheless worth reading for glimpses of harem life in the early years of the twentieth century.

PHOTOGRAPHS

Ann and Yann Arthus-Bertrand, *Morocco Seen From The Air* (Vendome Press, UK/US). Seek out this stunning, large-format book published in 1994 – it is a revelation – Moroccan cities, valleys, kasbahs, carpet souks captured from the air. Browse after a trip and odd, apparently impenetrable pockets of cities that you've walked through will begin to fall into place. Other photos simply have the appearance of abstract paintings.

Paul Bowles, *Photographs* (Scalo, US). Paul Bowles proved himself a talented photographer in this book of images from the 1930s to 1960s. The stunning black and white pictures are complemented by editor Simon Bishoff's recorded conversations with Bowles in Tangier between 1989 and 1991.

Margaret Courtney-Clarke, *Imazighen: The Vanishing Traditions of Berber Women* (Thames & Hudson, UK). The photographs here are of Berber communities across Morocco, Algeria and Tunisia. They are intimate portraits of communities at home and show the harsh nature of life and its constant work, as well as the beauty of the crafts and landscape.

Mary Cross, *Morocco: Sahara to the Sea* (Abbeville Press, US). A lavish book of images, with brief text from the photographer, a preface by Paul Bowles, and an introduction by the Moroccan novelist, Tahar Ben Jalloun.

Hugues Demeude, Jacques Bravo, Xavier Richer, *Morocco* (Taschen, Germany). This is a stunning assembly of photographs, published in 1998, and hard to beat (in quality and price) if you want a photo book to browse before or after a trip.

Alan Keohane, *Berbers of the Atlas* (Hamish Hamilton, UK, o/p). A marvellous collection of colour photos of daily life in the Atlas.

Published in the mid-1990s, it is well worth tracking down.

Jean-Marc Tingaud and Tahar Ben Jelloun, *Medinas: Morocco's Hidden Cities* (Assouline, France; Thames & Hudson, UK/US). These are wonderful photos of the mansions and palaces of Fes, Marrakesh and other cities, whose existence you could hardly imagine from the street outside. Tingaud's photos are accompanied by poems from the Moroccan novelist Ben Jelloun.

HISTORY

GENERAL

Barnaby Rogerson, *A Traveller's History of North Africa* (Windrush, UK/Interlink, US). Rogerson takes on a daunting task here, covering the history not just of Morocco, but Tunisia, Algeria and Libya, but pulls it off with style. This is an authoritative but very readable book, establishing a surprisingly clear vision of North African history from Carthage to the present. Rogerson sees his chosen area as a kind of island, isolated by sea and desert, and thus set apart from Europe and sub-Saharan Africa. Written in the 1990s, this is the only good, up-to-date, general history of Morocco.

SPECIFIC PERIODS

Moshe Gershovich, *French Military Rule in Morocco: Colonialism and its Consequences* (Frank Cass, UK/US). A detailed but not overly academic study of the French colonial period. The reputation of General Lyautey, still seen in France as the embodiment of "enlightened colonialism", is severely reassessed.

Roger Le Tourneau, *Fez in the Age of the Marinides* (University of Oklahoma Press, US, o/p). Interesting scholarly study of the Merenid capital of Morocco. Tourneau has also written on *The Almohad Movement* (Princeton University Press, US, 1981, o/p).

Gavin Maxwell, *Lords of the Atlas* (Cassell, UK). Drawing heavily on Walter Harris' accounts of the Moorish court (see p.607), this is the story of the Glaoui family – literally the "Lords" of the High Atlas, where they exercised almost complete control from the turn of the nineteenth century right through to Moroccan independence in 1956. Not an attractive tale but a compelling one, and superbly told. Originally published in 1966.

C.R. Pennell, *Morocco Since 1830* (C. Hurst, UK/Princeton University Press, US). This new paperback (published 2000) is the first general history of modern Morocco. It covers the major strands of power but also the social and cultural life of ordinary Moroccans and is strong on the country's pressing contemporary concerns of poverty, drought, and worsening agricultural land.

Douglas Porch, *The Conquest of Morocco* (Forward Movement, US). Accessible and fascinating account of the extraordinary manoeuvrings and characters of Morocco's turn-of-the-twentieth-century history.

Susan Raven, *Rome in Africa* (Routledge, UK/US). A well-illustrated survey of Roman (and Carthaginian) North Africa.

David Woolman, *Rebels in the Rif* (Stanford University Press, US, o/p). An academic but fascinating study of the Riffian war in the 1920s and of the tribes' uprising against the Moroccan government in 1956.

NORTH AFRICA/ARAB WORLD

J.M. Abun-Nasr, *History of the Maghreb in the Islamic Period* (Cambridge UP, UK/US). Morocco in the wider context of North Africa by a distinguished Arab historian.

Peter Mansfield, *The Arabs* (Penguin, UK/US). General introduction to the Arab world, from its beginnings through to the 1970s. Short final sections deal with each individual country.

R. Oliver and J. D. Fage, *A History of Africa* (Penguin, UK/US). Morocco within the context of its continent.

ANTHROPOLOGY

There is extensive anthropology literature on Morocco. Reviews below are just a selection of the more popular, not overly academic, books in print.

Donna Lee Bowen and Evelyn A. Early (**eds**), *Everyday Life in the Muslim Middle East* (Indiana University Press, US). Despite its broad title, around a third of this anthology deals with Morocco. It illustrates the experiences of ordinary men, women and children from Afghanistan to Morocco, through essays, short stories and poems. Highly recommended.

Michael Brett and Elizabeth Fentress, *The Berbers* (Blackwells, UK). A valuable recent (1997) overview of the Berber peoples of

Morocco, Algeria, and beyond, ranging through anthropology, history and literature.

Shlomo Deshen, *The Mellah Society: Jewish Community Life in Sherifian Morocco* (University of Chicago Press, US). A study of economic activity and political organization in the mellahs prior to the Protectorate.

Kevin Dwyer, *Moroccan Dialogues: Anthropology in Question* (Waveland Press, US). A series of recorded conversations with a farmer from near Taroudannt, ranging from attitudes to women, religion and village life to popular Moroccan perceptions of the Jews, the French and even the hippies.

Elizabeth Fernea, *A Street in Marrakesh* (Waveland Press, US). Highly readable account of a woman anthropologist's period of study and experiences in Marrakesh.

Ernest Gellner, *Saints of the Atlas* (University of Chicago Press, US). The bulk of this book is an in-depth study of a group of zaouia villages in the High Atlas, but there are excellent introductory chapters on Morocco's recent past and the concept and origins of Berbers.

David Hart, *Tribe and Society in Rural Morocco* (Frank Cass, UK/US). A collection of essays, dating from 1985–2000, around the themes of tribalism and Berberism in Morocco. More accessible than it sounds, with titles such as *Scratch a Moroccan, Find a Berber*.

Fatima Mernissi, *Doing Daily Battle: Interviews with Moroccan Women* (The Women's Press/Rutgers UP). Eleven women – carpet weavers, rural and factory workers, teachers – talk about all aspects of their lives, from work and housing to marriage. A fascinating insight into a resolutely private world.

ISLAM

The Koran (Oxford University Press, UK/US). The Word of God as handed down to the Prophet is the basis of all Islam, so essential reading for anyone interested. There are dozens of editions but the Oxford edition is probably the clearest and liveliest translation.

S. H. Nasr, *Ideas and Realities of Islam* (Collins, UK/US). A good general introduction.

Maxime Rodinson, *Muhammad* (Penguin, UK/Pantheon, US). Challenging account of the Prophet's life and the immediate impact of his ideology.

ART, ARCHITECTURE AND CRAFTS

In addition to the recommendations below, a number of large, glossy books on Moroccan jewellery, gardens, paintings, manuscripts, carpets, buildings, usually with French texts, are to be found in most of the larger bookshops in Morocco – notably at the excellent bookshop of the new Marrakesh Museum.

Pierre Bergé and Madison Cox, *Majorelle, A Moroccan Oasis* (Thames & Hudson, UK). This is one of a series of "small books on great gardens": a superbly photographed volume on the Marrakesh garden created by French furniture designer Louis Majorelle, and now maintained by Yves Saint-Laurent.

Michael Brett, *The Moors* (Orbis, o/p). A fine illustrated survey of the Moorish Empire, well thought out and with an understanding text.

Titus Burckhardt, *Fes: City of Islam* (Islamic Texts Society, UK); *Moorish Culture in Spain* (o/p). Burckhardt's *Moorish Culture* is a superb study of architecture, history, Islamic city-design and the mystical significance of its art – and as such it's entirely relevant to medieval Morocco. *Fes* is worth dipping into, if only for the photos; the conceptual approach and respect for tradition, however, are a bit hard going.

Salma Damluji, *Zillij: the Art of Moroccan Ceramics* (Garnet, UK). An expensive but beautifully illustrated study of the art of ceramic mosaic-work.

Lisl and Landt Dennis, *Living in Morocco* (Thames & Hudson, UK). An entrancing picture study of Moroccan craft and domestic design, both traditional and modern.

James F. Jereb, *Arts and Crafts of Morocco* (Thames & Hudson, UK/Chronicle Books, US; o/p). The arts and crafts of Morocco express the kaleidoscope of influences from Black Africa and Islam to the cultural alliance of the Moors and Spaniards. This recent (but currently out-of-print) book, with over 150 colour photographs, is a fascinating introduction to Moroccan arts and crafts and an excellent guide to the museums of the major cities.

Jack Cowart et al, *Matisse in Morocco* (Thames & Hudson, UK/Abrams, US; o/p). A gorgeous book of the paintings and drawings from the artist's stay in 1912–13. It has not been long out of print.

Lisa Houatt-Smith, *Moroccan Interiors* (Taschen, UK). This coffee-table tome may be aimed at the interior design market but it goes beyond that in its coverage of traditional crafts, and traditional and modern architecture. Given the mass of colour photography and high production values, it is also remarkably good value.

Andre Paccard, *Traditional Islamic Craft in Moroccan Architecture* (Editions Atelier, France, 2 vols). This hugely expensive coffee-table tome was written by an architect much favoured by King Hassan. The text is none too engaging but it is massively illustrated and – uniquely – includes photographs of Moroccan Royal Palaces currently in use.

Richard Parker, *A Practical Guide to Islamic Monuments in Morocco* (Baraka Press, Charlottesville, Virginia, US). Exactly what it claims to be – very helpful and well informed, with introductory sections on architectural forms and motifs, and craft traditions. Privately printed, the book is available at the American Bookstore in Rabat.

Brook Pickering et al, *Moroccan Carpets* (Laurence King, UK). Edited by a New York collector and dealer, this is the best book on Moroccan carpets – a large format, fully illustrated guide, showing examples region by region.

Herbert Ypma, *Morocco Modern* (Thames & Hudson, UK/Stewart, Tabori & Chang, US). This superbly illustrated book traces the origins of the great artisan traditions of Morocco (weavers, woodworkers, potters, zellij-makers) and looks at the way contemporary designers and architects reinterpret these influences to create surprisingly modern work.

FOOD

Robert Carrier, *Taste of Morocco* (Arrow, UK; o/p). Robert Carrier lived in Marrakesh for several months of each year and this beautifully illustrated cookbook reflects his love of Morocco and its distinctive cuisine – particularly the grand dishes of the south. Carrier considered Morocco to have (with France and China) one of the three greatest cuisines in the world. His focus is on wealthy kitchen dishes rather than anything very rustic.

Zette Guinaudeau, *Traditional Moroccan Cooking: Recipes from Fez* (Interlink, US). Madame Guinaudeau lived in Fes for over thirty years and first published her recipes in French in 1964. Now translated into English, they redress the imbalance of Robert Carrier's focus on Marrakesh cuisine. Some of her recipes echo Mrs Beeton's catering, for at least eight people and sometimes as many as twenty, but they can be adapted.

Anissa Helou, *Café Morocco* (Conran Octopus, UK/US). This sumptuous book is the best of the many recent Moroccan cookery guides. It combines good recipe writing with colourful background – and stunning photography – on the food (from street snacks to haute cuisine) and its origins.

Claudia Roden, *The Book of Jewish Food* (Penguin, UK/Knopf, US). An interesting and useful book that makes clear the distinctive dishes of the Sephardic Jews (of the Middle East and North Africa), showing that such specialities as couscous, tajine, harira, kefta and mechoui were to be found in both the medina and the mellah before the exodus to Israel.

Paula Wolfert, *Couscous and Other Good Foods from Morocco* (HarperCollins, US). This is a new edition of a book originally published in the 1960s, which at the time was groundbreaking in its emphasis on ordinary, rural cooking. Its recipes work and there's a nice line in anthropological background.

MOROCCAN FICTION/BIOGRAPHY

By far the largest body of Moroccan fiction/biography published in English is the translations by the American writer Paul Bowles, who lived in Tangier from the 1940s until his death in 1999. Many of the small press editions duck in and out of print but they are reasonably available if you do an Internet search; prices are now very high for first editions but reprints are reasonable.

TRANSLATIONS BY PAUL BOWLES

All of the books below are taped and translated from the Maghrebi by **Paul Bowles**. It's hard to generalize about them, except to say that they are mostly "tales" (even the biographies, which seem little different from the fiction), share a common fixation with intrigue and unexpected narrative twists, and are often punctuated by episodes of violence. None have particular characterization, though this hardly seems relevant as they have such a strong, vigorous narrative style – brilliantly matched by Bowles' sharp, economic language.

For a taste of the stories, see "Moroccan Storytelling" on pp.590–598.

Mohammed Mrabet, *Love with a Few Hairs* (City Lights, US); *The Boy Who Set the Fire & Other Stories* (City Lights, US); *The Lemon* (Peter Owen, UK/City Lights, US); *M'Hashish* (City Lights, US); *The Chest* (Tombouctou, US); *Marriage With Papers* (Tombouctou, US); *The Big Mirror* (Black Sparrow Press, US); *Harmless Poisons, Blameless Sins* (Black Sparrow Press, US); *The Beach Café and The Voice* (Black Sparrow Press, US); *Look and Move On: An Autobiography* (Peter Owen, UK/Black Sparrow Press, US).

Mohammed Mrabet's stories – *The Beach Café* is perhaps his best – are often *kif*-inspired, and this gives them a slightly paranoid quality, as Mrabet himself explained: "Give me twenty or thirty pipes . . . and an empty room can fill up with wonderful things, or terrible things. And the stories come from these things."

Mohamed Choukri, *For Bread Alone* (IB Tauris, UK). Now translated into more than ten languages, this first volume of Mohammed Choukri's autobiography speaks for an entire generation of North Africans. Born in the Rif, he moved with his family to Tangier at a time of great famine, spending his childhood in abject poverty. During his adolescence he worked for a time for a French family. He then returned to Tangier, where he experienced the violence of the 1952 independence riots. At the age of 20, and still illiterate, he took the decision to read and write classical Arabic – a decision which transformed his life.

Driss Ben Hamed Charhadi, *A Life Full of Holes* (Grove Press, US). This was Bowles' first Moroccan translation – in 1964 – a direct narrative of streetlife in Tangier. It was published under a pseudonym, the author being **Larbi Layachi** who, two decades later, published *Yesterday and Today* (Black Sparrow Press, US), a kind of sequel, describing in semi-fictionalized (and not very sympathetic) form his time with Paul and Jane Bowles.

Five Eyes, stories by *Mohammed Mrabet, Larbi Layachi, Mohamed Choukri, Ahmed Yacoubi and Abdesiam Boulaich* (Black Sparrow Press, US; o/p). An excellent introduction to these writers, sadly out of print.

OTHER TRANSLATIONS

Margot Badran and Miriam Cooke (eds), *Opening the Gates: A Century of Arab Feminist Writing* (Indian University Press, US). This anthology includes three Moroccan pieces, including a traditional women's tale, recounted by the Moroccan feminist, Fatima Mernissi.

Abdelkader Benali, *Wedding by the Sea* (Phoenix House, UK/Arcade Publishing, US). Moroccan magic realism? This is an impressive debut novel by a Moroccan-born author who has lived in The Netherlands since childhood. The story is about a young man who returns (from Holland) to his seaside village in Morocco for his sister's wedding, and during the festivities finds the bridegroom has made off to the local brothel. Sweet revenge lies in store from his sister.

Mohamed Choukri, *Streetwise* (Al Saqi Books, UK). The second volume of Choukri's autobiography (translated by Ed Emery) spans the 1960s and 70s and ranks among the best works of contemporary Arabic literature. Throughout his adversities, two things shine through: Choukri's determination to use literacy to surmount his desperate circumstances; and his compassion for the normally despised human beings who share this life of "the lowest of the low".

Driss Chraibi, *Heirs to the Past* (Heinemann, UK/US; o/p). A benchmark novel, written in French, this took the crisis of Moroccans' post-colonial identity as its theme; it is semi-autobiographical as the author-narrator (who has lived in France since the war) returns to Morocco for the funeral of his father. A number of other Chraibi novels are also available in translation.

Fatima Mernissi, *Dreams of Trespass: Tales of a Harem Girlhood* (Perseus Press, US). Part fairy tale, part feminist manifesto, this is a mix of biographical narrative, stories and fantasies from the renowned Moroccan sociologist, who was born in a harem in Fes in 1940.

Tahar Ben Jelloun, *The Sand Child* (John Hopkins University Press, US) and *Corruption* (New Press, US). Ben Jelloun, long resident mainly in Paris, and writing in French, is Morocco's most acclaimed writer. His is a deserved reputation and he has getting on for a dozen books translated into English. These two are probably the best. *The Sand Child*, which won the prestigious Prix Goncourt, is a tale of a girl brought up in southern Morocco as a boy in order to thwart Morocco's inheritance laws. *Corruption*, as its title suggests, explores the endemic corruption in contemporary Morocco, through the story of Mourad, the last honest man in the country, who attempts to stay clear of brown envelopes in Casablanca and Tangier.

Anouar Majid, *Si Yussef* (Quartet, UK). An interesting if somewhat tortuous narrative: the author writes as Lamin, a student in Fes, who presents the life story of an old man, born in Tangier in 1908, and his tales of the city.

Brick Ousaïd, *Mountains Forgotten by God* (Lynn Rienner, UK/Three Continents Press, US). Autobiographical narrative of an Atlas Berber family, which gives an impressive sense of the harshness of mountain life. As the author describes it, it is "not an exercise in literary style [but] a cry from the bottom of my heart, of despair and revolt".

Abdelhak Serhane, *Messaouda* (Carcanet, UK; o/p). Adventurous, semi-autobiographical novel about growing up in Azrou during the 1950s. The narrator's development parallels that of his country; his attempts to free himself from the patriarchy and authoritarianism of his father are used as an allegory for the struggle against French colonialism and its aftermath.

SET IN MOROCCO

Once again, the late Paul Bowles is the outstanding figure in American and European fiction set in Morocco, so no apologies for splitting this section into "Bowles" and "Others". Though the "Others" do include a couple of gems.

PAUL BOWLES

NOVELS: *The Sheltering Sky* (Penguin, UK/Ecco Press, US); *Let It Come Down* (Penguin, UK/Black Sparrow Press, US); *The Spider's House* (Arrow, UK/Black Sparrow Press, US).
STORIES: *Collected Stories of Paul Bowles 1939–76* (Black Sparrow Press, US) gathers together work from numerous editions, as does the more selective *Collected Stories* (Penguin, UK). Post-1976 collections include *Midnight Mass* (Peter Owen, UK/Black Sparrow Press,

US) and *Unwelcome Words* (Tombouctou, US).

Paul Bowles stands out as the most interesting and the most prolific writer using North African themes – and following Bertolucci's film of *The Sheltering Sky* he at last regained some of the recognition he was due (the novel had been a US bestseller on publication in 1955). Many of his stories are similar in vein to those of Mohammed Mrabet (see p.612), employing the same sparse forms, bizarre twists and interjections of violence. The novels are something different, exploring both Morocco (or, in *The Sheltering Sky*, Algeria) and the ways in which Europeans and Americans react to and are affected by it. If you read nothing else on the country, at least get hold of *The Spider's House* – one of the best political novels ever written, its backdrop the traditional daily life of Fes, its theme the conflicts and transformation at the last stages of the French occupation of the country.

The last few years have seen a flurry of **biographies and memoirs of Bowles** and his literary friends and acquaintances in **Tangier**. The best of these are:

Iain Finlayson, *Tangier: City of the Dreams* (Flamingo, UK/HarperCollins, UK; o/p). Good on the Moroccans whom Bowles has translated.

Michelle Green, *The Dream at the End of the World: Paul Bowles and the Literary Renegades of Tangier* (Bloomsbury, UK). Strong narrative, compulsively peopled: the best read if you're looking for one book on Tangier literary life.

Bowles' autobiography, *Without Stopping* (Peter Owen, UK/Ecco Press, US), is also of interest for its Moroccan episodes (though William Burroughs wryly dubbed it "Without Telling"), as is his *Two Years Beside the Strait* (Peter Owen, UK; published in US as *Days: A Tangier Journal, 1987–89*, Ecco Press).

In Touch: the Letters of Paul Bowles, edited by **Daniel Halpern** (HarperCollins, US; o/p) spans sixty years and reveals a little more, with letters (predominantly from Tangier) to intimates such as Burroughs and Aaron Copland.

OTHER FICTION SET IN MOROCCO

Arturo Barea, *The Forging of a Rebel* (Flamingo, UK reprint, 3 volumes, o/p). This is an autobiographical trilogy of the key Spanish events of the 1930s. The second volume, *The Track*, concerns the war and colonization of the Rif, the Spanish entry into Chaouen and life in Tetouan.

William Burroughs, *Naked Lunch* (Flamingo, UK/Grove Press, US). This Beat icon was written in a Tangier hotel room between 1954–57 and first published in France in 1959; its brazen obscenity prevented publication in the US until 1962 and in the UK until 1964. Put crudely, the book is about Burrough's addiction to hard drugs and young men. Its nonlinear, "cut-up" narrative was revolutionary, as was its twisted mix of allegory and slapstick. It is not, especially, about Morocco but if you are curious to read it for a first time, Tangier's the place.

William Bayer, *Tangier* (Dutton, US, 1971, o/p). Thinly disguised potboiler set amid the Tangier expat life of the 1960s.

Jane Bowles, *My Sister's Hand in Mine: The Collected Works of Jane Bowles* (Farrar Straus Giroux, US). Jane Bowles was resident in Morocco on and off, with her husband Paul, from the 1940s until her tragic death in 1973. Her work is strange and unique – really unlike anything else. She set a handful of stories (such as *Everything is Nice*) in Morocco. Millicent Dillon's biography, *A Little Original Sin: the Life of Jane Bowles* (University of California Press, US), includes some fascinating material.

Anthony Burgess, *Earthly Powers* (Penguin, UK/Carroll & Graf, US), *The Complete Enderby* (Carroll & Graf, US). Sporadic scenes in 1950s-decadent Tangier.

Aldo Busi, *Sodomies in Eleven Point* (Faber, UK). A (highly) picaresque tour of Morocco by the Italian novelist.

Elisa Chimenti, *Tales and Legends of Morocco* (Astor-Honor, US). Travelling in the 1930s and 1940s with her father, personal physician to Sultan Moulay Hassan, Chimenti learned many of these simple, fable-like tales from Berber tribesmen whose guest she was.

Rafael Chirbes, *Mimoun* (Serpent's Tail, UK/US). Compelling tale of a Spanish teacher, based south of Fes, adrift amid sexual adventures and bizarre local life and antagonisms.

Esther Freud, *Hideous Kinky* (Penguin, UK/WW Norton, US). You've seen the film? Well read the book – it's even better. An English hippy takes her two daughters to Marrakesh, where they live simply, as locals. The narrative – funny, sad, and full of informed insights – is told through the persona of the five-year-old.

Brion Gysin, *The Process* (The Overlook Press, US). Beat novel by ex-Tangier resident and friend of Paul Bowles and William Burroughs. Fun, if a little caught in its zany 1960s epoch.

John Haylock, *Body of Contention* (Arcadia, UK). An enjoyable romp set amid the expat community of Tangier in the months following Independence in 1957.

Richard Hughes, *In the Lap of Atlas* (Chatto, UK, o/p). Traditional Moroccan stories – cunning, humorous and ironic – reworked by the author of *A High Wind In Jamaica*. Also includes a narrative of Hughes' visit to Telouet and the Atlas in 1928.

Jane Kramer, *Honor to the Bride Like the Pigeon that Guards its Grain Under the Clove Tree* (Farrar, Straus & Giroux, US, 1970, o/p). Fictional narrative based on the true story of a Berber woman's kidnap in Meknes.

Amin Malouf, *Leo the African* (Abacus, UK); published as *Leo Africanus* (New Amsterdam, US). Superb historical novel, re-creating the life of Leo Africanus, the fifteenth-century Moorish geographer, in Granada and Fes and on later travels.

Robin Maugham, *The Wrong People* (Gay Men's Press, UK; o/p). Gay tragedy, set in Tangier.

Leonora Peets, *Women of Marrakesh* (C. Hurst, UK). Stories of domestic life in the city from the 1930s to 1970 by a long-term Estonian resident.

GLOSSARY

ADHAN the call to prayer

AGADIR fortified granary

AGDAL garden or park containing a pool

AGUELMANE lake

AÏN spring

AÏT tribe (literally, "sons of"); also *beni*

ALAOUITE ruling Moroccan dynasty from the seventeenth century to the present king, Mohammed VI

ALMOHAD the greatest of the medieval dynasties, ruled Morocco (and much of Spain) from c.1147 until the rise to power of the Merenids c.1224

ALMORAVIDS dynasty that preceded the Almohads, from c.1060 to c.1147

ANDALOUS Muslim Spain (a territory that centred on modern Andalucia)

ARABESQUE geometrical decoration or calligraphy

ASSIF river (often seasonal) in Berber

BAB gate or door

BABOUCHES slippers (usually yellow)

BALI (or **QDIM**) old

BARAKA sanctity or blessing, obtained through saints or marabouts

BARBARY European term for North Africa in the sixteenth to nineteenth centuries

BENI tribe (as *Aït*)

BERBERS native inhabitants of Morocco, and still the majority of the population

BLED countryside, or, literally "land"; **BLED ES MAKHZEN** – governed lands; **BLED ES SIBA** – land outside government control

BORDJ fort

CAID district administrator; **CADI** is an Islamic judge

CHLEUH southern Berber from the High or Anti-Atlas or plains

COL mountain pass (French)

DAR house or palace; **DAR EL MAKHZEN**, royal palace

DAYA, DEYET lake

DJEBEL mountain peak or ridge; a **DJEBALI** is someone from the mountains; the **DJEBALA** are the main tribe of the Western Rif

DJEDID, JDID new

DJELLABA wool or cotton hooded outer garment

DJEMAA, JAMAA mosque, or Friday (the main day of worship)

DJINN nature spirits (genies)

ERG sand dune

FAKIR Koranic schoolteacher or lawyer, or just an educated man

FANTASIA display of horsemanship performed at larger festivals or moussems

FASSI inhabitant of Fes

FILALI alternative name for the Alaouite dynasty – from the southern Tafilalt region

FONDOUK inn and storehouse, known as a caravanserai in the eastern part of the Arab world

GANDOURA man's cotton garment (male equivalent of a kaftan); also known as a *fokia*

GHARB coastal plain between Larache and Kenitra

GNAOUA itinerant musician, belonging to the Sufi brotherhood and of West African origin (from the same root as Guinea)

HABBOUS religious foundation or bequest of property for religious charities

HADJ pilgrimage to Mecca

HAMMADA stony desert of the sub-Sahara

HAMMAM Turkish-style steam bath

HARKA "burning" raid undertaken by sultans in order to raise taxes and assert authority

IDRISSID first Arab dynasty of Morocco – named after its founder, Moulay Idriss

IMAM prayer leader and elder of mosque

ISTIQLAL nationalist party founded during the struggle for independence

JOUTIA flea market

KASBAH palace centre and/or fortress of an Arab town; also used to mean a walled residential quarter around the Medina (eg Fes), or the citadel (eg Tangier and in Tunisia), or the whole medina (eg Algiers). In the south of Morocco, it is a feudal family castle – and it's the root of the Spanish *alcazar*.

KHETTARA underground irrigation canal

KIF marijuana, cannabis

KOUBBA dome; small marabout tomb

KSAR, KSOUR (pl.) village or tribal stronghold in the south

LALLA "madam", also a saint.

LITHAM veil

MAGHREB "West" in Arabic, used for Morocco and the North African countries

MAKHZEN government

MARABOUT holy man, and by extension his place of burial. These tombs, usually white-washed domes, play an important (and hetero-dox) role in the religion of country areas

MECHOUAR assembly place, court of judgement

MEDERSA student residence and, in part, a teaching annexe, for the old mosque universities

MEDINA literally, "city", now used for the original Arab part of any Moroccan town.

MELLAH Jewish quarter

MERENIDS dynasty from eastern plains who ruled from the thirteenth to fifteenth centuries

MIHRAB niche indicating the direction of Mecca (and for prayer)

MINARET tower attached to a mosque, used for call to prayer

MINZAH pavilion in a (usually palace) garden

MOULAY descendant of the Prophet Muhammad, a claim and title adopted by most Moroccan sultans

MOULOUD festival and birthday of the Prophet

MOUSSEM pilgrimage-festival

MSALLA prayer area

MUEZZIN, MUEDDIN singer who calls the faithful to prayer

NAZARENE, NSRANI Christian, or, more loosely, a European.

OUED river; can be seasonal or even dry on a permanent basis (a wadi in its anglicized form).

PISÉ mud and rubble building material

PISTE unsurfaced road or track, suitable for 4x4 or Renault 4L.

PROTECTORATE period of French and Spanish colonial occupation (1912–56)

QAHOUAJI café patron

RAMADAN month of fasting

RAS source or head

RAS EL MA water source

RIAD central courtyard within a home, open to the sky

RIBAT monastic fortress

SAADIAN southern dynasty from Drâa Valley, who ruled Morocco during the fifteenth century

SEBGHA lake or lagoon

SEGUIA irrigation canal

SHEIKH leader of religious brotherhood

SHEREEF descendant of the Prophet

SIDI, SI respectful title used for any man, like "Sir" or "Mister", also a saint

SOUK market, or market quarter

SUFI religious mystic; philosophy behind most of the religious brotherhoods

TABIA mud building material, as *pisé*

TIGHREMT similar to an agadir – fortified Berber home and storage place

TOUAREG nomadic Berber tribesmen of the disputed Western Sahara, fancifully known as "Blue Men" because of the blue dye of their cloaks (which gives a slight tinge to their skin)

TIZI mountain pass; as *col* in French

WATTASID fifteenth-century dynasty who replaced their cousins, the Merenids

ZAOUIA sanctuary established around a marabout tomb; seminary-type base for religious brotherhood

ZELLIJ geometrical mosaic tilework

GLOSSARY OF MOROCCAN STREET NAMES

Moroccan streets are often named after well-known historical figures, events and dates, and in recent years there has been a concerted drive to replace the old panoply of French and Spanish colonial names. As they're revealing of Moroccan interests and historical figures, a glossary follows of some of the most common.

Transliteration from Arabic into the Roman alphabet means that there are often many variations of the same name.

ABDELKRIM EL KATTABI Leader of the Rif war against the Spanish. In 1921, his Berber warriors defeated a Spanish army of 60,000 at Annoual. He formed the independent republic of the Rif, but was defeated by Spanish/French forces in 1926.

ALLAL BEN ABDALLAH On September 11, 1953, he tried to kill Sultan Ibn Aaraf who had been appointed by the French to succeed Mohammed V when he was sent into exile. Allal Ben Abdallah crashed an open car into the royal procession on its way to the mosque in Rabat and attacked the Sultan with a knife.

EL FARABI Born in Farab, now in Uzbekistan, he studied in Baghdad and taught as a Sufi in Aleppo, now in Syria. He lived from 870 to 950 and is one of the greatest Islamic philosophers; he harmonized Greek philosophy and Islamic thinking. He studied Aristotle, and was known as second only to him. Thus, he was known as Al Muallim Al Thani (the second teacher).

FERHAT HACHAD On December 7 and 8, 1952, there were massive riots in the streets of Casablanca and hundreds were killed. The overt cause of this was the assassination in Tunis of Ferhat Hachad, a Tunisian trade union leader and Arab nationalist.

HASSAN II The previous monarch and elder son of Mohammed V, whom he succeeded on **March 3, 1961**. He launched the Green March (see on p.535) on **November, 6 1975**. He died in **July 1999**.

IBN BATOUTA Born in Tangier (1304), he trained as a lawyer, made the pilgrimage to Mecca and was taken with a desire for further travel. He visited China and India, returning to Fes where he dictated his discoveries to a student. At the time, he was regarded as a romancer, but his reports turned out to be true.

IBN KHALDOUN Arab philosopher and historian, born in Tunis (1322) of an aristocratic family long resident in Muslim Spain, which he visited in 1362. He served as ambassador to Castile, Tamerlaine and the court at Fes. Study of North African history led him to his political theories about the natural life of a dynasty which he argued lasted only four generations.

IBN ROCHD Also known as Averroes, another of Islam's greatest philosophers. He was born in Córdoba (1126) and died in Marrakesh (1198). He introduced Christian monks to the works of Aristotle, but worked principally on astronomy, theology, mathematics and, particularly, medicine. Based in Marrakesh, he was doctor to Yacoub El Mansour.

IBN TACHFINE/YOUSSEF IBN TACHFINE A devout Muslim Berber from Adrar, now in Mauritania, and the first sultan of the Almoravid dynasty. He founded Marrakesh in 1060, captured Fes in 1069, fought against Alphonse IV and ruled Muslim Spain and the Maghreb as far east as Algiers.

IBN TOUMERT/MEHDI IBN TOUMERT Learned theologian, radical reformer and revolutionary leader, known as "The Torch". He was born around 1080, travelled to the Middle East in 1107, returned to Marrakesh in 1121, was expelled from there and took refuge with his warrior monks in the mountain stronghold of Tin Mal in 1124, where he died around 1130. He was believed by his followers to be the Mahdi – the "sinless one".

IBN ZAIDOUN Leading Andalucian poet of the eleventh century; like others, he followed the traditions of the east.

IBN ZIAD/TARIK BEN ZIAD/TARIK IBN ZIAD Berber chieftain who led the troops of Moussa Ibn Noussar across the Straits of Gibraltar. He defeated the Visigoths, near Tarifa, in 711, to bring seven centuries of civilization when the rest of Europe lived in the Dark Ages. He gave his name to Gibraltar – Djebel (mount) Tarik.

EL MANSOUR EDDAHBI The victory over the Portuguese at the Battle of the Three Kings in 1578 gave great prestige to El Mansour Eddahbi who succeeded his brother (who died in the battle). Mansour means "victorious"; Eddahbi means "golden".

MOHAMMED V Born in Fes in 1909, the third son of Sultan Moulay Youssef, he was chosen by the French to succeed his father on **November, 18 1927**. He was unprepared for his role, but gained strength with experience. He supported the joint manifesto of **January 11, 1944**, arguing for independence; he spoke openly for independence in Tangier, then in the International Zone, on **April 9, 1947**, and was deposed by the French on **August 20, 1953**. He returned from exile on **November 16, 1955**, to a hero's welcome and secured independence on **March 2, 1956**. He died in 1961 and was succeeded by his elder son, Hassan II.

MOHAMMED VI Hassan II's eldest son and current king, born in Rabat on August 21, 1963. He came to the throne on the death of his father in 1999.

MOHAMMED BEN ABDALLAH/SIDI MOHAMMED BEN ABDALLAH Grandson of Moulay Ismail, he gained the throne in 1757, and brought some order out of chaos. He established Essaouira in the 1760s, drove the Portuguese from El Jadida, armed the port of Larache and developed Tangier. Finally he contained the Spanish in their enclaves.

MOHAMMED ZERKTOUNI The most famous Moroccan freedom fighter. On December 24, 1953, in Casablanca's central market he placed a bomb in a shopping basket which killed twenty people and injured twenty-eight.

MOKHTAR SOUSSI Poet and nationalist figure during the French occupation. On independence, he became the government minister of *habous* (religious foundations which fund mosques, hospitals and schools). He also wrote a twelve-volume history of the Souss, his native province.

MOULAY ABDALLAH/PRINCE MOULAY ABDALLAH Younger son of Mohammed V. He married a Lebanese princess, Lamia Sohl and often deputized for his brother, Hassan II. He died in 1984.

MOULAY EL CHERIF/MOULAY RACHID First sultan (1666–1672) of the Alaouite dynasty –

originally an Arab family which settled in the Tafilalt in the twelfth century, where they lived modestly for centuries before seizing power. Er Rachidia (and its main street) are named after Moulay Rachid.

MOULAY HASSAN/HASSAN I The last notable Alaouite sultan (1873–1894) before the French Protectorate. He strived to damp down European-sponsored rebellion, attempting to reform his army with the help of a Scot, Caid Harry MacLean. He died suddenly and was succeeded by his son, Abd El Aziz, a profligate dreamer.

MOULAY IDRISS/MOULAY IDRISS I/ MOULAY IDRISS II Father and his posthumous son by a Berber mother. Moulay Idriss I (788–91) founded the first orthodox Muslim dynasty, ruling the northern Maghreb from Tlemcen, now in Algeria, to the Atlantic. After a regency, his son, Moulay Idriss II (804–28), came to the throne; he founded Fes and is regarded as the father of the Moroccan state.

MOULAY ISMAIL The second sultan of the Alaouite dynasty (1672–1727), but the first to establish complete rule over Morocco. His 55-year reign was one of the longest, and said to be the most brutal, in Moroccan history. He chose, and developed, Meknes as his capital. After his death, his sons fought over the succession and chaos ensued.

MOULAY YOUSSEF Appointed by the French as sultan (1912–27); he was the father of Mohammed V and grandfather of Hassan II.

MOUSSA IBN NOUSSAR Followed Oqba Ibn Nafi (see below) and converted the Berbers again to Islam. He conquered all the territory as far south as the Tafilalt, and launched Tarik Ibn Zaid across the Straits of Gibraltar.

OQBA IBN NAFI Military general and missionary who led the first Arab expedition westwards to convert the Berbers to Islam. He left Arabia in 666; founded Kairouan in present-day Tunisia in 670; and moved on into Morocco, reaching the Atlantic in 682. He was ambushed and killed by Berbers in (present-day) Algeria on his return to the east.

SALAH EDDINE EL AYOUBI (1137–90) Better known in the West as Salah Al Din or Saladin. He recaptured Jerusalem (then known, in Arabic, as Al Qods) from the Crusaders in 1187.

YACOUB EL MANSOUR/YACOUB EL MANSOUR AL MOUAHIDI Powerful sultan (1184–99) who created an empire comprising Muslim Spain and most of North Africa. He won the title "Mansour" (Victorious) when he defeated the Christians under Alfonso VIII of Castile at the battle of Alarcos on July 18, 1195. He was a generous patron of poets and philosophers.

DATES

Numerous dates, particularly those associated with Mohammed V and Hassan II (see their respective entries), have been commemorated as street names. The most common include:

January 11, 1944 Mohammed V backed the nationalist cause when the Istiqlal party issued its manifesto on January 11, 1944, demanding, for the first time, not just reform but independence.

February 29, 1960 The Agadir earthquake struck thirteen minutes before midnight, lasting fifteen seconds.

March 2, 1956 France renounced the Protectorate and, in a formal treaty, recognized Moroccan independence. It was the 45th anniversary of the entry of French troops into Fes.

July 5, 1999 Aïd El Arch (Festival of the Throne) is celebrated on the anniversary of the accession of the king.

August 16, 1953 Over three days (August 16–18, 1953) there were anti-French riots in Casablanca, Rabat, Marrakesh and Oujda. Over 45 people were killed and more than eighty injured in Oujda alone on August 16.

August 20, 1953 On this day, the eve of Aïd El Kebir, Mohammed V was deposed by the French and was exiled first in Corsica, then Madagascar. Mayhem followed.

November 6, 1975 The date of the Green March – Al Massira Al Khadra (see below).

November 16, 1955 Mohammed V returned from exile to a hero's welcome. He told crowds around the Rabat Palace that the Protectorate was over and independence would follow.

November 18, 1927/November 18, 1955 Mohammed V ascended the throne on November 18, 1927 and thus, during his reign, this was celebrated as Aïd El Arch (see March 3, above). In 1955, it was also celebrated as Independence Day and has been celebrated subsequently as such. The three days (November 16, 17 & 18) are taken as a holiday and are known as Les Trois Glorieuses.

EVENTS/ORGANIZATIONS

AL JAMIA AL ARABI The Arab League: formed in Egypt in 1945 and moved to Tunisia in 1979 following the Camp David peace accord between Egypt and Israel.

AL MASSIRA AL KHADRA/MARCHE VERTE The Green March into then Spanish Sahara was led by Ahmed Osman, Prime Minister at the time and brother-in-law to Hassan II. It began on November 6, 1975, and on November 14 Spain transferred administration of the territory to Morocco and Mauritania.

BIR ANZARANE Town in the Western Sahara and site of fierce battle between Moroccan and Polisario forces in 1979.

EL HOURIA Houria means freedom/liberté.

F.A.R./FORCES ARMÉES ROYALES After Mohammed V and Hassan II, the Armed Forces is the most popular name for avenues/boulevards, and their motto 'God, the Fatherland and the King' is to be found prominently displayed on many a hillside.

ISTIQLAL Istiqlal means **independence** and was adopted as its name by the nationalist party formed in Fes in 1943, with Allal Al Fasi as its first president. By 1951, the party had 100,000 members.

OUED EL MAKHAZINE Site of the Battle of the Three Kings (see El Mansour Eddahbi). The Portuguese found themselves trapped in a fork between the river Loukis and its tributary, the Oued El Makhazine. In European histories it is more often referred to as the battle of Ksar El Kebir.

LANGUAGE

Very few people who come to Morocco learn to speak a word of Arabic, let alone anything of the country's three distinct Berber dialects. This is a pity – you'll be treated in a very different way if you make even a small effort to master basic phrases – though not really surprising. Moroccans are superb linguists: much of the country is bilingual in French, and anyone who has significant dealings with tourists will know some English and maybe half-a-dozen other languages, too.

If you can speak French, you'll be able to get by almost anywhere you care to go; it is worth refreshing your knowledge before coming – and, if you're not too confident, bringing a good English–French phrasebook. Spanish is also useful, and widely understood in the old Spanish colonial zones around Tetouan and the Rif, and in the Deep South.

MOROCCAN ARABIC

Moroccan Arabic, the country's official language, is substantially different from classical Arabic, or from the modern Arabic spoken in Egypt and the Gulf States. If you speak any form of Arabic, however, you will be able to make yourself understood. Egyptian Arabic, in particular, is familiar to most Moroccans, through soap operas on TV, and many will adapt their speech accordingly.

PRONUNCIATION

There are no silent letters – you pronounce everything that's written – including double vowels. Letters and syllables **in bold** should be stressed.

Here are some keys to follow in pronouncing:

kh	like the "ch" in Scottish loch	ay	as in "say"
gh	like the French "r" (a slight gargling sound)	q	like "k" but further back in throat
ai	as in "eye"	j	like "s" in pleasure

BASICS

Yes	Na'**am**, E**ey**eh	(Very) good	Mezy**en**a (bz**ef**)
No	La	Bad/"ugly"	**Me**shee mezy**en**a/**kha**ib
Please	Minf**ad**lik/ Af**ek**	Beautiful	Zween/zweena
Thank you	Shokran/ Baraka**low**fik	Today	Ly**oom**/ lee**oom**
(polite response – **Blej**mccl)		Tomorrow	**Gh**edda

GREETINGS AND FAREWELLS

Hello	La **bes**	My name is	Ismee. . .
(informal, to one person)		What's your name?	S**mee**tik?
Response	Be**heer**	See you later.	N'**shoof**ik min bad
Hello	Sal**am** wa**lay**koom	. . . God willing	. . . In**shall**ah
(formal, to a group; response – Wa**lay**koom salam)		(response to "In**shall**ah" is In**shall**ah)	
		Good night	**Lee**la saieeda
Good morning	Sbah l'**khir**	Good-bye	B**slem**ah
Good afternoon	Msa l'**khir**	Bon voyage	Treq sal**ama**

continued overleaf

MOROCCAN ARABIC continued

DIRECTIONS, TRAVELLING, AND ACCOMMODATION

Where is . . . ?	Feen **kay**n . . . ?	When is the	Waq**tash** l'kar/tren?
. . . a (good) hotel?	. . . **O**tel (mizee**yen**)	bus/train?	
. . . a campsite?	. . . Moo**khai**yem	First/last/next	**Loo**wel/L'**akh**er/Lee
. . . a restaurant?	. . . Restaurant		minbad
. . . a bank?	. . . Bank	Write it (please).	Ktib ha (**Af**ek)
. . . the bus station?	. . . **Mah**atat d'lkee**ran**	Do you have a room?	Wesh **and**ik wahid
. . . the train station?	. . . l'Gare		beet?
. . . a toilet?	. . . Vaysay/ W.C.	Can I see it?	Wesh yimkin nshoof?
Straight	**Nee**shan/ tol	Is there. . . ?	Wesh kayn . . . ?
(To the) left,	(Al) Leeser,	. . . a (hot) shower?	. . . Doosh (skhoon)
right	Lee**min**	. . . a window?	. . . **Ser**jem
Near, far	Qreeb, Baieed	. . . a key?	. . . **Sar**oot
Junction	Rompwa	Can we camp here?	Wesh yimkin n**khai**moo
Here, there	Hn**na**, Tem**ma**		hanna

BUYING AND NUMBERS

How much (is that)?	Bsh **hal** (hadeek)	I want something. . .	Bgheet shi**haja** . . .
This isn't good	Hadee **me**shee mizee**yen**	. . . else	. . . **okh**ra
Too expensive	**Gha**lee bz**ef**	. . . better than this	. . . khir min hadee
. . . (for me)	(**ali**ya)	. . . like this	. . . bh**al** hadee
Still too expensive	Mazal **gha**lee bz**ef**	(but)	(walakeen)
Do you have. . . ?	wesh **and**ik. . . ?	. . . larger, smaller	. . . ke**bira**, seg**hira**
Okay	**Wak**ha	. . . cheaper	. . . r**khay**sa

1	wahed	12	tinach	40	arbaeen
2	tneen (Classical)	13	teltach	50	khamseen
	jooj (everyday)	14	arbatach	60	setteen
3	tlata	15	khamstach	70	seba'een
4	arba	16	settach	80	tmaneen
5	khamsa	17	sebatach	90	tsa'een
6	setta	18	tmentach	100	mia
7	sebaa	19	tsatach	200	miateen
8	tmenia	20	achreen	300	telt mia
9	tse'ud	21	wahed u achrin	400	arba mia
10	achra	22	tneen u achrin	1000	alef
11	hadach	30	tlateen		

USEFUL PHRASES/REACTIONS

I have . . .	Andee . . .	. . . key	. . . **sar**oot
That's all	Sahfee	. . . baggage	. . . bag**gaj**/how**ayj**
I don't have any money	Mandeesh floos	Help!	A**teqq**/ **Own**ee!
I've seen it already.	Shift ha baada	How do you say?	Keef t**kool**oo?
I don't want any.	Mabgheet**sh**	Excuse me	**Smeh** lee
I don't understand.	Mafhem**sh**	Sorry, I apologize	A**sif**
Do you understand?	Wesh f**hem**tee?	Never mind, so it goes	**Maa**lesh
Get lost!	Seer!	No problem	Meckee mush**keel**
Everything's fine.	**Kool**shee	Respect yourself	I**h**tarim na**fs**ak
	mizee**yen**	(a term of admonition)	
Let's go!	**Yallah!**	Calm down	**Taw**il **b**alak
Watch out!	**And**ak/ **Bal**ek!	(literally, "lengthen	
I've lost . . .	Msha leeya . . .	your mind")	
. . . passport	. . . passeport	You honour us	Too-shah-rif-na
. . . ticket	. . . **beeyay**/ warqa	Patience is a virtue	As-**sob**rmin Allah

BERBER WORDS AND PHRASES IN TASHELHAÏT

There are three Berber dialects which encompass roughly geographical areas. They are known by several names, of which these are the most common:
Riffi – The Rif mountains and Northern Morocco
Zaian, Tamazight – The Middle Atlas and Central Morocco
Tashelhaït, Soussi, Chleuh – The High and Anti-Atlas and the South
As the most popular Berber areas for visitors are the High Atlas and South, the following is a very brief guide to **Tashelhaït words and phrases**.

BASICS

Yes, no	Eyeh, Oho	Tomorrow	Sbah
Thank you, please	Barakalaufik	Yesterday	Eegdam
Good	Eefulkee/Eeshwa	Excuse me	Semhee
Bad	Khaib	Berbers	Shleuh
Today	Ghasad		

GREETINGS AND FAREWELLS (All Arabic greetings understood)

Hello	La bes darik (man)	See you later	Akrawes dah inshallah
(response – la bes)	La bes darim (woman)	Goodbye	Akayaoon Arbee
How are you?	Meneek antgeet?	Say hello to your	Sellum flfamilenik
(response – la bes Imamdulah)		family	

DIRECTIONS AND NAMES ON MAPS

Where is. . . ?	Mani heela . . . ?	I want to go to . . .	Reeh . . .
. . . the road to . . .	. . . aghares s . . .	(literally, "I want")	
. . . the village . . .	. . . doowar . . .		
. . . the river . . .	. . . aseet . . .	On survey maps you'll find these names:	
. . . the mountain . . .	. . . adrar . . .	Mountain	Adrar, Djebel
. . . the pass . . .	. . . tizee . . .	River	Assif, Oued
. . . your house	. . . teegimeenik	Pass (of)	Tizi (n.)
Is it far/close?	Ees yagoog/eeqareb?	Shepherd's hut	Azib
Straight	Neeshan	Hill, small mountain	Aourir
To the right/left	Fofaseenik/fozelmad	Ravine	Talat
Where are you going?	Manee treet? (s.)	Rock	Azrou
	Manee drem? (pl.)	("n" between words indicates the possessive,"of")	

BUYING AND NUMBERS

1	yen	8	tem	22	Ashreent d seen d mrawet
2	seen	9	tza	30	Ashreent d mrawet
3	krad	10	mrawet	40	Snet id ashreent
4	koz	11	yen d mrawet	50	Snet id ashreent d mrawet
5	smoos	12	seen d mrawet	100	Smoost id ashreent/meeya
6	sddes	20	Ashreent		
7	sa	21	Ashreent d yen d mrawet		

How much is it?	Minshk aysker?	. . . food	. . . teeremt
No good	oor eefulkee	. . . a mule	. . . aserdon
Too expensive	Eeghula bzef	. . . a place to sleep	. . . kra lblast mahengwen
Come down a little (in price)	Nuqs emeek	. . . water	. . . amen
Give me . . .	Feeyee . . .		

IMPERATIVES YOU MAY HEAR

I want . . .	Reeh . . .	Sit	Gawer, Skoos
Big/Small	Mqorn/Eemzee	Drink	Soo
A lot/little	Bzef/eemeek	Eat	Shta
Do you have . . . ?	Ees daroon . . . ?	Here	Rede (when handing
Is there . . . ?	Ees eela . . . ?		something to someone)

FRENCH ESSENTIALS

BASICS AND GREETINGS

Yes/no	Oui/non	Could you?	Pourriez-vous?
Hello, good day	Bonjour	Why?	Pourquoi?
Sorry, excuse me	Pardon	What?	Quoi?
How are you?	Ça va?	Open	Ouvert
Goodbye	Au revoir	Closed	Fermé
Please	S'il vous plaît	Go away!	Va-t-en
Thank you	Merci	Stop messing me about!	Arrête de m'emmerder!
I/you	Je/vous	No confidence!	Pas de confiance!

DIRECTIONS

Where is the	Quelle est la route	Far	Loin
road for . . . ?	pour . . . ?	When?	Quand?
Where is . . . ?	Où est . . . ?	At what time?	A quelle heure?
Do you have . . . ?	Avez vous . . . ?	Write it down, please	Ecrivez-le, s'il vous plaît
. . . a room?	. . . une chambre?	Now	Maintenant
Here, there	Ici, là	Later	Plus tard
Right	A droite	Never	Jamais
Left	A gauche	Today	Aujourd'hui
Straight on	Tout droit	Tomorrow	Demain
Near	Proche, près	Yesterday	Hier

THINGS

Bus	Car, autobus	Key	Clef
Bus station	Gare routière	Roof	Terrasse
Railway	Chemin de fer	Passport	Passeport
Airport	Aéroport	Exchange	Change
Railway station	Gare	Post office	Poste
Ferry	Ferry	Stamps	Timbres
Lorry	Camion	Left luggage	Consigne
Ticket (return)	Billet (de retour)	Visa	Visa
Bank	Banque	Money	Argent

BUYING

How much/many?	Combien?	Like this/that	Comme ceci/cela
How much does that cost?	Combien ça coute?	What is it?	Qu'est-ce que c'est?
Too expensive	Trop cher	Enough	Assez
More/less	Plus/moin	Big	Grand
Cheap	Bon marché	Little	Petit

NUMERALS

١	1	١٠	10	١٩	19	٨٠	80
٢	2	١١	11	٢٠	20	٩٠	90
٣	3	١٢	12	٢١	21	١٠٠	100
٤	4	١٣	13	٢٢	22	٢٠٠	200
٥	5	١٤	14	٣٠	30	٣٠٠	300
٦	6	١٥	15	٤٠	40	٤٠٠	400
٧	7	١٦	16	٥٠	50	١٠٠٠	1000
٨	8	١٧	17	٦٠	60		
٩	9	١٨	18	٧٠	70		

ARABIC/BERBER PHRASEBOOKS & LEARNING MATERIALS

Arabic phrasebooks
Moroccan Arabic Phrasebook (Lonely Planet, Australia). The most functional English–Moroccan Arabic phrasebook.
In Moroccan bookshops, you can pick up a *Guide de Conversation/Conversation Guide*, which covers basic phrases of English–French–Moroccan Arabic–Berber.

Arabic coursebooks
Ernest T. Abdel Massih, *An Introduction to Moroccan Arabic; Advanced Moroccan Arabic*. Both of these are published by University of Michigan Press, with accompanying tapes.
Richard S Harris and Mohammed Abn Tald, *Basic Course in Moroccan Arabic* (Georgetown UP).

Berber coursebooks
Ernest T. Abdel Massih, *A Course in Spoken Tamazight: Berber Dialects of the Middle Atlas, A Reference Grammar of Tamazight, Plus An Introduction to the Berber Language*. Again, both these are published by University of Michigan Press, with accompanying tapes.

Arabic lessons in Morocco
Contact the American Language Centre (head office: 1 Place de la Fraternité, Casablanca).

University of Michigan Publications
For **books** write to The Publications Secretary, Centre for Near Eastern and ANorth African Studies, 144 Lane Hall, University of Michigan, Ann Arbor, Michigan 48109. For **tapes** write to: Michigan Media Resource Centre (Tape Duplication Service), University of Michigan, 400 S. Fourth Street, Ann Arbor, Michigan 48103.

Bookshops
The following bookshops usually have language reference material:
Librairie des Colonnes, Bd. Pasteur, Tangier.
American Language Centre Bookstore, 1 Place de la Fraternite, just off Bd. Moulay Youssef, Casablanca.
American Bookstore, Rue Tangier, Rabat.
The Maghreb Review and Bookshop, 45 Bruton St, London WC1, England.

INDEX

A

Abbainou 526
Abd El Aziz 557
Abd El Krim 138, 558
Abd El Moumen 553
Abd Er Rahman 556
Abderrahmane Youssoufi 564
Abdessalam Yassine 565
Abou El Hassan 554
Abou Inan 554
accommodation 49
Ad Dakhla (Dakhla) 544
addresses 72
Adrar Mkorn 517
Afensou 411
Agadir 473–485
  Ancienne Talborjt 481
  arrival 476
  bars and nightlife 482
  beach 480
  campsite 479
  hotels 477
  Kasbah 481
  leaving 483
  listings 483
  restaurants 481
Agard Oudad 519
Agdz 426
Agoudal 453
Agoudim 265
Agoundis valley 402
Agouräi 198
Agouz 328
Aguelmame Azigza 249
Aguelmame Sidi Ali 250
Ahmed El Mansour 555
Ahouach 580
Aïd El Kebir 61
Aïd Es Seghir 61
Aïn Leuh 248
Aissaoua 571
Aït Arbi 444
Aït Atta 442, 433
Aït Baha 514
Aït Bekkou 526
Aït Benhaddou 408, 423
Aït Benimathar 171, 469
Aït Driss 411

Aït Hamed 500
Aït Hani 453
Aït Herbil 506
Aït Mansour 519
Aït Oufi 444
Aït Ourir 408
Aït Smageane-n-el Grara 435
Aït Souala 198
Aït Youb 403
Akhfame 501
Akhfenir 538
Akka 505
Aknoul 144
Al Hoceima 150–154
Al-Adl wal Ihsane 565
Alaouite dynasty 555
Almohad dynasty 553
Almoravid dynasty 552
Alnif 434
Amalou n'Mansour 443
Amazrou (Zagora) 429
Ameln valley 517
American Express agencies 26
Amizmiz 402
ammougars 62
Amsouzart 500
Amtoudi 507
Anameur 518
Andalous music 581
Anemiter 409
Angour traverse 398
animal welfare 72
Annoual 155
Annoual, Battle of 558
Anti-Atlas 514–520
Aoufouss 459
Aouili 252
Aourir 486
Arabic numerals 624
Arabic, Moroccan 621–622
Arboaua 112
Aremd (Aroumd) 394
Arg 403
Argan trees 487
Argana 412
Arhbala 258, 454
Arhbalou 384
Aroumd 394
Asif M'Goun 438
Asilah 102–106
  Asilah International Festival 102
Asni 387
Assaka 513

Assif n'Tifnout 499
Atlas mountain music 580
Atougha 501
Awlim 411
Azemmour 316
Azilal 263
Azrou 245
Azurki 264

B

Bab Berred 140
Bab n'Ali 443
Bab Taza 140
Banasa, Ancient 113
banks 25
Barbary apes 577
bargaining 69
bars 56
Battle of the Three Kings 554
Bayoud disease 457
BBC World Service 60
beer 56
Ben Barka, Mehdi 561
Beni Enzar 159
Beni Mellal 259
Berber language 623
Berber music 580
Berbers, High Atlas 382
Berbers, origins 549
Berkane 165
Bhalil 241
bibliography 607–615
Bin El Ouidane 262
birds 573
blankets 68
books on Morocco 607–615
Bou Ahmed 557
Bou Azzer 435
Bou Gafer 443
Bou Goumez valley 264
Bou Hamed 127
Bou Hamra 557
Bou Izakarn 507, 523
Bou Regreg Republic 555
Bouarfa 171, 468
Boudenib 468
Boujdor 544
Boulaich, Abdeslam 593
Boulaouane 315
Boumalne du Dades 438
Bouzmou 454
Bouznika Plage 297

Bowles, Paul 603, 607, 612, 614
British Moroccan Society 72
brotherhoods, religious 64, 571, 582
buses 41

C

Cabo Negro 126
Caid MacClean 557
campsites 52
Canetti, Elias 602, 607
cannabis 56
Cap Beddouza 324
Cap des Trois Forches 157
Cap Hadid 328
Cap Malabata 101
Cap Rhir 487
Cap Sim 339
Cap Spartel 100
car rental 43
carpets 68
Carthaginians 549
Casablanca 299–314
  accommodation 304
  Aïn Diab 309
  arrival 303
  bars and nightlife 312
  beach 309
  Cathedral 308
  Habous 308
  Hassan II Mosque 306
  history 299
  Jewish community 308
  leaving 314
  listings 313
  movie, the 307
  Old Medina 309
  restaurants 310
  transport 303
  Ville Nouvelle 308
Cascades Bou Mazouz 150
Cascades d'Ouzoud 263
Cascades de Ras El Oued 149
cassettes 587
Caves of Hercules 100
CD reviews 586
Ceuta 114–118
Chaabi music 583
Chaouen 127–133
Chefchaouen 127–133
Cheferat 140
chemists 27
Cherket 454

Chichaoua 410
Choukri, Mohammed 595, 612
chronology 566–568
Cirque Jaffar 253
city transport 48
climate xiv, xv
clothes, Moroccan 69
coaches to Morocco 10
Col du Kerdous 513
consulates (foreign) in Morocco 38
consulates, Moroccan abroad 23
contraceptives 72
costs 23
Cotta, Ancient 101
crafts 68
credit cards 25
CTM buses 41
currency 24
customs allowances 72
cycling in Morocco 46

D

Dadès gorge 444
Dadès valley 435–446
Dahomey Plage 297
Dakhla 544
Dar Caid Ouriki 384
Dayet Aouua 243
Dayet Er Roumi 197
Demnate 265
Diabat 337, 339
discography 586
Djebel Abad 241
Djebel Afougal 443
Djebel Amlal 443
Djebel Ayachi 250
Djebel Bani 432
Djebel Bou Gafer 443
Djebel Bou Iblane 241
Djebel Bou Nacceur 241
Djebel El Kest 517, 518
Djebel Erdouz 403
Djebel Igdat 403
Djebel Iguiguil 500
Djebel Kissane 426
Djebel Moussa 102
Djebel R'Nim 261
Djebel Sarhro 440–444
Djebel Sirwa 500
Djebel Tassemit 261

Djebel Tazzeka 148
Djebel Toubkal 387–399, 499, 500
Djebel Yagour 385
Djebel Zagora 429
Drâa valley 425–433
drinks 56
driving to Morocco 10
driving within Morocco 44
drugs regulations 57

E

Ech Chiana 296
El Ayoun (Laayoune) 539–543
El Hajeb 198
El Hammam 469
El Jadida 317–321
El Jebha 127
El Jorf 455
El Kelâa des Mgouna 438
El Ksiba 257
El Maiz 469
El Makhzen 403
El Mansour, Ahmed 555
El Moumen, Abd 553
electrical voltage 72
embassies (foreign) in Morocco 38
Er Rachidia 456–459
Erfoud 459–462
Erg Lakhbayta 539
Essaouira 328–338
expedition tours 6 (UK), 17 (US), 20 (Australia)

F

ferries to Morocco 11
Fes (Fez) 198–238
  accommodation 205
  Andalous mosque 227
  Andalous quarter 226
  arrival 202
  Attarin medersa 220
  Bab Boujeloud 212
  Bab Ftouh 227
  Bab Guissa 225
  bars and nightlife 234
  Bou Inania medersa 214
  Bou Inania water-clock 215
  Boujeloud Gardens 229
  campsite 209
  Cherabliyin mosque 217
  Cherratin medersa 223
  Dar Batha museum 212

Dar Saada 217
Dyers' souk 223
Fes El Bali 209
Fes El Djedid 227
Fondouk Guissa 225
guides 204
Hebrew cemetery 231
history 199
hotels 205
Jewellers' quarter 225
Kairaouine mosque 219
Kasbah Cherada 230
listings 235
Mechouars 229
Mellah 231
Merenid tombs 212
Misbahiya medersa 222
Moulay Idriss Zouia 217
Nejjarin souk 218
Palais de Fes 222
Palais Jamai hotel 206
Palais Jamai hotel 225
Place des Alaouites 232
Potters' quarter 227
restaurants 233
Royal Palace 232
Sahrija medersa 227
Seffarine medersa 223
shopping 236
Souk El Attarin 217
Souk El Henna 219
synagogues 231
Talâa Kebira 214
Talâa Seghira 213
tanneries 224
Tetouani fondouk 222
transport 203
festivals 61
fiction, Moroccan 590–598,
   612
Figuig 468
fishing 66
flash floods 383
flights to Morocco
   from Australia and
      New Zealand 18
   from Britain 3
   from Canada 15
   from Ireland 8
   from the US 14
flights within Morocco 39
flora 575
flowers 575
Fnideq 116, 126
food 52
football 65
Forbes, Malcolm 91
Fort Bou–Jerif 526

Foum El Hassan 506
Foum el Oued 543
Foum Zguid 434, 504
Freija 497
French, colonization and
   Protectorate 557–559
Friouato Cave 149

G

gay attitudes/laws 72
gendarmerie 38
geology 575
Gharnati 582
Glaoui, Madani El 557
Glaoui, T'Hami El 360, 408, 559
Glossary of Moroccan street
   names 618
Glossary of Moroccan terms
   616
Gnaoua music 583
golf 67, 317
Goulimine 523
Goulmima 454
Goundafi kasbahs 406
Gouraud's Cedar 244
Gouttitir 150
grands taxis 40
Green March 562
Grotte du Chameau 165
Grotte du Friouato
   (Friouato cave) 149
Guercif 150, 155
guidebooks (trekking) 33
guides 34
Guliz 501

H

Hadj 570
Haha 339
hammams 50
Hammat Moulay Ali Cherif 255
Harris, Walter 88, 102, 601,
   607
Hassan II 560–564
health 27
High Atlas 380–414
High Atlas trekking
   practicalities 388
High Atlas trekking seasons
   380
hiking 65, 382, 286, 388, 495
Hilali 552

history of Morocco 549–565
hitching within Morocco 43
holidays, public 62
horse-riding 486
hospitals 27
hotels 49
hustlers 34

I

Ibn Battuta 554
Ibn Khaldun 552, 554
Ibn Nafi, Oqba 551
Ibn Nasr, Moussa 551
Ibn Toumert 405, 553
Id Aïssa (Amtoudi) 507
Idni 404
Idrissid dynasty 551
Ifouriren (Tin Mal) 4045
Ifrane (Djebel Sirwa) 502
Ifrane (Middle Atlas) 243
Ifrane de l'Anti-Atlas 508
Igherm (Anti-Atlas) 502
Ighil Mgoun 264
Ihoukarn 502
Ijoukak 402
Ikassene 258
Ikkis valley 254
Iknioun 442
Ile de Mogador 336
Imenane valley 398
Imi n'Tanoute 410
Imi n'Waka 265
Imilchil 454
Imiter 446
Imlil (Toubkal) 391
Immouzer des Ida Outanane
   489
Immouzer du Kandar 242
Imoulas 413
independence 559
independence struggle 558
Inezgane 485
inoculations 27
insects 578
insurance, health/travel 29
Irherm (Tizi n'Tichka) 407
Islam 569–572
Islam, origins in Morocco 550
Islamist politics 564
Islas Chafarinas 158
Istiqlal 559
Itzer 250

Izerbi 514

J
Jaffar, Cirque 253
Jajouka,
   Master Musicians of 583
Jardins Exotiques 273
Jemaa Ida Oussemal 514
jewellery 68
Jewish music 589
Jilala music 583
Juba II 550

K
Kâaseras 127
Kalah Iris 141
Kariet Arkmane 158
Kasba Tadla 258
Kasbah Boulaouane 315
Kasbah Gharbia 323
Kasbah Hamidouch 328
Kasbah Tifoultoutte
   (Tifoultoutte) 421
kasbahs 425, 436, 444
Kasr El-Oudarhir 469
Kassita 155
Kenitra 269
Ketama 140
Khémisset 197
Khenifra 255
kif 56, 142
Kik Plateau 390
koubbas 71
Ksabi 252
Ksar (ksour) 425, 436, 444
Ksar el Kebir 111
Ksar es Seghir 102

L
Laayoune 539–543
Laayoune Plage 543
Lac d'Ifni 396
Lac du Sidi Bourhaba 273
Lac Izoughar 264
Lac Ouiouane 249
Lalla Fatma 324
Language 621–625
   Arabic 621
   Arabic numerals 624
   Berber 623
   Coursebooks 625
   French 624

Phrasebooks 625
Tashelhaït 623
Larache 107
laundries 73
Layachi, Larbi 612
Lemseyed 538
Lemsid 544
Lepiney refuge
   (Tazarhart refuge) 399
Lixus, Ancient 110
lorry transport 43
Lyautey, General Hubert 558

M
M'Hamid 433
Maadid 459
Madani El Glaoui 557
Maghreb society 72
mail 57
Mansouria 297
maps 30
Marabouts 570
markets 68
Marrakesh 342–379
   accommodation 348
   Agdal garden 370
   Almoravid koubba 359
   arrival 346
   Bab Debbagh 360
   Bab Doukkala 361
   Bab el Khemis 361
   bars and nightlife 376
   Ben Youssef medersa 358
   crafts 356
   Criée Berbère 357
   Dar el Glaoui 362
   Dar Si Said 369
   Djemaa el Fna 352
   Dyers' souk 357
   El Badi palace 365
   El Bahia palace 368
   Folklore Festival 366
   fondouks 361
   guides 356
   history 343
   kissarias 357
   Koutoubia 353
   La Mamounia hotel 372
   listings 376
   Maison Tiskiwin 370
   Majorelle garden 371
   Marrakesh Museum 359
   Mellah 367
   Menara garden 371
   restaurants 372
   Saadian tombs 362

shopping 356
Sidi Bel Abbes Zaouia 316
Souk el Khemis 360
Souks 354
tanneries 360
transport 347
Martil 125
Massa lagoon 490
Massif du Kandar 241
Mauritania, overland route 545
Mdiq 126
Meakin, Budgett 599, 607
medersas, function of 215
media, Moroccan 60
Mediterranean Coast, The
   136–171
Mehdiya Plage 272
Meknes 176–191
   Agdal basin 185
   arrival 177
   Bab Mansour 182
   bars and nightlife 190
   Bou Inania medersa 187
   campsite 181
   Dar el Kebira 184
   Dar el Makhzen 184
   Dar Jamai museum 185
   Haras de Meknes 184
   Heri as-Souani 185
   hotels 177
   Imperial City 181
   leaving 191
   listings 190
   Medina 185
   Moulay Ismail mausoleum 183
   restaurants 188
   Rouah 185
   Souks 186
   SPANA 184
Melilla 159–164
Mellab 455
menus 54
Merdja Zerga 113
Merenid dynasty 553
Merzouga 464
Meski 459
Mibladene 252
Middle Atlas 238–266
Midelt 250
Milhûn 582
minerals 453
Mirhleft 520
Mischliffen 245
Mohammed en Nasr 553
Mohammed esh Sheikh 554
Mohammed III 556

Mohammed V 559
Mohammedia 297
money 23
monkeys 577
Mont Araoui 155
monuments 70
Moroccan Tourist Board
(ONMT) 30
Morocco/Spanish border 116
mosques 70
motorbiking in Morocco 45
Moulay Abdallah 322
Moulay Bousselham 112
Moulay Brahim 387
Moulay Hafid 557
Moulay Hassan 556
Moulay Idriss 196, 551
Moulay Ismail 182, 555
Moulay Ismail 182, 555
Moulay Rashid 555
Moulay Slimane 556
Moulay Yacoub 237
mouloud 62
moussems 62
Mouvement Populaire 560
MPCD 565
Mrabet, Mohammed 590, 612
Msemrir 445
Msoun 150
music 580–589
musical instruments 584
Mzoura 107
Mzouzite 403

N
Nador 155
Neltner refuge (Toubkal refuge)
395
Nfis gorges 402
Nkob 434, 443
numerals, Arabic 624

O
ONMT (tourist board) 30
opening hours 74
Oualad Driss 433
Oualidia 322
Ouaouizaght 257
Ouarzazate 417–423
Oued Laou 127
Oued Moulouya 158
Oued Souss 498
Ouezzane 133

Ougdemt valley 403
Ouirgane 401
Oujda 166–171
Oukaïmeden 385
Ouled Berhil 499
Oulmès 257
Oum El Alek 506
Oum er Rbia, sources 249
Oumesnat 518
Ourika valley 383

P
package operators 5 (UK),
17 (US), 20 (Australia)
painted rocks (Tafraoute) 519
Paradise Valley 488
Paysage d'Ito 198
petits taxis 48
pharmacies 27
Phoenicians 549
phone calls 58
piracy 555
Plage Blanche 526
Plage des Nations 273
Pointe Imessouane 340
police 38
Port Blondin 297
Portuguese colonization 554
post offices 57
poste restante 58
prehistory 549
Ptolemy 550
public holidays 62
Puerto Cansado 538

R
Rabat 274–291
accommodation 278
Archeological Museum 286
arrival 275
Bab Er Rouah 286
bars and nightlife 290
buses 278
Chellah 286
embassies 291
Flea market 281
Hassan mosque and tower 284
history 274
hotels 278
Kasbah des Oudaïas 281
listings 290
Medina 279
Mellah 280
Mohammed V mausoleum 285

Museum of Moroccan Arts 284
restaurants 289
Royal Palace 286
Souks 280
Ville Nouvelle 285
Rafsaï 143
Raï music 589
Ramadan 61, 569
Ras El Ma 158
recordings 586
reptiles 577
Restinga–Smir 126
Rich 254
riding 66
Rif, The 137–155
Riffian revolt 138, 558
Rissani 465
rock carvings, prehistoric 385,
506, 520
Roman monuments 71
Roman Morocco 71, 101, 110,
113, 192, 550
Route de l'Unité 142
rugs 68
Rwais 581

S
Saadian dynasty 554
Safi 324–328
Saharan Provinces 535
Saïdia 165
Salé 292–295
Sebta (Ceuta) 114–118
security 38
Sefrou 238
Selouane 155
Sephardic music 589
Settat 314
Setti Fatma 384
sexual harassment 36
Sidi Abdallah El Jabar 514
Sidi Abderrahmane 315
Sidi Abed 322
Sidi Bibi 490
Sidi Bouknadel
(Plage des Nations) 273
Sidi Bouzid 324
Sidi Chamharouch 394
Sidi Harazem 237
Sidi Ifni 520
Sidi Kaouki 339
Sidi Mohammed 556
Sidi Moussa 322

Sidi Moussa d'Aglou 512
Sidi Rahhal 266
Sidi Yahia 170
Sijilmassa 466
Simmou 340
Skhirat Plage 296
skiing 66, 245, 385
Skoura oasis 435–438
Smara 534
Smir 126
Souk El Arba du Rharb 112
Souk el Djemaa 322
Souk El Hadd Issi 520
Souk Sebt Oulad Nemâa 259
Souk Sebt Talmakent 411
Souk Tnine de l'Ourika 384
Souk Inine Tigouga 414
souks 68
Sources Oum er Rbia 249
SPANA 72, 184
Spanish colonization 557–559
specialist operators 5 (UK),
   17 (US), 20 (Australia)
sports 65
Srempt 265
stones, semiprecious 69
street names 618
Sufi music 582
sûreté nationale 38
surfing 67, 337, 523
swimming pools 67

T

Tachdirt 397
Tachfine, Youssef bin 552
Taddert 407
Tafferete 242
Tafilalt 456
Taforalt 164
Tafraoute 514
Taghazoute 486
Taghbart 403
Taghia 265
Taghjicht 507
Tagmout 413
Tagoudiche 518
Tagoundaft 406
Tagounite 432
Tagouyamt 501
Talâat n'Yacoub 406
Taliouine 499
Tamanar 340

Tamdaght 409
Tamegroute 431
Tamgout 501
Tamnalt 444
Tamnougalt 427
tampons 74
Tamraght 486
Tamri 340, 487
Tamtatoucht 451
Tan Tan 531
Tan Tan Plage 534
Tangier (Tangiers) 79–100
   accommodation 84
   American Legation 89
   arrival 80
   bars 95
   beach 86
   cafés 95
   campsites 84
   Cap Malabata 101
   Cap Spartel 100
   Caves of Hercules 100
   Dar El Makhzen 91
   discos and clubs 96
   ferries 80
   gardens 93
   hotels 84
   Jews' Beach 92
   Kasbah 91
   leaving 99
   listings 97
   Medina 89
   Mountain, The 93
   Palace 91
   Petit Socco 90
   restaurants 93
   shopping 97
   Spanish Theatre 89
   St Andrew's Church 88
   Villa Harris 102
   Ville Nouvelle 88
Tansikht 434, 443
Taounate 143
Taourirt 150
Tarbat n'Tirsal 264
Tarfaya 538
Targannt gorge 505
Targuist 141
Tarhat 519
Tarkeddit 264
Taroudannt 491–497
Tashelhaït (language) 623
Tata 503
Tata circuit 502–509
taxis 40, 48
Taza 144–148

Tazarhart refuge 399
Tazenakht 435
Tazka 519
Tazoulte 518
Tazzarine 434
Tazzerte 266
Telouet 407–409
Temara Plage 295
Temguilcht 520
temperature xiv
Tendrara 171, 469
tennis 67
Tetouan 118–125
Thami El Glaoui 559
Thamusidia, Ancient 113
Tichka plateau 410–414
Tifnite 490
Tifoultoutte kasbah 421
Tighmi 513
Tijrhicht 403
time 74
Timesgadiouine 411
Timichi 397
Timiderte 427
Timoulay 507
Tin Mal 404
Tinejdad 455
Tinerghwet 411
Tinerhir 446–449
Tinfou 432
Tinzouline 227
Tioulit 514
Tioute 498
Tircht 506
Tirhboula 257
Tirnmatmat 518
Tisgui 501
Tissa 143
Tit 322
Tizerkine 520
Tizi Melloul 399
Tizi n'Aguensioual 398
Tizi n'Aït Ourit 265
Tizi n'Eddi 398
Tizi n'Isli 258
Tizi n'Likemt 396
Tizi n'Ouanoums 396
Tizi n'Tabghourt 411
Tizi n'Tafilalt 434
Tizi n'Talrhmeht 254
Tizi n'Tazazert 442
Tizi n'Terhaline 396
Tizi n'Test 399–406

Tizi n'Tichka 406–409
Tizi n'Timirout 412
Tizi n'Tinififft 426
Tizi n'Tirghyst 265
Tizi n'Uguent Zegasoun 453
Tizi n'Wannas 412
Tizi Oussem 398
Tiznit 509–512
Tleta Ketama 140
Tleta Tazrite 519
Todra gorge 449
Torres de Alcala 141
Toubkal massif 387–399
Toubkal refuge 395
Tounfite 254
tour operators 5 (UK), 17 (US),
    20 (Australia)
tourist offices 30
trains to Morocco 8
trains within Morocco 40
Treaty of Fes 557
trekking 65, 382, 286, 388, 495
trekking maps 32
trucks 43

U
UMA 563
UNFP 560
USFP 561

V
Vallée des Roses 438
visas 22
Volubilis 192–196

W
walking 65, 382, 386, 388,
    495
water 28
Wattasid dynasty 554
weather xiv, xv
Web sites about Morocco 32
Welles, Orson 329
Western Sahara 531–546,
    562
Western Saharan conflict 562
wildlife 573–579
windsurfing 67, 337, 339

work 74
work camps 74

X
Xaouen (Chaouen) 127–133

Y
Yacoub El Mansour 553
Youssef bin Tachfine 552
youth hostels 51

Z
Zagora 427–430
Zaouia Ahancal 261
Zaouia Sidi Ahmed ou Moussa
    513
zaouias 570
Zegzel gorge 164
Zenaga 469
Ziz gorges 255
Ziz palmery 459
Zoo, Temara 295

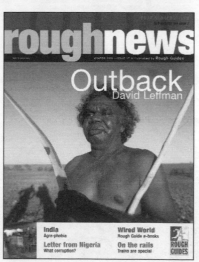

around the world

Alaska ★ Algarve ★ Amsterdam ★ Andalucía ★ Antigua & Barbuda ★
Argentina ★ Auckland Restaurants ★ Australia ★ Austria ★ Bahamas ★
Bali & Lombok ★ Bangkok ★ Barbados ★ Barcelona ★ Beijing ★ Belgium &
Luxembourg ★ Belize ★ Berlin ★ Big Island of Hawaii ★ Bolivia ★ Boston
★ Brazil ★ Britain ★ Brittany & Normandy ★ Bruges & Ghent ★ Brussels ★
Budapest ★ Bulgaria ★ California ★ Cambodia ★ Canada ★ Cape Town ★
The Caribbean ★ Central America ★ Chile ★ China ★ Copenhagen ★
Corsica ★ Costa Brava ★ Costa Rica ★ Crete ★ Croatia ★ Cuba ★ Cyprus ★
Czech & Slovak Republics ★ Devon & Cornwall ★ Dodecanese & East
Aegean ★ Dominican Republic ★ The Dordogne & the Lot ★ Dublin ★
Ecuador ★ Edinburgh ★ Egypt ★ England ★ Europe ★ First-time Asia ★
First-time Europe ★ Florence ★ Florida ★ France ★ French Hotels &
Restaurants ★ Gay & Lesbian Australia ★ Germany ★ Goa ★ Greece ★
Greek Islands ★ Guatemala ★ Hawaii ★ Holland ★ Hong Kong & Macau ★
Honolulu ★ Hungary ★ Ibiza & Formentera ★ Iceland ★ India ★ Indonesia
★ Ionian Islands ★ Ireland ★ Israel & the Palestinian Territories ★ Italy ★
Jamaica ★ Japan ★ Jerusalem ★ Jordan ★ Kenya ★ The Lake District ★
Languedoc & Roussillon ★ Laos ★ Las Vegas ★ Lisbon ★ London ★

in twenty years

London Mini Guide ★ London Restaurants ★ Los Angeles ★ Madeira ★ Madrid ★ Malaysia, Singapore & Brunei ★ Mallorca ★ Malta & Gozo ★ Maui ★ Maya World ★ Melbourne ★ Menorca ★ Mexico ★ Miami & the Florida Keys ★ Montréal ★ Morocco ★ Moscow ★ Nepal ★ New England ★ New Orleans ★ New York City ★ New York Mini Guide ★ New York Restaurants ★ New Zealand ★ Norway ★ Pacific Northwest ★ Paris ★ Paris Mini Guide ★ Peru ★ Poland ★ Portugal ★ Prague ★ Provence & the Côte d'Azur ★ Pyrenees ★ The Rocky Mountains ★ Romania ★ Rome ★ San Francisco ★ San Francisco Restaurants ★ Sardinia ★ Scandinavia ★ Scotland ★ Scottish Highlands & Islands ★ Seattle ★ Sicily ★ Singapore ★ South Africa, Lesotho & Swaziland ★ South India ★ Southeast Asia ★ Southwest USA ★ Spain ★ St Lucia ★ St Petersburg ★ Sweden ★ Switzerland ★ Sydney ★ Syria ★ Tanzania ★ Tenerife and La Gomera ★ Thailand ★ Thailand's Beaches & Islands ★ Tokyo ★ Toronto ★ Travel Health ★ Trinidad & Tobago ★ Tunisia ★ Turkey ★ Tuscany & Umbria ★ USA ★ Vancouver ★ Venice & the Veneto ★ Vienna ★ Vietnam ★ Wales ★ Washington DC ★ West Africa ★ Women Travel ★ Yosemite ★ Zanzibar ★ Zimbabwe

also look out for our maps, phrasebooks, music guides and reference books

Will you have enough stories to tell your grandchildren?

©2000 Yahoo! Inc.

Yahoo! Travel

Don't bury your head in the sand!

Take cover!

with Rough Guide Travel Insurance

Worldwide cover, for Rough Guide readers worldwide

UK Freefone **0800 015 09 06**

US Freefone **1 866 220 5588**

Worldwide **(+44) 1243 621 046**

Check the web at

www.roughguides.com/insurance

ROUGH GUIDES

Insurance organized by Torribles Insurance Brokers Ltd, 21 Prince Street, Bristol, BS1 4PH, England